1650	David Hume (1711–1776)
	Jean-Jacques Rousseau (1712–1778)
	Immanuel Kant (1724–1804)
	Jeremy Bentham (1748–1832)
	Georg Wilhelm Friedrich Hegel (1770–1831)
	Arthur Schopenhauer (1788–1860)
1800	John Stuart Mill (1806–1873)
	Harriet Taylor (1807–1858)
	Charles Darwin (1809–1882)
	Søren Kierkegaard (1813–1855)
	Frederick Douglass (1817–1895)
	Henry David Thoreau (1817–1862)
	Karl Marx (1818–1883)
	William James (1842–1910)
	Friedrich Nietzsche (1844–1900)
	Edmund Husserl (1859–1938)
1850	John Dewey (1859–1952)
	Mahatma Gandhi (1869–1948)
	Bertrand Russell (1872–1970)
	Albert Einstein (1879–1955)
	Ludwig Wittgenstein (1889–1951)
	Martin Heidegger (1889–1976)
	Charles Hartshorne (b. 1897)
1900	Gilbert Ryle (1900–1976)
	Kieji Nishitani (1900–1990)
	Jean-Paul Sartre (1905–1980)
	Maurice Merleau-Ponty (1908–1961)
	Simone de Beauvoir (1908–1986)
	Albert Camus (1913–1960)
	Nelson Mandela (b. 1918)
	Malcolm X (1925–1965)
1930	Martin Luther King, Jr. (1929–1968)

Introducing

Philosophy

A TEXT WITH
INTEGRATED READINGS

Seventh Edition

Introducing

Philosophy

A TEXT WITH
INTEGRATED READINGS

Seventh Edition

ROBERT C. SOLOMON
University of Texas at Austin

New York   Oxford
OXFORD UNIVERSITY PRESS

Oxford University Press

Oxford   New York
Auckland   Bangkok   Buenos Aires   Cape Town
Chennai   Dar es Salaam   Delhi   Hong Kong   Istanbul   Karachi
Kolkata   Kuala Lumpur   Madrid   Melbourne   Mexico City   Mumbai   Nairobi
São Paulo   Shanghai   Singapore   Taipei   Tokyo   Toronto

and an associated company in Berlin

Copyright © 2001 by Oxford University Press, Inc.

Published by Oxford University Press, Inc.
198 Madison Avenue, New York, New York 10016
http://www.oup-usa.org

Oxford is a registered trademark of Oxford University Press

ISBN: 0-19-515510-6

Printing number: 9 8 7 6 5 4 3 2

Printed in the United States of America
on acid-free paper

For Vita P. Solomon
She brought me into life
and taught me it was art.

PREFACE

Introducing Philosophy: A Text with Integrated Readings presupposes no background in the subject and no special abilities. Intended primarily as a textbook for a one- or two-semester introductory course, the book provides the course materials from which instructors and students can focus on a variety of problems and perspectives. The point of this textbook is to present students with alternatives on every issue and let them arrive at their own conclusions. These conclusions should be based on arguments in class and with friends or classmates, as well as on the discussions in this book. The purpose of philosophy is to encourage each person to think for himself or herself; no single source of arguments or information can take the place of personal dialogues and discussions. A textbook is ultimately a sourcebook; everything in it is to be taken as a cause for further argument, not as a final statement of results. This book does not attempt to sway students toward any particular philosophical positions, but rather presents basic philosophical problems and powerful philosophical arguments to encourage students to think for themselves.

This book derives from thirty years of teaching in very different schools in various cities and states. It is based on the belief that philosophy is a genuinely exciting subject, accessible not only to specialists and a few gifted undergraduate majors but to everyone. Everyone is a philosopher, whether enrolled in a philosophy course or not. Most of us are concerned with the same basic problems and use the same essential arguments. The difference is that someone who has studied philosophy has the advantage of having encountered stronger and more varied arguments than might have been available otherwise. In this book, the views of the major philosophers of the past twenty-five hundred years are used to give students these various arguments. This approach offers introductory students direct contact with substantial readings from significant works in the history of philosophy, but removes the unreasonable demand that they confront these often difficult works in full and without commentary or editing, as they would in the originals or in most anthologies. This book is not, however, a historical introduction but rather an introduction to the problems of philosophy and the various ways in which they have been answered. The history of philosophy thus serves to illuminate these problems and replies, not the other way around.

Although the language of philosophy is often specialized and sometimes difficult, this book is as free of jargon and special terminology as possible. Where necessary, the most important and widely used philosophical terms are carefully introduced within the text and also summarized in glossaries at the end of each chapter. Brief biographies of the philosophers discussed are provided at the end of the book. Although the book deals principally with the philosophers' ideas rather than with their lives, it is valuable to have the student learn their place in history.

Responses to the first six editions of *Introducing Philosophy* have been both gratifying and helpful in the preparation of this revision for a new generation of students. In this seventh edition, the most obvious change is a thorough editing and reorganization of the book and the readings. We decided that the best way to improve the book, in addition to bringing some of the "hotter" areas of philosophy up-to-date, was to put it through a rigorous weight-reduction regime. The readings have been edited for clarity and conciseness, the additions of feminist and "multicultural" material have been better integrated into the text, long chapters have been split apart, and sections have been more clearly defined. These improvements will give the instructor greater ease and flexibility in creating his or her own course with the text, using some sections of a chapter but not others, or rearranging the order of treatment from the one that appears here. A more descriptive table of contents should make the availability of such choices and arrangements more evident and efficient. The following section will make clear the various possibilities for using the seventh edition of *Introducing Philosophy* as a beginning philosophy textbook.

For the Instructor: How to Use This Book

Introducing Philosophy is written for a complete course, and the chapters build on one another in logical sequence. Nevertheless, each chapter has been written as an independent unit so that it is possible to use the book in a variety of ways and for a variety of courses. Within each chapter, too, various sections can be selected for shorter discussion. For example, some instructors may want to use only the first sections of Chapter 2 (Religion) or only a few key sections from Chapter 5 (Self) and Chapter 7 (Freedom). Some may want to emphasize the multicultural material. Others may choose to omit this material and focus on classical Western philosophy.

A full course might include the Introduction and all ten chapters, but this may be a heavy load for an average one-term course. At the other extreme, a short course (for example, a summer term or a class that meets only once a week, a quarter system, or a class that prefers to treat a few central issues in detail) might only use half the chapters. The following outlines are suggestions for a variety of uses of the book adapted to different lengths and kinds of classes:

MAXIMUM COURSE (one very full term):
Introduction; Chapters 1–10

MINIMUM COURSE (summer, part-time, quarter):
Introduction; Chapters 1, 2, 3, 5

TWO-TERM COURSE:
First term: Introduction; Chapters 1–6
Second term: Introduction; Chapters 7–10

AVERAGE COURSE (14–16 week term; chapters in parentheses are optional):
Introduction; Chapters 1, 2, (3), (4) 5,(6) 7, 8, (9), (10)

ETHIS AND RELIGION/VALUES COURSE
Introduction; Chapters 2, 5, 8, 9, (10),

METAPHYSICS AND EPISTEMOLOGY COURSE
Introduction; Chapters 1 (2) 3, 4, (5), 6, 7

Some classes may prefer to begin with either Chapter 2 (Religion) or Chapter 8 (Ethics) and reorder the sequence of chapters. The basic course—tailored to the average one-term, 14–16 week class meeting three times a week—would be:

Introduction; Chapters 1, 2, 3, 5, 6, 7, 8, 9

The remaining chapters can be added as time and interest permit.

In this edition, I have used alphabetic letters and numbers to designate sections and subsections within the chapters. Because some of the most important chapters (e.g., Knowledge, Self, Freedom, and Ethics) are longer and more involved, many instructors prefer to assign a few sections rather than an entire chapter. For instance, in Chapter 4 some instructors may prefer to deal only with the standard three theories of truth and dispense with the material on European philosophy (Kant and following) in the sections that follow. Others may prefer to delete the theories of truth and launch right into Kant following the discussion of Hume. So, too, some instructors may prefer to deal with the arguments concerning God's existence but dispense with the problem of evil; some may want to talk only about the basic problem of freedom versus determinism without subjecting students to the (comparative) subtleties and intrigue of the variations of "soft determinism." Other instructors may want to teach a brief history of ethics (Aristotle, Hume, Kant, Mill) without treating such general topics as ethical relativism. I am confident that this new edition makes all of this much easier to do.

For the Student: Doing Philosophy

Your attempt to develop your own thoughts—to "do" philosophy as well as to read what others have done—is central to any study of philosophy. Philosophy, more than any other field, is not so much a subject as it is a way of thinking, one that can be appreciated fully only by joining in. While reading each section, therefore, do not hesitate to put down the book at any time and do your own thinking and writing. When reading about metaphysics, for example, think about how you would develop your own view of reality and how you would answer the questions raised by the first philosophers of ancient Greece or the Orient. When confronted by an argument, consider how you might argue for or against a given position. When facing an idea that seems foreign, try to put it in your own terms and understand the vision that lies behind it. And when facing a problem, always offer your own answer as well as the answers offered by earlier thinkers. In philosophy, unlike physics or biology, your own answer may be just as legitimate as those given by the philosophers of the past, and there may be equally interesting answers from different traditions. That is what makes philosophy so difficult to learn at first, but it is also what make it so personally valuable and enjoyable.

Writing Philosophy

With the foregoing ideas in mind, it should be obvious why talking about philosophy with friends and classmates, raising important questions and objections in class, and writing down ideas are so very important. Articulation reinforces comprehension, and arguing against objections broadens understanding. Writing papers in philosophy is a particularly important part of any philosophy course, and there are certain general guidelines to keep in mind:

1. Begin your essay with a leading question. "Thinking about" some philosophical issue can be fun, but too easily loses direction and purpose. For instance, thinking about "freedom" involves far too many different problems and perspectives. Asking such questions as "Is freedom of action compatible with scientific determinism?" or "Can there be freedom in a socialist state?" gives your thinking a specific orientation and way of proceeding.

2. Be clear about the difficulties you face in tackling the question. Are the terms of the question clear? It is not always necessary or possible to define terms at the start of your essay. Indeed, defining the key term might be the basic and most difficult conclusion you reach. Also, it is often a poor idea to depend on a dictionary (even a good one) for clarifying your question. Dictionaries are not written by philosophers and generally reflect popular usage—which may include just such philosophical misunderstandings as you are attempting to correct.

3. Clarify the position you are arguing. Don't force the reader (your instructor) to guess where you are going. When you are clear about the question you ask, it will help you clarify the answer you intend to give, and vice versa. In fact, you may well change your mind—both about the question and the answer—several times while you are writing; this is the real danger of attempting a one-draft-the night-before approach to essay writing.

4. Argue your case. Demonstrate why you hold the position you do. The most frequent criticism of student papers is, "This is your assertion: where is the argument?" When an exam question asks you to discuss an idea or a quotation "critically," this does not mean that you must attack it or find fault with it, but rather that you need to consider the merits and possible inadequacies, consider the reasons given, and give your own reasons for what you say.

5. Anticipate objections to your position and to your arguments, and take the offensive against rival positions. If you don't know what your position is opposed to, it is doubtful you are clear about what your own position is. If you can't imagine how anyone could possibly disagree with you, you probably haven't thought through your position carefully.

6. Don't be afraid to be yourself, to be humorous, or charming, or sincere, or personal. The most powerful philosophical writings, those that have endured for centuries, often reflect the author's deepest concerns and attitudes toward life.

However, remember that no philosophical writing can be just humorous, or charming, or sincere, or personal. Make sure your jokes—and everything you write—is relevant to the topic at hand. What makes your writing philosophical is that it involves general concerns and careful arguments while attempting to prove an important point and answer one of the age-old questions.

Acknowledgments

This book and its six previous editions have been made possible through the encouragement and help of many people, most importantly the several thousand introductory students I have had the pleasure of meeting and teaching over the past decade. For the original edition, I thank Susan Zaleski for her very special insights and criticism of the manuscript in its early stages. I also thank Robert Fogelin, John McDermott, George Cronk, and Roland D. Zimany for their encouragement and helpful suggestions. And I thank Terry Boswell, Lisa Erlich, David Blumenfeld, Paul Woodruff, Harry O'Hara, Stephanie Lewis, and Barbara Barratt for their time and good advice. Revisions for the second edition were suggested by Paul Woodruff, Billy Joe Lucas, and Cheshire Calhoun. I benefited in the third edition from advice given by Peter Hutcheson, Richard Palmer, Norman Thomas, Greta Reed, Edward Johnson, Paul Woodruff, Don Branson, Hoke Robinson, Robert Fogelin, Meredith Michaels, Bruce Paternoster, Maxine Morphis, and Bruce Ballard. In the fourth edition, I was grateful for the constructive suggestions of Jeffery Coombs, Timothy Owen Davis, Conrad Gromada, Gregory Landini, Dan Bonevac, Paul Woodruff, Steven Phillips, Kathleen Higgins, and Kristy Bartlett. For the fifth edition, I owe a very special debt of gratitude to Janet McCracken, who once again combined her philosophical knowledge and enthusiasm, her talent for teaching and research, and her sensitivity to both students and the philosophical literature of other cultures to help me produce an improved textbook. I also received good advice from Marilyn Frye, Jonathan Westphal, David J. Paul, Edward Johnson, Fred Tabor, and Brian Kutin; my thanks to Clancy Martin for preparing the index. Again I thank Steve Phillips for his continuing help in my understanding of Indian texts and philosophy.

For the seventh, as for the sixth edition of *Introducing Philosophy*, I owe an enormous debt of gratitude to Karen Mottola for her creative, critical, and very knowledgeable reading, advice, and help in editing. Without her, this improved edition would not have been possible. I also want to thank John Rowell of Selkirk College, Christopher Melley and his introductory class in Landstuhl, Germany, and my own students in Plan II Honors at the University of Texas for their keen eye for details. I received helpful comments and suggestions for revision from John Carvallo, Villanova University; Michael Clifford, Mississippi State University; Timothy Davis, The Essex Campus of the Community College of Baltimore County; Ronald Glass, University of Wisconsin at LaCrosse; Isabel Luengo, Mira Costa College; Thomas Ryckman, Lawrence University; and William Smith, Millersville University.

At Harcourt College Publishers, my editors—David Tatom, Katie Frushour, and Katherine Dennis—have earned my appreciation for their work to give this edition its own distinctive character. Also deserving recognition are production manager Linda McMillan and designer Scott Baker. But I also want above all to once again thank my first philosophy teachers—Robert Hanson, Doris Yokum, Elizabeth Flower, James Ross, and C. G. Hempel—who provided me with the models and the materials for an ideal introductory philosophy course, and the many students who still continue to make the teaching of philosophy one of the more satisfying professions in a not easily satisfying world.

CONTENTS IN BRIEF

TABLE OF CONTENTS

TABLE OF CONTENTS
(WITH READING SELECTIONS)

INTRODUCTION:

PHILOSOPHY

The unexamined life is not worth living.

SOCRATES

A. SOCRATES

He was not the first philosopher, but he was, and is still, the ideal of philosophers. Once assured by the oracle at Delphi that he was the wisest man in Athens, **Socrates** (470–399 B.C.) borrowed his view of life from the inscription at Delphi, "Know Thyself." Mixing humility with arrogance, he boasted that his superiority lay in his awareness of his own ignorance, and he spent the rest of his life making fools of the self-proclaimed "wise men" of Athens.

In the opinion of Socrates and other critics of the time, the government of Athens was corrupt and notoriously bumbling, in marked contrast to the "Golden Age" of Pericles a few years before. Philosophical arguments had become all cleverness and demagoguery, rhetorical tricks to win arguments and legal cases; political ambition replaced justice and the search for the good life. Socrates believed that the people of Athens held their principles glibly, like banners at a football game, but rarely lived up to them and even more rarely examined them. Against this, he developed a technique of asking seemingly innocent questions, trapping his audience in their own confusions and hypocrisies, exploding the pretensions of his times. And against their easy certainties, he taught that "the unexamined life is not worth living." He referred to himself as a "gadfly" (an obnoxious insect with a painful bite), keeping his fellow citizens from ever becoming as smug and self-righteous as they would like to have been. Accordingly, he made many enemies and was satirized by **Aristophanes** in his play *The Clouds*.

1

FROM *THE CLOUDS*
BY **ARISTOPHANES**

STUDENT OF SOCRATES: Socrates asked Chaerephon how many of its own feet a flea could jump—one had bitten Chaerephon's brow and then jumped to Socrates' head.
STREPSIADES: And how did he measure the jump?
STUDENT: Most ingeniously. He melted wax, caught the flea, dipped its feet, and the hardened wax made Persian slippers. Unfastening these, he found their size.
STREPSIADES: Royal Zeus! What an acute intellect!
STUDENT: But yesterday a high thought was lost through a lizard.
STREPSIADES: How so? Tell me.
STUDENT: As he gaped up at the moon, investigating her paths and turnings, from off the roof a lizard befouled him.[1]

In the play, Aristophanes made Socrates and his students look utterly ridiculous, and the Athenian public enjoyed Aristophanes' sarcasm as a mild form of vengeance for Socrates' constant criticisms. Aristophanes' "clouds" refer to that confusion which we mean when we talk of someone "having his head in the clouds." Aristophanes probably expressed the general public opinion when he described Socrates as "shiftless" and merely a master at verbal trickery.

Socrates' students, however, virtually worshiped him. They described him as "the bravest, most wise and most upright man of our times" and perceived him as a martyr for the truth in a corrupted society. The price of his criticism was not merely the satire of the playwrights. Because he had been such a continual nuisance, the government arranged to have Socrates brought to trial for "corrupting the youth of Athens" and "not believing in the gods of the city." And for these trumped-up "crimes," Socrates was condemned to death. But at his trial, he once again became a gadfly to those who condemned him.

FROM *THE APOLOGY*
BY **PLATO**

He assesses the penalty at death. So be it. What counterassessment should I propose to you, gentlemen of the jury? Clearly it should be a penalty I deserve, and what do I deserve to suffer or to pay because I have deliberately not led a quiet life but have neglected what occupies most people: wealth, household affairs, the position of general or public orator or the other offices, the political clubs and factions that exist in the city? I thought myself too honest to survive if

---

[1] Aristophanes, *The Clouds,* in *The Complete Plays of Aristophanes,* trans. Moses Hadas (New York: Bantam, 1962).

I occupied myself with those things. I did not follow that path that would have made me of no use either to you or to myself, but I went to each of you privately and conferred upon him what I say is the greatest benefit, by persuading him not to care for any of his belongings before caring that he himself should be as good and as wise as possible, not to care for the city's possessions more than for the city itself, and to care for other things in the same way. What do I deserve for being such a man? Some good, gentlemen of the jury, if I must truly make an assessment according to my deserts, and something suitable.

Socrates here suggests that the state should give him a pension, rather than a punishment, for being a public benefactor and urging his students to be virtuous.

It is for the sake of a short time, gentlemen of the jury, that you will acquire the reputation and the guilt, in the eyes of those who want to denigrate the city, of having killed Socrates, a wise man, for they will say that I am wise even if I am not. If you had waited but a little while, this would have happened of its own accord. You see my age, that I am already advanced in years and close to death. I am saying this not to all of you but to those who condemned me to death, and to these same jurors I say: Perhaps you think that I was convicted for lack of such words as might have convinced you, if I thought I should say or do all I could to avoid my sentence. Far from it. I was convicted because I lacked not words but boldness and shamelessness and the willingness to say to you what you would most gladly have heard from me, lamentations and tears and my saying and doing many things that I say are unworthy of me but that you are accustomed to hear from others. I did not think then that the danger I ran should make me do anything mean, nor do I now regret the nature of my defense. I would much rather die after this kind of defense than live after making the other kind. Neither I nor any other man should, on trial or in war, contrive to avoid death at any cost. Indeed it is often obvious in battle that one could escape death by throwing away one's weapons and by turning to supplicate one's pursuers, and there are many ways to avoid death in every kind of danger if one will venture to do or say anything to avoid it. It is not difficult to avoid death, gentlemen of the jury, it is much more difficult to avoid wickedness, for it runs faster than death. Slow and elderly as I am, I have been caught by the slower pursuer, whereas my accusers, being clever and sharp, have been caught by the quicker, wickedness. I leave you now, condemned to death by you, but they are condemned by truth to wickedness and injustice. So I maintain my assessment, and they maintain theirs. This perhaps had to happen, and I think it is as it should be.

It is not difficult to avoid death, gentlemen of the jury, it is much more difficult to avoid wickedness, for it runs faster than death.

Now I want to prophesy to those who convicted me, for I am at the point when men prophesy most, when they are about to die. I say gentlemen, to those who voted to kill me, that vengeance will come upon you immediately after my death, a vengeance much harder to bear than that which you took in killing me. You did this in the belief that you would avoid giving an account of your life, but I maintain that quite the opposite will happen to you. There will be more people to test you, whom I now held back, but you did not notice it. They will be more difficult to deal with as they will be younger and you will resent them more. You are wrong if you believe that by killing people you will prevent anyone from reproaching you for not living in the right way. To escape such tests is neither possible nor good, but it is best and easiest not to discredit others but to prepare oneself to be as good as possible. With this prophecy to you who convicted me, I part from you.[2]

In prison, he was given the opportunity to escape. He refused it. He had always taught that "the really important thing is not to live, but to live well." And to "live well" meant, along with the more enjoyable things in life, to live according to your principles. When his friend Crito tried to persuade him otherwise, Socrates responded in this manner:

FROM *THE CRITO*
BY **PLATO**

SOCRATES: My good Crito, why should we care so much for what the majority think? The most reasonable people, to whom one should pay more attention, will believe that things were done as they were done.

CRITO: You see, Socrates, that one must also pay attention to the opinion of the majority. Your present situation makes clear that the majority can inflict not the least but pretty well the greatest evils if one is slandered among them.

SOCRATES: Would that the majority could inflict the greatest evils, for they would then be capable of the greatest good, and that would be fine, but now they cannot do either. They cannot make a man either wise or foolish, but they inflict things haphazardly.

CRITO: That may be so. But tell me this, Socrates, are you anticipating that I and your other friends would have trouble with the informers if you escape from here, as having stolen you away, and that we should be compelled to lose all our property or pay heavy fines and suffer other punishment besides? If you have any such fear, forget it. We would be justified in running this risk to save you, and worse, if necessary. Do follow my advice, and do not act differently.

SOCRATES: I do have these things in mind, Crito, and also many others.

CRITO: Have no such fear. It is not much money that some people require to save you and get you out of here. . . .

---

[2]Plato, *The Apology,* in *The Trial and Death of Socrates,* 2nd ed., trans. G. M. A. Grube (Indianapolis, IN: Hackett, 1974).

Besides, Socrates, I do not think that what you are doing is right, to give up your life when you can save it, and to hasten your fate as your enemies would hasten it, and indeed have hastened it in their wish to destroy you.

◆◆◆

SOCRATES: My dear Crito, your eagerness is worth much if it should have some right aim; if not, then the greater your keenness the more difficult it is to deal with. We must therefore examine whether we should act in this way or not, as not only now but at all times I am the kind of man who listens only to the argument that on reflection seems best to me. I cannot, now that this fate has come upon me, discard the arguments I used; they seem to me much the same. I value and respect the same principles as before, and if we have no better arguments to bring up at this moment, be sure that I shall not agree with you, not even if the power of the majority were to frighten us with more bogeys, as if we were children, with threats of incarcerations and executions and confiscation of property. How should we examine this matter more reasonably? Would it be by taking up first your argument about the opinions of men, whether it is sound in every case that one should pay attention to some opinions, but not to others? Or was that well-spoken before the necessity to die came upon me, but now it is clear that this was said in vain for the sake of argument, that it was in truth play and nonsense? I am eager to examine together with you, Crito, whether this argument will appear in any way different to me in my present circumstances, or whether it remains the same, whether we are to abandon it or believe it. It was said on every occasion that one should greatly value some opinions, but not others. Does that seem to you a sound statement?

> *. . . not only now but at all times I am the kind of man who listens only to the argument that on reflection seems best to me.*

◆◆◆

Examine the following statement in turn as to whether it stays the same or not, that the most important thing is not life, but the good life.

CRITO: It stays the same.

SOCRATES: And that the good life, the beautiful life, and the just life are the same; does that still hold, or not?

CRITO: It does hold.

SOCRATES: As we have agreed so far, we must examine next whether it is right for me to try to get out of here when the Athenians have not acquitted me. If it is seen to be right, we will try to do so; if it is not, we will abandon the idea. As for those questions you raise about money, reputation, the upbringing of children, Crito, those considerations in truth belong to those people who easily put men to death and would bring them to life again if they could, without thinking; I mean the majority of men. For us, however, since our argument leads to this, the only valid consideration, as we were saying just now, is whether we should be acting rightly in giving money and gratitude to those who will lead me out of here, and ourselves helping with the escape, or whether in truth we shall do wrong in doing all this. If it appears that we shall be acting unjustly, then we have no need at all to take into account whether we shall have to die, if we stay here and keep quiet, or suffer in another way, rather than do wrong.

CRITO: I think you put that beautifully, Socrates, but see what we should do.

SOCRATES: Let us examine the question together, my dear friend, and if you can make any objection while I am speaking, make it and I will listen to you, but if you have no objection to make, my dear Crito, then stop now from saying the same thing so often, that I must leave here against the will of the Athenians. I think it important to persuade you before I act, and not to act against your wishes. . . .

SOCRATES: Then . . . I ask you: when one has come to an agreement that is just with someone, should one fulfill it or cheat on it?

CRITO: One should fulfill it.

SOCRATES: See what follows from this: If we leave here without the city's permission, are we injuring people whom we should least injure? And are we sticking to a just agreement, or not?

CRITO: I cannot answer your question, Socrates, I do not know.

SOCRATES: Look at it this way. If, as we were planning to run away from here, or whatever one should call it, the laws and the state came and confronted us and asked: "Tell me, Socrates, what are you intending to do? Do you not by this action you are attempting intend to destroy us, the laws, and indeed the whole city, as far as you are concerned? Or do you think it possible for a city not to be destroyed if the verdicts of its courts have no force but are nullified and set at naught by private individuals?" What shall we answer to this and other such arguments? For many things could be said, especially by an orator on behalf of this law we are destroying, which orders that the judgments of the courts shall be carried out. Shall we say in answer, "The city wronged me, and its decision was not right." Shall we say that, or what?

CRITO: Yes, by Zeus, Socrates, that is our answer.

SOCRATES: Then what if the laws said, "Was that the agreement between us, Socrates, or was it to respect the judgments that the city came to?" And if we wondered at their words, they would perhaps add: "Socrates, do not wonder at what we say but answer, since you are accustomed to proceed by question and answer. Come now, what accusation do you bring against us and the city, that you should try to destroy us? Did we not, first, bring you to birth, and was it not through us that your father married your mother and begat you? Tell us, do you find anything to criticize in those of us who are concerned with marriage?" And I would say that I do not criticize them. "Or in those of us concerned with the nurture of babies and the education that you too received? Were those assigned to that subject not right to instruct your father to educate you in the arts and in physical culture?" And I would say that they were right. "Very well," they would continue, "and after you were

born and nurtured and educated, could you, in the first place, deny that you
are our offspring and servant, both you and your forefathers? If that is so,
do you think that we are on an equal footing as regards the right, and that
whatever we do to you it is right for you to do to us? You were not on an
equal footing with your father as regards the right, nor with your master if
you had one, so as to retaliate for anything they did to you, to revile them
if they reviled you, to beat them if they beat you, and so with many other
things. Do you think you have this right to retaliation against your country
and its laws? That if we undertake to destroy you and think it right to do so,
you can undertake to destroy us, as far as you can, in return? And will you
say that you are right to do so, you who truly care for virtue? Is your wisdom
such as not to realize that your country is to be honoured more than your
mother, your father, and all your ancestors, that it is more to be revered and
more sacred, and that it counts for more among the gods and sensible men,
that you must worship it, yield to it and placate its anger more than your father's? You must either persuade it or obey its orders, and endure in silence
whatever it instructs you to endure, whether blows or bonds, and if it leads
you into war to be wounded or killed, you must obey. To do so is right, and
one must not give way or retreat or leave one's post, but both in war and
in courts and everywhere else, one must obey the commands of one's city
and country, or persuade it as to the nature of justice. It is impious to bring
violence to bear against your mother or father, it is much more so to use it
against your country." What shall we say in reply, Crito, that the laws speak
the truth, or not?

CRITO: I think they do.

SOCRATES: "Reflect now, Socrates," the laws might say, "that if what we say is
true, you are not treating us rightly by planning to do what you are planning.

♦♦♦

"So decisively did you choose us and agree to be a citizen under us. Also,
you have had children in this city, thus showing that it was congenial to
you. Then at your trial you could have assessed your penalty at exile if you
wished, and you are now attempting to do against the city's wishes what you
could then have done with her consent. Then you prided yourself that you
did not resent death, but you chose, as you said, death in preference to exile.
Now, however, those words do not make you ashamed, and you pay no heed
to us, the laws, as you plan to destroy us, and you act like the meanest type
of slave by trying to run away, contrary to your undertakings and your agreement to live as a citizen under us. First then, answer us on this very point,
whether we speak the truth when we say that you agreed, not only in words
but by your deeds, to live in accordance with us." What are we to say to that,
Crito? Must we not agree?

CRITO: We must, Socrates.

SOCRATES: "Surely," they might say, "you are breaking the undertakings and
agreements that you made with us without compulsion or deceit, and under
no pressure of time for deliberation. You have had seventy years during

which you could have gone away if you did not like us, and if you thought our agreements unjust. You did not choose to go to Sparta or to Crete, which you are always saying are well governed, nor to any other city, Greek or foreign. You have been away from Athens less than the lame or the blind or other handicapped people. It is clear that the city has been outstandingly more congenial to you than to other Athenians, and so have we, the laws, for what city can please if its laws do not? Will you then not now stick to our agreements? You will, Socrates, if we can persuade you, and not make yourself a laughingstock by leaving the city.

"Be persuaded by us who have brought you up, Socrates. Do not value either your children or your life or anything else more than goodness, in order that you may have all this as your defense before rulers there. If you do this deed, you will not think it better or more just or more pious, nor will any one of your friends, nor will it be better for you when you arrive yonder. As it is, you depart, if you depart, after being wronged not by us, the laws, but by men; but if you depart after shamefully returning wrong for wrong and injury for injury, after breaking your agreement and contract with us, after injuring those you should injure least—yourself, your friends, your country and us— we shall be angry with you while you are still alive, and our brothers, the laws of the underworld, will not receive [you] kindly, knowing that you tried to destroy us as far as you could. Do not let Crito persuade you, rather than we, to do what he says."

◆◆◆

CRITO: I have nothing to say, Socrates.

SOCRATES: Let it be then, Crito, and let us act in this way, since this is the way the god is leading us.[3]

Socrates believed that the good of his "soul" was far more important than the transient pleasures of life. Accordingly, he preferred to die for his ideas than live as a hypocrite. An idea worth living for may be an idea worth dying for as well.

And while he was saying this, he was holding the cup, and then drained it calmly and easily. Most of us had been able to hold back our tears reasonably well up till then, but when we saw him drinking it and after he drank it, we could hold them back no longer; my own tears came in floods against my will. So I covered my face. I was weeping for myself—not for him, but for my misfortune in being deprived of such a comrade. Even before me, Crito was unable to restrain his tears and got up. Apollodorus had not ceased from weeping before, and at this moment his noisy tears and anger made

---

[3] Plato, *The Crito,* in *The Trial and Death of Socrates,* 2nd ed., trans. G. M. A. Grube (Indianapolis, IN: Hackett, 1974).

everybody present break down, except Socrates, "What is this," he said, "you strange fellows. It is mainly for this reason that I sent the women away, to avoid such unseemliness, for I am told one should die in good omened silence. So keep quiet and control yourselves. . . .

Such was the end of our comrade, Echecrates, a man who, we would say, was of all those we have known the best, and also the wisest and the most upright.[4]

Is there anything that you believe so passionately that you would die for it? Is there anything that you believe so passionately that it really makes your life worth living? For most people, now as always, life is rather a matter of "getting by." One of the more popular phrases of self-praise these days is "I'm a survivor." But, ironically, a person who is not willing to die for anything (for example, his or her own freedom) is thereby more vulnerable to threats and corruption. To be willing to die—as Socrates was—is to have a considerable advantage over someone for whom "life is everything."

If you look closely at your life, not only at your proclaimed ideals and principles but your desires and ambitions as well, do the facts of your life add up to its best intentions? Or are you too just drifting with the times, dissatisfied with ultimately meaningless jobs and mindless joyless entertainments, concerned with the price of tuition and some recent stupidity of your government, the petty competitions of school and society, the hassles of chores and assignments, car troubles and occasional social embarrassments, interrupted only by all too rare and too quickly passing pleasures and distractions? What we learn from Socrates is how to rise above all of this. Not that we should give up worldly pleasures—good food and fun, sex, sports and entertainment—and put our heads in the "clouds"; but we should see them in perspective and examine for ourselves that jungle of confused reactions and conditioned responses that we have unthinkingly inherited from our parents and borrowed from our peers. The point is not to give up what we have learned or to turn against our culture. Rather, the lesson to be learned from Socrates is that thinking about our lives and clarifying our ideals can turn it from a dreary series of tasks and distractions into a self-conscious adventure, one even worth dying for and certainly worth living for. It is a special kind of abstract thinking, rising above petty concerns and transforming our existence into a bold experiment in living. This special kind of thinking is called philosophy.

SOCRATES: Do you agree, or not, that when we say that a man has a passion for something, we shall say that he desires that whole kind of thing, not just one part of it and not the other?

GLAUCON: Yes, the whole of it.

---

[4] Plato, *The Phaedo,* in *The Trial and Death of Socrates,* 2nd ed., trans. G. M. A. Grube (Indianapolis, IN: Hackett, 1974).

But we shall rightly call a philosopher the man who is easily willing to learn every kind of knowledge, gladly turns to learning things, and is unsatiable in this respect.

SOCRATES: The lover of wisdom, we shall say, has a passion for wisdom, not for this kind of wisdom and not that, but for every kind of wisdom?

GLAUCON: True.

SOCRATES: As for one who is choosy about what he learns, especially if he is young and cannot yet give a reasoned account of what is useful and what is not, we shall not call him a lover of learning or a philosopher, just as we shall not say that a man who is difficult about his food is hungry or has an appetite for food. We shall not call him a lover of food but a bad feeder.

GLAUCON: And we should be right.

SOCRATES: But we shall rightly call a philosopher the man who is easily willing to learn every kind of knowledge, gladly turns to learning things, and is unsatiable in this respect. Is that not so?[5]

B. WHAT IS PHILOSOPHY?

Philosophy is not like any other academic subject; rather it is a critical approach to all subjects, the comprehensive vision within which all other subjects are contained. Philosophy is a style of life, a life of ideas or the life of reason, which a person like Socrates lives all of the time, which many of us live only a few hours a week. It is thinking, about everything and anything. But mainly, it is living thoughtfully. **Aristotle,** the student of **Plato,** who was the student of Socrates, called this "contemplative" or philosophical life the ideal life for humankind. He did not mean, however, that one should sit and think all of the time without doing anything. Aristotle, like the other Greek philosophers, was not one to abstain from pleasure or from political and social involvement for the sake of isolated thinking. Philosophy need not, as commonly believed, put our heads in the clouds, out of touch with everyday reality. Quite to the contrary, philosophy takes our heads out of the clouds, enlarging our view of ourselves and our knowledge of the world, allowing us to break out of prejudices and harmful habits that we have held since we were too young or too naive to know better. To say that philosophy is "critical" is not to say that it is negative or nihilistic; it is only to say that it is *reflective.* It looks at and thinks about ideas carefully, instead of unthinkingly accepting them.

Philosophy puts our lives and our beliefs in perspective by enabling us to see afresh the ways in which we view the world, to see what we assume, what we infer,

---

[5] Plato, *The Republic,* Bk. V, trans. G. M. A. Grube (Indianapolis, IN: Hackett, 1974).

and what we know for certain. It also allows us to appreciate *other* views of the world. It encourages us to see the consequences of our views and sometimes their hopeless inconsistencies. It allows us to see the justification (or lack of it) for our most treasured beliefs, and to separate what we will continue to believe with confidence from what we should consider doubtful or reject. It allows us the option of considering alternatives. Philosophy gives us the intellectual strength to defend what we do and what we believe to others and to ourselves. It forces us to be clear about the limits as well as the warrants for our acts and beliefs. Consequently, it gives us the intellectual strength to understand, tolerate, and even sympathize with or adopt views very different from our own.

Philosophy is first and foremost a discipline that teaches us how to articulate, hold, and defend beliefs that, perhaps, we have always held, but without having spelled them out and argued for them. For example, suppose you have been brought up in a deeply religious home; you have been taught respect for God and church, but you have never had to learn to justify or argue for your beliefs. You know that, although there are people who would disagree with you, your belief is a righteous and necessary one, but you have never had to explain this to anyone, nor have you tried to explain it to yourself. But now you enter college and immediately you are confronted by fellow students, some of whom you consider close friends and admire in many ways, who are openly skeptical about religion. Others accept very different doctrines and beliefs, and vociferously defend these. Your first reactions may be almost physical; you feel weak, flushed, and anxious. You refuse to listen, and if you respond at all, it is with a tinge of hysteria. You may get into fights as well as arguments. You feel as if some foundation of your life, one of its main supports, is slipping away. But slowly you gain some confidence; you begin to listen. You give yourself enough distance so that you will consider arguments about religion in just the same way you would consider arguments about some scientific or political dispute. You ask yourself *why* your friends don't believe what you believe. Are their arguments persuasive, their reasons *good* reasons? You begin asking yourself how you came to believe in your religion in the first place, and you may well come up with the answer (many freshmen do) that you were "conditioned" by your parents and by society in general. Consequently, you may, perhaps for a time, perhaps for a lifetime, question or reject the ideas you had once "naturally" accepted. Or you may reaffirm your faith with new commitment, determined that, whatever the source, your beliefs are right or, at least, right for you. But after further consideration and argument, perhaps with some new religious experience, you come to see both sides of the arguments. For the first time, you can weigh their merits and demerits against each other without defensively holding onto one and attacking the other. You may remain a believer; you may become an atheist or an agnostic (a person who admits not knowing whether there is a God or not). Some people convert to another faith. Or one can adopt a position in which he or she gives all religions (and nonreligion) equal weight, continuing to believe but not insisting that one belief is the only correct one or that a person is necessarily superior because of it. But whatever you decide, your position will no longer be naive and unthinking. You know the arguments, both for and against. You know how to defend yourself. And, most importantly, you have confidence that your position is secure, that you have considered its objections, and that you have mastered its strengths. So it is with all philosophical problems and positions. Philosophy does not pull us away from our lives; it clarifies them. It secures them on intellectual ground in place of the fragile supports provided by inherited prejudices, fragments of parental advice, and mindless slogans borrowed from television commercials.

"Philosophy" sounds like a new and mysterious discipline, unlike anything you have ever encountered. But the basic ideas of philosophy are familiar to all of us, even if we have not yet formally confronted the problems. In this sense, we are all philosophers already. Watch yourself in a crisis, or listen to yourself in an argument with a friend. Notice how quickly abstract concepts like "freedom," "mankind," "self-identity," "nature" and "natural," "relative," "reality," "illusion," and "truth" enter our thoughts and our conversations. Notice how certain basic philosophical principles—whether conservative or radical, pragmatic or idealistic, confident or skeptical, pedestrian or heroic—enter into our arguments and our thinking as well as our actions. We all have some opinions about God, about morality and its principles, about the nature of man and the nature of the universe. But because we haven't questioned them, they are merely the **assumptions** of our thinking. We believe many things without having thought about them, merely assuming them, sometimes without evidence or good reasons. What the study of philosophy does for us is to make our ideas explicit, to give us the means of defending our presuppositions, and to make alternative suppositions available to us as well. Where once we merely assumed a point of view, passively and for lack of alternatives, we now can argue for it with confidence, knowing that our acceptance is active and critical, systematic rather than merely a collection of borrowed beliefs (who knows from where). To be **critical** means to examine carefully and cautiously, willing, if necessary, to change one's own beliefs. It does not need to be nasty or destructive. There is "constructive criticism" as well. And to "argue" does not mean to "have a fight"; an **argument** may simply be the justification of our beliefs.

So what is philosophy? Literally, from the Greek (*philein, sophia*), it is "the love of wisdom."[6] It is an attitude of critical and systematic thoughtfulness rather than a particular subject matter. This makes matters very difficult for the beginner, who would like a definition of philosophy of the same kind received when he or she began biology, as "the study of living organisms." But the nature of philosophy is itself among the most bitter disputes in philosophy. Many philosophers say that it is a science, in fact, the "queen of the sciences," the womb in which physics, chemistry, mathematics, astronomy, biology, and psychology began their development before being born into their own distinguished worlds and separate university departments. Historically, this is certainly true. (Thus, in almost any scientific field, the highest degree is "doctor of philosophy" ["Ph.D."].) Insofar as one says that philosophy is

---

[6]The word was invented by Pythagoras (whom we shall meet in Chapter 1). When he was asked if he was already a wise man, he answered, "No, I am not wise, but I am a *lover* of wisdom."

the road to reality and that the goal of philosophy is truth, that would seem to make it the ultimate science as well.

But it has also been argued, as far back as Socrates, that the main business of philosophy is a matter of definitions—finding clear meanings for such important ideas as truth, justice, wisdom, knowledge, and happiness. Accordingly, many philosophers have taken advantage of the increasingly sophisticated tools of logic and linguistics in their attempts to find such definitions. Other philosophers, however, would insist that philosophy is rather closer to morality and religion, its purpose to give meaning to our lives and lead us down "the right path" to "the good life." Still others insist that philosophy is an art, the art of criticism and argumentation as well as the art of conceptual system building or, perhaps, the art of creating comprehensive and edifying visions, dazzling metaphors, new ways of thinking. So considered, philosophy may be akin to storytelling or mythology. Some philosophers place strong emphasis upon proof and argument; others place their trust in intuition and insight. Some philosophers reduce all philosophizing to the study of experience; other philosophers take it as a matter of principle not to trust experience. Also, some philosophers insist on being practical, in fact, insist that there are no other considerations but practicality; and then there are others who insist on the purity of the life of ideas, divorced from any practical considerations. But philosophy cannot, without distortion, be reduced to any one of these preferences. All enter into that constantly redefined critical and creative life of ideas that Socrates was willing to die for. In fact, Socrates himself insisted that it is the *seeking* of wisdom that is the essence of philosophy and that anyone who is sure that he or she has wisdom already is undoubtedly wrong. In *The Apology,* for example, he makes this famous disclaimer:

FROM *THE APOLOGY*
BY **PLATO**

The effect of these investigations of mine, gentlemen, has been to arouse against me a great deal of hostility, and hostility of a particularly bitter and persistent kind, which has resulted in various malicious suggestions, including the description of me as a professor of wisdom. This is due to the fact that whenever I succeed in disproving another person's claim to wisdom in a given subject, the bystanders assume that I know everything about that subject myself. But the truth of the matter, gentlemen, is pretty certainly this: that real wisdom is the property of God, and this oracle is his way of telling us that human wisdom has little or no value. It seems to me that he is not referring literally to Socrates, but has merely taken my name as an example, as if he would say to us "The wisest of you men is he who has realized, like Socrates, that in respect of wisdom he is really worthless."

That is why I still go about seeking and searching in obedience to the divine command, if I think that anyone is wise, whether citizen or stranger; and when I think that any person is not wise, I try to help the cause of God by proving that he is not. This occupation has kept me too busy to do much either in politics or in my own affairs; in fact, my service to God has reduced me to extreme poverty.[7]

Here is the true start of Western philosophy. But in Chinese philosophy, too, we find a similar message in the *Tao Te Ching:*

FROM *TAO TE CHING*
BY **LAO TSU**

My mind is that of a fool—how blank and how muddled. Vulgar people have clear ideas. They see clear-cut distinctions. I alone make no distinctions. They all have a purpose. I drift like a high wind and the ocean. They are alert and smart. I am uncouth and rustic.

> *The highest good is like water. Water is good; it benefits all things and does not compete with them.*

The highest good is like water. Water is good; it benefits all things and does not compete with them. It dwells in lowly places that all disdain. This is why it is so near to the Way.

◆◆◆

The best rulers are those with a shadowy presence to the people. Next comes the ruler they love and praise. Next comes one they fear. The next are those they despise.

Therefore the sage says: I take no action and the people of themselves are transformed. I engage in no activities and the people of themselves become prosperous.

Act without action. Do without ado.

Therefore the sage never strives for the great.

Such language may sound odd to the American reader—the idea of a wise ruler who does not (and should not) rule, the ideal of inaction ("act without action, do without ado"), the comparison of "the highest good" and lowly water—but you may well be able to think of analogs that are part of the Western tradition as well, for example, in the sports or artistic experience of doing things so "naturally" that it seems as if one is not really "doing" them, that is, putting an effort into them, at all. The comparison of "the highest good" and the lowly has often appeared in Western philosophy and religion in the guise of "the simple life" or what is often called **asceticism.** But, most of all, the comparison at stake here is a shared emphasis on humility, on the importance of the process of philosophy as well as its ultimate goals and products, the attainment of wisdom. For both Socrates and **Lao Tsu** (the reputed author of the *Tao*

---

[7] Plato, *The Last Days of Socrates,* trans. Hugh Tredennick (Harmondsworth, Middlesex: Penguin, 1954).

Te Ching), the important thing is beginning with a sense of your own inadequacies and ignorance, realizing how much you *do not* know, looking at the world, your life, and yourself with a sense of awe and mystery. *That* and the activity it engenders, is philosophy.

C. A MODERN APPROACH
TO PHILOSOPHY

The orientation to philosophy in this book is, inevitably, essentially a modern Western approach in which criticism plays a predominant role. Historically, modern European philosophy has its origins in the rise of science and technology. (As we shall see, philosophy and science both emerged in ancient Greece and Asia Minor and, about the same time, in South and East Asia.) We should understand science, however, not just as a particular discipline or subject matter, but rather as a state of mind, a way of looking at the world. In the European tradition, this means that the world is understandable and every event in the world is explainable. It sees the universe as *rational*—operating according to universal laws. And it sees the human mind as rational too—in the sense that it can grasp and formulate these laws for itself. European philosophy and science also put enormous emphasis on the mind of the individual.

Though science is essentially a team effort, requiring the labor and thinking of thousands of men and women, the great breakthroughs in science have often been the insights of one man or woman alone. The most famous modern example of this individual genius is the British philosopher-scientist **Isaac Newton.** In the eyes of his contemporaries and followers, he single-mindedly mastered the laws of the universe, while sitting (so the story goes) under an apple tree. The ideal of modern Western philosophy is, in a phrase, *thinking for yourself.* That is, philosophy is thinking for yourself about basic questions—about life, knowledge, religion, and what to do with yourself. It is *using* the rationality built into your brain to comprehend the rationality (or lack of it) in the world around you. In some cultures, however, the emphasis lies on the group or community, and thinking for yourself is not as important as maintaining group harmony and cohesiveness. In India and China, for example, it is the elusiveness of scientific knowledge that defines much of philosophy. In many of these traditions enlightenment rather than scientific knowledge is the main goal of philosophy. It is important to keep this difference in mind.

In much of Western tradition, the central demand of modern philosophy is *the autonomy of the individual person.* This means that each of us must be credited with the ability to ascertain what is true and what is right, through our own thinking and experience, without just depending upon outside authority: parents, teachers, popes, kings, or a majority of peers. This does not mean that you should not listen to or, where appropriate, obey other people. But what it means is that whether you believe in God must be decided by you, by appeal to your own reason and arguments that you can formulate and examine by yourself. Whether you accept a scientific theory, a doctor's diagnosis, a newspaper's version of the news, or the legitimacy of a new law are also matters to be decided by you on the basis of evidence, your evaluation of the testimony or authority of others, principles that you can accept, and arguments that you acknowledge as valid. This stress on individual autonomy stands at the very foundation of contemporary Western thought. We might say that it is our most basic assumption. (Accordingly, we shall have to examine it as well; but the obvious place to begin is to assume that we are—each of us—capable of carrying out the reflection and criticism that philosophy demands of us.)

Historically, the position of individual autonomy can be found most famously in Socrates, who went against the popular opinions of his day and, consequently, sacrificed his life for the "Laws" and principles he believed to be right. It also appears in many medieval philosophers, some of whom also faced grave danger in their partial rejection or questioning of the authority of the Church. It can also be found in those philosophers who, like the **Buddha**, struck out from established society to find a new way. The stress on individual autonomy comes to dominate Western thinking in that intellectually brilliant period of history called the **Enlightenment** (sometimes called "the Age of Reason"), which began in the late seventeenth century and continued through the French Revolution (1789). It appeared in different countries with varying speed and intensity, but ultimately it influenced the thinking of Europe, from England and France to Spain and Russia, and became the ideology of young America, which used Enlightenment doctrines in the formulation of a "Declaration of Independence," a war for its own autonomy, and a new government established on Enlightenment principles. Those principles were, whatever the variations from one country or party to another, the autonomy of the individual and each person's right to choose and to speak his [8] own religious, political, moral, and philosophical beliefs, to "pursue happiness" in his own way, and to lead the life that he, as a reasonable person, sees as right.

If these principles have often been abused, creating confusion and sometimes anarchy and encouraging ruthlessness in politics and strife in a mixed society, they are principles that can be challenged only with great difficulty and a sense of imminent danger. Once the individual's right or ability to decide such matters for himself or herself is denied, who shall decide? Society no longer agrees on any single unambiguous set of instructions from the Scriptures. Those in power are no longer trusted. We are rightfully suspicious of those who attack the individual, because it is not clear what else they have in mind. Whatever the abuses, and whatever political, social, or economic systems might be required to support it, philosophical autonomy is the starting point. Even in the most authority-minded societies, autonomy and the ability to think beyond prescribed limits, remain essential. (Think of the students in Tiananmen Square.)

The metaphor of enlightenment is common to many cultures. The comparison of clear thinking with illumination is to be found in ancient, Christian, and Eastern

---

[8] Not, at that point in history, *hers* as well. The concept of a woman's autonomy and right to choose is a late nineteenth-century idea that has only recently become accepted.

thought as well as in comic-book symbolism and modern philosophy. The seventeenth-century French philosopher **René Descartes** (1596–1650) was one of the founders of the Enlightenment, and he was particularly fond of the "illumination" metaphor. He is generally recognized as the father of modern philosophy. Like Socrates two thousand years before him, Descartes believed that each person was capable of ascertaining what beliefs were true and what actions were right. But whereas Socrates searched for the truth through dialogue and discussion, Descartes searched in the solitude of his own thinking. With considerable risk to his safety, he challenged the authority of the French government and the Catholic Church. He insisted that he would accept as true only those ideas that were demonstrably true to him. Against what he considered were obscure teachings of the Church and often opaque commands of his government, Descartes insisted upon "clear and distinct ideas" and arguments based upon "the light of reason." The modern philosophy of individual autonomy began with Descartes. As a matter of fact, his results were quite conservative. He retained much of his medieval teachings: he continued to believe in God and the Church, and he made it his first "moral maxim" to "obey the laws and customs of my country." His challenge to authority was rather his method, which signified one of the greatest revolutions in Western thought. From Descartes on, the ultimate authority was to be found in man's own thinking and experience, nowhere else.

None of this is meant to deny authority as such. Appeals are still made to authority, but authorities are never to be taken as absolutes. For example, none of us would particularly like to go out and establish on our own the figures of the 1990 census of the U. S. population. But it is up to the individual whether or not to accept the official "authoritative" figures, to question, if necessary, the integrity or motivation of the authorities, and to appeal, if necessary, to alternative sources of information.

For anyone beginning to study philosophy today, Descartes is a pivotal figure. His method is both easy to follow and very much in accord with our own independent temperaments. Descartes proceeded by means of logical arguments, giving his readers a long monologue of presentations and proofs of his philosophical doubts and beliefs. Like Socrates before him, Descartes used his philosophy to cut through the clouds of prejudice and unreliable opinions. He was concerned with their truth, no matter how many people already believed them—or, how few. Descartes' arguments were his tools for finding this truth and distinguishing it from falsehood and mere opinion.

Philosophy has always been concerned with truth and mankind's knowledge of reality. Not coincidentally, Descartes' new philosophy developed in the age of Galileo and the rise of modern science. In ancient Greece, the origins of philosophy and the birth of Greek science were one and the same. The truth, however, is not always what most people believe at any given time. (Most people once believed that the earth was flat and stationary, for example.) But, at the same time that they simply refuse to accept "common sense," philosophers try not to say things that common sense finds absurd. For example, a philosopher who denied that anyone existed besides himself would clearly be absurd. So too, the philosopher who argued that he knew that nobody ever knows anything. Nevertheless, philosophers often take such claims very seriously, if only to refute them and show us *why* they are absurd.

Accordingly, two of the most important challenges in the philosopher's search for truth are (1) skepticism and (2) paradox. In **skepticism,** the philosopher finds himself or herself unable to justify what every sane person knows to be the case; for example, that we are not merely dreaming all of the time. In Eastern as well as Western philosophy, skepticism has provided a valuable probe for our everyday presumptions of knowledge, and it sometimes becomes a philosophy in its own right. In a **paradox,** an absurd conclusion seems to result from perfectly acceptable ways of thinking. For example, there is the familiar paradox of **Epimenides the Cretan,** who claimed that "all Cretans are liars." (That sounds reasonable enough.) But if what he said was true, then he was lying and what he said, accordingly, was false. But how can the same statement be both true and false? What Epimenides said was true only if it was false at the same time. That is a paradox, and whenever a philosophical argument ends in paradox we can be sure that something has gone wrong. Again, in both East and West, philosophers have always been intrigued by paradoxes and have often been prompted by them to strike out in bold new directions in search of a resolution.

Skepticism begins with *doubt.* The philosopher considers the possibility that something that everyone believes is possibly mistaken. Some doubt is a healthy sign of intellectual autonomy, but excessive doubting becomes skepticism, which is no longer healthy. It has its obvious dangers: if you doubt whether you are ever awake or not, you might well do things that wouldn't have serious consequences in a dream but would be fatal in real life (jumping out of a plane, for example). Philosophers who have doubts about the most ordinary and seemingly unquestionable beliefs are called *skeptics.* For example, there was the Chinese philosopher who, when he once dreamed that he was a butterfly, started wondering whether he really were a butterfly—dreaming that he was a philosopher. But however challenging skeptics may be as philosophers, in practice their skepticism is impossible. Accordingly, one of the main drives in philosophy has been to refute the skeptic and return philosophy to common sense (to prove, for example, that we are *not* dreaming all of the time). Opposed to skepticism is an ancient philosophical ideal, the ideal of **certainty,** the ability to prove beyond a doubt that what we believe is true. Socrates and Descartes, in their very different ways, tried to provide precisely this certainty for the most important beliefs, and thus refute the skeptics of their own times.

In Western philosophy, the precision of mathematics has long served as an ideal of knowledge. In mathematics, we believe, we can be *certain.* For Descartes, certainty is the **criterion,** that is, the test according to which beliefs are to be evaluated. But do we ever find such certainty? It seems that we do, at least in one discipline Descartes suggested—mathematics. Who can doubt that two plus two equals four or that the interior angles of a triangle total 180 degrees? Using mathematics as his model, Descartes (and many generations of philosophers following him) attempted to apply a similar method in philosophy. First, he had to find, as in Euclidean geometry, a small set of "first principles" or **axioms** that were obvious or **self-evident.** They had to be assumed without proof or be so fundamental that they seemed not to allow any proof. These would serve as premises or starting points for the *arguments* that would take a person from the self-evident axioms to other principles that might not be self-evident at all. But if they could be deduced from other principles that were already certain, like the theorems of geometry, then they would share the certainty of the principles from which they have been derived.

Descartes was a scientist and a mathematician as well as a philosopher. With that in mind, we can understand his *Discourse on Method.* Descartes set out four basic rules that would define philosophy for many years:

The first of [my rules] was to accept . . . nothing more than what was presented to my mind so clearly and distinctly that I could have no occasion to doubt it.

FROM *DISCOURSE ON METHOD*
BY **RENÉ DESCARTES**

The first of these was to accept nothing as true which I did not clearly recognise to be so; that is to say, carefully to avoid precipitation and prejudice in judgments, and to accept in them nothing more than what was presented to my mind so clearly and distinctly that I could have no occasion to doubt it.

The second was to divide up each of the difficulties which I examined into as many parts as possible, and as seemed requisite in order that it might be resolved in the best manner possible.

The third was to carry on my reflections in due order, commencing with objects that were the most simple and easy to understand, in order to rise little by little, or by degrees, to knowledge of the most complex, assuming an order, even if a fictitious one, among those which do not follow a natural sequence relatively to one another.

The last was in all cases to make enumerations so complete and reviews so general that I should be certain of having omitted nothing.[9]

One might say that the essence of these rules is to be cautious and to think for oneself. The premises, upon which all else depends, must be utterly beyond doubt, "perfectly certain," otherwise all else is futile. The test or criterion of such a premise is that it be "a clear and distinct idea," self-evident, and "springing from the light of reason alone."

We shall see much more of Descartes in the following chapters. In Chapter 3, we shall see that Descartes' technique for assuring the certainty of his premises will be what he called the method of doubt (or *methodological doubt*). In order to make sure that he did not accept any principle too quickly ("too precipitously") before being convinced of its "perfect certainty," he resolved to doubt every belief until he could prove it true beyond question, and to show that the very act of doubting this belief

---

[9]René Descartes, *Discourse on Method,* in *The Philosophical Works of Descartes,* trans. Elizabeth S. Haldane and G. R. T. Ross (Cambridge: Cambridge University Press, 1911).

led to an intolerable paradox. The point of this kind of argument is not to become a skeptic, but, quite the contrary, to find those premises that even the skeptic cannot doubt. From those premises, Descartes and many generations of philosophers following him have attempted and will attempt to prove that we do indeed know what we think we know. Like Socrates, Descartes begins by questioning what no one but a philosopher would doubt and ends up changing the way we think about ourselves and our knowledge for several centuries. In other cultures too, entire societies have been dramatically altered by philosophers who challenged what seemed to be obvious; sometimes they challenged reality itself.

D. A BRIEF INTRODUCTION TO LOGIC

Descartes' strategy, and the technique of many philosophers, is to present arguments for what they believe. In Plato's *Crito,* Socrates and Crito offer arguments for their views, and Socrates wins because his arguments are better. An argument is a verbal attempt to get other people to accept a belief or opinion by providing reasons why they should accept it. We usually think of an argument as a confrontation between two people. When they try to convince each other, they usually resort to certain verbal means and it is with these means that a philosopher is concerned. Of course, there are other ways of getting people to agree with you—tricks, bribes, brainwashing, and threats of physical force. But the use of arguments is the most durable and trustworthy, as well as the most respectable, way of getting others to agree. Freedom of speech is the cornerstone of democracy (and the bane of totalitarianism) just because of our faith in the ability of arguments to determine the best among competing opinions. On the other hand, one should not think of an argument as a political weapon whose purpose is to shut down conversation or put other people and their opinions on the defensive. It is always reasonable to ask for arguments, but it may not be reasonable to push a person for arguments that he or she cannot provide. To fail to argue for a position is not necessarily to give up on it, and to refute the arguments for a position is not necessarily to reject the position.

You don't have to be arguing with anyone in particular in order to construct an argument. Editorials in newspapers, for example, argue for a position, but not necessarily against anyone. But whether your argument is a letter to a magazine, in which you are trying to convince the entire American population of your views, or a personal letter, in which you are trying to convince a friend not to do something foolhardy, the main point of argument is to demonstrate or establish a point of view. A scientist describing an experiment tries to demonstrate to other scientists the truth of his or her theory. A politician tries to demonstrate to his or her constituency the need for higher taxes. A philosopher tries to demonstrate to us the value of a certain view of life, a certain view of reality, a certain view of ourselves. In each case, these people try to give as many reasons as possible why other people should accept their view of things; in short, they use arguments to persuade others.

Argument involves at least two components: **logic** and **rhetoric.** Logic concerns those reasons that should hold for anyone, anywhere, without appealing to personal feelings, sympathies, or prejudices. Rhetoric, on the other hand, does involve such personal appeals. Personal charm may be part of rhetoric, in a writer as well as in a public speaker. Jokes may be part of rhetoric. Personal pleas are effective rhetorical tools; so is trying to be sympathetic to readers or playing off their fears. None of these personal tactics are part of logic, however. Logic is impersonal, and for this reason logic may be less flamboyant and personally exciting; but it has the advantage of being applicable to everyone. A logical argument goes beyond rhetorical appeal. But it is important to understand that logic and rhetoric virtually always function together. Although it is possible to be persuasive through pure rhetoric without being at all logical, such efforts often disappear as soon as readers have had a chance to think again about how they have been persuaded. One can also be logical without attention to rhetoric, but such arguments will be dry and unattractive, even if they do convince anyone who would take the time to read them. However, logic and rhetoric in combination can be very persuasive and are rarely separable in any great work of philosophy. In all of the readings of this book, you will notice the combination of impersonal logic and personal appeal, all aimed at getting the reader to agree with the author's point of view.

There are good arguments and there are bad arguments. Just as the success of a logically inadequate argument may depend upon the passing mood of a reader or the fact that he or she has not yet heard the other side, so a good argument must survive passing moods, reflection, and criticism. This requires good logic as well as effective rhetoric, and so it is important to master the basic rules of argument, as well as to be aware of the all too common pitfalls that lie in wait for those who ignore the rules. Knowing these rules and warnings will not only help you avoid what are called **fallacies**—it will allow you to criticize effectively other people's arguments as well. Have you ever heard someone say, "Well, there's something wrong with that argument, but I'm not sure what it is"? Knowing a little logic may help you see clearly what is wrong with an argument.

Standard logic textbooks emphasize two primary forms of logical argument:

1. **Deductive arguments** reason from one statement to another by means of accepted logical rules; anyone who accepts the premises is bound logically to accept the conclusion.
2. **Inductive arguments** infer one statement from another, but it is possible for the conclusion to be false even if all of the premises are true. The most familiar example of an inductive argument is a **generalization** from a set of particular observations to a general statement called a "hypothesis."

1. Deductive Arguments

A deductive argument is **valid** when it correctly conforms to the rules of deduction. The following are some examples of the most familiar rules:

1. It was either Phyllis or Fred. (It was Phyllis *or* it was Fred.)
   It wasn't Phyllis.
   Therefore it was Fred.

2. Both Tom and Jerry went to the circus last night. (Tom went to the circus last night *and* Jerry went to the circus last night.)
   Therefore Tom went to the circus last night.
3. *If* Carol did that all by herself, *then* she's courageous.
   Carol did it all by herself.
   Therefore Carol is courageous.

It is important to emphasize that whether or not an argument is valid depends only on the form of the argument. A valid argument—one in the correct form—can still have a conclusion that is false. Consider this:

4. If Carol did that all by herself, then elephants can fly.
   Carol did it all by herself.
   Therefore elephants can fly.

Notice that example 4 is identical in form to example 3. The conclusion is patently false, but the argument is still valid.

But what good is a deductive argument if its conclusion can be false? The answer is that if the initial statements are true, then the truth of the conclusion is guaranteed. The initial statements are called **premises,** and if the premises are true, then the conclusion must be true if the argument form is valid. It is important to remember that a deductive argument cannot prove its own premises. To be effective, you must be sure of the premises before beginning the deductive argument. Thus the following argument, although it is valid, is an appallingly bad argument.

5. If someone argues for socialized medicine, then he or she is a communist.
   Communists want to kill people.
   Therefore if someone is for socialized medicine, he or she wants to kill people.

This argument has the valid form:

5′. If p then q.
    If q then r.
    Therefore if p then r.

But although the argument is valid, its premises are not true, and therefore they provide no guarantee that the conclusion is true. A valid argument guarantees the truth of the conclusion only if the premises are true. Therefore, in using or evaluating any deductive argument, you must always ask yourself two things:

   a. Are the premises true?
   b. Is the argument valid?

If the answer to both of these is yes, then the argument is said to be **sound.**

An argument in an essay may not appear exactly in the form provided by the rules of deduction. This does not mean that the argument is invalid. In example 5, the second premise, "Communists want to kill people," must be restated in "If . . . then . . ." form. In fact, straightforward copying of the rules of deduction in an essay makes boring reading, so arguments usually must be restated in order to fit these forms exactly. When you are writing an argument, it is necessary to pay attention both to the validity of the argument and to the degree of interest with which it is stated. Sometimes it is permissible to leave out one of the premises, if it is so obvious to every reader that actually stating it would seem absurd. For example,

6. Men can't give birth.
   Therefore Robert can't give birth.

The missing premise, of course, is

Robert is a man.

But it would be unnecessary in most contexts to say this. When using deductive arguments effectively, rhetorical considerations are important too.

One of the best-known forms of deductive reasoning is called the **syllogism.** It refers to one kind in particular: deductive arguments, with two premises and a conclusion, usually involving membership in groups, and using the terms *all, some,* and *none.* The best-known example is

7. All men are mortal.
   Socrates is a man.
   Therefore Socrates is mortal.

The first statement, "All men are mortal," is called the *major premise;* the second statement, "Socrates is a man," is called the *minor premise.* The final statement, following from the other two, is the *conclusion* and is generally preceded by the word "therefore." In this example, the words "men" and "man" are called the *middle term,* the word "mortal" is called the *predicate,* and the name "Socrates" is called the *subject.* The middle term serves to link the subject and the predicate, both of which are joined in the conclusion. The form of this syllogism is

7′. All A's are B's.
    C is an A.
    Therefore C is a B.

Any nouns can be substituted for the A, B, and C in this deductive form. For example,

8. All cows are pigeons.
   George Washington is a cow.
   Therefore George Washington is a pigeon.

Argument 8 is valid, although its conclusion is false. The reason, of course, is that the premises are false. Again, a valid argument does not guarantee a true conclusion unless the premises are true. So always be certain that you have adequately defended the premises before beginning your deduction.

Valid arguments sometimes proceed from negative premises as well as positive assertions. For example,

9. No woman has ever been president.
   Eleanor Roosevelt was a woman.
   Therefore Eleanor Roosevelt was not president.

The form is

9'. No A's are B's.
    C is an A.
    Therefore C is not a B.

Another common argument is

10. Some elephants weigh more than two thousand pounds.
    Elephants are animals.
    Therefore some animals weigh more than two thousand pounds.

The form, with a little rephrasing, is

10'. Some A's are B's. (Some elephants are more than two thousand pounds in
     weight.)
     All A's are C's. (All elephants are animals. The "all" is implicit.)
     Therefore, some C's are B's. (Some animals are more than two thousand
     pounds in weight.)

Not all deductive arguments are syllogisms in this traditional sense. For example, the following is a valid deductive argument, but not a syllogism:

11. Jones is an idiot, and he (Jones) is also the luckiest man alive.
    Therefore Jones is an idiot.

The form of this argument is

11'. p and q.
     Therefore p.

In the discussion that follows, therefore, we will talk about deductive arguments in general and not worry whether they are properly to be called "syllogisms" or not.

It is impossible in this introduction to list all of the correct forms of deduction. We will, however, describe some of the most dangerous *fallacies,* mistakes in deductive form. The following example is one, for it looks dangerously like example 10':

12. Some elephants are domesticated.
    Some camels are domesticated.
    Therefore some elephants are camels.

This form

12'. Some A's are B's.
     Some C's are B's.
     Therefore some A's are C's.

is **invalid** (not valid), and is thus a fallacy. This fallacy often appears in political arguments. For example,

13. We all know that some influential Republicans are corrupt.
    And we all know that at least some Communists are corrupt.
    Therefore we know that at least some Republicans are Communists.

When stated so simply, the fallacy is obvious. But when this argument is spread through a long-winded speech, such fallacies are often accepted as valid arguments. Using the logician's symbolic forms to analyze a complex speech or essay will often make clear the validity or invalidity of an argument.

Another common fallacy closely resembles the deductive form in example 3:

14. If this antidote works then the patient will live.
    The patient lived.
    Therefore the antidote works.

This looks valid at first glance, but it is not. The patient may have recovered on his or her own, proving nothing about the antidote. The form of this argument is

14′. If p then q.
    q.
    Therefore p.

The correct deductive form of example 3 was

If p then q.
p.
Therefore q.

Be particularly careful of the difference between these two.

"If . . . then . . ." statements are often used in another pair of arguments, one valid, one invalid. The valid one is

15. If this antidote works then the patient will live.
    The patient didn't live.
    Therefore the antidote did not work.

The form is

15′. If p then q.
    Not q.
    Therefore not p.

This is valid, although one might insist on adding an explicit qualification to the first premise. The qualification is, "for nothing else whatever can save the patient," since one might argue that something else, perhaps a miracle, might save the patient rather than the antidote. Notice that this qualification doesn't save the invalid argument in example 14, however, nor does it save the invalid argument in the following example:

16. If this antidote doesn't work, then the patient will die.
The antidote works.
Therefore the patient won't die.

Again, the patient might very well die of other causes, despite the antidote. The form

16'. If p then q.
Not p.
Therefore not q.

is invalid.

Most valid and invalid deductive argument forms are a matter of common sense. What makes fallacies so common is not ignorance of logic so often as sloppy thinking or writing, or talking faster than one can organize thoughts in valid form. Most important, therefore, are careful thinking and writing. Yet even the greatest philosophers commit fallacies, and you will see some of them.

2. Inductive Arguments

In deduction, the conclusion never states more than the premises. (It is often said that the conclusion is already "contained in" the premises.) In an inductive argument, the conclusion *always* states more than the premises. It is, therefore, a less certain form of argument, but that does not mean that it is any less important. Many of the premises in deductive arguments will come from inductive ones, and most of our knowledge and almost all of science depends upon induction. Induction takes various forms and defies rigid characterization. One general form of an inductive argument is

Every A we have observed is a B.
Therefore A is a B.

The argument, in other words, is from an observed set of things to an entire class of things. For example

17. Every crow we have observed in the past twenty years is black.
Therefore all crows are black.

But induction, unlike deduction, does not guarantee the truth of the conclusion, even if we know that the observations are all correct. So the conclusion of example 17 should properly read

It is probable that all crows are black.

This tentative conclusion is called a **hypothesis.** A hypothesis is an educated guess on the basis of the evidence collected thus far. It is always possible, when we are using induction, that a new piece of evidence will turn up that will refute the hypothesis. This new piece of evidence is called a **counter-example.** Inductive arguments must always be ready for such counter-examples; it must be admitted that no inductive argument guarantees certainty. There is always the possibility that a counter-example will be found, or that a better hypothesis will be formulated. This is not to say, however, that we should not accept such arguments. Human beings have observed millions of rabbits, and never has a rabbit weighed more than two thousand pounds. This does not mean that it is impossible to find a two-thousand-pound rabbit, but neither does it mean that we should therefore hesitate to believe that no rabbits weigh more than two thousand pounds. Induction is never certain, but, on the basis of the evidence, we can nevertheless agree on the best hypothesis. It is worth noting, however, that some philosophers, following David Hume (see Chapter 2), have claimed that induction is without rational justification, no matter how undeniably useful it may be.

There are good (sound) and bad (**unsound**) inductive arguments. The most familiar reason why an inductive argument may be called unsound is generalization on the basis of too few examples. For instance, the following is clearly unsound:

18. Every U. S. president from the state of Pennsylvania has been a Democrat. Therefore we can suppose that every U. S. president from the state of Pennsylvania will be a Democrat.

There has only been one president from Pennsylvania, and the intricacies of politics are clearly such that the next president from Pennsylvania could as likely be a Republican as a Democrat. Similarly,

19. The driver of every Italian bus we rode had a beard. Therefore all Italian bus drivers have beards.

is unsound. Although the sampling involves more than one example, this is still not sufficient to make a sound inductive generalization. How many examples are required? It varies with the case. If a chemist, conducting an experiment, adds chemical g to chemical h and gets j, that in itself will probably warrant a hypothesis that

$$g + h \rightarrow j,$$

although this hypothesis, like all hypotheses, will have to be tested by further experiments and observations. (Deductions, on the contrary, do not have to be tested, assuming the truth of their premises.) A chemist can usually assume that one set of pure chemicals will react like any other set of the same chemicals. But when the hypothesis is about people, generalizations should be made with extreme caution, especially when writing about such a sensitive subject as "national character." For example, "Italians are . . . ," "Russians tend to be . . . ," "Americans are too . . ." require extreme care. But caution does not mean that it is impossible to write about such subjects. It has often been done brilliantly, and you might even agree that a person who refuses to see the general differences between different peoples and societies is even more foolish than someone who generalizes too quickly and carelessly. But all generalizations (even this one) must be made with care for the context and the subject matter.

A different kind of inductive unsoundness comes from generalizing to a hypothesis that goes too far beyond what the evidence will support. For example,

20. Every graduate we know of from Delmonico High School is an excellent athlete.
 Therefore we can suppose that the physical education teachers there must be very good.

The problem here is not too small a sampling; in fact, we might even look at *every* graduate of Delmonico High School. The problem is that this kind of evidence isn't sufficient to prove anything about the teachers. The students might come from athletic homes. Or the food in the student cafeteria might be loaded with extra vitamins and protein. Or the students may enjoy playing sports outside of school, even though their gym classes are badly taught. It is important to be sure that the hypothesis you defend is supported by the right kind of evidence. In this case, we need evidence about the physical education teachers, not just about the students.

Not every inductive argument proceeds from evidence to a generalization. For example, detectives use inductive arguments in moving from the evidence to the indictment of a particular individual. (What Sherlock Holmes refers to as his "powers of deduction" is in fact his remarkable ability with induction.) It is worth noting that not every philosopher thinks that induction is so important for knowledge. For example, the contemporary British philosopher **Karl Popper** believes that the logic of science (and police investigations) proceeds not by way of induction but by way of the *disconfirmation* of proposed hypotheses with counter-examples. In other words, knowledge proceeds from hypothesis to hypothesis, not from evidence to hypothesis by way of induction. But whatever one thinks of the justifiability of induction and its importance, it is essential not to think of induction as occurring in a vacuum. Inductive reasoning always goes on against a background of other hypotheses, theories, and scientific viewpoints as well as an abundance of other evidence that is taken for granted, built into the hypothesis itself or, perhaps, ignored as irrelevant, undependable, or unimportant. Because of its formality, deduction can deal with isolated arguments. But induction, even when subjected to the formal rigors of probability theory, can never be so understood out of context. Background conditions and the state of knowledge at the moment are always in some sense presupposed. Because of this informal (if not chaotic) complexity, induction is just as much a matter of insight as logic.

A very different kind of problem arises for induction when the hypothesis is *self-confirming*. A self-confirming hypothesis creates its own confirmation or, alternatively, blocks all possible counter-examples from the start. Two familiar examples: a policeman (in uniform) tries to evaluate the driving patterns of the cars that pass him, making sure that they all drive at the legal speed. Of course they do! But the same sort of self-confirmation often goes on in subtle ways in science, for example, where the equipment itself is designed to present precisely the evidence it is supposed to be looking for. The other example is the paranoid, who advances the hypothesis that "they're all out to get me." Given that way of looking at the world, indeed they are. Not only does the paranoid systematically interpret other people's behavior in a hostile way, he also behaves in such a way that people really do become wary of him, if not hostile to him. But again, this extreme case has thousands of more everyday instances; persons who feel friendless may easily work on a mild version of the paranoid hypothesis and confirm their own thesis. A person who entertains the hypothesis that "all people are basically selfish" will have little trouble finding what he or she is looking for, and, within that investigation, some selfish motive can always be found (for example, "in order not to feel guilty") for even the most generous and unselfish behavior. (We might note that there are also *self-defeating* hypotheses; the policeman may hypothesize that everyone breaks the law and goes out, in uniform, to catch them, thereby undermining his own hypothesis.)

3. Argument by Analogy

A form of inductive argument that is sometimes challenged unfairly is *argument by analogy*. An argument by analogy defends the similarity between some aspect of two things on the basis of their similarity in other respects. For example, a politician defends the need for more efficient government and fewer unnecessary jobs on the basis of an argument by analogy between government and business. A government is like a business, the politician argues. It has a certain product to turn out, namely, services to the people, and receives a certain income from the sale of that product, namely, taxes. It employs a certain number of people, whose job it is to turn out that product and who are paid with that income. Their business is to produce the product as cheaply but as well as possible, to keep the cost down, and make a profit in order to be able to offer new and better services. Thus, the politician argues, the more efficiently it is run and the fewer unnecessary employees it must support, the better a government will be.

Such an argument is valuable in getting people to see similarities and in clarifying complex and confusing issues. The danger, and the reason why many logicians reject arguments by analogy altogether, is that no two things are similar in every respect. (Otherwise, they would be the same.) And just because two things are similar in certain respects, it doesn't follow that they will be similar in others. But this objection is too strong. If two things are similar in several respects, it is at least plausible to suggest that they will be similar in others. For example, running the government is like running a business. Both involve managing an organization. Both require skill in handling money. The success of both depends on the quality of the products and services they produce. Therefore, the way to handle the city transportation problem, for instance, is to ask which plan will give the most service for the least money.

Arguments by analogy may employ both deductive and inductive arguments; insofar as A (government) is like B (a business) deductions appropriate in discussing A will be appropriate in discussing B as well. And if A and B are similar in so many ways, then it is inductively plausible that they will be similar in other ways as well. So arguments by analogy are at least a valuable form of reasoning, if not always a reliable form of proof. It is important, however, to pay careful attention to each particular analogy, to make sure that the two things compared are significantly similar and, most importantly, that the aspect that is argued about is significantly similar in both cases. Arguments by analogy are extremely valuable, but they must always be used with care. In traditional Western philosophy, analogies and metaphors play an enormous but often unappreciated role in the great philosophical classics. The assumption, or at least the expectation, is that these analogies and metaphors can be recast in terms of deductive and inductive arguments. But not all philosophical traditions make this assumption. In Chinese philosophy, for example, analogical reasoning is far more central to philosophical disputation than deductive arguments. What the philosopher does, in certain traditions, is to provide new ways of seeing things—a particular virtue of arguments by analogy. So, too, in many folk philosophies around the world, the use of myth and metaphor has not yet been replaced—and probably cannot be replaced—by the standard logics of Western reasoning. The place of logic itself can be an important philosophical problem.

The three kinds of arguments discussed above—deductive, inductive, and argument by analogy—attempt to defend a view or an opinion. But part of almost every argument is an attack on alternative views and opinions. In general, someone else's position can be attacked by asking the following questions:

a. What is he or she arguing? Is the position clear?

b. What are the arguments? Are they deductive? Inductive? Or by analogy?
    If deductive:
        What are the premises and are they all true?
        Are the deductive arguments valid?
If the answer to either of these questions is no, a good counter-argument exists to show that the adversary has not given us a reason for accepting his or her view.
    If inductive:
        Is there enough evidence to support the hypothesis?
        Does the evidence support the hypothesis?
        Is the hypothesis sufficiently clear?
        Is this the best hypothesis to explain the evidence?
If the answer to any of these is no, a good counter-argument exists to show that the adversary has not defended his or her general claim.
    If argument by analogy:
        Are the things compared similar?
        Are the things similar in the relevant respects in question?
If the answer to either of these is no, a good argument exists to show that the opponent's analogy is not a good one.

c. Does the conclusion mean what the opponent says it means?

4. Argument by Counter-Example

Whenever anyone makes a general claim, it is possible to attack with an example that seems to go against the claim. This is a *counter-example*. We mentioned counter-examples with respect to inductive generalizations. A counter-example that refutes an hypothesis, such as "here is an *a* that is not *b*," will always give trouble to someone who argues that "all *a*'s are *b*'s." For example, if a bigot says, "All people from

Poland are naturally unintelligent," the single counter-example of Copernicus, a Pole, is sufficient to undermine that claim. Counter-examples may also work in the face of deductively defended claims, however. Consider a common philosophical argument (which we shall discuss in Chapter 9):

21. All events in nature are determined by physical forces (gravity, chemistry, electromagnetic forces, and so on).
All human actions are events in nature.
Therefore all human actions are determined by physical forces.

This syllogism is a valid argument, of the form

21'. All A's are B's.
All C's are A's.
Therefore all C's are B's.

One way to attack this valid argument, even if you don't see any reasons to reject the premises as such, is to use the method of counter-examples: "Look. I decided to come to this college of my own free will. I thought about it for a few days, and I remember the exact moment when I made my decision—while eating pizza at Harry's restaurant. Now I made that decision. It wasn't caused in me by physical forces. Therefore, I reject your conclusion."

What has happened here is this: On the one hand, if we accept the premises as true and the argument as valid, it would seem that we have to accept the conclusion. But what the counter-example does in this case is force the person who has argued the syllogism to clarify what is meant by "determined by physical forces" in both the premise and the conclusion. Does this mean only that *some* forces must be present? If so, the argument is not nearly so interesting as we thought, for everyone will admit that when a person makes a decision there is an electrical charge or a chemical change in the brain. Does it mean rather that there are *only* physical causes present, in which case "free will" is indeed excluded? But what then of the counter-example (your college decision)? The burden of proof is on the person who argued the syllogism; he or she is forced to explain how it seems that you made a decision of your own free will when in fact there is no such thing as free will. You can see how this philosophical argument could become very complicated, but we only want to make a simple point. A single, well-placed counter-example can open up a whole new discussion, even when it might seem as if the matter had already been settled.

A general comment is necessary here. It might seem to you as if arguments are conclusive, one way or the other. In fact, this is almost never the case. An argument can be convincing and persuasive, but there is always room for further argument if someone is stubborn or persistent enough. A good counter-example can always be explained away, and even a large number of counter-examples might be explained away. What ultimately sinks a bad hypothesis or general claim is the weight of the extra explanations it needs. For example, someone argues that there are Martians currently living on the earth. You point out that no one has ever seen a Martian. Your opponent explains this away by suggesting that the Martians are invisible to the human eye. You argue that the atmosphere on Earth would not support Martian life. Your opponent argues that they are a different form of life, different from any that we can understand. You ask your opponent what these Martians do and how we might come to test his or her view. He or she says that the Martians don't want us to know that they are here, so that they are careful not to do anything that would let us discover their presence. At this point, you will probably walk away in disgust. You have not silenced your opponent. In fact, he or she might go on inventing new ways out of your arguments forever. But, at a certain point, your opponent's explanations will have become so complicated and based on so much dubious knowledge that you and everyone else will be completely justified in ignoring him or her. The point of argument, remember, is to persuade. Absolute proof is impossible. But this means too that persuading some people is also impossible. There are limits to argument—at least, practical limits.

5. Reductio ad Absurdum

One last argument deserves mention. It is usually called by its Latin name, **reductio ad absurdum,** and is a form of deductive argument. It is, however, an "indirect" argument. It consists of taking your opponent's view and showing that it has intolerable or contradictory consequences. For example, someone argues that one can never know whether minds exist other than one's own. You counter by pointing out that the very act of arguing this with you contradicts his point. He replies, no doubt, that he can't *know* that you exist. You show that he cannot even know that *he* exists. What you have done is reduce your opponent's view to absurdity, showing that it leads to consequences that no one could accept, in this case, the idea that he cannot have self-knowledge at all. A *reductio ad absurdum* argument, like a good counter-example, is often an excellent way of forcing other people to clarify their positions and explain more carefully exactly what they mean to argue.

6. The Worst Kinds of Fallacies

No brief survey of logic would be adequate without identifying other fallacies, more general than those we discussed previously under deductive arguments. Whatever kind of arguments you employ, be careful that you *never* use the following:

MERE ASSERTION   The fact that you accept a position is not sufficient for anyone else to believe it. Stating your view is not an argument for it, and unless you are just answering a public opinion survey, every opinion always deserves a supporting argument. There are statements, of course, that everyone would accept at face value, and you need not argue those. But that does not mean that they cannot be argued, for even the most obvious facts of common sense must be argued when challenged—this is what much of philosophy is about.

BEGGING THE QUESTION   Another fallacy is something that looks like an argument but simply accepts as a premise what is supposed to be argued for as a conclusion. For example, suppose you are arguing that one ought to be a Christian and your reason is that the Bible tells you so. This may, in fact, be conclusive for you, but if you are trying to convince someone who doesn't believe in Christ, he or she will probably not believe what the Bible says either. As an argument for becoming a Christian, therefore, referring to the Bible begs the question. Question begging often consists of a reworded conclusion, as in "this book will improve your grades because it will help you to do better in your courses."

VICIOUS CIRCLE   Begging the question is similar to another error, which is often called arguing in a "vicious circle." Consider a more elaborate version of the above fallacy. A person claims to know God exists because she has had a religious vision. Asked how she knows that the vision was religious rather than just the effect of something she ate, she replies that such an elaborate and powerful experience could not have been caused by anyone or anything but God. Asked how she knows this, she replies that God Himself told her—in the vision. Or, "he must be guilty because of the look on his face." "How do you know that he looks guilty rather than frightened or sad?" "Because he's the one who did it, that's why!" If you argue A because of B, and B because of C, but then C because of A, you have argued in a vicious circle. It is vicious because, as in begging the question, you have assumed just what you want to prove. But the following is worth remembering: Ultimately, all positions may come full circle, depending upon certain beliefs that can be defended only if you accept the rest of a great many beliefs. Debates between religious people and atheists are often like this, or arguments between free-marketeers and Marxists, where many hours of argument show quite clearly that each person accepts a large system of beliefs, all of which depend on the others. Some logicians call this a "virtuous circle," but this does not mean that there are no vicious circles. A virtuous circle is the development of an entire world view, and it requires a great deal of thinking and organizing. Vicious circles, like begging the question, are usually shortcuts to nowhere that result from careless thinking.

IRRELEVANCIES   You have seen people who argue a point by arguing everything else, throwing up charts of statistics and complaining about the state of the universe and telling jokes—everything but getting to the point. This may be a technique of wearing out your opponent; it is not a way of persuading him or her to agree with you. No matter how brilliant an argument may be, it is no good to you unless it is relevant to the point you want to defend.

AD HOMINEM ARGUMENTS   The most distasteful kind of irrelevancy is an attack on your opponent personally instead of arguing against his or her position. It may well be that the person you are arguing against is a liar, a sloppy dresser, bald and ugly, too young to vote or too old to work, but the only question is whether what he or she says is to be accepted. Harping on the appearance, reputation, manners, intelligence, friends, or possessions of your opponent may sometimes give your readers insight into why he or she holds a certain position, but it does not prove or disprove the position itself. As insight into an opponent's motives, personal considerations may, in small doses, be appropriate. But more than a very small dose is usually offensive, and it will usually weigh more against you than against your opponent.

Whenever possible, avoid this kind of argument completely. It usually indicates that you don't have any good arguments yourself.

UNCLEAR OR SHIFTING CONCLUSIONS   One of the most frustrating arguments to read is an argument that has a vague conclusion or that shifts conclusions with every paragraph. If something is worth defending at all, it is worth stating clearly and sticking with it. If you argue that drug users should be punished, but aren't clear whether you mean people who traffic in heroin or people who take aspirin, you are not worth listening to. If you say that you mean illegal drug offenders, don't argue that drugs are bad for your body, since this is equally true for both legal and illegal drugs. If you say that you mean amphetamine users, then don't switch to talking about the illegality of drugs when someone explains to you the several medical uses of amphetamines. Know what you are arguing, or your arguments will have no point.

CHANGING MEANINGS   It is easy to miss a fallacy when the words seem to form a valid argument. For example, consider this:

> People are free as long as they can think for themselves.
> Prisoners in jail are free to think for themselves.
> Therefore, prisoners in jail are free.

This paradoxical conclusion is due to the ambiguity of "free," first used to refer to a kind of mental freedom, second to refer to physical freedom. An interesting example is the argument often attributed to the famous British philosopher John Stuart Mill: "Whatever people desire, that is what is desirable." But notice that this argument plays with an ambiguity in the English language. Not everything that is in fact desired *should* be desired (for example, alcohol by alcoholics), so the argument is deductively invalid. (Mill makes the case, however, that the only evidence that x is desirable is that people in fact desire it.) Be careful that the key terms in your argument keep the same meaning throughout.

DISTRACTION   Another familiar form of fallacy is the "red herring," the sometimes long-winded pursuit of an argument leading away from the point at issue. For example, in the middle of an argument about the relation between the mind and the brain, a neurologist may well enjoy telling you, in impressive detail, any number of odd facts about neurology, about brain operations he or she has performed, about silly theories that neurology-ignorant philosophers have defended in the past. But if these do not bear on the issue at hand, they are only pleasant ways of spending the afternoon, not steps to settling a difference of opinion. Distraction is a fallacy that is especially advantageous when the time for argument is limited. (For this reason, it is particularly prevalent in the classroom.)

PSEUDO-QUESTIONS   Sometimes fallacious reasoning begins with the very question being asked. For example, some philosophers have argued that asking such questions as "How is the mind related to the body?" or "Could God create a mountain so heavy that even He could not move it?" are pseudo-questions; that is, they look like real questions—even profound questions—but are ultimately unanswerable because they are based on some hidden piece of nonsense. (In these two cases, it has been suggested that there is no legitimate distinction between mind and body, and therefore any question about how they are "related" is pointless; the second question presumes that God is "omnipotent" in the sense that He can do the logically impossible, which is absurd.) Pseudo-questions, like distractions, lead us down a lengthy path going nowhere, except that, with pseudo-questions, we start from nowhere as well.

DUBIOUS AUTHORITY   We mentioned earlier that modern philosophy is based on the assumption that we have a right—and sometimes a duty—to question authority. Yet, most of our knowledge and opinions are based on appeals to authorities— whether scientists or "the people" are particularly wise or not. It would be extremely foolish, if not fatal, not to so appeal to authorities, especially in a world that has grown so technologically and socially complicated. We ask an economist what will happen if interest rates fall. We ask Miss Manners which fork to use for the salad. The fallacy of dubious authority arises when we ask the *wrong* person, when we appeal to an expert who is not in fact an expert in the area of concern. For example, when physicians are asked questions about nuclear policy or physicists are asked questions about high school education, their expertise in one field does not necessarily transfer to the other. Appealing to opinions in books and newspapers depends on the authority of the authors and publications in question. What is in print is not necessarily authoritative.

SLIPPERY SLOPE   Metaphors often pervade arguments. One of the more common metaphors is the "slippery slope," the greased incline that, once trod, inevitably carries us to the bottom. (In politics, it is sometimes called "the chilling effect" or "the domino theory.") For example, it is argued that any interference with free speech whatsoever, even forbidding someone to scream "fire" in a crowded auditorium, will sooner or later lead to the eradication of free speech of every kind, including informed, responsible political discussion. But is it the case that, by attacking an extreme instance, we thereby endanger an entire institution? Sometimes, this may be so. But more often than not, the slippery slope metaphor leads us to think that there is such inevitability when in fact there is no such thing.

ATTACKING A STRAW MAN   Real opponents with real arguments and objections are sometimes difficult to refute, and so the easy way out is to attack an unreal opponent with easily refutable arguments and objections. This unreal fellow is called a "straw man," and he provides us with the extra advantage of not fighting back. For example, a writer of religion attacks those who have suggested that Mohammed never existed, when in fact his opponents have only questioned a particular interpretation of his claim to divinity. A writer discussing the mind-body problem lampoons those who believe that there is *no* possible correlation between mental events and some (perhaps unknown) physical events—a position that has been argued by virtually no one.

PITY (AND OTHER EMOTIONAL APPEALS)   Some forms of fallacy appeal to the better parts of us, even as they challenge our fragile logical abilities. The appeal to pity has always been such an argument. Photographs of suffering people may well be an incentive to social action, but the connection between our pity—which is an undeniable virtue—and the social action in question is not yet an argument. The appeal to pity—and all appeals to emotion—have a perfectly legitimate place in philosophical argument, but such appeals are not yet themselves arguments for any particular position. An orator may make us angry, but what we are to do about the problem must be the product of further argument.

APPEAL TO FORCE   Physical might never makes philosophical right. Sometimes a person can be intimidated, but he or she is not thus refuted. Sometimes one has to back up a philosophical conviction with force, but it is never the force that justifies the conviction.

INAPPROPRIATE ARGUMENTS   The last fallacy we will mention has to do with choice of methods. To insist on deductive arguments when there are powerful inductive arguments against you is a fallacy too—not a fallacious argument, perhaps, but a mistake in logic all the same. For example, if you are arguing deductively that there cannot be any torture going on in a certain country, since Mr. Q rules the country and Mr. Q is a good man (where the implicit premise is that "good men don't allow torture in their country"), you had better be willing to give up the argument when dozens of trustworthy eyewitnesses publicly describe the tortures they have seen or experienced. To continue with your deduction in the face of such information is foolish. This may not tell you where your argument has gone wrong: Perhaps Mr. Q is not such a good man. Or perhaps he has been overpowered. Or perhaps good men can't prevent torture if they aren't told about it. But in any case, the argument must now be given up.

The same may be true the other way around. Certain abstract questions seem to be answerable only by deduction. When arguing about religious questions, for example, looking for evidence upon which to build an inductive argument may be foolish. What is at stake are your basic concepts of religion and their implications. Evidence, in the sense of looking around for pertinent facts, may be irrelevant. Very abstract questions often require deductive arguments only.

To be caught in one of these fallacies is almost always embarrassing and damaging to your overall argument. If you have a case to make, then make it in the most powerfully persuasive way. An intelligent combination of deductive and inductive arguments, coupled with analogies and proper criticisms of alternative positions, is the most effective persuasion available. If you think your opinions are important, then they deserve nothing less than the best supporting arguments you can put together.

As you proceed with your course, you will have the opportunity to use many of these logical forms, not only on the great philosophers of the past but on your own thinking as well. You will find that philosophical criticism is a powerful tool in the arguments you have with your friends and the debates you carry on, whatever the topic. Most importantly, philosophy is a valuable aid to getting together your own thoughts about things, about the problems of philosophy that you will encounter in this book, and about life in general.

But then again, why should we assume that the truth is all that coherent or logical? As **Ralph Waldo Emerson** once wrote:

A foolish consistency is the hobgoblin of little minds, adored by little statesmen and philosophers and divines. With consistency a great soul has simply nothing to do. He may as well concern himself with his shadow on the wall. Speak what you think now in hard words and to-morrow speak what to-morrow thinks in hard words again, though it contradict every thing you said to-day.— "Ah, so you shall be sure to be misunderstood."—Is it so bad then to be misunderstood? Pythagoras was misunderstood, and Socrates and Jesus, and Luther, and Copernicus, and Galileo, and Newton, and every pure and wise spirit that ever took flesh. To be great is to be misunderstood.[10]

Nevertheless, it would be prudent to advise: do not contradict yourself. Even if you are "great" it is unpleasant to be misunderstood, especially by your instructor. A prudent consistency is the salvation of most students.

GLOSSARY

abstract Overly general, not concrete, independent of particular concerns or objects. For example, a philosopher may attempt to ascertain the nature of justice without particular reference to any concrete practical case.

ad hominem **argument** An argument against the person instead of the position; for example, attacking a philosopher's living habits instead of asking whether or not his theories are true.

argument The process of reasoning from one claim to another. An argument may, but need not, be directed against an explicit alternative. A philosophical argument does not require an opponent or a disagreement.

asceticism A life of self-denial and material simplicity, often to further philosophical or religious goals.

assertion A statement or declaration, taking a position. Mere assertion, when presented as an argument, is a fallacy; arguments consist not only of assertions but of reasons for them as well.

assumption A principle taken for granted, without argument or proof.

autonomy Intellectual independence and freedom from authority; the presumed ability to determine the acceptability of one's own beliefs and actions.

axiom A principle that is generally accepted from the beginning and so may be used without further debate as a starting point of argument.

begging the question Merely restating as the conclusion of an argument one of its premises. For example, "Why do oysters give me indigestion? Because they upset my stomach."

Cartesianism Concerning Descartes. In particular, concerning his philosophical method. (Descartes' followers are generally called "Cartesians" and their method "Cartesianism.")

---

[10] Ralph Waldo Emerson, "Self Reliance" (New York: Wise, 1929), pp. 143–44.

The Cartesian method is essentially a deductive method, as in geometry, starting with self-evident axioms and deducing the rest.

certainty Beyond doubt. But it is important to insist that certainty in the philosophical sense is more than the common psychological use of certain ("feeling certain"). One can feel certain and yet be wrong or foolish. One can be certain, in this philosophical sense, only if one can prove that the matter is beyond doubt, that no reasons for doubt could be raised.

coherence Logical connection. A statement by a witness in a courtroom coheres with other testimony and evidence when it fits in and follows from that other testimony and evidence. To say that a philosophy must be coherent is to say that its various principles must fit together in an orderly and logically agreeable fashion.

consistent Fitting together in an orderly logical way. Two principles are consistent if they do not contradict each other. A philosophy is consistent if none of its principles contradict each other.

contradiction The logical relation of two principles in which the truth of one requires the falsity of the other. A witness's statement in court contradicts other testimony if both statements cannot be true.

counter-example An example that contradicts a generalization, such as "all elephants have tusks." A counter-example would be an elephant without tusks.

criterion The test or standard according to which a judgment or an evaluation can be made. For example, a test for a substance being an acid is whether or not it turns litmus paper red.

critical Thinking so as to be mindful of mistakes in reasoning; to be critical is not necessarily to be unpleasant.

declarative sentence A sentence in which one takes a position, states a fact, asserts a proposition.

deduction (deductive argument) A process of reasoning from one principle to another by means of accepted rules of inference. In a deductive argument, a conclusion follows necessarily from the premises, and so if you are certain of the premises, you can be certain of the conclusion, too.

dialectic Argument through dialogue, disagreement, and successive revisions, out of which comes agreement.

doubt Lack of certainty; lack of reasons to believe and perhaps having reasons not to believe. It is important to distinguish doubt in this philosophical sense from doubt in the ordinary psychological sense. Mere personal uncertainty or distrust is not sufficient; there must be a demonstrable reason for doubt, that is, reasons for not accepting the beliefs in question.

Enlightenment A cultural and philosophical movement in the eighteenth century in Europe defined by a new confidence in human reason and individual autonomy. Some of the major figures of this movement were René Descartes, the metaphysician Baron Henri d'Holbach, the political philosopher Jean-Jacques Rousseau, and the political reformer-writer Voltaire in France. In Great Britain, Enlightenment philosophers were John Locke and David Hume; in Germany, Immanuel Kant.

fallacy An apparently persuasive argument that is really an error in reasoning; an unsound or invalid argument.

first principles Those axioms and assumptions from which a philosophy begins. These must be solid and indisputable principles; they need not be those principles that one happens to first believe.

formal logic A branch of logic that is concerned with the principles of reasoning as such, in which the relationships between symbols are studied and not their interpretation.

generalization Usually, a proposition about all of a group or set of things on the basis of a limited acquaintance with some of its members. In logic, however, a generalization may be universal ("all x's are y's") or existential ("there are some x's that are y's").

hypothesis A provisional conclusion, accepted as most probable in the light of the known facts or tentatively adopted as a basis for analysis.

implication One statement logically follows from another. Statements imply one another: We infer one from the other.

incoherent Not fitting together in an orderly or logically agreeable fashion. Using fancy jargon that has no precise meaning may be a source of incoherence. So is a mere list of random beliefs, without any order or logic to hold them together. (They may even contradict each other as well.) An incoherent philosophy may be insightful and true in parts, but because it never coheres into a single system, it may well appear to be nonsense or simply a jumble of words and phrases. In other cases, an incoherent philosophy may be one that makes no sense, whose terms are utter gibberish or whose principles are mere ramblings without intelligible connection or interpretation. (Opposite of coherent.)

inconsistent Not compatible; contradictory. One might also say that a person's actions are inconsistent with his or her principles. People as well as other principles can be inconsistent with a principle.

inductive argument A process of reasoning in which the characteristics of an entire class or set of things is inferred on the basis of an acquaintance with some of its members. In an inductive argument, although the conclusion is supported by the premises, it does not follow necessarily from the premises and its truth is not guaranteed by them.

inference Reasoning from one set of principles to another, as in an argument. Deductive inference is but a single kind of inference.

invalid Not correctly following agreed-upon rules of inference in an argument. Always applied to arguments, not to statements. (Opposite of valid.)

logic The study of the rules of valid inference and "rational argument." In general, a sense of order.

method (sometimes, **methodology**) An approach and strategy for resolving philosophical problems. For example, the appeal to experience, the appeal to divine revelation, the insistence upon mathematical logic, confidence in reason or trust in authority—all of these are aspects of philosophical methodology.

method of doubt (or **methodological doubt**) Descartes' technique for discovering those principles of which we can be "perfectly certain"; namely, doubt everything, until you discover those principles that cannot be doubted.

paradox A self-contradictory conclusion drawn from seemingly acceptable premises. For example, suppose you try to help all and only those people who do not help themselves. That sounds reasonable enough. But then, do you help yourself? If you do help everyone, then you would also help yourself. But if you don't help yourself, then you aren't helping all who don't help themselves. This is a paradox.

predicate That which is asserted or denied of a thing, which refers to a property of things. Some familiar predicates would be "is red," "is an animal."

premise The principle or one of those principles upon which an argument is based. The starting point of an argument.

presupposition A principle that is assumed as a precondition for whatever else one believes, which itself may remain unexamined and uncriticized throughout the argument. For example, a lawyer presupposes that the court aims at justice and has some idea what is just. It is the philosopher, not the lawyer, who challenges those claims.

proof In a deductive argument, a proof is a sequence of steps, each according to an acceptable rule of inference, to the conclusion to be proved.

proposition An assertion that is either true or false.

reason The ability to think abstractly, to form arguments and make inferences. Sometimes referred to as a "faculty" of the human mind (a leftover from eighteenth-century philosophy). More specialized meanings will be discussed in later chapters.

reasons Explanations, justifications, evidence, or some other basis for accepting a proposition.

reductio ad absurdum A form of argument in which one refutes a statement by showing that it leads to self-contradiction or an otherwise intolerable conclusion.

reflection To think about something, to "put it in perspective." We often do this with our beliefs and our emotions. For example, "This morning I was furious at you, but after reflecting on it at lunch, I decided that it was nothing to be angry about." One might say that philosophy is reflection about life and knowledge in general.

rhetoric The persuasive use of language to convince other people to accept your beliefs.

rule of inference A generally accepted principle according to which one may infer one statement from another. (We have not yet said anything about the nature of these "generally acceptable" rules; for now, we have simply presupposed that some such rules are acceptable to everyone; for example, "if *either* A is true *or* B is true, but we know that B is false, than we can conclude that A is true.")

self-contradictory A contradiction within one and the same statement or set of statements. What I say may contradict what you say; but what I say might also contradict something else that I said, in which case I am being self-contradictory. Moreover, in a few strange cases, my own statement may be self-contradictory; for example, "I do not exist."

self-evident Obvious without proof or argument; for Descartes, a "clear and distinct idea," one about which there could be no doubt and it is obvious that there could be no doubt.

skepticism A philosophical belief that knowledge is not possible, that doubt will not be overcome by any valid arguments. A philosopher who holds this belief is called a skeptic. Again, skepticism is not mere personal doubt; it requires systematic doubt with reasons for that doubt.

sound An argument whose premises are true and that is valid.

syllogism A three-line deductive argument; the best-known examples are those arguments of this form:

All P's are Q's. (Major premise)

S is a P. (Minor premise)

Therefore S is a Q. (Conclusion)

The major premise asserts something about the predicate of the conclusion (in this case, Q). The minor premise asserts something about the subject of the conclusion (in this case, S).

system An orderly formulation of principles (together with reasons, implications, evidence, methods, and presuppositions) that is comprehensive, consistent, and coherent and in which the various principles are interconnected as tightly as possible by logical implications.

trivial Obvious and not worth saying.

unsound An argument whose premises are false or that is invalid.

valid An argument that correctly follows agreed-upon rules of inference. Always applies to arguments, not statements.

vicious circle Use of two propositions or arguments to support one another with no other support. For example, "He must be guilty because he's got such a guilty look on his face. . . . Well, I can tell it's a guilty look because he's the one who is guilty."

BIBLIOGRAPHY AND FURTHER READING

A large number of alternative views of philosophy are available in Charles I. Bontempo and S. Jack Odell, eds., *The Owl of Minerva* (New York: McGraw-Hill, 1975). The trial, imprisonment, and death of Socrates are recounted by Plato in the dialogues *Apology, Crito,* and *Phaedo* in *The Last Days of Socrates,* trans. Hugh Tredennick (London: Penguin, 1954). An excellent account of Socrates' life is A. E. Taylor, *Socrates* (New York: Doubleday, Anchor, 1959). The best single book on the enlightenment is Peter Gay, *The Enlightenment: An Interpretation* (New York: Vintage, 1966); a simpler discussion is Robert Anchor, *The Enlightenment Tradition* (New York: Harper & Row, 1967); and a philosophical anthology of the period is Isaiah Berlin, *The Age of Enlightenment* (New York: Mentor, 1955). Two standard introductions to logic are I. Copi, *Introduction to Logic* (New York: Macmillan 1961), and Daniel Bonevac, *Simple Logic* (Fort Worth: Harcourt, Brace 1999).

I

THE WORLD AND BEYOND

REALITY

It must be that what can be spoken and thought is:
for it is possible for it to be,
and it is not possible for what is nothing to be.

PARMENIDES

Well over three thousand years ago, philosophers in India, in the *Rg Veda* (the oldest of those holy books called the *Vedas*), contemplated the nature and origins of the whole of reality ("**Brahman**"), concluding, with considerable skepticism, that reality as such was not, or at least not normally, known by us, and perhaps it could not be known at all. Now, at the end of the twentieth century, some philosophers and some of our best-known physicists have come to believe that ultimate reality, those evasive particles that seem to multiply as the experiments get more sophisticated and the origin of everything ("the big bang") gets more and more (rather than less and less) mysterious, and some theorists even suggest that we *create* reality through our observation of it and there is no independent reality at all.

These two questions about the ultimate nature of reality and the origins of the universe (or, from the Greek *cosmos,* thus, **cosmology**) have defined much of philosophy from most ancient times until today. (And we have no reason to suppose that the questions are getting any easier.) The way the question is asked, of course, varies considerably with the growth of science and among various religious and cultural contexts, but they are, in one sense, the most fundamental of philosophical questions.

A. "THE WAY THE WORLD REALLY IS"

Because it was a Greek who coined the term *philosophy* and in Greece where philosophy was first recognized as a formal discipline, Western philosophers today often refer to the first Greek thinkers as the first "philosophers." Philosophy in this sense is said to begin with a seemingly odd claim made by the Greek philosopher **Thales** on the coast of Turkey sometime around 580 B.C. He suggested that the source of everything was water. The earth floats upon water, and it and all things on it are made of water. Aristotle later called his theory "childish," but he also acknowledged that his was the "oldest view that has been transmitted to us" (in his essay "On the Heavens"). In his *Metaphysics,* **Aristotle** went on to consider Thales' view in some detail:

> *Most of the first philosophers thought that principles in the form of matter were the only principles of all things. For they say that the element and first principle of the things that exist is that from which they all are and from which they first come into being and into which they are finally destroyed, its substance remaining and its properties changing. . . . There must be some nature—either one or more than one—from which the other things come into being, it being preserved. But as to the number and form of this sort of principle, they do not all agree. Thales, the founder of this kind of philosophy, says that it is water (that is why he declares that the earth rests on water). He perhaps came to acquire this belief from seeing that the nourishment of everything is moist and that heat itself comes from this and lives by this (for that from which anything comes into being is its first principle)—he came to his belief both for this reason and because the seeds of everything have a moist nature, and water is the natural principle of moist things.*[1]

There must be some nature—either one or more than one—from which the other things come into being . . .

So too, the commentator **Simplicius** suggested that "Thales was the first to introduce the study of nature to the Greeks." His seemingly simple claim, that the world rests on water, was in fact one of the most remarkable claims of the ancient world, not because it is so implausible (as his own students pointed out to him) but because it was one of the first recorded attempts to describe "the way the world really is," beyond all appearances and day-to-day opinions. Accordingly, Thales' theory marks the beginning of Western science as well as philosophy. He was the first Greek thinker to break with common sense and religion and offer a general theory about the ultimate nature of reality. In place of mythological accounts of nature and human behavior in

---

[1] Aristotle, *Metaphysics* 983b6–11, pp. 17–27.

terms of divine agencies (gods, goddesses, and spirits), he and other thinkers of the period provided explanations in terms of laws and abstract generalizations. Knowledge became an end in itself, one of the noblest pursuits of humanity.

B. THE FIRST PHILOSOPHERS: THE "TURNING POINT OF CIVILIZATION"

We are all aware that the way the world really is may not correspond to our everyday views of the world, the way it seems to be. For example, we casually talk of "sunrises" and "sunsets," and surely it does seem as if the sun goes "up" and "down," while we and our earth stay in place. It took several thousand years for people in general to recognize that, despite appearances, our earth actually moves around the sun. We now accept that without question, even if there is little in our everyday experience to support it. Similarly, consider the chair on which you are sitting: Does it seem to you that it is composed mostly of empty space and tiny electrically charged colorless particles whirling about at fantastic speeds? Of course not, but modern science has taught you that "solid" objects are indeed made up of just such spaces and particles. The world is not as it seems, and the beginnings of both philosophy and science were the first attempts of men and women to see beyond their "commonsense" views of things and try to find the reality behind them.

Although the pre-Socratic Greeks were the first thinkers to call themselves "philosophers," we can look back from our modern vantage point to many ancient traditions we might want to call "philosophical," in the sense that they looked beyond ordinary experience for an understanding of "reality." The ancient philosophers did not have the advantage of either our scientific sophistication or a long history of philosophical thinking to give them support. Yet, there were lots of new and profoundly thoughtful opinions offered by the ancients about reality, whatever the differences in the ways different thinkers from different places thought about the world. The first investigations into the ultimate nature of reality, among which we include Thales' account, appeared in the middle of the first millennium B.C. Quite amazingly, several world-shattering views about reality appeared independently in different areas of the world during the same period. The twentieth-century philosopher **Karl Jaspers** described this as the "Axial Period"—the turning point of civilization.

FROM **THE "AXIAL PERIOD"**
BY **KARL JASPERS**

It would seem that this axis of history is to be found in the period around 500 B.C., in the spiritual process that occurred between 800 and 200 B.C. It is there that we meet with the most deep-cut dividing line in history. Man, as we know him today, came into being. For short we may style this the "Axial Period."

CHARACTERIZATION OF THE AXIAL PERIOD

The most extraordinary events are concentrated in this period. Confucius and Lao-tse were living in China, all the directions of Chinese philosophy came into being, including those of Mo-ti, Chuang-tse, Lieh-tsu, and a host of others; India produced the Upanishads and Buddha, and, like China, ran the whole gamut of philosophical possibilities down to skepticism, to materialism, sophism and nihilism; in Iran Zarathustra taught the challenging view of the world as a struggle between good and evil; in Palestine the prophets made their appearance, from Elijah, by way of Isaiah and Jeremiah, to Deutero-Isaiah; Greece witnessed the appearance of Homer, of the philosophers—Parmenides, Heraclitus, and Plato—of the tragedians, of Thucydides, and of Archimedes. Everything that is merely intimated by these names developed during these few centuries almost simultaneously in China, India, and the Occident without any one of these knowing of the others.

What is new about this age, in all three of these worlds, is that man becomes aware of Being as a whole, of himself and his limitations. He experiences the terrible nature of the world and his own impotence. He asks radical questions. Face to face with the void he strives for liberation and redemption. By consciously recognizing his limits he sets himself the highest goals. He experiences unconditionality in the depth of selfhood and in the clarity of transcendence.

This took place in reflection. . . .

In this age were born the fundamental categories within which we still think today, and the beginnings of the world religions, by which human beings still live, were created. The step into universality was taken in every sense.

As a result of this process, hitherto unconsciously accepted ideas, customs, and conditions were subjected to examination, questioned, and liquidated. Everything was swept into the vortex. Insofar as the traditional substance still possessed vitality and actuality, its manifestations were illuminated and thereby transmuted.

The *Mythical Age,* with its tranquility and self-evidence, was at an end. . . .

For the first time *philosophers* appeared. Human beings dared to rely on themselves as individuals. Hermits and wandering thinkers in China, ascetics in India, philosophers in Greece, and prophets in Israel all belong together, however much they may differ from each other in their beliefs, the contents of their thought, and their inner dispositions. Man proved capable of confronting inwardly the entire universe. He discovered within himself the origin from which to raise himself above his own self and the world.

In *speculative thought* he lifts himself up toward Being itself.[2]

---

[2] From Karl Jaspers: *Basic Philosophical Writings—Selections.* Ed., trans., and with introductions by Edith Ehrlich, Leonard H. Ehrlich, and George B. Pepper. (Athens, OH: Ohio University Press), pp. 382–87.

C. THE EARLY GREEK PHILOSOPHERS

What is this "Being"? What is the way the world really is? How do you answer that question? Very likely you will appeal to the authority of modern science, and that is probably a reasonable beginning. But you know that the "science" of one generation is seen as the superstitions of another. (Once people believed that the earth was flat.) You have probably, at least once in your school career, caught one of the "authorities"—perhaps a teacher, perhaps even a noted scientist—in a mistake. Can we simply accept what scientists tell us without question, any more than Descartes could accept the teachings of his teachers without question? Have you ever examined the evidence for the theory that the earth goes around the sun? If not, why should you believe it? Or, to take a very different example, scientists are generally agreed that some version of Darwin's theory of evolution is true. Does that mean that you have to believe it? Many people do not, because it seems to contradict the story of creation in the Bible. You have to decide which to believe. Even within science there are always disagreements and debates. There are different theories to answer the same questions, and you have to decide. Which are you to believe?

Your view of reality is influenced by modern science but it is also influenced by twenty-five hundred years of philosophy, even if you've never studied it before. We can say, with some confidence, that we know much more about the world than the ancient philosophers. But we must not be too confident. Not only are there still many scientific problems unsolved, there are and always will be conflicting views of how we are to see our world in more general terms. How much faith should we have in religion? How much should we see the world as a world of people and how much as a world of physical objects? How much should we accept "common sense" (which changes all the time) and how much should we indulge in scientific and philosophical speculation (which changes all the time also)?

1. The Ionian Naturalists

Thales' approach was somewhat different from that of the thinkers of other early traditions; he is rightly credited with being the first in the line of philosophers of which Socrates was the culmination (called the "pre-Socratics"). Thales' answer, that ultimate reality is water, should not surprise nearly so much as the fact that he attempted such a theory at all. Indeed, we should be impressed by the fact that he even asked "What is the world really like?" because as far as we know, no one had attempted to ask such a question in such a way before him.

Thales was not willing to accept the opinions and mythologies that had been handed down for generations. He insisted, instead, on observing the world for himself, on thinking out his own answer, and on discussing it with his friends and neighbors, many of whom, no doubt, thought that he was slightly peculiar. (It is also said, however, that his cosmic speculations helped him to make a fortune in the olive oil business. No doubt his neighbors respected that.)

Thales was the first of a group of philosophers—or rather, the first of several groups of philosophers—scattered around the various Greek islands and the coasts of Asia Minor, or Ionia, who lived in the sixth and fifth centuries B.C., just before the time of Socrates. Accordingly, they are called **Ionians,** one group of the pre-Socratics. Their opinions varied greatly. Among them they developed a wide range of systematic views of the universe and the ultimate nature of reality. Unlike Socrates and most later philosophers, they were not very concerned with questions of method. They went straight to the heart of the question, to the nature of the universe itself. As we shall see, some of them came strikingly close to our modern scientific conceptions.

The idea that everything was water did not satisfy Thales' friends and students. They appreciated his attempt to find the "One Reality," but they thought that it must be something else. Thales' first student, named **Anaximander,** argued against his teacher that some things, for example, the dry, dusty cliffs of Asia Minor, could not possibly be made of water, which was naturally wet and never dry. Anaximander was the first recorded student to talk back to his teacher (which in philosophy, unlike most other subjects, is considered a virtue rather than a discourtesy). Thales had made the first gigantic step, rejecting the "obvious" answers of common sense and trying to find out "the way the world really is." But notice that Thales' answer to that question still appeals to a commonsense ingredient, water, which is so familiar to us. Thales' defense of his thesis also depended on some very commonsensical claims: for example, the idea that if you dig deep enough into the earth, you will eventually hit water.

Once Thales had made the break with common sense and said that the way the world really is need not be at all like the way it seems to us, it was no longer necessary to suppose that reality was anything like our experiences. Anaximander, consequently, argued that ultimate reality could not be composed of any of the then-known elements—earth, air, fire, or water—since these were each so different from the others. They might be mixed together, as when earth and water are mixed to make mud or clay, but it made no sense to suppose that any of them might really be made up of any of the others. So Anaximander suggested that the ultimate nature of reality was something else—let us simply call it "primordial stuff"—that is not like anything we could ever experience.

The word Anaximander actually used was the *apeiron,* which is sometimes translated as "the indefinite" or "the unlimited." The *apeiron,* or "primordial stuff," was a chaos or void, which yielded the variety of things in the world. This notion of "stuff" was a second major step in philosophy and science. Today, we feel comfortable with the idea that things are made of "stuff" (atoms and molecules) that we never experience in everyday life. But in the ancient world, this suggestion must have seemed extremely exciting.

Anaximander's student, **Anaximenes,** thought his teacher's notion of "stuff" was too mysterious, but he also rejected Thales' theory and replaced it with the idea that air is the basic "stuff." Just as our soul, which is air, integrates us, so breath and air surround the whole cosmos. Air makes up the other elements and the various things of the world by becoming thicker and thinner. (Think of steam condensing to form water and then ice.) Anaximenes thus introduced the idea that changes in the quantity of basic elements can produce changes in quality as well—a key principle of modern science.

2. Monism, Materialism, and Immaterial "Stuff"

The attempt to reduce all of the varied things in the world to one kind of thing as Thales and his students did with water, air, and *apeiron,* is called **monism.** It is the search for ultimate reality, which might be very different from the appearance of everyday life, that has motivated philosophy and science for twenty-five hundred years. So the debate began: Was the world really made of water? Perhaps, thought Thales' students, it is some other kind of "stuff." Today, the debate continues: Is everything made up of matter, or energy, or matter-energy? Are there basic particles that cannot be reduced to anything else? Scientists once thought that atoms were such particles; then they discovered electrons, protons, and neutrons that made up atoms. Since then, they have discovered dozens of other particles, and today they are debating a mysterious particle called a quark, which physicists now think may provide the ultimate answer to Thales' ancient question. But notice that all of these views are strictly physical. That is, they are concerned about basic questions of what we now call physics and chemistry, concerned about the material "stuff" of which all things are composed. This was true of Thales; and it is still true of modern "quark" theorists. Accordingly, the philosophies of all of these thinkers can be called **materialism,** the view that reality is ultimately composed of some kind of material "stuff." (In this context, "materialism" does not mean concern about the material things in life—money, cars, jewelry, or getting a new garbage disposal every year.)

If you think like a physical scientist, the idea that the universe is made up of some kind of material "stuff" sounds very plausible. In fact, you might wonder, what else could it be made of? Consider this: There are some things in the universe that could not plausibly be made of material "stuff." For example, what about your thoughts and feelings? Are they simply bits of matter, or are they composed of some entirely different kind of "stuff," perhaps some kind of mental or spiritual "stuff"? Some early philosophers, particularly to the east of Greece, claimed that reality was not made of just physical elements, like water, air, or even the *apeiron,* but rather that reality was inherently spiritual. Many of these thinkers claimed that the primordial "stuff" was divine, or godly. We will see that in Greece as well, the pre-Socratic philosopher **Heraclitus** was already groping for a conception of an immaterial "stuff," something which was not material but rather spiritual or nonphysical. ("Immaterial," in a philosophical context, does not mean, as it does in law, "irrelevant.")

3. Heraclitus

Back in Greece, another pre-Socratic philosopher of the same period, named Heraclitus, quite independently defended the idea that fire was the fundamental "stuff" of reality. For Heraclitus, however, "fire" seemed to connote both the "natural element" it was for the Ionians and a "spiritual power." Heraclitus' philosophy was cryptically expressed, and his contemporaries and commentators did not understand him very well, calling him such things as "riddler." Indeed, Heraclitus seems to have been a very cynical person, hardly interested in sharing his thoughts with others. Nonetheless, Heraclitus' profound and provocative claims have been an inspiration to many philosophers since, especially during the nineteenth century.

Although Heraclitus claimed that everything in the world was a manifestation of fire, he did not understand fire as an eternal and unchanging origin. Quite the opposite; he claimed that everything that exists is fleeting and changeable. Fire was the element that best explained, or at least represented, the constant flux which Heraclitus claimed underlay nature. "It is in changing that things find repose," [23][3] he stated, indicating that the only thing in the world which is constant is change. "You cannot step into the same river, for other waters are continually flowing on," [21] he claimed. The fact that we refer to "the" river at all, however, shows that something is constant—the very change and flow itself.

"This world that is the same for all," one fragment of his work reads, ". . . ever was and is and shall be ever-living fire that kindles in regular measures and goes out by regular measures." [B 30] This fire, or on the other hand, the fluxuating flow of the river, itself seems to have measure, a rhythm, underlying it. Although the world never stops changing, the measure with which it does so can be understood. So, Heraclitus claimed, our ever-changing reality has a *form* that remains the same, which he called the *Logos*. The *Logos* is the deeper "nature" behind natural, changing things, but you cannot see it, or hear it, or touch it. Thus, "nature loves to hide" [17] beneath the constant flux of the ordinary world we perceive.

Heraclitus' doctrines were provocative, confusing, and sometimes maddening, as the following fragments indicate:

> *People do not understand how that which is at variance with itself agrees with itself. [117]*

> *Listen . . . not to me, but to the* Logos. *[118]*

4. Democritus, Atoms, and Pluralism

Not all materialists thought that there was only one ultimate component of reality. A number of philosophers appeared in the ancient world who believed in **pluralism,** that is, that more than one basic "stuff" made up the universe. The best known of the pluralists was **Democritus,** who suggested that the universe was made up of tiny bits of "stuff" that he called *atoms*. These combined together to form the many different things and qualities of the world. (The soul, he suggested, consists of smooth, round, unusually mobile atoms, disposed throughout the body.) Other pluralists stressed the idea that these different bits of "stuff" were very different in kind as well, so that the bits of "stuff" that composed water, for example, would be very different from

---

[3]This and all following fragments of Heraclitus were translated by Paul Woodruff (used by permission of Paul Woodruff).

that which composed fire. You can appreciate how modern these concepts are, given our current ideas in chemistry and physics. These ancient Greek issues and answers have not become obsolete; they have changed and become more refined. Some have been more in favor at one time and others at other times. But they are still very much with us.

5. Animism

These ancient attempts to find out the way the world really is should not be thought of as clumsy attempts to find out the things that modern scientists now know. All the theories of "stuff" were indeed the precursors of modern physics and chemistry. But you can already see that these philosophers were also concerned with what we would call the mental and the spiritual aspects of the world. Even the most materialistic among them, for example, Thales, did not believe that the basic matter of the universe was cold and lifeless "stuff." All of these philosophers believed that the universe itself, as well as everything in it, was alive in at least some limited way. That is, they all believed in **animism,** the doctrine that everything, volcanoes and stones as well as elephants and flowers, are living things. Furthermore, animism has not disappeared because of the advances of science, though in certain periods (like our own) it has been treated less favorably than in others. But even in the nineteenth century, when physics and chemistry were making some of their most spectacular advances, animism was an extremely popular doctrine, even among scientists. A great many people today still accept a modified version of it. So don't think that the problems discussed by these ancient philosophers have been solved by science or simply gone away. The place of mind and spirit in a world of matter and energy is still among our basic problems. The ancient search for the way the world really is is still very much with us.

6. Pythagoras

Another Greek pre-Socratic philosopher, **Pythagoras,** also attempted to defend a view of the world that did not depend upon the usual kinds of material "stuff." He believed, however, that numbers were the real nature of things, and he taught his students to worship the mathematical order of the universe. He was particularly inspired by new Greek discoveries in music and harmony, and he saw the universe itself as a grand *harmony.* (The term "the music of the spheres" was part of his teachings.) Unlike the other pre-Socratic Greek philosophers we have met, Pythagoras was much more of a religious figure. He was a mystic and the leader of a powerful underground cult that believed in reincarnation and the **immortality** of the soul which he understood as that part of man which is capable of abstract thought, such as mathematics. In accordance with his religion, he gave the mind and the soul a much more prominent place in his view of the world than did other pre-Socratic philosophers.

Despite the sometimes mysterious views of Pythagoras and his cult, he is still recognized as one of the most important thinkers of the ancient world. With Heraclitus, he was one of the first Greeks to defend a view of reality that depended more on logic and thought than purely material "stuff." (The "Pythagorean theorem" that students learn in high school is named after him.) It was his discovery and proof.

7. The Appearance/Reality Distinction

All of the thinkers we have considered so far, whatever their differing views and outlooks, have espoused an underlying reality that is different from the way the world appears in one's ordinary experiences. Many, as you will recall, claimed that this underlying reality was One: others claimed that it was diverse and changing. In Greece, the profound discrepancy between the way the world seems and the way it really must be grew wider and wider. The problem has come to be called, not surprisingly, the "appearance/reality distinction."

For Thales, water was the eternal and unchanging element, although the forms it took might be very different and change constantly. For Democritus, atoms were unchanging and indestructible, although the things they combined to compose might change and be destroyed.

Heraclitus' *Logos* and Pythagoras' notion of the immortal "soul" were right on the edge of an investigation into how the world can be both one and many, both changing and stable. Because he believed that the nature of reality was fire-like, Heraclitus appreciated the importance of change, as in the flickering of a flame. But he insisted that the *logos,* or logic, underlay the constant changes in the world. We shall see that the presupposition that reality cannot change, however much things seem to change, will remain one of the most important beliefs in Western culture. (In Christianity, for example, the eternal and unchanging nature of God and the human soul are built upon the same philosophical foundation.)

None of the early thinkers, however, offered an explanation as to why the world should appear so differently to people than their philosophical investigations led them to believe it really was. Nor did these thinkers present any convincing argument that this should be so. The conflict finally came to a head, and the argument was finally offered. The philosopher who brought it out most clearly was a pre-Socratic Greek, **Parmenides.**

8. Parmenides

Parmenides was an accomplished mathematician who thought far more of the eternal certainties of arithmetic than he did the transient things of everyday experience. He, too, was a monist and believed in a single reality, "the One." Because he shared the assumption that reality must be eternal and unchanging, he came to an astonishing conclusion: This world, the world of our experience, cannot be real! Our world is constantly changing: Objects are created and destroyed; organisms live and die; people grow old, change their appearance, and move from place to place. So this world, with all its changes, could not be the real world, nor could we ever know the real world, since we are as inconstant and changing as the other things of our experience. We are, at best, living in a kind of illusion, not in reality at all!

Parmenides gave us what is sometimes postulated to be the first full-scale philosophical argument:[4]

(The goddess addresses the young philosopher) Come, I will tell you—and you, take the story when you have heard it—about the only routes there are for seeking to know: One says is *and that there is no not being; this is the path of Persuasion (for she goes the way of Truth). The other says* is not, *and that not being is right. This I point out to you is an utterly ignorant footway. For you could not either get to know that which is not (for it is not attainable) or point to it.*

. . . because the same thing is for knowing (or "thinking about") that is for being.

It is right that what is for saying and knowing should be, *for it can be; but nothing can* not be.

It is right that what is for saying and knowing should *be,* for it can be; but nothing can *not be.*

. . . what is is unborn and imperishable, a whole of a single kind, unshakable and not incomplete. It neither was nor will be, because it is now, all of it together, one cohesive. For what birth will you seek for it? From what would it have grown? I will not let you say or think that it came from what is not. For "is not" cannot be said or thought.

The argument is: What really is cannot have come to be, for there is nothing outside of reality (what really is) that could have been its source. It is an argument that is the source of much of Western metaphysics. Naturally, no two scholars agree about what it means. But all agree on the main point: that philosophers should be interested only in *what is* in the fullest sense, and not in what is not, or in what sometimes is and sometimes is not. This means that philosophers should not be interested in anything that changes. The weather in Austin is cold one day, and not cold the next. Because it sometimes *is not* cold, it is not a proper subject for the pure philosopher. What is, according to Parmenides, is *unchanging and eternal.*

A simple way to understand the root of this argument is this: We cannot put nonexistent apples in a sack or nonexistent dollars in our wallet. By the same token, Parmenides assumes, we cannot put things that do not exist in our mind; we can only truly think about or know things that *are.* Moreover, only one kind of thought really contains knowledge of the thing we are thinking about. Suppose we are thinking about beer. It is no use thinking about all the things beer is not—like wine and orange juice. Really thinking about beer is thinking about what beer really is.

---

[4] Parmenides, *Fragments* (B 2; B 3; B 6, 11 1–2; B 8, 11 3–9), trans. Paul Woodruff (with permission of Paul Woodruff).

Since thinking about change involves thinking about things that are not always the same, it involves thinking, in a sense, about things that are not (as the weather is not cold today). But this, according to the Parmenides assumption, is impossible: We can only think about what is.

Since Thales, the main achievement of philosophy had been to break away from common sense and ordinary experience in order to find out the way the world really is. But now we can see how far away from common sense and ordinary experience this breaking away can lead us. In Parmenides' philosophy, if the results of his logic are incompatible with common sense and ordinary experience, so much the worse for common sense and ordinary experience. The followers of Parmenides, particularly the mathematician **Zeno of Elea,** carried these bizarre conclusions even further. Zeno argued, by means of a series of famous paradoxes, that all motion and change is nothing but an illusion.

9. The Sophists

The following generation of philosophers, who called themselves **sophists** (who have ever since given "sophistry" a bad name because of their rhetorical debating tricks), went even further. They argued that there is no reality, and even if there were, we couldn't know anything about it anyway. (So argued the sophist Gorgias.) The teaching of **Protagoras,** another sophist, is still well known today; he said, "Man is the measure of all things," which means that there is no reality except for what we take to be reality. We shall later see that the sophists, despite their bad reputation, anticipated many of the most important philosophical concerns of the twentieth century. In particular, they stressed *practical* questions rather than abstract questions, and thus anticipated our own American *pragmatists.* In suggesting that truth is *relative* to people, they anticipated the much-disputed question of *relativism,* the idea that truth might be different at different times for different people. Wandering around the countryside, giving lessons in debating and rhetoric, the sophists used the accomplishments of the earlier philosophers to ridicule philosophy and make fools of practically everyone. That is, until they met Socrates, whose arguments against them changed the course of philosophy and Western thought in general.

10. Metaphysics

These various theories about the way the world really is have a proper name. They are called metaphysical doctrines, and the attempt to develop such doctrines, in which we have been taking part for these past pages, is called **metaphysics.** The business of metaphysics is to ask and attempt to answer the most basic questions about the universe, its composition and the "stuff" of which it is composed, the rule of man and mind, and the nature of the immaterial aspects of the universe as well as its physical nature. But now that we are about to discuss metaphysics in its maturity, with Plato and Aristotle, let us also give "stuff" its proper name. It is called (first by Aristotle) **substance.** Accordingly, metaphysics, the study of "the way the world really is," begins with the answers to a series of questions about substance and how it is manifested in particular things (such as people and trees).

1. How many substances are there? (Monism versus pluralism.)
2. What are they? (Water, air, fire, numbers, something unknown, minds, spirit, atoms?)
3. How are individual things composed? (And how do we tell them apart, identify them, reidentify them?)
4. How do different things and (if there is more than one) different substances interact?
5. How did substance come into being? (Created by God? Or has it always been there?)
6. Are substances "in" space and time? Are space and time substances? (If not, what are they?)

The first four questions are usually referred to as **ontology,** the study of being as such. The last questions are referred to as **cosmology,** the study of the universe. (For the pre-Socratics, these were the same.) Cosmological questions are necessarily shared between philosophers, physicists, and astronomers, and it is impossible for us to give them more than a cursory review within a strictly philosophical book. Ontology, on the other hand, is still considered by many philosophers to be the heart of metaphysics. Therefore, this chapter will be primarily concerned with ontology.

(Ontology and cosmology are not all there is to metaphysics. A further set of problems must be singled out because it is of particular personal importance to us. [The division follows that of the great German metaphysician **Immanuel Kant,** whom we shall meet in later chapters.] Kant summarized this second set of problems with the abbreviation "God, Freedom, and Immorality," problems that "the human mind will never give up." The existence of God is both an ontological problem [God has been identified as the "substance of the universe"] and a cosmological problem [God as creator; God as eternal]. But the existence and nature of God quite obviously deserve separate study, however intricately bound up they may be with other ontological and cosmological problems. [We shall provide this separate study in Chapter 5.] The problem of the existence of the human soul is often tied to religious questions, particularly in the Christian tradition [which is the context Kant intended]. But it is more than this: We shall see how Plato used the concept of an immortal soul to explain our ability to know eternal truths. In a more secular and transient context, there is the metaphysical problem of the relationship between mind and body [Chapter 8]. Finally, the question of metaphysical freedom [the only one of these questions not deeply considered by any of the Greek philosophers] needs to be examined in detail before we can move on to any more "practical" questions involving human action [Chapter 9].)

D. ULTIMATE REALITY IN THE EAST: INDIA, PERSIA, AND CHINA

1. Reality as Spirit: The Upanishads

While the Ionian Naturalists were pursuing their protoscientific inquiries in Greece, sages in India were developing their own doctrines about the nature of reality which were essentially religious. The earliest articulation of the concept of God as reality appears in the ancient Indian Vedic literature, especially in the appendages called **Upanishads,** "secret doctrines," from which later Eastern religious and spiritual notions emerged. In addition to the innumerable sects and divisions of religious belief and practice traditionally termed Hindu or Buddhist, other Indic religions such as Jainism and Sikhism also owe a conceptual debt to the early Upanishads.

A passage from one of the oldest Upanishads (c. 800 B.C.) relates to the spiritual aspiration that sets the tone for much Upanishadic teaching (whom or what is invoked in this passage is not clear):

> From non-being (asat) to true being (sat) lead me.
> From darkness to light lead me.
> From death to immortality lead me.[5]

The "seeking" expressed in the early Upanishads centers on "**Brahman,**" considered the ultimate secret both of ourselves and of the universe. The Upanishadic notion of Brahman is a seeking of a Unity underlying all individual selves and things. So, too, the "Emptiness" and absolutist notions of much of Buddhist thought are concerned with "the One," this underlying unity. **Buddhism's** view of the supremely real as "Emptiness" or "Openness" is discussed in the following two ancient passages:

> An ocean, a single seer without duality becomes he whose world [of vision] is brahman. This is his supreme attainment. This is his highest fulfillment. This is his best world. This is his supreme bliss. Other creatures subsist on a small bit of this bliss.

This "Absolute" is considered to have a peculiar "logic," or "nature," unlike that of everyday, finite, physical things. It is important *not* to think of Buddhist "Emptiness" as merely *nothing,* the *absence* of all things. Paradoxically, it is rather a "fullness," but unlike anything in our ordinary experience.

---

[5] This passage and the following four passages are taken from *Brhadāranyaka* 1.3.28, *Brhadāranyaka* 4.3.32, *Īśā Upanisad* 4–6, *Brhadāranyaka* 5.1.1, *Brhadāranyaka* 3.7.3–3.7.23 passim. *Chāndogya* 6.11, and *Katha* 1.25–27, 2.11–12, and 2.20–23. Unless noted otherwise, all passages were translated by Stephen Phillips.

He who experiences all things in the Self and the Self in all things . . . does not fear.

Not moving the One is swifter than the mind. The gods do not reach That running [always] before. . . . That moves; That moves not. It is far, and It is near. It is within all this; It indeed is outside all this. He who experiences all things in the Self and the Self in all things thereupon does not fear.

Om. That is the Full. This is the Full. From the Full, the Full proceeds. Taking away the Full of the Full, it is just the Full that remains.

Indian conceptions of reality often invoke doctrines that are called "pantheism," an identification of God and Nature. Whether the following passage illustrates pantheism or not, it reveals a doctrine of divine immanence, of divine *indwelling* in all things. It also suggests an Inner Controller who is thought to be "other" than the things, and selves, in which it indwells.

Who standing in the earth is other than the earth, whom the earth knows not, whose body the earth is, who within controls the earth, that is this, the Self, the Inner Controller, the Immortal. Who standing in the waters is other than the waters, whom the waters know not, whose body the waters are, that is this, the Self, the Inner Controller. . . . Who standing in the wind is other than the wind, whom the wind knows not, whose body the wind is, who within controls the wind, that is this, the Self, the Inner Controller, the Immortal. . . . Who standing in all beings is other than all beings, whom all beings know not, whose body all beings are, that is this, the Self, the Inner Controller, the Immortal. . . . Who standing in the eye is other than the eye, whom the eye knows not, whose body the eye is, who within controls the eye, that is this, the Self, the Inner Controller, the Immortal. Who standing in the ear is other than the ear, whom the ear knows not, whose body the ear is, that is this, the Self, the Inner Controller, the Immortal. . . . Who standing in the understanding is other than the understanding, whom the understanding knows not, whose body the understanding is, who within controls the understanding, that is this, the Self, the Inner Controller, the Immortal. . . . Who standing in the seed of generation is other than the seed of generation, whom the seed of generation knows not, whose body the seed of generation is, that is this, the Self, the Inner Controller, the Immortal. Unseen, the seer, unheard, the hearer, unthought, the thinker, unknown, the knower; there is no other seer than this, no other hearer than this, no other thinker than this, no other knower than this. That is this, the Self, the Inner Controller, the Immortal; valueless is anything other.

The passage above—one that is quoted repeatedly over centuries of commentary and discussion—illustrates a "spiritually monist" view that has enjoyed substantial prominence in India, a view that finds the "self" (or *ātman*) as the key to life and reality. Clearly the "self" referred to here is not the individual, personal self. It is rather the "self" of all reality, an all-encompassing spirit that includes us all. Indian spiritualism in the Upanishads recognizes the small worth of worldly desires and attachments in the light of inevitable death and the possibility of an extraordinary knowledge, or experience, that can carry us beyond this great fear.

"Were someone to hack the root of this large tree, dear child, it would bleed but live; were someone to hack its trunk, it would bleed but live; were someone to hack its tops, it would bleed but live. Pervaded by the living self (ātmā), it stands continually drinking and exulting. If life were to leave one branch, then that branch would dry up; if a second, then that would dry up; a third, then that would dry up; if the whole, then the whole would dry up. Just in this way indeed, dear child," he [Śvetaketu's teacher] said, "understand: this endowed most surely with life dies; life does not die. That which is this, this is the most subtle, everything here has that as its soul (ātmā). That is the reality; that is the self (ātmā); you are that O Śvetaketu." "Please, sir, instruct me even further." "Alright, dear one," he said. . . .

[Yama, "Death":] "Whatever desires, (even) the most difficult to win in the world of mortals, have them all at your demand. Delightful females with chariots, with music—none like these may be won by mortal men—be entertained by them, O Naciketas, given by me. Do not inquire into dying." *[Naciketas:] Existing only until tomorrow are such desires of a mortal, and, O Bringer-of-the-end, they wear away the splendor and vigor of every sense and power one has. Even all that is alive is of small worth indeed. Yours alone are the chariots; yours the dancing and the singing. A person is not to be satisfied with wealth. Are we to have wealth once we have seen you? But the boon that I wish to choose is this (answer this question): 'Will we continue to exist while you rule?'"* . . . *[Death:] Having seen in your grasp, O Naciketas, the fulfillment of desire and the foundation of the world and an infinity of power, of self-will, and the safe shore of fearlessness, and great fame sung far and wide, you wisely let it all go. A person who is wise and steadfast, discerning the God through spiritual discipline and study—the one that is difficult to experience, who has plunged deep into the hidden and is established in the secret place, standing in the cavern, the ancient—leaves joy and sorrow behind. . . . Subtler than the subtle, grander than the grand, the self is set in the secret heart of the creature. One who is without self-will experiences this (and becomes) free of sorrow; through his clearness and purity towards material things [or, "through the grace of the Creator"[6]], one experiences the self's greatness and breadth. Seated he travels far; lying down he goes everywhere. Who other than I is fit to know this God, the one that has both maddening pleasure and freedom from maddening pleasure? The wise person, recognizing the bodiless in bodies, the settled in things unsettled, the great and pervasive self (ātmā), does not grieve nor suffer. This the self is not to be won by eloquent instruction, nor by intelligence, nor by much study. Just that person whom this chooses, by such a person is this to be won; to such a person this the self reveals, uncovers its very own form and body.*

---

[6] The Sanskrit text is ambiguous between these two meanings; the first suggests Buddhist doctrines, the alternative suggests Hindu theism.

2. Reality, Good, and Evil: Zarathustra

Greek materialism conceived of a world that was morally neutral (even if, as Thales said, "all things are filled with gods"). Not all early thinkers conceived of reality that way. In the sixth century B.C., a Persian reformer named **Zarathustra** broke away from the Indic peoples who were the progenitors of the Upanishads. He preached a **monotheism** over and against the early Indian polytheism. Zarathustra claimed that his god—called **Ahura Mazda**—was not just spiritual or divine nature, but a creator, the one origin of all that existed. Ahura Mazda was a personal and all-good god, who created all natural things. Thus, Zarathustra and the religion he began (called Zoroastrianism) was extremely influential on the later monotheistic religions of Christianity, Judaism, and Islam.

Zarathustra was the first to recognize and formulate a doctrine regarding the existence and origin of good and evil in the universe. Ahura Mazda, the One Lord, created first among all things two twin spirits, lower sorts of divinities. The character of the first, called **Spenta Mainyush,** drew him and everything that followed him to goodness and good acts. The character of the other, called **Angra Mainyush,** led him and everything in his service to do evil. The twins are described in this passage from the *Gathas* (the original portion of the **Zend Avesta,** the scripture of Zoroastrianism).

Thus are the primeval spirits who as a pair (combining their opposite strivings), and (yet each) independent in his action, have been famed (of old). (They are) a better thing, they two, and a worse, as to thought, word, and as to deed. And between these two let the wisely acting choose right. (Yasna, XLV: 2)[7]

Although Angra Mainyush and Spenta Mainyush are born with natural tendencies toward evil and good, respectively, they choose quite freely to express it in action. Thus, while Ahura Mazda is responsible for the creation of everything, Angra Mainyush is responsible for unleashing evil, whose forms are deceit, destructiveness, and death. The natural world, according to Zoroastrianism, is set against itself like two armies, in an eternal battle between good and evil. Everything that exists freely chooses its alliance in accordance with its tendencies. Human beings, however, are free and conscious decision makers, and so have more choice about their moral alliances than do other creatures.

It followed that all natural entities were things either to be worshiped or reviled. Fire, which represented the "Beneficient Immortal" spirit, **Asha** or "Righteousness," was especially to be worshiped, as the best of the "good creation." In fact, in their own time, Zoroastrians were referred to as "fire worshipers."

In the following passage, also from the *Gathas,* Ahura Mazda despairs for his creation, should Asha find no good guardian for it.

---

[7] All passages from the Yasna are taken from the Zend-Avesta, Part III, trans. L. H. Mills; part of the series, *The Sacred Books of the East,* ed. F. Max Muller (Westport, CT: Greenwood Press, 1972 [Oxford, 1887]). All passages from the Yashts are taken from the Zend-Avesta, Part II, trans. James Darmesteter; part of the series, *The Sacred Books of the East,* ed. F. Max Muller (Motilal Banarsidass: Delhi, 1965 [Oxford, 1883]).

Upon this the creator of the Kine (the holy herds) asked of Righteousness:
How (was) thy guardian for the Kine (appointed) by thee when, as having
power (over all her fate), ye made her? . . . Whom did ye select as her (life's)
master who might hurl back the fury of the wicked?

Asha: . . . (Great was our perplexity); a chieftain who was capable of
smiting back (their fury), and who was himself without hate (was not to be
obtained by us).

Zarathustra freely takes initiative on behalf of the herd. Recognizing his worthiness, God names Zarathustra its guardian. Zarathustra, then, takes a profoundly spiritual perspective on the question of the underlying nature of reality.

Although Zoroastrianism originally had no full-blown notion of "immaterial stuff," or thought, as the essential nature of reality, Zarathustra's Ahura Mazda is an immortal, conscious entity that creates from thought, and it is the human's ability to think, according to Zarathustra, that gives humankind its unique moral capacity. In addition, Zoroastrianism had a notion of eternity—of which our time here on earth is only a part. At the end of our time, so it was claimed, the evil creation would be eternally vanquished.

3. Confucius

In its earlier form in China, philosophy was not so concerned with the questions we have called "protoscientific" but rather with human beings, human relationships, and human actions. One Chinese thinker of the sixth century B.C., **Confucius,** insisted that thinking is our fundamental nature. He was concerned essentially for the human good, which he described as "gentlemanly," and he and his followers set the forms for Chinese society for millennia afterward. Confucian metaphysics, unlike the ontologies of the West, was primarily concerned with people.

Confucius and his followers claimed that human beings were divided within themselves—that the muddle of human passions, ambitions, and confused loyalties distracted people from their moral duty. Through conscious and attentive adherence to propriety, they claimed, human beings could overcome their "personal selves" and their desires and achieve a goodness that was "impersonal." This impersonal life— the life of propriety—however, was a person's more "real" way of living. Through thinking, a person gained a sense of "self" as a Good Man. To "think," in the Confucian sense, was to become a different, better, person; and Confucius believed that few if any men were capable of such profound thought, as these passages from the *Analects* (Confucius' collected sayings) attest:

The Master [Confucius] said, [in response to the saying] 'He who thinks but
does not learn, is in grave danger.' (XI:5)

'He who learns, but
does not think, is
lost.'

The Master said, I have never yet seen anyone
whose desire to build up his moral power was as
strong as sexual desire. (IX:17)

The Master said, I have never yet seen a man who was truly steadfast. Someone answered, 'Shen Ch'eng'. The Master said, Ch'eng! He is at the mercy of his desires. How can he be called steadfast? (V:10)[8]

Confucian "thinking" was a form of attention, in which the Good Man fixed upon his "inner self." Thus, the thinking of the "gentleman" did not so much involve contemplation as unerring attention to duty, where "duty" was understood essentially as social propriety. The Confucian "doctrine of the mean" directed that the "gentleman" always avoid extremity. "Moderation in all things" was the way of propriety. Thus, Confucius' dicta were often concerned with delineating proper dress, proper diet, proper manner, proper government, and proper respect for the examples set by the "Good Men" of past ages. This inner truth, attention to which led one always to act with propriety, was called the "Way" (or **Tao**) of Goodness.

Wealth and rank are what every man desires; but if they can only be retained to the detriment of the Way he possesses, he must relinquish them. . . . The gentleman who ever parts company with goodness does not fulfill that name. Never for a moment does a gentleman quit the way of Goodness. (IV:5)

For Confucius, harmony represented not only the unity that could be achieved in music, but also that between the inner person and his exterior self, which was distracted by so many concerns between the self and society and within society as such. For Confucius, propriety and singleness of spirit were practical, not merely contemplative, activities; but they pointed, at least in the realm of human affairs, to a path between oneness and dispersion, inner reality and exterior appearance.

[B]oth small matters and great depend upon it [harmony]. If things go amiss, he who knows the harmony will be able to attune them. But if harmony itself is not modulated by ritual, things will go amiss. (I:12)

4. Lao Tsu, or the Poets of the Tao Te Ching

In China during Confucius' own lifetime, or so the story goes, a religious mystic named Lao Tsu espoused a doctrine that rebelled against the powerful Chinese dynasty and the ancient heroes whom Confucius revered. This radical doctrine, which developed into the religion Taoism, also rejected the Confucian faith in ritual, or the exterior expression of moral goodness. More likely, the poems attributed to Lao Tsu, called the poems of the *Tao Te Ching* (or "Way of Life"), were composed by several authors who shared Confucius' frustration with unethical behavior and political corruption, but responded in a radically different way. They were mystic recluses who claimed that there was a nature of reality, called the **Tao,** or "Way," which they understood quite differently from Confucius. They claimed that the *Tao* could not be taught or understood through discourse or rules, nor mimicked through the constancy of gentlemanly conduct. Rather, they claimed, the *Tao* could be known only

---

[8] From *The Analects of Confucius,* trans. and annotated by Arthur Waley (New York: Vintage, 1938).

through direct acquaintance with it. The seeker after the *Tao* could only be prepared for its revelation to him through meditation—not ever through ritual. Thus, the poets of the *Tao Te Ching* shared Confucius' primarily practical and moral focus, including the impersonality of goodness. They believed, however, that "impersonal goodness" could be neither sought nor expressed in any visible, speakable, observable way. They claimed the *Tao* was "ineffable" and could not be known through words or thought.

> Existence is beyond the power of words
> To define:
> Terms may be used
> But are none of them absolute.[9]

> When people lost sight of the way to live
> Came codes of love and harmony,
> Learning came, charity came,
> Hypocrisy took charge; . . .

Thus, these mystics were monists. They believed that the nature of reality is one, and that this One is, in a sense, living or conscious. But they did not go the way of the scientific and animistic doctrines of Greece. The poets of the *Tao Te Ching* claimed that the One, living reality, is fully beyond the visible, sensible world of our ordinary experience. It was certainly not one of the physical elements, nor could it be known by way of the rules set down by our ancestors.

> What we look for beyond seeing
> And call the unseen
> Listen for beyond hearing,
> And call the unheard,
> Grasp for beyond reaching
> And call the withheld,
> Merge beyond understanding
> In a oneness. . . .

> Knowledge studies others,
> Wisdom is self-known; . . .

> A realm is governed by ordinary acts,
> A battle is governed by extraordinary acts,
> The world is governed by no acts at all.

5. Buddha

Buddhism's historical founder, Siddhārtha Gautama of the Śākya clan, was born a prince in India (or perhaps what is now southern Nepal) near the year 560 B.C. The

---

[9] From *The Way of Life: An American Version*, trans. Witter Bynner (New York: The John Day Co., 1944). Sections 1, 18, 14, 33, and 57, respectively.

Buddha (the Sanskrit term *buddha* means literally "the awakened one") did not write anything himself. Records of his teachings and sermons apparently were kept by his disciples.

Through the centuries—first in India and then in almost every Asian country east of India—Buddhist doctrines and practices evolved; in each culture and epoch in which Buddhism prospered, local customs and indigenous religious beliefs were assimilated, giving the religion everywhere a unique form and expression.

As a young prince, the Buddha-to-be led a life of pleasure and enjoyment. His father, fearing the prophecy that his son would become a religious mendicant, tried to protect him from the sight of anything unpleasant or evil. However, one day the young prince journeyed some distance from the royal enclave and encountered first a diseased person, then a wrinkled and decrepit old man, and then a corpse. Inquiring about each of these and being told that all persons are subject to such infirmities, the prince renounced his life of enjoyments and vowed to search tirelessly for the origin and cause of these evils—and for the power to root them up. Buddha's experience of enlightenment did not occur immediately, however; he had to try various paths before arriving at the "Middle Way," a way of life he later proclaimed to his disciples. Eventually, after a long ordeal of meditation under a Bodhi tree, Buddha achieved the *summum bonum*, *"nibbana"* (the Sanskrit *"nirvāna"*), an extinction of evil at its roots. The remainder of his life, Buddha spent traveling and preaching—helping others to reach this supreme good and developing a picture of reality to support this conception.

Among the most important of Buddha's teachings are the **Four Noble Truths:**

1. All is suffering (and transitory).
2. The root of suffering is desire, attachment, and personal clinging.
3. There is a way to eliminate desire, and thereby eliminate suffering, namely *nibbana*.
4. The way to this supreme good is The Eightfold Noble Path: right thought, right resolve, right speech, right conduct, right livelihood, right effort, right mindfulness, and right concentration or meditation.

The Buddhist vision of the universe was, in one sense, much like Parmenides', in that the world as we know it must be understood as *illusion*. But, like the Hindus of the *Upanishads,* the underlying reality was One, except that the Buddhists called this "emptiness" or "nothingness." Also like the Hindus, the Buddha proclaimed the "wheel of becoming," which shows the connectedness between life, craving, rebirth (rebirth seems never to have been doubted by the Buddha), and the causal interdependence of all things, their insubstantiality, and similarly the insubstantiality of the self or soul—there is "no soul" according to the Buddha.[10] Although each of these doctrines and others received much thought and elaboration in later years, it is the

---

[10]Some of these doctrines clearly have forerunners in the Upanishads; it is noteworthy that the Buddha upholds certain lines of continuity between his and previous spiritual perceptors' teachings. Others are distinctively Buddhist, in particular the "insubstantiality" doctrines.

practice-doctrines' emphases on meditation and compassion that underpin the main themes of the Buddha. What follows is one of the most famous of the many hundreds of sermons and discourses attributed to the Buddha.

THE **"FIRE-SERMON"**
ATTRIBUTED TO **BUDDHA**

Then the Blessed One, having dwelt in Uruvelā as long as He wished, proceeded on his wanderings in the direction of Gayā Head, accompanied by a great congregation of priests, a thousand in number, who had all of them aforetime been monks with matted hair. And there in Gayā, on Gayā Head, The Blessed One dwelt, together with the thousand priests.

And there The Blessed One addressed the priests:

"All things, O priests, are on fire. And what, O priests, are all these things which are on fire?

"The eye, O priests, is on fire; forms are on fire; eye-consciousness is on fire; impressions received by the eye are on fire; and whatever sensation, pleasant, unpleasant, or indifferent, originates in dependence on impressions received by the eye, that also is on fire.

"And with what are these on fire?

"With the fire of passion, say I, with the fire of hatred, with the fire of infatuation; with birth, old age, death, sorrow, lamentation, misery, grief, and despair are they on fire.

"The ear is on fire; sounds are on fire; . . . the nose is on fire; odors are on fire; . . . the tongue is on fire; tastes are on fire; . . . the body is on fire; things tangible are on fire; . . . the mind is on fire; ideas are on fire; . . . mind-consciousness is on fire; impressions received by the mind are on fire; and whatever sensation, pleasant, unpleasant, or indifferent, originates in dependence on impressions received by the mind, that also is on fire.

"And with what are these on fire?

"With the fire of passion, say I, with the fire of hatred, with the fire of infatuation; with birth, old age, death, sorrow, lamentation, misery, grief, and despair are they on fire.

"Perceiving this, O priests, the learned and noble discipline conceives an aversion for the eye, conceives an aversion for forms, conceives an aversion for eye-consciousness, conceives an aversion for the impressions received by the eye; and whatever sensation, pleasant, unpleasant, or indifferent, originates in dependence on impressions received by the eye, for that also he conceives an aversion. Conceives an aversion for the ear, conceives an aversion for sounds, . . . conceives an aversion for the nose, conceives an aversion for odors, . . . conceives an aversion for the tongue, conceives an aversion for tastes, . . . conceives an aversion for the body, conceives an aversion for things tangible, . . . conceives an aversion for the mind, conceives an aversion for ideas, conceives an aversion for mind-consciousness, conceives an aversion for the impressions received by

. . . the learned and noble discipline . . . becomes divested of passion, and by the absence of passion he becomes free . . .

the mind; and whatever sensation, pleasant, unpleasant, or indifferent, originates in dependence on impressions received by the mind, for this also he conceives an aversion. And in conceiving this aversion, he becomes divested of passion, and by the absence of passion he becomes free, and when he is free he becomes aware that he is free; and he knows that rebirth is exhausted, that he has lived the holy life, that he has done what it behooved him to do, and that he is no more for this world."

Now while this exposition was being delivered, the minds of the thousand priests become free from attachment and delivered from the depravities.[11]

E. TWO KINDS OF METAPHYSICS: PLATO AND ARISTOTLE

The term *metaphysics* is relatively new (from about 70 B.C. or so), but it is generally agreed that the first great systematic metaphysicians were Plato (428–348 B.C.) and Aristotle (384–322 B.C.). Plato had been a student of Socrates and his most faithful recorder. (Almost all that we have of Socrates' teachings comes to us through Plato.) Yet Socrates was a moralist, not a metaphysician, and most of the metaphysical doctrines that Plato discusses using Socrates as his mouthpiece are probably Plato's own. Aristotle never tried to be a faithful disciple of Plato, and he became his teacher's harshest and most famous critic. It has been said of each of them that the history of philosophy is nothing more than a series of footnotes to their brilliant dialogues and treatises of twenty-four hundred years ago.

Metaphysics is what Aristotle called "first philosophy," the investigation of "Being as Being," or ultimate reality. What does it mean for something to exist? What is it for something to change? What makes one thing like another? Sometimes these questions, or at least the answers to these questions, are presupposed in our everyday thinking, whether we actually think about them or not. For example, we "naturally" believe that a tree continues to exist when we aren't looking at it. But why do we believe this? Even when such questions are the creations of philosophers, they outline views of the world that nonphilosophers share with them. The problem is, as we shall see, that people disagree violently about these issues, even from one generation to the next (for example, from Plato to Aristotle). What seems to be clear and obvious to one philosopher will seem obscure, merely metaphorical, or downright paradoxical to another. But as we watch the warring history of metaphysics, we too should be humbled by it, for it cannot be that all of those geniuses got it wrong while we now

---

[11] From *Mahā-Vagga,* trans. Henry Clark Warren, *Buddhism in Translation* (Boston: Harvard, 1896).

have it right. We too, whether explicitly or not, have metaphysical views, and we too may have to be ready to give them up as we think more about them and face further arguments.

With Plato and Aristotle, metaphysics becomes a cautious consuming enterprise, producing monumental systems of many volumes that require a lifetime of study to master. All we can do here is present a thumbnail sketch, with some brief selections of Plato's metaphysics and a very brief introduction to Aristotle's philosophy, which seems, at first glance, to be primarily a refutation of Plato. But like so many philosophers who seem to be attacking each other from completely opposed viewpoints, Plato and Aristotle have much in common. Both attempted to resolve the problems they inherited from the pre-Socratics: to find the ultimate substance of the universe, to understand what was eternal and unchanging, to understand change, and to show that the universe as a whole is intelligible to human understanding. Plato, following Parmenides and the other pre-Socratics who trusted their reason more than common sense, gave reason a grander position in human life and in the universe in general than it had ever received before. Aristotle, although he too defended reason, insisted that philosophy return to common sense and have a respect for ordinary opinion, which many of the Greek philosophers seemed to have lost. But whatever their differences, it is the shared grandeur of their enterprise that should impress us most about Plato and Aristotle. Between them, they established what we today call "philosophy." And between them, they also laid the intellectual foundations for Christian theology. **St. Augustine,** for example, was very much a Platonist, and **St. Thomas Aquinas** was thoroughly indebted to Aristotle.

1. Plato

The most important single feature of Plato's philosophy is his theory of **Forms.** (The Greek word is *Eidos.*) Plato's Forms are sometimes referred to as **Ideas,** but Plato does not mean "ideas" in a person's mind, but rather *ideal forms* or perfect examples—the perfect circle or perfect beauty. To avoid confusion, we shall use not the word "Ideas," but "Forms."

Forms are the ultimate reality. Things change, people grow old and die, but Forms are eternal and unchanging. Thus Plato could agree with Heraclitus that the world of our experience is constantly changing; but he could also agree with Parmenides, who insisted that the real world, the eternal and unchanging world, was not the same as the world of our experience. According to Plato, it was a *world of Forms,* a world of eternal truths. There were, in other words, two worlds: (1) the world in which we live, a world of constant change or a *world of Becoming,* and (2) a world of Forms, an unchanging world, the real world or the *world of Being.* We can see here Plato's close connection with Parmenides, holding that ultimate reality (the Forms) must be changeless and eternal. Furthermore, also in accordance with Parmenides, it is only such changeless and eternal things that truly can be known. Our only access to this latter world, the real world, is through our reason, our capacity for intellectual thought. Plato's "two-worlds" view was to have a direct and obvious influence on Christian theology. It would also affect philosophers, mathematicians, mystics, poets, and romantics of all kinds until the present day. But in his own time it had a more immediate importance; it allowed him to reconcile Heraclitus and Parmenides, to resolve the problems of the pre-Socratics, and to finally give ideas their proper place in human thought.

Plato thought of the Forms as having the special features of *what is* according to Parmenides. The most exciting Form for Plato was the Form of beauty. Plato thought a person could get to know beauty by falling in love in the right way and by realizing that the excitement of love is really aimed not at the personality of the person loved but at the link between that person and eternal beauty:

> *You see, the man who has been thus far guided in matters of Love, who has beheld beautiful things in the right order and correctly, is coming now to the goal of Loving: All of a sudden he will catch sight of something wonderfully beautiful in its nature; that, Socrates, is the reason for all his earlier labors: First, [Beauty] always is, and neither comes to be nor passes away, neither waxes nor wanes. Second, it is not beautiful this way and ugly that way, nor beautiful at one time and ugly at another; nor beautiful in relation to one thing and ugly in relation to another; nor is it beautiful here but ugly there, as it would be if it were beautiful for some people and ugly for others. Nor will the beautiful appear to him in the guise of a face or hands or anything else that belongs to the body. It will not appear to him as one idea or one kind of knowledge. It is not anywhere in another thing, as in an animal, or in earth, or in heaven, or in anything else, but itself by itself with itself, it is always one in form; and all the other beautiful things share in that, in such a way that when those others come to be or pass away, this does not become the least bit smaller or greater nor suffer any change.* [12]

For Plato, it is the world of Forms, the world of being, that is real. But this is not to say (as Parmenides had argued) that the world we live in, the world of becoming, is unreal. It is, however, less than real, not an illusion, but without those qualities of eternity and necessity that are the marks of true reality. This might seem like a verbal trick; it is not. The idea of a hierarchy of realities was already familiar in religions that antedated Plato's philosophy by centuries. We still use such notions in our own thinking, comparing, for example, the world of film and novels to "the real world," or the dreary humdrum of working-day life to "really living." But the best illustration of Plato's two-worlds view is his own, which he offers us in a parable called the Myth of the Cave.

It is a parable about bringing people from the less real to the really real. Indeed, one of the most striking features of Plato's philosophy (and much of Greek philosophy in general) is its emphasis on the *love* of wisdom, the irresistibility of reality; and what is too easily lost in translation is the very erotic imagery Plato uses to describe our passion for the truth. The Myth of the Cave not only illustrates two kinds

---

[12] Plato, *The Symposium*, trans. Paul Woodruff and Alexander Nehamas (Indianapolis, IN: Hackett, 1989).

of knowledge, two kinds of worlds; it is also a parable about human timidity, the difficulties we have in facing the truth, and our resistance to the dazzling light of truth itself.

FROM **THE REPUBLIC**
BY **PLATO**

SOCRATES: Imagine men to be living in an underground cavelike dwelling place, which has a way up to the light along its whole width, but the entrance is a long way up. The men have been there from childhood, with their neck and legs in fetters, so that they remain in the same place and can only see ahead of them, as their bonds prevent them turning their heads. Light is provided by a fire burning some way behind them, and on a higher ground, there is a path across the cave and along this a low wall has been built, like the screen at a puppet show in front of the performers who show their puppets above it.

GLAUCON: I see it.

SOCRATES: See then also men carrying along that wall, so that they overtop it, all kinds of artifacts, statues of men, reproductions of other animals in stone or wood fashioned in all sorts of ways, and, as is likely, some of the carriers are talking while others are silent.

GLAUCON: This is a strange picture, and strange prisoners.

SOCRATES: They are like us, I said. Do you think, in the first place, that such men could see anything of themselves and each other except the shadows which the fire casts upon the wall of the cave in front of them?

GLAUCON: How could they, if they have to keep their heads still throughout life?

SOCRATES: And is not the same true of the objects carried along the wall?

GLAUCON: Quite.

SOCRATES: If they could converse with one another, do you not think that they would consider these shadows to be the real things?

GLAUCON: Necessarily.

SOCRATES: What if their prison had an echo which reached them from in front of them? Whenever one of the carriers passing behind the wall spoke, would they not think that it was the shadow passing in front of them which was talking? Do you agree?

GLAUCON: By Zeus, I do.

SOCRATES: Altogether then, I said, such men would believe the truth to be nothing else than the shadows of the artifacts?

GLAUCON: They must believe that.

SOCRATES: Consider then what deliverance from their bonds and the curing of their ignorance would be if something like this naturally happened to them. Whenever one of them was freed, had to stand up suddenly, turn his head, walk, and look up toward the light, doing all that would give him pain, the flash of the fire would make it impossible for him to see the objects of which he had earlier seen the shadows. What do you think he would say if he was told that what he saw was foolishness, that he was now somewhat closer to reality and turned to things that existed more fully, that he saw more correctly? If one then pointed to each of the objects passing by, asked him what each was, and forced him to answer, do you not think he would be at a loss and believe that the things which he saw earlier were truer than the things now pointed out to him?

GLAUCON: Much truer.

SOCRATES: If one then compelled him to look at the fire itself, his eyes would hurt, he would turn round and flee toward those things which he could see, and think that they were in fact clearer than those now shown to him.

GLAUCON: Quite so.

SOCRATES: And if one were to drag him thence by force up the rough and steep path, and did not let him go before he was dragged into the sunlight, would he not be in physical pain and angry as he was dragged along? When he came into the light, with the sunlight filling his eyes, he would not be able to see a single one of the things which are now said to be true.

GLAUCON: Not at once, certainly.

SOCRATES: I think he would need time to get adjusted before he could see things in the world above; at first he would see shadows most easily, then reflections of men and other things in water, then the things themselves. After this he would see objects in the sky and the sky itself more easily at night, the light of the stars and the moon more easily than the sun and the light of the sun during the day.

GLAUCON: Of course.

SOCRATES: Then, at last, he would be able to see the sun, not images of it in water or in some alien place, but the sun itself in its own place, and be able to contemplate it.

GLAUCON: That must be so.

SOCRATES: After this he would reflect that it is the sun which provides the seasons and the years, which governs everything in the visible world, and is also in some way the cause of those other things which he used to see.

GLAUCON: Clearly that would be the next stage.

SOCRATES: What then? As he reminds himself of his first dwelling place, of the wisdom there and of his fellow prisoners, would he not reckon himself happy for the change, and pity them?

GLAUCON: Surely.

SOCRATES: And if the men below had praise and honours from each other, and prizes for the man who saw most clearly the shadows that passed before them, and who could best remember which usually came earlier and which later, and which came together and thus could most ably prophesy the future, do you think our man would desire those rewards and envy those who were honoured and held power among the prisoners, or would he feel, as Homer put it, that he certainly wished to be "serf to another man without possessions upon the earth"[13] and go through any suffering, rather than share their opinions and live as they do?

GLAUCON: Quite so, I think he would rather suffer anything.

SOCRATES: Reflect on this too. If this man went down into the cave again and sat down in the same seat, would his eyes not be filled with darkness, coming suddenly out of the sunlight?

GLAUCON: They certainly would.

SOCRATES: And if he had to contend again with those who had remained prisoners in recognizing those shadows while his sight was affected and his eyes had not settled down—and the time for this adjustment would not be short—would he not be ridiculed? Would it not be said that he had returned from his upward journey with his eyesight spoiled, and that it was not worthwhile even to attempt to travel upward? As for the man who tried to free them and lead them upward, if they would somehow lay their hands on him and kill him, they would do so.

GLAUCON: They certainly would.

SOCRATES: This whole image, my dear Glaucon, must be related to what we said before. The realm of the visible should be compared to the prison dwelling, and the fire inside it to the power of the sun. If you interpret the upward journey and the contemplation of things above as the upward journey of the soul to the intelligible realm, you will grasp what I surmise since you were keen to hear it. Whether it is true or not only the god knows, but this is how I see it, namely that in the intelligible world the Form of the Good is the last to be seen, and with difficulty; when seen it must be reckoned to be for all the cause of all that is right and beautiful, to have produced in the visible world both the light and the fount of light, while in the intelligible world it is itself that which produces and controls truth and intelligence, and he who is to act intelligently in public or in private must see it.

GLAUCON: I share your thought as far as I am able.

SOCRATES: Come then, share with me this thought also: do not be surprised that those who have reached this point are unwilling to occupy themselves with human affairs, and that their souls are always pressing upward to spend their time there, for this is natural if things are as our parable indicates.

GLAUCON: That is very likely.

SOCRATES: Further, do you think it at all surprising that anyone coming to the evils of human life from the contemplation of the divine behaves awkwardly and appears very ridiculous while his eyes are still dazzled and before he is sufficiently adjusted to the darkness around him, if he is compelled to contend in court or some other place about the shadows of justice or the objects of which they are shadows, and to carry through the contest about these in the way these things are understood by those who have never seen Justice itself?

---

[13] *The Odyssey* 11, 489–90, where Achilles says to Odysseus, on the latter's visit to the underworld, that he would rather be a servant to a poor man on earth than king among the dead [transl. note].

GLAUCON: That is not surprising at all.

SOCRATES: Anyone with intelligence would remember that the eyes may be confused in two ways and from two causes, coming from light into darkness as well as from darkness into light. Realizing that the same applies to the soul, whenever he sees a soul disturbed and unable to see something, he will not laugh mindlessly but will consider whether it has come from a brighter life and is dimmed because unadjusted, or has come from greater ignorance into greater light and is filled with a brighter dazzlement. The former he would declare happy in its life and experience, the latter he would pity, and if he should wish to laugh at it, his laughter would be less ridiculous than if he laughed at the soul that has come from the light above.

GLAUCON: What you say is very reasonable.

SOCRATES: We must then, if these things are true, think something like this about them, namely that education is not what some declare it to be; they say that knowledge is not present in the soul and that they put it in, like putting sight into blind eyes.

. . . one must turn one's whole soul from the world of becoming until it can endure to contemplate reality, and the brightest of realities, which we say is the Good.

GLAUCON: They surely say that.

SOCRATES: Our present argument shows that the capacity to learn and the organ with which to do so are present in every person's soul. It is as if it were not possible to turn the eye from darkness to light without turning the whole body; so one must turn one's whole soul from the world of becoming until it can endure to contemplate reality, and the brightest of realities, which we say is the Good.

GLAUCON: Yes.

SOCRATES: Education then is the art of doing this very thing, this turning around, the knowledge of how the soul can most easily and most effectively be turned around; it is not the art of putting the capacity of sight into the soul; the soul possesses that already but it is not turned the right way or looking where it should. This is what education has to deal with.

GLAUCON: That seems likely.[14]

Our world is like a set of shadows of the real world; that does not make it an illusion, but it does make it a mere imitation of the bright originals. Notice, too, the saviorlike role of the philosopher that Plato is setting up here. (His famous argument that philosophers should be kings, and kings philosophers, is included here too.) Like Pythagoras, Plato believed that knowledge of pure Forms, knowledge of the world of "Being," is a person's only hope for salvation and the "good life."

---

[14] Plato, *The Republic*, Bk. VII, trans. G. M. A. Grube (Indianapolis, IN: Hackett, 1974).

Socrates had taught his students, Plato among them, that the truth, if we can know it at all, must be in us. Plato (using his teacher as his literary spokesman) gives this revelation a new twist. It begins with a puzzle. How is it possible to learn anything? If we don't already know it, how will we recognize it when we find it? And if we already do know it, it makes no sense to say that we "learn it." Now this puzzle sounds like nonsense if we think only of examples such as "what is the beer consumption rate in Omaha, Nebraska?" To answer such questions, obviously we can't simply "look into ourselves"; we have to go out into the world and get information. But Plato insists that he is after much bigger game than "information"; he wants Knowledge (with a capital K), knowledge of reality, to which we have access only through thinking. That world, unlike the world of change and "information" in which we live, is characterized by the fact that everything in it is eternal and necessary. In this eternal world, reality is not discoverable merely through observation and experience. For example, consider the simple truth, $2 + 2 = 4$; it never changes—no experience is necessary to know it; it is one of those eternal truths that deserves its place in Plato's world of Being.

Perhaps the best way to understand Plato's exciting but somewhat mysterious notion of the Forms is to think of them in terms of *definitions.* The Forms are what different things of the same kind have in common and what make them things of the same kind. For example, two horses have in common the Form horse, and you recognize a horse, Plato would say, because of its Form. Suppose that you've never seen a horse before. Is it possible for you to know what a horse is? The answer is, "of course." It is enough that you have learned what a horse is (from pictures or descriptions) even if you've never seen one. But how is such learning possible? According to Plato, it is possible because we know a definition and thus recognize the Form of a horse, like the ideal Form of a triangle, and with it we are able to know what a horse is, even if we have never seen one, and we recognize horses when we do see them. In Plato's terms, we can recognize all horses, no matter what their age, shape, color, or peculiarities, just because they "participate" in the Form horse. For Plato, the Form horse has even more reality than particular, flesh-and-blood horses.

The concept of Form allows Plato to explain what it is that one comes to understand when one learns that two or more things are of the same kind. But for Plato the notion of Form serves another purpose as well. In addition to what we know about things from experience, we also know some things independent of experience, and we know these things with certainty (the same certainty Descartes sought in our introduction). For example, we know that every horse is an animal. We know that not simply because every horse that we have seen has turned out to be an animal, but because we know, apart from any particular experiences with horses, that the very Form horse includes the Form animal. (In our times, we would say that the meaning of the English word "horse" already includes the concept of "being an animal"; accordingly, philosophers refer to this kind of truth as **conceptual truth.** But this term was not available to Plato.)

Definitions are essential because without them it is difficult to know exactly what one is talking about. But this quest for definitions should not be confused with the high school debating technique of asking your opponent to "define [your] terms." Rather, a definition is the *conclusion* of a philosophical argument—and it is very hard to come by. In his dialogue *The Meno,* Plato has Socrates push for a definition of "virtue"; his arguments here are a good illustration of the Socratic pursuit of the Forms as definitions.

FROM *THE MENO*
BY **PLATO**

MENO: Can you tell me, Socrates, can virtue be taught? Or is it not teachable but the result of practice, or is it neither of these, but men possess it by nature or in some other way?

SOCRATES: Before now, Meno, Thessalians had a high reputation among the Greeks and were admired for their horsemanship and their wealth, but now, it seems to me, they are also admired for their wisdom, not least the fellow citizens of your friend Aristippus of Larissa. The responsibility for this reputation of yours lies with Gorgias, for when he came to your city he found that the leading Aleuadae, your lover Aristippus among them, loved him for his wisdom, and so did the other leading Thessalians. In particular, he accustomed you to give a bold and grand answer to any question you may be asked, as experts are likely to do. Indeed, he himself was ready to answer any Greek who wished to question him, and every question was answered. But here in Athens, my dear Meno, the opposite is the case, as if there were a dearth of wisdom, and wisdom seems to have departed hence to go to you. If then you want to ask one of us that sort of question, everyone will laugh and say: "Good stranger, you must think me happy indeed if you think I know whether virtue can be taught or how it comes to be; I am so far from knowing whether virtue can be taught or not that I do not even have any knowledge of what virtue itself is."

I myself, Meno, am as poor as my fellow citizens in this matter, and I blame myself for my complete ignorance about virtue. If I do not know what something is, how could I know what qualities it possesses? Or do you think that someone who does not know at all who Meno is could know whether he is good-looking or rich or well-born, or the opposite of these? Do you think that is possible?

MENO: I do not; but, Socrates, do you really not know what virtue is? Are we to report this to the folk back home about you?

SOCRATES: Not only that, my friend, but also that, as I believe, I have never yet met anyone else who did know.

MENO: How so? Did you not meet Gorgias when he was here?

SOCRATES: I did.

MENO: Did you then not think that he knew?

SOCRATES: I do not altogether remember, Meno, so that I cannot tell you now what I thought then. Perhaps he does know; you know what he used to say, so you remind me of what he said. You tell me yourself, if you are willing, for surely you share his views.—I do.

Let us leave Gorgias out of it, since he is not here. But, Meno, by the gods, what do you yourself say that virtue is? Speak and do not begrudge us, so that I may have spoken a most unfortunate untruth when I said that I had never met anyone who knew, if you and Gorgias are shown to know.

MENO: It is not hard to tell you, Socrates. First, if you want the virtue of a man, it is easy to say that a man's virtue consists of being able to manage public affairs and in so doing to benefit his friends and harm his enemies and to be careful that no harm comes to himself; if you want the virtue of a woman, it is not difficult to describe: she must manage the home well, preserve its possessions, and be submissive to her husband; the virtue of child, whether male or female, is different again, and so is that of an elderly man, if you want that, or if you want that of a free man or a slave. And there are very many other virtues, so that one is not at a loss to say what virtue is. There is virtue for every action and every age, for every task of ours and every one of us—and Socrates, the same is true for wickedness.

SOCRATES: I seem to be in great luck, Meno; while I am looking for one virtue, I have found you to have a whole swarm of them. But, Meno, to follow up the image of swarms, if I were asking you what is the nature of bees, and you said that they are many and of all kinds, what would you answer if I asked you: "Do you mean that they are many and varied and different from one another in so far as they are bees? Or are they no different in that regard, but in some other respect, in their beauty, for example, or their size or in some other such way?" Tell me, what would you answer if thus questioned?

MENO: I would say that they do not differ from one another in being bees.

SOCRATES: If I went on to say: "Tell me, what is this very thing, Meno, in which they are all the same and do not differ from one another?" Would you be able to tell me?

MENO: I would.[15]

Meno continues to try to satisfy Socrates with a definition of virtue, but every time he either contradicts himself or argues in a circle. So how does one know a definition? The answer, according to Plato, is that we recognize the Forms. We know what a horse is because we recognize the Form of a horse. We recognize that $2 + 2 = 4$ because we know the Forms. But how do we *know* the Forms? If we do not and cannot learn of them from experience (the changing world of Becoming in everyday life), then how do we know them at all? The answer, according to Plato, is that they already are "in us."

The second principle of Plato's metaphysics, our bridge between the two worlds, is the immortality and immateriality of the human soul. Our souls contain knowl-

---

[15] Plato, *The Meno,* trans. G. M. A. Grube (Indianapolis, IN: Hackett, 1976). The subsequent quotation from Plato also was translated by Grube.

edge of the world of Being that is already in us at birth. Such knowledge and ideas are called **innate**. Experience only triggers them off and allows us to "remember" them. Here is the extravagant answer to Plato's puzzle, "How is it possible to learn a truth about the world of Being?" The answer is: We already "know" it; it's just a matter of recalling it. Consider his famous illustration of this second doctrine in *The Meno:*

MENO: How will you look for it, Socrates, when you do not know at all what it is? How will you aim to search for something you do not know at all? If you should meet with it, how will you know that this is the thing that you did not know?

SOCRATES: I know what you want to say, Meno. Do you realize what a debater's argument you are bringing up, that a man cannot search either for what he knows or for what he does not know? He cannot search for what he knows— since he knows it, there is no need to search—nor for what he does not know, for he does not know what to look for.

MENO: Does that argument not seem sound to you, Socrates?

SOCRATES: Not to me.

MENO: Can you tell me why?

SOCRATES: I can. I have heard wise men and women talk about divine matters. . . .

MENO: What did they say?

SOCRATES: What was, I thought, both true and beautiful.

MENO: What was it, and who were they?

SOCRATES: The speakers were among the priests and priestesses whose care it is to be able to give an account of their practices. Pindar too says it, and many others of the divine among our poets. What they say is this; see whether you think they speak the truth: They say that the human soul is immortal; at times it comes to an end, which they call dying, at times it is reborn, but it is never destroyed, and one must therefore live one's life as piously as possible:

Persephone will return to the sun above in the ninth year the souls of those from whom she will exact punishment for old miseries, and from these come noble kings, mighty in strength and greatest in wisdom, and for the rest of time men will call them sacred heroes.

As the soul is immortal, has been born often and has seen all things here and in the underworld, there is nothing which it has not learned; so it is in no way surprising that it can recollect the things it knew before, both about virtue and other things. As the whole of nature is akin, and the soul has learned every-thing, nothing prevents a man, after recalling one thing only—a process men call learning—discovering everything else for himself, if he is brave and does not tire of the search, for searching and learning are, as a whole, recollection. We must, therefore, not believe that debater's argument, for it would make us idle, and fainthearted men like to hear it, whereas my argument makes them energetic and keen on the search. I trust that this is true, and I want to inquire along with you into the nature of virtue.

. . . there is no teaching but recollection, in order to show me up at once as contradicting myself.

MENO: Yes, Socrates, but how do you mean that we do not learn, but that what we call learning is recollection? Can you teach me that this is so?

SOCRATES: As I said just now, Meno, you are a rascal. You now ask me if I can teach you, when I say there is no teaching but recollection, in order to show me up at once as contradicting myself.

MENO: No, by Zeus, Socrates, that was not my intention when I spoke, but just a habit. If you can somehow show me that things are as you say, please do so.

At this dramatic point in the dialogue, Socrates calls over an illiterate, uneducated slave boy and with minimal instructions leads him to discover an elementary geometrical proof. What is crucial is that Socrates does not tell the boy the answer but "draws it out of him." But then the question becomes, where was this answer "in him," and how did he recognize it? After the demonstration, Socrates draws his conclusions:

SOCRATES: What do you think, Meno? Has he, in his answers, expressed any opinion that was not his own?

MENO: No, they were all his own.

SOCRATES: And yet, as we said, he did not know a short time ago?

MENO: That is true.

SOCRATES: So these opinions were in him, were they not?

MENO: Yes.

SOCRATES: So the man who does not know has within himself true opinions about the things that he does not know?

MENO: So it appears.

SOCRATES: These opinions have now just been stirred up like a dream, but if he were repeatedly asked these same questions in various ways, you know that in the end his knowledge about these things would be as accurate as anyone's.

MENO: It is likely.

SOCRATES: And he will know it without having been taught but only questioned, and find the knowledge within himself?

MENO: Yes.

SOCRATES: And is not finding knowledge within oneself recollection?

MENO: Certainly.

SOCRATES: Must he not either have at some time acquired the knowledge he now possesses, or else have always possessed it?

MENO: Yes.

SOCRATES: If he always had it, he would always have known. If he acquired it, he cannot have done so in his present life. Or has someone taught him geometry? For he will perform in the same way about all geometry, and all other knowledge. Has someone taught him everything? You should know, especially as he has been born and brought up in your house.

MENO: But I know that no one has taught him.

SOCRATES: Yet he has these opinions, or doesn't he?

MENO: That seems indisputable, Socrates.

SOCRATES: If he has not acquired them in his present life, is it not clear that he had them and had learned them at some other time?

MENO: It seems so.

SOCRATES: Then that was the time when he was not a human being?

MENO: Yes.

SOCRATES: If then, during the time he exists and is not a human being he will have true opinions which, when stirred by questioning, become knowledge, will not his soul have learned during all time? For it is clear that during all time he exists either as a man or not.

MENO: So it seems.

SOCRATES: Then if the truth about reality is always in our soul, the soul would be immortal so that you should always confidently try to seek out and recollect what you do not know at present—that is, what you do not recollect?

MENO: Somehow, Socrates, I think that what you say is right.

SOCRATES: I think so too, Meno.[16]

The doctrine of the immortality of the soul did not originate with Plato, of course. The ancient Egyptians believed in it many centuries before the first Greek philosophers, and Pythagoras had taught it to his students. But Plato's doctrine had more than religious significance; it was his answer to the skeptics and our bridge to the eternal world of Being. Of course, as a student of Socrates, he also appreciated the advantages of believing in an afterlife. Socrates could face death so calmly, he told his students, just because he believed in life after death. But for Plato it signified something more; it provided us with knowledge in this life as well as continued existence in another.

Plato's doctrines of the world of Being and the immortality of the soul introduce a clearly immaterialist conception of reality, as opposed to all of the more or less materialist conceptions we have encountered so far (the world as "stuff"). Even Pythagoras' numbers and Heraclitus' *logos* had their materialistic foundations, for neither philosopher was willing to grant these things independent existence, independent, that is, of the material things of this world. The things of Plato's world of Being can exist apart from them.

What is in this "other world," this world of Being? We have already met one of its inhabitants: the simple truth, 2 + 2 = 4. Its inhabitants are Forms. Consider the following familiar example: Your geometry teacher asks you to prove that the internal angles of a triangle total 180°. Simple enough. You remember how: You extend the base of the triangle, draw a line parallel to the base through the apex, and then proceed with your proof. But now, how do you know that you have not only shown that the internal angles of *this* triangle total 180°? As a matter of fact, it is pretty obvious that what you have drawn isn't even a triangle; the sides sag, one of the angles is broken, and the lines are fat (after all, a real line has no width at all). But yet you claim to have proved something about all triangles. Well, it is clear that you needn't do the proof even twice, much less an infinite number of times, to make your claim.

---

[16] Plato, *The Meno*, trans. G. M. A. Grube (Indianapolis, IN: Hackett, 1976).

How come? Because, you will answer, what you have been working with is not this particular poorly drawn triangle in your notebook but an ideal triangle, the form of all and any triangles. And there it is—Plato's Form of a triangle. It is not identical to any particular triangle. (How could it be, for it would have to be acute, isosceles, right, and nonright all at the same time!) It is their ideal Form, which each particular triangle approximates, that has its own existence in the world of Being. Plato says that every triangle that we can draw participates in the ideal Form and that it is only through reason, not through observation of particular triangles, that we come into contact with these ideal Forms.

To know a Platonic Form is not just to "see" something. It is to fall in love with it; in fact, it is to fall madly in love. So Socrates, in nearly all of Plato's dialogues, repeats the claim that a philosopher is a kind of lover. Indeed, he says that to know the Forms is to want to reproduce, to propagate, to teach everyone else to see them and to love them too. The Myth of the Cave and the metaphor of the Sun and shadows have two sides. The first is that the changing world of our everyday experience is only a shadow, an imitation of reality. But the second side is that the world of our everyday experience is also an image of the divine and ultimate reality, and so in the things of everyday life we get at least a glimpse of perfection.

Among the Forms are those ideals of human perfection that we should not only recognize but try to realize here in the world of Becoming: Wisdom, Justice, Beauty, and Goodness. To these ideals of perfection each of us aspires, and it is the definition of these ideals that is the task of every philosopher. His or her job (Socrates' main task in all of Plato's dialogues) is to sort out the common confusions about such vital matters. The business of the philosopher, in short, is to make others recognize eternal Forms and make it possible to achieve that heroic wisdom to which Plato's teacher, Socrates, had devoted his life.

I hope that you can appreciate, even from this brief sketch, the power of the metaphysical doctrines Plato has developed. You may also be aware of some of their difficulties. Most importantly, the gap between our world and the real world makes us exceedingly uncomfortable; none of us likes to think of ourselves living merely in the shadows. (As Plato himself warns, "wouldn't the prisoners who had never been released . . . laugh at him and even . . . kill" the philosopher who thus instructs them?) The connection between the world of Being and our own world of Becoming is not at all clear. Plato does say that the things of this latter world "participate" in the Forms of the former, but one thing that we shall have to learn right away in philosophy (and in every other discipline) is that the words that pretend to be explanations are often only cosmetic cover-ups. It looks as if we have a theory when in fact we have only a word. This is particularly true of Plato's word "participates" (*methexis*), and he himself raises serious doubts about it in his later dialogues. But the real attack comes, as it should come in philosophy, from his own students, and in particular, from one, perhaps the greatest of them all, Aristotle.

2. Aristotle

Aristotle claimed that he did not understand Plato's concept of "participation." (When a philosopher claims "not to understand" something, it means that he is pushing for a better account of it, that he is not at all satisfied so far. Aristotle probably understood Plato as well as anybody ever has.) Aristotle's objection was, essentially, that Plato had failed to explain the relationship between the Forms and particular things, and that the word "participation" was no more than "a mere empty phrase and a poetic metaphor."[17] Furthermore, Plato's emphasis on the Forms made it impossible to appreciate the full reality of particular things, and the eternal permanence of the Forms made them useless for understanding how particular things could change. Indeed, the question "How do things change?" becomes the central theme of Aristotle's philosophy.

Aristotle also wanted to determine the nature of reality. But Plato had argued that reality was something other than the world of our experience. Aristotle, a practical man of the earth, a great biologist, physicist, and worldly tutor to Alexander the Great, would have none of this. This world, our world, is reality. He agreed with Plato that knowledge must be universal and concerned with what things have in common, but he rejected Plato's idea that these common universal ingredients—the Forms of things—could be separated from particular things. But this meant that Aristotle also rejected Plato's separation of the human soul from the body, and Aristotle, unlike Plato, saw human beings entirely as creatures of nature, "rational animals"—but still animals. Metaphysics, for Aristotle, was not the study of another world, recollected in our eternal souls; metaphysics was simply the study of nature (*physis*) and, as importantly, the study of ourselves. Accordingly, he brought metaphysics "back home." But it must not be thought that he made it any simpler. The beginning student of Aristotle—as well as the trained scholar—will attest to the fact that he is among the most difficult authors in philosophy.

There is a branch of knowledge that studies being qua *being, and the attributes that belong to it in virtue of its own nature. Now this is not the same as any of the so-called special sciences, since none of these enquires universally about being* qua *being. They cut off some part of it and study the attributes of this part—that is what the mathematical sciences do, for instance. But since we are seeking the first principles, the highest causes, it is of being* qua *being that we must grasp the first causes.*[18]

... since we are seeking the first principles, the highest causes, it is of being *qua* being that we must grasp the first causes.

The study of being *qua* being is metaphysics, which Aristotle was the first to isolate from other branches of philosophy. It is, first of all, the study of the different ways the word *be* can be used. This leads Aristotle to his famous theory of categories:

There are several senses in which a thing may be said to "be." In one sense the "being" meant is "what a thing is" or a "this," while in another sense it means

---

[17] Aristotle, *Metaphysics,* trans. W. D. Ross (Oxford: Oxford University Press, 1924).
[18] Aristotle, *Metaphysics* T.1.1003a21.

*a quality or a quantity or one of the other things that are predicted as these are.
While "being" has all these senses, the primary type of being is obviously the
"what," which indicates the substance of the thing. For when we say of what
quality something is, we say that it is good or bad, not that it is six feet long or
that it is a man; but when we say what it is, we do not say "white" or "hot" or
"six feet long," but "a man" or "a god." All other things are said to be because
they are quantities of that which is in this primary sense, or qualities of it, or in
some other way characteristics of it."* [19]

The primary use of "be" is to tell us what something *really is,* what it is in an unqualified sense: We are, in this sense, a certain individual human being. We are also
a certain number of inches tall; but that fact is secondary, it is something *about* us,
which could change without changing what we *are,* first and foremost, and belongs
to the category of *quantity.* We may also be pale or dark; that fact also is secondary
and belongs to the category of *quality.* The primary category is that of *substance.*
"Substance," as Aristotle defines it, is "that which stands alone." In other words,
"substance" is *independent* being. You would exist, for instance, even if you didn't
have hair. But *your* hair could not exist without you, and so it is not a substance. Substances are the basic elements in Aristotle's metaphysics. A horse, a tree, and a butterfly are substances.

Tables and chairs are not primary beings for Aristotle, because he thinks of primary beings as having their own natures. Something made by a human being, such
as a table, can only exist *along with* human beings. It cannot move or fulfill its nature—in this case, holding our foot—by itself. Our nature is what we will do if nothing stops us. A human being grows up and leads a human life, if nothing stops him;
that's his nature. But a wooden table will inevitably rot if no one stops it, since that is
the nature of the wood it is made of. Wood has a nature, tables do not. For that reason, Aristotle treats artifacts (things we make) as having a lower level of being than
we do ourselves.

*Some people think that the nature and real being of a natural object is the
primary material in it (material in itself unformed)—in a bed it would be the
wood, in a statue the bronze. It is an indication of this, according to Antiphon,
that if you bury a bed, and the rotting wood becomes able to send up a shoot,
what comes up will not be a bed, but wood—suggesting that the arrangement
in accordance with the rules of the art belongs only incidentally, and that the
reality—what the thing really is—is what actually persists through all those
changes.* [20]

*But there is another way of speaking, according to which the nature of a thing
is its shape or form as given in its definition . . . and this rather than its matter*

---

[19] Aristotle, *Metaphysics* Z.1.1028a10.
[20] Aristotle, *Physics* II.1.193a9.

is a thing's nature. For (i) each thing is called whatever it is, when it is that thing actually rather than just potentially [the wood or the seed, the matter, is not a table or a lettuce—though it may have the potentiality of being one— until it has actually been put together or has actually germinated and grown]. Further, (ii) men come to be from men, but not beds from beds. That is precisely why people say that the nature of a bed is not the shape but the wood; if it sprouts it is not a bed but wood that comes up. But if this shows that the wood is nature, form too is nature; for men come to be from men.[21]

The doctrines of Aristotle's metaphysics sound as simple as they could be. This world, the world of our experience, is reality; there is no other world. The ultimate things of reality, which he calls substances, are individual things—people, horses, trees, and butterflies. Change is real and much of reality is subject to change. Forms are real, but cannot exist separately from the particular substances whose forms they are. This is not as radical a departure from Plato as it may seem. Aristotle did believe that the highest level of reality was not subject to change. Gods, the heavens, and even the forms of biological species were changeless in his system. Aristotle did not believe in any form of evolution.

For Aristotle, the primary substances are individual things; secondary substances (less real than individuals) are what he called the "species" and the "genus" to which a thing belongs. To return to our equestrian example, this particular horse, for Aristotle, is the primary substance. The species, "horse," and the even broader genus, "animal," are less real than the horse itself. Aristotle, like Plato, has a hierarchy of reality. But he turns Plato's hierarchy upside down. Plato holds that the more abstract things are the more real; Aristotle argues that the more concrete things, individuals, are the more real. For Aristotle, as in common sense, the more tangible things are considered to be the most real things.

What is a substance? Aristotle spends many pages giving a number of definitions, enough to keep the philosophers of the Middle Ages busy for a thousand years sorting them out. For our purposes, it will be enough to mention three different descriptions of substance, each of which is important for Aristotle and for later philosophy. The first characterization of substance is presented in terms of grammar. Aristotle says, "a substance is that which is neither predictable of a subject nor present in a subject; for instance, the individual man or horse."[22] More simply, a substance is the thing referred to by a noun, which is the subject of a sentence; for example, "the man is . . ." or "Socrates is . . ." or "the horse is. . . ." (This characterization would have been less confusing in Greek.) A more ontological way of saying this, but unfortunately very confusing too, is to say that a substance is independent of anything else. (We shall see how important this becomes in the modern metaphysics of Spinoza and Leibniz.) Other things might depend upon a substance, but a substance does not depend upon them. This is an awkward way of saying, perhaps, that the color of a

---

[21] Aristotle, *Physics* II.1.193.
[22] Aristotle, *Categories,* trans. J. L. Ackrill (Oxford: Oxford University Press, 1963).

horse could not exist without the horse; indeed, nothing could be true of a horse if it did not exist.

A second way of characterizing substance is to say that substance is what underlies all of the properties and changes in something. In this sense, you can say that you are the same person (that is, the same substance) that you were ten years ago, despite the fact that you are, quite obviously, very different in a great many ways. (Aristotle says, "Substance, while remaining the same, is capable of admitting contrary properties.") Combining these two characterizations, we can say that a substance is whatever is most basic to reality, like the pre-Socratic philosophers' notion of "stuff." It is the concrete individual thing, which remains constant despite the fact that it changes and has different properties at different times. You are the same person before and after you've gotten a haircut, tried on a new suit of clothes, or had your appendix removed.

The third characterization of substance requires the introduction of another new term, which became a central concern of philosophers before this century. A substance can be defined in terms of what is *essential*. An **essence** (or an **essential property**) is that aspect of an individual that identifies it as a particular individual. For example, it is part of the essence of being Socrates that he is a human being, that he lived in the fourth century B.C., and that he was wise. Anything that does not have these properties could not possibly be Socrates. There are other properties that Socrates has, of course; for example, the fact that he had a wart on his nose. But this is not an essential property. (Aristotle calls it an *accident* or an *accidental property*.) Socrates still would have been Socrates without it. But Socrates could not have been a centipede, for it is part of his essence to be human.

A substance is a combination of form and matter. Aristotle's "form" is roughly the same as Plato's Form, except that for Aristotle, it does not exist apart from the individual things that have it; it is always *informing* some matter. **Matter** is a discovery of Aristotle's. It is, basically, what things are made out of; it is what is given shape and structure by the form. The matter of a boat is wood; its form is the design that the boatbuilder realized in the wood. (Notice that "form" is written with a small *f* here, although Aristotle uses the same word as Plato, *eidos*. His word for the matter is *hylē*.)

This enabled Aristotle to explain change. Earlier philosophers, he thought, believed only in matter that by itself would stay the same. Plato believed only in Forms that are eternally unchanging. But Aristotle believed in things that *combined* matter and form in a variety of ways. Substantial change, the "coming to be and passing away" of a substance, takes place when matter is given a new form.

With both concepts available, Aristotle thinks he can avoid the mistakes of his predecessors, especially the mistake of Parmenides, which he blames on inexperience:

> *The first people to philosophise about the nature and truth of things got sidetracked and driven off course by inexperience. They said that nothing comes to be or passes away, because whatever comes to be must do so either from what is, or from what is not—and neither of these is possible. For what is cannot come to be, since it is already; and nothing can come to be from what is*

not, *since there must [in all change and coming into being] be something underlying.*[23]

The essence of a thing cannot change (or it would no longer be the same thing), and it is of little metaphysical importance if accidents change. So what does change? Form and matter, Aristotle says, cannot exist separately, but they can be *distinguished* everywhere in nature. The best examples can be found in human craftsmanship. One can take a lump of clay, for example, and make it into a bowl of any number of shapes. Or one can take a piece of silver and make it into a fork, a spoon, a bracelet, or a couple of rings. The clay or the silver is the matter; the shape and the function define the form. Aristotle also says that the matter itself can be analyzed in terms of form and matter. The matter of the clay and the silver would be the basic elements—earth, air, fire, and water. The form would be the shape and proportion these elements assume to make clay or silver. Indeed, Aristotle even holds that the basic elements themselves can be analyzed in terms of more primitive matter—hotness, coldness, dryness, and wetness—which combine to give the form of the elements. It is the form of things that we can know and explain, according to Aristotle, never the matter. Thus, we can *talk* about form and matter separately, and so *understand* change. His predecessor, he thought, mistook the way we talk about reality for the way it is. The form, *by itself,* can never change, nor can the matter, but the way they combine can change. By changing their form, caterpillars turn into butterflies and seeds into fruits and flowers. Thus, Aristotle explains both change and stability.

You may already anticipate certain troubles that will plague later philosophers. How much can we change a person, for example, and still have him or her be the same? Provide a haircut? A college education? A ten-year jail sentence? A sex-change operation? But before we worry about such problems, let us appreciate the importance of this notion of essence in Aristotle's philosophy. With it, he can do everything that Plato wanted to do with his special notion of Forms, but without invoking anything otherworldly. According to Aristotle, we can know that Socrates is a man, for instance, just because the essence of Socrates includes the property of being a man. We can know that a horse is an animal because the essence of being a horse includes the property of being an animal. In Plato, a conceptual truth of this kind was a truth about eternal Forms; for Aristotle, it is the form that changes, and a conceptual truth is rather a statement about essences.

In both medieval and modern philosophy, the concepts of substance and essence will take on a particularly important role in debates about God and his relation to his creations as well as in the continuing controversies in ontology that accompanied the rise of modern science. But Aristotle's ontology, much more than the philosophy of his predecessors, was linked up with an exciting prescientific cosmology, an account of the nature and purpose of the universe. In the Middle Ages, these theories profoundly inspired the great Christian theologian St. Thomas Aquinas, who would refer to Aristotle as simply "The Philosopher."

---

[23] Aristotle, *Physics* I.8.191a24.

To understand Aristotle's cosmology, we have to begin with a notion that is extremely foreign to people today; it is that the universe as a whole, and all things in it, have a purpose, a goal. The Greek word for "purpose" or "goal" is *telos,* and Aristotle's view is called **teleology.** Teleology can be directly contrasted with our modern scientific view of reality, which is primarily a *causal* view. Teleology explains something by looking for its purpose, goal, or end; causal explanations seek to understand *how* something came about, not *why* it came about. If you were asked why a frog has a heart, for example, the teleological answer would be "in order to keep it alive, by pumping the blood through its body." The causal answer, on the other hand, would be an explanation of the genetics, the evolutionary process, the development of the frog. If you were asked why a plant turns its leaves toward the sunlight, the teleological answer would be "in order to face the sun." The causal explanation, instead, would refer you to the fact that the cells grow faster on one side of the stem and that certain light-sensitive chemicals do such-and-such, and so on. In modern science, a causal answer is always preferable, and if a teleological answer is allowed at all it is always with the qualification that either there is an underlying causal explanation or we do not yet have (but someday will have) an adequate causal explanation. In Aristotle's metaphysics, on the other hand, one does not have an explanation at all unless one knows what purpose a thing or an event serves. "Nature does nothing in vain" is the motto of the teleologist.[24]

Aristotle believed that every substance, every individual thing whether human, animal, vegetable, or mineral, had its own nature, its own internal principles, certain tendencies that were part of its essence. This was, for example, the basis of his famous theory of falling objects: Every object has its "place," and if that object is moved, it will return to its rightful place on its own power. That means that any object of sufficient size, whose place is on (or under) the ground, will fall toward the earth immediately if it is lifted into the air. And larger objects, which are not slowed down by the air's resistance, will fall faster than smaller ones. Indeed, this seemed so inherently reasonable to Aristotle and everyone around him that it never occurred to them to test it under experimental conditions. But gravitation, which Newton would not discover for another two millennia, is essentially a causal concept. Aristotle's explanation was a teleological one, which the Greeks found far more convincing. Moreover, even if they had had the equipment for a test, which they did not, the Greeks still might not have believed the answer. Aristotle could not understand how causation could possibly operate at a distance. Thus, Aristotle thought that the cause of an object falling had to be in the object and not in the earth.

A reader who begins Aristotle may be initially confused by his use of the word *cause* (*aition*) to include not only what we have been calling causal explanation but teleological accounts as well. In fact, Aristotle lists four different kinds of **cause,** all of which together explain why a thing is as it is at any given time. The first of these

---

[24] Aristotle rejected a theory of natural selection argued by Empedocles twenty-three hundred years before Darwin because it was not a teleological theory.

is the matter that makes it up, the *material cause,* the silver in the spoon or the flesh and blood that make up our bodies. The second is the principle or law by which it is made, the *formal cause,* the architect's blueprint or the craftsman's model. The third is what we would call "the cause," which Aristotle calls the *efficient cause,* the person or event that actually makes something happen by doing something—pushing a button, causing an explosion, calling the person in charge. Fourth, there is the purpose of the thing, its *final cause,* its *telos.* Now notice that Aristotle's four causes are better suited for explaining human activities than giving what we would call scientific explanations about things that happen in nature. But this is indeed Aristotle's paradigm, and he even says in *Physics,*[25] "If purpose is present in art, it must also be present in nature." It is the final cause that provides us with the most important explanation.

We can understand this without any difficulty when we are explaining human activities. We want to know, first of all, what purpose a person has in doing something. But when it comes to nature, we do not generally ask about purpose, but we are more likely to ask about (efficient) causes. We might ask of an animal, what purpose is served by a long neck, or certain features in its feet, or some kind of fur, but we are less likely to ask that of a plant and would find such a question unintelligible with reference to rocks, clouds, and stars. Aristotle and his fellow Greeks would not find this unintelligible at all. Indeed, he believed (and thousands of scientists followed him until the seventeenth century) that everything that existed had to be accounted for in terms of its inner purposes and the overall purpose it served in nature. Thus a magnet literally "attracts" little pieces of metal, and the stars really do have a purpose in their heavenly wanderings. Not only do all the things and creatures of the universe have their purposes, but the universe itself has its purpose too. Indeed, it is this ultimate purpose of the universe that gives all the particular things their significance. Indeed, for Aristotle, the idea that the universe as a whole might *not* have a purpose would have been absurd. One of his most famous arguments is aimed at showing why there must be an ultimate purpose, a "first (Final) cause," or what he calls, "the prime mover."

Moreover, it is obvious that there is some first principle, and that the causes of things are not infinitely many either in a direct sequence or in kind. For the material generation of one thing from another cannot go on in an infinite progression (e.g. flesh from earth, earth from air, air from fire, and so on without a stop); nor can the source of motion (e.g. man be moved by air, air by the sun, the sun by Strife, with no limit to the series). In the same way neither can the Final Cause [that is, purposes] recede to infinity—walking having health for its object, and health happiness, and happiness something else: one thing always being done for the sake of another. And it is just the same with the Formal Cause [that is, the essence]. For in the case of all intermediate terms

---

[25] Aristotle, *Physics,* trans. W. D. Ross (Oxford: Oxford University Press, 1936).

of a series which are contained between a first and last term, the prior term is necessarily the cause of those which follow it; because if we had to say which of the three is the cause, we should say "the first." At any rate it is not the last term, because what comes at the end is not the cause of anything. Neither, again, is the intermediate term, which is only the cause of one (and it makes no difference whether there is one intermediate term or several, nor whether they are infinite or limited in number). But of series which are infinite in this way, and in general of the infinite, all the parts are equally intermediate, down to the present moment. Thus if there is no first term, there is no cause at all.[26]

The argument, simply stated, is that teleological explanations cannot go on forever, or what philosophers sometimes call an **infinite regress.** For Aristotle, if *x* exists for the purpose of *y* and *y* exists for the purpose of *z*, there must be some ultimate purpose that will explain them all. A similar argument can be made with regard to efficient causes, that if *p* makes *q* happen and *r* makes *p* happen and so on, there must be an end to the "and so on," and so too with the material cause and the formal cause. But the most exciting aspect of this infinite regress argument is the idea that the universe itself must have a purpose, a Final cause, a "prime mover" that Aristotle characterizes as "pure thought, thinking about itself." It is an obscure but intriguing idea, which was taken up by Christian theology as an apt characterization of the Christian God (see Chapter 5). But Aristotle's prime mover has few of the characteristics of the Judeo-Christian-Islamic God; he (it) did not create the universe and has no special concern for man. The prime mover is more of a metaphysical necessity than a proper object of worship. But it is not too far-fetched to say that Aristotle, like most of the Greeks, viewed the universe as something like a cosmic organism, with an ultimate purpose, whose ultimate goal was thinking itself.

We can appreciate how this cosmology would become a source of inspiration for a great many philosophers, poets, and religious people. In more recent centuries, for example, it was used as a welcome alternative to the nuts and bolts materialism of modern Newtonian science (as we shall see in Leibniz). Tied to the technical details of Aristotle's ontology is an extremely imaginative cosmology: the picture of a purposeful universe, developing according to its own goals and principles. It is a fascinating picture and still an attractive alternative to the lifeless picture of the physical universe that is so central to our modern scientific outlook.

F. MODERN METAPHYSICS: DESCARTES, SPINOZA, AND LEIBNIZ

Throughout the Middle Ages, philosophers and theologians developed elaborate systems of metaphysics, many of them derived directly or indirectly from the

---

[26] Aristotle, *Metaphysics*, trans. Hugh Tredennick (Cambridge, MA: Harvard University Press, 1933).

thoughts and theories of Plato and Aristotle. Inherent in all such systems was the confidence that the world is ultimately intelligible, and that the truths that reason can discern about reality are not only true, but necessarily true. Throughout this rich millennium of philosophy (from the later days of the Roman Empire through the Renaissance and Reformation), philosophy and theology in Europe became pretty much a single subject, until the rise of the "new" science in the sixteenth and seventeenth centuries. At that time a series of revolutions took place that justify a discussion about the beginning of the "modern" era of philosophy. What distinguished these revolutions was not a separation from religion and theology (most of these philosophers were pious theists whose God played a central role in their thinking), but rather a new boldness of thought, often in contradiction with church authority and strikingly original in its form. The father of these revolutions was René Descartes (whom we met earlier in our introduction), whose philosophy represented a radically new turn in some very old ways of metaphysical thinking. (We should remind ourselves that no thinker, however bold or brilliant, carries off a revolution all alone. Generations paved the way for Descartes' revolution.)

Descartes' metaphysics was derived from ancient concerns, and in particular from the Aristotelian notion of *substance* as it had developed through the intervening centuries of Judeo-Christian and Arabic-Islamic theology during the Middle Ages. It was also a product of modern science, which was rapidly developing under the guidance of such geniuses as **Copernicus** and Galileo, and soon, under Sir Isaac Newton. And as with Aristotle, one of Descartes' central concerns was teleology, the purposiveness of the world, but in the new religious climate the question of purposiveness was focused wholly on the Being through whom all purposes were to be ultimately explained, the Judeo-Christian-Islamic God. But this sense of purpose (or final causality) started to run counter to the notions of efficient and material causality that had already come to rule modern science. With the birth of modern science and the modern world, the clash between the teleological visions of faith and the causal explanations of science became inevitable.

The most dramatic new ingredient in modern metaphysics, however, was a concept that played virtually no role in ancient metaphysics at all, and that was the notion of *mind* or *consciousness*. To be sure, the Greeks talked about their own psychological states. (Aristotle wrote long discussions of such emotions as anger, for example. Homer often described the psychology of his heroes, but almost always in physiological terms.) But the idea of a mind as a self-contained arena—what the contemporary philosopher **Daniel Dennett** has dubbed "the Cartesian theater"—is distinctively new. One can trace its development through the centuries by way of the ever-increasing Christian emphasis on the soul and inner personal experience, but it is only in modern metaphysics that we get the full-blown view that what the world is made of, the ultimate reality of things, is the mind. This view, in general, is called **idealism.** For a few eccentric philosophers, this might be taken to mean that the reality of the world is a function of one's individual mind, but most idealists had something much grander in mind, as we shall see. Deriving their views from medieval Christianity, for example, some philosophers suggested that there is ultimately only one mind, or one supreme mind, and that is the mind of God. Others suggested that mind pervades everything, both God and everything else. In one sense, this view is plausible: we realize that we know about the things of reality only by way of their effects (direct or indirect) on our minds. But whether they exist only because of our minds is a much more radical proposition, and whether our minds are "free" to conceive of things and determine our actions, in the light of modern science, will become one of the most pressing concerns of philosophy.

Descartes' metaphysical system was an amalgam of the latest theories in science and mathematics (some of which he discovered), established theology, and the new science of psychology. The method itself (discussed briefly in the introduction) was based on the model of mathematical proof, starting with premises that were self-evident and arguing deductively to conclusions that were therefore equally certain. We consider Descartes' contributions to knowledge—and the famous arguments beginning with his *Cogito* ("I think, therefore I am")—in the following chapter. Here we consider Descartes' equally famous metaphysical model of the world, one which has set the stage for much of philosophy ever since. (The basic idea that mind and body are distinct is still referred to as **Cartesian dualism**.) Next we look at Descartes' two most famous and brilliant followers, who developed elaborate metaphysical systems quite different from—and in opposition to—his own. The first is a Jewish philosopher, excommunicated for his heresies, who lived his life in poverty on the outskirts of Amsterdam. He is **Benedictus**[27] **de Spinoza** (1632–1677). The second is his slightly younger contemporary, **Gottfried Wilhelm von Leibniz** (1646–1716), Germany's first, great, modern philosopher. Together, they present us with the classics in modern Western metaphysics, three very different speculations on the nature of the world.

1. René Descartes

Modern metaphysics begins with Descartes' insistence upon perfect certainty and mathematical deduction as the legitimate methodology. But methodology aside, metaphysics is a continuous enterprise from the Greeks through medieval philosophy, with Descartes its direct heir. We should not be surprised, for example, to find that the central concept of Descartes' metaphysics is *substance,* and that his definition of it (and the term itself) comes straight from Aristotle: "a thing existing in such a manner that it has need of no other thing in order to exist." (Both Spinoza and Leibniz follow Descartes in taking substance as their central concept, and they follow him also in their method. The three philosophers are usually grouped together as a single school of thought called *Rationalism.*)

Descartes' metaphysics can be understood best in terms of a monumental historical conflict between the "new" science (developed by Galileo and others) and the established authority of the Roman Catholic Church. Descartes, like many of the most important philosophers to follow him, was both an enthusiast of the new science—in fact he was an important contributor to both science and its mathematical foun-

---

[27] Born Baruch, he changed his name after he was excommunicated from the Jewish faith.

dations—and a religious man. He could not tolerate the idea that science should replace the orderly, meaningful worldview of Christianity with a Godless, amoral universe of mere "matter in motion." Neither could Descartes ever agree that science should reduce human existence—in particular, the thinking self—to another mere machine. (It is often noted that Descartes did think that animals were mere machines: What we too generously attribute to them by way of learning and responding to the environment is in fact nothing but a mechanical adjustment.) Accordingly, his metaphysics divides the world into three sorts of "substances": God; the mind, or self; and physical, material being. The latter two sorts of substances are, of course, created by and dependent on God. Indeed, Descartes begins all his studies with a proof of the existence of the world (and one's knowledge of it) that rests on the presumption of God's goodness. Because God is rational and good, we can trust (within limits) our own limited knowledge of the world. (We examine some of these proofs and arguments in the following chapter.) But because the world (of minds and matter) depends on God, there is no danger that science should leave us with a Godless, meaningless, mechanical universe. In Aristotelian terms, the ultimate causes in the universe are "final" (or purposive) causes, not "efficient" (or mechanical) causes. The physical world is God's creation; and though it must be understood by science according to causal mechanisms, it is, nevertheless, within the domain of God's providence.

Within the domain of nature there are two (sorts of) substances, mind and body. Because these are substances, they are utterly distinct and independent. One immediate advantage of this "Cartesian dualism" is that the science of mind and the science of physical bodies (like theology and science) do not and cannot contradict one another. There is a science of the self and a science of physics, and there is no reason to suppose that science will deny the freedom of the self anymore than there is reason to fear that science will ultimately conflict with theology. What is true of physical bodies is not what is true of minds, and vice versa. Bodies may be wholly constrained by the laws of physics, but minds are free.

What is **substance,** according to Descartes? He deliniates three different kinds:

ON SUBSTANCE
BY RENÉ DESCARTES

PRINCIPLE LI

What substance is, and that it is a name which we cannot attribute in the same sense to God and to His creatures.

As regards these matters which we consider as being things or modes of things, it is necessary that we should examine them here one by one. By substance, we can understand nothing else than a thing which so exists that it needs no other thing in order to exist. And in fact only one single substance can be understood which clearly needs nothing else, namely, God. We perceive that all other things can exist only by the help of the concourse of God. That is why the word substance does not pertain *univoce* to God and to other things, as they say in the Schools, that is, no common signification for this appellation which will apply equally to God and to them can be distinctly understood.[28]

PRINCIPLE LII

That it may be attributed univocally to the soul and to body, and how we know substance.

Created substances, however, whether corporeal or thinking, may be conceived under this common concept; for they are things which need only the concurrence of God in order to exist. But yet substance cannot be first discovered merely from the fact that it is a thing that exists, for that fact alone is not observed by us. We may, however, easily discover it by means of any one of its attributes because it is a common notion that nothing is possessed of no attributes, properties, or qualities. For this reason, when we perceive any attribute, we therefore conclude that some existing thing or substance to which it may be attributed, is necessarily present.

PRINCIPLE LIII

That each substance has a principal attribute, and that the attribute of the mind is thought, while that of body is extension.

> *. . . extension in length, breadth and depth, constitutes the nature of corporeal substance; and thought constitutes the nature of thinking substance.*

But although any one attribute is sufficient to give us a knowledge of substance, there is always one principal property of substance which constitutes its nature and essence, and on which all the others depend. Thus extension in length, breadth and depth, constitutes the nature of corporeal substance; and thought constitutes the nature of thinking substance. For all else that may be attributed to body presupposes extension, and is but a mode of this extended thing; as everything that we find in mind is but so many diverse forms of thinking. Thus, for example, we cannot conceive figure but as an extended thing, nor movement but as in an extended space; so imagination, feeling, and will,

---

[28] René Descartes, *Principles of Philosophy,* in *The Philosophical Works of Descartes,* eds. E. Haldane and G. R. T. Ross (Cambridge: Cambridge University Press, 1911). All subsequent Cartesian Principles are from this edition.

only exist in a thinking thing. But, on the other hand, we can conceive extension without figure or action, and thinking without imagination or sensation, and so on with the rest; as is quite clear to anyone who attends to the matter.

This is to say, following Aristotle, everything is either a substance or an attribute of substance, and a substance (as opposed to an attribute) can be thought of independently and can exist independently. Strictly speaking, this is true only of God. But we can also so define physical and mental substances. What defines physical substance, Descartes tells us, is its *extension in space*. Mind, by contrast, is unextended; that is, a thought does not have (in the sense that a wooden box has) a location in the physical dimensions of space.

PRINCIPLE LIV

That the nature of body consists . . . in . . . extension alone.

The nature of matter or of body in its universal aspect, does not consist in its being hard, or heavy, or coloured, or one that affects our senses in some other way, but solely in the fact that it is a substance extended in length, breadth and depth. . . . If, whenever we moved our hands in some direction, all the bodies in that part retreated with the same velocity as our hands approached them, we should never feel hardness; and yet we have no reason to believe that the bodies which recede in this way would on this account lose what makes them bodies. It follows from this that the nature of body does not consist in hardness. The same reason shows us that weight, colour, and all the other qualities of the kind that is perceived in corporeal matter, may be taken from it, it remaining meanwhile entire: it thus follows that the nature of body depends on none of these.

PRINCIPLE XIII

What external place is . . .

The words place and space signify nothing different from the body which is said to be in a place, and merely designate its magnitude, figure, and situation as regards other bodies. . . . For example, if we consider a man seated at the stern of a vessel when it is carried out to sea, he may be said to be in one place if we regard the parts of the vessel . . . : and yet he will be found continually to change his position, if regard be paid to the neighbouring shores. . . . But if at length we are persuaded that there are no points in the universe that are really immovable, as will presently be shown to be probable, we shall conclude that there is nothing that has a permanent place except in so far as it is fixed by our thought.

Although physical nature is ruled by mechanical, causal laws, mental substance (the mind, the self) is defined by its freedom.

PRINCIPLE XXXIX

That freedom of the will is self-evident.

Finally it is so evident that we are possessed of a free will that can give or withhold its assent, that this may be counted as one of the first and most ordinary notions that are found innately in us. We had before a very clear proof of this, for at the same time as we tried to doubt all things and even supposed that He who created us employed His unlimited powers in deceiving us in every way, we perceived in ourselves a liberty such that we were able to abstain from believing what was not perfectly certain and indubitable. But that of which we could not doubt at such a time is as self-evident and clear as anything we can ever know.

But the mind not only "wills"; it also understands. We perceive the world and come to know its objects. But since the physical world and the mind are two distinct substances, how can there be a link between the two? The answer is that we have *ideas,* which are states of mind but nevertheless represent objects in the world that are their causes. However, this raises a number of ancient and more modern problems. Descartes, like Plato and Aristotle, has far more faith in reason and its favorite methods (e.g., mathematics) than he does in perception and the information gleaned from the senses. The senses can fool us, and we tend to rush to judgment prematurely on the basis of sensory experience. For instance:

> *When I feel pain in my foot, my knowledge of physics teaches me that this sensation is communicated by means of nerves dispersed through the foot, which, being extended like cords from there to the brain, when they are contracted in the foot, at the same time contract the inmost portions of the brain which is their extremity and place of origin, and then excite a certain movement which nature has established in order to cause the mind to be affected by a sensation of pain represented as existing in the foot. But because these nerves must pass through the tibia, the thigh, the loins, the back and the neck, in order to reach from the leg to the brain, it may happen that although their extremities which are in the foot are not affected, but only certain ones of their intervening parts, this action will excite the same movement in the brain that might have been excited there by a hurt received in the foot, in consequence of which the mind will necessarily feel in the foot the same pain as if it had received a hurt. And the same holds good of all the other perceptions of our senses. . . .*
>
> *From this it is quite clear that, notwithstanding the supreme goodness of God, the nature of man, inasmuch as it is composed of mind and body, cannot be otherwise than sometimes a source of deception.*[29]

But there is another source of ideas in addition to those caused in us by perception. There are also *innate* ideas, those implanted in us by God. Because of innate ideas

---

[29] Descartes, *Meditations,* pp. 196–98.

we can know certain propositions to be true *for certain* (e.g., the propositions of geometry, as Plato also had argued). It is because of innate ideas that we are able to *reason* and, in particular, to do philosophy, to know God, to know universal truths. But even here a dramatic difference must be noted between Descartes and his ancient predecessors. Plato and Aristotle would have claimed to know reality itself (whether this consisted of Forms or essences). But Descartes ultimately claims that we know only the ideas. There is always that gap between the mind and the world that the ancients never allowed and never entertained. Thus the doctrine of innate ideas might be said to play an even more essential role in Descartes' philosophy than in Plato's. Nevertheless, in his time Descartes was accused by the Roman Catholic Church of overreaching our claim to knowledge: His claim that the human mind has access to the truth through innate ideas was still a challenge to the church's claim to being the sole authority in all ultimate matters.

The most difficult problem facing Descartes' philosophy, however, was the relationship between the various substances. How could God create a substance if that so-called substance were then dependent on God? For example, how could one substance interact with another as physical objects must do if they are to cause in us a perception? In general, how do the mind and the body interact, as surely they must, on Descartes' account? By definition substances are distinct and independent; interaction would seem to be interdependence and not logically possible. These are the questions that most bothered Spinoza and Leibniz—the questions that would define much of philosophy for years to come.

With the rise of modern science, it became the generally accepted view that the universe was a giant machine, perhaps set up by God, but in any case a well-coordinated and predictable mechanism. Isaac Newton's discovery of the causal laws of motion and gravity only brought to a climax a scientific worldview that had been in the making for centuries. And though ancient animism was still alive and belief in God and spirituality was still virtually universal, the modern mechanical view of reality was an absolutely unavoidable consideration for any metaphysician.

Both Spinoza and Leibniz fully appreciated this modern scientific view, although they interpreted it very differently. They were both religious men. (Spinoza, ironically, was branded an atheist and his philosophy banned from most of Europe.) They both accepted Descartes' "rationalist," deductive method and both developed their thinking along the lines of a geometrical system. They both began by considering the concept of substance. Yet Spinoza emerged as a monist, Leibniz as a pluralist. In viewing their impressive systems of thought, it is important to keep in mind the long history we have quickly reviewed, the powerful influences of Christianity and science, and, most importantly, the various metaphysical problems to which we were introduced in the preceding chapter.

2. Benedictus de Spinoza

Spinoza's *Ethics* is one of the few modern works that is accepted as an unqualified classic by virtually everyone in philosophy. It is the author's only major work. Spinoza was an avid political reformer, particularly on the issue of religious toleration, and even in liberal Amsterdam that made him a dangerous person to know. The following work, which, as you will see, is much more than a study in ethics, was his most forceful contribution to the issue of tolerance. Spinoza introduced a shockingly radical reinterpretation of God and His relation to the universe. He also gave an equally shocking theory of our roles in the universe. So while you are attempting to comprehend these difficult statements and proofs about "substance," keep your mind open for the dramatic changes in the way Spinoza teaches us to look at our world and for his radical rethinking of Judaism.

Spinoza begins with a set of definitions:

FROM *ETHICS*
BY **BENEDICTUS DE SPINOZA**

DEFINITIONS

I. By that which is *self-caused,* I mean that of which the essence involves existence, or that of which the nature is only conceivable as existent.

II. A thing is called *finite after its kind,* when it can be limited by another thing of the same nature; for instance, a body is called finite because we always conceive another greater body. So, also, a thought is limited by another thought, but a body is not limited by thought, nor a thought by body.

III. By *substance,* I mean that which is in itself, and is conceived through itself: in other words, that of which a conception can be formed independently of any other conception.

IV. By *attribute,* I mean that which the intellect perceives as constituting the essence of substance.

V. By *mode,* I mean the modifications of substance, or that which exists in, and is conceived through, something other than itself.

VI. By *God,* I mean a being absolutely infinite—that is, a substance consisting in infinite attributes, in which each expresses eternal and infinite essentiality.

VII. That thing is called free, which exists solely by the necessity of its own nature, and of which the action is determined by itself alone. On the other hand, that thing is necessary, or rather constrained, which is determined by something external to itself to a fixed and definite method of existence or action.

VIII. By *eternity,* I mean existence itself, in so far as it is conceived necessarily to follow solely from the definition of that which is eternal.[30]

These definitions sound much more forbidding than they really are. Notice first how many of these terms and definitions are familiar to us from Aristotle: for example, the definition of substance as the basic "stuff" that has various properties but

---

[30] Benedictus de Spinoza, *Ethics,* in *The Rationalists,* trans. R. H. M. Elwes (New York: Doubleday, 1960). All subsequent quotations from Spinoza are from this edition of *Ethics.*

is dependent only on itself and can be thought of without thinking of anything else. **Attributes** and **modes,** on the other hand, are properties: attributes consist of essential characteristics of a substance; modes are modifications of attributes. (For example, having a body is an attribute of substance; being blond and blue-eyed are merely modes.) The **cause-of-itself** is like Aristotle's prime mover, but with some very important differences. Spinoza's "mover" turns out to be identical to the universe, and Spinoza's "God" is much more than "thought thinking itself," as in Aristotle. But the basic starting point of the entire system, as summarized in these definitions and axioms, is the Aristotelian notion of substance. Like the ancient metaphysicians, Spinoza insists that whatever really exists, exists eternally (Definition VIII). But that also means—there can be no Creation and no Creator!

As in geometry, the definitions are followed by a set of *axioms,* that is, principles that are so obvious that they need no defense. In plane geometry, such an axiom would be "the shortest distance between two points is a straight line." Spinoza's axioms may not seem quite so obvious at first glance, partly because of the unfamiliarity of his metaphysical terminology.

AXIOMS

Everything which exists, exists either in itself or in something else.

I. Everything which exists, exists either in itself or in something else.
II. That which cannot be conceived through anything else must be conceived through itself.
III. From a given definite cause an effect necessarily follows, and, on the other hand, if no definite cause be granted, it is impossible that an effect can follow.
IV. The knowledge of an effect depends on and involves the knowledge of a cause.
V. Things which have nothing in common cannot be understood, the one by means of the other; the conception of one does not involve the conception of the other.
VI. A true idea must correspond with its ideate or object.
VII. If a thing can be conceived as non-existing, its essence does not involve existence.

You can see that the axioms follow approximately the same sequence as the definitions, and the axioms in most cases are based on the definitions, although they do not strictly follow from them. For example, Axiom I, like Definition I, concerns the idea that everything has an explanation. Definition I, although stated in terms of "cause" ("self-caused"), concerns that which must exist if it can just be thought of. Axiom I says that everything must either be explainable through itself (that is, "self-caused") or through something else.

Similarly, Definition II uses a technical term ("finite after its kind") to talk about things that can be explained only by reference to something greater, while Axiom II says that anything that cannot be so explained must be explained simply in terms of itself ("self-caused" again). Axioms III and IV outline the basic principles of cause and effect; that is, that a cause makes its effect happen necessarily, and without the cause, there would be no effect, and that the knowledge of the effect depends on knowing the cause. (These principles have had a long and important history in both metaphysics and theories of science and knowledge. They will play a key role in Spinoza's theory of determinism [the idea that everything happens necessarily because of its causes] and in "deterministic" theories generally. These will be discussed in Chapter 9 in detail.) Axioms V–VII return to the central theme of explanation begun in Axioms I and II; Axiom V insists that one thing can be explained in terms of another only if they have "something in common." Thus you explain one physical event in terms of another physical event (since they have in common certain physical properties). Axiom VI repeats the important assumption we made explicit at the end of Chapter 1, namely, that our ideas are capable of grasping reality. (This axiom also states a seemingly innocent theory of truth, often called "the correspondence theory of truth," which says that "a true idea corresponds with some actual fact [*ideate* or *object*] in the world." This is discussed in Chapter 4.) Axiom VII returns to the idea of "essence involving existence," in other words, that which is self-caused, or substance or God. Axiom VII is stated negatively, however, and says that if we can think of something as not existing (for example, we can imagine what it would be like to live in a world without freeways, or without stars, or even without other people), then "its essence does not involve existence." That is, existing is not one of its essential characteristics and it is not "self-caused."

The general theme of the axioms is that everything has an explanation for its existence, either by reference to something else or because it is "self-caused" or self-explanatory, that is, its "essence involves its existence" or it is entirely "in itself and conceived through itself." This last phrase is from the definition of "substance" (Def. III), so you can see how, even in his axioms and definitions, Spinoza is setting up his main thesis—that there can only be one substance.

Starting with these definitions and axioms, which he takes to be unobjectionable, Spinoza begins the "proofs" of his "propositions," which follow like the theorems of Euclidean geometry from the definitions of terms such as "line," "point," and "parallel." Again, these look forbidding, but their philosophical relevance should be clear.

PROPOSITIONS

PROP. I. *Substance is by nature prior to its modifications.*

Proof.—This is clear from Def. iii. and v.

PROP. II. *Two substances, whose attributes are different, have nothing in common.*

Proof.—Also evident from Def. iii. For each must exist in itself, and be conceived through itself; in other words, the conception of one does not imply the conception of the other.

PROP. III. *Things which have nothing in common cannot be one the cause of the other.*

Proof.—If they have nothing in common, it follows that one cannot be apprehended by means of the other (Ax. v.), and, therefore, one cannot be the cause of the other (Ax. iv.). *Q.E.D.* [Latin, *quod erat demonstrandum,* a phrase used in traditional logic meaning "thus it is proven."]

PROP. IV. *Two or more distinct things are distinguished one from the other either by the difference of the attributes of the substances, or by the difference of their modifications.*

Proof.—Everything which exists, exists either in itself or in something else (Ax. i.),—that is (by Def. iii. and v.), nothing is granted in addition to the understanding, except substance and its modifications. Nothing is, therefore, given besides the understanding, by which several things may be distinguished one from the other, except the substances, or, in other words (see Ax. iv.), their attributes and modifications. *Q.E.D.*

PROP. V. *There cannot exist in the universe two or more substances having the same nature or attribute.*

Proof.—If several distinct substances be granted, they must be distinguished one from the other, either by the difference of their attributes, or by the difference of their modifications (Prop. iv.). If only by the difference of their attributes, it will be granted that there cannot be more than one with an identical attribute. If by the difference of their modifications—as substance is naturally prior to its modifications (Prop. i.),—it follows that setting the modifications aside, and considering substance in itself, that is truly (Deff. iii. and vi.), there cannot be conceived one substance different from another,—that is (by Prop. iv.), there cannot be granted several substances, but one substance only. *Q.E.D.*

PROP. VI. *One substance cannot be produced by another substance.*

Proof.—It is impossible that there should be in the universe two substances with an identical attribute, *i.e.,* which have anything common to them both (Prop. ii.), and, therefore (Prop. iii.), one cannot be the cause of another, neither can one be produced by the other. *Q.E.D.*

So far, the main point is quite simple: if there is more than one substance, the substances could have no possible relation to each other. Therefore, by a kind of *reductio ad absurdum* argument, there can only be one substance. In the propositions that follow (and especially the note to Prop. VIII) this is demonstrated again:

PROP. VII. *Existence belongs to the nature of substance.*

Proof.—Substance cannot be produced by anything external (Corollary, Prop. vi.), it must, therefore, be its own cause—that is, its essence necessarily involves existence, or existence belongs to its nature.

PROP. VIII. *Every substance is necessarily infinite.*

Proof.—There can only be one substance with an identical attribute, and existence follows from its nature (Prop. vii.); its nature, therefore, involves existence, either as finite or infinite. It does not exist as finite, for (by Def. ii.) it would then be limited by something else of the same kind, which would also necessarily exist (Prop. vii.); and there would be two substances with an identical attribute, which is absurd (Prop. v.). It therefore exists as infinite. *Q.E.D.*

Note.—No doubt it will be difficult for those who think about things loosely, and have not been accustomed to know them by their primary causes, to comprehend the demonstration of Prop. vii.: for such persons make no distinction between the modifications of substances and the substances themselves, and are ignorant of the manner in which things are produced; hence they attribute to substances the beginning which they observe in natural objects. Those who are ignorant of true causes, make complete confusion—think that trees might talk just as well as men—that men might be formed from stones as well as from seed; and imagine that any form might be changed into any other. So, also, those who confuse the two natures, divine and human, readily attribute human passions to the deity, especially so long as they do not know how passions originate in the mind. But, if people would consider the nature of substance, they would have no doubt about the truth of Prop. vii. In fact, this proposition would be a universal axiom, and accounted a truism. For, by substance, would be understood that which is in itself, and is conceived through itself—that is, something of which the conception requires not the conception of anything else; whereas modifications exist in something external to themselves, and a conception of them is formed by means of a conception of the thing in which they exist. Therefore, we may have true ideas of non-existent modifications; for, although they may have no *actual* existence apart from the conceiving intellect, yet their essence is so involved in something external to themselves that they may through it be conceived. Whereas the only truth substances can have, external to the intellect, must consist in their existence, because they are conceived through themselves. Therefore, for a person to say that he has a clear and distinct—that is, a true—idea of a substance, but that he is not sure whether such substance exists, would be the same as if he said that he had a true idea, but was not sure whether or not it was false (a little consideration will make this plain); or if anyone affirmed that substance is created, it would be the same as saying that a false idea was true—in short, the height of absurdity. It must, then, necessarily be admitted that the existence of substance as its essence is an eternal truth. And we can hence conclude by another process of reasoning—that there is but one such substance.

This last phrase summarizes the key doctrine of the entire *Ethics,* that there can be but one substance. The argument in this note, which insists that the essence of substance includes its existence, was a very popular argument throughout the Middle Ages. It means, quite simply, that if you can even imagine something whose essence includes existence, then you know that thing necessarily exists. In a further digression (but it is the digressions that often contain the most philosophy), Spinoza adopts Aristotle's insistence (see p. 87) that everything (or every event) must have its cause:

> There is necessarily for each individual existent thing a cause why it should exist.
> This cause of existence must either be contained in the nature and definition of the thing defined, or must be postulated apart from such definition.

Such an assertion gives Aristotle the basis for his "prime mover" argument. But Spinoza, unlike Aristotle, has no qualms about the idea of an "infinite regress"; in his view, the universe extends back in time forever, has always existed, and at no time ever came into existence.

What then follows is the working-out of the notion that there is one substance:

> PROP. IX. *The more reality or being a thing has, the greater the number of its attributes* (Def. iv.).
> PROP. X. *Each particular attribute of the one substance must be conceived through itself.*
> *Proof.*—An attribute is that which the intellect perceives of substance, as constituting its essence (Def. iv.), and, therefore, must be conceived through itself (Def. iii.). *Q.E.D.*

Spinoza goes on to explain that, although we might think of different attributes separately (for example, think of minds and bodies as totally different from each other), we must not conclude that they are different substances. They are rather separate properties of one and the same substance. He then concludes:

> Consequently it is abundantly clear, that an absolutely infinite being must necessarily be defined as consisting in infinite attributes, each of which expresses a certain eternal and infinite essence.
> If anyone now ask, by what sign shall he be able to distinguish different substances, let him read the following propositions, which show that there is but one substance in the universe, and that it is absolutely infinite, wherefore such a sign would be sought for in vain.

Now this looks complicated, but we can appreciate its straightforward significance by looking at it through our earlier questions in ontology and cosmology (p. 96): first, "How many substances does Spinoza say that there are (and must be)?" Only one—he is a monist, like the earliest pre-Socratics, Descartes, Spinoza's immediate predecessor, had argued that there are three kinds of substance: bodies, minds, and God. Spinoza, however, argues that the very definition of substance makes it necessary that there be only one substance and that bodies and minds are attributes of this one substance, not substances themselves.

So the answer to our second ontological question, "What kind of substances?" is "one infinite substance," the full nature of which we cannot know. But at least we know two of its properties, namely body and mind. Now notice that this gets around a problem that will plague Descartes (see Chapter 5): How can different substances, which by definition are independent, interact with one another (our fourth question)? If mind and body are separate substances, then how can they come together to form a person? For Spinoza, since there is only one substance, this problem does not arise. With regard to our third question, "How do we distinguish different things (attributes, bodies, and minds)?" Spinoza's answer is fantastic; there is ultimately only one body, namely the physical universe, and one mind, namely all of the thinking in the universe (which in turn are different attributes of the one substance). This means that distinctions between our bodies ("my" body and "your" body) and between our bodies and the rest of the physical universe are ultimately unwarranted, a humanistic pretension that has no basis in reality. But even more surprising is the idea that there is but a single mind and that our individual minds are somehow only "part of it" (that is, particular modes) but not individual minds at all! Your pride in your "individuality," therefore, has no foundation in reality. You are only a part of that one cosmic substance, the universe.

But the universe is also God. Here is where the innocent-looking obscurity of Spinoza's system becomes the heresy that was banned throughout Europe. By Proposition X, Spinoza has proved that God, substance, and the cause-of-itself are all identical. In the next few propositions, he proves that God necessarily exists (we shall see similar proofs in Chapter 2). Then, Proposition XIV: *"Besides God, no substance can be granted or conceived."* This means that God and the universe are one and the same. This position, called *pantheism* (literally, "everything is God"), was considered sacrilege, even in liberal Amsterdam. It means, against all traditional Judeo-Christian teachings, that God has no existence independent of the universe and that He therefore cannot be its Creator. Look again at the explanation to Definition VIII and then at Proposition XV and those that follow:

> PROP. XV. *Whatsoever is, is in God, and without God nothing can be, or be conceived.*
>
> PROP. XVI. *From the necessity of the divine nature must follow an infinite number of things in infinite ways—that is, all things which can fall within the sphere of infinite intellect.*
>
> PROP. XVII. *God acts solely by the laws of his own nature, and is not constrained by anyone.*
>
> PROP. XVIII. *God is the indwelling and not the transient cause of all things.*
>
> PROP. XIX. *God, and all the attributes of God, are eternal.*
>
> PROP. XX. *The existence of God and his essence are one and the same.*
>
> PROP. XXI. *All things which follow from the absolute nature of any attribute of God must always exist and be infinite, or, in other words, are eternal and infinite through the said attribute.*
>
> PROP. XXII. *Whatever follows from any attribute of God, in so far as it is modified by a modification, which exists necessarily and as infinite, through the said attribute, must also exist necessarily and as infinite.*
>
> PROP. XXIII. *Every mode which exists both necessarily and as infinite must necessarily follow either from the absolute nature of some attribute of God, or*

from an attribute modified by a modification which exists necessarily and as infinite.

PROP. XXIV. *The essence of things produced by God does not involve existence.*

PROP. XXV. *God is the efficient cause not only of the existence of things, but also of their essence.*

Yes, Spinoza believes in God. But God is nothing other than the universe. He has few of the characteristics traditionally attributed to Him and worshiped in Him. For example, Spinoza goes on to argue, on the basis of what he has said already, that God has no will, that He doesn't do anything, and, ultimately, He doesn't care about anything either, including humanity. Here is a scientific worldview that is so unrelenting that even Newton himself would be shocked by it. This does not mean that Spinoza is a materialist; quite to the contrary, the importance of his constant insistence upon "the infinite attributes of God," of which we are capable of knowing only two (could you imagine what some of the others might be like?) is to say that God has not only physical existence but (at least) mental existence as well.

But where the scientific outlook becomes most dramatic is in Spinoza's defense of the doctrine we shall call **determinism,** the thesis that every event in the universe necessarily occurs as the result of its cause. The ultimate cause is God, which is to say, the universe itself. Once again, the terms come from Aristotle, but it is therefore important to insist that Spinoza does not believe—with either Aristotle or Christendom—that the universe has any purpose whatsoever. Nor does he believe that the universe or God has any beginning or end, thus answering our two sets of cosmological questions with a single necessary truth, once again, derived directly from the definition of substance.

The ultimate meaning of Spinoza's arguments for determinism is that no action, whether of man or God, is ever free. Everything in the universe, according to Spinoza, is exactly as it must be; the universe couldn't be any other way. Nothing is so pointless as struggling against a universe in which everything, including our own natures and actions, is already determined.

PROP. XXVI. *A thing which is conditioned to act in a particular manner has necessarily been thus conditioned by God; and that which has not been conditioned by God cannot condition itself to act.*

PROP. XXVII. *A thing, which has been conditioned by God to act in a particular way, cannot render itself unconditioned.*

PROP. XXVIII. *Every individual thing, or everything which is finite and has a conditioned existence, cannot exist or be conditioned to act, unless it be conditioned for existence and action by a cause other than itself, which also is finite and has a conditioned existence; and likewise this cause cannot in its turn exist or be conditioned to act, unless it be conditioned for existence and action by another cause, which also is finite and has a conditioned existence, and so on to infinity.*

PROP. XXIX. *Nothing in the universe is contingent, but all things are conditioned to exist and operate in a particular manner by the necessity of the divine nature.*[31]

PROP. XXX. *Intellect, in function finite, or in function infinite, must comprehend the attributes of God and the modifications of God, and nothing else.*

PROP. XXXI. *The intellect in function, whether finite or infinite, as will, desire, love, & c., should be referred to passive nature and not to active nature.*

PROP. XXXII. *Will cannot be called a free cause, but only a necessary cause.*

PROP. XXXIII. *Things could not have been brought into being by God in any manner or in any order different from that which has in fact obtained. [God is determined too.]*

PROP. XXXIV. *God's power is identical with his essence.*

PROP. XXXV. *Whatsoever we conceive to be in the power of God, necessarily exists.*

PROP. XXXVI. *There is no cause from whose nature some effect does not follow.*

Part II of the *Ethics* discusses "the Nature and Origin of the Mind." It begins with a further set of definitions and axioms, most importantly, the definition of body as "extended thing," that is, extended in space (which Spinoza got directly from Descartes and the medieval philosophers) and idea, "the mental conception which is formed by the mind as a thinking thing." Mind, unlike body, is defined as **unextended** (that is, it has no spatial dimensions). It is in this part that Spinoza argues those surprising doctrines that we have already summarized: Mind and body are each one of an infinite number of attributes of God, not substance themselves (as they were for Descartes), and our individual minds are really indistinguishable modifications of the one Great Mind of the One Substance. And Spinoza joins with all of his metaphysical colleagues in insisting that "the order and connection of ideas is the same as the order and connection of things" (Prop. VII). Here again is Spinoza's affirmation of his confidence in thought to grasp reality. (Remember Heraclitus, "thought is Being.")

The upshot of Part II, and the subject that dominates the *Ethics* for the remaining three parts, is Spinoza's determinism.

PROP. XLVIII. *In the mind there is no absolute or free will; but the mind is determined to wish this or that by a cause, which has been determined by another cause, and this last by another cause, and so on to infinity.*

Spinoza has none of Aristotle's fears of an "infinite regress," and if he believes in a "cause-of-itself" that is not the same as a "first cause," for there is no such thing. We

---

[31] We are all determined by the nature of God or the universe. But then, here is a problem: Are we not then compelled to struggle and can't help doing so? If so, what is the point of Spinoza's urging us not to?

In the mind there is no absolute or free will; but the mind is determined to wish this or that by a cause, which has been determined by another cause, and this last by another cause, and so on to infinity.

shall talk more about this "free will and determinism" problem in Chapter 8; but it is worth noting, as a way of summing up, Spinoza's drastic answer to the problem. As an unyielding determinist, he rejects every attempt to save some space for freedom of human action. But he assures us that we can, with heroic effort (Prop. XLVII), understand the nature of this determinism, and accept it gracefully. The folly is in the fighting, he tells us. The remainder of the *Ethics* is given over to the attempt to draw out the logical consequences of this stoic conclusion.

Part III is a long argument against emotions and what we would call "emotional involvement" as the needless cause of suffering and vice. Against them, Spinoza argues the virtues of human reason, which penetrates the useless involvements of the emotions and allows us to understand the causes of our actions and feelings. To understand an emotion, Spinoza believes, is to change and eliminate it. For example, to understand why one is angry, according to Spinoza, is sufficient to let us get rid of our anger. To realize that we are unable to change, according to Spinoza, is the only freedom we can really be said to have.

What you have just seen is modern metaphysics at its most brilliant. The geometrical method, however, is no longer fashionable, and much of Spinoza's language is, to us, antiquated and unnatural. But the intricacies of his system, the way he ties so many different ideas together, the answers he gave to ancient philosophical problems, and the boldness with which he sets out a new vision of the universe, have made Spinoza's philosophy widely appreciated despite his difficult style. What you are about to read, though, is no less astonishing, no less brilliant, and its author no less remarkable a genius. The work from which these excerpts come is a very short work (of about ninety paragraphs) written by Leibniz, who begins with much the same concepts and definitions as Spinoza but ends up with a wholly different metaphysical system. (Leibniz and Spinoza met several times and discussed these issues. But Leibniz found Spinoza's opinions too shocking and acquaintanceship with him too dangerous.)

3. Gottfried Wilhelm von Leibniz

Leibniz begins with the same technical notion of substance, but from it he weaves an entirely different but equally fantastic picture of the universe. Where Spinoza's universe was mechanical and wholly dependent upon causes, Leibniz's universe is very much alive, and everything happens for a purpose (as in Aristotle's ancient teleology). The guiding principle of Leibniz's philosophy is called "The Principle of Sufficient Reason," which says, simply, that there must be a reason for everything. Even God, on this account, cannot act capriciously but must have a reason for whatever He has created. We shall see that this principle is among the most important guidelines to Leibniz's philosophy. From it, he develops a radical alternative to Isaac Newton's physics and a spectacularly optimistic view that, because God acts according to this principle, this world that He created must be "the best of all possible worlds."

Where Spinoza argues that there can be at most one substance, Leibniz argues that there are many. He calls them **monads.** Every monad is different from every other, and God (who is something of a supermonad and the only "uncreated monad") has created them all. The work presented here, accordingly, is called the *Monadology* ("the study of monads"), written in 1714. It is a very condensed summary of Leibniz's metaphysics:

FROM *MONADOLOGY*
BY **GOTTFRIED WILHELM VON LEIBNIZ**

1. The Monad, of which we will speak here, is nothing else than a simple substance, which goes to make up composites; by simple, we mean without parts.
2. There must be simple substances because there are composites; for a composite is nothing else than a collection or *aggregatum* of simple substances.[32]

A simple substance is one that cannot be divided. The argument is curious: any "composite" is obviously divisible. That means that every composite must be "composed" of some simple substances that make it up. (There is a hidden infinite regress argument here: If there weren't ultimately simple substances, then we could go on dividing things forever.) But if the simple substances were extended in space, then they too would be further divisible, for anything that has length, for example, no matter how small, can be cut in two (at least in theory). Therefore, Leibniz concludes, these basic simple substances or monads must be immaterial and have no extension. They can have neither parts, nor extension, nor divisibility:

3. Now, where there are no constituent parts there is possible neither extension, nor form, nor divisibility. These Monads are the true Atoms of nature, and, in fact, the Elements of things.

Here, in Leibniz's first three propositions, are the answers to our first two ontological questions: "How many substances are there?" Many. This answer makes Leibniz a pluralist. "What kind of substances are they?" Simple and immaterial substances, which makes Leibniz an *immaterialist.* (Don't be misled by the term "atoms": we are used to thinking of atoms as the smallest material substances, but Leibniz's atoms are *im*material.) Now, in three more propositions, Leibniz answers

---

[32] Gottfried W. von Leibniz, *Monadology,* in *The Rationalists,* trans. George Montgomery (New York: Doubleday, 1960). All subsequent quotations from Leibniz are from this edition of *Monadology.*

our first cosmological question: "Are these substances eternal, or do they come into being at some time? How do they come into being? Are they destructible?"

4. This dissolution, therefore, is not to be feared and there is no way conceivable by which a simple substance can perish through natural means.
5. For the same reason there is no way conceivable by which a simple substance might, through natural means, come into existence, since it cannot be formed by composition.
6. We may say then, that the existence of Monads can begin or end only all at once, that is to say, the Monad can begin only through creation and end only through annihilation. Composites, however, begin or end gradually.

Spinoza had argued that the one substance could neither be created nor destroyed; it had neither beginning nor end. Leibniz's substances, or "monads," can be created or destroyed, but not by any "natural" means. They can be created or destroyed only "all at once." Anticipating later propositions, we can guess that Leibniz will have God (who is something of a supermonad) create them. But notice that compounds of monads, for example, "material objects," can be created and destroyed "naturally."

Now our third question, "How do we distinguish different substances or monads?"

8. Still Monads must have some qualities, otherwise they would not even be existences. And if simple substances did not differ at all in their qualities, there would be no means of perceiving any change in things. Whatever is in a composite can come into it only through its simple elements and the Monads, if they were without qualities, since they do not differ at all in quantity, would be indistinguishable one from another. For instance, if we imagine *a plenum* or completely filled space, where each part receives only the equivalent of its own previous motion, one state of things would not be distinguishable from another.
9. Each Monad, indeed, must be different from every other. For there are never in nature two beings which are exactly alike, and in which it is not possible to find a difference either internal or based on an intrinsic property.

Only God could actually know everything about every monad in order to compare and contrast them. But even God can distinguish different monads only because they in fact have differences between them. This leads Leibniz to suggest one of his most controversial principles, the so-called "Principle of the Identity of Indiscernibles": no two monads can have the same properties (Prop. 9). Why is this? According to the "Principle of Sufficient Reason" (Prop. 32) nothing can be without good reason. Even God, therefore, would have no good reason for duplicating any monad. If two monads were identical, Leibniz argues, God could have no reason for putting one in one place and the other in another place, or for creating them both in the first place. Therefore, no two monads could be exactly alike. A strange kind of argument, but very much at the heart of Leibniz's philosophy, as we shall see later.

How does a monad, which is by definition "simple," alter or combine with other monads to form the changing and familiar universe of our experience? (Here you should be reminded of the similar problems that faced the ancient pre-Socratics and Plato.). Here is our fourth question, and the most difficult Leibniz has to answer: "How do substances interact?" By definition, monads cannot literally "interact." So Leibniz's answer is extremely speculative and imaginative:

7. There is also no way of explaining how a Monad can be altered or changed in its inner being by any other created thing, since there is no possibility of transposition within it, nor can we conceive of any internal movement which can be produced, directed, increased or diminished there within the substance, such as can take place in the case of composites where a change can occur among the parts. The Monads have no windows through which anything may come in or go out.

The problem is that different substances, by definition, are independent and cannot, therefore, have anything to do with one another. Descartes, as we shall see in Chapter 6, had a terrible time getting together his two substances of mind and body. Spinoza, as a monist, solved the problem in the simplest possible way; since there is only one substance, no question of "interaction" is applicable. But Leibniz is a pluralist; there are many substances. They cannot interact as such. They cannot even perceive each other in the usual sense. They "have no windows," in his peculiar but now famous expression; "nothing can come in or go out." Unlike the ancient (and modern) materialist atomists, Leibniz cannot have his monads simply combine and recombine to form new compounds in any usual sense. They cannot, in Leibniz's words, "be altered or changed in [their] inner being by any other created thing." So, how do monads change? They must have all changes already created (by God) within themselves.

Remember the animism that was so prevalent in the ancient Greek philosophers. For them, the phenomenon of life was the model for metaphysics. The idea of Newtonian mechanics would have been incomprehensible to them. Leibniz, we may now say, was vehemently anti-Newton. He was, we may also say, one of the outstanding modern animists. A monad is as different as can be from a Newtonian material atom; a monad is alive, and its changes come from within, never from without. (Except, that is, for its initial creation.) Think of a monad as a living being, "programmed" (to use a modern word) with all of the information and experiences it needs to develop in a certain way, like an acorn developing into an oak tree. Thus the changes in the monad are all internal, programmed by God at the creation. Now keep in mind that a monad is immaterial, and so its "growth" cannot be thought of as a development in the physical world. The growth too, therefore, must be internal, and the apparent interaction between monads must really be changes in the perceptions of the monads themselves.

10. I assume it as admitted that every created being, and consequently the created Monad, is subject to change, and indeed that this change is continuous in each.

11. It follows from what has just been said, that the natural changes of the Monad come from an internal principle, because an external cause can have no influence upon its inner being.

12. Now besides this principle of change there must also be in the Monad a manifoldness which changes. This manifoldness constitutes, so to speak, the specific nature and the variety of the simple substances.

13. This manifoldness must involve a multiplicity in the unity or in that which is simple. For since every natural change takes place by degrees, there must be something which changes and something which remains unchanged, and consequently there must be in the simple substance a plurality of conditions and relations, even though it has no parts.

14. The passing condition which involves and represents a multiplicity in the unity, or in the simple substance, is nothing else than what is called Perception. This should be carefully distinguished from Consciousness.

Leibniz argues that what we are really describing when we talk about a squirrel climbing a particular tree at a particular moment in time is ourselves. The perception of the squirrel is a permanent part of one unchanging monad—our perception as a whole. The apparent differences between parts of a monad are really changes in perception. Leibniz is arguing that the sense in which material things seem to exist in space in as different perceptions or experiences of a perceiving monad. What is ultimately real, therefore, is the perceiving monad. Perceptions change, within each monad, to create the appearance of a moving and changing material world. Notice that Leibniz carefully distinguishes "Perception" from what he calls "Consciousness." Perception is experience, in general, and is present, in some degree, in every monad. Consciousness, on the other hand, is a very special kind of experience, reflective and articulate, and is to be found only in a few monads. (It is worth noting that, with this distinction, Leibniz precociously introduces the concept of "the unconscious" into German philosophy two hundred years before Freud.)

Here is the attack on Newton's more materialist view of the universe. Such a view, Leibniz complains, cannot account for experience (perception), in other words, the immaterial aspects of the universe.

17. It must be confessed, however, that Perception, and that which depends upon it, are inexplicable by mechanical causes, that is to say, by figures and motions. Supposing that there were a machine whose structure produced thought, sensation, and perception, we could conceive of it as increased in size with the same proportions until one was able to enter into its interior, as he would into a mill. Now, on going into it he would find only pieces working upon one another, but never would he find anything to explain Perception.

   It is accordingly in the simple substance, and not in the composite nor in a machine that the Perception is to be sought. Furthermore, there is nothing besides perceptions and their changes to be found in the simple substance. And it is in these alone that all the internal activities of the simple substance can consist.

18. All simple substances or created Monads may be called Entelechies, because they have in themselves a certain perfection. There is in them a sufficiency which makes them the source of their internal activities, and renders them, so to speak, incorporeal Automations. [In other words, every monad is alive, to a certain extent.]

19. If we wish to designate as soul everything which has perceptions and desires in the general sense that I have just explained, all simple substances or created Monads could be called souls. But since feeling is something more than a mere perception I think that the general name of Monad or Entelechy should suffice for simple substances which have only perception, while we may reserve the term Soul for those whose perception is more distinct and is accompanied by memory. [Again, Leibniz insists that "Perception" is most primitive and is common to all monads.]

20. We experience in ourselves a state where we remember nothing and where we have no distinct perception, as in periods of fainting, or when we are overcome by a profound, dreamless sleep. In such a state the soul does not sensibly differ at all from a simple Monad. As this state, however, is not permanent and the soul can recover from it, the soul is something more.

21. Nevertheless it does not follow at all that the simple substance is in such a state without perception. This is so because of the reasons given above; for it cannot perish, nor on the other hand would it exist without some affection and the affection is nothing else than its perception. When, however, there are a great number of weak perceptions where nothing stands out distinctively, we are stunned; as when one turns around and around in the same direction, a dizziness comes on, which makes him swoon and makes him able to distinguish nothing. Among animals, death can occasion this state for quite a period.[!]

Every present state of a simple substance is a natural consequence of its preceding state, in such a way that its present is pregnant with its future.

22. Every present state of a simple substance is a natural consequence of its preceding state, in such a way that its present is pregnant with its future. [Here is Leibniz's version of the thesis that one cause necessarily follows another.]

23. Therefore, since on awakening after a period of unconsciousness we become conscious of our perceptions, we must, without having been conscious of them, have had perceptions immediately before; for one perception can come in a natural way only from another perception, just as a motion can come in a natural way only from a motion.

◆◆◆

29. It is the knowledge of eternal and necessary truths that distinguishes us from mere animals and gives us reason and the sciences, thus raising us to a knowledge of ourselves and of God. This is what is called in us the Rational Soul or the Mind.

30. It is also through the knowledge of necessary truths and through abstractions from them that we come to perform Reflective Acts, which cause us to think of what is called the I, and to decide that this or that is within us. It is thus, that in thinking upon ourselves we think of *being,* of *substance,* of the *simple* and *composite,* of a *material* thing and of *God* himself, conceiving that what is limited in us is in him without limits. These Reflective Acts furnish the principal objects of our reasonings.

As we have seen, the answer to our fourth question is, "Monads don't interact." Each is locked into itself and contains within itself its own view of the universe as a whole.

56. Now this interconnection, relationship, or this adaptation of all things to each particular one, and of each one to all the rest, brings it about that every simple substance has relations which express all the others and that it is consequently a perpetual living mirror of the universe.
57. And as the same city regarded from different sides appears entirely different, and is, as it were, multiplied respectively, so, because of the infinite number of simple substances, there are a similar infinite number of universes which are, nevertheless, only the aspects of a single one as seen from the special point of view of each monad.

But, of course, the perspective of any one monad is extremely one-sided and confused.

60. Besides, in what has just been seen can be seen the *a priori* reasons why things cannot be otherwise than they are. It is because God, in ordering the whole, has had regard to every part and in particular to each monad; and since the Monad is by its very nature *representative,* nothing can limit it to represent merely a part of things. It is nevertheless true that this representation is, as regards the details of the whole universe, only a confused representation, and is distinct only as regards a small part of them, that is to say, as regards those things which are nearest or greatest in relation to each Monad. If the representation were distinct as to the details of the entire universe, each Monad would be a Deity. It is not in the object represented that the Monads are limited, but in the modifications of their knowledge of the object. In a confused way they reach out to infinity or to the whole, but are limited and differentiated in the degree of their distinct perceptions.

Now Leibniz has an alternative to Newton: bodies (composite monads) only seem to interact; in fact, it all happens within each monad, programmed and created by God in "pre-established harmony."

61. In this respect composites are like simple substances, for all space is filled up; therefore, all matter is connected. And in a plenum or filled space every

> movement has an effect upon bodies in proportion to this distance, so that
> not only is every body affected by those which are in contact with it and
> responds in some way to whatever happens to them, but also by means of
> them the body responds to those bodies adjoining them, and their intercom-
> munication reaches to any distance whatsoever. Consequently every body
> responds to all that happens in the universe, so that he who saw all could
> read in each one what is happening everywhere, and even what has hap-
> pened and what will happen.
>
> 62. Thus although each created Monad represents the whole universe, it repre-
> sents more distinctly the body which specially pertains to it and of which
> it constitutes the entelechy. And as this body expresses all the universe
> through the interconnection of all matter in the plenum, the soul also repre-
> sents the whole universe in representing this body, which belongs to it in a
> particular way.

Every monad develops as a reflection of the development of all the other monads
in the universe as well. If, for example, we are watching a squirrel climb around a
tree, Leibniz's view is that the reality of the squirrel climbing around the tree is actually our perception of this. But you can see that this alone is not sufficient; we might
simply dream or hallucinate this view, and it would then not be "real" at all. The difference between the dream and the reality is the changes in the other monads, for instance, the monads that constitute the squirrel and any other observers of the same
scene, including God. Reality is composed of the totality of all monads, each perceiving from its own perspective (although God, Leibniz insists, perceives from all
perspectives at once). The "pre-established harmony" guarantees that all of these
views from all of these perspectives are in agreement, so that our view of the squirrel, for example, is matched by the squirrel's view of us.

This view of the pre-established harmony between monads allows Leibniz to
give a surprising answer to our fourth question, "How do different substances interact?" By definition, substances cannot interact as such. But they can seem to interact if their perceptions are coordinated. Thus, the collision of two billiard balls is in
fact a harmony of perceptions about the collision of two billiard balls. Two people
fighting is in fact a harmony of perceptions by each of the two people (and anyone else who is watching) about those two people fighting. This answer may seem
to be extreme, but given Leibniz's conception of the universe as composed of a great
number of immaterial substances, it is an answer that is necessary for his philosophy to be consistent. It is an answer that is also necessary, however, to enable him
to reject Newton's cosmology, which he and many of his contemporaries found
even more extreme and difficult to understand than Leibniz's own strange view of
interaction.

The last of our initial set of questions about substance and our second cosmological question is, "Are space and time themselves substances?" According to
Leibniz, the answer to this question is an emphatic no. It is on this question
that Leibniz makes his sharpest break with Newton's physics. Are monads "in"
space? Leibniz would have said no. But he also seems to give the surprising answer

that not only are monads not "in" space (since they are immaterial), they are, strictly speaking, not "in" time either. The monad does not change in time, but rather, time is in the monad. That is, time is a relation between experiences of the monad. It is not something independent. These views of space and time are intimately tied to Leibniz's analysis of the only seeming "interaction" between monads. Both are rejections of Newton's theory and an attempt to offer an alternative.

To our way of thinking, Leibniz's views seem bizarre, compared to the almost commonsense character of Newton's theory. Newton had argued that the universe was the motion of (material) atoms in empty space, acting against each other according to the laws of motion, force, and gravity that he had so elegantly formulated. But Newton's theories, which seem almost quaintly obvious to us now, contained what most people of his and Leibniz's time—including Newton himself—considered to be manifest absurdities. One, relating to our fourth ontological question, was the idea of **action-at-a-distance,** the idea that one object could affect another although the two were not even in contact. (For example, the idea that the moon and the earth have gravitational attraction for each other.) Thus Leibniz's conception of windowless monads, each seeming to interact with others but in fact only developing within itself, would have seemed to his contemporaries no more absurd than Newton's view of causality. Leibniz didn't need causality; he had his "pre-established harmony." Newton, meanwhile, had a great deal of trouble reconciling his mechanistic theories with the traditional ideas of God and Creation, which he continued to hold for the rest of his life.

The most famous disagreement between Leibniz and Newton concerns the nature of space and time, a topic that is still being debated because of the impact of Einstein's theory of relativity at the beginning of this century. Newton's mechanical theory seemed to presuppose the existence of some permanent container, namely space, in which the material atoms of his theory could mutually attract and bounce against each other. This container, which could exist independently of its contents, is called **absolute space.** In itself, this sounds entirely reasonable; we talk about things "moving in space" and "taking up space." But then, can we also talk about the entire universe being "in" space, the way a basketball can be said to be "in" the basket? This idea has some absurd consequences that led Leibniz and many of his contemporaries to reject it. The idea that space could exist apart from all things in it, perhaps even entirely empty (or what many philosophers called the **void**), would mean that it makes sense to talk about movement or location in space even when there isn't anything in space, not even points and rulers with which to measure distances or dimensions. **Bertrand Russell,** one of Leibniz's most famous followers, pointed out the absurdity of this idea by asking, "If space is absolute, then wouldn't it make sense to suggest that the universe might have doubled in size last night?" But what would it mean to say that the universe has gotten larger? An elephant or a planet or even a galaxy can get larger, but only in comparison to some measuring stick and a frame of reference. It is only by such comparisons that such "size" talk makes sense. But to say that the universe doubles in size is to say that our measuring stick, and we ourselves, double in size also. So all comparisons remain the same. Similarly, what would it mean to say that the universe in its entirety moved one foot to the left? All of the one-foot measurements are in the universe. There is no way to talk about the universe itself moving. On the basis of such considerations, Leibniz rejected Newton's idea of absolute space as absurd. In its place, he insisted that space is relative, that is, relative to measurements and things that are measured. There is no absolute space; there is only space relative to the various positions of the monads, that is, to observers.

The same is true of time. Newton believed in **absolute time** also, time as existing apart from anything happening "in" it. But the same consequences follow this initially reasonable idea. If time is absolute, it seems to make sense to ask, "When did the universe begin?" (In fact, astronomers are again asking this question.) But what could this "when" refer to? It can't refer to any measurement in the universe (clocks, the age of rocks or stars) for it is the universe itself that is being measured, and there aren't any measures of time outside of the universe. Consequently, Leibniz rejected absolute time along with absolute space. Both are relative to the monads and have no possible existence of their own. This means, among other things, that there could be no void or empty space, nor could there be any sense of time in which literally nothing happened. Space and time, according to Leibniz, are relative to our own perceptions.

Now I said many pages ago that such cosmological issues were never the domain of philosophy alone, and you are well aware that current physics and astronomy are still very much involved with these questions. Both alternatives, from Newton and from Leibniz, are still very much alive. Scientists do indeed still talk about the beginning of the universe, and with awesome sophistication; of course, they also talk in strictly relativistic terms, like Leibniz, but now à la Einstein. To delve into these issues any further, therefore, we should have to leave eighteenth-century metaphysics and move into twentieth-century physics. What is often relevant to these philosophical debates are the new and sometimes strange experimental findings that are always emerging from the sciences. Recently, for example, experiments with the speed of light have brought about startling changes in our views of space and time. One consequence of this changed view is the idea that we cannot talk intelligibly about two events happening "at the same time" if they are a sufficiently great distance apart, say several billion light years. The discovery of radiation from outer space and the expansion of galaxies has raised old issues about creation in a new way: whether the universe was created all at once and then started to expand and change (the "big-bang theory") or whether there is continuous creation going on even now (the "steady-state theory"). Because of recent theories in science, philosophers are now willing to say things that would have seemed like utter nonsense to both Newton and Leibniz—for example, that "space is curved."

These are not issues to be settled by scientists alone, however; it is philosophical theories that give structure and meaning to the scientific experiments. But neither can philosophers simply cut themselves off from science and pretend that they can solve these problems "just in their heads." At the outer reaches of science, you will find philosophy, just as, at the beginnings of philosophy, you will find the unanswered problems of science.

In an earlier chapter, we stressed the importance of a basic assumption of all metaphysics, that the universe is intelligible. In Leibniz's philosophy, this assumption is presented as one of the basic presuppositions of all thinking; he calls it

> 32. . . . *the Principle of Sufficient Reason,* in virtue of which we believe that no fact can be real and no statement true unless it has a sufficient reason why it should be thus and not otherwise. Most frequently, however, these reasons cannot be known to us.

They can, however, be known to God, who knows everything. It is on the basis of this principle, for example, that Leibniz defends the claim he made in Proposition 9, that two monads can never be identical ("the identity of indiscernibles"). The reasoning is this: Since God is the supremely rational Being (monad), He must have a reason for all that He does. But Leibniz also argues (Prop. 58) that God must have created the universe "with the greatest possible variety together with the greatest order that may be." Here is the reason why God would not have created any two monads alike. But the Principle of Sufficient Reason has a further implication; it also serves as a principle of divine ethics. Among the various possible worlds (that is, among the infinitely many ways in which the world might have been), God chooses the most perfect, that is, "the best of all possible worlds." Here is the doctrine of cosmic optimism that Voltaire so brilliantly lampooned in his novel *Candide.* But Leibniz took this concept of "the best of all possible worlds" very seriously. In the next century, it was to provide a foundation for much of the optimism of the Enlightenment. And in Leibniz's own metaphysics, it provides the concluding propositions of *Monadology,* a joyous optimism that creates as close to a happy ending as one can expect to find in a serious philosophical treatise.

> 85. Whence it is easy to conclude that the totality of all spirits must compose the city of God, that is to say, the most perfect state that is possible under the most perfect monarch.

◆◆◆

. . . it is easy to conclude that the totality of all spirits must compose the city of God, that is to say, the most perfect state that is possible under the most perfect monarch.

90. Finally, under this perfect government, there will be no good action unrewarded and no evil action unpunished; everything must turn out for the well-being of the good; that is to say, of those who are not disaffected in this great state, who, after having done their duty, trust in Providence and who love and imitate, as is meet, the Author of all Good, delighting in the contemplation of his perfections according to the nature of that genuine, pure love which finds pleasure in the happiness of those who are loved. It is for this reason that wise and virtuous persons work in behalf of everything

which seems conformable to presumptive or antecedent will of God, and are, nevertheless, content with what God actually brings to pass through his secret, consequent and determining will, recognizing that if we were able to understand sufficiently well the order of the universe, we should find that it surpasses all the desires of the wisest of us, and that it is impossible to render it better than it is, not only for all in general, but also for each one of us in particular, provided that we have the proper attachment for the author of all, not only as the Architect and the efficient cause of our being [our Creator] but also as our Lord and the Final Cause [purpose of our existence] who ought to be the whole goal of our will, and who alone can make us happy.

This theological "happy ending" is not an afterthought for Leibniz; it is the heart of his philosophy. Like his older contemporary Spinoza, his involvement in metaphysics is ultimately a very personal concern for religion and for his own view of himself and his place in the world. From this perspective, it is revealing to see the vast differences between the two philosophers. Spinoza's view of humanity is extremely anti-individualistic, and each individual is wholly submerged in the concept of the one substance. In Leibniz, however, his pluralism reinforces the view that each individual is a world in himself or herself, and his idealism places an emphasis on mind and thought that is in sharp contrast with Spinoza's balance between thought and body (although many critics have charged Spinoza with emphasizing body to an alarming degree). Spinoza's determinism and his view that ultimately we can do nothing but understand is surely a gloomy view compared to Leibniz's happy confidence that this is the "best of all possible worlds." Of course, Spinoza's heretical view of God as the one substance (sometimes called *pantheism*) is very different from Leibniz's more traditional and pious view.

But these considerations are far from being merely coincidental or curious implications of Descartes', Spinoza's, and Leibniz's metaphysical views. These religious concerns lie at the heart of their philosophical concerns, and one might well say that their metaphysics is constructed as an ingenious form of support for their religious convictions. Indeed, for most of the past two thousand years, and until very recently, the Judeo-Christian-Islamic religious tradition has provided much of the motivation and the structure of philosophy. So it is religion, as a philosophical enterprise, to which we must now turn our attention.

SUMMARY AND CONCLUSION

Metaphysics is the study of ultimate reality, the attempt to find out the way the world really is. The first recognized metaphysical theory in Western philosophy is Thales' suggestion that everything is ultimately made of water. After Thales, a number of schools of metaphysics suggested alternative theories, all of them depending on the speculative powers of human reason and diverging in various and important ways from "common sense." But these thinkers were not only the first significant Western philosophers; they were also the first theoretical scientists, anticipating in many ways some of the most sophisticated theories of contemporary physics, astronomy, and chemistry.

The first turning point in Western metaphysics came with Socrates, although Socrates himself was more interested in moral issues than in metaphysics as such. Socrates' student Plato and his student Aristotle in turn became the first great systematic metaphysicians, and philosophy ever since has been deeply indebted to them. Plato introduced an elaborate theory in which ultimate reality consisted of Forms, in contrast to the particular and changing things of everyday life. To support this "two-worlds" theory of Forms versus individual things, he offered a theory of learning, a "theory of recollection," in which he argued that the human soul is immortal and that each of us already knows, in some sense, what we appear to learn in our lives. Aristotle argues instead that only individual things deserve the ultimate claim to reality, for these individual things are the primary substances. Since Aristotle, metaphysicians have typically used the term *substance* as the name of the basic entities that compose reality.

We have also summarized the thought of some of the greatest metaphysical thinkers of modern times. In Europe, they begin from the concept of "substance" and attempt to use deduction as a method for proving the ultimate nature of reality. Their answers are extremely different. Spinoza argues that there can only be one substance; Leibniz argues that there are many. For Spinoza, God is identical to the universe, to the one substance; for Leibniz, God is distinct from all other substances, which He created. For Spinoza, mind and body are but two of an infinite number of attributes of God, the only two that we can know; for Leibniz, all substances are ultimately immaterial. But beneath these technical concerns is a struggle by both philosophers to answer the most important problems of human existence: the nature of God and proper religion, the place of man and woman in the universe, and the role and foundations of science.

GLOSSARY

absolute space and **absolute time** The view that space and time exist independently of objects and events "in" them, a view defended by Newton. In general, absolute, as used in philosophy, means independent and nonrelative, unqualified and all-inclusive.

action-at-a-distance The idea that one object can have a causal effect on another from a distance, as in Newton's laws of gravitational attraction. Leibniz's rejection of this idea as "absurd" led him to develop a noncausal interpretation of the same phenomena.

Ahura Mazda The God of Zoroastrianism.

Analects One of the major works of Confucius.

Angra Mainyush The evil spirit of Zoroastrianism.

animism The view that things (or, at the extreme, all things) are alive. It may also be the view that the universe as a whole is one gigantic organism.

apeiron in Anaximander, "the unlimited," the basic stuff of the universe.

Asha Immortal spirit or "righteousness" in Zoroastrianism.

attribute In Spinoza, an essential property of God; for example, having a physical nature, having thoughts. In general, an attribute is a property (as in Aristotle).

Becoming (in Plato) The "world of Becoming" is the changing world of our daily experience, in which things and people come into being and pass away.

Being (in Plato) The "world of Being" is the realm of eternal Forms, in which nothing ever changes. It is, for him, reality, and, in general, Being is used by philosophers to refer to whatever they consider ultimately real (substance, God).

best of all possible worlds Leibniz's view that God demands a perfect universe and makes it "the best possible," all things considered.

Bhagavadgita (Gita) The "Song of God" of ancient Hinduism; the epic poem of Krishna, the Hindu God.

Brahman In Hindu philosophy, the one, absolute reality.

Buddha "The awakened one"; the historical founder of Buddhism.

cause That which brings something about. Philosophers usually add, "as a matter of necessity." In Aristotle, "cause" means something like "reason," and he distinguishes four different kinds of "causes" of a change: (1) the *formal* cause, the principle or essential idea according to which a change comes about (think of a blueprint for a building, or the plans for a project); (2) the *material* cause, the matter that undergoes the change (think of the raw materials for building a house—lumber, bricks, cement); (3) the *efficient* cause, that which initiates the change (the construction workers and their tools); (4) the *final* cause, or the purpose of the change (to build a place where Socrates and his family can live, for example).

cause-of-itself (*causa sui*) That which explains its own existence, often said of God. It also follows from the usual definitions of substance.

conceptual truth A statement that is true and that we can see to be true by virtue of the meanings of the words (or we should say, the "concepts") that compose it. For example, "a horse is an animal" is a conceptual truth because anyone who speaks English and knows the meaning of the words "horse" and "animal" knows that such a statement must be true. (We shall discuss such statements in greater detail in Chapters 3 and 4.) In Plato, a conceptual truth is a truth about Forms. In Aristotle, a conceptual truth is a matter of describing the essence of a thing. (See *Form, essence.*)

cosmology The study of the universe in its entirety (from the Greek word for "universe"— *cosmos*).

determinism The view that every event in the universe is dependent upon other events, which are its causes. On this view, all human actions and decisions, even those which we would normally describe as "free" and "undetermined," are totally dependent on prior events that cause them. (This problem will be examined in Chapter 8.)

dharma In Hinduism, righteousness, the way of the good.

divine pre-ordination God's knowledge of and power over all that will happen, including our own future actions.

essence (or an **essential property**) The necessary or defining characteristics or properties of a thing. "That which makes a thing what it is," in other words, those features that one must list in a definition or uniquely identifying description. (For example, the fact that Socrates is a man is part of his essence, the fact that he never smoked on Saturdays is not.)

extended Having spatial dimensions. Philosophers (for example, Descartes, Leibniz, and Spinoza) often define bodies as "extended," minds and ideas as "unextended."

extended (substance) Physical matter in space and time, material objects.

Form (in Plato) An independently existing entity in the world of Being, which determines the nature of the particular things of this world. In Aristotle, forms have no independent existence.

Four Noble Truths among the most important teachings of the Buddha: All is suffering, the need to eliminate desire, the way to eliminate desire, and the right path to the good.

freedom of the will Actions undetermined by external causes, including the power of God (though how God can leave us this "indeterminacy" in spite of God's power and knowledge over us is and must be incomprehensible to us).

Idea In Plato, a Form.

idealism The metaphysical view that only minds and their ideas exist.

Identity of Indiscernibles A principle of Leibniz's philosophy according to which no two things can possibly have all of the same properties or be absolutely identical in all respects.

immaterialism The metaphysical view that accepts the existence of nonspatial, nonsensory entities such as numbers, minds, and ideas. The weak version asserts merely that there are such entities. The strong version asserts that there are *only* such entities (that is, there are no physical objects).

immortality The idea that the soul survives death (and, in some belief systems, precedes birth).

ineffable Impossible of expression in words.

infinite regress A sequence going back endlessly. For example, "A is caused by B, and B by C, and C by D . . . and so on to infinity." Aristotle believed such a regress to be an intellectual absurdity.

innate ideas Knowledge that is "programmed" into us from birth and need not be learned. Experience may be necessary to "trigger off" such ideas, but they are already "in" all of us. In Plato, the theory of innate ideas is part of a general theory of the immortality of the soul.

karma In Hinduism, the tendency of any course of action to be repeated; the limitation of one's own free will by one's own habits.

Krishna In Hinduism, God incarnate.

materialism The metaphysical view that only physical matter and its properties exist. Such intangible entities as numbers, minds, and ideas are really properties of physical bodies. To talk about energy, for example, is, in a way, to talk about physical potential; to talk about minds is, as a kind of shorthand, to talk about behavior; to talk about ideas is, in a misleading way, to talk about the various structures and interrelationships between objects. Numbers have no existence of their own but only represent sets of sets of objects (the set of all sets of eight things is the number eight, for example). Materialism has always been a powerful worldview in modern scientific culture. It is also the most common view among the pre-Socratic philosophers.

metaphysics Most simply, the study of the most basic (or "first") principles. Traditionally, the study of ultimate reality, or "Being as such." Popularly, any kind of very abstract or obscure thinking. Most philosophers today would define metaphysics as the study of the most general concepts of science and human life, for example, "reality," "existence," "freedom," "God," "soul," "action," "mind." In general, we can divide metaphysics into ontology, cosmology, and an ill-defined set of problems concerning God and the immortality of the human soul. (See *ontology, cosmology*.)

modes (in Spinoza) Inessential properties or modifications of attributes.

monad (in Leibniz) The simple immaterial substances that are the ultimate constituents of all reality. God, the one uncreated monad, created all of the others as self-enclosed ("windowless"), predetermined entities.

monism The metaphysical view that there is ultimately only one substance, that all reality is one. Less strictly, it may be applied to philosophers who believe in only one kind of substance.

monotheism Belief in one God.

mysticism The belief that immediate, intuitive knowledge of God is possible, and the attempt to achieve it.

naturalism The belief that ultimate reality is a natural property.

ontology The study of being. That is, that part of metaphysics that asks such questions as, "What is there?" "What is it for something to exist?" "What is an individual thing?" "How do things interact?" Traditionally, these questions were formulated as questions about substance. Today, much of ontology is part of logic and linguistics and is the study of the concepts we use to discuss such matters. Sometimes ontology is used as a synonym for metaphysics, but usually the latter is the broader discipline.

pantheism The belief that everything is divine, or that God is in everything.

participation Plato's obscure and unexplained relationship between the things of this world and the Forms of which they are manifestations. He tells us that individual things "participate" in their Forms.

pluralism The metaphysical view that there are many distinct substances in the universe and, perhaps, many different kinds of substances as well.

polytheism Belief in many gods.

pre-established harmony The belief that the order of the universe is prearranged by God. In Leibniz, this view allows him an alternative to Newton's theory of causal relationships.

prime mover (in Aristotle) The "cause-of-itself," the first cause, which (Who) initiates all changes but is not itself (Himself) affected by anything prior. Aristotle believes there must be a prime mover if we are to avoid an infinite regress, which he considers an absurdity. Aristotle also refers to the prime mover as "God," and medieval philosophers (for example, St. Thomas Aquinas) have developed these views into Christian theology.

Principle of Sufficient Reason (in Leibniz) The insistence that all events must have a justification and that ultimately all events must be justified by God's reasons. The principle is sometimes invoked to assert that everything must have some explanation, whether or not God is involved. (For example, scientists use such a principle in their work, as we shall see in Chapter 3.)

property Properties are generally distinguished from the substances in which they "inhere" by pointing to the fact that a property cannot exist without being a property of something; for example, there can be any number of red things but no redness that exists independently. (Many philosophers have challenged this idea, but this problem, which is called the "problem of universals," will not be discussed in this introductory course.)

reason In our introduction, we defined "reason" as simply "the ability to think abstractly." In metaphysics, however, it often has a more controversial meaning, namely, that human ability to go beyond experience to determine, through thought alone, what reality is really like.

sophists Ancient Greek philosophers and teachers who believed that no reality exists except for what we take to be reality.

Spenta Mainyush The good spirit of Zoroastrianism.

substance The essential reality of a thing or things that underlies the various properties and changes of properties. Its most common definitions: "that which is independent and can exist by itself" and "the essence of a thing which does not and cannot change." In traditional metaphysics, substance is the same as "ultimate reality," and the study of substance is that branch of metaphysics that studies reality, namely, ontology. (See *essence, ontology.*)

substance (in Descartes) A thing which so exists that it needs no other thing in order to exist (God). Created substances need only the occurrence of God to exist.

Tao The "Way"; in Confucianism, the "way" to be a gentleman, for example, following the rituals; in Taoism, the underlying and ineffable "way" of nature or reality.

teleology (teleological) The belief that all phenomena have a purpose, end, or goal (from the Greek *telos,* meaning "purpose"). Aristotle's metaphysics is a teleology, which means that he believes that the universe itself—and consequently everything in it—operates for purposes and can be explained according to goals.

unextended Not having spatial dimensions. Philosophers (for example, Descartes, Leibniz, and Spinoza) often define mind and ideas as unextended.

Upanishads The "secret doctrines" that form the basis of Hinduism and Buddhism.

void Empty space.

Zend Avesta The scripture of Zoroastrianism.

Zoroastrianism The religion of ancient Persia.

BIBLIOGRAPHY AND FURTHER READING

General surveys of ancient Greek philosophy can be found in J. Burnet, *Early Greek Philosophy* (London: Black, 1958), and W. K. C. Guthrie, *The Greek Philosophers: From Thales to Aristotle* (New York: Harper & Row, 1960). The most important texts from the pre-Socratics are in G. S. Kirk and J. E. Raven, *The Presocratic Philosophers* (Cambridge: Cambridge University Press, 1957). Plato's dialogues are collected in *Plato, Dialogues,* 4th ed., trans. Benjamin Jowett (Oxford: Oxford University Press, 1953); a helpful survey of his work is A. E. Taylor, *Plato: The Man and His Work* (New York: Dial, 1936). Aristotle's works are collected in R. McKeon, ed., *The Basic Works of Aristotle* (New York: Random House, 1941). An excellent survey of all Aristotle's works is W. D. Ross, *Aristotle* (New York: Meridian, 1959). Brief surveys of the pre-Socratics, Socrates, Plato, and Aristotle are D. J. O'Connor, ed., *A Critical History of Western Philosophy* (New York: Free Press, 1964), and P. Edwards, ed., *The Encyclopedia of Philosophy* (New York: Macmillan, 1967). Benedictus de Spinoza's *Ethics* is in *The Rationalists* (New York: Doubleday, 1960); an excellent account of Spinoza's philosophy is St. Hampshire, *Spinoza* (London: Penguin, 1951). A convenient collection of Gottfried W. von Leibniz's major works is Philip Wiener, ed., *Leibniz, Selections* (New York: Charles Scribner's Sons, 1951). Two recent studies of Leibniz are Hidé Ishiguro, *Leibniz's Philosophy of Logic and Language* (Ithaca, NY: Cornell University Press, 1972) and Robert Merrihew Adams, *Leibniz: Determinist, Theist, Idealist* (New York: Oxford University Press, 1994). An important but biased study is Bertrand Russell, *A Critical Exposition of the Philosophy of Leibniz* (London: George Allen and Unwin, 1937). To study more recent metaphysical systems, see A. Lovejoy, *The Great Chain of Being* (Cambridge, MA: Harvard University Press, 1936); Jacques Maritain, *A Preface to Metaphysics* (London: Sheed, 1948); Henri Bergson, *An Introduction to Metaphysics,* trans. T. E. Hulme (New York: Bobbs-Merrill, 1949); Martin Heidegger, *An Introduction to Metaphysics,* trans. Ralph Manheim (New Haven, CT: Yale University Press, 1959); Richard Taylor, *Metaphysics* (Englewood Cliffs, NJ:

Prentice-Hall, 1963); D. F. Pears, ed., *The Nature of Metaphysics* (London: Macmillan, 1957); and R. G. Collingwood, *An Essay on Metaphysics* (Oxford: Clarendon Press, 1940). For a discussion of medieval philosophy, see A. Hyman and J. Walsh, *Philosophy in the Middle Ages* (Indianapolis: Hackett, 1973). A broad selection of sources from non-Western cultures is found in R. Solomon and K. Higgins, *World Philosophy* (New York: McGraw-Hill, 1995).

RELIGION

Now faith is the substance of things hoped for, the evidence of things not seen.

HEBREWS I I : I

The age-old efforts of metaphysicians to know the way the world really is have rarely been motivated by curiosity or the scientific spirit alone. Most often, metaphysics and philosophy in general have been motivated by religious devotion. The search for truth and the concern with what we can know and how we ought to behave have often been tied to concern about the nature of the divine and its relationship to us. For many thoughtful people, there is no more powerful an experience than religious experience, and they have no more important beliefs than their religious beliefs. Religion defines their lives, and their religious views define reality. Although the issues of religion are philosophically within the domain of metaphysics, epistemology, and ethics, its importance demands special attention. It involves experiences of a kind that are not common to other ontological and cosmological concerns. Religious beliefs involve emotions that are not relevant to the technical concerns with substance and science. It is this emotional involvement in religion that has inspired some of the greatest art, the bloodiest wars, the kindest actions, and the most brilliant philosophy in history.

A. WHAT IS RELIGION?

Religion has played an important role in the history of philosophy. Indeed, many scholars would claim that philosophy grew out of religion and only occasionally has

philosophy from religion   123

turned against its religious heritage. But there have been many different religions. Some differ so drastically from one another that it is hard to say what they have in common. For instance, you might be inclined to cite "belief in God or gods" as a criterion for calling something a religion. But one of the biggest religious followings in the world—Buddhism—has no such concept. Or you might cite as a criterion some sort of social organization, a church, or a prayer gathering. But there are Christian Protestant sects who believe that religion is an entirely private affair for which no congregation is necessary.

Although we saw in Chapter 1 that many philosophical schools share their beginnings with religions, we would not necessarily want to call a Methodist minister a philosopher. Nor would we want to call a college teacher, who assigns the works of **Maimonides** (an important Jewish theologian), a rabbi. Although religion and philosophy are intimately linked, we hesitate to identify them. Central to both, however, is religious belief. A person who believes in a single, independent Being, God, who is the Creator of the universe, is a theist, a believer, whether Jewish, Catholic, Protestant, or Muslim. (To refuse to believe in God is to be an atheist. To admit one's ignorance, and simply accept the fact that one does not know and perhaps has no way of knowing whether there is such a being or not is to be an agnostic. We will discuss some atheistic and agnostic claims, as well as several different religious traditions, later in this chapter.)

Before we investigate specific religious-philosophical debates, however, let us take a look at how some philosophers have answered a preliminary question: What is religion? In a now famous symposium of thirty years ago, three British philosophers argued about just this problem. The three philosophers are **Antony Flew,** who pursued an argument derived from Hume; **R. M. Hare** (also following Hume), who argued that the attempt to explain the universe may not be the point of religion and that it doesn't matter if nothing could count against religious beliefs; and **Basil Mitchell,** who also argued that explanation is not primary to religion, but rather that the key ingredient must be "faith."

Flew's opening comments are a response to a famous article by the twentieth-century philosopher **John Wisdom,** a student of **Ludwig Wittgenstein,** in which Wisdom claims that the essential feature of religious belief is a certain "attitude" that the religious person has toward his or her surroundings, and that the gap between the religious "attitude" and that of the philosopher or scientist interested in explanation, is unbridgeable. All four, arguing entirely within a Christian context, assume that religious belief is a belief in God. On the assumption, however, that whatever belief— or faith— is, it is essential to all activities we would want to call religious, their debate is helpful in establishing a general academic definition of religion.

John Wisdom – religious belief = our attitude toward our surrounw
↳ the gap btwn this attitude's philosophers/scientists is unbridgea

FROM **"GODS"**
BY **JOHN WISDOM**

Two people return to their long neglected garden and find among the weeds a few of the old plants surprisingly vigorous. One says to the other "It must be that a gardener has been coming and doing something about these plants." Upon inquiry they find that no neighbor has ever seen anyone at work in their garden. The first man says to the other "He must have worked while people slept." The other says "No, someone would have heard him and besides, anybody who cared about the plants would have kept down these weeds." The first man says "Look at the way these are arranged. There is purpose and a feeling for beauty here. I believe that someone comes, someone invisible to mortal eyes. I believe that the more carefully we look the more we shall find confirmation of this." They examine the garden ever so carefully and sometimes they come on new things suggesting the contrary and even that a malicious person has been at work. Besides examining the garden carefully they also study what happens to gardens left without attention. Each learns all the other learns about this and about the garden. Consequently, when after all this, one says "I still believe a gardener comes" while the other says "I don't" their different words now reflect no difference as to what they have found in the garden, no difference as to what they would find in the garden if they looked further, and no difference about how fast untended gardens fall into disorder. At this stage, in this context, the gardener hypothesis has ceased to be experimental; the difference between one who accepts and one who rejects it is now not a matter of the one expecting something the other does not expect. What is the difference between them? The one says: "A gardener comes unseen and unheard. He is manifested only in his works with which we are all familiar." The other says "There is no gardener." And with this difference in what they say about the gardener goes a difference in how they feel toward the garden, in spite of the fact that neither expects anything of it which the other does not expect.

But is this the whole difference between them— that the one calls the garden by one name and feels one way toward it, while the other calls it by another name and feels in another way toward it? And if this is what the difference has become, then is it any longer appropriate to ask "Which is right?" or "Which is reasonable?"[1]

> *The one says: "A gardener comes unseen and unheard. He is manifested only in his works with which we are all familiar." The other says "There is no gardener."*

For Wisdom, religious belief is obviously different from the scientific quest for causal explanation. Since the scientific revolution of the sixteenth to eighteenth centuries, many philosophers have tried to define religion and science in contrast to one another, and many have tried to cast their lots with science. But there is plenty of resistance to such a move. Many scientists are deeply religious people, and many

---

[1] John Wisdom, "Gods," in *Proceedings of the Aristotelian Society,* XLV (London: Harrison & Sons, 1944–45).

religious thinkers accept the authority of science without compromising their religious faith. No less a scientist than **Albert Einstein,** for example, has argued that it is this religious awe and appreciation for the complex regularities of nature that has spawned the great efforts of science to understand it. Indeed, he says, science itself inspires a "cosmic religious feeling."

ON THE DESIGN OF THE UNIVERSE
BY ALBERT EINSTEIN

It is easy to see why the churches have always fought science and persecuted its devotees. On the other hand, I maintain that the cosmic religious feeling is the strongest and noblest motive for scientific research. Only those who realize the immense efforts and, above all, the devotion without which pioneer work in theoretical science cannot be achieved are able to grasp the strength of the emotion out of which alone such work, remote as it is from the immediate realities of life, can issue. What a deep conviction of the rationality of the universe and what a yearning to understand, were it but a feeble reflection of the mind revealed in this world, Kepler and Newton must have had to enable them to spend years of solitary labor in disentangling the principles of celestial mechanics! Those whose acquaintance with scientific research is derived chiefly from its practical results easily develop a completely false notion of the mentality of the men who, surrounded by a skeptical world, have shown the way to kindred spirits scattered wide through the world and the centuries. Only one who has devoted his life to similar ends can have a vivid realization of what has inspired these men and given them the strength to remain true to their purpose in spite of countless failures. It is cosmic religious feeling that gives a man such strength. A contemporary has said, not unjustly, that in this materialistic age of ours the serious scientific workers are the only profoundly religious people.[2]

> *... I maintain that the cosmic religious feeling is the strongest and noblest motive for scientific research.*

Einstein's statement of scientific faith is particularly important in times when science and religion seem once again at each other's throats. Current controversies over "Creation" versus "evolution," for example, have made it seem as if science and religion are utterly irreconcilable, with completely opposed visions of the world. But consider this response from **Keiji Nishitani,** a Japanese philosopher conversant in

---

[2] Albert Einstein, "Religion and Science," in *Ideas and Opinions,* trans. Sonia Bargmann (New York: Crown, 1954).

Keiji Nishitani — Japanese philosopher both Buddhist & Xti...
— each of us must give personally to th...
existence which WHAT IS RELIGION? **127**
we share w/ all the universe

both Christianity and Buddhism. Nishitani claims that the distinguishing feature of religion is the "personal/impersonal," or in other words, the deeply personal recognition that each of us must give to the existence which we share with all other things in the universe. To step outside of ourselves, to consider the world from an impersonal perspective—called "personal nihility" by Nishitani—is an intimate and unique activity. But it is a necessary one. Everyone, whether consciously or unconsciously, must engage in it at some point in his or her life.

FROM "WHAT IS RELIGION?"
BY KEIJI NISHITANI

"What is religion?" we ask ourselves, or, looking at it the other way around, "What is the purpose of religion for us? Why do we need it?" Though the question about the need for religion may be a familiar one, it already contains a problem. In one sense, for the person who poses the question, religion does not seem to be something he needs. The fact that he asks the question at all amounts to an admission that religion has not yet become a necessity for him. In another sense, however, it is surely in the nature of religion to be necessary for just such a person. Wherever questioning individuals like this are to be found, the need for religion is there as well. In short, the relationship we have to religion is a contradictory one: those for whom religion is *not* a necessity are, for that reason, the very ones for whom religion *is* a necessity. There is no other thing of which the same can be said.

When asked, "Why do we need learning and the arts?" we might try to explain in reply that such things are necessary for the advancement of mankind, for human happiness, for the cultivation of the individual, and so forth. Yet even if we can say why we need such things, this does not imply that we cannot get along without them. Somehow life would still go on. Learning and the arts may be indispensable to living well, but they are not indispensable to living. In that sense, they can be considered a kind of luxury.

Food, on the other hand, is essential to life. Nobody would turn to somebody else and ask him why he eats. Well, maybe an angel or some other celestial being who has no need to eat might ask such questions, but men do not. Religion, to judge from current conditions in which many people are in fact getting along without it, is clearly not the kind of necessity that food is. Yet this does not mean that it is merely something we need to live *well*. Religion has to do with life itself. Whether the life we are living will end up in extinction or in the attainment of eternal life is a matter of the utmost importance for life itself. In no sense is religion to be called a luxury. Indeed, this is why religion is an indispensable necessity for those very people who fail to see the need for it. Herein lies the distinctive feature of religion that sets it apart from the mere life of "nature" and from culture. Therefore, to say that we need religion for example, for the sake of social order, or human welfare, or public morals is a mistake, or at least a *religion is NOT a utility → It's something we need to live well, It's Life itself!*

confusion of priorities. Religion must not be considered from the viewpoint of its *utility,* any more than life should. A religion concerned primarily with its own utility bears witness to its own degeneration. One can ask about the utility of things like eating for the natural life, or of things like learning and the arts for culture. In fact, in such matters the question of utility should be of constant concern. Our ordinary mode of being is restricted to these levels of natural or cultural life. But it is in breaking through that ordinary mode of being and over-turning it from the ground up, in pressing us back to the elemental source of life where life itself is seen as useless, that religion becomes something we need—a *must* for human life.

Two points should be noted from what has just been said. First, religion is at all times the individual affair of each individual. This sets it apart from things like culture, which, while related to the individual, do not need to concern each individual. Accordingly, we cannot understand what religion is from the outside. The religious quest alone is the key to understanding it; there is no other way. This is the most important point to be made regarding the essence of religion.

> *. . . religion is at all times the individual affair of each individual.*

[margin notes: ...TION individual affair of each individual ... is ... for standing ...]

Second, from the standpoint of the essence of religion, it is a mistake to ask "What is the purpose of religion for us?" and one that clearly betrays an attitude of trying to understand religion apart from the religious quest. It is a question that must be broken through by another question coming from within the person who asks it. There is no other road that can lead to an understanding of what religion is and what purpose it serves. The counterquestion that achieves this breakthrough is one that asks, "For what purpose do I myself exist?" Of everything else we can ask its purpose for us, but not of religion. With regard to everything else we can make a *telos* of ourselves as individuals, as man, or as mankind, and evaluate those things in relation to our life and existence. We put ourselves as individuals/man/mankind at the center and weigh the signifi-cance of everything as the *contents* of our lives as individuals/man/mankind. But religion upsets the posture from which we think of ourselves as *telos* and center for all things. Instead, religion poses as a starting point the question: "For what purpose do I exist?"

[margin notes: ...ver ask "What's the ...se of ...ion for ... — you discover through journey. What se do I —? "]

We become aware of religion as a need, as a must for life, only at the level of life at which everything else loses its necessity and its utility. Why do we exist at all? Is not our very existence and human life ultimately meaningless? Or, if there is a meaning or significance to it all, where do we find it? When we come to doubt the meaning of our existence in this way, when we have become a ques-tion to ourselves, the religious quest awakens within us. These questions and the quest they give rise to show up when the mode of looking at and thinking about everything in terms of how it relates to *us* is broken through, where the mode of living that puts us at the center of everything is overturned. This is why

Nihility = that which renders meaningless the meaning of life.

Questioning ourselves & our existence

the question of religion in the form, "Why do we need religion?" obscures the way to its own answer from the very start. It blocks our becoming a question to ourselves.

The point at which the ordinarily necessary things of life, including learning and the arts, all lose their necessity and utility is found at those times when death, nihility, or sin—or any of those situations that entail a fundamental negation of our life, existence, and ideals, that undermine the roothold of our existence and bring the meaning of life into question—become pressing personal problems for us. This can occur through an illness that brings one face-to-face with death, or through some turn of events that robs one of what had made life worth living. . . .

Nihility refers to that which renders meaningless the meaning of life. When we become a question to ourselves and when the problem of why we exist arises, this means that nihility has emerged from the ground of our existence and that our very existence has turned into a question mark. The appearance of this nihility signals nothing less than that one's awareness of self-existence has penetrated to an extraordinary depth.

Normally we proceed through life, on and on, with our eye fixed on something or other, always caught up with something within or without ourselves. It is these engagements that prevent the deepening of awareness. They block off the way to an opening up of that horizon on which nihility appears and self-being becomes a question. This is even the case with learning and the arts and the whole range of other cultural engagements. But when this horizon does open up at the bottom of those engagements that keep life moving continually on and on, something seems to halt and linger before us. This something is the meaninglessness that lies in wait at the bottom of those very engagements that bring meaning to life. This is the point at which that sense of nihility, that sense that "everything is the same" we find in Nietzsche and Dostoevski, brings the restless, forward-advancing pace of life to a halt and makes it take a step back. In the Zen phrase, it "turns the light to what is directly underfoot."

In the forward progress of everyday life, the ground beneath our feet always falls behind as we move steadily ahead; we overlook it. Taking a step back to shed light on what is underfoot of the self—"stepping back to come to the self," as another ancient Zen phrase has it—marks a conversion in life itself. This fundamental conversion in life is occasioned by the opening up of the horizon of nihility at the ground of life. It is nothing less than a conversion from the self-centered (or man-centered) mode of being, which always asks what *use* things have for us (or for man), to an attitude that asks for what *purpose* we ourselves (or man) exist. Only when we stand at this turning point does the question "What is religion?" really become our own.[3]

---

[3] Keiji Nishitani, "What Is Religion?" from *Religion and Nothingness,* trans. Jan Van Bragt (Berkeley: University of California Press, 1982).

conversion from self centered—"what's the use of things" an attitude that asks for the purpose of why we exist.

Judaism, Christianity & Islam = "Abrahamic" →
share roots in Abraham of the Old testament
130 CHAPTER 2 ◆ RELIGION   *↳ aka: Western religions*

B. THE WESTERN RELIGIONS

Among the world religions, Judaism, Christianity, and Islam bear a special relationship to each other and to philosophy. They might be called the "Abrahamic" religions, because all three trace their roots to Abraham of the Old Testament. Thus, the God worshiped in all three of these religions is the "God of Abraham." We might also call these the three "Western" religions, in that they all originate among peoples living west of the Indus River (one traditional dividing line between East and West).

Judaism, Christianity, and Islam are closely associated together and with the West for another reason, as well. The early religious thinking of all three was heavily influenced by the Greek philosophy of Plato and Aristotle. Although some other religions make use of Greek philosophy, its influence in other faiths does not approach the status it holds in Christian, Jewish, and Muslim thought.

Yet the God who appears in the Old Testament is not readily understood in either Platonic or Aristotelian terms. (You might look back at our discussions of Plato and Aristotle in earlier chapters and see if you can find anything akin to the Judeo-Christian God described there.) Therefore, early thinkers, particularly in the Middle Ages, had their work cut out for them in offering defenses of their beliefs, or in arriving at rational religious beliefs, using the Greeks as their model. The medieval philosophers' attempts to do so are among the most monumental of efforts in the history of philosophy, with some of the most provocative and widely influential results.

In many cases, philosophy played a crucial role in the conversions of individuals, and whole countries, to one of these religions. In others, philosophical disputes were the primary cause of sectarian secessions. In all cases, philosophical arguments were a vital ingredient in the development of the doctrines that have come down to us today.

1. The Traditional Conception of God

The principal issues for all three of these great monotheisms, of course, are the existence and character of God. The God of Judaism, Christianity, and Islam has many characteristics that must be identified for our understanding. Most importantly, it is generally believed that God is an independent being, the Creator of the universe, and distinct from the universe He created. It is generally agreed that God is the supremely rational and moral being with concern for human justice and human suffering. It is agreed that He is all-powerful (**omnipotent**), all-knowing (**omniscient**), and that He is everywhere at once (**omnipresent**). In the Old Testament, it is made evident that God has emotions; for example, we read of God as "a jealous God" and we hear of the "wrath of God." It is the attempt to understand the being who has these characteristics that defines Western theology and a great deal of Western metaphysics.

To insist that God is an independent being, the Creator of the universe but distinct from that universe, is of the utmost importance for Western religion. When people try to reinterpret God so that He is nothing other than some universal quality, as in

God = independent being

"God is love" → belief no different from someone who might not believe in God, but just be in Love.

THE WESTERN RELIGIONS **131**

"God is love," or "God is ultimate force," or "God is life," or "God is the universe," there is a very real possibility that God's existence as an independent being is being denied. One can say "God is love" as shorthand for "God loves us and wants us to love each other" without this danger. But if one believes that God simply is identical to people's loving one another, then it is evident that this belief is no different from that of a person who might not believe in God at all but just believes in love. Similarly, it is one thing to believe that God is a "force," among other things, who created the universe; but if you believe that God is nothing other than a force that created the universe, without consciousness or concern, then your belief does not differ from that of someone who also believes that some force created the universe but does not believe in God.

In Judaism, Christianity, and Islam, the independence of God from the universe He created is an all-important belief. Philosophers and theologians refer to this independence as the **transcendence of God**. (Don't confuse this word with the adjective "transcendental" we used in Chapter 3.) We say that God "transcends" the universe and humankind. We also say that He "transcends" all human experience. It is this notion of transcendence that raises an immediate epistemological problem. If God transcends our experience, how can we know that He exists at all? If He is outside of our every possible experience—if we cannot see, hear, or touch Him—what possible evidence can we have for His existence, and how can we have any way of knowing what He must be like?

[margin: transcendance = independ; How c know that exist?]

In some ancient religions, gods and goddesses were very much like human beings. They were usually stronger and perhaps smarter. The Greek and Roman gods, for example, were like this. Although they were immortal, they often misbehaved and became jealous or furious at one another. Philosophers use the word **anthropomorphism** when they refer to the perception of gods more or less as human. It is quite natural, when people try to envision their deities, that they should endow them with those characteristics they understand best—human characteristics.

[margin: Anthrom mort Gods = hum]

The God of Judaism, Christianity, and Islam is much less anthropomorphic than the gods and goddesses of ancient Greece and Rome. But it would be a mistake to deny that God is conceived in certain anthropomorphic ways as well. The God of the Hebrews frequently took their side in battle in the Old Testament, helping them to fell the walls of Jericho, keeping the sun still for extra hours, and holding apart the waters of the Red Sea. The God of the Old Testament has many human emotions: He becomes jealous or angry when His commands are not carried out, having people swallowed by whales and sometimes destroying whole cities. Even the notion that God is a loving God carries with it anthropomorphism. It is often said that these are mere approximations, based on the idea that we can never really know or understand what God is like. (For example, it is said that we cannot understand divine love and that we use our all-too-human conception of love as the only example we can find.) But it must also be said that such anthropomorphic projections are in no way an objection to belief in God; it is only to be expected that people will try to understand religion in those terms that they know best.

The scriptural emphasis on God's sense of justice and His concern for humankind also demonstrates anthropomorphic characteristics, even if it is true, as we are so often told, that God's conception of justice may be very different from our own. These characteristics are so important that if a person does not believe that God is a merciful and concerned being with a strong sense of justice, then that person probably does not believe in God at all. (For example, Aristotle's "prime mover," despite the Western theologians' marvelous adaptation of the concept to their religions, is not on the face of it very much like the Judeo-Christian God.) Prayer is meaningful only on the assumption that God listens to us and understands us; faith is intelligible only on the assumption that God cares about us. Without these characteristics, God would not be a moral force in our lives.

Some sophisticated theists and theologians have tried to purge belief in God of all anthropomorphic characteristics, speaking, for example, only of "Being Itself" rather than the usual characterization of God as "Him." Still, although we might not actually believe that God, like Zeus, resembles some superhuman immortal being, it is clear that our traditional conception of God is far more anthropocentric than some theologians would no doubt prefer.

The Western religions' conception of God has been varied in so many ways that we can't even begin to consider them. The differences between the God of the Old Testament and the God of the New Testament have been often discussed. Then there are the obvious differences between the various sects of Judaism, Christianity, and Islam. And the differences between this God and other gods (Zeus, Krishna, Isis) are so enormous that traditional Christians, Jews, and Muslims would hesitate to call these "God" at all.

2. Can We Know That God Exists?

It is one thing to be taught that there is a God; it is another to believe in God for good reason, rationally, and to know what one believes. Of course, many people have insisted that belief in God is not a matter of rationality or knowledge at all but only of faith. But the turn to faith logically comes after attempts to know. So before we turn to examine other philosophical questions raised by religious belief, let us ask whether or not we can know that God exists.

The problem is a familiar one. Since God by definition transcends our experience, how can we have evidence for His existence? It is the same problem we faced with substance (for that reason God and substance are so intertwined in metaphysics, as for example in Spinoza). There are people who claim to have been direct witnesses to miracles or to have heard God's own voice. But, assuming that none of us is one of them, our problem remains: Should we believe their reports? Might they have been victims of imagination or hallucination? Is there any evidence in our experience that would allow us to know of God's existence? If not, what reasons can we give for a belief in God?

In the long history of Western theology, three major sets of "proofs" have emerged as attempts to demonstrate God's existence. Each has received various formulations, and all are still being discussed today. They are called (1) the **ontological argument,** (2) the **cosmological argument,** and (3) the **teleological argument.**

God's Existence:
① ontological argument
② cosmological argument
③ teleological argument

THE ONTOLOGICAL ARGUMENT   This is the most difficult, for it is a purely logical proof; it attempts to argue from the idea of God to His necessary existence. Descartes used this argument in his *Meditations* to prove God's existence. Similar arguments were to be found in both Spinoza and Leibniz. But the man who is generally credited with the invention of the argument is an eleventh-century monk named **St. Anselm.** Because the argument depends wholly on the idea of God's existence, it is called *ontological.* Here is how Anselm presents it:

THE ONTOLOGICAL ARGUMENT
BY **ST. ANSELM**

Some time ago, at the urgent request of some of my brethren, I published a brief work, as an example of meditation on the grounds of faith. I wrote it in the role of one who seeks, by silent reasoning with himself, to learn what he does not know. But when I reflected on this little book, and saw that it was put together as a long chain of arguments, I began to ask myself whether *one* argument might possibly be found, resting on no other argument for its proof, but sufficient in itself to prove that God truly exists, and that he is the supreme good, needing nothing outside himself, but needful for the being and well-being of all things. I often turned my earnest attention to this problem, and at times I believed that I could put my finger on what I was looking for, but at other times it completely escaped my mind's eye, until finally, in despair, I decided to give up searching for something that seemed impossible to find. But when I tried to put the whole question out of my mind, so as to avoid crowding out other matters, with which I might make some progress, by this useless preoccupation, then, despite my unwillingness and resistance, it began to force itself on me more persistently than ever. Then, one day when I was worn out by my vigorous resistance to the obsession, the solution I had ceased to hope for presented itself to me, in the very turmoil of my thoughts, so that I enthusiastically embraced the idea which in my disquiet, I had spurned.

◆◆◆

GOD TRULY IS

And so, O Lord, since thou givest understanding to faith, give me to understanding—as far as thou knowest it to be good for me—that thou dost exist, as we believe, and that thou art what we believe thee to be. Now we believe that thou art a being than which none greater can be thought. Or can it be that there is no such being, since "the fool hath said in his heart, 'There is no God'"? But when this same fool hears what I am saying—"A being than which none greater can be thought"—he understands what he hears, and what he understands is in his understanding, even if he does not understand that it exists. For it is one thing for an object to be in the understanding, and another thing to understand that it

[handwritten annotation: when he hears that there's a great being he understands & what's understood is in the understanding b/c if it's in the understanding It's thought of as existing in real]

exists. When a painter considers beforehand what he is going to paint, he has it in his understanding, but he does not suppose that what he has not yet painted already exists. But when he has painted it, he both has it in his understanding and understands that what he has now produced exists. Even the fool, then, must be convinced that a being than which none greater can be thought exists at least in his understanding, since when he hears this he understands it, and whatever is understood is in the understanding. But clearly that than which a greater cannot be thought cannot exist in the understanding alone. For if it is actually in the understanding alone, it can be thought of as existing also in reality, and this is greater. Therefore, if that than which a greater cannot be thought is in the understanding alone, this same thing than which a greater cannot be thought is that than which a greater can be thought. But obviously this is impossible. Without doubt, therefore, there exists, both in the understanding and in reality, something than which a greater cannot be thought. *(?)*

GOD CANNOT BE THOUGHT OF AS NONEXISTENT

[handwritten annotation: (?]

And certainly it exists so truly that it cannot be thought of as nonexistent. For something can be thought of as existing, which cannot be thought of as not existing, and this is greater than that which *can* be thought of as not existing. Thus, if that than which a greater cannot be thought can be thought of as not existing, this very thing than which a greater cannot be thought is *not* that than which a greater cannot be thought. But this is contradictory. So, then, there truly is a being than which a greater cannot be thought—so truly that it cannot even be thought of as not existing.

And *thou* art this being, O Lord our God. Thou so truly are, then, O Lord my God, that thou canst not even be thought of as not existing. And this is right. For if some mind could think of something better than thou, the creature would rise above the Creator and judge its Creator; but this is altogether absurd. And indeed, whatever is, except thyself alone, can be thought of as not existing. Thou alone, therefore, of all beings, has being in the truest and highest sense, since no other being so truly exists, and thus every other being has less being. Why, then, has "the fool said in his heart, 'There is no God,'" when it is so obvious to the rational mind that, of all beings, thou dost exist supremely? Why indeed, unless it is that he is a stupid fool?

HOW THE FOOL HAS SAID IN HIS HEART WHAT CANNOT BE THOUGHT

But how did he manage to say in his heart what he could not think? Or how is it that he was unable to think what he said in his heart? After all, to say in one's heart and to think are the same thing. Now if it is true—or, rather, since it is true—that he thought it, because he said it in his heart, but did not say it in his heart, since he could not think it, it is clear that something can be said in one's heart or thought in more than one way. For we think of a thing, in one sense, when we think of the word that signifies it, and in another sense, when we understand the very thing itself. Thus, in the first sense God can be thought of as nonexistent, but in the second sense this is quite impossible. For no one who understands what God is can think that God does not exist, even though he says these words in his heart—perhaps without any meaning, perhaps with some quite extraneous meaning. For God is that than which a greater cannot be thought, and whoever understands this rightly must understand that he exists in such a way that he cannot be non-existent even in thought. He, therefore, who understands that God thus exists cannot think of him as nonexistent.

Thanks be to thee, good Lord, thanks be to thee, because I now understand by thy light what I formerly believed thy gift, so that even if I were to refuse to believe in thy existence, I could not fail to understand its truth.[4]

> *For God is that than which a greater cannot be thought, and whoever understands this rightly must understand that he exists in such a way that he cannot be nonexistent even in thought.*

The logic of the argument is deceptively simple: The concept of "God" is defined, innocently enough, as "a being greater than which none can be thought." Then, Anselm asks, "which would be greater, a being who is merely thought, or a being who actually exists?" The answer, of course, is a being who actually exists. But since God is, by definition, the greatest being who can be thought, He must therefore exist. "God cannot be nonexistent even in thought." Anselm goes on to argue that the idea of an eternal being who either does not yet exist or no longer exists is self-contradictory, so that the very idea we have of such a being requires existence. It is worth noting that, while formulating the ontological argument, Anselm was also putting into place some of the final ingredients in the Christian conception of God, as not only a perfect or even the most perfect being but rather as the greatest (most perfect) *conceivable* being.

The argument has had a long, influential history, and logicians are still arguing about it. The argument was not seriously altered for five centuries, when Descartes took up Anselm's argument and gave it its modern formulation. In the seventeenth century, Descartes (in his *Meditations*) made explicit the presupposition of the argument, that existence is a property which, like color, shape, weight, and charm, a thing may either have or not have. Some properties, however, are essential to a thing: three angles are essential to a triangle, spots are essential to a Dalmatian. So too, Descartes suggests, perfection is essential to the most perfect being, and existence is a perfection. One can no more conceive of a most perfect being without existence than one can conceive of a triangle without three angles or a Dalmatian without spots.

perfection is essential to the most perfect bei[ng]

[4]St. Anselm, *Proslogion,* in *A Scholastic Miscellany,* Vol. 10. The Library of Christian Classics, ed. and trans. Eugene R. Fairweather (Philadelphia: Westminster Press, 1956).

existence is perfection!

THE ONTOLOGICAL ARGUMENT
BY RENÉ DESCARTES

But now, if just because I can draw the idea of something from my thought, it follows that all which I know clearly and distinctly as pertaining to this object does really belong to it, may I not derive from this an argument demonstrating the existence of God? It is certain that I no less find the idea of God, that is to say, the idea of a supremely perfect Being, in me, than that of any figure or number whatever it is; and I do not know any less clearly and distinctly that an [actual and] eternal existence pertains to this nature than I know that all that which I am able to demonstrate of some figure or number truly pertains to the nature of this figure or number, and therefore, although all that I concluded in the preceding Meditations were found to be false, the existence of God would pass with me as at least as certain as I have ever held the truths of mathematics (which concern only numbers and figures) to be. This indeed is not at first manifest, since it would seem to present some appearance of being a sophism. For being accustomed in all other things to make a distinction between existence and essence, I easily persuade myself that the existence can be separated from the essence of God, and that we can thus conceive God as not actually existing. But, nevertheless, when I think of it with more attention, I clearly see that existence can no more be separated from the essence of God than can its having its three angles equal to two right angles be separated from the essence of a [rectilinear] triangle, or the idea of a mountain from the idea of a valley; and so there is not any less repugnance to our conceiving a God (that is, a Being supremely perfect) to whom existence is lacking (that is to say, to whom a certain perfection is lacking), than to conceive of a mountain which has no valley.

But although I cannot really conceive of a God without existence any more than a mountain without a valley, still from the fact that I conceive a mountain with a valley, it does not follow that there is such a mountain in the world; similarly although I conceive of God as possessing existence, it would seem that it does not follow that there is a God which exists; for my thought does not impose any necessity upon things, and just as I may imagine a winged horse, although no horse with wings exists, so I could perhaps attribute existence to God, although no God existed.

But a sophism is concealed in this objection; for from the fact that I cannot conceive a mountain without a valley, it does not follow that there is any mountain or any valley in existence, but only that the mountain and the valley, whether they exist or do not exist, cannot in any way be separated one from the other. While from the fact that I cannot conceive God without existence, it follows that existence is inseparable from Him, and hence that He

. . . from the fact that I cannot conceive God without existence, it follows that existence is inseparable from Him, and hence that He really exists.

really exists; not that my thought can bring this to pass, or impose any necessity on things, but, on the contrary, because the necessity which lies in the thing itself, i.e. the necessity of the existence of God determines me to think in this way. For it is not within my power to think of God without existence (that is of a supremely perfect Being devoid of a supreme perfection) though it is in my power to imagine a horse either with wings or without wings.

And we must not here object that it is in truth necessary for me to assert that God exists after having presupposed that He possesses every sort of perfection, since existence is one of these, but that as a matter of fact my original supposition was not necessary, just as it is not necessary to consider that all quadrilateral figures can be inscribed in the circle; for supposing I thought of this, I should be constrained to admit that the rhombus might be inscribed in the circle since it is a quadrilateral figure, which, however, is manifestly false. Although it is not necessary that I should at any time entertain the notion of God, nevertheless whenever it happens that I think of a first and a sovereign Being, and, so to speak, derive the idea of Him from the storehouse of my mind, it is necessary that I should attribute to Him every sort of perfection, although I do not get so far as to enumerate them all, or to apply my mind to each one in particular. And this necessity suffices to make me conclude (after having recognised that existence is a perfection) that this first and sovereign Being really exists; just as though it is not necessary for me ever to imagine any triangle, yet, whenever I wish to consider a rectilinear figure composed only of three angles, it is absolutely essential that I should attribute to it all those properties which serve to bring about the conclusion that its three angles are not greater than two right angles, even although I may not then be considering this point in particular. But when I consider which figures are capable of being inscribed in the circle, it is in no way necessary that I should think that all quadrilateral figures are of this number; on the contrary, I cannot even pretend that this is the case, so long as I do not desire to accept anything which I cannot conceive clearly and distinctly. And in consequence there is a great difference between the false suppositions such as this, and the true ideas born within me, the first and principal of which is that of God. For really I discern in many ways that this idea is not something factitious, and depending solely on my thought, but that it is the image of a true and immutable nature; first of all, because I cannot conceive anything but God himself to whose essence existence [necessarily] pertains; in the second place because it is not possible for me to conceive two or more Gods in this same position; and, granted that there is one such God who now exists, I see clearly that it is necessary that He should have existed from all eternity and that He must exist eternally; and finally, because I know an infinitude of other properties in God, none of which I can either diminish or change.[5]

---

[5] René Descartes, "Meditation IV," in *Meditations on First Philosophy,* in *The Philosophical Works of Descartes,* trans. Elizabeth S. Haldane and G. R. T. Ross (Cambridge: Cambridge University Press, 1911).

Descartes' version is

> *I cannot conceive of a God without the property of existence.*
> *("His existence cannot be separated from His essence.")*
> *Therefore, God exists.*

Then he adds

> *My conception of God is such that He has every sort of perfection.*
> *Existence is a perfection.*
> *Therefore, God necessarily exists.*

These arguments are valid as stated, but are they also sound? Consider the following argument, which has been proposed in the same form as the above arguments. Define a "grenlin" as "the greenest imaginable creature." Now, which is greener, a green creature that does exist or one that does not? Obviously the one that exists. Therefore, at least one grenlin exists.

It is worth noting that this objection had been raised against Anselm too, by **Gaunilo of Marmoutier,** who suggested the existence of an island more perfect than any other, on the same grounds that it would be contradictory for the most perfect island not to exist. Anselm replied that the argument cannot be applied to islands (or grenlins) or anything else whose nonexistence is conceivable. The question, then, is what it means for nonexistence to be conceivable or for existence to be a necessary property of a thing.

Descartes faced a similar challenge to his formulation when a critic attacked his analogy with triangles and insisted that, while it may be true that *if* a triangle exists, then it must have three angles, it does not follow that triangles must exist, or that any in fact do exist. Descartes' answer is similar to Anselm's response to his critic: The essence of triangle does not include the perfection of existence, as God's surely does.

The ontological argument makes a special case for God, because He is the only "greatest conceivable" or "most perfect" being. Nevertheless, the argument has made many believers uneasy and has been dismissed as a clever trick by nonbelievers. But, whatever our unease, the argument is clearly valid.

The argument is a straightforward syllogism of the "All men are mortal/Socrates is a man/Socrates is mortal" type, the only real (but significant) difference being that, while there can be any number of men, there can be only one God, one "most perfect" being. But what we have so far taken for granted in the above presentations of the argument is the presupposition that existence is a property, like a color or shape. One way of attacking the logic of the argument, even while accepting its validity, is to challenge this presupposition, and thus the soundness of the argument. Should we be allowed to write, in our second premise, "Ex"? In other words, is "exists" a predicate, like "barks" and "is green"? Or is it rather a quantifier, like "all" and "none" and "some" (which is, essentially, "there exists at least one . . .")? The objection that "existence is not a predicate" was formulated against the ontological argument by Immanuel Kant.

The great philosopher Kant suggested that the problem lies in the central idea, shared by the ontological argument and the unacceptable arguments that follow the same form, that existence is one of the essential properties, that is, part of the defini-

Kant says existence can't be a part of a definition.

tion of a thing. But existence, Kant argues, is not a property and cannot be part of a definition. In an often quoted passage of his *Critique of Pure Reason,* he presents this argument:

AGAINST THE ONTOLOGICAL ARGUMENT
BY IMMANUEL KANT

I answer:—Even in introducing into the concept of a thing, which you wish to think in its possibility only, the concept of its existence, under whatever disguise it may be, you have been guilty of a contradiction. If you were allowed to do this, you would apparently have carried your point; but in reality you have achieved nothing, but have only committed a tautology. I simply ask you, whether the proposition, that *this* or *that thing* (which, whatever it may be, I grant you as possible) *exists,* is an analytical or a synthetical proposition? If the former, then by its existence you add nothing to your thought of the thing; but in that case, either the thought within you would be the thing itself, or you have presupposed existence, as belonging to possibility, and have according to your own showing deducted existence from internal possibility, which is nothing but a miserable tautology. The mere word *reality,* which in the concept of a thing sounds different from existence in the concept of the predicate, can make no difference. For if you call all accepting or positing (without determining what it is) reality, you have placed a thing, with all its predicates, within the concept of the subject, and accepted it as real, and you do nothing but repeat it in the predicate. If, on the contrary, you admit, as every sensible man must do, that every proposition involving existence is synthetical, how can you say that the predicate of existence does not admit of removal without contradiction, a distinguishing property which is peculiar to analytical propositions only, the very character of which depends on it?

I might have hoped to put an end to this subtle argumentation, without many words, and simply by an accurate definition of the concept of existence, if I had not seen that the illusion, in mistaking a logical predicate for a real one (that is the predicate which determines a thing), resists all correction. Everything can become a *logical predicate,* even the subject itself may be predicated of itself, because logic makes no account of any contents of concepts. *Determination,* however, is a predicate, added to the concept of the subject, and enlarging it, and it must not therefore be contained in it.

Being *is evidently not a real predicate, or a concept of something that can be added to the concept of a thing.*

Being is evidently not a real predicate, or a concept of something that can be added to the concept of a thing. It is merely the admission of a thing, and of certain determinations in it. Logically, it is merely the copula of a judgment. The proposition, *God is almighty,* contains two concepts, each having its object, namely, God and almightiness. The small word *is,* is not an additional predicate, but only serves to put the predicate *in relation* to the subject. If, then, I take the subject (God) with all its predicates (including that of almightiness), and say, *God is,* or there is a God, I do not put a new predicate to the concept of God, but I only put the subject by itself, with all its predicates, in relation to my concept, as its object. Both must contain exactly the same kind of thing, and nothing can have been added to the concept, which expresses possibility only, by my thinking its object as simply given and saying it is. And thus the real does not contain more than the possible. A hundred real dollars do not contain a penny more than a hundred possible dollars. For as the latter signify the concept, the former the object and its position by itself, it is clear that, in case the former contained more than the latter, my concept would not express the whole object, and would not therefore be its adequate concept. In my financial position no doubt there exists more by one hundred real dollars, than by their concept only (that is their possibility), because in reality the object is not only contained analytically in my concept, but is added to my concept (which is a determination of my state), synthetically; but the conceived hundred dollars are not in the least increased through the existence which is outside my concept.[6]

What Kant is arguing is that the existence of a thing can never be merely a matter of logic. (This is what he means when he says that the proposition that a thing exists cannot be analytic.) "Existence" or "being," he argues, isn't a "real predicate" (though it is a grammatical predicate) because it does not tell us anything more about whatever is said to have existence or being. In other words, there is something odd about the statement, "this apple is red, round, ripe, and exists." What is odd is that "exists" does not give a characteristic of the apple but rather says that there is an apple with these characteristics. The proper characterization of God, therefore, includes the various characteristics we discussed earlier in this chapter, but it should not include, according to Kant, any characteristic that implies God's existence. It is one thing to say that God, if He exists, has such-and-such characteristics; it is something more to say that such a God exists. (This is what Kant means by his example about the one hundred real versus one hundred possible dollars; they both have exactly the same number of cents, but only the one hundred real dollars are worth anything.)

Many contemporary philosophers agree with Kant's argument, but many do not. Furthermore, contemporary logicians have developed versions of the ontological argument that can even dispense with this controversial notion of existence as a property. For example, with just the seemingly innocent premise "if God exists, then He necessarily exists," some logicians have recently argued according to the sophisticated rules of modern logic that the conclusion that "God exists" does follow. The premise is innocent because you can grant that "if God exists" without in any way admitting that God in fact exists. **Charles Hartshorne,** for example, has argued that,

---

[6]Immanuel Kant, *The Critique of Pure Reason,* rev. 2nd ed., trans. Max Müller (London: Macmillan, 1927).

if our concept of God is of a being who is eternal and self-existent then the question of God's existence cannot be a contingent matter but must be a matter of logical necessity (or impossibility). An existent being, but one which we can imagine not existing, could not be God, for, following Anselm, God is the being of whom it must be said (by definition) that nothing greater is conceivable. But instead of employing the objectionable presupposition—that existence is a predicate—Hartshorne's argument simply goes on to demonstrate that there is nothing self-contradictory in the concept of such a being, and therefore we must conclude that God necessarily exists. (The presupposition here is that either a most perfect being necessarily exists or he necessarily does not exist—what logicians call "the law of the excluded middle"; in other words, there are no other possibilities.)

Whether or not the argument succeeds in its classical form, it can be understood in another way, which clearly distinguishes it from all the absurd arguments that apparently have the same form. If you believe in God, then the argument might be taken in a very different way, not as a "proof" but as an attempt to articulate your belief. The theologian **Karl Barth** has argued that this is what Anselm's argument really tries to do, and as you read over his argument a second or third time it becomes clear that he is expressing his faith as much as he is offering a logical proof. In general, the "proofs" of God's existence have been such articulations and expressions as well as proper logical arguments. Even if they fail as proofs, they often succeed in this other, and perhaps more important function. Descartes' and Anselm's argument is, ultimately, that we cannot think about God and at the same time doubt His existence.

It is clear that, considered simply as a logical argument, the ontological argument does not have the power to convert nonbelievers into believers. Or if you are a believer, it is clear that an objection to the "proof" is not going to shake your faith in any way whatsoever. So the significance of the proof is ambiguous; as a logical exercise it is brilliant, as an expression of faith it may be edifying, but as an actual proof that God exists or as a means of converting atheists it seems to have no power at all.

THE COSMOLOGICAL ARGUMENT   The second "proof" of God's existence is a set of arguments that date back to Aristotle's argument for the prime mover. The basis of all these arguments is the intolerability if not the unthinkability of an infinite regress and the need for some ultimate explanation. Together they are called the cosmological argument, and their best-known formulation is by St. Thomas Aquinas as the first three of his "five ways" of proving God's existence.

THE COSMOLOGICAL ARGUMENT
BY ST. THOMAS AQUINAS

The first and more manifest way is the argument from motion. It is certain, and evident to our senses, that in the world some things are in motion. Now whatever is moved is moved by another, for nothing can be moved except it is in potentiality to that towards which it is moved whereas a thing moves inasmuch as it is in act. For motion is nothing else than the reduction of something from potentiality to actuality. But nothing can be reduced from potentiality to actuality, except by something in a state of actuality. Thus that which is actually hot, as fire, makes wood, which is potentially hot, to be actually hot, and thereby moves and changes it. Now it is not possible that the same thing should be at once in actuality and potentiality in the same respect, but only in different respects. For what is actually hot cannot simultaneously be potentially hot; but it is simultaneously potentially cold. It is therefore impossible that in the same respect and in the same way a thing should be both mover and moved, i.e., that it should move itself. Therefore, whatever is moved must be moved by another. If that by which it is moved be itself moved, then this also must needs be moved by another, and that by another again. But this cannot go on to infinity, because then there would be no first mover, and consequently, no other mover, seeing that subsequent movers move only inasmuch as they are moved by the first mover, as the staff moves only because it is moved by the hand. Therefore, it is necessary to arrive at a first mover, moved by no other; and this everyone understands to be God.

The second way is from the nature of efficient cause.[7] In the world of sensible things we find there is an order of efficient causes. There is no case known (neither is it, indeed, possible) in which a thing is found to be the efficient cause of itself; for so it would be prior to itself, which is impossible. Now in efficient causes it is not possible to go on to infinity, because in all efficient causes following in order, the first is the cause of the intermediate cause, and the intermediate is the cause of the ultimate cause, whether the intermediate cause be several, or one only. Now to take away the cause is to take away the effect. Therefore, if there be no first cause among efficient causes, there will be no ultimate, nor any intermediate cause. But if in efficient causes it is possible to go on to infinity, there will be no first efficient cause, neither will there be an ultimate effect, nor any intermediate efficient causes; all of which is plainly false. Therefore it is necessary to admit a first efficient cause, to which everyone gives the name of God.

The third way is taken from possibility and necessity, and runs thus. We find in nature things that are possible to be and not to be, since they are found to be generated, and to be corrupted, and consequently, it is possible for them to be and not to be. But it is impossible for these always to exist, for that which can not-be at some time is not. Therefore, if everything can not-be, then at one time there was nothing in existence. Now if

> *. . . we cannot but admit the existence of some being having of itself its own necessity, and not receiving it from another, but rather causing in others their necessity.*

---

[7] An *efficient cause* is an event (or an agent) that brings something about. The term comes from Aristotle. See glossary to Chapter 1, "cause."

existence had to start somewhere

this were true, even now there would be nothing in existence, because that which does not exist begins to exist only through something already existing. Therefore, if at one time nothing was in existence, it would have been impossible for anything to have begun to exist; and thus even now nothing would be in existence—which is absurd. Therefore, not all beings are merely possible, but there must exist something the existence of which is necessary. But every necessary thing either has its necessity caused by another, or not. Now it is impossible to go on to infinity in necessary things which have their necessity caused by another, as has been already proved in regard to efficient causes. Therefore we cannot but admit the existence of some being having of itself its own necessity, and not receiving it from another, but rather causing in others their necessity. This all men speak of as God.

In his "fourth way," Aquinas combines the form of cosmological argument with some of the ideas from the ontological argument: *some better & some lesser than others*

God

causes to be be or lesser

The fourth way is taken from the gradation to be found in things. Among beings there are some more and some less good, true, noble, and the like. But *more* and *less* are predicated of different things according as they resemble in their different ways something which is the maximum, as a thing is said to be hotter according as it more nearly resembles that which is hottest; so that there is something which is truest, something best, something noblest, and, consequently, something which is most being, for those things that are greatest in truth are greatest in being, as it is written in [Aristotle's] *Metaphysics*. . . . Now the maximum in any genus is the cause of all in that genus, as fire, which is the maximum of heat, is the cause of all hot things, as is said in the same book. Therefore, there must also be something which is to all beings the cause of their being, goodness, and every other perfection; and this we call God.[8]

The cosmological argument, in all of these versions, is also both an attempt at "proof" and an expression of one's belief in God. Accordingly, it must be appreciated for its role in articulating the concept of God in traditional Christianity and evaluated as a logical argument. As a logical argument, two modern objections seem to have considerable weight. First, even if the argument is formally valid, it proves only that there is some "first mover" or "first cause" or "necessary being." It does not prove that this being has all of the other attributes that allow us to recognize God. (Aquinas' fourth "way," however, includes moral attributes of perfection as well.) Taken at face value, the first three versions of the cosmological argument are similar to Aristotle's argument for the "prime mover" (Chapter 1) except that Aquinas takes the "first cause" to be an "efficient" as well as "final" cause, that is, as the creator as well as the meaning of the universe.

---

[8] St. Thomas Aquinas, *Summa Theologica*, trans. Fathers of the English Dominican Province (New York: Benziger, Bruce & Glencoe, 1948).

Handwritten margin notes:

infinite regress ; universe always existed didn't have a beginning ↳ however this beginning required an act & would

Right margin: still need a prim mov

Furthermore, Aristotle (in his *Physics*) allows that there might be several prime movers, while Aquinas is clear that there can be only one. Nevertheless, one might accept the argument and believe only in a "first cause" and deny the existence of God. Or if it is accepted that there must be a first cause, why could the universe itself not be its own cause? In current physics, scientists would argue that this idea is just as plausible as the idea that there must have been something else that caused our universe to exist. This leads us to the second objection, which would have been unthinkable to Aquinas (or Aristotle) but is generally accepted today. The idea of an infinite regress, that the universe did not have a beginning but has always existed, seemed like an obvious absurdity until the nineteenth century. But now, even though scientists and mathematicians talk about the beginning of the universe and the relativity of time, they no longer consider an infinite regress as necessarily impossible. Without the idea that every infinite regress is an absurdity, the cosmological argument loses its main premise.

In fact, Aquinas admits that there is no valid argument against the claim that God and the universe existed for all eternity, but he has another argument to help him here. He says that the beginning of the universe required an *act*, which means that the universe could not have been the cause of itself. Furthermore, even if the universe existed eternally, it would still require a prime mover to keep it in motion. Therefore, he concludes, God must exist even if the infinite regress argument by itself does not prove this.

THE TELEOLOGICAL ARGUMENT The third "proof" of God's existence is the one that is probably most familiar to you. It is usually called **the argument from design.** Immanuel Kant called it the *teleological argument*. It is often the most universally appealing of the three arguments because it depends as much on our emotions and our sense of wonder as it does on logical principles. The classical form of the argument goes like this. Suppose you are walking across a deserted beach and come across a watch, lying in the sand. You immediately conclude, "people have been here." Why? Because it is highly unlikely that a mechanism as intricately designed as a watch might be thrown together by the chance forces of nature. A pebble on the beach might be curiously shaped, but anything approaching the complexity of a tool or a piece of sculpture, much less a complex mechanism, would strike us as proof of some intelligent being. Now, looking at the universe, it is easy to wonder at its complexity, the intricate workings of the heavens or even a single-celled organism and the grand variety and interconnection of all living things. From this, one concludes that the universe as a whole must have been rationally designed.

One classic version of the teleological argument is St. Thomas Aquinas' "fifth way":

THE "FIFTH WAY"
BY **ST. THOMAS AQUINAS**

The fifth way is taken from the governance of the world. We see that things which lack knowledge, such as natural bodies, act for an end, and this is

everything has an end → directed towards
God directs?

evident from their acting always, or nearly always in the same way, so as to obtain the best result. Hence it is plain that they achieve their end, not fortuitously, but designedly. Now whatever lacks knowledge cannot move towards an end, unless it be directed by some being endowed with knowledge and intelligence; as the arrow is directed by the archer. Therefore some intelligent being exists by whom all natural things are directed to their end; and this being we call God.[9]

The argument is powerful psychologically, but it too has its problems. Like the earlier two arguments, it may prove much less about God than the theist needs to have proven. The God who has rationally designed the universe need not have the slightest concern for humankind, for example. He may well consider us just one of those little curiosities of evolution that, for a few thousand years, interfered with His other interests. But there are other problems peculiar to this argument. It is easily mocked, and Voltaire, who was around when the argument was most popular, parodied its logic in *Candide* (by suggesting that, among other things, it was marvelous that God gave us noses so that we can wear eyeglasses). About the same time, the German Enlightenment writer Georg Christoph Lichtenberg commented that it was clever of God to put holes in the cat's skin right where his eyes are. These nonsensical comments make an important point, however. The "design" in nature appears as such only to one who is already predisposed to believe in a designer. This is most powerfully presented by David Hume in his blasphemous (and therefore posthumous) *Dialogues on Natural Religion:*

AN IMPERFECT UNIVERSE
BY **DAVID HUME**

This world, for aught he knows, is very faulty and imperfect compared to a superior standard and was only the first rude essay of some infant deity who afterwards abandoned it.

In a word, Cleanthes, a man who follows your hypothesis is able, perhaps, to assert or conjecture that the universe sometime arose from something like design; but beyond that position he cannot ascertain one single circumstance and is left afterwards to fix every point of his theology by the utmost license of fancy and hypothesis. This world, for aught he knows, is very faulty and imperfect compared to a superior standard and was only the first rude essay of some infant deity who afterwards abandoned it, ashamed of his lame performance; it is the work only of some dependent, inferior deity and is the object of derision to his superiors; it is the production of old age and dotage

---

[9] Aquinas, *Summa Theologica.*

in some superannuated deity and, ever since his death, has run on at adventures from the first impulse and active force which it received from him.[10]

Hume's argument is, quite simply, that this is not a perfect world, which means that the God who supposedly designed it cannot be perfect either. One can even wonder whether a universe that has been so badly designed has been designed at all. But Cleanthes replies that he rejects both the suppositions and the tone of these sarcastic remarks and even insists that the argument that the universe is badly designed presupposes a designer. There are more powerful replies, however: that the world is in fact designed as well as it could possibly be, or else that it is a design that has not yet been fully realized and has not yet come to see full perfection.

The credibility of the argument from design has suffered enormously (but perhaps needlessly) from the shock of Darwin's theory of evolution. Accordingly, the Christian Church has combated the latter with all of the resources at its command. But the battle has been largely unnecessary and, if anything, has falsely overemphasized the conflict between science and religion, weakening the credibility of the Church. For evolution need not deny the argument from design. It only changes the argument from the traditional idea that God created the universe all at once (though even in Genesis, He spread it out over several days) to the idea that He created it over a long period of time, using natural selection as one of His tools.

But the logic of evolution does undermine the appeal of the argument from design in a more subtle way. The power of the argument is, boiled down to essentials, "Isn't it marvelous that things are as they are!" But our "marvel" depends on our putting some premium on "the way things are." We place a high premium on "the way things are" because according to the laws of probability (or chance) the odds against this way are enormous. Now consider the following analogy: You are playing cards, stud poker, and the dealer gives you excellent hands twice in a row. You would be suspicious. The odds are against it. And, particularly if you lose both times, you will be certain that some "design" (namely, the dealer's) is behind it. But now, why would you not have the same suspicions given any two consecutive hands, for the odds are exactly the same against any combination of cards? (The odds against receiving any hand of the same five cards twice consecutively are 2.6 million to 1.) The answer, of course, has nothing to do with the "likelihood" of getting one set of hands rather than another but with the significance you place on the one combination rather than the other. So too, with the argument from design.

Evolution has given the world many different "ways that things are" and will give it many more. The reason for our marveling at this particular "way that things are" is that we suppose that the odds against it are uniquely high. But they are not. They are equally high against every other possible "way that things are," and so this "way" seems to deserve no special explanation. This does not deny "design," of course; it only emphasizes the importance of a certain way of seeing the world, a way shared

---

[10] David Hume, *Dialogues on Natural Religion,* ed. Norman Kemp Smith (Oxford: Oxford University Press, 1935).

by science and nature-lovers as well as theists. Wittgenstein summed up this view toward the argument from design in a phrase: "What is remarkable is not how things are, but that they are at all." (This turns us back to the cosmological argument.)

C. RELIGION, MORALITY, AND EVIL

The three traditional forms of "proof" don't seem to be adequate as literal proofs. In order to accept any of them, it looks as if one has to *begin* by believing in God. Moreover, what each of them proves is not the existence of *God,* but at most the existence of something; something that is defined by its existence, something that is a first cause, or something that is an intelligent "designer." But a very different view of God is defended, for example, by Immanuel Kant. On this view, the most important attribute of the traditional Western God—the reason why men and women have worshiped Him, prayed to Him, feared Him, fought wars, and died for Him—is their belief in God's divine justice. Thus the most important attributes of God in Western religion are His moral qualities. Without them, our belief in God would be very different than it is.

According to this view, the importance of God in Western thought is His role as the source of our moral laws, as the judge of our actions and feelings, and as the sanction that stands behind those laws and judgments. The preceding "proofs" of God's existence are not wholly convincing, even if they are valid, just because they leave out this all-important moral aspect of belief in God. What distinguishes theists from atheists is not a matter of mere theory or argument ("a mere hypothesis," the French philosopher **La Place** called it), but a difference in lifestyle and confidence. The theist believes in a divine source of morality, in a judgment of one's actions that transcends everyday life, and the promise of reward (or threat of punishment) after death. The atheist also believes in morality—but not in divine morality—and believes that all judgments of our actions and all rewards and punishments must take place in this life or not at all. Accordingly, the question of God's existence has a distinctly moral dimension. Our conception of the human good depends on, as believers, our conception of God.

1. Religion and "Practical Reason"

Immanuel Kant, after attempting to refute all three of the traditional arguments of God's existence, offered one of his own. He no longer tried to "prove" God's existence as such and even said that, strictly speaking, we could have no knowledge of God at all, since God, as transcendent, cannot be the object of any possible experience. So Kant, following a long tradition in Christianity, said that belief in God is a matter of faith. But this does not mean, as people so often take it to mean, that it is an irrational belief. Quite to the contrary, Kant insisted that it is the most rational belief of all. For without it, we would not have the anchor for our morality, nor would we have any reason to suppose that our good deeds would in fact be eventually rewarded or evil deeds punished. It was obvious to Kant, as it has been to every person with his or her eyes open since ancient times, that justice is not always delivered in this life. Innocent children are butchered in wars; evil men live grand lives well into old age. Therefore, according to Kant, it was rational to believe in God, rational to have faith, even if faith was not, strictly speaking, a matter of knowledge. It is, he says, a "Postulate of Practical Reason."

ON GOD AND MORALITY
BY IMMANUEL KANT

The moral law led, in the foregoing analysis, to a practical problem which is assigned solely by pure reason and without any concurrence of sensuous incentives. It is the problem of the completeness of the first and principal part of the highest good, viz., morality; since this problem can be solved only in eternity, it led to the postulate of immortality. The same law must also lead us to affirm the possibility of the second element of the highest good, i.e., happiness proportional to that morality; it must do so just as disinterestedly as heretofore, by a purely impartial reason. This it can do on the supposition of the existence of a cause adequate to this effect, i.e., it must postulate the existence of God as necessarily belonging to the possibility of the highest good (the object of our will which is necessarily connected with moral legislation of pure reason). We proceed to exhibit this connection in a convincing manner.

Happiness is the condition of a rational being in the world. In whose whole existence everything goes according to wish and will. It thus rests on the harmony of nature with his entire end and with the essential determining ground of his will. But the moral law commands as a law of freedom through motives wholly independent of nature and of its harmony·with our faculty of desire (as incentives). Still, the acting rational being in the world is not at the same time the cause of the world and of nature itself. Hence there is not the slightest ground in the moral law for a necessary connection between the morality and proportionate happiness of a being which belongs to the world as one of its parts and as thus dependent on it. Not being nature's cause, his will cannot by its own strength bring nature, as it touches on his happiness, into complete harmony with his practical principles. Nevertheless, in the practical task of pure reason, i.e., in the necessary endeavor after the highest good, such a connection is postulated as necessary: we *should* seek to further the highest good (which therefore must be at least possible). Therefore also the existence is postulated of a cause of the whole of nature, itself distinct from nature, which contains the ground of the exact coincidence of happiness with morality. This supreme cause, however, must contain the ground of the agreement of nature not merely with a law of the will of rational beings but with the idea of this law so far as they make it the supreme ground of determination of the will. Thus it contains the ground of the agreement of nature not merely with actions moral in their form but also with their morality as the motives to such actions, i.e., with their moral intention. Therefore, the highest good is possible in the world only on the supposition of a supreme cause of nature which has a causality corresponding to the moral intention. Now a being which is capable of actions by the idea of laws is an intelligence (a rational being), and the causality of such a being according to this idea of laws is his will., Therefore, the supreme cause of nature, in so far as it must be presupposed for the highest good, is a being which is the cause (and consequently the author) of nature through understanding and will, i.e., God. As a consequence, the postulate of the possibility of a highest derived good (the best world) is at the same time the postulate of the reality of a highest original good, namely, the existence of God. Now it was our duty to promote the highest good; and it is not merely our privilege but a necessity connected with duty as a requisite to presuppose the possibility of this highest good. This presupposition is made only under the condition of the existence of God, and this condition inseparably connects this supposition with duty. Therefore, it is morally necessary to assume the existence of God.[11]

The key to Kant's argument is the obvious fact that good deeds are not always rewarded in this life and evil deeds are often not punished. Why then, he asks, should a person be moral and do what is right? If we are to rationally decide to be moral, therefore, we must also believe that happiness and morality will be in harmony (what Kant calls "the highest good"), that good people will be rewarded with happiness and evil people will be punished. But if this does not happen in this life, then we must believe that it happens in another life ("this problem can be solved only in eternity"). Further, we must believe in some ultimate source of justice, a divine judge who will weigh good against evil and make certain that eternal happiness and punishment are meted out fairly. This argument is at one and the same time a defense of the Christian belief in the immortality of the human soul and in God. It is necessary to believe in both, according to Kant, in order to sustain our willingness to be moral. "Therefore, it is morally necessary to assume the existence of God."

A similar position was argued more recently by the pragmatist William James. His position is a "pragmatic" one; that is, believing in God is "rational" insofar as it doesn't conflict with our other beliefs (for example, our beliefs in science, a matter that Kant stressed also) and if it tends to make us lead better lives. He argues the following:

FROM **"THE WILL TO BELIEVE"**
BY **WILLIAM JAMES**

Science says things are; morality says some things are better than other things; and religion says essentially two things.

First, she says that the best things are the more eternal things, the overlapping things, the things in the universe that throw the last stone, so to speak, and say

---

[11] Immanuel Kant, *Critique of Practical Reason,* trans. Lewis White Beck (New York: Bobbs-Merrill, 1956).

the final word. "Perfection is eternal"—this phrase of Charles Secrétan seems a good way of putting this first affirmation of religion, an affirmation which obviously cannot yet be verified scientifically at all.

The second affirmation of religion is that we are better off even now if we believe her first affirmation to be true.

Now, let us consider what the logical elements of this situation are *in case the religious hypothesis in both its branches be really true.* (Of course, we must admit that possibility at the onset. If we are to discuss the question at all, it must involve a living option. If for any of you religion be a hypothesis that cannot, by any living possibility be true, then you need go no farther. I speak to the "saving remnant" alone.) So proceeding, we see, first, that religion offers itself as a *momentous* option. We are supposed to gain, even now, by our belief, and to lose by our nonbelief, a certain vital good. Secondly, religion is a *forced* option, so far as that good goes. We cannot escape the issue by remaining sceptical and waiting for more light, because, although we do avoid error in that way *if religion be untrue,* we lose the good, *if it be true,* just as certainly as if we positively chose to disbelieve. It is as if a man should hesitate indefinitely to ask a certain woman to marry him because he was not perfectly sure that she would prove an angel after he brought her home. Would he not cut himself off from that particular angel-possibility as decisively as if he went and married someone else? Scepticism, then, is not avoidance of option; it is option of a certain particular kind of risk. *Better risk loss of truth than chance of error*—that is your faith-vetoer's exact position. He is actively playing his stake as much as the believer is; he is backing the field against the religious hypothesis, just as the believer is backing the religious hypothesis against the field. To preach scepticism to us as a duty until "sufficient evidence" for religion be found, is tantamount therefore to telling us, when in presence of the religious hypothesis, that to yield to our fear of its being error is wiser and better than to yield to our hope that it may be true. It is not intellect against all passions, then; it is only intellect with one passion laying down its law. And by what, forsooth, is the supreme wisdom of this passion warranted? Dupery for dupery, what proof is there that dupery through hope is so much worse than dupery through fear? I, for one, can see no proof; and I simply refuse obedience to the scientist's command to imitate his kind of option, in a case where my own stake is important enough to give me the right to choose my own form of risk. If religion be true and the evidence for it be still insufficient, I do not wish, by putting your extinguisher upon my nature (which feels to me as if it had after all some business in this matter), to forfeit my sole chance in life of getting upon the winning side—that chance depending, of course, on my willingness to run the risk of acting as if my passional need of taking the world religiously might be prophetic and right.

All this is on the supposition that it really may be prophetic and right, and that, even to us who are discussing the matter, religion is a live hypothesis which may be true. Now, to most of us religion comes in a still further way that makes a veto on our active faith even more illogical. The more perfect and more eternal aspect of the universe is represented in our religions as having personal form.

The universe is no longer a mere *It* to us, but a *Thou,* if we are religious; and any relation that may be possible from person to person might be possible here. For instance, although in one sense we are passive por-

The universe is no longer a mere It to us, but a Thou, if we are religious; and any relation that may be possible from person to person might be possible here.

tions of the universe, in another we show a curious autonomy, as if we were small active centres on our own account. We feel, too, as if the appeal of religion to us were made to our own active good-will, as if evidence might be forever withheld from us unless we met the hypothesis half-way. To take a trivial illustration: just as a man who in a company of gentlemen made no advances, asked a warrant for every concession, and believed no one's word without proof, would cut himself off by such churlishness from all the social rewards that a more trusting spirit would earn—so here, one who should shut himself up in snarling logical-ity and try to make the gods extort his recognition willy-nilly, or not get it at all, might cut himself off forever from his only opportunity of making the gods' acquaintance. This feel-ing, forced on us we know not whence, that by obstinately believing that there are gods (although not to do so would be so easy both for our logic and our life) we are doing the universe the deepest service we can, seems part of the living essence of the religious hypothesis. If the hypothesis *were* true in all its parts, including this one, then pure intellectualism, with its veto on our making willing advances, would be an absurdity; and some participation of our sympathetic nature would be logically required. I, therefore, for one, cannot see my way to accepting the agnostic rules of truth-seeking, or willfully agree to keep my will-ing nature out of the game. I cannot do so for this plain reason, that *a rule of thinking which would absolutely prevent me from acknowledging certain kinds of truth if those kinds of truth were really there, would be an irrational rule.* That for me is the long and short of the formal logic of the situation, no matter what the kinds of truth might materially be.[12]

This "practical" argument for belief in God ruled philosophy from the time of Kant until the present century. It has its origins in a short but brilliant argument by the French philosopher **Blaise Pascal.** Pascal offered an argument that he called a wager, literally a bet about God. It isn't a proof of God's existence in any sense; in fact, one of its explicit terms is the fact that we can't know whether God exists or not. But then, he says, if God exists, and we believe in Him, we are entitled to an infinite reward. If He exists and we don't believe in Him, on the other hand, we are really in for it—eternal damnation. Even if he doesn't exist, we are still better off believing in

---

[12] William James, "The Will to Believe," in *The Will to Believe and Other Essays in Popular Philosophy* (New York: Longmans, Green, 1896).

God because of the qualities faith brings to life in us. In support of the decision to believe, Pascal asks:

> *Now, what harm will befall you in taking this side? You will be faithful, honest, humble, grateful, generous, a sincere friend, truthful. Certainly you will not have those poisonous pleasures, glory and luxury; but will you not have others? I will tell you that you will thereby gain in this life, and that, at each step you take on this road, you will see so great certainty of gain, so much nothingness in what you risk, that you will at last recognize that you have wagered for something certain and infinite, for which you have given nothing.*[13]

So, if we treat this as a betting situation, in which our option is simply to believe or not believe, our betting odds look like this:

"PASCAL'S WAGER"

	AND GOD EXISTS	AND GOD DOESN'T EXIST
If we believe:	Eternal reward.	We've wasted a little piety but perhaps been better people.
If we don't believe:	Eternal damnation.	No reward, no punishment.

Looking at the odds as a betting person, it is obvious which option we ought to choose. The risk of eternal damnation overwhelms the promise of a few "poisonous" pleasures; and the promise of eternal reward is well worth the risk that we may be wrong, considering what is gained even in this life. The conclusion, then, on strictly practical grounds, is that we ought to believe in God.

All three of these arguments by Kant, James, and Pascal are based on the same all-important assumption that "God is just." On the basis of this assumption, they then argue that it is rational to believe in God, even if it is not possible to prove (or even know) that He exists. Accordingly, belief in God is a matter of faith, but this faith can be argued and justified as rational belief. Just because it is faith and not knowledge, it does not follow that it is "blind faith" or irrational, beyond argument or arbitrary. To insist that belief in God is a matter of faith, therefore, is not to say that it is beyond the reach of philosophy or rational consideration.

2. The Problem of Evil

These "moral" arguments for believing in God are sound only as long as we accept the assumption that "God is just." There have been few sophisticated theists who

---

[13] Blaise Pascal, *Pensées*, #233 (New York: Modern Library, 1941).

have actually denied this, of course, but there have been a great many, particularly in modern times, who have worried about it considerably. The problem is called "the problem of evil." It can be stated very simply, but this solution, if you believe in God, is not simple at all. The problem is this: If God is all-powerful (omnipotent), all-knowing (omniscient), and just, then how is it possible that there is so much un-earned suffering and unpunished wickedness in the world? Or simply, if God exists, how can the world be so full of evil? It cannot be that He does not know of these mis-fortunes, for He is all-knowing. Nor can it be that He is unable to do anything about them, for He is all-powerful. And if He is just and has concern for human beings, then He must care about protecting the innocent and punishing or preventing evil.

The problem of evil is a problem because few believers in any religion are willing to give up their faith in the power of nature or of its Creator, its innate goodness, or the belief that there is real justice in it. The clearest and most widely known charac-terization of the problem of evil for the religious belief is probably still the one found in the Biblical Book of Job, in which Job, deeply pious yet undeservedly suf-fering, struggles to keep his faith:

> Then his wife said to him, "Are you still unshaken in your integrity? Curse God and die!" But he answered, ". . . If we accept good from God, shall we not accept evil?" (2:9–10)

But eventually, Job asks God:

> "Why should the sufferer be born to see the light? Why is life given to men who find it so bitter?" (3:20)

The most common solution to the problem of evil is offered to Job by his friend Eliphaz:

> "Mischief does not grow out of the soil
> nor trouble spring from the earth;
> man is born to trouble,
> as surely as birds fly upwards." (Job 5:6, New English Bible)

In other words, Eliphaz suggests that man has been created by God with the kind of nature which brings with it its own creation of troubles.

This has often been the solution offered by philosophers and theologians to the problem of evil. There are several versions even of this solution (that human beings have "free will"). The version most influential in Christianity was offered by **St. Au-gustine.** In his youth, Augustine had come under the influence of a religion called **Manichaeism,** which was branded as heresy by all of the great monotheisms (in-cluding, at that time, the Persian religion, Zoroastrianism, about whose founder we studied in Chapter 1) precisely because of the explanation of evil that it espoused. The Manichaeans claimed that there were two equally powerful gods, one of which was good and one evil. The good god ruled the spirit and mind, and the evil god ruled the body. According to the Manichaeans, then, neither god was all-powerful and human beings were not free, but rather at the mercy of one or the other of the gods. Only at death, claimed the Manichaeans, when the soul is separated forever from the body, could human beings achieve real moral goodness.

Augustine abandoned Manichaeism and embraced Christianity. As a Christian, he wrote eloquently about the freedom of the will and the ability of human beings to observe the moral obligations to which God has commanded them.

FROM *CONFESSIONS*
BY **ST. AUGUSTINE**

But although I declared and firmly believed that you, our Lord God, the true God who made not only our souls but also our bodies and not only our souls and bodies but all things, living and inanimate, as well, although I believed that you were free from corruption or mutation or any degree of change, I still could not find a clear explanation, without complications, of the cause of evil. Whatever the cause might be, I saw that it was not to be found in any theory that would oblige me to believe that the immutable God was mutable. If I believed this, I should myself become a cause of evil, the very thing which I was trying to discover. So I continued the search with some sense of relief, because I was quite sure that the theories of the Manichees were wrong. I repudiated these people with all my heart, because I could see that while they were inquiring into the origin of evil they were full of evil themselves, since they preferred to think that yours was a substance that could suffer evil rather than that theirs was capable of committing it.

I was told that we do evil because we choose to do so of our own free will, and suffer it because your justice rightly demands that we should. I did my best to understand this, but I could not see it clearly. I tried to raise my mental perceptions out of the abyss which engulfed them, but I sank back into it once more. Again and again I tried, but always I sank back. One thing lifted me up into the light of your day. It was that I knew that I had a will, as surely as I knew that there was life in me. When I chose to do something or not to do it, I was quite certain that it was my own self, and not some other person, who made this act of will, so that I was on the point of understanding that herein lay the cause of my sin. If I did anything against my will, it seemed to me to be something which happened to me rather than something which I did, and I looked upon it not as a fault, but as a punishment. And because I thought of you as a just God, I admitted at once that your punishments were not unjust.

But then I would ask myself once more: "Who made me? Surely it was my God, who is not only good but Goodness itself. How, then, do I come to possess a will that can choose to do wrong and refuse to do good, thereby providing a just reason why I should be punished? Who put this will into me? Who sowed this seed of bitterness in me, when all that I am was made by my God, who is Sweetness itself? If it was the devil who put it there, who made the devil? If he was a good angel who became a devil because of his own wicked will, how did he come to possess the wicked will which made him a devil, when the Creator, who is entirely good, made him a good angel and nothing else?"

These thoughts swept me back again into the gulf where I was being stifled. But I did not sink as far as that hell of error where no one confesses to you his own guilt, choosing to believe that you suffer evil rather than that man does it.

◆ ◆ ◆

"Where then is evil? What is its origin? How did it steal into the world? What is the root or stem from which it grew? Can it be that there simply is no evil? If so, why do we fear and guard against something which is not there? If our fear is unfounded, it is itself an evil, because it stabs and wrings our hearts for nothing. In fact the evil is all the greater if we are afraid when there is nothing to fear. Therefore, either there is evil and we fear it, or the fear itself is evil.

"Where then does evil come from, if God made all things and, because he is good, made them good too? It is true that he is the supreme Good, that he is himself a greater Good than these lesser goods which he created. But the Creator and all his creation are both good. Where then does evil come from?

"Can it be that there was something evil in the matter from which he made the universe? When he shaped this matter and fitted it to his purpose, did he leave in it some part which he did not convert to good? But why should he have done this? Are we to believe that, although he is omnipotent, he had not the power to convert the whole of this matter to good and change it so that no evil remained in it? Why, indeed, did he will to make anything of it at all? Why did he not instead, by this same omnipotence, destroy it utterly and entirely? Could it have existed against his will? If it had existed from eternity, why did he allow it to exist in that state through the infinite ages of the past and then, after so long a time, decide to make something of it? If he suddenly determined to act, would it not be more likely that he would use his almighty power to abolish this evil matter, so that nothing should exist besides himself, the total, true, supreme, and infinite Good? Or, if it was not good that a God who was good should not also create and establish something good, could he not have removed and annihilated the evil matter and replaced it with good, of which he could create all things? For he would not be omnipotent if he could not create something good without the help of matter which he had not created himself."

These were the thoughts which I turned over and over in my unhappy mind, and my anxiety was all the more galling for the fear that death might come before I had found the truth. But my heart clung firmly to the faith in Christ your Son, our Lord and Saviour, which it had received in the Catholic Church. There were many questions on which my beliefs were still indefinite and wavered from the strict rule of doctrine, yet my mind never relinquished the faith but drank it in more deeply day by day. . . .

I 2

It was made clear to me also that even those things which are subject to decay are good. If they were of the supreme order of goodness, they could not become corrupt; but neither could they become corrupt unless they were in some way good. For if they were supremely good, it would not be possible for them to be corrupted. On the other hand, if they were entirely without good, there would be nothing in them that could become corrupt. For corruption is harmful, but unless it diminished what is good, it could do no harm. The conclusion then must be either that corruption does no harm—which is not possible; or that everything which is corrupted is deprived of good—which is beyond doubt. But if they are deprived of all good, they will not exist at all. For if they still exist but can no longer be corrupted, they will be better than they were before, because they now continue their existence in an incorruptible state. But could anything be more preposterous than to say that things are made better by being deprived of all good?

... whatever is, is good; and evil ... is not a substance, because if it were a substance, it would be good.

So we must conclude that if things are deprived of all good, they cease altogether to be; and this means that as long as they are, they are good. Therefore, whatever is, is good; and evil, the origin of which I was trying to find, is not a substance, because if it were a substance, it would be good. For either it would be an incorruptible substance of the supreme order of goodness, or it would be a corruptible substance which would not be corruptible unless it were good. So it became obvious to me that all that you have made is good, and that there are no substances whatsoever that were not made by you. And because you did not make them all equal, each single thing is good and collectively they are very good, for our God made his whole creation *very good.*

13

For you evil does not exist, and not only for you but for the whole of your creation as well, because there is nothing outside it which could invade it and break down the order which you have imposed on it. Yet in the separate parts of your creation there are some things which we think of as evil because they are at variance with other things. But there are other things again with which they are in accord, and then they are good. In themselves, too, they are good. And all these things which are at variance with one another are in accord with the lower part of creation which we call the earth. The sky, which is cloudy and windy, suits the earth to which it belongs. So it would be wrong for me to wish that these earthly things did not exist, for even if I saw nothing but them, I might wish for something better, but still I ought to praise you for them alone. For all things give praise to the Lord on earth, *monsters of the sea and all its depths; fire and hail, snow and mist; and the storm-wind that executes his decree; all you mountains and hills, all you fruit trees and cedars; all you wild beasts and cattle, creeping things and birds that fly in air; all you kings and peoples of the world, all you that are princes and judges on earth; young men and maids, old men and boys together; let them all give praise to the Lord's name.* The heavens, too, ring with your praises, O God, for you are the god of us all. *Give praise to the Lord in heaven; praise him, all that dwells on high. Praise him, all you angels of his, praise him, all his armies. Praise him, sun and moon; praise him, every star that shines. Praise him, you highest heavens, you waters beyond the heavens. Let all these praise the Lord.* And since this is so, I no longer wished for a better world, because I was thinking of the whole creation, and in the light of this clearer discernment I had come to see that though the higher things are better than the lower, the sum of all creation is better than the higher things alone.[14]

The problem arises once again, however, if we ask "How could God have given people **free will,** knowing—as He must have—that they would misuse it so badly?" Would everyone be much better off if we had a bit less "free will," or at least if we would have more desires to do good and fewer impulses to cause trouble and suffering?

There are several traditional responses to this. One is that God has allowed us moral latitude to provide a test of our virtue, for if we were all "naturally" good, there would be little question of good versus evil or salvation versus damnation. But it is open to question whether these distinctions are themselves desirable; wouldn't it have been better for humanity to have stayed in the Garden of Eden? Why did God have to create temptation, and what would have been lost from the world if Adam and Eve had been created with a bit more fortitude and obedience?

Then there is the familiar defense, "but doesn't the world need some evil, in order that we recognize the good?" But it isn't at all obvious that we need anything like the amount of evil and suffering we have in the world in order to recognize what is good. But even if we were to agree on this "free will" defense of the traditional conception of God as omnipotent, omniscient, and perfectly just, laying the blame for suffering to people's own choices, that would not solve the problem of evil. This is why we said that this line of "free will" defense is, at best, a partial solution. For not all human hardships and sufferings seem to be our own doing; much of the evil in the world does not seem to depend on human action in any way. Even if we accept the claim that we cause evil through free choice, we still need to explain how the effects of our choices can seem so unrelated to the actions which are supposedly their cause. The Western religions' concept of "original sin" offers one such explanation, and it too finds its first expression in the Book of Job. When Job insists that he has done nothing to warrant his suffering, his friend Bildad suggests: "Inquire now of older generations and consider the experience of their fathers" (8:8), implying that the "sins of the fathers," the original sin of the whole human race, justifies Job's punishment. The punishment by God of any individual person, so goes the claim, is just, even though that particular individual did nothing to deserve it. Thus, God remains both Just and Good.

But this solution, rejected by Job himself, undermines our hopes that right action will be rewarded, and so again it belies the moral force that God is supposed to play in our lives. For if we were destined to suffer anyway for sins committed by others,

---

[14] St. Augustine, *Confessions,* Bk. VII, trans. R. S. Pine-Coffin (Harmondsworth, England: Penguin Books, 1961), pp. 136–49.

then God would not appear to be just, and there would be little incentive for us to be faithful and follow God's commandments.

3. Hinduism, Buddhism, Karma, and Compassion

The difficulties stemming from the "free will" solution to the problem of evil may indicate to some that the Western religions' conceptions of God and of human nature are just not adequate. The Western religions characterize human beings as so limited in our understanding of God's justice that we can never predict the evil or good effects of our actions. But then how can we have any meaningful moral theory at all? Similarly, these religions claim that the wrongdoings we engage in during our short life here on earth are punished eternally by God and our occasional good actions are rewarded eternally. The view that each and every human lifetime belongs to a unique eternal soul would seem to make all of God's rewards and punishments intrinsically unjust—way out of proportion to the insignificant actions which are supposedly their cause.

One interesting alternative to these conceptions of humans and God is offered by the Hindu religion, whose solution to the problem of evil is unique in its use of the notion of **karma.**

Hinduism is not actually a single religion. At best it is a family of religious beliefs and practices united, among other things, by a belief in the notion of social caste and a shared lineage from the Indic religions, such as Upanishadism, which we discussed in Chapter 1. There are no identifiable "core" Hindu *beliefs*—beyond a "reverence" for the Veda, though it is rarely read, and a participation in a social organization. Nevertheless, one may speak of "scriptures" and of ideas that over the centuries have been more at the center of Hindu culture than others. In general, a theistic worldview has more than any other dominated Hindu belief and guided religious practices. However, the Hindu conception of God is radically different from that shared by Judaism, Christianity, and Islam. The Hindu notion of human nature also radically differs from the Western notion. For most Hindus, human beings do have free will, but the free exercise of that will *changes* the human being. This is the doctrine of karma, which claims that any course of action that one undertakes creates a psychological tendency, or habit, to repeat it. One's free will thus becomes limited by one's own dispositions to action, or habits, dispositions that according to much ancient Indian thought continue even into a new birth. The inveterate smoker, for instance, is drawn to the taste of tobacco at a young age in her next incarnation.

Of all the many, many "scriptures" and sacred texts that over the centuries have moved the hearts of the faithful in India, the **Bhagavadgītā** (or "Gītā"), the "Song of God" (ca. 200 B.C.), clearly stands out as the most important. The *Gītā* is a small portion of a long epic poem. The central theme of the passages given below is the unique Hindu response to the "problem of evil." The warrior **Krishna** is the ruler of a neighboring state. Throughout most of the long poem Krishna is an ordinary person though an able, just, clever, and politically astute one. The key event of the entire epic is a battle over political succession. The political issues involved are complex; only one side of the warring family has a just claim. Five brothers are the principal representatives of the just family (although many noble and venerable sages and heroes fight against them). Krishna joins the battle line as charioteer for the third o. five brothers, a champion archer named Arjuna. The *Gītā* is a dialogue between Krishna and Arjuna that occurs just minutes before the battle begins. In the dialogue, Krishna ceases to be a mere mortal and reveals Himself to Arjuna as God incarnate. So His advice to Arjuna, at least according to Hindu theists, is not simply the encouragement of a friend or the wise teachings of a guru; His words are the voice of God speaking to a human being in a time of personal moral crisis. Arjuna insists that it cannot be the morally right thing to do to fight and kill his kinsmen, teachers, friends, and loved ones who face him on the far side of the field of KurukSetra.

> *"No good do I see in killing my own family in battle. I desire not victory,nor rule, nor pleasures, Krishna; what is power to us, enjoyments, or life, Govinda? Those who make rulership desirable for us, and enjoyments and pleasures, it is they that are arrayed in battle (against us), abandoning life and wealth. Teachers, fathers, sons, grandfathers, uncles, inlaws—these I do not wish to kill even if it means that I must die, Krishna—not even to rule the three worlds, why then for the earth?"*[15]

Despite the passion and sincerity of moral feeling that Arjuna expresses, Krishna insists that the right thing to do in the circumstances is to fight, to kill the opposing warriors, and to win the battle.

There are several dimensions to Krishna's explanation why fighting is the right course of action for Arjuna, and more commentary has been elicited by His response to Arjuna's plea for guidance than by any other comparably brief text, except perhaps the Torah and the Gospels. In the verses that follow (part of Krishna's reply), Krishna first explains the cosmic foundations of human action. Next He states His own motive as God for assuming mortal birth. Krishna goes on to talk again about human action and closes with a refrain recurring throughout the *Gītā*—injunctions about the practice of *yoga,* (i.e., spiritual "discipline"). Through such self-discipline in general—whether *karmayoga, jñānayoga,* or *bhaktiyoga* (the yoga of action, the yoga of knowledge and meditation, the yoga of love and devotion)—Krishna lays out the three "paths" by which one may live a spiritually transformed life.

> *[Krishna:] Without personal attachment undertake action, Arjuna, for just one purpose, for the purpose of sacrifice. From work undertaken for purposes other than sacrifice, this world is bound to the law of **karma.***[16] *Having loosed forth creatures along with sacrifice, the Creator said of old, "With this may you bring forth fruit, let it be your horn-of-plenty.*[17] *Make the gods flourish with this and may the gods make you flourish. Mutually fostering one another, you will attain the supreme good. For made to flourish by sacrifice, the gods will give you the enjoyments you desire. One who not giving to them enjoys their gifts is nothing but a thief."* . . . *Know action to have its origin in the Absolute, Brahman, and*

---

[15] *Gītā* 1.31b–35.

[16] Ibid.

[17] Literally, "wish-fulfilling cow."

its foundation in the Immutable. Therefore is the omnipresent ...shed through all time in sacrifice. . . . Although I exist as the)erishable self (ātmā), and although I exist as the Lord of beings, ...d controlling my own nature I come into (phenomenal) being ...agical power of self-delimitation. Whenever there is a crisis of ...,hteousness, the good, the cosmic direction], Arjuna, and a rising up ..., then I loose myself forth. For the protection of good people and for the ae... *ction of evil-doers, for the establishment of* dharma, *I take birth age after age. . . . Just in the ways in which I am approached, so do I receive to my love. People on all sides follow the path that is mine, Arjuna. . . . Actions do not stain me; nor do I have desire for the fruits of works. The person who recognizes me as this way is himself not bound by dispositions of action. So knowing, very ancient seekers of liberation and enlightenment carried out works. Therefore simply do actions as were done of old by the ancients. What action is (and all its implications), and what inaction, even the seer-sages are confused on this score. To you I will explain that kind of action which when understood you will be free from the untoward and evil. . . . For action must be understood, and wrong action as well; inaction must be understood—deep, dark, and dense is the nature of action. Were one to see inaction in action and action in inaction, that person among mortals would be the one with wisdom; he, spiritually disciplined, would be the agent of all works. One whose instigations and undertakings are all free from the motive of personal desire, the wise see that person as the truly learned, as one whose personal dispositions have been burned up in the fire of knowledge. . . . Satisfied with whatever gain comes by him, passed beyond oppositions and dualities, untouched by jealousy, equal-minded and balanced in the face of both success and failure, such a person though he acts is not bound (by karmic dispositions). All dispositions dissolve and wash away when a person is free from attachment, "liberated," and has his mind firmly fixed in knowledge—acting in a spirit of sacrifice. . . . This world does not belong to one who fails to sacrifice, so how could the next, Arjuna? In this way, numerous diverse sacrifices are spread wide in the mouth of Brahman. Know them all as born in action. Thus knowing, you will be "liberated" and enlightened. The sacrifice that is knowledge, O you who are a great warrior, is superior to any sacrifice involving material things. All work and action in its entirety, Arjuna, culminates and is fulfilled in (spiritual) knowledge. . . . Even if of all sinners you are now the very worst evil-doer, once in the boat of knowledge you will safely cross over the crookedness of evil. As a fire kindled reduces its fuel to ashes, Arjuna, so the fire of knowledge makes ashes all* karma. . . . *In yoga, in "spiritual discipline," take your stand; son of Bharata, stand up and fight.*[18]

Yet another approach to religion and the problem of evil is offered in Buddhism, whose Indian roots and spread throughout Asia was discussed in Chapter 1. In Buddhism, the problem of evil is avoided entirely, since Buddhism abandons any

---

[18] *Gītā* 3.9–12, 3.15, 4.6–8, 4.11, 4.14–19, 4.22–24, 4.31–33, 4.36–37, and 4.42b.

conception of an anthropomorphic God. Yet Buddhism retains a belief in moral obligation and in reason. The highest form of Buddhism confronts evil—or, rather, human suffering—by working to help others in need. The answer to "the problem of evil," in other words, is *compassion.* This is particularly true of the Northern, or **Mahāyāna**, doctrines. Against those Buddhists who encourage a course of spiritual discipline toward a solely personal end, the Mahāyāna argue that such an end is not the best and the highest. If we strive for our own personal salvation alone and if we intend to follow no career (*"yāna"*) helping others to the supreme good of *nirvāna,* we would belong to the "Hīnayāna," literally "a being with no career" (a term used by Mahāyānists in deprecation of such a "path"). Mahāyānists, "beings with wide and great careers," however, seek not only personal salvation but "deliverance of all sentient beings from suffering and ignorance." A follower of this "wide path" attempts to acquire the six moral, intellectual, and spiritual perfections (*pāramitā*) possessed by Siddhārtha Gautama who, in this conception, is less "the Buddha" than a *Bodhisattva*—one who has one foot in the bliss of *nirvāna,* so to say, but whose being is turned naturally through compassion toward achieving the welfare of all beings. Thus Mahāyāna is more world-affirming than "Hīnayāna," in that the development of individual perfections is the goal, not an extinction of individuality and personality in an other-worldly bliss. One does not aim at extinction of individ-ual form; one needs individual form and body as a medium with which to help others.

The six personal perfections sought by Mahāyānists are liberality or charity, good moral character, patience or peace in the face of anger or desires, energy (energy to strive for the good), ability to maintain deep meditation, and last, the most important, insight or wisdom (*prajñā*).

Thus the Mahāyānists do not view the natural world as an evil place to be abandoned but as—could we only perceive it as such—the "Body of the Buddha," the *dharmakāya.* But even though nature comes to be viewed in such a positive way, Buddhist philosophy throughout the long history of Mahāyāna tends to be thoroughly "idealistic," and the answer to evil lies not in the world but in us.

D. REASON AND FAITH

A popular response at this point is to refer to "God's mysterious ways" and to argue that we cannot possibly understand God's ultimate purposes. This is the eventual conclusion of the Book of Job. This response does succeed in answering the problem of evil, but only at considerable cost. In all of the arguments we have considered so far, and in most of the history of Western religion, belief in God, and belief in God's omnipotence, omniscience, and perfect justice, has been a matter of rational belief (whether this was considered a matter of knowledge or of faith). But with the reference to "God's mysterious ways," we mark a major breach with this rational tradition, and we admit that not only can we not know about God, but we cannot even understand or rationally argue these matters. In other words, the phrase "God's mysterious ways" solves the problem of evil only at the cost of ending discussion altogether.

Many philosophers and religious people do not object to this costly consequence. It is costly, they would argue, only to the interests of those who insist on arguing and rationalizing these religious matters; it need have no effect on religious belief itself. In the next section, we discuss some of these nonrational alternatives to the philosophy of religion. But it is first important to appreciate that there is a long history of efforts to demonstrate rationally the tenets of faith and to save a more or less traditional conception of God.

Remember St. Anselm's heart-felt plea to reconcile faith and reason:

And so, O Lord, since thou givest understanding to faith, give me to understanding—as far as thou knowest it to be good for me—that thou dost exist, we believe . . .

The discrepancy between the claims of reason and the claims of faith was a particular concern for Islamic theologians, because of the role that the prophet **Mohammed** played in the Muslim faith. The Islamic scripture, the Qur'an, is believed by Muslims to be the actual word of God, or Allah, as revealed to Mohammed. Still, there were disputes after the prophet's death about the interpretation of scripture. How can the direct word of God be understood in different ways, some right and some wrong? How can mere human beings, uninformed by revelation, decide between competing interpretations? Islamic theology begins with these questions, which were understood as disputes between the authority of reason versus that of revelation in knowing the truth revealed by God.

The first Muslims to favor a rationalistic method in Qur'anic studies—called the Kalam—were the **Mu'tazilites,** considered a heretical sect when they first began their school. Despite their radical method, however, the Mu'tazilites gained popularity. They were eventually challenged, however, and largely overshadowed, by the Ash'arites, who advocated applying rational method to Qur'anic interpretation, but only as an elucidation of the literal word of the Qur'an.

The Spanish Muslim, **ibn-Rushd** (called **Averroës** in the West) (1126—1198), is generally thought to be the culmination of Aristotelianism in Islamic theology. He advocated an Aristotelian metaphysics against the Platonism of earlier Islamic theologians. In the following passage, from *The Decisive Treatise Determining the Nature of the Connection Between Religion and Philosophy,* he claims that the pursuit of rational explanation is actually commanded by God. Somewhat ironically, but quite within the tradition set by the Ash'arites, ibn-Rushd justified his claim with scriptural authority.

ON THE PHILOSOPHIC STUDY OF GOD
BY IBN-RUSHD

CHAPTER ONE. THE LAW MAKES PHILOSOPHIC STUDIES OBLIGATORY.

If teleological study of the world is philosophy, and if the Law commands such a study, then the Law commands philosophy. . . .

That the Law summons to reflection on beings, and the pursuit of knowledge about them, by the intellect is clear from several verses of the Book of God,

If teleological study of the world is philosophy, and if the Law commands such a study, then the Law commands philosophy.

Blessed and Exalted, such as the saying of the Exalted, 'Reflect, you have vision' (Koran, LIX, 2): this is textual authority for the obligation to use intellectual reasoning, or a combination of intellectual and legal reasoning (VII, 185). . . .

Since it has now been established that the Law has rendered obligatory the study of beings by the intellect, and reflection on them, and since reflection is nothing more than inference and drawing out of the unknown from the known, and since this is reasoning or at any rate done by reasoning, therefore we are under an obligation to carry on our study of beings by intellectual reasoning. It is further evident that this manner of study, to which the Law summons and urges, is the most perfect kind of study using the most perfect kind of reasoning; and this is the kind called 'demonstration.'

To master this instrument the religious thinker must make a preliminary study of logic, just as the lawyer must study legal reasoning. This is no more heretical in the one case than in the other. And logic must be learned from the ancient masters, regardless of the fact that they were not Muslims.

The Law, then, has urged us to have demonstrative knowledge of God the Exalted and all the beings of His creation. But it is preferable and even necessary for anyone, who wants to understand God the Exalted and the other beings demonstratively, to have first understood the kinds of demonstration and their conditions [of validity], and in what respects demonstrative reasoning differs from dialectical, rhetorical and fallacious reasoning. But this is not possible unless he has previously learned what reasoning as such is, and how many kinds it has, and which of them are valid and which invalid. This in turn is not possible unless he has previously learned the parts of reasoning, of which it is composed, i.e. the premises and their kinds. Therefore he who believes in the Law, and obeys its command to study beings, ought prior to his study to gain a knowledge of these things, which have the same place in theoretical studies as instruments have in practical activities.[19]

The problem is that the emphasis on *faith* in religion often threatens the sometimes skeptical use of reason in understanding such matters. Accordingly, attempts to reconcile reason and faith often lead to unorthodox or even heretical conceptions of religion. For example, Spinoza's **pantheism** was one of these many attempts to save belief in God while maintaining a rational picture of nature. More radical versions of pantheism deny that God is just and that He has any moral characteristics at all. In Spinoza's theory, however, which has often been compared to that of the Eastern religions, God is identical to the universe. He is not its creator. He is not a moral

---

[19] From *Philosophy in the Middle Ages: The Christian, Islamic, and Jewish Traditions,* ed. Arthur Hyman and James J. Walsh (Indianapolis: Hackett, 1973, 1983).

agent, so He has neither concern nor ability for the misfortunes and suffering of the world. He has no special concern for people. If one defends an extreme determinism in which no one—not even God—has "free will," questions of moral responsibility, reward, and punishment become irrelevant, a matter of human vanity, nothing more. Not surprisingly, Spinoza, though devout, was long branded an atheist and his books were proscribed.

This way of avoiding the problem of evil by advocating a more purely rational religious belief was quite common in the Enlightenment, that period of Western thought in which people were rebelling against medieval authority. The best example of this attitude was the French genius **Voltaire.** He was a vehement opponent of Christianity. ("I have heard enough how it took only twelve men to establish Christianity; I should like to prove that only one can destroy it.") But he wouldn't give up God, so he invented a new religion (that he in many ways borrowed from the English), which sheared the concept of God of all His moral attributes, thus avoiding the problem of evil by denying God His attribute of "justice." "It makes no more sense to say that God is just or unjust than it does to say that he is blue or green." For Voltaire, God was just a "hypothesis," the creator who turned on the giant Newtonian machine but then left it to go on its own. This peculiarly truncated version of theism is usually called **deism.** It believes in God, but not much of one. It is essentially an appeal to the cosmological argument; and it is satisfied with a minimal deity, which stops far short of our traditional conception of God. Needless to say, Voltaire despised the "argument from design" with all of its hidden moralizing. The world is full of evil, Voltaire insisted, and there is no denying it. And since there is evil, there cannot be an all-powerful, all-knowing God who is also just, and there can be no appeal to His "mysterious ways." He has no "mysterious ways"; in fact, He has no "ways" at all. Thus Voltaire made his point against Leibniz and his "best of all possible worlds" hypothesis by imagining a whole book full of disasters and tragedies and evils of the most sadistic sort, all greeted rather foolishly by a Leibnizian character named Dr. Pangloss. The book was called *Candide,* and it remains one of the classics of Western literature.

The seeming irrationality of God's actions also haunted the great Russian novelist, **Fyodor Dostoyevski,** a devout Christian whose faith had been shaken many times, not least by the cruelty that he often witnessed (and of which he was occasionally the victim) in feudal Tsarist Russia. In his novel *The Brothers Karamazov,* he portrays a conversation between two of the three Karamazov brothers, Ivan who like the author is wracked with doubts—and Alyosha—who has joined a monastery and aspires to be a true Christian. Ivan presents us with a vivid picture of how instances of patently unjust evil pit reason against faith, especially for someone who wants desperately to believe in God, but for the most vindictive, even violent reasons.

FROM *THE BROTHERS KARAMAZOV*
BY **FYODOR DOSTOYEVSKI**

"I want you to understand me," he said, "I spoke only of [the suffering of] small children to make my point more obvious. I didn't mention the other human tears with which our earth is soaked from crust to core, because I was deliberately narrowing the subject. I'm nothing but a bug and I most humbly admit that it's quite beyond me why things are arranged the way they are. I suppose that men themselves are to blame for it: they were given a paradise on earth, but they wanted freedom and they stole fire from heaven, although they knew that it would bring them unhappiness. So there's no reason to be sorry for them. All that my puny, Euclidean, earthling's mind can grasp is that there is such a thing as suffering, that no one can be blamed for it, that quite uncomplicatedly cause precedes effect, that everything that flows finds its proper level—but then all that is just Euclidean gibberish, and, being aware of that fact, I cannot agree to live by it! What good does it to do me to know that no one is to blame, that every effect is determined by a cause, which itself is an effect of some other cause, and so on, and that, therefore, no one should ever be blamed for anything? For, even though I may know it, I still need retribution. Without it I'd rather destroy myself. And I must have that retribution not somewhere far off in infinity but here, on earth. I want to see it myself. I believe in justice and I want to see justice done with my own eyes; if I should be dead by that time, I want to be brought back to life, because the idea that, when justice finally does triumph, I won't even be there to witness it is too abhorrent to me. No, I want to see with my own eyes the lamb lie down with the lion and the resurrected victim rise and embrace his murderer. I want to be here when everyone understands why the world has been arranged the way it is. It is on that craving for understanding that all human religions are founded, so I am a believer. But then, what about the children? . . . If the suffering of little children is needed to complete the sum total of suffering required to pay for the truth, I don't want that truth, and I declare in advance that all the truth in the world is not worth the price! . . . It isn't that I reject God; I am simply returning Him most respectfully the ticket that would entitle me to a seat."[20]

> *If the suffering of little children is needed to complete the sum total of suffering required to pay for the truth, I don't want that truth, and I declare in advance that all the truth in the world is not worth the price!*

E. FAITH AND IRRATIONALITY

Whenever you can defend your belief rationally it is obviously desirable to do so. The move from rationality to irrationality in the defense of religion, therefore, is a

---

[20] Fyodor Dostoyevski, *The Brothers Karamazov*, trans. Andrew R. MacAndrew (New York: Bantam, 1970).

serious step. Kant, who defended belief in God as a matter of faith, nevertheless defended this belief as rational. But there have always been religious people who have defended faith against reason, emphasizing the impossibility of rational justification and the irrelevance of the usual forms of understanding and knowledge where religion is concerned. In some cases, particularly in modern times, this step away from rationality may be a convenient escape from arguments and doubts that have become too overpowering. But it is not always, or even usually, taken for this reason. As we've seen, there has always been an enthusiastic movement within the sometimes overly formal confines of all the organized religions and dogmas to emphasize the experience of religious belief, called **"mysticism."** Such experience may well be indescribable and incommunicable. (Philosophers would thereby say it is **ineffable.**) But it is precisely the fact that it defies description and contradicts our everyday rational beliefs that makes such experiences so important to those who have had them.

1. God as Experience

Elsewhere in the text we discuss the rationalist notion of intuition, a special kind of experience that allows us to know some things for certain without argument and without abstraction from experience in the usual sense. According to the rationalists, we know the basic principles of logic and arithmetic in this way, and perhaps the basic principles of metaphysics as well. But when we introduced intuition, however, we emphasized that not everyone believed that intuition was part of rationality. In addition to rational insight, there may also be, according to most religious mystics, extra-rational or even irrational insight. Their epistemology is often ambiguous at this point. On the one hand, mystics want to deny the rational nature of their intuitions. But at the same time, they want to insist that what they experience is true. You can see how this will generate considerable confusion. When the mystic insists that his experience is true, he has made a claim that is on a par with the rationalist's claim (whether they agree or disagree in their conclusions). If they disagree, that is, if the mystic insists that there is a God (perhaps he has even "seen" Him) and the rationalist denies it, it should be obvious that little room for constructive argument exists. The mystic considers the rationalist's arguments irrelevant; the rationalist considers the mystic obstinate and unwilling to argue rationally. At this point, assuming the discussion does not degenerate to name-calling and fisticuffs, the rationalist will probably storm out of the room in frustration and the mystic, like a Zen master, may just shrug his shoulders. In such a case, that is probably the most rational response for both of them.

The mystic need not argue that what he has experienced is true, however. He might insist only that what he has "seen" is extremely important to him personally. If he does so, it is clear that he need have no disagreement whatsoever with the rationalist, either in conclusions or in methods. They are different, of course, but not at odds. This is rare, of course, since it is a rare person indeed who does not yield to the temptation to insist that his or her experience is the truth about reality as well. Or the mystic could argue, as the Islamic mystics (or **Sufis**) from al-Ghazali on have done, that rationalist and mystical experience lead to the same truths by different "paths."

But whether the mystical experience is an intuition of the (more or less) traditional Judeo-Christian God, whether it is a vision of the Virgin or simply a "feeling of oneness with the universe," whether the experience is the result of twenty years of prayer and meditation or induced in an evening with peyote or mescaline, the philosophical question that follows is always one of interpretation. Without denying the reality of the experience, the question is always whether one ought to interpret the experience as the knowledge of reality. Is it just an experience—perhaps beautiful, worth repeating, even worth building your life around? It is very different to claim that the experience is true, a breakthrough in our normal perceptions (or, perhaps, our everyday illusions) to the reality behind them. This is not to say that the mystic must be wrong. It is only to say that, given the impossibility of argument, there is no way to decide the issue. Just because the mystic is "irrational" doesn't mean that he is wrong.

Following the Enlightenment, particularly in Germany, religion took a dramatic swing to the subjective. Attempts at rational defense were given up entirely. The German Romantic philosopher **Friedrich Schleiermacher** insisted that religion was simply a matter of intense feelings of dependence, nothing more. (His contemporary, Hegel, wryly retorted that this would make a dog a better Christian than most of us.) Other philosophers turned to modernized mysticism, including very contemporary experiments with drug-induced experiences, in an attempt to save their religion from rational criticism. The American philosopher William James, for example, wrote about mysticism in his book *The Varieties of Religious Experience* and defended the idea that personal religious experience has a central place in religion and that mysticism is the root of such experience. He too insists that mystical experiences are essentially "ineffable," that is, impossible to describe to anyone else, and he compares this experience with the experience of listening to a symphony or being in love. But he also insists that mystical experiences provide us with knowledge, "states of insight into depths of truth unplumbed by the discursive intellect." James concludes that "the existence of mystical states absolutely overthrows the pretension of nonmystical states to be the sole and ultimate dictators of what we may believe." "The mystic," he writes, "is *invulnerable,* and must be left, whether we like it or not, in undisturbed enjoyment of his creed."[21] Consider, for example, the following argument by the Sufi philosopher **Mohammad al-Ghazali,** a medieval mystic.

FROM *THE DELIVERANCE FROM ERROR*
BY **MOHAMMAD AL-GHAZALI**

When I had finished with [philosophy and theology], I next turned with set purpose to the method of mysticism (or Sufism). I knew that the complete mystic 'way' includes both intellectual belief and practical activity; the latter consists in

---

[21] William James, "The Varieties of Religious Experience," in *The Writings of William James,* ed. John J. McDermott (New York: Random House, 1967).

getting rid of the obstacles in the self and in stripping off its base characteristics and vicious morals, so that the heart may attain to freedom from what is not God and to constant recollection of Him.

The intellectual belief was easier to me than the practical activity. I began to acquaint myself with their belief by reading their books, such as *The Food of the Hearts* by Abū Tālib al-Makkī (God have mercy upon him), the works of al-Hārith al-Muhāsibī, the various anecdotes about al-Junayd, ash-Shiblī and Abū Yazīd al-Bistāmī (may God sanctify their spirits), and other discourses of their leading men. I thus comprehended their fundamental teachings on the intellectual side, and progressed, as far as is possible by study and oral instruction, in the knowledge of mysticism. It became clear to me, however, that what is most distinctive of mysticism is something which cannot be apprehended by study, but only by immediate experience (*dhawq*—literally 'tasting'), by ecstasy and by a moral change. What a difference there is between *knowing* the definition of health and satiety, together with their causes and presuppositions, and *being* healthy and satisfied! What a difference between being acquainted with the definition of drunkenness—namely, that it designates a state arising from the domination of the seat of the intellect by vapours arising from the stomach—and being drunk! Indeed, the drunken man while in that condition does not know the definition of drunkenness nor the scientific account of it; he has not the very least scientific knowledge of it. The sober man, on the other hand, knows the definition of drunkenness and its basis, yet he is not drunk in the very least. Again the doctor, when he is himself ill, knows the definition and causes of health and the remedies which restore it, and yet is lacking in health. Similarly there is a difference between knowing the true nature and causes and conditions of the ascetic life and actually leading such a life and forsaking the world.

> *. . . what is most distinctive of mysticism is something which cannot be apprehended by study, but only by immediate experience . . . by ecstasy and by a moral change.*

I apprehended clearly that the mystics were men who had real experiences, not men of words, and that I had already progressed as far as was possible by way of intellectual apprehension. What remained for me was not to be attained by oral instruction and study but only by immediate experience and by walking in the mystic way.[22]

2. The Leap of Faith

The best and most famous of all of these "new" Christians was an eccentric Danish philosopher, **Søren Kierkegaard,** who is often claimed as the father of both the

---

[22] Hyman and Walsh, *Philosophy in the Middle Ages.*

"new" Christianity and that nonreligious philosophy called **existentialism.** Kierkegaard was born into a society in which everyone was a Christian; they all believed the same dogmas, without thinking about them. They all went to the same (Lutheran) churches for Sunday services and Friday afternoon bingo games and enjoyed these social gatherings immensely. They were all entitled to call themselves "Christians" just by virtue of the fact that they had been born of certain parents, brought as children to certain churches, and continued to mouth certain doctrines that they didn't understand or care to understand in the slightest. What they all lacked was passion. Their religion and they themselves, according to Kierkegaard, were boring through and through. Whatever happened to the phrase "the fear of God in their hearts"? These people felt no "fear," just the security of a comfortable and self-righteous society and warm swill of beer in their bellies, he complained. Kierkegaard, who had been brought up in an unusually devout Lutheran home, was disgusted with them. This isn't Christianity, he insisted, and the sophisticated disputes over doctrine and dogma had nothing more to do with being religious than the calculations of an accountant at tax time.

Accordingly Kierkegaard offered his alternative—a new (in fact, very old) way of seeing oneself as a Christian. Rational argument was irrelevant. The doctrines of Christianity, he admitted, were absolutely absurd. But that didn't matter. In fact, it was the very absurdity of these beliefs that made the passion of Christianity possible. After all, if it were simply a matter of accepting some proposition, why should we feel anything? And "proofs" of God's existence, needless to say, were as irrelevant—in fact, offensive—as you could imagine. "Christianity is passion!" he insisted. "Religion is feeling and commitment." No talk of "truth"—unless you mean simply **subjective truth,** truth for me alone. No talk of "proof" and no talk of "rationality." There is simply, to use his most famous phrase, *the leap of faith,* across the borders of rationality and thinking to the passion-filled life of old-fashioned Christian fear and awe of God. "My only analogy is Socrates. My task is a Socratic task—to revise the conception of what it means to be a Christian.

Kierkegaard's move away from rationality is characterized as a rejection of "objectivity." Being a Christian, he says, is not a matter of "objective faith" (consisting of reason, doctrines, and "proofs") but of subjectivity, passion, and "inwardness."

ON SUBJECTIVE TRUTH
BY **SØREN KIERKEGAARD**

The objective faith, what does that mean? It means a sum of doctrinal propositions. But suppose Christianity were nothing of the kind; suppose on the contrary it were inwardness, and hence also the paradox, so as to thrust the individual away objectively, in order to obtain significance for the existing individual in the inwardness of his existence, in order to place him as decisively as no judge can place an accused person, between time and eternity in time, between heaven and hell in the time of salvation. The objective faith—it is as if Christianity also had been promulgated as a little system, if not quite so good as the Hegelian; it is as if Christ—aye, I speak without offense—it is as if Christ were a professor, and as if the Apostles had formed a little scientific society. Verily, if it was once difficult to become a Christian, now I believe it becomes increasingly difficult year by year, because it has now become so easy that the only ambition which stirs any competition is that of becoming a speculative philosopher. And yet the speculative philosopher is perhaps at the farthest possible remove from Christianity, and it is perhaps far preferable to be an offended individual who nevertheless sustains a relation to Christianity than a speculative philosopher who assumes to have understood it.

♦ ♦ ♦

Suppose, on the other hand, that subjectivity is the truth, and that subjectivity is an existing subjectivity, then, if I may so express myself, Christianity fits perfectly into the picture. Subjectivity culminates in passion, Christianity is the paradox, paradox and passion are a mutual fit, and the paradox is altogether suited to one whose situation is, to be in the extremity of existence. Aye, never in all the world could there be found two lovers so wholly suited to one another as paradox and passion, and the strife between them is like the strife between lovers, when the dispute is about whether he first aroused her passion, or she his. And so it is here; the existing individual has by means of the paradox itself come to be placed in the extremity of existence. And what can be more splendid for lovers than that they are permitted a long time together without any alteration in the relationship between them, except that it becomes more intensive in inwardness?[23]

Religion is a confrontation with the unknown, not something knowable.

But what is this unknown something with which the Reason collides when inspired by its paradoxical passion, with the result of unsettling even man's knowledge of himself? It is the Unknown. It is not a human being, in so far as we know what man is; nor is it any other known thing. So let us call this unknown something: *the God*. It is nothing more than a name we assign to it. The idea of demonstrating that this unknown something (the God) exists, could scarcely suggest itself to the Reason. For if the God does not exist it would of course be impossible to prove it; and if he does exist it would be folly to attempt it. For at the very outset, in beginning my proof, I would have presupposed it, not as doubtful but as certain (a presupposition is never doubtful, for the very reason that it is a presupposition), since otherwise I would not begin, readily understanding that the whole would be impossible if he did not exist. But if when I speak of proving the God's existence I mean that I propose to prove that the Unknown, which exists, is the God, then I express myself unfortunately. For in that case I do not prove anything, least of all an existence, but merely develop

---

[23] Søren Kierkegaard, *Concluding Unscientific Postscript,* trans. David F. Swenson and Walter Lowrie (Princeton, NJ: Princeton University Press, 1941).

the content of a conception. Generally speaking, it is a difficult matter to prove that anything exists; and what is still worse for the intrepid souls who undertake the venture, the difficulty is such that fame scarcely awaits those who concern themselves with it. The entire demonstration always turns into something very different and becomes an additional development of the consequences that flow from my having assumed that the object in question exists. Thus I always reason from existence, not toward existence, whether I move in the sphere of palpable sensible fact or in the realm of thought. I do not for example prove that a stone exists, but that some existing thing is a stone. The procedure in a court of justice does not prove that a criminal exists, but that the accused, whose existence is given, is a criminal. Whether we call existence an *accessorium* [something predicated] or the eternal *prius* [first given or assumed], it is never subject to demonstration. Let us take ample time for consideration. We have no such reason for haste as have those who from concern for themselves or for the God or for some other thing, must make haste to get existence demonstrated. Under such circumstances there may indeed to need for haste, especially if the prover sincerely seeks to appreciate the danger that he himself, or the thing in question, may be nonexistent unless the proof is finished and does not surreptitiously entertain the thought that it exists whether he succeeds in proving it or not.

If it were proposed to prove Napoleon's existence from Napoleon's deeds, would it not be a most curious proceeding? His existence does indeed explain his deeds, but the deeds do not prove *his* existence, unless I have already understood the word "his" so as thereby to have assumed his existence. But Napoleon is only an individual, and in so far there exists no absolute relationship between him and his deeds; some other person might have performed the same deeds. Perhaps this is the reason why I cannot pass from the deeds to existence. If I call these deeds the deeds of Napoleon the proof becomes superfluous, since I have already named him; if I ignore this, I can never prove from the deeds that they are Napoleon's, but only in a purely ideal manner that such deeds are the deeds of a great general, and so forth. But between the God and his works there is an absolute relationship; God is not a name but a concept. Is this perhaps the reason that his *essentia involvit existentiam* [essence entails existence]? The works of God are such that only the God can perform them. Just so, but where then are the works of the God? The works from which I would deduce his existence are not directly and immediately given. The wisdom in nature, the goodness, the wisdom in the governance of the world—are all these manifest, perhaps, upon the very face of things? Are we not here confronted with the most terrible temptations to doubt, and is it not impossible finally to dispose of all those doubts? But from such an order of things I will surely not attempt to prove God's existence; and even if I began I would never finish, and would in addition have to live constantly in suspense, lest something so terrible should suddenly happen that my bit of proof would be demolished. From what works then do I propose to derive the proof? From the works as apprehended through an ideal interpretation, i.e., such as they do not immediately reveal themselves. But in that case it

In beginning my proof I presuppose the ideal interpretation, and also that I will be successful in carrying it through; but what else is this but to presuppose that the God exists, so that I really begin by virtue of confidence in him?

is not from the works that I make the proof; I merely develop the ideality I have presupposed, and because of my confidence in *this* I make so bold as to defy all objections, even those that have not yet been made. In beginning my proof I presuppose the ideal interpretation, and also that I will be successful in carrying it through; but what else is this but to presuppose that the God exists, so that I really begin by virtue of confidence in him?[24]

You can see how little Kierkegaard thinks of the ingenious "proofs" of God's existence, as well as all attempts to "know" Him. The point of religion, he says, is precisely not to know, but rather to feel. It is the absurdity and the irrationality of Christian doctrines, he insists, that makes this rare intensity of feeling possible.

The **absurd** is precisely by its objective repulsion the measure of the intensity of faith in inwardness. Suppose a man who wishes to acquire faith; let the comedy begin. He wishes to have faith, but he wishes also to safeguard himself by means of an objective inquiry and its approximation-process. What happens? With the help of the approximation-process the absurd becomes something different; it becomes probable, it becomes increasingly probable, it becomes extremely and emphatically probable. Now he is ready to believe it, and he ventures to claim for himself that he does not believe as shoemakers and tailors and simple folk believe, but only after long deliberation. Now he is ready to believe it; and lo, now it has become precisely impossible to believe it. Anything that is almost probable, or probable, or extremely and emphatically probable, is something he can almost know, or as good as know, or extremely and emphatically almost *know*—but it is impossible to *believe*. For the absurd is the object of faith, and the only object that can be believed.[25]

Christianity, Kierkegaard concludes, is suffering, the suffering that comes with the anticipation of our own death and our feeling of smallness and insignificance when we consider the eternal order of things. For those who try to minimize this suffering through professional "understanding" and knowledge, Kierkegaard has little but sarcasm: "*The two ways.* One is to suffer; the other is to become a professor of the fact that another suffered."

---

[24] Søren Kierkegaard, *Philosophical Fragments,* trans. David Swenson (Princeton, NJ: Princeton University Press, 1936).

[25] Kierkegaard, *Concluding Unscientific Postscript.*

3. God as Ultimate Concern

Following Kierkegaard, Christian "irrationalism" changed the complexion of Western religion and gave faith a meaning that is not vulnerable to rational arguments. Recently **Paul Tillich** proposed an extremely powerful form of Christianity that also gives up the traditional view of God and moves the focus of the religion to purely personal concerns and commitments. These are our religion, and we don't need anything more.

THE ULTIMATE CONCERN
BY **PAUL TILLICH**

RELIGIOUS SYMBOLS

We have discussed the meaning of symbols generally because, as we said, man's ultimate concern must be expressed symbolically! One may ask: Why can it not be expressed directly and properly? If money, success, or the nation is someone's ultimate concern, can this not be said in a direct way without symbolic language? Is it not only in those cases in which the content of the ultimate concern is called "God" that we are in the realm of symbols? The answer is that everything which is a matter of unconditional concern is made into a god. If the nation is someone's ultimate concern, the name of the nation becomes a sacred name and the nation receives divine qualities which far surpass the reality of the being and functioning of the nation. The nation then stands for and symbolizes the true ultimate, but in an idolatrous way. Success as ultimate concern is not the natural desire of actualizing potentialities, but its readiness to sacrifice all other values of life for the sake of a position of power and social predominance. The anxiety about not being a success is an idolatrous form of the anxiety about divine condemnation. Success is grace; lack of success, ultimate judgment. In this way concepts designating ordinary realities become idolatrous symbols of ultimate concern.

The reason for this transformation of concepts into symbols is the character of ultimacy and the nature of faith. That which is the true ultimate transcends the realm of finite reality infinitely. Therefore, no finite reality can express it directly and properly. Religiously speaking, God transcends his own name. This is why the use of his name easily becomes an abuse or a blasphemy. Whatever we say about that which concerns us ultimately, whether or not we call it God, has a symbolic meaning. It points beyond itself while participating in that to which it points. In no other way can faith express itself adequately. The language of faith is the language of symbols. If faith were what we have shown that it is not, such an assertion could not be made. But faith, understood as the state of being ultimately concerned, has no language other than symbols. When saying this I always expect the question: Only a symbol? He who asks this question shows that he has not understood the difference between signs and symbols nor the power of symbolic language, which surpasses in quality and strength the power of any nonsymbolic language. One should never say "only a symbol," but one should say "not less than a symbol." With this in mind we can now describe the different kinds of symbols of faith.

The fundamental symbol of our ultimate concern is God. It is always present in any act of faith, even if the act of faith includes the denial of God. Where there is ultimate concern, God can be denied only in the name of God. One God can deny the other one. Ultimate concern cannot deny its own character as ultimate. Therefore, it affirms what is meant by the word "God." Atheism, consequently, can only mean the attempt to remove any ultimate concern—to remain unconcerned about the meaning of one's existence. Indifference toward the ultimate question is the only imaginable form of atheism. Whether it is possible is a problem which must remain unsolved at this point. In any case, he who denies God as matter of ultimate concern affirms God, because he affirms ultimacy in his concern. God is the fundamental symbol for what concerns us ultimately. Again, it would be completely wrong to ask: So God is nothing but a symbol? Because the next question has to be: A symbol for what? And then the answer would be: For God! God is symbol for God. This means that in the person of God we must distinguish two elements: the element of ultimacy, which is a matter of immediate experience and not symbolic in itself, and the element of concreteness, which is taken from our ordinary experience and symbolically applied to God. The man whose ultimate concern is a sacred tree has both the ultimacy of concern and the concreteness of the tree which symbolizes his relation to the ultimate. The man who adores Apollo is ultimately concerned, but not in an abstract way. His ultimate concern is symbolized in the divine figure of Apollo. The man who glorifies Jahweh, the God of the Old Testament, has both an ultimate concern and a concrete image of what concerns him ultimately. This is the meaning of the seemingly cryptic statement that God is the symbol of God. In this qualified sense God is the fundamental and universal content of faith.

God as the ultimate in man's ultimate concern is more certain than any other certainty, even that of oneself.

It is obvious that such an understanding of the meaning of God makes the discussions about the existence or nonexistence of God meaningless. It is meaningless to question the ultimacy of an ultimate concern. This element in the idea of God is in itself certain. The symbolic expression of this element varies endlessly through the whole history of mankind. Here again it would be meaningless to ask whether one or another of the figures in which an ultimate concern is symbolized does "exist." If "existence" refers to something which can be found within the whole of reality, no divine being exists.

The question is not this, but: Which of the innumerable symbols of faith is most adequate to the meaning of faith? In other words, which symbol of ultimacy expresses the ultimate without idolatrous elements? This is the problem, and not the so-called "existence of God"—which is in itself an impossible combination of words. God as the ultimate in man's ultimate concern is more certain than any other certainty, even that of oneself. God as symbolized in a divine figure is a matter of daring faith, of courage and risk.

God is the basic symbol of faith, but not the only one. All the qualities we attribute to him, power, love, justice, are taken from finite experiences and applied symbolically to that which is beyond finitude and infinity. If faith calls God "almighty," it uses the human experience of power in order to symbolize the content of its infinite concern, but it does not describe a highest being who can do as he pleases. So it is with all the other qualities and with all the actions, past, present, and future, which men attribute to God. They are symbols taken from our daily experience, and not information about what God did once upon a time or will do sometime in the future. Faith is not the belief in such stories, but it is the acceptance of symbols that express our ultimate concern in terms of divine actions.

Another group of symbols of faith are manifestations of the divine in things and events, in persons and communities, in words and documents. This whole realm of sacred objects is a treasure of symbols. Holy things are not holy in themselves, but they point beyond themselves to the source of all holiness, that which is of ultimate concern.[26]

Notice how far Tillich has moved from the traditional Judeo-Christian-Islamic conception of God. Yet he is still a theist and a Christian. But it is not clear that "God" means the same for Tillich as it does in the Old and New Testaments. God is a symbol of "ultimate concern." Nevertheless, is this God as Christians are supposed to think of Him? The belief in God is now expanded to represent the fact that one finds his or her life meaningful. Tillich says that this "makes the discussions about the existence or nonexistence of God meaningless." It also undercuts the Western idea that God is a single kind of being with the characteristics we discussed earlier and brings Tillich's theism very close to the *general* idea of religion, which Nishitani described in the passage we looked at earlier. God is whatever concerns us ultimately, whatever is most important in our lives. This is even true, Tillich says, when one denies the existence of God. "Where there is ultimate concern, God can be denied only in the name of God."

F. THE ATTACK ON RELIGION: MARX, NIETZSCHE, AND FREUD

But even if religion is a matter of personal viewpoint, beyond rational argument and mere passion or "experience," this is not to say that it is immune from attack. The truth and falsity of religious doctrines may not be subject to rational scrutiny, but the motivation of religious thinking might be. Why do people turn to religion? Is it just

---

[26] Paul Tillich, *Dynamics of Faith* (New York: Harper & Row; London: George Allen and Unwin, 1957).

for edification, is it to give them hope, or is it a rationalization for the lack of justice in this world? Or is it an escape, a kind of irresponsible reaction to a world we cannot cope with, perhaps a childish unwillingness to give up an illusion of security we ought to have outgrown in adolescence?

Karl Marx is often quoted for his incisive critique of religion. His point is simple, and he makes it powerfully. Humans invent religion to escape their intolerable social conditions. And once we see this, we should reject religion as an escape and turn instead to the correction of those conditions that make such an escape necessary.

FROM *CRITIQUE OF HEGEL'S PHILOSOPHY OF RIGHT* BY **KARL MARX**

The basis of irreligious criticism is this: *man makes religion;* religion does not make man. Religion is indeed man's self-consciousness and self-awareness so long as he has not found himself or has lost himself again. But *man* is not an abstract being, squatting outside the world. Man is *the human world,* a state, society. This state, this society, produce religion which is an *inverted world consciousness,* because they are an *inverted world.* Religion is the general theory of this world, its encyclopedic compendium, its logic in popular form, its spiritual *point d'honneur,* its enthusiasm, its moral sanction, its solemn complement, its general basis of consolation and justification. It is *the fantastic realization* of the human being inasmuch as the *human being* possesses no true reality. The struggle against religion is, therefore, indirectly a struggle against *that world* whose spiritual *aroma* is religion.

Religious suffering is at the same time an *expression* of real suffering and a *protest* against real suffering. Religion is the sigh of the oppressed creature, the sentiment of a heartless world, and the soul of soulless conditions. It is the *opium* of the people.

The abolition of religion as the *illusory* happiness of men, is a demand for their *real* happiness. The call to abandon their illusions about their condition is a *call to abandon a condition which requires illusions.* The criticism of religion is, therefore, *the embryonic criticism of this vale of tears* of which religion is the *halo.*

Criticism has plucked the imaginary flowers from the chain, not in order that man shall bear the chain without caprice or consolation but so that he shall cast off the chain and pluck the living flower. The criticism of religion disillusions man so that he will think, act and fashion his reality as a man who has lost his illusions and regained his reason; so that he will revolve about himself as his own true sun. Religion is only the illusory sun about which man revolves so long as he does not revolve about himself. . . .

It is clear that the arm of criticism cannot replace the criticism of arms. Material force can only be overthrown by material force; but theory itself becomes a material force when it has seized the masses. Theory is capable of seizing the masses when it demonstrates *ad hominem,* and it demonstrates *ad hominem* as soon as it becomes radical. To be radical is to grasp things by the root. But for man the root is man himself. What proves beyond doubt the radicalism of German theory, and thus its practical energy, is that it begins from the resolute *positive* abolition of religion. The criticism of religion ends with the doctrine that *man is the supreme being for man.* It ends, therefore, with the *categorical imperative to overthrow all those conditions* in which man is an abased, enslaved, abandoned, contemptible being—conditions which can hardly be better described than in the exclamation of the Frenchman on the occasion of a proposed tax upon dogs: "Wretched dogs! They want to treat you like men!"[27]

Fifty years later, Friedrich Nietzsche opened an even more blistering attack on religion in general, on Christianity in particular. Christianity is accused of being nothing other than rationalizations for impotence, an expression of everything that is most contemptible in human nature.

FROM ***BEYOND GOOD AND EVIL*** AND ***THE ANTICHRIST***
BY **FRIEDRICH NIETZSCHE**

In the Jewish "Old Testament," the book of divine justice, there are men, things, and speeches in so grand a style that Greek and Indian literature have nothing to compare with it. One stands in awe and reverence before these tremendous remnants of what man once was, and sad thoughts come to one about ancient Asia and its jutting peninsula, Europe, which wants so definitely to signify, as against Asia, the "progress of man." Of course, those who are merely wretched tame domestic animals and know only the wants of domestic animals (like our cultivated people of today, including the Christians of "cultivated" Christianity) need neither be amazed nor even sorry when faced with these ruins: the taste for the Old Testament is a touchstone of "greatness" and "smallness." Perhaps they will even find the New Testament, the book of grace, more to their taste (it is full of the odor of the real, effeminate, stupid canter and petty soul). To have glued this New Testament, a kind of rococo of taste in every respect, to the Old Testament to form one book—the "Bible," *the* book—that is perhaps the greatest audacity and "sin against the spirit" which literary Europe has on its conscience.[28]

◆◆◆

Christianity should not be beautified and embellished: it has waged deadly war against this higher type of man; it has placed all the basic instincts of this type under the ban; and out of these instincts it has distilled evil and the Evil One: the strong man as the typically reprehensible man, the "reprobate."

---

[27] Karl Marx, *Critique of Hegel's Philosophy of Right,* in *Early Writings,* trans. T. Bottomore (New York: McGraw-Hill, 1963).

[28] Friedrich Nietzsche, *Beyond Good and Evil,* trans. Walter Kaufmann (New York: Random House, 1966).

Christianity has sided with all that is weak and base, with all failures; it has made an ideal of what *contradicts* the instinct of the strong life to preserve itself; it has corrupted the reason even of those strongest in spirit . . . it has in fear of them bred the opposite type—the domestic animal, the herd animal, the sick human animal—the Christian.

As long as the priest is considered a *higher* type of man—this *professional* negator, slanderer, and poisoner of life—there is no answer to the question: what *is* truth? For truth has been stood on its head when the conscious advocate of nothingness and negation is accepted as the representative of "truth."

In Christianity neither morality nor religion has even a single point of contact with reality.

. . . This *world of pure fiction* is vastly inferior to the world of dreams insofar as the latter *mirrors* reality, whereas the former falsifies, devalues, and negates reality. . . . Who alone has good reason to lie his way out of reality? He who suffers from it . . .

The Christian conception of God—God as god of the sick, God as a spider, God as spirit—is one of the most corrupt conceptions of the divine ever attained on earth. It may even represent the low-water mark in the descending development of divine types. . . .

This pitiful god of Christian monotono-theism! This hybrid product of decay, this mixture of zero, concept, and contradiction, in which all the instincts of decadence, all cowardices and wearinesses of the soul, find their sanction![29]

Not surprisingly, Nietzsche sees the decline of Christianity, and religion in general, with great enthusiasm. It is Nietzsche who popularized the old Lutheran phrase, "God is dead," but with an antireligious twist and a shout of delight that declared open war on all remaining forms of religious "weaknesses."

FROM ***THE JOYFUL WISDOM***
BY **NIETZSCHE**

The most important of more recent events—that "God is dead," that the belief in the Christian God has become unworthy of belief—already begins to cast its first shadows over Europe. To the few at least whose eye, whose *suspecting* glance, is strong enough and subtle enough for this drama, some sun seems to have set, some old, profound confidence seems to have changed into doubt: our old world must seem to them daily more darksome, distrustful, strange and "old." In the main, however, one may say that the event itself is far too great, too remote, too much beyond most people's power of apprehension, for one to suppose that so much as the report of it could have *reached* them; not to speak of

---

[29] Friedrich Nietzsche, *The Antichrist,* in *The Portable Nietzsche,* ed. and trans. Walter Kaufmann (New York: Viking, 1954).

many who already knew *what* had taken place, and what must all collapse now that this belief had been undermined—because so much was built upon it, so much rested on it, and had become one with it: for example, our entire European morality. This lengthy, vast and uninterrupted process of crumbling, destruction, ruin and overthrow which is now imminent: who has realised it sufficiently to-day to have to stand up as the teacher and herald of such a tremendous logic of terror, as the prophet of a period of gloom and eclipse, the like of which has probably never taken place on earth before? . . . Even we, the born riddle-readers, who wait as it were on the mountains posted 'twixt to-day and tomorrow, and engirt by their contradiction, we, the firstlings and premature children of the coming century, into whose sight especially the shadows which must forthwith envelop Europe *should* already have come—how it is that even we, without genuine sympathy for this period of gloom, contemplate its advent without any *personal solicitude* or *fear?* Are we still, perhaps, too much under the *immediate effects* of the event—and are these effects, especially as regards *ourselves,* perhaps the reverse of what was to be expected—not at all sad and depressing, but rather like a new and indescribable variety of light, happiness, relief, enlivenment, encouragement, and dawning day? . . . In fact, we philosophers and "free spirits" feel ourselves irradiated as by a new dawn by the report that the "old God is dead"; our hearts overflow with gratitude, astonishment, presentiment and expectation. At last the horizon seems open once more, granting even that it is not bright; our ships can at least put out to sea in face of every danger; every hazard is again permitted to the discerner; the sea, *our* sea, again lies open before us; perhaps never before did such an "open sea" exist.[30]

Finally, in our own century, the attack has been given a psychoanalytic foundation by **Sigmund Freud,** who also reduces the grand aspirations of religion to mere illusions, but, even worse, the illusions of an insecure child who has never properly grown up.

FROM *THE FUTURE OF AN ILLUSION*
BY **SIGMUND FREUD**

. . . the psychical origin of religious ideas. These, which are given out as teachings, are not precipitates of experience or end results of thinking: they are illusions, fulfilments of the oldest, strongest and most urgent wishes of mankind. The secret of their strength lies in the strength of those wishes. As we already know, the terrifying impression of helplessness in childhood aroused the need for protection—for protection through love—which was provided by the father; and the recognition that this helplessness lasts throughout life made it necessary

---

[30] Friedrich Nietzsche, *The Joyful Wisdom,* trans. Thomas Common, in *The Complete Works of Friedrich Nietzsche,* Oscar Levy, general editor (1909–11) (New York: Russell & Russell, 1964).

to cling to the existence of a father, but this time a more powerful one. Thus the benevolent rule of a divine Providence allays our fear of the dangers of life; the establishment of a moral world-order ensures the fulfilment of the demands of justice, which have so often remained unfulfilled in human civilization; and the prolongation of earthly existence in a future life provides the local and temporal framework in which these wish-fulfilments shall take place. Answers to the riddles that tempt the curiosity of man, such as how the universe began or what the relation is between body and mind, are developed in conformity with the underlying assumptions of this system. It is an enormous relief to the individual psyche if the conflicts of its childhood arising from the father-complex—conflicts which it has never wholly overcome—are removed from it and brought to a solution which is universally accepted.

When I say that these things are all illusions, I must define the meaning of the word. An illusion is not the same thing as an error; nor is it necessarily an error. Aristotle's belief that vermin are developed out of dung (a belief to which ignorant people still cling) was an error; so was the belief of a former generation of doctors that *tabes dorsalis* is the result of sexual excess. It would be incorrect to call these errors illusions. On the other hand, it was an illusion of Columbus's that he had discovered a new searoute to the Indies. The part played by his wish in this error is very clear. One may describe as an illusion the assertion made by certain nationalists that the Indo-Germanic race is the only one capable of civilization; or the belief, which was only destroyed by psycho-analysis, that children are creatures without sexuality. What is characteristic of illusions is that they are derived from human wishes. In this respect they come near to psychiatric delusions. But they differ from them, too, apart from the more complicated structure of delusions. In the case of delusions, we emphasize as essential their being in contradiction with reality. Illusions need not necessarily be false—that is to say, unrealizable or in contradiction of reality. . . . Thus we call a belief an illusion when a wish-fulfilment is a prominent factor in its motivation, and in doing so we disregard its relations to reality, just as the illusion itself sets no store by verification.[31]

Illusions need not necessarily be false—that is to say, unrealizable or in contradiction of reality.

In conclusion, Freud agrees with Marx and Nietzsche that the only proper concern of man is humanity. But is this necessarily an indictment of religion? Freud was fascinated by Jewish mysticism, and Nietzsche offered extravagant praise of Buddhism. Many Christians, Muslims, and Jews have used their religion as a metaphysical support for concerted social activism and humanism (as well as "holy" wars), and for many people religion is an emotional support without which they could not

---

[31] Sigmund Freud, *The Future of an Illusion*, ed. and trans. James Strachey (New York: Norton, 1961).

even function as human beings. The balance is precarious. No one can deny that there have been thousands of atrocities—to both spirit and body—in the name of religion. But neither has it been proved that such cruelty is necessary for religion nor that religion is as easily dispensable as some of its critics have suggested. (Even Nietzsche had his serious doubts.)

SUMMARY AND CONCLUSION

Religion is one of the most important, and therefore one of the most controversial and sensitive, parts of our lives. It is therefore also one of the most important, controversial, and sensitive areas of philosophy. Initially, religion seems to be part of metaphysics, an examination of the way the world really is, and the answer of religion is that reality is, in a word, divine. But we have seen that religion is much more than a search for knowledge; it is also a search for meaning, for morality, for ultimate justice, and for a type of experience that is like no other. Philosophy of religion begins as a metaphysical discipline, attempting to define a supreme entity of a certain type (God) and to demonstrate His existence through rational arguments and proofs. But many philosophers and religious people deny that such a metaphysical approach is either possible or appropriate. Some philosophers deny that we can *know* God but insist that it is necessary to have faith. But while some philosophers interpret this faith as a form of rationality, others claim that it is strictly an emotional commitment beyond the domain of rational argument and understanding.

These various approaches to the philosophy of religion are all very much alive, and so too are the doubts that accompany each approach. Those who believe that we can know God are at odds with those who deny that we can know Him. Those who insist on faith disagree among themselves whether this faith can be or ought to be justified. There are those who want to believe in God but find that certain problems (for example, the problem of evil) make it difficult or impossible for them to do so. There are those who see belief in God as an outmoded belief, left over from the inadequate science and metaphysics of previous centuries. And there are those who attack religion as not only outmoded but as insidious, as a symptom of decadence, weakness, or immaturity. But in the face of these various doubts and attacks, the traditional religious beliefs of Judaism and Christianity continue to grow and to raise new questions. Religion is humanity's oldest philosophy, and it is still the most controversial area of philosophical concern.

GLOSSARY

Abrahamic religions The Western monotheisms: Judaism, Christianity, and Islam (they all trace their roots from the prophet Abraham).

agnosticism The refusal to believe either that God exists or that He does not exist, usually on the grounds that there can be no sufficient evidence for either belief.

anthropomorphic Humanlike. An anthropomorphic conception of God ascribes human attributes to Him.

argument from design See *teleological argument.*

atheism The belief that there is no God. A person who believes that there is no God is an *atheist.*

Batin, Batinya In Islamic mysticism, the "hidden truth" of the Qur'an and those who know it or seek it.

Bhagavadgītā ("Gītā") The "Song of God" of ancient Hinduism; the epic poem of Krishna, who is God incarnate.

Brahma ("Brahman") Precursor of God in Hindu theism; the idea of the One, the unity underlying all things.

Buddha "The awakened one"; the historical founder of Buddhism.

cosmological argument An argument (or set of arguments) that undertakes to "prove" that God exists on the basis of the idea that there must have been a first cause or an ultimate reason for the existence of the universe (the cosmos).

deism A variation of the Judeo-Christian religion that was extremely popular in the science-minded eighteenth century. Deism holds that God must have existed to create the universe with all of its laws (and thereby usually accepts some form of the cosmological argument) but also holds that there is no justification for our belief that God has any special concern for man, any concern for justice, or any of those anthropomorphic attributes for which we worship Him, pray to Him, and believe in biblical stories about Him.

dharma In Hinduism, righteousness, the good.

faith In the popular sense, believing in something for which you have inadequate evidence or little good reason. In theology, faith usually refers to the trust that a believer should have in God's ultimate grace and fairness. Sometimes, faith is defended as a rational belief in God (for example, in Kant). More often, faith is defended against rationality (as in Kierkegaard).

Four Noble Truths Among the most important teachings of the Buddha: "All is suffering (and transitory)," the need to eliminate desire, the way to eliminate desire, and the right path to the good.

God In traditional Judeo-Christian theology, that being who created the universe and exists independently of it, who is all-powerful, all-knowing, everywhere at once, and concerned with justice and the ultimate welfare of humankind. When spelled with a small "g" the word refers to any supernatural being worthy of worship or at least extraordinary respect.

illusion A false belief motivated by intense wishes. According to Marx, religion is an illusion that is intended to compensate for an intolerable social situation. According to Freud, religion is an illusion that attempts to hold onto our childhood desires for fatherly protection and security.

ineffable Indescribable.

karma In Hinduism, the tendency of any course of action to be repeated; the limitation of one's free will by one's own habits and dispositions (even into the next life).

Krishna In Hinduism, God incarnate.

mysticism The belief that one can come to grasp certain fundamental religious truths (the existence of God, the oneness of the universe) through direct experience, but of a very special kind, different from ordinary understanding and often at odds with reason.

nihility "The Nothing," "nothingness."

omnipotent All-powerful, usually said of God.

omnipresent Everywhere at once, usually said of God.

omniscient All-knowing, usually said of God.

ontological argument An argument (or set of arguments) that tries to "prove" the existence of God from the very concept of "God." For example, "God," by definition, is that being with all possible perfection; existence is a perfection; therefore, God exists.

pantheism The belief that God is identical to the universe as a whole. Spinoza, for example, was a pantheist. Hinduism is a form of pantheism in that it includes a conception of the divine in all things, rather than as a separate Creator.

problem of evil The dilemma that emerges from trying to reconcile the belief that God is omnipotent, omniscient, and just with the suffering and evil in the world.

subjective truth In Kierkegaard, the "truth" of strong feelings and commitment.

Sufism Islamic mysticism.

teleological argument (for God's existence) An argument that attempts to "prove" that God exists because of the intricacy and "design" of nature. It is sometimes called the "argument from design," since the basis of the argument is that since the universe is evidently designed, it must have a designer. The analogy most often used is our inference from finding a complex mechanism on the beach (for example, a watch) that some intelligent being must have created it.

theism Belief in God.

Theology of Liberation Christian Marxism; especially in Latin America, the religious motivated search for political freedoms.

transcendent Independent of. In the philosophy of religion, a *transcendent God* is one who is distinct and separate from the universe he created. This is contrasted with the concept of an immanent God, for example, in pantheism, where God is identical with his creation, or, to take a different example, in certain forms of humanism, in which God is identical with humankind. (Hegel argued such a thesis.)

BIBLIOGRAPHY AND FURTHER READING

Several good anthologies on the philosophy of religion are S. Cahn, ed., *Philosophy of Religion* (New York: Harper & Row, 1970); J. Hick, ed., *Faith and the Philosophers* (New York: St. Martin's Press, 1964); and N. Smart, ed., *Historical Selections in the Philosophy of Religion* (New York: Harper & Row, 1962). A general discussion of religious issues is J. Hick, *Faith and Knowledge,* 2nd ed. (Ithaca, NY: Cornell University Press, 1966). A good series of studies on the problem of evil is N. Pike, ed., *Good and Evil* (Englewood Cliffs, NJ: Prentice-Hall, 1964). David Hume's *Dialogues on Natural Religion* (New York: Bobbs-Merrill, 1963) makes excellent and provocative reading. A convenient collection of Søren Kierkegaard's writings is W. H. Auden, *The Living Thoughts of Kierkegaard* (Bloomington, IN: Indiana University Press, 1963). Two good studies of Kierkegaard are J. Collins, *The Mind of Kierkegaard* (Chicago: Regnery, 1953) and Louis Mackey, *Kierkegaard: A Kind of Poet* (Philadelphia: University of Pennsylvania Press, 1972). The selections from Karl Marx, Friedrich Nietzsche, and Sigmund Freud are developed in Karl Marx, *Early Writings,* trans. T. Bottomore (New York: McGraw-Hill, 1963); Friedrich Nietzsche, *The Antichrist* in *The Viking Portable Nietzsche,* trans. Walter Kaufmann (New York: Viking, 1959); and Sigmund Freud, *The Future of an Illusion,* trans. W. D. Robson-Scott (New York: Doubleday, Anchor, 1953). On medieval religions, see A. Hyman and J. Walsh, *Philosophy in the Middle Ages* (Indianapolis: Hackett, 1973). On Nishitani see, *Religion and Nothingness* (Berkeley: University of California Press) and D. T. Suzuki, *Zen Buddhism* (New York: Doubleday, 1956).

KNOWLEDGE

Once upon a time, I, Chuang Tzu, dreamt I was a butterfly, fluttering hither and thither, to all intents and purposes a butterfly. I was conscious only of following my fancies as a butterfly, and was unconscious of my individuality as a man. Suddenly, I waked, and there I lay, myself again. Now I do not know whether I was then a man dreaming I was a butterfly, or whether I am now a butterfly dreaming I am a man.

CHUANG-TZU[1]

After an evening of heated but fruitless metaphysical debate with a number of his friends, the British physician **John Locke** turned to them and asked, "Shouldn't we first determine whether we are capable of answering such questions?" They agreed. Perhaps you are thinking much the same thing. These great metaphysical systems are surely monuments to human intelligence. But do they achieve what they are intended to? Do they tell us "the way the world really is"? Since each of the contending systems claims that it does, how can it be that they disagree? Which is right? And how can we decide?

In 1690 Locke took philosophy around a sharp turn, one that had been suggested by Descartes a half century before. But Descartes had broached the question, "What can we know?" only as a preface to his metaphysics. Locke, on the other hand,

---

[1] From Herbert A. Giles, trans. *Chuang-Tzu: Taoist Philosopher and Chinese Mystic.* London: George Allen and Unwin, 1961 [1889], p. 47.

decided to put questions about reality on the shelf until he could develop an adequate theory of human knowledge. Accordingly, his great book is not primarily an inquiry into substance or reality or God or truth (although all of these enter in); it is *An Essay Concerning Human Understanding*. From metaphysics, the study of ultimate reality, we now turn to **epistemology**, the study of human knowledge—how we get it, what it is, whether we have it, or why we don't.

Even before Plato, Parmenides had seen that between a false belief and knowledge of reality are many opinions and appearances of reality, which might be very different from the reality itself. Plato's "Myth of the Cave" is a graphic illustration of this distinction. Descartes, although he distrusted his senses and wasn't certain that they gave accurate representations of reality, at least could be certain of the appearances themselves—he could not be mistaken about them. And here is the problem that has defined epistemology, the seeming abyss between reality and mere appearance. Perhaps we know the appearances of things, but how can we know that we know the reality "behind" them?

Let us return for a moment to the central idea of traditional metaphysics, that of substance. Substance is that which underlies all of the various properties of a thing (or things); and it is the properties, never the substance itself, that are experienced by us. Now, presumably, there can be no properties unless they are properties of something. That seems to be a platitude. But yet, we cannot experience the nature of the substance itself. And here begins the embarrassment of metaphysics.

The problem was stated succinctly by the best-known British philosopher of this century, Bertrand Russell, in a little volume called *The Problems of Philosophy,* in which he says the following:

FROM *THE PROBLEMS*
OF PHILOSOPHY
BY **BERTRAND RUSSELL**

In daily life, we assume as certain many things which, on a closer scrutiny, are found to be so full of apparent contradictions that only a great amount of thought enables us to know what it is that we really may believe. In the search for certainty, it is natural to begin with our present experiences, and in some sense, no doubt, knowledge is to be derived from them. But any statement as to what it is that our immediate experiences make us know is very likely to be wrong. It seems to me that I am now sitting in a chair, at a table of a certain shape, on which I see sheets of paper with writing or print. By turning my head I see out of the window buildings and clouds and the sun. I believe that the sun is about ninety-three million miles from the earth; that it is a hot globe many times bigger than the earth; that, owing to the earth's rotation, it rises every morning, and will continue to do so for an indefinite time in the future. I believe that, if any other normal person comes into my room, he will see the same chairs and tables and books and papers as I see, and that the table which I see is the same as the table which I feel pressing against my arm. All this seems to be so evident as to be hardly worth stating, except in answer to a man who doubts whether I know anything. Yet all this may be reasonably doubted, and all of it requires much careful discussion before we can be sure that we have stated it in a form that is wholly true.

To make our difficulties plain, let us concentrate attention on the table. To the eye it is oblong, brown and shiny, to the touch it is smooth and cool and hard; when I tap it, it gives out a wooden sound. Any one else who sees and feels and hears the table will agree with this description, so that it might seem as if no difficulty would arise; but as soon as we try to be more precise our troubles begin. Although I believe that the table is "really" of the same colour all over, the parts that reflect the light look much brighter than the other parts, and some parts look white because of reflected light. I know that, if I move, the parts that reflect the light will be different, so that the apparent distribution of colours on the table will change. It follows that if several people are looking at the table at the same moment, no two of them will see exactly the same distribution of colours, because no two can see it from exactly the same point of view, and any change in the point of view makes some change in the way the light is reflected.

For most practical purposes the differences are unimportant, but to the painter they are all-important: the painter has to unlearn the habit of thinking that things seem to have the colour which common sense says they "really" have, and to learn the habit of seeing things as they appear. Here we have already the beginning of one of the distinctions that cause most trouble in philosophy—the distinction between "appearance" and "reality," between what things seem to be and what they are. The painter wants to know what things seem to be, the practical man and the philosopher want to know what they are; but the philosopher's wish to know this is stronger than the practical man's, and is more troubled by knowledge as to the difficulties of answering the question.

To return to the table. It is evident from what we have found, that there is no colour which preeminently appears to be *the* colour of the table, or even of any one particular part of the table—it appears to be of different colours from different points of view, and there is no reason for regarding some of these as more really its colour than others. And we know that even from a given point of view the colour will seem different by artificial light, or to a colour-blind man, or to a man wearing blue spectacles, while in the dark there will be no colour at all, though to touch and hearing the table will be unchanged. This colour is not something which is inherent in the table, but something depending upon the table and the spectator and the way the light falls on the table. When, in ordinary life, we speak of *the* colour of the table, we only mean the sort of colour which it will seem to have to a normal spectator from an ordinary point of view under usual conditions of light. But the other colours which appear under other conditions have just as good a right to be considered real; and therefore, to avoid favouritism, we are compelled to deny that, in itself, the table has any one particular colour.

The same thing applies to the texture. With the naked eye one can see the grain, but otherwise the table looks smooth and even. If we looked at it through a microscope, we should see roughnesses and hills and valleys, and all sorts of differences that are imperceptible to the naked eye. Which of these is the "real" table? We are naturally tempted to say that what we see through the microscope is more real, but that in turn would be changed by a still more powerful microscope. If, then, we cannot trust what we see with the naked eye, why should we trust what we see through a microscope? Thus, again, the confidence in our sense with which we began deserts us.

The *shape* of the table is not better. We are all in the habit of judging as to the "real" shapes of things, and we do this so unreflectingly that we come to think we actually see the real shapes. But, in fact, as we all have to learn if we try to draw, a given thing looks different in shape from every different point of view. If our table is "really" rectangular, it will look, from almost all points of view, as if it had two acute angles and two obtuse angles. If opposite sides are parallel, they will look as if they converged to a point away from the spectator; if they are of equal length, they will look as if the nearer side were longer. All these things are not commonly noticed in looking at a table, because experience has taught us to construct the "real" shape from the apparent shape, and the "real" shape is what interests us as practical men. But the "real" shape is not what we see; it is something inferred from what we see. And what we see is constantly changing in shape as we move about the room; so that here again the senses seem not to give us the truth about the table itself, but only about the appearance of the table.

Similar difficulties arise when we consider the sense of touch. It is true that the table always gives us a sensation of hardness, and we feel that it resists pressure. But the sensation we obtain depends upon how hard we press the table and also upon what part of the body we press with; thus the various sensations due to various pressures or various parts of the body cannot be supposed to reveal *directly* any definite property of the table, but at most to be *signs* of some property, which *causes* all the sensations, but is not actually apparent in any of them. And the same applies still more obviously to the sounds which can be elicited by rapping the table.

The real table, if there is one, is not immediately known to us at all, but must be an inference from what is immediately known.

Thus it becomes evident that the real table, if there is one, is not the same as what we immediately experience by sight or touch or hearing. The real table, if there is one, is not *immediately* known to us at all, but must be an inference from what is immediately known. Hence, two very difficult questions at once arise; namely, (1) Is there a real table at all? (2) If so, what sort of object can it be?[2]

In these few pages, Russell succeeds in summarizing the problems that have dominated British philosophy since Locke's original epistemological studies. But why say "British philosophy"? Why should this problem have been more serious there

---

[2] Bertrand Russell, *The Problems of Philosophy* (Oxford: Oxford University Press, 1912).

than on the continent of Europe, where most of the great metaphysicians were working? Why should it have had more impact on Locke and his followers than on Descartes, Spinoza, Leibniz, and their latter-day followers? Because of a single profound difference, which has always created a general gap in understanding between British-American philosophy and European philosophy. Descartes, Spinoza, and Leibniz retained their faith in human reason's ability to give us knowledge of reality, despite the fact that reality was beyond our every possible experience. Because of their confidence in the powers of reason, they are usually called **rationalists.** Because it happens that all three were Europeans (Descartes was French; Spinoza, Dutch; and Leibniz, German), they are often called *continental rationalists.* The movement developed by John Locke, on the other hand, is generally called **empiricism,** because of its insistence upon the data of experience (or *empirical* data) as the source of all knowledge. (A **datum** [plural, *data*] is a bit of "given" information; modern empiricist philosophers sometimes talk of *sense-data,* that is, the information immediately given by the senses.) Also included in this group of empiricists are **Bishop George Berkeley**[3] and **David Hume,** whom we shall also meet in this chapter. Because they were all from Great Britain, they are often called *British empiricists.* (Berkeley was Irish; Hume, Scottish; Russell is generally considered a more contemporary member of this same movement.)

Although epistemology received a renewed attention and a new kind of treatment in the era after Descartes, the rift between the claims of rationalists and those of empiricists was not new. The basics of the debate were laid out by Plato, in his dialogue *Theatetus:*

FROM THE *THEATETUS*
BY **PLATO**

SOCRATES: But the question you were asked, Theatetus, was not, what are the objects of knowledge, nor yet how many sorts of knowledge there are. We did not want to count them, but to find out what the thing itself—knowledge—is.

◆◆◆

Perception, you say, is knowledge?
THEATETUS: Yes.
SOCRATES: The account you give of the nature of knowledge is not, by any means, to be despised. It is the same that was given by Protagoras, though he stated it in a somewhat different way. He says, you will remember, that "man is the measure of all things—alike of the being of things that are and of the not-being of things that are not." No doubt you have read that.
THEATETUS: Yes, often.
SOCRATES: He puts it in this sort of way, doesn't he, that any given thing is "is to me such as it appears to me and is to you such as it appears to you," you and I being men?

---

[3] Bishop Berkeley traveled to the United States; Berkeley, California, is named after him.

THEATETUS: Yes, that is how he puts it.

SOCRATES: Well, what a wise man says is not likely to be nonsense. So let us follow his meaning. Sometimes, when the same wind is blowing, one of us feels chilly, the other does not, or one may feel slightly chilly, the other quite cold.

THEATETUS: Certainly.

SOCRATES: Well, in that case are we to say that the wind in itself is cold or not cold? Or shall we agree with Protagoras that it is cold to the one who feels chilly and not to the other?

◆◆◆

... [I]ndeed the doctrine is a remarkable one. It declares that nothing is *one* thing just by itself, nor can you rightly call it by one definite name, nor even say it is of any definite sort.

In this way, Socrates claims that the empiricist cannot have any knowledge at all. He defends the rationalist's claim earlier in the dialogue:

SOCRATES: You do not suppose a man can understand the name of a thing when he does not know what the thing is?

THEATETUS: Certainly not.

SOCRATES: Then, if he has no idea of knowledge, "knowledge about shoes" conveys nothing to him?

THEATETUS: No.

SOCRATES: "Cobblery" in fact, or the name of any other art has no meaning for anyone who has no conception of knowledge.[4]

Russell, like Theatetus, associates knowledge with perception, or "sense-data." Thus, he had assumed that any notion of "substance" we might have must be *derived* from our perceptions. Socrates claimed that our varied perceptions can never give us a notion of substance. All we would be able to get out of a bunch of differing perceptions is a bunch of differing perceptions. Since we *have* a notion of substance, however, (in Russell's example, for instance, of a "table") we must have gotten it from something other than our perceptions. Knowledge, concludes Socrates, must be something other than perception. The continental rationalists in a sense, agreed with Socrates on this point and claimed that the nonperceptual source of knowledge must be "reason" itself. The British empiricists went the other way, claiming that there simply wasn't any other source of ideas other than perception. ("Perception" actually can mean both "sense-data" and "understanding." We mean the first sense here.)

So, how are we to know reality? By retaining confidence in our own powers of abstract reason? Or by appeal to experience, which carries with it the threat that we may never know reality beyond our experience at all? In the pages that follow, you will see one of the most vigorous and long-lasting dialogues in philosophy, not

---

[4] Translated by F. M. Cornford, reprinted in *The Collected Dialogues of Plato,* ed. Edith Hamilton and Huntington Cairnes, Bollingen series (Princeton: Princeton University Press, 1980), p. 61.

only between the rationalists and the empiricists but (as we saw in the juxtaposition of Spinoza and Leibniz in Chapter 1) between various rationalists and empiricists as well.

Is the choice between reason and experience a "false dilemma" (a kind of pseudo-question)? Among the issues in dispute are not only the emphasis and faith in reason versus experience but also the nature of reason and the nature of experience. What is an idea that can be known to be true by reasons alone—a "truth of reason"? How can we infer from the nature of our private experience what the world "outside" is like? How do we even know that there *is* an "external" world? How is it possible to have "abstract" ideas, that is, ideas that are not simply based on the concrete particulars of experience, such as *this* dog, *this* table, *that* star over there to the left of the Big Dipper? How do we get the idea, for example, of "dog" in general, not this dog or that dog or big dog or little dog or Chihuahua or German Shepherd but just "dog," which includes all of them?

The question of *substance* comes up again and again; what is a substance? How do we know of substances? So does the notion of *cause*. Is an idea *caused* by an object of which it is the idea, or do we make the idea up, and so "cause" it ourselves? And, a more specific set of questions: What aspects of a thing are *in it?* What aspects of a thing are rather *in us,* that is, in the way we perceive it, in the mental apparatus that we use in our knowledge? But beneath the welter of questions and debates, there is a singular shared concern. All of the rationalists and empiricists are men of science who appreciate the advances of modern physics and its kindred disciplines, who think of knowledge as one of the highest human attributes, and who want to understand knowledge and its foundations as a way of justifying their faith in science. At the bottom of all of these disputes, in other words, is that basic admiration and concern for knowledge as such, as the question "How is this knowledge possible?" is itself an extension of that same admiration and concern.

A. THE RATIONALIST'S CONFIDENCE: DESCARTES

Let's return to the philosopher who began the modern emphasis on methodology, René Descartes. We have already mentioned his "method of doubt," but the goal of this method is not to defend the doubts but, quite to the contrary, to move from doubt to knowledge and certainty. Descartes' doubt is intended only to separate what is doubtful from what is not. He never doubted, nor did his followers, that he would be able to find beliefs about reality. These beliefs would be "clear and distinct" and "perfectly certain." (Spinoza refers to such ideas as "adequate ideas"; Leibniz calls them "truths of reason.") Once Descartes had found even one such belief, he could use it as a premise from which he could deduce all of his other beliefs about reality. And none of this depends upon the data of experience; it is entirely a process of reason, of examining the clarity of his beliefs and the logical connections between them.

Once again, it is important to remind ourselves that these problems and their sometimes radical complications and solutions do not appear in a vacuum. Descartes lived in the time of **Galileo,** and Galileo's new science is always in the background of Descartes' method of doubt. In undermining the traditional science of Aristotle and the Middle Ages, Galileo raised the doubt that what we think that we see we might not really see at all. Colors, for example, seemed to be more in the minds of men and women than in the objects themselves. But if we could be mistaken about something so seemingly certain as the color of objects, Descartes reasons, could we not be mistaken about much else besides? Indeed, could we not be mistaken in our perceptions *in general?* For this reason Descartes appeals to reason rather than to experience (although, as we shall see, he dangerously calls reason into question as well). We might also add that, although he was a devout Catholic, Descartes could not help but be affected by **Martin Luther**'s challenge to church authority the century before. Thus the insistence of resolving these doubts for oneself, instead of appealing to established authority, was very much a part of the radical temperament of the time.

In six famous "meditations," Descartes begins with the resolve to doubt everything that he believes, that is, until he can find a first premise that is beyond doubt, from which he can then argue for the truth of other beliefs, which he can then use as premises to prove more beliefs, and so on. In the first meditation, he states his method of doubt and begins to eliminate all of those beliefs about which he could possibly be mistaken. He doubts his senses; could they not mislead him, as they do in an optical illusion or a hallucination? He examines his belief in God; could it be that his Jesuit teachers had been fooling him? He even doubts the existence of the world; is it not conceivable that he is merely dreaming? Here is the first of the meditations.

. . . I was convinced that I must once and for all seriously undertake to rid myself of all the opinions which I had formerly accepted, and commence to build anew from the foundation, if I wanted to establish any firm and permanent structure in the sciences.

FROM **"MEDITATION I"**
BY **RENÉ DESCARTES**

OF THE THINGS WHICH MAY BE BROUGHT WITHIN THE SPHERE OF THE DOUBTFUL

It is now some years since I detected how many were the false beliefs that I had from my earliest youth admitted as true, and how doubtful was everything I had since constructed on this basis; and from that time I was convinced that I must once and for all seriously undertake to rid myself of all the opinions which I had formerly accepted, and commence to build anew from the foundation, if I wanted to establish any firm and permanent structure in the sciences.

In order to "build anew" his system of beliefs and eliminate his false beliefs, Descartes resolves to doubt everything that he believes. But this does not mean that he has to list every belief he has; that might take forever. Instead, it is necessary only for him to examine those "first principles" upon which all of his other beliefs are based.

> Now for this object it is not necessary that I should show that all of these are false—I shall perhaps never arrive at this end. But inasmuch as reason already persuades me that I ought no less carefully to withhold my assent from matters which are not entirely certain and indubitable than from those which appear to me manifestly to be false, if I am able to find in each one some reason to doubt, this will suffice to justify my rejecting the whole. And for that end it will not be requisite that I should examine each in particular, which would be an endless undertaking; for owing to the fact that the destruction of the foundations of necessity brings with it the downfall of the rest of the edifice, I shall only in the first place attack those principles upon which all my former opinions rested.

The first set of principles to be doubted is that "commonsense" set of beliefs that relies upon the senses: seeing, hearing, tasting, smelling, and touching. Descartes argues that, despite our commonsense reliance on these, it is nevertheless possible that we could be deceived by our senses.

> All that up to the present time I have accepted as most true and certain I have learned either from the senses or through the senses; but it is sometimes proved to me that these senses are deceptive, and it is wiser not to trust entirely to any thing by which we have once been deceived.
>
> But it may be that although the senses sometimes deceive us concerning things which are hardly perceptible, or very far away, there are yet many others to be met with as to which we cannot reasonably have any doubt, although we recognise them by their means. For example, there is the fact that I am here, seated by the fire, attired in a dressing gown, having this paper in my hands and other similar matters. And how could I deny that these hands and this body are mine, were it not perhaps that I compare myself to certain persons, devoid of sense, whose cerebella are so troubled and clouded by the violent vapours of black bile, that they constantly assure us that they think they are kings when they are really quite poor, or that they are clothed in purple when they are really without covering, or who imagine that they have an earthenware head or are nothing but pumpkins or are made of glass. But they are mad, and I should not be any the less insane were I to follow examples so extravagant.

Now Descartes makes one of his most famous philosophical moves: He wonders whether he could possibly be dreaming all of his experience; for in a dream, as we all know, it is possible that everything can still seem perfectly real, as if we were actually awake:

At the same time I must remember that I am a man, and that consequently I am in the habit of sleeping, and in my dreams representing to myself the same things or sometimes even less probable things, than do those who are insane in their waking moments. How often has it happened to me that in the night I dreamt that I found myself in this particular place, that I was dressed and seated near the fire, whilst in reality I was lying undressed in bed! At this moment it does indeed seem to me that it is with eyes awake that I am looking at this paper; that this head which I move is not asleep, that it is deliberately and of set purpose that I extend my hand and perceive it; what happens in sleep does not appear so clear nor so distinct as does all this. But in thinking over this I remind myself that on many occasions I have in sleep been deceived by similar illusions, and in dwelling carefully on this reflection I see so manifestly that there are no certain indications by which we may clearly distinguish wakefulness from sleep that I am lost in astonishment. And my astonishment is such that it is almost capable of persuading me that I now dream.

Thus Descartes has brought himself to the point where he doubts the existence of the whole of nature, even the existence of his own body. After all, one can dream that one's body has changed grotesquely, and on rare occasions it is even possible to dream that one leaves one's body altogether. So isn't it possible, according to this strict method of doubt, to wonder whether one does indeed have a body, just as it is possible to wonder how one knows of the existence of the "external world" in general?

But there is one sphere of knowledge that would seem to be immune even to Descartes' radical doubting—the principles of arithmetic and geometry:

Arithmetic, Geometry and other sciences of that kind which only treat of things that are very simple and very general, without taking great trouble to ascertain whether they are actually existent or not, contain some measure of certainty and an element of the indubitable. For whether I am awake or asleep, two and three together always form five, and the square can never have more than four sides, and it does not seem possible that truths so clear and apparent can be suspected of any falsity [or uncertainty].

But these can be doubted, too. To do so, Descartes turns his attention to God, his Creator, and asks whether God might be able to deceive him, even about these apparently certain principles:

Nevertheless I have long had fixed in my mind the belief that an all-powerful God existed by whom I have been created such as I am. But how do I know that He has not brought it to pass that there is no earth, no heaven, no extended body, no magnitude, no place, and that nevertheless [I possess the perceptions of all these things and that] they seem to me to exist just exactly as I now see them? And, besides, as I sometimes imagine that others deceive themselves in the things which they think they know best, how do I know that I am not deceived every time that I add two and three, or count the sides of a square, or judge of things yet simpler, if anything simpler can be imagined? But possibly God has not desired that I should be thus deceived, for He is said to be supremely good. If, however, it is contrary to His goodness to have made me such that I constantly deceive myself, it would also appear to be contrary to His goodness to permit me to be sometimes deceived, and nevertheless I cannot doubt that He does permit this.

Descartes' argument, which he will use again later in his *Meditations,* is that God is good and would not deceive him. But suppose, just suppose, that God did not exist?

There may indeed be those who would prefer to deny the existence of a God so powerful, rather than believe that all other things are uncertain. But let us not oppose them for the present, and grant that all that is here said of a God is a fable; nevertheless in whatever way they suppose that I have arrived at the state of being that I have reached—whether they attribute it to fate or to accident, or make out that it is by a continual succession of antecedents, or by some other method—since to err and deceive oneself is a defect, it is clear that the greater will be the probability of my being so imperfect as to deceive myself ever, as is the Author to whom they assign my origin the less powerful. To these reasons I have certainly nothing to reply, but at the end I feel constrained to confess that there is nothing in all that I formerly believed to be true, of which I cannot in some measure doubt, and that not merely through want of thought or through levity, but for reasons which are very powerful and maturely considered; so that henceforth I ought not the less carefully to refrain from giving credence to these opinions than to that which is manifestly false, if I desire to arrive at any certainty [in the sciences].

To bring his method to its extreme conclusion, Descartes now introduces a drastic supposition, namely, that not a good God but an evil genius, a malicious demon, is constantly deceiving him, even about those things of which he seems to be most certain:

I shall then suppose, not that God who is supremely good and the fountain of truth, but some evil genius not less powerful than deceitful, has employed his whole energies in deceiving me; I shall consider that the heavens, the earth, colours, figures, sound, and all other external things are nought but the illusions and dreams of which this genius has availed himself in order to lay traps for my credulity; I shall consider myself as having no hands, no eyes, no flesh, no blood, nor any senses, yet falsely believing myself to possess all these things; I shall remain obstinately attached to this idea, and if by this means it is not in my power to arrive at the knowledge of any truth, I may at least do what is in my power [i.e., suspend my judgment], and with firm purpose avoid giving credence to any false thing, or being imposed upon by this arch deceiver, however powerful and deceptive he may be. But this task is a laborious one, and insensibly a certain lassitude leads me into the course of my ordinary life. And just as a captive who in sleep enjoys an imaginary liberty, when he begins to suspect that this liberty is but a dream, fears to awaken, and conspires with these agreeable illusions that the deception may be prolonged, so insensibly of my own accord I fall back into my former opinions, and I dread awakening from this slumber, lest the laborious wakefulness which would follow the tranquility of this repose should have to be spent not in daylight, but in the excessive darkness of the difficulties which have just been discussed.[5]

Descartes has taken his doubt as far as he can possibly go; he now doubts everything, until, that is, he finds the one principle that is beyond all doubt and perfectly certain. That principle is the fact of his own existence. That he cannot doubt, for if he doubts it, he still knows that he must exist to doubt. Thus, he can be certain of one thing, at least, that he himself exists. From this first principle, Descartes proceeds, through the "Meditations" that follow, to reestablish his confidence in other things he believes as well—the existence of God, the existence of the "external world," and the existence of his own body.

Many philosophers have challenged the extremity of Descartes' method and have often objected that once you begin to doubt things so thoroughly, you will never again be able to argue your way back to certainty. One way of making this objection is to ask, how can Descartes possibly get rid of an "evil genius" who is deceiving him about everything once he has introduced this possibility? Indeed, the supposition of an evil genius was so extreme that even Descartes, in the years that followed the publication and many disputes about his *Meditations,* insisted that no one should take his argument too seriously. But in the "Meditations" themselves he tried to show that we could indeed get rid of the evil genius. Having watched Descartes work his way into the depth of Plato's cave, let us now watch him work his way out again.

FROM **"MEDITATION II"**
BY **DESCARTES**

OF THE NATURE OF THE HUMAN MIND; AND THAT IT IS MORE
EASILY KNOWN THAN THE BODY

The Meditation of yesterday filled my mind with so many doubts that it is no longer in my power to forget them. And yet I do not see in what manner I can resolve them; and, just as if I had all of a sudden fallen into very deep water, I am so disconcerted that I can neither make certain of setting my feet on the bottom, nor can I swim and so support myself on the surface. I shall nevertheless make

---

[5] Descartes, *Meditations on First Philosophy,* in *The Philosophical Works of Descartes,* trans. Elizabeth S. Haldane and G. R. T. Ross (Cambridge: Cambridge University Press, 1911). All subsequent "Meditations" by Descartes are from this edition.

an effort and follow anew the same path as that on which I yesterday entered, i.e. I shall proceed by setting aside all that in which the least doubt could be supposed to exist, just as if I had discovered that it was absolutely false; and I shall ever follow in this road until I have met with something which is certain, or at least, if I can do nothing else, until I have learned for certain that there is nothing in the world that is certain. Archimedes, in order that he might draw the terrestrial globe out of its place, and transport it elsewhere, demanded only that one point should be fixed and immovable; in the same way I shall have the right to conceive high hopes if I am happy enough to discover one thing only which is certain and indubitable.

I suppose, then, that all the things that I see are false; I persuade myself that nothing has ever existed of all that my fallacious memory represents to me. I consider that I possess no senses; I imagine that body, figure, extension, movement and place are but the fictions of my mind. What, then, can be esteemed as true? Perhaps nothing at all, unless that there is nothing in the world that is certain.

But how can I know there is not something different from those things that I have just considered, of which one cannot have the slightest doubt? Is there not some God, or some other being by whatever name we call it, who puts these reflections into my mind? That is not necessary, for is it not possible that I am capable of producing them myself? I myself, am I not at least something? But I have already denied that I had senses and body. Yet I hesitate, for what follows from that? Am I so dependent on body and senses that I cannot exist without these? But I was persuaded that there was nothing in all the world, that there was no heaven, no earth, that there were no minds, nor any bodies; was I not then likewise persuaded that I did not exist? Not at all; of a surety I myself did exist since I persuaded myself of something [or merely because I thought of something]. But there is some deceiver or other, very powerful and very cunning, who ever employs his ingenuity in deceiving me. Then without doubt I exist also if he deceives me, and let him deceive me as much as he will, he can never cause me to be nothing so long as I think that I am something. So that after having reflected well and carefully examined all things, we must come to the definite conclusion that this proposition: I am, I exist, is necessarily true each time that I pronounce it, or that I mentally conceive it.

> *. . . I am, I exist, is necessarily true each time that I pronounce it, or that I mentally conceive it.*

Here it is, the one, certain truth that Descartes needs to start his argument. The more famous formulation of this truth, *cogito, ergo sum,* "I think, therefore I am," occurs in his earlier *Discourse on Method* (1637). (It may be worth pointing out that a similar argument appears in St. Augustine, more than one thousand years earlier.)

But now that Descartes knows that he exists, what is he? His answer: "a thing which thinks."

But I do not yet know clearly enough what I am, I who am certain that I am; and hence I must be careful to see that I do not imprudently take some other object in place of myself, and thus that I do not go astray in respect of this knowledge that I hold to be the most certain and most evident of all that I have formerly learned. That is why I shall now consider anew what I believed myself to be before I embarked upon these last reflections; and of my former opinions I shall withdraw all that might even in a small degree be invalidated by the reasons which I have just brought forward, in order that there may be nothing at all left beyond what is absolutely certain and indubitable.

What then did I formerly believe myself to be? Undoubtedly I believed myself to be a man. But what is a man? Shall I say a reasonable animal? Certainly not; for then I should have to inquire what an animal is, and what is reasonable; and thus from a single question I should insensibly fall into an infinitude of others more difficult; and I should not wish to waste the little time and leisure remaining to me in trying to unravel subtleties like these. But I shall rather stop here to consider the thoughts which of themselves spring up in my mind, and which were not inspired by anything beyond my own nature alone when I applied myself to the consideration of my being. In the first place, then, I considered myself as having a face, hands, arms, and all that system of members composed of bones and flesh as seen in a corpse which I designated by the name of body. In addition to this I considered that I was nourished, that I walked, that I felt, and that I thought, and I referred all these actions to the soul: but I did not stop to consider what the soul was, or if I did stop, I imagined that it was something extremely rare and subtle like a wind, a flame, or an ether, which was spread throughout my grosser parts. As to body I had no manner of doubt about its nature, but thought I had a very clear knowledge of it; and if I had desired to explain it according to the notions that I had then formed of it, I should have described it thus: By the body I understand all that which can be defined by a certain figure: something which can be confined in a certain place, and which can fill a given space in such a way that every other body will be excluded from it; which can be perceived either by touch, or by sight, or by hearing, or by taste, or by smell: which can be moved in many ways not, in truth, by itself, but by something which is foreign to it, by which it is touched [and from which it receives impressions]: for to have the power of self-movement, as also of feeling or of thinking, I did not consider to appertain to the nature of body: on the contrary, I was rather astonished to find that faculties similar to them existed in some bodies.

But what am I, now that I suppose that there is a certain genius which is extremely powerful, and, if I may say so, malicious, who employs all his power in deceiving me? Can I affirm that I possess the least of all those things which I have just said pertain to the nature of body? I pause to consider, I revolve all these things in my mind, and I find none of which I can say that it pertains to me. It would be tedious to stop to enumerate them. Let us pass to the attributes of soul and see if there is any one which is in me? What of nutrition or walking [the first mentioned]? But if it is so that I have no body it is also true that I can neither walk nor take nourishment. Another attribute is sensation. But one cannot feel without body, and besides I have thought I perceived many things during sleep that I recognized in my waking moments as not having been experienced at all. What of thinking? I find here that thought is an attribute that belongs to me; it alone cannot be separated from me. I am, I exist, that is certain. But how often? Just when I think; for it might possibly be the case if I ceased entirely to think, that I should likewise cease altogether to exist. I do not now admit anything which is not necessarily true: to speak accurately I am not more than a thing which thinks, that is to say a mind or a soul, or an understanding, or a reason, which are terms whose significance was formerly unknown to me. I am, however, a real thing and really exist; but what thing? I have answered: a thing which thinks. . . . What is a thing which thinks? It is a thing which doubts, understands, [conceives], affirms, denies, wills, refuses, which also imagines and feels.

In other words, Descartes cannot know for certain that he has a body, much less a particular kind of body, since the evil genius could fool him about that. The only thing that the evil genius could not possibly fool him about is his own thinking, and therefore, the "I" that he knows to exist can only be a thinking "I," not a person or a man in the more usual sense. Later on, this will cause Descartes to raise a gigantic problem, namely, how to explain the connection between this thinking self and the body with which it is associated. But for now, we are more interested in the way he will use his discovery of a single, certain truth. (His discussion of the "mind-body" connection occurs in "Meditation VI," which we shall discuss in Chapter 5, pp. 323–324.)

Descartes has his premise, the fact of his own existence as a "thinking thing." What must follow, then, is the use of this premise in an argument that will "prove" the beliefs he began by doubting: the existence of his own body, the existence of the "external" world, and the existence of God. Finally, he must somehow get rid of his tentative supposition of the evil demon. But first, he raises once again the old metaphysical question of substance. In a famous example from "Meditation II" he argues:

Let us begin by considering the commonest matters, those which we believe to be the most distinctly comprehended, to wit, the bodies which we touch and see; not indeed bodies in general, for these general ideas are usually a little more confused, but let us consider one body in particular. Let us take, for example, this piece of wax: it has been taken quite freshly from the hive, and it has not yet lost the sweetness of the odour of the honey which it contains; it still retains somewhat of the odour of the flowers from which it has been culled; its colour, its figure, its size are apparent; it is hard, cold, easily handled, and if you strike it with the finger, it will emit a sound. Finally all the things which are requisite to cause us distinctly to recognize a body, are met with in it. But notice that while I speak and approach the fire what remained of the taste is exhaled, the smell evaporates, the colour alters, the figure is destroyed, the size increases, it becomes liquid, it heats, scarcely can one handle it, and when one strikes it, no sound is emitted. Does the same wax remain after this change? We must confess that it remains; none would judge otherwise. What then did I know so distinctly in this piece of wax? It could certainly be nothing of all that the senses brought to my notice, since all these things which fall under taste, smell, sight, touch and hearing, are found to be changed, and yet the same wax remains.

Perhaps it was what I now think, viz. that this wax was not that sweetness of honey, nor that agreeable scent of flowers, nor that particular whiteness, nor that figure, nor that sound, but simply a body which a little while before appeared to me as perceptible under these forms, and which is now perceptible under others. But what, precisely, is it that I imagine when I form such conceptions? Let us attentively consider this, and, abstracting from all that does not belong to the wax, let us see what remains. Certainly nothing remains excepting a certain extended thing which is flexible and movable. But what is the meaning of flexible and movable? Is it not that I imagine that this piece of wax being round is capable of becoming square and of passing from a square to a triangular figure? No, certainly it is not that, since I imagine it admits of an infinitude of similar changes, and I nevertheless do not know how to compass the infinitude of my imagination, and consequently this conception which I have of the wax is not brought about by the faculty of imagination. What now is this extension? Is it not also unknown? For it becomes greater when the wax is melted, greater when it is boiled, and greater still when the heat increases; and I should not conceive [clearly] according to truth what wax is, if I did not think that even this piece that we are considering is capable of receiving more variations in extension than I have ever imagined. We must then grant that I could not even understand through the imagination what this piece of wax is, and that it is my mind alone which perceives it. I say this piece of wax in particular, for as to wax in general it is yet clearer. But what is this piece of wax which cannot be understood excepting by the [understanding or] mind? It is certainly the same that I see, touch, imagine, and finally it is the same which I have always believed it to be from the beginning. But what must particularly be observed is that its perception is neither an act of vision, nor of touch, nor of imagination, and has never been such although it may have appeared formerly to be so, but only an intuition of the mind, which may be imperfect and confused as it was formerly, or clear and distinct as it is at present, according as my attention is more or less directed to the elements which are found in it, and of which it is composed.

This "intuition of mind" is the key to all rationalist thinking. Intuition is where the rationalist obtains his premises, from which he argues to all other conclusions. The difference between the rationalist and the empiricist, at least in what they say that they are doing, is the rationalist's heavy reliance on nonempirical intuition. Both would agree on the legitimacy of the deductions that follow; it is the source of the premises that is in dispute. And intuition, according to the rationalists, has its source in reason alone. (Notice that "reason" refers not only to the activity of reasoning but to unreasoned intuitions and insights as well.) Accordingly it is this source of intuition that will be the center of the dispute rather than the actual arguments that Descartes then uses to "prove" his other beliefs. The strategy of Descartes' argument is as follows. First, there is the premise, which you have seen:

I exist *(as a thinking thing).*

Then (in "Meditation III"), Descartes uses this premise to prove the existence of God. This is the second key move in the argument. (The first is the establishment of the premise, "I exist.") The argument itself is a version of two arguments called "the cosmological argument" and "the ontological argument for God's existence." We will discuss them in detail in Chapter 5 ("Religion"), but the basic logic of both arguments is this: If a finite, dependent, and merely contingent being like myself can even think of an infinite, independent, and necessary being, then such a being must exist. The details of these arguments, however, are not so much the concern of epistemology or the theory of knowledge as they are of the special logical considerations necessary when talking about the Supreme Being. For now, therefore, let us simply grant Descartes his second step, with the promissory note that the proofs will be explained in the later chapter on the philosophy of religion. So, we have

I exist *(as a thinking thing). (premise)*
God exists *(because I could not exist without Him).*

Now we can say that, by His very nature (another intuition), God is good, in fact, perfectly good. So, as Descartes says in "Meditation VI,"

FROM **"MEDITATION VI"**
BY **DESCARTES**

Since He has given me a very strong inclination to believe that these ideas (of trees, houses, etc.) arise from corporeal objects, I do not see how he could be vindicated from the charge of deceit, if in truth they proceeded from any other source, or were produced by other causes than corporeal things? (For example, by the evil demon, or in dreams.)

Therefore,

We *cannot be deceived* [whether by the evil demon or whatever else].

. . . I cannot doubt but that there is in me a certain passive faculty of perception, that is, of receiving and taking knowledge of the ideas of sensible things; but this would be useless to me, if there did not also exist in me, or in some other thing, another active faculty capable of forming and producing those ideas. But this active faculty cannot be in me [in as far as I am but a thinking thing], seeing that it does not presuppose thought, and also that those ideas are frequently produced in my mind without my contributing to it in any way, and even frequently contrary to my will. This faculty must therefore exist in some substance different from me, in which all the objective reality of the ideas that are produced by this faculty is contained formally or eminently, as I before remarked: and this substance is either a body, that is to say, a corporeal nature in which is contained formally [and in effect] all that is objectively [and by representation] in those ideas; or it is God himself, or some other creature, of a rank superior to body, in which the same is contained eminently. But as God is no deceiver, it is manifest that he does not of himself and immediately communicate those ideas to me, nor even by the intervention of any creature in which their objective reality is not formally, but only eminently, contained. For as he has given me no faculty whereby I can discover this to be the case, but, on the contrary, a very strong inclination to believe that those ideas arise from corporeal objects, I do not see how he could be vindicated from the charge of deceit, if in truth they proceeded from any other source, or were produced by other causes than corporeal things: and accordingly it must be concluded, that corporeal objects exist. Nevertheless they are not perhaps exactly such as we perceive by the senses, for their comprehension by the senses is, in many instances, very obscure and confused; but it is at least necessary to admit that all which I clearly and distinctly conceive as in them, that is, generally speaking, all that is comprehended in the object of speculative geometry, really exists external to me.

The argument is not convincing, as Descartes' critics were quick to point out. Where does Descartes get his confidence in reason to begin with, such that he feels confident in his own abilities to prove God's existence? Descartes' answer is that we get that confidence from God Himself. But with this answer he has begged the question; that is, he has presumed the existence of God in order to get the confidence with which he then proves God's existence. (This circularity of argument is often called "the Cartesian Circle.") Another way of criticizing the same strategy is to say that, having once introduced the evil demon, Descartes has no way of getting rid of him, since that supposition undermines his confidence in his own reason just as thoroughly as his confidence in God bolsters it.

Our primary concern, however, is with Descartes' claim that certain beliefs are self-evident or "clear and distinct" on the basis of intuition and reason alone. These are beliefs that we don't have to learn—in fact, couldn't learn—from experience. It is not just Descartes' "I exist" premise that is such a belief; all of the rules of inference, which he uses in his arguments, are also beliefs of this kind. Ultimately, his confidence in reason itself is one, too. But how does one defend these beliefs, for not every philosopher agrees with them. In particular, John Locke, in his disillusionment with metaphysics, begins his philosophy with an assault on the very idea of knowledge that is independent of experience. Thus he begins with an attack on the heart of the rationalist methodology.

B. INNATE IDEAS CONCERNING HUMAN UNDERSTANDING: JOHN LOCKE

Regarding metaphysics, John Locke is reported to have commented to a friend, "you and I have had enough of this kind of fiddling." Against the sometimes fantastic claims of the metaphysicians, Locke sought a restoration of common sense.[6] Just as Aristotle had acted as a critic of Plato's extravagant two-worlds view, Locke acted as a corrective to the metaphysical enthusiasm of the medieval and modern worlds. He accepted Descartes' method of tentative skepticism, but he questioned his French predecessor's urge to metaphysics as well as his confidence in the insights of pure reason. He rejected the unsupportable "intuitions" that provided Descartes with his rules and his premises, and he turned instead to the data of experience as the ultimate source of all knowledge. He therefore rejected Descartes' exclusively deductive method and supplanted it with a method appropriate to generalizations from experience, or **induction.** In inductive reasoning, the conclusion always goes beyond the premises and therefore, unlike deductions, is always less certain than they are. (For example, from the observed fact that all the philosophy professors that you have met have been absent-minded [the premise] you conclude by **inductive generalization** that all philosophy professors are probably absent-minded.) Accordingly, Locke also modified Descartes' demand for "perfect certainty" and allowed for probability and "degrees of assent." But it must not be thought that Locke therefore rejected reason as such. He still accepted the certainty of mathematical reasoning and the validity of deductive inferences; but he also expanded the concept of rationality to include inductive reasoning and probability as well as deduction and certainty.

Locke's *Essay Concerning Human Understanding* (1689) is built on a single premise, namely, that all our knowledge comes from experience. This means, in his view, that there cannot possibly be ideas that are prior to experience, ideas that are "born into" us, as suggested so vividly by Plato. In other words, Locke refuses to accept the notion of innate ideas, by which he means not only those ideas that are literally "born into us" but all ideas that are derived without appeal to experience. This includes, in his opinion, Descartes' "clear and distinct ideas," Spinoza's "adequate ideas" and Leibniz's "truths of reason."

FROM *AN ESSAY CONCERNING
HUMAN UNDERSTANDING*
BY **JOHN LOCKE**

1. *The way shown how we come by any knowledge, sufficient to prove it not innate.*—It is an established opinion among some men, that there are in the understanding certain innate principles; some primary notions, κοιναί ἔννοιαι, characters, as it were, stamped upon the mind of man which the soul receives in its very first being, and brings into the world with it. It would be sufficient to convince unprejudiced readers of the falseness of this supposition, if I should only show (as I hope I shall in the following parts of this discourse) how men, barely by the use of their natural faculties, may attain to all

---

[6]British empiricism traditionally has considered itself the defender of "common sense" against the excesses of metaphysics. This was even true of Berkeley and Hume, who reached conclusions more outrageous than any metaphysician. It is also true of Bertrand Russell and G. E. Moore in the twentieth century.

the knowledge they have, without the help of any innate impressions, and may arrive at certainty, without any such original notions or principles. . . .

2. *General Assent the great Argument.*—There is nothing more commonly taken for granted, than that there are certain principles, both speculative and practical (for they speak of both), universally agreed upon by all mankind, which therefore, they argue, must needs be constant impressions which the souls of men receive in their first beings, and which they bring into the world with them, as necessarily and really as they do any of their inherent faculties.

3. *Universal Consent proves nothing innate.*—This argument, drawn from universal consent, has this misfortune in it, that if it were true in matter of fact that there were certain truths wherein all mankind agreed, it would not prove them innate, if there can be any other way shown how men may come to that universal agreement in the things they do consent in, which I presume may be done.

4. *"What is, is," and "it is impossible for the same Thing to be and not to be," not universally assented to.*—But, which is worse, this argument of universal consent, which is made use of to prove innate principles, seems to me a demonstration that there are none such; because there are none to which all mankind give an universal assent. I shall begin with the speculative, and instance in those magnified principles of demonstration, "Whatsoever is, is" and "It is impossible for the same thing to be, and not to be"; which, of all others, I think, have the most allowed title to innate. These have so settled a reputation of maxims universally received that it will no doubt be thought strange if anyone should seem to question it. But yet I take liberty to say that these propositions are so far from having an universal assent that there are a great part of mankind to whom they are not so much as known.

5. *Not on the Mind naturally imprinted, because not known to Children, Idiots, &c.*—For, first, it is evident that all children and idiots have not the least apprehension or thought of them; and the want of that is enough to destroy that universal assent which must needs be the necessary concomitant of all innate truths: it seeming to me near a contradiction to say that there are truths imprinted on the soul which it perceives or understands not; imprinting, if it signify anything, being nothing else but the making certain truths to be perceived. For to imprint anything on the mind without the mind's perceiving it, seems to me hardly intelligible. If therefore children and idiots have souls, have minds, with those impressions upon them, they must unavoidably perceive them, and necessarily know and assent to these truths; which since they do not, it is evident that there are no such impressions. For if they are not notions naturally imprinted, how can they be innate, and if they are notions imprinted, how can they be unknown? To say a notion is imprinted on the mind, and yet at the same time to say that the mind is ignorant of it, and never yet took notice of it, is to make this impression nothing. No proposition

No proposition can be said to be in the mind which it never yet knew, which it was never yet conscious of.

can be said to be in the mind which it never yet knew, which it was never yet conscious of.[7]

The argument is straightforward; there is, in fact, no universal agreement regarding supposedly "innate" principles, and even if there were, that would not prove their "innateness." Rather, he argues:

Let us suppose the mind to be, as we say, a blank tablet (*tabula rasa*) of white paper, void of all characters, without any ideas; how comes it to be furnished? Whence comes it by that vast store, which the busy and boundless fancy of man has painted on it with almost endless variety? Whence has it all the materials of reason and knowledge? To this I answer in one word, from *experience:* in that all our knowledge is founded, and from that it ultimately derives itself.

It is this premise that Locke is concerned to defend and use, and his attack on innate ideas is by way of introduction. But Locke fails to prove that the human mind does not have inborn potentials and limitations, and more importantly, he fails to recognize that inference from experience might itself require principles that are not drawn from experience. In fact, Leibniz, one of the chief targets of Locke's attack, was not long in providing what we might call "the rationalist's reply." Turning Locke against himself, Leibniz argued that, by his own principles, he could not attack the concept of innate ideas.

LEIBNIZ'S REBUTTAL
FROM *NEW ESSAYS*
ON THE HUMAN UNDERSTANDING
BY **GOTTFRIED WILHELM VON LEIBNIZ**

The question at issue is whether the soul in itself is entirely empty, like the tablet upon which nothing has yet been written (*tabula rasa*), as is the view of Aristotle and the author of the *Essay* (Locke), and whether all that is traced on it comes solely from the senses and from experience; or whether the soul contains originally the principles of various notions and doctrines which external objects merely awaken from time to time, as I believe, with Plato and even with the Schoolmen, and with all those who take in this sense the passage of St. Paul (Romans, 2:15) where he remarks that the law of God is written in the heart. . . . From this there arises another question, whether all truths depend on experience, that is to say, on induction and examples, or whether there are some that have

---

[7] John Locke, *An Essay Concerning Human Understanding,* A. C. Fraser (Oxford: Clarendon Press, 1894). All subsequent quotations from Locke are from this edition.

some other basis. For if some events can be foreseen before any trial has been made of them, it is clear that we must here contribute something of our own. The senses, although necessary for all our actual knowledge, are not sufficient to give us the whole of it, since the senses never give anything except examples, that is to say, particular or individual truths. All examples which confirm a general truth, however numerous they may be, are not enough to establish the universal necessity of this same truth; for it does not follow that what has happened will happen again in the same way.

. . . It would seem that necessary truths, such as are found in pure mathematics, and especially in arithmetic and in geometry, must have principles the proof of which does not depend on examples, nor, consequently, on the testimony of the senses, although without the senses it would never have occurred to us to think of them.This ought to be well recognised; Euclid has so well understood it that he often demonstrates by reason what is obvious enough through experience and by sensible images. Logic also, together with metaphysics and ethics, one of which forms natural theology and the other natural jurisprudence, are full of such truths; and consequently their proof can only come from internal principles, which are called innate. It is true that we must not imagine that these eternal laws of the reason can be read in the soul as in an open book, as the edict of the praetor can be read in his *album* without difficulty or research; but it is enough that they can be discovered in us by dint of attention, for which opportunities are given by the senses. The success of experiments serves also as confirmation of the reason, very much as proofs serve in arithmetic for better avoiding error of reckoning when the reasoning is long. . . .

It seems that our able author claims that there is nothing potential in us and nothing even of which we are not at any time actually conscious; but he cannot mean this strictly, or his opinion would be too paradoxical; for acquired habits and the contents of our memory are not always consciously perceived and do not even always come to our aid at need, although we often easily bring them back to mind on some slight occasion which makes us remember them, just as we need only the beginning of a song to remember the song. Also he modifies his assertion in other places by saying that there is nothing in us of which we have not been at least formerly conscious. But besides the fact that no one can be sure by reason alone how far our past apperceptions, which we may have forgotten, may have gone, especially in view of the Platonic doctrine of reminiscence, which, mythical as it is, is not, in part at least, incompatible with bare reason; in addition to this, I say, why is it necessary that everything should be acquired by us through the perceptions of external things, and that nothing can be unearthed in ourselves? Is our soul, then, such a blank that, besides the images borrowed from without, it is nothing? . . . there are a thousand indications that lead us to think that there are at every moment numberless perceptions in us, but without apperception and without reflections; that is to say, changes in the soul itself of which we are not conscious, because the impressions are either to slight and too numerous, or too even, so that they have nothing sufficient to distinguish them one from the other; but, joined to others, they do not fail to produce their effect and to make themselves felt at least confusedly in the mass.[8]

Locke himself did not continue the debate; he was already convinced of his position and had more urgent problems to worry about (the political chaos in London following the "Glorious Revolution" of 1688). But the debate continued in different forms. The rise of anthropology in the nineteenth century, with the discoveries of societies whose basic ideas were radically different from our own, seemed to support Locke's claim that no one will believe in innate universal principles if they "ever look beyond the smoke of their own chimneys." But in the nineteenth century a great many philosophers still argued for the existence of universal principles not learned through experience. (Immanuel Kant did this in a very powerful set of arguments that we will view in the next several chapters.) In the early twentieth century, opinion was in general accord with Locke, but recently it has taken another swing back to Leibniz, this time, ironically, supported by anthropology. A major movement in the social sciences, usually called structuralism (whose main proponent is Claude Lévi-Strauss in France), has argued that underneath the many superficial differences between very different societies there are certain basic "structures" that are universal and innate. In America, the notion of innate ideas has appeared once again in the work of the well-known linguist Noam Chomsky. According to Chomsky, certain capacities for language are built into us from birth, and this allows him to explain not only the similarities of human thinking (which was the view that Locke attacked) but also the enormous capacity for learning different languages quickly. (The average three-year-old learns a language in six months.) The Locke-Leibniz debate is still very much alive.

C. THE EMPIRICIST THEORY
OF KNOWLEDGE

The *tabula rasa* or "blank tablet" view of the mind is Locke's most famous epistemological concept. Leaving aside those special concerns that involve only "the relations between ideas" (as in mathematics, logic, and trivial conceptual truths such as "a horse is an animal"), all of our ideas are derived from experience. Epistemology (and philosophy in general) now became a kind of psychology (indeed, the two disciplines were not yet distinguished), a study of the history of our common experiences in order to discover where we get our ideas, particularly such ideas as substance, God, and our various conceptions of reality. In his theory, Locke uses three familiar terms: **sensation** (or what more modern empiricists call sense-data), **ideas** (not in the Platonic

---

[8] Gottfried W. von Leibniz, *New Essays on the Human Understanding,* trans. A. G. Langley (La Salle, IL: Open Court, 1949).

sense but simply "the immediate object of perception, thought, or understanding"), and **quality** (or what we have so far been calling property, for example, being red, being round, being heavy).

FROM THE *ESSAY*
BY **LOCKE**

1. Concerning the simple ideas of Sensation, it is to be considered—that whatsoever is so constituted in nature as to be able, by affecting our senses, to cause any perception in the mind, doth thereby produce in the understanding a simple idea; which, whatever be the external cause of it, when it comes to be taken notice of by our discerning faculty, it is by the mind looked on and considered there to be a real positive idea in the understanding, as much as any other whatsoever; though, perhaps, the cause of it be but a privation of the subject.

2. Thus the ideas of heat and cold, light and darkness, white and black, motion and rest, are equally clear and positive ideas in the mind; though perhaps, some of the causes which produce them are barely privations, in those subjects from whence our senses derive those ideas. These the understanding, in its view of them, considers all as distinct positive ideas, without taking notice of the causes that produce them: which is an inquiry not belonging to the idea, as it is in the understanding, but to the nature of the things existing without us. These are two very different things, and carefully to be distinguished; it being one thing to perceive and know the idea of white or black, and quite another to examine what kind of particles they must be, and how ranged in the superficies, to make any object appear white or black. . . .

7. To discover the nature of our *ideas* the better, and to discourse of them intelligibly, it will be convenient to distinguish them *as they are ideas or perceptions in our minds;* and *as they are modifications of matter in the bodies that cause such perceptions in us:* that so we may not think (as perhaps usually is done) that they are exactly the images and resemblances of something inherent in the subject; most of those of sensation being in the mind no more the likeness of something existing without us, than the names that stand for them are the likeness of our ideas, which yet upon hearing they are apt to excite in us.

8. Whatsoever the mind perceives *in itself,* or is the immediate object of perception, thought, or understanding, that I call *idea;* and the power to produce any idea in our mind, I call *quality* of the subject wherein that power is. Thus a snowball having the power to produce in us the ideas of white, cold, and round—the power to produce those ideas in us, as they are in the snowball, I call qualities; and as they are sensations or perceptions in our understanding, I call them ideas; which *ideas,* if I speak of sometimes as in the things themselves, I should be understood to mean those qualities in the objects which produce them in us.

Notice that the basis of Locke's theory is the "commonsense" distinction between physical objects in the world and sensations and ideas in our minds. Accordingly, we may talk of the qualities or properties inherent in the objects in the world, such as size and shape, and the qualities or properties they merely appear to have, such as color or texture, but they do not exist independently of the objects' effects on our sense organs. Locke refers to those properties of the objects themselves as **primary qualities;** he calls those "properties" of the objects, which we merely see them as having, **secondary qualities.**

PRIMARY QUALITIES:

Qualities thus considered in bodies are, *First,* such as are utterly inseparable from the body, in what state soever it be; and such as in all the alterations and changes it suffers, all the force can be used upon it, it constantly keeps; and such as sense constantly finds in every particle of matter which has bulk enough to be perceived; and the mind finds inseparable from every particle of matter, though less than to make itself singly be perceived by our senses: e.g. Take a grain of wheat, divide it into two parts; each part has still solidity, extension, figure, and mobility: divide it again, and it retains still the same qualities; and so divide it on, till the parts become insensible; they must retain still each of them all those qualities. For division (which is all that a mill, or pestle, or any other body, does upon another, in reducing it to insensible parts) can never take away either solidity, extension, figure, or mobility from any body, but only makes two or more distinct separate masses of matter, of that which was but one before; all which distinct masses, reckoned as so many distinct bodies; after division, make a certain number. These I call *original* or *primary qualities* of body, which I think we may observe to produce simple ideas in us, viz. solidity, extension, figure, motion or rest, and number.

◆◆◆

SECONDARY QUALITIES:

Secondly, such qualities which in truth are nothing in the objects themselves but powers to produce various sensations in us by their primary qualities, i.e., by the bulk, figure, texture, and motion of their insensible parts, as colours, sounds, tastes, &c. These I call *secondary qualities.* To these might be added a *third* sort, which are allowed to be barely powers; though they are as much real qualities in the subject as those which I, to comply with the common way of speaking, call qualities, but for distinction, secondary qualities. For the power in fire to produce a new colour, or consistency, in *wax* or *clay*—by its primary qualities, is as much a quality in fire, as the power it has to produce in *me* a new idea or sensation of warmth or burning, which I felt not before—by the same primary qualities, viz. the bulk, texture, and motion of its insensible parts.

The question, then, is how physical objects cause us to have sensations and ideas. Locke's answer (which, like his theory as a whole, is very strongly influenced by the physical theories of his contemporary Isaac Newton) is, by impulse. This might not seem illuminating until you try to think of the Newtonian theory of force as a product of particles and masses in motion. It is on this model that Locke develops what is now called his "Causal Theory of Perception." First, for the primary qualities:

> If then external objects be not united to our minds when they produce ideas therein; and yet we perceive these *original* qualities in such of them as singly fall under our senses, it is evident that some motion must be thence continued by our nerves, or animal spirits, by some parts of our bodies, to the brains or the seat of sensation, there to produce in our minds the particular ideas we have of them. And since the extension, figure, number, and motion of bodies of an observable bigness, may be perceived at a distance by the sight, it is evident some singly imperceptible bodies must come from them to the eyes, and thereby convey to the brain some motion; which produces these ideas which we have of them in us.

Then, for secondary qualities:

> After the same manner that the ideas of these original qualities are produced in us, we may conceive that the ideas of *secondary* qualities are also produced, viz. by the operation of insensible particles on our senses. For, it being manifest that there are bodies and good store of bodies, each whereof are so small, that we cannot by any of our senses discover either their bulk, figure, or motion—as is evident in those particles of the air and water, and others extremely smaller and those; perhaps as much smaller than the particles of air and water, as the particles of air and water are smaller than peas or hail-stones;—let us suppose at present that the different motions and figures, bulk and number, of such particles, affecting the several organs of our senses, produce in us those different sensations which we have from the colours and smells of bodies; e.g. that a violet, by the impulse of such insensible particles of matter, of peculiar figures and bulks, and in different degrees and modifications of their motions, causes the ideas of the blue colour, and sweet scent of that flower to be produced in our minds. It being no more impossible to conceive that God should annex such ideas to such motions, with which they have no similitude, than that he should annex the idea of pain to the motion of a piece of steel dividing our flesh, with which that idea hath no resemblance.
>
> What I have said concerning colours and smells may be understood also of tastes and sounds, and other the like sensible qualities; which, whatever reality we by mistake attribute to them, are in truth nothing in the objects themselves, but powers to produce various sensations in us; and depend on those primary qualities, viz. bulk, figure, texture, and motion of parts [as I have said].

Therefore,

> I think it easy to draw this observation—that the ideas of primary qualities of bodies are resemblances of them, and their patterns do really exist in the bodies themselves, but the ideas produced in us by these secondary qualities have no

. . . the ideas of primary qualities of bodies are resemblances of them, and their patterns do really exist in the bodies themselves, but the ideas produced in us by these secondary qualities have no resemblance of them at all.

resemblance of them at all. There is nothing like our ideas, existing in the bodies themselves. They are, in the bodies we denominate from them, only a power to produce those sensations in us: and what is sweet, blue, or warm in idea, is but the certain bulk, figure, and motion of the insensible parts, in the bodies themselves, which we call so.

Flame is denominated hot and light; snow, white and cold; and manna, white and sweet, from the ideas they produce in us. Which qualities are commonly thought to be the same in those bodies that those ideas are in us, the one the perfect resemblance of the other, as they are in a mirror, and it would by most men be judged very extravagant if one should say otherwise. And yet he that will consider that the same fire that, at one distance produces in us the sensation of warmth, does, at a nearer approach, produce in us the far different sensation of pain, ought to bethink himself what reason he has to say—that this idea of warmth, which was produced in him by fire, is *actually in the fire;* and his idea of pain, which the same fire produced in him the same way, is *not* in the fire. Why are whiteness and coldness in snow, and pain not, when it produces the one and the other idea in us; and can do neither, but by the bulk, figure, number, and motion of its solid parts?

The particular bulk, number, figure, and motion of the parts of fire or snow are really in them—whether any one's senses perceive them or no: and therefore they may be called *real* qualities, because they really exist in those bodies. But light, heat, whiteness, or coldness, are no more really in them than sickness or pain is in manna. Take away the sensation of them; let not the eyes see light or colours, nor the ears hear sounds; let the palate not taste, nor the nose smell, and all colours, tastes, odours, and sounds, *as they are such particular ideas,* vanish and cease, and are reduced to their causes, i.e., bulk, figure, and motion of parts.

This is the basic empiricist theory as Locke presented it. The logical consequences of empiricism, as we shall see when we study Berkeley and Hume, are not nearly so palatable. But how does the "causal theory of perception" allow Locke to approach the traditional questions of metaphysics? Significantly, the first two steps in the argument are identical with those we traced in Descartes—one's own existence and the existence of God—and Locke even includes the problematic notion of "intuition."

1. The knowledge of our own being we have by intuition. The existence of God, reason clearly makes known to us.

But then, the strict empiricist reemerges and insists:

The knowledge of the existence of *any other thing* we can have only by *sensation:* for there being no necessary connexion of real existence with any *idea* a man hath in his memory; nor of any other existence but that of God with the existence of any particular man: no particular man can know the existence of any other being, but only when, by actual operating upon him, it makes itself perceived by him. For, the having the idea of anything in our mind, no more proves the existence of that thing, than the picture of a man evidences his being in the world, or the visions of a dream make thereby a true history.

2. It is therefore the *actual receiving* of ideas from without that gives us notice of the existence of other things, and makes us know, that something doth exist at that time without us, which causes that idea in us; though perhaps we neither know nor consider how it does it. For it takes not from the certainty of our senses, and the ideas we receive by them, that we know not the manner wherein they are produced: e.g. whilst I write this, I have, by the paper affecting my eyes, that idea produced in my mind, which, whatever object causes, I call *white;* by which I know that that quality or accident (i.e. whose appearance before my eyes always causes that idea) doth really exist, and hath a being without me. And of this, the greatest assurance I can possibly have, and to which my faculties can attain, is the testimony of my eyes, which are the proper and sole judges of this thing; whose testimony I have reason to rely on as so certain, that I can no more doubt, whilst I write this, that I see white and black, and that something really exists that causes that sensation in me, than that I write or move my hand; which is a certainty as great as human nature is capable of, concerning the existence of anything, but a man's self alone, and of God.

Here Locke asserts his alternative to the strict Cartesian limitation of knowledge to matters of certainty and deduction:

3. The notice we have by our senses of the existing of things without us, though it be not altogether so certain as our intuitive knowledge, or the deductions of our reason employed about the clear abstract ideas of our own minds; yet it is an assurance that deserves the name of *knowledge.* If we persuade ourselves that our faculties act and inform us right concerning the existence of those objects that affect them, it cannot pass for an ill-grounded confidence: for I think nobody can, in earnest, be so sceptical as to be uncertain of the existence of those things which he sees and feels. At least, he that can doubt so far, (whatever he may have with his own thoughts,) will never have any controversy with me; since he can never be sure I say anything contrary to his own opinion. As to myself, I think God has given me assurance enough of the existence of things without me: since, by their different application, I can produce in myself both pleasure and pain, which is one great concernment of my present state. This is certain: the confidence that our faculties do not herein deceive us, is the greatest assurance we are capable of concerning the

existence of material beings. For we cannot act anything but by our faculties; nor talk of knowledge itself, but by the help of those faculties which are fitted to apprehend even what knowledge is.

Locke then answers Descartes:

8. But yet, if after all this any one will be so sceptical as to distrust his senses, and to affirm all that we see and hear, feel and taste, think and do, during our whole being, is but the series and deluding appearance of a long dream, whereof there is no reality; and therefore will question the existence of all things, or our knowledge of anything: I must desire him to consider, that, if all be a dream, then he doth but dream that he makes the question, and so it is not much matter that a waking man should answer him. But yet, if he pleases, he may dream that I make him this answer, that the certainty of things existing in *rerum natura* when we have the testimony of our senses for it is not only as great as our frame can attain to, but as our condition needs. For, our faculties being suited not to the full extent of being, nor to a perfect, clear, comprehensive knowledge of things free from all doubt and scruple; but to the preservation of us, in whom they are; and accommodated to the use of life: they serve to our purpose well enough, if they will but give us certain notice of those things, which are convenient or inconvenient to us. For he that sees a candle burning, and hath experimented the force of its flame by putting his finger in it, will little doubt that this is something existing without him, which does him harm, and puts him to great pain: which is assurance enough, when no man requires greater certainty to govern his actions by than what is as certain as his actions themselves. And if our dreamer pleases to try whether the glowing heat of a glass furnace be barely a wandering imagination in a drowsy man's fancy, by putting his hand into it, he may perhaps be wakened into a certainty greater than he could wish, that it is something more than bare imagination. So that this evidence is as great as we can desire, being as certain to us as our pleasure or pain, i.e., happiness or misery; beyond which we have no concernment, either of knowing or being. Such an assurance of the existence of things without us is sufficient to direct us in the attaining the good and avoiding the evil which is caused by them, which is the important concernment we have of being made acquainted with them.

9. In summary, then, when our senses do actually convey into our understanding any idea, we cannot but be satisfied that there doth something *at that time* really exist without us, which doth affect our senses, and by them give notice of itself to our apprehensive faculties, and actually produce that idea which we then perceive.

We are now ready to return to the traditional metaphysical notion of substance—that which underlies both the primary and the secondary qualities of a thing.

1. *Ideas of Substances, how made.*—The mind being, as I have declared, furnished with a great number of the simple ideas conveyed in by the senses, as

they are found in exterior things, or by reflection on its own operations, takes notice, also, that a certain number of these simple ideas go constantly together; which being presumed to belong to one thing, and words being suited to common apprehensions, and made use of for quick dispatch, are called, so united in one subject, by one name; which, by inadvertency, we are apt afterward to talk of and consider as one simple idea, which indeed is a complication of many ideas together: because, as I have said, not imagining how these simple ideas can subsist by themselves, we accustom ourselves to suppose some substratum wherein they do subsist, and from which they do result; which therefore we call "substance."

2. *Our Ideas of Substance in general.*—So that if anyone will examine himself concerning his notion of pure substance in general, he will find he has no other idea of it at all, but only a supposition of he knows not what support of such qualities which are capable of producing simple ideas in us; which qualities are commonly called "accidents." If anyone should be asked, "What is the subject wherein colour or weight inheres?" he would have nothing to say but, "The solid extended parts." And if he were demanded, "what is it that solidity and extension inhere in?" he would not be in a much better case than the Indian . . . who, saying that the world was supported by a great elephant, was asked what the elephant rested on? to which his answer was, "a great tortoise"; but being again pressed to know what gave support to the broad-backed tortoise, replied—something, he knew not what. And thus here, as in all other cases where we use words without having clear and distinct ideas, we talk like children, who, being questioned what such a thing is which they know not, readily give this satisfactory answer, that it is something, which in truth signifies no more, when so used, either by children or men, but that they know not what; and that the thing they pretend to know and talk of is what they have no distinct idea of at all, and so are perfectly ignorant of it, and in the dark. The idea, then, we have, to which we give the general name "substance" being nothing but the supposed, but unknown, support of those qualities we find existing, which we imagine cannot subsist *sine re substante,* "without something to support them," we call that support *substantia;* which, according to the true import of the word, is, in plain English, "standing under," or "upholding."

♦♦♦

Hence, when we talk or think of any particular sort of corporeal substances, as horse, stone, &c., though the idea we have of either of them be but the complication or collection of those several simple ideas of sensible qualities which we used to find united in the thing called "horse" or "stone"; yet because we cannot conceive how they should subsist alone, nor one in another, we suppose them existing in, and supported by some common subject; which support we denote by the name "substance," though it be certain we have no clear or distinct idea of that thing we suppose a support.

Substance is "we know not what." Yet Locke hesitates to reject the notions, for he cannot escape the suspicion that talk of "qualities" makes no sense unless the qualities are the qualities of something. But this suspicion is dispensable according to Locke's own principles. So, it turns out, is his central distinction between primary and secondary qualities, as Bishop Berkeley is soon to point out. The consequence of these simple, technical moves will be shocking, to say the least.

D. COMMON SENSE UNDONE: BISHOP BERKELEY

Beginning from John Locke's "commonsense" philosophy, Bishop Berkeley developed the most provocative thesis in all philosophy. Berkeley's thesis is called **subjective idealism**. It is the doctrine that there are no material substances, no physical objects, only minds and ideas in mind. (His concept of "idea" comes directly from Locke.) This surprising position emerges directly from Locke's thesis by three simple steps. First, it accepts the argument that we have no idea whatsoever what a substance might be, and it agrees that all that we can ever know of a thing are its sensible properties (or "qualities"). Second, it is shown that the distinction between primary and secondary qualities cannot be, as Locke had argued, a distinction between properties inherent in the objects themselves as opposed to properties that the objects simply cause in us. Third, once one has agreed that all knowledge of the world (except for knowledge of one's own existence and of God) must be based upon experience, the question becomes why we should ever think that there is anything other than our experiences. Locke had argued that our experiences were caused by the physical objects; but how could this claim be justified by experience? Since we have no experience of either the objects themselves or their causation, but only of their effects (that is, the ideas they cause in us), a consistent empiricist must give up not only the causal theory of perception but the notion of physical objects as well.

Berkeley is an exceptionally clear writer, and the following excerpts from his *Treatise Concerning the Principles of Human Knowledge* (1710) should not be difficult to understand:

FROM THE ***TREATISE CONCERNING***
THE PRINCIPLES
OF HUMAN KNOWLEDGE
BY **BISHOP GEORGE BERKELEY**

1. It is evident to anyone who takes a survey of the objects of human knowledge, that they are either ideas (1) actually imprinted on the senses, or else such as are (2) perceived by attending to the passions and operations of the mind, or lastly (3) ideas formed by help of memory and imagination, either compounding, dividing, or barely representing those originally perceived in the aforesaid ways. By sight I have the ideas of lights and colors, with their several degrees and variations. By touch I perceive hard and soft, heat and

cold, motion and resistance, and of all these more and less either as to quantity or degree. Smelling furnishes me with odors, the palate with tastes, and hearing conveys sounds to the mind in all their variety of tone and composition. And as several of these are observed to accompany each other, they come to be marked by one name, and so to be reputed as one thing. Thus, for example, a certain color, taste, smell, figure, and consistence, having been observed to go together, are accounted one distinct thing, signified by the name "apple." Other collections of ideas constitute a stone, a tree, a book, and the like sensible things; which, as they are pleasing or disagreeable, excite the passions of love, hatred, joy, grief, and so forth.

2. But besides all that endless variety of ideas or objects of knowledge, there is likewise something which knows or perceives them, and exercises divers operations, as willing, imagining, remembering, about them. This perceiving, active being is what I call *mind, spirit, soul,* or *myself.* By which words I do not denote any one of my ideas, but a thing entirely distinct from them wherein they exist, or, which is the same thing, whereby they are perceived, for the existence of an idea consists in being perceived.

3. That neither our thoughts, nor passions, nor ideas formed by the imagination, exist without the mind, is what everybody will allow. And it seems no less evident that the various sensations or ideas imprinted on the sense, however blended or combined together (that is, whatever objects they compose), cannot exist otherwise than in a mind perceiving them. I think an intuitive knowledge may be obtained of this by anyone that shall attend to what is meant by the term "exist" when applied to sensible things. The table I write on I say exists—that is, I see and feel it; and if I were out of my study I should say it existed— meaning thereby that if I was in my study I might perceive it, or that some other spirit actually does perceive it. There was an odor, that is, it was smelt; that was a sound, that is, it was heard; a color or figure, and it was perceived by sight or touch. This is all that I can understand by these and the like expressions. For as to what is said of the absolute existence of unthinking things without any relation to their being perceived, that seems perfectly unintelligible. Their *esse* is *percipi,*[9] nor is it possible they should have any existence out of the minds or thinking things which perceive them.

> *There was an odor, that is, it was smelt; that was a sound, that is, it was heard; a color or figure, and it was perceived by sight or touch. . . . Their* esse *is* percipi.

4. It is indeed an opinion strangely prevailing amongst men, that houses, mountains, rivers, and in a word all sensible objects, have an existence, natural or real, distinct from their being perceived by the understanding. But with how

---

[9] *To be* is *to be perceived.*

great an assurance and acquiescence so ever this principle may be entertained in the world, yet whoever shall find in his heart to call it in question may, if I mistake not, perceive it to involve a manifest contradiction. For what are the forementioned objects but the things we perceive by sense? And what do we perceive *besides our own ideas or sensations?* And is it not plainly repugnant that any one of these, or any combination of them, should exist unperceived?

This is Berkeley's central thesis—that "to be is to be perceived" (*esse est percipi*). In what follows, Berkeley argues that there is nothing other than these perceptions, or "ideas," and it is nonsense to suppose that there are things outside of the mind "like" our ideas—for "nothing is like an idea but another idea."

6. Some truths there are so near and obvious to the mind that a man need only open his eyes to see them. Such I take this important one to be, to wit, that all the choir of heaven and furniture of the earth, in a word all those bodies which compose the mighty frame of the world, have not any subsistence without a mind, that their *being* is to be perceived or known; that consequently so long as they are not actually perceived by me, or do not exist in my mind or that of any other created spirit, they must either have no existence at all, or else subsist in the mind of some Eternal Spirit; it being perfectly unintelligible, and involving all the absurdity of abstraction, to attribute to any single part of them an existence independent of a spirit. To be convinced of which, the reader need only reflect and try to separate in his own thoughts the *being* of a sensible thing from its *being perceived.*

7. From what has been said it follows there is not any other substance than *spirit,* or that which perceives. But for the fuller proof of this point, let it be considered the sensible qualities are color, figure, motion, smell, taste, etc.—that is, the ideas perceived by sense. Now, for an idea to exist in an unperceiving thing is a manifest contradiction, for to have an idea is all one as to perceive; that therefore wherein color, figure, and the like qualities exist must perceive them; hence it is clear there can be no unthinking substance or *substratum* of those ideas.

8. But, say you, though the ideas themselves do not exist without the mind, yet there may be things *like* them, whereof they are copies or resemblances, which things exist without the mind in an unthinking substance. I answer, an idea can be like nothing but an idea; a color or figure can be like nothing but another color or figure. If we look but never so little into our thoughts, we shall find it impossible for us to conceive a likeness except only between our ideas. Again, I ask whether those supposed originals or external things, of which our ideas are the pictures or representations, be themselves perceivable or no? If they are, then they are ideas and we have gained our point; but if you say they are not, I appeal to anyone whether it be sense to assert a color is like something which is invisible, hard or soft, like something which is intangible; and so of the rest.

At this point Berkeley takes up Locke's distinction between "primary and secondary qualities," and maintains that the arguments Locke put forward regarding the latter also can be applied to the former. Primary qualities too can be ideas only, and not properties of matter.

9. Some there are who make a distinction betwixt *primary* and *secondary* qualities. By the former they mean extension, figure, motion, rest, solidity or impenetrability, and number; by the latter they denote all other sensible qualities, as colors, sounds, tastes, and so forth. The ideas we have of these they acknowledge not to be the resemblances of anything existing without the mind, or unperceived, but they will have our ideas of the primary qualities to be patterns or images of things which exist without the mind, in an unthinking substance which they call *matter*. By *matter*, therefore, we are to understand an inert, senseless substance, in which extension, figure, and motion do actually subsist. But it is evident from what we have already shown, that extension, figure, and motion are only ideas existing in the mind, and that an idea can be like nothing but another idea, and that consequently neither they nor their archetypes can exist in an unperceiving substance. Hence, it is plain that the very notion of what is called *matter*, or *corporeal substance*, involves a contradiction in it.

10. They who assert that figure, motion, and the rest of the primary or original qualities do exist without the mind in unthinking substances, do at the same time acknowledge that color, sounds, heat, cold, and suchlike secondary qualities, do not; which they tell us are sensations existing in the mind alone, that depend on and are occasioned by the different size, texture, and motion of the minute particles of matter. This they take for an undoubted truth, which they can demonstrate beyond all exception. Now, if it be certain that those original qualities are inseparably united with the other sensible qualities, and not, even in thought, capable of being abstracted from them, it plainly follows that they exist only in the mind. But I desire anyone to reflect and try whether he can, by any abstraction of thought, conceive the extension and motion of a body without all possible sensible qualities. For my own part, I see evidently that it is not in my power to frame an idea of a body extended and moving, but I must withal give it some color or other sensible quality which is acknowledged to exist only in the mind. In short, extension, figure, and motion, abstracted from all other qualities, are inconceivable. Where therefore the other sensible qualities are, there must be these also, to wit, in the mind and nowhere else. . . .

14. I shall farther add that, after the same manner as modern philosophers prove certain sensible qualities to have no existence in matter, or without the mind, the same thing may be likewise proved of all other sensible qualities whatsoever. Thus, for instance, it is said that heat and cold are affections only of the mind, and not at all patterns of real beings, existing in the corporeal substances which excite them, for that the same body which appears cold to one

hand seems warm to another. Now, why may we not as well argue that figure and extension are not patterns or resemblances of qualities existing in matter, because to the same eye at different stations, or eyes of a different texture at the same station, they appear various, and cannot therefore be the images of anything settled and determinate without the mind? Again, it is proved that sweetness is not really in the sapid thing, because the thing remaining unaltered the sweetness is changed into bitter, as in case of a fever or otherwise vitiated palate. Is it not as reasonable to say that motion is not without the mind, since if the succession of ideas in the mind become swifter, the motion, it is acknowledged, shall appear slower without any alteration in any external object?

15. In short, let anyone consider those arguments which are thought manifestly to prove that colors and taste exist only in the mind, and he shall find they may with equal force be brought to prove the same thing of extension, figure, and motion—though it must be confessed this method of arguing does not so much prove that there is no extension or color in an outward object, as that we do not know by sense which is the true extension or color of the object. But the arguments foregoing plainly show it to be impossible that any color or extension at all, or other sensible quality whatsoever, should exist in an unthinking subject without the mind, or in truth, that there should be any such thing as an outward object.

Must there be substances apart from the mind? Berkeley asks. It is true that we are somehow "affected," but it does not follow that there must be material objects. How would we know of any such objects?

18. But though it were possible that solid, figured, movable substances may exist without the mind, corresponding to the ideas we have of bodies, yet how is it possible for us to know this? Either we must know it by sense or by reason. As for our senses, by them we have the knowledge only of our sensations, ideas, or those things that are immediately perceived by sense, call them what you will; but they do not inform us that things exist without the mind, or unperceived, like to those which are perceived. This the materialists [10] themselves acknowledge. It remains therefore that if we have any knowledge at all of external things, it must be by reason, inferring their existence from what is immediately perceived by sense. But what reason can induce us to believe the existence of bodies without the mind, from what we perceive, since the very patrons of matter themselves do not pretend there is any necessary connection betwixt them and our ideas? I say it is granted on all hands (and what happens in dreams, frenzies, and the like, puts it beyond

---

[10] Berkeley uses "materialists" to refer to those who believe in the existence of matter, not to those who believe in only matter, its usual meaning.

dispute) that *it is possible we might be affected with all the ideas we have now, though there were no bodies existing without, resembling them.* Hence, it is evident the supposition of external bodies is not necessary for the producing our ideas; since it is granted they are produced sometimes, and might possibly be produced always in the same order we see them in at present, without their concurrence.

19. But, though we might possibly have all our sensations without them, yet perhaps it may be thought easier to conceive and explain the manner of their production by supposing external bodies in their likeness rather than otherwise; and so it might be at least probable there are such things as bodies that excite their ideas in our minds. But neither can this be said; for though we give the materialists their external bodies, they by their own confession are never the nearer knowing how our ideas are produced, since they own themselves unable to comprehend in what manner body can act upon spirit, or how it is possible it should imprint any idea in the mind. Hence it is evident the production of ideas or sensations in our minds can be no reason why we should suppose matter or corporeal substances, since that is acknowledged to remain equally inexplicable with or without this supposition. If therefore it were possible for bodies to exist without the mind, yet to hold they do so, must needs be a very precarious opinion; since it is to suppose, without any reason at all, that God has created innumerable things that are entirely useless, and serve to no manner of purpose.

20. In short, if there were external bodies, it is impossible we should ever come to know it; and if there were not, we might have the very same reasons to think there were that we have now. Suppose (what no one can deny possible) an intelligence without the help of external bodies, to be affected with the same train of sensations or ideas that you are, imprinted in the same order and with like vividness in his mind. I ask whether that intelligence hath not all the reason to believe the existence of corporeal substances, represented by his ideas, and exciting them in his mind, that you can possibly have for believing the same thing? Of this there can be no question; which one consideration were enough to make any reasonable person suspect the strength of whatever argument he may think himself to have for the existence of bodies without the mind. . . .

23. But, say you, surely there is nothing easier than for me to imagine trees, for instance, in a park, or books existing in a closet, and nobody by to perceive them. I answer, you may so, there is no difficulty in it; but what is all this, I beseech you, more than framing in your mind certain ideas which you call books and trees, and the same time omitting to frame the idea of anyone that may perceive them? But do not you yourself perceive or think of them all the while? This therefore is nothing to the purpose; it only shews you have the power of imagining or forming ideas in your mind: but it doth not shew that you can conceive it possible the objects of your thought may exist without the mind. To make out this, it is necessary that you conceive them existing

unconceived or unthought of, which is a manifest repugnancy. When we do our utmost to conceive the existence of external bodies, we are all the while only contemplating our own ideas.[11]

But what, then, can explain the fact that we cannot simply "think" things into existence by imagining them? And how can we say that a thing exists when no one is there to perceive it? ("If a tree falls in the forest, and there's no one there to hear it, does it make a sound?") It is here that God enters the picture as a matter of necessity.

> *But, whatever power I may have over my own thoughts, I find the ideas actually perceived by Sense . . . are not creatures of my will. There is therefore some* other *Will or Spirit that produces them.*

29. But, whatever power I may have over my own thoughts, I find the ideas actually perceived by Sense have not a like dependence on my will. When in broad daylight I open my eyes, it is not in my power to choose whether I shall see or no, or to determine what particular objects shall present themselves to my view; and so likewise as to the hearing and other senses, the ideas imprinted on them are not creatures of my will. There is therefore some *other* Will or Spirit that produces them.

30. The ideas of Sense are more strong, lively, and distinct than those of the Imagination; they have likewise a steadiness, order, and coherence, and are not excited at random, as those which are the effects of human wills often are, but in a regular train or series—the admirable connexion whereof sufficiently testifies the wisdom and benevolence of its Author. Now the set rules or established methods wherein the Mind we depend on excites in us the ideas of sense, are called the *laws of nature;* and these we learn by experience, which teaches us that such and such ideas are attended with such and such other ideas, in the ordinary course of things.

31. This gives us a sort of foresight which enables us to regulate our actions for the benefit of life. And without this we should be eternally at a loss; we could not know how to act anything that might procure us the least pleasure, or remove the least pain of sense. That food nourishes, sleep refreshes, and fire warms us; that to sow in the seedtime is the way to reap in the harvest; and in general that to obtain such or such ends, such or such means are conducive—all this we know, not by discovering any *necessary connexion* between our ideas, but only by the *observation* of the settled laws of nature, without which we should be all in uncertainty and confusion, and a grown

---

[11] George Berkeley, *Treatise Concerning the Principles of Human Knowledge* (New York: Bobbs-Merrill, 1957).

man no more know how to manage himself in the affairs of life than an infant just born. . . .

33. The ideas imprinted on the senses by the Author of nature are called *real things;* and those excited in the imagination being less regular, vivid, and constant, are more properly termed *ideas,* or *images* of *things,* which they copy and represent. But then our sensations, be they never so vivid and distinct, are nevertheless ideas, that is, they exist in the mind, or are perceived by it, as truly as the ideas of its own framing. The ideas of sense are allowed to have more reality in them, that is, to be more strong, orderly, and coherent than the creatures of the mind; but this is no argument that they exist without the mind. They are also less dependent on the spirit, or thinking substance which perceives them, in that they are excited by the will of another and more powerful spirit; yet still they are *ideas,* and certainly no idea, whether faint or strong, can exist otherwise than in a mind perceiving it.[12]

There was a young man who said, "God
Must think it exceedingly odd
   If he finds that this tree
   Continues to be
When there's no one about in the Quad."

         REPLY
Dear Sir:
   Your astonishment's odd:
I am always about in the Quad.
   And that's why the tree
   Will continue to be,
Since observed by
   Yours faithfully,
       GOD.

Finally, the defense against common sense:

38. But after all, say you, it sounds very harsh to say we eat and drink ideas, and are clothed with ideas. I acknowledge it does so; the word "idea" not being used in common discourse to signify the several combinations of sensible qualities which are called "things"; and it is certain that any expression which varies from the familiar use of language will seem harsh and ridiculous. But this doth not concern the truth of the proposition, which in other words is no more than to say, we are fed and clothed with those things which we perceive immediately by our senses.

39. If it be demanded why I make use of the word "idea," and do not rather in compliance with custom call them "thing"; I answer, I do it for two

---

[12] This final formulation, that the things of the world are nothing other than ideas in the mind of God, is the subject of a limerick by Ronald Knox, quoted for us by Bertrand Russell.

reasons—first, because the term "thing" in contradistinction to "idea," is generally supposed to denote somewhat existing without the mind; secondly, because "thing" hath a more comprehensive signification than "idea," including spirit or thinking things as well as ideas. Since therefore the objects of sense exist only in the mind, and are withal thoughtless and inactive, I chose to mark them by the word "idea," which implies those properties.[13]

Is this where Locke was leading us? If so, it looks as if the "new metaphysics" is every bit as fantastic as the old ones. But the controversial development of Locke's empiricism has still another step to go.

E. THE CONGENIAL SKEPTIC: DAVID HUME

It isn't very far from Berkeley's subjective idealism to David Hume's outrageous, but seemingly irrefutable, skepticism. Russell, writing about Hume two hundred years later (1945), says,

> To refute him has been, ever since he wrote, a favorite pastime among metaphysicians. For my part, I find none of their refutations convincing; nevertheless, I cannot but hope that something less skeptical than Hume's system may be discoverable.

And

> Hume's skeptical conclusions . . . are equally difficult to refute and to accept. The result was a challenge to philosophers, which, in my opinion, has still not been adequately met.[14]

There have been philosophers who have said—or feared—that Hume's skepticism is the last word in philosophy. In any case, it is one of those positions that no philosophy student can avoid taking seriously.

Hume's *Treatise of Human Nature* (1739) was written when he was in his early twenties; his ambition was no less than to be the Isaac Newton of philosophy and psychology, following but outdoing John Locke. The book failed to attract much attention (he said "it fell stillborn from the press"), and Hume turned his attention to other matters, making himself famous as a historian. Later, in 1748, he wrote a more popular version of his earlier *Treatise,* which he called *An Enquiry Concerning Human Understanding.* It was extremely successful, and Hume became widely known as a "devil's advocate" during his lifetime, a position he generally enjoyed. Both the

---

[13] Berkeley, *Treatise Concerning the Principles of Human Knowledge.*

[14] Bertrand Russell, *A History of Western Philosophy* (New York: Simon and Schuster, 1945)

Treatise and the *Enquiry* are firmly committed to Locke's empiricist methodology, but where Locke was generous with doubtful ideas with no clear experiential basis (notably, substance and God), Hume was ruthless. In a famous threatening passage, he bellowed

> *When we run over libraries, persuaded of these [empiricist] principles, what havoc must we make? If we take in our hand any volume of divinity or school metaphysics, for instance, let us ask, Does it contain any abstract reasoning concerning quantity or number? No. Does it contain any experimental reasoning concerning matter of fact and existence? No, Commit it to the flames, for it can contain nothing but sophistry and illusion.*[15]

In this unveiled threat to traditional metaphysics we can see in a glance Hume's formidable tactics—the insistence that every justifiable belief must be either a "relation of ideas," for example, a statement of mathematics, logic, or a trivial conceptual truth, or a "matter of fact," which can be confirmed by appeal to our experience. (This "either-or" is sometimes called "Hume's fork.") Of course, most of the modern philosophers we have discussed shared this insistence upon justifiability either by reason ("relation of ideas") or by experience. But it is only Hume who realizes the severity of this demand and the embarrassing number of our fundamental beliefs that do not allow justification either by reason or experience.

Like his empiricist predecessor, Hume insists that all knowledge begins with basic units of sensory experience. Hume's "impressions" (Locke's "sensations") are these basic units (what we would still call "sensations" or "sense-data").

FROM *A TREATISE*
OF HUMAN NATURE
BY **DAVID HUME**

All the perceptions of the human mind resolve themselves into two distinct kinds, which I shall call *impressions* and *ideas*. The difference betwixt these consists in the degrees of force and liveliness with which they strike upon the mind, and make their way into our thought or consciousness. Those perceptions, which enter with most force and violence, we may name *impressions;* and under this name I comprehend all our sensations, passions and emotions, as they make their first appearance in the soul. By *ideas* I mean the faint images of these in thinking and reasoning; such as, for instance, are all the perceptions excited by the present discourse, excepting only, those which arise from the sight and touch, and excepting the immediate pleasure or uneasiness it may occasion. I believe it will not be very necessary to employ many words in explaining this

---

[15]David Hume, *An Enquiry Concerning Human Understanding,* 2nd ed., ed. L. A. Selby-Bigge (Oxford: Oxford University Press, 1902). All subsequent quotations from Hume's *Enquiry* are from this edition unless otherwise noted.

distinction. Every one of himself will readily perceive the difference betwixt feeling and thinking. The common degrees of these are easily distinguished; tho' it is not impossible but in particular instances they may very nearly approach to each other. Thus in sleep, in a fever, in madness, or in any very violent emotions of soul, our ideas may approach to our impressions: As on the other hand it sometimes happens, that our impressions are so faint and low, that we cannot distinguish them from our ideas. But notwithstanding this near resemblance in a few instances, they are in general so very different, that no-one can make a scruple to rank them under distinct heads, and assign to each a peculiar name to mark the difference.

There is another division of our perceptions, which it will be convenient to observe, and which extends itself both to our impressions and ideas. This division is into *simple* and *complex*. Simple perceptions or impressions and ideas are such as admit of no distinction nor separation. The complex are the contrary to these, and may be distinguished into parts. Tho' a particular colour, taste, and smell are qualities all united together in this apple, 'tis easy to perceive they are not the same, but are at least distinguishable from each other.

Having by these divisions given an order and arrangement to our objects, we may now apply ourselves to consider with the more accuracy their qualities and relations. The first circumstance, that strikes my eye, is the great resemblance betwixt our impressions and ideas in every other particular, except their degree of force and vivacity. The one seem to be in a manner the reflexion of the other; so that all the perceptions of the mind are double, and appear both as impressions and ideas. When I shut my eyes and think of my chamber, the ideas I form are exact representations of the impressions I felt, nor is there any circumstance of the one, which is not to be found in the other. In running over my other perceptions, I find still the same resemblance and representation. Ideas and impressions appear always to correspond to each other. This circumstance seems to me remarkable, and engages my attention for a moment.

Upon a more accurate survey I find I have been carried away too far by the first appearance, and that I must make use of the distinction of perceptions into *simple and complex,* to limit this general decision, *that all our ideas and impressions are resembling.* I observe, that many of our complex ideas never had impressions, that corresponded to them, and that many of our complex impressions never are exactly copied in ideas. I can imagine to myself such a city as the *New Jerusalem,* whose pavement is gold and walls are rubies, tho' I never saw any such. I have seen *Paris;* but shall I affirm I can form such an idea of that city, as will perfectly represent all its streets and houses in their real and just proportions?

I perceive, therefore, that tho' there is in general a great resemblance betwixt our *complex* impressions and ideas, yet the rule is not universally true, that they are exact copies of each other. We may next consider how the case stands with our *simple* perceptions. After the most accurate examination, of which I am capable, I venture to affirm, that the rule here holds without any exception, and that every simple idea has a simple impression, which resembles it; and every simple impression a correspondent idea. That idea of red, which we form in the dark, and that impression, which strikes our eyes in sun-shine, differ only in degree, not in nature. That the case is the same with all our simple impressions and ideas, 'tis impossible to prove by a particular enumeration of them. Every one may satisfy himself in this point by running over as many as he pleases. But if any one should deny this universal resemblance, I know of no way of convincing him, but by desiring him to show a simple impression that has not a correspondent idea, or a simple idea, that has not a correspondent impression. If he does not answer this challenge, as 'tis certain he cannot, we may from his silence and our own observation establish our conclusion.

> *That idea of red, which we form in the dark, and that impression, which strikes our eyes in sun-shine, differ only in degree, not in nature.*

Thus we find, that all simple ideas and impressions resemble each other; and as the complex are formed from them, we may affirm in general, that these two species of perception are exactly correspondent. Having discover'd this relation, which requires no farther examination, I am curious to find some other of their qualities. Let us consider how they stand with regard to their existence, and which of the impressions and ideas are causes, and which effects.

The *full* examination of this question is the subject of the present treatise; and therefore we shall here content ourselves with establishing one general proposition. *That all our simple ideas in their first appearance are deriv'd from simple impressions, which are correspondent to them, and which they exactly represent.*[16]

According to Hume, simple ideas are derived from simple impressions. A simple idea would be something like a red, round image; the simple impression would be seeing a red, round image. More complex ideas, for example, the idea of an apple, are complex arrangements and associations of simple ideas. To justify a belief as knowledge, therefore, we must break up its complex ideas into simple ideas and then find the impressions upon which those ideas are based. If I claim to see an apple, for example, I analyze my experience; my idea that there is an apple out there depends upon my seeing several red, round images from different angles, feeling something smooth, tasting something fruity and tart, and so on. If I claim that there are objects of a certain kind (apples, for example), I must identify the simple ideas and impressions upon which my supposed knowledge is based. And if I make a metaphysical claim, about the existence of God or substances, I must either be preapproved to identify the ideas and impressions upon which such a claim is based, or I must show that it is nothing other than a "relation of ideas"; otherwise, the claim cannot be justified ("commit it to the flames").

---

[16] David Hume, *A Treatise of Human Nature*, ed. L. A. Selby-Bigge (Oxford: Oxford University Press, 1888).

But, to the embarrassment of most metaphysical doctrines, they cannot be defended by either of the methods allowed by Hume. They are, by their very nature, about things beyond everyday experience (for example, God, substance) and so are not based upon "impression"; nor are they "relations of ideas" that can be demonstrated by a simple logical or mathematical proof. Therefore, they cannot be justified. The problem, however, is that the same argument extends far beyond the debatable claims of metaphysics and undermines some of the beliefs that are most essential to our everyday experiences as well.

In Hume's philosophy, three such beliefs in particular are singled out for analysis. On the one hand, they are so fundamental to our daily experience and common knowledge that no sane man or woman could possibly doubt them; on the other hand, they are completely without justification. As Hume argues, first, there is our idea of **causation** (or causality), of one event bringing about or causing another event.

From this idea, which provides what Hume calls "the strongest connections" of our experience and, elsewhere, "the cement of the universe," we derive a most important principle, the **principle of universal causation,** which states that every event has its cause (or causes). It is evident that we invoke such a principle every time we explain anything; for example, the car won't start. We search for the cause, but everything seems to check out—the carburetor, the electrical system, and so on. Now we might search for hours without finding the cause, but there is one thing that we know for certain and that is that there must be a cause somewhere—even if it is a very complex cause. What is not possible is that there be no cause. Presupposed in our everyday thinking is this principle, that every event has its cause. (You may recognize this principle as a version of Leibniz's Principle of Sufficient Reason, which substitutes the more Newtonian notion of "cause" for the notion of "reason.")

Second, because of our presupposed belief in causation and its universal applicability, we are able to think beyond our immediate "ideas" and predict the future and explain the past. But to do so, we must also believe that our observations of the present will have some relevance in the future, that we can in fact draw valid inductive generalizations from our experience. Of course, we do so all of the time; for example, when I wake up at 6:00 in the morning, I expect the sun to rise within the hour. Why? Because it has always done so, and because it is February 26th and the almanac says it will. In making every such prediction, we presuppose a **principle of induction,** that is, that the laws of nature that have always held in the past will continue to hold in the future. The principle of induction is sometimes summarized as "the future will be like the past," which is all right only so long as it is not taken too literally; for of course the future is never just like the past—you are now fifteen seconds older, for example, you have added a whole expression to your knowledge, and (unless you are eating while you read) you have lost a tiny bit of weight as well. But the laws of nature, at least, do not change from moment to moment.

Third, there is our belief in the "external world," that is, a physical or material world that exists independently of our impressions and ideas, which it presumably causes in us. Bishop Berkeley had already done Hume's work for him here. Hume, following Berkeley, also rejects all notions of substance as unintelligible, including even that minimal "we know not what" of John Locke. But where Berkeley turned the rejection of matter and substance into a metaphysics (namely, his subjective idealism) and used it to defend the existence of God, Hume rejects this idealist metaphysics as well and remains wholly skeptical, refusing to accept the existence of God. He remains firm in his insistence that our belief in the existence of anything is no different from "the idea of what we conceive to be existent."

We can see that these three basic beliefs are intimately tied together; the notion of cause supports the principle of induction,[17] and the causal theory of perception supports our belief in the "external world." Accordingly, Hume takes causation to be the central idea of all reasoning,[18] that is, all attempts to connect separate ideas together in a single belief. Hume's arguments are both elegant and simple to follow. He refutes both the principle of universal causation and the principle of induction by showing that neither can be defended either as a "relation of ideas" or as a "matter of fact." He begins with a statement that all human knowledge must be one or the other, explains what he means by "relations of ideas" and "matters of fact," shows how it is that "cause and effect" are the basis of all reasoning, and then proceeds to show that such reasoning can be neither a relation of ideas nor a simple matter of fact.

FROM THE *ENQUIRY*
BY **HUME**

All the objects of human reason or enquiry may naturally be divided into two kinds, to wit, *Relations of Ideas,* and *Matters of Fact.* Of the first kind are the sciences of Geometry, Algebra, and Arithmetic; and in short, every affirmation which is either intuitively or demonstratively certain. *That the square of the hypotenuse is equal to the square of the two sides,* is a proposition which expresses a relation between these figures. *That three times five is equal to the half of thirty,* expresses a relation between these numbers. Propositions of this kind are discoverable by the mere operation of thought, without dependence on what is anywhere existent in the universe. Though there never were a circle or triangle in nature, the truths demonstrated by Euclid would for ever retain their certainty and evidence.

Matters of fact, which are the second objects of human reason, are not ascertained in the same manner; nor is our evidence of their truth, however great, of a like nature with the foregoing. The contrary of every matter of fact is still possible; because it can never imply a contradiction, and is conceived by the mind with the same facility and distinctness, as if ever so conformable to reality. *That*

---

[17] Modern philosophers have given a great deal of attention to inductive inferences that are not based upon any obvious causes, for example, statistical probabilities (as in genetics or gambling).

[18] It is important to remember that Hume, like Locke, models his philosophy-psychology after Newton's physics. So even if he rejects Locke's "causal theory of perception," the Newtonian model, in which causality is central, remains at the heart of his theories.

the sun will not rise tomorrow is no less intelligible a proposition, and implies no more contradiction than the affirmation, *that it will rise.* We should in vain, therefore, attempt to demonstrate its falsehood. Were it demonstratively false, it would imply a contradiction, and could never be distinctly conceived by the mind.

It may, therefore, be a subject worthy of curiosity, to enquire what is the nature of that evidence which assures us of any real existence and matter of fact, beyond the present testimony of our senses, or the records of our memory. This part of philosophy, it is observable, has been little cultivated, either by the ancients or moderns; and therefore our doubts and errors, in the prosecution of so important an enquiry, may be the more excusable; while we march through such difficult paths without any guide or direction. They may even prove useful, by exciting curiosity, and destroying that implicit faith and security, which is the bane of all reasoning and free enquiry. The discovery of defects in the common philosophy, if any such there be, will not, I presume, be a discouragement, but rather an incitement, as is usual, to attempt something more full and satisfactory than has yet been proposed to the public.

All reasonings concerning matter of fact seem to be founded on the relations of *Cause and Effect.* By means of that relation alone we can go beyond the evidence of our memory and senses. If you were to ask a man, why he believes any matter of fact, which is absent; for instance, that his friend is in the country, or in France; he would give you a reason; and this reason would be some other fact; as a letter received from him, or the knowledge of his former resolutions and promises. A man finding a watch or any other machine in a desert island, would conclude that there had once been men in that island. All our reasonings concerning fact are of the same nature. And here it is constantly supposed that there is a connexion between the present fact and that which is inferred from it. Were there nothing to bind them together, the inference would be entirely precarious. The hearing of an articulate voice and rational discourse in the dark assures us of the presence of some person: Why? because these are the effects of the human make and fabric, and closely connected with it. If we anatomize all the other reasonings of this nature, we shall find that they are founded on the relation of cause and effect, and that this relation is either near or remote, direct or collateral. Heat and light are collateral effects of fire, and the one effect may justly be inferred from the other.

Hume's argument, which we shall see again and again, is that we explain our experiences and events by appeal to other experiences and events. If I burn my finger and wonder how, I look down and see that I have just placed my hand too near the stovetop burner. I explain that the heat of the burner is the cause and the burn is the effect of the hot burner. Indeed, we are perplexed whenever we cannot find some causal explanation, and the suggestion that there might not be one ("there was no cause; you just burned yourself, that's all") is all but unintelligible to us. But now, Hume asks, where do we get this knowledge of causes and effects?

If we would satisfy ourselves, therefore, concerning the nature of that evidence, which assures us of matters of fact, we must enquire how we arrive at the knowledge of cause and effect.

I shall venture to affirm, as a general proposition, which admits of no exception, that the knowledge of this relation is not, in any instance, attained by reasonings *a priori;* but arises entirely from experience, when we find that any particular objects are constantly conjoined with each other. Let an object be presented to a man of ever so strong natural reason and abilities; if that object be entirely new to him, he will not be able, by the most accurate examination of its sensible qualities, to discover any of its causes or effects. Adam, though his rational faculties be supposed, at the very first, entirely perfect, could not have inferred from the fluidity and transparency of water that it would suffocate him, or from the light and warmth of fire that it would consume him. No object ever discovers, by the qualities which appear to the senses, either the causes which produced it, or the effects which will arise from it; nor can our reason, unassisted by experience, ever draw any inference concerning real existence and matter of fact.

This proposition, *that causes and effects are discoverable, not by reason but by experience,* will readily be admitted with regard to such objects, as we remember to have once been altogether unknown to us; since we must be conscious of the utter inability, which we then lay under, of foretelling what would arise from them. Present two smooth pieces of marble to a man who has no tincture of natural philosophy; he will never discover that they will adhere together in such a manner as to require great force to separate them in a direct line, while they make so small a resistance to lateral pressure. Such events, as bear little analogy to the common course of nature, are also readily confessed to be known only by experience; nor does any man imagine that the explosion of gunpowder, or the attraction of a lodestone, could ever be discovered by arguments *a priori.* In like manner, when an effect is supposed to depend upon an intricate machinery or secret structure of parts, we make no difficulty in attributing all our knowledge of it to experience. Who will assert that he can give the ultimate reason, why milk or bread is proper nourishment for a man, not for a lion or a tiger?

But the same truth may not appear, at first sight, to have the same evidence with regard to events, which have become familiar to us from our first appearance in the world, which bear a close analogy to the whole course of nature, and which are supposed to depend on the simple qualities of objects, without any secret structure of parts. We are apt to imagine that we could discover these effects by the mere operation of our reason, without experience. We fancy, that were we brought on a sudden into this world, we could at first have inferred that one Billiard-ball would communicate motion to another upon impulse; and that we needed not to have waited for the event, in order to pronounce with certainty concerning it. Such is the influence of custom, that, where it is strongest, it not only covers our natural ignorance, but even conceals itself, and seems not to take place, merely because it is found in the highest degree.

But to convince us that all the laws of nature, and all the operations of bodies without exception, are known only by experience, the following reflections may, perhaps, suffice. Were any object presented to us, and were we required to pronounce concerning the effect, which will result from it, without consulting past observation; after what manner, I beseech you, must the mind proceed in this operation? It must invent or imagine some event, which it ascribes to the object as its effect; and it is plain that this invention must be entirely arbitrary. The mind can never possibly find the effect in the supposed cause, by the most accurate scrutiny and examination. For the effect is totally different from the cause, and consequently can never be discovered in it. Motion in the second Billiard-ball is a quite distinct event from motion in the first; nor is there anything in the one to suggest the smallest hint of the other. A stone or piece of metal raised into the air, and left without any support, immediately falls: but to consider the matter *a priori,* is there anything we discover in this situation which can beget the idea of a downward, rather than an upward, or any other motion in the stone or metal?

The mind can never possibly find the effect in the supposed cause, by the most accurate scrutiny and examination. For the effect is totally different from the cause, and consequently can never be discovered in it.

And as the first imagination or invention of a particular effect, in all natural operations, is arbitrary, where we consult not experience; so must we also esteem the supposed tie or connexion between the cause and effect, which binds them together, and renders it impossible that any other effect could result from the operation of that cause. When I see, for instance, a Billiard-ball moving in a straight line towards another; even suppose motion in the second ball should by accident be suggested to me, as the result of their contact or impulse; may I not conceive, that a hundred different events might as well follow from that cause? May not both these balls remain at absolute rest? May not the first ball return in a straight line, or leap off from the second in any line or direction? All these suppositions are consistent and conceivable. Why then should we give the preference to one, which is no more consistent or conceivable than the rest? All our reasonings *a priori* will never be able to show us any foundations for this preference.

Hume's argument so far is that we do not know particular causes and effects through reason, but only through experience. Because you have seen it so many times, you know that a billiard ball moving toward and striking another billiard ball sets the second in motion on a predictable path. But if you had never seen anything like it before—perhaps if you were Adam or Eve (pool tables were not created until the eighth day of creation)—you would not have any idea of what to expect. Both balls might stop dead. Both might explode. The second might start a lawsuit. Prediction of cause and effect, in other words, depends upon prior experience, and no amount of mere reasoning will suffice by itself.

In a word, then, every effect is a distinct event from its cause. It could not, therefore, be discovered in the cause, and the first invention or conception of it, *a priori,* must be entirely arbitrary. And even after it is suggested, the conjunction of it with the cause must appear equally arbitrary; since there are always many other effects, which, to reason, must seem fully as consistent and natural. In vain, therefore, should we pretend to determine any single event, or infer any cause or effect, without the assistance of observation and experience. . . .

When we reason *a priori,* and consider merely any object or cause, as it appears to the mind, independent of all observation, it never could suggest to us the notion of any distinct object, such as its effect; much less, show us the inseparable and inviolable connexion between them. A man must be very sagacious who could discover by reasoning that crystal is the effect of heat, and ice of cold, without being previously acquainted with the operations of these qualities.

In this argument, we see Hume applying the first half of his "fork" to the idea of causation. The idea of cause and effect cannot be a relation of ideas, because, for example, no matter how closely we examine the idea of fire, we will never discover the idea of its causing gunpowder to explode. Reasoning alone cannot reveal the causes or effects of particular events. At the outset of this argument, Hume also suggests that the idea of causation is not discoverable through perception either: Although we perceive many different qualities of fire, we never perceive its power to cause gunpowder to explode. Hume concludes that the idea of cause and effect must be derived from our experience of the constant conjunction of two events. We observe, for example, that every time we set a match to gunpowder it explodes; and because we expect the future to be like the past, we infer that the application of fire is the cause of the gunpowder's exploding. In short, our knowledge of causes is arrived at through induction from past experiences.

Hume's argument against induction, and in particular against the inductive principle that the future will be like the past, takes exactly the same form. Again he begins with his "fork" between "relations of ideas" and "matters of fact," and again he proves that one of the basic assumptions of all our thinking, the principle of induction, cannot be established either way:

But we have not yet attained any tolerable satisfaction with regard to the question first proposed. Each solution still gives rise to a new question as difficult as the foregoing, and leads us on to further enquiries. When it is asked, *What is the nature of all our reasonings concerning matter of fact?* the proper answer seems to be, that they are founded on the relation of cause and effect. When again it is asked, *What is the foundation of all our reasonings and conclusions concerning that relation?* it may be replied in one word, Experience. But if we still carry on our shifting humour, and ask, *What is the foundation of all conclusions from experience?* this implies a new question, which may be of more difficult solution and explication. Philosophers, that give themselves airs of superior wisdom and sufficiency, have a hard task when they encounter persons of inquisitive dispositions, who push them from every corner to which they retreat, and who are sure at last to bring them to some dangerous dilemma. The best expedient to prevent this confusion, is to be modest in our pretensions; and even to discover the difficulty ourselves before it is objected to us. By this means, we may make a kind of merit of our very ignorance.

I shall content myself, in this section, with an easy task, and shall pretend only to give a negative answer to the question here proposed. I say then, that, even after we have experience of the operations of cause and effect, our conclusions from that experience are *not* founded on reasoning, or any process of the understanding. This answer we must endeavour both to explain and to defend.

It must certainly be allowed, that nature has kept us at a great distance from all her secrets, and has afforded us only the knowledge of a few superficial qualities of objects; while she conceals from us those powers and principles on which the influence of those objects entirely depends. Our senses inform us of the colour, weight, and consistence of bread; but neither sense nor reason can ever inform us of those qualities which fit it for the nourishment and support of a human body. Sight or feeling conveys an idea of the actual motion of bodies; but as to that wonderful force or power, which would carry on a moving body for ever in a continued change of place, and which bodies never lose but by communicating it to others; of this we cannot form the most distant conception. But notwithstanding this ignorance of natural powers and principles, we always presume, when we see like sensible qualities, that they have like secret powers, and expect that effects, similar to those which we have experienced, will follow from them. If a body of like colour and consistence with that bread, which we have formerly eat, be presented to us, we make no scruple of repeating the experiment, and foresee, with certainty, like nourishment and support. Now this is a process of the mind or thought, of which I would willingly know the foundation. It is allowed on all hands that there is no known connexion between the sensible qualities and the secret powers; and consequently, that the mind is not led to form such a conclusion concerning their constant and regular conjunction, by anything which it knows of their nature. As to past *Experience,* it can be allowed to give *direct* and *certain* information of those precise objects only, and that precise period of time, which fell under its cognizance: but why this experience should be extended to future times, and to other objects, which for aught we know, may be only in appearance similar; this is the main question on which I would insist. The bread, which I formerly eat, nourished me; that is, a body of such sensible qualities was, at that time, endued with such secret powers: but does it follow, that other bread must also nourish me at another time, and that like sensible qualities must always be attended with like secret powers? The consequence seems nowise necessary. At least, it must be acknowledged that there is here a consequence drawn by the mind; that there is a certain step taken; a process of thought, and an inference, which wants to be explained. These two propositions are far from being the same, *I have found that such an object has always been attended with such an effect,* and *I foresee, that other objects, which are, in appearance, similar, will be attended with similar effects.*

The argument so far is just like the argument regarding cause and effect, namely, that it is only from experience that we know the properties and effects of things and events, that moving bodies cause others to move, for instance, or that eating bread gives me nourishment. But now Hume distinguishes two propositions: (1) I have recognized a certain cause-and-effect relationship in my past experience, and (2) I predict that a similar cause-and-effect relationship will hold in the future also. The reference is surely reasonable, Hume says, but again he forces us to say why such an inference is reasonable, and he argues that we cannot do so.

I shall allow, if you please, that the one proposition may justify be inferred from the other: I know, in fact, that it always is inferred. But if you insist that the inference is made by a chain of reasoning, I desire you to produce the reasoning. The connexion between these propositions is not intuitive. There is required a medium, which may enable the mind to draw such an inference, if indeed it be drawn by reasoning and argument. What that medium is, I must confess, passes my comprehension; and it is incumbent on those to produce it, who assert that it really exists, and is the origin of all our conclusions concerning matter of fact.

This negative argument must certainly, in process of time, become altogether convincing, if many penetrating and able philosophers shall turn their enquiries this way and no one be ever able to discover any connecting proposition or intermediate step, which supports the understanding in this conclusion. But as the question is yet new, every reader may not trust so far to his own penetration, as to conclude, because an argument escapes his enquiry, that therefore it does not really exist. For this reason it may be requisite to venture upon a more difficult task; and enumerating all the branches of human knowledge, endeavour to show that none of them can afford such an argument.

Here is "Hume's fork": the division of all knowledge into reasoning about relations of ideas (which he here calls "demonstrative") and reasoning about matters of fact (which he here calls "moral"). He says that it is clear from the above arguments that no demonstrative reasoning is available to justify our predictions of the future. But then he goes on to argue that no reasoning about matters of fact—no appeal to experience—can justify our propensity to make predictions either. For in order to justify our belief that the future will resemble the past on the basis of our experience, we would in effect be arguing that we know that the future will be like the past because in the past the future has always been like the past, and this is "begging the question" and a "vicious circle," in which one defends a proposition by referring it back to itself. (Like asking a suspected liar, "Are you lying to me?") Therefore our propensity for predicting can't be justified by appealing to experience either, which leaves us without any justification at all.

All reasonings may be divided into two kinds, namely, demonstrative reasoning, or that concerning relations of ideas, and moral reasoning, or that concerning matter of fact and existence. That there are no demonstrative arguments in the case seems evident; since it implies no contradiction that the course of nature may change, and that an object, seemingly like those which we have experienced, may be attended with different or contrary effects. May I not clearly and distinctly conceive that a body, falling from the clouds, and which, in all other respects, resembles snow, has yet the taste of salt or feeling of fire? Is there any more intelligible proposition than to affirm, that all the trees will flourish in December and January, and decay in May and June? Now whatever is intelligible, and can be distinctly conceived, implies no contradiction, and can never be proved false by any demonstrative argument or abstract reasoning *a priori.*

If we be, therefore, engaged by arguments to put trust in past experience, and make it the standard of our future judgement, these arguments must be probable only, or such as regard matter of fact and real existence, according to the division above mentioned. But that there is no argument of this kind, must appear, if our explication of that species of reasoning be admitted as solid and satisfactory. We have said that all arguments concerning existence are founded on the relation of cause and effect; that our knowledge of that relation is derived entirely from experience; and that all our experimental conclusions proceed upon the supposition that the future will be conformable to the past. To endeavour, therefore, the proof of this last supposition by probable arguments, or arguments regarding existence, must be evidently going in a circle, and taking that for granted, which is the very point in question.

. . . When a man says, *I have found, in all past instances, such sensible qualities conjoined with such secret powers:* And when he says, *Similar sensible qualities will always be conjoined with similar secret powers,* he is not guilty of tautology, nor are these propositions in any respect the same. You say that the one proposition is an inference from the other. But you must confess that the inference is not intuitive; neither is it demonstrative: Of what nature is it, then? To say it is experimental, is begging the question. For all inferences from experience suppose, as their foundation, that the future will resemble the past, and that similar powers will be conjoined with similar sensible qualities. If there be any suspicion that the course of nature may change, and that the past may be no rule for the future, all experience becomes useless, and can give rise to no inference or conclusion. It is impossible, therefore, that any arguments from experience can prove this resemblance of the past to the future; since all these arguments are founded on the supposition of that resemblance. Let the source of things be allowed hitherto ever so regular; that alone, without some new argument or inference, proves not that, for the future, it will continue so. In vain do you pretend to have learned the nature of bodies from your past experience. Their secret nature, and consequently all their effects and influence may change, without any change in their sensible qualities. This happens sometimes, and with regard to some objects: Why may it not happen always, and with regard to all objects? What logic, what process of argument secures you against this position? My practice, you say, refutes my doubts. But you mistake the purport of my question. As an agent, I am quite satisfied in the point; but as a philosopher, who has some share of curiosity, I will not say scepticism, I want to learn the foundation of this inference. No reading, no enquiry has yet been able to remove my difficulty, or give me satisfaction in a matter of such importance. Can I do better than propose the difficulty to the public, even though, perhaps, I have small hopes of obtaining a solution? We shall at least, by this means, be sensible of our ignorance, if we do not augment our knowledge.

Hume's arguments against the principle of universal causation and the principle of induction are also arguments against rationalism in general. What he is saying is that reasoning alone, without information from experience, cannot tell us anything whatever about the world. Reasoning *a priori,* that is, thinking without any appeal to experience, is incapable of proving any of those theorems so important to the rationalists, such as the existence of substances, a God, and causes, as well as the conformity of future events to past ones. His arguments are at the same time skeptical ones, since he reasons that even an appeal to experience cannot prove the reality of any of these things.

What is the solution to these skeptical doubts? If we seek a justification or defense, there is none, according to Hume. But in everyday life, such philosophical doubts need have no effect at all, for though there is no justification of our beliefs, we can yet remain confident that at least there is an explanation for them.

Suppose a person, though endowed with the strongest faculties of reason and reflection, to be brought on a sudden into this world; he would, indeed, immediately observe a continual succession of objects and one event following another, but he would not be able to discover anything further. He would not at first, by any reasoning, be able to reach the idea of cause and effect, since the particular powers by which all natural operations are performed never appear to the senses; nor is it reasonable to conclude, merely because one event in one instance precedes another, that therefore the one is the cause, the other the effect. The conjunction may be arbitrary and casual. There may be no reason to infer the existence of one from the appearance of the other: and, in a word, such a person without more experience could never employ his conjecture or reasoning concerning any matter of fact or be assured of anything beyond what was immediately present to his memory or senses.

Suppose again that he has acquired more experience and has lived so long in the world as to have observed similar objects or events to be constantly conjoined together—what is the consequence of this experience? He immediately infers the existence of one object from the appearance of the other, yet he has not, by all his experience, acquired any idea or knowledge of the secret power by which the one object produces the other, nor is it by any process of reasoning he is engaged to draw this inference; but still he finds himself determined to draw it, and though he should be convinced that his understanding has no part in the operation, he would nevertheless continue in the same course of thinking. There is some other principle which determines him to form such a conclusion.

This principle is *custom* or *habit*. For wherever the repetition of any particular act or operation produces a propensity to renew the same act or operation without being impelled by any reasoning or process of the understanding, we always say that this propensity is the effect of *custom*. By employing that word we pretend not to have given the ultimate reason of such a propensity. We only point out a principle of human nature which is universally acknowledged, and which is well known by its effects. Perhaps we can push our inquiries no further or pretend to give the cause of this cause, but must rest contented with it as the ultimate principle which we can assign of all our conclusions from experience. It is sufficient satisfaction that we can go so far without repining at the narrowness of our faculties, because they will carry us no further. And it is certain we here advance a very intelligible proposition at least, if not a true one, when we assert that after the constant conjunction of two objects, heat and flame, for instance, weight and solidity, we are determined by custom alone to expect the one from the appearance of the other. This hypothesis seems even the only one which explains the difficulty why we draw from a thousand instances an inference which we are not able to draw from one instance that is in no respect different from them. Reason is incapable of any such variation. The conclusions which it draws from considering one circle are the same which it would form upon surveying all the circles in the universe. But no man, having seen only one body move after being impelled by another, could infer that every other body will move after a like impulse. All inferences from experience, therefore, are effects of custom, not of reasoning.

> *All inferences from experience . . . are effects of custom, not of reasoning.*

In other words, there is no "solution to these skeptical doubts," but, at most, what Hume calls "a skeptical solution." It means an end, not only to philosophy, but to all rational inquiry and all claims that we can know anything (even that the sun will rise tomorrow, or that there is a typewriter now in front of me). You might think that such conclusions would have driven Hume mad or caused him such confusion that he would have been incapable of coping with the most everyday chores. Yet we know that he was the most practical and jolliest sort of fellow. As a philosopher, he has been driven right up against the wall of Plato's Cave. But he remains unperturbed. In a famous passage at the end of the *Treatise*, he simply remarks:

> *Most fortunately it happens, that since reason is incapable of dispelling these clouds, nature herself suffices to that purpose, and cures me of this philosophical melancholy and delirium, either by relaxing this bent of mind, or by some avocation, and lively impression of my senses, which obliterate all these chimeras. I dine, I play a game of backgammon, I converse, and am merry*

with my friends; and when after three or four hours' amusement, I wou'd return to these speculations, they appear so cold, and strain'd, and ridiculous, that I cannot find in my heart to enter into them any farther.

Perhaps you too find "these speculations cold, strained and ridiculous." If so, however, this is not the time to run off to dinner and an evening of games and conversation. Something has gone very wrong. The empiricist attempt to restore common sense to philosophy has ended in the least commonsensical philosophy imaginable. A person who really believed that there might be no material world or that the future will not resemble the past (and therefore, having been hit by a truck last week, steps into the street convinced that it will not happen again) would be crazy! How can our intellects be so out of joint with our experience or our philosophy so far away from practical life? How serious is Hume's skepticism?

F. AN ANCIENT SKEPTIC: NĀGĀRJUNA

As we mentioned above, the epistemological questions raised by the modern rationalists and empiricists were not original to the modern era. One ancient empiricist continued the philosophical effort that Hume abandoned. **Nāgārjuna,** an Indian Buddhist philosopher (probably a Mahayana Buddhist of the late second century A.D.), *begins* his philosophy with a denial of our knowledge of causation. The very first verse (after the dedication) of his *Mādhyamaka-Kārikās* reads:

No existents whatsoever are evident anywhere that are arisen from themselves, from another, from both, or from a non-cause.[19]

Thus, Nāgārjuna has a logic that includes four concepts of cause: self-causation, external causation, joint causation, and noncausation (or eternality). But there is no perception of anything being caused by any of them. In other words, Nāgārjuna claims, just as Hume does, that we have no impression of cause; indeed like Hume he says that without cause, we have no impression of "things" (or substances) at all.

In fact, Nāgārjuna denies the existence of substance entirely. And without the notion of substance, the question of the possibility of knowledge is very different than it was for the other thinkers at whom we have looked in this chapter. So far, the sense in which "knowledge" has been understood is as knowledge *of* whether and how a *thing* exists. When Hume proved to his satisfaction that we couldn't know the nature and existence of substances, he concluded that knowledge was impossible. Nāgārjuna, instead, pursues an epistemology in the absence of substance and causation. Where Hume says that we simply must, as is our custom, rely on the concept of cause, Nāgārjuna says we are bound, if we are dedicated empiricists, to change our custom.

---

[19]All passages from the *Mādhyamaka-Kārikās* are from *Nāgārjuna: The Philosophy of the Middle,* trans. by David J. Kalupuhana (Albany: SUNY Press, 1986).

A condition of an effect that is either non-existent or existent is not proper. Of what non-existent [effect] is a condition? Of what use is a condition of the existent [effect]? (I:6)

Since a thing that is existent or non-existent or both existent and non-existent is not produced, how pertinent in that context would a producing cause be? (I:7)

Thus, Nāgārjuna advocates pursuing a more "appropriate" logic, which he calls— after the Buddhist doctrine—an "analysis in terms of *emptiness (sūnyata)*." Such an analysis involves limiting our claims to what we can know, that is, impressions.

Seeing does not perceive itself, its own form. How can that which does not perceive itself, see others?

Seeing, hearing, smelling, tasting, touching, and mind are the six faculties. Their spheres consist of the object of seeing, etc. (III:1)

Seeing does not perceive itself, its own form. How can that which does not perceive itself, see others? (III:2)

We have no knowledge and should make no claims, therefore, to the effect that we see, hear, taste, touch, smell, or *intellect* a substance. There exist only instances of seeing-being seen, hearing-being heard, and so on, even in the case of thinking-being thought.

Seeing does not perceive (i.e., "know a thing"), nor does non-seeing perceive. One should admit that a seer is explained by [the analysis of] seeing itself. (III:5)

Thus, neither the seer nor the form seen are independent substances. Rather, they are "empty" of substance. Since our experience is ample evidence of the mutual dependence of sensation and sensed-form, Nāgārjuna felt that the burden of proof lay upon the believer in substance. Thus, his "emptiness" was not, as it was for Hume, a dark and threatening realization that demanded the end of his investigation, but rather, an opportunity for a wealth of valuable analyses of experience. The believer in substance, in a sense, has dug his own pit whether he is an empiricist or a rationalist, because all the evidence of experience is unavailable to him.

When an analysis is made in terms of emptiness, whosoever were to address a refutation, all that is left unrefuted by him will be equal to what is yet to be proved. (IV:8)

When an explanation in terms of emptiness is given, whosoever were to address a censure, all that is left uncensured by him will be equal to what is yet to be proved. (IV:9)

G. DOUBLE VISION: A NON-WESTERN FEMINIST PERSPECTIVE

The example of Nāgārjuna shows that what counts for knowledge may differ from culture to culture. It seems that religious background, national ancestry, and other social distinctions may affect the epistemological project. (In the case of Nāgārjuna, for example, his access to the Buddhist concepts of "emptiness" and "nonself" gave him the opportunity to think about knowledge in different terms than were apparently available to the modern European rationalists and empiricists.) One important distinction which has recently come to epistemologists' attention is the difference between the sexes.

To an empiricist, goes one feminist claim, if women can be shown to have different sense-experiences from men (which they surely do), then women must have a very different sort of knowledge. To a rationalist, if women have a different "nature" or way of reasoning than do men, then one must admit that women have a very different sort of knowledge. Different interests and different backgrounds, perhaps, lead different people to set different criteria for knowledge.

But if gender makes a difference and cultural heritage makes a difference, imagine the combination. **Uma Narayan,** a feminist philosopher from Bombay, does just that.

ON FEMINIST EPISTEMOLOGY
BY **UMA NARAYAN**

A fundamental thesis of feminist epistemology is that our location in the world as women makes it possible for us to perceive and understand different aspects of both the world and human activities in ways that challenge the male bias of existing perspectives. Feminist epistemology is a particular manifestation of the general insight that the nature of women's experiences as individuals and as social beings, our contributions to work, culture, knowledge, and our history and political interests have been systematically ignored or misrepresented by mainstream discourses in different areas.

Women have been often excluded from prestigious areas of human activity (for example, politics or science) and this has often made these activities seem clearly "male." In areas where women were not excluded (for example, subsistence work), their contribution has been misrepresented as secondary and inferior to that of men. Feminist epistemology sees mainstream theories about various human enterprises, including mainstream theories about human knowledge, as one-dimensional and deeply flawed because of the exclusion and misrepresentation of women's contributions.

Feminist epistemology suggests that integrating women's contribution into the domain of science and knowledge will not constitute a mere adding of details; it will not merely widen the canvas but result in a shift of perspective enabling us to see a very different picture. The inclusion of women's perspective will not merely amount to women participating in greater numbers in the existing practice of science and knowledge, but it will change the very nature of these activities and their self-understanding.

It would be misleading to suggest that feminist epistemology is a homogenous and cohesive enterprise. Its practitioners differ both philosophically and politically in a number of significant ways (Harding 1986). But an important theme on its agenda has been to undermine the abstract, rationalistic, and universal image of the scientific enterprise by using several different strategies. It has studied, for instance, how contingent historical factors have colored both scientific theories and practices and provided the (often sexist) metaphors in which scientists have conceptualized their activity (Bordo 1986; Keller 1985; Harding and O'Barr 1987). It has tried to reintegrate values and emotions into our account of our cognitive activities, arguing for both the inevitability of their presence and the importance of the contributions they are capable of making to our knowledge. . . . It has also attacked various sets of dualisms characteristic of western philosophical thinking—reason versus emotion, culture versus nature, universal versus particular—in which the first of each set is identified with science, rationality, and the masculine and the second is relegated to the nonscientific, the nonrational, and the feminine. . . .

At the most general level, feminist epistemology resembles the efforts of many oppressed groups to reclaim for themselves the value of their own experience. The writing of novels that focused on working-class life in England or the lives of black people in the United States shares a motivation similar to that of feminist epistemology—to depict an experience different from the norm and to assert the value of this difference.

In a similar manner, feminist epistemology also resembles attempts by third-world writers and historians to document the wealth and complexity of local economic and social structures that existed prior to colonialism. These attempts are useful for their ability to restore to colonized peoples a sense of the richness of their own history and culture. These projects also mitigate the tendency of intellectuals in former colonies who are westernized through their education to think that anything western is necessarily better and more "progressive." In some cases, such studies help to preserve the knowledge of many local arts, crafts, lore, and techniques that were part of the former way of life before they are lost not only to practice but even to memory.

These enterprises are analogous to feminist epistemology's project of restoring to women a sense of the richness of their history, to mitigate our tendency to see the stereotypically "masculine" as better or more progressive, and to preserve for posterity the contents of "feminine" areas of knowledge and expertise—medical lore, knowledge associated with the practices of childbirth and child rearing, traditionally feminine crafts, and so on. Feminist epistemology, like these other enterprises, must attempt to balance the assertion of the value of a different culture or experience against the dangers of romanticizing it to the extent that the limitations and oppressions it confers on its subjects are ignored.

◆ ◆ ◆

I think that one of the most interesting insights of feminist epistemology is the view that oppressed groups, whether women, the poor, or racial minorities, may derive an "epistemic advantage" from having knowledge of the practices of both their own contexts and those of their oppressors. The practices of the dominant groups (for instance, men) govern a society; the dominated group (for instance, women) must acquire some fluency with these practices in order to survive in that society.

There is no similar pressure on members of the dominant group to acquire knowledge of the practices of the dominated groups. For instance, colonized people had to learn the language and culture of their colonizers. The colonizers seldom found it necessary to have more than a sketchy acquaintance with the language and culture of the "natives." Thus, the oppressed are seen as having an "epistemic advantage" because they can operate with two sets of practices and in two different contexts. This advantage is thought to lead to critical insights because each framework provides a critical perspective on the other.

The oppressed are seen as having an "epistemic advantage" because they can operate with two sets of practices and in two different contexts. This advantage is thought to lead to critical insights because each framework provides a critical perspective on the other.

I would like to balance this account with a few comments about the "dark side," the disadvantages, of being able to or of having to inhabit two mutually incompatible frameworks that provide differing perspectives on social reality. I suspect that nonwestern feminists, given the often complex and troublesome interrelationships between the contexts they must inhabit, are less likely to express unqualified enthusiasm about the benefits of straddling a multiplicity of contexts. Mere access to two different and incompatible contexts is not a guarantee that a critical stance on the part of an individual will result. There are many ways in which she may deal with the situation.

First, the person may be tempted to dichotomize her life and reserve the framework of a different context for each part. The middle class of nonwestern countries supplies numerous examples of people who are very westernized in public life but who return to a very traditional lifestyle in the realm of the family. Women may choose to live their public lives in a "male" mode, displaying characteristics of aggressiveness, competition, and so on, while continuing to play dependent and compliant roles in their private lives. The pressures of jumping between two different lifestyles may be mitigated by justifications of how each pattern of behavior is appropriate to its particular context and of how it enables them to "get the best of both worlds."

Second, the individual may try to reject the practices of her own context and try to be as much as possible like members of the dominant group. Westernized intellectuals in the nonwestern world often may almost lose knowledge of their own cultures and practices and be ashamed of the little that they do still know. Women may try both to acquire stereotypically male characteristics, like aggressiveness, and to expunge stereotypically female characteristics, like emotionality. Or the individual could try to reject entirely the framework of the dominant group and assert the virtues of her own despite the risks of being marginalized from the power structures of the society; consider, for example, women who seek a certain sort of security in traditionally defined roles.

The choice to inhabit two contexts critically is an alternative to these choices and, I would argue, a more useful one. But the presence of alternative contexts does not by itself guarantee that one of the other choices will not be made. Moreover, the decision to inhabit two contexts critically, although it may lead to an "epistemic advantage," is likely to exact a certain price. It may lead to a sense of totally lacking roots or any space where one is at home in a relaxed manner.

This sense of alienation may be minimized if the critical straddling of two contexts is part of an ongoing critical politics, due to the support of others and a deeper understanding of what is going on. When it is not so rooted, it may generate ambivalence, uncertainty, despair, and even madness, rather than more positive critical emotions and attitudes. However such a person determines her locus, there may be a sense of being an outsider in both contexts and a sense of clumsiness or lack of fluency in both sets of practices. Consider this simple linguistic example: most people who learn two different languages that are associated with two very different cultures seldom acquire both with equal fluency; they may find themselves devoid of vocabulary in one language for certain contexts of life or be unable to match real objects with terms they have acquired in their vocabulary. For instance, people from my sort of background would know words in Indian languages for some spices, fruits, and vegetables that they do not know in English. Similarly, they might be unable to discuss "technical" subjects like economics or biology in their own languages because they learned about these subjects and acquired their technical vocabularies only in English.

The relation between the two contexts the individual inhabits may not be simple or straightforward. The individual subject is seldom in a position to carry out a perfect "dialectical synthesis" that preserves all the advantages of both contexts and transcends all their problems. There may be a number of different "syntheses," each of which avoids a different subset of the problems and preserves a different subset of the benefits.

No solution may be perfect or even palatable to the agent confronted with a choice. For example, some Indian feminists may find some western modes of dress (say trousers) either more comfortable or more their "style" than some local modes of dress. However, they may find that wearing the local mode of dress is less socially troublesome, alienates them less from more traditional people they want to work with, and so on. Either choice is bound to leave them partly frustrated in their desires.

Feminist theory must be temperate in the use it makes of this doctrine of "double vision"—the claim that oppressed groups have an epistemic advantage and access to greater critical conceptual space. Certain types and contexts of oppression certainly may bear out the truth of this claim. Others certainly do not seem to do so; and even if they do provide space for critical insights, they may also rule out the possibility of actions subversive of the oppressive state of affairs.

Certain kinds of oppressive contexts, such as the contexts in which women of my grandmother's background lived, rendered their subjects entirely devoid of skills required to function as independent entities in the culture. Girls were married off barely past puberty, trained for nothing beyond household tasks and the rearing of children, and passed from economic dependency on their fathers to economic dependency on their husbands to economic dependency on their sons in old age. Their criticisms of their lot were articulated, if at all, in terms that precluded a desire for any radical change. They saw themselves sometimes as personally unfortunate, but they did not locate the causes of their misery in larger social arrangements.

I conclude by stressing that the important insight incorporated in the doctrine of "double vision" should not be reified into a metaphysics that serves as a substitute for concrete social analysis. Furthermore, the alternative to "buying" into an oppressive social system need not be a celebration of exclusion and the mechanisms of marginalization. The thesis that oppression may bestow an epistemic advantage should not tempt us in the direction of idealizing or romanticizing oppression and blind us to its real material and psychic deprivations.[20]

SUMMARY AND CONCLUSION

Epistemology is the study of human knowledge—what we can know, how we can know it, and what we cannot know. In this sense, epistemology and metaphysics are complementary disciplines. Epistemology becomes the method of approach to the knowledge of the way the world really is. For some philosophers, for example, Descartes, this approach places its primary trust in reason; accordingly, they are called rationalists. For other philosophers, for example, Locke, the preferred approach is to trust the senses and experience; they are called empiricists. The problem for both the rationalists and the empiricists is to get beyond the mere appearance of things to the reality behind them. The rationalist tries to do this by appealing to intuition and certain principles from which he or she can deduce the way the world really is. The empiricist, on the other hand, appeals to his or her experiences, trying to find there evidence for the nature of reality. For both views, however, the danger is that their methods do not always seem to achieve as much as they would like. Rationalists disagree about which principles to start with and which intuitions to trust. Empiricists find that their own method of experience makes it impossible to say anything about what lies beyond experience. Thus Berkeley argues that only our ideas (including God) and the minds that have these ideas exist, and Hume concludes that we can never know anything about reality, but only about our own associations of ideas. Epistemologists are still working on more satisfactory answers to the questions of knowledge, and still trying to defeat or defend once and for all the

---

[20] Uma Narayan, "The Project of Feminist Epistemology: Perspectives from a Nonwestern Feminist," in *Gender/Body/Knowledge,* ed. Alison M. Jaggar and Susan R. Bordo (New Brunswick: Rutgers University Press, 1989).

skeptical conclusions so brilliantly argued by Hume and other skeptics centuries ago. But some are turning to other traditions in an attempt to understand alternative approaches to knowledge and the limitations that may be built into our way of seeing the world. The differences between the sexes have also been added to our questions about knowledge. Do women and men know the world differently? How personal is knowledge—how relative to the individual and his or her cultural context and biology?

GLOSSARY

appearance The way something seems to us, through our senses. Usually philosophers worry about something's being a mere appearance, such that it bears no faithful resemblance to the reality of which it is the appearance.

a priori (knowledge) "Before experience," or more accurately, independent of all experience. A priori knowledge is always necessary, for there can be no imaginable instances that would refute it and no intelligible doubting of it. One might come to know something a priori through experience (for example, you might find out that no parallel lines ever touch each other by drawing tens of thousands of parallel lines) but what is essential to a priori knowledge is that no such experience is needed. Knowledge is a priori if it can be proven independently of experience. The most obvious examples of a priori knowledge are analytic sentences, such as "a horse is an animal," and "if all men are mammals and Socrates is a man, then Socrates is a mammal."

association of ideas A central idea of empiricist philosophy, according to which all knowledge is composed of separate ideas that are connected by their resemblance to one another (e.g., "this one looks exactly like that one"), by their contiguity in space and time (e.g., "every time I see this, I see that as well"), and by their causality (e.g., "every time a thing of that sort happens it is followed by something of this sort"). (The three different "associations" here are Hume's.)

causal theory of perception The view that our experience (our sensations and ideas) are the effects of physical objects acting upon our sense organs (which are thereby the causes).

causation or causality The relation of cause and effect, one event's bringing about another according to natural law. In Hume, (1) one event's following another necessarily (or so it seems to us); (2) one type of event regularly following another (see *association of ideas*).

cause That which produces an effect; an event (or state of affairs, object, act, or person) that brings about another event.

cogito, ergo sum Or "I think, therefore I am" is Descartes' only principle that he finds "beyond doubt" and "perfectly certain." ("Think" here refers to any kind of idea or experience in the mind, not just what we would call "thinking.") It is the premise of his entire philosophy.

datum Latin, literally, "what is given." (plural, *data*)

empiricism The philosophy that demands that all knowledge, except for certain logical truths and principles of mathematics, comes from experience. British empiricism is often used to refer specifically to the three philosophers Locke, Berkeley, and Hume. It is still very much alive, however, and includes Bertrand Russell in our own century and a great many philosophers of the past forty years who have called themselves "logical empiricists" (better known as logical positivists).

emptiness In Buddhism, in Nāgārjuna, being without substance: the proper understanding of being as without substance.

epistemology The study of human knowledge, its nature, its sources, its justification.

explanation An account—usually a causal account—of something; it is opposed to *justification,* which also defends. One can, for example, explain one's action (say, by claiming that he or she was drunk) without thereby justifying it, that is, showing it to be right. Hume ultimately explains our knowledge but does not justify it.

generalization from experience (*or* **inductive generalization**) Inference from observation, experience, and experiment to a generalization about all members of a certain class. For example, in a laboratory, a researcher finds that certain experiments on tobacco plants always have the same result. He or she generalizes, through induction, from experimental observations to a claim (or *hypothesis*) about all tobacco plants. But notice that this generalization is never certain (like the generalization in geometry from a proof of a theorem about this triangle to a theorem about all triangles). It might always turn out that there was a fluke in the experiment or that he/she chose a peculiar sample of plants.

Hume's fork Hume's insistence that every belief be justified either as a "relation between ideas" or as a "matter of fact."

idea In epistemology, almost any mental phenomenon (not, as in Plato, with existence independent of individual minds). The terminology varies slightly; Locke uses "idea" to refer to virtually any "mental content"; Hume reserves "idea" for those mental atoms that are derived by the mind from impressions.

impression Hume's word for sensations or sense-data, that which is given to the mind through the senses.

induction; inductive reasoning; inductive generalization Induction is the process of inferring general conclusions (for example, "all swans are white") from a sufficiently large sample of particular observations ("this swan is white, that swan is white, and that one, and that one, and that one . . ."). It is usually contrasted with *deduction* (see Chapter 1), in that, while deductive reasoning guarantees that the conclusion shall be as certain as the premises, induction never gives us a conclusion as certain as the premises. Its conclusions are, at most, merely probable. ("There might always be some black swan somewhere"; and there are, in Western Australia.) (See "A Brief Introduction to Logic," pp. 20–37.)

innate ideas Literally, ideas that are "born into the mind." Locke's famous attack on such ideas took them to be literally ideas that all men share from birth. The rationalist philosophers he was supposedly attacking, however, held a much more sophisticated notion; they did not believe that ideas were literally "born into us," but they did believe that we are born with certain "innate" capacities and dispositions, which will develop with proper education (and mental health). And these ideas, most importantly, can be defended or justified without appeal to any particular experiences or experiments. This is the claim that Locke ultimately rejected.

intuition Immediate knowledge, without the aid of reasoning or inference. It must be stressed, however, that intuition is often (even usually) argued to be a function of reason and capable of rational insights even if they are, by their very nature, not defensible by any arguments.

justification An attempt to defend a position or an act, to show that it is correct (or at least reasonable). (Compare with *explanation.*)

masculinist From the point of view of men's interests and advantage, as opposed to those of women.

perception A kind of knowledge, sense experience.

primary qualities In Locke, those properties ("qualities") that inhere in the object.

principle of induction The belief that the laws of nature will continue to hold in the future as they have in the past. (Crudely, "the future will be like the past".)

principle of universal causation The belief that every event has its cause (or causes). In scientific circles, it is usually added, "its sufficient natural cause," in order to eliminate the possibility of miracles and divine intervention (which are allowed in Leibniz's similar but broader Principle of Sufficient Reason).

probable Likely; or supported by the evidence (but not conclusively). The empiricist's middle step between the extremities of certainty and doubt. (Probability is the measure of how probable something is.)

quality In Locke (and other authors), a property.

rationalism The philosophy that is characterized by its confidence in reason, and intuition in particular, to know reality independently of experience. (See *reason* and *intuition.*) Continental rationalism is usually reserved for three European philosophers, Descartes, Spinoza, and Leibniz.

reason In rationalism the faculty that allows us to know reality, through intuition. In empiricism, simply the ability to recognize certain principles that are "relations of ideas," for example, trivial truths ("a cat is an animal") and, more complicated, principles of arithmetic and geometry. Empiricists deny that reason allows us special insight into reality, however; it tells us only relations between ideas.

relations of ideas In empiricism, knowledge that is restricted to the logical and conceptual connections between ideas, not to the correspondence of those ideas to experience or to reality.

secondary qualities In Locke, those properties ("qualities") that are caused in us by objects, but do not inhere in the objects themselves (for example, color).

sensation The experimental result of the stimulation of a sense organ, for example, *seeing* red, *hearing* a ringing noise, *smelling* something burning. The simplest of mental phenomena.

sense-data That which is given to the senses, prior to any reasoning or organization on our part.

skepticism The philosophical belief (or fear) that knowledge is not possible, and that no rational arguments will succeed in overcoming our doubts.

subjective idealism The view that only ideas and mind exist, and that there are no substances, matter, or material objects. In particular, the philosophy of Bishop Berkeley.

substance A "unit" of existence, a being; something which "stands by itself."

Sunyata Buddhist term for emptiness; see *emptiness.*

tabula rasa In Locke's philosophy, the "blank tablet" metaphor of the mind, in opposition to the doctrine that there are innate ideas. In other words, the mind is a "blank" at birth, and everything we know must be "stamped in" through experience.

BIBLIOGRAPHY AND FURTHER READING

Several studies of the various problems in René Descartes' epistemology are in Willis Doney, ed., *Descartes* (New York: Doubleday, Anchor, 1967). Gottfried W. von Leibniz's reply to John Locke is spelled out at length in Leibniz's *New Essays on Human Understanding,* trans. A. G. Langley (La Salle, IL: Open Court, 1949). Locke's *Essay Concerning Human Understanding* is published by Dover Publications (New York, 1959). Bishop Berkeley's *Treatise* is printed in full in T. E. Jessop, ed., *Berkeley, Philosophical Writings* (Austin, TX: University of Texas Press, 1953). Of special interest is Berkeley's *Three Dialogues Between Hylas and Philonous* (La Salle, IL: Open Court, 1935), in which the arguments of his *Treatise* are worked out in entertaining dialogue form. David Hume's *Treatise of Human Nature* is available, edited by L. A. Selby-Bigge (Oxford: Oxford University Press, 1888), but most beginners will find Hume's *Enquiry Concerning Human Understanding* (Oxford: Oxford University Press, 1902) much easier reading. Bertrand Russell, *Problems of Philosophy* (London: Oxford University Press, 1912) is an excellent introduction to the problems of epistemology and some of the problems of metaphysics. Two more modern epistemological studies are A. J. Ayer, *The Problem of Knowledge* (New York: St. Martin's Press, 1956) and Roderick Chisholm, *Theory of Knowledge* (Englewood Cliffs, NJ: Prentice-Hall, 1956). A modern series of studies is R. J. Swartz, ed., *Perceiving, Sensing, Knowing* (New York: Doubleday, Anchor, 1965). For a comprehensive anthology on epistemology, see E. Nagel and R. Brandt, eds., *Meaning and Knowledge* (New York: Harcourt Brace Jovanovich, 1965). A modern defense of skepticism is Peter Unger, *Ignorance* (London: Oxford University Press, 1975). On feminist theories of knowledge, see Ann Garry and Marilyn Pearsall, *Women, Knowledge and Reality* (Boston: Unwin Hyman, 1989). For a concise overview of Indian skepticism, see Stephen Phillips, "Indian Philosophy," in R. Solomon and K. Higgins, *From Africa to Zen* (Savage, Md.: Rowman and Littlefield, 1993).

TRUTH

4

The limits of my language mean the limits of my world.

LUDWIG WITTGENSTEIN

We turned from metaphysics to epistemology because we began to question our ability to know "the way the world really is." Hence, we thought we should first find out what we can know. But then after Hume, it seemed that not only were we incapable of doing metaphysics but we could not justify even the most ordinary and obvious principles of our everyday lives. If we can't even know with certainty that there is an "external" world, then how can we claim to know anything—except, perhaps, our own isolated and limited experiences? But then, what is the *truth?* Surely it cannot be solely a function of our ideas. If it is true that there is a bald-headed man in the governor's mansion, then there must *be* a bald-headed man in the governor's mansion, not just our impression or idea of him. Furthermore, if our knowledge of reality is colored by our ideas and "habits" of understanding and interpretation, could it be possible that reality will be different for different people, who have different ideas and different intellectual and perceptual habits? Did Aristotle and the ancient animists live in the same world as John Locke and modern scientists? Did Confucius share a world with Lao Tsu and the Buddha? Or were their ideas about the world so different that the worlds they lived in were different as well? Is there, in that case, any such thing as "the Truth"? Or does it make sense to say that what is true for one person might nevertheless be false for someone else?

The problem of truth has always been central to philosophy. In asking "What is reality *really* like?" the ancient philosophers were trying to ascertain the truth behind the appearances of reality. Some of them, such as Parmenides and Plato, quite clearly distinguished between the True World—or simply "the Truth"—and the world of our everyday experiences. Descartes and Locke were both looking for the truth, but in different ways, and the difference in their approaches signified a difference in their sense of what the truth should be. But they both believed that there was such a thing as the Truth, that their preferred philosophical methods would get them the Truth. It is with the skeptics—and Hume in particular—that this assurance has broken down.

The multiplicity of cultures and philosophies—and different *types* of philosophy—also throw open the question of truth. If different cultures and philosophies only disagree in their perspective and style, then despite their differences it may nonetheless be true that there is a truth that all of them describe, but they orient themselves to that truth in different ways. It is like the old Persian story about the several blind men fondling an elephant, one of whom claims that the beast is as big as a barrel, another that the elephant is more like a snake, two others that it is like a rope or an ivory sword. But in this familiar story it is obvious that the blind men could, by moving around the animal, come to agree.

The real problem arises if it turns out that our various perspectives and the language in which we describe them render us immobile, incapable of appreciating (except in the abstract) other orientations. It is as if we never experience reality itself—the thesis shared by various idealists and the skeptics alike—but know only our own interpretations. Or, to take a different metaphor, it is as if we were reading a book, a translation of an ancient text into English, which itself was translated from another ancient language, which was in turn translated from another ancient language, which was copied from some ancient scrolls which now no longer exist and, just possibly, never existed in the first place. Do other cultures share our world but just see it differently, or do they live in some sense in a different world? If so, as Nietzsche writes, there may be many kinds of "truth," and thus no truth at all (in his book, *The Will to Power*).

The view of the Truth as "out there," in the world, is the basis of both common sense and much of the history of philosophy. Even Bishop Berkeley, who argued that the world consists of ideas, insisted that these ideas were caused by God, who is the Truth. But skepticism challenges God as Truth just as it challenges our assumption that most of what we know is the Truth. The idea that the Truth is outside of us becomes no longer a matter of common sense but the source of serious paradoxes. If it is outside of us, how will we ever know it? If it is not outside of us, is there anything at all to know?

What now comes into question are the very assumptions that have ruled metaphysics and common sense since the time of the first philosophers. Consider again Plato's "two-worlds" view: "the world of Being," which is the true world, and "the world of Becoming," the world of our daily experience that, though perhaps not unreal, is less real than the world of Being. Now, the actual model Plato uses (the real world as the world of Forms as over against our world as the world of material objects and change) has not been accepted by all modern philosophers, and it is certainly out of line with common sense. Many philosophers, of both East and West, *have* accepted the distinction between appearance and reality. The empiricists, for example, held precisely the reverse of Plato's view. According to modern empiricism, it is the material world that becomes the real world, and the world of ideas— our mental "ideas" and experiences—becomes the less real world. The problem, in Descartes, Locke, Hume, and Russell, is always how to know that our "ideas" or experiences in fact match up to the real world. The fact that Descartes is confident that he can know that his experiences "match up," while Hume believes that we can never know even if there is such a world, must not hide from us the "two-worlds" model that both of them presuppose: reality (if there is one) on the one side, our experience on the other. How do we move from experience to reality?

The most serious complication in our making this move is our recognition that our experience of reality is **mediated,** that is, it is filtered through our mental/ neurological apparatus—our senses, our concepts, our ways of understanding, and our language. But this means that we must assume that our senses do not distort reality, that our concepts are "faithful" to the things they conceptualize, that our ways of understanding are themselves true or faithful to what we claim to understand, that our language is adequate to describe the world without oversimplification or distortion. Or, at any rate, we must take into account the possibility that there may be such distortion. Could the words we use to pick out individual objects in fact distort the truth for us, forcing things into categories not inherent in them and blinding us to other kinds of things or processes or events that cannot be captured by our language? Could it be that ancient Greek described a different world than the one we live in today? Could it be that Chinese describes a different world than the one we describe in English? Are there different truths for different people at different times speaking different languages? This is the difficult problem of **relativism,** the thesis that truth varies from context to context, from culture to culture, that truth is relative to a context, a culture, a language, a set of circumstances, a way of looking at the world. If so, is it possible to say anything about reality that we have not ourselves imposed through language and our own experience?

Once again, the issue of multiculturalism crashes in on traditional Western philosophy with a vengeance. Could it be that the structure Western philosophers and scientists posit in the world is in fact a projection of their language and methods? Could it be that the emphasis on abstract theory is an oversimplification or even a distortion of the truth? African folk traditions, for example, explain the ways of the world in what we would call metaphorical or mythological language. Is it correct or fair to insist, as Western philosophers and scientists have for nearly three thousand years, that those folk traditions are false or misleading, rather than an equally but extremely different way of trying to express one of several possible visions of the world?

Descartes had insisted that any belief worth the honorific title "knowledge" had to be certain ("perfectly certain," he said). But now, let us ask, wasn't he demanding a bit too much? In fact, much too much! Surely I have the right to say that I know that I'm not dreaming right now, even if it's true that I might be wrong. The assumption that knowledge consists of necessary truths has already begun to bother us, since Locke and his empiricist followers insisted that all of our knowledge of the world must consist of truths based upon experience, and since, by the very nature of inductive arguments from experience, we could not actually be certain of anything. In other words, it is time to weaken our demands. Perhaps it will be enough if we believe what is **rational** to believe, even if it is not certain and even if it does not "match up" with some unexperienceable reality. You might even say, "perhaps it is not necessary to believe what is true," but notice that you would have already presupposed that what makes our belief true is some reality beyond our experience. It is just this notion of truth we must examine in this chapter.

A. TWO KINDS OF TRUTHS

Not all truths depend upon the facts of the case, upon the proper matching of our experience and reality. Some truths seem to be true no matter what is the case, truths that seem to be, as Descartes hoped, known to be true with certainty, no matter what, even if an evil demon were fooling us. Even Hume, for example, granted that some of our beliefs are beyond the range of his skeptical doubts, namely, those that he calls "relations of ideas," such as the basic principles of arithmetic. Nothing could make us doubt that two plus two equals four. Descartes may have suggested that it was possible that an evil demon was fooling him about even this; but what would it mean to be "fooled" about such matters? How could he have been wrong about that? Of course, he could always say that he might be wrong about two plus two equalling four, just as we could always say that two plus two equals five. But what could we possibly mean by that? We can understand what it would be like to be wrong about some factual belief, such as "there are no Chinese paratroopers in Cuba"; perhaps it even makes sense, however implausible, to suggest that we might be dreaming right now. But one can't even imagine, no matter how hard one tries, what it would be for "two plus two equals four" to be false.

Beliefs that we cannot even imagine being false and that lie beyond the range of all possible doubt and refutation are called **necessary truths.** In short, they must be true. Plato and Aristotle thought that their metaphysical doctrines were necessary truths. So did Descartes, Spinoza, and Leibniz. Necessary truth is contrasted with **contingent truth,** which is a belief that is in fact true but might not have been. It is true, for example, that I am now wearing a sweater, but we can easily imagine what it would be for me not to wear one. That is a contingent truth. Necessary truths, because we cannot even imagine what it would be like for them to be false, are always "perfectly certain"; contingent truths, because we can always imagine that they might be false (and that we are possibly fooled or misled in believing them) are never "perfectly certain" but always merely probable. We can always think of some way, no matter how implausible, in which we might be wrong. (I might be dreaming that I'm wearing a sweater, for example.) But one cannot be mistaken about a necessary truth. (A curious but important exception to this distinction is already familiar to you: Descartes' "I exist" is both necessary [it can't be intelligibly doubted] and contingent [since it is possible that he might not have existed].) But since metaphysical doctrines conflict, we might well wonder whether they can be necessary truths after all.

A partial distinction between necessary truth and contingent truth is this: Contingent truths are based upon experience and necessary truths are not. Accordingly, contingent truths allow for some further experience that would change our minds. We may be sure that there are no armadillos on the upper east side of Manhattan, but because that is a contingent truth, it is always possible that we shall see an armadillo crossing 86th Street, and thereby have to give up our belief.

Because of this essential link between contingent truths and experience, philosophers often refer to our knowledge of them as **empirical** knowledge. Necessary truths, on the other hand, are not based upon experience, and no possible experience—real or imagined—could change our minds about them. For this reason, philosophers talk about these truths as being prior to experience or **a priori** and knowledge of them is also considered to be a priori, in other words, to be knowledge that is independent of experience. It is important to stress that the word *prior,* which means "before," does not mean "earlier in time." For example, it does not mean that we know a priori that "two plus two equals four" before we ever have experience of two things adding up with two other things to give us four things. It means rather that the justification of a priori knowledge does not depend on any possible experience. You cannot refute "two plus two equals four" through experience. But neither can you justify it through experience. You could spend a year adding up different pairs of things: walnuts, elephants, pieces of chalk, people, and scoops of ice cream. You would then have the general claim that "whenever I add two things to two things I get four things," but you would fail to prove the necessity of that truth.

There are philosophers, as we have seen, who do take a priori to mean literally "before"; that is, those philosophers who believe in innate ideas believe that we actually do have certain knowledge before we have any experience at all. We are born with it, and that would explain, if you accept this theory, how it is that a priori knowledge is possible. But it is important to emphasize that the belief in innate ideas is not essential to the notion of either necessary truth or a priori knowledge, and most philosophers talk about the latter without ever mentioning the former.

What then is the source of a priori knowledge? For those philosophers who believe in innate ideas, the answer is that we are born with it. But even this is not enough, for it is necessary to say how it is that we are born with such knowledge. Even if it is "stamped in our minds by God," as some philosophers have held, how do we recognize it? The traditional answer, for those who believe in innate ideas and for those who do not, is through reason. In fact, reason is traditionally defined (for example, by Plato, Aristotle, Spinoza, and Leibniz) as our ability to know necessary truths. But our account is circular; we are told that we can know necessary truths because of reason, but reason is defined as our ability to know necessary truths. So, we must ask, what is this ability? How do we have it? How is a priori knowledge possible?

Although we shall be exclusively concerned with necessary and contingent truths, it is important to say that there is a similar distinction between necessary and contingent falsehoods. "Every triangle has at least five sides" is a necessary falsehood—it could not possibly be true. "There are no eagles in America," is a contingent falsehood—it is in fact false, but we can (too easily) imagine that it might be true.

1. Analytic Truths

Consider the utterly trivial statement, "all bachelors are unmarried." Not very interesting, to be sure, but it is obviously a necessary truth. We can be perfectly certain that this statement is true, and we know in advance that no study of bachelors could possibly turn up an instance of one who was married. We cannot even imagine a situation in which this statement would be false, and there is no sense in wondering, "well, we've only looked at the bachelors in our neighborhood, what about the bachelors in southern California?" All we have to know to know that "all bachelors are unmarried" is the meaning of the English sentence, nothing else.

Now consider the contingent claim, "all bachelors are happy." Of course, in order to find out whether that is true or not you have to know the meanings of the words, but you cannot tell whether or not it is true just by looking at the words. This statement raises an empirical question. In order to know whether or not it is true you have to go interview bachelors. To falsify the claim that all bachelors are happy, you would have to find only one unhappy bachelor. But even if you never found one, you could never be perfectly certain of the truth of the claim. There might always be one unhappy bachelor, living in a cave off the coast of Madagascar. A contingent claim, therefore, is never perfectly certain. One can always at least imagine some circumstance that would prove it false, even if it seems, on the basis of the present evidence, to be true.

The example "all bachelors are unmarried" is an analytic truth. Its truth can be demonstrated just by referring to the meanings of the words in the sentence. This particular example is what we referred to in earlier chapters as a conceptual truth (such as, "a horse is an animal"). **Conceptual truths** are a special class of analytic truths. Aristotle discussed such truths in terms of essences. He would say that "the essence of a bachelor is to be unmarried." More modern philosophers would talk about concepts. They would say that "the concept 'bachelor' includes the concept of being unmarried." Today most philosophers would rather say that "bachelor means unmarried person." But these different formulations all point to the same fact, that conceptual truths are necessary truths because of meanings and not because of facts.

Not all analytic truths are conceptual truths, however. Consider the statement, "either it is raining or it is not raining." Now obviously you don't have to look out the window to see whether this is true or not. It is true just because of the form of the sentence, which is "*P or not P.*" Such sentences are called **tautologies.** They are true by virtue of the form of the sentence alone, and it doesn't matter what phrase you substitute for *P.* For example, you know that "either there are exactly 7,500 comets in our galaxy or there are not," even if you don't know anything about astronomy, or exactly what a "comet" or a "galaxy is. ("*P or not P*" is called the **law of the excluded middle**—either a sentence or its denial must be true.)

Tautologies are not very interesting. They are the most boring and uninformative sentences in our language, but they are also very important. Every tautology gives us what we called (in the Introduction) a **rule of inference,** one of those basic rules that we use in all our thinking. (This is true even for people who claim "not to be logical" or who actually attack logic.) According to these rules of inference, we define the validity of our arguments. But here a problem arises. How can we defend a rule of inference itself? We cannot say that it is valid, since we have to use such rules in order to say that anything is valid. And we can't use a rule to prove itself. (That would be the same as appointing a magistrate to judge his or her own alleged corruption.) To answer this question, many philosophers appeal to **intuition** as a defense of fundamental rules of inference. Rationalists feel comfortable with this since they have confidence in reason to show us such basic truths through intuition. Empiricists tend to feel very uncomfortable, however, for they would rather these rules be based upon experience (but they are not) or that they be matters of reasoning (but this can't be either, since they are the foundation of all reasoning). So, empiricists try to find as small a set of basic rules as possible, from which they can derive all of the others. The problem then becomes, how do you defend that basic set of rules?

The most fundamental of these rules is called the **law of contradiction,** which says, a statement and its denial cannot both be true. For example, it cannot be true that it is raining and that it is not raining at the same place at the same time. This law has been used by many philosophers (for example, Leibniz and Hume) to define analytic truths in general. They say that a statement is analytic if when you deny it you get a contradiction. The recognition of the importance of this law, however, goes as far back as Aristotle, who worried about this law and what makes it true. After considerable thought, he concluded:

FROM *METAPHYSICS*
BY **ARISTOTLE**

This is the most certain of all principles, for it is impossible for anyone to suppose that the same thing is and is not . . . then clearly it is impossible for the same man to suppose at the same time that the same thing is and is not; for the man who made this error would entertain two contrary opinions at the same time. Hence all men who are demonstrating anything refer back to this as an ultimate belief; for it is by nature the starting-point of all the other axioms as well. . . .

> *This is the most certain of all principles, for it is impossible for anyone to suppose that the same thing is and is not.*

Some, indeed, demand to have the law proved, but this is because they lack education; for it shows lack of education not to know of what we should require proof, and of what we should not. For it is quite impossible that everything should have a proof; the process would go on to infinity, so that even so there would be no proof. If on the other hand there are some things of which no proof need be sought, they cannot say what principle they think to be more self-evident. Even in the case of this law, however, we can demonstrate the impossibility of refutation, if only our opponent makes some statement. If he makes none, it is absurd to seek for an argument against one who has no arguments of his own about anything, in so far as he has none; for such a person, in so far as he is such, is really no better than a vegetable.[1]

---

[1] Aristotle, *Metaphysics,* Bk. IV, trans. High Tredennick (Cambridge, MA: Harvard University Press, 1933).

Aristotle's answer is still accepted by most philosophers. This one principle, at least, cannot be defended except to say that it would be utterly absurd to deny it. Even if a philosopher will not accept the appeal to intuition in any other case, it seems that he must at least in this one.

There are many other kinds of analytic truths, but it would take a course of logic to discuss them adequately. What they all have in common is that they are necessary truths that can be known simply by the analysis of the form of the sentence or the meanings of words or concepts. This raises a huge question, however, which has been of special concern to mathematics-oriented philosophers for many years. We used "two plus two equals four" as a paradigm example of a necessary truth, and so most philosophers would agree. But whether it is also an *analytic* proposition is a matter on which some of the greatest philosophers of modern times would disagree. Immanuel Kant, in particular, argued that such propositions were not analytic but rather **synthetic a priori truths.** What makes this claim of particular philosophical significance is the fact that Kant also claimed this status for just those metaphysical or foundational truths that Hume, for example, had called into question.

FROM *THE CRITIQUE*
OF PURE REASON
BY **IMMANUEL KANT**

THE DISTINCTION BETWEEN PURE (*A PRIORI*) AND EMPIRICAL
(*A POSTERIORI*) KNOWLEDGE

That all our knowledge begins with experience there can be no doubt. For how should the faculty of knowledge be called into activity, if not by objects which affect our senses, and which either produce representations by themselves, or rouse the activity of our understanding to compare, or connect, or to separate them, and thus to convert the raw material of our sensuous impressions into a knowledge of objects, which we call experience? In respect of time, therefore, no knowledge within us is antecedent to experience, but all knowledge begins with it.

But although all our knowledge begins with experience, it does not follow that it arises from experience. For it is quite possible that even our empirical experience is a compound of that which we receive through impressions, and of that which our own faculty of knowledge (incited only by sensuous impressions), supplies from itself, a supplement which we do not distinguish from that raw material, until long practice has roused our attention and rendered us capable of separating one from the other.

It is therefore a question which deserves at least closer investigation, and cannot be disposed of at first sight, whether there exists a knowledge independent of experience, and even of all impressions of the senses? Such *knowledge* is called *a priori,* and distinguished from *empirical* knowledge, which has its source *a posteriori,* that is, in experience.

But now we are getting ahead of our story. The problem of truth is not just a question about necessary or *a priori* truth. It is, first of all, a question about empirical truth, about how we can have confidence that our experience and beliefs are faithful to the way the world itself (reality) is. And that is, by no means, a simple matter either.

2. Truths about the World

"What is truth?" That familiar question was raised by Pontius Pilate as he dismissed Christ's case from his court. He was just a politician; he did not take the question seriously. Philosophers do. It is their business to find the truth, to expose fraudulent beliefs and superstitions, and to assure us that we can know, at least most of the time, what is true from what is false.

What indeed is truth? Should we say, as we have so far, that our beliefs are true if and only if they "match up" with reality? Or, in accordance with our present suspicions, should we not perhaps hold out for some different conception of "truth," one that does not place such emphasis on "matching up" and the separation of reality on the one hand from our beliefs and experiences on the other?

The proper philosophical name for this notion of "matching up" our beliefs and experiences with reality is the **correspondence theory of truth.** On the one hand, it is an obvious truism: for example, when I tell you "there is a grapefruit in the refrigerator," what I tell you is true if and only if there is in fact a grapefruit in the refrigerator. So obvious is this "correspondence" criterion of truth—that a belief or a statement is true if and only if it corresponds to the facts—that no one would have thought of calling it a "theory" at all until recently. In his *Metaphysics,* Aristotle dismissed the whole "problem of truth" in a single sentence: "To say of what is that it is not, or of what is not that it is, is false, while to say of what is that it is, or of what is not that it is not, is true." As long as philosophers (and everyone else) believed themselves unquestionably capable of knowing reality as such, this commonsense platitude was as appropriate for the investigations of metaphysics as it was for the daily task of checking to see whether there was a grapefruit in the refrigerator. But as empiricism and Hume's skepticism grew in persuasiveness and the confidence that we could know reality was thrown into question, the platitude became a problem.

For Descartes, the correspondence between our ideas and reality had to be demonstrated. Locke expressed his doubts; Berkeley rejected the "external world" altogether, leaving only God (and other minds like Berkeley's own); and Hume left us with the seemingly irrefutable argument that we could never know reality outside of us, or even if there was a reality to be known. Hume had given us a *reductio ad absurdum* argument; one of his premises—perhaps not an explicit one—has brought us to the absurdity of not being able to defend the most commonsense beliefs. But all of these philosophers presuppose the correspondence theory of truth, the idea that knowledge is the correspondence of our ideas to reality and that the only knowledge worthy of the name is our being certain of this correspondence. It is here that Kant returns to the beginnings of Hume's arguments, and everyone else's, and roots out the correspondence theory of truth as the implicit premise that is the cause of all the trouble.

Now it will probably seem odd to you to even question something so obviously "true" as the correspondence theory of truth. Of course, we cannot deny that "there is a grapefruit in the refrigerator" is true if and only if there is a grapefruit in the refrigerator. But let us note immediately that the correspondence theory is not so obviously adequate for all true statements. What does "two plus two equals four" correspond to that makes it true? One might suggest that it corresponds to all combinations in the world of two things (walnuts, elephants, acres, or apples) and two other things of the same kind. "Two plus two equals four" would still be true even if there were no such combinations in the universe. A tautology such as "either it is snowing or it is not snowing" does not correspond to anything; it "tells us nothing about the world." A conceptual truth such as "blue is a color" tells us only about the meanings of the words in our language. A rule of inference tells us how to think. But none of these "correspond" to anything. So, at most, we shall have to say that the correspondence theory is good as an account of empirical knowledge only! (This is the conclusion of most empiricists, including more contemporary "logical positivists.")

But there are more serious problems, even within the domain of empirical knowledge. Let's look again at the truism, " 'there's a grapefruit in the refrigerator' is true if and only if there is a grapefruit in the refrigerator." Let's ask, first of all, in what sense the noises you utter (the sounds, "there's a grapefruit in the refrigerator . . .") correspond to the fact that there is a grapefruit in the refrigerator. If you think of one thing corresponding to another, you might think of a map corresponding to the terrain it is a map of: smaller scale with many omissions, but at least it is the same shape, same proportions, and has representations of things in that terrain that you can recognize. But how do those sounds coming out of your mouth (which, now that you listen to them, might sound strange indeed) "correspond" to that grapefruit in the kitchen? Now you will say that it is not merely "the sounds" that correspond but rather what you are saying or meaning. Of course, this is correct. But notice that what those words mean is not a matter of their use in this particular instance; they depend upon their role in a language (American English), which you happen to speak. (If you spoke only Eskimo and pronounced the same sounds, it would be a remarkable coincidence, but wouldn't mean anything.) And the "correspondence" between those words with their meanings and the fact that there is a grapefruit in the refrigerator depends not only on the whole American-English language and your knowledge of it but also on a set of conventions that both you and your friend must understand as referring to the grapefruit in the refrigerator.

In class, for example, your teacher says, "there is a grapefruit in the refrigerator" as an example of an English sentence. But you do not get up and look for a refrigerator. You know that although your teacher has said the same words that you say to your friend when offering a grapefruit he or she is not directly referring to anything. The statement does not "correspond" to a fact that there is a grapefruit in the refrigerator. It is clear that what you've said (and the same is true of what you've thought) cannot correspond to anything by itself. In a sense, you might say that what corresponds to the fact that there is a grapefruit in the refrigerator when you offer your friend a grapefruit is the whole of the English language, with all of its conventions and everything that you and your friend know that is relevant to the meaning of your statement in this particular case.

From the other side of this "correspondence," matters are no less complicated. What is "the fact" that there is a grapefruit in the refrigerator? Sounds like an easy question. The answer is that there is a grapefruit in the refrigerator! But how do we pick out this fact, except by using our language to distinguish this fact from any number of others. Suppose, instead of saying anything, you were simply to point toward the refrigerator for your friend. Now, of course, knowing you, your friend knows what you mean. In this case, the pointing is shorthand for the statement, and presupposes it. But suppose your friend is a time-traveler from thirteenth-century China who had no idea what a refrigerator was, or a grapefruit for that matter? Would he pick out the right "fact"? How would he know whether you were pointing to the kitchen, to the door of the refrigerator, or to its contents? Is the "grapefruit" to be eaten or to be dropped on one's feet? How do we even understand the pointing gesture? (When I point my finger toward the cat food, my cats smell my finger!) So, if it seems obvious to you that "the facts" are simply there, waiting to be corresponded to by our verbal or gestural pointing, think again. One distinguishes the facts of the world only by picking them out by language. The language then can't be said to "correspond" to the world, for it is language that "carves up" our world into those individually identifiable "facts."

Now none of this is to say that your statement, "there's a grapefruit in the refrigerator" isn't true if and only if there is a grapefruit in the refrigerator. It is rather to say that this simple "correspondence" is possible only because of the enormous number of systematic assumptions we share within our language and about the world and about the way we refer to particular "facts" in the world by use of certain statements. In everyday life we don't have to think about such things. But in philosophy, they make us marvel at what complex and clever creatures we are. Bertrand Russell, certainly one of the smartest among us, spent forty years trying to make sense out of the "commonsense" correspondence theory. He never did. He never succeeded in formulating an adequate defense of the idea that some single unit of language could "correspond" to discrete "facts" in the world. Today, most philosophers would agree, no matter what kind of method they follow, that the correspondence theory alone cannot make sense of the notion of truth. A statement means something only within a language, and a "fact" is "corresponded to" only after it has been picked out by language. That means that truth can't be simple correspondence.

So the seemingly simple act of "saying what is true" turns out to be enormously complicated, and against the "correspondence theory of truth," there are three telling arguments:

1. It is, at best, limited. All cases of necessary truth, and perhaps some others, cannot be accounted for by it at all.

2. There is no such thing as a statement or a belief that by itself is capable of "corresponding" to anything.
3. There is no such thing as a "fact" that can be picked out independently of the language used to describe it.

Next time you say or think that there is a grapefruit in the refrigerator, you might marvel at the complex that has just come into action. That won't, unfortunately, guarantee that your statement or thought will be true. For despite all this sophisticated, intellectual apparatus we still occasionally forget to buy the grapefruit.

B. THEORIES OF TRUTH

Now what? We find ourselves with some ill-defined complex in which our language and reality are tied together and mutually depend on each other. But what we have been leading up to, finally, is that we need something more than the naive commonsense "correspondence theory of truth," one which takes into account this complexity of interrelations. Three such theories have achieved prominence in this century, although all three of them were anticipated by Immanuel Kant, whom we shall meet later in this chapter. The three theories are the following:

1. The **coherence theory of truth,** which says that a statement or a belief is true if and only if it "coheres" or ties in with other statements and beliefs.
2. The **pragmatic theory of truth,** which says that a statement or a belief is true if and only if "it works," if it allows us to predict certain results, if it allows us to function effectively in everyday life, and if it encourages further inquiry or helps us lead better lives.
3. The **semantic theory of truth,** which says that a statement or a belief is true because the rules of our language set up a correspondence between certain statements and "the facts" that our language picks out in the world. Superficially this theory looks like the correspondence theory, but it is very different. The correspondence theory accepts facts as "already there," independent of our language. The semantic theory explains this apparent correspondence by telling us that it is our language that sets it up in the first place.

1. The Coherence Theory

The coherence theory of truth does not necessarily oppose the commonsense idea that true statements "correspond" to facts in the world, but it does shift the focus of the discussion away from this correspondence—if there is one—to the interdependence of the statements themselves. In other words, it seizes on the observation made in our discussion of the correspondence theory, that a simple statement of fact ("there's a grapefruit in the refrigerator") involves, in some sense, the whole English language. The words in that simple sentence would not mean much if they did not also have the same meaning in an unlimited number of other sentences, and their ability to refer to the world therefore depends on their role in a language.

Furthermore, when we try to ascertain the truth of a statement, how do we do it? By ascertaining the truth of other statements and arguing, deductively or inductively, for the consequent truth of this one. Thus the coherence theory places its emphasis on the ways in which we find out the truth, and it rightly points out that knowledge is not just a matter of establishing the truth of one statement after another; it is a matter of getting more and more statements to cohere in a unified body of knowledge. This coherence makes them true, whether or not there is some metaphysical sense in which they cohere because, in fact, they are true.

To represent the coherence theory, here is a selection from the American philosopher, **Brand Blanshard.**

ON THE COHERENCE THEORY
BY **BRAND BLANSHARD**

To think is to seek understanding. And to seek understanding is an activity of mind that is marked off from all other activities by a highly distinctive aim. This aim . . . is to achieve systematic vision, so to apprehend what is now unknown to us as to relate it, and relate it necessarily, to what we know already.

But may it not be that what satisfies thought fails to conform to the real world? Where is the guarantee that when I have brought my ideas into the form my ideal requires, they should be *true?* . . . In our long struggle with the relation of thought to reality we saw that if thought and things are conceived as related only externally, then knowledge is luck; there is no necessity whatever that what satisfies intelligence should coincide with what really is. It may do so, or it may not; on the principle that there are many misses to one bull's-eye, it more probably does not. But if we get rid of the misleading analogies through which this relation has been conceived, of copy and original, stimulus and organism, lantern and screen, and go to thought itself with the question what reference to an object means, we get a different and more hopeful answer. To think of a thing is to get that thing itself in some degree within the mind. To think of a color or an emotion is to have that within us which if it *were developed and completed,* would identify itself with the object. In short, if we accept its own report, thought is related to reality as the partial to the perfect fulfillment of a purpose. The more adequate its grasp the more nearly does it approximate, the more fully does it realize in itself, the nature and relations of its objects.

. . . We may look at the growth of knowledge, individual or social, either as an attempt by our own minds to return to union with things as they are in their ordered wholeness, or the affirmation through our minds of the ordered whole

> *Where is the guarantee that when I have brought my ideas into the form my ideal requires, they should be* **true?**

itself. And if we take this view, our notion of truth is marked out for us. Truth is the approximation of thought to reality. It is thought on its way home. Its measure is the distance thought has travelled, under guidance of its inner compass, toward that intelligible system which unites its ultimate object with its ultimate end. Hence at any given time the degree of truth in our experience as a whole is the degree of system it has achieved. The degree of truth of a particular proposition is to be judged in the first instance by its coherence with experience as a whole, ultimately by its coherence with that further whole, all-comprehensive and fully articulated, in which thought can come to rest.[2]

The coherence theory of truth, according to Blanshard, begins with the observation that we test the truth of a belief by seeing its implications and other logically connected beliefs. But the theory is not confined to this test. Truth itself, he insists, is nothing other than the interconnectedness of our various beliefs. The truth of a particular belief is nothing other than how well it fits in with everything else we believe.

2. The Pragmatic Theory

Pragmatism is the one major philosophical movement to originate and remain more or less completely in the United States. The three philosophers most easily identified with this movement are Charles Peirce, William James, and John Dewey, all of them Americans (Peirce and James in Massachusetts, Dewey in Chicago and New York). We shall see more of pragmatism later in this chapter, but for now, what is important to us is the pragmatists' theory or theories of truth (for they did not entirely agree with one another). As one might expect, both from the name "pragmatism" and the characteristic American concern for what is "practical," a pragmatic theory of truths begins with a certain impatience for the abstractions and obscurities of traditional metaphysics and epistemology. In particular, the inadequacies of the correspondence theory of truth struck them not just as a philosophical dilemma, but a genuine source of scandal. How is it possible, they asked, that the traditional theories of truth ended up in skepticism?

Charles Peirce found the traditional discussions absurd just because they tried to conceive of truth without any concern or reference whatsoever to the practical circumstances in which we worry about the truth. Truth is not a relationship between sentences and the world, nor is it a complex relationship among sentences. Truth is the answer to questions that we ask, because we are uncertain, because we have doubts. The truth is what we all, eventually, agree upon. According to Peirce, "The opinion which is fated to be ultimately agreed to by all who investigate, is what we mean by the truth." The emphasis thus gets shifted from truth as a property of sentences and beliefs and their relationships to facts and each other to truth as a function of asking questions, carrying on investigations, and clearing up actual mysteries and

---

[2] Brand Blanshard, *The Nature of Thought* (New York: Macmillan, 1941).

disagreements. The test of truth is neither correspondence nor coherence but agreement, what in fact solves our problems and answers our inquiries.

Peirce was deeply concerned with the practices of scientific investigation, and his theory of truth was aimed primarily at questions of truth in science, where experimentation and observation should lead, eventually, to agreement on one hypothesis or theory or another. **William James,** on the other hand, had much broader interests in philosophy. While he was interested in science (and, indeed, was one of America's leading physicians and psychologists), he was also interested in the less scientific aspects of human life, in which truth was also a critical issue. For example, he wrote extensively on the topic of religious belief in which questions of experimentation and observation play virtually no role at all. (One of his best known essays is included in Chapter 5.)

Accordingly, James places very little emphasis on agreement as the test of truth. However appropriate this might be in science, it is surely not even plausible in the subject of religion. Instead, he stressed the advantages of a certain belief in life. By "practical," James meant the concrete, the effective, not that which leads to scientific agreement. Thus a religious belief can be said to be true, for example, according to its effects on us. Believing in a good, just God makes us optimistic and happy; believing that life is meaningless makes us miserable. Thus truth refers to what significance a belief has in our lives, not correspondence, coherence or, we can add, the limited success of scientific hypotheses and theories. Scientific truth still has its place in James' philosophy, of course. But that kind of truth is defined by the restricted context of an investigation; it should not be generalized as a concept of truth in all contexts. (It should be noted that Peirce so radically disagreed with James' generalization of his theory that he actually changed the name of his philosophy, from "pragmatism" to "pragmaticism," which he noted was a word "sufficiently ugly" to avoid popularization.)

John Dewey returned the pragmatic theory to its narrower focus. He did not restrict truth to scientific truth, but he did restrict it to *experiential* truth. But whereas James would include, for example, religious experience, Dewey insists that the only meaningful notion of "experience" must be limited to empirically verifiable matters. That eliminates questions of theology. Like Peirce, Dewey emphasizes the context of investigation, in particular, the intellectually painful experience of doubt. Like James and unlike Peirce, Dewey does not emphasize the notion of general agreement as the test of truth so much as he emphasizes its efficacy in ending doubts and closing an investigation. A police case, for example, comes to an end when "all the pieces fall into place." But that is not a matter of coherence so much as it is a matter of resolving doubts and "tying together loose ends," satisfying all of our questions and quieting critics and skeptics. A scientific hypothesis is said to be true when all attempts to falsify it have failed and every attempt to confirm it comes out successfully. Again, it is an end to the inquiry, a solution to the problem. Where traditional philosophy gets into trouble is in trying to understand "truth" in a vacuum, without reference to any inquiry or investigation, without any reference to the context in which truth makes a difference.

The following selections are from Charles Peirce, "How to Make Our Ideas Clear," and William James, *Pragmatism*.

FROM **"HOW TO MAKE OUR IDEAS CLEAR"** BY **CHARLES PEIRCE**

Let us now approach the subject of logic, and consider a conception which particularly concerns it, that of *reality*. Taking clearness in the sense of familiarity, no idea could be clearer than this. Every child uses it with perfect confidence, never dreaming that he does not understand it. As for clearness in its second grade, however, it would probably puzzle most men, even among those of a reflective turn of mind, to give an abstract definition of the real. Yet such a definition may perhaps be reached by considering the points of difference between reality and its opposite, fiction. A figment is a product of somebody's imagination; it has such characters as his thought impresses upon it. That those characters are independent of how you or I think is an external reality. There are, however, phenomena within our own minds, dependent upon our thought, which are at the same time real in the sense that we really think them. But though their characters depend on how we think, they do not depend on what we think those characters to be. Thus, a dream has a real existence as a mental phenomenon. If somebody has really dreamt it; that he dreamt so and so, does not depend on what anybody thinks was dreamt, but is completely independent of all opinions on the subject. On the other hand, considering, not the fact of dreaming, but the thing dreamt, it retains its peculiarities by virtue of no other fact than that it was dreamt to possess them. Thus we may define the real as that whose characters are independent of what anybody may think them to be.

But, however satisfactory such a definition may be found, it would be a great mistake to suppose that it makes the idea of reality perfectly clear. Here, then, let us apply our rules. According to them, reality, like every other quality, consists in the peculiar, sensible effects which things partaking of it produce. The only effect which real things have is to cause belief, for all the sensations which they excite emerge into consciousness in the form of beliefs. The question, therefore, is, how is true belief (or belief in the real) distinguished from false belief (or belief in fiction). Now, as we have seen in the former paper, the ideas of truth and falsehood, in their full development, appertain exclusively to the scientific method of settling opinion. A person who arbitrarily chooses the propositions which he will adopt can use the word truth only to emphasize the expression of his determination to hold on to his choice. Of course, the method of tenacity never prevailed exclusively; reason is too natural to men for that. But in the literature of the Dark Ages we find some fine examples of it. . . . It is noticeable that where different faiths flourish side by side, renegades are looked upon with contempt even by the party whose belief they adopt; so completely has the idea of loyalty replaced that of truth-seeking. Since the time of Descartes, the defect in the conception of truth has been less apparent. Still, it will sometimes strike a scientific man that philosophers have been less intent on finding out what the facts are than on inquiring what belief is most in harmony with their system. It is hard to convince a follower of the *a priori* method by adducing facts; but show him that an opinion he is defending is inconsistent with what he has laid down elsewhere, and he will be very apt to retract it. These minds do not seem to believe that disputation is ever to cease; they seem to think that the opinion which is natural for one man is not so for another, and that belief will, consequently, never be settled. In contenting themselves with fixing their own opinions by a method which would lead another man to a different result, they betray their feeble hold of the conception of what truth is.

On the other hand, all the followers of science are fully persuaded that the processes of investigation, if only pushed far enough, will give one certain solution to each question to which they can be applied. One man may investigate the velocity of light by studying the transits of Venus and the aberration of the stars; another by the oppositions of Mars and the eclipses of Jupiter's satellites; a third by the method of Fizeau; a fourth by that of Foucault; a fifth by the motions of the curves of Lissajous; a sixth, a seventh, an eighth, and a ninth, may follow the different methods of comparing the measures of statical and dynamical electricity. They may at first obtain different results, but, as each perfects his method and his processes, the results will move steadily together toward a destined center. So with all scientific research. Different minds may set out with the most antagonistic views, but the progress of investigation carries them by a force outside of themselves to one and the same conclusion. This activity of thought by which we are carried, not where we wish, but to a foreordained goal, is like the operation of destiny. No modification of the point of view taken, no selection of other facts for study, no natural bent of mind even, can enable a man to escape the predestinate opinion. This great law is embodied in the conception of truth and reality. The opinion which is fated[3] to be ultimately agreed to by all who investigate is what we mean by the truth, and the object represented in this opinion is real. That is the way I would explain reality.

But it may be said that this view is directly opposed to the abstract definition which we have given of reality, inasmuch as it makes the characters of the real

> *Different minds may set out with the most antagonistic views, but the progress of investigation carries them by a force outside of themselves to one and the same conclusion.*

---

[3] Fate means merely that which is sure to come true and cannot be avoided. It is a superstition to suppose that a certain sort of events are ever fated, and it is another to suppose that the word *fate* can never be freed from its superstitious taint. We are all fated to die.

depend on what is ultimately thought about them. But the answer to this is that, on the one hand, reality is independent, not necessarily thought of in general, but only of what you or I or any finite number of men may think about it; and that, on the other hand, though the object of the final opinion depends on what that opinion is, yet what that opinion is does not depend on what you or I or any man thinks. Our perversity and that of others may indefinitely postpone the settlement of opinion; it might even conceivably cause an arbitrary proposition to be universally accepted as long as the human race should last. Yet even that would not change the nature of the belief, which alone could be the result of investigation carried sufficiently far; and if, after the extinction of our race, another should arise with faculties and disposition for investigation, that true opinion must be the one which they would ultimately come to. "Truth crushed to earth shall rise again," and the opinion which would finally result from investigation does not depend on how anybody may actually think. But the reality of that which is real does depend on the real fact that investigation is destined to lead, at last, if continued long enough, to a belief in it.[4]

ON THE PRAGMATIC THEORY
BY **WILLIAM JAMES**

I fully expect to see the pragmatist view of truth run through the classic stages of a theories career. First, you know, a new theory is attacked as absurd; then it is admitted to be true, but obvious and insignificant; finally it is seen to be so important that its adversaries claim that they themselves discovered it. Our doctrine of truth is at present in the first of these three stages, with symptoms of the second stage having begun in certain quarters. . . . Truth, as any dictionary will tell you, is a property of certain of our ideas. It means their "agreement," as falsity means their disagreement, with "reality." Pragmatism and intellectualists both accept this definition as a matter of course. They begin to quarrel only after the question is raised as to what may precisely be meant by the term "agreement," and what by the term "reality," when reality is taken as something for our ideas to agree with.

In answering these questions the pragmatists are more analytic and painstaking, the intellectualists more offhand and irreflective. The popular notion is that a true idea must copy its reality. Like other popular views, this one follows the analogy of the most usual experience. Our true ideas of sensible things do indeed copy them. Shut your eyes and think of yonder clock on the wall, and you get just such a true picture or copy of its dial. But your ideas of its "works" (unless you are a clock-maker) is much less of a copy, yet it passes muster, for it in no way clashes with the reality. Even though it should shrink to the mere word "works," that word still serves you truly; and when you speak of the

---

[4] Charles S. Peirce, "How to Make Our Ideas Clear," in *Popular Science Monthly* (January 1878).

"time-keeping function" of a clock, or of its spring's "elasticity," it is hard to see exactly what your ideas can copy.

You perceive that there is a problem here. Where our ideas cannot copy definitely their object, what does agreement with that object mean? Some idealists seem to say that they are true whenever they are what God means that we ought to think about that object. Others hold the copy-view all through, and speak as if our ideas possessed truth just in proportion as they approach to being copies of the Absolute's eternal way of thinking.

These views, you see, invite pragmatistic discussion. But the great assumption of the intellectualists is that truth means essentially an inert static relation. When you've got your true idea of anything, there's an end of the matter. You're in possession: you *know;* you have fulfilled your thinking destiny. You are where you ought to be mentally; you have obeyed your categorical imperative; and nothing more need follow on that climax of your rational destiny. Epistemologically you are in stable equilibrium.

Pragmatism, on the other hand, asks its usual question, "Grant an idea or belief to be true," it says, "what concrete different will its being true make in any one's actual life? How will the truth be realized? What experiences will be different from those which would obtain if the belief were false? What, in short, is the truth's cash-value in experiential terms?"

The moment pragmatism asks this question, it sees the answer: *True ideas are those that we can assimilate, validate, corroborate and verify. False ideas are those that we can not.* That is the practical difference it makes to us to have true ideas; that therefore, is the meaning of truth, for it is all that truth is known as.

This thesis is what I have to defend. The truth of an idea is not a stagnant property inherent in it. Truth *happens* to an idea. It *becomes* true, is *made* true by events. Its verity *is* in fact an event, a process: the process namely of its verifying itself, its veri-*fication*. Its validity is the process of its valid*ation*.

But what do the words verification and validation themselves pragmatically mean? They again signify certain practical consequences of the verified and validated idea. It is hard to find any one phrase that characterizes these consequences better than the ordinary agreement-formula—just such consequences being what we have in mind whenever we say that our ideas "agree" with reality. They lead us, namely, through the acts and other ideas which they instigate, into or up to, or towards, other parts of experience with which we feel all the while—such feeling being among our potentialities—that the original ideas remain in agreement. The connexions and transitions come to us from point to point as being progressive, harmonious, satisfactory. This function of agreeable leading is what we mean by an idea's verification. Such an account is vague and it sounds at first quite trivial, but it has results which it will take the rest of my hour to explain.

Let me begin by reminding you of the fact that the possession of true thoughts means everywhere the possession of invaluable instruments of action; and that our duty to gain truth, so far from being a blank command from out of the blue, or a "stunt" self-imposed by our intellect, can account for itself by excellent practical reasons.

The importance to human life of having true beliefs about matters of fact is a thing too notorious. We live in a world of realities that can be infinitely useful or infinitely harmful. Ideas that tell us which of them to expect count as the true ideas in all this primary sphere of verification, and the pursuit of such ideas is a primary human duty. The possession of truth, so far from being here an end in itself, is only a preliminary means towards other vital satisfactions. If I am lost in the woods and starved, and find what looks like a cow-path, it is of the utmost importance that I should think of a human habitation at the end of it, for if I do so and follow it, I save myself. The true thought is useful here because the house which is its object is useful. The practical value of true ideas is thus primarily derived from the practical importance of their objects to us. Their objects are, indeed, not important at all times. I may on another occasion have no use for the house; and then my idea of it, however verifiable, will be practically irrelevant, and had better remain latent. Yet since almost any object may some day become temporarily important, the advantage of having a general stock of *extra* truths, of ideas that shall be true of merely possible situations, is obvious. We store such extra truths away in our memories, and with the overflow we fill our books of reference. Whenever such an extra truth becomes practically relevant to one of our emergencies, it passes from cold storage to do work in the world and our belief in it grows active. You can say of it then either that "it is useful because it is true" or that "it is true because it is useful." Both these phrases mean exactly the same thing, namely that here is an idea that gets fulfilled and can be verified. True is the name for whatever idea starts the verification-process, useful is the name for its completed function in experience. True ideas would never have been singled out as such, would never have acquired a class-name, least of all a name suggesting value, unless they had been useful from the outset in this way.

◆◆◆

"The true," to put it very briefly, is only the expedient in the way of our thinking, just as "the right" is only the expedient way of our behaving.

To "agree" in the widest sense with a reality *can only mean to be guided either straight up to it or into its surroundings, or to be put into such working touch with it as to handle either it or something connected with it better than if we disagreed. . . .*

"The true," to put it very briefly, is only the expedient in the way of our thinking, just as "the right" is only the expedient way of our behaving.[5]

---

[5] William James, *Pragmatism: A New Name for Some Old Ways of Thinking* (New York: Longmans, Green, 1907).

In other words, truth, according to the pragmatic theory, is what allows us to handle situations better, what is expedient, what "works." This includes, however, not isolated tasks (in which a "false" belief might occasionally work better) but the entire process of scientific verification, so that the truth of a belief depends not only on its workability on some particular occasion, but, as in the coherence theory, on its connection with scientific testing and the whole of our lives.

3. The Semantic Theory

The semantic theory is most difficult of all, partly because of its misleading, superficial resemblance to the correspondence theory, but mainly because it has been a purely formal theory. That is, it is neutral regarding the other theories and the ordinary, "natural" languages (for example, English or French). In a sense, it is a theory that has been developing in many ways since the linguistic turn in philosophy. In its formal "semantic" version, however, it is generally credited to the American logician **Alfred Tarski.**

FROM **"THE SEMANTIC THEORY OF TRUTH"** BY **ALFRED TARSKI**

[W]e must always relate the notion of truth, like that of a sentence, to a specific language; for it is obvious that the same expression which is a true sentence in one language can be false or meaningless in another.

Let us start with a concrete example. Consider the sentence *"snow is white."* We ask the question under what conditions this sentence is true or false. It seems clear that if we base ourselves on the classical conception of truth, we shall say that the sentence is true if snow is white, and that it is false if snow is not white. Thus, if the definition of truth is to conform to our conception, it must imply the following equivalence:

The sentence "snow is white" is true, if, and only if, snow is white.

We shall now generalize the procedure which we have applied above.

(T) X is true if, and only if, p.

We shall call any such equivalence (with *"p"* replaced by any sentence of the language to which the word *"true"* refers, and *"X"* replaced by a name of this sentence) an *"equivalence of the form (T)."*

Now at last we are able to put into a precise form the conditions under which we will consider the usage and the definition of the term *"true"* as adequate from the material point of view: we wish to use the term *"true"* in such a way that all equivalences of the form (T) can be asserted, and *we shall call a definition of truth "adequate" if all these equivalences follow from it.*

I should like to propose the name *"the semantic conception of truth"* for the conception of truth which has just been discussed.

Semantics is a discipline which, speaking loosely, *deals with certain relations between expressions of a language and the objects* (or "states of affairs") *"referred to"* by those expressions. As typical examples of semantic concepts we may mention the concepts of *designation, satisfaction,* and *definition* as these occur in the following examples:

> The expression *"the father of his country"* designates (denotes)
> George Washington;
> Snow satisfies the sentential function (the condition) "x is white";
> The equation "2 · x = 1" defines (uniquely determines) the number ½

While the words *"designates," "satisfies,"* and *"defines"* express relations (between certain expressions and the object "referred to" by these expressions), the word *"true"* is of a different logical nature: it expresses a property (or denotes a class) of certain expressions, viz., of sentences. However, it is easily seen that all the formulations which were given earlier and which aimed at the meaning of this word ("true") referred not only to sentences themselves, but also to objects "talked about" by these sentences, or possibly to "states of affairs" described by them. . . . A definition of truth can be obtained in a very simple way from that of another semantic notion, namely, of the notion of *satisfaction.*[6]

Very simply explained, Tarski's semantic theory picks out a "class" of "individuals" (objects, states of affairs, or "facts") and specifies, for every sentence in the language, which individuals will or will not "satisfy" it, that is, make it "true" or not. But since the logician must "set up" each pair of sentences and individuals that will satisfy it, it is obvious that this formula will work only for a relatively small number of basic sentences with a manageable class of individuals. Here is the problem in extending the theory to natural languages (such as American English), which have a potentially infinite number of sentences and have to deal with an indefinite number of individuals. (This extension is being attempted today, however, by several leading philosophers, particularly **Donald Davidson.**) But for our purposes, the theory comes to this: We must set up the rules of satisfaction according to which our sentences become true or false. "Correspondence" is not a relation for which we supply only the appropriate sentences. In developing a language, we must also specify the relation of the language to the world, and thus "set up" the world to correspond to our language.

The semantic theory certainly resembles the correspondence theory. (Some philosophers, such as **Karl Popper,** have insisted that it *is* a version of the correspondence theory.) But in the development of the semantic theory of truth, Tarski and his

---

[6] Alfred Tarski, "The Semantic Theory of Truth," in *Philosophy and Phenomenological Research* 4, no. 3 (March 1944).

followers have avoided traditional talk of "facts"; indeed, facts are in disfavor. Instead, the emphasis is on the semantic conception of "satisfaction" (and the related notion of "reference"). *Something* outside of the language makes statements true—that is, satisfies them, but the semantic theory, unlike the traditional correspondence theory, does not insist or suggest that this "something" consists of already discrete and complete units of reality. The "something" too is defined through language by its stipulative role in our statements. (It is an open question, for the semantic theory, whether the same references, the same *somethings,* are available in every language or whether reference and satisfaction are limited to particular languages; in other words, it is still being argued—vigorously—whether or not the semantic theory leads to relativism.)

Taken individually, each of these theories has its opponents. We have attacked the correspondence theory sufficiently. Against the coherence theory, other philosophers have objected that a system of statements and beliefs can be "coherent" but yet not be true. For example, take a simple system of true beliefs and deny them all. They will still form a coherent system, but they will all be false. Similarly, we said in Chapter 1 that an argument can be valid (which makes it coherent) yet have false premises and false conclusions.

Two opposed systems of statements and beliefs can be equally "coherent," but surely both cannot be true, for they claim opposite things about the world. (Think of the metaphysical systems of Spinoza and Leibniz.) So, truth must be more than mere coherence.

Against the pragmatic theory, philosophers have objected that a belief might "work" but not be true. Scientists have often made great headway with false hypotheses. Political demagogues have often obtained great power and even achieved positive results with lies, and false beliefs often make us happier than the truth. ("What you don't know won't hurt you" and "the truth hurts.") The reason some beliefs "work" better than others, it has been argued (for example, by Bertrand Russell), is that they are true. They are true, therefore, not because they "work," but they work because they are true to the facts.

Against the semantic theory, philosophers have objected that ultimately, it is still a restatement of the correspondence theory ("'snow is white' is true if and only if snow is white"). Although the semantic theory is an improvement because it emphasizes the role of language in picking out the facts that make our statements true, it still leaves the nature of the "picking out" as obscure as ever. We are not in the position of a logician, who can make up his semantic models and languages at will. (Consider the following silly but profoundly philosophical joke: Eve says to Adam: "Let's call that one a hippopotamus." Adam: "Why 'hippopotamus'?" Eve: "Because it looks more like a hippopotamus than anything else we've seen so far.")

An adequate semantic theory of truth must be far more than merely formal. It must specify how such a theory would apply to natural (unformalized and open-ended) languages. Truth cannot be only formally defined. If the semantic theory is true, then translations between languages are impossible since the rules of satisfaction are unique to each language.

The debate between these theories continues, but the likeliest outcome is usually a combination of theories rather than the exclusive victory of any particular one. Each makes up for the deficiencies in the others. But one of the most important consequences of this debate, ironically, has been the loss of interest in the very concept of Truth (with a capital "T"). In everyday contexts, of course, philosophers, like everyone else, will talk about statements and beliefs being "true" and "false" on the basis of a primitive "correspondence" notion, that is, "correspondence to the facts." But philosophically, the power of the word "Truth" has always dwelled in its strong metaphysical linkage to "the way the world really is." Having given up on that grandiose conception of Truth, many philosophers are sometimes inclined to give up the word "truth" altogether. They concern themselves only with what we ordinarily mean when we say that a statement is "true."[7] Other philosophers, however, refuse to give up the traditional search for truth, and new and improved versions of the traditional and newer theories are still appearing.

C. KANT'S REVOLUTION

What, then, is truth? It seems that either it is "out there," independent of us but perhaps therefore unknowable, or else it is, in some sense, "in us"—in the language we speak or the practical concerns we bring to our inquiries. The correspondence and semantic theories of truth accept this dualism of language and world; the coherence and pragmatic theories challenge it but, however hesitantly, find themselves uneasy about denying correspondence altogether, and with it, "the real world." But there is another tradition—one of which the coherence theory and the pragmatic theory are partial heirs—in which this very distinction between language and world, between us and Truth, is rejected. The prime mover of this other tradition is the German philosopher Immanuel Kant. Here is the importance of his conception of synthetic a priori truth.

Immanuel Kant is considered by a great many philosophers to be the greatest thinker since Plato and Aristotle. He stands at the beginning of almost every modern movement in philosophy in the United States and Europe, as an inspiration and as a kind of founder. Existentialism would not be possible without him; nor would phenomenology, pragmatism, or many of the varieties of linguistic philosophy that have dominated English and American philosophy for most of this century. He brings together the often opposed threads of rationalism and empiricism and weaves them into a single monumental philosophical system, which he published primarily in three "critiques" (*The Critique of Pure Reason, The Critique of Practical Reason,* and *The Critique of Judgment*) in the last two decades of the eighteenth century. His writing

---

[7] J. L. Austin, for example, begins an essay on "Truth" by declaring, *"In vino veritas,* ('in wine, truth') perhaps, but in a sober symposium, *verum* ('true')."

is notoriously difficult, but it is possible for even a beginning philosophy student to appreciate the main theme of his self-proclaimed "revolution" in philosophy. It is, in one sense, a total reorientation of what we mean when we talk about the Truth.

Ever since the ancient Greeks, almost all philosophers had accepted the idea that there is a reality "out there," which we could come to know through reason, through experience, or perhaps which we could not come to know at all, according to a skeptic such as David Hume. The idea of an "external world" seemed innocent enough, until metaphysicians began to find that their contradictory views about this world could not be reconciled. This dilemma prompted John Locke to turn away from metaphysics and pay more attention to the way we acquire knowledge. The shift of attention to knowledge led Hume to argue that we couldn't even know that the sun would rise tomorrow, or that one billiard ball in fact causes the movement of another, or that there is indeed a world outside of our own ideas.

This skeptical conclusion seemed utterly absurd to Kant, who was, in his own words, "awakened from his dogmatic slumbers" by Hume. Kant had been a metaphysician (a follower of Leibniz), but reading Hume convinced him that there was a serious problem, not only for metaphysics, but for our claims to know the world at all. And Kant, who was also a scientist and an enthusiastic supporter of Isaac Newton and the new physics, saw that he had to refute Hume if he was going to keep claiming that scientists (and everyone else) could know anything at all. But the problem, as he diagnosed it, turned out to be the unquestioned idea that there was a distinction to be made between our beliefs and experience of the world, on the one hand, and the world itself, Reality or Truth, on the other.

What Kant suspected, and what many philosophers believe today, is that our "ideas"—our concepts and our language—do not just correspond to reality but in some sense "set up" the world, impose upon the world the structures we experience. We see material objects instead of just patterns of light and colors (as seen perhaps by a newborn baby), and this is our contribution to experience. We experience events in a cause-and-effect relationship, instead of as mere sequences of events, and this is not because of experience alone, but because we *make* our experience conform to causal rules. We expect certain events in the future on the basis of what we have experienced in the past; and this too is not mere habit, but a set of rules we impose necessarily on every experience. According to Kant, space and time do not exist "out there," independent of our experience; we impose the forms of three-dimensional space and one-dimensional time on our experience, and through these forms come to know the world. So too, Kant argues, all of our knowledge of the world is in part a product of the various forms and rules that we impose upon, or use to "set up," our experience. The word Kant uses for "set up" is "constitutes." A "constitution" sets up a government, provides it with its rules and structures. We **constitute** our own experience in the sense that we provide the rules and structures according to which we experience objects, as objects in space and time, as governed by the laws of nature and the relations of cause and effect. Kant writes, "the understanding does not derive its laws from, but prescribes them to, nature."

According to Kant's philosophy, reality has no existence that we can understand except as we constitute it through our basic concepts. Kant took these concepts—or what he called "categories"—to be the basic rules of the human mind as such, common to all peoples in all places at all times. Today, many philosophers would rather say that these concepts through which we constitute the world are part of a language, which raises the intriguing but controversial possibility that the world might be quite different for people who speak different languages. (Kant himself did not believe this.) Truth, in other words, is a function of our concepts. It is not correspondence, it is not mere coherence, and it is not just a matter of what "works" or satisfies our investigations. Kant's revolution rejects the very idea of an external Reality and instead looks to the concepts through which we "constitute" Reality. Thus there is no point to wondering whether our concepts match up to Reality, since there would be no Reality without our concepts. Our concepts not only cohere with each other; they "set up" a corresponding reality as well. Of course those concepts "work"—it is as if someone were to wonder how it is that a ceramic mold exactly fits a piece of jewelry, when the mold gave shape to the jewelry in the first place.

Previous philosophers had asked, "How can we know that our ideas correspond with the way the world really is?" Kant rejected that question. Instead, he asked, *"How do our ideas constitute the world?"* "What is the structure and what are the rules (the *concepts* or *categories*) of the human mind according to which we 'set up' our world, the world of our experience?"

The project of Kant's *Critique of Pure Reason* is to analyze and prove the necessity of these concepts, which we can know a priori—independently of all experience and with certainty, just because they are the rules within which all of our knowledge is possible. Think of it this way: You take a number of pieces of wood and a checkerboard and "set up" the game by making up rules about what can be moved where, how, and when. Then, within the game, you are free to make any number of moves, some brilliant, some stupid, but you are always bound by the rules that you yourself have "set up." And since you yourself have established these rules, it would be absurd to wonder whether or not they are "true."

Kant's revolution changed our conception of truth and, along with it, our conception of reality, our conception of knowledge, and, most importantly, our conception of ourselves. Truth is no longer correspondence between our ideas and reality, but our own system of rules (concepts or categories) by which we constitute our reality. Knowledge, accordingly, is no longer the comprehending of a reality beyond our experience, but knowledge of our experience. But this does not mean knowledge of experience, distinct from knowledge of objects, for the objects of our experience are all there is to reality. Moreover, in making this move, Kant gives the philosophers something which they thought they had lost, a renewed ideal of certainty, for, he argued, we can be certain of the rules of our own experience. Kant defended the necessity of the truths of arithmetic and geometry as those rules that have to do with the a priori forms of our intuitions of space and time. According to Kant's philosophy in general, reality is the world of our experience, as we constitute it through the concepts of our understanding. Therefore, we can know it with certainty, for truth, in general, is our own construction.

You might at first think that there is some trick here, as if Kant is saying, "Well, if we can't have knowledge in the hard sense, then I'll simply redefine the words *knowledge, reality,* and *truth.*" But what he has done is to point to the difficulty of the picture that other philosophers had accepted; he has shown that what we normally mean by "truth," "knowledge," and "reality" is not an insatiable appeal to a world beyond our experience. My everyday statement, "there's a grapefruit in the refrigerator," is true, whatever any philosopher might say, if there is a grapefruit in the refrigerator—if I can go and look, see it, pick it up, slice it open, and eat it. As for some grapefruit beyond my experience that is the real grapefruit, what kind of absurdity is that? Underneath Kant's spectacular pronouncements there is, once again, a return to common sense. This world, the one I stand in, touch, and see, is the real world. But what makes it real, according to Kant, is not just that I stand in, touch, and see it, but that I actively constitute it as the way it is, apply my own rules for understanding it, and structure it through my own experience.

In 1781 Kant already anticipated the three "theories of truth" that would become so powerful in the twentieth century. In his emphasis on our constitution of reality through interconnected rules and concepts, Kant anticipates the coherence theory of truth, which stresses precisely these interconnections. In his emphasis on the workability of these rules, he anticipates the pragmatic theory. And in his theory that it is our concepts and rules that "set up" reality, Kant anticipates Tarski's semantic theory. But what is of equal importance is that Kant does not endorse any single one of these theories, but embraces them all.

Kant gives us a general way of giving an account of all those truths that metaphysicians have always argued about. Using Kant's terminology, we can say they are forms of **synthetic** a priori knowledge. Such knowledge is, briefly characterized, knowledge of our own rules with which we (necessarily) constitute reality. If a truth is not true because of our experiences, nor is it true because of the grammar or meanings of the sentences of our language, how else could it be defended? This was Hume's dilemma, and with this two-test system of justification, he eliminated many of our most important beliefs as "unjustifiable," as neither "truths of reason" nor "matters of fact." But now, we have our third way: A belief can be true, necessarily true, if it is one of those rules that we impose to constitute our experience. Thus we saw that Kant defended the truths of arithmetic and geometry by showing that they were the "(a priori) forms of intuition," the ways in which we must experience our world. So too will he defend all of those truths that Hume had claimed to be unjustifiable.

The principle of universal causation is neither a generalization from experience nor an analytic truth, but rather a *rule* for "setting up" our world. That rule is, "Always look for regular (or 'lawlike') connections between events, so that you can explain an event as an *effect* of previous events, and therefore predict future events as well." Like a rule in chess, this is not a move within the game but one of those rules that defines the game. So too with the principle of induction; it is neither based upon experience nor a trivial truth but a rule with which we govern all of our experience. So too for our belief in the "external" or material world, which Berkeley and Hume found so problematic. Our experience alone will not tell us whether we are dreaming or not, and the idea of the material ("external") world is not a tautology or a conceptual truth. It too is one of the rules that we use to constitute our experience, namely, that we shall *always* interpret our experience of objects in space as external to us and as material or *substantial*. But notice, our metaphysical notion of substance is no longer that which is, by definition, outside of our experience. It is now part of the rules by which we set up our experience.

My purpose is to persuade all those who think metaphysics worth studying that it is absolutely necessary to . . . propose first the preliminary question, "Whether such a thing as metaphysics can be even possible at all?

FROM **PROLEGOMENA TO ANY FUTURE METAPHYSICS** BY **IMMANUEL KANT**

My purpose is to persuade all those who think metaphysics worth studying that it is absolutely necessary to pause a moment and, regarding all that has been done as though undone, to propose first the preliminary question, "Whether such a thing as metaphysics can be even possible at all?"

If it be science, how is it that it cannot, like other sciences, obtain universal and lasting recognition? If no, how can it maintain its pretensions and keep the human mind in suspense with hopes never ceasing, yet never fulfilled? Whether then we demonstrate our knowledge or our ignorance in this field, we must come one and for all to a definite conclusion respecting the nature of this so-called science, which cannot possibly remain on its present footing. It seems almost ridiculous, while every other science is continually advancing, that in this, which pretends to be wisdom incarnate, for whose oracle everyone inquires, we should constantly move round the same spot, without gaining a single step. And so its votaries having melted away, we do not find men confident of their ability to shine in other sciences venturing their reputation here, where everybody, however ignorant in other matters, presumes to deliver a final verdict, because in this domain there is actually as yet no standard weight and measure to distinguish sound knowledge from shallow talk.

◆ ◆ ◆

Hume started chiefly from a single but important concept in metaphysics, namely, that of the connection of cause and effect (including its derivatives force and action, and so on). He challenged reason, which pretends to have given birth to this concept of herself, to answer him by what right she thinks anything could be so constituted that if that thing be posited, something else also must necessarily be posited; for this is the meaning of the concept of cause. He demonstrated irrefutably that it was perfectly impossible for reason to think *a priori* and by means of concepts such a combination, for it implies necessity. We cannot at all see why, in consequence of the existence of one thing, another must necessarily exist or how the concept of such a combination can arise *a priori.* Hence he inferred that reason was altogether deluded with reference to this concept, which she erroneously considered as one of her own children, whereas in reality it was nothing but a bastard of imagination, impregnated by experience, which subsumed certain representations under the law of association and mistook a subjective necessity (habit) for an objective necessity arising from insight. Hence he inferred that reason had no power to think such combinations, even in general, because her concepts would then be purely fictitious and all her pretended *a priori* cognitions nothing but common experiences marked with a false stamp. In plain language, this means that there is not and cannot be any such thing as metaphysics at all.

◆ ◆ ◆

I openly confess my recollection of David Hume was the very thing which many years ago interrupted my dogmatic slumber and gave my investigations in the field of speculative philosophy a quite new direction. I was far from following him in the conclusions at which he arrived by regarding, not the whole of his problem, but a part, which by itself can give us no information. If we start from a well-founded, but undeveloped, thought which another has bequeathed to us, we may well hope by continued reflection to advance farther than the acute man to whom we owe the first spark of light.

I therefore first tried whether Hume's objection could not be put into a general form, and soon found that the concept of the connection of cause and effect was by no means the only concept by which the understanding thinks the connection of things *a priori,* but rather that metaphysics consists altogether of such concepts. I sought to ascertain their number; and when I had satisfactorily succeeded in this by starting from a single principle, I proceeded to the deduction of these concepts, which I was now certain were not derived from experience,as Hume had attempted to derive them, but sprang from the pure understanding. This deduction (which seemed impossible to my acute predecessor, which had never even occurred to anyone else, though no one had hesitated to use the concepts without investigating the basis of their objective validity) was the most difficult task which ever could have been undertaken in the service of metaphysics; and the worst was that metaphysics, such as it is, could not assist me in the least because this deduction alone can render metaphysics possible. But as soon as I had succeeded in solving Hume's problem, not merely in a particular case, but with respect to the whole faculty of pure reason, I could proceed safely, though slowly, to determine the whole sphere of pure reason completely and from universal principles, in its boundaries as well as in its contents. This was required for metaphysics in order to construct its system according to a safe plan.[8]

---

[8] Immanuel Kant, *Prolegomena to Any Future Metaphysics,* trans. Lewis White Beck (New York: Bobbs-Merrill, 1950).

Kant gives us a way of resolving the age-old disputes of metaphysics—questions concerning reality as such. Since the claims of the metaphysicians are all synthetic a priori, Kant provides us with the following policy:

1. Those claims that are rules by which we must interpret our experience are true—necessarily true.
2. Those claims that contradict rules by which we must interpret our experience are false—necessarily false.
3. Those that are not rules by which we must interpret our experience are either analytic, contingently true, or contingently false.
4. Finally, those claims that cannot be decided by appeal to the rules of our experiences and make no difference to our experience one way or the other are to be rejected as possible topics of knowledge.

The logical positivists in this century took this last part of Kant's policy as a program for a devastating attack on metaphysics in general. Although the logical positivists, as empiricists in the tradition of David Hume, did not accept much of Kant's theory, they wholeheartedly endorsed his rejection of claims that made no difference whatever to our experience. They said that any claim that makes no difference to our experience—that cannot be tested in any way—is meaningless.

Some of the metaphysician's claims will be upheld. For example, Kant saves Newton's (and Spinoza's) determinism in his rule of causality, thus rejecting Leibniz's "pre-established harmony" view as necessarily false. With some revisions, he accepts a large part of Leibniz's view of space and time as relative, that is, relative to our experience. He saves the notion of substance because he says that one of the most important rules of our experience is that we see objects as substantial (that is, as "real"). But he does not accept the view that substance is something independent of human experience, for such a view, by definition, means that substance would be irrelevant to our experience. Nor does he accept the central dispute between Spinoza and Leibniz, whether there is but one substance or many, for no rule of our experience is concerned one way or another. It makes no difference to our experience. It is a metaphysician's game and not a possible topic for knowledge.

Kant's revolution is the elimination of "reality" and "truth" as external to ourselves. Since Kant, many philosophers no longer view human knowledge as the passive reception of sensations or intuitions. And, needless to say, the problems of philosophy have become radically changed.

Kant destroyed the old problems, resolved the old disputes, and answered Hume's skepticism, at least for a while. In rejecting the correspondence theory of truth and the idea of an "external" reality, he eliminated the basis of those problems, disputes, and doubts. But I expect that you can already see a new and even more virulent version of those problems, disputes, and doubts on the horizon. By denying us our anchor in reality, Kant launches philosophy in a bold new direction, and he creates the dilemma that still defines philosophy today: If we supply our own rules for experience, is there any uniquely correct way of describing the way the world is?

The basis of Kant's theory is that we supply the rules according to which we constitute our experience. Truth can be talked about only within our experience and according to those rules. But you can see what happens when we raise the following question: What about people (or creatures) who are very different from us? Will they use the same rules? Will they have the same experiences? And, if we do differ from them, who is "right"? Whose rules are "better"? Whose experience is "true"? You can see here the problems of the coherence theory of truth coming to haunt Kant's philosophy. Suppose there are two (or more) sets of rules, equally coherent? Can they both be "true"? And the problems of the semantic theory, too: What if there are different languages with different basic concepts or categories, constituting different "facts"? Are they all "true"? You can appreciate how easily the German Romantic philosophers who immediately followed Kant replaced his notion of "constitution" with the more exciting notion of "creation." We create our realities, they announced. We are all artists, building our worlds. Notice the words reali*ties*" and "world*s*"; there is no longer confidence, much less a guarantee, that there is only one reality or one world.

Kant's most immediate follower, a German named **Johann Gottlieb Fichte,** used the pragmatic theory of truth to come to the same conclusion; the truth is, according to him, that which is most practical, most conducive to the good life, and the evaluation of different realities depends wholly on the practical consequences. (He said, in his most famous dictum: "The kind of philosophy a man chooses depends upon the kind of man he is.") With Kant's revolution, the Truth seems destined to be replaced by many truths.

But before we go on to explore these intriguing complications, let us make it clear that Kant himself never accepted a word of all this. According to him, there was still but one possible set of rules and therefore only one way of constituting our experience, whoever we are, wherever we're from, and no matter what kind of conscious creature we happen to be. This means: one world, one science, one reality, and one truth. Kant tries to prove this in the central section of his *Critique of Pure Reason* in a formidable argument that he calls a "transcendental deduction."

Like so much philosophical jargon, Kant's term is easily explained and is used often enough to make it worth explaining. You already know that a deduction is an inference from one statement to another according to a set of rules of inference. In this case, Kant attempts to infer from various statements that we believe, the basic rules (concepts, categories) of human experience. This is what "transcendental" means, the basic rules of human experience. But a transcendental deduction is not satisfied with simply deducing some such rules; it also proves that they are the *only* rules that we are able to use to constitute our experience. That is why it is so important to Kant. It allows him his revolution without its anarchist consequences.

The argument itself is enormously complicated and scholars who have studied it for half their lives still do not agree what it is or whether it is a valid argument. So, obviously, we won't try to summarize it for you here. What can and must be said is this, however: Kant believed that such a transcendental deduction would prove that, although it is we ourselves who supply the rules of our experience and determine what can be true for us, we don't have a choice in the matter. There is still only one truth for all of us.

Philosophers are still arguing whether any such transcendental argument (Kant's or not) might succeed. If one does, then people must, in their basic rules, all agree. (Of course, they will always disagree about particular matters; no two chess players make all the same moves.) But if there is no successful transcendental argument, then there need be no such universal agreement. It then makes sense to talk about different truths for different people. This, we may say, is the dominant battle of twentieth-century philosophy in the United States and in Europe. But obviously, it is not new to the twentieth century. Those who believe that there is only one set of rules and one truth are often called **absolutists** (though many philosophers find that name repulsive because it sounds so dogmatic). Others, who believe that there are different rules for different people and therefore different "truths," are called **relativists.** You have probably already figured out that Plato, and Descartes, for example, were absolutists and that Protagoras and the Sophists were relativists. Kant was an absolutist. Most of his followers were relativists. (This is obscured by the confusing fact that many of them talked about "the Absolute" all the time. But, they were still relativists, and to avoid confusion, we shall not talk about "the Absolute" at all in this book.)

D. THE BATTLE IN EUROPE AFTER KANT: RELATIVISM AND ABSOLUTISM

The story of philosophy in Europe since Kant is largely the story of a war between relativism and absolutism, in which even the politics and arts of the times play a continuing role. The philosophers immediately following Kant, as we have already mentioned, pursued relativism with relish, developing alternative systems of philosophy as fast as they could find publishers. The philosopher **Friedrich Schelling,** for example, produced about one system a year at the turn of the century. He became the best-known "Romantic" philosopher of a large group of "Romantic" intellectuals, poets, and critics throughout Europe who turned to the virtual worship of individual "genius" and competed for the most extravagant and creative views of the world. The virtually undisputed winner of this contest, however, was not Schelling but one of his schoolmates, **Georg Wilhelm Friedrich Hegel.**

1. Hegel

Hegel was in college (Tübingen Lutheran seminary) when the French revolution was raging just across the border. He was just starting to put together his mature philosophy when Napoleon was attempting to take over all of Europe. This international turmoil helps us understand the global reach of Hegel's philosophy and his bold effort to proclaim an "absolute" position with reference to knowledge. Like many young German intellectuals in that exciting period, he was trying to get outside his provincial perspective and to understand the world from a larger, even a "divine" point of view. Accordingly, Hegel's theory of truth is part and parcel of his all-embracing system of thought.

Hegel begins by rejecting many key metaphors that have ruled modern philosophy, especially all the "correspondence" metaphors in which the world in itself (or "the Absolute") is on one side and our knowledge (beliefs, sentences, utterances) are on the other, separated by some distorting filter (our senses) or actively altered by the machinery of our understanding. In place of such metaphors (and the skepticism they inevitably engender), Hegel suggests a holistic worldview in which consciousness and the world are not separate but inseparably integrated. In traditional terms, this means that there is no world, no reality-in-itself apart from consciousness.

It also means that we must give up our view of consciousness and the self as self-enclosed and, in some sense, "inside" us. Indeed, Hegel also suggests that we give up the view that the self is essentially a feature of the individual: the self—or "Spirit"—is shared by all of us; or rather, in more Platonic language, we all "participate" in Spirit. Not surprisingly, Hegel was familiar with some Oriental thinkers and incorporated some Eastern views into his notion of truth. However, the truth, according to Hegel, "is the whole"—that is, the unity of all our consciousnesses and the world. This means that there is no saying (and no point in attempting to say) what the world might be apart from our conceptions of it. But neither is this to invite skepticism, for the world is nothing but the synthesis of all our possible conceptions of it.

Hegel, like Kant, is an idealist. He calls himself an "absolute idealist" (in contrast to Kant's "transcendental idealism"). This means, simply stated, that reality is the product of mind (not individual minds, of course)—the cosmic mind, "Spirit." Yet this opens the way for the most radical departure from Kant, who argued at great length that there could be but one possible way of conceiving the world—that is, one a priori set of forms of intuition (space and time) and one set of categories (substance, causality, etc.). Hegel's predecessor (Kant's immediate successor) Fichte had already argued that there are at least two basically different ways of envisioning the world—the scientific, objective ("dogmatic") way and the practical, moral, activist ("idealist") way—and rather than being simply "right" or "wrong," Fichte had declared famously that "The philosophy a man chooses depends upon the kind of man that he is." Hegel goes a giant step further and provides a long series of possible conceptions of the world—or "forms of consciousness"—conceptions that are not divided into "practical" and "theoretical" but, Hegel tells us, all of which have both their practical and their theoretical aspects. (Once again Hegel rejects an age-old dichotomy.) Such views are not simply alternative options, as if we could each simply chose one or another (as Kierkegaard would argue some years later). The way we view the world is already determined by our place in history, our language, and our society. Nor is the variety of forms of consciousness a demonstration of the now-popular view that there is no "correct" way of knowing. The various forms of consciousness emerge one from another by way of improvement or by way of opposition (as, for example, scientific theories tend to follow one another), and (again, as in science) there is always the necessary sense that they are all moving toward some final end—the correct view. So, too, Hegel insists that all these different conceptions and ways of viewing the world are leading up to something—to a viewpoint that is not relative to any particular viewpoint or perspective. This is the standpoint he calls "absolute knowing."

This idea that the various forms of consciousness emerge one from another and lead us eventually to the absolute is perhaps Hegel's most exciting philosophical contribution to Western thinking. Virtually every other philosopher we have discussed, whether metaphysician or epistemologist, essentially offered us a static view of knowledge, a concept of the understanding that—except for education from childhood and the detailed knowledge gained by the sciences—did not change, did not grow, did not develop. Hegel provides philosophy (and humanity) with a historical perspective. Truth is not, as many philosophers had insisted ever since ancient times, what is. Truth develops, as the human mind develops. Truth is not being but becoming. Truth develops through conflict and confrontation, or what Hegel famously calls a **dialectic** (a term he borrowed from Kant but which goes back to the Greeks).

In an important sense, it is Hegel who discovers (or invents) the history of philosophy. Other philosophers had talked about their predecessors, of course. (Aristotle, for instance, provided us with much of what we know about the pre-Socratic philosophers.) But what Hegel suggests is that something more is to be gleaned than a mere sequence of refutations, additions, and improvements to thought; it is reality itself that is being converted. The history of philosophy, accordingly, is but one aspect of an incredible cosmic odyssey, a "phenomenology of spirit"—the development through time not only of consciousness but of reality too.

The selection that follows is from the Introduction of Hegel's 1807 masterpiece, *The Phenomenology of Spirit.* In this book, Hegel presents a dialectic of various forms of consciousness, from the most primitive sensory perception to the most sophisticated views of the Enlightenment and "Revealed Religion" (Christianity), culminating in that final stage of "Absolute Knowing." In these paragraphs, Hegel rejects the traditional metaphors of epistemology and argues that skepticism should not be taken at all seriously. He then suggests the holistic form of his overall system. (There is more on Hegel's notion of "Spirit" in Chapter 5, pp. 360–362.)

FROM *THE PHENOMENOLOGY OF SPIRIT*
BY **G. W. F. HEGEL**

It is a natural assumption that in philosophy, before we start to deal with its proper subject-matter, *viz.* the actual cognition of what truly is, one must first of all come to an understanding about cognition, which is regarded either as the instrument to get hold of the Absolute, or as the medium through which one discovers it. A certain uneasiness seems justified, partly because there are different types of cognition, and one of them might be more appropriate than another for the attainment of this goal, so that we could make a bad choice of means; and partly because cognition is a faculty of a definite kind and scope, and thus, without a more precise definition of its nature and limits, we might grasp clouds of error instead of the heaven of truth. This feeling of uneasiness is surely bound to be transformed into the conviction that the whole project of securing for consciousness through cognition what exists in itself is absurd, and that there is a boundary between cognition and the Absolute that completely separates form. For, if cognition is the instrument for getting hold of absolute being, it is obvious that the use of an instrument on a thing certainly does not let it be what it is for itself, but rather sets out to reshape and alter it. If, on the other hand, cognition is not an instrument of our activity but a more or less passive medium through which the light of truth reaches us, then again we do not receive the truth as it is in itself, but only as it exists through and in this medium. Either way we employ a means which immediately brings about the opposite of its own end; or rather, what is really absurd is that we should make use of a means at all.

It would seem, to be sure, that this evil could be remedied through an acquaintance with the way in which the *instrument* works; for this would enable us to eliminate from the representation of the Absolute which we have gained through it whatever is due to the instrument, and thus get the truth in its purity. But this "improvement" would in fact only bring us back to where we were before. If we remove from a reshaped thing what the instrument has done to it, then the thing—here the Absolute—becomes for us exactly what it was before this (accordingly) superfluous effort. On the other hand, if the Absolute is supposed merely to be brought nearer to us through this instrument, without anything in it being altered, like a bird caught by a lime-twig, it would surely laugh our little ruse to scorn, if it were not with us, in and for itself, all along, and of its own volition. For a ruse is just what cognition would be in such a case, since it would, with its manifold exertions, be giving itself the air of doing something quite different from creating a merely immediate and therefore effortless relationship. Or, if by testing cognition, which we conceive of as a *medium,* we get to know the law of its refraction, it is again useless to subtract this from the end result. For it is not the refraction of the ray, but the ray itself whereby truth reaches us, that is cognition; and if this were removed, all that would be indicated would be a pure direction or a blank space.

Meanwhile, if the fear of falling into error sets up a mistrust of Science, which in the absence of such scruples gets on with the work itself, and actually cognizes something, it is hard to see why we should not turn round and mistrust this very mistrust. Should we not be concerned as to whether this fear of error is not just the error itself? Indeed, this fear takes something—a great deal in fact—for granted as truth, supporting its scruples and inferences on what is itself in need of prior scrutiny to see if it is true. To be specific, it takes for granted certain ideas about cognition as an *instrument* and as a *medium,* and assumes that there is a *difference between ourselves and this cognition.* Above all, it presupposes that the Absolute stands on one side and cognition on the other, independent and separated from it, and yet is something real; or in other words, it presupposes that cognition which, since it is excluded from the Absolute, is surely outside of the truth as well, is nevertheless true, an assumption whereby what calls itself fear of error reveals itself rather as fear of the truth.

> *. . . the Absolute alone is true, or the truth alone is absolute.*

This conclusion stems from the fact that the Absolute alone is true, or the truth alone is absolute.

◆ ◆ ◆

Now, because it has only phenomenal knowledge for its object, this exposition seems not to be Science, free and self-moving in its own peculiar shape; yet from this standpoint it can be regarded as the path of the natural consciousness which presses forward to true knowledge; or as the way of the Soul which journeys through the series of its own configurations as though they were the stations appointed for it by its own nature, so that it may purify itself for the life of the Spirit, and achieve finally, through a completed experience of life itself, the awareness of what it really is in itself.

Natural consciousness will show itself to be only the Notion of knowledge, or in other words, not to be real knowledge. But since it directly takes itself to be real knowledge, this path has a negative significance for it, and what is in fact the realization of the Notion, counts for it rather as the loss of its own self; for it does lose its truth on this path. The road can therefore be regarded as the pathway of *doubt,* or more precisely as the way of despair. For what happens on it is not what is ordinarily understood when the word "doubt" is used: shilly-shallying about this or that presumed truth, followed by a return to that truth again, after the doubt has been appropriately dispelled—so that at the end of the process the matter is taken to be what it was in the first place. On the contrary, this path is the conscious insight into the untruth of phenomenal knowledge, for which the supreme reality is what is in truth only the unrealized Notion. Therefore this thoroughgoing scepticism is also not the scepticism with which an earnest zeal for truth and Science fancies it has prepared and equipped itself in their service: the *resolve,* in Science, not to give oneself over to the thoughts of others, upon mere authority, but to examine everything for oneself and follow only one's conviction, or better still, to produce everything oneself, and accept only one's deed as what is true.

The series of configurations which consciousness goes through along this road is, in reality, the detailed history of the *education* of consciousness itself to the standpoint of Science. That zealous resolve represents this education simplistically as something directly over and done with in the making of the resolution; but the way of the Soul is the actual fulfillment of the resolution, in contrast to the untruth of that view. Now, following one's own conviction is, of course, more than giving oneself over to authority; but changing an opinion accepted on authority into an opinion held out of personal conviction, does not necessarily alter the content of the opinion, or replace error with truth. The only difference between being caught up in a system of opinions and prejudices based on personal conviction, and being caught up in one based on the authority of others, lies in the added conceit that is innate in the former position. The scepticism that is directed against the whole range of phenomenal consciousness, on the other hand, renders the Spirit for the first time competent to examine what truth is. For it brings about a state of despair about all the so-called natural ideas, thoughts, and opinions, regardless of whether they are called one's own or someone else's, ideas with which the consciousness that sets about the examination (of truth) *straight away* is still filled and hampered, so that it is, in fact, incapable of carrying out what it wants to undertake.

The necessary progression and interconnection of the forms of the unreal consciousness will by itself bring to pass the *completion* of the series. To make this more intelligible, it may be remarked, in a preliminary and general way, that the exposition of the untrue consciousness in its untruth is not a merely *negative* procedure. The natural consciousness itself normally takes this one-sided view of it; and a knowledge which makes the one-sidedness its very essence is itself one of the patterns of incomplete consciousness which occurs on the road itself, and will manifest itself in due course. This is just the scepticism which only ever sees pure nothingness in its result and abstracts from the fact that this nothingness is specifically the nothingness of that *from which it results.* For it is only when it is taken as the result of that from which it emerges, that it is, in fact, the true result; in that case it is itself a *determinate* nothingness, one which has a *content.* The scepticism that ends up with the bare abstraction of nothingness or emptiness cannot get any further from there, but must wait to see whether something new comes along and what it is, in order to throw it too into the same empty abyss. But when, on the other hand, the result is conceived as it is in truth, namely, as a *determinate* negation, a new form has thereby immediately arisen, and in the negation the transition is made through which the progress through the complete series of forms comes about of itself.

◆◆◆

This contradiction and its removal will become more definite if we call to mind the abstract determinations of truth and knowledge as they occur in consciousness. Consciousness simultaneously *distinguishes* itself from something, and at the same time *relates* itself to it, or, as it is said, this something exists *for* consciousness; and the determinate aspect of the *relating,* or of the *being* of something for a consciousness, is *knowing.* But we distinguish the being-for-another from *being-in-itself;* whatever is related to knowledge or knowing is also distinguished from it, and posited as existing outside of this relationship; this *being-in-itself* is called *truth.* Just what might be involved in these determinations is of no further concern to us here. Since our object is phenomenal knowledge, its determinations too will at first be taken directly as they present themselves; and they do present themselves very much as we have already apprehended them.

Now, if we inquire into the truth of knowledge, it seems that we are asking what knowledge is *in itself.* Yet in this inquiry knowledge is *our* object, something that exists *for us;* and the *in-itself* that would supposedly result from it would rather be the being of knowledge *for us.* What we asserted to be its essence would be not so much its truth but rather just our knowledge of it. The essence or criterion would lie within ourselves, and that which was to be compared with it and about which a decision would be reached through this comparison would not necessarily have to recognize the validity of such a standard.[9]

Starting from a clearly Kantian perspective, Hegel taught that we have to stop talking about "true" and "false" philosophies, and "true" and "false" religions, political systems, societies, scientific theories, and values. There are only different "forms of consciousness," some more sophisticated and perspicacious than others, but none wholly true (or false) to the exclusion of others. Hegel wholly endorsed the Kantian thesis that the world is nothing other than the way in which we constitute it.

Hegel's dialectic was essentially a dialectic of ideas, a series of confrontations of various forms of consciousness so that we could see how they all form an interlocking view of reality. But although philosophy and human history improve through time—eventually reaching a form of absolute knowledge and (Hegel hoped) world peace and universal freedom—the movement itself is by no means a smooth progression. It was often violent, both in the intellectual realm and in the flesh-and-blood world of human politics, which Hegel grimly referred to as "the slaughter-bench of history."

One of Hegel's most enthusiastic followers, a young student in Berlin named **Karl Marx,** thought that Hegel had the dialectic of history turned upside down. It is not ideas that determine world history, Marx argued, but rather the details of history—in particular the economic details—that determine the ideas, including the ideas of philosophers. From this notion of dialectic Marx developed his powerful and influential view of history as class conflict, replacing Hegel's abstract "forms of consciousness" with the day-to-day battles of wages, jobs, exploitation, and profits.[10]

In what follows, Hegel presents an overview of his all-embracing notion of "spirit" (also called "the Idea"). Spirit, in one sense, is God, but the concept embraces all of humanity, all of history, and all of nature as well. The point of the argument is that the world itself *develops* and *changes,* and so the virtues and truths of one generation may well become inadequate to the next generation. Yet this is not relativism in the crude sense, such that a truth, for example, is only true for a particular person or people. First, truth is not, in this sense, subjective; it is to be found in the world and not just in the minds of individuals or groups. Second, and even more important, to say that a truth is inadequate from a later, probably more expansive, point of view is not to say that it "was true but now is false;" rather, it shows that we are slowly approaching an ever more adequate conception of the truth, a truth which, in the following selection, Hegel calls "Freedom." Freedom is God's purpose developing through history and humanity.

---

[9] G. W. F. Hegel, *The Phenomenology of Spirit,* trans. A. V. Miller (New York: Oxford University Press, 1977).

[10] The familiar doctrine of Hegel's dialectic is often known only in terms of "thesis-antithesis-synthesis." In fact these categories are rarely used by either Hegel or Marx.

FROM *REASON IN HISTORY*
("INTRODUCTION: LECTURES ON
THE PHILOSOPHY OF HISTORY")
BY **HEGEL**

THE IDEA AND THE INDIVIDUAL

The question of the *means* whereby Freedom develops itself into a world leads us directly to the phenomenon of history. Although Freedom as such is primarily an internal idea, the means it uses are the external phenomena which in history present themselves directly before our eyes. The first glance at history convinces us that the actions of men spring from their needs, their passions, their interests, their characters, and their talents. Indeed, it appears as if in this drama of activities these needs, passions, and interests are the sole springs of action and the main efficient cause. It is true that this drama involves also universal purposes, benevolence, or noble patriotism. But such virtues and aims are insignificant on the broad canvas of history. We may, perhaps, see the ideal of Reason actualized in those who adopt such aims and in the spheres of their influence; but their number is small in proportion to the mass of the human race and their influence accordingly limited. Passions, private aims, and the satisfaction of selfish desires are, on the contrary, tremendous springs of action. Their power lies in the fact that they respect none of the limitations which law and morality would impose on them; and that these natural impulses are closer to the core of human nature than the artificial and troublesome discipline that tends toward order, self-restraint, law, and morality.

When we contemplate this display of passions and the consequences of their violence, the unreason which is associated not only with them, but even—rather we might say *especially*—with *good* designs and righteous aims; when we see arising therefrom the evil, the vice, the ruin that has befallen the most flourishing kingdoms which the mind of man ever created, we can hardly avoid being filled with sorrow at this universal taint of corruption. And since this decay is not the work of mere nature, but of human will, our reflections may well lead us to a moral sadness, a revolt of the good will (spirit)—if indeed it has a place within us. Without rhetorical exaggeration, a simple, truthful account of the miseries that have overwhelmed the noblest of nations and polities and the finest exemplars of private virtue forms a most fearful picture and excites emotions of the profoundest and most hopeless sadness, counter-balanced by no consoling result. We can endure it and strengthen ourselves against it only by thinking that this is the way it had to be—it is fate; nothing can be done. And at last, out of the boredom with which this sorrowful reflection threatens us, we draw back into the vitality of the present, into our aims and interests of the moment; we retreat, in short, into the selfishness that stands on the quiet shore and thence enjoys in safety the distant spectacle of wreckage and confusion.

But in contemplating history as the slaughter-bench at which the happiness of peoples, the wisdom of states, and the virtue of individuals have been sacrificed, a question necessarily arises: To what principle, to what final purpose, have these monstrous sacrifices been offered?

From here one usually proceeds to the starting point of our investigation: the events which make up this picture of gloomy emotion and thoughtful reflection are only the means for realizing the essential destiny, the absolute and final purpose, or, what amounts to the same thing, the true result of world history. We have all along purposely eschewed that method of reflection which ascends from this scene of particulars to general principles. Besides, it is not in the interest of such sentimental reflections really to rise above these depressing emotions and to solve the mysteries of Providence presented in such contemplations. It is rather their nature to dwell melancholically on the empty and fruitless sublimities of their negative result. For this reason we return to our original point of view. What we shall have to say about it will also answer the questions put to us by this panorama of history.

The first thing we notice—something which has been stressed more than once before but which cannot be repeated too often, for it belongs to the central point of our inquiry—is the merely general and abstract nature of what we call principle, final purpose, destiny, or the nature and concept of Spirit. A principle, a law is something implicit, which as such, however true in itself, is not completely real (actual). Purposes, principles, and the like, are at first in our thoughts, our inner intention. They are not yet in reality. That which is in itself is a possibility, a faculty. It has not yet emerged out of its implicitness into existence. A second element must be added for it to become reality, namely, activity, actualization. The principle of this is the will, man's activity in general. It is only through this activity that the concept and its implicit ("being-in-themselves") determinations can be realized, actualized; for of themselves they have no immediate efficacy. The activity which puts them in operation and in existence is the need, the instinct, the inclination, and passion of man. When I have an idea I am greatly interested in transforming it into action, into actuality. In its realization through my participation I want to find my own satisfaction. A purpose for which I shall be active must in some way be my purpose; I must thereby satisfy my own desires, even though it may have ever so many aspects which do not concern me. This is the infinite right of the individual to find itself satisfied in its activity and labor. If men are to be interested in anything they must have "their heart" in it. Their feelings of self-importance must be satisfied. But here a misunderstanding must be avoided. To say that an individual "has an interest" in something is justly regarded as a reproach or blame; we imply that he seeks only his private advantage. Indeed, the blame implies not only his disregard of the common interest, but his taking advantage of it and even his sacrificing it to his own interest. Yet, he who is active for a cause is not simply "interested," but "interested *in it.*" Language faithfully expresses this distinction. Nothing therefore happens, nothing is accomplished, unless those concerned with an issue find their own satisfaction in it. They are particular individuals; they have their special needs, instincts, and interests. They have their own particular desires and volitions, their own insight and conviction, or at least their own attitude and opinion, once the aspirations to reflect, understand, and reason have been awakened. Therefore people demand that a cause for which they should be active accord with their ideas. And they expect their opinion—concerning its goodness, justice, advantage, profit—to be taken into account. This is of particular importance today when people are moved to support a cause not by faith in other people's authority, but rather on the basis of their own independent judgment and conviction.

We assert then that nothing has been accomplished without an interest on the part of those who brought it about. And if "interest" be called "passion"—because the whole individuality is concentrating all its desires and powers, with every fiber of volition, to the neglect of all other actual or possible interests and aims, on one object—we may then affirm without qualification that *nothing great in the world* has been accomplished without passion.

◆◆◆

. . . [O]ne may indeed question whether those manifestations of vitality on the part of individuals and peoples in which they seek and satisfy their own purposes are, at the same time, the means and tools of a higher and broader purpose of which they know nothing, which they realize unconsciously. This purpose has been questioned, and in every variety of form denied, decried, and denounced as mere dreaming and "philosophy." On this point, however, I announced my view at the very outset, and asserted our hypothesis—which eventually will appear as the result of our investigation—namely, that Reason governs the world and has consequently governed its history. In relation to this Reason, which is universal and substantial, in and for itself, all else is subordinate, subservient, and the means for its actualization. Moreover, this Reason is immanent in historical existence and reaches its own perfection in and through this existence. The union of the abstract universal, existing in and for itself, with the particular or subjective, and the fact that this union alone constitutes truth are a matter of speculative philosophy which, in this general form, is treated in logic. But in its historical development (*the subjective side, consciousness, is not yet able to know what is*) the abstract final aim of history, the idea of Spirit, for it is then itself in process and incomplete. The idea of Spirit is not yet its distant object of desire and interest. Thus desire is still unconscious of its purpose; yet it already exists in the particular purposes and realizes itself through them. The problem concerning the union of the general and the subjective may also be raised under the form of the union of freedom and necessity. We consider the immanent development of the Spirit, existing in and for itself, as necessary, while we refer to freedom the interests contained in men's conscious volitions.[11]

> *Reason governs the world and has consequently governed its history.*

---

[11] G. W. F. Hegel, *Reason in History,* trans. Robert S. Hartman (New York: Bobbs-Merrill, 1953).

2. Schopenhauer

Arthur Schopenhauer claimed to be a faithful student of Kant. Indeed, he claimed to be the only faithful interpreter of what he took to be Kant's central idea, the distinction between the constituted world of our experience and an underlying reality, which could be found in the realm of the **Will**. But Schopenhauer, who was one of the great eccentrics in the history of philosophy, gave Kant's philosophy a dramatic twist, encouraged by his readings of Eastern philosophy. In place of Kant's confidence in the truth of the world of our experience, Schopenhauer invokes the Buddhist conception of the "veil of Maya" and declares our experience of the world to be largely illusion. Meanwhile the Will, which Kant takes to be inherently rational, becomes an irrational, impersonal, inner force for Schopenhauer, exerting itself to no particular purpose within us. The most evident manifestation of the Will, in us and in all creatures, Schopenhauer suggests, is sexual desire, the often urgent and foolish desire to reproduce ourselves, so that our offspring can reproduce themselves, and so on and so on, to no end whatever. Thus Schopenhauer, like the Buddha, stresses the futility of desire, and his whole philosophy is aimed at giving us some relief from the Will. (In our final chapter on aesthetics, "Beauty," we will see that Schopenhauer invokes the power of art to give us this relief.) But the Will is ultimate reality, and within its purposeless striving dwell all of the peoples and all of the creatures of nature. The following selection is from Schopenhauer's great book, *The World as Will and Representation.*

FROM ***THE WORLD AS WILL AND REPRESENTATION***
BY **ARTHUR SCHOPENHAUER**

The will, considered purely in itself, is devoid of knowledge, and is only a blind, irresistible cure, as we see it appear in inorganic and vegetable nature and in their laws, and also in the vegetative part of our own life. Through the addition of the world as representation, developed for its service, the will obtains knowledge of its own willing and what it wills, namely that this is nothing but this world, life, precisely as it exists. We have therefore called the phenomenal world the mirror, the objectivity, of the will; and as what the will wills is always life, just because this is nothing but the presentation of that willing for the representation, it is immaterial and a mere pleonasm if, instead of simply saying "the will," we say "the will-to-live."

As the will is the thing-in-itself, the inner content, the essence of the world, but life, the visible world, the phenomenon, is only the mirror of the will, this world will accompany the will as inseparably as a body is accompanied by its shadow; and if will exists, then life, the world, will exist. Therefore life is certain to the will-to-live, and as long as we are filled with the will-to-live we need not be apprehensive for our existence, even at the sight of death. It is true that we see the individual come into being and pass away; but the individual is only phenomenon, exists only for knowledge involved in the principle of sufficient reason, in the *principium individuationis*. Naturally, for this knowledge, the individual receives his life as a gift, rises out of nothing, and then suffers the loss of this gift through death, and returns to nothing. We, however, wish to consider life philosophically, that is to say, according to its Ideas, and then we shall find that neither the will, the thing-in-itself in all phenomena, nor the subject of knowing, the spectator of all phenomena, is in any way affected by birth and death. Birth and death belong only to the phenomenon of the will, and hence to life; and it is essential to this that is manifest itself in individuals that come into being and pass away, as fleeting phenomena, appearing in the form of time, of that which in itself knows no time, but must be manifested precisely in the way aforesaid in order to objectify its real nature. Birth and death belong equally to life, and hold the balance as mutual conditions of each other, or, if the expression be preferred, as poles of the whole phenomenon of life. The wisest of all mythologies, the Indian, expresses this by giving to the very god who symbolizes destruction and death (just as Brahma, the most sinful and lowest god of the Trimurti, symbolizes generation, origination, and Vishnu preservation), by giving, I say, to Shiva as an attribute not only the necklace of skulls, but also the lingam, that symbol of generation which appears as the counterpart of death. In this way it is intimated that generation and death are essential correlatives which reciprocally neutralize and eliminate each other. It was precisely the same sentiment that prompted the Greeks and Romans to adorn the costly sarcophagi, just as we still see them, with feasts, dances, marriages, hunts, fights between wild beasts, bacchanalia, that is with presentations of life's most powerful urge. This they present to us not only through such diversions and merriments, but even in sensual groups, to the point of showing us the sexual intercourse between satyrs and goats. The object was obviously to indicate with the greatest emphasis from the death of the mourned individual the immortal life of nature, and thus to intimate, although without abstract knowledge, that the whole of nature is the phenomenon, and also the fulfillment, of the will-to-live. The form of this phenomenon is time, space, and causality, and through these individuation, which requires that the individual must come into being and pass away. But this no more disturbs the will-to-live—the individual being only a particular example or specimen, so to speak, of the phenomenon of this will—than does the death of an individual injure the whole of nature. For it is not the individual that nature cares for, but only the species; and in all seriousness she urges the preservation of the species, since she provides for this so lavishly through the immense surplus of the seed and the great strength of the fructifying impulse. The individual, on the contrary, has no value for nature, and can have none, for infinite time, infinite space, and the infinite number of possible individuals therein are her kingdom. Therefore nature is always ready to let the individual fall, and the individual is accordingly not only exposed to destruction in a thousand ways from the most insignificant accidents, but is even destined for this and is led towards it by nature herself, from the moment that individual has served the maintenance

Now man is nature herself, and indeed nature at the highest grade of her self-consciousness, but nature is only the objectified will-to-live.

of the species. In this way, nature quite openly expresses the great truth that only the Ideas, not individuals, have reality proper, in other words are a complete objectivity of the will. Now man is nature herself, and indeed nature at the highest grade of her self-consciousness, but nature is only the objectified will-to-live; the person who has grasped and retained this point of view may certainly and justly console himself for his own death and for that of his friends by looking back on the immortal life of nature, which he himself is.[12]

3. Nietzsche

After Hegel, relativism became ever more sophisticated. In Marx, differences in philosophical worldviews were explained in terms of different economic and social circumstances. The question was no longer "which view of the world is true?" but rather, "what circumstances would make a person believe that?" Hegel's rival Arthur Schopenhauer defended the radical idea that what we called reality was in fact an illusion; and a few years later, following Schopenhauer, a similar view was defended by the eccentric but brilliant iconoclast, **Friedrich Nietzsche.** He too attacked the traditional notions of truth with a vengeance and argued that there could be as many equally "true" (or equally "false"—it doesn't matter) worldviews as there were creative people and societies. He also urged that every person adopt for himself or herself as many different worldviews as possible, at one time or another, as a matter of "experiment."

Like Schopenhauer, he considered all such views as dictated by the Will and not merely as knowledge as such, and, like Marx, he replaced the old question, "which view of the world is true?" with a question of circumstances. But Nietzsche was not interested in economic or social circumstances so much as psychological factors. So he asked, "What kind of personality would need to believe that?" Truth is no longer even an issue. In fact, even rationality is starting to feel the threat of relativism. For, with Nietzsche, not only is truth out the window, but coherence and pragmatism are forced to take second place as well. What comes first? Excitement, adventure, heroism, creativity, and what Nietzsche generally calls "the will to power." Of course, one must still act rationally if one is to achieve these things, but thinking, in Nietzsche's view, plays at most a secondary role in our lives.

Nietzsche's view of truth was, to put it mildly, startling. His basic claim was a paradox: "truth is error." This can be interpreted in many different ways, and Nietzsche himself interprets and reinterprets it from many different perspectives—which is quite in line with his view of truth itself. "There are no facts," he tells us, "only

---

[12] Arthur Schopenhauer, *The World as Will and Representation,* pp. 275 *et supra.*

interpretations." Elsewhere he tells us that there are only "perspectives," various ways of viewing the world and no ultimately correct (or incorrect) way. The very idea of "Truth," he writes, and the curious obsession with truth enjoyed by the scholars, is a kind of pathology, or at least a real curiosity, that requires examination. Why are we so enamored with the idea of "the Truth"? How and why did philosophers ever get the idea that there is another world, more real and "better" than this one?

FROM **VARIOUS WORKS**
BY **FRIEDRICH NIETZSCHE**

Chemistry of concepts and sensations.—Almost all the problems of philosophy once again pose the same form of question as they did 2,000 years ago: how can something originate in its opposite, for example rationality in irrationality, the sentient in the dead, logic in illogic, disinterested contemplation in covetous desire, living for others in egoism, truth in errors? Metaphysical philosophy has hitherto surmounted this difficulty by denying that the one originates in the other and assuming for the more highly valued thing a miraculous source in the very kernel and being of the "thing in itself." Historical philosophy, on the other hand, which can no longer be separated from natural science, the youngest of all philosophical methods, has discovered in individual cases (and this will probably be the result in every case) that there are no opposites, except in the customary exaggeration of popular or metaphysical interpretations, and that a mistake in reasoning lies at the bottom of this antithesis: according to this explanation there exists, strictly speaking, neither an unegoistic action nor completely disinterested contemplation; both are only sublimations, in which the basic element seems almost to have dispersed and reveals itself only under the most painstaking observation. All we require, and what can be given us only now that the individual sciences have attained their present level, is a chemistry of the moral, religious, and aesthetic conceptions and sensations, likewise of all the agitations we experience within ourselves in cultural and social intercourse and indeed even when we are alone: what if this chemistry would end up by revealing that in this domain, too, the most glorious colors are derived from base, indeed from despised materials? Will there be many who desire to pursue such researches? Mankind likes to put questions of origin and beginnings out of its mind: must one not be almost inhuman to detect in oneself a contrary inclination?—

Metaphysical world.—It is true, there could be a metaphysical world; the absolute possibility of it is hardly to be disputed. We behold all things through the human head and cannot cut off this head; while the question nonetheless remains what of the world would still be there if one had cut it off. This is a purely scientific problem and one not very calculated to bother people overmuch; but all that has hitherto made metaphysical assumptions *valuable, terrible, delightful* to them, all that has begotten these assumptions, is passion, error and self-deception; the worst of all methods of acquiring knowledge, not the best of all, have taught belief in them. When one has disclosed these methods as the foundation of all extant religions and metaphysical systems one has refuted them! Then that possibility still remains over; but one can do absolutely nothing with it, not to speak of letting happiness, salvation and life depend on the gossamer of such a possibility.—For one could assert nothing at all of the metaphysical world except that it was a being-other, an inaccessible, incomprehensible being-other; it would be a thing with negative qualities.—Even if the existence of such a world were never so well demonstrated, it is certain that knowledge of it would be the most useless of all knowledge: more useless even than knowledge of the chemical composition of water must be to the sailor in danger of shipwreck.[13]

♦ ♦ ♦

Now, we praise and censure, however, only under this false presupposition that there are *identical* facts, that there exists a graduated order of *classes* of facts which corresponds to a graduated world-order: thus we *isolate,* not only the individual fact, but also again groups of supposedly identical facts (good, evil, sympathetic, envious actions, etc.)—in both cases erroneously.—The word and the concept are the most manifest ground for our belief in this isolation of groups of actions: we do not only *designate* things with them, we think originally that through them we grasp the *true* in things. Through words and concepts we are still continually misled into imagining things as simpler than they are, separate from one another, indivisible, each existing in and for itself. A philosophical mythology lies concealed in *language* which breaks out again every moment, however careful one may be otherwise. Belief in freedom of will—that is to say in *identical* facts and in *isolated* facts—has in language its constant evangelist and advocate.

Source of knowledge.—Throughout tremendous periods of time the intellect begot nothing but errors; some of them proved useful and preservative of the species: he who came upon them or inherited them fought his fight for himself and his posterity with greater good fortune. These articles of belief, which have been repeatedly handed down and have finally become almost a basic component of the human species, are for example the following: that there are enduring things, that there are identical things, that there are things, material, bodies, that a thing is what it appears to be, that our willing is free, that what is good for me is good in itself. Deniers and doubters of these propositions appeared only very late—truth, as the feeblest form of knowledge, appeared only very late. It seemed one was incapable of living with truth, our organism was adapted to the opposite; all its higher functions, the perceptions of the senses and every kind of sensation in general worked in concert with those primevally incorporated fundamental errors. More: those propositions became even within the domain

---

[13] Friedrich Nietzsche, *Human-All-Too-Human,* trans. R. J. Hollingdale in *The Nietzsche Reader* (New York: Penguin, 1977).

of knowledge the norms according to which one meted out "true" and "untrue"—right into the remotest regions of pure logic. Thus the *strength* of items
of knowledge lies, not in their degree of truth, but in their age, their incorpor-
atedness, their character as a condition of life. Where life and knowledge seem
to come into contradiction there is never any serious contest; doubt and denial
here count as madness. Those exceptions as thinkers, the Eleatics, who nonetheless advanced and maintained the antithesis of these natural errors, believed it
was possible to *live* this opposite, too: they invented the sage as the man of un-
changeability, impersonality, universality of perception, as one and at the same
time all, with a special capacity for that inverted knowledge; they held the belief
that their knowledge was at the same time the principle of *life*. [. . .] The evolution of honesty and scepticism in greater refinement at length rendered these
people, too, impossible. [. . .] This more refined honesty and scepticism everywhere had its origin when two antithetical propositions seemed to be *applicable*
to life because both were compatible with those fundamental errors, when, that
is to say, there could be dispute as to the greater or less degree of *utility* for life
of these propositions; likewise wherever novel propositions, though not useful
to life, were at any rate not harmful to it, being expressions of an intellectual
instinct for play, at the same time innocent and happy, like all play. Gradually
the human brain was filled with such judgments and convictions; fermentation,
struggle and lust for power arose within this throng. Not only utility and pleasure, every kind of drive took sides in the struggle over "truth"; the intellectual
struggle became an occupation, excitement, profession, duty, dignity: knowledge and the striving after the true finally ordered itself as a need among the
other needs. From then on not only belief and conviction, but examination,
denial, mistrust, contradiction, too, were a *power,* all the "evil" instincts were
subordinated to knowledge and placed in its service and acquired the lustre of
the permitted, honoured, useful and finally the eye and innocence of the *good*.
Knowledge thus becomes a piece of life itself and, as life, a perpetually increasing power: until at last knowledge and those primeval fundamental errors come
into collision, both as life, both as power, both in the same man. The thinker:
this is now the being within whom the drive to truth and those life-preservative
errors fight their first fight, after which the drive to truth, too, has proved itself
a life-preservative power. In comparison with the importance of this fight everything else is a matter of indifference: the ultimate question as to the conditions
of life is posed here, and the first attempt to answer this question by experiment
is made here. To what extent can truth endure incorporation?—that is the question, that is the experiment.[14]

◆ ◆ ◆

The falseness of a judgement is to us not necessarily an objection to a judgement [. . .] The question is to what extent it is life-advancing, life-preserving,

---

[14]Friedrich Nietzsche, *Gay Science,* trans. R. J. Hollingdale in *The Nietzsche Reader*
(New York: Penguin, 1977).

The falseness of a judgement is to us not necessarily an objection to a judgement . . .

species-preserving, perhaps even species-breeding; and our fundamental tendency is to assert that the falsest judgements (to which synthetic *a priori* judgements belong) are the most indispensable to us, that without granting as true the fictions of logic, without measuring reality against the purely invented world of the unconditional and self-identical, without continual falsification of the world by means of numbers, mankind could not live—that to renounce false judgements would be to renounce life, would be to deny life [. . .][15]

Although Nietzsche wrote in the last half of the nineteenth century, his works were ignored until this century, when they made an enormous impact (not all of it positive), first in Germany and, only recently, in Europe and in the United States. Nietzsche's relativistic view of truth, while very much at home with many current thinkers, was still quite alien to the ideas of the nineteenth century, when thinkers— following Hegel or Kant or natural science—were still trying to develop a unified and "true" picture of the world. However, one of Nietzsche's German colleagues did have an impact, just at the end of the last century, and though his relativistic view of truth was not nearly so extreme as Nietzsche's, he provoked extensive activity and comment. We speak of **Wilhelm Dilthey.** The doctrine he promoted, which is still tremendously influential in both Europe and the United States, is called **historicism.** Historicism is Hegel's dialectic of forms of consciousness, pinned down to precise social and historical periods. It is the thesis, simply, that truth and rationality are relative to particular peoples at particular times in history and that overall comparison of them, with the intention of finding out which is "true," is totally mistaken. It is, obviously, a very strong relativist doctrine, so strong and so influential that the absolutists in philosophy, who had had much less publicity and success than the relativists for the last century, starting looking around for a champion. They found him in the "phenomenologist" **Edmund Husserl.**

E. PHENOMENOLOGY

Phenomenology is a self-consciously "scientific" and "rigorous" discipline, modeled after mathematics (as it was for Descartes and the ancient Greeks). Phenomenology is the study of the essential structures of the human mind, and because these are essential, they can be known to be true, universally and necessarily. Husserl was a new kind of rationalist, who believed that the truths of arithmetic and geometry are

---

[15] Friedrich Nietzsche, *Beyond Good and Evil*, trans. R. J. Hollingdale in *The Nietzsche Reader* (New York: Penguin, 1977).

known—and known with certainty—by appeal to a certain kind of intuition, which he called "essential" intuition. Believing that such intuitions are adequate for arithmetic and geometry, Husserl turned his theory elsewhere, to philosophy in general. Husserl, as much as any philosopher of his time (the early twentieth century), was horrified by what he saw as rampant relativism. He saw it, in fact, not only as a crisis in philosophy but as "a crisis in European civilization." So he turned his phenomenology to attack it. Turning against Dilthey, for example, he argued that

> *Historicism takes its position in the factual sphere of the empirical life of the spirit. To the extent that it posits this latter absolutely, without exactly naturalizing it (the specific sense of nature in particular lies far from historical thinking and in any event does not influence it by determining it in general), there arises a relativism that has a close affinity to naturalistic psychologism and runs into similar sceptical difficulties.*
>
> *. . . In view of this constant change in scientific views we would actually have no right to speak of sciences as objectively valid unities instead of merely as cultural formations. It is easy to see that historicism, if consistently carried through, carries over into extreme sceptical subjectivism. The ideas of truth, theory, and science would then, like all ideas, lose their absolute validity. That an idea has validity would mean that it is a factual construction of spirit which is held as valid and which in its contingent validity determines thought. There would be no unqualified validity, or validity-in-itself, which is what it is even if no one has achieved it and though no historical humanity will ever achieve it. Thus too there would then be no validity to the principle of contradiction nor to any logic, which latter is nevertheless still in full vigor in our time. The result, perhaps, will be that the logical principles of noncontradiction will be transformed into their opposites.*[16]

Using both Kant's terminology and his absolutist intentions, Husserl attacked all forms of relativism and attempted to develop a *transcendental phenomenology,* in other words, a phenomenology that discovers the basic rules of all experience (just as he had discovered them for arithmetic and geometry before). Because these rules (or "ideal laws") were discovered to be essential, they were, Husserl concluded, the only rules possible. In Husserl as in Kant, the word *transcendental* means the basic and the only rules with which we "constitute" our world. (Husserl used the notion of "constitution" also, with much the same meaning that Kant did.) But what is *phenomenology*? It is the study of human consciousness. These essential rules of experience, in other words, were to be found in consciousness, not in a mysterious Platonic "world of Being" nor simply in our language. Consciousness itself, with the objects of its own constitution, becomes our new anchor. Starting from Descartes, Husserl suggests that we go back to that "subjective" starting point—and that we look again.

---

[16]Edmund Husserl, "Philosophy as Rigorous Science," in *Phenomenology and the Crisis of Philosophy,* trans. Quentin Lauer (New York: Harper & Row, 1965).

FROM *THE 1929 PARIS LECTURES*
BY **EDMUND HUSSERL**

The splintering of contemporary philosophy and its aimless activity makes us pause. Must this situation not be traced back to the fact that the motivations from which Descartes' meditations emanate have lost their original vitality? Is it not true that the only fruitful renaissance is one which reawakens these meditations, not in order to accept them, but to reveal the profound truth in the radicalism of a return to the *ego cogito* with the eternal values that reside therein? . . .

We thus begin, everyone for himself and in himself, with the decision to disregard all our present knowledge. We do not give up Descartes' guiding goal of an absolute foundation for knowledge. At the beginning, however, to presuppose even the possibility of that goal would be prejudice. . . . Science demands proof *by reference to the things and facts themselves, as these given in actual experience and intuition.* Thus guided, we, the beginning philosophers, make it a rule to judge only by the evidence. . . .

Here, specifically following Descartes, we make the great shift which, when properly carried out, leads to *transcendental subjectivity.* . . . Let us consider: as radically meditating philosophers we now have neither knowledge that is valid for us nor a world that exists for us. . . . However, whatever be the veracity of the claim to being made by phenomena, whether they represent reality or appearance, phenomena in themselves cannot be disregarded as mere "nothing." On the contrary, it is precisely the phenomena themselves which, without exception, render possible for me the very existence of both reality and appearance. This epistemological abstention is still what it is: it includes the whole stream of experienced life and all its particulars, the appearances of objects, other people, cultural situations, etc. Nothing changes, except that I no longer accept the world simply as real; I no longer judge regarding the distinction between reality and appearance. . . . This ubiquitous detachment from any point of view regarding the objective world we term the *phenomenological epoché.* It is the methodology through which I come to understand myself as that ego and life of consciousness in which and through which the entire objective world exists for me, and is for me precisely as it is. . . . Through the phenomenological *epoché* the natural human ego, specifically my own, is reduced to the transcendental ego. This is the meaning of the phenomenological reduction.[17]

Husserl's battle, from beginning to end, was a battle against relativism, against all of those philosophies that held that there can be different equally true or equally rational worldviews. And it must be said that his phenomenology, for all of its internal struggles, was immensely successful and still attracts the attention of a great many philosophers today. But phenomenology was not the solution to relativism. Husserl thought that phenomenology could be transcendental and prove that certain

---

[17] Edmund Husserl, *The 1929 Paris Lectures,* trans. Peter Koestenbaum (Hague: Nijhoff, 1975).

rules were basic and essential to all human thinking. But just as Kant opened the door to relativism with his view that we constitute our world, Husserl opened it wider with his view that a study of consciousness was the way to do philosophy. For were there not, his followers asked, many different forms of consciousness? (Thus returning to Hegel rather than Kant.) And phenomenology as it developed in France, rather than Germany, became the source of a new relativism, which is extremely fashionable today.

F. HERMENEUTICS, PRAGMATISM, AND FEMINISM: RELATIVISM RECONSIDERED

Absolutism seems to deny the obvious fact that people are different and disagree, not only in superficial ways but in terms of their most basic beliefs. Relativism, on the other hand, seems to deny the obvious similarities among people and imply that we will never be able to understand one another—or find the truth—at all. One attempt to bridge the gap between dogmatic absolutism and solipsistic relativism is **hermeneutics.**

"Hermeneutics" is an old name for "interpretation," with an eye to getting at the Truth. For many centuries, this formidable word was applied exclusively to the interpretation of the Bible, with the aim of understanding the Word of God. Today, however, the term has a much broader meaning. It is often used in literary criticism to talk about the interpretation of texts—not only the Bible, but any text. But it is now used in philosophy too to refer to the discipline of interpreting and understanding the world, which becomes, in effect, our text, and different cultures' views of the world, which may seem initially to be mutually incommensurable.

The modern father of hermeneutics is the German "historicist" Wilhelm Dilthey, whom we encountered in the previous section. Dilthey came to realize that the methods of the physical sciences were not very successful when applied to the "human sciences," in part because history played such enormous importance in human life. He also realized that there was a very real danger in the Kantian attempt to overcome traditional philosophical distinctions between appearance and reality, subjectivity, and objective truth. While his historicism lent itself to relativism, Dilthey himself was vehemently antirelativist. The problem, he argued, was to develop a method for *understanding* human differences. But he believed that all of these were ultimately superficial and thus not incommensurable at all.

Contemporary hermeneutics is just this attempt to provide a way of understanding viewpoints other than our own. It is simply dogmatic to insist—as Kant and many other philosophers have insisted—that the structures of the human mind are everywhere the same and, consequently, that we all share a common basis of knowledge. But is it simple-minded, on the other hand, to insist that we are all different and have different truths, since there is at least enough overlap for us to understand that we do disagree. For example, the medievals saw God and the earth as the spiritual and spatial centers of the universe. How can a twentieth-century scientist understand them? Well, not just by dismissing their views as nonsense, nor can we sensibly say, "Well, they have their opinions and we have ours." Hermeneutics is just this attempt to step into someone else's shoes (but without taking off our own shoes first).

In this century, hermeneutics has been turned into a powerful style of philosophizing by the German metaphysician **Martin Heidegger.** It was Heidegger, in his monumental book *Being and Time* (1928), who suggested that life is like a text, and the purpose of our lives is to understand that text. Heidegger was a student of Husserl and was thus a phenomenologist. But in his hermeneutical phenomenology he tries to "uncover" the hidden meanings in our experience. He rejects the scientific tone of Husserl's phenomenology and prefers to talk about the structures of life itself, including our profound sense of history, which defines human life.

The most important proponent of hermeneutics, however, is a student of Heidegger, **Hans Georg Gadamer.** In fact, Gadamer is so wary of the fact that method—and not only the scientific method—may distort our understanding that he insists that hermeneutics must resist the temptation to become another method. It is rather the attempt to overcome methods, to dispense with the overemphasis on proofs and arguments and the quest for certainty and emphasize instead the shared understandings that we already have with one another. The substance of philosophy then becomes dialogue rather than individual phenomenology or abstract proofs. Interpretation thus becomes not an abstract function of the intellect but a process that permeates our every activity.

Gadamer's hermeneutics does not reject the notion of truth, but it does give up entirely the idea that there is a Truth wholly outside of us which we need a method (rationalism, empiricism, scientific psychology) to discover. Like the coherence theorist and the pragmatist, he gives up the idea of secure *foundations* for our knowledge—such as the raw experiences or "sense data" discussed by some empiricists, or the a priori principles defended by Kant. But where both the coherence theorist and the pragmatist tend to interpret truth as a function of the present—coherence of beliefs and workability, respectively—the hermeneuticist insists that truth must be understood *historically,* in terms of a *tradition.* Thus the philosophical tradition, ironically, has tended to ignore the importance of its own tradition and look for strictly eternal truths. Gadamer's hermeneutics hold rather that it is only within a tradition, and by looking at our tradition, that philosophical truth is possible at all. Does this mean that we must accept whatever our tradition may be, even if it is wrong? But what would it be, Gadamer asks, for a tradition to be wrong? We can criticize ourselves, of course, and that is just the point of hermeneutics. But does it mean that we must also justify ourselves and what we have always believed? "Do we need to justify," he asks rhetorically, "that which has always supported us?"

Does relativism mean that there can be no truth? Does relativism apply only to philosophical views, not to *real* theories? Could there be *really* different views of the world—and different worlds? But does it even make sense to talk about relative truth, that is, a truth that is only "true for" one person or group and not another?

If such a phrase even makes sense, it must mean that a statement is true for a person or group by virtue of the scheme or conceptual framework they employ; thus it is true for a certain society that the witchdoctor embodies the power of the devil, but true for another society that the powers of the so-called witchdoctor are nothing but the combination of natural pharmaceuticals plus the power of suggestion. But we must not fall into the radical trap of Protagoras and claim that "man is the measure of all things"—if we are to continue using the word *truth* at all. A statement or a belief cannot be true just by virtue of its being believed, in other words, if there is no possibility that a person or a group can believe what is false (or, not believe some statement that is nevertheless true). Furthermore, as in hermeneutics, it is essential that we do not close off the possibility that one truth might be understandable—perhaps in different terms—by those who believe another, apparently contradictory truth. This would be to deny the possibility of cross-cultural communication—to cut people of different cultures off from each other completely.

Hermeneutics has had a recent resurgence in American philosophy, particularly in discussions of relativism and multiculturalism. In the following essay, the contemporary American philosopher, **Richard Rorty,** who claims a profound debt to hermeneutics, defends a vision of "solidarity"—which he contrasts with the traditional notion of "objectivity," which he associates with "pragmatism." His claim is that the pragmatic theory of truth, which we outlined previously, is essentially the theory that truth has a moral standard—the solidarity of a community—rather than a metaphysical one—objectivity. In other words, he claims that pragmatism defines "truth" as "what it is morally best for our community to believe," and using this definition, he can claim that it is morally best for us to believe in pragmatism.

FROM "SOLIDARITY OR OBJECTIVITY?"
BY RICHARD RORTY

There are two principal ways in which reflective human beings try, by placing their lives in a larger context, to give sense to those lives. The first is by telling the story of their contribution to a community. This community may be the actual historical one in which they live, or another actual one, distant in time and place, or a quite imaginary one, consisting perhaps of a dozen heroes and heroines selected from history or fiction or both. The second way is to describe themselves as standing in immediate relation to a nonhuman reality. This relation is immediate in the sense that it does not derive from a relation between such a reality and their tribe, or their nation, or their imagined band of comrades. I shall say that stories of the former kind exemplify the desire for solidarity, and that stories of the latter kind exemplify the desire for objectivity. Insofar as a person is seeking solidarity, he or she does not ask about the relation between the practices of the chosen community and something outside that community. Insofar as he seeks objectivity, he distances himself from the actual persons around him not by thinking of himself as a member of some other real or imaginary group, but rather by attaching himself to something which can be described without reference to any particular human beings.

◆◆◆

Those who wish to ground solidarity in objectivity—call them "realists"—have to construe truth as correspondence to reality. So they must construct a metaphysics which has room for a special relation between beliefs and objects which will differentiate true from false beliefs. They also must argue that there are procedures of justification of belief which are natural and not merely local. So they must construct an epistemology which has room for a kind of justification which is not merely social but natural, springing from human nature itself, and made possible by a link between that part of nature and the rest of nature. On their view, the various procedures which are thought of as providing rational justification by one or another culture may or may not really *be* rational. For to be truly rational, procedures of justification *must* lead to the truth, to correspondence to reality, to the intrinsic nature of things.

By contrast, those who wish to reduce objectivity to solidarity—call them "pragmatists"—do not require either a metaphysics or an epistemology. They view truth as, in William James' phrase, what it is good for *us* to believe. So they do not need an account of a relation between beliefs and objects called "correspondence," nor an account of human cognitive abilities which ensures that our species is capable of entering into that relation. They see the gap between truth and justification not as something to be bridged by isolating a natural and transcultural sort of rationality which can be used to criticize certain cultures and praise others, but simply as the gap between the actual good and the possible better. From a pragmatist point of view, to say that what is rational for us now to believe may not be *true,* is simply to say that somebody may have come up with a better idea. It is to say that there is always room for improved belief, since new evidence, or new hypotheses, or a whole new vocabulary, may come along. For pragmatists, the desire for objectivity is not the desire to escape the limitations of one's community, but simply the desire for as much intersubjective agreement as possible, the desire to extend the reference of "us" as far as we can. Insofar as pragmatists make a distinction between topics on which such agreement is relatively easy to get and topics on which agreement is relatively hard to get.

"Relativism" is the traditional epithet applied to pragmatism by realists. Three different views are commonly referred to by this name. The first is the view that every belief is as good as every other. The second is the view that "true" is an equivocal term, having as many meanings as there are procedures of justification. The third is the view that there is nothing to be said about either truth or rationality apart from descriptions of the familiar procedures of justification which a given society—*ours*—uses in one or another area of inquiry. The pragmatist holds the ethnocentric third view. But he does not hold the self-refuting first view, nor the eccentric second view. He thinks that his views are better than the realists, but he does not think that his views correspond to the nature of things. He thinks that the very flexibility of the word "true"—the fact that it is merely an expression of commendation—insures its univocity. The term "true," on his account, means the same in all cultures, just as equally flexible terms like "here," "there," "good," "bad," "you," and "me" mean the same in all cultures. But the identity of meaning is, of course, compatible with diversity of reference, and with diversity of procedures for assigning the terms. So he feels free to use the term "true" as a general term of commendation in the same way as his realist opponent does—and in particular to use it to commend his own view.

However, it is not clear why "relativist" should be thought an appropriate term for the ethnocentric third view, the one which the pragmatist *does* hold. For the pragmatist is not holding a positive theory which says that something is relative to something else. He is, instead, making the purely *negative* point that we should drop the traditional distinction between knowledge and opinion, construed as the distinction between truth as correspondence to reality and truth as a commendatory term for well-justified beliefs. The reason that the realist calls this negative claim "relativistic" is that he cannot believe that anybody would seriously deny that truth has an intrinsic nature. So when the pragmatist says that there is nothing to be said about truth save that each of us will commend as true those beliefs which he or she finds good to believe, the realist is inclined to interpret this as one more positive theory about the nature of truth: a theory according to which truth is simply the contemporary opinion of a chosen individual or group. Such a theory would, of course, be self-refuting. But the pragmatist does not have a theory of truth, much less a relativistic one. As a partisan of solidarity, his account of the value of cooperative human inquiry has only an ethical base, not an epistemological or metaphysical one. Not having *any* epistemology, *a fortiori* he does not have a relativistic one.

> *The question is not about how to define words like "truth" or "rationality" or "knowledge" or "philosophy," but about what self-image our society should have of itself.*

. . . [T]he question is not about how to define words like "truth" or "rationality" or "knowledge" or "philosophy," but about what self-image our society should have of itself. The ritual invocation of the "need to avoid relativism" is most comprehensible as an expression of the need to preserve certain habits of contemporary European life. These are the habits nurtured by the Enlightenment, and justified by it in terms of an appeal of Reason, conceived as a transcultural human ability to correspond to reality, a faculty whose possession and use is demonstrated by obedience to explicit criteria. So the real question about relativism is whether these same habits of intellectual, social, and political life can be justified by a conception of rationality as criterionless muddling through, and by a pragmatist conception of truth.

I think that the answer to this question is that the pragmatist cannot justify these habits without circularity, but then neither can the realist. The pragmatists' justification of toleration, free inquiry, and the quest for undistorted communication can only take the form of a comparison between societies which exemplify these habits and those which do not, leading up to the suggestion that nobody who has experienced both would prefer the latter. It is exemplified by Winston

Churchill's defense of democracy as the worst form of government imaginable, except for all the others which have been tried so far.

◆◆◆

My suggestion that the desire for objectivity is in part a disguised form of the fear of the death of our community echoes Nietzsche's charge that the philosophical tradition which stems from Plato is an attempt to avoid facing up to contingency, to escape from time and chance. Nietzsche thought that realism was to be condemned not only by arguments from its theoretical incoherence, the sort of argument we find in Putnam and Davidson, but also on practical, pragmatic grounds. Nietzsche thought that the test of human character was the ability to live with the thought that there was no convergence. He wanted us to be able to think of truth as:

a mobile army of metaphors, metonyms, and anthromorphisms—in short a sum of human relations, which have been enhanced, transposed, and embellished poetically and rhetorically and which after long use seem firm, canonical, and obligatory to a people.

Nietzsche hoped that eventually there might be human beings who could and did think of truth in this way, but who still liked themselves, who saw themselves as *good* people for whom solidarity was *enough.*

I think that pragmatism's attack on the various structure-content distinctions which buttress the realist's notion of objectivity can best be seen as an attempt to let us think of truth in this Nietzschean way, as entirely a matter of solidarity. That is why I think we need to say, despite Putnam, that "there is only the dialogue," only *us,* and to throw out the last residues of the notion of "transcultural rationality." But this should not lead us to repudiate, as Nietzsche sometimes did, the elements in our movable host which embody the ideas of Socratic conversation, Christian fellowship, and Enlightenment science. Nietzsche ran together his diagnosis of philosophical realism as an expression of fear and resentment with his own resentful idiosyncratic idealizations of silence, solitude, and violence. Post-Nietzschean thinkers like Adorno and Heidegger and Foucault have run together Nietzsche's criticisms of the metaphysical tradition on the one hand with his criticisms of bourgeois civility, of Christian love, and of the nineteenth century's hope that science would make the world a better place to live, on the other. I do not think that there is any interesting connection between these two sets of criticisms. Pragmatism seems to me, as I have said, a philosophy of solidarity rather than of despair. From this point of view, Socrates' turn away from the gods, Christianity's turn from an Omnipotent Creator to the man who suffered on the Cross, and the Baconian turn from science as contemplation of eternal truth to science as instrument of social progress, can be seen as so many preparations for the act of social faith which is suggested by a Nietzschean view of truth.

The best argument we partisans of solidarity have against the realistic partisans of objectivity is Nietzsche's argument that the traditional Western metaphysico-epistemological way of firming up our habits simply isn't working anymore. It isn't doing its job. It has become as transparent a device as the postulation of deities who turn out, by a happy coincidence, to have chosen *us* as their people. So the pragmatist suggestion that we substitute a "merely" ethical foundation for our sense of community—or, better, that we think of our sense of community as having no foundation except shared hope and the trust created by such sharing—is put forward on practical grounds. It is *not* put forward as a corollary of a metaphysical claim that the objects in the world contain no intrinsically action-guiding properties, nor of an epistemological claim that we lack a faculty of moral sense, nor of a semantical claim that truth is reducible to justification.[18]

Rorty makes the point that our metaphysical theory of "truth" has political overtones. The belief that there is one, single, truth can lead to condescension and disrespect toward people who believe differently from oneself. Only, however, if the absolutist believes, in addition to his or her absolutism, that he or she or his or her culture is closer to that one truth than are others. Need the absolutist always think that the objective truth is his or her sole dominion? This seems to cut off the possibility of communication and learning between cultures.

Is "solidarity *enough*"? In the following reading, Japanese philosopher **Isamu Nagami** looks phenomenologically at the communication between individuals and cultures, which he calls "intersubjectivity," and suggests that neither "solidarity" nor "objectivity" is politically "enough."

FROM **"CULTURAL GAPS:
WHY DO WE MISUNDERSTAND?"**
BY **ISAMU NAGAMI**

A well-known Japanese psychologist, Takeo Doi, expressed his frustration and puzzlement with American ways of life in his book, *The Anatomy of Dependence:*

> *From time to time I began to feel an awkwardness arising from the difference between my ways of thinking and feeling and those of my hosts (that is, Americans). For example, not long after my arrival in America I visited the house of someone to whom I had been introduced by a Japanese acquaintance, and was talking to him when he asked me, "Are you hungry? We have some ice cream if you'd like it." As I remember, I was rather hungry, but finding myself asked point-blank if I was hungry by someone whom I was visiting for the first time, I could not bring myself to admit it, and ended by denying the suggestion. I probably cherished a mild hope that he would press me again; but my host, disappointingly, said "I see" with no*

---

[18]Richard Rorty, "Solidarity or Objectivity?" from *Consequences of Pragmatism: Essays 1972–1980* (Minneapolis: University of Minnesota Press, 1982).

further ado, leaving me regretting that I had not replied more honestly. And I found myself thinking that a Japanese would almost never ask a stranger unceremoniously if he was hungry, but would produce something to give him without asking.

Those who have lived in foreign countries have experienced more or less the sort of cultural shock Doi expressed so well. These kinds of intercultural experiences have led many thinkers to probe into the core elements of culture for comparative study. In Japan, for example, we find many popular writers who explain the difference between Japanese culture and that of the Western nations including the U.S.A. in terms of group orientation and individual identity. The thesis for this type of argument is that while Japanese behavior in general can be explained by orientation within the group, Americans behave on the basis of individual freedom. There is no doubt that this reveals a meaningful comparison between the two cultures to those who have journalistic interests. But if we start by inquiring into various modalities of the experiential world of daily life in culture, we find we cannot follow the above approach primarily for three reasons. 1) Those who accept the group versus individual thesis tend to explain every cultural phenomenon in terms of this and as a result they conceal many other rich possibilities which every culture may contain. 2) Certain features are common to all social worlds. In this respect every culture can share a kind of symbolic common denominator through which we can compare differences. Yet, this approach of contrast ignores the universality in human existence. 3) The very fact that people understand and describe different cultures reveals a kind of cultural ethos in which their thinking is embedded. That is to say, their ways of thinking are inescapably and necessarily cultural. This thought process is not self-critically oriented in the sense that it is not able to show its historico-cultural character and, therefore, tends to be ideological.

The most striking characteristic of these approaches is based on their inability to provide any critical perspective and at the same time on a sort of false legitimacy in our actual human life. Thus it is crucial for us to find another way to understand culture in its most sensible manners. In this respect, we would propose a method of phenomenological reflection, for phenomenology can reveal the various dimensions of human life which, I believe, symbolize culture and thereby can help us to overcome the aforementioned difficulties.

◆ ◆ ◆

INTERSUBJECTIVITY, LANGUAGE AND TAKEN-FOR-GRANTEDNESS

When, for instance a boy and his mother see a cedar, she is most likely to call it a tree rather than a cedar. After a while if he happens to see an oak tree and asks her "What's that?" she will call it a tree. At that time he might be very confused with that term simply because there is a difference between a cedar and an oak and yet they partake of the same name, tree. But gradually he realizes that the word or sound "tree" implies a certain group of characteristics which belong to the same category. It is clear that a word "tree" signifies an abstract expression in the sense that it represents certain characteristics and ignores others such as those that belong to the category "flower." In this respect, concreteness in common sense is not concrete in reality, but rather abstract. The reason why people mistake abstract expressions for concrete reality is due to the fact that they unconsciously accept the expressions as taken-for-granted, rooted in a specific-temporal world. Hence some concrete meanings in one culture are not concrete but very enigmatic, non-concrete expressions in another. In English, people distinguish tree from parts of tree which are used for architectural and other purposes, that is "wood." But in Japanese we don't do so. We express the idea of tree and wood both with one term, *Ki*. Yet, the dictionary usually describes *Ki* as having the same meaning as tree. Languages also differ in their built-in grammatical signals, that is in semantics, syntax and phonetics. In English people are very conscious of specifying the number of people involved in what they are discussing. But in Japanese the contrary is often true. Here we can see that the very nature of language through which we comprehend the world and understand ourselves inevitably involves us in the cultural context of language. Hence languages differ immensely from one another not only in pronunciation, vocabulary and grammar, but also in the way they recognize certain things and ignore others, thereby reflecting the society and culture they serve. Experience and language are reciprocal in the sense that human beings can experience outside reality only in terms of the meanings disclosed by language. Human beings are thrown into language worlds in which they learn to identify things as well as to understand reality. In this sense it is obvious that our ways of understanding and interpreting reality are already conditioned by the socially given knowledge.

If we accept that our knowledge is socially given, it seems that we are caught in the relativistic position of suggesting that there is no such thing as objectivity. Hence, we may ask a further question: How can we affirm something as an objective entity on which everybody can agree? In this question we again need to reflect on what I will call the intersubjective world which language as well as our everyday life thinking always presupposes. Situationally we unconsciously put ourselves as the center of spatio-temporal coordinates in the world. This means that I usually see the position I occupy as "here," distinguished from "there" taken by a fellow human being. Yet we can interchange our positions freely, as if we can place ourselves in the other's situation. A saying such as "Do unto others as you would have them do unto you," implies this interchangeability. This interchangeability is possible because there is an intersubjectively acknowledged spatio-temporal world in which both s/he and I are embedded and therefore can exchange, as well as share, our positions in essentially the same fashion with essentially the same possibilities and consequences. The concept of intersubjectivity signifies this intersubjectively acknowledged spatio-temporal world. Each socio-cultural environment presupposes an intersubjective world which historically develops various conceptions of the world as symbolized in language. Those who have been living in American society share various typicalities as a horizon of familiarity and of unquestioned pre-experience. Through the use of these we can converse with one another and understand the objects of the world as the reality of the taken-for-granted. The meanings of words such as tree or flower are simply taken for granted and therefore are self-evident. In other words, we are speaking, acting and understanding within an intersubjective world in which we share our perspectives through knowledge gained by previous experience. The fact that I am able to express my thinking to a fellow human being already presupposes an intersubjective world in which both s/he and I are embedded and, therefore, s/he can share my thinking and I hers/his. This sharing is the very basis with which we can affirm objective reality for we are able to identify an entity within the same perspective. Understanding, hence, always presupposes a common social heritage of an intersubjective world with the participation of Mystery. It is in this intersubjectivity that we can understand our ways of perceiving outside reality as the objective one.

THE PROBLEM OF INTERSUBJECTIVITY

Up till this point in our discussion, intersubjectivity has not seemed to present a crucial problem to our cultural concerns. However, when we consider cases in which there are two distinctive groups responding differently according to their own intersubjective worlds, the problem of intersubjectivity can be seen. In order to reveal this problem, let me follow Alfred Schutz's notion of "in-group" and "out-group." The in-group, as defined by Schutz, are those who accept the ready-made standardized scheme of a socio-cultural environment, that is, an intersubjective world as an unquestioned and unquestionable system of knowledge. For them the system of knowledge in everyday life situation as manifested in language, tradition, habits and various social systems appears to have sufficient coherence, clarity and consistency. In contrast those who stand outside of that world are defined as the out-group. Members of the out-group sometimes feel that what is taken-for-granted by the in-group is actually an ambiguous and enigmatic reality since the out-group have not had any sharing experience with the in-group's historical traditions. Suppose, for instance, that an American who has never lived in any foreign country has to live in Japan, without first learning about the culture or studying the language, and to work at a Japanese factory in a Japanese style. Being astonished by the Japanese employee's daily singing of the company's song or quoting the company's slogan in a militaristic manner, s/he would as a result have considerable difficulty in understanding the Japanese way of life simply because s/he does not share his/her intersubjective world with that of the Japanese. The self-evidence of everyday life for the members of an in-group may not be self-evident for those of the out-group. It is this gap that creates misunderstandings.

I explained a sharing world of an in-group in distinction to that of out-groups. Actually this characterization does not really indicate the true meaning of sharing because the sharing world of an in-group eventually destroys the sharing world in the global sense. A sharing world of an in-group becomes a kind of confinement in which we tend to glorify ourselves as a sharing people, as exemplified in Germany and Japan during the Second World War. As long as we understand "sharing a world" in terms of in-group and out-group, we in a sense validate a dualism of the human condition in which in-group stands apart from out-group. This does not really signify the true meaning of sharing. To share various human concerns in the world means not to differentiate in-group from out-group, but to take part in every possible activity in the world. This participation can create a sort of "fusion of horizons" in which the differences between in-group and out-group eventually disappear, creating a new horizon of understanding which involves a broadening of the present horizon.

FUSION OF HORIZON: OPENNESS AND LISTENING

The encounter between in-group and out-group usually creates tension. How can we overcome this tension and at the same time attain a respectful understanding of each other, allowing every individual and every culture to their own dignity? Indeed this is an important question. Let us recall Gadamer's attempt to explain the encounter between text and interpreter in his *magnum opus, Truth and Method,* for his analysis is helpful in understanding the question of the encounter between in-group and out-group. He states:

> *The concept of the 'horizon' suggests itself because it expresses the wide, superior vision that the person who is seeking to understand must have. To acquire a horizon means that one learns to look beyond what is close at hand—not in order to look away from it, but to see it better within a larger whole and in truer proportion.*

"To acquire a horizon means that one learns to look beyond what is close at hand." What does that mean? It means that we need to learn to understand the out-group's own dignity enabling them to disclose their true nature. This requires from us an openness towards out-groups, a willingness to listen to what the members of out-groups would say. Earlier I discussed the example of the notions of tree and *Ki;* so long as we are caught up within the taken-for-grantedness of our notions in language, we will never be able to understand the real meanings of out-groups' expressions. But if we are able to admit that our understanding is historically conditioned and therefore to allow ourselves to be open to what an out-group says, then a new horizon between us may come into being in the sense that everybody will become able to realize the limitedness of both tree and *Ki* in a larger context.

Openness and listening are keys to understanding other cultures as well as other human beings.

Openness and listening are keys to understanding other cultures as well as other human beings. It is true that an understanding of other cultures involves issues more complex than the difference between tree and *Ki.* Yet, if we lose a sense of listening and openness, there is no possibility for us to understand different cultures and people.

At present we are confronted by the nuclear crisis. This came about because we lost the attitude of listening to others, because we forgot that human beings are rooted in the common destiny of the world, because we manipulated others at our disposal, and because we lost the original meaning of the Biblical story about human beings on earth: human beings were created to bring to light and to protect the world in the context of relationships within which different people and things belong together with mutual dependency.

In the question of fusion of horizons between different cultures and people, language reveals very mysterious powers. Since every language is tied up to a particular historical setting, various languages differ from one another. Language is also the medium through which human beings are able to identify various historico-cultural phenomena in their settings. Hence, historico-cultural differences can be understood as differences among languages. In this regard, language always discloses particular characteristics of its own historico-cultural setting.

But how can we mediate these differences of language? Clearly it is also through language that differences can be fused or compared. In this respect, language discloses the universal dimension through which differences can be overcome. It is true that the English language is different from Japanese. But if English discloses totally different characteristics from Japanese, is it possible for any Japanese to understand the various meanings of English? The very fact that I can translate different English expressions into Japanese already presupposes that there are universally shared meanings between the two languages. Thus language discloses not only particular modes of being, but also the universal dimensions of our existence.

Language, furthermore, has the immanently transcending power by which I mean that language is able to overcome its own limited meaning in its historical condition. Here, paradoxically speaking, our fateful situation is not fateful when we reflect on, and open ourselves to, the fatefulness of our existence. When I say that the tree of the English language is different from the *Ki* of Japanese, I note that the meanings of tree and *Ki* are limited. Yet, in so pointing out, language can open much larger possibilities than those of tree and *Ki*. Because any society signifies linguistically its historical heritage in which human relationality dwells, human relationships, too, disclose particular modes of being as well as universality. Human relationality contains something common to all humanity. Everywhere we find language, cultural objects, playthings for children, family life through which human beings live and celebrate such great events of life as birth, initiation, marriage and death. These are given universally. Human beings are different and yet we share various dimensions of human existence as universally shared meanings. It is in this human sharing that we can appreciate and understand different people.

We cannot escape the "taken-for-grantedness" of our world. We are fatefully thrown into that world where we must find meanings for our existence. It is impossible for us to have meaningful dialogue with others if we do not take our language for granted. For example, it is impossible for us to bring our sick baby to a doctor if we do not take some medical knowledge for granted. In this regard "taken-for-grantedness" discloses appreciative human meanings in addition to its ideological dimensions. One of the fundamental mistakes utopian theorists often make is to assume that they themselves are the vanguard as they claim *a-priori* powers to transcend the ideological power of culture. But, in so doing, they themselves become ideological in the sense that they negate the ultimate human condition: human beings are historical beings who disclose a fateful as well as a transformative mode of life and thought. It seems to me that every human being at certain points has to share in the ideological power of existence. We are, in a sense, living within original sin. However, this does not mean that we cannot transcend various modes of ideological power in our respective cultures. We are living in a constant transformative process within the horizon of encounters between different people. If we are open and responsive to other people in dialogue, then Mystery can lead humans to learn to trust and find a way of reconciling the differences of culture and existence. This awareness opens up much richer possibilities of shaping various modes of our existence in more meaningful ways. The genuine work of education, it seems to me, is to provide and teach this dialogical-critical ability to human beings so that we can create and develop meaningful societies in a global sense.[19]

Like Nagami, feminist philosopher **Elizabeth Grosz** argues for a multiplicity of meaning. In her view, feminism allows for the acknowledgement of multiple points of view without thereby equating their value or prohibiting critique.

ON FEMINIST KNOWLEDGE
BY **ELIZABETH GROSZ**

There is considerable disagreement among feminists about which approach to take in questioning philosophy's sexist, patriarchal and phallocentric assumptions. They are divided over whether to accept philosophy on its own terms, to undertake a revision of it in the light of feminist knowledges, to abandon it or actively to undermine it. Radical feminists challenge philosophy's orientation around *oneness,* unity, or identity—one truth, one method, one reality, one logic, and so on. Many have insisted that there are a plurality of perspectives and a multiplicity of models on which philosophy could base itself.

In their endorsement of plurality and multiplicity, feminists such as Le Doeuff, Irigaray, and Lloyd are not, however, committed to relativism. Relativism is the belief that there are no absolute positions of judgment or knowl-

---

[19] Isamu Nagami, "Cultural Gaps: Why Do We Misunderstand?" from *Liberation Ethics: Essays in Religious and Social Ethics in Honor of Gibson Winter,* eds. Charles Amjad-Ali and W. Alvin Pitcher (Chicago: Center for Scientific Study of Religion, 1985).

edge. There are many positions, each of which is *equally valid.* Relativism or pluralism implies the existence of frameworks and positions which each have their own validity and standards; and the belief that none of these positions is comprehensive or all-inclusive.

Pluralism and relativism imply abandoning the right to criticize actively other positions, even those we find offensive and disturbing—phallocentric or racist statements, for example—and to accept them as having equal validity to our own positions. Radical feminists instead aim to expand and multiply the criteria for what is considered true, rational, or valid and to reject or condemn those they perceive to be discriminatory. They insist on retaining the right to judge other positions, to criticize them, and also to supersede them. Radical feminists are not absolutists nor objectivists nor relativists nor subjectivists. They advocate a *perspectivism* which acknowledges other points of view but denies them equal value.

It is at this time impossible to specify what a philosophy compatible with feminism would be like; given that it does not exist as a definite body of texts, any definition or description would be overly prescriptive. Nevertheless, some general tendencies can be briefly outlined.

Among the features a feminist philosophy may develop are the following.

(a) Instead of a commitment to truth and objectivity, it can openly accept its own status (and that of all discourses) as context-specific. It accepts its *perspectivism,* that fact that all discourses represent a point of view, have specific aims and objectives, often not coinciding with those of their authors. Rather than seeing itself as disinterested knowledge, it can openly avow its own political position: all texts speak from or represent particular positions within power relations.

(b) Instead of regarding philosophy as the unfolding of reason, a sure path of progress towards truth, a feminist philosophy can accept itself as the product of a specific socio-economic and textual-discursive history. Neither relativist nor subjectivist, it aims to render these and other binary oppositions problematic. A feminist philosophy defies modes of conventional evaluation. This is not, however, to claim that it cannot be evaluated in any terms; simply that the criteria used must be different. A theory's validity is not judged simply according to its adoption of a fixed or pre-given form, but it may be judged according to its *intersubjective* effects, that is, its capacity to be shared, understood, and communicated by those occupying similar positions; and also by its *intertextual* effects, that is, its capacity to affirm or undermine various prevailing or subordinated discursive systems, and the effects it has on other discourses.

(c) Instead of separating the subject and object of knowledge, a feminist philosophy may instead assert a continuity or contiguity between them. The gulf necessary for objectivity is an attempt to guarantee a knowing subject free of personal, social, political, and moral interests (a Cartesian subject), unimplicated in a social context, and uninfluenced by prior ideas and knowledges. A feminist philosophy would need to reconceptualize their interrelations so that reason and knowledge include history, context, and specificity. A feminist philosophy could accept, as patriarchal discourses cannot, that subjects occupying different positions may develop different types of theory and have different investments in their relation to the object. Above all, it can accept that all knowledge is *sexualized,* that it occupies a sexually coded and structured position. However, the sexual position of the text cannot be readily identified with the sexual identity of its author; a female author, for example, does not in any way guarantee a feminine text.

(d) Instead of the dichotomous, oppositional structure, which separates subject and object, teacher and pupil, truth and falsity, etc., a feminist philosophy may regard these terms as continuities or *differences.* Distinctions or oppositions imply that two binary terms are mutually exclusive and exhaustive of the field; that one term defines the other as its negative; that this other can have a place in the binary structure; however, when terms are conceived as two among many others, they are neither contradictory nor all-inclusive. If anything, the relation of difference is based on contrariety not contradiction.

(e) Instead of aspiring to the status of truth, a feminist philosophy prefers to see itself as a form of *strategy.* Strategies are not abstractions, blueprints, or battle-plans for future action. Rather, they involve a provisional commitment to goals and ideals; a recognition of the prevailing situation, in opposition to which these ideals are erected; and an expedient relation to terms, arguments, and techniques which help transform the prevailing order into the ideal. To deny that a feminist philosophy aspires to truth is not to claim it is content with being regarded as false; rather, the opposition between truth and falsity is largely irrelevant for a strategic model.

(f) Instead of dividing theory from practice—so that practice is located chronologically before and after theory (construed as either a plan or a *post facto* reflection, respectively)—a feminist philosophy may regard theory as a form of practice, a textual, conceptual, and educational practice, one involved in struggles for theoretical ascendancy, where dominant and subordinated discourses battle with each other. Theory is not privileged by its isolation from practice and its relegation to a pure conceptual level. When it is seen as a material process, theory can be seen as a practice like any other, neither more nor less privileged in its ability to survey and assess other practices. As a material labour or practice, theory relies on concepts, words, and discursive 'raw materials', processes of theoretical production (e.g. the form of argument, narrative, or linguistic structure needed to make coherent discourses) and a determined product (a text or theory). It is not hierarchically privileged over other practices, reserving the right of judgement; rather it is itself capable of being assessed by other practices.

(g) Instead of opposing reason to its others, a feminist philosophy expands the concept of reason. It has analyzed how reason as we know it is allied with masculinity and relegates feminine attributes to a repressed or subordinated status. A feminist philosophy would not reverse the relation between reason and its others, but would expand reason so that its expelled others are now included. In beginning with women's lived experiences in the production of knowledge it seeks a reason that is not separated from experience but based upon it, that is not opposed to the body but accepts it, not distinct from everyday life but cognisant of it.

(h) Instead of accepting dominant models of knowledge (with their logic, binary structure, desire for precision and clarity) a feminist philosophy can accept its status as material, textual, and institutional. As such, it can accept the provisional, not eternal, status of its postulates. It aims for the production of new methods of knowing, new forms of analysis, new modes of writing, new kinds of textual objects, new texts. No *one* method, point of view, position for subjects and objects is the norm or model for all philosophy.[20]

> *No* **one** *method, point of view, position for subjects and objects is the norm or model for all philosophy.*

SUMMARY AND CONCLUSION

Philosophers have always seen their main business as the search for truth. But the notion of truth has itself become a problem, and there are at least two very different kinds of truth and several competing theories of truth. There is necessary and there is contingent (empirical) truth. The traditional theory of empirical truth is the correspondence theory of truth, which claims that a belief (or statement) is true if it "matches up" or corresponds to the facts of reality. But there have been many arguments to show that this view is inadequate. Accordingly, philosophers have defended the coherence theory of truth, which says that a belief or statement is true if it is logically connected to other beliefs and statements; the pragmatic theory of truth, which says that a belief or statement is true if it helps us in practice with our work and our lives; and a semantic theory of truth, which says that truth is a function of our language as well as a question about the "facts" of the world.

Since the writings of Immanuel Kant, truth is sometimes discussed in terms of our "constitution" of reality, but this also tends to lead to "relativism," the view that there is no reality—no truth—independent of our consciousness and "constitution" of the world. The history of philosophy since Kant is very much bound up with this challenge.

---

[20] Elizabeth Grosz, "Philosophy" in *Feminist Knowledge: Critique and Construct,* ed. Sneja Gunew (London: Routledge, 1990).

GLOSSARY

absolutism The thesis that there is but one correct view of reality. Opposed to *relativism*.

analytic (of a sentence or truth) Demonstrably true (and necessarily true) by virtue of the logical form or the meanings of the component words. The concept was introduced by Kant, who defined it in terms of a sentence (he called it a "judgment") in which the "predicate was contained in the subject" and "added nothing to it." For example, in "a horse is an animal," he would say that the concept of "horse" already includes the concept of being an animal; we would say that "horse" means "an animal which . . ." and thus "is an animal" adds nothing to what we already know just from "horse." Kant also says that the *criterion* or test for analytic sentences (or *analyticity*) is the principle of contradiction; an analytic sentence is one for which denial yields a self-contradiction.

analytic philosophy The movement in twentieth-century philosophy, particularly in the United States and Britain, that focuses its primary attention on language and linguistic analysis. Also called "linguistic philosophy."

a posteriori (knowledge) "After experience," or empirical. (See *empirical*.)

a priori (knowledge) Independent of all experience. A priori knowledge is always necessary, for there can be no imaginable instances that would refute it and no intelligible doubting of it. One might come to know something a priori through experience (for example, you might find out that no parallel lines ever touch each other by drawing tens of thousands of parallel lines), but what is essential to a priori knowledge is that no such experience is needed. Knowledge is a priori if it can be proven independently of experience. The most obvious examples of a priori knowledge are analytic sentences, such as "a horse is an animal" and "if all men are mammals and Socrates is a man, then Socrates is a mammal."

categories Kant's word (borrowed from Aristotle) for those most basic and a priori concepts of human knowledge, for example, "causality," and "substance."

coherence theory of truth A statement or a belief is true if and only if it "coheres" with a system of statements or beliefs. A truth of mathematics is "true" because if forms part of the nexus in the complex of mathematical truths. A geometrical theorem is "true" because it can be proven from other theorems (axioms, definitions) of the geometrical system. A "factual" statement is "true" insofar as other "factual" statements, including general statements about experience that are logically relevant to the original statement, support it. Since we can never get "outside" our experience, the only sense in saying that a belief is true (according to this theory) is that it "coheres" with the rest of our experience.

conceptual truth An analytic sentence that is true by virtue of the meanings of its component words, or concepts. The example, "a horse is an animal," is a conceptual truth because part of the definition of the word *horse* is "an animal. "All sisters are females" is a conceptual truth because part of the meaning of "sister" is "female."

constitute To put together, "set up," or synthesize experience through categories or concepts. First used by Kant, later by Husserl.

contingent (truth) Dependent on the facts; neither logically necessary nor logically impossible. A contingent state of affairs could have been otherwise. One test to see if a state of affairs is contingent is to see if it is conceivable that it could be other than it is. It is contingent, for example, that heavy objects fall toward the earth, since it is easily imaginable what it would be like if they did not. This is so even though, in another sense, we say that it is (physically) necessary that heavy objects fall. The philosophical terms *contingent* and *necessary* refer to logical possibility, not to the factual question whether a statement is true or not.

correspondence theory of truth A statement or belief is true if and only if it "corresponds" with "the facts." Even when restricting our attention to statements of fact, however, this commonsensical "theory" gets into trouble as soon as it tries to pick out what corresponds to what. How can we identify a "fact," for example, apart from the language we use to identify it? And what does it mean to say that a statement "corresponds" to a fact?

dialectic A "logic" developed by Hegel in which different forms or philosophies are arranged according to increasing sophistication and scope. The "logic" is a development from one form, whose inadequacies are demonstrated, to another, which corrects these inadequacies, and so on. Marx borrows this "dialectic" and gives it a social interpretation. (The "logic" need not be anything like the form "thesis-antithesis-synthesis.")

empirical (knowledge) Derived from and to be defended by appeal to experience. Empirical knowledge can only be so derived and so defended (as opposed to a priori knowledge, which need not be).

essence or **essential intuition** In Husserl, those ideal objects and laws that constitute necessary truths. The term *essence* is borrowed from Aristotle (and the medieval philosophers) and used in much the same way, except that Husserl's notion of essence is always tied to "intuition" and consciousness.

hermeneutics The discipline of interpretation of texts. Broadly conceived (as by Heidegger, Gadamer) it is the "uncovering" of meanings in everyday life, the attempt to understand the signs and symbols of one's culture and tradition in juxtaposition with other cultures and traditions.

historicism A philosophy that localizes truth and different views of reality to particular times, places, and peoples in history. It is generally linked to a very strong relativist thesis as well, that there is no truth apart from these various historical commitments.

intuition Immediate knowledge of the truth, without the aid of any reasoning and without appeal to experience. Intuition, as rational intuition (there are other kinds), is a central concern of the rationalist philosophers, who consider intuition one of the main functions of reason. But because of its very nature, intuition cannot be argued for, nor can it be defended by experience. Accordingly, many philosophers, especially empiricists, reject the notion of intuition and accept it only when absolutely unavoidable. In this century, Edmund Husserl has defended the appeal to intuition in his phenomenology.

law of contradiction That basic rule of logic that demands that a sentence and its denial cannot both be true. "Not (P and not P)." This law is used by many philosophers (Kant, Leibniz, and Hume, for example) as criterion for analyticity or analytic truth.

law of the excluded middle That rule of logic that says either a sentence or its denial must be true: "Either P or not P." In formal logic, this law, together with the law of contradiction, forms the basis of a great many arguments (for example, that form of *reductio ad absurdum* argument in which the consequences of one premise are shown to be absurd, and therefore its denial is accepted. Many logicians are now reconsidering this law, for it is becoming evident that not all sentences are either true or false. For example, consider Russell's famous example, "the King of France is bald" (when there is no king of France); is that true or false? It surely isn't true, but neither can it be false, for there is no king of France who is not bald. Or what of, "green ideas sleep furiously"? Many philosophers would say that these are neither true nor false, thus rejecting the law of the excluded middle.

logical truth A sentence that can be shown to be true by virtue of its logical form alone (by virtue of the connectives, "and," "or," etc.).

matter of fact (In Hume), an empirical claim, to be confirmed or falsified through experience.

necessary (truth) Cannot be otherwise and cannot be imagined to be otherwise. In philosophy, it is not enough that something be "necessary" according to physical laws (for example, the law of gravity), or "necessary" according to custom or habit (for example, the "necessity" of laws against rape or the felt necessity of having a cigarette after dinner). Necessary allows for not even imaginary counter-examples; thus it is a necessary truth that two plus two equals four. Not only do we believe thus with certainty and find ourselves incapable of intelligibly doubting it, but we cannot even suggest what it might be for it to be false, no matter how wild our imaginations.

necessity In accordance with a necessary truth.

phenomenology A contemporary European philosophy, founded by the German-Czech philosopher Edmund Husserl, that begins with a "pure description of consciousness." Originally developed as an answer to certain questions of necessary truth in the foundations of arithmetic, it was later expanded to answer more general philosophical questions and, in the hands of its later practitioners, it became a "philosophy of man" as well as a theory of knowledge.

pragmatic theory of truth A statement or a belief that is true if and only if it "works," that is, if it allows us to predict certain results and function effectively in everyday life, and if it encourages further inquiry and helps us lead better lives.

pragmatism A distinctly American philosophical movement founded by Charles Sanders Peirce at the turn of this century and popularized by William James and John Dewey. Its central thesis is obvious in its name, that truth (etc.) is always to be determined by reference to practical (pragmatic) considerations. Only those metaphysical distinctions that make some difference in practice are worth considering, and the only ultimate defense of any belief is that "it works."

rational In accordance with the rules of effective thought: coherence, consistency, practicability, simplicity, comprehensiveness, looking at the evidence and weighing it carefully, not jumping to conclusions, and so forth. Rationality may not guarantee truth; all of the evidence and everything we believe may point to one conclusion, while later generations, who know things that we do not, may see that our conclusion was incorrect. Yet it would still be, for us, the rational conclusion. Rationality points to the manner of thinking rather than its ultimate conclusions. Philosophically, the stress on rationality takes the emphasis off reality and places it on our manner of philosophizing.

realism The thesis that reality exists in itself and it is independent of our consciousness of it.

relation of ideas In traditional empiricist philosophy, analytic truths, which can be demonstrated without appeal to experience. Arithmetic and geometry were taken to be paradigm examples of "relations of ideas."

relativism The thesis that there is no single correct view of reality, no single truth. Relativists often talk about the possibility of "different conceptual frameworks," "alternative lifestyles," and various "forms of consciousness." They are opposed, often violently, to realists and absolutists.

rules of inference Those rules of logic according to which validity is defined. All such rules are analytic, but there is considerable disagreement whether all are so by virtue of their own logical form or whether some are so because they are derived from other, more basic rules. There is also the following question: Given that these rules define correct logical form, how is it possible to say that they have correct logical form?

semantics The meanings of a sentence and its various components. Also, the study of those meanings. (So, we can talk about the semantics of a sentence, and we can talk about doing semantics.) "Merely semantic" is a nasty way of referring to conceptual truths, analytic sentences that are true just by virtue of meanings.

semantic theory of truth A formal theory, best known from the work of Alfred Tarski, that defines "true" in terms of a technical notion of *satisfaction*. According to the theory, every sentence in the language is either satisfied or not by a distinct class of individuals. This is adequate, however, only for artificially constructed languages. Generalizing the theory to natural language (for example, American English), we can say that the theory suggests that we (but not each of us personally) set up the rules according to which our sentences do or do not "correspond with the facts" of the world.

synonym "Meaning the same." Two words are synonymous if they are interchangeable in a sentence, without losing the meaning of the sentence. For example, "criminal" and "felon" are synonyms in most contexts. The test of a supposedly conceptual truth is to replace certain words with synonyms and then see if its denial yields a self-contradiction. In other words, substituting synonyms turns a conceptual truth into an analytic truth. For example, "ferns are plants"; substituting for "fern" its synonym (or, in this case, also its definition) "a primitive plant that bears spores, etc." we have "a plant is a plant," whose denial is a contradiction ("a plant is not a plant") and thus is analytic.

synthetic (statement) A noncontradictory proposition in which the predicate is not entailed by the subject, for example, "horses are generally obstinate." ("Synthetic" is opposed, in this sense, to "analytic.") A synthetic sentence cannot be shown to be true by appeal to the logical form or the meanings of the component words. Kant defined a "synthetic" sentence as one that "adds an idea to the subject which is not already contained in it." For example, "a horse is the source of a large income for some people" is a strictly synthetic sentence. No appeal to the meaning of "horse" will help you find out whether it is true or not, and its denial surely does not result in self-contradiction. But, according to Kant, it must not be concluded that all synthetic sentences can be shown to be true solely by appeal to experience. Some, he claimed, are known a priori.

synthetic a priori (knowledge) Knowledge that is necessary and known independently of experience (and thus a priori), but that does not derive its truth from the logic or meaning of sentences (thus synthetic). This is the focal concept of Kant's philosophy.

tautology A trivial truth that is true by virtue of logical form alone and tells us nothing about the world. (Popularly, a bit of repetitive nonsense, for example, "a rose is a rose is a rose." Technically, [in logic] a sentence that can be shown to be true no matter what the truth or falsity of its component parts.)

transcendental Referring to the basic rules of human knowledge, usually with an absolutist suggestion that there can be but a single set of such basic rules. Thus Kant's "transcendental deduction" attempted to deduce the one possible set of basic rules for human understanding, and Husserl's transcendental phenomenology attempted to lay bare the one set of basic ("essential") laws of human consciousness. Contemporary philosophers sometimes talk about "the transcendental turn" in philosophy, in other words, the attempt to move beyond claims that might apply only to ourselves and our way of viewing things to the way that things must be viewed.

transcendental deduction Kant's elaborate attempt to prove that there is but one set of categories (basic rules or a priori concepts) that all rational creatures must use in constituting their experience.

truth of reason In traditional rationalism, a belief that can be justified solely by appeal to intuition or deduction from premises based upon intuition. Arithmetic and geometry were, for the rationalists as for the empiricists, a paradigm case of such truths. They disagreed mainly on the scope of such truths, and the restrictions to be placed on the problematic appeal to intuition.

BIBLIOGRAPHY AND FURTHER READING

Discussion and criticism of the various theories of truth can be found in Alan R. White, *Truth* (New York: Doubleday, Anchor, 1970). A discussion of Alfred Tarski's theory is in W. V. O. Quine, *Philosophy of Logic* (Englewood Cliffs, NJ: Prentice-Hall, 1970). Brand Blanshard's argument is developed in his *Nature of Thought* (New York: Macmillan, 1941). William James develops his pragmatic theory in his *Pragmatism: A New Name for Some Old Ways of Thinking* (New York: Longmans Green, 1907). Two brief but helpful introductions to Immanuel Kant's philosophy are J. Kemp, *The Philosophy of Kant* (London: Oxford University Press, 1968) and G. J. Warnock, "Kant," in *A Critical History of Western Philosophy*, ed. D. J. O'Connor (New York: Free Press, 1964). A short introduction to German idealism is R. Solomon, *Introducing the German Idealists* (Indianapolis, IN: Hackett, 1981). The best basic discussion of hermeneutics is David Hoy, *The Critical Circle* (Berkeley: University of California Press, 1978). A compendium of writings by Gadamer is *Philosophical Hermeneutics*, trans. D. Linge (Berkeley: University of California Press, 1976). *Relativism* is the subject of the essays collected by M. Kraucze and J. Meiland, eds. (Notre Dame, IN: University of Notre Dame Press, 1982). A controversial discussion of the whole problem of truth and its complications is Richard Rorty, *Philosophy and the Mirror of Nature* (Princeton: Princeton University Press, 1979). Two anthologies on necessary truth are Robert Sleigh, ed., *Necessary Truth* (Englewood Cliffs, NJ: Prentice-Hall, 1972) and L. W. Sumner and John Woods, *Necessary Truth: A Book of Readings* (New York: Random House, 1970).

II

KNOW THYSELF

SELF

"I'm not myself today, you see," Alice said to the caterpillar.

"I don't see," said the caterpillar.

LEWIS CARROLL

"Just be yourself!" How often have you heard that? What is it to be a "self"? And what does it mean to be a particular self? In the abstract, these questions seem obscure. But in everything that we do, we adopt some conception of our identity, both as a person and as an individual, whether we are called upon to articulate it or not. As a student, you walk into a classroom with certain conceptions of your own abilities and intelligence, your status among other students, your role vis-à-vis the professor, some haunting memories, perhaps some embarrassment or a certain vanity about your looks, your clothes, your grades, or just your new pair of shoes.

If you had to identify yourself as an individual, describe what makes you you, how would you do it? What features are essential to being a person? What are essential to being the person you are and what features distinguish you from other persons? Think for a moment of yourself in an office, applying for a job or a scholarship for professional school or just filling out one of those dozens of forms that bombard you during the year. You dutifully fill in your birthdate, where you were born, your grades in school, your service in the military if any, awards you have received, arrests and other troubles, whether you're married or not, male or female, perhaps your race and religion. This list of facts about yourself would be one way of identifying "you." But at some point, I am sure you have felt that sense of absurdity and rebellion, "this isn't me!" or "this is all irrelevant!" What may seem more relevant to your self-identity are your political views, your tastes in art and music, your favorite books and movies, your loves and hates, habits and beliefs, or just the fact, perhaps, that you think your own thoughts. These more personal, or "internal," features as well as the "cold facts," or "external" features, about yourself are important for identifying you as an individual different from other individuals.

In one sense, your **self-identity** is the way you characterize yourself as an individual. The philosophical problem of self-identity is thus concerned in part with what these characterizing qualities are. Are they just concerned with status and roles among other people? Or is there something that can truly be called "your self," your "essence," or maybe even your soul, without reference to anyone else? Should we think of ourselves as individuals? Or should we instead view ourselves as mere components of a larger organism—society, mankind, or perhaps the world as a whole? How should we identify ourselves?

There is another sense in which we might talk about a person's self-identity. You may know someone who has experienced a religious conversion, or who has just undergone treatment for alcoholism; or perhaps you can think of someone you see again after a long time who says, "I'm not the same person." What does this mean, and how is it possible to say you are not the same person? When someone says, "I'm not the same person I was," he or she is pointing to the fact that some significant aspects of himself or herself have changed; this person has a new self-identity. Yet, in another sense, this is still the same person; the old identity and the new identity are both identities of the same person.

So we have a second sense of "self-identity." Here your self-identity is what makes you the same person over time. Thus, the second philosophical problem, which is the one that has most concerned philosophers, is how to identify an individual as the *same* individual over time. What is it about you without which you wouldn't be you? Presumably you would still be you if you changed your religious beliefs or tastes in music. But what if you had a sex-change operation? Or what if you completely lost your memory, all recollection of your family and friends? Or what if you physically disappeared altogether, remaining only a wispy consciousness, a spirit, or a ghost without a body? Would it then make sense to say that you are still you?

There is yet a third sense in which we talk about self-identity. What is it that *allows* us to be individual people at all? Interestingly, the fact of consciousness—of having thoughts and feelings—seems the most private and individual thing a person possesses, and yet is the very thing that we tend to believe *all* people possess. Whatever our attempts to answer the problems of self-identity, they begin with a single "fact"—our own consciousness. We will see that this was the logical beginning for Descartes, who used the fact of his own consciousness as the starting point for his whole philosophy. It was true for Locke, as well, who argued that our identity is to be found in the continuity of our consciousness rather than in the continuity of our bodies. We will see that it was even used by Hume, who used his own consciousness as the basis of his denial that there is any such thing as the self!

Of course, these questions assume some metaphysical claims that can and have been questioned. Later in this chapter, we will look at some of these assumptions and some criticisms of them. Is self-identity a matter of nature? Are we born with an identity? Or is it a matter of personal choice or of environmental factors such as our upbringing or education? Must a person have only one "self," or might he or she in fact have several or many selves? Is there a "self" at all? Or is the self, as many Eastern philosophers have argued, an illusion? Should self-lessness be our ideal self-identity? Ought we even to conceive of ourselves as individuals? Or ought we instead think of ourselves as organic components of a larger community or society?

In this chapter, we explore a number of different questions and conceptions about self-identity. We consider the question of what makes you *you,* both in the sense of what makes you a person, and in the sense of what makes you the particular person you are. Freud, the great nineteenth-century psychologist, once said that every man is in some ways like all other men, in some ways like some other men, and in some ways like no other man. Philosophers who investigate the problem of self-identity attempt to figure out exactly how and why this might be so. We begin with an all-important and still influential tradition in philosophy, from Descartes and Locke to Hume and Kant, which focuses on self-consciousness as the sole key to personal identity.

A. CONSCIOUSNESS AND THE SELF: FROM DESCARTES TO KANT

Sometimes we act out our identities without being aware of it at all. At other times, particularly when we talk about ourselves or are placed in a situation where we are forced to "look at ourselves as others see us," we are very much aware—even painfully aware—of our identities. At such times we say we are **self-conscious.** In general, most modern philosophers and psychologists would argue that you can't have a concept of who you are unless you are also sometimes (not necessarily always) self-conscious. Conversely, you can't even be self-conscious unless you have some sense of identity, no matter how crude. The two concepts, in other words, go hand in hand and cannot be separated from each other.

Many philosophers have argued that not only is self-consciousness crucial to having a concept of one's own individuality, but it is also crucial for establishing that one is an enduring self, that is, the same person over time. Descartes is an example. Remember how he characterized himself:

> *But what then am I? A thing which thinks. What is a thing which thinks? It is a thing which doubts, understands, affirms, denies, wills, refuses, which also imagines and feels.*

He goes on to say, I am a thing with desires, who perceives light and noise and feels heat. Clearly, Descartes' concept of "self" is of thought, or consciousness—a human essence—which each person has and with which each person identifies himself or herself. He also claims to show by his method of doubt that all of this might be so even if he were not to have a body at all. Perhaps, he argues, I am fooled about my "having" a body just as I might be fooled about all sorts of other things. Therefore, he concludes, it is not my body that provides me with an identity or with the self from which I begin my philosophy. It follows from this that the particular aspects of my self—whether I am male or female, black or white, tall or short, handsome or ugly, strong or weak—are associated with my body only and cannot be essential to my identity. My self-identity is in my mind, in my thinking, doubting, feeling, perceiving, imagining, and desiring. I am, essentially, "a thing which thinks."

FROM "MEDITATION VI" BY RENÉ DESCARTES

Therefore, just because I know certainly that I exist, and that meanwhile I do not remark that any other thing necessarily pertains to my nature or essence, excepting that I am a thinking thing, I rightly conclude that my essence consists solely in the fact that I am a thinking thing [or a substance whose whole essence or nature is to think]. And although possibly (or rather certainly, as I shall say in a moment) I possess a body with which I am very intimately conjoined, yet because, on the one side, I have a clear and distinct idea of myself inasmuch as I am only a thinking and unextended thing, and as, on the other, I possess a distinct idea of body, inasmuch as it is only an extended and unthinking thing, it is certain that this I [that is to say, my soul by which I am what I am], is entirely and absolutely distinct from my body, and can exist without it.[1]

It is important to appreciate the kind of step Descartes has taken here. What he is saying is that self-identity depends on consciousness. Our identity does not depend in any way on our body remaining the same, and so human identity is different from the identity of anything else in the world.

John Locke, like Descartes, sees self-consciousness as the key to self-identity. But unlike Descartes, he argues that this identity does not depend on our remaining the same thinking substance, that is, on our having the same soul. Indeed, in the course of our life our soul might be replaced with new souls just as in the course of a tree's growth its cells are replaced with new cells. What makes the tree the same tree is the fact that the same life is present in spite of changes in its physical structure; and what makes a person the same person is that the same *consciousness* and memories are present. Thus Locke differs from Descartes in distinguishing between the soul (a substance) and consciousness. It is our consciousness that we call our "self." In *An Essay Concerning Human Understanding*, Locke argues:

ON PERSONAL IDENTITY BY JOHN LOCKE

To find wherein personal identity consists, we must consider what *person* stands for;—which, I think, is a thinking intelligent being, that has reason and reflec-

---

[1] René Descartes, "Meditation VI," in Meditations on First Philosophy, in *The Philosophical Works of Descartes,* trans. Elizabeth S. Haldane and G. R. T. Ross (Cambridge: Cambridge University Press, 1911).

tion, and can consider itself as itself, the same thinking thing, in different times and places; which it does only by that consciousness which is inseparable from thinking, and as it seems to me, essential to it: it being impossible for any one to perceive without *perceiving* that he does perceive. When we see, hear, smell, taste, feel, meditate, or will anything, we know that we do so. Thus it is always as to our present sensations and perceptions: and by this every one is to himself that which he calls *self:*—it not being considered, in this case, whether the same self be continued in the same or divers substances. For, since consciousness always accompanies thinking, and it is that which makes every one to be what he calls self, and thereby distinguishes himself from all other thinking things, in this alone consists personal identity, i.e. the sameness of a rational being: and as far as this consciousness can be extended backwards to any past action or thought, so far reaches the identity of that person; it is the same self now it was then; and it is by the same self with this present one that now reflects on it, that that action was done.

Consciousness makes personal Identity.—But it is further inquired, whether it be the same identical substance. This few[2] would think they had reason to doubt of, if these perceptions, with their consciousness, always remained present in the mind, whereby the same thinking thing would be always consciously present, and, as would be thought, evidently the same to itself. But that which seems to make the difficulty is this, that this consciousness being interrupted always by forgetfulness, there being no moment of our lives wherein we have the whole train of all our past actions before our eyes in one view, but even the best memories losing the sight of one part whilst they are viewing another; and we sometimes, and that the greatest part of our lives, not reflecting on our past selves, being intent on our present thoughts, and in sound sleep having no thoughts at all, or at least none with that consciousness which remarks our waking thoughts,—I say, in all these cases, our consciousness being interrupted, and we losing the sight of our past selves, doubts are raised whether we are the same thinking thing, i.e. the same *substance* or no. Which, however reasonable or unreasonable, concerns not *personal* identity at all. The question being what makes the same person; and not whether it be the same identical substance, which always thinks in the same person, which, in this case, matters not at all: different substances, by the same consciousness (where they do partake in it) being united into one person, as well as different bodies by the same life are united into one animal, whose identity is preserved in that change of substances by the unity of one continued life. For, it being the same consciousness that makes a man be himself to himself, personal identity depends on that only, whether it be annexed solely to one individual substance, or can be continued in a succession of several substances. For as far as any intelligent being *can* repeat the idea of any past action with the same consciousness it had of it at first, and with the same consciousness it has of any present action; so far it is the same personal self. For it is by the consciousness it has of its present thoughts and actions, that it is *self to*

---

[2] Locke refers here to Descartes.

itself now, and so will be the same self, as far as the same consciousness can extend to actions past or to come; and would be by distance of time, or change of substance, no more two persons, than a man be two men by wearing other clothes to-day than he did yesterday, with a long or a short sleep between: the same consciousness uniting those distant actions into the same person, whatever substances contributed to their production.

Personal Identity in Change of Substance.—That this is so, we have some kind of evidence in our very bodies, all whose particles, whilst vitally united to this same thinking conscious self, so that *we feel* when they are touched, and are affected by, and conscious of good or harm that happens to them, are a part of ourselves; i.e. of our thinking conscious self. Thus, the limbs of his body are to every one a part of himself; he sympathizes and is concerned for them. Cut off a hand, and thereby separate it from that consciousness he had of its heat, cold, and other affections, and it is then no longer a part of that which is himself, any more than the remotest part of matter. Thus, we see the *substance* whereof personal self consisted at one time may be varied at another, without the change of personal identity; there being no question about the same person, though the limbs which but now were a part of it, be cut off.

◆◆◆

If the same consciousness (which, as has been shown, is quite a different thing from the same numerical figure or motion in body) can be transferred from one thinking substance to another, it will be possible that two thinking substances may make but one person. For the same consciousness being preserved, whether in the same or different substances, the personal identity is preserved. Whether the same immaterial being, being conscious of the action of its past duration, may be wholly stripped of all the consciousness of its past existence, and lose it beyond the power of ever retrieving it again: and so as it were beginning a new account from a new period, have a consciousness that *cannot* reach beyond this new state. All those who hold pre-existence are evidently of this mind; since they allow the soul to have no remaining consciousness of what it did in the pre-existing state, either wholly separate from body, or informing any other body; and if they should not, it is plain experience would be against them. So that personal identity, reaching no further than consciousness reaches, a pre-existent spirit not having continued so many ages in a state of silence, must needs make different persons. Suppose a Christian Platonist or a Pythagorean should, upon God's having ended all his works of creation the seventh day, think his soul hath existed ever since; and should imagine it has revolved in several human bodies; as I once met with one, who was persuaded his had been the *soul* of Socrates (how reasonably I will not dispute; this I know, that in the post he filled, which was no inconsiderable one, he passed for a very rational man, and the press has shown that he wanted not parts of learning;)—would any one say, that he, being not conscious of any of Socrates' actions or thoughts, could be the same *person* with Socrates? Let any one reflect upon himself, and conclude that he has in himself an immaterial spirit, which is that which thinks in him, and, in the constant change of his body keeps him the same: and is that which he calls *himself.*

The body, as well as the soul, goes to the making of a Man.—And thus may we be able, without any difficulty, to conceive the same person at the resurrection, though in a body not exactly in make or parts the same which he had here,—the same consciousness going along with the soul that inhabits it. But yet the soul alone, in the change of bodies, would scarce to any one but to him that makes the soul the man, be enough to make the same man. For should the soul of a prince, carrying with it the consciousness of the prince's past life, enter and inform the body of a cobbler, as soon as deserted by his own soul, every one sees he would be the same *person* with the prince, accountable only for the prince's actions: but who would say it was the same *man?* The body too goes to the making the man, and would, I guess, to everybody determine the man in this case, wherein the soul, with all its princely thoughts about it, would not make another man: but he would be the same cobbler to every one besides himself. I know that, in the ordinary way of speaking, the same person, and the same man, stand for one and the same thing.

Consciousness alone unites actions into the same Person.—But though the same immaterial substance or soul does not alone, wherever it be, and in whatsoever state, make the same *man;* yet it is plain, consciousness, as far as ever it can be extended—should it be to ages past—unites existences and actions very remote in time into the same *person,* as well as it does the existences and actions of the immediately preceding moment: so that whatever has the consciousness of present and past actions, is the same person to whom they both belong. Had I the same consciousness that I saw the ark and Noah's flood, as that I saw an overflowing of the Thames last winter, or as that I write now, I could no more doubt that I who write this now, that saw the Thames overflowed last winter, and that viewed the flood at the general deluge, was the same *self,*—place that self in what *substance* you please—than that I who write this am the same *myself* now whilst I write (whether I consist of all the same substance, material or immaterial, or no) that I was yesterday. For as to this point of being the same self, it matters not whether this present self be made up of the same or other substances—I being as much concerned, and as justly accountable for any action that was done a thousand years since, appropriated to me now by this self-consciousness, as I am for what I did the last moment.

Self depends on Consciousness, not on Substance.—*Self* is that conscious thinking thing,—whatever substance made up of, (whether spiritual or material, simple or compounded, it matters not)—which is sensible or conscious of pleasure and pain, capable of happiness or misery, and so is concerned for itself, as far as that consciousness extends. Thus every one finds that, whilst comprehended under that consciousness, the little finger is as much a

Self *is that conscious thinking thing . . . which is sensible or conscious of pleasure and pain, capable of happiness or misery, and so is concerned for itself, as far as that consciousness extends.*

part of himself as what is most so. Upon separation of this little finger, should this consciousness go along with the little finger, and leave the rest of the body, it is evident the little finger would be the person, the same person; and self then would have nothing to do with the rest of the body. As in this case it is the consciousness that goes along with the substance, when one part is separate from another, which makes the same person, and constitutes this inseparable self: so it is in reference to the substances remote in time. That with which the consciousness of this present thinking thing *can* join itself, makes the same person, and is one self with it, and with nothing else; and so attributes to itself, and owns all the actions of that thing, as its own, as far as that consciousness reaches, and no further.[3]

The main thesis of Locke's argument is this: Personal self-identity is based upon self-consciousness, in particular, upon memories about one's former experiences. In this, he argues, man is different from animals, whose identity (that is, "the same dog" or "the same horse") is based on the continuity of the body, just as you would say that you have had "the same car" for ten years even if almost every part except the chassis has been replaced during that time. The identity of a "person," that is, "personal" identity, depends on self-consciousness.

Locke's idea that memory is what constitutes a self-identity is inspired by the distinctly Cartesian notion that a person's relationship to her own thoughts is unique. You cannot think my thoughts and I cannot think yours. Since memory is a species of thought, it follows that you cannot remember my experiences, nor I yours. For example, you may remember your first day of school. Because *you* are remembering that experience as one that happened to *you,* you are self-identical to the person who had the earlier experience. According to Locke, then, memory provides an infallible link between what we might call different "stages" of a person. Memory seems to guarantee the identity of the person who is now remembering with the person who was then having the experience.

While Locke's theory has the advantage over Descartes' of allowing us to understand self-identity in terms of consciousness without requiring that we posit the existence of a persisting immaterial soul, it is not without its own difficulties. First, much of what we experience, we later forget. Do you remember everything that has ever happened to you? Undoubtedly, the answer is no. Even a person who has a very good memory does not remember being born, learning to walk, or what he had for breakfast on June 3, 1982. Probably you have completely forgotten some fairly long stretches of your past. What are we to make of these forgotten periods, with regard to our personal identity? How mistaken can we be in our memories and beliefs about ourselves? At what point of remembering would we want to say that "those memories cannot be our memories at all?"

Second, our memories are not always accurate. Sometimes we remember things that never happened. For example, you might remember very clearly lending your

---

[3] John Locke, *An Essay Concerning Human Understanding,* ed. A. C. Fraser (Oxford: Clarendon Press, 1894).

copy of *Introducing Philosophy* to a friend, only to find later that you had, in fact, been using it as a doorstop. Even more disturbing, though fortunately less frequent, cases of inaccurate memory occur when a person sincerely remembers experiences which, in fact, happened, but didn't happen to him. There are people who now remember delivering the Gettysburg Address, discovering radium, or singing "I wanna hold your hand" with George, John, Paul, and Ringo at Carnegie Hall. What are we to say of the memories of the deluded and the deranged? They are not *genuine* memories, but are only *apparent* memories. Clearly, Locke did not intend merely apparent memories to count among those which guarantee identity. We must, then, find a way to distinguish between those cases in which a memory is genuine and those in which it is not. But to do this, it seems that we would have to say that the memories are in fact the correct memories *of that person*. If this is so, it would appear that the Memory Theory is circular.

A genuine memory, as opposed to a merely apparent one, is, of course, a memory of an experience the rememberer actually had. The person who is having the memory must be the one who had the experience. Now you can see that in distinguishing genuine from apparent memory, we have presupposed the existence of a persisting, self-identical person. That would be all very well were it not for the fact that the concept of self-identity is precisely what we are trying to explain. We cannot use the concept of memory to explain self-identity and then use the concept of self-identity to explain memory. Moreover, once we reflect on the nature of genuine memory, we can see that Locke was, indeed, putting the cart before the horse. When a person says, "I remember when I learned to ride my bike," the truth of his statement presupposes, rather than establishes, that he is self-identical to the little boy with the scabby knees.

Nevertheless, modern theories of personal identity have by and large appealed to some notion of memory, self-consciousness, or psychological continuity. It is worth mentioning that ancient philosophers, Aristotle for example, did not believe this and probably would not even have understood much of what Descartes and Locke were arguing about. For Aristotle, self-identity was essentially bodily identity, without any particular reference to self-consciousness. But neither must it be thought that the modern thesis has been without its critics, in fact, its devastating critics.

Hume completely undercuts Descartes' and Locke's view of self-identity. Relying on his belief that any idea must be derived from an impression, Hume argues that when we are self-conscious we are only aware of fleeting thoughts, feelings, and perceptions; we do not have an impression of the self or a thinking substance. He concludes that the idea of the self is simply a fiction. Moreover, since we are never aware of any enduring self, we are never justified in claiming we are the same person we were a year or a minute ago.

"THERE IS NO *SELF*"
BY DAVID HUME

There are some philosophers, who imagine we are every moment intimately conscious of what we call our SELF, that we feel its existence and its continuance in existence and are certain, beyond the evidence of a demonstration, both of its perfect identity and simplicity. The strongest sensation, the most violent passion, say they, instead of distracting us from this view, only fix it the more intensely, and make us consider their influence on *self* either by their pain or pleasure. To attempt a farther proof of this were to weaken its evidence; since no proof can be deriv'd from any fact, of which we are so intimately conscious; nor is there any thing of which we can be certain, if we doubt of this.

Unluckily all these positive assertions are contrary to that very experience, which is pleaded for them, nor have we any idea of *self,* after the manner it is here explain'd. For from what impression cou'd this idea be deriv'd? This question 'tis impossible to answer without a manifest contradiction, and absurdity; and yet 'tis a question, which must necessarily be answer'd, if we wou'd have the idea of self pass for clear and intelligible. It must be some one impression, that gives rise to every real idea. But self or person is not any one impression, but that to which our several impressions and ideas are suppos'd to have a reference. If any impression gives rise to the idea of self, that impression must continue invariably the same, thro' the whole course of our lives; since self is suppos'd to exist after that manner. But there is no impression constant and invariable. Pain and pleasure, grief and joy, passions and sensations succeed each other, and never all exist at the same time. It cannot, therefore, be from any of these impressions, or from any other, that the idea of self is deriv'd; and consequently there is no such idea.

But farther, what must become of all our particular perceptions upon this hypothesis? All these are different, and distinguishable, and separable from each other and may be separately consider'd, and may exist separately, and have no need of any thing to support their existence. After what manner, therefore, do they belong to self and how are they connected with it? For my part, when I enter most intimately into what I call *myself,* I always stumble on some particular perception or other, of heat or cold, light or shade, love or hatred, pain or pleasure. I never can catch *myself* at any time without a perception, and never can observe any thing but the perception. When my perceptions are remov'd for any time, as by sound sleep; so long am I insensible of myself, and may truly be said not to exist. And were all my perceptions remov'd by death, and cou'd I neither think, nor feel, nor see, nor love, nor hate after the dissolution of my body, I shou'd be entirely annihilated, nor do I conceive what is further requisite to make me a perfect nonentity. If any one upon serious and unprejudiced reflexion, thinks he has a different notion of *himself,* I must confess I can reason no longer with him. All I can allow him is, that he may be in the right as well as I, and that we are essentially different in this particular. He may, perhaps, perceive something simple and continu'd, which he calls *himself;* tho' I am certain there is no such principle in me.

But setting aside some metaphysicians of this kind, I may venture to affirm of the rest of mankind, that they are nothing but a bundle or collection of different perceptions, which succeed each other with an inconceivable rapidity, and are in a perpetual flux and movement. Our eyes cannot turn in their sockets without varying our perceptions. Our thought is still more variable than our sight; and all

. . . I may venture to affirm of the rest of mankind, that they are nothing but a bundle or collection of different perceptions, which succeed each other with an inconceivable rapidity, and are in a perpetual flux and movement.

our other senses and faculties contribute to this change; nor is there any single power of the soul, which remains unalterably the same, perhaps for one moment. The mind is a kind of theatre, where several perceptions successively make their appearance; pass, repass, glide away, and mingle in an infinite variety of postures and situations. There is properly no *simplicity* in it at one time, nor *identity* in different; whatever natural propension we may have to imagine that simplicity and identity. The comparison of the theatre must not mislead us. They are the successive perceptions only, that constitute the mind: nor have we the most distant notion of the place, where these scenes are represented, or of the materials, of which it is compos'd.

What then gives us so great a propension to ascribe an identity to these successive perceptions, and to suppose ourselves possest of any invariable and uninterrupted existence thro' the whole course of our lives?[4]

To answer this question, Hume draws an analogy between the fictitious identity we ascribe to persons and the equally fictitious identity we ascribe to things. Just as we can never find an impression of the self that will explain human identity, so we can never find an impression of an object or substance to explain the identity of plants, animals, and things. According to Hume, then, we are never justified in claiming that, for example, a tree we see now is the same tree we saw five years ago or even five minutes ago. The cells and parts of the tree are continuously being replaced so that at no time is it ever literally the same tree. But Hume's argument goes further than this; even if that were not so, we would still have no way of justifying our belief that this tree is the same one we saw some time ago, rather than another, reasonably similar to it, but yet different. How do we know, for example, that someone has not come along and replaced it with another?

The temptation to ascribe identity to things and persons, Hume thinks, arises in part from the spatiotemporal continuity of the thing; the tree is in the same place at different times. People, however, have the troublesome habit of moving around, going to Europe for the summer or college for the semester; we still see the continuity of his or her movement, receive postcards from the appropriate places at the appropriate times, and so we conclude that it is the same person. In addition to spatiotemporal continuity, we ordinarily rely on resemblance as a criterion of identity. We tolerate small changes, a haircut or a new scar, perhaps even a lost leg or a bit of

---

[4]David Hume, *A Treatise of Human Nature,* ed. L. A. Selby-Bigge (Oxford: Oxford University Press, 1888).

plastic surgery. As long as there is a strong resemblance between two individuals, for example before and after a haircut, we think of them as the same. Only when there is a great change, as from Dr. Jekyll to Mr. Hyde, do we question the identity of the two individuals.

Hume, however, argues that spatiotemporal continuity and resemblance do not in fact guarantee identity:

> The identity, which we ascribe to the mind of man, is only a fictitious one, and of a like kind with that which we ascribe to vegetables and animal bodies. It cannot, therefore, have a different origin, but must proceed from a like operation of the imagination upon his objects.
>
> We have a distinct idea of an object, that remains invariable and uninterrupted thro' a suppos'd variation of time; and this idea we call that of *identity* or *sameness*. We have also a distinct idea of several different objects existing in succession, and connected together by a close relation; and this to an accurate view affords as perfect a notion of *diversity,* as if there was no manner of relation among the objects. But tho' these two ideas of identity, and a succession of related objects be in themselves perfectly distinct, and even contrary, yet 'tis certain, that in our common way of thinking they are generally confounded with each other. That action of the imagination, by which we consider the uninterrupted and invariable object, and that by which we reflect on the succession of related objects, are almost the same to the feeling, nor is there much more effort to thought requir'd in the latter case than in the former. The relation facilitates the transition of the mind from one object to another, and renders its passage as smooth as if it contemplated one continu'd object. This resemblance is the cause of the confusion and mistake, and makes us substitute the notion of identity, instead of that related objects.
>
> Our last resource is to . . . boldly assert that these different related objects are in effect the same, however interrupted and variable. In order to justify to ourselves this absurdity, we often feign some new and unintelligible principle, that connects the objects together, and prevents their interruption or variation. Thus we feign the continu'd existence of the perceptions of our senses, to remove the interruption; and run into the notion of a *soul,* and *self,* and *substance,* to disguise the variation. But we may farther observe, that where we do not give rise to such a fiction, our propension to confound identity with relation is so great, that we are apt to imagine something unknown and mysterious connecting the parts, beside their relation; and this I take to be the case with regard to the identity we ascribe to plants and vegetables. And even when this does not take place, we still feel a propensity to confound these ideas, tho' we are not able fully to satisfy ourselves in that particular, nor find any thing invariable and uninterrupted to justify our notion of identity. . . .
>
> Suppose any mass of matter, of which the parts are contiguous and connected, to be plac'd before us; 'tis plain we must attribute a perfect identity to this mass, provided all the parts continue uninterruptedly and invariably the same, whatever motion or change of place we may observe either in the

whole or in any of the parts. But supposing some very *small* or *inconsiderable* part to be added to the mass, or subtracted from it; tho' this absolutely destroys the identity of the whole, strictly speaking; yet as we seldom think so accurately, we scruple not to pronounce a mass of matter the same, where we find so trivial an alteration. The passage of the thought from the object before the change to the object after it, is so smooth and easy, that we scarce perceive the transition, and are apt to imagine, that 'tis nothing but a continu'd survey, of the same object.[5]

Hume's argument is familiar to us from our discussion of empiricism in Chapter 2. All we perceive, he says, is a sequence of impressions, and nowhere do we encounter an impression either of a substance (an enduring object) or of the self. What right do we have, therefore, to identify the object of this impression with the object of another? What right do we have to identify the person we are now with someone in the past?

But Hume's argument that "I never can catch myself" suffers from a peculiar but obvious form of self-contradiction. He can't even deny that there is a self without in some sense pointing to himself in order to do it. This point was not missed by Kant. Kant agrees with Hume that the enduring self is not to be found in self-consciousness. The enduring self is not an object of experience—Hume was right on this point and both Descartes and Locke were mistaken. In Kant's words, the enduring self is not empirical. It is transcendental.

By "transcendental" Kant means what is a necessary condition for the possibility of *any* experience. Kant saw that if there were a different self at each moment of consciousness, we would not be able to perceive anything. In order to experience an object, we must be able to combine our various impressions of it in a unified consciousness. Thus, if we do in fact experience objects, we must assume that we have a unified consciousness that combines these impressions into the perception of an object. Or, to take a different example, Hume talks of different sorts of relations of impressions, for example, succession. In order for an individual to perceive two impressions as successive, these impressions must have been perceived by the *same* consciousness.

The self of "I" for Kant, then, is the necessary logical subject of any thought, perception, feeling, and so on. It is not an object of experience but transcends and is presupposed by all experience.

Hume's error, as in other matters, was in confusing the supposed experience of self-consciousness with the transcendental rules with which we tie these various experiences together. Accordingly, Kant argues, Descartes and Locke are both correct in equating self-identity and self-consciousness, but it must not be thought that the self is therefore a "thing" (as Descartes said) that we find in experience.

According to Kant, the self is the activity of consciousness, in particular the activity of organizing our various experiences. Kant borrows Hume's argument, but he

---

[5] Hume, *A Treatise of Human Nature.*

turns it toward the opposite conclusion: True, I never find a self "in" my experiences, but I can always find myself in that "I" that has the experience. Kant's "self," in other words, is the act of having experiences rather than anything that we experience itself. But for Kant this self is not merely the passive recipient of experiences, and here is where the notion of self as activity becomes all-important. The self is the activity of applying the rules by which we organize our experience. Moreover, Kant argues that one of the most basic rules of this activity is that the self organize its experience as its own experience. The rule is that we must always "synthesize" our various experiences into a unity, for we could not come to have any knowledge whatever of a scattering of various impressions and sensations without this synthesis. (Think, for example, of the slightly painful and generally meaningless sensations you have when someone sets off a camera flashbulb in your eyes.) This basic rule of synthesis allows Kant to say that not only is the self the activity that applies the various rules to experience but its existence as a unified self with a unified synthesis of experiences is itself a rule.

Kant gives this curious idea of the self as a rule a formidable name, "the transcendental unity of apperception." What is important in this concept is that the self for Kant is indeed essential to self-consciousness, but it is not "in" self-consciousness. Metaphorically, it is often said that it is "behind" self-consciousness, that is, it is the activity of bringing our various experiences together in accordance with the basic rules of our experience. Accordingly, Kant refers to this self as the **transcendental ego**, "transcendental" because, as we discussed in Chapter 4, it is basic and necessary for all possible human experience. The difference between Hume and Kant is sometimes illustrated in this way: Hume looks for the self among our experiences and doesn't find it; Kant agrees with Hume but argues that he looked in the wrong place. The self, Kant says, is the thread that ties together our various experiences. Accordingly, the self is not in the bundle of our experiences; it is rather the "transcendental" thread that holds them all together and is as real as any experience.

Kant returns to Descartes and challenges his main theses, even while agreeing with parts of them. First, while Descartes thought that we had to be self-conscious all the time, Kant insists that it is only necessary for "the 'I think' to be able to accompany all experiences." It is not necessary to be always conscious of our selves but only to be, at any point in our experience, capable of becoming self-conscious; we can turn our attention when we want to from whatever we are doing and watch ourselves doing what we are doing. This is an important point: Our concern with self-consciousness is given impetus just because we are often not self-conscious. In fact, several philosophers (and many mystics) have argued that self-consciousness is bad, a useless thing, and should be avoided as much as possible. According to Descartes, this is not possible, for to exist at all as a human being is to exist self-consciously. According to Kant, on the other hand, to exist as a human being is "to be able" to be self-conscious.

Second, Kant objects to Descartes' belief that the thinking self is a thinking thing. He objects to this, first of all, because of his insistence (as a result of Hume's argument) that the self (or "transcendental ego") is not in our experience but rather "behind" it and responsible for it. More literally, he says that the self must be thought of as an activity. You can see what a radical move this is when you recall the traditional doctrine of the soul in Plato, in Christianity, and in much of modern thought. The soul, quite simply, is the self conceived of as a thing, an enduring thing that can survive the death of the body. By saying that the self is an activity, Kant undermines (as Hume had intended to undermine) the traditional concept of soul.[6]

AGAINST THE SOUL
BY **IMMANUEL KANT**

Pure reason requires us to seek for every predicate of a thing its own subject, and for this subject, which is itself necessarily nothing but a predicate, its subject, and so on indefinitely (or as far as we can reach). But hence it follows that we must not hold anything at which we can arrive to be an ultimate subject.

Now we appear to have this substance in the consciousness of ourselves (in the thinking subject), and indeed in an immediate intuition; for all the predicates of an internal sense refer to the *ego,* as a subject, and I cannot conceive myself as the predicate of any other subject. Hence completeness in the reference of the given concepts as predicates to a subject—not merely an Idea, but an object— that is, the absolute subject itself, seems to be given in experience. But this expectation is disappointed. For the ego is not a concept, but only the indication of the object of the inner sense, so far as we know it by no further predicate. Consequently it cannot indeed be itself a predicate of any other thing; but just as little can it be a definite concept of an absolute subject, but is, as in all other cases, only the reference of the inner phenomena to their unknown subject. Yet this idea (which serves very well as a regulative principle totally to destroy all materialistic explanations of the internal phenomena of the soul) occasions by a very natural misunderstanding a very specious argument, which infers its nature from this supposed knowledge of the substance of our thinking being. This is specious so far as the knowledge of it falls quite without the complex of experience.

But though we may call this thinking self (the soul) "substance," as being the ultimate subject of thinking which cannot be further represented as the predicate of another thing, it remains quite empty and without significance if permanence—the quality which renders the concept of substances in experience fruitful—cannot be proved of it.

But permanence can never be proved of the concept of a substance as a thing in itself, but for the purposes of experience only.

If, therefore, from the concept of the soul as a substance we would infer its permanence, this can hold good as regards possible experience only, not of the

---

[6] It is worth mentioning that Kant held onto the Christian concept of soul; to do so, he defended it as a "postulate of practical reason," in other words, as a strictly moral claim, much as he had defended his belief in God. Later philosophers borrowed Kant's arguments to get rid of the concept of the soul altogether.

Life is the subjective condition of all our possible experience; consequently we can only infer the permanence of the soul in life, for the death of a man is the end of all experience . . .

soul as a thing in itself and beyond all possible experience. Life is the subjective condition of all our possible experience; consequently we can only infer the permanence of the soul in life, for the death of a man is the end of all experience which concerns the soul as an object of experience, except the contrary be proved—which is the very question in hand. The permanence of the soul can therefore only be proved (and no one cares to do that) during the life of man, but not, as we desire to do, after death. The reason for this is that the concept of substance, so far as it is to be considered necessarily with the concept of permanence, can be so combined only according to the principles of possible experience, and therefore for the purposes of experience only.[7]

Third, Kant argued that we need two very different conceptions of self. He saw that this conception of self as self-consciousness was not sufficient to do the whole job that philosophers had wanted it to do. One part of Descartes' enterprise was to find out what was essential to his existence, what could not be doubted and so could serve as a first premise for his *Meditations.* So too Locke and Hume had tried to find (though Locke did and Hume didn't) that self that defined us through our various changes, which identified Jekyll and Hyde and identifies us from year to year, day to day, and mood to mood. But the function of the self was also to serve as a way of identifying ourselves in distinction from other people and other things. Thus Descartes' concept of the self as a thinking thing was not sufficient to tell us what made one person different from another, and he found it necessary to supplement his concept of self with an account of how a person was composed of a self and a body in some special way.

Similarly, Locke distinguishes between personal identity and identity as a man (that is, as a biological example of the species Homo sapiens) and tells us that both are necessary for us to understand how one particular person is different from another particular person. We can now clearly see that the question of self-identity divides into two questions: (1) What is essential to being a self? and (2) What is essential to being a particular self? Kant's conception of self as that which has experiences, the transcendental self, only answers the first question. Nothing in the notion of transcendental self allows us to distinguish between different people and tell them apart.

---

[7] Immanuel Kant, *Prolegomena to Any Future Metaphysics,* trans. Lewis White Beck (New York: Bobbs-Merrill, 1950). Ludwig Wittgenstein, for example, used a Kantian thesis to deny the existence of the subject altogether. In his *Tractatus Logico-Philosophicus,* he tells us: The thinking, presenting subject—there is no such thing. *In an important sense* there is no subject. The subject does not belong to the world, but is a limit of the world. There is [therefore] really a sense in which in philosophy we can talk nonpsychologically of the I. The I occurs in philosophy through the fact that the "world is my world." The philosophical I is not the man, not the human body, or the human soul of which psychology treats, but the metaphysical subject, the limit—not a part of the world.

Accordingly, he identifies another "self" that he calls the **empirical ego,** which includes all of those particular things about us that make us different people. Differences in our bodies, our looks, our size, our strength would be such differences. So too would our different personalities, our different thoughts and memories. It is the empirical self that identifies us as individual persons. The transcendental self makes us human.

These have been the traditional answers to the philosophical problem of self-identity. What is it that makes one "the same person" from moment to moment and year to year? The spatiotemporal **continuity** of the body would seem to be a part of the answer. But philosophers since (and before) Descartes have seen quite clearly that this is never enough, that it is also self-consciousness that provides the key to self-identity. But even this has not solved the problem. To see this, consider these bizarre but illuminating examples:

Jones has an emergency brain operation. His own brain is removed and replaced by the brain of Brown (who is recently deceased). "Jones" still looks like Jones, still carries the same driver's license and lives in the same house, but all of his memories and personality traits are those of Brown. Is he still Jones? Or is he Brown in Jones's body? Suppose you had been (or are) Brown, could you claim to be still alive in Jones's body?

Or, suppose Smith undergoes a personality split of the most radical kind imaginable. Like the one-celled animal, the amoeba, Smith splits, head to toe, each half of him forming an exact duplicate of the original—same memories and personality, same habits, knowledge, likes and dislikes, skills, and so on. Which of the two is Smith? Does it make any sense to say that both are? Suppose that you are one of the two resultant Smiths. Would you—could you—intelligibly say that the other Smith is also you? But, given your common origins and exact similarities, could you say that the other Smith was merely someone else?

In the movie *All of Me,* the soul of a woman who has recently died (played by Lily Tomlin) winds up occupying the body of a male lawyer (played by Steve Martin). The resulting character, played by Martin, still looks, acts, and thinks like the Steve Martin character, but now also possesses the memories and personality traits of Lily Tomlin's original character. Who is this dual character?

To consider the bizarre complications, here is Massachusetts philosopher **Meredith Michaels,** who has written extensively on the problem of personal identity:

"PERSONAL IDENTITY"
BY **MEREDITH MICHAELS**

While they are illuminating, particularly in relation to one another, these traditional answers to the philosophical problem of self-identity raise as many questions as they answer. To see this, let us travel to a not very distant make-believe world.

One night, after a serious bout with the library, you and your best friend Wanda Bagg (or Walter, if you prefer) decide to indulge yourselves at the College Haven. Before you can stop her, Wanda steps out in front of a steamroller that happens to be moving down Main Street. Wanda is crushed. Witnessing the horror of the accident, you have a stroke. Fortunately, Dr. Hagendaas, the famous neurosurgeon who has been visiting the campus, is also on the way to the College Haven. Taking charge, he rushes you and Wanda to the Health Center, where he performs a "body transplant." He takes Wanda's brain, which miraculously escaped the impact of the steamroller, and puts it in the place of yours, which was, of course, severely damaged by the stroke. After several days, the following battle ensues: Wanda's parents claim that they are under no obligation to continue paying tuition. After all, Wanda was killed by a steamroller. Your parents claim that they are under no obligation to continue paying tuition. After all, you died of a stroke. It is clear, then, that a basic question is in need of an answer: who is the person lying in bed in the Health Center? Is it Wanda? Is it you? Is it someone else altogether? For the sake of discussion, let us call the person lying in the bed Schwanda. What reasons do we have for believing that Schwanda is Wanda? Given that one's self-consciousness, one's thoughts, beliefs and feelings are all mental phenomena, we might naturally conclude that a person goes wherever her brain goes (on the assumption that our mental characteristics are more likely "located" in the brain than in, say, our smallest left toe). Schwanda will remember having set off for the College Haven with you; she will remember receiving the college acceptance letter addressed: "Dear Wanda, We are happy to inform you that . . ."; she'll remember being hugged by Wanda's mother on the afternoon of her first day of school. That is, Schwanda will *believe* that she's Wanda.

Nevertheless, the fact that Schwanda believes herself to be Wanda does not in itself guarantee that she is. Do we have any basis for insisting that Schwanda is Wanda and not someone who is *deluded* into thinking that she's Wanda? How can we determine whether Schwanda's Wanda memories are genuine and not merely apparent? As we came to realize in our discussion of Locke's Memory Theory, it is not legitimate at this point to appeal to the self-identity of Schwanda and Wanda, since that is precisely what we're trying to determine. In other words, in attempting to establish that Schwanda's Wanda memories are genuine memories, we cannot argue that they are genuine on the grounds that Schwanda *is* Wanda.

Perhaps it is possible to stop short of circularity. Why couldn't we say that Schwanda's Wanda memories are genuine because the *brain* that is remembering is the same as the brain that had the original experiences. Thus, the experiences are preserved in the very organ that underwent them. Though there is an initial plausibility to this response, it fails to solve our problem. Suppose that Schwanda is Wanda—remembering the experience of learning to ride a bicycle. Though the brain in question is indeed the same, it is nonetheless clear to all of us that brains alone do not learn to ride bicycles. Nor, indeed, do brains alone remember having done so. *People* learn to ride bicycles and *people* remember having done so. And the question we are trying to answer is whether Schwanda (who is remembering) is the same person as Wanda (who did the bicycling). The appeal to the fact that the same brain is involved in each event does not provide us with a way out of the Lockean circle.

It is at this point that philosophers begin to reconsider the Aristotelian position, mentioned earlier, that self-identity is essentially *bodily* identity. If the Body Theory of Personal Identity is true, then the person lying in bed at the Health Center is you, deluded into believing that you are Wanda. That is, Schwanda is self-identical to you.

You might wonder, at this point, whether there are any positive reasons for endorsing the Body Theory, or whether it is simply a place to which one retreats only in defeat? The following case is designed to persuade you that there is at least *some* plausibility to the Body Theory. Suppose that an evil scientist, Dr. Nefarious, has selected you as his prime subject for a horrible experiment. You are dragged into his office. He says, "Tomorrow at 5:00, you will be subjected to the most terrible tortures. Your nails will be pulled out one by one. Rats will be caged around your head. Burning oil will drip slowly on your back. The remainder I leave as a surprise."

Are you worried about what will happen to you at 5:00 tomorrow? If you have any sense, you are. You think of the excruciating pain and suffering you will undergo and would surely do just about anything to avoid it.

But now, Dr. Nefarious says, "Tomorrow at 4:55, I will use my Dememorizer to erase your memory of this conversation." Are you still anxious about what is going to happen to you tomorrow at 5:00? Surely you are. After all the fact that you won't, between 4:55 and 5:00, be anticipating your torture doesn't entail that the torture itself will be any less painful. When you forget that your Calculus professor told the class there would be a test on Friday, you aren't thereby spared the experience of taking the test (in fact, in that case the experience is made worse by your not having had the opportunity to anticipate it).

Now, Dr. Nefarious says, "Tomorrow at 4:57, I will use my Dememorizer to erase *all* of your memories." Are you still anxious about what will happen tomorrow at 5:00? Isn't it natural to describe the situation as one in which you will undergo horrible torture, though you won't know who you are or why this is happening to you? *You* will still experience *your* fingernails being pulled out, *your* back being burned, *your* face being eaten up by rats. Surely, those experiences are ones you would like to avoid.

Finally, Dr. Nefarious says to you, "Tomorrow at 4:58, I am going to use my Rememorizer to implant in your brain all of Ronald Reagan's memories." Though this may not please you for personal or political reasons, the relevant question remains this: are you still worried about what is going to happen tomorrow at 5:00? Isn't it again perfectly natural to describe the situation as one in which you will undergo horrible torture, all the while believing that you are Ronald Reagan. Do you not *now* remain concerned that you are Ronald Reagan. Do you not *now* remain concerned that you will experience excruciating pain and intolerable suffering? Look at your fingernails while you consider your answer to this question.

What this story demonstrates is not the conclusive superiority of the Body Theory over the Memory (or Brain) Theory, but rather the importance of our bodies to our self-identity. This is something that tends to get lost in the traditional conceptions of personal identity. Furthermore, returning to the case of

Schwanda, we can now see that it is not altogether preposterous to argue that Schwanda is indeed you, deluded into believing that she is Wanda. In other words, anyone who wishes to dismiss the possibility must also dismiss the possibility that the person who undergoes the torture is indeed you, deluded into believing that you are Ronald Reagan.

. . . we lack a concept of self-identity that allows us to predict when we would or wouldn't persist through time.

While it is true that we tend to identify ourselves with and by our thoughts, beliefs, inclinations and feelings, our discussion of the Body Theory should remind us that there are reasons for believing that our bodies are, at the very least, important to who we are. Some philosophers would argue that our bodies *are* who we are, that self-identity *is* bodily identity.

In considering these admittedly fanciful problem cases, we have seen that we lack a concept of self-identity that allows us to predict when we would or wouldn't persist through time. This might suggest to us that our concept of self-identity is not an all-or-nothing one, that, in fact, our concept is one which admits of degrees. If so, we are no longer talking about identity *per se,* which is an all-or-nothing concept, but rather about some other relation of psychological and physical connectedness. Nevertheless, we can now see first, that the answer to the question "Who ought to pay Schwanda's tuition?" will depend upon which theory of personal identity we are inclined to endorse and second, that the answer may not be as clear and unequivocal as we would like it to be.[8]

B. EXISTENTIALISM: SELF-IDENTITY AND THE RESPONSIBILITY OF CHOICE

The idea of a multiple, or nonself introduced a very important alternative to Western, essentially Judeo-Christian conceptions. In addition to the concern for survival in Heaven or Hell, this Western conception is typically concerned with striving and ambition, status and planning for the future, "making something of yourself." Existentialism is one form of this conception. The American dream and the Protestant and capitalist ethics in general are another. But from the conception of nonself comes a very different picture—of unqualified acceptance of things as they are rather than struggling to change them, which involves a rejection of such notions as "status" and "making something of yourself."

Once again we must not confuse this rejection of traditional Western conceptions of the self with a rejection of the philosophical question of self-identity. "Who am I?" is as important a question for the mystic as it is for the Western philosopher. It is

---

[8] This essay was written by Meredith Michaels for the third edition of *Introducing Philosophy.*

just that the mystic's answer to the question is radically different. Does it make sense to say that the one is more "correct" than the other? This too is part of the question of self-identity. Must there be a single "correct" answer for everyone? There is nothing necessary about this, or even desirable. The problem of self-identity, both in each individual case and as a general problem, is the problem of deciding which of the many possible characteristics (not necessarily one) should be chosen as our own standards for self-identity, and that choice is not just one that philosophers make, but one which each person makes at some point or points during his or her life.

A self-identity isn't simply a label you throw on yourself in the casual discussion of a philosophy class. It is a mask and a role that you wear in every social encounter (though perhaps slightly different masks and roles for significantly different encounters). It is the way you think of yourself and the standards by which you judge yourself in every moment of reflection and self-evaluation. It is the self-image you follow in every action, when you decide that one thing is "worth doing" more than another or when you decide how to act in a given circumstance. Because of it, you feel proud, guilty, ashamed, or delighted after you have done something. The problem of self-identity is not just a problem for philosophers; it is a problem we all face, either explicitly or implicitly, every self-conscious minute of our lives.

But, you might say, why make it sound as if there is any single notion or goal of a correct self-identity? The way in which a contemporary Chinese farmer thinks of himself and judges himself is very different from that of a contemporary American college student. And a very handsome but stupendously dumb bully will surely have a very different conception of self-identity than an extremely intelligent and talented college mathematics major. This may not stop the medieval scholastic, who will immediately declare all of that irrelevant and insist that "before God" all of us are the same and our identities are to be judged accordingly. And most of us, despite the glib relativism we usually defend, would insist on a category that transcends all such individual considerations; we call it "being a good person." Ultimately we would judge the dumb bully and the budding young artist according to the same criterion, and, in doing so, we would think that they should share the criterion "being a good person." Even where cultural differences would seem to demand entirely different conceptions of self-identity, we might still insist on applying the same criterion. For example, a South Sea Islander might well think of himself or herself in terms that would be wholly unacceptable to us, but we can always reduce any variance from our norms to mere "accidental differences," insisting that we are essentially the same. Of course people are different and think differently of themselves; but it does not follow that those differences are essential, nor does it follow that relativism is true. Ultimately when you say that all people are "essentially the same," then you believe that there are, indeed, universal criteria for self-identity and that the differences between people, though we need not deny them, are merely superficial.

One of the most powerful schools of contemporary thought, however, has been dedicated to the idea that self-identity, in every case, is a matter of individual choice. This school, which we have briefly met before, is existentialism. Its most powerful advocate is the French philosopher **Jean-Paul Sartre**. According to Sartre, there are no set standards for self-identity, either for individuals or for people in general. There is, he argues, no such thing as "human nature," and what we are—and what it means to be a human being—are always matters of decision. There is no correct choice; there are only choices, he claims. In a well-known essay from the late 1940s, he argues:

ON EXISTENTIALISM
BY JEAN-PAUL SARTRE

What existentialists have in common is simply the fact that they believe that *existence* comes before *essence*—or, if you will, that we must begin from the subjective. What exactly do we mean by that?

If one considers an article of manufacture—as, for example, a book or paper-knife—one sees that it has been made by an artisan who had a conception of it; and he has paid attention, equally, to the conception of a paper-knife and to the pre-existent technique of production which is a part of that conception and is, at bottom, a formula. Thus the paper-knife is at the same time an article producible in a certain manner and one which, on the other hand, serves a definite purpose, for one cannot suppose that a man would produce a paper-knife without knowing what it was for. Let us say, then, of the paper-knife that its essence—that is to say the sum of the formulae and the qualities which made its production and its definition possible—precedes its existence. The presence of such-and-such a paper-knife or book is thus determined before my eyes. Here, then, we are viewing the world from a technical standpoint, and we say that production precedes existence.

When we think of God as the creator, we are thinking of him, most of the time, as a supernal artisan. Whatever doctrine we may be considering, whether it be a doctrine like that of Descartes, or of Leibniz himself, we always imply that the will follows, more or less, from the understanding or at least accompanies it, so that when God creates he knows precisely what he is creating. Thus, the conception of man in the mind of God is comparable to that of the paper-knife in the mind of the artisan: God makes man according to a procedure and a conception, exactly as the artisan manufactures a paper-knife, following a definition and a formula. Thus each individual man is the realisation of a certain conception which dwells in the divine understanding. In the philosophic atheism of the eighteenth century, the notion of God is suppressed, but not, for all that, the idea that essence is prior to existence; something of that idea we still find everywhere, in Diderot, in Voltaire and even in Kant. Man possesses a human nature; that "human nature," which is the conception of human being, is found in every man; which means that each man is a particular example of an universal conception, the conception of Man. In Kant, this universality goes so far that the wild man of the woods, man in the state of nature and the bourgeois are all contained in the same definition and have the same fundamental qualities. Here again, the essence of man precedes that historic existence which we confront in experience.

◆◆◆

What do we mean by saying that existence precedes essence? We mean that man first of all exists, encounters himself, surges up in the world—and defines himself afterwards. If man as the existentialist sees him is not definable, it is because to begin with he is nothing. He will not be anything until later, and then he will be what he makes of himself. Thus, there is no human nature, because there is no God to have a conception of it. Man simply is. Not that he is simply what he conceives himself to be, but he is what he wills, and as he conceives himself after already existing—as he wills to be after that leap towards existence. Man is nothing else but that which he makes of himself. That is the first principle of existentialism. And this is what people call its "subjectivity," using the word as a reproach against us. But what do we mean to say by this, but that man is of a greater dignity than a stone or a table? For we mean to say that man primarily exists—that man is, before all else, something which propels itself towards a future and is aware that it is doing so. Man is, indeed, a project which possesses a subjective life, instead of being a kind of moss, or a fungus or a cauliflower. Before that projection of the self nothing exists; not even in the heaven of intelligence: man will only attain existence when he is what he purposes to be. Not, however, what he may wish to be. For what we usually understand by wishing or willing is a conscious decision taken—much more often than not—after we have made ourselves what we are. I may wish to join a party, to write a book or to marry—but in such a case what is usually called my will is probably a manifestation of a prior and more spontaneous decision. If, however, it is true that existence is prior to essence, man is responsible for what he is. Thus, the first effect of existentialism is that it puts every man in possession of himself as he is, and places the entire responsibility for his existence squarely upon his own shoulders. And, when we say that man is responsible for himself, we do not mean that he is responsible only for his own individuality, but that he is responsible for all men.

> *. . . when we say that man is responsible for himself, we do not mean that he is responsible only for his own individuality, but that he is responsible for all men.*

When we say that man chooses himself, we do mean that every one of us must choose himself; but by that we also mean that in choosing for himself he chooses for all men. For in effect, of all the actions a man may take in order to create himself as he wills to be, there is not one which is not creative, at the same time, of an image of man such as he believes he ought to be.[9]

But this existentialist doctrine of choice doesn't make the problem of self-identity any easier. In fact, it complicates it enormously. Earlier in this section, we began by

---

[9] Jean-Paul Sartre, *Existentialism as a Humanism,* trans. Phillip Mairet (New York: Philosophical Library, 1949).

asking whether the facts about a person are sufficient to determine his or her identity. We said surely not all of them are necessary; some are more essential than others. But this isn't yet an answer to the question, for it may be that all the essential facts are still not sufficient to determine a person's identity.

According to the existentialist, this is made even more complex by the fact that a person chooses which facts are to be considered as essential. Are the facts alone ever sufficient to determine our identity? Sartre's answer, which he adapted from German existentialist Martin Heidegger, is "never!" The facts that are true of a person are always, at least so long as a person is alive, only indicative of what a person has been and done so far. In judging a person's identity, we must always consider more than the facts that are true of him or her (which Sartre and Heidegger collectively name, somewhat technically, a person's **facticity**); we must also consider their projections into the future, their ambitions, plans, intentions, hopes, and fantasies. (Sartre calls these considerations a person's **transcendence.** Notice that this is the third different way in which "transcendence" has been used, so be careful.) This way of viewing the person makes the question of self-identity impossibly complex, in fact, irresolvable. For example, consider Sartre's example of what he calls "bad faith" in one of his most important works, *Being and Nothingness* (1943).

Bad faith, quite simply, is refusing to accept yourself.[10] This can happen in two different ways. Either you can refuse to accept the facts and actions as relevant to your self-identity (for example, denying that your repeated cowardly behavior establishes your identity as a coward). Or you can go too far in the opposite direction, believing that your actions conclusively and unalterably establish your self-identity (for example, denying that you could ever alter your cowardly self-identity through an act of heroism).

ON BAD FAITH
BY SARTRE

Let us take an example: A homosexual frequently has an intolerable feeling of guilt, and his whole existence is determined in relation to this feeling. One will readily foresee that he is in bad faith. In fact it frequently happens that this man, while recognizing his homosexual inclination, while avowing each and every particular misdeed which he has committed, refuses with all his strength to consider himself "*a homosexual.*" His case is always "different," peculiar; there enters into it something of a game, of chance, of bad luck; the mistakes are all in the past; they are explained by a certain conception of the beautiful which women cannot satisfy; we should see in them the results of a restless search, rather than the manifestations of a deeply rooted tendency, *etc., etc.* Here is assuredly a man in bad faith who borders on the comic since, acknowledging all

---

[10] This is, however, the main concept of *Being and Nothingness* and takes well over seven hundred pages to analyze correctly.

the facts which are imputed to him, he refuses to draw from them the conclusion which they impose. His friend, who is his most severe critic, becomes irritated with this duplicity. The critic asks only one thing—and perhaps then he will show himself indulgent: that the guilty one recognize himself as guilty, that the homosexual declare frankly—whether humbly or boastfully matters little— "I am a homosexual." We ask here: Who is in bad faith? The homosexual or the champion of sincerity?

The homosexual recognizes his faults, but he struggles with all his strength against the crushing view that his mistakes constitute for him a *destiny*. He does not wish to let himself be considered as a thing. He has an obscure but strong feeling that a homosexual is not a homosexual as this table is a table or as this red-haired man is red-haired. It seems to him that he has escaped from each mistake as soon as he has posited it and recognized it; he even feels that the psychic duration by itself cleanses him from each misdeed, constitutes for him an undetermined future, causes him to be born anew. Is he wrong? Does he not recognize in himself the peculiar, irreducible character of human reality? His attitude includes then an undeniable comprehension of truth. But at the same time he needs this perpetual rebirth, this constant escape in order to live; he must constantly put himself beyond reach in order to avoid the terrible judgment of collectivity. Thus he plays on the word *being*. He would be right actually if he understood the phrase, "I am not a homosexual" in the sense of "I am not what I am." That is, if he declared to himself, "To the extent that a pattern of conduct is defined as the conduct of a paederast and to the extent that I have adopted this conduct, I am a homosexual. But to the extent that human reality cannot be finally defined by patterns of conduct, I am not one." But instead he slides surreptitiously toward a different connotation of the word "being." He understands "not being" in the sense of "not-being-in-itself." He lays claim to "not being a homosexual" in the sense in which this table *is not* an inkwell. He is in bad faith.[11]

Sartre then lays bare the heart of his theory. Bad faith points to the most important single fact about personal self-identity—there isn't any. In somewhat paradoxical terminology, Sartre tells us, "one is what one is not, and one is not what one is." In other words, whatever the facts about you, you are always something more than those facts. The homosexual in Sartre's example *is* a homosexual to the extent that all his past actions and desires are those of a homosexual. He falls into bad faith by refusing to see that his past actions point to his having a self-identity as a homosexual. Yet at the same time, there is a genuine sense in which he is *not* a homosexual: In the future, he may radically alter his lifestyle. It would, then, also be bad faith were he to totally accept his self-identity as a homosexual, denying that he could be anything else. As long as a person is alive, he or she is identified by intentions, plans,

---

[11] Jean-Paul Sartre, *Being and Nothingness,* trans. Hazel E. Barnes (New York: Philosophical Library, 1956).

dreams, and hopes as much as by what is already true by virtue of the facts. Given this complexity, the problem of deciding "who I am" takes on dramatic and extravagant complications. Consider the following scene from Sartre's famous play, *No Exit*, in which one of the characters (now dead and "living" in hell) tries to justify his image of himself as a hero, despite the facts of his life, which would indicate that he was a coward.

FROM *NO EXIT*
BY **SARTRE**

GARCIN: They shot me.

ESTELLE: I know. Because you refused to fight. Well, why shouldn't you?

GARCIN: I—I didn't exactly refuse. [*In a far-away voice*] I must say he talks well, he makes out a good case against me, but he never says what I should have done instead. Should I have gone to the general and said: "General I decline to fight"? A mug's game; they'd have promptly locked me up. But I wanted to show my colors, my true colors, do you understand? I wasn't going to be silenced. [*To* ESTELLE] So I—I took the train. . . . They caught me at the frontier.

ESTELLE: Where were you trying to go?

GARCIN: To Mexico. I meant to launch a pacifist newspaper down there. [*A short silence.*] Well, why don't you speak?

ESTELLE: What could I say? You acted quite rightly, as you didn't want to fight. [GARCIN *makes a fretful gesture.*] But, darling, how on earth can I guess what you want me to answer?

INEZ: Can't you guess? Well, *I* can. He wants you to tell him that he bolted like a lion. For "bolt" he did, and that's what's biting him.

GARCIN: "Bolted," "went away"—we won't quarrel over words.

ESTELLE: But you *had* to run away. If you'd stayed they'd have sent you to jail, wouldn't they?

GARCIN: Of course. [*A pause.*] Well, Estelle, am I a coward?

ESTELLE: How can I say? Don't be so unreasonable, darling. I can't put myself in your skin. You must decide that for yourself.

GARCIN: [*wearily*]: I can't decide.

ESTELLE: Anyhow, you must remember. You must have had reasons for acting as you did.

GARCIN: I had.

ESTELLE: Well?

GARCIN: But were they the real reasons?

ESTELLE: You've a twisted mind, that's your trouble. Plaguing yourself over such trifles!

GARCIN: I'd thought it all out, and I wanted to make a stand. But was that my real motive?

INEZ: Exactly. That's the question. Was that your real motive? No doubt you argued it out with yourself, you weighed the pros and cons, you found good reasons for what you did. But fear and hatred and all the dirty little instincts one keeps dark—they're motives too. So carry on, Mr. Garcin, and try to be honest with yourself—for once.

GARCIN: Do I need you to tell me that? Day and night I paced my cell, from the window to the door, from the door to the window. I pried into my heart, I sleuthed myself like a detective. By the end of it I felt as if I'd given my whole life to introspection. But always I harked back to the one thing certain—that I had acted as I did, I'd taken that train to the frontier. But why? Why? Finally I thought: My death will settle it. If I face death courageously, I'll prove I am no coward.

INEZ: And how did you face death?

GARCIN: Miserably. Rottenly. [INEZ *laughs.*] Oh, it was only a physical lapse—that might happen to anyone; I'm not ashamed of it. Only everything's been left in suspense, forever. [*To* ESTELLE] Come here, Estelle. Look at me. I want to feel someone looking at me while they're talking about me on earth. . . . I like green eyes.

INEZ: Green eyes! Just hark to him! And you, Estelle, do you like cowards?

ESTELLE: If you knew how little I care! Coward or hero, it's all one—provided he kisses well.

GARCIN: There they are, slumped in their chairs, sucking at their cigars. Bored they look. Half-asleep. They're thinking: "Garcin's a coward." But only vaguely, dreamily. One's got to think of something. "That chap Garcin was a coward." That's what they've decided, those dear friends of mine. In six months' time they'll be saying: "Cowardly as that skunk Garcin." You're lucky, you two; no one on earth is giving you another thought. But I—I'm long in dying.

GARCIN: [*putting his hands on* (INEZ*'s*) *shoulders*]: Listen! Each man has an aim in life, a leading motive; that's so, isn't it? Well, I didn't give a damn for wealth, or for love. I aimed at being a real man. A tough, as they say. I staked everything on the same horse. . . . Can one possibly be a coward when one's deliberately courted danger at every turn? And can one judge a life by a single action?

INEZ: Why not? For thirty years you dreamt you were a hero, and condoned a thousand petty lapses—because a hero, of course, can do no wrong. An easy method obviously. Then a day came when you were up against it, the red light of real danger—and you took the train to Mexico.

It's what one does, and nothing else, that shows the stuff one's made of.

GARCIN: I "dreamt," you say. It was no dream. When I chose that hardest path, I made my choice deliberately. A man is what he wills himself to be.

INEZ: Prove it. Prove it was no dream. It's what one does, and nothing else, that shows the stuff one's made of.

GARCIN: I died too soon. I wasn't allowed time to—to do my deeds.

INEZ: One always dies too soon—or too late. And yet one's whole life is complete at that moment, with a line drawn neatly under it, ready for the summing up. You are—your life, and nothing else.[12]

C. THE INDIVIDUAL AND THE COMMUNITY

So far, both our defenses and criticisms of the Cartesian model have focused on the individual. We have considered the individual and individual consciousness, asking whether or not it conforms to the Cartesian picture of the self. There is a wholly different alternative, however, which we haven't discussed yet (although Sartre's *No Exit* does touch upon it).

Even within discussions of the individual self, it becomes evident that the individual self is largely, if not entirely, a social product and a self defined by society. We have all had the experience of finding ourselves in company in which we "could not be ourselves" or, even worse, in which we acted according to an identity that was wholly imposed upon us by other people. When going to school, for example, we played the role of "student," ingratiating and oppressed, long before we started to recognize that it is a role, and not a very pleasant one at that. Now we see it as a role that has been formulated solely for the advantage of other people—teachers, administrators, parents—so that we could be forced to "behave." Have you started to wonder how many other aspects of your identity have been similarly imposed upon you, not chosen at all, much less created by you? How much of your behavior has been "programmed" or "conditioned" by parents, society, television, movies, friends, and schoolmates? The suspicion deepens, and soon you start to see a split developing in your thinking about yourself: First, there is your conception of your own identity; second, there is the identity that has been imposed upon you. The two drift apart like boat and dock, and you find yourself falling between.

No wonder, then, that one of the leading psychiatrists of our times, **R. D. Laing,** has looked at this problem not only as the basis of much of our everyday unhappiness but as the cause of some of our most serious psychological breakdowns as well. Laing describes what he calls "ontological insecurity" as just this split between your awareness of yourself by yourself and the awareness that is imposed upon yourself as an object of other people's attention. Guilt is an example of this split; in excess (as Freud often argued) such emotions tend to be pathological. One definition of guilt is that it is a kind of self-consciousness that is caught between the need for approval and recognition by others and the feeling that you must be "yourself." Thus we tend to get the idea of a "true self" that lies concealed behind the masks that we present in

---

[12] Jean-Paul Sartre, *No Exit and Other Plays,* trans. Stuart Gilbert (Hamish Hamilton, Ltd., 1961).

public, even to our closest friends. We get the sense that our real selves are known only to ourselves, but at the same time we do not really exist except with other people.

But this is an extremely negative view of a tension that is in fact central to our whole Western notion of self, the tension between individuality and social self-identity. In most societies, Plato and Aristotle's Greece, for example, a person would always see his or her own identity in terms of the society of which one was a member. The idea of a self that was antagonistic to society would have been completely foreign to them (Consider, for instance, Socrates' speech in the *Crito,* in our Introduction, in which he says, in effect, that he cannot serve his own interests against the state without betraying himself.) Yet our own idea of self-identity has become so individualistic that the very idea that self-identity is really social-identity flies in the face of that whole Cartesian tradition—and much of Western thinking—that begins with the autonomy of the self and self-consciousness. Nietzsche, for example, goes so far as to suggest that self-consciousness is simply superfluous.

ON THE DISPENSABILITY OF CONSCIOUSNESS
BY **FRIEDRICH NIETZSCHE**

The *"Genius of the Species."*—The problem of consciousness (or more correctly: of becoming conscious of oneself) meets us only when we begin to perceive in what measure we could dispense with it: and it is at the beginning of this perception that we are now placed by physiology and zoology (which have thus required two centuries to overtake the hint thrown out in advance by Leibniz). For we could in fact think, feel, will and recollect, we could likewise "act" in every sense of the term, and nevertheless nothing of it all need necessarily "come into consciousness" (as one says metaphorically). The whole of life would be possible without its seeing itself as it were in a mirror: as in fact even at present the far greater part of our life still goes on without this mirroring— and even our thinking, feeling, volitional life as well, however painful this statement may sound to an older philosopher. *What* then is the *purpose* of consciousness generally, when it is in the main *superfluous? . . . Consciousness generally has only been developed under the pressure of the necessity for communication,*—that from the first it has been necessary and useful only between man and man (especially between those commanding and those obeying), and has only developed in proportion to its utility. Consciousness is properly only a connecting network between man and man,—it is only as such that it has had to develop; the recluse and wild-beast species of men would not have needed it. The very fact that our actions, thoughts, feelings and motions come within the range of our consciousness—at least a part of them—is the result of a terrible, prolonged "must" ruling man's destiny: as the most endangered animal he *needed* help and protection; he needed his fellows, he was obliged to express his distress, he had to know how to make himself understood—and for all this he needed "consciousness" first of all: he had to "know" himself what he lacked, to "know" how he felt, and to "know" what he thought. For, to repeat it once more, man, like every living creature, thinks unceasingly, but does not know it; the thinking which is becoming *conscious of itself* is only the smallest part thereof, we may say, the most superficial part, the worst part. . . . As is obvious, my idea is that consciousness does not properly belong to the individual existence of man, but rather to the social and gregarious nature in him; that, as follows therefrom, it is only in relation to communal and gregarious utility that it is finely developed; and that consequently each of us, in spite of the best intention of *understanding* himself as individually as possible, and of "knowing himself," will always just call into consciousness the non-individual in him, namely, his "averageness";—that our thought itself is continuously as it were *outvoted* by the character of consciousness—by the imperious "genius of the species" therein—and is translated back into the perspective of the herd. Fundamentally our actions are in comparable manner altogether personal, unique, and absolutely individual—there is no doubt about it; but as soon as we translate them into consciousness, they *do not appear so any longer.* . . . This is the proper phenomenalism and perspectivism as I understand it: the nature of *animal consciousness* involves the notion that the world of which we can become conscious is only a superficial and symbolic world, a generalised and vulgarised world;— that everything which becomes conscious *becomes* just thereby shallow, meagre, relatively stupid,—a generalisation, a symbol, a characteristic of the herd; that with the evolving of consciousness there is always combined a great, radical perversion, falsification, superficialisation and generalisation.[13]

> *. . . man, like every living creature, thinks unceasingly, but does not know it; the thinking which is becoming* **conscious of itself** *is only the smallest part thereof, we may say, the most superficial part, the worst part.*

Our response to this split between what some philosophers call the "self for itself" and the "self for others" has been varied. For some, particularly those who have been called existentialists, such as Sartre, whom we read about earlier, the response has been wholesale rebellion, the demand that we break away from "the masses" and our given social identities and create our selves. Nietzsche, for example, attacks what he calls "the herd" in the above passage and urges us to develop ourselves as unique individuals. Indeed, this is the main point of Nietzsche's entire philosophy and underlies his attack on religion and morality.

---

[13] Friedrich Nietzsche, *The Joyful Wisdom,* trans. Thomas Common, in *The Complete Works of Friedrich Nietzsche,* Oscar Levy, gen. ed. (1909–11) (New York: Russell & Russell, 1964).

A similar attempt at individual rebellion was launched even earlier by Kierkegaard, the Christian philosopher who has often been claimed as the father of existentialism. Like Nietzsche, he deplores what he sarcastically called "the public" and urges an end to collective identity and social roles in favor of renewed respect for the individual.

ON "THE PUBLIC"
BY SØREN KIERKEGAARD

In spite of all his exertion the subjective thinker enjoys only a meager reward. The more the collective idea comes to dominate even the ordinary consciousness, the more forbidding seems the transition to becoming a particular existing human being instead of losing oneself in the race, and saying "we," "our age," "the nineteenth century." That it is a little thing merely to be a particular existing human being is not to be denied; but for this very reason it requires considerable resignation not to make light of it. For what does a mere individual count for? Our age knows only too well how little it is, but here also lies the specific immorality of the age. Each age has its own characteristic depravity. Ours is perhaps not pleasure of indulgence or sensuality, but rather a dissolute pantheistic contempt for the individual man. In the midst of all our exultation over the achievements of the age and the nineteenth century, there sounds a note of poorly conceived contempt for the individual man; in the midst of the self-importance of the contemporary generation there is revealed a sense of despair over being human. Everything must attach itself so as to be a part of some movement; men are determined to lose themselves in the totality of things, in world-history, fascinated and deceived by a magic witchery; no one wants to be an individual human being.

In fact, so adamant is Kierkegaard on this issue that he argues that a person who "follows the crowd" and does not choose his or her own identity and live passionately as an individual cannot even be said to really exist.

ON SELF AND PASSION
BY KIERKEGAARD

It is impossible to exist without passion, unless we understand the word "exist" in the loose sense of a so-called existence. Every Greek thinker was therefore essentially a passionate thinker. I have often reflected how one might bring a man into a state of passion. I have thought in this connection that if I could get him seated on a horse and the horse made to take fright and gallop wildly, or better still, for the sake of bringing the passion out, if I could take a man who wanted to arrive at a certain place as quickly as possible, and hence already had some passion, and could set him astride a horse that can scarcely walk—and yet this is what existence is like if one is to become consciously aware of it. Or if a driver were otherwise not especially inclined toward passion, if someone hitched a team of horses to a wagon for him, one of them a Pegasus and the other a worn-out jade, and told him to drive—I think one might succeed. And it is just this that it means to exist, if one is to become conscious of it. Eternity is the winged horse, infinitely fast, and time is a worn-out jade; the existing individual is the driver. That is to say, he is such a driver when his mode of existence is not an existence loosely so called; for then he is no driver, but a drunken peasant who lies asleep in the wagon and lets the horse take care of themselves. To be sure, he also drives and is a driver; and so there are perhaps many who—also exist.[14]

And in this century, borrowing from both Kierkegaard and Nietzsche, the German existentialist Martin Heidegger has argued against collective social identity in terms of what he (also ironically) calls *das Man,* an extremely useful German expression that roughly translates as "they" in "*they* say that garlic cures colds." Who are "they"? No one at all, Heidegger says, just an anonymous no one. In dense philosophical prose, he presents the following argument: [15]

"DASEIN" AND THE "THEY"
BY **MARTIN HEIDEGGER**

Dasein, as everyday Being-with-one-another, stands in *subjection* to Others. It itself *is* not; its Being has been taken away by the Others. Dasein's everyday possibilities of Being are for the Others to dispose of as they please. These Others, moreover, are not *definite* Others. On the contrary, any Other can represent them. What is decisive is just that inconspicuous domination by Others which has already been taken over unawares from Dasein as Being-with. One belongs to the Others oneself and enhances their power. "The Others" whom one thus designates in order to cover up the fact of one's belonging to them essentially oneself, are those who proximally and for the most part "*are there*" in everyday Being-with-one-another. The "who" is not this one, not that one, not oneself, not some people, and not the sum of them all. The "who" is the neuter, the "*they*" [*das Man*]. . . .

Everyone is the other, and no one is himself.

Everyone is the other, and no one is himself. The "*they*," which supplies the answer to the question of the "who" of everyday Dasein, is the "*nobody*" to whom every Dasein has already surrendered itself in Being-among-one-other.

---

[14] Søren Kierkegaard, *Concluding Unscientific Postscript,* trans. David F. Swenson and Walter Lowrie (Princeton, NJ: Princeton University Press, 1941).

[15] For "Dasein," read "individual human being"; for "Being-with," read "being around other people."

Against this "surrender," Heidegger urges us to "take hold of ourselves" as individuals and find our "authentic" selves.

> The Self of everyday Dasein is the *they-self,* which we distinguish from the *authentic Self*—that is, from the Self which has been taken hold of in its own way.[16]

This **individualist** movement is not unique to existentialism; it is in the mainstream of Western thinking, from ancient Socrates through Reformation Christianity to contemporary capitalism. Socrates' rebellion was, in a very important way, an existential rebellion. He stood up for his principles against the opinions of the age. Luther's Reformation was, among other things, very much a reassertion of the individual (individual conscience, individual actions) against the all-embracing spirit of the Catholic Church. Today, virtually every American would agree that every individual deserves at least some individual rights and respect. But individualism has always had its doubters. Individualism arises largely as a reaction against the awareness of how socially conditioned we really are. As an instrument of personal growth and as a defense against excessive socialization, individualism is extremely valuable. But when individualism becomes so powerful that personal interests eclipse the interests of everyone else and individual values begin to destroy the community, then it may be time to bring the limits of individualism into question as well. Furthermore, an excessive emphasis on individuality may lead us to forget that there are other human ways of living that are not individualistic at all. There are limits to the degree to which we can challenge the values and customs of our upbringing. Some rebellion is required for growth and change of the society as well as of the individual. But too much rebellion can be self-destructive as well as destructive to the community. For our self-identities, no matter how hard we try to think of ourselves as total individuals, are inextricably tied to the communities and values in which we were raised.

The American sociologist **David Reisman** looks again at individualism in the light of these considerations and defends it as follows:

ON INDIVIDUALISM
BY **DAVID REISMAN**

Social science has helped us become more aware of the extent to which individuals, great and little, are the creatures of their cultural conditioning; and so we neither blame the little nor exalt the great. But the same wisdom has sometimes led us to the fallacy that, since all men have their being in culture and as the result of the culture, they owe a debt to that culture which even a lifetime of

---

[16] Martin Heidegger, *Being and Time,* trans. J. MacQuarrie and E. Robinson (New York: Harper & Row, 1962).

altruism could not repay. (One might as well argue, and in fact many societies in effect do, that since we are born of parents, we must feel guilt whenever we transcend their limitations!) Sometimes the point is pushed to the virtual denial of individuality: since we arise in society, it is assumed with a ferocious determinism that we can never transcend it. All such concepts are useful correctives of an earlier solipsism. But if they are extended to hold that conformity with society is not only a necessity but also a duty, they destroy that margin of freedom which gives life its savor and its endless possibility for advance.[17]

1. Voices of Protest

In contemporary times, the question of how individuals are defined by or in society is a deeply political issue. It is tied to questions of how we categorize our society ethnically, sexually, and racially. In our pluralist American society, we tend to believe that individual freedoms play more of a role in defining us within society than do, say, our family lineage or professional organizations. We are particularly sensitive, then, to racial or sexual stereotyping and to strict enforcement of social roles, because we feel that our identities are thereby taken out of our own control and our individuality is overlooked. This concern is similar to the concern that dualists have about materialism. We worry that if we "are" just our bodies—or similarly if we "are" just what our society makes us—then we are not the free, rational creatures we would like to be.

In the passage that follows, the Black Nationalist leader Malcolm X argues the extent to which African-Americans' self-identities are defined for them by American society in which whites are a majority.

ON BEING "AFRICAN"
BY **MALCOLM X**

Right now, in this country, if you and I, 22 million African-Americans—that's what we are—Africans who are in America. You're nothing but Africans. Nothing but Africans. In fact, you'd get farther calling yourself African instead of Negro. Africans don't catch hell. You're the only one catching hell. They don't have to pass civil-rights bills for Africans. An African can go anywhere he wants right now. All you've got to do is tie your head up. That's right, go anywhere you want. Just stop being a Negro. Change your name to Hoogagagooba. That'll show you how silly the white man is. You're dealing with a silly man. A friend of mine who's very dark put a turban on his head and went into a restaurant in Atlanta before they called themselves desegregated. He went into a white restaurant, he sat down, they served him, and he said, "What would happen if a Negro came in here?" And there he's sitting, black as night, but because he had his

---

[17] David Reisman, *Individualism Reconsidered* (New York: Doubleday, 1954).

head wrapped up the waitress looked back at him and says, "Why, there wouldn't no nigger dare come in here." [18]

Malcolm X explains the moral of the story in another famous speech:

FROM "AT THE AUDOBON"
BY **MALCOLM X**

You'll be surprised how fast, how easy it is for someone to steal your and my mind. You don't think so? We never like to think in terms of being dumb enough to let someone put something over on us in a very deceitful and tricky way. But you and I are living in a very deceitful and tricky society, in a very deceitful and tricky country, which has a very deceitful and tricky government. *All* of them in it aren't tricky and deceitful, but *most* of them are. And any time you have a government in which *most* of them are deceitful and tricky, you have to be on guard at all times. You have to know how they work this deceit and how they work these tricks. Otherwise you'll find yourself in a bind.

> *One of the best ways to safeguard yourself from being deceived is always to form the habit of looking at things for yourself, listening to things for yourself, thinking for yourself, before you try and come to any judgment.*

One of the best ways to safeguard yourself from being deceived is always to form the habit of looking at things for yourself, listening to things for yourself, thinking for yourself, before you try and come to any judgment. Never base your impression of someone on what someone else has said. Or upon what someone else has written. Or upon what you read about someone that somebody else wrote. Never base your judgment on things like that. Especially in this kind of country and in this kind of society which has mastered the art of very deceitfully painting people whom they don't like in an image that they know you won't like. So you end up hating your friends and loving their enemies. [19]

Obviously, social roles have been binding to the "free individuality" of other groups, too, like women. Many contemporary feminists have analyzed how sex roles, perhaps more than anything else, falsely define us and undermine our individuality. In a now-famous article, **Sherri Ortner** considers the way society identifies women.

---

[18]Malcolm X, "The Ballot or the Bullet," rpt. in *Malcolm X Speaks,* ed. George Breitman (New York: Grove Press, 1965).

[19]Malcolm X, "At the Audobon," *Malcolm X Speaks.*

FROM "IS FEMALE TO MALE AS NATURE IS TO CULTURE?"
BY SHERRI ORTNER [20]

Much of the creativity of anthropology derives from the tension between two sets of demands: that we explain human universals, and that we explain cultural particulars. By this canon, woman provides us with one of the more challenging problems to be dealt with. The secondary status of woman in society is one of the true universals, a pan-cultural fact. Yet within that universal fact, the specific cultural conceptions and symbolizations of woman are extraordinarily diverse and even mutually contradictory. Further, the actual treatment of women and their relative power and contribution vary enormously from culture to culture, and over different periods in the history of particular cultural traditions. Both of these points—the universal fact and the cultural variation—constitute problems to be explained.

My interest in the problem is of course more than academic: I wish to see genuine change come about, the emergence of a social and cultural order in which as much of the range of human potential is open to women as is open to men. The universality of female subordination, the fact that it exists within every type of social and economic arrangement and in societies of every degree of complexity, indicates to me that we are up against something very profound, very stubborn, something we cannot rout out simply by rearranging a few tasks and roles in the social system, or even by reordering the whole economic structure. In this paper I try to expose the underlying logic of cultural thinking that assumes the inferiority of women; I try to show the highly persuasive nature of the logic, for if it were not so persuasive, people would not keep subscribing to it. But I also try to show the social and cultural sources of that logic, to indicate wherein lies the potential for change.

THE UNIVERSALITY OF FEMALE SUBORDINATION

What do I mean when I say that everywhere, in every known culture, women are considered in some degree inferior to men? First of all, I must stress that I am talking about *cultural* evaluations; I am saying that each culture, in its own way and on its own terms, makes this evaluation. But what would constitute evidence that a particular culture considers women inferior?

Three types of data would suffice: (1) elements of cultural ideology and informants' statements that *explicitly* devalue women, according them, their roles, their tasks, their products, and their social milieux less prestige than are

---

[20] Sherry B. Ortner, "Is Female to Male as Nature Is to Culture?" reprinted in *Woman, Culture, and Society,* edited by Michelle Z. Rosaldo and Louise Lamphere (Stanford: Stanford University Press, 1974).

accorded men and the male correlates; (2) symbolic devices, such as the attribution of defilement, which may be interpreted as *implicitly* making a statement of interior valuation; and (3) social-structural arrangements that exclude women from participation in or contact with some realm in which the highest powers of the society are felt to reside. These three types of data may all of course be interrelated in any particular system, though they need not necessarily be. Further, any one of them will usually be sufficient to make the point of female inferiority in a given culture. Certainly, female exclusion from the most sacred rite or the highest political council is sufficient evidence. Certainly, explicit cultural ideology devaluing women (and their tasks, roles, products, etc.) is sufficient evidence. Symbolic indicators such as defilement are usually sufficient, although in a few cases in which, say, men and women are equally polluting to one another, a further indicator is required—and is, as far as my investigations have ascertained, always available.

On any or all of these counts, then, I would flatly assert that we find women subordinated to men in every known society.

◆ ◆ ◆

NATURE AND CULTURE

How are we to explain the universal devaluation of women? We could of course rest the case on biological determinism. There is something genetically inherent in the male of the species, so the biological determinists would argue, that makes them the naturally dominant sex; that "something" is lacking in females, and as a result women are not only naturally subordinate but in general quite satisfied with their position, since it affords them protection and the opportunity to maximize maternal pleasures, which to them are the most satisfying experiences of life. Without going into a detailed refutation of this position, I think it fair to say that it has failed to be established to the satisfaction of almost anyone in academic anthropology. This is to say, not that biological facts are irrelevant, or that men and women are not different, but that these facts and differences only take on significance of superior/inferior within the framework of culturally defined value systems.

If we are unwilling to rest the case on genetic determinism, it seems to me that we have only one way to proceed. We must attempt to interpret female subordination in light of other universals, factors built into the structure of the most generalized situation in which all human beings, in whatever culture, find themselves. For example, every human being has a physical body and a sense of nonphysical mind, is part of a society of other individuals and an inheritor of a cultural tradition, and must engage in some relationship, however mediated, with "nature," or the nonhuman realm, in order to survive. Every human being is born (to a mother) and ultimately dies, all are assumed to have an interest in personal survival, and society/culture has its own interest in (or at least momentum toward) continuity and survival, which transcends the lives and deaths of particular individuals. And so forth. It is in the realm of such universals of the human condition that we must seek an explanation for the universal fact of female devaluation.

I translate the problem, in other words, into the following simple question. What could there be in the generalized structure and conditions of existence, common to every culture, that would lead every culture to place a lower value upon women? Specifically, my thesis is that woman is being identified with—or, if you will, seems to be a symbol of—something that every culture devalues, something that every culture defines as being of a lower order of existence than itself. Now it seems that there is only one thing that would fit that description, and that is "nature" in the most generalized sense. Every culture, or, generically, "culture," is engaged in the process of generating and sustaining systems of meaningful forms (symbols, artifacts, etc.) by means of which humanity transcends the givens of natural existence, bends them to its purposes, controls them in its interest. We may thus broadly equate culture with the notion of human consciousness, or with the products of human consciousness (i.e., systems of thought and technology), by means of which humanity attempts to assert control over nature.

◆◆◆

Returning now to the issue of women, their pan-cultural second-class status could be accounted for, quite simply, by postulating that women are being identified or symbolically associated with nature, as opposed to men, who are identified with culture. Since it is always culture's project to subsume and transcend nature, if women were considered part of nature, then culture would find it "natural" to subordinate, not to say oppress, them. Yet although this argument can be shown to have considerable force, it seems to oversimplify the case. The formulation I would like to defend and elaborate on in the following section, then, is that women are seen "merely" as being *closer* to nature than men. That is, culture (still equated relatively unambiguously with men) recognizes that women are active participants in its special processes, but at the same time sees them as being more rooted in, or having more direct affinity with, nature.

... even if women are not equated with nature, they are nonetheless seen as representing a lower order of being, as being less transcendental of nature than men are.

The revision may seem minor or even trivial, but I think it is a more accurate rendering of cultural assumptions. Further, the argument cast in these terms has several analytic advantages over the simpler formulation; I shall discuss these later. It might simply be stressed here that the revised argument would still account for the pan-cultural devaluation of women, for even if women are not equated with nature, they are nonetheless seen as representing a lower order of being, as being less transcendental of nature than men are.

◆◆◆

In short, the postulate that woman is viewed as closer to nature than man has several implications for further analysis, and can be interpreted in several different ways. If it is viewed simply as a *middle* position on a scale from culture down to nature, then it is still seen as lower than culture and thus accounts for the pan-cultural assumption that woman is lower than man in the order of things. If it is read as a *mediating* element in the culture-nature relationship, then it may account in part for the cultural tendency not merely to devalue woman but to circumscribe and restrict her functions, since culture must maintain control over its (pragmatic and symbolic) mechanisms for the conversion of nature into culture. And if it is read as an *ambiguous* status between culture and nature, it may help account for the fact that, in specific cultural ideologies and symbolizations, woman can occasionally be aligned with culture, and in any event is often assigned polarized and contradictory meanings within a single symbolic system. Middle status, mediating functions, ambiguous meaning—all are different readings, for different contextual purposes, of woman's being seen as intermediate between nature and culture.

But how would a society *without* clear social and sexual roles function? Is it even possible that we could interact with each other as entirely free individuals? Some feminists, like **Ann Ferguson,** believe so. She believes, however, that in order to achieve such an ideal, we must all embrace an "androgynous" sexuality.

ON ANDROGYNY
BY ANN FERGUSON

There is good evidence that human babies are bisexual, and only *learn* a specific male or female identity by imitating and identifying with adult models. This evidence comes from the discovery that all human beings possess both male and female hormones (androgen and estrogen respectively), and also from concepts first developed at length by Freud. Freud argued that heterosexual identity is not achieved until the third stage of the child's sexual development. Sex identity is developed through the resolution of the Oedipus complex, in which the child has to give up a primary attachment to the mother and learn either to identify with, or love, the father. But Shulamith Firestone suggests that this process is not an inevitable one, as Freud presents it to be. Rather, it is due to the power dynamics of the patriarchal nuclear family. Note that, on this analysis, if the sexual division of labor were destroyed, the mechanism that trains boys and girls to develop heterosexual sexual identities would also be destroyed. If fathers and mothers played equal nurturant roles in child-rearing and had equal social, economic, and political power outside the home, there would be no reason for the boy to have to reject his emotional side in order to gain the power associated with the male role. Neither would the girl have to assume a female role in rejecting her assertive, independent side in order to attain power indirectly through manipulation of males. As a sexual identity, bisexuality would then be the norm rather than the exception. . . .

I believe that only androgynous people can attain the full human potential possible given our present level of material and social resources (and this only if society is radically restructured). Only such people can have ideal love relationships; and without such relationships, I maintain that none can develop to the fullest potential. . . . Furthermore, recent studies have shown that the human brain has two distinct functions: one associated with analytic, logical, sequential thinking (the left brain), and the other associated with holistic, metaphorical, intuitive thought (the right brain). Only a person capable of tapping both these sides of him/herself will have developed to full potential. We might call this characteristic of the human brain "psychic bisexuality," since it has been shown that women in fact have developed skills which allow them to tap the abilities of the right side of the brain more than men, who on the contrary excel in the analytic, logical thought characteristic of the left side. The point is that men and women have the potential for using both these functions, and yet our socialization at present tends to cut off from one or the other of these parts of ourselves.[21]

2. Beyond "Individualism"

As we can see from the examples above, the argument for individualism is often stated as a form of mutual conflict (as in the existentialists and Reisman), which many philosophers would not accept. Why need there be a conflict? Kant, for example, while very much the champion of individual autonomy, insisted that the only individuality worth defending was the ability of the individual to participate in universal morality. The same argument is to be found in the writings of Socrates, Plato, and Aristotle. In more recent times, this argument has found a large following among thinkers who have seen the disastrous results of overly individual thinking (what Reisman refers to as "solipsism"). The German philosopher Hegel, for example, writing in the midst of the great international movements of the early nineteenth century, argued the following:

"SPIRIT" AND THE INDIVIDUAL
BY G. W. F. HEGEL

At a time when the universal nature of spiritual life has become so very much emphasized and strengthened, and the mere individual aspect has become, as it should be, correspondingly a matter of indifference, when, too, that universal

---

[21] Ann Ferguson, "Androgyny as a Progressive Ideal for Human Development," rpt. in *Feminism and Philosophy,* ed. Mary Vetterling-Braggin, Frederick A. Elliston, and Jane English (Lanham, MD: Littlefield, Adams, 1977).

aspect holds, by the entire range of its substance, the full measure of the wealth it has built up, and lays claim to it all, the share in the total work of mind that falls to the activity of any particular individual can only be very small. Because this is so, the individual must all the more forget himself, as in fact the very nature of science implies and requires that he should; and he must, moreover, become and do what he can. But all the less must be demanded of him, just as he can expect the less from himself, and may ask the less for himself.[22]

Elsewhere, in a famous passage, he argues that individuals in history are significant only insofar as they contribute to movements far greater than themselves:

> In contemplating history as the slaughter-bench at which the happiness of peoples, the wisdom of states, and the virtue of individuals have been sacrificed, a question necessarily arises: To what principle, to what final purpose, have these monstrous sacrifices been offered?
>
> . . . human agents have before them limited aims, special interests. But they are also intelligent, thinking beings. Their purposes are interwoven with general and essential considerations of law, the good, duty, etc. For mere desire, volition in its raw and savage form, falls outside the scene and sphere of world history. These general considerations, which at the same time form norms for directing purposes and actions, have a definite content. For such empty abstractions as "good for its own sake" have no place in living actuality.
>
> . . . Each individual has his position; he knows, on the whole, what a lawful and honorable course of conduct is. To assert in ordinary private relations that it is difficult to choose the right and good, and to regard it as mark of an exalted morality to find difficulties and raise scruples on that score indicates an evil and perverse will. It indicates a will that seeks to evade obvious duties or, at least, a petty will that gives its mind too little to do. The mind, then, in idle reflection, busies itself with itself and indulges in moral smugness.
>
> *. . . each individual is also the child of a people at a definite stage of its development. One cannot skip over the spirit of his people any more than one can skip over the earth. The earth is the center of gravity; a body imagined as leaving this center can only be imagined as exploding into the air. So it is with an individual. But only through his own effort can he be in harmony with his substance; he must bring the will demanded by his people to his own consciousness, to articulation. The individual does not invent his own content; he is what he is by acting out the universal as his own content.*
>
> *In the course of history two factors are important. One is the preservation of a people, a state, or the well-ordered spheres of life. This is the activity of*

---

[22] G. W. F. Hegel, *The Phenomenology of Spirit,* trans. A. N. Miller (Oxford: Oxford University Press, 1977).

individuals participating in the common effort and helping to bring about its particular manifestations. It is the preservation of ethical life. The other important factor, however, is the decline of a state. The existence of a national spirit is broken when it has used up and exhausted itself. World history, the World Spirit, continues on its course. . . .

This universal is an essential phase in the development of the creating Idea, of truth striving and urging toward itself. The historical men, *world-historical individuals,* are those [*who grasp just such a higher universal, make it their own purpose, and realize this purpose in accordance with the higher law of the spirit*].[23]

In the midst of the international upheavals led by Napoleon, you can appreciate the appropriateness of such a brutal philosophy. "The slaughter-bench of history" is not a pleasant concept! The idea that each of us is virtually insignificant in our tiny place in history also hurts our grander conceptions of ourselves. But Hegel argues that no other view of ourselves is defensible. Even the greatest among us is nothing more than an expression of the "universal," the monumental forces of society and humankind as a whole (these are what Hegel refers to as "spirit" and "the Creating Idea" and elsewhere as "the cunning of Reason").

But however appropriate in times of international warfare, Hegel's conception is bound to raise hackles among the individualists in peacetime. Consider Kierkegaard's ironic retort to Hegel's philosophy:

A RETORT
BY **KIERKEGAARD**

Hence perhaps the many attempts to continue clinging to Hegel, even by men who have reached an insight into the questionable character of his philosophy. It is a fear that if they were to become particular existing human beings, they would vanish tracelessly, so that not even the daily press would be able to discover them, still less critical journals, to say nothing at all of speculative philosophers immersed in world-history. As particular human beings they fear that they will be doomed to a more isolated and forgotten existence than that of a man in the country; for if a man lets go of Hegel he will not even be in a position to have a letter addressed to him.[24]

Karl Marx was a student of Hegel's philosophy. In his "early writings" of 1844, he too argues for a view of self as essentially social, a part of a community, a "species-being":

---

[23]G. W. F. Hegel, *Reason in History,* trans. Robert S. Hartman (New York: Bobbs-Merrill, 1953).

[24]Kierkegaard, *Concluding Unscientific Postscript.*

ON THE SOCIAL SELF
BY KARL MARX

It follows from the character of this relationship [the human family] how far *man* has become, and has understood himself as, a *species-being,* a *human being.* . . .

Activity and mind are social in their content as well as in their *origin;* they are *social* activity and social mind. . . .

It is above all necessary to avoid postulating "society" once again as an abstraction confronting the individual. The individual *is* the *social being.* The manifestation of his life—even when it does not appear directly in the form of a communal manifestation, accomplished in association with other men—is, therefore, a manifestation, and affirmation of *social life.* Individual human life and species-life are not different things, even though the mode of existence of individual life is necessarily either a more *specific* or a more *general* mode of species-life, or that of species-life a *specific* or more *general* mode of individual life.

In his *species-consciousness* man confirms his real *social life,* and reproduces his real existence in thought; while conversely, species-life confirms itself in species-consciousness and exists for itself in its universality as a thinking being. Though man is a unique individual—and it is just his particularity which makes him an individual, a really *individual* communal being— he is equally the *whole,* the ideal whole, the subjective existence of society as thought and experienced. He exists in reality as the representation and the real mind of social existence, and as the sum of human manifestations of life.[25]

> *Activity and mind are social in their* **origin;** *they are* **social** *activity and social* **mind.** . . .

In the twentieth century, under the mixed influences of existentialism, especially as espoused by the German Martin Heidegger, and of German Idealism, especially Hegel and Marx, a new philosophical school became very popular. It is called "**deconstruction,**" a name coined by its founder, the Frenchman **Jacques Derrida.** Deconstruction is the attempt to offer a social analysis and criticism which recognizes its own identification with the culture it criticizes. To "deconstruct" a theory or a belief or a tradition, then, is neither to destroy it nor to rebuild it, but rather to "reread" it, and thereby change it, see into it, add to it, *make* it our own, perhaps more plural, more disperse, action. In his early work, Derrida argues that the school of deconstruction itself—of rereading, criticizing, and dispersing our cultural institutions and the philosophers who come from them—is itself an epitomal product of our cultural institutions. His claim is that the "unified self" is just a product of Western culture,

---

[25] Karl Marx, *Early Writings,* trans. T. Bottomore (New York: McGraw-Hill, 1963).

and that it is now dying at the hands of its own creator. If there is "self," he suggests, "it must be *plural*."[26]

Some contemporary political thinkers—especially feminist and African-American philosophers—have found deconstruction attractive. Some of the contemporary philosophical debate about individual freedoms has evolved into criticisms and defenses of the "Western philosophy" Derrida describes. If only "Western philosophy" were so univocally definable, then perhaps all its mistakes and cruelties could be identified and avoided. As we've seen, however, and as Derrida admits, these very modern criticism form an integral part of the complex, culturally interwoven philosophical debate around the world.

It is important to emphasize that none of these philosophers actually denies the individual, or individual respect, or individual rights. They are, however, insisting that an individual derives his or her rights only insofar as he or she is a member of a community. This does not mean that a person cannot be eccentric, like the weirdo artist or the spaced-out rock musician, but it does mean that even their eccentricity, as well as their talents, must be viewed as social contributions. What they are denying, in other words, is what has sometimes been called "vulgar individualism," that form of self-identity that denies all social relevance and social obligations.

D. ONE SELF? ANY SELF? QUESTIONING THE CONCEPT OF PERSONAL "ESSENCE"

So far, we have talked as if self-identity is something singular, a unified set of ideals and characteristics according to which one identifies himself or herself. But need we think of the "self" in this way?

In his novel *Steppenwolf,* **Hermann Hesse** presents a character whose "self" is something quite different. Hesse's Harry Haller is a *multiple* or *pluralistic* self, a collection of "selves," with no one of them "real" or "essential." Like many of us, he lives with the myth of "two selves," one human, rational, and well behaved, the other beastly, wild, and wolflike. He is torn between the two. But, Hesse tells us, Harry's unhappiness is not, as he thinks, a result of his "war between the selves" at all but rather the result of an oversimplified notion of self. "The Steppenwolf is a fiction," writes Hesse, a "mythological simplification." The idea of two selves, one wolf, one man, is as old as the mind-body distinction, as the Christian division between the body and the soul—even older, in fact, dating back to Pythagoras and Plato. Hesse's argument is that this simple self is a strictly "bourgeois convention," a middle-class argument for the simplicity and unity of the self; indeed, Harry is

---

[26] Jacques Derrida, "The Ends of Man," trans. Alan Bass in *Margins of Philosophy* (Chicago: University of Chicago Press, 1982).

unhappy because of the tension and complexity of only two selves: the "human" who has culture and cultivated thoughts and feelings and the "wolf" who is savage and cruel, the dark world of Freud's unconscious instincts and raw, untamed nature. He argues the following:

FROM *STEPPENWOLF*
BY **HERMANN HESSE**

Suppose that Harry tried to ascertain in any single moment of his life, any single act, what part the man had in it and what part the wolf, he would find himself at once in a dilemma, and his whole beautiful wolf theory would go to pieces. For there is not a single human being . . . not even the idiot, who is so conveniently simple that his being can be explained as the sum of two or three principal elements; and to explain so complex a man as Harry by the artless division into wolf and man is a hopelessly childish attempt. Harry consists of a hundred or a thousand selves, not of two. His life oscillates, as everyone's does, not merely between two poles, such as the body and the spirit, the saint and the sinner, but between thousand and thousands.

Why is it, Hesse asks, that we all seem to have this need to think of ourselves in such deceptive terms and regard the self as a single unit? Because, he suggests, we are deluded by an analogy; since each of us has but one body, it is assumed that each of us has a single soul too. From this analogy we assume that there must be one self within each body. But it is here that Hesse contrasts our view with the views of ancient India and notes with admiration that there is no trace of such a notion in the poems of the ancient Asiatics. He then offers us his own analogy:

Man is an onion made up of a hundred integuments, a texture made up of many threads. The ancient Asiatics knew this well enough, and in the Buddhist Yoga an exact technique was devised for unmasking the illusion of the personality. The human merry-go-round sees many changes: The illusion that cost India the efforts of thousands of years to unmask is the same illusion that the West has labored just as hard to maintain and strengthen.[27]

Hesse refers to Buddhist concepts of the self with praise. Although he remains entrenched in Western ideas as well, Hesse is already more than halfway to one of the ancient Eastern conceptions of self, which is essentially a denial of the self as we think of it. As we've seen in Chapter 1, the Buddhist says, "give up your self-identity," "give up your self-consciousness," and finally, "give up your self." This is a familiar refrain among many Eastern mystics. It may also be an ideal secular aspiration, however. For instance, the contemporary French philosopher and feminist

---

[27] Hermann Hesse, *Steppenwolf,* trans. Basil Creighton and Rev. Joseph Mileck (New York: Holt, Rinehart and Winston, 1929).

Luce Irigaray claims that the unified, "essential" self is a limiting and oppressive notion, particularly when applied to women. In her book *The Sex Which Is Not One* she claims that the genuine and free identity of a woman is a multiplicity or plurality of characters. Note the deliberate play on words in her title: "the sex which is not one." With it, she implies a multiplicity of meanings: The female sex is not singular and unified; women are not unified together; the female is not *a sex* at all. With this last reading, we see that Irigaray is not only claiming that a woman has multiple selves instead of a single body and a single soul, but also that all human beings, men included, may have multiple sexualities, multiple identities—that there may not be any natural masculinity or femininity at all in the plural "self" from which we sort them out. Thus, Irigaray is making a feminist criticism of all our social and sexual roles at the same time as she offers a theory of self-identity.

FROM *THIS SEX WHICH IS NOT ONE*
BY **LUCE IRIGARAY**

. . . not knowing what she wants, ready for anything, even asking for more, so long as he will "take" her as his "object" when he seeks his own pleasure. Thus she will not say what she herself wants; moreover, she does not know, or no longer knows, what she wants. As Freud admits, the beginnings of the sexual life of a girl child are so "obscure," so "faded with time," that one would have to dig down very deep indeed to discover beneath the traces of this civilization, of this history, the vestiges of a more archaic civilization that might give some clue to woman's sexuality. That extremely ancient civilization would undoubtedly have a different alphabet, a different language . . . Woman's desire would not be expected to speak the same language as man's; woman's desire has doubtless been submerged by the logic that has dominated the West since the time of the Greeks.

◆◆◆

"She" is indefinitely other in herself. This is doubtless why she is said to be whimsical, incomprehensible, agitated, capricious . . . not to mention her language, in which "she" sets off in all directions leaving "him" unable to discern the coherence of any meaning. Hers are contradictory words, somewhat mad from the standpoint of reason, inaudible for whoever listens to them with ready-made grids, with a fully elaborated code in hand. For in what she says, too, at least when she dares, woman is constantly touching herself. She steps ever so slightly aside from herself with a murmur, an exclamation, a whisper, a sentence left unfinished . . . When she returns, it is to set off again from elsewhere. From another point of pleasure, or of pain. One would have to listen with another ear, as if hearing *an "other meaning" always in the process of weaving itself, of embracing itself with words, but also of getting rid of words in order not to become fixed, congealed in them.* For if "she" says something, it is not, it is already no longer, identical with what she means. What she says is never identical with anything, moreover; rather, it is contiguous. *It touches (upon).* And when it strays too far from that proximity, she breaks off and starts over at "zero," her body-sex.

It is useless, then, to trap women in the exact definition of what they mean, to make them repeat (themselves) so that it will be clear; they are already elsewhere in that discursive machinery where you expected to surprise them. They have returned within themselves. Which must not be understood in the same way as within yourself. They do not have the interiority that you have, the one *you* perhaps suppose they have. Within themselves means *within the intimacy of that silent, multiple, diffuse touch.* And if you ask them insistently what they are thinking about, they can only reply: Nothing. Everything.

Thus what they desire is precisely nothing, and at the same time everything. Always something more and something else besides that *one*—sexual organ, for example—that you give them, attribute to them. Their desire is often interpreted, and feared, as a sort of insatiable hunger, a voracity that will swallow you whole. Whereas it really involves a different economy more than anything else, one that upsets the linearity of a project, undermines the goal-object of a desire, diffuses the polarization toward a single pleasure, disconcerts fidelity to a single discourse . . .

Must this multiplicity of female desire and female language be understood as shards, scattered remnants of a violated sexuality? A sexuality denied? The question has no simple answer. The rejection, the exclusion of a female imaginary certainly puts woman in the position of experiencing herself only fragmentarily, in the little-structured margins of a dominant ideology, as waste, or excess, what is left of a mirror invested by the (masculine) "subject" to reflect himself, to copy himself. Moreover, the role of "femininity" is prescribed by this masculine specularization and corresponds scarcely at all to woman's desire, which may be recovered only in secret, in hiding, with anxiety and guilt.

> *. . . the role of "femininity" is prescribed by this masculine specularization and corresponds scarcely at all to woman's desire, which may be recovered only in secret, in hiding, with anxiety and guilt.*

But if the female imaginary were to deploy itself, if it could bring itself into play otherwise than as scraps, uncollected debris, would it represent itself, even so, in the form of *one* universe? Would it even be volume instead of surface? No.

♦♦♦

(Re-)discovering herself, for a woman, thus could only signify the possibility of sacrificing no one of her pleasures to another, of identifying herself with none of them in particular, *of never being simply one.* A sort of expanding universe to which no limits could be fixed and which would not be incoherence . . . nonetheless—nor that polymorphous perversion of the child in which the erogenous zones would lie waiting to be regrouped under the primacy of the phallus.

Woman always remains several, but she is kept from dispersion because the other is already within her and is autoerotically familiar to her. Which is not to say that she appropriates the other for herself, that she reduces it to her own property. Ownership and property are doubtless quite foreign to the feminine. At least sexually. But not *nearness*. Nearness so pronounced that it makes all discrimination of identity, and thus all forms of property, impossible.[28]

Irigaray is not the only feminist philosopher to criticize the notion of "self" that was assumed by Descartes and adopted by many of his successors. Many feminists are critical of the Cartesian notion "self" particularly because of the way the mind-body distinction is related to stereotypes of gender. Because our society has come to accept the "masculinity" of the mind and the "femininity" of the body, these feminists claim, the philosophical notion of the "self" as consciousness or mind incorporates sexism right into our notions of human nature.

In the following passage, **Genevieve Lloyd,** a contemporary feminist and philosopher, criticizes the mind-body distinction over its whole history from a feminist perspective.

FROM "THE MAN OF REASON"
BY GENEVIEVE LLOYD

By the Man of Reason I mean the ideal of rationality associated with the rationalist philosophies of the seventeenth century. And, secondly, something more nebulous—the residue of that ideal in our contemporary consciousness, our inheritance from seventeenth century rationalism. This is, I think, a substantial component in what reason has come to be. But it is not, of course, the only component. In focusing on it to the exclusion of any other developments in the notion of reason since the seventeenth century, this paper inevitably presents an incomplete picture of reason, but one that does highlight, I think, some aspects of reason that are of considerable relevance to philosophical aspects of feminism.

The main feature of the Man of Reason that I am concerned to bring into focus is his maleness. This in itself, I think, is a matter of philosophical interest. More is involved here than the supposedly "neutral" sense of "man" to include women. We are all familiar with the fact that linguistic usage commonly fails to recognize that humanity comprises two sexes. But there is something deeper to the maleness of the Man of Reason; something more deeply engrained in consciousness. He is after all a creation of reflective consciousness. When the Man of Reason is extolled, philosophers are not talking about idealizations of human beings. They are talking about ideals of manhood.

---

[28] Luce Irigaray, "The Sex Which Is Not One," chapter 2 of *The Sex Which Is Not One* (Ithaca: Cornell University Press, 1985).

What I want to do in this paper is to bring this undoubted maleness of the Man of Reason into clearer focus. There are, I think, reasons that belong in the history of philosophy for the association between reason and masculinity. Some parts of the history of philosophy can throw light here on a very confused and tension-ridden area of human experience. Past philosophical reflection has after all helped form our present thought structures. And the creature I am calling the Man of Reason embodies some of the fundamental ideals of our culture. Let us try then to bring him into sharper focus.

THE ASSOCIATION OF "MALE" WITH "RATIONAL"

The associations between "male" and "rational" and between "female" and "non-rational" have, of course, a very long history. The idea that the rational is somehow specially associated with masculinity goes back to the Greek founding fathers of rationality as we know it. Aristotle thought that woman was "as it were an impotent male, for it is through a certain incapacity that the female is female." This intrinsic female incapacity was a lack in the "principle of soul" and hence associated with an incapacity in respect of rationality. The claim is not of course that women do not have rationality, but they have it in an inferior, fainter way. They have rationality; they are distinguished from the animals by being rational. Yet they are not equal to men. They are somehow *lesser* men, lesser in respect of the all-important thing; rationality.

◆◆◆

REASON IN THE SEVENTEENTH CENTURY

One of the most striking things that happens to reason in the seventeenth century is the attempt to encapsulate it in a systematic method for attaining certainty. The paradigm of this approach to reason is Descartes's *Regulae,* the *Rules for the Direction of the Mind,* written in 1628. Here there emerges a new conception of what is involved in knowledge. The acquisition of knowledge is a matter of the systematic pursuit of an orderly method. The essence of the method is to break down all the complex operations involved in reasoning into their most basic constituents and to render the mind adept in performing these simple operations—intuition and deduction. Intuition is the undoubting conception of an unclouded and attentive mind which comes from the light of reason alone. This is the basis for Descartes's later influential doctrine of clear and distinct ideas. Deduction is the process by which we extend knowledge beyond intuitions by connecting them in series. These are the only mental operations Descartes will admit into his method; but the proper understanding and use of them will, he thinks, yield all that lies within the province of knowledge. Anything else is in fact an impediment to knowledge:

> *nothing can be added to the pure light of reason which does not in some way obscure it.*

The method is universally applicable, regardless of any difference in subject matter:

> we must not fancy that one kind of knowledge is more obscure than another, since all knowledge is of the same nature throughout, and consists solely in combining what is self evident.

This universality of Cartesian method is emphasized in the *Discourse on Method,* published in 1637:

> provided only that we abstain from receiving anything as true which is not so, and always retain the order which is necessary in order to deduce the one conclusion from the other, there can be nothing so remote that we cannot reach to it, nor so recondite that we cannot discover it.

For Descartes, then, all knowledge consists in self-evident intuition and necessary deduction. We are to break down the complex and obscure into what is simple and self-evident, then combine the resultant units in an orderly manner. In order to know we must isolate the "simple natures," the objects of intuition, and "scrutinise them separately with steadfast mental gaze." We then combine them in chains of deductions. The whole of human knowledge consists in a distinct perception of the way in which these simple natures combine in order to build up other objects.

There is a deeper, metaphysical, dimension to the Cartesian treatment of reason. In the course of elaborating a method for attaining certain knowledge Descartes thinks he is uncovering the unity of all the sciences, the unity of knowledge. For him this is identical with the order of thought itself, with the very structure of the knowing mind. And this order of thought is taken as transparently reflecting the order of things. In the *Regulae* there is no gap between intuitions and the simple natures that are their objective correlates. In the later *Meditations* (1641) the possibility of radical doubt opens a gap between ideas and the material world, between the structure of the mind and the structure of the reality it attempts to know. But this gap is then closed by the existence of a veracious God. Introspection of the nature of thought in an individual mind ultimately yields access to universal reason, God given and God guaranteed, and hence to the structure of reality itself, conceived by Cartesian rationalism to be identical with that of the mind.

This isomorphism, between reason and reality, founded on a veracious God, gives reason a quasi-divine character. Reason is God imbued, the divine spark in man. This is the seventeenth century version of the treatment of man's rational faculty as reflecting the godhead, as that in virtue of which man is made in God's image.

Another feature of Descartes's treatment of reason that is crucial here is its connection with his antithesis between mind and matter. The basic units of Cartesian method are discrete, sharp edged and self-contained mental items. This becomes even more pronounced in his later works. The vehicles of knowledge are clear, precisely bordered mental states, sharply separated from one another:

The distinct is that which is so precise and different from all other objects that it contains within itself nothing but what is clear.

And this discrete, delineated character of the units of knowledge is grounded in Descartes's distinction between mind and matter. The absolute certainty that accompanies clear and distinct ideas derives from their purely mental character. Intuition, as Descartes puts it, is free of the "fluctuating testimony of the senses" and the "blundering constructions of imagination." Cartesian method is essentially a matter of forming the "habit of distinguishing intellectual from corporeal matters." It is a matter of shedding the sensuous from thought.

The search for the "clear and distinct," the separating out of the emotional, the sensuous, the imaginative, now makes possible polarizations of previously existing contrasts—intellect versus the emotions; reason versus imagination; mind versus matter. We have seen that the claim that women are somehow lacking in respect of rationality, that they are more impulsive, more emotional, than men is by no means a seventeenth century innovation. But these contrasts were previously contrasts *within* the rational. What ought to be dominated by reason had not previously been so sharply delineated from the intellectual. The conjunction of Cartesian down-grading of the sensuous with the use of the mind-matter distinction to establish the discrete character of Cartesian ideas introduces possibilities of polarization that were not there before.

Another relevant factor here is that shedding the non-intellectual from our mental states is something that demands training. In earlier centuries too, of course, it was thought appropriate to give the education of women a different character from that of men. And it was possible to present this as justified by their being different in respect of rationality. But with the seventeenth century there is a new dimension. Women can now be excluded from training *in* reason, that is, from the acquisition of method. And since this training is explicitly a matter of learning to leave one's emotions, imagination, etc., out of account, there now emerges a new dimension to the idea that women are more emotional or more impulsive, etc., than men. If they are excluded from training in rationality, women are perforce *left* emotional, impulsive, fancy ridden. They are not trained out of the "blundering constructions of the imagination" to enter the rarified air of reason. So thought styles, that are in the seventeenth century sense pre-rational, can survive in women. This *makes* it true, in a way it need not have been before, that women are less rational than men.

Also, it now becomes possible, as it was not before, to have a reasoned basis for assigning the emotions, the imagination, the sensuous in general, to women as their special area of responsibility. The training of a Man of Reason does after all involve getting him to shed many of his normal characteristics. It can now be seen as woman's role to preserve for him the areas of warmth and sensuousness that training in reason demands that he himself transcend. A great deal happens of course between the time of Descartes and that of Rousseau. But we can see this theme, elaborated almost to the point of parody, in Rousseau's views on the education of women in *Emile,* which so outraged Mary Wollstonecraft in the *Vindication of the Rights of Women:*

To be pleasing in his sight, to win his respect and love, to train him in childhood, to tend him in manhood, to counsel and console, to make his life pleasant and happy, these are the duties of woman for all time, and this is what she should be taught while she is young.

Given an already existing situation of sexual inequality, reason — the godlike, the spark of the divine in man — is assigned to the male. The emotions, the imagination, the sensuous are assigned to women.

The contrast involved in the idea that man was made in God's image and woman was made to be a companion for man thus takes on a new dimension in the seventeenth century. We now have a separation of functions backed by a theory of mind. Given an already existing situation of sexual inequality, reason—the godlike, the spark of the divine in man—is assigned to the male. The emotions, the imagination, the sensuous are assigned to women. They are to provide comfort, relief, entertainment and solace for the austerity that being a Man of Reason demands. Something like this had of course been the case before. Different training was given to men and women to fit them for different life styles. But now the transcending of the sensuous can be seen as an end in itself. It is not in order to fit him for the heroic that the Man of Reason is to be trained out of his soft emotions and his sensuousness, but because that is precisely what it is to be rational. The division between reason and the non-rational can now be seen as reflexing and as being reenacted in the division between the sexes—in a way it was not before.

The stage is now set for the emergence of the Man of Reason as a male character ideal.[29]

Although these feminist criticisms are contemporary, there has long been criticism of the notion of the unified "self" in the Eastern religions, as Hesse noted. Around the world, in fact, mystic sects of all faiths have tended toward a different conception of self-identity from that which has been dominant in Western philosophy. Of course, even these mystics admit that people have "personalities" and "egos" in some sense; most people most of the time think of "themselves." Some Eastern religions claim, however, that this vision of "ourselves" is a false image. It is just an illusion which one accepts out of moral weakness or backwardness. Thus, in these Eastern religions the multiple self or the non-self is an ideal understanding which can be achieved only with enlightenment.

An early Buddhist work, for instance, the *Dhammapada* (ca. 250 B.C.), contains several passages about this ideal.

---

[29]Genevieve Lloyd, "The Man of Reason," first published in *Metaphilosophy* 10, 1 (January 1979): 18–37; rpt. in *Women, Knowledge, and Reality: Explorations in Feminist Philosophy,* ed. Ann Garry and Marilyn Pearsall (Boston: Unwin, Hyman, 1989).

FROM **THE *DHAMMAPADA***

CHAPTER XII SELF

Let each man first direct himself to what is proper, then let him teach others; thus a wise man will not suffer.

If a man make himself as he teaches others to be, then, being himself well-subdued, he may subdue others; for one's own self is difficult to subdue.

Self is the lord of self, who else could be the lord? With self well-subdued, a man finds a lord such as few can find.

The evil done by one's self, born of one's self, begotten by one's self, crushes the foolish, as a diamond breaks even a precious stone. . . .

The foolish man who scorns the instruction of the saintly, of the elect [*ariya*], of the virtuous, and follows a false doctrine—he bears fruit to his own destruction, like the fruits of the *Katthaka* reed.

By one's self the evil is done, by one's self one suffers; by one's self evil is left undone; by one's self one is purified. The pure and the impure stand and fall by themselves; no one can purify another.

Let no one forget his own duty for the sake of another's, however great; let a man after he has discerned his own duty, be faithful to his duty.

All forms are unreal—he who knows and sees this is at peace though in a world of pain; this is the way that leads to purity.

He who does not rouse himself when it is time to rise, who, though young and strong, is full of sloth, whose will and thought are weak, that lazy and idle man never finds the way to wisdom.

Watching his speech, well-restrained in mind, let a man never commit any wrong with his body! Let a man but keep these three roads of action clear, and he will achieve the way which is taught by the wise.

Through zeal knowledge is gained, through lack of zeal knowledge is lost; let a man who knows this two-fold path of gain and loss thus place himself that knowledge may grow.

Cut down the whole forest of desires, not a tree only! Danger comes out of the forest of desires. When you have cut down both the forest of desires and its undergrowth, then, *bhikshus,* you will be rid of the forest and of desires!

So long as the desire of man toward women, even the smallest, is not destroyed, so long is his mind in bondage; as the calf that drinks milk is to its mother.

Cut out the love of self, like an autumn lotus with your hand! Cherish the road to peace. Nirvana has been shown by the Blessed One.[30]

The thirteenth poem of the *Tao Te Ching* touches on the same theme:

---

[30] From the *Dhammapada,* parts rpt. in *The Teachings of the Compassionate Buddha: Early Discourses, the Dhammapada, and Later Basic Writings* ed. E. A. Burtt (New York: New American Library, 1955).

TAO TE CHING, 13

Favor and disfavor have been called equal worries,
Success and failure have been called equal ailments.
How can favor and disfavor be called equal worries?

Because winning favor burdens a man
With the fear of losing it.

One who recog-
nizes all men
as members of
his own body
Is a sound man
to guard them.

How can success and failure be called equal ailments?
Because a man thinks of the personal body as self.
When he no longer thinks of the personal body as self,
Neither failure nor success can ail him.
One who knows his lot to be the lot of all other men
Is a safe man to guide them.
One who recognizes all men as members of his own body
Is a sound man to guard them.[31]

These Eastern examples are certainly not the only alternatives to the early modern European notion of the self accepted by Descartes. Islamic, Christian, and Jewish mystics in the West as well as other Eastern traditions also offered alternatives to this conception. There have always been challenges to the notion of a unified self.

SUMMARY AND CONCLUSION

Self-identity is a question of essential properties: What is it about you that makes you a particular person and the same person over time? In this chapter we have reviewed a series of different answers to this question. The tradition from Descartes and Locke to Kant stresses the importance of consciousness in our conception of ourselves, that is, the importance of our minds over our bodies. (Even Hume, who denies that there is a self, is part of this tradition.) Then there is the general question, how much is the self something that we can choose, and how much is it something that is determined for us? Does each person have just one self, one set of essential properties, or might a single "person" be several people, with several selves? Or might there really be no self at all? And how much should we conceive of ourselves as individuals, and how much as organic components of a larger community? None of these questions has any firmly agreed-upon answers, but all of us adopt one view or another, even if just for a short time, every time we attempt to define ourselves or just "be ourselves."

---

[31] From *The Way of Life According to Lao Tzu: An American Version,* trans. Witter Bynner (New York: John Day, 1944).

GLOSSARY

bad faith Sartre's characterization of a person's refusal to accept himself or herself; this sometimes means not accepting the facts that are true about you. More often it means accepting the facts about you as conclusive about your identity, as in the statement "Oh, I couldn't do that, I'm too shy."

continuity (spatiotemporal continuity) The uninterrupted identifiability of an object over time in the same location or in a sequence of tangent locations.

criterion Test or standard.

deconstruction Initiated by Jacques Derrida, a current school of philosophical thought (especially popular among some feminist and African-American thinkers) that encourages critical reading for "cultural bias" and that rejects the idea of the "unified self."

dualism In general, the distinction between mind and body as separate substances, or very different kinds of states and events with radically different properties.

empirical ego All those characteristics of a person that can be discovered through experience and that distinguish each of us from other persons qualitatively; that which makes each of us a particular man or woman and gives us a particular "character." Compare *transcendental ego*.

essence That which is necessary for something to be what it is. The essence of a person is that without which we would not say one is *that* particular person (Fred rather than Mary, for example).

existentialism In Sartre's terms, the philosophy that teaches that "man's existence precedes his essence." That is, people have no given self-identity, they have to choose their identities and work for them through their actions. (Neglect and omission, however, are also actions. One can be a certain type of person just by not bothering to do the appropriate activities.)

facticity Sartre's term (borrowed from Heidegger) for the totality of facts that are true of a person at any given time.

immediate For certain and without need for argument.

incorrigibility Impossible to correct; cannot be mistaken. It has long been argued that our claims about our own mental states are incorrigible—we cannot be mistaken about them.

resemblance Having the same features. All people resemble each other (or at least most do) in having one and only one head; you resemble yourself five years ago in (perhaps) having the same texture hair, the same color eyes, the same fear of spiders, and the same skill at chess.

self-consciousness Being aware of oneself, whether "as others see you" (looking in a mirror or "watching yourself play a role" at a party) or just "looking into yourself" (as when you reflect on your goals in life or wonder, in a moment of philosophical perversity, whether you really exist or not.) Self-consciousness requires having some concept of your "self." Accordingly, it is logically tied to questions of self-identity.

self-identity The way you characterize yourself, either in general (as a human being, as a man or as a woman, as a creature before God or as one among many animals) or in particular (as the person who can run the fastest mile, as an all-"C" student, or as the worst-dressed slob in your class). Self-identity, on this characterization, requires self-consciousness. The self-identity of a person, in other words, is not merely the same as the identity of a "thing," for example, the identity of a human body.

transcendence Sartre's term for a person's plan, ambitions, intentions, and hopes for the future (Do not confuse this use of the word with those introduced in Chapters 3 and 5.)

transcendental ego The bare, logical fact of one's own self-consciousness: Descartes "I think"; the self "behind" all of our experiences; the mental activity that unifies our various thoughts and sensations. (The term comes from Kant's *Critique of Pure Reason*.)

unconscious Freud's famous way of referring to the fact that there are ideas, desires, memories, and experiences in our minds to which we do not have privileged access, which we may be wrong about (and, therefore, about which our claims are not incorrigible), and which may be more evident to other people than to oneself. He also distinguishes a *preconscious* ("the antechamber of consciousness"). Preconscious ideas can be made conscious simply by being attended to. (For example, you do know what the capital of California is, but you weren't conscious of it before I mentioned it; it was preconscious.) Truly unconscious ideas, however, cannot be made conscious, even when one tries to do so.

BIBLIOGRAPHY AND FURTHER READING

A recent anthology on the question of self-identity is J. Perry, *Personal Identity* (New York: Lieber-Atherton, 1975). An extended study of this traditional problem is Sidney Shoemaker, *Self-Knowledge and Self-Identity* (Ithaca, NY: Cornell University Press, 1963). Jean-Paul Sartre's existentialist view of the self is developed in his essay *Transcendence of the Ego* (New York: Noonday, 1957). Hermann Hesse's complex theory of the self is best developed in *Steppenwolf*, rev. ed., trans. Basil Creighton (New York: Holt, Rinehart and Winston, 1970), but it is most simply portrayed in *Siddhartha*, trans. H. Rosner (New York: New Directions, 1951). Further reading in Eastern conceptions of the self may begin with D. Suzuki, *Zen Buddhism*, ed. W. Barrett (New York: Doubleday, 1956) or C. Moore, ed., *The Individual in East and West* (Honolulu: East-West Center Press, 1967). A good introduction of G. W. F. Hegel's very difficult philosophy is the introduction to his lectures on the philosophy of history in his *Reason in History*, trans. R. Hartman (New York: Bobbs-Merrill, 1953).

MIND AND BODY

It is certain that I (that is, my mind, by which I am what I am) is entirely and truly distinct from my body, and may exist without it.

RENÉ DESCARTES

Whatever our attempts to answer the problems of self-identity, they begin with a single "fact," our own consciousness. This was the logical beginning for Descartes, who used the fact of his own consciousness as the starting point for his whole philosophy. It was true for Locke, who argued that our identity is to be found in the continuity of our consciousness rather than in the continuity of our bodies. It was even used by Hume, who used his own consciousness as the basis of his denial that there was any such thing as the self. It was the starting point of Kant's philosophy; his transcendental ego, like Descartes's "I think," gave him the basis for the rest of his philosophy. Even those philosophers who have not been interested in these logical arguments—Buddhists, Marxists, and existentialists—have begun with at least one of a variety of considerations of consciousness; the fact of our own self-consciousness, the facts of consciousness, or just the fact that only people seem capable of or interested in asking the question "Who am I?" But now what is this "consciousness"? As soon as we ask the question, we find ourselves once again up to our eyeballs in the labyrinth of traditional metaphysics.

A. WHAT IS CONSCIOUSNESS?

We can begin to appreciate the problems of consciousness by returning to the attempts of the eighteenth-century rationalist metaphysicians to be clear about their notion of "substance." Descartes said that there were two different kinds of substances; mind or mental substance, and body or physical substance. Accordingly, he is usually called a *dualist* and the position, in general, that mind and body are different substances is called **Cartesian dualism.**[1] You remember that Descartes insisted that his identity was as a "thinking thing," in other words, a mental substance. But now, what of his body? We have seen that he believed that he could intelligibly doubt the existence of his body but not of his mind. But what is so special about this body that, unlike other bodies (the chair in front of him, the body of the king), was so intimately connected to his mind? It moved when he willed it to move, it walked when he decided to walk, it wrote what he wanted to write. In the last of his six *Meditations,* he returns to this problem.

FROM **"MEDITATION VI"**
BY **RENÉ DESCARTES**

Firstly, then, I perceived that I had a head, hands, feet, and other members composing that body which I considered as part, or perhaps even as the whole, of myself. I perceived further, that that body was placed among many others, by which it was capable of being affected in diverse ways, both beneficial and hurtful; and what was beneficial I remarked by a certain sensation of pleasure, and what was hurtful by a sensation of pain. And, besides this pleasure and pain, I was likewise conscious of hunger, thirst, and other appetites, as well as certain corporeal inclinations towards joy, sadness, anger, and similar passions.

◆ ◆ ◆

Nor was I altogether wrong in likewise believing that that body which, by a special right, I called my own, pertained to me more properly and strictly than any of the others; for in truth, I could never be separated from it as from other bodies: I felt in it and on account of it all my appetites and affections, and in fine I was affected in its parts by pain and the titillation of pleasure, and not in the parts of the other bodies that were separated from it. But when I inquired into the reason why, from this I know not what sensation of pain, sadness of mind should follow, and why from the sensation of pleasure joy should arise, or why this indescribable twitching of the stomach, which I call hunger, should put me in mind of taking food, and the parchedness of the throat of drink, and so in other cases, I was unable to give any explanation, unless that I was so taught by nature; for there is assuredly no affinity, at least none that I am able to comprehend, between this irritation of the stomach and the desire of food, any more than between the perception of an object that causes pain and the consciousness of sadness which springs from the perception. And in the same way it seems

---

[1] Named after Descartes. As a matter of fact, Descartes believed that there were three kinds of substances, the third being God. But we need not worry about that third substance at this point. For our purposes, Descartes is simply a dualist.

to me that all the other judgments I had formed regarding the objects of sense, were dictates of nature; because I remarked that those judgments were formed in me, before I had leisure to weigh and consider the reasons that might constrain me to form them.

But, afterwards, a wide experience by degrees sapped the faith I had reposed in my senses; for I frequently observed that towers, which at a distance seemed round, appeared square when more closely viewed, and that colossal figures, raised on the summits of these towers, looked like small statues, when viewed from the bottom of them; and, in other instances without number, I also discovered error in judgments founded on the external senses; and not only in those founded on the external, but even in those that rested on the internal senses; for is there aught more internal than pain? and yet I have sometimes been informed by parties whose arm or leg had been amputated, that they still occasionally seemed to feel pain in that part of the body which they had lost,—a circumstance that led me to think that I could not be quite certain even that any one of my members were affected when I felt pain in it. And to these grounds of doubt I shortly afterwards also added two others of very wide generality: the first of them was that I believed I never perceived anything when awake which I could not occasionally think I also perceived when asleep, and as I do not believe that the ideas I seem to perceive in my sleep proceed from objects external to me, I did not any more observe any ground for believing this of such as I seem to perceive when awake; the second was that since I was as yet ignorant of the author of my being, or at least supposed myself to be so, I saw nothing to prevent my having been so constituted by nature as that I should be deceived even in matters that appeared to me to possess the greatest truth.

♦♦♦

But now that I begin to know myself better, and to discover more clearly the author of my being, I do not, indeed, think that I ought rashly to admit all which the senses seem to teach, nor, on the other hand, is it my conviction that I ought to doubt in general of their teachings.

And, firstly, because I know that all which I clearly and distinctly conceive can be produced by God exactly as I conceive it, it is sufficient that I am able clearly and distinctly to conceive one thing apart from another, in order to be certain that the one is different from the other, seeing they may at least be made to exist separately, by the omnipotence of God; and it matters not by what power this separation is made, in order to be compelled

> *. . . because, on the one hand, I have a clear and distinct idea of myself . . . as . . . only a thinking and unextended thing, and as, on the other hand, I possess a distinct idea of body . . . only an extended and unthinking thing, it is certain that I am entirely and truly distinct from my body, and may exist without it.*

to judge them different; and, therefore, merely because I know with certitude that I exist, and because, in the meantime, I do not observe that aught necessarily belongs to my nature or essence beyond my being a thinking thing, I rightly conclude that my essence consists only in my being a thinking thing [or a substance whose whole essence or nature is merely thinking]. And although I may, or rather, as I will shortly say, although I certainly do possess a body with which I am very closely conjoined; nevertheless, because, on the one hand, I have a clear and distinct idea of myself, in as far as I am only a thinking and unextended thing, and as, on the other hand, I possess a distinct idea of body, in as far as it is only an extended and unthinking thing, it is certain that I [that is, my mind, by which I am what I am] am entirely and truly distinct from my body, and may exist without it.

Then comes Descartes's proof that, in general, he could not be fooled about the existence of bodies "outside" of him.

But there is nothing which that nature teaches me more expressly [or more sensibly] than that I have a body which is ill affected when I feel pain, and stands in need of food and drink when I experience the sensations of hunger and thirst, etc. And therefore I ought not to doubt but that there is some truth in these informations.

Nature likewise teaches me by these sensations of pain, hunger, thirst, etc., that I am not only lodged in my body as a pilot in a vessel, but that I am besides so intimately conjoined, and as it were intermixed with it, that my mind and body compose a certain unity. For if this were not the case, I should not feel pain when my body is hurt, seeing I am merely a thinking thing, but should perceive the wound by the understanding alone, just as a pilot perceives by sight when any part of his vessel is damaged; and when my body has need of food or drink, I should have a clear knowledge of this, and not be made aware of it by the confused sensations of hunger and thirst: for, in truth, all these sensations of hunger, thirst, pain, etc., are nothing more than certain confused modes of thinking, arising from the union and apparent fusion of mind and body.

Besides this, nature teaches me that my own body is surrounded by many other bodies. . . . some are agreeable, and others disagreeable, there can be no doubt that my body, or rather my entire self, in as far as I am composed of body and mind, may be variously affected, both beneficially and hurtfully, by surrounding bodies.[2]

But how can two different substances, particularly two such different kinds of substances, interact? We know what it is for two bodies to interact, but how can a body make contact with a mind, which seems so intangible and "ghostly"? Descartes

---

[2] René Descartes, "Meditation VI," in *Meditations on First Philosophy,* in *The Philosophical Works of Descartes,* trans. Elizabeth S. Haldane and G. R. T. Ross (Cambridge: Cambridge University Press, 1911).

never answers this problem to his or to his critics' satisfaction. Spinoza, seeing Descartes's troubles, insists that there is only one substance and that body and mind are but different "attributes" of that one substance. That avoids the metaphysical question, for there is no trouble about interaction within a substance. But it still leaves a sizable problem, namely, how these two attributes are coordinated. That is a question Spinoza never answers; and Leibniz, attacking the same problem, finds it preferable to deny the reality of physical substance altogether. There are only mental substances, monads, each locked into its own experience. The extravagance of these two solutions should give you some idea of the difficulty of the problem.

We can get a more specific clue to the mysterious quality of "consciousness" if we consider the following. Descartes, Spinoza, and Leibniz, you recall, define mind as "unextended," that is, unextended in space. (Bodies, on the other hand, are defined as extended in space.) In other words, it is essential that minds, unlike bodies, cannot be said to be "this large" or to be located in such and such a place. But despite this definition, notice how much of our talk about consciousness consists of metaphors of spatial form; we talk about something being "in" our minds. We talk about something "slipping (out of) our minds." Philosophers often talk about the "contents" of consciousness, and a popular phrase from William James is the "stream of consciousness." Now we might say, "those are just metaphors"; but why are such metaphors necessary?

How would you answer the question "What is it to be conscious?" You might say something about "awareness" or "feelings," but that only restates the problem with different words. When we try to describe an image we do so in terms appropriate to physical things (namely, what it is an image *of*). We try to describe a pain and come out with metaphors ("it's as if a vice were closing on my head") or comparisons ("it feels the same as when . . ."). The retreat to spatial metaphors reflects this difficulty. We talk about our experiences as if we were describing other things but then qualify our descriptions by saying that they are "in" consciousness rather than in the world.

How can we describe consciousness itself? There is a further difficulty: If I can talk about my mind only with difficulty, how can I talk about your mind at all? I can experience only what is "in" my mind, I can't feel your pain. Even if I feel "sympathy pains" with you, it is my pain I feel. So I can't describe your mind at all, and evidently I have difficulty describing my mind as well. Therefore, how can we talk about "mind" at all? Not surprisingly, many psychologists and philosophers have rejected the idea of "mind" altogether, preferring to talk only about what is mutually observable and "extended" in physical space (for example, neurology and overt behavior).

We shall later consider some of these attempts to reject the idea of "mind" altogether. But what should seem fairly obvious to you is that this idea can be rejected only with reference to other people, not with reference to ourselves. *Why? Because of Descartes's first premise, to put it bluntly.* The same logic that allows him to assert with certainty "I am thinking" and "I exist as a thinking thing" now forces us to admit that "I am not thinking" and "I am not a thinking thing" are utterly absurd and unintelligible statements. They are self-refuting in exactly the same sense that "I am thinking" is self-confirming. (This isn't to say that you are thinking clearly, or well, or enjoying it; only that, in some minimal sense, you are thinking.) Therefore, you must have a mind. In one's own case, the fact that a person is conscious is the last thing one could ever deny.

It is important to appreciate the fact that Descartes did not defend the idea of a radical difference between mind and body only as a metaphysical or scientific thesis. There is much in "common sense" that supports it, and the separation of mind or soul from physical body obviously serves a long-standing religious concern as well. It makes sense of the thesis that the soul might survive the body after death, and it safely separates the realms of religion and science. It even provides an argument for the necessity of God's existence. Descartes points out (in Meditation III) that his various fleeting thoughts could not be unified into a coherent, enduring self without the intervention of a higher power.

FROM "MEDITATION III" BY DESCARTES

Because the entire period of one's life can be divided into countless parts, each of which in no way depends on the others, it does not follow from the fact that I existed a short while ago that I now ought to exist, unless some cause creates me once again, as it were, at this moment—that is to say, preserves me. For it is obvious to one who is cognizant of the nature of time that the same force and action is needed to preserve anything at all during the individual moments that it lasts as is needed to create that same thing anew—if it should happen not yet to exist. It is one of those things that is manifest by the light of nature that preservation differs from creation solely by virtue of a distinction of reason.

Therefore I ought now to ask myself whether I have some power through which I can bring it about that I myself, who now am, will also exist a little later? Because I am nothing but a thing that thinks—or at least because I am now dealing only with precisely that part of me that is a thing that thinks—if such a power were in me, then I would certainly be aware of it. But I observe that there is no such power; from this fact I know most evidently that I depend upon a being other than myself.

And in the dedication of the same work, he writes,

And as to the soul: although many have regarded its nature as incapable of easy inquiry, and some have gone so far as to say that human reasoning convinces them that the soul dies with the body, and that the contrary is to be held on faith alone; nevertheless, because the Lateran Council under Leo X, in Session 8, condemned these people and explicitly enjoined Christian philosophers to refute their arguments and to use all their abilities to make the truth known, I too have not hesitated to go forward with this.[3]

---

[3] René Descartes, "Letter of Dedication to the Dean and Doctors of the Faculty of Sacred Theology of Paris," in *Meditations on First Philosophy,* trans. Donald A. Cress (Indianapolis: Hackett, 1979).

B. THE PROBLEM OF DUALISM

How is consciousness connected to your body? You decide to raise your hand, and your hand goes up. You formulate an answer to your friend's question, and it comes out of your mouth. How does what takes place "in your mind" determine what happens with your body? A familiar image, borrowed from untold numbers of cartoons, is the little man (or woman) in your head, operating your body as a construction worker operates a giant steam shovel. But this is no answer at all. First, there is no little man. But even if there were, the same problem would then focus on him (or her). How does he or she move a body by making certain mental decisions? The same problem arises in the other direction, from body to mind. A friend steps on your toe—your physiology teacher can explain to you what happens: nerves are pinched and signals are sent through your central nervous system into that huge complex of fat cells called your brain. But then, at some point, there is something else, the feeling, the pain. How does this happen? How does a feeling emerge from that complex and still unknown network of neurological reactions going on in your body?

You can see that this problem of **mind-body interaction** is no longer just a technical metaphysical problem having to do with the special notion of substance. The problem of "interaction" is the same for Spinoza and his one substance as it is for Descartes and his dualism. Even if you don't want to talk of substances at all, there is still the problem of explaining how your mind affects your body and how your body affects your mind. For whether or not you accept the special problems of the eighteenth-century metaphysicians, you have to admit that your mind is very different from your body, and that is the source of the trickiest of all modern philosophy problems—the **mind-body problem.** How are mind and body related?

The human body, like any other physical body, can be described in terms of its size, weight, chemical composition, and movements in space. The workings of the human nervous system, although very complex and not yet adequately understood, can be described just like any other biological reaction, in terms of the changes in cell membranes and chemical reactions, the procession of chemoelectric nerve "impulses," and the computer-like network of different nerve components that are stimulated at any given time. The human brain can be seen as a complex machine, like a gooey computer. The human mind, however, is not to be characterized in any such spatial or chemical terms. The mind is not the same as the brain. It has no shape, no weight, and has the awkward property of being observable—in any particular case—by one and only one person. (Anyone can see my brain if they can get inside my skull.) We can understand how a body might interact with another body, even when the "forces" involved are hard to picture (for example, the gravitational attraction between two distant planets). But how does a body interact with something that has none of the crucial characteristics of a body? You might think of "energy" here, for energy would seem to have at least some of the intangible and "unextended" features of mind. It too, in a very limited sense, "has no size or weight." But energy is a function of physical bodies, force is a function of mass and acceleration. They are not, like our experiences, "private": a lightning bolt is observable to anyone who looks. And no one has ever claimed that descriptions of energy states, like descriptions of our ideas, are incorrigible. While it has often been demonstrated (by

Einstein) that energy and mass are interconvertible, any such "interconvertibility" of mind and matter is still at the highly speculative stage, limited to freak performances by a few isolated and not wholly dependable "psychics" and such. We may well talk about "mental energy," but it is far from clear what we mean. (The fact that transcendental meditation gives us more of "whatever it is" only proves that we don't yet know what meditation is either.)

How can something so different as ideas and sensations interact with nervous systems and brain cells? Philosophers have proposed a number of solutions, all of them controversial and none of them yet satisfactory. But even before we look at some of them, it is important to stress the following point: The "mind-body problem" is not simply a matter of how little we still know about the human nervous system. No matter how our knowledge develops, we will still be faced with that mysterious gap between the last known neurological occurrence and the experience. Right now we can trace our neural impulses only so far, and the "last known neurological occurrence" is not very far along. But even when we have complete "brain maps" and can say for every mental occurrence what is going on in the brain at the same time, the problem will still remain: How are the two related?[4]

Here is a recent review of the problem from *The Economist:*

"A TOUR OF THE BRAIN"
FROM *THE ECONOMIST*

Raise a glass to René Descartes, who was born 400 years ago in the village of La Haye below the vineyards of the Loire. If provocation is a test of great philosophy, Descartes belongs with the elect. By the time he died of pneumonia in Stockholm in 1650 he had bequeathed the modern version of two deep but simple questions. Are minds and bodies distinct? If so, how do they interact? There are still no good answers. But spurred by recent work in neuroscience and artificial intelligence today's philosophers are trying harder than ever to find some. . . .

A TOUR THROUGH THE BRAIN

Suppose in the year 3001, your science museum offers a show, "The Mystery of Consciousness Revealed." You take a virtual-reality tour through a model brain showing how electroneural activity creates subjective experiences. "Look," says the guide, "those sparks there are déjà-vu. The pink lights are memories

---

[4] Scientific research could show, although it is extremely unlikely, that the brain and our mind have very little to do with each other, that the presumed coordination between the two does not exist. It once was thought, for example, that the heart had to do with emotions (Aristotle and Descartes, for example). Science has proved them wrong. But science cannot do more than lay the groundwork for the problem. It cannot solve it.

of eating papaya, the green ones, guava." You can wire yourself up to deep brain scans and watch yourself think: those 65-hertz oscillations are "Oops, I forgot the gas bill" and that tremor of grey stuff is your fretting about consciousness. Amazingly, anything in your mind shows up somehow on the screen.

After the tour, the guide hands out comment cards asking, "Did our tour explain consciousness to your satisfaction?" You have to answer yes or no and you cannot, for the moment, fuss about the assumptions behind the question or the details of the show. In your reply you will inevitably gravitate to one of the two great poles on the mind-body problem: yea-saying, physics-can-explain-mind materialism and nay-saying, mind-is-special dualism.

Memory is not contemporary philosophy's strong point. The world has not always believed in the superiority of the spirit. Modern as it sounds, the idea that "*Mind* is second-class matter" (as the American postal information for Britain's best-known philosophy magazine nicely had it) is very old. The belief that matter is basic and that mind comes after or on top was a favourite of the early Greeks. It irked Plato who insisted that people had souls that survived bodily death. Aristotle countered that separating mind and body was like trying to prise a coin's imprint from its wax—a potent image, suggestively equating mind with form or structure. Yet Aristotle recoiled from the atomism of Democritus, who held that the soul was made of matter. To him and to the Epicureans, the universe contained just matter in different mixtures. Epicureanism, which entailed denial of an afterlife, became notorious to Christians and its adepts were confined to living graves in Dante's sixth circle of hell.

Yet it was not fear of the inferno that led Descartes to dualism. He was a man of science and mathematics. People's bodies, he said, were machines. He would have liked to say the same about minds. Yet he was true also to a profound and seemingly universal conviction. When you look into yourself you are aware of something special and private, something with no position in space and something whose contents cannot be gainsaid but are known to you directly and have a distinct, subjective feel: your mind.[5]

If materialism attracts you—remember, these are rough-and-ready labels— you are in the company of many of the grand figures of modern English-speaking philosophy. Their outlook is rooted in a philosophical naturalism: as part of nature, humans are objects of science and any human phenomenon, including "the phenomenal" (subjective experience), has a material cause. Despite its successes elsewhere, as regards the mind this outlook is still a programme, not a result. Unfortunately, not all materialists admit this. Partly from the sensible philosophical habit of testing a good insight to breaking point and partly from sheer technohype, philosophers like Paul Churchland and Mr. Dennett often talk as if victory were already at hand: brains are to minds, they have said in effect, as computers are to processing; the mystery of consciousness is solved.

---

[5] "Science Does It With Feeling," *The Economist,* July 20, 1996, pp. 71–73.

So if materialism repels you or if you think that the museum "explanation" of the mind leaves something vital out, you are also in good company. Must sound explanations of the mind come from hard science? Even if computing does prove a good model for thinking, can it be right for feeling and experience? How can brain activity be all there is to twinges of pain or sensations of colour? Questions like that are being put with new sharpness as some of the snags with earlier or cruder versions of materialism are re-exposed.

The classic attempt to resolve the problem of dualism is by Descartes. The following selection is from his essay "The Passions of the Soul."

FROM **"THE PASSIONS OF THE SOUL"**
BY **DESCARTES**

But in order to understand all these things more perfectly, we must know that the soul is really joined to the whole body, and that we cannot, properly speaking, say that it exists in any one of its parts to the exclusion of the others, because it is one and in some manner indivisible, owing to the disposition of its organs, which are so related to one another that when any one of them is removed, that renders the whole body defective; and because it is of a nature which has no relation to extension, nor dimensions, nor other properties of the matter of which the body is composed, but only to the whole conglomerate of its organs, as appears from the fact that we could not in any way conceive of the half or the third of a soul, nor of the space it occupies, and because it does not become smaller owing to the cutting off of some portion of the body, but separates itself from it entirely when the union of its assembled organs is dissolved.

> *. . . the soul is really joined to the whole body, and . . . we cannot, properly speaking, say that it exists in any one of its parts to the exclusion of the others . . .*

It is likewise necessary to know that although the soul is joined to the whole body, there is yet in that a certain part in which it exercises its functions more particularly than in all the others; and it is usually believed that this part is the brain, or possibly the heart: the brain, because it is with it that the organs of sense are connected, and the heart because it is apparently in it that we experience the passions. But, in examining the matter with care, it seems as though I had clearly ascertained that the part of the body in which the soul exercises its functions immediately is in nowise the heart, nor the whole of the brain, but merely the most inward of all its parts, to wit, a certain very small gland which is situated in the middle of its substance and so suspended above the duct whereby the animal spirits in its anterior cavities have communication with those in the posterior, that the slightest movements which take place in it may alter very greatly the course of these spirits; and reciprocally that the smallest changes which occur in the course of the spirits may do much to change the movements of this gland.[6]

◆◆◆

Let us then conceive here that the soul has its principal seat in the little gland that exists in the middle of the brain, from whence it radiates forth through all the remainder of the body by means of the animal spirits, nerves, and even the blood, which, participating in the impressions of the spirits, can carry them by the arteries into all the members. Recollecting what has been said above about the machine of our body, that is, that the little filaments of our nerves are so distributed in all its parts, that on the occasion of the diverse movements which are there excited by sensible objects, they open in diverse ways the pores of the brain, which causes the animal spirits contained in these cavities to enter in diverse ways into the muscles, by which means they are capable of being moved; and also that all the other causes which are capable of moving the spirits in diverse ways suffice to conduct them into diverse muscles; let us here add that the small gland which is the main seat of the soul is so suspended between the cavities which contain the spirits that it can be moved by them in as many different ways as there are sensible diversities in the object, but that it may also be moved in diverse ways by the soul, whose nature is such that it receives in itself as many diverse impressions, that is to say, that it possesses as many diverse perceptions as there are diverse moments in this gland. Reciprocally, likewise, the machine of the body is so formed that from the simple fact that this gland is diversely moved by the soul, or by such other cause, whatever it is, it thrusts the spirits which surround it towards the pores of the brain, which conduct them by the nerves into the muscles, by which means it causes them to move the limbs.[7]

The technical name given to this theory is **causal interactionism,** in other words, mental changes cause bodily changes and vice versa. Unlike his followers, Descartes did not take seriously the problem of separate substances or radically different changes causally affecting one another. He apparently felt satisfied if not exactly comfortable, with such a causal account. He was vigorously attacked in this by most of his immediate followers, including Spinoza, Leibniz, and many of the empiricists. "Different substances cannot interact," they insisted. Or, in more modern dress, they argued that only physical bodies can causally interact, not anything so different as physical bodies and minds. Yet one thing remains obvious, and that is that the

---

[6] The gland Descartes is referring to is what is now called the Pineal Gland, a small endocrine gland at the base of the brain. It had only recently been discovered in Descartes's time, and its functions are still not adequately understood. It is currently hypothesized that it controls mating cycles in higher animals and possibly any number of other activity cycles.

[7] René Descartes, "The Passions of the Soul," in *The Philosophical Works of Descartes.*

familiar coordination of our mental activities and the movements of our bodies must be accounted for. To do so, without bringing in causal interaction, required considerable ingenuity on the part of Descartes' critics.

We have already seen the two metaphysical alternatives that immediately followed Descartes. The first was formulated by Leibniz as part of his overall theory of monads. He insisted that there could be no causal interaction between monads, and specifically, there could be no sense made out of the claim that mental substances interacted with anything that we call "physical bodies." So what could he suggest as an alternative? His answer to the problem was that God, who had created monads in the first place, had also "programmed" them in such a way that our mental activities and what we call our bodily activities are exactly coordinated. Leaving aside the rest of Leibniz's theory and looking just at the mind—body problem, we can restate his solution as a form of what is called **parallelism.** His "pre-established harmony" between monads can now be viewed as the somewhat strange theory that our mental lives and the movements of our bodies are exactly coordinated (so that I feel pain when you step on my toe and so that my hand goes up just when I "decide" that it should). Yet there is no causal interaction between them whatsoever. It is like the sound and visual tracks of a movie film, moving along exactly parallel but never in fact interacting. (That is, the character who appears to be talking in the movie does not cause the sounds that you hear as if he or she were producing them. The sounds are actually produced separately and would continue even if the projector bulb burned out and the figure on the screen disappeared altogether.) Of course, to accept this theory you must also accept the considerable metaphysical and theological supports that it requires. If you don't believe in a God who could set up this complex system, there is absolutely no way of explaining the remarkable coordination of mind and body. Even if you do believe in God, you may well think that the mind-body problem requires some more plausible and secular solution.

Spinoza's theory need not be kept in the "one substance" metaphysics that he used to present it. In fact, much the same theory was defended only a few years ago by Bertrand Russell, without reference to the metaphysical notion of substance at all. Russell said, as Spinoza had said centuries before, that mind and body, mental events and physical changes, were different aspects of one and the same "something." For Spinoza, the "something" was "the one substance" and the aspects were what he called "attributes." Russell claimed only that our experiences and ideas were one aspect of some events or activities of which the various chemical reactions of the brain were another aspect. Accordingly, the theory has often been called the **dual aspect theory,** whether or not it is specifically addressed to the problem of substances and their attributes. Since we are now talking about two "aspects" of the same thing rather than two different things, the problem of interaction doesn't arise. But, as we complained before, this only hides the problem rather than solves it. What is this mysterious "something" of which mind and body are merely "aspects"? It is neither brain nor mind, so what could it be? By the nature of the case, we can't find out, which leaves us with the equally embarrassing question, "How could one and the same thing have such different aspects?" You might say, "Well, a hot coal has both 'aspects' of being heavy and being hot." But that we can explain. What are we to say of a "something" that is neither brain nor mind but both?

C. THE REJECTION OF DUALISM

If the problem is dualism, then perhaps the answer is the rejection of dualism. Of course, we still have to account for the obvious facts of the case: that we feel something when certain things happen to our bodies, that we do something when we mentally decide to. But philosophers of recent years—and nearly all psychologists—have taken a dim view toward dualism in all of the above forms.

A first, still timid step towards eliminating dualism consists of minimizing, though not rejecting, the mental side of dualism. This theory is usually called **epiphenomenalism,** and William James was one of its best-known defenders. Epiphenomenalism allows for causal interaction, but only in one direction. Bodies and changes in bodies cause mental events. You might think of a boiler system or automobile engine equipped with various gauges to tell us how the machine is functioning at any given time. The machine works on, registering certain results on the attached gauges. But notice that the gauge is relatively unimportant to the working of the machine. In fact, the gauge can break and the machine can function for years. What is the significance of such a theory? Many philosophers and psychologists are interested primarily in the continuity of physical and physiological laws without the problematic disruption of mysterious "mental causes." For them, such a theory allows them to concentrate wholly on the physical side of the matter and ignore "the mind" completely. If an objection is raised one can always insist: "Oh, I'm not denying that you feel something too." But this is an unimportant detail, a side-product, an epiphenomenon, that need not be taken all that seriously.

1. Radical Behaviorism

Epiphenomenalism is a timid rejection of dualism. It doesn't actually reject dualism, but it minimizes one half the duality. Other forms of attack are not so timid. In psychology, many authors have long accepted that all talk of "the mental" is a hopeless tangle of confusions that, by the nature of the case, cannot be resolved through any experiment whatsoever. (That is, only one person could observe the results of the experiment in any given case, and the very nature of a scientific experiment is that it must be observable by anyone.) Accordingly, many psychologists have followed the American theorist **John Watson** in practicing what they call **behaviorism.**

Today the best-known behaviorist is the late psychologist **B. F. Skinner.** Behaviorism, as a form of science, refuses to even consider any events that cannot be publicly witnessed. That immediately and logically excludes mental events. Behaviorism is primarily a scientific method and need not deny the existence of mental events. Most behaviorists, however, have gone beyond the method—which only says that they will not scientifically study such events—and have done a bit of meta-physics as well; they also deny that there can be any mental events. Watson, for example, goes so far as to suggest that belief in consciousness goes back to the ancient days of superstition and magic. He insists that any good behaviorist can catch the average undergraduate student in a mess of tongue-tied contradictions but concludes from this not that our concept of consciousness is complicated and confused but rather that there could not possibly be any such thing. His argument is self-consciously "scientific," the alternative to which is being a mere "savage and still believing in magic." His test is simply whether the soul (philosophers and psychologists often shift too easily between "soul" and "consciousness") can be experienced; "no one has ever touched a soul, or seen one in a test tube, or has in any other way come into relationship with it as he has with the other objects of his daily experience."[8] Thus Watson shifts from his view as a scientist, able to write about only what he can measure and observe, to a view as a metaphysician, insisting that there cannot be any such thing as consciousness and that no rational person should believe that there is.

2. Logical Behaviorism

Philosophers too have turned to behaviorism as a way of escaping the problems of Cartesian dualism. Oxford philosopher **Gilbert Ryle,** following some suggestions by Ludwig Wittgenstein, established a new form of behaviorism—*logical* behaviorism—in his book *The Concept of Mind* (1949). Its first chapter is appropriately called "Descartes' Myth." First he describes what he calls "the official doctrine":

"DESCARTES' MYTH"
BY **GILBERT RYLE**

There is a doctrine about the nature and place of minds which is so prevalent among theorists and even among laymen that it deserves to be described as the official theory. Most philosophers, psychologists and religious teachers subscribe, with minor reservations, to its main articles and, although they admit certain theoretical difficulties in it, they tend to assume that these can be overcome without serious modifications being made to the architecture of the theory. It will be argued here that the central principles of the doctrine are unsound and conflict with the whole body of what we know about minds when we are not speculating about them.

The official doctrine, which hails chiefly from Descartes, is something like this. With the doubtful exceptions of idiots and infants in arms every human being has both a body and a mind. Some would prefer to say that every human being has both a body and a mind. His body and his mind are ordinarily

---

[8] John Watson, *Behaviorism* (New York: Norton, 1930).

harnessed together, but after the death of the body his mind may continue to exist and function.

Human bodies are in space and are subject to the mechanical laws which govern all other bodies in space. Bodily processes and states can be inspected by external observers. So a man's bodily life is as much a public affair as are the lives of animals and reptiles and even as the careers of trees, crystals and plants.

But minds are not in space, nor are their operations subject to mechanical laws. The workings of one mind are not witnessable by other observers; its career is private. Only I can take direct cognisance of the states and processes of my own mind. A person therefore lives through two collateral histories, one consisting of what happens in and to his body, the other consisting of what happens in and to his mind. The first is public, the second private. The events in the first history are events in the physical world, those in the second are events in the mental world.

It has been disputed whether a person does or can directly monitor all or only some of the episodes of his own private history; but, according to the official doctrine, of at least some of these episodes he has direct and unchallengeable cognisance. In consciousness, self-consciousness and introspection he is directly and authentically apprised of the present states and operations of his mind. He may have great or small uncertainties about concurrent and adjacent episodes in the physical world, but he can have none about at least part of what is momentarily occupying his mind.

It is customary to express this bifurcation of his two lives and of his two worlds by saying that the things and events which belong to the physical world, including his own body, are external, while the workings of his own mind are internal. This antithesis of outer and inner is of course meant to be construed as a metaphor, since minds, not being in space, could not be described as being spatially inside anything else, or as having things going on spatially inside themselves. But relapses from this good intention are common and theorists are found speculating how stimuli, the physical sources of which are yards or miles outside a person's skin, can generate mental responses inside his skull, or how decisions framed inside his cranium can set going movements of his extremities.

Even when "inner" and "outer" are construed as metaphors, the problem of how a person's mind and body influence one another is notoriously charged with theoretical difficulties. What the mind wills, the legs, arms and the tongue execute; what affects the ear and the eye has something to do with what the mind perceives; grimaces and smiles betray the mind's moods and bodily castigations lead, it is hoped, to moral improvement. But the actual transactions between the episodes of the private history and those of the public history remain mysterious, since by definition they can belong to neither series. They could not be reported among the happenings described in a person's autobiography of his inner life, but nor could they be reported among those described in someone else's biography of that person's overt career. They can be inspected neither by introspection nor by laboratory experiment. They are theoretical shuttlecocks which are forever being bandied from the physiologist back to the psychologist and from the psychologist back to the physiologist.

Underlying this partly metaphorical representation of the bifurcation of a person's two lives there is a seemingly more profound and philosophical assumption. It is assumed that there are two different kinds of existence or status. What exists or happens may have the status of physical existence, or it may have the status of mental existence. Somewhat as the faces of coins are either heads or tails, or somewhat as living creatures are either male or female, so, it is supposed, some existing is physical existing, other existing is mental existing. It is a necessary feature of what has physical existence that it is in space and time; it is a necessary feature of what has mental existence that it is in time but not in space. What has physical existence is composed of matter, or else is a function of matter; what has mental existence consists of consciousness, or else is a function of consciousness. . . .

What sort of knowledge can be secured of the workings of a mind? On the one side, according to the official theory, a person has direct knowledge of the best imaginable kind of the workings of his own mind. Mental states and processes are (or are normally) conscious states and processes, and the consciousness which irradiates them can engender no illusions and leaves the door open for no doubts. A person's present thinkings, feelings and willings, his perceivings, rememberings and imaginings are intrinsically "phosphorescent"; their existence and their nature are inevitably betrayed to their owner. The inner life is a stream of consciousness of such a sort that it would be absurd to suggest that the mind whose life is that stream might be unaware of what is passing down it. . . .

On the other side, one person has no direct access of any sort to the events of the inner life of another. He cannot do better than make problematic inferences from the observed behaviour of the other person's body to the states of mind which, by analogy from his own conduct, he supposes to be signalised by that behaviour. Direct access to the workings of a mind is the privilege of that mind itself; in default of such privileged access, the workings of one mind are inevitably occult to everyone else. For the supposed arguments from bodily movements similar to their own to mental workings similar to their own would lack any possibility of observational corroboration. Not unnaturally, therefore, an adherent of the official theory finds it difficult to resist this consequence of his premises, that he has no good reason to believe that there do exist minds other than his own. Even if he prefers to believe that to other human bodies there are harnessed minds not unlike his own, he cannot claim to be able to discover their individual characteristics, or the particular things that they undergo and do. Absolute solitude is on this showing the ineluctable destiny of the soul. Only our bodies can meet.

Then, in section 2, Ryle argues that the "official doctrine" is "absurd" and is based upon what he calls "a category mistake":

Such in outline is the official theory. I shall often speak of it with deliberate abusiveness, as "the dogma of the Ghost in the Machine." I hope to prove that it is entirely false, and false not in detail but in principle. It is not merely an assemblage of particular mistakes. It is one big mistake and a mistake of a special kind. It is, namely, a category-mistake. It represents the facts of mental life as if they belonged to one logical type of category (or range of types or categories), when they actually belong to another. The dogma is therefore a philosopher's myth. In attempting to explode the myth I shall probably be taken to be denying well-known facts about the mental life of human beings, and my plea that I aim to do nothing more than rectify the logic of mental-conduct concepts will probably be disallowed as mere subterfuge.

I must first indicate what is meant by the phrase "Category-mistake." This I do in a series of illustrations.

A foreigner visiting Oxford or Cambridge for the first time is shown a number of colleges, libraries, playing fields, museums, scientific departments and administrative offices. He then asks "But where is the university? I have seen where the members of the Colleges live, where the Registrar works, where the scientists experiment and the rest. But I have not yet seen the University in which reside and work the members of your University." It has then to be explained to him that the University is not another collateral institution, some ulterior counterpart to the colleges, laboratories and offices which he has seen. The University is just the way in which all that he has already seen is organized. When they are seen and when their coordination is understood, the University has been seen. His mistake lay in his innocent assumption that it was correct to speak of Christ Church, the Bodleian Library, the Ashmolean Museum *and* the University, to speak, that is, as if "the University" stood for an extra member of the class of which these other units are members. He was mistakenly allocating the University to the same category as that to which the other institutions belong. . . .

One more illustration. A foreigner watching his first game of cricket learns what are the functions of the bowlers, the batsmen, the fielders, the umpires and the scorers. He then says "But there is no one left on the field to contribute the famous element of team-spirit. I see who does the bowling, the batting and the wicket-keeping; but I do not see whose role it is to exercise *esprit de corps.*" Once more, it would have to be explained that he was looking for the wrong type of thing. Team-spirit is not another cricketing-operation supplementary to all of the other special tasks. It is, roughly, the keenness with which each of the special tasks is performed, and performing a task keenly is not performing two tasks. Certainly exhibiting team-spirit is not the same thing as bowling or catching, but nor is it a third thing such that we can say that the bowler first bowls *and* then exhibits team-spirit or that a fielder is at a given moment *either* catching *or* displaying *esprit de corps.*

These illustrations of category-mistakes have a common feature which must be noticed. The mistakes were made by people who did not know how to wield the concepts *University . . .* and *team-spirit.* Their puzzles arose from inability to use certain items in the English vocabulary.[9]

A **category mistake,** in general, is mistaking one *type* of thing for another. For example, it would be a category mistake to ask, "what color is the number 3?" The philosophically interesting mistakes, of course, are neither so obvious nor so silly as the above examples. They are mistakes made when we try to think abstractly. Most important are the category mistakes that philosophers make when they talk about "the mind":

> My destructive purpose is to show that a family of radical category-mistakes is the source of the double-life theory. The representation of a person as a ghost mysteriously ensconced in a machine derives from this argument. Because, as is true, a person's thinking, feeling and purposive doing cannot be described solely in the idioms of physics, chemistry and physiology, therefore they must be described in counterpart idioms. As the human body is a complex organised unit, so the human mind must be another complex organized unit, though one made of a different sort of stuff and with a different sort of structure. Or, again, as the human body, like any other parcel of matter, is a field of causes and effects, so the mind must be another field of causes and effects, though not (Heaven be praised) mechanical causes and effects.

This disastrous category mistake, which Ryle attributes primarily to Descartes, is thinking that "the mind" and its events are some strange and mysteriously private sort of *thing* behind our behavior, when, in fact, mind is the *pattern* of our behavior and not "behind" behavior at all.

. . . the phrase "there occur mental processes" does not mean the same sort of thing as "there occur physical processes," and, therefore . . . it makes no sense to conjoin or disjoin the two.

When two terms belong to the same category, it is proper to construct conjunctive propositions embodying them. Thus a purchaser may say that he bought a left-hand glove and a right-hand glove, but not that he bought a left-hand glove, a right-hand glove and a pair of gloves. "She came home in a flood of tears and a sedan-chair" is a well-known joke based on the absurdity of conjoining terms of different types. It would have been equally ridiculous to construct the disjunction "She came home either in a flood of tears or else in a sedan-chair." Now the dogma of the Ghost in the Machine does just this. It maintains that there exist both bodies and minds; that there occur physical processes and mental processes; that there are mechanical causes of corporeal movements and

---

[9] Gilbert Ryle, *The Concept of Mind* (New York: Barnes & Noble, 1949).

mental causes of corporeal movements. I shall argue that these and other analogous conjunctions are absurd; but, it must be noticed, the argument will not show that either of the illegitimately conjoined propositions is absurd in itself. I am not, for example, denying that there occur mental processes. Doing long division is a mental process and so is making a joke. But I am saying that the phrase "there occur mental processes" does not mean the same sort of thing as "there occur physical processes," and, therefore, that it makes no sense to conjoin or disjoin the two.[10]

The key to Ryle's analysis is what he calls a disposition. A **disposition** is a tendency for something to happen given certain conditions. For example, we say that "if the lever is disturbed, the mousetrap will snap closed." The key is the "*if . . . then*" (or "hypothetical") form of the statement. Ryle explains this in the following way:

There are at least two quite different senses in which an occurrence is said to be "explained"; and there are correspondingly at least two quite different senses in which we ask "why" it occurred and two quite different senses in which we say that it happened "because" so and so was the case. The first sense is the causal sense. To ask why the glass broke is to ask what caused it to break, and we explain, in this sense, the fracture of the glass when we report that a stone hit it. The "because" clause in the explanation reports an event, namely the event which stood to the fracture of the glass as cause to effect.

But very frequently we look for and get explanations of occurrences in another sense of "explanation." We ask why the glass shivered when struck by the stone and we get the answer that it was because the glass was brittle. Now "brittle" is a dispositional adjective; that is to say, to describe the glass as brittle is to assert a general hypothetical proposition about the glass. So when we say that the glass broke when struck because it was brittle, the "because" clause does not report a happening or a cause; it states a law-like proposition. People commonly say of explanations of this second kind that they give the "reason" for the glass breaking when struck.

How does the law-like general hypothetical proposition work? It says, roughly, that the glass, *if* sharply struck or twisted, etc. *would* not dissolve or stretch or evaporate but fly into fragments. The matter of fact that the glass did at a particular moment fly into fragments, when struck by a particular stone, is explained, in this sense of "explain," when the first happening, namely the impact of the stone, satisfies the protasis of the general hypothetical proposition, and when the second happening, namely the fragmentation of the glass, satisfies its apodosis.

He then applies this concept of disposition to his analysis of "mind." (This occupies him for most of his book.) The main idea is this: Everything "mental" is really a

---

[10] Ryle, *The Concept of Mind.*

disposition to behave in certain ways. Consider, for example, his brief analysis of acting from vanity:

> The statement "he boasted from vanity" ought, on one view, to be construed as saying that "he boasted and the cause of his boasting was the occurrence in him of a particular feeling or impulse of vanity." On the other view, it is to be construed as saying "he boasted on meeting the stranger and his doing so satisfies the law-like proposition that whenever he finds a chance of securing the admiration and envy of others, he does whatever he thinks will produce this admiration and envy."

Then the general argument:

> To say that a person knows something, or aspires to be something, is not to say that he is at a particular moment in process of doing or undergoing anything, but that he is able to do certain things, when the need arises, or that he is prone to do and feel certain things in situations of certain sorts. . . .
> Abandonment of the two-worlds legend involves the abandonment of the idea that there is a locked door and a still to be discovered key. Those human actions and reactions, those spoken and unspoken utterances, those tones of voice, facial expressions and gestures, which have always been the data of all the other students of men, have, after all, been the right and the only manifestations to study. They and they alone have merited, but fortunately not received, the grandiose title "mental phenomena." [11]

Ryle's (and Wittgenstein's) logical behaviorism differs from the radical behaviorism of the psychologists in that it is not a theory about behavior and its causes so much as it is a theory about the language of mind, about the meaning of "mentalistic" terms such as "wants," "believes," "hurts," "loves," "feels," and "thinks." Ryle's basic thesis, stripped of his polemic against "the ghost in the machine," is that applying a mental term—attributing a mental property to a person—is logically equivalent to saying that the person will act in a certain way. The advantage of this is that it eliminates all mysterious things mental by translating the mental terminology into statements about behavior, not "inner events." Instead of thinking of love as "a feeling deep inside," for example, the logical behaviorist would say, unromantically perhaps, that "John loves Mary" means that John will be with Mary every chance he gets, he will buy her flowers if flowers are available, he will take her to the movies if she utters the stimulating words, "Let's go to the movies!" As you can see from this example, the number of acts and possible acts involved in the translation of a mentalistic term can be indefinitely large, since, in various circumstances and with various opportunities, a person in love might do almost anything. (The case is not so complicated, usually, with such mental predicates as "is thirsty" and "has an itch.") But however complicated the translation from mental language to behavioral disposition, the problem of dualism does not arise. The causal interaction between mind

---

[11] Ryle, *The Concept of Mind.*

and body has been reformulated as the causal connection between a physical state—a disposition to behave in certain ways—and the actual consequent behavior. Saying "he will marry her because he loves her" is therefore no more metaphysically problematic than saying "the glass will break because it is brittle."

There is a problem with all forms of behaviorism—both radical and logical. However tempting such a theory might be when we are studying other people at a distance, it seems utterly absurd when we try to think behavioristically while talking to a friend or listening to someone talk to us. And behaviorism becomes pure nonsense in one's own case, when we are trying to understand and talk about our own mental states. My pain is not the same as my behavior, and no matter how easy it may be for you to infer from my behavior that I am in pain, that is certainly not how *I* know that I am in pain, and it is not what I mean by my report, "I am in pain." Indeed, when I tell you "I am in pain," I am not predicting my behavior. I am telling you what I *feel*, quite apart from anything I might *do*. Whatever the logic of mental language, that undeniable feeling seems to remind us that behaviorism, however therapeutic in psychology and however powerful as an antidote to Cartesianism, cannot be the whole story. Watson's behaviorism helped correct an absurd amount of mentalistic theorizing about the behavior of animals ("the rat is trying to figure out how to get the door open"). So too, Ryle's behaviorism is a vital challenge to the too-easy supposition that our "minds" are ghostly containers filled with equally ghostly entities and processes. But as an alternative account of the mind, behaviorism inevitably bangs up against that ultimate mark of the mental, Descartes's "I think." There is no way you can think consistently that you never think or think that your thinking is nothing but your tendency to behave. As one of Watson's early critics commented, "What behaviorism shows is that psychologists do not always think very well, not that they don't think at all."

The rejection of dualism need not be a rejection of the mental side of the duality, although that is the obvious preference of most scientists. We have seen at least one philosopher, however, who escapes the problems of Cartesian dualism by rejecting the physical side of the problem. That is Bishop Berkeley, who quite clearly, in attacking Locke and defending his own "subjective idealism," provides a radical solution to the mind-body problem as well. His theory is that there are only minds and their ideas, no physical bodies. Therefore, there is no problem of interaction. He too (like Leibniz), however, needs God to hold his system together. But idealism has not been as rare an answer to the mind-body problem as you might think, although we see little of it nowadays. The religious idealists of the past century, in the United States as well as in England and Europe, were so powerful that they virtually ruled philosophy for a number of decades.

3. The Identity Theory

The most powerful and most plausible rejection of dualism, however, consists neither of denying consciousness nor of denying physical bodies. To deny dualism by denying mind or body strikes us as a bit simple-minded. There is a better way. Why not say that there are not two things at all, as there appear to be, but only one. In other words, mind and body, or more accurately, mental events and certain bodily events (presumably brain events) are identical. This theory, accordingly, is called the **identity theory,** and it once was one of the hottest controversies in American philosophy. You can see that it was anticipated, in a sense, by Spinoza and Russell with their dual aspect theory. But the identity theory, unlike the others, tries to tie itself as closely as possible with current scientific research, and although it is not a scientific theory itself, it will allow no such mysterious "something" such as we found in Spinoza and Russell. Accordingly, it is usually considered a form of materialism (although it does not deny the existence—only the ontological independence—of mental events).

The identity theory says that there are mental events, but they are identical to— the same thing as—certain physical events, that is, processes in the brain. Unlike behaviorism (radical or logical), the identity theory does not deny that mentalistic terms refer to something. The identity theory rather denies dualism by insisting that what mentalistic terms such as "wants," "believes," and "loves" refer to is not only some further unspecifiable mental state; it is also a neurological process that scientists, someday, will be able to specify precisely. Dualism is eliminated because there are no longer two things to interact; there is just a single event, a mental-neurological event, which can be described in either of two ways, in either of two quite different languages. One can (truthfully) say, "I have a headache" or, if one knows an extensive amount of neurology, one could just as well say, "such and such (the details are not for a philosophy book) is going on in my brain."

The following essay is one of the classic statements of the identity theory by Australian philosopher **J. J. C. Smart:**

"SENSATIONS AND BRAIN PROCESSES"
BY J. J. C. SMART

It seems to me that science is increasingly giving us a viewpoint whereby organisms are able to be seen as physico-chemical mechanisms: it seems that even the behavior of man himself will one day be explicable in mechanistic terms. There does seem to be, so far as science is concerned, nothing in the world but increasingly complex arrangements of physical constituents. All except for one place: in consciousness. That is, for a full description of what is going on in a man you would have to mention not only the physical processes in his tissue, glands, nervous system, and so forth, but also his states of consciousness: his visual, auditory, and tactual sensations, his aches and pains. That these should be *correlated* with brain processes does not help, for to say that they are *correlated* is to say that they are something "over and above." You cannot correlate something with itself. You correlate footprints with burglars, but not Bill Sikes the burglar with Bill Sikes the burglar. So sensations, states of consciousness, do seem to be the one sort of thing left outside the physicalist picture, and for various reasons I just cannot believe that this can be so. That everything should be explicable in terms of physics (together of course with descriptions of the ways in which the parts are put together—roughly, biology is to physics as radio-engineering is to electromagnetism) except the occurrence of sensations seems to me to be frankly unbelievable. Such sensations would be "nomological danglers," to use Feigl's expression. It is not often realized how odd would be the laws whereby these nomological danglers would dangle. It is sometimes asked, "Why can't there be psycho-physical laws which are of a novel sort, just as the laws of electricity and magnetism were novelties from the standpoint of Newtonian mechanics?" Certainly we are pretty sure in the future to come across new ultimate laws of a novel type, but I expect them to relate simple constituents: for example, whatever ultimate particles are then in vogue. I cannot believe that ultimate laws of nature could relate simple constituents to configurations consisting of perhaps billions of neurons (and goodness knows how many billion billions of ultimate particles) all put together for all the world as though their main purpose in life was to be a negative feedback mechanism of a complicated sort. Such ultimate laws would be like nothing so far known in science. They have a queer "smell" to them. I am just unable to believe in the nomological danglers themselves, or in the laws whereby they would dangle. If any philosophical arguments seemed to compel us to believe in such things, I would suspect a catch in the argument. In any case it is the object of this paper to show that there are no philosophical arguments which compel us to be dualists.

◆◆◆

Why should sensations just be brain processes of a certain sort? There are, of course, well-known (as well as lesser-known) philosophical objections to the view that reports of sensations are reports of brain-processes, but I shall try to argue that these arguments are by no means as cogent as is commonly thought to be the case.

Let me first try to state more accurately the thesis that sensations are brain processes. It is not the thesis that, for example, "after-image" or "ache" means the same as "brain process of sort X" (where "X" is replaced by a description of a certain sort of brain process). It is that, in so far as "after-image" or "ache" is a report of a process, it is a report of a process that *happens to be* a brain process. It follows that the thesis does not claim that sensation statements can be *translated* into statements about brain processes. Nor does it claim that the logic of a sensation statement is the same as that of a brain-process statement. All it claims is that in so far as a sensation statement is a report of something, that something is in fact a brain process. Sensations are nothing over and above brain processes. Nations are nothing "over and above" citizens, but this does not prevent the logic of nation statements being very different from the logic of citizen statements, nor does it insure the translatability of nation statements into citizen statements. (I do not, however, wish to assert that the relation of sensation statements to brain-process statements is very like that of nation statements to citizen statements. Nations do not just *happen to be* nothing over and above citizens, for example. I bring in the

Sensations are nothing over and above brain processes.

"nations" example merely to make a negative point: that the fact that the logic of A-statements is different from that of B-statements does not insure that A's are anything over and above B's.)

Remarks on identity (When I say that a sensation is a brain process or that lightning is an electric discharge, I am using "is" in the sense of strict identity. Just as in the—in this case necessary—proposition "7 is identical with the smallest prime number greater than 5.") When I say that a sensation is a brain process or that lightning is an electric discharge I do not mean just that the sensation is somehow spatially or temporally continuous with the brain process or that the lightning is just spatially or temporally continuous with the discharge. When on the other hand I say that the successful general is the same person as the small boy who stole the apples I mean only that the successful general I see before me is a time slice of the same four-dimensional object of which the small boy stealing apples is an earlier time slice. However, the four-dimensional object which has the general-I-see-before-me for its late time slice is identical in the strict sense with the four-dimensional object which has the small-boy-stealing-apples for an early time slice. I distinguish these two senses of "is identical with" because I wish to make it clear that the brain-process doctrine asserts identity in the *strict* sense.[12]

As compatible as the identity theory may seem with contemporary science and as plausible as it may seem as a way of rejecting dualism without rejecting the obvious facts about feelings and thinking, the identity theory too runs up against its share of paradoxes. The idea that one thing (a brain event = a mental event) can be referred to and described in two different languages sounds plausible and impressive. But, in this case, the two languages are so very different that there is very good reason to suppose that the thing(s) they refer to is/are very different as well. To pursue this line of criticism, here is a reevaluation of the identity theory by the American philosopher Jerome Shaffer.

AGAINST THE IDENTITY THEORY
BY **JEROME SHAFFER**

The sense of "identity" relevant here is that in which we say, for example, that the morning star is "identical" with the evening star. It is not that the expression "morning star" means the same as the expression "evening star"; on the contrary, these expressions mean something different. But the object referred to by the two expressions is one and the same; there is just one heavenly body, namely, Venus, which when seen in the morning is called the morning star and when

---

[12]From J. J. C. Smart, "Sensations and Brain Processes," *Philosophical Review* 68 (1959), pp. 141–56.

seen in the evening is called the evening star. The morning star is identical with the evening star; they are one and the same object.[13]

Of course, the identity of the mental with the physical is not exactly of this sort, since it is held to be simultaneous identity rather than the identity of a thing at one time with the same thing at a later time. To take a closer example, one can say that lightning is a particularly massive electrical discharge from one cloud to another or to the earth. Not that the word "lightning" *means* "a particularly massive electrical discharge . . ."; when Benjamin Franklin discovered that lightning was electrical, he did not make a discovery about the meaning of words. Nor when it was discovered that water was H_2O was a discovery made about the meanings of words; yet water is identical with H_2O.

In a similar fashion, the identity theorist can hold that thoughts, feelings, wishes, and the like are identical with physical states. Not "identical" in the sense that mentalistic terms are synonymous in meaning with physicalistic terms but "identical" in the sense that the actual events picked out by mentalistic terms are one and the same events as those picked out by physicalistic terms.

◆ ◆ ◆

What are the advantages of the identity theory? As a form of materialism, it does not have to cope with a world which has in it both mental phenomena and physical phenomena, and it does not have to ponder how they might be related. There exist only the physical phenomena, although there do exist two different ways of talking about such phenomena: physicalistic terminology and, in at least some situations, mentalistic terminology. We have here a dualism of language, but not a dualism of entities, events or properties.

But do we have merely a dualism of languages and no other sort of dualism? In the case of Venus, we do indeed have only one object, but the expression "morning star" picks out one phase of that object's history, where it is in the mornings, and the expression "evening star" picks out another phase of the object's history, where it is in the evenings. If that object did not have these two distinct aspects, it would not have been a *discovery* that the morning star and the evening star were indeed one and the same body, and, further, there would be no point to the different ways of referring to it.

Now it would be admitted by identity theorists that physicalistic and mentalistic terms do not refer to different phases in the history of one and the same object. What sort of identity is intended? Let us turn to an allegedly closer analogy, that of the identity of lightning and a particular sort of electrical phenomenon. Yet here again we have two distinguishable aspects, the appearance to the naked eye on the one hand and the physical composition on the other. And this is also not the kind of identity which is plausible for mental and physical events. The appearance *to the naked eye* of a neurological event is utterly different from the experience of having a thought or a pain.

---

[13] Both refer to the planet Venus, one as seen in the morning, the other at night. But it took many years for this identity to be discovered.

It is sometimes suggested that the physical aspect results from looking at a particular event "from the outside," whereas the mental results from looking at the same event "from the inside." When the brain surgeon observes my brain he is looking at it from the outside, whereas when I experience a mental event I am "looking" at my brain "from the inside."

Such an account gives us only a misleading analogy, rather than an accurate characterization of the relationship between the mental and the physical. The analogy suggests the difference between a man who knows his own house from the inside, in that he is free to move about within, seeing objects from different perspectives, touching them, etc., but can never get outside to see how it looks from there, and a man who cannot get inside and therefore knows only the outside appearance of the house, and perhaps what he can glimpse through the windows. But what does this have to do with the brain? Am I free to roam about inside my brain, observing what the brain surgeon may never see? Is not the "inner" aspect of my brain far more accessible to the brain surgeon than to me? He has the X rays, probes, electrodes, scalpels, and scissors for getting at the inside of my brain. If it is replied that this is only an analogy, not to be taken literally, then the question still remains how the mental and the physical are related. . . .

One of the leading identity theorists, J. J. C. Smart, holds that mentalistic discourse is simply a vaguer, more indefinite way of talking about what could be talked about more precisely by using physiological terms. If I report a red afterimage, I mean (roughly) that something is going on which is like what goes on when I really see a red patch. I do not actually *mean* that a particular sort of brain process is occurring, but when I say something is going on I refer (very vaguely, to be sure) to just that brain process. Thus the thing referred to in my report of an afterimage is a brain process. Hence there is no need to bring in any nonphysical features. Thus even the taint of dualism is avoided.

Does this ingenious attempt to evade dualistic implications stand up under philosophical scrutiny? I am inclined to think it will not. Let us return to the man reporting the red afterimage. He was aware of the occurrence of something or other, of some feature or other. Now it seems to me obvious that he was not necessarily aware of the state of his brain at that time (I doubt that most of us are ever aware of the state of our brain) nor, in general, necessarily aware of any physical features of his body at that time. He might, of course, have been incidentally aware of some physical feature but not insofar as he was aware of the red afterimage as such. Yet he was definitely aware of something, or else how could he have made that report? So he must have been aware of some nonphysical feature. That is the only way of explaining how he was aware of anything at all.

Of course, the thing that our reporter of the afterimage was aware of might well have had further features which he was *not* aware of, particularly, in this connection, physical features. I may be aware of certain features of an object without being aware of others. So it is not ruled out that the event our reporter is aware of might be an event with predominantly physical features—he just does not notice those. But he must be aware of some of its features, or else it would not be proper to say he was aware of *that* event. And if he is not aware of any physical features, he must be aware of something else. And that shows that we cannot get rid of those nonphysical features in the way that Smart suggests. ... If by X rays or some other means we were able to see every event which occurred in the brain, we would never get a glimpse of a thought. If, to resort to fantasy, we could so enlarge a brain or so shrink ourselves that we could wander freely through the brain, we would still never observe a thought. All we could ever observe in the brain would be the *physical* events which occur in it. If mental events had location in the brain, there should be some means of detecting them there. But of course there is none. The very idea of it is senseless.[14]

Shaffer disagrees with the identity theory, but both his presentation and his criticism of it are central to ongoing debate. In defending the identity theory, it is most important to stress that the identity of brain processes and thoughts is an empirical identity, that is, an identity that must be discovered through experiment and experience. It is not a logical identity, as if the two terms "brain process" and "thought" are synonymous. The latter suggestion is obviously false, and modern defenders of the identity theory are always emphasizing that future neurophysiological research will prove them right. Shaffer's criticism, however, is based on a principle that must be distinguished from the all-too-easy attack on the logical identity suggestion. The principle is that if two things are identical, then they must have all the same properties. But, Shaffer argues, no amount of research could possibly show that brain processes and thought have the same properties. Most importantly, brain processes take place in the brain and can be traced like any other physical processes; thoughts, on the other hand, have no spatial location, and there is nothing that research can "discover" that will show that they do. Of course, research can and has shown that certain thoughts are correlated with certain brain processes, but correlation is not yet identity.

4. Eliminative Materialism

To most materialists, the identity theory seemed promising, even if its arguments proved inadequate. The real question was whether there might be some other version of the thesis—that mental states were "nothing but" brain states—that did not claim the kind of "one-to-one match" required by the identity theory. One suggestion (still popular in many quarters) is the thesis called **eliminative materialism,** which proposes to defend materialism without claiming an identity between what we call "mental states" and the workings of the brain. Rather, the argument goes, our increasing knowledge of the workings of the brain will make outmoded our "folk-psychology" talk about the mind and we will all learn to talk the language of neurology instead.

---

[14] Jerome Shaffer, *The Philosophy of Mind* (Englewood Cliffs, NJ: Prentice-Hall, 1968).

In the following excerpt, **Paul Churchland** defends the opposition (rather than the complementarity) of neurological explanations of human behavior and the familiar mentalistic accounts. With increased knowledge of neurology, our ordinary language will be replaced or, at least, seriously revised:

ON ELIMINATIVE MATERIALISM
BY **PAUL M. CHURCHLAND**

The identity theory was called into doubt not because the prospects for a materialist account of our mental capacities were thought to be poor, but because it seemed unlikely that the arrival of an adequate materialist theory would bring with it the nice one-to-one match-ups, between the concepts of folk psychology and the concepts of theoretical neuroscience, that intertheoretic reduction requires. The reason for that doubt was the great variety of quite different physical systems that could instantiate the required functional organization. *Eliminative materialism* also doubts that the correct neuroscientific account of human capacities will produce a neat reduction of our common-sense framework, but here the doubts arise from a quite different source.

As the eliminative materialists see it, the one-to-one match-ups will not be found, and our common-sense psychological framework will not enjoy an intertheoretic reduction, *because our commonsense psychological framework is a false and radically misleading conception of the causes of human behavior and the nature of cognitive activity.* On this view, folk psychology is not just an incomplete representation of our inner natures; it is an outright *mis*-representation of our internal states and activities. Consequently, we cannot expect a truly adequate neuroscientific account of our inner lives to provide theoretical categories that match up nicely with the categories of our common-sense framework. Accordingly, we must expect that the older framework will simply be eliminated, rather than be reduced, by a matured neuroscience.

HISTORICAL PARALLELS

As the identity theorist can point to historical cases of successful intertheoretic reduction, so the eliminative materialist can point to historical cases of the outright elimination of the ontology of an older theory in favor of the ontology of a new and superior theory. . . .

It used to be thought that when a piece of wood burns, or a piece of metal rusts, a spiritlike substance called "phlogiston" was being released: briskly, in the former case, slowly in the latter. Once gone, that "noble" substance left only a base pile of ash or rust. It later came to be appreciated that both processes involve, not the loss of something, but the *gaining* of a substance taken from the atmosphere: oxygen. Phlogiston emerged, not as an incomplete description of what was going on, but as a radical misdescription. Phlogiston was therefore not suitable for reduction to or identification with some notion from within the new oxygen chemistry, and it was simply eliminated from science.

◆ ◆ ◆

The concepts of folk psychology—belief, desire, fear, sensation, pain, joy, and so on—await a similar fate, according to the view at issue. And when neuroscience has matured to the point where the poverty of our current conceptions is apparent to everyone, the superiority of the new framework is established, we shall then be able to set about *re*conceiving our internal states and activities, within a truly adequate conceptual framework at last. Our explanations of one another's behavior will appeal to such things as our neuropharmacological states, the neural activity in specialized anatomical areas, and whatever other states are deemed relevant by the new theory. Our private introspection will also be transformed, and may be profoundly enhanced by reason of the more accurate and penetrating framework it will have to work with—just as the astronomer's perception of the night sky is much enhanced by the detailed knowledge of modern astronomical theory that he or she possesses.

The magnitude of the conceptual revolution here suggested should not be minimized: it would be enormous. And the benefits to humanity might be equally great. If each of us possessed an accurate neuroscientific understanding of (what we now conceive dimly as) the varieties and causes of mental illness, the factors involved in learning, the neural basis of emotions, intelligence, and socialization, then the sum total of human misery might be much reduced. The simple increase in mutual understanding that the new framework made possible could contribute substantially toward a more peaceful and humane society. Of course, there would be dangers as well: increased knowledge means increased power, and power can always be misused.

ARGUMENTS FOR ELIMINATIVE MATERIALISM

The arguments for eliminative materialism are diffuse and less than decisive, but they are stronger than is widely supposed. The distinguishing feature of this position is its denial that a smooth intertheoretic reduction is to be expected—even a species-specific reduction—of the framework of folk psychology to the framework of a matured neuroscience. The reason for this denial is the eliminative materialist's conviction that folk psychology is a hopelessly primitive and deeply confused conception of our internal activities. But why this low opinion of our common-sense conceptions?

There are at least three reasons. First, the eliminative materialist will point to the widespread explanatory, predictive, and manipulative failures of folk psychology. So much of what is central and familiar to us remains a complete mystery from within folk psychology. We do not know what *sleep* is, or why we have to have it, despite spending a full third of our lives in that condition. (The answer, "For rest," is mistaken. Even if people are allowed to rest continuously, their need for sleep is undiminished. Apparently, sleep serves some deeper functions, but we do not yet know what they are.) We do not understand how *learning* transforms each of us from a gaping infant to a cunning adult, or how differences in *intelligence* are grounded. We have not the slightest idea how *memory* works, or how we manage to retrieve relevant bits of information instantly from the awesome mass we have stored. We do not know what *mental illness* is, nor how to cure it.

In sum, the most central things about us remain almost entirely mysterious from within folk psychology. . . .

This argument from explanatory poverty has a further aspect. So long as one sticks to normal brains, the poverty of folk psychology is perhaps not strikingly evident. But as soon as one examines the many perplexing behavioral and cognitive deficits suffered by people with *damaged* brains, one's descriptive and explanatory resources start to claw the air. . . . As with other humble theories asked to operate successfully in unexplored extensions of their old domain (for example, Newtonian mechanics in the domain of velocities close to the velocity of light, and the classical gas law in the domain of high pressures or temperatures), the descriptive and explanatory inadequacies of folk psychology become starkly evident.

> *. . . the most central things about us remain almost entirely mysterious from within folk psychology.*

The second argument tries to draw an inductive lesson from our conceptual history. Our early folk theories of motion were profoundly confused, and were eventually displaced entirely by more sophisticated theories. Our early folk theories of the structure and activity of the heavens were wildly off the mark, and survive only as historical lessons in how wrong we can be. Our folk theories of the nature of fire, and the nature of life, were similarly cockeyed. And one could go on, since the vast majority of our past folk conceptions have been similarly exploded. All except folk psychology, which survives to this day and has only recently begun to feel pressure. But the phenomenon of conscious intelligence is surely a more complex and difficult phenomenon than any of those just listed. So far as accurate understanding is concerned, it would be a *miracle* if we had got *that* one right the very first time, when we fell down so badly on all the others. Folk psychology has survived for so very long, presumably, not because it is basically correct in its representations, but because the phenomena addressed are so surpassingly difficult that any useful handle on them, no matter how feeble, is unlikely to be displaced in a hurry. . . .

ARGUMENTS AGAINST ELIMINATIVE MATERIALISM

The initial plausibility of this rather radical view is low for almost everyone, since it denies deeply entrenched assumptions. That is at best a question-begging complaint, of course, since those assumptions are precisely what is at issue. But the following line of thought does attempt to mount a real argument.

Eliminative materialism is false, runs the argument, because one's introspection reveals directly the existence of pains, beliefs, desires, fears, and so forth. Their existence is as obvious as anything could be.

The eliminative materialist will reply that this argument makes the same mistake that an ancient or medieval person would be making if he insisted that he could just see with his own eyes that the heavens form a turning sphere, or that witches exist. The fact is, all observation occurs within some system of concepts, and our observation judgments are only as good as the conceptual framework in which they are expressed. In all three cases—the starry sphere, witches, and the familiar mental states—precisely what is challenged is the integrity of the background conceptual frameworks in which the observation judgments are expressed. To insist on the validity of one's experiences, *traditionally interpreted,* is therefore to beg the very question at issue. For in all three cases, the question is whether we should *re*conceive the nature of some familiar observational domain.

♦♦♦

A final criticism draws a much weaker conclusion, but makes a rather stronger case. Eliminative materialism, it has been said, is making mountains out of molehills. It exaggerates the defects in folk psychology, and underplays its real successes. Perhaps the arrival of a matured neuroscience will require the elimination of the occasional folk-psychological concept, continues the criticism, and a minor adjustment in certain folk-psychological principles may have to be endured. But the large-scale elimination forecast by the eliminative materialist is just an alarmist worry or a romantic enthusiasm.

Perhaps this complaint is correct. And perhaps it is merely complacent. Whichever, it does bring out the important point that we do not confront two simple and mutually exclusive possibilities here: pure reduction versus pure elimination. Rather, these are the end points of a smooth spectrum of possible outcomes, between which there are mixed cases of partial elimination and partial reduction. Only empirical research . . . can tell us where on that spectrum our own case will fall. Perhaps we should speak here, more liberally, of "revisionary materialism," instead of concentrating on the more radical possibility of an across-the-board elimination.[15]

Churchland's primary aim in this final section of argument is to present as at least intelligible his position that "our collective conceptual destiny lies substantially toward the revolutionary end of the spectrum."

5. Functionalism: The Mind and the Computer

Despite the claims of Cartesians that "minds are nonphysical," at least in the obvious sense, Churchland and other materialists based their notion of the "self" on what they felt to be scientific fact, the physical basis of minds—the brain and the central nervous system. It is the brain that makes minds possible.

On the one hand, this was a rather remarkable discovery in the history of biology. It is by no means obvious, looking at the cauliflower-like mound inside the skull, that

---

[15] Paul M. Churchland, *Matter and Consciousness: A Contemporary Introduction to the Philosophy of Mind* (Cambridge, MA: MIT Press, 1988, pp. 43–49).

in that space is packed billions of tiny neural networks that control our very experience, our every action, including the inner actions of our bodies of which we may not even be aware (control of metabolism and blood flow, for example). But since the introduction of computers, scientific criticisms of dualism have taken another line. Is it so obvious that minds could *only* be the product of brains? Could mental processes be based on physical processes that are not brain processes? Could, for example, mental processes be based upon a network of electronic signals in a properly designed complex of transistors and circuit boards? In other words, could mental processes be the product of a computer? Could the brain be nothing but an organic computer? Could computers—the kind that we make out of metal and minerals—have minds?

It is no coincidence that the past decade or so of computer breakthroughs has produced a revolution in the way some philosophers think about selves and minds. The philosophical position is called **functionalism,** and its basic insight is that minds are produced not so much by particular kinds of materials (for example, brains) but rather by the *relations* between parts. In another few decades, it may in fact be possible, according to the most optimistic functionalists, to build a human mind out of computer parts. But whether or not computer scientists achieve such a (frightening) miracle, less optimistic functionalists hold that the mind is, in effect, a *function* of the patterns of neurological activity in the brain.

In computer technology (now at least in part included in our everyday language), there is a crucial distinction between "hardware" and "software." Hardware is the actual computer with its circuits. In the case of human minds, the hardware would be the brain and its neurological circuits. Software is the program that gives the computer specific instructions. (Sometimes, specific instructions can be "hard-wired," as in the case of instinct, but these are not the exciting cases that inspire most functionalists and computer scientists.) The view of the functionalists is that the mind is nothing other than an elaborate program of sorts, which is the product of a spectacularly complicated pattern embodied in the physical workings of the brain.

The idea that the computer will someday provide a single model of mental states and information processes has been called into question recently. It is not at all clear that the mind works like a computer, or whether instead it works on different parallel levels in a manner substantially more complicated and considerably faster than any known computer.

Nevertheless, like any bold new hypothesis, the functionalist-analogy analysis of the mind as a computer has crashed head-on into some of the most entrenched ideas and experiences of common sense. In defense of common sense, **John Searle**—one of the leading analysts of ordinary human language and the special features of human communication—attacks the notion that computers are sufficiently intelligent to threaten or to challenge human intelligence anytime soon.

FROM **"THE MYTH OF THE COMPUTER"**
BY **JOHN R. SEARLE**

The details of how the brain works are immensely complicated and largely unknown, but some of the general principles of the relations between brain functioning and computer programs can be stated quite simply. First, we know that brain processes cause mental phenomena. Mental states are caused by and realized in the structure of the brain. From this it follows that any system that produced mental states would have to have powers equivalent to those of the brain. Such a system might use a different chemistry, but whatever its chemistry it would have to be able to cause what the brain causes. We know from the [previous] argument digital computer programs by themselves are never sufficient to produce mental states. Now since brains do produce minds, and since programs by themselves can't produce minds, it follows that the way the brain does it can't be by simply instantiating a computer program. (Everything, by the way, instantiates some program or other, and brains are no exception. So in that trivial sense brains, like everything else, are digital computers.) And it also follows that if you wanted to build a machine to produce mental states, a thinking machine, you couldn't do it solely in virtue of the fact that your machine ran a certain kind of computer program.

> *... since brains do produce minds, and since programs by themselves can't produce minds, it follows that the way the brain does it can't be by simply instantiating a computer program.*

The thinking machine couldn't work solely in virtue of being a digital computer but would have to duplicate the specific causal powers of the brain.

A lot of the nonsense talked about computers nowadays stems from their relative rarity and hence mystery. As computers and robots become more common, as common as telephones, washing machines, and forklift trucks, it seems likely that this aura will disappear and people will take computers for what they are, namely useful machines.[16]

6. Connectionism

Not all criticisms of functionalism are nonmaterialist. Recently, objections have been brought against functionalism from neurophysiologists who claim that functionalism is just too simplistic in its vision of the brain and of computers. **Connectionists** complain that functionalism is a "top-down," "software" approach, which can never be accurate in its representation of the "hardware" of either the brain or the computer. In other words, say the connectionists, a functionalist starts with behavior—either human behavior or computer behavior—and claims that understanding human consciousness is just a matter of finding the "program" for that behavior. The functionalist claims that to understand the "program" is to understand the behavior, regardless of the mechanical and physical interactions which make the program run. The connectionist, on the other hand, claims that the mechanical and physical interactions that occur in the brain determine the kinds of behavior—which kinds of

---

[16] John R. Searle, "The Myth of the Computer," in the *New York Review of Books,* 1982.

software—that computers are capable of processing. Connectionists therefore advocate a "bottom-up" approach to understanding the mind. Connectionists are still materialists, but not in the simple, reductionist, way of their predecessors. They believe that consciousness—in its full color and quality—is a result of the complicated "connections" that really do go on in the brain. There is no one-to-one correspondence between neurons and thoughts or perceptions; rather, they claim, the "hardware" of the brain is an immensely complex mechanism to which the functionalists do not do justice.

D. THE PROBLEM OF CONSCIOUSNESS

Descartes claimed he knew what was going on in his mind with an immediate certainty that he could never have about what was going on in the world "outside" him. In his first "Meditation," he talks about his seeming to be sitting in front of the fire and the fact that he might be wrong (if he were in bed asleep at the time). But what he could not be wrong about is his seeming to be sitting in front of the fire. Similarly, you think you see a friend walking across the street. You are wrong, for your friend is in fact in Alaska this week. But you can still be certain that you thought that you saw him, even if you didn't. Philosophers often refer to this special kind of "immediate" certainty in the case of our own conscious experiences as **incorrigibility.** You might make a mistake in any factual claim about the world, for you might be hallucinating, or dreaming, or simply fooled by circumstances. But nothing could lead you to suspect that you might be mistaken about your own experiences. Given enough evidence against you, you might be willing to change from "but I know that I saw it" to "well, I thought I saw it." But nothing could convince you that you were wrong in thinking that you saw whatever it was. That claim, the claim about your experience, is incorrigible. Your claim about what you saw, however, is always open to further questioning.

For many years, this notion of incorrigibility served as part of the definition of "mind" and therefore, as Churchland implies, also defense against materialism. Whatever was mental could be described incorrigibly and this is very different than is the case with physical things. But doubts have begun to creep in recently. Part of the problem was Freud's introduction of the notion of the **unconscious.** According to his famous "psychoanalytic" theory, not everything mental is knowable, and therefore surely not everything "in the mind" can be described incorrigibly. In a famous passage from his "Introductory Lectures," Freud says the following:

ON THE "UNCONSCIOUS"
BY **SIGMUND FREUD**

There is no need to discuss what is to be called conscious: it is removed from all doubt. The oldest and best meaning of the word "unconscious" is the descriptive one; we call a psychical process unconscious whose existence we are obliged to assume—for some such reason as that we infer it from its effects—, but of which we know nothing. In that case we have the same relation to it as we have to a physical process in another person, except that it is in fact one of our own. If we want to be still more correct, we shall modify our assertion by saying that we call a process unconscious if we are obliged to assume that it is being activated *at the moment* though *at the moment* we know nothing about it.[17]

Notice that Freud starts from a Cartesian position, the idea that "conscious is removed from all doubt." But then he suggests what no Cartesian can tolerate, the idea that there are ideas (experiences, intentions) in our minds that we do not and sometimes cannot know, much less know with certainty. And if we accept this notion of "the unconscious" (or even the weaker notion of "preconscious"), the traditional notion of the "incorrigibility" of the mental is seriously challenged.

The argument, however, cuts both ways. Many philosophers have rejected Freud just because his notion of "the unconscious" goes against the notion of incorrigibility. "If it isn't knowable incorrigibly," these philosophers have said, "then it can't be mental at all." Even Freud himself was forced to admit that his theory flew in the face of our normal "manner of speaking." The debate continues. Can you be wrong about what is going on in your own mind? For a long time, it was generally agreed that you could not be. Now we aren't so sure. You are certain that you are over an old love affair, but, without too much difficulty, a friend or a psychologist convinces you that you have been thinking about it constantly. You are certain that you are angry, but on closer examination, and in retrospect, you decide that you really felt guilty. You thought that you were thinking about your professor, when suddenly you realize that in fact it was the face of your father!

Is there anything about which we could not be mistaken? What of those basic bits of data that the empiricists talked about—sensations or impressions? Could we possibly be wrong in our confidence that "right now, I am experiencing a cold feeling in my hand"? The empiricists assumed that one could not be wrong about this, for it was on the basis of such certainties that we were able to construct, through inductive reasoning, our theories about the world. Could we be wrong even about our own sensations? Consider this example (it comes from Bishop Berkeley): A mischievous friend tells you that he is going to touch your hand with a very hot spoon. When you aren't looking, he touches you with a piece of ice. You scream and claim, with seeming certainty, that he has given you an uncomfortable sensation of heat. But you're wrong. What you felt was cold. What you seemed to feel was heat. But even your "seeming," in this case, was mistaken.

Philosophers have also pointed out that what is unique to mind as opposed to body is the fact that one and only one person can (and must) experience what is going on. I can (and must) feel only my pains, I can't experience your pains. Philosophers have referred to this as **privileged access,** sometimes as the **privacy** of mental events. The "privilege" is the fact that, whatever is going on in your mind, you are

---

[17] Sigmund Freud, *New Introductory Lectures on Psychoanalysis,* ed. and trans. James Strachey (New York: Norton, 1964).

not only the first but the only one to know of it directly. The "privacy" refers to the fact that if you decide not to tell anyone or betray yourself (through your facial expressions or your behavior), no one else need ever know. If you have a wart on your thigh, you can keep it contingently "private" by choosing suitable clothing. But if you have a "dirty little secret" in your mind, you have a logical guarantee of its privacy—it is private necessarily.

"Incorrigible" means "beyond correction"; "privileged access" means "known in a special way." (These concepts must be kept separate.) Because of privileged access and the "privacy" of consciousness, our states of mind have the very peculiar status of being always knowable to ourselves (though whether or not we want to say "knowable with certainty" depends on our views about incorrigibility) and yet possibly unknowable to anyone else. That is why, as you learned in grade school, you could always fake a headache to stay home for the day but you couldn't fake a fever or a sore. As long as it was purely mental, it was also purely private. Your success depended wholly upon how good (or bad) an actor you were. But when it comes to your body, you were in no privileged position. It was the thermometer, not your opinions, that told whether you had a fever or not. And it was the doctor, not you, who decided how serious your sore really was. But when it came to your own consciousness, you were in a truly privileged and irrefutable position.

This peculiarity of the first-person position, of our relationship to our own consciousness, is one of the things that makes the notion of "self" so difficult and that makes the problem so seemingly unresolvable. It makes the way that we establish our own identity seem categorically different from how others know it. Against all forms of reductionism and materialism, philosopher **Thomas Nagel** has argued in an ingenious fashion that it is consciousness, or what he calls "subjectivity," that makes the problem so "intractable." If "subjectivity" can be loosely defined as "what it's like" to be something, Nagel introduces his concern about the mind-body problem with the intriguing question: "What is it like to be a bat?"

. . . fundamentally an organism has conscious mental states if and only if there is something that it is like to be that organism — something it is like for the organism.

"WHAT IS IT LIKE TO BE A BAT?"
BY **THOMAS NAGEL**

Conscious experience is a widespread phenomenon. It occurs at many levels of animal life, though we cannot be sure of its presence in the simpler organisms, and it is very difficult to say in general what provides evidence of it. (Some extremists have been prepared to deny it even of mammals other than man.) No doubt it occurs in countless forms totally unimaginable to us, on other planets in other solar systems throughout the universe. But no matter how the form may vary, the fact that an organism has conscious experience *at all* means, basically, that there is something it is like to *be* that organism. There may be further implications about the form of the experience; there may even (though I doubt it) be implications about the behavior of the organism. But fundamentally an organism has conscious mental states if and only if there is something that it is like to *be* that organism—something it is like *for* the organism.

We may call this the subjective character of experience. It is not captured by any of the familiar, recently devised reductive analyses of the mental, for all of them are logically compatible with its absence. It is not analyzable in terms of any explanatory system of functional states, or intentional states, since these could be ascribed to robots or automata that behaved like people though they experienced nothing. It is not analyzable in terms of the causal role of experiences in relation to typical human behavior—for similar reasons. I do not deny that conscious mental states and events cause behavior, nor that they may be given functional characterizations. I deny only that this kind of thing exhausts their analysis. Any reductionist program has to be based on an analysis of what is to be reduced. If the analysis leaves something out, the problem will be falsely posed. It is useless to base the defense of materialism on any analysis of mental phenomena that fails to deal explicitly with their subjective character.

◆◆◆

I assume we all believe that bats have experience. After all, they are mammals, and there is no more doubt that they have experience than that mice or pigeons or whales have experience. I have chosen bats instead of wasps or flounders because if one travels too far down the phylogenetic tree, people gradually shed their faith that there is experience there at all. Bats, although more closely related to us than those other species, nevertheless present a range of activity and a sensory apparatus so different from ours that the problem I want to pose is exceptionally vivid (though it certainly could be raised with other species). Even without the benefit of philosophical reflection, anyone who has spent some time in an enclosed space with an excited bat knows what it is to encounter a fundamentally *alien* form of life.

I have said that the essence of the belief that bats have experience is that there is something that it is like to be a bat. Now we know that most bats (the microchiroptera, to be precise) perceive the external world primarily by sonar, or echolocation, detecting the reflections, from objects within range, of their own rapid, subtly modulated, high-frequency shrieks. Their brains are designed to correlate the outgoing impulses with the subsequent echoes, and the information thus acquired enables bats to make precise discriminations of distance, size, shape, motion, and texture comparable to those we make by vision. But bat sonar, though clearly a form of perception, is not similar in its operation to any sense that we possess, and there is no reason to suppose that it is subjectively like anything we can experience or imagine. This appears to create difficulties for the notion of what it is like to be a bat. We must consider whether any method will permit us to extrapolate to the inner life of the bat from our own case, and if not, what alternative methods there may be for understanding the notion.

Our own experience provides the basic material for our imagination, whose range is therefore limited. It will not help to try to imagine that one has webbing on one's arms, which enables one to fly around at dusk and dawn catching insects in one's mouth; that one has very poor vision, and perceives the surrounding world by a system of reflected high-frequency sound signals; and that one spends the day hanging upside down by one's feet in an attic. Insofar as I can imagine this (which is not very far), it tells me only what it would be like for *me* to behave as a bat behaves. But that is not the question. I want to know what it is like for a *bat* to be a bat. Yet if I try to imagine this, I am restricted to the resources of my own mind, and those resources are inadequate to the task. I cannot perform it either by imagining additions to my present experience, or by imagining segments gradually subtracted from it, or by imagining some combination of additions, subtractions, and modifications.

To the extent that I could look and behave like a wasp or a bat without changing my fundamental structure, my experiences would not be anything like the experiences of those animals. On the other hand, it is doubtful that any meaning can be attached to the supposition that I should possess the internal neurophysiological constitution of a bat. Even if I could by gradual degrees be transformed into a bat, nothing in my present constitution enables me to imagine what the experiences of such a future stage of myself thus metamorphosed would be like. The best evidence would come from the experiences of bats, if we only knew what they were like.[18]

1. Changing Our Minds: Holism and Consciousness

When Aristotle wrote about "the soul," he meant nothing other than "the form of the body":

FROM **DE ANIMA**
BY **ARISTOTLE**

One can no more ask if the body and the soul are one than if the wax and the impression it receives are one, or speaking generally the matter of each thing and the form of which it is the matter; for admitting that the terms unity and existence are used in many senses, the paramount sense is that of actuality. We have, then, given a general definition of what the soul is: it is substance expressed as form. It is this which makes a body what it is.[19]

This is not behaviorism. Aristotle is not denying the existence of anything that we normally believe in. Yet it is clearly not a dualism of the Cartesian variety, and this raises the following question: Are there ways of conceiving of ourselves without falling into the Cartesian trap of talking about minds and bodies?

We can only suggest a few possibilities here. The first, perhaps, was advanced by Ludwig Wittgenstein in his *Philosophical Investigations*. Although he is usually considered to be an unconfessed behaviorist, a more recent and perhaps more plausible interpretation is that Wittgenstein wanted to deny the very idea that human beings

---

[18] Thomas Nagel, *Mortal Questions* (Cambridge: Cambridge University Press, 1979).

[19] Aristotle, *De Anima,* trans. W. S. Hett (Cambridge, MA: Harvard University Press, 1936).

are a curious combination of two very different substances or kinds of entities or events. Rather, there are just people, not minds plus bodies.

A very different kind of answer comes to us from Husserl's phenomenology. Although Husserl was not particularly concerned with the mind-body problem as such, he was obviously very interested in the nature of consciousness, since consciousness provides the subject matter of his entire life's work. What Husserl argued began with a violent attack on the spatial metaphors we use in talking about consciousness. At the beginning of the chapter, we mentioned these, suggesting that they were "just metaphors," symptoms of a problem but not a problem themselves. Well, Husserl shows that they are a problem, that philosophers have not used them merely as metaphors, and that it is because of their taking these metaphors literally that our problems about consciousness arise in the first place.

What Husserl attacks is the very idea of consciousness as a mysterious container, "in" which one finds ideas, thoughts, feelings, desires, and so on. The same objection holds of such metaphors as "the stream of consciousness," with emotions, thoughts, and feelings floating by like so much flotsam and jetsam. Consciousness must rather be viewed in two parts (though Husserl insists these must not be thought of as a separate "dualism"): There are acts of consciousness, and there are the objects of those acts.

Simply stated, a phenomenologist would analyze my seeing a tree into (1) my act of seeing and (2) the tree as seen. So far, this looks innocent enough. But its consequences are not so innocent. First, just in passing, notice what this does to Berkeley's idealism. Berkeley's whole argument rested on his thesis that all we can experience are ideas. But this is a confusion, Husserl insists, of our act of experiencing with the objects experienced. The object experienced (the tree) is not merely my idea. Accordingly, Husserl concludes that Berkeley's idealism is "absurd." And in general, Husserl's phenomenological theory insists that philosophers have been neglectful of this crucial distinction. Many attributes of the act of experiencing do not hold of the object; for example, the object, unlike the act, is not "private." One and only one person, namely, myself, can perform my act of seeing. But any number of people can see the object of my seeing, the tree. Moreover, there can be no such thing, Husserl argues, as a conscious act without an object. You can see how this might provide a powerful argument against many traditional forms of skepticism.

Our concern here is Husserl's conception of consciousness, which he calls **intentionality.** (Accordingly, the act is often called the "intentional act," and the object is called the "intentional object.") To say that consciousness is intentional means (among other things, which are irrelevant to this chapter) that our conscious acts are always directed toward objects and that we should not, therefore, talk about conscious acts as self-contained "contents" that are mysteriously coordinated with the movements of our bodies. Rather, we can simply say that among our various acts as persons are intentional conscious acts as well as physical actions. We can look at a tree and we can kick a tree. But there is no problem of "coordination" or interaction.

This theory was never actually developed by Husserl himself, but it was worked out in great detail by one of his "existential" followers in France, **Maurice Merleau-Ponty** (a close friend and student of Sartre). Coming from a very different starting point, Merleau-Ponty arrives at a position surprisingly close to that of Wittgenstein.

It must not be called "behaviorist," but like Wittgenstein, Merleau-Ponty does reject the traditional way of dividing up mind and body and thereby suggests a very different conception of persons in which such problematic distinctions are not allowed to arise.

Merleau-Ponty attacks dualism from the side that has so far seemed least controversial—the idea that the human body is just another "bit of matter." He introduces the notion of a "dialectic" between mind and body, by which he means that there is no ultimate distinction between them. From one point of view, he argues, it is possible to see the body as "the cause of the structure of consciousness," for example, as a physiologist interested in the workings of the brain and the sense organs. From another point of view, it is possible to see the body as a mere "object of knowledge," for example, when a medical student dissects a body in his anatomy class. But it is a mistake, Merleau-Ponty argues, to confuse either of these viewpoints with the "correct" view of the body, either as a cause of consciousness or as something wholly distinct from it. Only the *living* body can count as *my* body, except in a very special and not everyday sense, namely, the sense in which I can talk about what will happen to my body after I die.

"The body is not a self-enclosed mechanism" he argues, nor does it makes sense to treat "the soul" or consciousness as a distinct entity with some mysterious relationship with the body. "There is not a duality of substances," he writes, but only "the dialectic of living being in its biological milieu." Merleau-Ponty sometimes says the consciousness is nothing but "the meaning of one's body," all of which is to say, in extremely difficult prose, that mind and body are nothing other than a single entity, and the distinctions we make between them are always special cases. "I live my body," he says; there is no enigma of "my body" to be explained.[20]

In his difficult "dialectical" language, Merleau-Ponty defends a thesis that is strikingly similar to that defended by Wittgenstein: One cannot treat a person as an uneasy conglomerate of mental parts and body parts but must begin with the whole person. But where Wittgenstein and Strawson proceed by attacking the mental side of Cartesian dualism, Merleau-Ponty attacks anyone who would treat the human as "just another body." The body itself is not only alive but, in an important sense, conscious. This does not mean, as in Descartes, that it is connected with a consciousness. It is itself aware, as we often notice when we talk of "bodily awareness" or "feeling our way." The difference between the body of a living person and a corpse is not just a difference in physiology, nor is it the difference between an "inhabited" body and an "uninhabited" body. My body and myself are essentially one, and to try to separate them, as Descartes had done, is to make the relationship between "me and my body" into an unnecessary mystery.

A view that is strikingly similar to the phenomenological theory was defended in the United States by William James. But instead of giving consciousness the attention it receives in Husserl, he argues that there is no such thing as consciousness as an entity, only different functions of experience:

---

[20]Maurice Merleau-Ponty, *The Structure of Behavior,* trans. Alden L. Fisher (Boston: Beacon Press, 1963).

FROM **"DOES CONSCIOUSNESS EXIST?"**
BY **WILLIAM JAMES**

"Thoughts" and "things" are names for two sorts of objects, which common sense will always find contrasted and will always practically oppose to each other. Philosophy, reflecting on the contrast, has varied in the past in her explanations of it, and may be expected to vary in the future. At first, "spirit and matter," "soul and body," stood for a pair of equipollent substances quite on a par in weight and interest. But one day Kant undermined the soul and brought in the transcendental ego, and ever since then the bipolar relation has been very much off its balance. The transcendental ego seems nowadays in rationalist quarters to stand for everything, in empiricist quarters for almost nothing. In the hands of . . . writers . . . the spiritual principle attenuates itself to a thoroughly ghostly condition, being only a name for the fact that the "content" of experience *is known*. It loses personal form and activity—these passing over to the content—and becomes a bare [consciousness], of which in its own right absolutely nothing can be said.

I believe that "consciousness," when once it has evaporated to this estate . . . is on the point of disappearing altogether. It is the name of a nonentity, and has no right to a place among first principles. Those who still cling to it are clinging to a mere echo, the faint rumor left behind by the disappearing "soul" upon the air of philosophy. During the past year, I have read a number of articles whose authors seemed just on the point of abandoning the notion of consciousness, and substituting for it that of an absolute experience not due to two factors. But they were not quite radical enough, not quite daring enough in their negations. For twenty years past I have mistrusted "consciousness" as an entity; for seven or eight years past I have suggested its non-existence to my students, and tried to give them its pragmatic-equivalent in realities of experience. It seems to me that the hour is ripe for it to be openly and universally discarded.

To deny plumply that "consciousness" exists seems so absurd on the face of it—for undeniably "thoughts" do exist—that I fear some readers will follow me no farther. Let me then immediately explain that I mean only to deny that the word stands for an entity, but to insist most emphatically that it does stand for a function. There is, I mean, no aboriginal stuff or quality of being, contrasted with that of which material objects are made, out of which our thoughts of them are made; but there is a function in experience which thoughts perform, and for the performance of which this quality of being is invoked. That function is *knowing*. "Consciousness" is supposed necessary to explain the fact that things not only are, but get reported, are known. Whoever blots out the notion of consciousness from his list of first principles must still provide in some way for that function's being carried on. . . .

My thesis is that if we start with the supposition that there is only one primal stuff or material in the world, a stuff of which everything is composed, and if we call that stuff "pure experience," then knowing can easily be explained as a particular sort of relation towards one another into which portions of pure experience may enter. The relation itself is a part of pure experience; one of its "terms" becomes the subject or bearer of the knowledge, the knower, the other becomes the object known.

. . . I am as confident as I am of anything that, in myself, the stream of thinking (which I recognize emphatically as a phenomenon) is only a careless name for what, when scrutinized, reveals itself to consist chiefly of the stream of my breathing. The "I think" which Kant said must be able to accompany all my objects, is the "I breathe" which actually does accompany them. There are other internal facts besides breathing (intracephalic muscular adjustments, etc., of which I have said a word in my larger Psychology), and these increase the assets of "consciousness," so far as the latter is subject to immediate perception; but breath, which was ever the original of "spirit," breath moving outwards, between the glottis and the nostrils, is, I am persuaded, the essence out of which philosophers have constructed the entity known to them as consciousness. *That entity is fictitious, while thoughts in the concrete are fully real. But thoughts in the concrete are made of the same stuff as things are.*[21]

> **. . . *consciousness* . . . is fictitious, while thoughts in the concrete are fully real. But thoughts in the concrete are made of the same stuff as things are.**

SUMMARY AND CONCLUSION

Since Descartes's discussion of mind and body as two separate and different substances, philosophers have struggled with a number of theories to explain how mind and body worked together to constitute a complete human being. Certain properties of mind—its lack of "extension" and seeming "privileged access," and the "incorrigibility" of mental claims—made the connection between mind and body extremely problematic. Therefore, philosophers suggested that mental events and bodily events are different aspects of some other event (dual aspect theory), or that they occur in parallel, like the sound and visual tracks on a film (parallelism or pre-established harmony), or that bodily events cause mental events but not the other way around (epiphenomenalism), or that mental events and bodily events are in fact identical (identity theory). Many philosophers and psychologists embraced behaviorism, arguing that "mental event" is in fact only shorthand for a complex description of patterns of behavior. More recently, many philosophers have come to reject the distinction between mind and body altogether, insisting on the primacy and indivisibility of the concept of a person. Other philosophers have come to embrace func-

---

[21] William James, "Does Consciousness Exist?" in *Journal of Philosophy, Psychology and Scientific Methods,* September 1, 1904.

tionalism, which holds that the brain is in fact an extremely sophisticated computer, and the mind is causally but not logically dependent on the brain.

GLOSSARY

behaviorism In psychology, the radical methodological thesis that insists that only what is publicly observable can be used as subject matter or as evidence in scientific research regarding human beings. In particular, all talk of "minds" and "mental events," "desires," "purposes," "ideas," "perceptions," and "experiences" is to be given up in favor of terms that refer only to the experimental situation or the behavior of the creature (or person) in question (for example, "stimulus," "response," "reinforcements"). In philosophy and metaphysics, behaviorism is the logical thesis that there are no "covert" or "private" mental events, only patterns of behavior and psychological ways of talking about behavior as "intelligent," "deceitful," "calculating," or "inattentive." All of these must be understood not in terms of some process ("intelligence," "deceitful thinking," "calculating," or "lack of attending") going on "in the mind" but rather as ways of interpreting, predicting, and otherwise describing and evaluating behavior.

causal interactionism The theory that mind and body causally interact, that mental events (for example, an "act of will") can cause a bodily consequence (for example, raising one's arm), and that a bodily change (for example, a puncture of the skin) can cause a mental consequence (for example, a pain).

dual aspect theory The theory (for example, in Spinoza) that mind and body are simply different aspects (or "attributes") of one and the same substance, thus avoiding the problem of interaction between substances.

dualism In general, the distinction between mind and body as separate substances, or very different kinds of states and events with radically different properties.

eliminative materialism The thesis that increasing knowledge of neurology eventually will allow us to give up our "folk psychological" terminology of mental states.

epiphenomenalism The thesis that mental events are epiphenomena, that is, side effects of various physical processes in the brain and nervous system but of little importance themselves. The model is a one-way causal model: Body states cause changes in the mind, but mental states have no effect in themselves on the body.

functionalism The view that the mind is the product of a pattern in the brain, as in a computer, rather than a product of the matter of the brain as such.

identity theory The thesis that the mind and brain are ontologically one and the same, or, more accurately, that mental states and events are in fact certain brain and nervous system processes. The theory is usually presented as a form of materialism, but it is important to emphasize that, unlike many materialistic theories, it does not deny the existence of mental events. It denies only that they have independent existence. Mental events are nothing other than certain bodily events.

immediate For certain and without need for argument.

incorrigibility Impossible to correct, cannot be mistaken. It has long been argued that our claims about our own mental states are incorrigible—we cannot be mistaken about them.

inference-ticket Ryle's term for referring to the proper function of a mental state: talk, as a description of a pattern of behavior and, therefore, as an "inference-ticket" that allows us to infer what a person will do in the future. (To say "George wants an olive" is to give us an inference-ticket regarding his future behavior around olives.)

intentionality In phenomenology, the thesis that every conscious act has an object. (The act is therefore called the "intentional act" and the object the "intentional object.") The importance of this concept is that it undercuts the metaphor of mental "contents" (as in a theater, an image explicitly used by Hume, for example). The concept was used by Husserl's teacher, Franz Brentano, who borrowed it from some medieval philosophers, before Husserl used it and made it famous.

parallelism The thesis that mental events and bodily events parallel each other and occur in perfect coordination but do not interact.

pre-established harmony Leibniz's view that the coordination between our ideas and the physical events of the world and our bodies was set up by God in perfect order.

privacy The seeming inaccessibility of mental states and events to anyone other than the person who "has" them.

private language argument Wittgenstein's argument that even if there were such "private objects" as mental states and events, it would be impossible for us to talk about them and impossible for us to identify them, even in our own case.

privileged access The technical term used by philosophers to refer to the curious fact that a person usually (if not always) can immediately know, simply by paying attention, what is going on in his own mind, while other people can find out what is going on—if they can at all—only by watching the person's behavior, listening to what he or she says, or asking (and hoping they get a truthful answer). It is important to distinguish privileged access from incorrigibility. The first means that a person knows directly what is "in his mind" without having to observe his behavior; the second means that he knows for certain and beyond the possibility of error.

unconscious Freud's famous way of referring to the fact that there are ideas, desires, memories, and experiences in our minds to which we do not have privileged access, which we may be wrong about (and, therefore, about which our claims are not incorrigible), and which may be more evident to other people than to oneself. He also distinguishes a *preconscious* ("the antechamber of consciousness"). Preconscious ideas can be made conscious simply by being attended to. (For example, you do know what the capital of California is, but you weren't conscious of it before I mentioned it; it was preconscious.) Truly unconscious ideas, however, cannot be made conscious, even when one tries to do so.

BIBLIOGRAPHY AND FURTHER READING

A good short survey of the "mind-body problem" is Keith Campbell, *Body and Mind* (New York: Doubleday, Anchor, 1970); a helpful introduction to the problem and the various alternatives is J. Shaffer, *The Philosophy of Mind* (Englewood Cliffs, NJ: Prentice-Hall, 1968). A good historical discussion of the reactions against Cartesian dualism is A. Lovejoy, *The Revolt Against Dualism* (La Salle, IL: Open Court, 1955). Two more recent anthologies, with special attention to the "identity theory," are David Rosenthal, ed., *Materialism and the Mind-Body Problem* (Englewood Cliffs, NJ: Prentice-Hall, 1971) and C. V. Borst, ed., *The Mind-Brain Identity Theory* (New York: St. Martin's Press, 1970). Two delightful presentations of the functionalist position is the collection of essays by Dan Dennett, *Brainstorms* (Newton Center, MA: Bradford Books, 1979) and his *Consciousness Explained* (Boston: Little Brown, 1991). See also J. Margolis, *The Philosophy of Psychology* (Englewood Cliffs, NJ: Prentice-Hall, 1983), Jay L. Garfield, *Foundations of Cognitive Science* (New York: Paragon House, 1990), and David Chalmers, *The Conscious Mind* (New York: Oxford Unity Press, 1996).

FREEDOM

"Two plus two equals four"—as if freedom means that!

FYODOR DOSTOYEVSKI

"The murderer had been raised in a slum. His father abandoned him when he was seven months old; he was beaten by his older siblings and constantly abused by his mother. He never had the chance to attend school; he never could get or hold a job. By the time he robbed the store, he was near starvation, addicted to hard drugs, without friends, and without help of any kind. His sister said, 'I've known since he was a child that he would do this some day.' His mother complained, 'I don't understand!' The prosecutor called it a 'cold-blooded, premeditated act.' The defense accused the whole of society, claiming that it had, through its neglect as well as its negative conditioning, made this man an inevitable killer." We know the rest of the arguments; what we don't know is their resolution. Should a man be held responsible for an act for which he has been conditioned the whole of his life? Or must we not hold out that no matter what the circumstances, he could have resisted, he could have decided not to commit the crime, and therefore he must be held responsible?

Of all the abstract problems of philosophy, the problem of **freedom** has the most obvious practical consequences. If we believe a person is free to choose his or her actions and destiny, we tend to load the person with moral responsibility, praise or blame; if we believe a person is simply a victim of the fates, a cog in a mechanical universe, or a pawn in the abstract hands of society, then our attitude toward his or her actions can be no different than our attitudes toward the movement of glaciers and the growth of flowers. "It happens that way," that's all.

A. FATALISM AND KARMA

Are we cogs in the universe? Are we pawns of the fates? People have often thought so. Our tendency to believe in fate goes back to the ancient Greeks. Most of the ancient Greeks believed that our destinies were already decided for us; no matter what our actions, the outcome was settled. Today, many people believe our actions and character are the causal result of our genes and our upbringing, and perhaps also the result of unconscious fears and desires that we may never even recognize. Then too, astrology and other theories of external determination have always been popular. (For instance, "*Virgo:* It's going to be a bad day: don't get out of bed and don't talk to anyone.") And we can see why they would be. The more our actions are the results of other forces and not our own doing, the less we need feel responsible for them, and the less we need worry about deciding what to do. It is already decided, and not by us.

Consider for example, the following news article that appeared throughout the United States in April 1980:[1]

> The way lawyer John Badger saw it, he was giving the judge a chance to "follow the flow into the brotherhood of man" by entertaining the notion that his client's life of crime was ordained by the stars.
>
> But Circuit Judge Ruben Costa, who said he was "inclined to believe there is a certain verity" to astrology, threw out the proposed defense at a pretrial hearing Monday for 23-year-old John Matthew Gopel, who is charged with rape, robbery and assault.
>
> Badger had planned to argue Gopel was insane by virtue of his astrological destiny.
>
> Badger said his client, born at 8:14 p.m. on Aug. 8, 1956, was literally "a born loser."
>
> "There is a force in the life of this young man that forced him to go on transmission fluid, sniff gasoline, cocaine, anything he could get his hands on," he said.
>
> Badger said he intended to present testimony from astrologers, scientists and mental health experts, as well as a bartender who would describe the effects of the full moon on human behavior.
>
> The list of defense evidence included the song "When You Wish Upon A Star," Spiderman comic books and the plays King Lear and Hamlet.

The ancient Greek tragedies, like *Oedipus the King,* depend upon **fatalism,** the view that whatever a person's actions and circumstances, however free they may seem, his or her predetermined end is inevitable. The story of Oedipus most famously

---

[1]All names in this article have been invented to protect the individuals involved.

recounted in the tragedy by Sophocles is perhaps the most stirring picture of Greek determinism. Oedipus and his wife, Iocasta, both scoffed at the prophets and made efforts to avoid their prophesied destinies.

FROM *OEDIPUS THE KING*
BY **SOPHOCLES**

OEDIPUS: I went to Delphi. Phoebus . . . declared
A thing most horrible: he foretold that I
Should mate with my own mother, and beget
A brood that men would shudder to behold,
And that I was to be the murderer
Of my own father.
              Therefore, back to Corinth
I never went—the stars alone have told me
Where Corinth lies—that I might never see
Cruel fulfillment of that oracle. [107–116]

IOCASTA: Listen to me
And you will hear the prophetic art
Touches our human fortunes not at all.
I soon can give you proof.—An oracle
Once came to [my husband] . . .
His fate it was, that he should have a son
By me, that son would take his father's life.
But he was killed—or so they said—by
Strangers.
By brigands, at a place where three ways meet.
As for the child, it was not three days old
When [my husband] fastened both its feet together
And had it cast off a precipice.
Therefore Apollo failed . . .
So much for what prophetic voices have uttered.[2]

    Unbeknown to either of them, of course, the "brigand" who killed Iocasta's husband was Oedipus himself, Iocasta's son, saved as a baby from the precipice and adopted by the man he had thought was his father, from whom he had fled. Thus, both their destinies had been fulfilled. Neither had any control over—nor even knowledge of—what happened to them, and so neither acted freely at all. Thus, the Chorus of observers declares:

---

[2]From Sophocles, *Oedipus the King,* trans. H. D. F. Kitto, rpt. in Barnet, Berman, Burto, *Types of Drama,* 3rd ed. (Boston: Little, Brown).

I pray that I might pass my life in reverent holiness of word and deed
For there are laws enthroned above,
Heaven created them,
Olympus was their father,
And mortal men had no part in their birth.

How should we deal with our fate? Should we try to know our fate? Iocasta advocates that "ignorance is bliss," and tries hard throughout the play not to acknowledge her growing suspicions. If we can't do anything about our fate, she reasons, then we shouldn't even think about it. But Oedipus insists on finding out the truth, and as a whole the play seems to advocate facing the fact of our destinies.

IOCASTA: Why should we fear, seeing that man is ruled
    By chance, and there is room for no clear forethought?
    No: live at random, live as best one can.
    . . .   Whoever thinks
    The least of this, he lives most comfortably. [80]
OEDIPUS: Alas! you generations of men!
    Even while you live you are next to nothing!
    Has any man won for himself
    More than the shadow of happiness?
    . . .
    Time sees all, and Time, in your despite
    Disclosed and punished your unnatural marriage
CREON [OEDIPUS'S UNCLE/BROTHER-IN-LAW]:
    Seek not to have your way in all things.
    Where you had your way before,
    Your mastery broke before the end.

The anthropomorphic Greek gods were integral to the ancient Greek notion of "fate." Human choices were considered impotent to change one's fate, because human beings were thought to be at the mercy of the gods' whims. But another conception of fate, the Buddhist conception, sees human choices as tremendously important—not because they are free, but precisely the opposite. In Buddhism, all human choices are gestures of *attachment* to the physical world, each one binding its maker more and more to a difficult fate. The effects of one's choices, as we have seen in Chapter 1, are called his or her *karma,* which one can only escape by paying the long-term debt that he or she has built up. Thus, there is a concept of freedom here, called *nirvana,* but it is not a freedom of the self or the individual. In fact, it is a freedom *from* the self and the individual, achieved only when there is no longer a self at all. It is our foolish attachment to this world, the Buddhist claims, which fosters the illusion that we are individuals at all. In a sense then, our fate is entirely determined; yet ironically, if we submit ourselves to fate and accept its authority, if we can stop making choices which further delude us into believing we are free, then and only then, can we ultimately become really free.

Consider the following excerpt from a contemporary Japanese philosopher, Keiji Nishitani, who has written extensively on the Buddhist concept of "nothingness" and the Western concept of "nihilism," which he says has now infected Japan.

ON FATE
BY KEIJI NISHITANI

From that viewpoint [the standpoint of nothingness] the world of karma is a world where each individual is determined by its ties and causal kinship within an endless world nexus, and yet each instance of individual existence and behavior, as well as each moment of their time, arises as something totally new, possessed of freedom and creativity.

Although the ebb and flow of the total nexus "since time past without beginning" is conceived as an infinite chain of causal necessity, its having no beginning implies, conversely, a *before* previous to any and all conceivable pasts. For such time to have no end means that it has an *after* that is future even to the most remote of possible futures. Any such before and after (beyond any definite before and after) lies in the present of every man and makes the present into free and creative activity.

◆ ◆ ◆

The karmic deeds that make manifest this restless, incessant becoming always return thereby at the same time to the home-ground of karma, to the home-ground of the present. In other words, doing opens itself up on each occasion to the openness of nihility and thus preserves the dimension of ecstatic transcendence.

This means that the self is at all times itself. Even as in my karma I constantly constitute my existence as a becoming *qua* being, in the home-ground of that karma I am ever in my own homeground: I am always myself. This is why restless, incessant becoming within time is at all times *my* existence. Karma is at all times *my* karma. And this means that it is free karma, that it implies an ecstatic transcendence to nihility.

Of course, although we call it freedom or creativity, it is not at this point true freedom or creativity. Freedom here is one with an inner necessity compelling us constantly to be doing something. It is in unison with that infinite drive and that infinite drive in turn is in unison with freedom. To be within the limitless world-nexus ceaselessly relating to something or other, and to be conditioned and determined in these relations by the world-nexus, is, seen from the other side, a self-determination. While the present karma is here the free work of the self, it appears at the same time to be possessed of the character of fate. Fate arises to awareness in unison with that freedom. Here the present karma reaches awareness under its form of infinity as infinite drive, in its "willful" essence.

The self's relation with something, seen as a self-determination, is the self's exercise of free will. Of its own accord, the self accepts a thing as good or rejects it as bad. But insofar as it is determined through causal kinship within the total nexus, this free will is a fate, a causal necessity, without thereby ceasing to be free will. To accept or reject something implies a simultaneous "attachment" to it. The karma that relates to something by lusting after it is at once voluntary and compulsory. The being of the self that comes about in that karma is at once a freedom and a burden. Here spontaneity becomes a burden and a debt.

◆ ◆ ◆

All of this indicates how deeply rooted self-centeredness is. So deeply underground do the roots of the self extend that no karmic activity can ever reach them. The karma of the self at all times returns to its own home-ground, namely, to the self itself, but it cannot get back to the home-ground of the self as such. Karma can do no more than go back to its own home-ground in the self and there reinstate its debt-laden existence. In karma, the self is constantly oriented inward to the home-ground of the self; and yet the only thing it achieves by this is the constant reconstitution of being *qua* becoming in a time without beginning or end. To transit endlessly through time in search of the home-ground of the self is the true form of our karma, that is, of our being in time, our life.

The karma of "time past without beginning" is the true form of our life. It implies a sense of essential "despair." Karma is what Kierkegaard calls the "sickness unto death." Its despair rises to awareness from directly underfoot of the work of our present deed, word, and thought, from the fountainhead of time without beginning or end, and of being within that time, in short from our self-centeredness. We can see an awareness of that despair also underlying the confession of the Buddhist *Verse of Repentance,* which suggests that every sort of karma stemming from the body, mouth, and mind of the self is grounded in a greed, anger, and folly without beginning. . . .

Karma here comes to bear the marks of guilt and sin. In a certain sense, it takes on the character of original sin, namely, sin that is as equally elemental as the free work and existence of man. Karma is freedom determined by causal necessity within the whole infinite nexus, a freedom of spontaneity in "attachment" and, therefore, a freedom totally *bound* by fate. At the same time, having reduced the whole causal nexus to its own center, it is a freedom altogether *unbound.* In karma these two aspects of freedom and causal necessity become one. Consequently, as a freedom that derives entirely from the determining force of causal necessity, as a freedom chased out and driven away from necessity, karma binds itself in attachment to the other, while at the same time it remains an altogether unbound freedom, gathering every other into the center of the self. This freedom is in the mode of an original sin.[3]

> *Karma is freedom determined by causal necessity within the whole infinite nexus, a freedom of spontaneity in "attachment" and, therefore, a freedom totally bound by fate.*

---

[3] Keiji Nishitani, *Religion and Nothingness,* trans. Jan Van Bragt (Berkeley: University of California Press, 1982).

B. PREDESTINATION

Fatalism, in its Greek or Buddhist sense, is the claim that our future is determined by a play of forces beyond our understanding. But what if these forces are understood and in fact *created* by one, superhuman being? **Predestination** has been the view of many theologians, according to whom our every action (and every event in the universe) is known, if not also caused in advance, by God. Predestination, like fatalism, does not depend upon any particular antecedent conditions, unless we want to say that God is an antecedent condition.

All the Western theologians have had to ponder the problem of predestination and freedom, since all the Western religions' scriptures claim that God created, or caused, everything. As we saw in Chapter 5, this is of particular concern when considering evil. There, the "problem of evil" was described as the question of how evil could be caused by a good God. We now can see that the crux of the "problem of evil" is the question of freedom. It would be easy to explain much evil if human beings were free—in that case, we are the cause of evil, and not an all-good God. But if, as is stated in scripture, God created and caused everything, then surely, God creates our human actions, too. Humans sin—and so it seems we are back to the drawing board. How can an all-good God cause us or let us be free to sin?

The following lines from St. Augustine summarize the problem of freedom and one Christian solution to it. God made human beings free, because He is all good, and free actions are better than unfree ones. However, since freedom allows us to sin, we are responsible for bringing evil into the world.

ON FREE CHOICE OF THE WILL, BOOK II
BY **ST. AUGUSTINE**

I.
WHY DID GOD GIVE FREEDOM OF THE WILL TO MEN,
SINCE IT IS BY THIS THAT MEN SIN?

EVODIUS. Now, if possible, explain to me why God gave man free choice of the will since if he had not received it he would not be able to sin.

AUGUSTINE. Are you perfectly sure that God gave to man what you think ought not to have been given?

EVODIUS. As far as I seem to understand the discussion in the first book, we have freedom of will, and could not sin if we were without it.

AUGUSTINE. I, too, remember that this was made clear to us. But I just asked you whether you know that it was God who gave us that which we possess, through which it is clear that we commit sin.

EVODIUS. No one else. For we are from Him, and whether we sin or whether we do right, we earn reward or punishment from Him.

AUGUSTINE. I want to ask, as well: do you know this clearly, or do you believe it willingly without really knowing it, because you are prompted by authority?

EVODIUS. I admit that at first I trusted authority on this point. But what can be more true than that all good proceeds from God, that everything just is good, and that it is just to punish sinners and to reward those who do right? From this it follows that through God sinners are afflicted with unhappiness, and those who do right endowed with happiness.

AUGUSTINE. I do not object, but let me ask another question: how do you know that we are from God? You did not answer that; instead, you explained that we merit punishment and reward from God.

EVODIUS. The answer to *that* question, too, is clear, if for no other reason than the fact that, as we have already agreed, God punished sins. All justice is from God, and it is not the role of justice to punish foreigners, although it is the role of goodness to bestow benefits on them. Thus it is clear that we belong to God, since He is not only most generous in bestowing benefits upon us, but also most just in punishing us. Also, we can understand that man is from God through the fact, which I proposed and you conceded, that every good is from God. For man himself, insofar as he is a man, is a good, because he can live rightly when he so wills.

AUGUSTINE. If this is so, the question that you proposed is clearly answered. If man is a good, and cannot act rightly unless he wills to do so, then he must have free will, without which he cannot act rightly. We must not believe that God gave us free will so that we might sin, just because sin is committed through free will. It is sufficient for our question, why free will should have been given to man, to know that without it man cannot live rightly. That it was given for this reason can be understood from the following: if anyone uses free will for sinning, he incurs divine punishment. This would be unjust if free will had been given not only that man might live rightly, but also that he might sin. For how could a man justly incur punishment who used free will to do the thing for which it was given? When God punishes a sinner, does He not seem to say, "Why have you not used free will for the purpose for which I gave it to you, to act rightly?" Then too, if man did not have free choice of will, how could there exist the good according to which it is just to condemn evildoers and reward those who act rightly? What was not done by will would be neither evildoing nor right action. But punishment and reward would be unjust if man did not have free will. Moreover, there must needs be justice both in punishment and in reward, since justice is one of the goods that are from God. Therefore, God must needs have given free will to man.[4]

One's opinion on the question of freedom was a crucial determinant of one's sectarian alliance in early Islam. Islam is sometimes understood in the West as a "fatalist" religion; in other words, it is thought that all Muslims believe that human beings are not free. However, the Mu'tazilites, one of the first Islamic sects, claimed

---

[4] St. Augustine, *On Free Choice of the Will*, trans. Anna S. Benjamin and L. H. Hackstaff (Indianapolis: Bobbs-Merrill, 1964).

that the human will is free, despite passages in scripture which would lead one to believe the contrary, such as the following:

"No misfortune befalls except by Allah's [God's] will. He guides the hearts of those who believe in him. Allah has knowledge of all things." (64:11)

"Every misfortune that befalls the earth or your own persons, is ordained before we bring it into being." (57:22–23)

Thus, Islam provides an interesting breadth of argument on the question of freedom. The Mu'tazilites claimed that human freedom is consistent with God's power, by distinguishing between two types of action, or causality. God's actions are "necessary," or lawlike. They *must* happen. Human actions, however, are "intentional," they are contingent upon God's actions, which are their necessary conditions and consequences. Thus, a person is free, for instance, to hit a billiard ball with his or her pool cue. But he or she is *not* free to hit the ball and have it stay still, or to hit it in one direction and have it go in another. Only God is "free" to make necessary, physical, laws. For the Mu'tazilites, human freedom amounts to *directing* God's actions along various possible paths. We are responsible for how we direct God's creations, and so we are rightly rewarded or punished by God for our choices.

Another very important Islamic school, the **Ash'arites,** reacted against the Mu'tazilites in favor of a more liberal interpretation of scriptural passages like the ones above. The Ash'arites, however, wound up making a distinction with regard to the question of freedom which was similar to that of the Mu'tazilites. The Ash'arites claimed that only God is free, and that all human actions are determined by God. God's "predestination" here, however, is more like an offer of a gift. God offers to human beings various actions, which they can accept, acquire, or pass. Only God, therefore, can create an action, according to the Ash'arites. Human beings merely acquire them, "secondhand" so to speak. When we acquire good actions, we deserve our reward. When we acquire bad ones, we deserve our punishment.

Although one may take it overall, then, that Islamic tradition does seem to believe more in God's predestination than does Christianity, the Islamic stance on the question of freedom is really a very complex one. The debate within Islam about freedom continues to this day. Here is an example from an important twentieth-century Islamic theologian, **Sir Mohammad Iqbal:**

FROM "**THE HUMAN EGO:
ITS FREEDOM AND IMMORTALITY**"
BY **MOHAMMAD IQBAL**

Does the ego then determine its own activity? If so, how is the self-determination of the ego related to the determination of the spatio-temporal order? Is personal causality a special kind of causality, or only a disguised form of the mechanism of Nature? It is claimed that the two kinds of determinism are not mutually exclusive and that the scientific method is equally applicable to human action. The human act of deliberation is understood to be a conflict of motives which are conceived, not as the ego's own present or inherited tendencies of action or inaction, but as so many external forces fighting one another, gladiator-like, on the arena of the mind. Yet the final choice is regarded as a fact determined by the *strongest* force, and not by the resultant of contending motives, like a purely physical effect. I am, however, firmly of the opinion that the controversy between the advocates of Mechanism and Freedom arises from a wrong view of intelligent action which modern psychology, unmindful of its own independence as a science, possessing a special set of facts to observe, was bound to take on account of its slavish imitation of physical sciences.

◆◆◆

Thus the element of guidance and directive control in the ego's activity clearly shows that the ego is a free personal causality. He shares in the life and freedom of the Ultimate Ego who, by permitting the emergence of a finite ego, capable of private initiative, has limited this freedom of His own free will. This freedom of conscious behaviour follows from the view of ego-activity which the Quran takes. There are verses which are unmistakably clear on this point:

'And say: The truth is from your Lord: Let him, then, who will, believe: and let him who will, be an unbeliever.' (18:28.)

'If ye do well to your own behoof will ye do well: and if ye do evil against yourselves will ye do it.' (17:7.)

[Fatalism] is life and boundless power which recognizes no obstruction, and can make a man calmly offer his prayers when bullets are showering around him.

Indeed Islam recognizes a very important fact of human psychology, i.e., the rise and fall of the power to act freely, and is anxious to retain the power to act freely as a constant and undiminished factor in the life of the ego. The timing of the daily prayer which according to the Quran restores 'self-possession' to the ego by bringing it into closer touch with the ultimate source of life and freedom, is intended to save the ego from the mechanizing effects of sleep and business. Prayer in Islam is the ego's escape from mechanism to freedom.

The fatalism implied in this attitude is not negation of the ego . . . it is life and boundless power which recognizes no obstruction, and can make a man calmly offer his prayers when bullets are showering around him.[5]

A very different example of determinism comes from the African Yoruba nation. In the Yoruba version, there is a place for human freedom within a larger determinist context. Here it is described by Texas philosopher **Jacqueline Trimier:**

---

[5] Sir Mohammad Iqbal, *The Reconstruction of Religious Thought in Islam* (London: Oxford University Press, 1934).

ON THE YORUBA *ORI*
BY **JACKIE TRIMIER**

In Yoruba philosophy, the *ori* [or "inner head"] determines one's fate, and, contrary to most alternative cultural accounts of the soul, the Yoruba actually **chooses** his *ori*. In the creation myth *Ajala,* the "potter of heads," provides each body with a head. But before a person arrives on earth, he or she must go to the house of *Ajala* to choose a head. To make matters more complicated, *Ajala* has a reputation for being irresponsible and careless. As a result, *Ajala* molds many bad heads; he sometimes forgets to fire some, misshapes others, and overburns still others. Because it is said that he owes money to many people, *Ajala* commonly hides in the ceiling to avoid creditors and neglects some of the heads he put on the fire, leaving them to burn. But beneath this earthy and all-too-human depiction of the deity, certain classic concepts of fate and freedom are evident. People choose their destinies, but it is a choice that is fraught with dangers and uncertainties. *Ajala* molds many bad heads and only a few good ones. When a person gets to *Ajala*'s storehouse of heads, he or she does not know which heads are bad or good—all people choose heads in ignorance. If a person picks a bad head, he or she is doomed to failure in life. Moreover, before a person reaches earth with a body, head, and soul, rain can erode an imperfectly made head. On earth, hard work would be useless to affect one's fortune because all of one's energy would have been used for repairing the damaged, useless head. yet, if a person picks a really good head, the person is destined to have a good, prosperous life. With hard work, he or she will surely be successful, since little or no energy need be expended in costly head repairs.

The concept of the *ori* or inner head carries with it a profound belief in predestination. The life one leads depends upon the head one chooses. One myth from *Ifa* literary corpus tells about three friends *Oriseeku, Orileemere,* and *Afuwape* who needed heads to travel from heaven to earth. They went to find the house of *Ajala* to choose their heads. Before leaving heaven, they were told not to stop at any place along the way. However, *Afuwape* did not listen; he visited his father, and his two friends left him behind. When the latter reached *Ajala*'s house, they did not find him because, as usual, he was hiding in the rafters from creditors. Instead of waiting for *Ajala* to appear, the two friends picked their heads without knowing which ones were properly made; and as they descended to earth, rain wore out their heads. Consequently, they lived unsuccessful lives on earth.

Afuwape got to the home of his father, *Orunmila* (god of wisdom), who was consulting his *Ifa* (divination texts). When *Afuwape* told his father of his plan to see *Ajala,* the *Ifa* priests consulted for *Afuwape* and said *Orunmila* should offer money and salt as a sacrifice and that *Afuwape* should carry part of these offerings on his journey. *Afuwape* left his father's home and, along the way, asked a gatekeeper for the way to *Ajala*'s house. The gatekeeper had never used salt before and was cooking his soup over a flame and salting it with ashes. *Afuwape* offered the gatekeeper some salt which he liked. To return the kindness, the gatekeeper took *Afuwape* to the house of *Ajala.*

When *Afuwape* found *Ajala*'s house, *Ajala* was not at home but one of the creditors was waiting for him. The gatekeeper had advised *Afuwape* to help *Ajala* pay part of his debt so that *Ajala* would help him choose the best head possible. *Afuwape* paid the debt, and the creditor left. When *Ajala* came home, he was so grateful that he took *Afuwape* to his storehouse and helped him choose the best head. Consequently, *Afuwape*'s head withstood the hazards of a journey to earth, and he had a good life on earth.[6]

To Americans, the most familiar version of belief in predestination comes from that school of Protestant Christianity called Calvinism. In the following passage, the famous American Calvinist theologian, **Jonathan Edwards** (1703–1758), gives a defense of his belief in predestination.

FROM **"FREEDOM OF THE WILL"**
BY **JONATHAN EDWARDS**

WHEREIN IT IS CONSIDERED WHETHER THERE IS OR CAN BE ANY SUCH SORT OF FREEDOM OF WILL, AS THAT WHEREIN ARMINIANS[7] PLACE THE ESSENCE OF THE LIBERTY OF ALL MORAL AGENTS; AND WHETHER ANY SUCH THING EVER WAS OR CAN BE CONCEIVED OF. . . .

First, I am to prove, that God has an absolute and certain foreknowledge of the free actions of moral agents.

One would think, it should be wholly needless to enter on such an argument with any that profess themselves Christians: but so it is; God's certain fore-knowledge of the free acts of moral agents, is denied by some that pretend to believe the Scriptures to be the word of God; and especially of late. I therefore shall consider the evidence of such a prescience in the Most High, as fully as the designed limits of this essay will admit of; supposing myself herein to have to do with such as own the truth of the Bible.

ARG I. My first argument shall be taken from God's *prediction* of such events. Here I would, in the first place, lay down these two things as axioms.

(1.)   If God does not foreknow, he cannot foretell such events; that is, he can-
        not peremptorily and certainly foretell them. If God has no more than an

---

[6] Jacqueline Trimier, "African Philosophy," from *World Philosophy,* ed. R. C. Solomon and K. Higgins (reprinted by permission of the editors).

[7] Jacobus Arminius (1560–1609) was a Dutch theologian who claimed that although God has foreknowledge of our actions, human beings nonetheless act freely. Edwards aims his arguments against Arminius' followers throughout.

uncertain guess concerning events of this kind, then he can declare no more than an uncertain guess. Positively to foretell, is to profess to foreknow, or to declare positive foreknowledge.

(2.) If God does not certainly foreknow the future volitions of moral agents, then neither can he certainly foreknow those events which are consequent and dependent on these volitions. The existence of the one depending on the existence of the other; the knowledge of the existence of the one depends on the knowledge of the existence of the other; and the one cannot be more certain than the other.

Therefore, how many, how great and how extensive soever the consequences of the volitions of moral agents may be; though they should extend to an alteration of the slate of things through the universe, and should be continued in a series of successive events to all eternity, and should in the progress of things branch forth into an infinite number of series, each of them going on in an endless line or chain of events; God must be as ignorant of all these consequences, as he is of the volitions whence they take their rise: all these events, and the whole slate of things depending on them, how important, extensive and vast soever, must be hid from him.

SECTION XII.

God's certain Foreknowledge of the future Volitions of moral
Agents, inconsistent with such a Contingence of those Volitions
as is without all Necessity.

Having proved that God has a certain and infallible prescience of the act of the Will of moral agents, I come now, in the *second* place, to show the consequence; to show how it follows from hence, that these events are *necessary,* with a Necessity of connection or consequence.

The chief Arminian divines, so far as I have opportunity to observe, deny this consequence; and affirm, that if such Foreknowledge be allowed, it is no evidence of any Necessity of the event foreknown. Now I desire, that this matter may be particularly and thoroughly inquired into. I cannot but think that, on particular and full consideration, it may be perfectly determined, whether it be indeed so or not.

In order to a proper consideration of this matter, I would observe the following things.

I. It is very evident, with regard to a thing whose existence is infallibly and indissolubly connected with something which already hath or has had existence, the existence of that thing is necessary. Here may be noted:

1. I observed before, in explaining the nature of Necessity, that in things which are past, their existence is now necessary: having already made sure of existence, it is too late for any possibility of alteration in that respect: it is now impossible that it should be otherwise than true, that that thing has existed.

If there be any such thing as a divine Foreknowledge of the volitions of free agents, that Foreknowledge . . . is a thing which already has, and long ago had, existence; and so, now its existence is necessary; it is now utterly impossible to be otherwise than that this Foreknowledge should be, or should have been.

2. If there be any such thing as a divine Foreknowledge of the volitions of free agents, that Foreknowledge, by the supposition, is a thing which already has, and long ago had, existence; and so, now its existence is necessary; it is now utterly impossible to be otherwise than that this Foreknowledge should be, or should have been.

3. It is also very manifest, that those things which are indissolubly connected with other things that are necessary, are themselves necessary. As that proposition whose truth is necessarily connected with another proposition, which is necessarily true, is itself necessarily true. To say otherwise, would be a contradiction: it would be in effect to say, that the connection was indissoluble, and yet was not so, but might be broken. If that, whose existence is indissolubly connected with something whose existence is now necessary, is itself not necessary, then it may possibly not exist, notwithstanding that indissoluble connection of its existence.— Whether that absurdity be not glaring, let the reader judge.

4. It is no less evident, that if there be a full, certain, and infallible Foreknowledge of the future existence of the volitions of moral agents, then there is a certain infallible and indissoluble connection between those events and that Foreknowledge; and that therefore, by the preceding observations, those events are necessary events; being infallibly and indissolubly connected with that whose existence already is, and so is now necessary, and cannot but have been.

To say the Foreknowledge is certain and infallible, and yet the connection of the event with that Foreknowledge is not indissoluble, but dissoluble and fallible, is very absurd. To affirm it, would be the same thing as to affirm that there is no necessary connection between a proposition's being infallibly known to be true, and its being true indeed. So that it is perfectly demonstrable, that if there be any infallible knowledge of future volitions, the event is necessary; or, in other words, that it is impossible but the event should come to pass. For if it be not impossible but that it may be otherwise, then it is not impossible but true. But how absurd is that, on the supposition that there is now an infallible knowledge (i.e. knowledge which it is impossible should fail) that it is true. There is this absurdity in it, that it is not impossible but that there now should be no truth in that proposition which is now infallibly known to be true.

II. That no future event can be certainly foreknown, whose existence is contingent, and without all necessity, may be proved thus; it is impossible for a thing to be certainly known to any intellect without evidence. To suppose otherwise, implies a contradiction: because, for a thing to be certainly known to any understanding, is for it to be evident to that understanding: and for a thing to be evident to any understanding, is the same thing as for that understanding to see evidence of it: but no understanding, created or uncreated, can see evidence where there is none: for is the same thing as to see that to be which is not. And therefore, if there by any truth which is absolutely without evidence, that truth is absolutely unknowable, insomuch that it implies a contradiction to suppose that it is known. . . .

III. To suppose the future volitions of moral agents not to be necessary events; or, which is the same thing, events which it is not impossible but that they may not come to pass; and yet to suppose that God certainly foreknows them, and knows all things, is to suppose God's knowledge to be inconsistent with itself. For to say, that God certainly, and without all conjecture, knows that a thing will infallibly be, which at the same time he knows to be so contingent that it may possibly not be, is to suppose his knowledge inconsistent with itself; or that one thing that he knows, is utterly inconsistent with another thing that he knows.[8]

C. DETERMINISM

As we have seen, the problem of freedom occurs in different contexts, from pagan fatalism to Christian predestination. The problem occurs in terms of the most abstract thesis that the universe as a whole is a single great machine or "substance" (as in Newton or Spinoza) and in very localized theories about the psychology of the human personality. At all levels, however, the problem has usually been identified with a single claim, **determinism.** We were briefly introduced to determinism in Chapter 1: Spinoza defended it in his metaphysical system; Newton gave it a convincing scientific interpretation with his physical theories. In a phrase, **determinism** can be characterized by a principle already familiar to us from Chapter 2, the "principle of universal causation." "Every event has its cause(s)." Determinism is the thesis that everything that happens in the universe is determined according to the *laws of nature.* The problem is that human actions, whatever else they might be, are also events in the physical universe. But if human action is just another law-determined natural occurrence, can it also be free? It is as if we were to start praising people (or blaming them) for obeying the law of gravity. What else could they possibly do?

Determinism as we have defined it is related, but different from fatalism and predestination. According to fatalism, despite what happens, the end is inevitable. In

---

[8] Jonathan Edwards, "Freedom of the Will," from *The Works of President Edwards, In Four Volumes,* Vol. 2 (New York: Leavitt and Allen, 1856).

predestination, God's will has power over *both* human choices and natural law. According to determinism, however, an event will necessarily happen if its antecedent conditions are fulfilled. Determinism, on the other hand, need not say that any event is inevitable, it insists only that *if* certain conditions exist, *then* a certain kind of event will take place (for example, if a pot of water is heated sufficiently, then it will boil; or if a person is forced to choose between losing his life and killing an insect, then he will take the life of the insect). This "if . . . then" structure is essential to determinism. (There need be no such "ifs" or "thens" to fatalism or predestination.)

Determinism is the theory that every event in the universe, including every human action, has its natural causes; given certain antecedent conditions, then an event will take place necessarily, according to the laws of nature. But we must fill out the determinist's premise by at least one more step. It is not enough to say, "every event has its natural cause(s)," since this would leave open the possibility that although every event requires certain **antecedent conditions** in order to take place, the event might still be a matter of chance, at least to some extent, or a matter of human choice. We must say that "every event has its sufficient natural cause(s)." **Sufficient** means capable of bringing the event about by itself. Then there is no room for chance and no room for choice. This view, which we shall call "hard" determinism ("hard" as in "hardhearted" as well as a "hard" conclusion to accept), clearly leaves no room for human freedom. Without choice, there can be no freedom, and without freedom, there is no reason to hold a person responsible for his action, no matter how virtuous or how vicious it might be. According to the hard determinist thesis, we can barely be said to be "acting" at all, for our "actions" are nothing but the result of antecedent conditions and laws of nature that leave no room for our "doing something" at all.

1. Hard Determinism

The hard determinist premise received its greatest impetus from Newton's physics and his picture of the universe as "matter in motion," determined according to the laws of motion and gravitation that he so elegantly formulated. But his followers applied these laws not only to the movements of the planets and the stars or to the ball rolling down an inclined plane. According to them, we too are "matter in motion," physical bodies that are subject to all of the laws of nature. What we "do" is just as determined by these laws as any other event in nature.

This "hardheaded" determinism has maintained a powerful hold on philosophers ever since Isaac Newton published his theories in the seventeenth century. The philosopher **Pierre Simon La Place** had such confidence in the Newtonian system that he claimed that if he knew the location and motion of every object in the universe, he could predict the location and motion of every object in the universe at any time in the future. (He could also *retrodict,* or look, back to, every past state of the universe.) This means that if he had a proper map of the universe, including the material parts of our own bodies, he could predict everything that would ever happen, and of course, everything that we would ever do. If this is so, what possible sense could we make of our vain claims to have choices of actions, to decide what to do, or to hold ourselves and others responsible for what we have done?

La Place's confidence in the hard determinist thesis was common among the immediate successors and enthusiasts of Newton. For example, one of the philosophers of the French Enlightenment, **Baron Paul Henri d'Holbach,** defended the hard determinist viewpoint so uncompromisingly that he shocked even his colleagues as well as the many traditionalists.

FROM *SYSTEM OF NATURE*
BY **PAUL HENRI D'HOLBACH**

In whatever manner man is considered, he is connected to universal nature, and submitted to the necessary and immutable laws that she interposes on all beings she contains, according to their peculiar essences or to the respective properties with which, without consulting them, she endows each particular species. Man's life is a line that nature commands him to describe upon the surface of the earth, without his ever being able to swerve from it, even for an instant. He is born without his own consent; his organization does in nowise depend upon himself; his ideas come to him involuntarily; his habits are in the power of those who cause him to contract them; he is unceasingly modified by causes, whether visible or concealed, over which he has no control, which necessarily regulate his mode or existence, give the hue to his way of thinking, and determine his manner of acting. He is good or bad, happy or miserable, wise or foolish, reasonable or irrational, without his will being for anything in these various states. Nevertheless, in spite of the shackles by which he is bound, it is pretended he is a free agent, or that independent of the causes by which he is moved, he determines his own will, and regulates his own condition.

However slender the foundation of his opinion, of which everything ought to point out to him the error, it is current at this day and passes for an incontestable truth with a great number of people, otherwise extremely enlightened; it is the basis of religion, which supposing relations between man and the unknown being she has placed above nature, has been incapable of imagining how man could merit reward or deserve punishment from this being, if he was not a free agent. Society has been believed interested in his system; because an idea has gone abroad, that if all the actions of man were to be contemplated as necessary, the right of punishing those who injure their associates would no longer exist. At length human vanity accommodated itself to a hypothesis which, unquestionably, appears to distinguish man from all other physical beings, by assigning to him the special privilege of a total independence of all other causes, but of which a very little reflection would have shown him the impossibility.

The will, as we have elsewhere said, is a modification of the brain, by which it is disposed to action, or prepared to give play to the organs. This will be necessarily determined by the qualities, good or bad, agreeable or painful, of the object or the motive that acts upon his sense, or of which the idea remains with him, and is resuscitated by his memory. In consequence, he acts necessarily, his action is the result of the impulse he receives either from the motive, from the object, or from the idea which has modified his brain, or disposed his will. When he does not act according to his impulse, it is because there comes some new cause, some new motive, some new idea, which modified his brain in a different manner, gives him a new impulse, determines his will in another way, by which the action of the former impulse is suspended: thus, the sight of an agreeable object, or its idea, determines his will to set him in action to procure it; but if a new object or a new idea more powerfully attracts him, it gives a new direction to his will, annihilates the effect of the former, and prevents the action by which it was to be procured. This is the mode in which reflection, experience, reason, necessarily arrests or suspends the action of man's will: without this he would of necessity have followed the anterior impulse which carried him toward a then desirable object. In all this he always acts according to necessary laws from which he has no means of emancipating himself.

◆◆◆

In short, the actions of man are never free; they are always the necessary consequence of his temperament, of the received ideas, and of the notions, either true or false, which he has formed to himself of happiness; of his opinions, strengthened by example, by education, and by daily experience. So many crimes are witnessed on the earth only because every thing conspires to render man vicious and criminal; the religion he has adopted, his government, his education, the examples set before him, irresistibly drive him on to evil: under these circumstances, morality preaches virtue to him in vain. In those societies where vice is esteemed, where crime is crowned, where venality is constantly recompensed, where the most dreadful disorders are punished only in those who are too weak to enjoy the privilege of committing them with impunity, the practice of virtue is considered nothing more than a painful sacrifice of happiness. Such societies chastise, in the lower orders, those excesses which they respect in the higher ranks; and frequently have the injustice to condemn those in the penalty of death, whom public prejudices, maintained by constant example, have rendered criminal.

Man, then, is not a free agent in any one instant of life; he is necessarily guided in each step by those advantages, whether real or fictitious, that he attaches to the objects by which his passions are roused: these passions themselves are necessary in a being who unceasingly tends towards his own happiness; their energy is necessary, since that depends on his temperament; his temperament is necessary, because it depends

> *In short, the actions of man are never free; they are always the necessary consequence of his temperament, of the received ideas, and of the notions, either true or false, which he has formed to himself of happiness; of his opinions, strengthened by example, by education, and by daily experience.*

on the physical elements which enter into his composition; the modification of his temperament is necessary, as it is the infallible and inevitable consequence of the impulse he receives from the incessant action of moral and physical beings.[9]

2. Determinism versus Indeterminism

Should we accept the determinist's premise? Without it, determinism cannot get to first base. Well, we have already seen the arguments traditionally advanced in earlier chapters, even by philosophers who are not themselves "hard determinists." The most general argument is that only by assuming from the outset that every event has its (sufficient natural) cause(s) can we ever understand anything. Otherwise, we should have auto mechanics always giving us back our cars (and our bills) with the unhelpful statement that "there's no cause for our troubles." We could expect the same from doctors whenever a diagnosis gave them the least bit of trouble, and we would use it ourselves every time a problem began to get difficult.

A much stronger argument is made by Kant, who says that the basic rule of determinism, the principle of universal causation, is one of the rules by which we must interpret every experience. But even Hume, who denies that this principle can be justified either through reason or through experience, insists that it is a "natural habit" or custom that is indispensable to us and that we could not give up even if we wanted to. The consensus, then, has been that the principle itself is inescapable. Even Leibniz, who rejected the idea of causation altogether, insisted on his "Principle of Sufficient Reason," which came to the same end, that is, "every event has its sufficient reason."

The agreement of so many philosophers indicates the strength of the hard determinist position. Without the assumption that "every event has its sufficient natural cause(s)," human knowledge would seem to be without one of its most vital presuppositions. Not only scientific research but even our most ordinary, everyday beliefs would be forced to an intolerable skeptical standstill. Our every experience would be unintelligible, and our universe would appear to be nothing but a disconnected stream of incoherent happenings from which nothing could be predicted and nothing understood. So the answer to the question, "Why should we accept the determinist's premise?" seems to be, "We cannot give it up; how could we possibly do without it?" For no matter how it is rephrased or philosophically altered (for example, by Leibniz, who eliminates the concept of "cause" from it), the assumption that every event in the universe, including our own actions, can be explained and understood, if only one knows enough about it and its antecedent conditions, is a presupposition of all human thinking that we cannot imagine doing without.

Even if the hard determinist's premise seems undeniable, it is not yet clear how we are to understand that premise. The older determinists of the Newtonian period (La Place, d'Holbach) understood the idea of a cause as a literal push or compulsion, as if one were given a shove down the stairs. On this model, our actions are no different, except in complexity, from the "actions" of billiard balls on a felt-covered table,

---

[9] Baron Paul Henri d'Holbach, *System of Nature* (London: Kearsley, 1797).

the motion of each wholly determining the motion of the next. The exact movements of every ball, of course, are not always evident. In the opening break, for example, even the most expert player cannot predict with accuracy where each ball will go. But we can be sure that each one is absolutely determined by the movements of the other balls that make contact with it, just as with the simple predictable case of a single ball hitting another straight on.

If we view human beings as nothing more than physical bodies—bones, muscles, nerve cells, and the like—then this mechanical billiard ball model might make some sense. But a much weaker interpretation of the hard determinist premise does not require us to so radically reduce people to mere bodies. Instead of talking about actual physical pushes and compulsions, we can interpret the determinist premise in the following: To say that every event has its cause(s) is to say that if certain antecedent conditions are satisfied, then we can predict that such and such will occur. On the stronger mechanistic determinist interpretation, causes are actual pushes and, on such an interpretation, the notion of freedom is clearly impossible. But the weaker interpretation, of determinism as predictability, may yet offer room for us to talk about freedom of action. For example, we may be able to predict our friend's decision, but that does not seem to mean that he was forced to make it. We may be able to predict his action, but only because, knowing him, we know what he will probably do. On the second interpretation, perhaps we can have determinism and freedom.

Many philosophers defend determinism only as predictability on the basis of probability. We might easily be wrong. To say that every event is determined, on this view, means only that it is predictable if we know enough about antecedent conditions. But it has been objected, against the determinist, that the fact of such predictability is not sufficient to defend determinism in anything like the "hard" sense. It is one thing to say that all events, including human actions, are actually caused or compelled by physical forces. It is something quite different to say that all events including human actions, are predictable. They might be predictable, for example, only on the basis of certain statistical probabilities. "Most people in this circumstance would do that." "The odds are for it," in other words. Or, in the case of human actions, the predictability might still be due to human choices; we can predict each other's actions because we know how we would probably choose in the same circumstances. But there is no need here to talk about "causes" or compulsions. Nor, it has been argued, should we even talk any longer about "determinism," if this is all that we mean by it.

In contrast, the antideterminist thesis, called **indeterminism,** rejects both versions of determinism. Indeterminism claims that not every event has its sufficient natural cause(s). This theory at least appears to leave room for free will, for as soon as we allow that there are some events that are uncaused, human actions might be among them. Thus it would seem that we can be held properly responsible for our actions. But is the indeterminist thesis plausible?

The indeterminist argument has recently received a boost from physics, the very science that gave rise to the determinist threat in the first place. It was Newtonian physics that gave determinism its strongest claims. Remember La Place boasting that if he knew the location and motion of every particle in the universe, he could predict every future state of the universe at any time. But it has been shown in recent physics that such knowledge is impossible. One of the most important discoveries of modern physics is the **Heisenberg Uncertainty Principle** (named after its discoverer, **Werner Heisenberg**), which says that we cannot know both the location and the momentum of a subatomic particle. In coming to know the one, we make it impossible for us to know the other at the same time.

From this principle, the British physicist-philosopher **Sir Arthur Eddington** advanced the indeterminist argument that determinism is false on physical grounds. Not every event in the universe is predictable. Furthermore, many scientists now agree, on the basis of such considerations, that the concept of "cause" does not apply to certain subatomic particles either. The determinist premise that "every event in the universe has its sufficient natural cause" is false. Some events, namely those involving some subatomic particles, are not caused, not predictable, and therefore not determined, on any interpretation. But if not all events are determined, then perhaps human actions are not determined but free; if they are predictable, it is not because they are caused.

The object of indeterminism is to deny the determinist position in order to make room for human freedom. But there are, unfortunately, two serious objections to this indeterminist argument. First, even if we suppose that the conclusions of modern physical ("quantum") theory are correct (a matter still in dispute among physicists), it is clear that determinism is of importance to us primarily as a theory of macroscopic bodies (that is, visible size—people, trees, cars) not subatomic particles. No one has ever concluded that quantum theory and modern physics actually refute Newton's theories. Rather, it supplements them, put them in their place, and qualifies them in ways that would have been unthinkable in the eighteenth century. But as for the determinism of the gravitation of the planets or the rolling of a ball down an inclined plane, the spectacular discoveries of modern particle physics don't affect them in the least. With regard to the physical determinism of our own bodies, the case remains as before. It might be true that it is impossible to predict what a subatomic particle in our bodies might do. But it does not follow that it is impossible to predict what our bodies will do. Falling out of a plane, we still fall at exactly the same speed as a sack of potatoes, which is all the determinist needs to continue his attack on our concept of freedom. Second, even if there should be such indeterminism, indeterminism is not the same as freedom. Suppose there should be a "gap" in the causal determinism of our decisions by the various neurological processes of our brains; that would mean, at most, that what we do is not determined at all—or is determined only randomly. Suppose all of a sudden your legs started moving and you found yourself kicking a fire hydrant; surely this is not what we mean by a "free action." Freedom means, at least, that we are free to choose what we shall do and that our decisions are effective. Indeterminism robs us of our freedom, therefore, just as much as determinism. And the argument against determinism, in any case, is not yet sufficiently persuasive to allow the indeterminist his conclusions.

Here, presenting this argument, is philosopher **Robert Kane:**

ON INDETERMINISM
BY **ROBERT KANE**

Yet such thoughts only lead to a further problem that has haunted free will debates for centuries: if this deeper freedom is not compatible with determinism, it does not seem to be compatible with *indeterminism* either. An event which is undermined might occur or might not occur, given the entire past. (A determined event *must* occur, given the entire past.) Thus, whether or not an undetermined event actually occurs, given its past, is a matter of chance. But chance events occur spontaneously and are not under the control of anything, hence not under the control of agents. How then could they be free actions? If, for example, a choice occurred by virtue of a quantum jump or other undetermined event in one's brain, it would seem a fluke or accident rather than a responsible choice. Undetermined events in the brain or body it seems would inhibit or interfere with our freedom, occurring spontaneously and not under our control. They would turn out to be a nuisance—or perhaps a curse, like epilepsy—rather than an enhancement of our freedom.

Or look at the problem in another way that goes a little deeper. If my choice is really undetermined, that means I could have made a different choice *given exactly the same past* right up to the moment when I did choose. That is what indeterminism and the denial of determinism mean: exactly the same past, different outcomes. Imagine, for example, that I had been deliberating about where to spend my vacation, in Hawaii or Colorado, and after much thought and deliberation had decided I preferred Hawaii and chose it. If the choice was undetermined, then exactly the same deliberation, the same thought processes, the same beliefs, desires and other motives—not a sliver of difference—that led up to my favoring and choosing Hawaii over Colorado, might by chance have issued in my choosing Colorado instead. That is very strange. If such a thing happened it would seem a fluke or accident, like that quantum jump in the brain just mentioned, not a rational choice. Since I had come to favor Hawaii and was about to choose it, when by chance I chose Colorado, I would wonder what went wrong and perhaps consult a neurologist. For reasons such as these, people have argued that undetermined free choices would be "arbitrary," "capricious," "random," "irrational," "uncontrolled," and "inexplicable," not really free and responsible choices at all. If free will is not compatible with determinism, it does not seem to be compatible with indeterminism either.[10]

3. The Role of Consciousness

Hard determinism is true of us as physical bodies. But, you might insist, we are not just physical bodies, we are also conscious. We can make decisions. We have a will of our own. The problem of freedom is often called "the free will problem." But we shall not use this terminology here.

---

[10] Robert Kane, from the essay "Free Will: Old Dispute, New Themes."

The question of whether we are free or not is intimately joined to the question of who "we" are, as discussed in Chapter 6. Are we the meeting place of a body *and* a mind, or is our consciousness "just" brain processes? Whatever we are besides physical bodies, our physical bodies are still subject to all of the laws of Newtonian physics. You can see the problem. If our bodies are just cogs in the universe, what does it matter whether we are conscious or not? If you fall out of an airplane, you fall and accelerate at exactly the same rate as a sack of potatoes. The fact that you, unlike the potatoes, are aware of your falling, scared out of your mind, and wishing or praying like crazy that some miracle will save you makes not a bit of difference. But perhaps this is so with all of our actions as well. Our bodies are composed of bits of matter, various molecules undergoing chemical interactions and acted upon by the various laws of physics. No one can deny that they are subject to all the laws of physical nature. But once all the parts are determined in their various movements and activities, what is left for consciousness to do?

Suppose one insists that consciousness, unlike our physical bodies, is not part of the scheme of determinism. Consciousness, unlike our bodies, is free, free to make decisions, free to choose what to do. But if our bodies are determined in their movements, then what can consciousness do even if it is "free"? Whatever consciousness decides, it cannot have any possible effect on the movements of our bodies; in other words, it cannot affect our actions. Our "decisions," then, would be mere vanities, like fancy switches on a machine that in fact don't do anything at all. Consciousness, on this view, is nothing but a sideshow, for whatever it "decides," what we will do and what will happen are already determined by other antecedent conditions that have nothing to do with the "decision." In crude form, this was Spinoza's ethical position, and also that of some of the early Stoic philosophers. Everything is determined by the laws of nature; it is absurd to fight against nature. All that can be done is to accept the necessity of whatever happens and recognize our consciousness and our apparent freedom as a luxurious vanity. Every human action has its sufficient natural causes apart from consciousness, so consciousness can make no difference whatsoever.

Most hard determinists, however, would probably not agree with the idea that any event, even a nonphysical event such as an act of consciousness, could be "outside" the determinism of nature. Most hard determinists would argue that our thoughts and feelings, even our decisions, are caused by the states of our brains and nervous systems. Our "decisions" are nothing but the conscious effects of complex causal antecedents—most of which we still don't understand—but are definitely part of the deterministic scheme of things. How consciousness enters this deterministic scheme is open to all of the questions that we asked in the previous chapter—whether, for example, there can be causal connections between consciousness and our bodies, whether consciousness is merely an "epiphenomenon" of our brain states or identical to them, or whether we should no longer speak of "consciousness" at all. But, however those disputes are resolved, the hard determinist will insist that consciousness cannot be an exception to determinism.

If consciousness is part of the deterministic scheme of things, could we not say that what happens in consciousness, particularly our decisions, thereby causes movements of our bodies, and therefore controls our actions? This attractive compromise, however, faces an overwhelming problem. If one accepts the determinist's premise, then our decisions cannot cause our actions unless it is also true that our decisions, as part of the deterministic scheme, are caused in turn. Our decisions, therefore, are also determined, and no matter that it might seem as if we have a choice of actions, what we decide is already determined by those antecedent conditions that determine our decision.

Suppose, for example, you are deciding whether or not to go to the movies. Whether or not you go depends upon your decision. But your decision, in turn, depends upon its causal antecedents. Now suppose that we knew enough about your upbringing and tastes, your character and the workings of your brain, that we could see that your decision—let's say to go to the movies—is nothing more than the result of all of these conditions. What sense would it make, then, to say that you decided to go? Of course, it is true that you went through all of the motions of "making a decision." But the outcomes of that decision, even if it was the causal result of the decision, was nevertheless nothing more than the result of conditions that preceded and had nothing to do with the decision. It is as if I gave you a choice of two alternatives, only one of which was possible anyway. That is hardly a choice. Therefore, if a decision enters into our actions, it might be a decision whose outcome is already determined in advance. The hard determinist thus wins in either case. If consciousness is not part of the deterministic scheme, it can have no possible effects on our actions. If it is part of the deterministic scheme of things, then it cannot be free. In either case, hard determinism is undeniable and freedom turns out to be an illusion.

4. Soft Determinism

The philosophers of the Newtonian tradition, those "hard" determinists who believe that determinism precludes the possibility of freedom of choice and action, have always had a powerful and simple argument on their side. But because of the urgency of our demand that we hold ourselves and each other responsible for our actions, most philosophers have not accepted "hard" determinism, even though they have accepted the determinist argument. Accordingly, many philosophers have espoused what has been called **soft determinism.** (The name was coined by William James.) Soft determinists, unlike the uncompromising hard determinists, believe that human freedom and determinism are compatible positions. On the one hand, they accept the determinist's argument, but, on the other, they refuse to give up the all-important demand for human freedom and responsibility. (Accordingly, they are often called *compatibilists,* and their position, **compatibilism.**)

The key to the "soft determinist" position is that an action or a decision, though fully determined, is free if it "flows from the agent's character." **John Stuart Mill,** for example, defends such a position in the following way:

ON CAUSATION AND NECESSITY
BY **JOHN STUART MILL**

The question, whether the law of causality appears in the same strict sense to human actions as to other phenomena, is the celebrated controversy concerning the freedom of the will; which, from at least as far back as the time of Pelagius, has divided both the philosophical and the religious world. The affirmative opinion is commonly called the doctrine of Necessity, as asserting human volitions and actions to be necessary and inevitable. The negative maintains that the will is not determined, like other phenomena, by antecedents, but determines itself; that our volitions are not, properly speaking, the effects of causes, or at least no causes which they uniformly and implicitly obey.

I have already made it sufficiently apparent that the former of these opinions is that which I consider the true one; but the misleading terms in which it is often expressed, and in the indistinct manner in which it is usually apprehended, have both obstructed its reception, and perverted its influence when received. The metaphysical theory of free-will, as held by philosophers (for the practical feeling of it, common in a great or less degree to all mankind, is in no way inconsistent with the contrary theory), was invented because the supposed alternative of admitting human actions to be *necessary* was deemed inconsistent with every one's instinctive consciousness, as well as humiliating to the pride and even degrading to the moral nature of man. Nor do I deny that the doctrine, as sometimes held, is open to these imputations; for the misapprehension in which I shall be able to show that they originate, unfortunately is not confined to the opponents of the doctrine, but is participated in by many, perhaps we might say by most, of its supporters.

Correctly conceived, the doctrine called Philosophical Necessity is simply this: that, given the motives which are present to an individual's mind, and given likewise the character and disposition of the individual, the manner in which he will act might be unerringly inferred; that if we knew the person thoroughly, and knew all the inducements which are acting upon him, we could foretell his conduct with as much certainty as we can predict any physical event. This proposition I take to be a mere interpretation of universal experience, a statement in words of what every one is internally convinced of. No one who believed that he knew thoroughly the circumstances of any case, and the characters of the different persons concerned, would hesitate to foretell how all of them would act. Whatever degree of doubt he may in fact feel, arises from the uncertainty whether he really knows the circumstances, or the character of some one or other of the persons, with the degree of accuracy required; but by no means from thinking that if he did know these things, there could be any uncertainty what the conduct would be. Nor does this full assurance conflict in the smallest degree with what is called our feeling of freedom. We do not feel ourselves the less free, because those to whom we are intimately known are well assured how we shall will to act in a particular case. We often, on the contrary, regard the doubt

> *. . . given the motives which are present to an individual's mind, and given likewise the character and disposition of the individual, the manner in which he will act might be unerringly inferred . . .*

what our conduct will be, as a mark of ignorance of our character, and sometimes even resent it as an imputation. The religious metaphysicians who have asserted the freedom of the will, have always maintained it to be consistent with divine foreknowledge of our actions: and if with divine, then with any other foreknowledge. We may be free, and yet another may have reason to be perfectly certain what use we shall make of our freedom. It is not, therefore, the doctrine that our volitions and actions are invariable consequents of our antecedent states of mind, that is either contradicted by our consciousness, or felt to be degrading.

But the doctrine of causation, when considered as obtaining between our volitions and their antecedents, is almost universally conceived as involving more than this. Many do not believe, and very few practically feel, that there is nothing in causation but invariable, certain, and unconditional sequence. There are few to whom mere constancy of succession appears a sufficient stringent bond of union for so peculiar a relation as that of cause and effect. Even if the reason repudiates, the imagination retains, the feeling of some more intimate connection, of some peculiar tie, or mysterious constraint exercised by the antecedent over the consequent. Now this it is which, considered as applying to the human will, conflicts with our consciousness, and revolts our feelings. We are certain that, in the case of our volitions, there is not this mysterious constraint. We know that we are not compelled, as by a magical spell, to obey any particular motive. We feel, that if we wished to prove that we have the power of resisting the motive, we could do so (that wish being, it needs scarcely be observed, a *new antecedent*); and it would be humiliating to our pride, and (what is of more importance) paralyzing to our desire of excellence, if we thought otherwise. But neither is any such mysterious compulsion now supposed, by the best philosophical authorities, to be exercised by any other cause over its effect. Those who think that causes draw their effects after them by a mystical tie, are right in believing that the relation between volitions and their antecedents is of another nature. But they should go farther, and admit that this is also true of all other effects and their antecedents. If such a tie is considered to be involved in the word Necessity, the doctrine is not true of human actions; but neither is it then true of inanimate objects. It would be more correct to say that matter is not bound by necessity, than that mind is so.

◆◆◆

A fatalist believes, or half believes (for nobody is a consistent fatalist), not only that whatever is about to happen will be the infallible result of the causes which produce it (which is the true necessitarian doctrine), but moreover that there is no use in struggling against it; that it will happen however we may strive to prevent it. Now, a necessitarian, believing that our actions follow from our characters, and that our characters follow from our organization, our education, and our circumstances, is apt to be, with more or less of consciousness on his part, a fatalist as to his own actions, and to believe that his nature is such, or that his education and circumstances have so moulded his character, that nothing can now prevent him from feeling and acting in a particular way, or at least that no effort of his own can hinder it. In the words of the sect which in our own day has most perseveringly inculcated and most perversely misunderstood this great doctrine, his character is formed *for* him, and not *by* him; therefore his wishing that it had been formed differently is of no use; he has no power to alter it. But this is a grand error. He has, to a certain extent, a power to alter his character. Its being, in the ultimate resort, formed for him, is not inconsistent with its being, in part formed *by* him as one of the intermediate agents. His character is formed by his circumstances (including among these his particular organization); but his own desire to mould it in a particular way, is one of those circumstances, and by no means one of the least influential. We can not, indeed, directly will to be different from what we are. But neither did those who are supposed to have formed our characters directly will that we should be what we are. Their will had no direct power except over their own actions. They made us what they did make us, by willing, not the end, but the requisite means; and we, when our habits are not too inveterate, can, by similarly willing the requisite means, make ourselves different. If they could place us under the influence of certain circumstances, we, in like manner, can place ourselves under the influence of other circumstances. We are exactly as capable of making our own character, *if we will,* as others are of making it for us.

Yes (answers the Owenite),[11] but these words, "if we will," surrender the whole point: since the will to alter our own character is given us, not by any efforts of ours, but by circumstances which we can not help, it comes to us either from external causes, or not at all. Most true: if the Owenite stops here, he is in a position from which nothing can expel him. Our character is formed by us as well as for us; but the wish which induces us to attempt to form it is formed for us; and how? Not, in general, by our organization, nor wholly by our education, but by our experience; experience of the painful consequences of the character we previously had; or by some strong feeling of admiration or aspiration, accidentally aroused. But to think that we have no power of altering our character, and to think that we shall not use our power unless we desire to use it, are very different things, and have a very different effect on the mind. A person who does not wish to alter his character, can not be the person who is supposed to feel discouraged or paralyzed by thinking himself unable to do it. The depressing effect of the fatalist doctrine can only be felt where there *is* a wish to do what that doctrine represents as impossible. It is of no consequence what we think forms our character, when we have no desire of our own about forming it; but it is of great consequence that we should not be prevented from forming such a desire by thinking the attainment impracticable, and that if we have the desire, we should know that the work is not so irrevocably done as to be incapable of being altered.

---

[11] From Robert Owen (1771–1858), a political reformer.

And indeed, if we examine closely, we shall find that this feeling, of our being able to modify our own character *if we wish,* is itself the feeling of moral freedom which we are conscious of. A person feels morally free who feels that his habits or his temptations are not his masters, but he theirs; who, even in yielding to them, knows that he could resist; that were he desirous of altogether throwing them off, there would not be required for the purpose a stronger desire than he knows himself to be capable of feeling. It is of course necessary, to render our consciousness of freedom complete, that we should have succeeded in making our character all we have hitherto attempted to make it; for if we have wished and not attained, we have, to that extent, not power over our own character; we are not free. Or at least, we must feel that our wish, if not strong enough to alter our character, is strong enough to conquer our character when the two are brought into conflict in any particular case of conduct. And hence it is said with truth, that none but a person of confirmed virtue is completely free.[12]

In this section, Mill glides between the harsh alternatives of "hard determinism" and indeterminism. He begins by accepting determinism and the idea that all human actions are "necessary and inevitable," given their causes. But he then goes on to say that these causes are themselves within human control, that we can alter the causes of events and even, by taking certain steps, alter our own characters. But this is not in the least to deny determinism; nor does it deny that we are in control and have "free will" in an important sense. Human actions, following from their various causes (including "character" or personality), are as predictable as any other events. But predictability is not incompatible with freedom, for freedom means, according to Mill, nothing other than acting in accordance with one's own character, desires, and wishes. Since these are the causes of our actions, that means that Mill can defend both determinism and freedom at the same time.

David Hume is also a "soft determinist," and he too argues that the reconciliation of "liberty and necessity" is to be found in the fact that a person's actions "flow from one's character or disposition." In defending soft determinism, Hume argues that we cannot mean by a free action one that is uncaused, a matter of chance, for this flies in the face of our common assumption that every event must have a cause. Such a view of freedom is also incoherent: The free-will advocate wants to ensure that we can hold people responsible for their actions; but if people's actions were merely a matter of chance, over which they have no control, we surely would not hold them responsible. On the contrary, actions that we praise or blame are precisely those determined by the person's character.

Although Hume defends a soft determinist position, there is a sense in which Hume is not a determinist at all. Recall from Chapter 3 that Hume thinks that causality is a fiction and our penchant for seeking out causes merely a habit. Thus he can argue that just as we are never rationally justified in claiming that a particular

---

[12] John Stuart Mill, *A System of Logic,* 8th ed. (New York: Harper & Row, 1874).

event has a cause, so we are never fully justified in claiming that human actions have causes.

ON CAUSATION AND CHARACTER
BY **DAVID HUME**

But to proceed in this reconciling project with regard to the question of liberty and necessity; the most contentious question of metaphysics, the most contentious science; it will not require many words to prove, that all mankind have ever agreed in the doctrine of liberty as well as in that of necessity, and that the whole dispute, in this respect also, has been hitherto merely verbal. For what is meant by liberty, when applied to voluntary actions? We cannot surely mean that actions have so little connexion with motives, inclinations, and circumstances, that one does not follow with a certain degree of uniformity from the other, and that one affords no inference by which we can conclude the existence of the other. For these are plain and acknowledged matters of fact. By liberty, then, we can only mean *a power of acting or not acting according to the determinations of the will;* that is, if we choose to remain at rest, we may; if we choose to move, we also may. Now this hypothetical liberty is universally allowed to belong to everyone who is not a prisoner and in chains. Here then is no subject of dispute.

> *By liberty, . . . we can only mean* a power of acting or not acting according to the determinations of the will . . .

Whatever definition we may give of liberty, we should be careful to observe two requisite circumstances: *first,* that it be consistent with plain matter of fact; *secondly,* that it be consistent with itself. If we observe these circumstances and render our definition intelligible, I am persuaded that all mankind will be found of one opinion with regard to it.

It is universally allowed that nothing exists without a cause of its existence, and that chance, when strictly examined, is a mere negative word and means not any real power which has anywhere a being in nature. But it is pretended that some causes are necessary, some not necessary. Here then is the advantage of definitions. Let anyone *define* a cause without comprehending it, as part of the definition, a *necessary connexion* with its effect, and let him show distinctly the origin of the idea expressed by the definition, and I shall readily give up the whole controversy. But if the foregoing explication of the matter be received, this must be absolutely impracticable. Had not objects a regular conjunction with each other, we should never have entertained any notion of cause and effect; and this regular conjunction produces that inference of the understanding which is the only connexion that we can have any comprehension of. Whoever attempts a definition of cause exclusive of these circumstances will be obliged either to employ unintelligible terms or such as are synonymous to the term which he endeavours to define. And if the definition above mentioned be admitted, liberty, when opposed to necessity, not to constraint, is the same thing with chance, which is universally allowed to have no existence. . . .

All laws being founded on rewards and punishments, it is supposed as a fundamental principle, that these motives have a regular and uniform influence on the mind, and both produce the good and prevent the evil actions. We may give to this influence what name we please; but, as it is usually conjoined with the action, it must be esteemed a *cause,* and be looked upon as an instance of that necessity, which we would here establish.

The only proper object of hatred or vengeance is a person or creature, endowed with thought and consciousness; and when any criminal or injurious actions excite that passion, it is only by their relation to the person, or connexion with him. Actions are, by their very nature, temporary and perishing; and where they proceed not from some *cause* in the character and disposition of the person who performed them, they can neither redound to his honour, if good; nor infamy, if evil. The actions themselves may be blameable; they may be contrary to all the rules of morality and religion: But the person is not answerable for them; and as they proceeded from nothing in him that is durable and constant, and leave nothing of that nature behind them, it is impossible he can, upon their account, become the object of punishment or vengeance. According to the principle, therefore, which denies necessity, and consequently causes, a man is as pure and untainted, after having committed the most horrid crime, as at the first moment of his birth, nor is his character anywise concerned in his actions, since they are not derived from it, and the wickedness of the one can never be used as a proof of the depravity of the other.

Men are not blamed for such actions as they perform ignorantly and casually, whatever may be the consequences. Why? but because the principles of these actions are only momentary, and terminate in them alone. Men are less blamed for such actions as they perform hastily and unpremeditatedly than for such as proceed from deliberation. For what reason? but because a hasty temper, though a constant cause or principle in the mind, operates only by intervals, and infects not the whole character. Again, repentance wipes off every crime, if attended with a reformation of life and manners. How is this to be accounted for? but by asserting that actions render a person criminal merely as they are proofs of criminal principles in the mind; and when, by an alteration of these principles, they cease to be just proofs, they likewise cease to be criminal. But, except upon the doctrine of necessity, they never were just proofs, and consequently never were criminal.

It will be equally easy to prove, and from the same arguments, that *liberty,* according to that definition above mentioned, in which all men agree, is also essential to morality, and that no human actions, where it is wanting, are susceptible of any moral qualities, or can be the objects either of approbation or dislike. For as actions are objects of our moral sentiment, so far only as they are indications of the internal character, passions, and affections; it is impossible that they can give rise either to praise or blame, where they proceed not from these principles, but are derived altogether from external violence.[13]

In other words, Hume too suggests that not only is freedom of choice and action possible within the framework of determinism, but determinism is even necessary if we are to make sense out of the notion of freedom of choice and responsibility. His language is convoluted, but his point is plain: We can make sense of the notion of voluntary action only because there is a uniform ("necessary") connection between our motives, inclinations, circumstances, and characters and what we do. But "soft determinism" raises the same old questions yet once again. Can we be said to be responsible even for those acts that are caused by our character? Can we choose our character, as Mill suggests? Could we have done other than what we did, even if we had wanted to? Consider the following argument from Robert Kane:

"WIGGLE ROOM"
BY **ROBERT KANE**

Frequently in everyday life we act from our existing motives without having to think or deliberate about what to do. At such times, we may very well be determined by our existing characters and motives. Yet we may also be acting "of our own free wills" to the extent that we formed our present characters and motives (our wills) by earlier choices or actions that were not themselves determined. Let us call these earlier choices or actions "self-forming" choices or actions.

Now I believe that such undetermined self-forming choices or actions occur at those difficult times of life when we are torn between competing visions of what we should do or become; and they are more frequent than we think. Perhaps we are torn between doing the moral thing or acting from ambition, or between powerful present desires and long term goals, or we are faced with difficult tasks for which we have aversions. In all such cases, we are faced with competing motivations and have to make an effort to overcome temptation to do something else we also strongly want. There is tension and uncertainty in our minds about what to do at such times that, I suggest, is reflected in appropriate regions of our brains by movement away from thermodynamic equilibrium—in short, a kind of stirring up of chaos in the brain that makes it sensitive to micro-indeterminacies at the neuronal level. The uncertainty and inner tension we feel at such soul-searching moments of self-formation would thus be reflected in the indeterminacy of our neural processes themselves. What is experienced personally as uncertainty would correspond physically to the opening of a window of opportunity that temporarily screens off complete determination by influences of the past. (By contrast, when we act from predominant motives or settled dispositions,

---

[13] David Hume, *An Enquiry Concerning Human Understanding,* 2nd ed., ed. L. A. Selby-Bigge (Oxford: Oxford University Press, 1902).

the uncertainty or indeterminacy is muted. If it did play a role in such cases, it *would* be a mere nuisance or fluke.)

When we do decide under such conditions of uncertainty, the outcome is not determined because of the preceding indeterminacy—and yet it can be willed (and hence rational and voluntary) either way owing to the fact that in such self-formation, the agents' prior wills are divided by conflicting motives. Consider a businesswoman who faces a conflict of this kind. She is on the way to a business meeting important to her career when she observes an assault taking place in an alley. An inner struggle ensues between her moral conscience, to stop and call for help, and her career ambitions which tell her she cannot miss this meeting. She has to make an effort of will to overcome the temptation to go on to her meeting. If she overcomes this temptation, it will be the result of her effort, but if she fails, it will be because she did not *allow* her effort to succeed. And this is due to the fact that, while she wanted to overcome temptation, she also wanted to fail, for quite different and incommensurable reasons. When we, like the businesswoman, decide in such circumstances, and the indeterminate efforts we are making become determinate choices, we *make* one set of competing reasons or motives prevail over the others at that moment *by deciding*.[14]

D. COMPULSION AND IGNORANCE

The basis of compatibilism or "soft determinism" is that we somehow carve a space within determinism for those actions that we insist on calling "free" and for which we hold ourselves and other people responsible. But this means that "free actions" must also be actions that are determined by antecedent conditions and causes. Free as well as unfree acts (like falling down the stairs) are caused according to the determinist argument. The distinction, therefore, as we saw in both Mill and Hume, depends upon whether the determining factors are within the agent or "outside" of him or her. In the latter case, we say that the act was not free but *compelled* or "done under compulsion." This distinction, of course, has important moral implications. We often say a person is *not morally responsible* for an action that he or she was *not free not* to do. This distinction is not a new one. Aristotle, for example, many centuries ago defined a voluntary action as one that was (1) not done under compulsion and (2) not done from ignorance.

ON VOLUNTARY ACTION
BY **ARISTOTLE**

It is only voluntary feelings and actions for which praise and blame are given; those that are involuntary are condoned, and sometimes even pitied. Hence it seems to be necessary for the student of ethics to define the difference between

---

[14] Robert Kane, from the essay "Free Will: Old Dispute, New Themes."

the Voluntary and the Involuntary; and this will also be of service to the legislator in assigning rewards and punishments.

It is then generally held that actions are involuntary when done (a) under compulsion or (b) through ignorance, and that (a) an act is compulsory when its origin is from without, being of such a nature that the agent, or person compelled, contributes nothing to it: for example, when a ship's captain is carried somewhere by stress of weather, or by people who have him in their power. But there is some doubt about actions done through fear of a worse alternative, or for some noble object—as for instance if a tyrant having a man's parents and children in his power commands him to do something base, when if he complies their lives will be spared but if he refuses they will be put to death. It is open to question whether such actions are voluntary or involuntary. A somewhat similar case is when cargo is jettisoned in a storm; apart from circumstances, no one voluntarily throws away his property, but to save his own life and that of his shipmates any sane man would do so. Acts of this kind, then, are "mixed" or composite; but they approximate rather to the voluntary class. For at the actual time when they are done they are chosen or willed; and the end or motive of an act varies with the occasion, so that the terms "voluntary" and "involuntary" should be used with reference to the time of action; now the actual deed in the cases in question is done voluntarily, for the origin of the movement of the parts of the body instrumental to the act lies in the agent; and when the origin of an action is in oneself, it is in one's own power to do it or not. Such acts therefore are voluntary, though perhaps involuntary apart from circumstances—for no one would choose to do any such action in and for itself.

◆◆◆

What kind of actions then are to be called "compulsory"? Used without qualification, perhaps this term applies to any case where the cause of the action lies in things outside the agent, and when the agent contributes nothing. But when actions intrinsically involuntary are yet in given circumstances deliberately chosen in preference to a given alternative, and when their origin lies in the agent, these actions are to be pronounced intrinsically involuntary but voluntary in the circumstances, and in preference to the alternative. They approximate however rather to the voluntary class, since conduct consists of particular things done, and the particular things done in the cases in question are voluntary. But it is not easy to lay down rules for deciding which of two alternatives is to be chosen, for particular cases differ widely.

To apply the term "compulsory" to acts done for the sake of pleasure or for noble objects, on the plea that these exercise constraint on us from without, is to make every action compulsory. For (1) pleasure and nobility between them supply the motives of all actions whatsoever. Also (2) to act under compulsion and involuntarily is painful, but actions aiming at something pleasant or noble are pleasant. And (3) it is absurd to blame external things, instead of blaming ourselves for falling an easy prey to their attractions; or to take the credit of our noble deeds to ourselves, while putting the blame for our disgraceful ones upon the temptations of pleasure. It appears therefore that an act is compulsory when its origin is from outside, the person compelled contributing nothing to it.

Everything that is done by reason of ignorance is *not* voluntary; it is only what produces pain and repentance that is *in*voluntary. For the man who has done something owing to ignorance, and feels not the least vexation at his action, has not acted voluntarily, since he did not know what he was doing, nor yet involuntarily, since he is not pained. Of people, then, who act by reason of ignorance he who repents is thought an involuntary agent, and the man who does not repent may, since he is different, be called a not voluntary agent; for, since he differs from the other, it is better that he should have a name of his own.

Acting by reason of ignorance seems also to be different from acting *in* ignorance; for the man who is drunk or in a rage is thought to act as a result not of ignorance but of one of the causes mentioned, yet not knowingly but in ignorance.

Now every wicked man is ignorant of what he ought to do and what he ought to abstain from, and it is by reason of error of this kind that men become unjust and in general bad . . .

Now every wicked man is ignorant of what he ought to do and what he ought to abstain from, \and it is by reason of error of this kind that men become unjust and in general bad; but the term 'involuntary' tends to be used not if a man is ignorant of what is to his advantage—for it is not mistaken purpose that causes involuntary action (it leads rather to wickedness), nor ignorance of the universal (for *that* men are *blamed*), but ignorance of particulars, i.e. of the circumstances of the action and the objects with which it is concerned. For it is on these that both pity and pardon depend, since the person who is ignorant of any of these acts involuntarily.[15]

What is compulsion? According to Aristotle, an act is compulsory "when its origin is without" such that the person who acts "contributes nothing to it." Thus a person who is literally pushed into doing something is compelled rather than free. But what are we to say, for example, of the person who is neurotic, who acts compulsively or "irrationally" because of mental illness? It might once have been said that such a person was "possessed," as if something "external" (a demon or an evil spirit) had "taken over" and compelled certain actions.

This, in a sense, is what Aristotle means by "ignorance." Factors unknown to the agent influence his or her choice.

But today we talk about "compulsions" and "denial" of the facts within the person and not "external" at all. In fact, psychologists would say that the neurotic always contributes to the neurosis as well as suffers from it, and thus, according to Aristotle's criterion, such acts are not really compelled at all, but voluntary, like the acts of a drunkard.

To take a much more difficult kind of case, what are we to say of those celebrated "brain-washing" cases (as the Chinese did to UN prisoners of war during the Korean

---

[15] Aristotle, *Nicomachean Ethics,* Bk. III, trans. H. Rackham (Cambridge, MA: Harvard University Press, 1934).

War) in which a person seemingly performs an action voluntarily, but only after he or she has been "conditioned" in a dramatic and sometimes brutal way? Sometimes even the person's "character" itself is changed. Should we hold a person responsible for such actions? (This question has been an issue in some war-crimes cases, for example.) Similarly, should we go against Aristotle and hold a person responsible for actions performed under great stress or as the result of a violent emotion (rage or infatuation, for example)? Should we hold a person responsible for actions performed under the influence of drugs or alcohol (assuming that we might well hold them responsible for taking the drugs or drinking in the first place)? You can see that the distinction between "free" actions and acts that are "compelled" is not nearly as clear as it first seemed. We can easily distinguish between a person who breaks into a store and a person who is pushed through the front window. But in many cases where freedom is most in question, in cases of neurosis, brainwashing, great passion, and chemical "influences," the distinction between what is "external" to the person and what is within his or her character is not clear at all.

There are more serious problems with the notion of "compulsion," however. Even if we admit that some problematic examples of actions are not clearly either "free" or "compelled" (neurosis and brainwashing, great passion and drugs), we would want to insist that at least some actions are clearly free and not compelled. For example, I write a check to the American Cancer Society just because I believe that it is an important organization and I want to make a contribution. No one has solicited me, no one has encouraged me to do it, and no one need know that I do it. Can even this act so seemingly performed "of my own free will" be counted as a "free action"? The "soft determinist" would say that this action is "free" because it flows from my generous character. But what goes into *making* my character? My education and upbringing? My social class? What about my national origin or my gender? Perhaps even my height and weight affect my choices.

Even in our "freest" acts, it can be argued that the desires and decisions, in short, our "personality" is wholly determined by forces outside of us and beyond our control. Consider the following argument, for example, by Professor **John Hospers,** who uses Freud and psychoanalysis as the basis for his claim that all of our acts are compelled and not free, insofar as all of our acts are brought about by a set of psychological determinants over which we have no control:

FROM **"WHAT MEANS THIS FREEDOM?"**
BY **JOHN HOSPERS**

[Are we] in the final analysis, *responsible for any of our actions at all.* The issue may be put this way: How can anyone be responsible for his actions, since they grow out of his character, which is shaped and molded and made what it is by influences—some hereditary, but most of them stemming from early parental environment—that were not of his own making or choosing? This question, I believe, still troubles many people who would agree to all the distinctions we have just made but still have the feeling that "this isn't all." They have the uneasy suspicion that there is a more ultimate sense, a "deeper" sense, in which we are *not* responsible for our actions, since we are not responsible for the character out of which those actions spring. . . .

Let us take as an example a criminal who, let us say, strangled several persons and is himself now condemned to die in the electric chair. Jury and public alike hold him fully responsible (at least they utter the words "he is responsible"), for the murders were planned down to the minutest detail, and the defendant tells the jury exactly how he planned them. But now we find out how it all came about; we learn of parents who rejected him from babyhood, of the childhood spent in one foster home after another, where it was always plain to him that he was not wanted; of the constantly frustrated early desire for affection, the hard shell of nonchalance and bitterness that he assumed to cover the painful and humiliating fact of being unwanted, and his subsequent attempts to heal those wounds to his shattered ego through defensive aggression. . . . The poor victim is not conscious of the inner forces that exact from him this ghastly toll; he battles, he schemes, he revels in pseudo-aggression, he is miserable, but he does not know what works within him to produce these catastrophic acts of crime. His aggressive actions are the wriggling of a worm on a fisherman's hook. And if this is so, it seems difficult to say any longer, "He is responsible." Rather, we shall put him behind bars for the protection of society, but we shall no longer flatter our feeling of moral superiority by calling him personally responsible for what he did.

Let us suppose it were established that a man commits murder only if sometime during the previous week, he has eaten a certain combination of foods— say, tuna fish salad at a meal also including peas, mushroom soup, and blueberry pie. What if we were to track down the factors common to all murders committed in this country during the last twenty years and found this factor present in all of them, and only in them? The example is of course empirically absurd; but may it not be that there is *some* combination of factors that regularly leads to homicide, factors such as are described in general terms in the above quotation? (Indeed the situation in the quotation is less fortunate than in our hypothetical example, for it is easy to avoid certain foods once we have been warned about them, but the situation of the infant is thrust on him; something has already happened to him once and for all, before he knows it has happened.) When such specific factors are discovered, won't they make it clear that it is foolish and pointless, as well as immoral, to hold human beings responsible for crimes? Or, if one prefers biological to psychological factors, suppose a neurologist is called in to testify at a murder trial and produces X-ray pictures of the brain of the criminal; anyone can see, he argues, that the *cella turcica* was already calcified at the age of nineteen; it should be a flexible bone, growing, enabling the gland to grow. All the defendant's disorders might have resulted from this early calcification. Now, this particular explanation may be empirically false; but who can say that no such factors, far more complex, to be sure, exist?

When we know such things as these, we no longer feel as much tempted to say that the criminal is responsible for his crime; and we tend also (do we not?)

to excuse him—not legally (we still confine him to prison) but morally; we no longer call him a monster or hold him personally responsible for what he did. Moreover, we do this in general, not merely in the case of crime: "You must excuse Grandmother for being irritable; she's really quite ill and is suffering some pain all the time." Or: "The dog always bites children after she's had a litter of pups; you can't blame her for it: she's not feeling well, and besides she naturally wants to defend them." Or: "She's nervous and jumpy, but do excuse her: she has a severe glandular disturbance." . . .

But one may still object that so far we have talked only about neurotic behavior. Isn't nonneurotic or normal or not unconsciously motivated (or whatever you want to call it) behavior still within the area of responsibility? There are reasons for answering "No" even here, for the normal person no more than neurotic one has caused his own character, which makes him what he is. Granted that neurotics are not responsible for their behavior (that part of it which we call neurotic) because it stems from undigested infantile conflicts that they had no part in bringing about, and that are external to them just as surely as if their behavior had been forced on them by a malevolent deity (which is indeed one theory on the subject); but the so-called normal person is equally the product of causes in which his volition took no part. And if, unlike the neurotic's, his behavior is changeable by rational considerations, and if he has the will power to overcome the effects of an unfortunate early environment, this again is no credit to him; he is just lucky. If energy is available to him in a form in which it can be mobilized for constructive purposes, this is no credit to him, for this too is part of his psychic legacy. Those of us who can discipline ourselves and develop habits of concentration of purpose tend to blame those who cannot, and call them lazy and weak-willed; but what we fail to see is that they literally cannot do what we expect; if their psyches were structured like ours, they could, but as they are burdened with a tyrannical super-ego (to use psychoanalytic jargon for the moment), and a weak defenseless ego whose energies are constantly consumed in fighting endless charges of the super-ego, they simply cannot do it, and it is irrational to expect it of them. We cannot with justification blame them for their inability, any more than we can congratulate ourselves for our ability. This lesson is hard to learn, for we constantly and naïvely assume that other people are constructed as we ourselves are. . . .

> *. . . if we can overcome the effects of early environment, the ability to do so is itself a product of the early environment.*

The position, then, is this: if we *can* overcome the effects of early environment, the ability to do so is itself a product of the early environment. We did not give ourselves this ability; and if we lack it we cannot be blamed for not having it. Sometimes, to be sure, moral exhortation brings out an ability that is there but not being used, and in this lies its *occasional* utility; but very often its use is pointless, because the ability is not there. The only thing that can overcome a desire, as Spinoza said, is a stronger contrary desire; and many times there simply is no wherewithal for producing a stronger contrary desire. Those of us who do have the wherewithal are lucky.[16]

While Hospers' example of eating a tuna sandwich as a kind of physiological compulsion may seem exaggerated, we might more easily accept many physical factors as having a decisive influence on our character. Many have argued, for instance, that a person's sex or race are inescapable physical factors that compel him or her to make certain decisions. Determinist arguments of this sort have been made even among members of oppressed groups seeking tolerance. In a recent well-publicized example, a lawyer defended her client against charges of assault by claiming that her client's actions were determined by her overwhelming case of premenstrual syndrome!

> A Brooklyn woman who had contended that charges against her should be dismissed because stress from the approach of her menstrual period had caused her to beat her child dropped that claim in Criminal Court yesterday.
> Instead, the 25-year-old woman, Shirley Santos, pleaded guilty to a harassment charge.
> Elizabeth Holtzman, the Brooklyn District Attorney, said the plea marked the end of the first known case in the United States in which "premenstrual syndrome" had been used as a defense. "The withdrawal of this defense," she said, "is a signal that PMS is a defense without merit."
> Miss Santos, of 621 Rutland Road, had originally been charged with assault in the beating of her 4-year-old daughter, Quadina, last Dec. 16. In an agreement with the District Attorney's office, Miss Santos dropped the premenstrual-stress argument and pleaded to the lesser charge of harassment.

CRITICIZED BY FEMINISTS

> The premenstrual-syndrome defense has been used to mitigate the sentences of at least two women in British trials, but it has drawn the fire of feminists, who say it is discriminatory and degrades women.[17]

TO THE EDITOR

> I am the attorney for Shirley Santos, whose arrest for felonious assault and endangering the welfare of a child ended in no criminal conviction, no jail, no fine and no probation (news story Nov. 4).
> Your article says that Miss Santos "dropped" the claim of premenstrual stress syndrome (P.M.S.). She did so only with the reciprocal promise that all

---

[16] John Hospers, "What Means This Freedom?" in *Determinism and Freedom in the Age of Modern Science,* ed. Sidney Hook (New York: New York University Press, 1958).

[17] David Bird, "Defense Linked to Menstruation Dropped in Case," *New York Times,* Nov. 4, 1982.

criminal charges would be dropped. They were. Miss Santos entered a plea of guilty to a violation (which is not a crime), that of harassment. Upon completion of her conditional discharge, the court papers will be sealed.

As to District Attorney Holtzman's assertion that the "withdrawal of this defense is a signal that P.M.S. is a defense without merit," I respectfully disagree. I wholeheartedly believe that without the P.M.S. arguments Miss Santos would still be facing criminal charges. The fact that they were all dropped is, instead, a testament to its validity.

In addition, there has been some confusion as to the nature of the defense in this case. It was never an insanity case.

My hope is that in the future women with such difficulties will be able to recognize and receive appropriate treatment for them—free of social stigma or ill-conceived fear of economic reprisals.[18]

Despite the optimism of the defense attorney, what emerges from the foregoing arguments is not an attractive conclusion. If we believe that most of our actions are physiologically compelled, then no matter how we try to wriggle free of total determinism, it seems as if we keep finding ourselves enmeshed back in "hard" determinism. We suggested that perhaps an act is free if one of its causes is a decision, but if the decision itself is caused in turn, ours is not really a decision at all. We suggested that an action is free if it "flows from a person's character"; but then we saw that it can be argued that an act that "flows from a person's character" is no more within his or her control and no more his or her responsibility than any other act. We might want to say that a person's act is free if, in this case, he or she could have done otherwise, but what does this mean, given the previous arguments, except that the act would have been different if the circumstances had been different or if the person had been, in effect, another person?

For example, it is true that you could have changed the course of World War II— but *if what?* If you had been born Winston Churchill, perhaps. But that is a nonsensical "if." Does it make any more sense, however, to say that "you could have been a professional football player?" If what? If circumstances had been different? If you had been born with a different body, or raised in a different environment? But isn't this to say, for each of these "ifs," that you would be (slightly but significantly) a different person than you are? It looks as if we are trapped by the tautology that each of us is whoever he or she is. It is true of the geranium that if it had been planted in better soil, it would be larger; and if the ball had been dropped from the greater height it would have landed harder; and if you were raised differently, placed in different circumstances, then you might have acted other than you did. But does this have anything to do with "freedom"? Are your actions any more free than the growth of the plant or the falling of the ball? Of course, there is a difference: You think that you've made some decision. But why should what you think change the way things are determined? You might pretend to be flying after you've fallen out of the plane. But you're still falling, and whatever you think or do doesn't slow you down at all.

---

[18] Stephanie Benson, Letter to the *New York Times,* November 15, 1982.

Conditioning

Not everyone views determinism with horror. The eminent American psychologist
B. F. Skinner, for example, applauds the determinist's argument as a means of controlling human behavior and changing it for the better. In his best-seller *Beyond
Freedom and Dignity*, Skinner argues that we have made a fetish of freedom and that
we should replace this with an acceptance of determinism. Behavioral scientists can
and should be given the power to "engineer" human behavior in accordance with an
agreed-upon set of ideals (social harmony, individual happiness, and productivity).

BEYOND FREEDOM
BY **B.F. SKINNER**

Perhaps the most crucial part of our democratic philosophy to be reconsidered is
our attitude toward freedom—or its reciprocal, the control of human behavior.
We do not oppose all forms of control because it is "human nature" to do so.
The reaction is not characteristic of all men under all conditions of life. It is an
attitude which has been carefully engineered, in large part by what we call the
"literature" of democracy. With respect to some methods of control (for example, the threat of force), very little engineering is needed, for the techniques
or their immediate consequences are objectionable. Society has suppressed these
methods by branding them "wrong," "illegal," or "sinful." But to encourage
these attitudes toward objectionable forms of control, it has been necessary to
disguise the real nature of certain indispensable techniques, the commonest
examples of which are education, moral discourse, and persuasion. The actual
procedures appear harmless enough. They consist of supplying information, presenting opportunities for action, pointing out logical relationships, appealing to
reason or "enlightened understanding," and so on. Through a masterful piece
of misrepresentation, the illusion is fostered that these procedures do not involve
the control of behavior; at most, they are simply ways of "getting someone to
change his mind." But analysis not only reveals the presence of well-defined
behavioral processes, it demonstrates a kind of control no less inexorable, though
in some ways more acceptable, than the bully's threat of force.

   Let us suppose that someone in whom we are interested is acting unwisely—
he is careless in the way he deals with his friends, he drives too fast, or he holds
his golf club the wrong way. We could probably help him by issuing a series of
commands: don't nag, don't drive over sixty, don't hold your club that way. Much
less objectionable would be "an appeal to reason." We could show him how
people are affected by his treatment of them, how accident rates rise sharply at
higher speeds, how a particular grip on the club alters the way the ball is struck
and corrects a slice. In doing so we resort to verbal mediating devices which
emphasize and support certain "contingencies of reinforcement"—that is, certain relations between behavior and its consequences—which strengthen the
behavior we wish to set up. The same consequences would possibly set up the

behavior without our help, and they eventually take control no matter which form of help we give. The appeal to reason has certain advantages over the authoritative command. A threat of punishment, no matter how subtle, generates emotional reactions and tendencies to escape or revolt. Perhaps the controllee merely "feels resentment" at being made to act in a given way, but even that is to be avoided. When we "appeal to reason," he "feels freer to do as he pleases." The fact is that we have exerted *less* control than in using a threat; since other conditions may contribute to the result, the effect may be delayed or, possibly in a given instance, lacking. But if we have worked a change in his behavior at all, it is because we have altered relevant environmental conditions, and the processes we have set in motion are just as real and just as inexorable, if not as comprehensive, as in the most authoritative coercion.

"Arranging an opportunity for action" is another example of disguised control. The power of the negative form has already been exposed in the analysis of censorship. Restriction of opportunity is recognized as far from harmless. As Ralph Barton Perry said in an article which appeared in the Spring, 1953, *Pacific Spectator,* "Whoever determines what alternatives shall be made known to man controls what that man shall choose *from.* He is deprived of freedom in proportion as he is denied access to *any* ideas, or is confined to any range of ideas short of totality of relevant possibilities." But there is a positive side as well. When we present a relevant state of affairs, we increase the likelihood that a given form of behavior will be emitted. To the extent that the probability of action has changed, we have made a definite contribution. The teacher of history controls a student's behavior (or, if the reader prefers, "deprives him of freedom") just as much in *presenting* historical facts as in suppressing them. Other conditions will no doubt affect the student, but the contribution made to his behavior by the presentation of material is fixed and, within its range, irresistible.

The methods of education, moral discourse, and persuasion are acceptable not because they recognize the freedom of the individual or his right to dissent, but because they make only *partial* contributions to the control of his behavior. The freedom they recognize is freedom from a more coercive form of control. The dissent which they tolerate is the possible effect of other determiners of action. Since these sanctioned methods are frequently ineffective, we have been able to convince ourselves that they do not represent control at all. When they show too much strength to permit disguise, we give them other names and suppress them as energetically as we suppress the use of force. Education grown too powerful is rejected as propaganda or "brain-washing," while really effective persuasion is decried as "undue influence," "demagoguery," "seduction," and so on.

If we are not to rely solely upon accident for the innovations which give rise to cultural evolution, we must accept the fact that some kind of control of human behavior is inevitable. We cannot use good sense in human affairs unless someone engages in the design and construction of environmental conditions which affect the behavior of men. Environmental changes have always been the condition for the improvement of cultural patterns, and we can hardly use the more

We are all controlled by the world in which we live, and part of the world has been and will be constructed by men. The question is this: Are we to be controlled by accident, by tyrants, or by ourselves in effective cultural design?

effective methods of science without making changes on a grander scale. We are all controlled by the world in which we live, and part of the world has been and will be constructed by men. The question is this: Are we to be controlled by accident, by tyrants, or by ourselves in effective cultural design?

The danger of the misuse of power is possibly greater than ever. It is not allayed by disguising the facts. We cannot make wise decisions if we continue to pretend that human behavior is not controlled, or if we refuse to engage in control when valuable results might be forthcoming. Such measures weaken only ourselves, leaving the strength of science to others. The first step in a defense against tyranny is the fullest possible exposure of controlling techniques. A second step has already been taken successfully in restricting the use of physical force. Slowly, and as yet imperfectly, we have worked out an ethical and governmental design in which the strong man is not allowed to use the power deriving from his strength to control his fellow men. He is restrained by a superior force created for that purpose—the ethical pressure of the group, or more explicit religious and governmental measures. We tend to distrust superior forces, as we currently hesitate to relinquish sovereignty in order to set up an international police force. But it is only through such countercontrol that we have achieved what we call peace—a condition in which men are not permitted to control each other through force. In other words, control itself must be controlled.

Science has turned up dangerous processes and materials before. To use the facts and techniques of a science of man to the fullest extent without making some monstrous mistake will be difficult and obviously perilous. It is no time for self-deception, emotional indulgence, or the assumption of attitudes which are no longer useful. Man is facing a difficult test. He must keep his head now, or he must start again—a long way back.[19]

In his novel *Walden II*, Skinner gives us a prototype for his deterministic utopia:

". . . When a particular emotion is no longer a useful part of a behavioral repertoire, we proceed to eliminate it."
"Yes, but how?"
"It's simply a matter of behavioral engineering," said Frazier.
"Behavioral engineering?"

---

[19] B. F. Skinner, "Freedom and the Control of Men," in *The American Scholar,* 1955–56.

"Each of us," Frazier began, "is engaged in a pitched battle with the rest of mankind."

"A curious premise for a Utopia," said Castle. "Even a pessimist like myself takes a more hopeful view than that."

"You do, you do," said Frazier. "But let's be realistic. Each of us has interests which conflict with the interests of everybody else. That's our original sin, and it can't be helped. Now, 'everybody else' we call 'society.' It's a powerful opponent, and it always wins. Oh, here and there an individual prevails for a while and gets what he wants. Sometimes he storms the culture of a society and changes it slightly to his own advantage. But society wins in the long run, for it has the advantage of numbers and of age. Many prevail against one, and men against a baby. Society attacks early, when the individual is helpless. It enslaves him almost before he has tasted freedom. The 'ologies' will tell you how it's done. Theology calls it building a conscience or developing a spirit of selflessness. Psychology calls it the growth of the super-ego.

"Considering how long society has been at it, you'd expect a better job. But the campaigns have been badly planned and the victory has never been secure. The behavior of the individual has been shaped according to revelations of 'good conduct,' never as the result of experimental study. But why not experiment? The questions are simple enough. What's the best behavior for the individual so far as the group is concerned? And how can the individual be induced to behave in that way? Why not explore these questions in a scientific spirit?" [20]

Philosopher Robert Kane thinks about Skinner this way:

BEYOND SKINNER
BY ROBERT KANE

The problem is brought out in a striking way by twentieth-century utopian novels, like Aldous Huxley's *Brave New World* and B. F. Skinner's *Walden Two*. In the fictional societies described in these famous works, people can have and do what they will or choose, but only to the extent that they have been conditioned by behavioral engineers or neuro-chemists to will or choose what they can have and do. In *Brave New World,* the lower-echelon workers are under the influence of powerful drugs so that they do not dream of things they cannot have. They are quite content to play miniature golf all weekend. They can do what they want, though their wants are meager and controlled by drugs.

The citizens of *Walden Two* have a richer existence than the workers of *Brave New World*. Yet their desires and purposes are also covertly controlled, in this case by behavioral engineers. Walden Two-ers live collectively in a kind of rural commune; and because they share duties of farming and raising children, they

---

[20] B. F. Skinner, *Walden II* (New York: Macmillan, 1965).

have plenty of leisure. They pursue arts, sciences, crafts, engage in musical performances and enjoy what appears to be a pleasant existence. The fictional founder of Walden Two, a fellow named Frazier, forthrightly says that their pleasant existence is brought about by the fact that, in his community, persons can do whatever they want or choose because they have been behaviorally conditioned since childhood to want and choose only what they can have and do. In other words, they have maximal *surface freedom* of action and choice (they can choose or do anything they want), but they lack a *deeper freedom* of the will because their desires and purposes are created by their behavioral conditioners or controllers. Their wills are not of "their own" making. Indeed, what happens in Walden Two is their surface freedom to act and choose *as* they will is maximized by minimizing the deeper freedom to have the ultimate say in what they will.

Thus Frazier can say that Walden Two "is the freest place on earth," since he has surface freedoms in mind. For there is no *coercion* in Walden Two and no *punishment* because no one has to be forced to do anything against his or her will. The citizens can have anything they want because they have been conditioned not to want anything they cannot have. As for the deeper freedom, or free will, it does not exist in Walden Two, as Frazier himself admits. But this is no loss, according to Frazier. Echoing *Walden Two*'s author, B. F. Skinner (a foremost defender of behaviorism in psychology), Frazier thinks the deeper freedom of the will is an illusion in the first place. We do not have it anyway, inside or outside Walden Two. In our ordinary lives, he argues, we are just as much the products of upbringing and social conditioning as the citizens of Walden Two, though we may delude ourselves into thinking otherwise. In our case, the conditioners are parents, teachers, coaches, schoolmates, peers, makers of TV programs, films, videos and other creators of the cultures and societies in which we live. The difference is that, unlike Walden Two, such everyday conditioning is often haphazard, incompetent and harmful.

Why then, Skinner asks, reject the maximal surface freedom and happiness of Walden Two for a deeper freedom of the will that is something we do not and cannot have anyway? Along with many other scientists, he thinks the idea that we could be *ultimate* determiners of our own ends or purposes (which is what the deeper freedom of the will would require) is an impossible ideal that cannot fit into the modern scientific picture of the world. To have such freedom, we would have to have been the original creators of our own wills—of ourselves. But if we trace the psychological springs of action back further and further to childhood, we find that we were less free back then, not more, and more subject to conditioning. We thus delude ourselves into thinking that we have sacrificed some real (deeper) freedom for the happiness of Walden Two. Rather we have gained a maximum amount of the only kind of freedom we really can have (surface freedom), while giving up an illusion (free will).

Seductive as these arguments may be, there are many people who continue to believe that something important is missing in Walden Two and that the deeper freedom is not a mere illusion. Such persons want to be the ultimate designers of their own lives as Frazier was for the lives of Walden Two. They want to be the creators, as he was, not the pawns—at least for their own lives. What they long for is what was traditionally meant by "free will."[21]

Not every visionary has looked upon determinism with delight. More often determinism has appeared in novels as a nightmare, as the philosophical basis of societies more oppressive and authoritarian than any we have ever seen. The most famous examples are **George Orwell**'s *1984* and **Aldous Huxley**'s *Brave New World*. In both novels, psychology and drugs are used to manipulate the inhabitants of entire societies and force them to conform to a single set of behavioral standards, concerning which they have no choice whatsoever. In a more recent novel, *A Clockwork Orange*, **Anthony Burgess** presents a nightmarish fantasy in which a young hoodlum named Alex is "reconditioned" to be "good" through a series of experiments in which his viewing of violent movies is accompanied by a drug that makes him violently ill. It works (after a fashion), but the prison chaplain summarizes the philosophical difficulties this raises:

FROM *A CLOCKWORK ORANGE*
BY **ANTHONY BURGESS**

[The Prison Chaplain tells him:] "Very hard ethical questions are involved," he went on. "You are to be made into a good boy, 6655321. Never again will you have the desire to commit acts of violence or to offend in any way whatsoever against the State's Peace. I hope you take all that in. I hope you are absolutely clear in your own mind about that." I said:

"Oh, it will be nice to be good, sir." But I had a real horrorshow smeck at that inside, brothers. He said:

"It may not be nice to be good, little 6655321. It may be horrible to be good. And when I say that you I realize how self-contradictory that sounds. I know I shall have many sleepless nights about this. What does God want? Does God want goodness or the choice of goodness? Is a man who chooses the bad perhaps in some way better than a man who has the good imposed upon him? Deep and hard questions, little 6655321. But all I want to say to you now is this: if at any time in the future you look back to these times and remember me, the lowest and humblest of all God's servitors, do not, I pray, think evil of me in your heart, thinking me in any way involved in what is now about to happen to you. And now, talking of praying, I realize sadly that there will be little point in praying for you. You are passing now to a region where you will be beyond the reach of the power of prayer. A terrible terrible thing to consider. And yet, in a sense, in choosing to be deprived of the ability to make an ethical choice, you have in a sense really chosen the good. So I shall like to think. So, God help us all, 6655321, I shall like to think." And he began to cry.[22]

---

[21] Robert Kane, from the essay "Free Will: Old Dispute, New Themes."

[22] Anthony Burgess, *A Clockwork Orange*, unabridged ed. (New York: Norton, 1987).

The claims of behavioral scientists like Skinner have provoked among contemporary ethicists similar responses to those that have provoked religious determinists. The repercussions are frightening. What if, for instance, instead of associating illness and repulsion with violent movies, the scientists in *A Clockwork Orange* were to associate pleasure? Well, that is exactly what our society does, claims **Catherine MacKinnon,** an American feminist philosopher. MacKinnon claims that advertisers, moviemakers, pornographers, and others in the media in our society *make* men's treatment of women fundamentally violent.

ON COERCION OF WOMEN'S SEXUALITY
BY CATHERINE MACKINNON

"Representation of the world," de Beauvoir writes, "like the world itself, is the work of men; they describe it from their own point of view, which they confuse with the absolute truth." The parallel between representation and construction should be sustained: men *create* the world from their own point of view, which then *becomes* the truth to be described. This is a closed system, not anyone's confusion. *Power to create the world from one's point of view is power in its male form.* The male epistemological stance, which corresponds to the world it creates, is objectivity: the ostensibly noninvolved stance, the view from a distance and from no particular perspective, apparently transparent to its reality. It does not comprehend its own perspectivity, does not recognize what it sees as subject like itself, or that the way it apprehends its world is a form of its subjugation and presupposes it. The objectively knowable is object. Woman through male eyes is sex object, that by which man knows himself at once as man and as subject. What is objectively known corresponds to the world and can be verified by pointing to it (as science does) because the world itself is controlled from the same point of view. Combining, like any form of power, legitimation with force, male power extends beneath the representation of reality to its construction: it makes women (as it were) and so verifies (makes true) who women "are" in its view, simultaneously confirming its way of being and its vision of truth. The eroticism that corresponds to this is "the use of things to experience self." As a coerced pornography model put it, "You do it, you do it, and you do it; then you become it." The fetish speaks feminism.

Objectification makes sexuality a material reality of women's lives, not just a psychological, attitudinal, or ideological one. It obliterates the mind/matter distinction that such a division is premised upon. Like the value of a commodity, women's sexual desirability is fetishized: it is made to appear a quality of the object itself, spontaneous and inherent, independent of the social relation which creates it, uncontrolled by the force that requires it. It helps if the object cooperates: hence, the vaginal orgasm; hence, faked orgasms altogether. Women's sexualness, like male prowess, is no less real for being mythic. It is embodied. Commodities do have value, but only because value is a social property arising from the totality of the same social relations which, unconscious of their determination, fetishize it. Women's bodies possess no less real desirability—or,

Sexual objectification is the primary process of the subjection of women.

probably, desire. Sartre exemplifies the problem on the epistemological level: "But if I desire a house, or a glass of water, or a woman's body, how could this body, this glass, this piece of property reside in my desire and how can my desire be anything but the consciousness of these objects as desirable?" Indeed. Objectivity is the methodological stance of which objectification is the social process. Sexual objectification is the primary process of the subjection of women. It unites act with word, construction with expression, perception with enforcement, myth with reality. Man [*expletive deleted*] woman; subject verb object.[23]

Note that MacKinnon's argument, despite its opposition to the media conditioning of sexual oppression, is thoroughly determinist. She believes that our traditions and media *cause* violence and oppression. Do we really want to believe, however, that human actions are just conditioned reflexes?

It seems like a slippery slope: If any of our actions can really be compelled through psychological conditioning, then why not all our actions? And if our actions, good or bad, are compelled, then it doesn't seem to make sense to hold anyone responsible for his or her actions (even the people doing the conditioning). If Skinner is right, then moral education and political activity can be reduced to the results of multiple conditions and reinforcements.

E. FREEDOM IN PRACTICE

As many of the foregoing arguments show, it isn't enough just to answer the metaphysical question about the causes of human action. The demand for freedom and responsibility is not going to be satisfied by different variations of determinism, no matter how "soft" they pretend to be. If we are to understand the role of freedom in our daily lives, what we need is a breach in determinism, a conception of our actions, or at least our decisions, as truly free and not determined in any of the ways discussed previously.

The classic statement of this claim to freedom and responsibility is to be found in the philosophy of Immanuel Kant. (I am sure that you now appreciate how truly monumental Kant's philosophy has been. We shall see more of him in the next chapter as well.) We have already seen that Kant gave an unqualified endorsement of determinism, arguing that the principle (of universal causation) upon which it is based is nothing less than a necessary rule of all human experience. This includes human actions:

Actions of men are determined in conformity with the order of Nature, by their empirical character and other causes; if we could exhaust all the appearances,

---

[23] Catherine MacKinnon, by permission of the University of Chicago Press.

there would not be found a single human action which would not be predicted with certainty.[24]

This is surely a statement of the hardest of "hard" determinism. But Kant also appreciated, as much as any philosopher ever has, the importance of unqualified freedom for human responsibility. (He called freedom, as he had called God, a "postulate" [or presupposition] of practical reason.) But how could he defend both universal determinism and human freedom? Determinism is true of every possible event and object of human knowledge, Kant says, but it does not follow that it is also applicable to human acts of will or decisions to act. Action is a wholly different matter than knowledge. The metaphysics with which Kant defends this view is far too complicated to even summarize here. But the basic principle is simple enough: Kant says that we adopt two different standpoints toward the world, one theoretical, one practical. Insofar as we want to know something, we adopt the standpoint of science and determinism. Within that standpoint, every event, including human actions, is determined, brought about by sufficient natural causes (including the states of our brains and various psychological factors). But when we are ready to do something, we switch to the practical standpoint. The main point is this: Insofar as we are acting or deciding to act, we *must* consider our own acts of will and decisions as the sufficient causes of our actions, and we cannot continue the causal chain backward to consider whether those acts of will are themselves caused. When we act, in other words, we cannot think of ourselves except as acting freely.

Suppose that you are about to make a decision: You are finally going to give up smoking. A friend offers you a cigarette on the second day. Yes or no? Do you smoke it? Now it might very well be that, given your personality, your weakness for past habits, and any number of other psychological factors, you are clearly determined to accept and thus break your resolution. Your friend, who knows you quite well, may even know this. But you can't think of yourself in this deterministic way, for insofar as you have to make a decision, you can't simply "find out" what you will do. In other words, you can't simply predict your own behavior, no matter how much you know about the various causes and factors that allow your friend to predict your behavior. If you were to predict, "I'm going to start smoking again anyway," you would not be simply predicting; you would be, in that very act, breaking your resolution, that is, deciding to break it. So, when your own acts and decisions are concerned, you have to act as if you were totally free. This in a way denies determinism. It says, as you are the one that has to make the decision, determinism isn't relevant. (Kant says, "and to have to think yourself free is to *be* free.")

Kant defends both freedom and determinism, and so he undermines the distinction that philosophers had drawn between them. Kant implies that a careful reconsideration of human action from the point of view of practice may put the metaphysicians' insistence on freedom as a type of causation in a new light and may

---

[24] Immanuel Kant, *The Critique of Pure Reason*, trans. Norman Kemp Smith (New York: St. Martin's Press, 1933).

allow us to think of freedom in a new way. For Kant, freedom is a certain *type of experience,* not an "internal cause." In a similar vein, the contemporary American philosopher **Harry Frankfurt** rethinks the meaning of coercion (or compulsion) in terms of the experience of the agent. His claim is that coercion is not properly understood as an "external cause" of an action. Rather, the question of what counts as coercion (and similarly what counts as freedom) is bound up inseparably with the question of what it means to be a person.

"COERCION AND MORAL RESPONSIBILITY"
BY HARRY FRANKFURT

The courts may refuse to admit in evidence, on the grounds that it was coerced, a confession which the police have obtained from a prisoner by threatening to beat him. But the prisoner's accomplices, who are compromised by his confession, are less likely to agree that he was genuinely coerced into confession. They may feel, perhaps justifiably, that he made a reprehensible choice and that he acted badly: he ought to have accepted the beating rather than to have betrayed them. Thus sometimes, though not always, the use of the term "coercion" conveys an exclusion of moral responsibility. A person who acts under coercion is for that reason regarded as not having acted freely, or of his own free will. It may be established that a person is not to be credited or blamed for what he has done, then, by showing that he was "coerced" into doing it.

A person is sometimes said to have been coerced even when he has performed no action at all. Suppose that one man applies intense pressure to another man's wrist, forcing him to drop the knife in his hand. In this case, which involves what may be called "physical coercion," the victim is not made to act; what happens is that his fingers are made to open by the pressure applied to his wrist. It may in certain situations be difficult, or even impossible, to know whether or not an action has been performed. Perhaps it will be unclear whether the man dropped the knife because his fingers were forced open or because he wished to avoid a continuation of the pressure on his wrist. Or suppose that a man is being severely tortured in order to compel him to reveal a password, and that at a certain point he utters the word. There may be no way of discovering whether he spoke the word in submission to the threat of further pain, or whether—his will having been overcome by the agony which he had already suffered—the word passed involuntarily through his lips.

I propose to consider those cases of coercion in which the victim is made to perform an action, by being provided with a certain kind of motive for doing so, but which resemble cases of physical coercion in that the victim is not to be regarded as morally responsible for what he has been coerced into doing. We might say that in instances of physical coercion the victim's body is used as an instrument, whose movements are made subject to another person's will. In those instances of coercion that concern me, on the other hand, it is the victim's will which is subjected to the will of another. How, in those cases, does coercion affect its victim's freedom? What basis does it provide for the judgment that he is not morally responsible for doing what he is made to do?

II

But what is coercion? Coercing someone into performing a certain action cannot be, if it is to imply his freedom from moral responsibility, merely a matter of getting him to perform the action by means of a threat. A person who is coerced is *compelled* to do what he does. He has *no choice* but to do it. This is at least part of what is essential if coercion is to relieve its victim of moral responsibility—if it is to make it inappropriate either to praise him or to blame him for having done what he was coerced into doing. Now it is not necessarily true of a person who decides to avoid a penalty with which he has been threatened that he is compelled to do so or that he has no other choice. Nor is it true that a person bears no moral responsibility for what he has done just because he does it in submission to a threat. Such a person may be described as acting "under duress"; but not all duress is coercion.

It might be suggested that someone is coerced if, in addition to his acting in order to avoid a threatened penalty, two further conditions are satisfied: (1) the penalty with which he is threatened renders the action against which the threat is issued *substantially* less attractive to him than it would have been otherwise; and (2) he believes that he would be left worse off by defying the threat than by submitting to it. Adding these conditions does not, however, serve adequately to identify instances of coercion.

Suppose that P threatens to step on Q's toe unless Q sets fire to a crowded hospital, and that Q sets the fire in order to keep P off his toe. This does not satisfy the first condition, which excludes trivial threats: the penalty Q seeks to avoid by submitting to P's demand is not a substantial one. Suppose instead, then, that P threatens to break Q's thumb unless Q sets fire to the hospital, and that Q submits to this threat. Here the penalty with which P threatens Q is substantial: any course of action is rendered substantially less attractive to a person if it leads him to a broken thumb than it would if it did not involve this consequence. Thus the first condition is now satisfied. It may be, moreover, that the second condition is satisfied too. Suppose that Q thinks he will not be apprehended or punished for setting fire to the hospital, and that he does not expect to be troubled very greatly by his conscience for doing so. Then he may well believe that he would be left worse off by defying P's threat and having his thumb broken than by doing what P demands of him. Even if both conditions are satisfied in this way, however, it does not seem appropriate to describe Q as being coerced into setting the fire.

Why are we disinclined to regard Q as being coerced even when we suppose that he believes he will suffer substantially more by defying P's threat than by submitting to it? One suggestion would be that it is because we think that since Q must realize that it is better to suffer even a broken thumb than to set fire to a hospital, he cannot believe that his submission to P's threat is justifiable or reasonable. We might, accordingly, consider revising the second condition to make it require that Q believes it would be unreasonable for him to defy P's threat, or believes that he is justified in submitting to it.

Now the satisfaction of this revised condition would ensure that a person who has been coerced into performing a certain action *believes* that he cannot properly be *blamed* for having performed it. But the criterion of coercion for which we are looking must do more than this. It must ensure that a coerced person cannot properly be held *morally* responsible at all for what he has been coerced into doing. And this would not be accomplished even by strengthening (2) still further so that it required Q to believe *correctly* that he is justified in submitting to P's threat, or that it would be unreasonable for him to defy it. In fact the satisfaction of the second condition in any plausible version is neither necessary for coercion nor, even in conjunction with the satisfaction of the first condition, sufficient for it.

◆◆◆

A person's evaluations may not only affect his judgments concerning what it is reasonable for him to do. They may also have an effect upon what he is capable of doing.

> *Faced with a coercive threat, the victim has no choice but to submit: he cannot prevent his desire to avoid the penalty in question from determining his response.*

Faced with a coercive threat, the victim has no choice but to submit: he cannot prevent his desire to avoid the penalty in question from determining his response. When he decides that it is reasonable for him to submit to a threat which is not coercive, his submission is not in this way made inescapable by forces within himself which he is unable to overcome. Sometimes we speak of threats as coercive even when we have no particular evidence that their victims are incapable of defying them. This is because there are certain penalties which we do not expect anyone to be able to choose to incur. A person who surpasses this expectation thereby performs not merely rightly or wrongly but with a certain heroic quality.

We do on some occasions find it appropriate to make an adverse judgment concerning a person's submission to a threat, even though we recognize that he has genuinely been coerced and that he is therefore not properly to be held morally responsible for his submission. This is because we think that the person, although he was in fact quite unable to control a certain desire, ought to have been able to control it.

◆◆◆

Consider the following two situations. Suppose first that a man comes to a fork in the road, that someone on a hillside adjoining the left-hand fork threatens to start an avalanche which will crush him if he goes that way, and that the man takes the fork to the right in order to satisfy a commanding desire to preserve his own life. Next, suppose that when the man comes to the fork he finds no one issuing threats but instead notices that on account of the natural conditions of things he will be crushed by an avalanche if he takes the left-hand fork, and that he is moved irresistibly by his desire to live to proceed by the fork to the right. There are interesting differences between these situations, to be sure, but there is no basis for regarding the man as acting more or less freely or of his own free will in the one case than in the other. Whether he is morally responsible for his decision or action in each case depends not on the source of the injury he is motivated to avoid but on the way in which his desire to avoid it operates within him.

We do tend, of course, to be more resentful when another person places obstacles in our way than when the environment does so. What accounts for this greater resentment is not, however, the love of liberty. It is pride; or, what is closely related to pride, a sense of injustice. Only another person can *coerce* us, or interfere with our *social* or *political* freedom, but this is no more than a matter of useful terminology. When a person chooses to act in order to acquire a benefit or in order to escape an injury, the degree to which his choice is autonomous and the degree to which he acts freely do not depend on the origin of the conditions which lead him to choose and to act as he does. A man's will may not be his own even when he is not moved by the will of another.[25]

The call for a reevaluation of freedom as a reevaluation of personhood is essential to the American civil rights advocate **Dr. Martin Luther King, Jr.** His stance is quite Kantian. While maintaining that freedom is integral to personhood and inalienable by law or psychological compulsion, Reverend King claims that freedom cannot be *given* by law or psychological compulsion, either. Rather, freedom is acquired only through a restoration of personhood, which, in the case of persons so long oppressed and demeaned as African-Americans, may take a long and concerted effort on all our parts.

"THE DILEMMA OF NEGRO AMERICANS" BY MARTIN LUTHER KING, JR.

Negro life! Being a Negro in America means being scarred by a history of slavery and family disorganization. Negroes have grown accustomed now to hearing unfeeling and insensitive whites say: "Other immigrant groups such as the Irish, the Jews and the Italians started out with similar handicaps, and yet they made it. Why haven't the Negroes done the same?" These questioners refuse to see that the situation of other immigrant groups a hundred years ago and the situation of the Negro today cannot be usefully compared. Negroes were brought here in chains long before the Irish decided *voluntarily* to leave Ireland or the Italians

---

[25] Harry Frankfurt, "Coercion and Moral Responsibility," from *The Importance of What We Care About* (Cambridge: Cambridge University Press, 1988).

thought of leaving Italy. Some Jews may have left their homes in Europe involuntarily, but they were not in chains when they arrived on these shores. Other immigrant groups came to America with language and economic handicaps, but not with the stigma of color. Above all, no other group has been a slave on American soil, and no other group has had its family structure deliberately torn apart. This is the rub.

◆◆◆

The Negro family for three hundred years has been on the tracks of the racing locomotives of American history, dragged along mangled and crippled. Pettigrew has pointed out that American slavery is distinguished from all other forms of slavery because it consciously dehumanized the Negro. In Greece and Rome, for example, slaves preserved dignity and a measure of family life. Our institution of slavery, on the other hand, began with the break-up of families on the coasts of Africa. Because the middle passage was long and expensive, African families were torn apart in the interest of selectivity, as if the members were beasts. In the ships' holds, black captives were packed spoon fashion to live on a voyage often lasting two to six months in a space for each the size of a coffin. If water ran short, or famine threatened, or a plague broke out, whole cargoes of living and dead were thrown overboard. The sheer physical torture was sufficient to murder millions of men, women, and children. But even more incalculable was the psychological damage.

The Negro family for three hundred years has been on the tracks of the racing locomotives of American history, dragged along mangled and crippled.

Of those families who survived the voyage, many more were ripped apart on the auction block as soon as they reached American shores. Against this ghastly background the Negro family began life in the United States. On the plantation the institution of legal marriage for slaves did not exist. The masters might direct mating, or if they did not intervene, marriage occurred without sanctions.

◆◆◆

The liberation from slavery in 1863, which should have initiated the birth of a stable Negro family life, meant a formal legal freedom but, as Henrietta Buckmaster put it, "With Appomattox, four million black people in the South owned their skins and nothing more." With civil war still dividing the nation, a new inferno engulfed the Negro and his family. Thrown off the plantations, penniless, homeless, still largely in the territory of their enemies and in the grip of fear, bewilderment and aimlessness, hundreds of thousands became wanderers. For security they fled to Union Army camps that were unprepared to help. One writer describes a mother carrying a child in one arm, a father holding another child, and eight other children with their hands tied to one rope held by the mother, who struggled after Sherman's army and traveled hundreds of miles to safety. All were not so fortunate. In the starvation-induced madness some Negroes killed their children to free them of their misery.

These are historical facts. If they cause the mind to reel with horror, it is still necessary to realize that this is but a tiny glimpse of the reality of the era, and it does justice neither to the enormous extent of the tragedy nor to the degree of human suffering and sorrow.

Following the Civil War, millions returned to a new form of slavery, once again imprisoned on plantations devoid of human rights and plunged into searing poverty generation after generation. Some families found their way to the North, in a movement E. Franklin Frazier aptly describes as "into the city of destruction." Illiterate, afraid and crushed by want, they were herded into the slums. The bewildering complexity of the city undermined the confidence of fathers and mothers, causing them to lose control of their children, whose bewilderment was even more acute.

◆◆◆

Most people are totally unaware of the darkness of the cave in which the Negro is forced to live. A few individuals can break out, but the vast majority remain its prisoners. Our cities have constructed elaborate expressways and elevated skyways, and white Americans speed from suburb to inner city through vast pockets of black deprivation without ever getting a glimpse of the suffering and misery in their midst.

But while so many white Americans are unaware of conditions inside the ghetto, there are very few ghetto dwellers who are unaware of the life outside. Their television sets bombard them day by day with the opulence of the larger society. From behind the ghetto walls they see glistening towers of glass and steel springing up almost overnight. They hear jet liners speeding over their heads at six hundred miles an hour. They hear of satellites streaking through outer space and revealing details of the moon.

Then they begin to think of their own conditions. They know that they are always given the hardest, ugliest, most mental work to do. They look at these impressive buildings under construction and realize that almost certainly they cannot get those well-paying construction jobs, because building trade unions reserve them for whites only. They know that people who built the bridges, the mansions and docks of the South could build modern buildings if they were only given a chance for apprenticeship training. They realize that it is hard, raw discrimination that shuts them out. It is not only poverty that torments the Negro; it is the fact of poverty amid plenty. It is a misery generated by the gulf between the affluence he sees in the mass media and the deprivation he experiences in his everyday life.

◆◆◆

Here the democratic process breaks down, for the rights of the individual voter are impossible to organize without adequate funds, while the business community supplies the existing political machine with enough funds to organize massive campaigns and control mass media.

Here, too, the North reveals its true ambivalence on the subject of civil rights. When, in the last session of Congress, the issue came home to the North through a call for open housing legislation, white Northern Congressmen who had enthusiastically supported the 1964 and 1965 civil rights bills now joined in a mighty chorus of anguish and dismay reminiscent of Alabama and Mississippi. So the first piece of legislation aimed at rectifying a shocking evil in the North went down to crushing defeat.

Nothing today more clearly indicates the residue of racism still lodging in our society than the responses of white America to integrated housing. Here the tides of prejudice, fear and irrationality rise to flood proportions. This is not a new backlash caused by the Black Power movement; there had been no ominous riots in Watts when white Californians defeated a fair housing bill in 1964. The present resistance to open housing is based on the same premises that came into being to rationalize slavery. It is rooted in the fear that the alleged depravity or defective nature of the out-race will infiltrate the neighborhood of the in-race.[26]

Both King and Frankfurt argue a quasi-Kantian view of freedom. In practice, they claim, actions are free to the extent that their agent is a dignified, capable, rational human being. The ability to act freely, then, is not *determined* by "outside" influences, but such influences—like the economy, the society, the media, our friends and families—can and do *affect* freedom. Outside influences debilitate and/or enhance an agent's freedom and humanity.

F. RADICAL FREEDOM: EXISTENTIALISM

Kant's suggestion, however, has been taken up in a very different way in European philosophy, particularly by the existentialists. Like Kant, they accept (or at least do not bother to reject) determinism in science. But they insist that even if determinism is true, one must always view *him* or *herself as agent* as necessarily free. When you have to decide what to do, all the knowledge of the possible factors determining your decision are not sufficient to cause you to decide. For you cannot predict your own decision without at the same time making it.

Jean-Paul Sartre, the late French existentialist, has defended the Kantian claim for human freedom as far as it can possibly be defended. In his mammoth book *Being and Nothingness,* Sartre argued that we are, always, absolutely free. This means, as Kant had insisted, that insofar as we act (and Sartre says that we are always acting) our decisions and our actions cannot be viewed as having any causes whatsoever. We must make decisions, and no amount of information and no number of causal circumstances can ever replace our need to make them. We can, of course, refuse to make decisions, acting as if they were made for us, as if circumstances already determined them, as if the fates had already established the outcome. But even in these cases, we are making decisions, "choosing not to choose," in a classic

---

[26] Martin Luther King, Jr., *Where Do We Go From Here? Chaos or Community?* (Boston: Beacon Press, 1967).

Sartrian phrase. We are "condemned to be free," he says, in a phrase that has since become famous. Again, desires may enter into consideration, but only as "consideration." We can always act against a desire, any desire, no matter how strong, if only we are sufficiently decided that we shall do so. A starving man may yet refuse food if, for example, he is taking part in a hunger strike for a political cause to which he is dedicated. A mother may refuse to save her own life if it would be at the expense of her children. A student may miss his favorite television show if he has resolved to study for tomorrow's test. Whether trivial or grandiose, our every act is a decision, and our every decision is free. Even if we fail to live up to them or find that we "cannot" make them, we are responsible nevertheless. There is no escape from freedom or responsibility.

FROM **"ABSOLUTE FREEDOM"**
BY **JEAN-PAUL SARTRE**

Although the considerations which are about to follow are of interest primarily to the ethicist, it may nevertheless be worthwhile after these descriptions and arguments to return to the freedom of the for-itself and try to understand what the fact of this freedom represents for human destiny.

The essential consequence of our earlier remarks is that man being condemned to be free carries the weight of the whole world on his shoulders; he is responsible for the world and for himself as a way of being. We are taking the word "responsibility" in its ordinary sense as "consciousness" (of) being the incontestable author of an event or of an object." In this sense the responsibility of the for-itself is overwhelming since he is the one by whom it happens that *there is* a world; since he is also the one who makes himself be, then whatever may be the situation in which he finds himself, the for-itself must wholly assume this situation with its peculiar coefficient of adversity, even though it be insupportable. He must assume the situation with the proud consciousness of being the author of it, for the very worst disadvantages or the worst threats which can endanger my person have meaning only in and through my project; and it is on the ground of the engagement which I am that they appear. It is therefore senseless to think of complaining since nothing foreign has decided what we feel, what we live, or what we are.

Furthermore this absolute responsibility is not resignation; it is simply the logical requirement of the consequences of our freedom. What happens to me happens through me, and I can neither affect myself with it nor revolt against it nor resign myself to it. Moreover everything which happens to me is *mine*. By this we must understand first of all that I am always equal to what happens to me *qua* man, for what happens to a man through other men and through himself can be only human. The most terrible situations of war, the worst tortures do not create a non-human state of things; there is no non-human situation. It is only through fear, flight, and recourse to magical types of conduct that I shall decide on the non-human, but this decision is human, and I shall carry the entire responsibility for it. But in addition the situation is *mine* because it is the image of my free choice of myself, and everything which it presents to me is *mine* in that this represents me and symbolizes me. Is it not I who decide the coefficient of adversity in things and even their unpredictability by deciding myself?

Thus there are no *accidents* in life; a community event which suddenly burst forth and involves me in it does not come from the outside. If I am mobilized in a war, this war is *my* war; it is in my image and I deserve it. I deserve it first because I could always get out of it by suicide or by desertion; these ultimate possibles are those which must always be present for us when there is a question of envisaging a situation. For lack of getting out of it, I have *chosen* it. This can be due to inertia, to cowardice in the face of public opinion, or because I prefer certain other values to the value of the refusal to join in the war (the good opinion of my relatives, the honor of my family, *etc.*). Any way you look at it, it is a matter of choice. This choice will be repeated later on again and again without a break until the end of the war. Therefore we must agree with the statement by J. Romains, "In war there are no innocent victims." If therefore I have preferred war to death or to dishonor, everything takes place as if I bore the entire responsibility for this war. Of course others have declared it, and one might be tempted perhaps to consider me as a simple accomplice. But this notion of complicity has only a juridical sense, and it does not hold here. For it depended on me that for me and by me this war should not exist, and I have decided that it does exist. There was no compulsion here, for the compulsion could have got no hold on a freedom. I did not have any excuse; . . . the peculiar character of human-reality is that it is without excuse. Therefore it remains for me only to lay claim to this war.

But in addition the war is *mine* because by the sole fact that it arises in a situation which I cause to be and that I can discover it there only by engaging myself for or against it, I can no longer distinguish at present the choice which I make of myself from the choice which I make of the war. To live this war is to choose myself through it and to choose it through my choice of myself. There can be no question of considering it as "four years of vacation" or as "reprieve," as a "recess," the essential part of my responsibilities being elsewhere in my married, family, or professional life. In this war which I have chosen I choose myself from day to day, and I make it mine by making myself. If it is going to be four empty years, then it is I who bear the responsibility for this.

Finally, . . . each person is an absolute choice of self from the standpoint of a world of knowledges and of techniques which this choice both assumes and illumines; each person is an absolute upsurge at an absolute date and is perfectly unthinkable at another date. It is therefore a waste of time to ask what I should have been if this war had not broken out, for I have chosen myself as one of the possible meanings of the epoch which imperceptibly led to war. I am not distinct from this same epoch; I could not be transported to another epoch without contradiction. Thus *I am* this war which restricts and limits and makes comprehensible the period which preceded it. In this sense we may define more precisely, the responsibility of the for-itself if to the earlier quoted statement, "There are no innocent victims," we added the words, "We have the war we deserve." Thus, totally free, undistinguishable from the period for which I have chosen to be the meaning, as profoundly responsible for the war as if I had myself declared it, unable to live without integrating it in *my* situation, engaging myself in it wholly and stamping it with my seal, I must be without remorse or regrets as I am without excuse; for from the instant of my upsurge into being, I carry the weight of the world by myself alone without anything or any person being able to lighten it.

... from the instant of my upsurge into being, I carry the weight of the world by myself alone without anything or any person being able to lighten it.

Yet this responsibility is of a very particular type. Someone will say, "I did not ask to be born." This is a naïve way of throwing greater emphasis on our facticity. I am responsible for everything, in fact, except for my very responsibility, for I am not the foundation of my being. Therefore everything takes place as if I were compelled to be responsible. I am *abandoned* in the world, not in the sense that I might remain abandoned and passive in a hostile universe like a board floating on the water, but rather in the sense that I find myself suddenly alone and without help, engaged in a world for which I bear the whole responsibility without being able, whatever I do, to tear myself away from this responsibility for an instant. For I am responsible for my very desire of fleeing responsibilities. To make myself passive in the world, to refuse to act upon things and upon Others is still to choose myself, and suicide is one mode among others of being-in-the-world. Yet I find an absolute responsibility for the fact that my facticity (here the fact of my birth) is directly inapprehensible and even inconceivable, for this fact of my birth never appears as a brute fact but always across a projective reconstruction of my for-itself. I am ashamed of being born or I am astonished at it or I rejoice over it, or in attempting to get rid of my life I affirm that I live and I assume this life as bad. Thus in a certain sense I *choose* being born. This choice itself is integrally affected with facticity since I am not able not to choose, but this facticity in turn will appear only in so far as I surpass it toward my ends. Thus facticity is everywhere but inapprehensible; I never encounter anything except my responsibility. That is why I can not ask, "*Why* was I born?" or curse the day of my birth or declare that I did not ask to be born, for these various attitudes toward my birth—i.e., toward the *fact* that I realize a presence in the world—are absolutely nothing else but ways of assuming this birth in full responsibility and of making it *mine*. Here again I encounter only myself and my projects so that finally my abandonment—i.e., my facticity—consists simply in the fact that I am condemned to be wholly responsible for myself. I am the being which *is* in such a way that in its being its being is in question. And this "is" of my being *is* as present and inapprehensible.

Under these conditions since every event in the world can be revealed to me only as an *opportunity* (an opportunity made use of, lacked, neglected, etc.) or better yet since everything which happens to us can be considered as a *chance* (i.e., can appear to us only as a way of realizing this being which is in question in our being) and since others as transcendences-transcended are themselves only *opportunities* and *chances,* the responsibility of the for-itself extends to the entire world as a peopled-world. It is precisely thus that the for-itself apprehends itself in anguish; that is, as a being which is neither the foundation of its own being nor of the Other's being nor of the in-itselfs which form the world, but a being which is compelled to decide the meaning of being—within it and everywhere outside of it. The one who realizes in anguish his condition as *being* thrown into a responsibility which extends to his very abandonment has no longer either remorse or regret or excuse; he is no longer anything but a freedom which perfectly reveals itself and whose being resides in this very revelation. But as we pointed out . . . , most of the time we flee anguish in bad faith.[27]

Sartre's position is the culmination of a full century of existentialist thought, beginning with Søren Kierkegaard in the 1840s. Kierkegaard too argued that one is responsible for whatever one is and that self-conscious choice and commitment were the factors that made a person most human. Sartre's very strong sense of responsibility goes even so far as to ascribe an act of choice to those situations in which we seem clearly to be only victims, for example, in war. "There are no accidents in life," he argues. It is always my choice as to how I shall act in and deal with a situation. One can always complain, "I didn't ask to be born," Sartre says, but this is only one of many ways we have of trying to avoid responsibility. Given the fact that we have been born, raised in certain conditions, and so forth, it is now entirely up to us as to what we shall make of all this. Instead of looking at the events of the world as problems and intrusions, Sartre ultimately says, we should learn to look at everything as an opportunity. Here is the optimistic note to his very strong defense of human freedom.

What all of these arguments demand is the following: In one's own case, in making your decision, there can be no appeal to determinism even if determinism is true. Whatever might be theoretically determined, in practice, you must choose. Since freedom is the key to our self-esteem and our pride in ourselves, some people will demand it at any cost.

The most brilliant, if bizarre, example of this existentialist demand is formulated by the strange character in Dostoyevski's short novel *Notes from the Underground.* The argument is simple. Any prediction can be thwarted as long as you know about it. If they say, "you'll do *x*"; do *y*. Now, suppose that determinism is true. In particular, suppose that psychological determinism is true and that its basic law is this: "people always act to their own advantage." Now, what does this have to do with the predictability of a person's actions? Absolutely nothing, if you are sufficiently determined not to be predictable. Accordingly, the character in this novel is, more than

---

[27] Jean-Paul Sartre, *Being and Nothingness,* trans. Hazel E. Barnes (New York: Philosophical Library, 1956).

anything else, spiteful. His main concern is not being predictable, in proving his freedom even if it means making himself miserable. Now you might say that his spite itself is the determinant of his behavior, and of course it is. But the very point of the argument is that causes and explanations of any kind are simply beside the point. Let the underground man know what you expect him to do, and he'll do precisely the opposite. If you predict he'll act spiteful, he'll be as agreeable as can be—just out of spite!

FROM **"THE MOST ADVANTAGEOUS ADVANTAGE"**
BY **FYODOR DOSTOYEVSKI**

I am a sick man . . . I am a spiteful man. I am an unpleasant man. I think my liver is diseased. However, I don't know beans about my disease, and I am not sure what is bothering me. I don't treat it and never have, though I respect medicine and doctors. Besides, I am extremely superstitious, let's say sufficiently so to respect medicine. (I am educated enough not to be superstitious, but I am.) No, I refuse to treat it out of spite. You probably will not understand that. Well, but *I* understand it. . . .

. . . Why, in the first place, when in all these thousands of years has there ever been a time when man has acted only for his own advantage? What is to be done with the millions of facts that bear witness that men, *knowingly,* that is, fully understanding their real advantages, have left them in the background and have rushed headlong on another path, to risk, to chance, compelled to this course by nobody and by nothing, but, as it were, precisely because they did not want the beaten track, and stubbornly, wilfully, went off on another difficult, absurd way seeking it almost in the darkness. After all, it means that this stubbornness and wilfulness were more pleasant to them than any advantage. Advantage! What is advantage? And will you take it upon yourself to define with perfect accuracy in exactly what the advantage of man consists of? And what if it so happens that a man's advantage *sometimes* not only may, but even must, consist exactly in his desiring under certain conditions what is harmful to himself and not what is advantageous. And if so, if there can be such a condition then the whole principle becomes worthless.

. . . The fact is, gentlemen, it seems that something that is dearer to almost every man than his greatest advantages must really exist, or (not to be illogical) there is one most advantageous advantage (the very one omitted of which we spoke just now) which is more important and more advantageous than all other advantages, for which, if necessary, a man is ready to act in opposition to all laws, that is, in opposition to reason, honor, peace, prosperity—in short, in opposition to all those wonderful and useful things if only he can attain that fundamental, most advantageous advantage which is dearer to him than all.

What is that "advantageous advantage?" Nothing other than

One's own free unfettered choice, one's own fancy, however wild it may be, one's own fancy worked up at times to frenzy. That is the "most advantageous advantage," which is always overlooked.[28]

Freedom in other words, is itself what we most demand, whatever the cost, whatever the difficulties, and whatever the arguments against it. Whatever else may be true, we will refuse to see ourselves as anything but free. For it is freedom that makes us human. Dostoyevski's picture of this radical, desperate freedom is perhaps not a very uplifting one. A similar sentiment, however, can give a very joyous image of freedom. Here is a sample from **Thich Nhat Hanh,** a Vietnamese Buddhist monk. It is a prayer to say when turning on the television:

FROM **"TURNING ON THE TELEVISION"**
BY **THICH NHAT HANH**

> The mind is a television
> with thousands of channels.
> I choose a world that is tranquil and calm
> so that my joy will always be fresh.

Mind is consciousness. Consciousness includes the subject which knows and the object which is known. The two aspects, subject and object, depend on each other in order to exist. As the Vietnamese meditation master, Huong Hai, said, "In seeing matter, you are at the same time seeing mind. Without the arising of the object, the subject does not arise." When our mind is conscious of something, we *are* that thing. When we contemplate a snow-covered mountain, we are that mountain. When we watch a noisy film, we are that noisy film.

> *Our mind is like a television set with thousands of channels, and the channel we switch on is the channel we are at that moment.*

Our mind is like a television set with thousands of channels, and the channel we switch on is the channel we are at that moment. When we turn on anger, we are anger. When we turn on peace and joy, we are peace and joy. We have the ability to select the channel. *We are what we choose to be.* We can select any channel of the mind. Buddha is a channel, Mara is a channel, remembering is a channel, forgetting is a channel, calm is a channel, agitation is a channel. Changing from one state of being to another is as simple as the change from a channel showing a film to a channel playing music.

---

[28] Fyodor Dostoyevski, *Notes from the Underground,* in *Notes from the Underground and The Grand Inquisitor,* trans. Ralph Matlaw (New York: E. P. Dutton, 1960).

There are people who cannot tolerate peace and quiet, who are afraid of facing themselves, so they turn on the television in order to be preoccupied with it for a whole evening. In contemporary culture, people rarely like to be with themselves, and they frequently seek forgetfulness—downtown at the theater or other places of amusement. People rarely like to look deeply and compassionately at themselves. Young people in America watch television more than five hours per day, and they also have all sorts of electronic games to occupy them. Where will a culture in which people do not have the chance to face themselves or form real relationships with others lead us?

There are many interesting, instructive programs on television, and we can use the TV guide to select programs which encourage mindfulness. We should decide to watch only the programs we have selected and avoid becoming a victim of the television.[29]

SUMMARY AND CONCLUSION

To say that a person's act is free is to be able to ascribe responsibility. The defense of freedom therefore becomes extremely important to us. Our confidence in the universality of scientific explanations, however, seems to imply the thesis of determinism, which holds that every event has its sufficient natural cause. Human actions, as events, thus seem to be determined and thus not free. In this chapter, we have explored the various ways in which philosophers have attempted to reconcile these two vital beliefs—that at least some human acts are free and that science can ultimately (at least in principle) explain everything.

Some philosophers have defended determinism ("hard determinism") to the exclusion of freedom. Others have defended freedom to the exclusion of determinism ("indeterminists"). Most philosophers, however, have tried to defend both theses (and so are often called "compatibilists"). They have argued that determinism does not preclude freedom if an act flows from a person's decision or character ("soft determinists"), that we can be more and less susceptible to determinists (Frankfurt, King), or that even if determinism is true, we cannot help but think of ourselves as free (Kant and the existentialists).

GLOSSARY

antecedent conditions Those circumstances, states of affairs, or events that regularly precede and can be said to cause an event. The antecedent conditions of boiling water, for example, are the application of heat to water under normal atmospheric pressure, and so

---

[29] Thich Nhat Hanh, #47, "Turning on the Television," from *Present Moment, Wonderful Moment* (Berkeley: Parallax Press, 1990).

on. A determinist would say that the antecedent conditions of a human action would be the state of his or her nervous system, a developed character (with personality traits), certain desires and beliefs, and the circumstances (or "stimulus") in which the action takes place.

cause That which brings something about. On the hard determinist interpretation, a cause is an antecedent condition that, together with other antecedent conditions, is sufficient to make the occurrence of some event necessary, according to the laws of nature. On a weaker interpretation, a cause may simply be an event (or condition) that regularly precedes another event and thus can be used to predict when the latter will occur. (For example, if we say "a cause of forest fires is lightning," we mean "whenever lightning strikes a sufficiently dry forest, fire will occur.") (The concept of a "cause" is also discussed in Chapters 1, 3, and 4.)

compatibilism The thesis that both determinism (on some interpretations) and free action can be true. Determinism does not rule out free action and the possibility of free action does not require that determinism be false. They are compatible positions.

compulsion "Being forced to do something." One acts from compulsion (or is compelled to act) when he or she could not have done otherwise. Some philosophers distinguish between *external* compulsions (for example, being pushed) and *internal* compulsions (for example, a neurotic obsession).

determinism The thesis that every event has its sufficient natural cause(s), that every event is caused by its antecedent conditions, or that every event is predictable on the basis of such conditions.

fatalism The thesis that certain events (or perhaps all events) are going to happen inevitably, regardless of what efforts we take to prevent them.

free will Among philosophers, a somewhat antiquated expression (as in "he did it of his own free will") that means that a person is capable of making decisions that are not determined by antecedent conditions. Of course there may be antecedent considerations, such as what a person wants, what a person believes, but free will means that such considerations never determine a person's decision. At most they "enter into the decision."

freedom The idea that a human decision or action is a person's own responsibility and that praise and blame may be appropriately ascribed. The most extreme interpretation of "freedom" is the absence of any causes or determinations. Thus an indeterminist would say that an event was free if it had no causes; a libertarian would say that a human act was free if it was only self-caused, but not determined by anything else (including a person's character). Certain determinists, however ("soft determinists"), would say that an act is free if only it is "in character" and based upon a person's desire and personality. Most generally, we say that a person's act was free whether or not it was the result of a conscious decision and whether or not certain causes may have been involved, if we would say that he or she could have done otherwise.

Heisenberg Uncertainty Principle An important principle of recent physics that demonstrates that we cannot know both the position and the momentum of certain subatomic particles, for in our attempts to know one, we make it impossible to know the other. This principle has been used to attack the very idea of "determinism" in its classical formulations, for determinism requires just the "certainty" of possible prediction that the Heisenberg Principle rejects.

indeterminism The thesis that at least some events in the universe are not determined, are not caused by antecedent conditions, and may not be predictable.

predestination The thesis (usually in a theological context) that every event is destined to happen (as in fatalism) whatever efforts we make to prevent it. The usual version is that

God knows and perhaps causes all things to happen, and therefore everything must happen precisely as He knows (and possibly causes) it to happen.

prediction To say that some event will happen before it happens. Determinism normally includes the thesis that if we know enough about the antecedent conditions of an event, we can always predict that it will occur. But prediction does not require determinism. One might predict the outcome of some state of affairs on the basis of statistical probabilities without knowing any antecedent conditions and perhaps even without assuming that there are any such conditions (in quantum physics, for example). It is also possible that a person might predict the future on the basis of lucky guesses or E.S.P., again without necessarily accepting determinism.

responsibility Answerability or accountability for some act or event presumed to be within a person's control.

retrodiction To say, on the basis of certain present evidence, what must have happened in the past. For example, the astronomer who looks at the present course of a comet can retrodict certain facts about its history. For the determinist, retrodiction is as important to his thesis as prediction.

soft determinism A thesis that accepts determinism but claims that certain kinds of causes, namely, a person's character, still allow us to call his or her actions "free." The soft determinist is therefore a compatibilist, for he believes in both freedom and determinism.

sufficient cause Capable of bringing something about by itself (for example, four healthy people are sufficient to push a Volkswagen up a hill).

BIBLIOGRAPHY AND FURTHER READING

General anthologies are Sidney Hook, ed., *Determinism and Freedom in the Age of Modern Science* (New York: Macmillan, Collier, 1961); B. Berofsky, ed., *Free Will and Determinism* (New York: Harper & Row, 1966); and H. Morris, ed., *Freedom and Responsibility* (Stanford, CA: Stanford University Press, 1961). See also D. F. Pears, ed., *Freedom and the Will* (New York: St. Martin's Press, 1963), and, much more recent, Robert Kane, *The Significance of Free Will* (New York: Oxford University Press, 1996).

III

THE GOOD AND
THE BEAUTIFUL

ETHICS

"From now on I'm thinking only of me."

Major Danby replied indulgently with a superior smile,

"But Yossarian, suppose everyone felt that way?"

"Then I'd certainly be a—fool to feel any other way, wouldn't I?"

JOSEPH HELLER, *CATCH 22*

What should we do, and what should we not do? What acts should we praise? What acts should we condemn and blame? These are questions of **ethics,** the concern for which Socrates was willing to give up his life. The core of ethics is **morality.** Morality is a set of fundamental rules that guide our actions; for example, they may forbid us to kill each other, encourage us to help each other, tell us not to lie, command us to keep our promises.

Most of the moral rules we accept and follow are ones that we have learned and adopted from parents, friends, teachers, and our own society. At times, though, others may challenge our moral rules, demanding that we defend them. Why should we help each other? Why shouldn't we ever cheat? What reasons can we give to defend one sexual ethic rather than another? New social and technological developments may also force us to reevaluate our morality. Since minorities and women have participated more and more in public debates on moral issues, we now find ourselves constantly confronted with the injustices of discrimination on the basis of race or sex. The development of sophisticated life-sustaining devices has forced both physicians and philosophers to question whether it is always a moral duty to preserve life whenever possible.

Whenever we try to defend or criticize a moral belief we enter the realm of ethics. Ethics is not concerned with specific moral rules but with the foundation of morality and with providing general principles that will both help us evaluate the validity of a moral rule and choose between different moralities (different sets of moral rules). For example, some ethical theorists called **utilitarians** hold that any good moral rule should promote the greatest happiness for the greatest number. Other theorists, for example, Aristotle and Kant, have argued that a good moral rule helps us act in the most rational way possible.

Ethics is also concerned with whether or not to take into account others' or our own interests and desires when deciding what we ought to do. For some ethicists, morality is tied to self-interest at least in an abstract way, and they argue that morality is the best way of satisfying everyone's interests. Other philosophers retain the rigid distinction between morality and self-interest and insist that obedience to morality is good for its own sake, or equivalent to being rational, or simply required in order to make us human. Finally some authors have argued that morality is only one among many sets of principles, which we may but need not choose to obey.

In this chapter, we will begin by raising some of the perennial problems of ethics, including the nature of morality and the problem of moral relativism. Then, we will address the familiar claim that the basis of all human behavior—moral behavior included—is selfishness, or **egoism**. Finally we will examine several different ethical theories, different ways of conceiving of morals and (or) justifying moral beliefs:

- The ethics of Aristotle, who based his view of morality on the concept of "virtue" and his idea that man is by nature a social and rational animal. Aristotle argues that being virtuous—controlling our feelings and acting rationally—enables us to become fully human. In this discussion, we have the opportunity to examine a moral system that is significantly different from our own, but still sufficiently similar for us to understand it.
- The view that morality is essentially a matter of feeling; David Hume and Jean-Jacques Rousseau are its representatives.
- The monumental ethical theory of Immanuel Kant, who insisted that morality is strictly a matter of practical reason, divorced from our personal interests and desires and based solely on universal principles or laws. Thus, according to Kant, we cannot justify the morality of our actions simply by appealing to the good consequences of our actions for others or ourselves. We will also consider subsequent efforts to support or criticize Kant's view.
- The ethical theories of the utilitarians, who argued (in contrast to Kant) that moral rules are merely rules of thumb for achieving the greatest good for the greatest number of people, and who thereby tried to reconcile the interests of each individual with the interests of everyone else.
- The radical theories of Nietzsche and the existentialists, who insist that, in an important sense, we choose our moralities and that this choice cannot be justified in any of the ways argued by other modern philosophers. For Nietzsche, at least, this view also included a retrospective appreciation of the morality of the ancient Greeks, and he argued that we should inject some

of their conceptions into our own. We will also look at subsequent efforts to support the idea that morality is conventional—a matter of custom in certain sorts of societies.

◆ Recent feminist gay-lesbian theories and the implications for practical and personal ethics.

A. MORALITY

Morality gives us the rules by which we live with other people. It sets limits to our desires and our actions. It tells us what is permitted and what is not. It gives us guiding principles for making decisions. It tells us what we ought and what we ought not to do. But what is this "morality" that sounds so impersonal and "above" us? It is important to begin with an appreciation for the metaphor, which so well characterizes moral rules. Nietzsche describes it this way: "A tablet of virtues hangs over every people."

The "tablet of virtues" is morality. The prototype of morality, in this view, is those ancient codes, carved in stone, with commands that are eternal and absolute, such as the two tablets inscribed by God in front of Moses that we call the Ten Commandments. And they are indeed *commandments*. "Thou shalt" and "Thou shalt not" is all they say. This is the essence of morality. It consists of commands. These commands do not appeal to individual pleasures or desires. They do not make different demands on different individuals or societies. Quite to the contrary, they are absolute rules that tell us what we must or must not do, no matter who we are, no matter what we want and regardless of whether or not our interests will be served by the command. "Thou shalt not kill" means that even if you want to, even if you have the power to, and even if you can escape all punishment, you are absolutely forbidden to kill.

The image of morality as coming "from above" is appropriate. First, because moral laws are often said, and not only in our society, to come from God. Second, because we learn these laws from our parents, who literally "stand over us" and indoctrinate us with them through their shouts, commands, examples, threats, and gestures. Finally and most importantly, morality itself is "above" any given individual or individuals, whether it is canonized in the laws of society or not. Morality is not just another aid in getting us what we want; it is entirely concerned with right and wrong. And these considerations are "above" tampering by any individual, no matter how powerful, as if they have a life of their own.

This characteristic of morality as independent of individual desires and ambitions has led many people to characterize morality simply in terms of some absolute and independent agency. Most often, this absolute and independent agency is God. St. Augustine, for example, talks about morality in this way:

Unless you turn to Him and repay the existence that He gave you, you won't be "nothing"; you will be wretched. All things owe to God, first of all, what they are insofar as they are natures. Then, those who have received a will owe to

Him whatever better thing they can will to be, and whatever they ought to be. No man is ever blamed for what he has not been given, but he is justly blamed if he has not done what he should have done; and if he has received free will and sufficient power, he stands under obligation. When a man does not do what he ought, God the Creator is not at fault. It is to His glory that a man suffers justly; and by blaming a man for not doing what he should have done, you are praising what he ought to do. You are praised for seeing what you ought to do, even though you see this only through God, who is immutable Truth.[1]

St. Thomas Aquinas noted, "It is apparent that things prescribed by divine law are right, not only because they are put forth by law, but also because they are in accord with nature." Or "Therefore by divine law precepts had to be given, so that each man would give his neighbor his due and would abstain from doing injuries to him."[2] And in the Bible we read, "When thou shalt harken—to the voice of the Lord thy God, to keep all his commandments, which I command thee this day, to do that which is right in the eyes of the Lord thy God."[3]

But whether or not one believes in God, it is clear that something further is needed to help us define morality. Even assuming that there is a God, we need a way of determining what His moral commands must be. One might say that He has given these commands to various individuals, but the fact is that different people seem to have very different ideas about the morality that God has given them. Some, for example, would say that it explicitly rules out abortion and infanticide. Others would argue that God does not rule these out but makes it clear that they are, like other forms of killing (a "holy war," for example), justifiable only in certain circumstances. In view of such disagreements, we cannot simply appeal to God but must, for reasons that we can formulate and defend, define our morality for ourselves. There is the further question, which has often been debated, but was raised originally by Plato, in his dialogue, *Euthyphro*. Should we follow God's laws just because they are His or rather, because His laws are good? If the latter, then we have to decide what is good in order to know that God is good. If the former, then one has to decide whether or not to believe in God precisely on the basis of whether we can accept those laws. Either way, we have to decide for ourselves what laws of morality we are willing to accept.

Similar considerations hold true for that familiar appeal to conscience in determining what we ought or ought not do. Even if one believes that conscience is God-given, the same problems emerge again. Should we follow our consciences just because "conscience tells us to"? Or do we follow our conscience just because we know that what our conscience commands is good? How does one decide whether a nagging thought is or is not the prompting of God? Probably on the basis of whether

---

[1] St. Augustine, *On Freedom* (New York: Bobbs-Merrill, 1956).

[2] St. Thomas Aquinas, *Summa Contra Gentiles,* Bk. III (New York: Doubleday, 1955).

[3] Deuteronomy 13:18.

what it demands is good or not. (Thus one readily attributes to conscience the nagging reminder that one shouldn't have cheated an unsuspecting child, but one does not attribute to conscience the nagging thought that one could have gotten away with shoplifting if only one had had the daring to do it.) If one believes that conscience is simply the internalization of the moral teachings of one's parents and society, then the question takes an extra dimension: Should we accept or reject what we have been taught? Since our consciences often disagree, we must still decide whose conscience and which rules of conscience one ought to obey. Identifying morality with the promptings of one's conscience is both plausible and valuable, but philosophically it only moves the question one step back: How do we know what is, and what is not, the prompting of conscience? And is it always right to follow one's conscience? But these two questions are in fact just another way of asking what is moral. What should I do?

Morality is not just obedience—whether obedience to a king, a pope, the law, or one's conscience. Morality is doing what is *right,* whether or not it is commanded by any person or law and whether or not one "feels" it in one's conscience. One way of putting this—defended later by Immanuel Kant—is to say that morality involves **autonomy,** that is, the ability to think for oneself and decide, for oneself, what is right and what is wrong, whom to obey and whom to ignore, what to do and what not to do. The danger is that this conception of morality as autonomy seems to leave us without a place to learn morality in the first place. How do we learn to judge right and wrong but from our parents, our friends, our teachers, and our society and its models? But if we try to tie morality too closely to our upbringing and our society, then it looks as if there is no room for autonomy, no way in which we could disagree with our family or society, no way to criticize the way in which we have been raised. Furthermore, tying morality to particular societies raises an additional question, and that is whether morality (or morali*ties*) might not be relative to particular societies and cultures.

B. IS MORALITY RELATIVE?

Moralities, like lifestyles, vary from culture to culture and even from person to person. But while there is nothing surprising about the fact that lifestyles vary, there is a problem in the variation of moralities. Morality, by its very nature, is supposed to be a set of universal principles, principles that do not distinguish between cultures or peoples or lifestyles. If it is morally reprehensible to kill for fun, then it is morally reprehensible in every society, in every culture, for every lifestyle, and for every person, no matter who he or she is. This will be true even if the society or person in question does not agree with that moral principle.

Aristotle, for example, discusses at length what he calls "the wicked man," who does evil because he believes in immoral principles and therefore acts without regret, unlike the person who acts badly from momentary weakness, force of circumstances, desperation, or misinformation. But on what grounds can one society or person claim that another society's or person's principles are immoral? How could European Christians, for example, be justified in criticizing the sexual morality of Polynesians in the South Pacific? The Polynesians were a separate society, with their own mores and principles that worked quite well for them, possibly even better in certain ways than the European customs worked in Europe. Yet European missionaries felt no hesitation whatever in condemning their sexual practices as "immoral." Similarly but more seriously, what gives us the right to criticize a culture across the world that still believes in genocide as a legitimate consequence of war or in torture as a way of keeping civil order? We surely feel that we have the right to speak up in such cases, but then we too are asserting the universality of our morality, extending it even to people who might explicitly reject our principles. How can we do this? What justifies such an extension?

The problem of **relativism** has become extremely controversial since the nineteenth century, when anthropologists began telling us of exotic societies with moralities so different from ours. In a sense, relativism has always been a threat to established morality, for even the Greeks came into contact with societies that were much different from theirs. (Thus they tended to immediately label anything non-Greek "barbarian," so that they didn't have to consider the possibility of relativism.) Kant was the most vigorous opponent of relativism, for his conception of morality was such that if a human being was to count as rational at all, he or she had to agree to at least the basic principles of a universal morality. There were people and societies that did not, but that, according to Kant, only proved that they were less than rational (and therefore less than human as well). Today we tend to be more liberal in our acceptance of different styles of life, but few people would deny that at least some moral principles hold for every society. The principle that unnecessary cruelty is wrong, for example, would be such a principle, although people might well disagree about what is "cruel" and what is "unnecessary."

Philosophers generally distinguish two theses. First, there is the factual claim that different societies have different moralities. This is called **cultural relativism.** The difficult question is whether these different moralities are only different superficially or whether they are fundamentally different. For example, Eskimos of certain tribes kill their elders by leaving them to freeze on the ice; we consider that grossly immoral (we send most of our elders to frigid "old-age homes" instead). But the question of cultural relativity is whether this difference is merely the reflection of different interpretations of some basic moral principle (such as, don't kill anyone unless it is absolutely necessary for the survival of the rest) or whether it really is a wholly different morality. This is among the most controversial anthropological questions of our time. But philosophers are interested in a somewhat different question: Assuming that two moralities really are fundamentally different, is it possible that each is as correct as the other? The philosopher who says "yes" is an **ethical relativist,** and ethical relativism is what occupies us here.

In the following selection, the English-American philosopher **Walter Stace** presents the ethical relativist position and its traditional opponent, **ethical absolutism,** the view that there is only one correct morality. Stace's own answer to the problem is more of an absolutist solution; later in the same work he says that "happiness" is a universal and absolute value, and therefore cross-cultural evaluations are possible.

ON ETHICAL RELATIVISM
BY **WALTER STACE**

There is an opinion widely current nowadays in philosophical circles which passes under the name of "ethical relativity." Exactly what this phrase means or implies is certainly far from clear. But unquestionably it stands as a label for the opinions of a group of ethical philosophers whose position is roughly on the extreme left wing among the moral theorizers of the day. And perhaps one may best understand it by placing it in contrast with the opposite kind of extreme view against which, undoubtedly, it has arisen as a protest. For among moral philosophers one may clearly distinguish a left and a right wing. Those of the left wing are the ethical relativists. They are the revolutionaries, the clever young men, the up to date. Those of the right wing we may call the ethical absolutists. They are the conservatives and the old-fashioned.

According to the absolutists there is but one eternally true and valid moral code. This moral code applies with rigid impartiality to all men. What is a duty for me must likewise be a duty for you. And this will be true whether you are an Englishman, a Chinaman, or a Hottentot. If cannibalism is an abomination in England or America, it is an abomination in central Africa, notwithstanding that the African may think otherwise. The fact that he sees nothing wrong in his cannibal practices does not make them for him morally right. They are as much contrary to morality for him as they are for us. The only difference is that he is an ignorant savage who does not know this. There is not one law for one man or race of men, another for another. There is not one moral standard for Europeans, another for Indians, another for Chinese. There is but one law, one standard, one morality, for all men. And this standard, this law, is absolute and unvarying.

Moreover, as the one moral law extends its dominion over all the corners of the earth, so too it is not limited in its application by any considerations of time or period. That which is right now was right in the centuries of Greece and Rome, nay, in the very ages of the cave man. That which is evil now was evil then. If slavery is morally wicked today, it was morally wicked among the ancient Athenians, notwithstanding that their greatest men accepted it as a necessary condition of human society. Their opinion did not make slavery a moral good for them. It only showed that they were, in spite of their otherwise noble conceptions, ignorant of what is truly right and good in this matter.

♦♦♦

The ethical absolutist recognizes as a fact that moral customs and moral ideas differ from country to country and from age to age. This indeed seems manifest and not to be disputed. We think slavery morally wrong, the Greeks thought it morally unobjectionable. The inhabitants of New Guinea certainly have very different moral ideas from ours. But the fact that the Greeks or the inhabitants of New Guinea think something right does not make it right, even for them. Nor does the fact that we think the same things wrong make them wrong. They are *in themselves* either right or wrong. What we have to do is to discover which they are. What anyone thinks makes no difference. It is here just as it is in matters of physical science. We believe the earth to be a globe. Our ancestors may have thought it flat. This does not show that it *was* flat, and is *now* a globe. What it shows is that men having in other ages been ignorant about the shape of the earth have now learned the truth. So if the Greeks thought slavery morally legitimate, this does not indicate that it was for them and in that age morally legitimate, but rather that they were ignorant of the truth of the matter. . . .

Now ethical absolutism was, in its central ideas, the product of Christian theology. The connection is not difficult to detect. For morality has been conceived, during the Christian dispensation, as issuing from the will of God. That indeed was its single and all-sufficient source. There would be no point, for the naïve believer in the faith, in the philosopher's questions regarding the foundations of morality and the basis of moral obligation. Even to ask such questions is a mark of incipient religious scepticism. For the true believer the author of the moral law is God. What pleases God, what God commands—that is the definition of right. What displeases God, what he forbids—that is the definition of wrong. Now there is, for the Christian monotheist, only one God ruling over the entire universe. And this God is rational, self-consistent. He does not act upon whims. Consequently his will and his commands must be the same everywhere. They will be unvarying for all peoples and in all ages. If the heathen have other moral ideas than ours—inferior ideas—that can only be because they live in ignorance of the true God. If they knew God and his commands, their ethical precepts would be the same as ours.

◆◆◆

This explains why ethical absolutism, until very recently, was not only believed by philosophers but *taken for granted without any argument.* The ideas of philosophers, like the ideas of everyone else, are largely moulded by the civilizations in which they live. Their philosophies are largely attempts to state in abstract terms and in self-consistent language the stock of ideas which they have breathed in from the atmosphere of their social environment. This accounts for the large number of so-called "unrecognized presuppositions" with which systems of philosophy always abound. These presuppositions are simply the ideas which the authors of the systems have breathed in with the intellectual atmospheres by which they happen to be surrounded—which they have taken over therefore as a matter of course, without argument, without criticism, without even a suspicion that they might be false. . . .

We can now turn to the consideration of ethical relativity which is the proper subject of this chapter. The revolt of the relativists against absolutism is, I believe, part and parcel of the general revolutionary tendency of our times. In particular it is a result of the decay of belief in the dogmas of orthodox religion. Belief in absolutism was supported, as we have seen, by belief in Christian monotheism. And now that, in an age of widespread religious scepticism, that support is withdrawn, absolutism tends to collapse. Revolutionary movements are as a rule, at any rate in their first onset, purely negative. They attack and destroy. And ethical relativity is, in its essence, a purely negative creed. It is simply a denial of ethical absolutism. That is why the best way of explaining it is to begin by explaining ethical absolutism. If we understand that what the latter asserts the former denies, then we understand ethical relativity.

> *Any ethical position which denies that there is a single moral standard which is equally applicable to all men at all times may fairly be called a species of ethical relativity.*

Any ethical position which denies that there is a single moral standard which is equally applicable to all men at all times may fairly be called a species of ethical relativity. There is not, the relativist asserts, merely one moral law, one code, one standard. There are many moral laws, codes, standards. What morality ordains in one place or age may be quite different from what morality ordains in another place or age. The moral code of Chinamen is quite different from that of Europeans, that of African savages quite different from both. Any morality, therefore, is relative to the age, the place, and the circumstances in which it is found. It is in no sense absolute.

This does not mean merely—as one might at first sight be inclined to suppose—that the very same kind of action which is *thought* right in one country and period may be *thought* wrong in another. This would be a mere platitude, the truth of which everyone would have to admit. Even the absolutist would admit this—would even wish to emphasize it—since he is well aware that different peoples have different sets of moral ideas, and his whole point is that some of these sets of ideas are false. What the relativist means to assert is, not this platitude, but that the very same kind of action which *is* right in one country and period may *be* wrong in another. And this, far from being a platitude, is a very startling assertion.

It is very important to grasp thoroughly the difference between the two ideas. For there is reason to think that many minds tend to find ethical relativity attractive because they fail to keep them clearly apart. It is so very obvious that moral ideas differ from country to country and from age to age. And it is so very easy, if you are mentally lazy, to suppose that to say this means the same as to say that no universal moral standard exists—or in other words that it implies ethical relativity. We fail to see that the word "standard" is used in two different senses. It is perfectly true that, in one sense, there are many variable moral standards. We speak of judging a man by the standard of his time. And this implies that different times have different standards. And this, of course, is quite true. But when the word "standard" is used in this sense it means simply the set of moral ideas current during the period in question. It means what people *think* right, whether as a matter of fact it *is* right or not. On the other hand when the absolutist asserts that there exists a single universal moral "standard," he is not using the word in this sense at all. He means by "standard" what *is* right as distinct from what people merely think right. His point is that although what people think right varies in different countries and periods, yet what actually is right is everywhere and always the same. And it follows that when the ethical relativist disputes the position of the absolutist and denies that any universal moral standard exists he too means by "standard" what actually is right. But it is exceedingly easy, if we are not careful, to slip loosely from using the word in the first sense to using it in the second sense; and to suppose that the variability of moral beliefs is the same thing as the variability of what really is moral. And unless we keep the two senses of the word "standard" distinct, we are likely to think the creed of ethical relativity much more plausible than it actually is.

The genuine relativist, then, does not merely mean that Chinamen may think right what Frenchmen think wrong. He means that what *is* wrong for the French-man may *be* right for the Chinaman. And if one enquires how, in those circumstances, one is to know what actually is right in China or in France, the answer comes quite glibly. What is right in China is the same as what people think right in China; and what is right in France is the same as what people think right in France. So that, if you want to know what is moral in any particular country or age all you have to do is to ascertain what are the moral ideas current in that age or country. Those ideas are, *for that age or country,* right. Thus what is morally right is identified with what is thought to be morally right, and the distinction which we made above between these two is simply denied. To put the same thing in another way, it is denied that there can be or ought to be any distinction between the two senses of the word "standard." There is only one kind of standard of right and wrong, namely, the moral ideas current in any particular age or country.[4]

One of the subjects about which we feel the strongest call of conscience or morality is sex. Judgments about "what's right" and "what's wrong" seem to accompany all our beliefs about sex and sexual relationships. Sexual morality would seem to be a "natural" candidate for absolutism in morality: There are only two sexes, after all, no matter what culture one considers. Surely, one might think, there are "natural" standards for how members of the sexes should behave toward one another. There are men and women in every culture: Surely, one might think, every culture distinguishes its proper moral treatment in roughly the same way.

The American anthropologist **Margaret Mead** made an extensive cross-cultural study of sex distinctions and sexual morality in her famous work, *Sex and Temperament.* There she suggests that distinctions between the sexes themselves are culturally relative. Contrary to the absolutist view, she argues that sex distinctions are created by and dependent upon the social mores of particular cultures.

---

[4] Walter Stace, *Concept of Morals* (New York: Macmillan, 1937).

SEX AND TEMPERAMENT
BY **MARGARET MEAD**

The material suggests that we may say that many, if not all, of the personality traits which we have called masculine or feminine are as lightly linked to sex as are the clothing, the manners, and the form of headdress that a society at a given time period assigns to either sex when we consider the behaviour of the typical Arapesh man or woman as contrasted with the behaviour of the typical Mundugumor man or woman, the evidence is overwhelmingly in favour of the strength of social conditioning. In no other way can we account for the almost complete uniformity with which Arapesh children develop into contented, passive, secure persons, while Mundugumor children develop as characteristically into violent, aggressive, insecure persons. Only to the impact of the whole of the integrated culture upon the growing child can we lay the formation of the contrasting types. There is no other explanation of race, or diet, or selection that can be adduced to explain them. We are forced to conclude that human nature is almost unbelievably malleable, responding accurately and contrastingly to contrasting cultural conditions. The differences between individuals who are members of different cultures, like the differences between individuals within a culture, are almost entirely to be laid to differences in conditioning, especially during early childhood, and the form of this conditioning is culturally determined. Standardized personality differences between the sexes are of this order, cultural creations to which each generation, male and female, is trained to conform. There remains, however, the problem of the origin of these socially standardized differences.

While the basic importance of social conditioning is still imperfectly recognized—not only in lay thought, but even by the scientist specifically concerned with such matters—to go beyond it and consider the possible influence of variations in hereditary equipment is a hazardous matter. The following pages will read very differently to one who has made a part of this thinking a recognition of the whole amazing mechanism of cultural conditioning—who has really accepted the fact that the same infant could be developed into a full participant in any one of these three cultures—than they will read to one who still believes that the minutiae of cultural behaviour are carried in the individual germ-plasm. If it is said, therefore, that when we have grasped the full significance of the malleability of the human organism and the preponderant importance of cultural conditioning, there are still further problems to solve, it must be remembered that these problems come *after* such a comprehension of the force of conditioning; they cannot precede it. The forces that make children born among the Arapesh grow up into typical Arapesh personalities are entirely social, and any discussion of the variations which do occur must be looked at against this social background.

With this warning firmly in mind, we can ask a further question. Granting the malleability of human nature, whence arise the differences between the standardized personalities that different cultures decree for all of their members, or which one culture decrees for the members of one sex as contrasted with the members of the opposite sex? If such differences are culturally created, as this material would most strongly suggest that they are, if the new-born child can be shaped with equal ease into an unaggressive Arapesh or an aggressive Mundugumor, why do these striking contrasts occur at all? If the clues to the different personalities decreed for men and women in Tchambuli do not lie in the physical constitution of the two sexes—an assumption that we must reject both for the Tchambuli and for our own society—where can we find the clues upon which the Tchambuli, the Arapesh, the Mundugumor, have built? Cultures are manmade, they are built of human materials; they are diverse but comparable structures within which human beings can attain full human stature. Upon what have they built their diversities?

Cultures are man-made, they are built of human materials; they are diverse but comparable structures within which human beings can attain full human stature.

We recognize that a homogeneous culture committed in all of its gravest institutions and slight usages to a co-operative unaggressive course can bend every child to that emphasis, some to a perfect accord with it, the majority to an easy acceptance, while only a few deviants fail to receive the cultural imprint. To consider such traits as aggressiveness or passivity to be sex-linked is not possible in the light of the facts. Have such traits, then, as aggressiveness or passivity, pride or humility, objectivity or a preoccupation with personal relationships, an easy response to the needs of the young and the weak or a hostility to the young and the weak, a tendency to initiate sex-relations or merely to respond to the dictates of a situation or another person's advances—have these traits any basis in temperament at all? Are they potentialities of all human temperaments that can be developed by different kinds of social conditioning and which will not appear if the necessary conditioning is absent?[5]

C. EGOISM AND ALTRUISM

Most moral rules, whether about sexuality or otherwise, enjoin us to take into account the interests, feelings, or welfare of other people. The commands not to lie, not to kill, and not to steal, as well as the commands to keep our promises, treat others fairly, and be generous are all commands that concern our relations to other persons. (There can, of course, be moral rules that require us to take into account our own

---

[5] Margaret Mead, *Sex and Temperament* (New York: Mentor, 1958 [1935]).

interests; for example, the prohibition of suicide or, as Kant thought, the obligation to develop our talents.)

One of the important assumptions of any morality, then, is that it is possible for us to act in the interests of other people. In addition, morality assumes that it is possible for us to do so *because* we are concerned about others' welfare or because we recognize that we ought to be. Someone who refrains from cheating, for example, simply because he or she is afraid of being caught acts purely self-interestedly; we would not think this person is morally praiseworthy. Again, a person who visits a dying relative in the hospital because he or she wants to ensure a substantial inheritance is not acting morally. Only if actions are motivated by a concern for others' interests do we call them truly moral actions.

One important theory, though, denies that we can be motivated simply by a concern for others. This is psychological egoism. **Psychological egoism** is the thesis that everyone, in fact, acts for his or her own advantage, and the only reason why people act respectfully or kindly toward each other is that that too, for one reason or another, is to their advantage. It might be fear of punishment that makes them act "correctly." Some have "ulterior motives"; that is, they expect other things later on, perhaps a favor in return or reward in heaven after they die, or they are trying to avoid guilt or want a feeling of self-satisfaction. In popular language, the egoist position is often called **selfishness**.

One should be careful, though, to distinguish psychological egoism from ethical egoism. Psychological egoism asserts that our psychology is such that we cannot help but act in our own interests. In contrast, **ethical egoism** claims that even though we can act in others' interests because we are concerned for others, we *ought* always to act in our own interest. One of the most widely read contemporary ethical egoists is the late **Ayn Rand,** who wrote of "the virtue of selfishness."

It is psychological, not ethical, egoism that challenges the very possibility of any morality. One of Socrates' opponents in *The Republic* states the psychological egoist's view with brutal clarity:

FROM *THE REPUBLIC*
BY **PLATO**

They say that to do wrong is naturally good, to be wronged is bad, but the suffering of injury so far exceeds in badness the good of inflicting it that when men have done wrong to each other and suffered it, and have had a taste of both, those who are unable to avoid the latter and practise the former decide that it is profitable to come to an agreement with each other neither to inflict injury nor to suffer it. As a result they begin to make laws and covenants, and the law's command they call lawful and just. This, they say, is the origin and essence of justice; it stands between the best and the worst, the best being to do wrong without paying the penalty and the worst to be wronged without the power of revenge. The just then is a mean between two extremes; it is welcomed and honoured because of men's lack of the power to do wrong. The man who has that power, the real man, would not make a compact with anyone not to inflict injury or suffer it. For him that would be madness. This then, Socrates, is, according to their argument, the nature and origin of justice.

Even those who practise justice do so against their will because they lack the power to do wrong. This we could realize very clearly if we imagined ourselves granting to both the just and the unjust the freedom to do whatever they liked. We could then follow both of them and observe where their desires led them, and we would catch the just man redhanded travelling the same road as the unjust. The reason is the desire for undue gain which every organism by nature pursues as a good, but the law forcibly sidetracks him to honour equality. The freedom I just mentioned would most easily occur if these men had the power which they say the ancestor of the Lydian Gyges possessed. The story is that he was a shepherd in the service of the ruler of Lydia. There was a violent rainstorm and an earthquake which broke open the ground and created a chasm at the place where he was tending sheep. Seeing this and marvelling, he went down into it. He saw, besides many other wonders of which we are told, a hollow bronze horse. There were window-like openings in it; he climbed through them and caught sight of a corpse which seemed of more than human stature, wearing nothing but a ring of gold on its finger. This ring the shepherd put on and came out. He arrived at the usual monthly meeting which reported to the king on the state of the flocks, wearing the ring. As he was sitting among the others he happened to twist the hoop of the ring towards himself, to the inside of his hand, and as he did this he became invisible to those sitting near him and they went on talking as if he had gone. He marvelled at this and, fingering the ring, he turned the hoop outward again and became visible. Perceiving this he tested whether the ring had this power and so it happened: if he turned the hoop inwards he became invisible, but was visible when he turned it outwards. When he realized this, he at once arranged to become one of the messengers to the king. He went, committed adultery with the king's wife, attacked the king with her help, killed him, and took over the kingdom.

Now if there were two such rings, one worn by the just man, the other by the unjust, no one, as these people think, would be so incorruptible that he would stay on the path of justice or bring himself to keep away from other people's property and not touch it, when he could with impunity take whatever he wanted from the market, go into houses and have sexual relations with anyone he wanted, kill anyone, free all those he wished from prison, and do the other things which would make him like a god among men. His actions would be in no way different from those of the other and they would both follow the same path. This, some would say, is a great proof that no one is just willingly but under compulsion, so that justice is not one's private good, since wherever either thought he could do wrong with impunity he would do so. Every man believes that injustice is much more profitable to himself than justice, and any exponent of this argument will say that he is right. The man who did not wish to do wrong with that opportunity, and did not touch other people's property, would be thought by those who knew it to be very foolish and miserable. They would praise him in public, thus deceiving one another, for fear of being wronged. So much for my second topic.[6]

Both egoist positions are contrasted with what is usually called **altruism, that is,** acting for the sake of other people's interests. There are degrees of altruism. One may be altruistic because one acts morally, because he or she recognizes an obligation to other people. Or one may be altruistic in actually taking another person's interests as important or even more important than one's own interests, such as one often finds between lovers or brothers and sisters. Altruism can also be divided into two distinct theses, although these are not so often distinguished. *Psychological altruism* says that people "naturally" act for each other's sakes. (We shall see this thesis defended by several important philosophers in later sections.) It has rarely been argued, however, that people are compelled to act altruistically. Thus psychological egoism is usually defended for all cases; psychological altruism, in contrast, is only defended for some cases. *Ethical altruism,* on the other hand, says that people ought to act with each other's interests in mind. This is, of course, a basic statement of morality, best summarized in the so-called **Golden Rule:** "Do unto others as you would have them do unto you." (We shall see a modern version of this ancient teaching in the philosophy of Kant.)

The most familiar and most difficult question is about psychological egoism: Is it true that people only act for their own self-interest? A famous story about Abraham Lincoln is an apt illustration of the thesis. As he was arguing the psychological egoist position with a friend, his coach was passing a mud slide where a mother pig was squealing as her piglets were drowning. Lincoln stopped the coach, saved the piglets, then moved on. His friend asked him whether that wasn't a clear case of altruism. Lincoln replied: "Why that was the very essence of selfishness. I should have had no peace of mind all day had I gone on and left that suffering old sow worrying over those piglets. I did it to get peace of mind, don't you see?"[7]

Many actions are based upon self-interest and are "selfish" without any question. The question is, are there any actions that are not based on self-interest? Lincoln's response is an excellent example because it would seem as if his action is not for selfish reasons at all. Yet, according to him, there was a selfish reason behind his actions—his own sense of satisfaction and "peace of mind." Could this be true of all our actions?

The arguments that are still considered to be the most powerful and definitive against psychological egoism were formulated as sermons by an English bishop, **Joseph Butler.** Bishop Butler argued that such reasoning as Lincoln's turned on a number of fallacies. Butler begins by accepting the distinction between "private good and a person's own preservation and happiness" and "respect to society and the promotion of public good and the happiness of society." But then he insists that these

---

[6] Plato, *Republic,* Bk. II, trans. G. M. A. Grube (Indianapolis, IN: Hackett, 1974).

[7] Quoted in F. Sharp, *Ethics* (New York: Appleton-Century-Crofts, 1928).

are not, as the egoists argue, always in conflict and fighting against each other. To the contrary, they are almost always in perfect harmony.

AGAINST EGOISM
BY JOSEPH BUTLER

From this review and comparison of the nature of man as respecting self and as respecting society, it will plainly appear that there are as real and the same kind of indications in human nature that we were made for society and to do good to our fellow creatures, as that we were intended to take care of our own life and health and private good; and that the same objections lie against one of these assertions as against the other.

First, there is a natural principle of *benevolence* in man, which is in some degree to *society* what *self-love* is to the *individual*. And if there be in mankind any disposition to friendship; if there be any such thing as compassion, for compassion is momentary love; if there be any such thing as the paternal or filial affections; if there be any affection in human nature the object and end of which is the good of another—this is itself benevolence or the love of another. Be it ever so short, be it in ever so low a degree, or ever so unhappily confined, it proves the assertion and points out what we were designed for, as really as though it were in a higher degree and more extensive. I must however remind you that though benevolence and self-love are different, though the former tends most directly to public good, and the latter to private, yet they are so perfectly coincident that the greatest satisfactions to ourselves depend upon our having benevolence in a due degree, and that self-love is one chief security of our right behavior toward society. It may be added that their mutual coinciding, so that we can scarce promote one without the other, is equally a proof that we were made for both.

◆◆◆

Secondly, this will further appear, from observing that the *several passions and affections,* which are distinct both from benevolence and self-love, do in general contribute and lead us to *public* good as really as to *private*. It might be thought too minute and particular, and would carry us too great a length, to distinguish between and compare together the several passions or appetites distinct from benevolence, whose primary use and intention is the security and good of society; and the passions distinct from self-love, whose primary intention and design is the security and good of the individual. It is enough to the present argument that desire of esteem from others, contempt and esteem of them, love of society as distinct from affection to the good of it, indignation against successful vice—that these are public affections or passions, have an immediate respect to others, naturally lead us to regulate our behavior in such a manner as will be of service to our fellow creatures. If any or all of these may be considered likewise as private affections, as tending to private good, this does not hinder them from being public affections, too, or destroy the good influence of them upon society, and their tendency to public good. It may be added that as persons without any conviction from reason of the desirableness of life would yet of course preserve it merely from the appetite of hunger, so by acting merely from regard (suppose) to reputation, without any consideration of the good of others, men often contribute to public good. In both these instances they are plainly instruments in the hands of another, in the hands of Providence, to carry on ends, the preservation of the individual and good of society, which they themselves have not in their view or intention. The sum is, men have various appetites, passions, and particular affections, quite distinct both from self-love and from benevolence—all of these have a tendency to promote both public and private good, and may be considered as respecting others and ourselves equally and in common; but some of them seem most immediately to respect others, or tend to public good, others of them most immediately to respect self, or tend to private good; as the former are not benevolence, so the latter are not self-love; neither sort are instances of our love either to ourselves or others, but only instances of our Maker's care and love both of the individual and the species, and proofs that He intended we should be instruments of good to each other, as well as that we should be so to ourselves.

If it be said that there are persons in the world who are in great measure without the natural affections toward their fellow creatures, there are likewise instances of persons without the common natural affections to themselves; but the nature of man is not to be judged of by either of these, but by what appears in the common world, in the bulk of mankind.

Thirdly, there is a principle of reflection in men by which they distinguish between, approve and disapprove, their own actions. We are plainly constituted such sort of creatures as to reflect upon our own nature. The mind can take a view of what passes within itself, its propensions, aversions, passions, affections, as respecting such objects and in such degrees, and of the several actions consequent thereupon. In this survey it approves of one, disapproves of another, and toward a third is affected in neither of these ways, but is quite indifferent. This principle in man by which he approves or disapproves his heart, temper, and actions, is conscience. . . . That this faculty tends to restrain men from doing mischief to each other, and leads them to do good, is too manifest to need being insisted upon. Thus a parent has the affection of love to his children; this leads him to take care of, to educate, to make due provision for them; the natural affection leads to this, but the reflection that it is his proper business, what belongs to him, that it is right and commendable so to do—this added to the affection becomes a much more settled principle and carries him on through more labor and difficulties for the sake of his children than he would undergo from that affection alone, if he thought it, and the course of action it led to, either indifferent or criminal. This indeed is impossible, to do that which is good and not to approve of it; for which reason they are frequently not considered as distinct, though they really are, for men often approve of the actions of others which they will not imitate, and likewise do that which they approve not. It cannot possibly be denied that there is this principle of reflection or conscience in human nature. Suppose a man to relieve an innocent person in great distress, suppose the same man afterwards, in the fury of anger, to do the greatest mischief to a person who had given no just cause of offense; to aggravate the injury, add the circumstances of former friendship and obligation from the injured person, let the man who is supposed to have done these two different actions coolly reflect upon them afterwards, without regard to their consequences to himself; to assert that any common man would be affected in the same way toward these different actions, that he would make no distinction between them, but approve or disapprove them equally, is too glaring a falsity to need being confuted. There is therefore this principle of reflection or conscience in mankind. . . .

If it be said that there are persons in the world who are in great measure without the natural affections toward their fellow creatures, there are likewise instances of persons without the common natural affections to themselves; but the nature of man is not to be judged of by either of these, but by what appears in the common world, in the bulk of mankind.[8]

In short, Butler argues that merely acting on one's own desires does not make an action selfish, for all actions are, in some sense, based on our desires, but at least some of those desires are desires to serve someone else's interests. Thus the "object" of desire is what makes an act selfish or unselfish, not merely the fact that one's own desire is acted upon. Nor can simply acting with some benefit to oneself make an action selfish, for even if we agreed that an act gives us some benefit (for example, peace of mind), it may still be the case that most of the benefit is for someone else. Even if peace of mind typically follows virtuous actions, that does not show that our motivation is selfish. The satisfaction that accompanies good acts is itself not the motivation of the act. Here is the answer to Lincoln. His act was, despite his philosophical claims, an altruistic one; his satisfaction was not the motive of the act but only its consequence.

D. MORALITY AS VIRTUE: ARISTOTLE

Aristotle's *Ethics* (properly called *The Nicomachean Ethics*) is the best systematic guide to ancient Greek moral and ethical thinking. The significant feature of Greek

---

[8] Bishop Joseph Butler, *Five Sermons* (New York: Bobbs-Merrill, 1950).

ethics is its stress on being virtuous as opposed to merely following moral rules. Aristotle's concept of virtue is based on a very special conception of man as a rational being. **Virtue, accordingly, is rational activity, activity in accordance with a rational principle.** Having defined virtue in this way, Aristotle can then defend, for example, courage as a virtue by showing that the courageous man is more rational than the coward.

Aristotle arrives at his conception of man as an essentially rational being by asking what "the natural good for man" is. This, he argues, will be discovered by finding what all men desire "for its own sake" and not "for the sake of anything else."

FROM *THE NICOMACHEAN ETHICS*
BY **ARISTOTLE**

Every art and every kind of inquiry, and likewise every act and purpose, seems to aim at some good; and so it has been well said that the good is that at which everything aims. But a difference is observable among these aims or ends. What is aimed at is sometimes the exercise of a faculty, sometimes a certain result beyond that exercise. And where there is an end beyond that act, there the result is better than the exercise of the faculty. Now since there are many kinds of actions and many arts and sciences, it follows that there are many ends also; *e.g.* health is the end of medicine, ships of shipbuilding, victory of the art of war, and wealth of economy. But when several of these are subordinated to some one art or science,—as the making of bridles and other trappings to the art of horsemanship, and this in turn, along with all else that the soldier does, to the art of war, and so on,—then the end of the master art is always more desired than the end of the subordinate arts, since these are pursued for its sake. And this is equally true whether the end in view be the mere exercise of a faculty or something beyond that, as in the above instances.

If then in what we do there be some end which we wish for on its own account, choosing all the others as means to this, but not every end without exception as a means to something else (for so we should go on *ad infinitum,* and desire would be left void and objectless),—this evidently will be the good or the best of all things.[9]

We see here the same logical strategy that Aristotle used in Chapter 1—the idea that every act is for the sake of something else (we want to earn a dollar to buy ourselves some food, and we want that to satisfy our hunger). But since there can be no "infinite regress," there must be some ultimate end. Aristotle examines two popular conceptions of this ultimate end that is the natural good for man: pleasure and

---

[9] Aristotle, *Nicomachean Ethics,* trans. by F. H. Peters, 8th ed. (1901). All subsequent quotations from Aristotle are from this edition.

success. He rejects both because neither pleasure nor success is desired for its own sake. Rather, happiness is what all men desire for its own sake and is the natural good for man.

It seems that men not unreasonably take their notions of the good or happiness from the lives actually led, and that the masses who are the least refined suppose it to be pleasure, which is the reason why they aim at nothing higher than the life of enjoyment. For the most conspicuous kinds of life are three: this life of enjoyment, the life of the statesman, and, thirdly, the contemplative life. The mass of men show themselves utterly slavish in their preference for the life of brute beasts, but their views receive consideration because many of those in high places have the tastes of Sardanapalus. Men of refinement with a practical turn prefer honour; for I suppose we may say that honour is the aim of the statesman's life. But this seems too superficial to be the good we are seeking: for it appears to depend upon those who give rather than upon those who receive it; while we have a presentiment that the good is something that is peculiarly a man's own and can scarce be taken away from him. Moreover, these men seem to pursue honour in order that they may be assured of their own excellence,—at least, they wish to be honoured by men of sense, and by those who know them, and on the ground of their virtue or excellence. It is plain, then, that in their view, at any rate, virtue or excellence is better than honour; and perhaps we should take this to be the end of the statesman's life, rather than honour. But virtue or excellence also appears too incomplete to be what we want; for it seems that a man might have virtue and yet be asleep or be inactive all his life, and, moreover, might meet with the greatest disasters and misfortunes; and no one would maintain that such a man is happy, except for argument's sake. But we will not dwell on these matters now, for they are sufficiently discussed in the popular treatises. The third kind of life is the life of contemplation: we will treat of it further on. As for the money-making life, it is something quite contrary to nature; and wealth evidently is not the good of which we are in search, for it is merely useful as a means to something else. So we might rather take pleasure and virtue or excellence to be ends than wealth; for they are chosen on their own account. But it seems that not even they are the end, though much breath has been wasted in attempts to show that they are.

. . . Let us return once more to the question, what this good can be of which we are in search. It seems to be different in different kinds of action and in different arts,—one thing in medicine and another in war, and so on. What then is the good in each of these cases? Surely that for the sake of which all else is done. And that in medicine is health, in war is victory, in building is a house,—a different thing in each different case, but always, in whatever we do and in whatever we choose, the end. For it is always for the sake of the end that all else is done. If then there be one end of all that man does, this end will be the realizable good,—or these ends, if there be more than one.

By this generalization our argument is brought to the same point as before. This point we must try to explain more clearly. We see that there are many ends.

But some of these are chosen only as means, as wealth, flutes, and the whole class of instruments. And so it is plain that not all ends are final. But the best of all things must, we conceive, be something final. If then there be only one final end, this will be what we are seeking—or if there be more than one, then the most final of them. Now that which is pursued as an end in itself is more final than that which is pursued as means to something else, and that which is never chosen as means than that which is chosen both as an end in itself and as means, and that is strictly final which is always chosen as an end in itself and never as means.

Happiness seems more than anything else to answer to this description: for we always choose it for itself, and never for the sake of something else; while honour and pleasure and reason, and all virtue or excellence, we choose partly indeed for themselves (for, apart from any result, we should choose each of them), but partly also for the sake of happiness, supposing that they will help to make us happy. But no one chooses happiness for the sake of these things, or as a means to anything else at all. We seem to be led to the same conclusion when we start from the notion of self-sufficiency. The final good is thought to be self-sufficing [or all-sufficing]. In applying this term we do not regard a man as an individual leading a solitary life, but we also take account of parents, children, wife, and, in short, friends and fellow-citizens generally, since man is naturally a social being. Some limit must indeed be set to this; for if you go on to parents and descendants and friends of friends, you will never come to a stop. But this we will consider further on: for the present we will take self-sufficing to mean what by itself makes life desirable and in want of nothing. And happiness is believed to answer to this description. And further, happiness is believed to be the most desirable thing in the world, and that not merely as one among other good things: if it were merely one among other good things [so that other things could be added to it], it is plain that the addition of the least of other goods must make it more desirable; for the addition becomes a surplus of good, and of two goods the greater is always more desirable. Thus it seems that happiness is something final and self-sufficing, and is the end of all that man does.

We need some idea of what happiness is, and Aristotle here gives us his idea: Happiness is living according to rationality, the exercise of our most vital faculties.

But perhaps the reader thinks that though no one will dispute the statement that happiness is the best thing in the world, yet a still more precise definition of it is needed. This will best be gained, I think, by asking, What is the function of man? For as the goodness and the excellence of a piper or a sculptor, or the practiser of any art, and generally of those who have any function or business to do, lies in that function, so man's good would seem to lie in his function, if he has one. But can we suppose that, while a carpenter and a cobbler has a function and a business of his own, man has no business and no function assigned him by nature? Nay, surely as his several members, eye and hand and foot, plainly have each his own function, so we must suppose that man also has some function over and above all these.

What then is it? Life evidently he has in common even with the plants, but we want that which is peculiar to him. We must exclude, therefore, the life of mere nutrition and growth. Next to this comes the life of sense; but this too he plainly shares with horses and cattle and all kinds of animals. There remains then the life whereby he acts—the life of his rational nature, with its two sides or divisions, one rational as obeying reason, the other rational as having and exercising reason. But as this expression is ambiguous, we must be understood to mean thereby the life that consists in the exercise [not the mere possession] of the faculties; for this seems to be more properly entitled to the name.

The function of man, then, is exercise of his vital faculties [or soul] on one side in obedience to reason, and on the other side with reason. But what is called the function of a man of any profession and the function of a man who is good in that profession are, generically the same, *e.g.* of a harper and of a good harper; and this holds in all cases without exception, only that in the case of the latter his superior excellence at his work is added; for we say a harper's function is to harp, and a good harper's to harp well. Man's function then being, as we say, a kind of life—that is to say, exercise of his faculties and action of various kinds with reason—the good man's function is to do this well and beautifully [or nobly]. But the function of anything is done well when it is done in accordance with the proper excellence of that thing. If this be so the result is that the good of man is exercise of his faculties in accordance with excellence or virtue, or, if there be more than one, in accordance with the best and most complete virtue. But there must also be a full term of years for this exercise; for one swallow or one fine day does not make a spring, nor does one day or any small space of time make a blessed or happy man.

> *. . . the good of man is exercise of his faculties in accordance with excellence or virtue, or, if there be more than one, in accordance with the best and most complete virtue.*

It is important to notice the structure of Aristotle's argument here, for we shall see it emerge often in philosophy as well as in our own thought. The argument is an argument on the basis of what is "natural" to man. The good for man is that which is "natural" to him, and that means, according to Aristotle, what is special or unique to him as well. Thus mere "nutrition and growth," that is, eating and keeping physically healthy, cannot in themselves be happiness (although it is necessary for happiness) because even plants, Aristotle says, have this "goal." Nor can happiness lie in simple experience, even exciting experiences, since even a cow has this as the "end" of its life. What is unique to man, Aristotle concludes, is his rationality, his ability to act on rational principles. But action according to rational principles, is, as we shall see, precisely what Aristotle thinks virtue is. Thus happiness turns out to be an "activity of the soul in accordance with perfect virtue." (This is the key phrase of his work.) This "perfect virtue" is also called "excellence," and thus Aristotle's ethics is often called an ethics of self-realization, the goal of which is to make each individual as perfect as possible in all ways:

> Indeed, in addition to what we have said, a man is not good at all unless he takes pleasure in noble deeds. No one would call a man just who did not take pleasure in doing justice, nor generous who took no pleasure in acts of generosity, and so on. If this be so, the manifestations of excellence will be pleasant in themselves. But they are also both good and noble, and that in the highest degree—at least, if the good man's judgment about them is right, for this is his judgment. Happiness, then, is at once the best and noblest and pleasantest thing in the world. . . .

So far, however, it sounds as if virtue and happiness are strictly individual matters. But this is not the case. Aristotle's well-known belief that man is a social animal is as important as these other principles. Thus, the principles of reason and rationality that enter into his *Ethics* will have the interests of society as well as the individual built into them. (Aristotle even says that there is no real distinction between ethics and politics and that the proper end of ethics is politics.) Virtue, accordingly, is also a social conception, and most of the virtues Aristotle discusses, for example, justice and courage, have much to do with one's role in society. Happiness in general, therefore, has its social dimensions. For example, Aristotle argues that both respect and honor are ingredients in the good life. For Aristotle, the happy person, the virtuous person, is mainly a good citizen. It is necessary to add, however, that the only people who could qualify for Aristotle's good life were Greek citizens, which meant that women, children, slaves, and anyone who did not have the good fortune to be born Greek did not even have a chance at being happy, in Aristotle's sense.[10]

Not only does happiness have a social dimension and not only are the virtues socially defined, but the good life, according to Aristotle, must be taught us by society. Accordingly, Aristotle talks a great deal about the need for "good education," and he goes so far as to say that if a person has not been brought up "properly," then no amount of philosophy will be able to make him either virtuous or happy. He also says that young people, because they are "inexperienced in the actions of life" and are "so ruled by their passions," should not try to learn moral philosophy, which depends upon maturity and rationality. On this point, however, we will ignore Aristotle's warnings. For we have seen that growing older and more "mature" is certainly no guarantee of wisdom, and the passions of youth are sometimes more virtuous than the "rationality" of established maturity.

We have already seen Aristotle's beginning: Every act has its goal (or "good"), and ultimately there is a goal (or "chief good") toward which all human acts aim, and

---

[10] It is necessary to say something about Aristotle's special notion of *happiness;* it is not at all like our conception of "feeling happy." Aristotle's term (*eudaimonia*) means more like "living well," and it includes such matters as one's status in society and virtuous acts as well as good feelings. No matter how good you feel about yourself—even if you are in a state of ecstasy all of the time—you would not be happy in Aristotle's sense unless you had these other advantages and acted virtuously as well.

that is generally called happiness (**eudaimonia**). But, Aristotle adds, this is not much help, for people give very different accounts of what they take to be the ingredients in happiness. Some say that it is pleasure, others say it is wealth or honor. We have seen Aristotle's arguments against these views and his conclusion that happiness must be "activity in accordance with rational principle," and that means, virtuous activity. The key to Aristotle's ethics, then, lies in his concept of virtue.

Aristotle distinguishes two kinds of virtues, the practical or moral virtues (courage, generosity, and so on) and the intellectual virtues (skill at mathematics and philosophy). Although Aristotle thinks the highest virtue is the intellectual virtue of philosophic contemplation, most of his discussion of virtue centers on the moral virtues. We will now take a closer look at how moral virtues are acquired, what Aristotle means by a moral virtue, and what the moral virtues are.

Excellence, then, being of these two kinds, intellectual and moral, intellectual excellence owes its birth and growth mainly to instruction, and so requires time and experience, while moral excellence is the result of habit or custom and has accordingly in our language received a name formed by a slight change from the word for custom. From this it is plain that none of the moral excellences or virtues is implanted in us by nature; for that which is by nature cannot be altered by training. For instance, a stone naturally tends to fall downwards, and you could not train it to rise upwards, though you tried to do so by throwing it up ten thousand times, nor could you train fire to move downwards, nor accustom anything which naturally behaves in one way to behave in any other way. The virtues, then, come neither by nature nor against nature, but nature gives the capacity for acquiring them, and this is developed by training.

Again, where we do things by nature we get the power first, and put this power forth in act afterwards: as we plainly see in the case of the senses; for it is not by constantly seeing and hearing that we acquire those faculties, but, on the contrary, we had the power first and then used it, instead of acquiring the power by the use. But the virtues we acquire by doing the acts, as is the case with the arts too. We learn an art by doing that which we wish to do when we have learned it; we become builders by building, and harpers by harping. And so by doing just acts we become just, and by doing acts of temperance and courage we become temperate and courageous. . . .

Again, both the moral virtues and the corresponding vices result from and are formed by the same acts; and this is the case with the arts also. It is by harping that good harpers and bad harpers alike are produced: and so with builders and the rest; by building well they will become good builders, and bad builders by building badly. Indeed, if it were not so, they would not want anybody to teach them, but would all be born either good or bad at their trades. And it is just the same with the virtues also. It is by our conduct in our intercourse with other men that we become just or unjust, and by acting in circumstances of danger, and training ourselves to feel fear or confidence, that we become courageous or cowardly. So, too, with our animal appetites and the passion of anger; for by behaving in this way or in that on the occasions with which these passions are concerned, some become temperate and gentle, and others profligate and ill-tempered. In a word, acts of any kind produce habits or characters of the same kind. Hence we ought to make sure that our acts be of a certain kind; for the resulting character varies as they vary. It makes no small difference, therefore, whether a man be trained from his youth up in this way or in that, but a great difference, or rather all the difference.

Aristotle's point here is not just that the virtues are acquired by practice; he is also arguing that virtue is a state of character. The virtuous person wants to do virtuous acts and he does them "naturally." We sometimes think that we are moral just because we believe in moral principles. But believing isn't enough, virtuous action is required. But not even virtuous action by itself is enough to make us virtuous. We sometimes think a person is virtuous because he "forces himself" to do what he is supposed to. Not according to Aristotle. The virtuous person is one who does what he is supposed to do because he wants to, because it is built into his very character. It is even essential, according to Aristotle, that the virtuous man enjoys being virtuous:

> And, further, the life of these men is in itself pleasant. For pleasure is an affection of the soul, and each man takes pleasure in that which he is said to love,—he who loves horses in horses, he who loves sight-seeing in sight-seeing, and in the same way he who loves justice in acts of justice, and generally the lover of excellence or virtue in virtuous acts or the manifestation of excellence. And while with most men there is a perpetual conflict between the several things in which they find pleasure, since these are not naturally pleasant, those who love what is noble take pleasure in that which is naturally pleasant. For the manifestations of excellence are naturally pleasant, so that they are both pleasant to them and pleasant in themselves. Their life, then, does not need pleasure to be added to it as an appendage, but contains pleasure in itself.

Here Aristotle gives us perhaps his most famous doctrine, the idea that virtues are "means between the extremes." This is often misinterpreted, however, to read, "everything in moderation." In a way, what Aristotle teaches is very different from this; he tells us that we can't do too much of a good thing, that is, if it is a virtue. One can't be too courageous (as opposed to being rash or cowardly), or too just. What he intends by "the means between the extremes" is this:

> By the absolute mean, or mean relatively to the thing itself, I understand that which is equidistant from both extremes, and this is one and the same for all. By the mean relatively to us I understand that which is neither too much nor too little for us; and this is not one and the same for all. For instance, if ten be too large and two too small, six is the mean relatively to the thing itself: for it exceeds one extreme by the same amount by which it is exceeded by the other extreme: and this is the mean in arithmetical proportion. But the mean relatively to us cannot be found in this way. If ten pounds of food is too much for a given man to eat, and two pounds too little, it does not follow that the trainer will order

him six pounds: for that also may perhaps be too much for the man in question, or too little; too little for Milo, too much for the beginner. The same holds true in running and wrestling. And so we may say generally that a master in any art avoids what is too much and what is too little, and seeks for the mean and chooses it—not the absolute but the relative mean.

If, then, every art or science perfects its work in this way, looking to the mean and bringing its work up to this standard (so that people are wont to say of a good work that nothing could be taken from it or added to it, implying that excellence is destroyed by excess or deficiency, but secured by observing the mean; and good artists, as we say, do in fact keep their eyes fixed on this in all that they do), and if virtue, like nature, is more exact and better than any art, it follows that virtue also must aim at the mean—virtue of course meaning moral virtue or excellence; for it has to do with passions and actions, and it is these that admit of excess and deficiency and the mean. For instance, it is possible to feel fear, confidence, desire, anger, pity, and generally to be affected pleasantly and painfully, either too much or too little, in either case wrongly; but to be thus affected at the right times, and on the right occasions, and towards the right persons, and with the right object, and in the right fashion, is the mean course and the best course, and these are characteristics of virtue. And in the same way our outward acts also admit of excess and deficiency, and the mean or due amount. Virtue, then, has to deal with feelings or passions and with outward acts, in which excess is wrong and deficiency also is blamed, but the mean amount is praised, and is right—both of which are characteristics of virtue. Virtue, then, is a kind of moderation inasmuch as it aims at the mean.

> *Virtue, then, has to deal with feelings or passions and with outward acts, in which excess is wrong and deficiency also is blamed, but the mean amount is praised, and is right—both of which are characteristics of virtue. Virtue, then, is a kind of moderation inasmuch as it aims at the mean.*

Again, there are many ways of going wrong (for evil is infinite in nature, to use a Pythagorean figure, while good is finite), but only one way of going right; so that the one is easy and the other hard—easy to miss the mark and hard to hit. On this account also, then, excess and deficiency are characteristic of vice, hitting the mean is characteristic of virtue.

◆◆◆

Virtue, then, is a habit or trained faculty of choice, the characteristic of which lies in moderation or observance of the mean relatively to the persons concerned, as determined by reason, *i.e.* by the reason by which the prudent man would determine it. And it is a moderation, firstly, inasmuch as it comes in the middle or mean between two vices, one on the side of excess, the other on the side of defect; and, secondly, inasmuch as, while these vices fall short of or exceed the due measure in feeling and in action, it finds and chooses the mean, middling, or moderate amount. Regarded in its essence, therefore, or according to the definition of its nature, virtue is a moderation or middle state, but viewed in its relation to what is best and right it is the extreme of perfection.

But it is not all actions nor all passions that admit of moderation; there are some whose very names imply badness, or malevolence, shamelessness, envy, and, among acts, adultery, theft, murder. These and all other like things are blamed as being bad in themselves, and not merely in their excess or deficiency. It is impossible therefore to go right in them; they are always wrong: rightness and wrongness in such things (*e.g.* in adultery) does not depend upon whether it is the right person and occasion and manner, but the mere doing of any one of them is wrong. It would be equally absurd to look for moderation or excess or deficiency in unjust cowardly or profligate conduct; for then there would be moderation in excess or deficiency, and excess in excess, and deficiency in deficiency. The fact is that just as there can be no excess or deficiency in temperance or courage because the mean or moderate amount is, in a sense, an extreme, so in these kinds of conduct also there can be no moderation or excess or deficiency, but the acts are wrong however they be done. For, to put it generally, there cannot be moderation in excess or deficiency, nor excess or deficiency in moderation.

We see that Aristotle defines "moral virtue" as a mean both in feeling and action. Thus courage is a virtue because the courageous man feels neither too little nor too much fear. His fear is appropriate to the dangerousness of his situation. Because the courageous person feels the right amount of fear, he acts in the right way, neither plunging rashly into danger nor fleeing from it in terror. Now, finally, Aristotle gives us his examples of virtue:

Moderation in the feelings of fear and confidence is courage: of those that exceed, he that exceeds in fearlessness has no name (as often happens), but he that exceeds in confidence is foolhardy, while he that exceeds in fear, but is deficient in confidence, is cowardly. Moderation in respect of certain pleasures and also (though to a less extent) certain pains in temperance, while excess is profligacy. But defectiveness in the matter of these pleasures is hardly ever found, and so this sort of people also have as yet received no name: let us put them down as "void of sensibility." In the matter of giving and taking money, moderation is liberality, excess and deficiency are prodigality and illiberality. But both vices exceed and fall short in giving and taking in contrary ways: the prodigal exceeds in spending, but falls short in taking; while the illiberal man exceeds in taking, but falls short in spending. . . . But, besides these, there are other dispositions in the matter of money: there is a moderation which is called magnificence (for the magnificent is not the same as the liberal man: the former deals with large sums, the latter with small), and an excess which is called bad taste or vulgarity, and a deficiency which is called meanness. . . . With respect to honour and disgrace, there is a moderation which is pride, an excess which may be called vanity, and a deficiency which is humility.

But just as we said that liberality is related to magnificence, differing only in that it deals with small sums, so here there is a virtue related to high-mindedness, and differing only in that it is concerned with small instead of great honours. A man may have a due desire for honour, and also more or less than a due desire: he that carries this desire to excess is called ambitious, he that has not enough of it is called unambitious, but he that has the due amount has no name. . . . In the matter of anger also we find excess and deficiency and moderation. The characters themselves hardly have recognized names, but as the moderate man is here called gentle, we will call his character gentleness; of those who go into extremes, we may take the term wrathful for him who exceeds, with wrathfulness for the vice, and wrathless for him who is deficient, with wrathlessness for his character. . . .

In the matter of truth, then, let us call him who observes the mean a true [or truthful] person, and observance of the mean truth [or truthfulness]: pretence, when it exaggerates, may be called boasting, and the person a boaster; when it understates, let the names be irony and ironical. With regard to pleasantness in amusement, he who observes the mean may be called witty, and his character wittiness; excess may be called buffoonery, and the man a buffoon; while boorish may stand for the person who is deficient, and boorishness for his character. With regard to pleasantness in the other affairs of life, he who makes himself properly pleasant may be called friendly, and his moderation friendliness; he that exceeds may be called obsequious if he have no ulterior motive, but a flatterer if he has an eye to his own advantage; he that is deficient in this respect, and always makes himself disagreeable, may be called a quarrelsome or peevish fellow.

Moreover, in mere emotions and in our conduct with regard to them, there are ways of observing the mean; for instance, shame is not a virtue, but yet the modest man is praised. For in these matters also we speak of this man as observing the mean, of that man as going beyond it (as the shamefaced man whom the least thing makes shy), while he who is deficient in the feeling, or lacks it altogether, is called shameless; but the term modest is applied to him who observes the mean. Righteous indignation, again, hits the mean between envy and malevolence. These have to do with feelings of pleasure and pain at what happens to our neighbours. A man is called righteously indignant when he feels pain at the sight of undeserved prosperity, but your envious man goes beyond him and is pained by the sight of any one in prosperity, while the malevolent man is so far from being pained that he actually exults in the misfortunes of his neighbours.

It is worth making a short list of Aristotle's moral virtues. Many of them are our own virtues also, but some of them are far more appropriate to an aristocratic, warrior society than they are to our own. To illustrate Aristotle's idea that virtues are the means between the extremes, I have included "the extremes" in parentheses for contrast:

Courage, *particularly courage in battle* (extremes: cowardice, rashness). *What motivates courage, Aristotle tells us, is a sense of honor, not fear of punishment nor desire for reward, nor merely a sense of duty. The courageous man is afraid, he adds, because without fear there would be no courage. The man who feels no fear in the face of danger is rather rash.*

Temperance, *particularly concerning bodily pleasures, such as sex, food, and drinking (extremes: self-indulgence or piggishness, insensitivity). Notice that Aristotle does not say, along with many modern moralists, that pleasures are either "bad" or unimportant; in fact, he attacks the man who does not enjoy sex, food, and drinking as much as he attacks the man who overindulges himself. He says that such people "are not even human."*

Liberality, *we would say, charity (extremes: prodigality or waste, meanness or stinginess). It is worth noting that Aristotle ridicules the man who gives more than he can afford to charity as much as he chastizes the man who will not give at all.*

Magnificence, *in other words, how extravagantly you live (extremes: vulgarity, miserliness). Aristotle says that one ought to live "like an artist" and spend lavishly. (There is little of the ascetic in Aristotle.)*

Pride (extremes: humility, vanity). It is worth noting that pride is one of the seven deadly sins in Christian morality while humility is a virtue. In Aristotle's ethics, this is reversed.

Good temper *(extremes: irascibility or bad temper, being too easygoing). It is important to get angry, according to Aristotle, about the right things, but not too much (which "makes a person impossible to live with").*

Friendliness *(extremes: obsequiousness, churlishness). Friendship, for Aristotle, is one of the most important ingredients in the good life, and being friendly, therefore, is an extremely important virtue. But Aristotle does not say that we should be friendly to everyone; the person who is indiscriminately friendly toward everyone is not worth being a friend with at all.*

Truthfulness *(extremes: lying, boasting). Especially telling the truth about oneself.*

Wittiness *(extremes: buffoonery, boorishness). We think of wittiness as a personal asset, but rarely as a virtue. Aristotle thinks that people who are incapable of telling a joke or who tell bad jokes are actually inferior. Fun is an important ingredient in Greek virtuousness.*

Shame: *Aristotle calls this a "quasi-virtue" (extreme: shamelessness). We all make mistakes and it is a sign of virtue, according to Aristotle, that the good man feels shame when he does them. Shamelessness is a sign of wickedness. Aristotle does not even talk of the other extreme, which he did not consider a problem. (We certainly would. We call it excessive guilt.)*

Justice, *the cardinal virtue of the Greeks. The need for lawful and fair (which does not mean equal) treatment of other men. (The sense in which justice is a mean between extremes is too complex to discuss here. Aristotle spends a full chapter explaining it.)*

Finally, Aristotle gives us his view of the good life for humankind; it is the life of activity in accordance with virtue, but it is also, ideally, a life of intellectual activity, or what he calls "the life of contemplation." In other words, the happiest person is the philosopher:

We said that happiness is not a habit or trained faculty. If it were, it would be within the reach of a man who slept all his days and lived the life of a vegetable, or of a man who met with the greatest misfortunes. As we cannot accept this conclusion, we must place happiness in some exercise of faculty, as we said before. But as the exercises of faculty are sometimes necessary (*i.e.* desirable for the sake of something else), sometimes desirable in themselves, it is evident that happiness must be placed among those that are desirable in themselves, and not among those that are desirable for the sake of something else: for happiness lacks nothing; it is sufficient in itself.

Now, the exercise of faculty is desirable in itself when nothing is expected from it beyond itself. Of this nature are held to be (1) the manifestations of excellence; for to do what is noble and excellent must be counted desirable for itself: and (2) those amusements which please are more apt to be injured than to be benefited by them, through neglect of their health and fortunes. Now, most of those whom men call happy have recourse to pastimes of this sort. And on this account those who show a ready wit in such pastimes find favour with tyrants; for they make themselves pleasant in that which the tyrant wants, and what he wants is pastime. These amusements, then, are generally thought to be elements of happiness, because princes employ their leisure in them. But such persons, we may venture to say, are no criterion. For princely rank does not imply the possession of virtue or of reason, which are the sources of all excellent exercise of faculty. And if these men, never having tasted pure and refined pleasure, have recourse to the pleasures of the body, we should not on that account think these more desirable; for children also fancy that the things which they value are better than anything else. It is only natural, then, that as children differ from men in their estimate of what is valuable, so bad men should differ from good.

As we have often said, therefore, that is truly valuable and pleasant which is so to the perfect man. Now, the exercise of those trained faculties which are proper to him is what each man finds most desirable; what the perfect man finds most desirable, therefore, is the exercise of virtue. Happiness, therefore, does not consist in amusement; and indeed it is absurd to suppose that the end is amusement, and that we toil and moil all our life long for the sake of amusing ourselves. We may say that we choose everything for the sake of something else, excepting only happiness; for it is the end. But to be serious and to labour for the sake of amusement seems silly and utterly childish; while to amuse ourselves in order that we may be serious, as Anacharsis says, seems to be right; for amusement is a sort of recreation, and we need recreation because we are unable to work continuously. Recreation then, cannot be the end; for it is taken as a means to the exercise of our faculties.

Again, the happy life is thought to be that which exhibits virtue; and such a life must be serious and cannot consist in amusement. Again, it is held that things of serious importance are better than laughable and amusing things, and that the better the organ or the man, the most important is the function; but we have already said that the function or exercise of that which is better is higher and more conducive to happiness. Again, the enjoyment of bodily pleasures is within the reach of anybody, of a slave no less than the best of men; but no one supposes that a slave can participate in happiness, seeing that he cannot participate in the proper life of man. For indeed happiness does not consist in pastimes of this sort, but in the exercise of virtue, as we have already said.

But if happiness be the exercise of virtue, it is reasonable to suppose that it will be the exercise of the highest virtue; and that will be the virtue or excellence of the best part of us. Now, that part or faculty—call it reason or what you will—which seems naturally to rule and take the lead, and to apprehend things noble and divine—whether it be itself divine, or only the divinest part of us—is the faculty the exercise of which, in its proper excellence, will be perfect happiness. . . . this consists in speculation or theorizing.

This conclusion would seem to agree both with what we have said above, and with known truths. This exercise of faculty must be the highest possible; for the reason is the highest of our faculties and of all knowable things those that reason deals with are the highest. Again, it is the most continuous; for speculation can be carried on more continuously than any kind of action whatsoever. We think too that pleasure ought to be one of the ingredients of happiness; but of all virtuous exercises it is allowed that the pleasantest is the exercise of wisdom. At least philosophy is thought to have pleasures that are admirable in purity and steadfastness; and it is reasonable to suppose that the time passes more pleasantly with those who possess, than with those who are seeking knowledge. Again, what is called self-sufficiency will be most of all found in the speculative life. The necessaries of life, indeed, are needed by the wise man as well as by the just man and the rest; but, when these have been provided in due quantity, the just man further needs persons towards whom, and along with whom, he may act justly; and so does the temperate and the courageous man and the rest; while the wise man is able to speculate even by himself, and the wiser he is the more is he able to do this. He could speculate better, we may confess, if he had others to help him, but nevertheless he is more self-sufficient than anybody else. Again, it would seem that this life alone is desired solely for its own sake; for it yields no result beyond the contemplation, but from the practical activities we get something more or less besides action.

. . . it follows that the exercise of reason will be the complete happiness of man, *i.e.* when a complete term of days is added; for nothing incomplete can be admitted into our idea of happiness. But a life which realized this idea would be something more than human; for it would not be the expression of man's nature, but of some divine element in that nature—the exercise of which is as far superior to the exercise of the other kind of virtue, as this divine element is superior

> *Since . . . it is the reason that in the truest sense is the man, the life that consists in the exercise of the reason is the best and pleasantest for man—and therefore the happiest.*

to our compound human nature. If then reason be divine as compared with man, the life which consists in the exercise of reason will also be divine in comparison with human life. Nevertheless, instead of listening to those who advise us as men and mortals not to lift our thoughts above what is human and mortal, we ought rather, as far as possible, to put off our mortality and make every effort to live in the exercise of the highest of our faculties; for though it be but a small part of us, yet in power and value it far surpasses all the rest. And indeed this part would even seem to constitute our true self, since it is the sovereign and the better part. It would be strange, then, if a man were to prefer the life of something else to the life of his true self. Again, we may apply here what we said above—for every being that is best and pleasantest which is naturally proper to it. Since, then, it is the reason that in the truest sense is the man, the life that consists in the exercise of the reason is the best and pleasantest for man—and therefore the happiest.

But it must not be thought that Aristotle's ideal philosopher does nothing but contemplate. He may also enjoy pleasure, wealth, honor, success, and power. As a man among men, he is also virtuous and chooses to act virtuously like all good men. But in addition, he has an understanding and an appreciation of reason that makes him "dearest to the Gods and presumably the happiest among men." This is surely a flattering portrait of the place of the philosopher! But if we ignore this final self-congratulation, we can see in Aristotle a powerful conception of morality, with its emphasis on virtue, excellence, and a kind of heroism (whether intellectual or moral) that is in some ways very different from our own conception of morality and the good life.

E. MORALITY AND SENTIMENT: HUME AND ROUSSEAU

Morality for Aristotle depended upon rules embedded and learned in a particular society, an elite society of the privileged males of the Greek aristocracy. Modern conceptions of morality, on the other hand, are usually thought to be universal, that is, not restricted to a particular society or a particular elite. It applies to women, men, poor people, rich people, adults, and children, even if they are only a few years old. At the same time, however, most modern conceptions of morality minimize Aristotle's emphasis on society and upbringing, preferring to place morals on some individual basis. In Kant's moral philosophy, the key to morality is *individual autonomy,* the idea that every person can find for himself or herself, just through the use of reason, what acts are moral and what acts are not. Before Kant, the ruling conception of morality was based upon a conception of personal feelings of a special moral kind, a "natural desire" to help one's fellow man. (As in Aristotle, this philosophy insisted that morality had to be viewed as a part of nature.)

It should be clear how this conception of morality has a distinct advantage in reconciling personal interests and moral principles. Since strong moral feelings are a kind of personal interest, one can satisfy his personal feelings and the demands of morality at the same time. (Again, this lies in the heart of Bishop Butler's arguments.) Of course, other personal feelings—jealousy, greed, and envy—can act against these moral feelings. But at least some of our feelings are satisfied by moral action. According to these philosophers, such moral feelings can be found in virtually all of us.

The two most famous philosophers to argue this position are David Hume and the French philosopher **Jean-Jacques Rousseau.** The key to both of their philosophies is the notion of **sentiment** ("feeling") and the notion of **sympathy** ("fellow feeling" or feeling pity for other people and taking their interests into account as well as our own). Hume says:

> *The hypothesis which we embrace is plain. It maintains that morality is determined by sentiment. It defines virtue to be whatever mental action or quality gives to a spectator the pleasing sentiment of approbation; and vice the contrary.*[11]

The central concern in Hume's moral philosophy distinguishes those who defend morality as a function of reason from those who say that it is rather a matter of sentiment and passion. Elsewhere Hume gives us his very strong opinion that "reason is, and ought to be, the slave of the passions." Here is his argument:

ON "REASON AS SLAVE OF THE PASSIONS"
BY DAVID HUME

There has been a controversy started of late, much better worth examination, concerning the general foundation of *morals;* whether they be derived from *reason* or from *sentiment;* whether we attain the knowledge of them by a chain of argument and induction or by an immediate feeling and finer internal sense; whether, like all sound judgment of truth and falsehood, they should be the same to every rational, intelligent being, or whether, like the perception of beauty and deformity, they be founded entirely on the particular fabric and constitution of the human species.

The ancient philosophers, though they often affirm that virtue is nothing but conformity to reason, yet, in general, seem to consider morals as deriving their

---

[11] David Hume, *Enquiry Concerning the Principles of Morals* (La Salle, IL: Open Court, 1912).

existence from taste and sentiment. On the other hand, our modern inquirers, though they also talk much of the beauty of virtue and deformity of vice, yet have commonly endeavored to account for these distinctions by metaphysical reasonings and by deductions from the most abstract principles of the understanding. Such confusion reigned in these subjects that an opposition of the greatest consequence could prevail between one system and another, and even in the parts of almost each individual system, and yet nobody, till very lately, was ever sensible of it.

◆ ◆ ◆

It must be acknowledged that both sides of the question are susceptible of specious arguments. Moral distinctions, it may be said, are discernible by pure *reason;* else, whence the many disputes that reign in common life, as well as in philosophy with regard to this subject, the long chain of proofs often produced on both sides, the examples cited, the authorities appealed to, the analogies employed, the fallacies detected, the inferences drawn, and the several conclusions adjusted to their proper principles? Truth is disputable, not taste: what exists in the nature of things is the standard of our judgment: what each man feels within himself is the standard of sentiment. Propositions in geometry may be proved, systems in physics may be controverted, but the harmony of verse, the tenderness of passion, the brilliancy of wit must give immediate pleasure. No man reasons concerning another's beauty, but frequently concerning the justice or injustice of his actions. In every criminal trial, the first object of the prisoner is to disprove the facts alleged and deny the actions imputed to him; the second, to prove that, even if these actions were real, they might be justified as innocent and lawful. It is confessedly by deductions of the understanding that the first point is ascertained; how can we suppose a different faculty of the mind is employed in fixing the other?

On the other hand, those who would resolve all moral determinations into *sentiments* may endeavor to show that it is impossible for reason ever to draw conclusions of this nature. To virtue, say they, it belongs to be *amiable* and vice *odious*. This forms their very nature or essence. But can reason or argumentation distribute these different epithets to any subjects and pronounce beforehand that this must produce love and that hatred? Or what other reason can we ever assign for these affections but the original fabric and formation of the human mind, which is naturally adapted to receive them?

The end of all moral speculations is to teach us our duty, and, by proper representations of the deformity of vice and beauty of virtue, beget correspondent habits and engage us to avoid the one and embrace the other. But is this ever to be expected from inferences and conclusions of the understanding, which of themselves have no hold of the affections or set in motion the active powers of men? They discover truths. But where the truths which they discover are indifferent and beget no desire or aversion, they can have no influence on conduct and behavior. What is honorable, what is fair, what is becoming, what is noble, what is generous takes possession of the heart and animates us to embrace and maintain it. What is intelligible, what is evident, what is probable, what is true procures only the cool assent of the understanding and, gratifying a speculative curiosity, puts an end to our researches. . . .

Extinguish all the warm feelings and prepossessions in favor of virtue, and all disgust or aversion to vice; render men totally indifferent toward these distinctions, and morality is no longer a practical study nor has any tendency to regulate our lives and actions.

These arguments on each side (and many more might be produced) are so plausible that I am apt to suspect they may, the one as well as the other, be solid and satisfactory and that *reason* and *sentiment* concur in almost all moral determinations and conclusions. The final sentence, it is probable, which pronounces characters and actions amiable or odious, praiseworthy or blamable; that which stamps on them the mark of honor or infamy, approbation or censure; that which renders morality an active principle and constitutes virtue our happiness, and vice our misery—it is probable, I say, that this final sentence depends on some internal sense of feeling which nature has made universal in the whole species.

It is worth noting here that Hume's moral philosophy, like his philosophy of knowledge, is strictly empiricist:

Men are now cured of their passion for hypotheses and systems in natural philosophy and will hearken to no arguments but those which are derived from experience. It is full time they should attempt a like reformation in all moral disquisitions and reject every system of ethics, however subtle or ingenious, which is not founded on fact and observation.

Reason, Hume argues, may be of use in deciding how we can get what we want, but it is incapable of ever telling us what we ultimately want. Notice the familiar argument against an infinite regress; notice also Hume's sharp distinction between reason (which is concerned with knowledge, truth, and falsehood) and taste or sentiment (that judges values, which ultimately depend upon pleasure and pain):

It appears evident that the ultimate ends of human actions can never, in any case, be accounted for by *reason,* but recommend themselves entirely to the sentiments and affections of mankind without any dependence on the intellectual faculties. Ask a man *why he uses exercise;* he will answer, *because he desires to keep his health.* If you then inquire *why he desires health,* he will readily reply, *because sickness is painful.* If you push your inquiries further and desire a reason *why he hates pain,* it is impossible he can ever give any. This is an ultimate end and is never referred to any other object.

Perhaps to your second question, *why he desires health,* he may also reply that *it is necessary for the exercise of his calling.* If you ask *why he is anxious on that head,* he will answer, *because he desires to get money.* If you demand, *why? It is the instrument of pleasure,* says he. And beyond this, it is an absurdity to ask for a reason. It is impossible there can be a progress *in infinitum* and that one thing can always be a reason why another is desired. Something must be desirable on its own account and because of its immediate accord or agreement with human sentiment and affection.

Now, as virtue is an end and is desirable on its own account, without fee or reward, merely for the immediate satisfaction which it conveys, it is requisite that there should be some sentiment which it touches—some internal taste or feeling, or whatever you please to call it, which distinguishes moral good and evil and which embraces the one and rejects the other.

> *. . . the distinct boundaries and offices of* **reason** *and of* **taste** *are easily ascertained. The former conveys the knowledge of truth and falsehood; the latter gives the sentiment of beauty and deformity, vice and virtue.*

Thus, the distinct boundaries and offices of *reason* and of *taste* are easily ascertained. The former conveys the knowledge of truth and falsehood; the latter gives the sentiment of beauty and deformity, vice and virtue. The one discovers objects as they really stand in nature, without addition or diminution; the other has a productive faculty; and gliding or straining all natural objects with the colors borrowed from internal sentiment, raises, in a manner, a new creation. Reason, being cool and disengaged, is no motive to action and directs only the impulse received from appetite or inclination by showing us the means of attaining happiness or avoiding misery. Taste, as it gives pleasure or pain, and thereby constitutes happiness or misery, becomes a motive to action and is the first spring or impulse to desire and volition. From circumstances and relations, known or supposed, the former leads us to the discovery of the concealed and unknown. After all circumstances and relations are laid before us, the latter makes us feel from the whole a new sentiment of blame or approbation.[12]

Elsewhere Hume argues a razor-sharp distinction between facts and values. He argues with characteristic conciseness that "it is impossible to derive an 'ought' from an 'is,' " that is, any notions of value or what we *ought to do* cannot be derived from any statements of fact. One can know, as a matter of fact, that pushing this button will kill a thousand innocent children, but from that fact alone, it does not follow that I ought not push the button. What I ought to do—or ought not to do—depends on something that is not a matter of fact or reason at all, my moral feelings or sentiments. Without these sentiments, no action is either moral or immoral, praiseworthy or blameworthy, or of any value whatever. Accordingly, in one of his most shocking statements Hume says that it would not be irrational for him to prefer the death of half the world to the pricking of his little finger. This is not to say that he would prefer this, but there is *nothing in reason* to forbid it. Values are a matter of sentiment, not of reason.

---

[12] Hume, *Enquiry Concerning the Principles of Morals.*

A similar theory of sentiment is defended by Jean-Jacques Rousseau. Although he is often characterized as the first great "Romantic," it is worth noting that Rousseau is not nearly so antagonistic to reason as his reputation suggests. Sentiment, by his theory, is tied to a kind of "natural reason." The key to his theory, therefore, is the concept of **conscience,** a powerful kind of moral feeling that has its own kind of divine reason. As in Hume, detached reason offers us no guidance. Notice that he too reconciles "self-love" and "moral goodness" as ultimately having the same goals:

FROM *EMILE*
BY **JEAN-JACQUES ROUSSEAU**

Let us lay it down as an incontrovertible rule that the first impulses of nature are always right; there is no original sin in the human heart, the how and why of the entrance of every vice can be traced. The only natural passion is self-love or selfishness taken in a wider sense. This selfishness is good in itself and in relation to ourselves; and as the child has no necessary relations to other people he is naturally indifferent to them; his self-love only becomes good or bad by the use made of it and the relations established by its means. Until the time is ripe for the appearance of reason, that guide of selfishness, the main thing is that the child shall do nothing because you are watching him or listening to him; in a word, nothing because of other people, but only what nature asks of him; then he will never do wrong.

I do not mean to say that he will never do any mischief, never hurt himself, never break a costly ornament if you leave it within his reach. He might do much damage without doing wrong, since wrong-doing depends on the harmful intention which will never be his. If once he meant to do harm, his whole education would be ruined; he would be almost hopelessly bad. . . .

The morality of our actions consists entirely in the judgments we ourselves form with regard to them. If good is good, it must be good in the depth of our heart as well as in our actions; and the first reward of justice is the consciousness that we are acting justly. If moral goodness is in accordance with our nature, man can only be healthy in mind and body when he is good. If it is not so, and if man is by nature evil, he cannot cease to be evil without corrupting his nature, and goodness in him is a crime against nature. If he is made to do harm to his fellow-creatures, as the wolf is made to devour his prey, a humane man would be as depraved a creature as a pitiful wolf; and virtue alone would cause remorse.

My young friend, let us look within, let us set aside all personal prejudices and see whither our inclinations lead us. Do we take more pleasure in the sight of the sufferings of others or their joys? Is it pleasanter to do a kind action or an unkind action, and which leaves the more delightful memory behind it? Why do you enjoy the theatre? Do you delight in the crimes you behold? Do you weep over the punishment which overtakes the criminal? They say we are indifferent to everything but self-interest; yet we find our consolation in our sufferings in the charms of friendship and humanity, and even in our pleasures we should be too lonely and miserable if we had no one to share them with us. If there is no such thing as morality in man's heart, what is the source of his rapturous admiration of noble deeds, his passionate devotion to great men? What connection is there between self-interest and this enthusiasm for virtue?

◆ ◆ ◆

Take from our hearts this love of what is noble and you rob us of the joy of life. The mean-spirited man in whom these delicious feelings have been stifled among vile passions, who by thinking of no one but himself comes at last to love no one but himself, this man feels no raptures, his cold heart no longer throbs with joy, and his eyes no longer fill with the sweet tears of sympathy, he delights in nothing; the wretch has neither life nor feeling, he is already dead.

There are many bad men in this world, but there are few of these dead souls, alive only to self-interest, and insensible to all that is right and good. We only delight in injustice so long as it is to our own advantage; in every other case we wish the innocent to be protected. If we see some act of violence or injustice in town or country, our hearts are at once stirred to their depths by an instinctive anger and wrath, which bids us go to the help of the oppressed; but we are restrained by a stronger duty, and the law deprives us of our right to protect the innocent. On the other hand, if some deed of mercy or generosity meets our eye, what reverence and love does it inspire! Do we not say to ourselves, "I should like to have done that myself"? What does it matter to us that two thousand years ago a man was just or unjust? and yet we take the same interest in ancient history as if it happened yesterday. What are the crimes of Cataline to me? I shall not be his victim. Why then have I the same horror of his crimes as if he were living now? We do not hate the wicked merely because of the harm they do to ourselves, but because they are wicked. Not only do we wish to be happy ourselves, we wish others to be happy too, and if this happiness does not interfere with our own happiness, it increases it. In conclusion, whether we will or not, we pity the unfortunate; when we see their suffering we suffer too. Even the most depraved are not wholly without this instinct, and it often leads them to self-contradiction. The highwayman who robs the traveller, clothes the nakedness of the poor; the fiercest murderer supports a fainting man.

Men speak of the voice of remorse, the secret punishment of hidden crimes, by which such are often brought to light. Alas! who does not know its unwelcome voice? We speak from experience and we would gladly stifle this imperious feeling which causes us such agony. Let us obey the call of nature; we shall see that her yoke is easy and that when we give heed to her voice we find a joy in the answer of a good conscience. The wicked fears and flees from her; he delights to escape from himself; his anxious eyes look around him for some object of diversion; without bitter satire and rude mockery he would always be sorrowful; the scornful laugh is his one pleasure. Not so the just man, who finds his peace within himself; there is joy not malice in his laughter, a joy which springs from his own heart; he is as cheerful alone as in company, his satisfaction does not depend on those who approach him; it includes them.

◆ ◆ ◆

It is no part of my scheme to enter at present into metaphysical discussions which neither you nor I can understand, discussions which really lead nowhere.

I have told you already that I do not wish to philosophise with you, but to help you to consult your own heart. If all the philosophers in the world should prove that I am wrong, and you feel that I am right, that is all I ask.

For this purpose it is enough to lead you to distinguish between our acquired ideas and our natural feelings; for feeling precedes knowledge; and since we do not learn to seek what is good for us and avoid what is bad for us, but get this desire from nature, in the same way the love of good and the hatred of evil are as natural to us as our self-love. The decrees of conscience are not judgments but feelings. Although all our ideas come from without, the feelings by which they are weighed are within us, and it is by these feelings alone that we perceive fitness or unfitness of things in relation to ourselves, which leads us to seek or shun these things.

To exist is to feel; our feeling is undoubtedly earlier than our intelligence, and we had feelings before we had ideas. Whatever may be the cause of our being, it has provided for our preservation by giving us feelings suited to our nature; and no one can deny that these at least are innate. These feelings, so far as the individual is concerned, are self-love, fear, pain, the dread of death, the desire for comfort. Again, if, as it is impossible to doubt, man is by nature sociable, or at least fitted to become sociable, he can only be so by means of other innate feelings, relative to his kind; for if only physical well-being were considered, men would certainly be scattered rather than brought together. But the motive power of conscience is derived from the moral system formed through this twofold relation to himself and to his fellow-men. To know good is not to love it; this knowledge is not innate in man; but as soon as his reason leads him to perceive it, his conscience impels him to love it; it is this feeling which is innate.

> *To know good is not to love it; this knowledge is not innate in man; but as soon as his reason leads him to perceive it, his conscience impels him to love it; it is this feeling which is innate.*

So I do not think, my young friend, that it is impossible to explain the immediate force of conscience as a result of our own nature, independent of reason itself. And even should it be impossible, it is necessary; for those who deny this principle, admitted and received by everybody else in the world, do not prove that there is no such thing; they are content to affirm, and when we affirm its existence we have quite as good grounds as they, while we have moreover the witness within us, the voice of conscience, which speaks on its own behalf. If the first beams of judgment dazzle us and confuse the objects we behold, let us wait till our feeble sight grows clear and strong, and in the light of reason we shall soon behold these very objects as nature has already showed them to us. Or rather let us be simpler and less pretentious; let us be content with the first feelings we experience in ourselves, since science always brings us back to these, unless it has led us astray.

Conscience! Conscience! Divine instinct, immortal voice from heaven; sure guide for a creature ignorant and finite indeed; yet intelligent and free; infallible judge of good and evil, making man like to God! In these consists the excellence of man's nature and the morality of his actions; apart from thee, I find nothing in myself to raise me above the beasts—nothing but the sad privilege of wandering from one error to another, by the help of an unbridled understanding and a reason which knows no principle.[13]

But, as we pointed out before, there is a problem with this notion of conscience and with all appeals of morality to personal feeling. What if different people disagree? Whose conscience or whose feelings should we accept? And even if we find ourselves in agreement, how do we know that our consciences or feelings are right? It is with these questions in mind that we turn to the moral philosophy of Kant.

F. MORALITY AND PRACTICAL REASON: KANT

Aristotle, Hume, and Rousseau all give feeling an important place in their conceptions of morality. For Aristotle, the virtuous man wants to act virtuously and enjoys doing so. For Hume and Rousseau, sentiment defines morality. On all such accounts, our concept of *duty*—what we ought to do—is derivative, at least in part, from such feelings and from our upbringing. But what if feelings disagree? What if people are brought up to value different things? What are we to say of a person who is brought up by criminals to value what is wicked and to enjoy cruelty? And what are we to say, most importantly of all, in those familiar cases in which a person's feelings all draw him or her toward personal interests but duty calls in the opposite direction? This is the problem that Kant considered, and because of it, he rejected all attempts to base morality on feelings of any kind. Morality, he argued, must be based solely on reason and reason alone. Its central concept is the concept of **duty,** and so morality is a matter of **deontology** (from the Greek word *dein,* or "duty").

Hume had restricted the notion of reason to concern with knowledge, truth, and falsity; Kant replies that reason also has a practical side, one that is capable of telling us what to do as well as how to do it. Rousseau had said that morality must be universal, common to all men, even in a presocietal "state of nature"; Kant (who very much admired Rousseau) agrees but says that the nature of this universality cannot lie in people's feelings, which may vary from person to person and society to society, but only in reason, which by its very nature must be universal. And Aristotle had insisted that morality must be taught within society and that morals were very much a matter of public opinion and practices; but unlike most modern philosophers, Kant insisted on the independence of morality from society. What is most important, he argues, is that morality be autonomous, a function of individual reason, such that every rational person is capable of finding out what is right and what is wrong for

---

[13] Jean-Jacques Rousseau, *Emile,* trans. Barbara Foxley (New York: E. P. Dutton, 1968).

himself or herself. Where Hume and Rousseau had looked for morality in individual feeling, Kant again insists that it must be found through an examination of reason, nothing else. This is the key to Kant's moral philosophy: Morality consists solely of *rational* principles.

Since morality is based on reason, according to Kant, it does not depend on particular societies or particular circumstances; it does not depend on individual feelings or desires (Kant summarizes all such personal feelings, desires, ambitions, impulses, and emotions as **inclinations**). The purpose of moral philosophy, therefore, is to examine our ability to reason practically and to determine from this examination the fundamental principles that lie at the basis of every morality, for every person, and in every society. In direct contrast to Aristotle, Kant begins by saying that what is ultimately good is none of those benefits and virtues that make up Greek happiness, but rather what he calls a good will. And a good will, in turn, is the will that exercises pure practical reason.

FROM *FUNDAMENTAL PRINCIPLES
OF THE METAPHYSICS OF MORALS*
BY **IMMANUEL KANT**

Nothing can possibly be conceived in the world, or even out of it, which can be called good without qualification, except a *good will.* Intelligence, wit, judgment, and other *talents* of the mind, however they may be named, or courage, resolution, perseverance, as qualities of temperament, are undoubtedly good and desirable in many respects; but these gifts of nature may also become extremely bad and mischievous if the will which is to make use of them, and which, therefore, constitutes what is called *character,* is not good. It is the same with the *gifts of fortune.* Power, riches, honor, even health, and the general well being and contentment with one's condition which is called *happiness,* inspire pride and often presumption, if there is not a good will to correct the influence of these on the mind, and with this also to rectify the whole principle of acting, and adapt it to its end. The sight of a being who is not adorned with a single feature of a pure and good will, enjoying unbroken prosperity, can never give pleasure to an impartial rational spectator. Thus a good will appears to constitute the indispensable condition even of being worthy of happiness.[14]

The argument behind this opening move is this: It makes no sense to blame or praise a person for his or her character or abilities or the consequences of his or her actions. Many factors contribute to a person's circumstances. Whether or not a person is wealthy, intelligent, courageous, witty, and so on (Aristotle's virtues) is often due to his or her upbringing and heredity rather than any personal choice. But what

---

[14] Immanuel Kant, *Fundamental Principles of the Metaphysics of Morals,* trans. T. K. Abbott (New York: Longmans, Green, 1898). All subsequent quotations from Kant are from this edition.

we *will,* that is, what we try to do, is wholly within our control. Therefore it is the only thing that is ultimately worth moral consideration. Notice that Kant is concerned with questions of morality and not questions of the good life in general. What makes us happy is not particularly his concern. He is only concerned with what makes a person morally *worthy* of being happy.

> A good will is good not because of what it performs or effects, not by its aptness for the attainment of some proposed end, but simply by virtue of the volition— that is, it is good in itself, and considered by itself is to be esteemed much higher than all that can be brought about by it in favor of any inclination, nay, even of the sum-total of all inclinations. Even if it should happen that, owing to special disfavor of fortune, or the niggardly provision of a step-motherly nature, this will should wholly lack power to accomplish its purpose, if with its greatest efforts it should yet achieve nothing, and there should remain only the good will (not, to be sure, a mere wish, but the summoning of all means in our power), then, like a jewel, it would still shine by its own light, as a thing which has its whole value in itself. Its usefulness or fruitlessness can neither add to nor take away anything from this value. It would be, as it were, only the setting to enable us to handle it the more conveniently in common commerce, or to attract it to the attention of those who are not yet connoisseurs, but not to recommend it to true connoisseurs, or to determine its value.
>
> There is, however, something so strange in this idea of the absolute value of the mere will, in which no account is taken of its utility, that notwithstanding the thorough assent of even common reason to the idea, yet a suspicion must arise that it may perhaps really be the product of mere high-flown fancy, and that we may have misunderstood the purpose of nature in assigning reason as the governor of our will. Therefore we will examine this idea from this point of view.

Kant's argument here is surprisingly similar to Aristotle's argument in his *Ethics.* You remember that Aristotle argues that the good for man must be found in man's nature, in that which is unique to him. The assumption is that since man is singularly endowed with reason, then reason must have a special significance in human life. Kant's argument also begins with the observation that man, unlike other creatures, is capable of reasoning. But why should he have such a capacity? Not in order to make him happy, Kant argues, because any number of instincts would have served that end more effectively. (Remember that Kant is presupposing God as Creator here, so he believes, like Leibniz, that everything exists for some sufficient reason.)

> . . . our existence has a different and far nobler end, for which and not for happiness, reason is properly intended, and which must, therefore, be regarded as the supreme condition to which the private ends of man must, for the most part, be postponed.

This "far nobler end" and "supreme condition" is what Kant calls *duty.* "The notion of duty," he tells us, "includes that of a good will," but a good will that subjects itself to rational principles. Those rational principles are moral laws, and it is action in accordance with such laws that alone makes a man good.

It is important, however, to make a distinction, which Aristotle makes too: It is one thing to do what duty requires for some personal interest, and it is something else to do one's duty just because it is one's duty. For example, a grocer might refuse to cheat his customers (which is his duty) because it would be bad for business; then he is not acting for the sake of duty, but for personal interests. But he may refuse to cheat his customers just because he knows that he ought not to. This does count as doing his duty and thereby makes him morally worthy.

I omit here all actions which are already recognized as inconsistent with duty, although they may be useful for this or that purpose, for with these the question whether they are done *from duty* cannot arise at all, since they even conflict with it. I also set aside those actions which really conform to duty, but to which men have *no* direct *inclination,* performing them because they are impelled thereto by some other inclination. For in this case we can readily distinguish whether the action which agrees with duty is done *from duty* or from a selfish view. It is much harder to make this distinction when the action accords with duty, and the subject has besides a *direct* inclination to it. For example, it is always a matter of duty that a dealer should not overcharge an inexperienced purchaser; and wherever there is much commerce the prudent tradesman does not overcharge, but keeps a fixed price for everyone, so that a child buys of him as well as any other. Men are thus *honestly* served; but this is not enough to make us believe that the tradesman has so acted from duty and from principles of honesty; his own advantage required it; it is out of the question in this case to suppose that he might besides have a direct inclination in favor of the buyers, so that, as it were, from love he should give no advantage to one over another. Accordingly the action was done neither from duty nor from direct inclination, but merely with a selfish view.

On the other hand, it is a duty to maintain one's life; and, in addition, everyone has also a direct inclination to do so. But on this account the often anxious care which most men take for it has no intrinsic worth, and their maximum has no moral import. They preserve their life *as duty requires,* no doubt, but not *because duty requires.* On the other hand, if adversity and hopeless sorrow have completely taken away the relish for life, if the unfortunate one, strong in mind, indignant at his fate rather than desponding or dejected, wishes for death, and yet preserves his life without loving it—not from inclination or fear, but from duty—then his maxim has a moral worth.

To be beneficent when we can is a duty; and besides this, there are many minds so sympathetically constituted that, without any other motive of vanity or self-interest, they find a pleasure in spreading joy around them, and can take delight in the satisfaction of others so far as it is their own work. But I maintain that in such a case an action of this kind, however proper, however amiable it may be, has nevertheless no true moral worth, but is on a level with other inclinations, for example, the inclination to honor, which, if it is happily directed to that which is in fact of public utility and accordant with duty, and consequently honorable, deserves praise and encouragement, but not esteem. For the maxim lacks the moral import, namely, that such actions be done *from duty,* not from inclination. Put the case that the mind of that philanthropist was clouded by sorrow of his own extinguishing all sympathy with the lot of others, and that while he still has the power to benefit others in distress he is not touched by their trouble because he is absorbed with his own; and now suppose that he tears himself out of this dread insensibility and performs the action without any inclination to it, but simply from duty, then first has his action its genuine moral worth. Further still, if nature has put little sympathy in the heart of this or that man, if he, supposed to be an upright man, is by temperament cold and indifferent to the sufferings of others, perhaps because in respect of his own he is provided with the special gift of patience and fortitude and supposes, or even requires, that others should have the same—and such a man would certainly not be the meanest product of nature—but if nature had not specially framed him for a philanthropist, would he not still find in himself a source from whence to give himself a far higher worth than that of a good-natured temperament could be? Unquestionably. It is just in this that the moral worth of the character is brought out which is incomparably the highest of all, namely, that he is beneficent, not from inclination, but from duty.

In a curious two short paragraphs, Kant tells us that we have a duty to make ourselves happy, not because we want to be happy (wants are never duties) but because it is necessary for us to do our other duties. Then, with reference to the Bible, Kant makes a famous (or infamous) distinction between two kinds of love: practical love, which is commanded as a duty, and pathological love, in other words, what we would call the *emotion* of love.

To secure one's own happiness is a duty, at least indirectly; for discontent with one's condition, under a pressure of many anxieties and amidst unsatisfied wants, might easily become a great *temptation to transgression of duty.* But here again, without looking to duty, all men have already the strongest and most intimate inclination to happiness, because it is just in this idea that all inclinations are combined in one total. But the precept of happiness is often of such a sort that it greatly interferes with some inclinations, and yet a man cannot form any definite and certain conception of the sum of satisfaction of all of them which is called happiness. It is not then to be wondered at that a single inclination, definite both as to what it promises and as to the time within which it can be gratified, is often able to overcome such a fluctuating idea, and that a gouty patient, for instance, can choose to enjoy what he likes, and to suffer what he may, since, according to his calculation, on this occasion at least, he has [only] not sacrificed the enjoyment of the present moment to a possibly mistaken expectation of a happiness which is supposed to be found in health. But even in this case, if the general desire for happiness did not influence his will, and supposing that in his particular case health was not a necessary element in this calculation, there yet remains in this, as in all other cases, this law—namely, that he should promote his happiness not from inclination but from duty, and by this would his conduct first acquire true moral worth.

It is in this manner, undoubtedly, that we are to understand those passages of Scripture also in which we are commanded to love our neighbor, even our enemy. For love, as an affection, cannot be commanded, but beneficence for duty's sake may, even though we are not impelled to it by any inclination—nay, are even repelled by a natural and unconquerable aversion. This is *practical* love, and not *pathological*—a love which is seated in the will, and not in the propensions of sense—in principles of action and not of tender sympathy; and it is this love alone which can be commanded.

Having thus defended his primary proposition that what is ultimately good is a good will acting in accordance with practical reason, in other words, from duty, Kant moves on to two corollary propositions:

The second proposition is: That an action done from duty derives its moral worth, *not from the purpose* which is to be attained by it, but from the maxim by which it is determined, and therefore does not depend on the realization of the object of the action, but merely on the *principle of volition* by which the action has taken place, without regard to any object of desire. It is clear from what precedes that the purposes which we may have in view in our actions, or their effects regarded as ends and springs of the will cannot give to actions any unconditional or moral worth. In what, then, can their worth lie if it is not to consist in the will and in reference to its expected effect? It cannot lie anywhere but in the *principle of the will* without regard to the ends which can be attained by the action. For the will stands between its *a priori* principle, which is formal, and its *a posteriori* spring which is material, as between two roads, and as it must be determined by something, it follows that it must be determined by the formal principle of volition when an action is done from duty, in which case every material principle has been withdrawn from it.

The third proposition, which is a consequence of the two preceding, I would express thus: *Duty is the necessity of acting from respect for the law.* I may have *inclination* for an object as the effect of my proposed action, but I cannot have *respect* for it just for this reason that it is an effect and not an energy of will. Similarly, I cannot have respect for inclination, whether my own or another's; I can at most, if my own, approve it; if another's, sometimes even love it, that is, look on it as favorable to my own interest. It is only what is connected with my will as a principle, by no means as an effect—what does not subserve my inclination, but overpowers it, or at least in case of choice excludes it from its calculation—in other words, simply the law of itself, which can be an object of respect, and hence a command. Now an action done from duty must wholly exclude the influence of inclination, and with it every object of the will, so that

Now an action done from duty must wholly exclude the influence of inclination, and with it every object of the will, so that nothing remains which can determine the will except objectively the **law**, *and subjectively* **pure** respect *for this practical law, and consequently the maxim that I should follow this law even to the thwarting of all my inclinations.*

nothing remains which can determine the will except objectively the *law,* and subjectively *pure respect* for this practical law, and consequently the maxim that I should follow this law even to the thwarting of all my inclinations.

Thus the moral worth of an action does not lie in the effect expected from it, nor in any principle of action which requires to borrow its motive from this expected effect. For all these effects—agreeableness of one's condition, and even the promotion of the happiness of others—could have been also brought about by other causes, so that for this there would have been no need of the will of a rational being; whereas it is in this alone that the supreme and unconditional good can be found. The pre-eminent good which we call moral can therefore consist in nothing else than *the conception of law* in itself, *which certainly is only possible in a rational being,* in so far as this conception, and not the expected effect, determines the will. This is a good which is already preset in the person who acts accordingly, and we have not to wait for it to appear first in the result.

By what sort of law can that be the conception of which must determine the will, even without paying any regard to the effect expected from it, in order that this will may be called good absolutely and without qualification? As I have deprived the will of every impulse which could arise to it from obedience to any law, there remains nothing but the universal conformity of its actions to law in general, which alone is to serve the will as a principle.

This conception of "universal conformity to law" is Kant's central notion of duty. He defines it, as we shall see, as a generalized version of the Golden Rule: "Do unto others as you would have them do unto you." The point is, decide what you ought to do by asking yourself the question, "What if everyone were to do that?" The rule, as he states it, is

I am never to act otherwise than so, *that I could also will that my maxim should become a universal law.* Here, now, it is the simple conformity to law in general, without assuming any particular law applicable to certain actions, that serves the will as its principle, and must so serve it if duty is not to be a vain delusion and a chimerical notion. The common reason of men in its practical judgments perfectly coincides with this, and always has in view the principle here suggested.

Let the question be, for example: May I when in distress make a promise with the intention not to keep it? I readily distinguish here between the two significations which the question may have: whether it is prudent or whether it is right to make a false promise? The former may undoubtedly often be the case. I see clearly indeed that it is not enough to extricate myself from a present difficulty by means of this subterfuge, but it must be well considered whether there may not hereafter spring from this lie much greater inconvenience than that from which I now free myself, and as, with all my supposed *cunning,* the consequences cannot be so easily foreseen but that credit once lost may be much more injurious to me than any mischief which I seek to avoid at present, it should be considered whether it would not be more *prudent* to act herein according to a universal maxim, and to make it a habit to promise nothing except with the intention of keeping it. But it is soon clear to me that such a maxim will still only be based on the fear of consequences. Now it is a wholly different thing to be truthful from duty, and to be so from apprehension of injurious consequences. In the first case, the very notion of the action implies a law for me; in the second case, I must first look about elsewhere to see what results may be combined with it which would affect myself. For to deviate from the principle of duty is beyond all doubt wicked; but to be unfaithful to my maxim of prudence may often be very advantageous to me, although to abide by it is certainly safer. The shortest way, however, and an unerring one, to discover the answer to this question whether a lying promise is consistent with duty, is to ask myself, Should I be content that my maxim (to extricate myself from difficulty by a false promise) should hold good as a universal law, for myself as well as for others; and should I be able to say to myself, "Every one may make a deceitful promise when he finds himself in a difficulty from which he cannot otherwise extricate himself"? Then I presently become aware that, while I can will the lie, I can by no means will that lying should be a universal law. For with such a law there would be no promises at all, since it would be in vain to allege my intention in regard to my future actions to those who would not believe this allegation, or if they over-hastily did so, would pay me back in my own coin. Hence my maxim, as soon as it should be made a universal law, would necessarily destroy itself.

The impressive name Kant gives to this general formulation of his notion of duty is the **categorical imperative.** An imperative, however, is just what we called a command in our preliminary discussion of morality. It is of the form "do this!" or "don't do this!" The word that distinguishes moral commands in general is the word **ought,** and this tells us something about the term *categorical.* Some imperatives tell us to "do this!" but only in order to get or do something else. Kant calls these "hypothetical imperatives." For example, "go to law school" (if you want to be a lawyer) or "don't eat very hot curry" (unless you don't mind risking an ulcer). But imperatives with a moral *ought* in them are not tied to any such "if" or "in order to" conditions. They are simply "do this" or "don't do this," whatever the circumstances, whatever you would like or enjoy personally; for example, "don't lie" (no matter what). This is what Kant means by "categorical."

Now all *imperatives* command either *hypothetically* or *categorically.* The former represent the practical necessity of a possible action as means to something else that is willed (or at least which one might possibly will). The categorical imperative would be that which represented an action as necessary of itself without reference to another end, that is, as objectively necessary.

Since every practical law represents a possible action as good, and on this account, for a subject who is practically determinable by reason as necessary, all imperatives are formulae determining an action which is necessary according to the principle of a will good in some respects. If now the action is good only as a means *to something else,* then the imperative is *hypothetical;* if it is conceived as good *in itself* and consequently as being necessarily the principle of a will which of itself conforms to reason, then it is *categorical.*

With hypothetical imperatives, what is commanded depends upon particular circumstances. With moral or categorical imperatives, there are universal laws that tell us what to do in every circumstance. (A **maxim,** according to Kant, is a "subjective principle of action," or what we would call an *intention.* It is distinguished from an "objective principle," that is, a universal law of reason.)

There is therefore but one categorical imperative, namely, this: *Act only on that maxim whereby thou canst at the same time will that it should become a universal law.*

Now if all imperatives of duty can be deduced from this one imperative as from their principle, then, although it should remain undecided whether what is called duty is not merely a vain notion, yet at least we shall be able to show what we understand by it and what this notion means.

Since the universality of the law according to which effects are produced constitutes what is properly called *nature* in the most general sense (as to form)—that is, the existence of things so far as it is determined by general laws—the imperative of duty may be expressed thus: *Act as if the maxim of thy action were to become by thy will a universal law of nature.*

We will now enumerate a few duties, adopting the usual division of them into duties to ourselves and to others, and into perfect and imperfect duties.

1. A man reduced to despair by a series of misfortunes feels wearied of life, but is still so far in possession of his reason that he can ask himself whether it would not be contrary to his duty to himself to take his own life. Now he inquires whether the maxim of his action could become a universal law of nature. His maxim is: From self-love I adopt it as a principle to shorten my life when its longer duration is likely to bring more evil than satisfaction. It is asked then simply whether this principle founded on self-love can become a universal law of nature. Now we see at once that a system of nature of which it should be law to destroy life by means of the very feeling whose special nature it is to impel to the improvement of life would contradict itself, and therefore could not exist as a system of nature; hence that maxim cannot

possibly exist as a universal law of nature, and consequently would be wholly inconsistent with the supreme principle of all duty.

2. Another finds himself forced by necessity to borrow money. He knows that he will not be able to repay it, but sees also that nothing will be lent to him unless he promises stoutly to repay it in a definite time. He desires to make this promise, but he has still so much conscience as to ask himself: Is it not unlawful and inconsistent with duty to get out of a difficulty in this way? Suppose, however, that he resolves to do so, then the maxim of his action would be expressed thus: When I think myself in want of money, I will borrow money and promise to repay it, although I know that I never can do so. Now this principle of self-love or of one's own advantage may perhaps be consistent with my whole future welfare; but the question now is, Is it right? I change then the suggestion of self-love into a universal law, and state the question thus: How would it be if my maxim were a universal law? Then I see at once that it could never hold as a universal law of nature, but would necessarily contradict itself. For supposing it to be a universal law that everyone when he thinks himself in a difficulty should be able to promise whatever he pleases, with the purpose of not keeping his promise, the promise itself would become impossible, as well as the end that one might have in view in it, since no one would consider that anything was promised to him, but would ridicule all such statements as vain pretenses.

3. A third finds in himself a talent which with the help of some culture might make him a useful man in many respects. But he finds himself in comfortable circumstances and prefers to indulge in pleasure rather than to take pains in enlarging and improving his happy natural capacities. He asks, however, whether his maxim of neglect of his natural gifts, besides agreeing with his inclination to indulgence, agrees also with what is called duty. He sees then that a system of nature could indeed subsist with such a universal law, although men (like the South Sea islanders) should let their talents rest and resolve to devote their lives merely to idleness, amusement, and propagation of their species—in a word, to enjoyment; but he cannot possibly *will* that this should be a universal law of nature, or be implanted in us as such by a natural instinct. For, as a rational being, he necessarily wills that his faculties be developed, since they serve him, and have been given him, for all sorts of possible purposes.

4. A fourth, who is in prosperity, while he sees that others have to contend with great wretchedness and that he could help them, thinks: What concern is it of mine? Let everyone be as happy as Heaven pleases, or as he can make himself; I will take nothing from him nor even envy him, only I do not wish to contribute anything to his welfare or to his assistance in distress! Now no doubt, if such a mode of thinking were a universal law, the human race might very well subsist, and doubtless even better than in a state in which everyone talks of sympathy and good-will, or even takes care occasionally to put it into practice, but, on the other side, also cheats when he can, betrays the rights of men, or otherwise violates them. But although it is possible that a universal

law of nature might exist in accordance with that maxim, it is impossible to *will* that such a principle should have the universal validity of a law of nature. For a will which resolved this would contradict itself, inasmuch as many cases might occur in which one would have need of the love and sympathy of others, and in which, by such a law of nature, sprung from his own will, he would deprive himself of all hope of the aid he desires.

These are a few of the many actual duties, or at least what we regard as such, which obviously fall into two classes on the one principle that we have laid down. We must be *able to will* that a maxim of our action should be a universal law. This is the canon of the moral appreciation of the action generally. Some actions are of such a character that their maxim cannot without contradiction be even *conceived* as a universal law of nature, far from it being possible that we should *will* that it *should* be so. In others, this intrinsic impossibility is not found, but still it is impossible to *will* that their maxim should be raised to the universality of a law of nature, since such a will would contradict itself. It is easily seen that the former violate strict or rigorous (inflexible) duty; the latter only laxer (meritorious) duty. Thus it has been completely shown by these examples how all duties depend as regards the nature of the obligation (not the object of the action) on the same principle.

Another way of describing the categorical imperative, using a term from Kant that we've already encountered, is to say that it is an a priori principle, in this case, independent of any particular circumstances. Moral principles are necessary for the same reason that certain principles of knowledge are necessary, according to Kant, that is, because they are essential to human nature. It is important, therefore, for Kant to insist that moral principles, as a priori principles of reason, hold for every human being, in fact, even more generally, for every rational creature. (There is an extremely important point hidden in this phrase; traditionally, morality has always been defended on the basis of God's will, that is, we ought to be moral because God gave us the moral laws. According to Kant, however, God does not give the laws but as a rational creature He is bound to them just as we are. Thus, in answer to the question, "Are the laws of morality good because God is good or is God good because he obeys the laws of morality?" Kant would accept the latter.)

Kant's discussion of the categorical imperative is made confusing because after he has told us that "there is but one categorical imperative," he then goes on to give us others. He calls these "alternative formulations of the categorical imperative," but their effect on most readers is to confuse them unnecessarily. In actuality, for Kant there are a great many categorical imperatives. The first one Kant gave us is merely the most general. More specific examples are "don't lie!" and "keep your promises!" Another general categorical imperative is "never use people!" There is, however, a sense in which "using people" may be perfectly innocent. For example, I "use" you in order to play tennis, since I could not play alone. In such a case, you derive as much benefit from my "using you" as I do, and we could say that you are "using me" as well. But there are cases in which we are tempted to "use" people for our own benefit without any regard to their interests. This is what Kant forbids.

Now I say: man and generally any rational being *exists* as an end in himself, *not merely as a means* to be arbitrarily used by this or that will, but in all his actions, whether they concern himself or other rational beings, must be always regarded at the same time as an end. All objects of the inclinations have only a conditional worth; for if the inclinations and the wants founded on them did not exist, then their object would be without value. But the inclinations themselves, being sources of want, are so far from having an absolute worth for which they should be desired that, on the contrary, it must be the universal wish of every rational being to be wholly free from them. Thus the worth of any object which is *to be acquired* by our action is always conditional. Beings whose existence depends not on our will but on nature's, have nevertheless, if they are not rational beings, only a relative value as means, and are therefore called *things;* rational beings, on the contrary, are called *persons,*

> *. . . rational beings, on the contrary, are called* **persons,** *because their very nature points them out as ends in themselves, that is, as something which must not be used merely as means . . .*

because their very nature points them out as ends in themselves, that is, as something which must not be used merely as means, and so far therefore restricts freedom of action (and is an object of respect). These, therefore, are not merely subjective ends whose existence has a worth *for us* as an effect of our action, but *objective ends,* that is, things whose existence is an end in itself—an end, moreover, for which no other can be substituted, which they should subserve *merely* as means, for otherwise nothing whatever would possess *absolute worth;* but if all worth were conditioned and therefore contingent, then there would be no supreme practical principle of reason whatever.

If then there is a supreme practical principle or, in respect of the human will, a categorical imperative, it must be one which, being drawn from the conception of that which is necessarily an end for everyone because it is *an end in itself,* constitutes an *objective* principle of will, and can therefore serve as a universal practical law. The foundation of this principle is: *rational nature exists as an end in itself.* Man necessarily conceives his own existence as being so; so far then this is a *subjective* principle of human actions. But every other rational being regards its existence similarly, just on the same rational principle that holds for me; so that it is at the same time an objective principle from which as a supreme practical law all laws of the will must be capable of being deduced. Accordingly the practical imperative will be as follows: *So act as to treat humanity, whether in thine own person or in that of any other in every case as an end withal, never as means only.* We will now inquire whether this can be practically carried out.

To abide by the previous examples:

First, under the head of necessary duty to oneself: He who contemplates suicide should ask himself whether his action can be consistent with the idea of humanity *as an end in itself.* If he destroys himself in order to escape from painful circumstances, he uses a person merely as *a mean* to maintain a tolerable condition up to the end of life. But a man is not a thing, that is to say, something which can be used merely as means, but must in all his actions be always considered as an end in himself. I cannot, therefore, dispose in any way of a man in my own person so as to mutilate him, to damage or kill him. (It belongs to ethics proper to define this principle more precisely, so as to avoid all misunderstanding, for example, as to the amputation of the limbs in order to preserve myself; as to exposing my life to danger with a view to preserve it, etc. This question is therefore omitted here.)

Secondly, as regards necessary duties, or those of strict obligation, towards others: He who is thinking of making a lying promise to others will see at once that he would be using another man *merely as a mean,* without the latter containing at the same time the end in himself. For he whom I propose by such a promise to use for my own purpose cannot possibly assent to my mode of acting towards him, and therefore cannot himself contain the end of this action. This violation of the principle of humanity in other men is more obvious if we take in examples of attacks on the freedom and property of others. For then it is clear that he who transgresses the rights of men intends to use the person of others merely as means, without considering that as rational beings they ought always to be esteemed also as ends, that is, as beings who must be capable of containing in themselves the end of the very same action.

Thirdly, as regards contingent (meritorious) duties to oneself: It is not enough that the action does not violate humanity in our own person as an end in itself, it must also *harmonize with it.* Now there are in humanity capacities of greater perfection which belong to the end that nature has in view in regard to humanity in ourselves as the subject; to neglect these might perhaps be consistent with the *maintenance of* humanity as an end in itself, but not with the *advancement* of this end.

Fourthly, as regards meritorious duties towards others: The natural end which all men have is their own happiness. Now humanity might indeed subsist although no one should contribute anything to the happiness of others, provided he did not intentionally withdraw anything from it; but after all, this would only harmonize negatively, not positively, with *humanity as an end in itself,* if everyone does not also endeavor, as far as in him lies, to forward the ends of others. For the ends of any subject which is an end in himself ought as far as possible to be *my* ends also, if that conception is to have its *full* effect with me.

This principle that humanity and generally every rational nature is *an end in itself* (which is the supreme limiting condition of every man's freedom of action), is not borrowed from experience, *first,* because it is universal, applying as it does to all rational beings whatever, and experience is not capable of determining anything about them; *secondly,* because it does not present humanity as an end to men (subjectively), that is, as an object which men do of themselves actually adopt as an end; but as an objective end which must as a law constitute the supreme limiting condition of all our subjective ends, let them be what we will; it must therefore spring from pure reason.

In Kant's own terms, every human will is a will capable of acting according to universal laws of morality, not based upon any personal inclinations or interests but obeying rational principles that are categorical. Using this as a definition of morality, Kant then looks back at his predecessors:

> Looking back now on all previous attempts to discover the principle of morality, we need not wonder why they all failed. It was seen that man was bound to laws by duty, but it was not observed that the laws to which he is subject are *only those of his own giving,* though at the same time they are *universal,* and that he is only bound to act in conformity with his own will—a will, however, which is designed by nature to give universal laws. For when one has conceived man only as subject to a law (no matter what), then this law required some interest, either by way of attraction or constraint, since it did not originate as a law from *his own will,* but this will was according to a law obliged by *something else* to act in a certain manner. Now by this necessary consequence all the labor spent in finding a supreme principle of *duty* was irrevocably lost. For men never elicited duty, but only a necessity of acting from a certain interest.

Any morality worthy of the name, in other words, must be a product of a person's own autonomous reason yet universal at the same time, as a product of rational will and independent of personal feeling or interest. All previous philosophy, however, has insisted upon appealing to such personal feelings and interests and thus ended up with principles that were in every case hypothetical and not, according to Kant, categorical or moral. Thus morality for Aristotle depended upon a person's being a male Greek citizen. For Kant, morality and duty are completely set apart from such personal circumstances and concerns. Morality and duty have no qualifications, and, ultimately, they need have nothing to do with the good life or with happiness. In a perfect world, perhaps, doing our duty might also bring us happiness. But this is not such a world, Kant observes, and so happiness and morality are two separate concerns, with the second always to be considered the most important. (It is at this point, however, that Kant introduces his "Postulates of Practical Reason," and God in particular, in order to give us some assurance that, at least in the [very] long run, doing our duty will bring us some reward.)

Kant's conception of morality is so strict that it is hard for most people to accept. What is most difficult to accept is the idea that morality and duty have nothing to do with our personal desires, ambitions, and feelings, which Kant called our inclinations. We can agree that at least sometimes our duties and our inclinations are in conflict. But many philosophers have felt that Kant went much too far the other way in separating them entirely. Furthermore, Kant's emphasis on the categorical imperative systematically rules out all reference to particular situations and circumstances. In response to Kant, one may ask: Isn't the right thing to do often determined only within the particular context or situation? (A very recent moral philosophy called "situation ethics" has renewed this ancient demand.) Don't we have to know the particular problems and persons involved? What is right in one situation might very well be wrong in another, just because of different personalities, for example. Some people may be extremely hurt if we tell them the "truth" about themselves. On the other hand, a little "white" lie will make them feel much better. Other people are offended at any lie, however, and prefer even hurtful truths to the "ignorant bliss" of not knowing. Must not all moral rules be tempered to the particular situation?

The Kantian response to this objection would be that there are many ways to avoid hurting people other than telling lies. One can say, "no comment." One can cough conveniently, or drop the platter in one's hand. The fact that certain deceptions are institutionalized in our society (such as "regrets" for a dinner party) does not mean that a Kantian should defend them. The question, then, becomes how one formulates an accurate description of the options in such cases. Is it ever simply the case that one has a choice—hurt someone or tell a lie?

In a more general way, it has been objected that Kant's unqualified concept of morality is much too general to help us decide what to do in any particular situation. As an example, take the categorical imperative "don't steal!" Although the imperative itself, as a categorical one, must be unqualified, in order to apply it at all, we have to understand the kinds of circumstances to which it applies. Can't we have a right to steal in certain circumstances? Or, to put the same point differently, aren't there some circumstances in which "stealing" isn't really stealing at all? But what then of the situation in which a starving man steals a loaf of bread from an extremely wealthy baker. Surely he is stealing, but wouldn't we say that under the circumstances he is justified in doing so? The Kantian reply here is to distinguish between the question whether that person is *wrong* in stealing and the question of whether (or how) he should be punished. In this case, we can presume, Kant would insist that the man did wrong, but nevertheless agree that he should not be punished.

How do we decide "under which circumstances" a moral law is to be applied? Kant's formulation of the categorical imperative only tells us that we must act in such a way that anyone in similar circumstances would act the same way. What defines these "similar" circumstances? Suppose I were to say that "anyone in these circumstances, namely, being five-foot-seven and born in Detroit in 1942, having blond hair and blue eyes, and being a graduate of C. High School, may steal." Anyone in the same circumstances can steal, but, of course, I have defined the circumstances in such a way that it is extremely unlikely that anyone but myself will ever qualify. How can we avoid such trickery? Not by any considerations within the categorical imperative itself, for by its very nature it is incapable of telling us under what circumstances a moral law applies. Another way of making the same objection is to complain that there is no way of deciding how detailed the imperative must be. For example, should we simply say, "don't steal!" or rather "don't steal unless you're starving and the other person is not!" or else, "don't steal unless you're blond and blue-eyed!" and so on? Kant's reply, to prevent such abuses, is to quite clearly leave out all mention of particular circumstances in the formulation of principles. Nevertheless we have to decide in what circumstances to apply what principles, and here the question comes up once again: How narrowly must we define the circumstances? Which circumstances are relevant to the formulation of a categorical imperative? Surely it won't be to say that *none* is relevant; at least we must know enough to know whether or not this act is an instance of stealing.

There have been other objections to Kant's severe philosophy. For example, if moral principles are categorical, then what do we do when two different moral principles conflict? The rule that tells us "don't lie!" is categorical; so is the rule that tells us "keep your promises!" Suppose that I promise not to tell anyone where you will be this weekend. Then some people wishing to kill you force me to tell. I have to say something. Either I break the promise or I lie. Kant gives us no adequate way of choosing between the promise and the lie. He has ruled out any appeal to the consequences of our actions. In Kant's argument, even if your enemies are trying to kill you, it is not morally relevant. Most importantly, Kant has ruled out any appeal to what will make people happy, not only the person who must either lie or break a promise but everyone else who is involved as well. Kant would reply, presumably, that such cases of apparent conflict are due to a misrepresentation of the case. For example, one could respond to the intruders by playing dumb, or refusing to say anything, or trying to make them go away with force. The question of moral conflict thus becomes critical for Kant's moral philosophy. If moral principles conflict, we need a way of choosing between them. If they do not conflict, then we need a way of accounting for apparent conflicts and resolving them. But it is not clear that the Kantian theory gives us either a satisfactory criterion for getting out of moral quandaries or for explaining away some of the very painful moral conflicts in which we occasionally find ourselves.

G. UTILITARIANISM

In response to the harsh Kantian view of morality, with its neglect of happiness and the good life, a number of British philosophers, chiefly **Jeremy Bentham, James Mill,** and his son John Stuart Mill, developed a conception of morality that is called **utilitarianism.** It was an attempt to bring back personal inclinations and interests into moral considerations. Utilitarians wished to reconsider the consequences as well as the "will" of an action and to consider the particular circumstances of an action in an attempt to determine what is morally right. Most importantly, it was an attempt to return morality to the search for the personally satisfying life which Kant had neglected.

The basis of utilitarianism is a form of **hedonism,** the conception of the good life that says the ultimate good is pleasure and that in the final analysis we want and ought to want this pleasure. But where traditional hedonism is concerned only with one's personal pleasure, utilitarianism is concerned with pleasure in general; that is, with one's own pleasure and the pleasure of other people. In many utilitarian writings, the notions of pleasure and happiness are used interchangeably. From our earlier discussions (and especially our discussion of Aristotle), we know that we must be cautious of such an exchange. Many short-lived pleasures do not make us happy, and happiness is much more than mere pleasure. But this is a major concern for the utilitarians; their whole theory revolves around a single aim, to make the most people as happy as possible, sometimes sacrificing short-term pleasures for enduring ones. Their central principle is often summarized as "the greatest good for the greatest number."

Jeremy Bentham was motivated to formulate his utilitarian theories not so much by the strict moralism of Kant's philosophy as by the absurd complexity of the British legal system. Just as Kant sought a single principle that would simplify all morality, Bentham looked for a single principle that would simplify the law. Bentham began with the fact that people seek pleasure and avoid pain and developed the "principle of utility" on just this basis:

FROM *THE PRINCIPLES OF MORALS AND LEGISLATION* BY **JEREMY BENTHAM**

I. Nature has placed mankind under the governance of two sovereign masters, pain and pleasure. It is for them alone to point out what we ought to do, as well as to determine what we shall do. On the one hand the standard of right and wrong, on the other the chain of causes and effects, are fastened to their throne. They govern us in all we do, in all we say, in all we think; every effort we can make to throw off our subjection, will serve but to demonstrate and confirm it. In words a man may pretend to abjure their empire; but in reality he will remain subject to it all the while. The principle of utility recognizes the subjection, and assumes it for the foundation of that system, the object of which is to tear the fabric of felicity by the hands of reason and of law. Systems which attempt to question it, deal in sounds instead of sense, in caprice instead of reason, the darkness instead of light.

But enough of metaphor and declamation: it is not by such means that moral science is to be improved.

II. The principle of utility is the foundation of the present work; it will be proper therefore at the outset to give an explicit and determinate account of what is meant by it. By the principle of utility is meant that principle which approves or disapproves of every action whatsoever, according to the tendency which it appears to have to augment or diminish the happiness of the party whose interest is in question; or, what is the same thing in other words, to promote or to oppose that happiness. I say of every action whatsoever; and therefore not only of every action of a private individual, but of every measure of government.

III. By utility is meant that property in any object, whereby it tends to produce benefit, advantage, pleasure, good, or happiness, (all this in the present case comes to the same thing) or (what comes again to the same thing) to prevent the happening of mischief, pain, evil, or unhappiness to the party whose interest is considered: if that party be the community in general, then the happiness of the community: if a particular individual, then the happiness of that individual.

IV. The interest of the community is one of the most general expressions that can occur in the phraseology of morals: no wonder that the meaning of it is often lost. When it has a meaning, it is this. The community is a fictitious body, composed of the individual persons who are considered as constituting as it were its members. The interest of the community then is, what?—the sum of the interests of the several members who compose it.

V. It is in vain to talk of the interest of the community, without understanding what is the interest of the individual. A thing is said to promote the interest, or to be for the interest, of an individual, when it tends to add to the sum total of his pleasures: or, what comes to the same thing, to diminish the sum total of his pains.

> *An action ...*
> *may be said to be*
> *conformable ...*
> *to utility ... when*
> *the tendency it*
> *has to augment*
> *the happiness of*
> *the community is*
> *greater than any it*
> *has to diminish it.*

VI. An action then may be said to be conformable to the principle of utility, or, for shortness' sake, to utility, (meaning with respect to the community at large) when the tendency it has to augment the happiness of the community is greater than any it has to diminish it.

VII. A measure of government (which is but a particular kind of action, performed by a particular person or persons) may be said to be conformable to or dictated by the principle of utility, when in like manner the tendency which it has to augment the happiness of the community is greater than any which it has to diminish it.[15]

Morality, according to Bentham's principle of utility, means nothing other than action that tends to increase the amount of pleasure rather than diminish it.

X. Of an action that is conformable to the principle of utility, one may always say either that it is one that ought to be done, or at least that it is not one that ought not to be done. One may say also, that it is right it should be done; at least that it is not wrong it should be done: that it is a right action; at least that it is not a wrong action. When thus interpreted, the words ought, and right and wrong, and others of that stamp, have a meaning: when otherwise, they have none.

How does one defend this principle of utility? One cannot. To try to prove the principle is "as impossible as it is needless." People quite "naturally," whether they admit to it or not, act on the basis of it. This is not to say that they always act on it, but that is only because, according to Bentham, people do not always know what is best for them. That is the reason for formulating the principle in philosophy.

---

[15] Jeremy Bentham, *An Introduction to the Principles of Morals and Legislation* (New York: Hafner, 1948). All subsequent quotations from Bentham are from this edition.

The heart of Bentham's theory is the formulation of a procedure for deciding, in every possible case, the value of alternative courses of action. The procedure simply involves the determination of alternative amounts of pleasures and pain, according to what has appropriately been called the **happiness calculus.**

I. Pleasures then, and the avoidance of pains, are the *ends* which the legislator has in view; it behoves him therefore to understand their *value*. Pleasures and pains are the *instruments* he has to work with: it behoves him therefore to understand their force, which is gain, in other words, their value.

II. To a person considered *by himself,* the value of a pleasure or pain considered *by itself,* will be greater or less, according to the four following circumstances.

    1. Its *intensity.*
    2. Its *duration.*
    3. Its *certainty* or *uncertainty.*
    4. Its *propinquity* or *remoteness.*

III. These are the circumstances which are to be considered in estimating a pleasure or a pain considered each of them by itself. But when the value of any pleasure or pain is considered for the purpose of estimating the tendency of any *act* by which it is produced, there are two other circumstances to be taken into the account; these are,

    5. Its *fecundity,* or the chance it has of being followed by sensations of the *same* kind: that is, pleasures, if it be a pleasure: pains, if it be a pain.
    6. Its *purity,* or the chance it has of *not* being followed by sensations of the *opposite* kind: that is, pains, if it be a pleasure: pleasures, if it be a pain.

Then the test itself:

V. To take an exact account then of the general tendency of any act by which the interests of a community are affected, proceed as follows. Begin with any one person of those whose interests seem most immediately to be affected by it; and take an account,

    1. Of the value of each distinguishable *pleasure* which appears to be produced by it in the *first* instance.
    2. Of the value of each *pain* which appears to be produced by it in the *first* instance.
    3. Of the value of each pleasure which appears to be produced by it *after* the first. This constitutes the *fecundity* of the first *pleasure* and the *impurity* of the first *pain.*
    4. Of the value of each *pain* which appears to be produced by it after the first. This constitutes the *fecundity* of the first *pain,* and the *impurity* of the first pleasure.
    5. Sum up all the values of all the *pleasures* on the one side, and those of all the pains on the other. The balance, if it be on the side of pleasure,

will give the *good* tendency of the act upon the whole, with respect to the interests of that *individual* person; if on the side of pain, the *bad* tendency of it upon the whole.

6. Take an account of the *number* of persons whose interests appear to be concerned; and repeat the above process with respect to each. *Sum up* the numbers expressive of the degrees of *good* tendency, which the act has, with respect to each individual, in regard to whom the tendency of it is *good* upon the whole: do this again with respect to each individual, in regard to whom the tendency of it is *bad* upon the whole. Take the balance; which, if on the side of *pleasure,* will give the general *good tendency* of the act, with respect to the total number of community of individuals concerned; if on the side of pain the general *evil tendency,* with respect to the same community.

Let us take an example. Bentham himself discusses the problem of lust (Prop. XXX), which he says is always bad. Why? "Because if the effects of the motive are not bad, then we do not call it lust." Lust, in other words, is sexual desire that is so excessive that it brings about more pain than pleasure. Suppose you are sexually attracted to another person. How do you decide (assuming that there is already mutual agreement) whether to follow through or not? First, you estimate the amount of pleasure each person will gain. An important question is whether the pleasure of only these two people should be estimated or the pleasure of others besides. If it is a question of adultery, then the interests of at least a third person should be considered. But assuming that no such direct complications are involved, even the indirect interests of the rest of society must be considered. (If you and your potential lover are sufficiently young, should the happiness of your parents enter into your decision?) Then, after you have considered its initial pleasure, estimate the initial pain. (In this case, we may presume it will be slight.) Then ask about the longer term pleasures and pains for each person involved. If a sexual relationship will leave you feeling happy about yourself and the other person, then the subsequent pleasure will be considerable. If either person will feel regrets, or degraded, or embarrassed, or if sex will spoil a good friendship, or if a sexual relationship will set up expectations that one or both of you is unwilling to fulfill, the amount of subsequent pain may be overwhelming. Then add up the pleasures and pains for each person, match the total amount of pleasure against the total pain, and if the balance is positive, go ahead. If the balance is negative, don't do it.

Suppose, for example, you each expect a great deal of initial pleasure, and one of you expects nothing but good feelings afterward while the other expects only mild regrets. No one else need even know, and so the balance, clearly, is very positive. But suppose neither of you expects to enjoy it all that much, and the subsequent hassles will be a prolonged and troublesome bother, then, very likely the balance will be negative. We don't often make this kind of decision in this way; we simply do what we want to do at the time. And this is precisely what Bentham says we shouldn't do. He argues that it is because we so often act on the basis of impulses without rational calculations that we end up unhappy. In other words, the fact that we are usually irrational is not an argument against Bentham's principles. Their purpose is precisely to make us rational, to help us get what we really want.

There are problems with Bentham's theory. All that is considered, according to his "happiness calculus," is solely the amount of pleasure and pain. But some of you, in response to our preceding example, might well say, "It doesn't matter how much pleasure and how little pain two people will gain if they get into a sexual relationship. Under certain circumstances (if it is adultery, or simply if they are not married) such behavior is wrong! Mere happiness is not enough!" Here we see the beginning of a swing back toward Kant. To see why such a move is necessary, let us examine the following objection to Bentham.

Suppose a great many people would get a great deal of pleasure out of seeing some innocent person tortured and slaughtered like a beast. Of course the victim would suffer a great deal of pain, but by increasing the size of the crowd we could eventually obtain an amount of pleasure on the part of everyone else that more than balanced the suffering of the victim. Bentham's calculus has no way of rejecting such a gruesome outcome. A less horrible example is this: If a person gets great pleasure from some activity and no pain, there are no other considerations that apply to him or her (assuming that his or her actions do not affect others). Are we then to say that a life of sloth and self-indulgence, if it satisfies everyone and gives them a lot of pleasure and no pain, is to be preferred to any other life of any kind? Does Bentham give us any reason to try for anything "better" than being happy pigs? This was the problem that bothered Bentham's godson, John Stuart Mill.

Mill's version of utilitarianism added an important qualification to Bentham's purely quantitative calculus. He said that it is not only the quantity of pleasure that counts, but the quality as well. Needless to say, this makes the calculations much more complicated. In fact, it makes them impossible, for there cannot be precise calculations of quality, even though there can be precise calculations of quantity. Mill's now-famous example is the following: If a pig can live a completely satisfied life, while a morally concerned and thoughtful individual like Socrates cannot ever be so satisfied, is the life of the pig therefore preferable? Mill's answer is this:

> *It is better to be a human being dissatisfied than a pig satisfied; better to be Socrates dissatisfied than a fool satisfied.*

On what grounds can he say this? Aren't the pig and the fool happier?

> *If the fool, or the pig, are of a different opinion, it is because they only know their own side of the question. The other party [Socrates] knows both sides.*[16]

Some problems emerge from this theory. How are we to evaluate different "qualities" of pleasure, even if we have tried them all? But first let us look to Mill's revision of utilitarianism, as summarized in his popular pamphlet, appropriately called *Utilitarianism*. (It was Mill, not Bentham, who invented this term.) It begins with a general consideration of morality and of Kant's moral philosophy in particular.

---

[16] John Stuart Mill, *Utilitarianism* (New York: Bobbs-Merrill, 1957).

FROM *UTILITARIANISM*
BY **JOHN STUART MILL**

Our moral faculty, according to all those of its interpreters who are entitled to
the name of thinkers, supplies us only with the general principles of moral judgments; it is a branch of our reason, not of our sensitive faculty; and must be
looked to for the abstract doctrines of morality, not for perception of it in the
concrete. The intuitive, no less than what may be termed the inductive, school of
ethics insists on the necessity of general laws. They both agree that the morality
of an individual action is not a question of direct perception, but of the application of a law to an individual case. They recognize also, to a great extent, the
same moral laws but differ as to their evidence and the source from which they
derive their authority. According to the one opinion, the principles of morals are
evident *a priori,* requiring nothing to command assent except that the meaning
of the terms be understood. According to the other doctrine, right and wrong,
as well as truth and falsehood, are questions of observation and experience. But
both hold equally that morality must be deduced from principles; and the intuitive school affirm as strongly as the inductive that there is a science of morals.
Yet they seldom attempt to make out a list of the *a priori* principles which are
to serve as the premises of the science; still more rarely do they make any effort
to reduce those various principles to one first principle, or common ground of
obligation. They either assume the ordinary precepts of morals as of *a priori*
authority, or they lay down as the common groundwork of those maxims, some
generality much less obviously authoritative than the maxims themselves, and
which has never succeeded in gaining popular acceptance. Yet to support their
pretensions there ought either to be some one fundamental principle or law at
the root of all morality, or, if there be several, there should be a determinate
order of precedence among them; and the one principle, or the rule for deciding
between the various principles when they conflict, ought to be self-evident.

  To inquire how far the the bad effects of this deficiency have been mitigated
in practice, or to what extent the moral beliefs of mankind have been vitiated or
made uncertain by the absence of any distinct recognition of an ultimate standard, would imply a complete survey and criticism of past and present ethical
doctrine. It would, however, be easy to show that whatever steadiness or consistency these moral beliefs have attained has been mainly due to the tacit influence
of a standard not recognized. Although the nonexistence of an acknowledged
first principle has made ethics not so much a guide as a consecration of men's
actual sentiments, still, as men's sentiments, both in favor and of aversion, are
greatly influenced by what they suppose to be the effect of things upon their happiness, the principle of utility, or, as Bentham latterly called it, the greatest happiness principle, has had a large share in forming the moral doctrines even of
those who most scornfully eject its authority. Nor is there any school of thought
which refuses to admit that the influence of actions on happiness is a most material and even predominant consideration in many of the details, of morals, however unwilling to acknowledge it as the fundamental principle of morality and
the source of moral obligation. I might go much further and say that to all those

a priori moralists who deem it necessary to argue at all, utilitarian arguments are indispensable. It is not my present purpose to criticize these thinkers; but I cannot help referring, for illustration, to a systematic treatise by one of the most illustrious of them, the *Metaphysics of Ethics* by Kant. This remarkable man, whose system of thought will long remain one of the landmarks in the history of philosophical speculation, does, in the treatise in question, lay down a universal first principle as the origin and ground of moral obligation; it is this: "So act that the rule on which thou actest would admit of being adopted as a law by all rational beings." But when he begins to deduce from this precept any of the actual duties of morality, he fails, almost grotesquely, to show that there would be any contradiction, and logical (not to say physical) impossibility, in the adoption by all rational beings of the most outrageously immoral rules of conduct. All he knows is that the *consequences* of their universal adoption would be such as no one would choose to incur.

Then Mill gets down to the business of redefining utilitarianism. Like Bentham, he insists that the principle of utility cannot be proven as such, for it is the ultimate end in terms of which everything else is justified. But there is, Mill tells us, a "larger sense of the word 'proof' ":

On the present occasion, I shall, without further discussion of the other theories, attempt to contribute something towards the understanding and appreciation of the "utilitarian" or "happiness" theory, and towards such proof as it is susceptible of. It is evident that this cannot be proof in the ordinary and popular meaning of the term. Questions of ultimate ends are not amendable to direct proof. Whatever can be proved to be good must be so by being shown to be a means to something admitted to be good without proof. The medical art is proved to be good by its conducing to health; but how is it possible to prove that health is good? The art of music is good, for the reason, among others, that it produces pleasure; but what proof is it possible to give that pleasure is good? If, then, it is asserted that there is a comprehensive formula, including all things which are in themselves good, and that whatever else is good is not so as an end but as a means, the formula may be accepted or rejected, but is not a subject of what is commonly understood by proof. We are not, however, to infer that its acceptance or rejection must depend on blind impulse, or arbitrary choice. There is a larger meaning of the word "proof," in which this question is as amenable to it as any other of the disputed questions of philosophy. The subject is within the cognizance of the rational

> *Questions of ultimate ends are not amendable to direct proof. Whatever can be proved to be good must be so by being shown to be a means to something admitted to be good without proof.*

faculty; and neither does that faculty deal with it solely in the way of intuition. Considerations may be presented capable of determining the intellect either to give or withhold its assent to the doctrine; and this is equivalent to proof.

WHAT UTILITARIANISM IS

A passing remark is all that needs be given to the ignorant blunder of supposing that those who stand up for utility as the test of right and wrong use the term in that restricted and merely colloquial sense in which utility is opposed to pleasure. An apology is due to the philosophical opponents of utilitarianism, for even the momentary appearance of confounding them with anyone capable of so absurd a misconception; which is the more extraordinary, inasmuch as the contrary accusation, of referring everything to pleasure, and that, too, in its grossest form, is another of the common charges against utilitarianism: and, as has been pointedly remarked by an able writer, the same sort of persons, and often the very same persons, denounce the theory "as impracticably dry when the word 'utility' precedes the word 'pleasure,' and as too practicably voluptuous when the word 'pleasure' precedes the word 'utility.'" Those who know anything about the matter are aware that every writer, from Epicurus to Bentham, who maintained the theory of utility, meant by it, not something to be contradistinguished from pleasure, but pleasure itself, together with exemption from pain; and instead of opposing the useful to the agreeable to the ornamental, have always declared that the useful means these, among other things. Yet the common herd, including the herd of writers, not only in newspapers and periodicals, but in books of weight and pretension, are perpetually falling into this shallow mistake. Having caught up the word "utilitarian," while knowing nothing whatever about it but its sound, they habitually express by it the rejection or the neglect of pleasure in some of its forms: of beauty, of ornament, or of amusement. Nor is the term thus ignorantly misapplied solely in disparagement, but occasionally in compliment, as though it implied superiority to frivolity and the mere pleasures of the moment. And this perverted use is the only one in which the word is popularly known, and the one from which the new generation are acquiring their sole notion of its meaning. Those who introduced the word, but who had for many years discontinued it as a distinctive apellation, may well feel themselves called upon to resume it if by doing so they can hope to contribute anything towards rescuing it from this utter degradation.

The creed which accepts as the foundation of morals "utility" or the "greatest happiness principle" holds that actions are right in proportion as they tend to promote happiness, wrong as they tend to produce the reverse of happiness. By happiness is intended pleasure, and the absence of pain; by unhappiness, pain, and the privation of pleasure. To give a clear view of the moral standard set up by the theory, much more requires to be said; in particular, what things it includes in the ideas of pain and pleasure; and to what extent this is left an open question. But three supplementary explanations do not affect the theory of life on which this theory of morality is grounded—namely, that pleasure and freedom from pain are the only things desirable as ends, and that all desirable things (which are as numerous in the utilitarian as in any other scheme) are desirable either for the pleasure inherent in themselves, or as means to the promotion of pleasure and the prevention of pain.

Now such a theory of life excites in many minds, and among them in some of the most estimable in feeling and purpose, inveterate dislike. To suppose that life has (as they express it) no higher end than pleasure—no better and nobler object of desire and pursuit—they designate as utterly mean and groveling; as a doctrine worthy only of swine, to whom the followers of Epicurus were, at a very early period, contemptuously likened; and modern holders of the doctrine are occasionally made the subject of equally polite comparisons by its German, French, and English assailants.

When thus attacked, the Epicureans have always answered that it is not they, but their accusers, who represent human nature in a degrading light, since the accusation supposes human beings to be capable of no pleasures except those of which swine are capable. If this supposition were true, the charge could not be gainsaid, but would then be no longer an imputation; for if the sources of pleasure were precisely the same to human beings and to swine, the rule of life which is good enough for the one would be good enough for the other. The comparison of the Epicurean life to that of beasts is felt as degrading, precisely because a beast's pleasures do not satisfy a human being's conception of happiness. Human beings have faculties more elevated than the animal appetites and, when once made conscious of them, do not regard anything as happiness which does not include their gratification. I do not, indeed, consider the Epicureans to have been by any means faultless in drawing out their scheme of consequences from the utilitarian principle. To do this in any sufficient manner, many Stoic, as well as Christian, elements require to be included. But there is no known Epicurean theory of life which does not assign to the pleasures of the intellect, of the feelings and imagination, and of the moral sentiments, a much higher value of pleasures than to those of mere sensation. It must be admitted, however, that utilitarian writers in general have placed the superiority of mental over bodily pleasures chiefly in the greater permanency, safety, uncostliness, etc., of the former—that is, in their circumstantial advantages rather than in their intrinsic nature. And on all these points utilitarians have fully proved their case; but they might have taken the other and, as it may be called, higher ground with entire consistency. It is quite compatible with the principle of utility to recognize the fact that some kinds of pleasure are more desirable and more valuable than others. It would be absurd that, while, in estimating all other things, quality is considered as well as quantity, the estimation of pleasures should be supposed to depend on quantity alone.

If I am asked what I mean by difference of quality in pleasures, or what makes one pleasure more valuable than another, merely as a pleasure, except its being greater in amount, there is but one possible answer. Of two pleasures, if there be one to which all or almost all who have experience of both give a decided preference, irrespective of a feeling of moral obligation to prefer it, that is

Of two pleasures, if there be one to which all or almost all who have experience of both give a decided prefer- ence, irrespective of a feeling of moral obligation to prefer it, that is the more desir- able pleasure.

the more desirable pleasure. If one of the two is, by those who are competently acquainted with both, placed so far above the other that they prefer it, even though knowing it to be attended with a greater amount of discontent, and would not resign it for any quantity of the other pleasure which their nature is capable of, we are justified in ascribing to the pre- ferred enjoyment a superiority in quality so far out- weighing quantity as to render it, in comparison, of small account.

Now it is an unquestionable fact that those who are equally acquainted with and equally capable of appreciating and enjoying both, do give a most marked preference to the manner of existence which employs their higher faculties. Few human creatures would consent to be changed into any of the lower animals for a promise of the fullest allowance of a beast's pleasures; no intelligent human being would consent to be a fool, no instructed person would be an ignoramus, no person of feeling and conscience would be selfish and base, even though they should be persuaded that the fool, the dunce, or the rascal is better satisfied with his lot than they are with theirs. They would not resign what they possess more than he for the most complete satisfaction of all the desires which they have in common with him. If they ever fancy they would, it is only in cases of unhappiness so ex- treme that to escape from it they would exchange their lot for almost any other, however undesirable in their own eyes. A being of higher faculties requires more to make him happy, is capable probably of more acute suffering, and certainly accessible to it at more points, than one of an inferior type; but in spite of these liabilities, he can never really wish to sink into what he feels to be a lower grade of existence. We may give what explanation we please of this unwillingness; we may attribute it to pride, a name which is given indiscriminately to some of the most and to some of the least estimable feelings of which mankind are capable: we may refer it to the love of liberty and personal independence, an appeal to which was with the Stoics one of the most effective means for the inculcation of it; to the love of power or to the love of excitement, both of which do really enter into and contribute to it; but its most appropriate appellation is a sense of dignity, which all human beings possess in one form or other, and in some, though by no means in exact, proportion to their higher faculties, and which is so essential a part of the happiness of those in whom it is strong that nothing which conflicts with it could be otherwise than momentarily an object of desire to them. Whoever supposes that this preference takes place at a sacrifice of hap- piness—that the superior being, in anything like equal circumstances, is not happier than the inferior—confounds the two very different ideas of happiness and content. It is indisputable that the being whose capacities of enjoyment are low has the greatest chance of having them fully satisfied; and a highly endowed being will always feel that any happiness which he can look for, as the world is constituted, is imperfect. But he can learn to bear its imperfections, if they are at all bearable; and they will not make him envy the being who is indeed unconscious of the imperfections, but only because he feels not at all the good which those imperfections qualify. It is better to be a human being dissatisfied than a pig satisfied; better to be Socrates dissatisfied than a fool satisfied. And if the fool, or the pig, are of a different opinion, it is because they only know their own side of the question. The other party to the comparison knows both sides.

It may be objected that many who are capable of the higher pleasures occasionally, under the influence of temptation, postpone them to the lower. But this is quite compatible with a full appreciation of the intrinsic superiority of the higher. Men often, from infirmity of character, make their election for the nearer good, though they know it to be the less valuable; and this no less when the choice is between two bodily pleasures than when it is between bodily and mental. They pursue sensual indulgences to the injury of health, though perfectly aware that health is the greater good. It may be further objected that many who begin with youthful enthusiasm for everything noble, as they advance in years, sink into indolence and selfishness. But I do not believe that those who undergo this very common change voluntarily choose the lower description of pleasures in preference to the higher. I believe that, before they devote themselves exclusively to the one, they have already become incapable of the other. Capacity for the nobler feelings is in most natures a very tender plant, easily killed, not only by hostile influences, but by mere want of sustenance; and in the majority of young persons it speedily dies away if the occupations to which their position in life has devoted them, and the society into which it has thrown them, are not favorable to keeping that higher capacity in exercise. Men lose their high aspirations as they lose their intellectual tastes, because they have no time or opportunity for indulging them; and they addict themselves to inferior pleasures, not because they deliberately prefer them, but because they are either the only ones to which they have access, or the only ones which they are any longer capable of enjoying. It may be questioned whether any one who has remained equally susceptible to both classes of pleasures, ever knowingly and calmly preferred the lower, though many, in all ages, have broken down in an ineffectual attempt to combine both.

I have dwelt on this point, as being a necessary part of a perfectly just conception of utility or happiness considered as the directive rule of human conduct. But it is by no means an indispensable condition to the acceptance of the utilitarian standard; for that standard is not the agent's own greatest happiness, but the greatest amount of happiness altogether; and if it may possibly be doubted whether a noble character is always the happier for its nobleness, there can be no doubt that it makes other people happier, and that the world in general is immensely a gainer by it. Utilitarianism, therefore, could only attain its end by the general cultivation of nobleness of character, even if each individual were only benefited by the nobleness of others, and his own, so far as happiness is concerned, where a sheer deduction from the benefit. But the bare enunciation of such an absurdity as this last renders refutation superfluous.

According to the greatest happiness principle, as above explained, the ultimate end, with reference to and for the sake of which all other things are desirable—whether we are considering our own good or that of other people—is an existence exempt as far as possible from pain, and as rich as possible in enjoyments, both in point of quantity and quality, the test of quality and the rule for measuring it against quantity being the preference felt by those who, in their opportunities of experience, to which must be added their habits of self-consciousness and self-observation, are best furnished with the means of comparison. This, being, according to the utilitarian opinion, the end of human action, is necessarily also the standard of morality, which may accordingly be defined "the rules and precepts for human conduct," by the observance of which an existence such as has been described might be, to the greatest extent possible, secured to all mankind; and not to them only, but, so far as the nature of things admits, to the whole sentient creation.[17]

H. THE CREATION OF MORALITY: NIETZSCHE AND EXISTENTIALISM

The single term *morality* must not mislead us. We have been discussing not simply different theories of morality (ethics) but different conceptions of morality, and that means different moralities, even if they should have many principles in common. The problem of relativism, in other words, is not confined to the comparison of exotically different cultures. It faces us in a far more urgent form in our own conceptions of morality. We might agree that killing without extreme provocation is wrong. But why do we believe that it is wrong? One person claims that it is wrong because the Ten Commandments (and therefore God) forbid it. Another says it is wrong because it is a mark of insensitivity and therefore a flaw in character. Another says it is wrong because it violates peoples' rights, while still another says it increases the amount of pain in the world without equally adding to happiness. They all agree that killing is wrong, but the different reasons point to different circumstances in which each would kill: the first, if God commanded him or her to; the second, if the killing could be seen as a sign of strength and heroism; the third, if he or she found a way to take away people's right to live or found another right that was overriding; the fourth, as a utilitarian, would only have to find a circumstance in which the death of one person was more than balanced by the increased welfare of the others (as in a criminal execution).

From the three great moral philosophies we have studied, four such conceptions emerge. They all agree on many principles, but the reasons differ widely, and some of the principles do also. But most dramatic is the difference between Aristotle's

---

[17] Mill, *Utilitarianism.*

ancient Greek morality and Kant's modern morality of duty. Kant's morality may be taken as a fair representation of the modern Judeo-Christian morality in its strictest form: the emphasis on moral principle and laws, the emphasis on reason and individual autonomy, the emphasis on good intentions ("a good will") and doing one's duty. There are small differences that we have already pointed out: the Greek emphasis on pride as a virtue in contrast to the Christian condemnation of pride as a "deadly sin" (or at least a personality flaw) and its emphasis on humility. One of Aristotle's first virtues was courage in battle, while most modern moralities consider that as a special case, not as a matter of being an everyday "good person" at all. This difference might well be attributed to the different political climates of the two societies. But that is not enough. As we shall see, the differences are much deeper than that.

There are crucial differences between ancient and modern moral perspectives; the most striking is the difference in the scope of their applicability. In Aristotle's moral philosophy, only a small elite is thought to be capable of true happiness (*eudaimonia*) through virtuous action and contemplation. Other people (women, slaves, noncitizens) may live comfortably enough and do their duties and chores efficiently, but they cannot be called "happy." The elite, however, are characterized by their excellence, by their individual achievements, including wealth, power, honor, intelligence, wit, and all of those rewards that come with an aristocratic upbringing, the best of education and a life that is guaranteed in basic comforts from birth. In Kant's conception of morality, by contrast, all people who are rational (that is, everyone except morons, very young children, and popular musicians) are to be judged by the same moral standards, the standards of duty. There are no elites. And since the judgments of moral worth are made solely on the basis of good intentions, no "external" advantages are relevant to a person's goodness or badness. In fact, it is possible that a perfectly "good" person would, with only the best intentions, cause chaos and unhappiness around him wherever he goes. And the harder he tries to make amends, the more he fouls them up. Dostoyevski wrote one of his greatest novels, *The Idiot,* about just this—a perfectly good man, with all the right intentions, causes suffering and even death every time he tries to do good. Yet the point is, he is, by this modern conception, still the perfectly good man. Aristotle would find this laughable. How could we call a man virtuous just because of his intentions? How can a perfect failure be an example of ideal goodness?

In Aristotle's morality, the only people who operate on the basis of duty are those who are incapable of being truly good and truly happy. Duty is a morality for women and servants. For the elite, it is rather a question of personal excellence—in battle, in games, in business, in love, in debate, and in all things, especially philosophy. And where Kant's morality mostly consists (like the Ten Commandments) of "thou shalt not . . ." Aristotle's morality appropriately consists of personal desires and ambitions, not commands to achieve, and certainly not negative commands. The key element of Kant's philosophy, duty, is treated minimally in Aristotle, where the emphasis is on personal growth and achievement. On the other side, the image of the well-rounded, successful man, excellent in all things and the envy of his fellow men, plays only a secondary role in Kant's philosophy (for example, in his *Doctrine of Virtue,* the second part of the *Metaphysics of Morals*). For him, what is important is the person who does what he or she is supposed to do. For Aristotle, the ideal is to strive for personal excellence, and doing what a person is supposed to do is simply taken for granted along the way.

Now notice that both moralities have many of the same results. Aristotle's morality will praise many and condemn most of the same acts as Kant's morality: Killing needlessly and stealing are wrong; telling the truth and keeping promises are right. But their conceptions of morality, and consequently, their conceptions of people are distinctively different. As we appreciate the nature of this difference, we will be in a position to understand one of the most dramatic moral revolutions of modern times, initiated by Friedrich Nietzsche. Nietzsche called himself an **immoralist,** and he attacked morality as viciously as he attacked Christianity. But though he has often been interpreted as saying that we should give up morality and feel free to kill, steal, and commit crimes of all kinds, his moral philosophy does not in fact say that at all. What he did was to attack modern morality, as summarized by Kant and Christianity, and urge us to return to ancient Greek morality as summarized by Aristotle. He also attacked utilitarianism, which he considered "vulgar." Like a great many philosophers of the nineteenth century (particularly German philosophers: Fichte, Hegel, Marx), Nietzsche saw in the ancient Greeks a sense of personal harmony and a sense of excellence that had been lost in the modern world. Nietzsche, like Aristotle, saw the concept of duty as fit for servants and slaves, but such a morality was wholly inadequate to motivate us to personal excellence and achievement. And Nietzsche, like Aristotle, was an unabashed elitist. Only a few people were capable of this "higher" morality. For the rest, the "slave morality" of duty would have to suffice. But for those few, nothing was more important than to give up the "thou shalt not . . ." of Judeo-Christian morality and seek out one's own virtues and abilities. This does not mean that such a person need ever violate the laws of morality although it must be said that Nietzsche's belligerent style and often warlike terminology certainly suggests that his master morality will include a good amount of cruelty and immorality. But it is clear that Nietzsche does not consider obedience to laws as the most important thing in life. Nor does this mean that Nietzsche is (as he is often thought to be) an ethical egoist. To say that a person should develop his or her own virtues and become excellent in as many ways as possible is not at all to say that one must act only in one's own interests. As in Aristotle, the excellence of the individual is part of and contributes to the excellence of mankind as a whole.

Nietzsche takes his central project as a philosopher to be what he calls "the creation of values." In this he is rightly listed as one of the existentialist philosophers, or at least as one of their most important predecessors. The phrase is perhaps misleading, however. What Nietzsche is doing is not inventing new values so much as reasserting very old ones. Furthermore, Nietzsche, like Aristotle, takes ethics to be based solely upon human nature, and so it is not a question of "creating values" so much as finding them in oneself. But where such a philosophy for Aristotle was in agreement with most of the thinking of his times, Nietzsche's thought was a radical disruption of the usual Kantian style of thinking of the modern period and so takes on the tone of violent destructiveness rather than—as in Aristotle—the self-satisfied tones of a gentleman. Since Nietzsche, unlike Aristotle, did not believe that every human "nature" was the same, he taught that different individuals would most assuredly find and follow different values, different conceptions of excellence and thus have different moralities. For this reason, students who read Nietzsche looking for concrete moral advice, a set of principles to act on, are always disappointed. His central teaching is rather "follow yourself, don't follow me." Consequently, he can't—and won't—try to tell you how to live. But he does tell you to live and to give up the servile views that we have held of ourselves for many centuries.

Nietzsche's moral philosophy is largely critical, and most of his efforts have gone into the rejection of Kant's conception of morality in order to make room for individual self-achieving as found in Aristotle. His argument, however, is not a refutation in the usual sense. Instead, he undermines morality by showing that the motivation behind it is decrepit and weak. categories of Nietzsche's philosophy are strength and weakness, and he considers the Greek tradition of personal excellence a source of strength, the modern conception of morality a facade for weakness. Accordingly, he calls the first a "master morality," the second, a "slave morality" or, with reference to modern mass movements, a "herd instinct." The excerpts that follow, therefore, illustrate Nietzsche's general attack on morality. But never forget that his purpose is not merely destructive but, in his eyes, creative, and the point is to get us to look to ourselves for values and to excel, each in our own ways (the phrase "will to power" refers to just this effort to excel as individuals).

By morality the individual is taught to become a function of the herd, and to ascribe to himself value only as a function.

ON "MASTER AND SLAVE MORALITY"
BY **FRIEDRICH NIETZSCHE**

What does your conscience say? "You should become him who you are."

Herd-Instinct.—Wherever we meet with a morality we find a valuation and order of rank of the human impulses and activities. These valuations and orders of rank are always the expression of the needs of a community or herd: that which is in the first place to *its* advantage—and in the second place and third place—is also the authoritative standard for the worth of every individual. By morality the individual is taught to become a function of the herd, and to ascribe to himself value only as a function. As the conditions for the maintenance of one community have been very different from those of another community, there have been very different moralities; and in respect to the future essential transformations of herd and communities, states and societies, one can prophesy that there will still be very divergent moralities. Morality is the herd-instinct in the individual.[18]

---

[18]Friedrich Nietzsche, *Joyful Wisdom,* trans. Thomas Common, in *Complete Works of Friedrich Nietzsche,* Oscar Levy, gen. ed. (1909–11) (New York: Russell & Russell, 1964).

Apart from the value of such assertions as "there is a categorical imperative in us," one can always ask: What does such an assertion indicate about him who makes it? There are systems of morals which are meant to justify their author in the eyes of other people; other systems of morals are meant to tranquillise him, and make him self-satisfied; with other systems he wants to crucify and humble himself; with others he wishes to take revenge; with others to conceal himself; with others to glorify himself and gain superiority and distinction;— this system of morals helps its author to forget, that system makes him, or something of him, forgotten; many a moralist would like to exercise power and creative arbitrariness over mankind; many another, perhaps, Kant especially, gives us to understand by his morals that "what is estimable in me, is that I know how to obey—and with you it *shall* not be otherwise than with me!" In short, systems of morals are only a *sign-language of the emotions*. . . .

In a tour through the many finer and coarser moralities which have hitherto prevailed or still prevail on the earth, I found certain traits recurring regularly together and connected with one another, until finally two primary types revealed themselves to me, and a radical distinction was brought to light. There is *master-morality* and *slave-morality;*—I would at once add, however, that in all higher and mixed civilisations, there are also attempts at the reconciliation of the two moralities; but one finds still oftener the confusion and mutual misunderstanding of them, indeed sometimes their close juxtaposition—even in the same man, within one soul. The distinctions of moral values have either originated in a ruling caste, pleasantly conscious of being different from the ruled—or among the ruled class, the slaves and dependents of all sorts. In the first case, when it is the rulers who determine the conception "good," it is the exalted, proud disposition which is regarded as the distinguishing feature, and that which determines the order of rank. The noble type of man separates from himself the beings in whom the opposite of this exalted, proud disposition displays itself: he despises them. Let it at once be noted that in this first kind of morality the antithesis "good" and "bad" means practically the same as "noble" and "despicable";—the antithesis "good" and "*evil*" is of a different origin. The cowardly, the timid, the insignificant, and those thinking merely of narrow utility are despised; moreover, also, the distrustful, with their constrained glances, the self-abasing, the dog-like kind of men who let themselves be abused, the mendicant flatterers, and above all the liars:—it is a fundamental belief of all aristocrats that the common people are untruthful. "We truthful ones"—the nobility in ancient Greece called themselves. It is obvious that everywhere the designations of moral value were at first applied to *men,* and were only derivatively and at a later period applied to *actions;* it is a gross mistake, therefore, when historians of morals start questions like, "Why have sympathetic actions been praised?" The noble type of man regards *himself* as a determiner of values; he does not require to be approved of; he passes the judgment: "What is injurious to me is injurious in itself"; he knows that it is he himself only who confers honour on things; he is a *creator of values.* He honours whatever he recognises in himself: such morality is self-glorification. In the foreground there is the feeling of plenitude, of power, which seeks to overflow, the happiness of high tension, the consciousness of a wealth which would fain give and bestow:—the noble man also helps the unfortunate, but not—or scarcely—out of pity, but rather from an impulse generated by the super-abundance of power. The noble man honours in himself the powerful one, him also who has power over himself, who knows how to speak and how to keep silence, who takes pleasure in subjecting himself to severity and hardness, and has reverence for all that is severe and hard. "Wotan placed a hard heart in my breast," says an old Scandinavian Saga: it is thus rightly expressed from the soul of a proud Viking. Such a type of man is even proud of *not* being made for sympathy; the hero of the Saga therefore adds warningly: "He who has not a hard heart when young, will never have one." The noble and brave who think thus are the furthest removed from the morality which sees precisely in sympathy, or in acting for the good of others, or in *désintéressement,* the characteristic of the moral; faith in oneself, pride in oneself, a radical enmity and irony towards "selflessness," belong as definitely to noble morality, as do a careless scorn and precaution in presence of sympathy and the "warm heart."—It is the powerful who *know* how to honour, it is their art, their domain for invention. The profound reverence for age and for tradition—all law rests on this double reverence,—the belief and prejudice in favour of ancestors and unfavourable to newcomers, is typical in the morality of the powerful; and if, reversely, men of "modern ideas" believe almost instinctively in "progress" and the "future," and are more and more lacking in respect for old age, the ignoble origin of these "ideas" has complacently betrayed itself thereby. A morality of the ruling class, however, is more especially foreign and irritating to present-day taste in the sternness of its principle that one has duties only to one's equals; that one may act towards beings of a lower rank, towards all that is foreign, just as seems good to one, or "as the heart desires," and in any case "beyond good and evil": it is here that sympathy and similar sentiments can have a place. The ability and obligation to exercise prolonged gratitude and prolonged revenge—both only within the circle of equals,—artfulness in retaliation, *raffinement* of the idea in friendship, a certain necessity to have enemies (as outlets for the emotions of envy, quarrelsomeness, arrogance—in fact, in order to be a good *friend*): all these are typical characteristics of the noble morality, which, as has been pointed out, is not the morality of "modern ideas," and is therefore at present difficult to realise, and also to unearth and disclose.—It is otherwise with the second type of morality, _slave-morality._ Supposing that the abused, the oppressed, the suffering, the unemancipated, the weary, and those uncertain of themselves, should moralise, what will be the common element in their moral estimates? Probably a pessimistic suspicion with regard to the entire situation of man will find expression, perhaps a condemnation of man, together with his situation. The slave has an unfavourable eye for the virtues of the powerful; he has a scepticism and distrust, a *refinement* of distrust of everything "good" that is there honoured—he would fain persuade himself that the very happiness there is not genuine. On the other hand, *those* qualities which serve to alleviate the existence of sufferers are brought into prominence and flooded with light; it is here that sympathy, the kind, helping hand, the warm heart, patience, diligence, humility, and friendliness attain to honour for here these are the most useful qualities, and almost the only means of supporting the burden of existence. Slave-morality is essentially the morality of utility. Here is the seat of the origin of the famous antithesis "good" and "evil":—power and dangerousness are assumed to reside in the evil, a certain dreadfulness, subtlety, and strength, which do not admit of being despised. According to slave-morality, therefore, the "evil" man arouses fear; according to master-morality, it is precisely the "good" man who arouses fear and seeks to arouse it, while the bad man is regarded as the despicable being. The contrast attains its maximum when, in accordance with the logical consequences of slave-morality, a shade of depreciation—it may be slight and well-intentioned—at last attaches itself to the "good" man of this morality; because, according to the servile mode of thought, the good man must in any case be the *safe* man: he is good-natured, easily deceived, perhaps a little stupid, *un bonhomme.* Everywhere that slave-morality gains the ascendency, language shows a tendency to approximate the significations of the words "good" and "stupid."—At last fundamental difference: the desire for *freedom,* the instinct for happiness and the refinements of the feeling of liberty belong as necessarily to slave-morals and morality, as artifice and enthusiasm in reverence and devotion are the regular symptoms of an aristocratic mode of thinking and estimating.—Hence we can understand without further detail why love *as a passion*—it is our European specialty—must absolutely be of noble origin.

And on the philosopher:

The philosophical workers, after the excellent pattern of Kant and Hegel, have to fix and formalise some great existing body of valuations—that is to say, former *determinations of value,* creations of value, which have become prevalent, and are for a time called "truths"—whether in the domain of the *logical,* the *political* (moral), or the *artistic.* It is for these investigators to make whatever has happened and been esteemed hitherto, conspicuous, conceivable, intelligible, and manageable, to shorten everything long, even "time" itself, and to *subjugate* the entire past; an immense and wonderful task, in the carrying out of which all refined pride, all tenacious will, can surely find satisfaction. *The real philosophers, however, are commanders and law-givers;* they say: "Thus *shall* it be!" They determine first the Whither and the Why of mankind, and thereby set aside the previous labour of all philosophical workers and all subjugators of the past— they grasp at the future with a creative hand, and whatever is and was, becomes for them thereby a means, an instrument, and a hammer. Their "knowing" is *creating,* their creating is a law-giving, their will to truth is—*Will to Power.*— Are there at present such philosophers? Have there ever been such philosophers? *Must* there not be such philosophers some day?[19]

---

[19] Friedrich Nietzsche, *Beyond Good and Evil,* trans. Helen Zimmern, in *Complete Works of Friedrich Nietzsche,* Oscar Levy, gen. ed. (1909–11) (New York: Russell & Russell, 1964).

Nietzsche is often viewed as the most extreme of the antimoralists, those who attack the traditional duty-bound Kantian-Christian conception of morality. In fact, he is but one among many philosophers who have rejected that morality in exchange for a more personal and individual set of principles. Given his emphasis on human "nature," we can say that even Nietzsche is much more traditional than is usually supposed (though it is the Aristotelian, not the Kantian tradition). In the past few decades, however, morality has become far more personalized than even Nietzsche suggested. In Anglo-American philosophy, largely in the wake of logical positivism, ethics has been reduced to a matter of emotions, prescriptions, and attitudes rather than principles and rational laws. (Ironically, Nietzsche has always been in extreme disfavor among such philosophers while Kant has been considered with extreme favor.)

The attack on the absolute moral principles of reason, which are the same for everyone, has been one of the most vigorous philosophical movements of the twentieth century, so much so that many philosophers, religious leaders, and moralists have become alarmed at the destruction of uniform moral codes and have attempted to reassert the old moral laws in new ways. The problem is one of relativism. Is there a single moral code? Or are there possibly as many moralities as there are people? There are intermediary suggestions, such as relativizing morals to particular groups or societies, but the question is still the same: "Is there ultimately any way of defending one moral code against any other?"

The most extreme relativist position of all has emerged from Nietzsche's existentialist successors, particularly Jean-Paul Sartre. In Sartre's philosophy, not only the idea of a uniform morality but the idea of a human nature upon which this morality might be based is completely rejected. Not because different people might have different "natures," as in Nietzsche, but because for Sartre our values are quite literally a question of creation, of personal commitment. In answer to any question about morality, the only ultimate answer is "because I choose to accept these values." But what is most fascinating about Sartre's conception of morality as choice is that he does not therefore abandon general principles as Nietzsche does. Quite the contrary, he adopts an almost Kantian stance about the need to choose principles for all mankind, not just oneself. The difference is that Sartre, unlike Kant, makes no claims about the singular correctness of these principles. All he can say is "this is what I choose mankind to be." Thus Sartre's moral philosophy is a curious mixture of the most radical relativism and the most traditional moralizing.

FROM **"EXISTENTIALISM"**
BY **JEAN-PAUL SARTRE**

Man is nothing else but that which he makes of himself. That is the first principle of existentialism. And this is what people call its "subjectivity," using the word as a reproach against us. But what do we mean to say by this, but that man is of a greater dignity than a stone or a table? For we mean to say that man primarily exists—that man is, before all else, something which propels itself towards a future and is aware that it is doing so. Man is, indeed, a project which possesses a subjective life, instead of being a kind of moss, or a fungus or a cauliflower. Before that projection of the self nothing exists; not even in the heaven of intelligence; man will only attain existence when he is what he purposes to be. Not, however, what he may wish to be. For what we usually understand by wishing or willing is a conscious decision taken—much more often than not—after we have made ourselves what we are. I may wish to join a party, to write a book or to marry—but in such a case what is usually called my will is probably a manifestation of a prior and more spontaneous decision. If, however, it is true that existence is prior to essence, man is responsible for what he is. Thus, the first effect of existentialism is that it puts every man in possession of himself as he is, and places the entire responsibility for his existence squarely upon his own shoulders.

. . . when we say that man is responsible for himself, we do not mean that he is responsible only for his own individuality, but that he is responsible for all men.

And, when we say that man is responsible for himself, we do not mean that he is responsible only for his own individuality, but that he is responsible for all men. The word "subjectivism" is to be understood in two senses, and our adversaries play upon only one of them. Subjectivism means, on the one hand, the freedom of the individual subject and, on the other, that man cannot pass beyond human subjectivity. It is the latter which is the deeper meaning of existentialism. When we say that man chooses himself, we do mean that every one of us must choose himself; but by that we also mean that in choosing for himself he chooses for all men. For in effect, of all the actions a man may take in order to create himself as he wills to be, there is not one which is not creative, at the same time, of an image of man such as he believes he ought to be. To choose between this or that is at the same time to affirm the value of that which is chosen; for we are unable ever to choose the worse. What we choose is always the better and nothing can be better for us unless it is better for all. If, moreover, existence precedes essence and we will to exist at the same time as we fashion our image, that image is valid for all and for the entire epoch in which we find ourselves. Our responsibility is thus much greater than we had supposed, for it concerns mankind as a whole. If I am a worker, for instance, I may choose to join a Christian rather than a Communist trade union. And if, by that membership, I choose to signify that resignation is, after all, the attitude that best becomes a man, that man's kingdom is not upon this earth, I do not commit myself alone to that view. Resignation is my will for everyone, and my action is, in consequence, a commitment on behalf of all mankind. Or if, to take a more personal case, I decide to marry and to have children, even though this decision proceeds simply from my situation, from my passion or my desire, I am thereby committing not only myself, but humanity as a whole, to the practice of monogamy. I am thus responsible for myself and for all men, and I am creating a certain image of man as I would have him to be. In fashioning myself I fashion man. . . .

. . . Who can prove that I am the proper person to impose, by my own choice, my conception of man upon mankind? I shall never find any proof whatever; there will be no sign to convince me of it. . . .

If I regard a certain course of action as good, it is only I who choose to say that it is good and not bad. . . . nevertheless I also am obliged at every instant to perform actions which are examples. Everything happens to every man as though the whole human race had its eyes fixed upon what he is doing and regulated its conduct accordingly. . . .

As an example by which you may the better understand this state of abandonment, I will refer to the case of a pupil of mine, who sought me out in the following circumstances. His father was quarrelling with his mother and was also inclined to be a "collaborator"; his elder brother had been killed in the German offensive of 1940 and this young man, with a sentiment somewhat primitive but generous, burned to avenge him. His mother was living alone with him, deeply afflicted by the semi-treason of his father and by the death of her eldest son, and her only consolation was in this young man. But he, at this momemt, had the choice between going to England to join the Free French Forces or of staying near his mother, and helping her to live. He fully realized that this woman lived only for him and that his disappearance—or perhaps his death—would plunge her into despair. He also realized that, concretely and in fact, every action he performed on his mother's behalf would be sure of effect in the sense of aiding her to live, whereas anything he did in order to go and fight would be an ambiguous action which might vanish like water into sand and serve no purpose. For instance, to set out for England he would have to wait indefinitely in a Spanish camp on the way through Spain; or, on arriving in England or in Algiers he might be put into an office to fill up forms. Consequently, he found himself confronted by two very different modes of action; the one concrete, immediate, but directed towards only one individual; and the other an action addressed to an end infinitely greater, a national collectivity, but for that very reason ambiguous—and it might be frustrated on the way. At the same time, he was hesitating between two kinds of morality; on the one side the morality of sympathy, of personal devotion and, on the other side, a morality of wider scope but of more debatable validity. He had to choose between those two. What could help him to choose? Could the Christian doctrine? No. Christian doctrine says: Act with charity, love your neighbour, deny yourself for others, choose the way which is hardest, and so forth. But which is the harder road? To whom does one owe the more brotherly love, the patriot or the mother? Which is the more useful aim, the general one of fighting in and for the whole community, or the precise aim of helping one particular person to live? Who can give an answer to that *a priori?* No one. Nor is it given in any ethical scripture. The Kantian ethic says, Never regard another as a means, but always as an end. Very well; if I remain with my mother, I shall be regarding her as the end and not as a means: but by the same token I am in danger of treating as means those who are fighting on my behalf; and the converse is also true, that if I go to the aid of the combatants I shall be treating them as the end at the risk of treating my mother as a means.

If values are uncertain, if they are still too abstract to determine the particular, concrete case under consideration, nothing remains but to trust in our instincts. That is what this young man tried to do; and when I saw him he said, "In the end, it is feeling that counts; the direction in which it is really pushing me is the one I ought to choose. If I feel that I love my mother enough to sacrifice everything else for her—my will to be avenged, all my longings for action and adventure—then I stay with her. If, on the contrary, I feel that my love for her is not enough, I go." But how does one estimate the strength of a feeling? The value of his feeling for his mother was determined precisely by the fact that he was standing by her. I may say that I love a certain friend enough to sacrifice such or such a sum of money for him, but I cannot prove that unless I have done it. I may say, "I love my mother enough to remain with her," if actually I have remained with her. I can only estimate the strength of this affection if I have performed an action by which it is defined and ratified. But if I then appeal to this affection to justify my action, I find myself drawn into a vicious circle. . . .

In other words, feeling is formed by the deeds that one does; therefore I cannot consult it as a guide to action. And that is to say that I can neither seek within myself for an authentic impulse to action, nor can I expect, from some ethic, formulae that will enable me to act. You may say that the youth did, at least, go to a professor to ask for advice. But if you seek counsel—from a priest, for example—you have selected that priest; and at bottom you already knew, more or less, what he would advise. In other words, to choose an adviser is nevertheless to commit oneself by that choice. If you are a Christian, you will say, Consult a priest; but there are collaborationists, priests who are resisters and priests who wait for the tide to turn: which will you choose? Had this young man chosen a priest of the resistance, or one of the collaboration, he would have decided beforehand the kind of advice he was to receive. Similarly, in coming to me, he knew what advice I should give him, and I had but one reply to make. You are free, therefore choose—that is to say, invent. No rule of general morality can show you what you ought to do.

To say that it does not matter what you choose is not correct. In one sense choice is possible, but what is not possible is not to choose. I can always choose but I must know that if I do not choose, that is still a choice. This although it may appear merely formal, is of great importance as a limit to fantasy and caprice. For, when I confront a real situation—for example, that I am a sexual being, able to have relations with a being of the other sex and able to have children—I am obliged to choose my attitude to it, and in every respect I bear the responsibility of the choice which, in committing myself, also commits the whole of humanity. . . . Man finds himself in an organized situation in which he is himself involved: his choice involves mankind in its entirety, and he cannot avoid choosing. Either he must remain single, or he must marry without having children, or he must marry and have children. In any case, and whichever he may choose, it is impossible for him, in respect of this situation, not to take complete responsibility. Doubtless he chooses without reference to any pre-established values, but it is unjust to tax him with caprice. Rather let us say that the moral choice is comparable to the construction of a work of art.

◆◆◆

No one can tell what the painting of tomorrow will be like; one cannot judge a painting until it is done. What has that to do with morality: We are in the same creative situation. We never speak of a work of art as irresponsible; when we are discussing a canvas by Picasso, we understand very well that the composition became what it is at the time when he was painting it, and that his works are part and parcel of his entire life.

There is this in common between art and morality, that in both we have to do with creation and invention. We cannot decide a priori what it is that should be done.

It is the same upon the plane of morality. There is this in common between art and morality, that in both we have to do with creation and invention. We cannot decide a priori what it is that should be done. I think it was made sufficiently clear to you in the case of that student who came to see me, that to whatever ethical system he might appeal, the Kantian or any other, he could find no sort of guidance whatever; he was obliged to invent the law for himself. Certainly we cannot say that this man, in choosing to remain with his mother—that is, in taking sentiment, personal devotion and concrete charity as his moral foundations—would be making an irresponsible choice, nor could we do so if he preferred the sacrifice of going away to England. Man makes himself; he is not found ready-made; he makes himself by the choice of his morality, and he cannot but choose a morality, such is the pressure of circumstances upon him.[20]

Sartre says that "man makes himself." He believes this to be true both individually and collectively. It is through my actions that I commit myself to values, not through principles I accept a priori or rules that are imposed upon me by God or society. If you accept the voice of some authority, you have chosen to accept that authority rather than some other. If you appeal for advice or help, you have chosen to seek that kind of advice rather than some other kind. If you refuse to choose between alternatives, then you are responsible for neglecting both or all the alternatives, for "copping-out." In any case, you must do something, even if what you do is "doing nothing" (that is, not taking one of the important alternatives before you).

Here is Sartre's reply to his predecessors: We are no longer in the position of Aristotle, in which morality appears to us as a given, as "natural," and without alternatives of the most irresolvable kind. We can no longer trust our "sentiments," as Hume did, for we now find ourselves torn with conflicting sentiments of every kind. We can no longer accept the a priori moralizing of Kant, for we now see that the circumstances in which we must act are never so simple that they will allow for a

---

[20] Jean-Paul Sartre, *Existentialism As a Humanism,* trans. Philip Mairet (New York: Philosophical Library, 1949).

simple "categorical" imperative. And even "the greatest good for the greatest number" no longer provides a guide for our actions, for we no longer pretend that we can calculate the consequences of our actions with any such accuracy. Besides, who is to say what "the greatest good" or, for that matter, "the greatest number" is today? Against all of this, Sartre argues that there is simply our choice of actions and values, together with their consequences, whatever they are. There is no justification for these and no "right" or "wrong." But this does not mean that we need not choose or that it is all "arbitrary." To the contrary, the upshot of Sartre's thesis is precisely that we are always choosing and that morality is nothing other than our commitments, at least for the present, to those values we choose to follow through our actions.

I. ETHICS AND GENDER

One of the most obvious features of so much of the moral philosophy we have been examining is its focus on (or occasionally the denial of) the centrality of abstract principles of reason. Kant, most obviously, celebrates the a priori dictates of practical reason as the core of morality, and Mill, though the nature of his utilitarian principles may be quite different, nevertheless emphasizes the importance of a calculative impersonal principle in the determination of right and wrong. In recent decades, however, an enormous volume of literature has appeared challenging this view of morality as something essentially rational, principled, and impersonal. Twenty years ago, the Harvard psychologist Carol Gilligan argued at some length that women tended to think about moral issues differently than men did, and ever since, there has been a booming business in trying to define and sort out the differences between the two. Of course, many of the features emphasized in feminist ethics, for instance, a healthy attention to personal feelings as well as (or rather than) impersonal reason, were anticipated by earlier male philosophers, such as Hume and Rousseau. Some of the features of feminist ethics are indeed distinctively female, such as the ability to give birth to a child and the experience of motherhood. In the following essay, **Virginia Held,** philosopher and feminist, attempts to spell out some of these differences and suggests new directions for moral thinking on the basis of them. Then philosopher **John Corvino** challenges the idea that homosexuality is "unnatural."

ON FEMINIST ETHICS
BY VIRGINIA HELD

The history of philosophy, including the history of ethics, has been constructed from male points of view, and has been built on assumptions and concepts that are by no means gender-neutral. Feminists characteristically begin with different concerns and give different emphases to the issues we consider than do non-feminist approaches. And, as Lorraine Code expresses it, "starting points and focal points shape the impact of theoretical discussion." Within philosophy, feminists often start with, and focus on, quite different issues than those found in standard philosophy and ethics, however "standard" is understood. Far from providing mere additional insights which can be incorporated into traditional theory, feminist explorations often require radical transformations of existing fields of inquiry and theory. From a feminist point of view, moral theory along with almost all theory will have to be transformed to take adequate account of the experience of women. . . .

THE HISTORY OF ETHICS

Consider the ideals embodied in the phrase "the man of reason." As Genevieve Lloyd has told the story, what has been taken to characterize the man of reason may have changed from historical period to historical period, but in each, the character ideal of the man of reason has been constructed in conjunction with a rejection of whatever has been taken to be characteristic of the feminine. "Rationality," Lloyd writes, "has been conceived as transcendence of the 'feminine,' and the 'feminine' itself has been partly constituted by its occurrence within this structure.

This has of course fundamentally affected the history of philosophy and of ethics. The split between reason and emotion is one of the most familiar of philosophical conceptions. And the advocacy of reason "controlling" unruly emotion, of rationality guiding responsible human action against the blindness of passion, has a long and highly influential history, almost as familiar to non-philosophers as to philosophers. We should certainly now be alert to the ways in which reason has been associated with male endeavor, emotion with female weakness, and the ways in which this is of course not an accidental association. As Lloyd writes, "From the beginnings of philosophical thought, femaleness was symbolically associated with what Reason supposedly left behind—the dark powers of the earth goddesses, immersion in unknown forces associated with mysterious female powers. The early Greeks saw women's capacity to conceive as connecting them with the fertility of Nature. As Plato later expressed the thought, women 'imitate the earth.' " . . .

The associations, between Reason, form, knowledge, and maleness, have persisted in various guises, and have permeated what has been thought to be moral knowledge as well as what has been thought to be scientific knowledge, and what has been thought to be the practice of morality. The associations between the philosophical concepts and gender cannot be merely dropped, and the concepts retained regardless of gender, because gender has been built into them in such a way that without it, they will have to be different concepts. As feminists repeatedly show, if the concept of "human" were built on what we think about "woman" rather than what we think about "man," it would be a very different concept. Ethics, thus, has not been a search for universal, or truly human guidance, but a gender-biased enterprise.

Other distinctions and associations have supplemented and reinforced the identification of reason with maleness, and of the irrational with the female; on this and other grounds "man" has been associated with the human, "woman" with the natural. Prominent among distinctions reinforcing the latter view has been that between the public and the private, because of the way they have been interpreted. Again, these provide as familiar and entrenched a framework as do reason and emotion, and they have been as influential for non-philosophers as for philosophers. It has been supposed that in the public realm, man transcends his animal nature and creates human history. As citizen, he creates government and law; as warrior, he protects society by his willingness to risk death; and as artist or philosopher, he overcomes his human mortality. Here, in the public realm, morality should guide human decision. In the household, in contrast, it has been supposed that women merely "reproduce" life as natural, biological matter. Within the household, the "natural" needs of man for food and shelter are served, and new instances of the biological creature that man is are brought into being. But what is distinctively human, and what transcends any given level of development to create human progress, are thought to occur elsewhere.

This contrast was made highly explicit in Aristotle's conceptions of polis and household; it has continued to affect the basic assumptions of a remarkably broad swath of thought ever since. In ancient Athens, women were confined to the household; the public sphere was literally a male domain. In more recent history, though women have been permitted to venture into public space, the associations of the public, historically male sphere with the distinctively human, and of the household, historically a female sphere, with the merely natural and repetitious, have persisted. These associations have deeply affected moral theory, which has often supposed the transcendent, public domain to be relevant to the foundations of morality in ways that the natural behavior of women in the household could not be. To take some recent and representative examples, David Heyd, in his discussion of supererogation, dismisses a mother's sacrifice for her child as an example of the supererogatory because it belongs, in his view, to "the sphere of natural relationships and instinctive feelings (which lie outside morality)." J. O. Urmson had earlier taken a similar position. In his discussion of supererogation, Urmson said, "Let us be clear that we are not now considering cases of natural affection, such as the sacrifice made by a mother for her child; such cases may be said with some justice not to fall under the concept of morality . . ." And in a recent article called "Distrusting Economics," Alan Ryan argues persuasively about the questionableness of economics and other branches of the social sciences built on the assumption that human beings are rational, self-interested calculators; he discusses various examples of non self-interested behavior, such as of men in wartime, which show the assumption to be false, but nowhere in the article is there any mention of the activity of mothering, which would seem to be a fertile locus for doubts about the usual picture of rational man. Although Ryan does not provide the kind of explicit reason offered by Heyd and Urmson for omitting the context of mothering from consideration as relevant to his discussion, it is difficult to understand the omission without a comparable assumption being implicit here, as it so often is elsewhere. Without feminist insistence on the relevance for morality of the experience in mothering, this context is largely ignored by moral theorists. And yet, from a gender-neutral point of view, how can this vast and fundamental domain of human experience possibly be imagined to lie "outside morality"?

The result of the public/private distinction, as usually formulated, has been to privilege the points of view of men in the public domains of state and law, and later in the marketplace, and to discount the experience of women. Mothering has been conceptualized as a primarily biological activity, even when performed by humans, and virtually no moral theory in the history of ethics has taken mothering, as experienced by women, seriously as a source of moral insight, until feminists in recent years have begun to. Women have been seen as emotional rather than as rational beings, and thus as incapable of full moral personhood. Women's behavior has been interpreted as either "natural" and driven by instinct, and thus as irrelevant to morality and to the construction of moral principles, or it has been interpreted as, at best, in need of instruction and supervision by males better able to know what morality requires and better able to live up to its demands.

> *Mothering has been conceptualized as a primarily biological activity, even when performed by humans, and virtually no moral theory in the history of ethics has taken mothering, as experienced by women, seriously as a source of moral insight . . .*

The Hobbesian conception of reason is very different from the Platonic or Aristotelian conceptions before it, and from the conceptions of Rousseau or Kant or Hegel later; all have in common that they ignore and disparage the experience and reality of women. Consider Hobbes' account of man in the state of nature contracting with other men to establish society. These men hypothetically come into existence fully formed and independent of one another, and decide on entering or staying outside of civil society. As Christine Di Stefano writes, "What we find in Hobbes's account of human nature and political order is a vital concern with the survival of a self conceived in masculine terms . . . This masculine dimension of Hobbes's atomistic egoism is powerfully underscored in his state of nature, which is effectively built on the foundation of denied maternity." In *Citizen,* where Hobbes gave his first systematic exposition of the state of nature, he asks us to "consider men as if but even now sprung out of the earth, and suddenly, like mushrooms, come to full maturity, without all kinds of engagement with each other." As Di Stefano says, it is a most incredible and problematic feature of Hobbes's state of nature that the men in it "are not born of, much less nurtured by, women, or anyone else." To abstract from the complex web of human reality an abstract man for rational perusal, Hobbes has, Di Stefano continues, "expunged human reproduction and early nurturance, two of the most basic and typically female-identified features of distinctively human life, from his account of basic human nature. Such a strategy ensures that he can present a thoroughly atomistic subject . . ." From the point of view of women's experience, such a subject or self is unbelievable and misleading, even as a theoretical construct. The Leviathan, Di Stefano writes, "is effectively comprised of a body politic of orphans who have reared themselves, whose desires are situated within and reflect nothing but independently generated movement . . . These essential elements are natural human beings conceived along masculine lines."

Rousseau, and Kant, and Hegel, paid homage to the emotional power, the aesthetic sensibility, and the familial concerns, respectively, of women. But since in their views morality must be based on rational principle, and women were incapable of full rationality, or a degree or kind of rationality comparable to that of men, women were deemed, in the view of these moralists, to be inherently wanting in morality. For Rousseau, women must be trained from childhood to submit to the will of men lest their sexual power lead both men and women to disaster. For Kant, women were thought incapable of achieving full moral personhood, and women lose all charm if they try to behave like men by engaging in rational pursuits. For Hegel, women's moral concern for their families could be admirable in its proper place, but is a threat to the more universal aims to which men, as members of the state, should aspire.

These images, of the feminine as what must be overcome if knowledge and morality are to be achieved, of female experience as naturally irrelevant to morality, and of women as inherently deficient moral creatures, are built into the history of ethics. Feminists examine these images, and see that they are not the incidental or merely idiosyncratic suppositions of a few philosophers whose views on many topics depart far from the ordinary anyway. Such views are the nearly uniform reflection in philosophical and ethical theory of patriarchal attitudes pervasive throughout human history. Or they are exaggerations even of ordinary male experience, which exaggerations then reinforce rather than temper other patriarchal conceptions and institutions. They distort the actual experience and aspirations of many men as well as of women. Annette Baier recently speculated about why it is that moral philosophy has so seriously overlooked the trust between human beings that in her view is an utterly central aspect of moral life. She noted that "the great moral theorists in our tradition not only are all men, they are mostly men who had minimal adult dealings with (and so were then minimally influenced by) women." They were for the most part "clerics, misogynists, and puritan bachelors," and thus it is not surprising that they focus their philosophical attention "so single-mindedly on cool, distanced relations between more or less free and equal adult strangers . . ."

As feminists, we deplore the patriarchal attitudes that so much of philosophy and moral theory reflect. But we recognize that the problem is more serious even than changing those attitudes. For moral theory as so far developed is incapable of correcting itself without an almost total transformation. It cannot simply absorb the gender that has been "left behind," even if both genders would want it to. To continue to build morality on rational principles opposed to the emotions and to include women among the rational will leave no one to reflect the promptings of the heart, which promptings can be moral rather than merely instinctive. To simply bring women into the public and male domain of the polis will leave no one to speak for the household. Its values have been hitherto unrecognized, but they are often moral values. Or to continue to seek contractual restraints on the pursuits of self-interest by atomistic individuals, and to have women join men in devotion to these pursuits, will leave no one involved in the nurturance of children and cultivation of social relations, which nurturance and cultivation can be of greatest moral import.

There are very good reasons for women not to want simply to be accorded entry as equals into the enterprise of morality as so far developed. In a recent survey of types of feminist moral theory, Kathryn Morgan notes that "many women who engage in philosophical reflection are acutely aware of the masculine nature of the profession and tradition, and feel their own moral concerns as women silenced or trivialized in virtually all the official settings that define the practice." Women should clearly not agree, as the price of admission to the masculine realm of traditional morality, to abandon our own moral concerns as women.

And so we are groping to shape new moral theory. Understandably, we do not yet have fully worked out feminist moral theories to offer. But we can suggest some directions our project of developing such theories is taking. As Kathryn Morgan points out, there is not likely to be a "star" feminist moral theorist on the order of a Rawls or Nozick: "There will be no individual singled out for two reasons. One reason is that vital moral and theoretical conversations are taking place on a large dialectical scale as the feminist community struggles to develop a feminist ethic. The second reason is that this community of feminist theoreticians is calling into question the very model of the individualized autonomous self presupposed by a star-centered male-dominated tradition . . . We experience it as a common labour, a common task."

The dialogues that are enabling feminist approaches to moral theory to develop are proceeding. As Alison Jaggar makes clear in her useful overview of them, there is no unitary view of ethics that can be identified as "feminist ethics." Feminist approaches to ethics share a commitment to "rethinking ethics with a view to correcting whatever forms of male bias it may contain." While those who develop these approaches are "united by a shared project, they diverge widely in their views as to how this project is to be accomplished."

Not all feminists, by any means, agree that there are distinctive feminist virtues or values. Some are especially skeptical of the attempt to give positive value to such traditional "feminine virtues" as a willingness to nurture, or an affinity with caring, or reluctance to seek independence. They see this approach as playing into the hands of those who would confine women to traditional roles. Other feminists are skeptical of all claims about women as such, emphasizing that women are divided by class and race and sexual orientation in ways that make any conclusions drawn from "women's experience" dubious.

Still, it is possible, I think, to discern various important focal points evident in current feminist attempts to transform ethics into a theoretical and practical activity that could be acceptable from a feminist point of view. In the glimpse I have presented of bias in the history of ethics, I focused on what, from a feminist point of view, are three of its most questionable aspects: 1) the split between reason and emotion and the devaluation of emotion; 2) the public/private distinction and the relegation of the private to the natural; and 3) the concept of the self as constructed from a male point of view.

FROM *SAME SEX: DEBATING THE ETHICS, SCIENCE, AND CULTURE OF HOMOSEXUALITY* BY **JOHN CORVINO**

HOMOSEXUAL SEX IS "UNNATURAL"

Many contend that homosexual sex is "unnatural." But what does that mean? Many things that people value—clothing, houses, medicine, and government, for example—are unnatural in some sense. On the other hand, many things that people detest—disease, suffering, and death, for example—are "natural" in the sense that they occur "in nature." If the unnaturalness charge is to be more than empty rhetorical flourish, those who levy it must specify what they mean. Borrowing from Burton Leiser, I will examine several possible meanings of "unnatural."

WHAT IS UNUSUAL OR ABNORMAL IS UNNATURAL

One meaning of "unnatural" refers to that which deviates from the norm, that is, from what most people do. Obviously, most people engage in heterosexual relationships. But does it follow that it is wrong to engage in homosexual relationships? Relatively few people read Sanskrit, pilot ships, play the mandolin, breed goats, or write with both hands, yet none of these activities is immoral simply because it is unusual. As the Ramsey Colloquium, a group of Jewish and Christian scholars who oppose homosexuality, writes, "The statistical frequency of an act does not determine its moral status." So while homosexuality might be unnatural in the sense of being unusual, that fact is morally irrelevant.

WHAT IS NOT PRACTICED BY OTHER ANIMALS IS UNNATURAL

Some people argue, "Even animals know better than to behave homosexually; homosexuality must be wrong." This argument is doubly flawed. First, it rests on a false premise. Numerous studies—including Anne Perkins's study of "gay" sheep and George and Molly Hunt's study of "lesbian" seagulls—have shown that some animals do form homosexual pair-bonds. Second, even if animals did not behave homosexually, that fact would not prove that homosexuality is immoral. After all, animals don't cook their food, brush their teeth, participate in religious worship, or attend college; human beings do all of these without moral censure. Indeed, the idea that animals could provide us with our standards—especially our sexual standards—is simply amusing.

WHAT DOES NOT PROCEED FROM INNATE DESIRES IS UNNATURAL

Recent studies suggesting a biological basis for homosexuality have resulted in two popular positions. One side proposes that homosexual people are "born that way" and that it is therefore natural (and thus good) for them to form homosexual relationships. The other side maintains that homosexuality is a lifestyle choice, which is therefore unnatural (and thus wrong). Both sides assume a connection between the origin of homosexual orientation, on the one hand, and the moral value of homosexual activity, on the other. And insofar as they share that assumption, both sides are wrong.

Consider first the pro-homosexual side: "They are born that way; therefore it's natural and good." This inference assumes that all innate desires are good ones (i.e., that they should be acted upon). But that assumption is clearly false. Research suggests that some people are born with a predisposition toward violence, but such people have no more right to strangle their neighbors than anyone else. So while people like Tommy and Jim may be born with homosexual tendencies, it doesn't follow that they ought to act on them. Nor does it follow that they ought *not* to act on them, even if the tendencies are not innate. I probably do not have any innate tendency to write with my left hand (since I, like everyone else in my family, have always been right-handed), but it doesn't follow that it would be immoral for me to do so. So simply asserting that homosexuality is a lifestyle choice will not show that it is an immoral lifestyle choice.

Do people "choose" to be homosexual? People certainly don't seem to choose their sexual *feelings,* at least not in any direct or obvious way. (Do you? Think about it.) Rather, they find certain people attractive and certain activities arousing, whether they "decide" to or not. Indeed, most people at some point in their lives wish that they could control their feelings more—for example, in situations of unrequited love—and find it frustrating that they cannot. What they *can* control to a considerable degree is how and when they act upon those feelings. In that sense, both homosexuality and heterosexuality involve lifestyle choices. But in either case, determining the origin of the feelings will not determine whether it is moral to act on them.

WHAT VIOLATES AN ORGAN'S PRINCIPAL PURPOSE IS UNNATURAL

Perhaps when people claim that homosexual sex is unnatural they mean that it cannot result in procreation. The idea behind the argument is that human organs have various natural purposes: eyes are for seeing, ears are for hearing, genitals are for procreating. According to this argument, it is immoral to use an organ in a way that violates its particular purpose.

Many of our organs, however, have multiple purposes. Tommy can use his mouth for talking, eating, breathing, licking stamps, chewing gum, kissing women, or kissing Jim; and it seems rather arbitrary to claim that all but the last use are "natural." (And if we say that some of the other uses are "unnatural, but not immoral," we have failed to specify a morally relevant sense of the term "natural.")

Just because people can and do use their sexual organs to procreate, it does not follow that they should not use them for other purposes. Sexual organs seem very well suited for expressing love, for giving and receiving pleasure, and for celebrating, replenishing, and enhancing a relationship—even when procreation is not a factor. Unless opponents of homosexuality are prepared to condemn heterosexual couples who use contraception or individuals who masturbate, they must abandon this version of the unnaturalness argument. Indeed, even the Roman Catholic Church, which forbids contraception and masturbation, approves of sex for sterile couples and of sex during pregnancy, neither of which can lead to procreation. The Church concedes here that intimacy and pleasure are morally legitimate purposes for sex, even in cases where procreation is impossible. But since homosexual sex can achieve these purposes as well, it is inconsistent for the Church to condemn it on the grounds that it is not procreative.

One might object that sterile heterosexual couples do not *intentionally* turn away from procreation, whereas homosexual couples do. But this distinction doesn't hold. It is no more possible for Tommy to procreate with a woman whose uterus has been removed than it is for him to procreate with Jim. By having sex with either one, he is intentionally engaging in a nonprocreative sexual act.

Yet one might press the objection further and insist that Tommy and the woman *could* produce children if the woman were fertile: whereas homosexual relationships are essentially infertile, heterosexual relationships are only incidentally so. But what does that prove? Granted, it might require less of a miracle for a woman without a uterus to become pregnant than for Jim to become pregnant, but it would require a miracle nonetheless. Thus it seems that the real difference here is not that one couple is fertile and the other not, nor that one couple "could" be fertile (with the help of a miracle) and the other not, but rather that one couple is male-female and the other male-male. In other words, sex between Tommy and Jim is wrong because it's male-male—i.e., because it's homosexual. But that, of course, is no argument at all.

WHAT IS DISGUSTING OR OFFENSIVE IS UNNATURAL

It often seems that when people call homosexuality "unnatural" they really just mean that it's disgusting. But plenty of morally neutral activities—handling snakes, eating snails, performing autopsies,

> *It often seems that when people call homosexuality "unnatural" they really just mean that it's disgusting. But plenty of morally neutral activities—handling snakes, eating snails, performing autopsies, cleaning toilets, and so on—disgust people.*

cleaning toilets, and so on—disgust people. Indeed, for centuries, most people found interracial relationships disgusting, yet that feeling—which has by no means disappeared—hardly proves that such relationships are wrong. In sum, the charge that homosexuality is unnatural, at least in its most common forms, is longer on rhetorical flourish than on philosophical cogency. At best it expresses an aesthetic judgment, not a moral judgment.[21]

SUMMARY AND CONCLUSION

In this chapter, we have reviewed a half dozen or so theories of morality. (1) Aristotle takes the key to morality to be the concept of "virtue," which he argues to be activity in accordance with rational principles. He bases this argument on a concept of what is "natural" for man, but his discussion is clearly limited to a small class of Greek male citizens, whom he views as the ideal specimens of humanity. (2) Hume and Rousseau both argue that morality must be based on certain kinds of feelings or "sentiments." "Reason is and ought to be the slave of the passions," Hume argues, and Rousseau similarly argues that man is "naturally" good. (3) Kant insists that morality is strictly a matter of rational principle divorced from all personal interests and desires ("inclinations"). This includes a rejection of Hume and Rousseau, who base morality on feelings (which are inclinations in Kant's sense). This also includes a rejection of Aristotle. Although both philosophers use the notion of a "rational principle," Kant intends his notion to apply to every human being, and therefore every person has the same duties and obligations. (4) The utilitarians, Bentham and Mill, reject Kant's divorce between morality and personal interest and argue that morality is our guide to the satisfaction of the greatest number of interests of the greatest number of people. (5) Nietzsche rejects both Kant and the utilitarians, preferring a return to the elitism and "virtue" orientation of Aristotle's ethics. He argues that we create our values and live with them according to our personal needs. Following him, the existentialists, particularly Jean-Paul Sartre, argue that all values are chosen by us; there is no "true" morality, only those values to which we have voluntarily committed ourselves. (6) Finally, recent feminists have challenged the "male bias" of these traditional theories and challenges to sexual orientation bias suggest the possibility of a different *kind* of moral view.

GLOSSARY

a priori In moral philosophy, independent of particular circumstances. In Kant's philosophy, moral laws are said to be a priori in this sense.

---

[21] John Corvino, *Same Sex: Debating the Ethics, Science, and Culture of Homosexuality* (Lanham, MA: Rowman & Littlefield, 1997), pp. 4–7.

altruism The thesis that one ought to act for the sake of the interests of others.

autonomy Independence. Moral autonomy is the ability of every rational person to reach his or her own moral conclusions about what is right and what is wrong. (This does not mean that they will therefore come to different conclusions.)

categorical imperative In Kant's philosophy, a moral law, a command that is unqualified and not dependent on any conditions or qualifications. In particular, that rule that tells us to act in such a way that we would want everyone else to act the same way.

commitment To form a binding obligation voluntarily. In Sartre's moral philosophy, a commitment is a freely chosen adoption of a moral principle or project which one thereby vows to defend and practice, even in the absence of any other reasons for doing so. Since, according to Sartre, there are never conclusive reasons for adopting any particular moral position, one must always defend his or her position through commitment and nothing else.

conscience A sense or feeling about what is right and wrong, usually without argument. (It is like intuition in matters of knowledge.) In Christian moral theory, it is a moral sense instilled in us by God. In Freudian psychology, it is the internalization of the moral lessons given us as children by our parents and teachers.

contemplation (the life of) According to Aristotle (and other philosophers), the happiest life, the life of thought and philosophy.

cultural relativism The descriptive anthropological thesis that different societies have different moralities. It is important to stress that these moralities must be fundamentally different, not only different in details. Some societies consider an act as stealing while others do not, but a society that does not have a conception of private property might be fundamentally different from one that does.

deontology Ethics based on duty (Gk: *dein*). Kant's ethic is deontological in that it stresses obedience to principle rather than attention to consequences (including happiness).

duty What one is morally bound to do.

egoism The thesis that people act for their own interests. *Psychological egoism* is merely the thesis that they in fact act in their own interests; *ethical egoism* is the thesis that people ought to act in their own interests.

ethical absolutism The thesis that there is one and only one correct morality.

ethical egoism The thesis that people ought to act in their own interests.

ethical relativism The thesis that different moralities should be considered equally correct even if they directly contradict each other. A morality is "correct," by this thesis, merely if it is correct according to the particular society that accepts it.

ethics A system of general moral principles and a conception of morality and its foundation. Or, the study of moral principles.

eudaimonia Aristotle's word for "happiness," or, more literally, "living well."

existentialism The modern movement in philosophy that puts great emphasis on individual choice and the voluntary acceptance of all values.

Golden Rule "Do unto others as you would have them do unto you."

happiness The achievement of the good life. In Aristotle, the name we all agree to give to the good life, whatever it is. Happiness, in this sense, must not be confused with pleasure, which is but one (among many) concerns and conceptions of the good life.

happiness calculus (also *felicity calculus*) Bentham's technique for quantifying and adding up pleasures and pains as a way of deciding what to do.

hedonism The conception of the good life that takes pleasure to be the ultimate good. Hedonism is the premise of most forms of utilitarianism. It is often the premise—though sometimes a consequence—of ethical egoism. (These two are not the same: hedonism refers to the *end;* egoism refers to *whose* ends.)

hypothetical imperative In Kant, a command that is conditional, depending upon particular aims or inclinations. For example, "if you want to be a doctor, then go to medical school." According to Kant, all other philosophers (Aristotle, Hume, Rousseau) took morality to be a hypothetical imperative. He does not.

immoralist A person who rejects the ultimate claims of morality. An immoralist need not actually break the rules of morality; he or she does not consider them absolute rules and claims that other considerations (even personal considerations) may override them.

imperative A command.

inclination Kant's term for all personal considerations: desires, feelings, emotions, attitudes, moods, and so on.

law An objective rule that is binding on individuals whether they personally accept it or not. Contrasted with *maxim*.

master morality In Nietzsche, a morality that takes personal self-realization as primary, so-called because it was the morality of the "masters" in the slave states of the ancient world (including Greece).

maxim In Kant, a personal rule or intention. Contrasted with *law*.

mean (between the extremes) In Aristotle, the middle course, not too much, not too little. Courage, for example, is a mean because a person with courage is neither too timid to fight nor so lacking in fear that he or she is rash or reckless in the face of danger.

morality In general, the rules for right action and prohibitions against wrong acts. Sometimes morality is that single set of absolute rules and prohibitions that are valid for all men at all times and all societies. More loosely, a morality can be any set of ultimate principles, and there might be any number of moralities in different societies.

obligation Bound by duty. For example, "you have an obligation to keep your promises."

ought The term most often used to express moral duty or obligation. Sometimes "should" is used, but this is ambiguously between "ought" and merely "preferable." Sometimes "must" or "have to" is used, but this is ambiguously between "ought to" and "forced to." In Hume's ethics (and in many others as well), "ought" is contrasted with "is" as the hallmark of value (esp. moral) judgment.

principle of utility In Bentham, the principle that one ought to do what gives the greatest pleasure to the greatest number of people.

psychological egoism The thesis that people always act for their own self-interest, even when it seems as if they are acting for other people's benefit (for example, in giving to charity, the egoist would say, the person is simply making himself or herself feel self-righteous).

rationality Acting in the best possible way; according to reason. Sometimes, rationality means simply doing what is best under the circumstances, without insisting that there is only one rational way of acting. In other words, rationality is considered relative to particular interests and circumstances. In Kant's philosophy, however, rationality refers to that faculty that allows us to act in the correct way, without reference to particular interests and circumstances.

relativism The thesis that morals are relative to particular societies, particular interests, particular circumstances, or particular individuals. (See *cultural relativism, ethical relativism*.)

selfishness Acting in one's own interest to the exclusion of others' interests. The word has a nasty connotation and so should be separated from the more neutral claims of the psychological egoist. To say that a person is acting selfishly is to condemn him or her and say that the action is blameworthy. It is possible to act for one's own interests, however, and not be selfish, for one may also act for the benefit of others. A selfish act is to the exclusion of other people's interests; an act may be both in one's own interests and in the interests of others, however.

sentiment Feeling, emotion; particularly moral feelings (as in Hume, Rousseau).

slave morality In Nietzsche's moral philosophy, a morality that takes duties and obligations as primary, so called because it was the morality of the slaves who were not allowed to aspire any higher than mere efficiency and personal comfort.

sympathy Fellow feeling; felt concern for other people's welfare. In the ethics of Hume and Rousseau, the necessary and universal sentiment without which morals—and society—would be impossible.

utilitarianism The moral philosophy that says that we should act in such ways as to make the greatest number of people as happy as possible.

virtue Moral excellence. In Aristotle's philosophy, a state of character according to which we enjoy doing what is right. In Kant, willing what is right (whether or not we enjoy it, in fact, especially if we don't enjoy it).

will The power of mind that allows us to choose our own actions, or, at least, what we shall try to do. In Kant, a good will is the only thing that is good "without qualification," in other words, acting for the right reasons and good intentions.

will to power In Nietzsche's philosophy, the thesis that every act is ultimately aimed at superiority, sometimes over other people, but, more importantly, superiority according to one's own standards. In other words, it is what Aristotle meant by excellence. (Nietzsche has often been interpreted, however, to mean political power.)

BIBLIOGRAPHY AND FURTHER READING

A comprehensive but brief history of ethics is A. MacIntyre, *A Short History of Ethics* (New York: Macmillan, 1966). A general schematic discussion of the problems of ethics is W. Fankena, *Ethics* (Englewood Cliffs, NJ: Prentice-Hall, 1963). A much more detailed survey of the problems and the recent history of ethics is Richard R. Brandt, *Ethical Theory* (Englewood Cliffs, NJ: Prentice-Hall, 1959). Also available is a companion anthology, Richard R. Brandt, *Value and Obligation* (New York: Harcourt Brace Jovanovich, 1961). The classic arguments against egoism are in J. Butler, *Fifteen Sermons Upon Human Nature* (London: Macmillan, 1900). A more modern and technical set of arguments is in T. Nagel, *The Possibility of Altruism* (New York: Oxford University Press, 1970). Textbooks that include various discussions of ethical options are R. N. Beck and J. B. Orr, *Ethical Choice* (New York: Free Press, 1970) and John Hospers, *Human Conduct* (New York: Harcourt Brace Jovanovich, 1962). Aristotle's *Nicomachean Ethics* is translated by W. D. Ross (Oxford: Oxford University Press, 1925). Ross also has a good summary of the arguments in his *Aristotle* (New York: Meridian, 1959). Some excellent articles on Aristotle's ethics are collected in J. Walsh and H. Shapiro, eds., *Aristotle's Ethics* (Belmont, CA: Wadsworth, 1967) and J. Moravscik, ed., *Aristotle* (New York: Doubleday, Anchor, 1966). David Hume's moral philosophy is most accessible in his *Enquiry Concerning the Principles of Morals* (La Salle, IL: Open Court, 1912). Jean-Jacques Rousseau's moral theories are to be found in his second discourse "On the Origins of Inequality" in The *Social Contract* (New York: Dutton, 1950) and in *Emile* (New York: Dutton, 1970). The best summary of Immanuel Kant's moral philosophy is his own *Foundations of the Metaphysics of Morals,* available in various translations, the most helpful, because of the commentary, being *Groundwork of the Metaphysics of Morals,* trans. H. J. Paton (New York: Harper & Row, 1957). See also Immanuel Kant, *Lectures in Ethics,* trans. L. Infield (New

York: Harper & Row, 1963). John Stuart Mill's utilitarianism is well summarized in his pamphlet *Utilitarianism* (New York: Dutton, 1910). A good summary of Friedrich Nietzsche's ethics is in Walter Kaufmann, *Nietzsche* (Princeton, NJ: Princeton University Press, 1950). A good summary of existentialist ethics is M. Warnock, *Existentialist Ethics* (New York: St. Martin's Press, 1967). A good collection of essays on feminist ethics is Alison M. Jaggar and Paula S. Rothenberg, eds., *Feminist Frameworks,* 3rd ed. (New York: McGraw-Hill, 1993). An excellent historical overview is Janet McCracken, *Thinking About Gender: A Historical Anthology* (Fort Worth: Harcourt Brace, 1997).

JUSTICE

We hold these truths to be self-evident, that all men are created equal,

that they are endowed by their creator with certain unalienable Rights,

that among these are Life, Liberty and the Pursuit of Happiness.

THOMAS JEFFERSON, ET AL.

"Man is a social animal," wrote Aristotle. Therefore, he is a political animal as well. We live with other people, not just our friends and families but thousands and millions of others, most of whom we will never meet and many of whom we come across in only the most casual way—passing them as we cross the street or buying a ticket at the movie theater. Yet we have to be concerned about them, and they about us, for there is a sense in which we are all clearly dependent upon each other. For example, we depend on them not to attack us without reason or steal our possessions. Of course, our confidence varies from person to person and from city to city. But it is clear that, in general, we have duties toward people we never know, for example, the duty not to contaminate their water or air supplies or to place their lives in danger. And they have similar duties to us. We also claim certain rights for ourselves: for example, the right not to be attacked as we walk down the street, the right to speak our mind about politically controversial issues without being thrown in jail, the right to believe in this religion or that religion or no religion without having our jobs, our homes, or our freedom taken from us.

Political and social philosophy is the study of people in societies with particular attention to the abstract claims they have on each other in the form of "rights," "duties," and "privileges," and their demands for "justice," "equality," and "freedom."

(It is important to distinguish this sense of *political* freedom from the causal or metaphysical freedom that we discussed earlier. These can be discussed independently of each other). At least ideally, politics is continuous with morality. Our political duties and obligations, for example, are often the same as our moral duties and obligations. Our claims to certain "moral rights" are often claims to political rights as well, and political rights—particularly those very general and absolute rights which we call human rights (for example, the right not to be tortured or degraded, the right not to be exploited by powerful institutions or persons)—are typically defended on the basis of moral principles. The virtues of government are ideally the virtues of individuals: Government should be just, temperate, courageous, honest, humane, considerate, and reasonable.

Plato and Aristotle, for example, portrayed their visions of the ideal state in precisely these terms. (Both Plato and Aristotle, unlike most modern philosophers, actually had the opportunity to set up such governments; both failed, but for reasons that were hardly their fault.) This is not to say that all politics or all politicians are moral; we know much better than that. But it is to say that our politics are constrained and determined by our sense of morality. Morality is concerned more with relations between particular people while politics is concerned more with large and impersonal groups. But the difference is one of degree. In ancient Greece, Plato and Aristotle lived in relatively small "city-states" (each called a *polis*), with fewer citizens than even most U.S. towns. It was much easier for them to treat morality and politics together. But even today, we still speak hopefully of "the human family" and "international brotherhood," which is to reassert our enduring belief that politics—even at the international level—ought to be based on interpersonal moral principles.

The key to a successful society is cooperation. If people do not cooperate, the success of society requires that some authority have the power to bring individual interests into line with the public interest. This authority is generally called the state. The state passes laws and enforces them; its purpose is to protect the public interest. But is it only this? We would probably say *no*. Its purpose is also to protect individual rights, for example, against powerful corporations and against strongly mobilized pressure groups that try to interfere with individual lives. In general, we might say that the function of the state is to protect justice. But there has been disagreement ever since ancient times about what that means and how much the primary emphasis should be placed on the public interest and how much on individual rights and interests.

Our concept of the state and the extent of its power and **authority** depends very much on our conception of human nature and of people's willingness to cooperate without being forced to do so. At one extreme are those who place such strong emphasis on the smooth workings of society that they are willing to sacrifice most individual rights and interests; they are generally called **"authoritarians,"** and their confidence in willing individual cooperation is very slight compared to their confidence in a strong authoritarian state. ("He makes the trains run on time" was often said of the fascist Italian dictator Benito Mussolini.) At the other extreme are people with so much confidence in individual cooperation and so little confidence in the state that they argue that the state should be eliminated altogether. They are called **anarchists.** Between these extremes are more moderate positions, for example, people who have some confidence both in individual cooperation and in the possibility of a reasonably just state, but don't have complete confidence in either. Democrats and Republicans, for example, both believe in a government that is at least partially run by the people themselves but with sufficient power to enforce its laws over individual interests whenever necessary. All these people believe in varying solutions to the same central problem: the problem of a balance between the public interest and the need for cooperation on the one hand and individual rights and interests on the other—in other words, the problem of **justice.**

A. THE PROBLEM OF JUSTICE

When we think of justice, we first tend to think of criminal cases and of punishment. Justice, in this sense, is catching the criminal and "making him pay for his crime." The oldest sense of the word *justice,* therefore, is what philosophers call **retributive justice,** or simply, "getting even." Retribution for a crime is making the criminal suffer or pay an amount appropriate to the severity of the crime. In ancient traditions, the key phrase was "an eye for an eye, a tooth for a tooth." If a criminal caused a person to be blind, he was in turn blinded. We now view this as brutal and less than civilized. But is it so clear that we have in fact given up this retributive sense of justice? Do we punish our criminals (that is, demand retribution), or do we sincerely attempt to reform them? Or is the purpose of prison simply to keep them off the street? Should we ever punish people for crimes, or should we simply protect ourselves against their doing the same thing again? If a man commits an atrocious murder, is it enough that we guarantee that he won't do another one? Or does he deserve punishment even if we know that he won't do it again?

But retributive justice and the problems of punishment are really only a small piece of a much larger concern. Justice is not just "getting even" for crimes and offenses. It concerns the running of society as a whole in day-to-day civil matters as well as the more dramatic criminal concerns. Given the relative scarcity of wealth and goods, how should they be distributed? Should everyone receive exactly the same amount? Should the person who works hard at an unpleasant job receive no more than the person who refuses to work at all and prefers to watch TV all day and just amuse himself or herself? Should the person who uses his wealth to the benefit of others receive no more than the person who "throws away" his or her money on gambling, drinking, and debauchery? If a class of people has historically been deprived of its adequate share because of the color of their skin, their religious beliefs, or their sex or age, should that class now be given more than its share in compensation, or is this too an injustice against other people?

Not only are wealth and goods at issue here, however. Distribution of privileges and power are equally important. Who will vote? Will everyone's vote count exactly the same? Should the opinions of an illiterate who does not even know the name of his political leaders have as much say in the government as the political scientist or economist who has studied these matters for years? Should everyone be allowed to drive? Or to drink? Should everyone receive exactly the same treatment before the law? Or are there concerns that would indicate that some people (for example, congressmen or foreign diplomats) should receive special privileges?

Enjoyment of society's cultural gifts is also at issue. Should everyone receive the same education? What if that turns out to be "impractical" (since job training is much more efficient than "liberal arts")? But doesn't that mean that some—the workers and career persons who are trained to do a job—are deprived of the education necessary to enjoy great books, music, poetry, philosophy, intellectual debate, or proficiency in foreign languages, which give considerable enjoyment to those who have been taught to appreciate them?

There are also questions of status. Should there be social classes? What if it could be proved that such divisions make a society run more smoothly? How minimal should distinctions in status be? This in turn leads to the more general question: Shouldn't all members of society be able to expect equal treatment and respect not only by the law but in every conceivable social situation? All of these are the concerns of justice. But what is just? Who decides? And how?

1. Two Ancient Theories of Justice: Plato and Aristotle

Theories of justice, in one sense, are as old as human society. The ancient codes of the Hebrews, the Persians, and the Babylonians were theories of justice in the sense that they tried, in their various ways, to develop rules to cover fair dealing and distribution of goods, the punishment of criminals, and the settling of disputes. A fully developed theory of justice, however, should go beyond this and try to analyze the nature of justice itself. The first great theories of justice to try to do this were those of Plato and Aristotle. In *The Republic,* Plato argues that justice in the state is precisely the same as justice in the individual, that is, a harmony between the various parts for the good of the whole. In other words, cooperation among all for the sake of a successful society is the key to justice. But this means that the interests of the individual take a clearly secondary role to the interests of society. In ancient Greece, this may have been only rarely true for the wealthy and powerful, but for the majority of people—especially the slaves—this secondary role was the norm. Because their docile submission was seen as necessary to the overall success of society, their individual interests and rights were extremely minimal. They expected to be rewarded and satisfied only insofar as their efforts benefited their betters, and then they expected their betters to reap far more reward from their labor than they themselves. In Plato's universe, everyone has his or her "place," and justice means that they act and are treated accordingly:

FROM *THE REPUBLIC*
BY **PLATO**

I think that justice is the very thing, or some form of the thing which, when we were beginning to found our city, we said had to be established throughout.

We stated, and often repeated, if you remember, that everyone must pursue one occupation of those in the city, that for which his nature best fitted him.

Yes, we kept saying that.

Further, we have heard many people say, and have often said ourselves, that justice is to perform one's own task, and not to meddle with that of others.

We have said that.

This then, my friend, I said, when it happens, is in some way justice, to do one's own job. And do you know what I take to be a proof of this?

No, tell me.

I think what is left over of those things we have been investigating, after moderation and courage and wisdom have been found, was that which made it possible for those three qualities to appear in the city and to continue as long as it was present. We also said that what remained after we found the other three was justice.

It had to be.

And surely, I said, if we had to decide which of the four will make the city good by its presence, it would be hard to judge whether it is a common belief among the rulers and the ruled, or the preservation among the soldiers of a law-inspired belief as to the nature of what is, and what is not, to be feared, or the knowledge and guardianship of the rulers, or whether it is, above all, the presence of this fourth in child and woman, slave and free, artisan, ruler and subject, namely that each man, a unity in himself, performed his own task and was not meddling with that of others.

How could this not be hard to judge?

It seems then that the capacity for each in the city to perform his own task rivals wisdom, moderation, and courage as a source of excellence for the city.

It certainly does.

You would then describe justice as a rival to them for excellence in the city?

Most certainly.

Look at it this way and see whether you agree: you will order your rulers to act as judges in the courts of the city?

Surely.

And will their exclusive aim in delivering judgment not be that no citizen should have what belongs to another or be deprived of what is his own?

That would be their aim.

That being just?

Yes.

In some way then possession of one's own and the performance of one's own task could be agreed to be justice.

That is so.

Consider then whether you agree with me in this: if a carpenter attempts to do the work of a cobbler, or a cobbler that of a carpenter, and they exchange their tools and the esteem that goes with the job, or the same man tries to do both, and all the other exchanges are made, do you think that this does any great harm to the city?

No.

But I think that when one who is by nature a worker or some other kind of moneymaker is puffed up by wealth, or by the mob, or by his own strength, or some other such thing, and attempts to enter the warrior class, or one of the soldiers tries to enter the group of counselors or guardians, though he is unworthy of it, and these exchange their tools and the public esteem, or when the same man tries to perform all these jobs together, then I think you will agree that these exchanges and this meddling bring the city to ruin.

> *... the doing of one's own job by the moneymaking, auxiliary, and guardian groups, when each group is performing its own task in the city ... is justice and makes the city just.*

They certainly do.

The meddling and exchange between the three established orders does very great harm to the city and would most correctly be called wickedness.

Very definitely.

And you would call the greatest wickedness worked against one's own city injustice?

Of course.

That then is injustice. And let us repeat that the doing of one's own job by the moneymaking, auxiliary, and guardian groups, when each group is performing its own task in the city, is the opposite, it is justice and makes the city just.

I agree with you that this is so.[1]

Plato's rigid hierarchy of social classes and insistence on the inequality of people offends our sense of universal equality, but it is important to see that equality (or, more properly, **egalitarianism,** the view that all men and women are equal just by virtue of their being human) is a position that must be argued and is not a "natural" state of affairs or a belief that has always been accepted by everyone. The same is true of Aristotle's theory of justice.

In his *Politics,* Aristotle gives an unabashed defense of slavery, not only on the grounds that slaves are efficient and good for society as a whole, but because those who are slaves are "naturally" meant to be slaves and would be unhappy and unable to cope if they were granted freedom and made citizens. (This is not just an ancient argument, however, I am sure you have heard similar arguments about other groups of people in your own lifetime.) For Aristotle as for Plato, different people have different roles, and to treat unequals equally is as unjust, according to them, as it is to treat equals unequally. They would consider the view that morons and children and foreigners deserve the same respect and treatment as citizens ridiculous. So too would they find the contemporary argument that we should treat men and women as equals.[2] But despite these opinions, Plato and Aristotle laid the foundations of much

---

[1] Plato, *The Republic,* Bk. VI, trans. G. M. A. Grube (Indianapolis, IN: Hackett, 1974).

[2] Plato did venture that women as well as men ought to be rulers.

of our own conceptions of justice. The idea that equals must be treated as equals is the foundation of our sense of justice just as much as theirs. The difference is that we are taught to believe that everybody is an equal. Similarly, the theory of what is called **distributive justice,** the fair distribution of wealth and goods among the members of society, is a current international as well as national concern that owes much to Aristotle's original formulations. The idea that individuals are due certain rewards for their labor is also Aristotle's idea. But despite his aristocratic opinions and his harsh elitism, Aristotle saw quite clearly that the members of society who depended most upon an adequate theory of justice were the poorer and less powerful members. It was for them that the just society was most vital (since the powerful and wealthy had a much better chance of taking care of themselves). It was also Aristotle who made the vital distinction, with which we began this section, between that restricted concern for justice that rights certain wrongs (in crimes, in bad business deals, and in public misfortunes) and the general concern of justice for a well-balanced and reasonable society.

FROM *THE NICOMACHEAN ETHICS* BY **ARISTOTLE**

Let us take as a starting-point, then, the various meanings of "an unjust man." Both the lawless man and the greedy and unfair man are thought to be unjust, so that evidently both the law-abiding and the fair man will be just. The just, then, is the lawful and the fair, the unjust the unlawful and the unfair.

Since the lawless man was seen to be unjust and the law-abiding man just, evidently all lawful acts are in a sense just acts; for the acts laid down by the legislative art are lawful, and each of these, we say, is just. Now the laws in their enactments on all subjects aim at the common advantage either of all or of the best of those who hold power, or something of the sort; so that in one sense we call those acts just that tend to produce and preserve happiness and its components for the political society. And the law bids us do both the acts of a brave man (*e.g.* not to desert our post nor take to flight nor throw away our arms), and those of a temperate man (*e.g.* not to commit adultery nor to gratify one's lust), and those of a good-tempered man (*e.g.* not to strike another nor to speak evil), and similarly with regard to the other virtues and forms of wickedness, commanding some acts and forbidding others; and the rightly-framed law does this rightly, and the hastily conceived one less well.

This form of justice, then, is complete virtue, but not absolutely, but in relation to our neighbour. And therefore justice is often thought to be the greatest of virtues, and "neither evening nor morning star" is so wonderful; and proverbially "in justice is every virtue comprehended." And it is complete virtue in its fullest sense, because it is the actual exercise of complete virtue. It is complete because he who possesses it can exercise his virtue not only in himself but towards his neighbour also; for many men can exercise virtue in their own affairs, but not in their relations to their neighbour.

◆◆◆

But at all events what we are investigating is the justice which is a *part* of virtue; for there is a justice of this kind, as we maintain. Similarly it is with injustice in the particular sense that we are concerned.

That there is such a thing is indicated by the fact that while the man who exhibits in action the other forms of wickedness acts wrongly indeed, but not graspingly (*e.g.* the man who throws away his shield through cowardice or speaks harshly through bad temper or fails to help a friend with money through meanness), when a man acts graspingly he often exhibits none of these vices— no, nor all together, but certainly wickedness of some kind (for we blame him) and injustice. There is, then, another kind of injustice which is a part of injustice in the wide sense, and a use of the word "unjust" which answers to a part of what is unjust in the wide sense of "contrary to the law." Again, if one man commits adultery for the sake of gain and makes money by it, while another does so at the bidding of appetite though he loses money and is penalized for it, the latter would be held to be self-indulgent rather than grasping, but the former is unjust, but not self-indulgent; evidently, therefore, he is unjust by reason of his making gain by his act. Again, all other unjust acts are ascribed invariably to some particular kind of wickedness, for example adultery to self-indulgence, the desertion of a comrade in battle to cowardice, physical violence to anger; but if a man makes gain, his action is ascribed to no form of wickedness but injustice. Evidently, therefore, there is apart from injustice in the wide sense another, "particular," injustice which shares the name and nature of the first, because its definition falls within the same genus; for the significance of both consists in a relation to one's neighbour, but the one is concerned with honour or money or safety—or that which includes all these, if we had a single name for it—and its motive is the pleasure that arises from gain; while the other is concerned with all the objects with which the good man is concerned.

It is clear, then, that there is more than one kind of justice, and that there is one which is distinct from virtue entire; we must try to grasp its genus and differentia. . . .

Of particular justice and that which is just in the corresponding sense, (A) one kind is that which is manifested in distributions of honour or money or the other things that fall to be divided among those who have a share in the constitution (for in these it is possible for one man to have a share either unequal or equal to that of another), and (B) one is that which plays a rectifying part in transactions between man and man. Of this there are two divisions; of transactions (1) some are voluntary, and (2) others involuntary—voluntary such transactions as sale, purchase, loan for consumption, pledging, loan for use, depositing, letting (they are called voluntary because the origin of these transactions is voluntary), while of the involuntary (a) some are clandestine, such as theft, adultery, poisoning, procuring, enticement of slaves, assassination, false witness, and (b) others are violent, such as assault, imprisonment, murder, robbery with violence, mutilation, abuse, insult.

◆◆◆

(A) We have shown that both the unjust man and the unjust act are unfair or unequal; now it is clear that there is also an intermediate between the two unequals involved in either case. And this is the equal; for in any kind of action in which there is a more and a less there is also what is equal. If, then, the unjust is unequal, the just is equal, as all men suppose it to be, even apart from argument. And since the equal is intermediate, the just will be an intermediate. Now equality implies at least two things. The just, then, must be both intermediate and equal and relative (*i.e.* for certain persons). And *qua* intermediate it must be between certain things (which are respectively greater and less); *qua* equal, it involves *two* things; *qua* just, it is for certain people. The just, therefore, involves at least four terms; for the persons for whom it is in fact just are two, and the things in which it is manifested, the objects distributed, are two. And the same equality will exist between the persons and between the things concerned; for as the latter—the things concerned—are related, so are the former; if they are not equal, they will not have what is equal, but this is the origin of quarrels and complaints—when either equals have and are awarded unequal shares, or unequals equal shares. Further, this is plain from the fact that awards should be "according to merit"; for all men agree that what is just in distribution must be according to merit in some sense, though they do not all specify the same sort of merit, but democrats identify it with the status of freeman, supporters of oligarchy with wealth (or with noble birth), and supporters of aristocracy with excellence.

This, then, is what the just is—the proportional; the unjust is what violates the proportion. Hence one term becomes too great, the other too small, as indeed happens in practice, for the man who acts unjustly has too much, and the man who is unjustly treated too little, of what is good. In the case of evil the reverse is true; for the lesser evil is reckoned a good in comparison with the greater, and what is worthy of choice is good, and what is worthier of choice a greater good.

This, then, is one species of the just.

◆◆◆

(B) The remaining one is the rectificatory, which arises in connexion with transactions both voluntary and involuntary. This form of the just has a different specific character from the former. For the justice which distributes common possessions is always in accordance with the kind of proportion mentioned above (for in the case also in which the distribution is made from the common funds of a partnership it will be according to the same ratio which the funds put into the business by the partners bear to one another); and the injustice opposed to this kind of justice is that which violates the proportion. But the justice in transactions between man and man is a sort of equality indeed, and the injustice a sort of inequality; not according to that kind of proportion, however, but according to arithmetical proportion. For it makes no difference whether a good man has defrauded a bad man or a bad man a good one, nor whether it is a good or a bad man that has committed adultery; the law looks only to the distinctive character of the injury, and treats the parties as equal, if one is in the wrong and the other is being wronged, and if one inflicted injury and the other has received it. Therefore, this kind of injustice being an inequality, the judge tries to equalize it; for in the case also in which one has received and the other has inflicted a wound, or one has slain and the other has been slain, the suffering and the action have been unequally distributed; but the judge tries to equalize things by means of the penalty, taking away from the gain of the assailant. For the term "gain" is applied generally to such cases, even if it be not a term appropriate to certain cases, for example to the person who inflicts a wound—and "loss" to the sufferer; at all events when the suffering has been estimated, the one is called loss and the other gain.

> *To go to the judge is to go to justice; for the nature of the judge is to be a sort of animate justice.*

Therefore the equal is intermediate between the greater and less in contrary ways; more of the good and less of the evil are gain, and the contrary is loss; intermediate between them is, as we saw, the equal, which we say is just; therefore corrective justice will be the intermediate between loss and gain. This is why, when people dispute, they take refuge in the judge; and to go to the judge is to go to justice; for the nature of the judge is to be a sort of animate justice; and they seek the judge as an intermediate; and in some states they call judges mediators, on the assumption that if they get what is intermediate they will get what is just. The just, then, is an intermediate, since the judge is so. The judge restores equality.[3]

2. Two Modern Theories of Justice: Hume and Mill on Utility and Rights

In contrast to the Greeks, the premise of most modern theories of justice has been the equality of everyone with everyone else. No one is "better" than anyone else, whatever his or her talents, achievements, wealth, family, or intelligence. This view rules out slavery on principle, whatever the benefits to society as a whole and whatever the alleged benefits to the slaves. Slavery is inequality and is thus to be condemned. But this egalitarian principle has its problems too. It is obvious that, as a matter of fact, all people are not equally endowed with intelligence or talent, good looks or abilities. Is it therefore to the good of all that everyone should be treated equally? One person is a doctor, capable of saving many lives; another is a chronic profligate and drunkard. If they were to commit exactly the same crime, would it be to the public interest to give them equal jail terms? Obviously not. But would it be just to give them different terms? It doesn't appear so. One problem that recent theorists have tried to answer is connected with cases in which the public interest seems at odds with the demands for equal treatment. A similar problem gives rise to one of the "paradoxes of democracy," which we mentioned before. Does it make sense to treat the opinions of an ignorant person whose only knowledge of current events comes from fifteen minutes (at best) of television news a day in the way that we treat

---

[3] Aristotle, *Nicomachean Ethics*, trans. W. D. Ross (Oxford: Oxford University Press, 1925).

the opinions of a skilled political veteran? But the ballots we vote on make no such distinction. And it is obvious that our society, despite its egalitarian principles, treats people who are cleverer at business or power-brokering much better than everyone else. Is this an example of systematic injustice? Or are there cases, even for us, in which inequality can still be justified as justice?

The theory of justice has been one of the central concerns of British philosophy for several centuries. **Thomas Hobbes** developed a theory that began with equality as a "natural fact" and took justice to be that which "assured peace and security to all" enforced by the government. There is no justice in "the state of nature," Hobbes argued; justice like law comes into existence only with society, through a "social compact" in which everyone agrees to abide by certain rules and to cooperate rather than compete—all for their mutual benefit. Several years later, John Locke and then David Hume argued a similar theory of justice; again, equality was the premise, and mutual agreement the basis of government authority. For both philosophers, the ultimate criterion of justice was utility, the public interest, and therefore the satisfaction of the interests of at least most citizens. This would have been rejected by Plato and Aristotle.

Hume exemplifies this modern view—that justice is to be characterized not just in terms of the structure of the overall society and everyone's "place" in it, but by the interests and well-being of each and every individual. But what about an instance, Hume asks, in which a particular act of justice clearly is contrary to the public interests, such as the case in which an obviously guilty criminal is released for technical reasons or a disgusting pornographer is allowed to publish and sell his or her wares under the protection of "free speech"? Hume replies that there is a need to distinguish between the utility of a single act and the utility of an overall system; that although a specific act of justice might go against the public interest, the system of justice necessarily will be in the public interest. This means that a single unjust act is to be challenged not as an isolated occurrence but as an example of a general set of rules and practices.

ON "JUSTICE AND UTILITY"
BY **DAVID HUME**

To make this more evident, consider, that though the rules of justice are established merely by interest, their connection with interest is somewhat singular, and is different from what may be observed on other occasions. A single act of justice is frequently contrary to *public interest;* and were it to stand alone, without being followed by other acts, may, in itself, be very prejudicial to society. When a man of merit, of a beneficent disposition, restores a great fortune to a miser, or a seditious bigot, he has acted justly and laudably, but the public is a real sufferer. Nor is every single act of justice, considered apart, more conducive to private interest, than to public; and it is easily conceived how a man may impoverish himself by a single instance of integrity, and have reason to wish that with regard to that single act, the laws of justice were for a moment suspended in the universe. But however single acts of justice may be contrary, either to public or private interest, it is certain, that the whole plan or scheme is highly conducive, or indeed absolutely requisite, both to the support of society, and the well-being of every individual.[4]

The most explicitly "utilitarian" statement of justice as utility is found, however, in John Stuart Mill's influential pamphlet, *Utilitarianism.*

FROM *UTILITARIANISM*
BY **JOHN STUART MILL**

In the case of this, as of our other moral sentiments, there is no necessary connexion between the question of its origin and that of its binding force. That a feeling is bestowed on us by nature does not necessarily legitimate all its promptings. The feeling of justice might be a peculiar instinct, and might yet require, like our other instincts, to be controlled and enlightened by a higher reason. If we have intellectual instincts leading us to judge in a particular way, as well as animal instincts that prompt us to act in a particular way, there is no necessity that the former should be more infallible in their sphere than the latter in theirs; it may as well happen that wrong judgments are occasionally suggested by those, as wrong actions by those.

◆◆◆

In the first place, it is mostly considered unjust to deprive anyone of his personal liberty, his property, or any other thing which belongs to him by law. Here, therefore, is one instance of the application of the terms "just" and "unjust" in a perfectly definite sense, namely, that it is just to respect, unjust to violate, the *legal rights* of anyone. But this judgment admits of several exceptions, arising from the other forms in which the notions of justice and injustice present themselves. For example, the person who suffers the deprivation may (as the phrase is) have forfeited the rights which he is so deprived of—a case to which we shall return presently. . . .

Secondly, the legal rights of which he is deprived may be rights which *ought* not to have belonged to him; in other words, the law which confers on him these rights may be a bad law. When it is so or when (which is the same thing for our purpose) it is supposed to be so, opinions will differ as to the justice or injustice of infringing it. Some maintain that no law, however bad, ought to be disobeyed by an individual citizen; that his opposition to it, if shown at all, should only be shown in endeavoring to get it altered by competent authority. This opinion (which condemns many of the most illustrious benefactors of mankind, and would often protect pernicious institutions against the only weapons which, in the state of things existing at the time, have any chance of succeeding against them) is defended by those who hold it on grounds of expediency, principally on

---

[4]David Hume, *Enquiry Concerning the Principles of Morals* (La Salle, IL: Open Court, 1912).

that of the importance to the common interest of mankind, of maintaining inviolate the sentiment of submission to law. Other persons, again, hold the directly contrary opinion that any law, judged to be bad, may blamelessly be disobeyed, even though it be not judged to be unjust but only inexpedient, while others would confine the license of disobedience to the case of unjust laws; but, again, some say that all laws which are inexpedient are unjust, since every law imposes some restriction on the natural liberty of mankind, which restriction is an injustice unless legitimated by tending to their good. Among these diversities of opinion it seems to be universally admitted that there may be unjust laws, and that law, consequently, is not the ultimate criterion of justice, but may give to one person a benefit, or impose on another an evil, which justice condemns. When, however, a law is thought to be unjust, it seems always to be regarded as being so in the same way in which a breach of law is unjust, namely, by infringing somebody's right, which, as it cannot in this case be a legal right, receives a different appellation and is called a moral right. We may say, therefore, that a second case of injustice consists in taking or withholding from any person that to which he has a *moral right.*

Thirdly, it is universally considered just that each person should obtain that (whether good or evil) which he *deserves,* and unjust that he should obtain a good or be made to undergo an evil which he does not deserve. This is, perhaps, the clearest and most emphatic form in which the idea of justice is conceived by the general mind. As it involves the notion of desert, the question arises what constitutes desert? Speaking in a general way, a person is understood to deserve good if he does right, evil if he does wrong; and in a more particular sense, to deserve good from those to whom he does or has done good, and evil from those to whom he does or has done evil. The precept of returning good for evil has never been regarded as a case of the fulfillment of justice, but as one in which the claims of justice are waived, in obedience to other considerations.

Fourthly, it is confessedly unjust to *break faith* with anyone: to violate an engagement, either express or implied, or disappoint expectations raised by our own conduct, at least if we have raised those expectations knowingly and voluntarily. Like the other obligations of justice already spoken of, this one is not regarded as absolute, but as capable of being overruled by a stronger obligation of justice on the other side, or by such conduct on the part of the person concerned as is deemed to absolve us from our obligation to him and to constitute a *forfeiture* of the benefit which he has been led to expect.

Fifthly, it is, by universal admission, inconsistent with justice to be *partial*— to show favor or preference to one person over another in matters to which favor and preference do not properly apply. Impartiality, however, does not seem to be regarded as a duty in itself, but rather as instrumental to some other duty; for it is admitted that favor and preference are not always censurable, and, indeed, the cases in which they are condemned are rather the exception than the rule. A person would be more likely to be blamed than applauded for giving his family or friends no superiority in good offices over strangers when he could do so without violating any other duty; and no one thinks it unjust to seek one person in preference to another as a friend, connection, or companion. Impartiality where rights are concerned is of course obligatory, but this is involved in the more general obligation of giving to everyone his right. A tribunal, for example, must be impartial because it is bound to award, without regard to any other consideration, a disputed object to the one of two parties who has the right to it. There are other cases in which impartiality means being solely influenced by desert, as with those who, in the capacity of judges, preceptors, or parents, administer reward and punishment as such. There are cases, again, in which it means being solely influenced by consideration for the public interest, as in making a selection among candidates for a government employment. Impartiality, in short, as an obligation of justice, may be said to mean being exclusively influenced by the considerations which it is supposed ought to influence the particular case in hand, and resisting solicitation of any motives which prompt to conduct different from what those considerations would dictate.

Nearly allied to the idea of impartiality is that of *equality,* which often enters as a component part both into the conception of justice and into the practice of it, and, in the eyes of many persons, constitutes its essence. But in this, still more than in any other case, the notion of justice varies in different persons, and always conforms in its variations to their notion of utility. Each person maintains that equality is the dictate of justice, except where he thinks that expediency requires inequality. The justice of giving equal protection to the rights of all is maintained by those who support the most outrageous inequality in the rights themselves. Even in slave countries it is theoretically admitted that the rights of the slave, such as they are, ought to be as sacred as those of the master, and that a tribunal which fails to enforce them with equal strictness is wanting in justice; while, at the same time, institutions which leave to the slave scarcely any rights to enforce are not deemed unjust because they are not deemed inexpedient. Those who think that utility requires distinctions of rank do not consider it unjust that riches and social privileges should be unequally dispensed; but those who think this inequality inexpedient think it unjust also. Whoever thinks that government is necessary sees no injustice in as much inequality as is constituted by giving to the magistrate powers not granted to other people. Even among those who hold leveling doctrines, there are differences of opinion about expediency. Some communists consider it unjust that the produce of the labor of the community should be shared on any other principle than that of exact equality; others think it just that those should receive most whose wants are greatest; while others hold that those who work harder, or who produce more, or whose services are more valuable to the community, may justly claim a larger quota in the division of the produce. And the sense of natural justice may be plausibly appealed to in behalf of every one of the opinions.

Mill then goes on to define a **right:**

When we call anything a person's right, we mean that he has a valid claim on society to protect him in the possession of it, either by the force of law or by that of education and opinion. If he has what we consider a sufficient claim,

When we call any-thing a person's right, we mean that he has a valid claim on society to protect him in the possession of it, either by the force of law or by that of education and opinion.

on whatever account, to have something guar-anteed to him by society, we say that he has a right to it.

To have a right, then, is, I conceive, to have something which society ought to defend me in the possession of. If the objector goes on to ask why it ought, I can give him no other reason than general utility. If that expression does not seem to convey a sufficient feeling of the strength of the obligation, nor to account for the peculiar energy of the feeling, it is because there goes to the com-position of the sentiment, not a rational only but also an animal element—the thirst for retaliation; and this thirst derives its intensity, as well as its moral justification, from the extraordinarily impor-tant and impressive kind of utility which is con-cerned. The interest involved is that of security, to everyone's feelings the most vital of all interests. All other earthly benefits are needed by one person, not needed by another; and many of them can, if necessary, be cheerfully foregone or replaced by something else; but security no human being can possibly do without; on it we depend for all our immunity from evil and for the whole value of all and every good, beyond the passing moment, since nothing but the grati-fication of the instant could be of any worth to us if we could be deprived of everything the next instant by whoever was momentarily stronger than our-selves. Now this most indispensable of all necessaries, after physical nutriment, cannot be had unless the machinery for providing it is kept unintermittedly in active play. Our notion, therefore, of the claim we have on our fellow creatures to join in making safe for us the very groundwork of our existence gathers feel-ings around it so much more intense than those concerned in any of the more common cases of utility that the difference in degree (as is often the case in psy-chology) becomes a real difference in kind. The claim assumes that character of absoluteness, that apparent infinity and incommensurability with all other considerations which constitute the distinction between the feeling of right and wrong and that of ordinary expediency and inexpediency. The feelings con-cerned are so powerful, and we count so positively on finding a responsive feel-ing in others (all being alike interested) that *ought* and *should* grow into *must,* and recognized indispensability becomes a moral necessity, analogous to physi-cal, and often not inferior to it in binding force.[5]

Mill's utilitarian theory of justice is a logical extension of his ethical theories: What is good and desirable is what is best for the greatest number of people. But although it might at first seem as if the greatest happiness of the greatest number leaves no

---

[5] John Stuart Mill, *Utilitarianism* (New York: Bobbs-Merrill, 1957).

room for such abstract concerns as justice, Mill argues that, to the contrary, only utility can give that abstract sense of justice some concrete basis in human life.

The problem with the utilitarian theory of justice is identical to the problem we saw with the utilitarian theory of morals. Could there not be a case in which the public interest and general utility would be served only at the clearly unjust expense of a single unfortunate individual? Suppose we lived in a society that ran extremely well, such that we had few if any complaints about our government and the way it was run, when a single muckraking journalist started turning the peace upside down with his insistence that something was very wrong in the government. We might easily suppose that, at least in the short run, the public confusion and trauma would be much more harmful to the public interest than the slight correction that would result from public exposure. Should the government forcefully silence the journalist? We would say no. He has a right to his inquiries and a right to speak his mind. Or suppose that the most efficient way to solve a series of ongoing crimes was to torture a recently captured suspect and hold him without evidence? Here again public interest and justice are at odds. Or more generally, should the government have the authority to throw people in jail just because it has reason (even good reason) to believe that they will create a public disturbance or commit certain crimes? Public interest says yes; justice says no.

This is the problem with utilitarian theories of justice in general: although we may well agree that justice *ought* to serve the public interest and every individual's interests as well, the utilitarian view is always in an awkward position when it must choose to serve the public interest at the intolerable expense and injustice of a small number of individuals or even a single individual. Consider the extreme example of an entire city that would prosper if it would sacrifice the life of one innocent child. Arguably, utilitarianism would seem to defend the sacrifice; justice, however, says that such a sacrifice is inexcusable.

3. The Social Contract

The single most influential conception of justice in modern times has been called the "social contract theory." The **social contract** is an agreement among people to share certain interests and make certain compromises for the good of them all. It is a "consent of the governed theory." In one form or another, it existed even in ancient times. For example, read Socrates' argument in the *Crito,* in which he says that by staying in Athens he had implicitly agreed to abide by its laws, even when those laws unfairly condemned him to death. What is most important in understanding the nature of this social contract is that, as in Socrates' argument, there need not have been any actual, physical contract or even oral agreement in order to talk about it. We are bound by social contract, in other words, even if we never signed or saw such a contract. Moreover, it may not be the case that there was ever such a contract, even in past history. It happens, however, that Americans are among the few people in the world whose state was actually formed explicitly by such a contract, namely, our *Constitution.* But the actual existence of such a piece of paper is not necessary to a discussion about a social contract. Simply to live in a society, according to these philosophers, is to have agreed, at least implicitly, to such an agreement. (Thus, living in a society you are expected to obey its laws; "ignorance is no excuse," and you cannot get out of an arrest by saying "I don't really live here," much less "I don't recognize your right to arrest me.")

Two very different pictures of the original social contract are presented to us by the English philosopher Thomas Hobbes and the French philosopher Jean-Jacques Rousseau. Both begin by considering man in "the state of nature," without laws and without society, before men and women came together to accept the social contract. Hobbes bases his conception of the social contract, however, on an extremely unfavorable conception of human nature. He attacks the idealistic political philosophies of Plato and Aristotle for being unrealistic and assuming wrongly that people are naturally capable of virtue and wisdom. Like **Machiavelli,** whom he follows with praise, he considers himself a "realist." As with most realists, this meant seeing the nasty side of things. So, according to his theory of human nature, natural man is a selfish beast, fighting for his own interests against everyone else. Human life is a "war of all against all" and a person's life, consequently, is "nasty, brutish and short." He dismisses reason and appeals to human passions, particularly the passion for self-preservation. The social contract, therefore, is mainly an agreement of equally selfish and self-seeking persons not to commit mutual murder.

FROM *LEVIATHAN*
BY **THOMAS HOBBES**

OF THE NATURAL CONDITION OF MANKIND AS
CONCERNING THEIR FELICITY, AND MISERY

Men by nature equal. Nature hath made men so equal, in the faculties of the body, and mind; as that though there be found one man sometimes manifestly stronger in body, or of quicker mind than another; yet when all is reckoned together, the difference between man, and man, is not so considerable, as that one man can thereupon claim to himself any benefit, to which another may not pretend, as well as he. For as to the strength of the body, the weakest has strength enough to kill the strongest, either by secret machination or by confederacy with others, that are in the same danger with himself.

◆◆◆

For such is the nature of men, that howsoever they may acknowledge many others to be more witty, or more eloquent, or more learned; yet they will hardly believe there be many so wise as themselves; for they see their own wit at hand, and other men's at a distance. But this proveth rather that men are in that point equal, than unequal. For there is not ordinarily a greater sign of the equal distribution of any thing, than that every man is contented with his share.

From equality proceeds diffidence. From this equality of ability, ariseth equality of hope in the attaining of our ends. And therefore if any two men desire the same thing, which nevertheless they cannot both enjoy, they become enemies; and in the way to their end, which is principally their own conservation, and sometimes their delectation only, endeavour to destroy, or subdue one another. And from hence it comes to pass, that where an invader hath no more to fear, than another man's single power; if one plant, sow, build, or possess a convenient seat, others may probably be expected to come prepared with forces united, to dispossess, and deprive him, not only of the fruit of his labour, but also of his life, or liberty. And the invader again is in the like danger of another.

> *... if any two men desire the same thing, which nevertheless they cannot both enjoy, they become enemies; and in the way to their end, which is principally their own conservation, and sometimes their delectation only, endeavour to destroy, or subdue one another.*

From diffidence war. And from this diffidence of one another, there is no way for any man to secure himself, so reasonable, as anticipation; that is, by force, or wiles, to master the persons of all men he can, so long, till he see no other power great enough to endanger him: and this is no more than his own conservation requireth, and is generally allowed. Also because there be some, that taking pleasure in contemplating their own power in the acts of conquest, which they pursue farther than their security requires; if others, that otherwise would be glad to be at ease within modest bounds, should not by invasion increase their power, they would not be able, long time, by standing only on their defence, to subsist. And by consequence, such augmentation of dominion over men being necessary to a man's conservation, it ought to be allowed him.

Again, men have no pleasure, but on the contrary a great deal of grief, in keeping company, where there is no power able to overawe them all. For every man looketh that his companion should value him, at the same rate he sets upon himself: and upon all signs of contempt, or undervaluing, naturally endeavors, as far as he dares (which amongst them that have no common power to keep them in quiet, is far enough to make them destroy each other), to extort a greater value from his contemners, by damage; and from others, by the example.

So that in the nature of man, we find three principal causes of quarrel. First, competition; secondly, diffidence; thirdly, glory.

The first, maketh men invade for gain; the second, for safety; and the third, for reputation. The first use violence, to make themselves masters of other men's persons, wives, children, and cattle; the second, to defend them; the third, for trifles, as a word, a smile, a different opinion, and any other sign of undervalue, either direct in their persons, or by reflection in their kindred, their friends, their nation, their profession, or their name.

Out of civil states, there is always war of every one against every one. Hereby it is manifest, that during the time men live without a common power to keep them all in awe, they are in that condition which is called war; and such a war, as is of every man, against every man. For war, consisteth not in battle only, or the act of fighting, but in a tract of time, wherein the will to contend by battle is sufficiently known. . . .

The incommodities of such a war. Whatsoever therefore is consequent to a time of war, where every man is enemy to every man; the same is consequent to the time, wherein men live without other security, than what their own strength, and their own invention shall furnish them withal. In such condition, there is no place for industry; because the fruit thereof is uncertain: and consequently no culture of the earth; no navigation, nor use of the commodities that may be imported by sea; no commodious building; no instruments of moving, and removing, such things as require much force; no knowledge of the face of the earth; no account of time; no arts; no letters; no society; and which is worst of all, continual fear, and danger of violent death; and the life of man, solitary, poor, nasty, brutish, and short.

It may seem strange to some man, that has not well weighed these things; that nature should thus dissociate, and render men apt to invade, and destroy one another: and he may therefore, not trusting to this inference, made from the passions, desire perhaps to have the same confirmed by experience. Let him therefore consider with himself, when taking a journey, he arms himself, and seeks to go well accompanied; when going to sleep, he locks his doors; when even in his house he locks his chests; and this when he knows there be laws, and public officers, armed to revenge all injuries shall be done him; what opinion he has of his fellow-subjects, when he rides armed; of his fellow citizens, when he locks his doors; and of his children, and servants, when he locks his chests. Does he not there as much accuse mankind by his actions, as I do by my words? But neither of us accuse men's nature in it. The desires, and other passions of man, are in themselves no sin. No more are the actions, that proceed from those passions, till they know a law that forbids them: which till laws be made they cannot know: nor can any law be made, till they have agreed upon the person that shall make it.

It may peradventure be thought, there was never such a time, nor condition of war as this; and I believe it was never generally so, over all the world: but there are many places, where they live so now. For the savage people in many places of America, except the government of small families, the concord whereof dependeth on natural lust, have no government at all; and live at this day in that brutish manner, as I said before. Howsoever, it may be perceived what manner of life there would be, where there were no common power to fear, by the manner of life, which men that have formerly lived under a peaceful government, use to degenerate into, in a civil war.

OF THE FIRST AND SECOND NATURAL LAWS, AND OF CONTRACTS

Right of nature what. The right of nature, which writers commonly call *jus naturale,* is the liberty each man hath, to use his own power, as he will himself, for the preservation of his own nature; that is to say, of his own life; and consequently, of doing any thing, which in his own judgment, and reason, he shall conceive to be the aptest means thereunto.

Liberty what. By liberty, is understood, according to the proper signification of the word, the absence of external impediments: which impediments, may oft take away part of a man's power to do what he would; but cannot hinder him from using the power left him, according as his judgment, and reason shall dictate to him.

A law of nature what. A law of nature, *lex naturalis,* is a precept or general rule, found out by reason, by which a man is forbidden to do that, which is destructive of his life, or taketh away the means of preserving the same; and to omit that, by which he thinketh it may be best preserved.

Difference of right and law. For though they that speak of this subject, use to confound *jus,* and *lex, right* and *law:* yet they ought to be distinguished; because right, consisteth in liberty to do, or to forbear: whereas law, determineth, and bindeth to one of them: so that law, and right, differ as much, as obligation, and liberty; which in one and the same matter are inconsistent.

Naturally every man has right to every thing. And because the condition of man, as hath been declared in the precedent chapter, is a condition of war of every one against every one; in which case every one is governed by his own reason; and there is nothing he can make use of, that may not be of help unto him, in preserving his life against his enemies; it followeth, that in such a condition, every man has a right to every thing; even to one another's body. And therefore, as long as this natural right of every man to every thing endureth, there can be no security to any man, how strong or wise soever he be, of living out the time, which nature ordinarily alloweth men to live.

The fundamental law of nature. And consequently it is a precept, or general rule of reason, *that every man, ought to endeavour peace, as far as he has hope of obtaining it; and when he cannot obtain it, that he may seek, and use, all helps, and advantages of war.*

◆◆◆

The second law of nature. From this fundamental law of nature, by which men are commanded to endeavour peace, is derived this second law; *that a man be willing, when others are so too, as far-forth, as for peace, and defence of himself he shall think it necessary, to lay down this right to all things; and be contented with so much liberty against other men, as he would allow other men against himself.* For as long as every man holdeth this right, of doing any thing he liketh; so long are all men in the condition of war. But if other men will not lay down their right, as well as he; then there is no reason for any one, to divest himself of his: for that were to expose himself to prey, which no man is bound to, rather than to dispose himself to peace. This is that law of the Gospel; *whatsoever you require that others should do to you, that do ye to them.*

◆◆◆

What it is to lay down a right. To *lay down* man's *right to* any thing, is to *divest* himself of the *liberty,* of hindering another of the benefit of his own right to the same. For he that renounceth, or passeth away his right, giveth not to any other man a right which he had not before; because there is nothing to which every man had not right by nature: but only standeth out of his way, that he may enjoy his own original right, without hindrance from him; not without hindrance from another. So that the effect which redoundeth to one man, by another man's defect of right, is but so much diminution of impediments to the use of his own right original.

◆◆◆

Not all rights are alienable. Whensoever a man transferreth his right, or renounceth it; it is either in consideration of some right reciprocally transferred to himself; or for some other good he hopeth for thereby. For it is a voluntary act: and of the voluntary acts of every man, the object is some *good to himself.*

If a covenant be made, wherein neither of the parties perform presently, but trust one another; in the condition of mere nature, which is a condition of war of every man against every man, upon any reasonable suspicion, it is void: but if there be a common power set over them both, with right and force sufficient to compel performance, it is not void.

And therefore there be some rights, which no man can be understood by any words, or other signs, to have abandoned, or transferred. As first a man cannot lay down the right of resisting them, that assault him by force, to take away his life; because he cannot be understood to aim thereby, at any good to himself. The same may be said of wounds, and chains, and imprisonment; both because there is no benefit consequent to such patience; as there is to the patience of suffering another to be wounded, or imprisoned: as also because a man cannot tell, when he seeth men proceed against him by violence, whether they intend his death or not. And lastly the motive, and end for which this renouncing, and transferring of right is introduced, is nothing else but the security of man's person, in his life, and in the means of so preserving life, as not to be weary of it. And therefore if a man by words, or other signs, seem to despoil himself of the end, for which those signs were intended; he is not to be understood as if he meant it, or that it was his will; but that he was ignorant of how such words and actions were to be interpreted.

Contract what. The mutual transferring of right, as that which men call CONTRACT.

◆◆◆

Covenants of mutual trust, when invalid. If a covenant be made, wherein neither of the parties perform presently, but trust one another; in the condition of mere nature, which is a condition of war of every man against every man, upon any reasonable suspicion, it is void: but if there be a common power set over them both, with right and force sufficient to compel performance, it is not void. For he that performeth first, has no assurance the other will perform after; because the bonds of words are too weak to bridle men's ambition, avarice, anger, and other passions, without the fear of some coercive power; which in the condition of mere nature, where all men are equal, and judges of the justness of their own fears, cannot possibly be supposed. And therefore he which performeth first, does but betray himself to his enemy; contrary to the right, he can never abandon, of defending his life, and means of living.

But in a civil estate, where there is a power set up to constrain those that would otherwise violate their faith, that fear is no more reasonable; and for that cause, he which by the covenant is to perform first, is obliged so to do.

The cause of fear, which maketh such a covenant invalid, must be always something arising after the covenant made; as some new fact, or other sign of the will not to perform: else it cannot make the covenant void. For that which could not hinder a man from promising, ought not to be admitted as a hindrance of performing.

Right to the end, containeth right to the means. He that transferreth any right, transferreth the means of enjoying it, as far as lieth in his power. As he that selleth land, is understood to transfer the herbage, and whatsoever grows upon it: nor can he that sells a mill turn away the stream that drives it. And they that give to a man the right of government in sovereignty, are understood to give him the right of levying money to maintain soldiers; and of appointing magistrates for the administration of justice.[6]

Hobbes begins his argument with the perhaps surprising observation that people are basically equal in nature. He is not talking here about legal equality or equal rights (for there are no laws and no legal rights) but rather equality in abilities, talents, and power. This seems strange, because the problem of equality usually pays attention to the great differences between people. Instead Hobbes points out our similarities. In particular, he points out that almost everyone is strong and smart enough to kill or inflict grievous injury on others. Even a puny moron can, with a knife or a handgun, kill the strongest and smartest person on earth. Accordingly, the basis of the social contract (or "covenant") according to Hobbes is our mutual protection. Everyone agrees not to kill other people and in return is guaranteed that he or she won't be killed. Although it is a cynical view of human nature, it also continues to be one of the most powerful arguments for strong governments. (Hobbes himself was a conservative monarchist.)

Rousseau, quite to the contrary, had an extremely optimistic view of human nature, as we saw in the preceding chapter. He believed that people were "naturally good," and it was only the corruptions of society that made them selfish and destructive.

---

[6] Thomas Hobbes, *Leviathan* (New York: Hafner, 1926).

Rousseau does not take the social contract, therefore, to be simply a doctrine of protection between mutually brutish individuals. The function of the state is rather to allow people to develop the "natural goodness" that they had in the absence of any state at all. This is not to say (although Rousseau is often interpreted this way) that he was nostalgic and wanted to "go back to the state of nature." That is impossible. (It is not even clear that Rousseau believed that there ever was a "state of nature" as such; his example, like Hobbes' example, is a way of giving a picture of "human nature," whether or not it is historically accurate.) We are already in society; that is a given fact. So Rousseau's aim is to develop a conception of the state that will allow us to live as morally as possible. This is important, for Rousseau, unlike most social contract theorists, is not at all a utilitarian; it is not happiness that is most important but goodness. (Hobbes, by way of contrast, took utility, pleasure and well-being, in addition to self-preservation, to be the purpose of the social contract.)

Rousseau's ambition, therefore, is not to "get us back to nature" but rather to revise our conception of the state. His "revision," however, is one of the most radical documents in modern history and has rightly been said to be one of the causes of both the American and French revolutions. The main thesis is one that Rousseau inherits from Locke: The state has legitimate power only so long as it serves the people it governs. The revolutionary corollary is that when a state ceases to serve its citizens, the citizens have a right to overthrow that government. This was a radical claim, again reminiscent of Locke. Even Rousseau was not comfortable with it. (Locke had made his statement *after* the English Revolution.) He called revolution "the most horrible alternative," to be avoided wherever possible. But subsequent French history took his theories quite literally and demonstrated too the "horror" that may follow too radical and abrupt a change in the authority that citizens accept as legitimate.

In earlier works, Rousseau argued his famous thesis that "natural man" is "naturally good" and that contemporary society has corrupted him (and her). He went on to say that competition and the artificiality of our lust for private property are responsible for this corruption, and he even included marriage and romantic love as forms of this "lust for private property." In the state of nature, he suggests, people mated when they felt like it, with whomever they felt like, and duels fought between rivals were unheard of. Rousseau does not suggest that we return to that prehistoric custom, but he does use it as a wedge to pry open even the most sacred of our modern civil institutions. All of these, he argues, must be reexamined, and the tool for that reexamination is the social contract.

The key to his most famous book, appropriately called *The Social Contract,* is that man must regain his freedom within society. This does not mean, however, that a person can do whatever he or she would like to do. Quite the contrary—to be a citizen, according to Rousseau, is to want and do what is good for the society as well. To be free is precisely to want to do what is good for the society. In fact, in one of the most problematic statements of the social contract, Rousseau says that a person who does not so act for the good of the society may have to "be forced to be free." Here is the basis for a strange paradox. On the one hand, Rousseau has properly been regarded as the father of the most liberal and revolutionary political theories of our time. (Marx, for example, claims a great debt to Rousseau). His political philosophy stresses individual freedom and rights above all, even above the state itself. But another side to Rousseau emerges in his paradoxical phrase; his stress on the state as an entity in itself ("the sovereign," presumably the king, but essentially any government) and the subservience of the individual to the state has also caused him to be labeled an authoritarian and the forerunner of totalitarian and fascist governments.

This paradox is not easily resolved, but we can at least explain how it comes about. Rousseau believes that the state is subject to and receives its legitimacy from the people it governs. But that does not mean that individual people need have any real power in determining the form or functions of government. Rousseau is not a democrat. What he says instead is that the state is subject to what he calls the general will, which is not simply a collection of individuals but something more. For example, we talk about "the spirit of the revolution" or "the discontent of the working class," but this spirit or discontent is not simply the product of each individual person. A poll of workers or revolutionaries would not show it either way. The revolution may have spirit even though some participants do not; indeed, they may even dislike the whole idea. Here is the source of the paradox: Legitimacy is given to the state by the general will, not by every individual person. The person who does not agree with the general will, therefore, may very well find himself or herself forced into compliance with the state (as Rousseau says, "forced to be free"). How much force, however, is a matter about which Rousseau is not very clear; nor have his many followers agreed on that crucial point either. On one extreme, Rousseau's authoritarian followers have insisted that all dissent from the general will must be stifled; on the other extreme, Rousseau's most libertarian and anarchist followers have insisted that the rights of the individual to be free from government intervention and to live according to his or her own "natural goodness" outweigh any claims that the state may have. What follows are a few selections from *The Social Contract*, beginning with one of Rousseau's best-known slogans.

FROM *THE SOCIAL CONTRACT*
BY **JEAN-JACQUES ROUSSEAU**

Man is born free; and everywhere he is in chains. One thinks himself the master of others, and still remains a greater slave than they. How did this change come about? I do not know. What can make it legitimate? That question I think I can answer.

If I took into account only force, and the effects derived from it, I should say: "As long as a people is compelled to obey, and obeys, it does well; as soon as it can shake off the yoke, and shakes it off, it does still better; for, regaining its liberty by the same right as took it away, either it is justified in resuming it, or there was no justification for those who took it away." But the social order is a sacred right which is the basis of all other rights. Nevertheless, this right does not come from nature, and must therefore be founded on conventions. Before coming to that, I have to prove what I have just asserted.

THE FIRST SOCIETIES

The most ancient of all societies, and the only one that is natural, is the family: and even so the children remain attached to the father only so long as they need him for their preservation. As soon as this need ceases, the natural bond is dissolved. The children, released from the obedience they owed to the father, and the father, released from the care he owed his children, return equally to independence. If they remain united, they continue so no longer naturally, but voluntarily; and the family itself is then maintained only by convention.

This common liberty results from the nature of man. His first law is to provide for his own preservation, his first cares are those which he owes to himself; and, as soon as he reaches years of discretion, he is the sole judge of the proper means of preserving himself, and consequently becomes his own master.

The family then may be called the first model of political societies; the ruler corresponds to the father, and the people to the children; and all, being born free and equal, alienate their liberty only for their own advantage. The whole difference is that, in the family, the love of the father for his children repays him for the care he takes of them, while, in the State, the pleasure of commanding takes the place of the love which the chief cannot have for the peoples under him.

◆◆◆

THE SOCIAL CONTRACT

I suppose men to have reached the point at which the obstacles in the way of their preservation in the state of nature show their power of resistance to be greater than the resources at the disposal of each individual for his maintenance in that state. That primitive condition can then subsist no longer; and the human race would perish unless it changed its manner of existence.

But, as men cannot engender new forces, but only unite and direct existing ones, they have no other means of preserving themselves than the formation, by aggregation, of a sum of forces great enough to overcome the resistance. These they have to bring into play by means of a single motive power, and cause to act in concert.

This sum of forces can arise only where several persons come together: but, as the force and liberty of each man are the chief instruments of his self-preservation, how can he pledge them without harming his own interests, and neglecting the care he owes to himself? This difficulty, in its bearing on my present subject, may be stated in the following terms:

"The problem is to find a form of association which will defend and protect with the whole common force the person and goods of each associate, and in which each, while uniting himself with all, may still obey himself alone, and remain as free as before." This is the fundamental problem of which the *Social Contract* provides the solution.

The clauses of this contract are so determined by the nature of the act that the slightest modification would make them vain and ineffective; so that, although they have perhaps never been formally set forth, they are everywhere the same and everywhere tacitly admitted and recognized, until, on the violation of the social compact, each regains his original rights and resumes his natural liberty, while losing the conventional liberty in favour of which he renounced it.

These clauses, properly understood, may be reduced to one—the total alienation of each associate, together with all his rights, to the whole community; for, in the first place, as each gives himself absolutely, the conditions are the same for all; and, this being so, no one has any interest in making them burdensome to others.

Moreover, the alienation being without reserve, the union is as perfect as it can be, and no associate has anything more to demand: for, if the individuals retained certain rights, as there would be no common superior to decide between them and the public, each, being on one point his own judge, would ask to be so on all; the state of nature would thus continue, and the association would necessarily become inoperative or tyrannical.

Finally, each man, in giving himself to all, gives himself to nobody; and as there is no associate over which he does not acquire the same right as he yields others over himself, he gains an equivalent for everything he loses, and an increase of force for the preservation of what he has.

If then we discard from the social contract what is not of its essence, we shall find that it reduces itself to the following terms:

"Each of us puts his person and all his power in common under the supreme direction of the general will, and, in our corporate capacity, we receive each member as an indivisible part of the whole."

At once, in place of the individual personality of each contracting party, this act of association creates a moral and collective body, composed of as many members as the assembly contains voters, and receiving from this act its unity, its common identity, its life, and its will. This public person, so formed by the union of all other persons, formerly took the name of *city,* and now takes that of *Republic* or *body politic;* it is called by its members *State* when passive, *Sovereign* when active, and *Power* when compared with others like itself. Those who are associated in it take collectively the name of *people,* and severally are called *citizens,* as sharing in the sovereign power, and *subjects,* as being under the laws of the State. But these terms are often confused and take one for another: it is enough to know how to distinguish them when they are being used with precision.

THE SOVEREIGN

This formula shows us that the act of association comprises a mutual understanding between the public and the individuals, and that each individual, in making a contract, as we may say, with himself, is bound in a double capacity; as a member of the Sovereign he is bound to the individuals, and as a member of the State to the Sovereign. But the maxim of civil right, that no one is bound by undertakings made to himself, does not apply in this case; for there is a great difference between incurring an obligation to yourself and incurring one to a whole of which you form a part.

. . . each individual, in making a contract, as we may say, with himself, is bound in a double capacity; as a member of the Sovereign he is bound to the individuals, and as a member of the State to the Sovereign.

Attention must further be called to the fact that public deliberation, while competent to bind all the subjects to the Sovereign, because of the two different capacities in which each of them may be regarded, cannot, for the opposite reason, bind that Sovereign to itself; and that it is consequently against the nature of the body politic for the Sovereign to impose on itself a law which it cannot infringe. Being able to regard itself in only one capacity, it is in the position of an individual who makes a contract with himself; and this makes it clear that there neither is nor can be any kind of fundamental law binding on the body of the people—not even the social contract itself. This does not mean that the body politic cannot enter into undertakings with others, provided the contract is not infringed by them; for in relation to what is external to it, it becomes a simple being, an individual.

But the body politic or the Sovereign, drawing its being wholly from the sanctity of the contract, can never bind itself, even to an outsider, to do anything derogatory to the original act, for instance, to alienate any part of itself, or to submit to another Sovereign. Violation of the act by which it exists would be self-annihilation; and that which is itself nothing can create nothing.

As soon as this multitude is so united in one body, it is impossible to offend against one of the members without attacking the body, and still more to offend against the body without the members resenting it. Duty and interest therefore equally oblige the two contracting parties to give each other help; and the same men should seek to combine, in their double capacity, all the advantages dependent upon that capacity.

Again, the Sovereign, being formed wholly of the individuals who compose it, neither has nor can have any interest contrary to theirs; and consequently the sovereign power need give no guarantee to its subjects, because it is impossible for the body to wish to hurt all its members. . . .

In fact, each individual, as a man, may have a particular will contrary or dissimilar to the general will which he has as a citizen. His particular interest may speak to him quite differently from the common interest: his absolute and naturally independent existence may make him look upon what he owes to the common cause as a gratuitous contribution, the loss of which will do less harm to others than the payment of it is burdensome to himself; and, regarding the moral person which constitutes the State as a *persona ficta,* because not a man, he may wish to enjoy the rights of citizenship without being ready to fulfil the duties of a subject. The continuance of such an injustice could not but prove the undoing of the body politic.

In order then that the social compact may not be an empty formula, it tacitly includes the undertaking, which alone can give force to the rest, that whoever refuses to obey the general will shall be compelled to do so by the whole body. This means nothing less than that he will be forced to be free; for this is the condition which, by giving each citizen to his country, secures him against all personal dependence. In this lies the key to the working of the political machine; this alone legitimizes civil undertakings, which, without it, would be absurd, tyrannical, and liable to the most frightful abuses.

THE CIVIL STATE

The passage from the state of nature to the civil state produces a very remarkable change in man, by substituting justice for instinct in his conduct, and giving his actions the morality they had formerly lacked. Then only, when the voice of duty takes the place of physical impulses and right of appetite, does man, who so far had considered only himself, find that he is forced to act on different principles, and to consult his reason before listening to his inclinations. Although, in this state, he deprives himself of some advantages which he got from nature, he gains in return others so great, his faculties are so stimulated and developed, his ideas so extended, his feelings so ennobled, and his whole soul so uplifted, that, did not the abuses of this new condition often degrade him below that which he left, he would be bound to bless continually the happy moment which took him from it for ever, and, instead of a stupid and unimaginative animal, made him an intelligent being and a man.

Let us draw up the whole account in terms easily commensurable. What man loses by the social contract is his natural liberty and an unlimited right to everything he tries to get and succeeds in getting; what he gains is civil liberty and the proprietorship of all he possesses. If we are to avoid mistake in weighing one against the other, we must clearly distinguish natural liberty, which is bounded only by the strength of the individual, from civil liberty, which is limited by the general will; and possession, which is merely the effect of force or the right of the first occupier, from property, which can be founded only on a positive title.

We might, over and above all this, add, to what man acquires in the civil state, moral liberty, which alone makes him truly master of himself; for the mere impulse of appetite is slavery, while obedience to a law which we prescribe to ourselves is liberty.[7]

Although Rousseau shares with Hobbes a belief in the social contract theory, the differences between them could not be more striking. Where Hobbes begins with a brutal view of human nature forced into agreement by fear of mutual violence,

---

[7] Jean-Jacques Rousseau, *The Social Contract and Discourses,* trans. G. D. H. Cole (New York: Everyman's Library Edition, E. P. Dutton, 1947).

Rousseau begins by saying that "man is born free." For Rousseau, the social contract is not an instrument of mutual protection but a means of improving people and bringing out what is best in them. His central theme is not antagonism but humanity's "natural goodness." With unmistakable clarity, Rousseau rejects all might-makes-right theories and insists that legitimacy must always be a matter of the consent of the governed. "The general will" is not a general compromise but the creation of a new power, the power of the people, which for Rousseau is the ultimate voice of authority.

The most famous example of social contract theory at work is in our own Declaration of Independence. In that document, social contract theory combined with a theory of "natural" ("unalienable") rights provided an epoch-making announcement of the right of a people to overthrow an established government:

FROM **THE DECLARATION OF INDEPENDENCE**
BY **THOMAS JEFFERSON** ET AL.

We hold these Truths to be self-evident, that all Men are created equal, that they are endowed by their Creator with certain unalienable Rights, that among these are Life, Liberty, and the pursuit of Happiness—That to secure these rights, Governments are instituted among Men, deriving their just Powers from the Consent of the Governed, that whenever any Form of Government becomes destructive of these Ends, it is the Right of the People to alter or to abolish it, and to institute new Government, laying its Foundation on such Principles, and organizing its Powers in such Form, as to them shall seem most likely to effect their Safety and Happiness. Prudence, indeed, will indicate that Governments long established should not be changed for light and transient causes; and accordingly all Experience hath shewn, that Mankind are more disposed to suffer, while Evils are sufferable, than to right themselves by abolishing the Forms to which they are accustomed. But when a long Train of Abuses and Usurpations, pursuing invariably the same Object, evinces a Design to reduce them under absolute Despotism, it is their Right, it is their Duty, to throw off such Government, and to provide new Guards for their future Security.

4. Two Contemporary Theories of Justice: Rawls and Nozick

It is because of increased sensitivity to the unacceptability of such scenarios that a very different conception of justice has once again begun to dominate—a set of views that recognizes the desirability of serving every individual's interests while having a primary concern for justice, not in terms of utility but in terms of *rights*. Thus, public interest is important but respect for every individual's rights is even more important. This view dates back (at least) to Kant, who defended the notions of "duty" and "obligation" as morally basic to any concern for utility. In its modern conception, this view is most ably defended by Harvard philosopher **John Rawls** in his profound work entitled *Theory of Justice*. For nearly six hundred pages, Rawls essentially defends two principles in order of priority. The first (and more funda-mental) principle asserts that we all have basic rights and equal rights, in particular with reference to our personal freedom. The second principle (which assumes the first) asserts that although we cannot expect everyone in society to enjoy equal wealth, equal health, and equal opportunities, we can and should insist that all in-equalities are to every individual's advantage. For example, it should not be such that society allows that "the rich get richer and the poor get poorer." Rawls' actual state-ment from *Theory of Justice* is as follows:

First: each person is to have an equal right to the most extensive basic liberty compatible with a similar liberty for others.

Second: social and economic inequalities are to be arranged so that they are both (a) reasonably expected to be to everyone's advantage, and (b) attached to positions and offices open to all.

Rawls' justification for establishing the rationality and necessity of these "lib-eral" principles derives from his view that all of us (or our ancestors) might be in "the original position"—like Hobbes' "State of Nature"—and "unencumbered" by any of our particular traits or interests. In such a situation, what would be rational for us to choose by way of the principles according to which society would be run? Be-cause we do not know, in the essential sense, who we will be in that society, it does us no good to adopt principles that benefit the persons we are now. For example, in a society composed entirely of purple people and green people (remembering that in the original position we do not know which we will be), it would only be rational, Rawls argues, to enact a law that would treat all people equally, whether purple or green. It is much like (but much more complicated and uncertain than) the childhood example involving one of us being asked to cut a pie into sections, giving everyone else first choice. The only rational decision—even if you suspect that the other chil-dren are dullards, is to divide the pie equally. So too, the aim of Rawls' dual prin-ciples is to cut for all of us—if not equal pieces of the social pie, at least pieces that are as equal as possible.

The following selection is from one of Rawls' early essays.

FROM "JUSTICE AS FAIRNESS"
BY JOHN RAWLS

Throughout I consider justice only as a virtue of social institutions, or what I shall call practices.[8] The principles of justice are regarded as formulating restrictions

---

[8] I use the word *practice* throughout as a sort of technical term meaning any form of activity specified by a system of rules which defines offices, roles, moves, penalties, defences, and so on, and which gives the activity its structure. As examples one may think of games and rituals, trials and parliaments, markets and systems or property. I have attempted a partial analysis of the notion of a practice in a paper, "Two Concepts of Rules," *Philosophical Review* 64 (1955), pp. 3–32 [Rawls' note].

as to how practices may define positions and offices, and assign thereto powers and liabilities, rights and duties. Justice as a virtue of particular actions or of persons I do not take up at all. It is important to distinguish these various subjects of justice, since the meaning of the concept varies according to whether it is applied to practices, particular actions, or persons.

The conception of justice which I want to develop may be stated in the form of two principles as follows: first, each person participating in a practice, or affected by it, has an equal right to the most extensive liberty compatible with a like liberty for all; and second, inequalities are arbitrary unless it is reasonable to expect that they will work out for everyone's advantage, and provided the positions and offices to which they attach, or from which they may be gained, are open to all.

These meanings are, indeed, connected, but they are not identical. I shall confine my discussion to the sense of justice as applied to practices, since this sense is the basic one. Once it is understood, the other senses should go quite easily.

The conception of justice which I want to develop may be stated in the form of two principles as follows: first, each person participating in a practice, or affected by it, has an equal right to the most extensive liberty compatible with a like liberty for all; and second, inequalities are arbitrary unless it is reasonable to expect that they will work out for everyone's advantage, and provided the positions and offices to which they attach, or from which they may be gained, are open to all. These principles express justice as a complex of three ideas: liberty, equality, and reward for services contributing to the common good.

The term "person" is to be construed variously depending on the circumstances. On some occasions it will mean human individuals, but in others it may refer to nations, provinces, business firms, churches, teams, and so on. The principles of justice apply in all these instances, although there is a certain logical priority to the case of human individuals. As I shall use the term "person," it will be ambiguous in the manner indicated.

The first principle holds, of course, only if other things are equal: that is, while there must always be a justification for departing from the initial position of equal liberty (which is defined by the pattern of rights and duties, powers and liabilities, established by a practice), and the burden or proof is placed on him who would depart from it, nevertheless, there can be, and often there is, a justification for doing so. Now, that similar particular cases, as defined by a practice, should be treated similarly as they arise, is part of the very concept of a practice; it is involved in the notion of an activity in accordance with rules. The first principle expresses an analogous conception, but as applied to the structure of practices themselves. It holds, for example, that there is a presumption against the distinctions and classifications made by legal systems and other practices to the extent that they infringe on the original and equal liberty of the persons participating in them. The second principle defines how this presumption may be rebutted.

It might be argued at this point that justice requires only an equal liberty. If, however, a greater liberty were possible for all without loss or conflict, then it would be irrational to settle on a lesser liberty. There is no reason for circumscribing rights unless their exercise would be incompatible, or would render the practice defining them less effective. Therefore no serious distortion of the concept of justice is likely to follow from including within it the concept of the greatest equal liberty.

The second principle defines what sorts of inequalities are permissible; it specifies how the presumption laid down by the first principle may be put aside. Now by inequalities it is best to understand not *any* differences between offices and positions, but differences in the benefits and burdens attached to them either directly or indirectly, such as prestige and wealth, or liability to taxation and compulsory services. Players in a game do not protest against there being different positions, such as batter, pitcher, catcher, and the like, nor to there being various privileges and powers as specified by the rules; nor do the citizens of a country object to there being the different offices of government such as president, senator, governor, judge, and so on, each with their special rights and duties. It is not differences in the resulting distribution established by a practice, or made possible by it, of the things men strive to attain or avoid. Thus they may complain about the pattern of honors and rewards set up by a practice (*e.g.* the privileges and salaries of government officials) or they may object to the distribution of power and wealth which results from the various ways in which men avail themselves of the opportunities allowed by it (*e.g.* the concentration of wealth which may develop in a free price system allowing large entrepreneurial or speculative gains).

It should be noted that the second principle holds that an inequality is allowed only if there is reason to believe that the practice with the inequality, or resulting from it, will work for the advantage of *every* party engaging in it. Here it is important to stress that *every* party must gain from the inequality. Since the principle applies to practices, it implies that the representative man in every office or position defined by a practice, when he views it as a going concern, must find it reasonable to prefer his condition and prospects with the inequality to what they would be under the practice without it. The principle excludes, therefore, the justification of inequalities on the grounds that the disadvantages of those in one position are outweighed by the greater advantages of those in another position. This rather simple restriction is the main modification I wish to make in the utilitarian principle as usually understood.[9]

---

[9] John Rawls, "Justice as Fairness," in *The Philosophical Review* 67 (April 1958).

Rawls, like Hume in particular, ties the concept of "justice" to the concept of "equality." The main theme of his work is an attempt to develop this connection and to state precisely the kind of "equality" that is most important for justice. Against the conservative suggestion that people are equal in legal rights and "opportunities" alone, without any right to material goods and social services, he argues that a just society will consider the welfare of the worst-off members of society as an obligation. Here he differs with Mill and the utilitarians, who would say that such help is a matter of utility; for Rawls, it is more like a Kantian duty. Moreover, Rawls clearly distinguishes himself from socialists as well, who would argue that all property should be shared; he says only that it is obligatory to help out the worst-off members of society, but nowhere does he suggest that all people therefore ought to have equal wealth and property. Justice, in other words, does not equate fair distribution with equal distribution. Equality becomes a far more complex notion, therefore, than simple egalitarianism, often takes it to be.

Is equality the primary concern of justice? Even Rawls admits that a society in which everyone had exactly equal shares of social goods is impossible. But why is it impossible? We can all imagine a situation—and some radical thinkers even propose it—in which all material goods (at least) would be collected and cataloged by the state, then redistributed to every citizen in precisely equal shares. Most of us, including Rawls, find this suggestion intolerable. Yet why, if it realizes the equality that justice demands? Something stops us, and it is not simply the idea that we might lose our own goods, for many of us would in fact benefit from such a redistribution scheme. What bothers us initially is the very idea of anyone, including (perhaps especially) the government, intruding into our lives and exerting such power. However, we also sense that such a scheme for redistributing the wealth violates something very basic to justice—namely, the rights we have to our possessions. Rawls, of course, gives rights top priority in his theory; but they are rights having to do with liberty in general, not rights having to do with possession as such. We all feel, with whatever reservations, that we have a right to what we earn and that we have a right to keep what we already possess. We resent that the government takes from us a substantial percentage of our earnings to use in ways not directly (or perhaps even indirectly) under our control. And we believe we have the right, for instance, to the modest sum that grandfather left us in his will (presumably the residue of earlier taxation), even though we did not earn it in any sense. Thus many philosophers have become increasingly aware of another kind of right that is not treated adequately by such liberal theories of Rawls'— in fact, a right that goes against the modest scheme of redistribution (for example, through taxation) encouraged by his principles. This other kind of right, known as **entitlement,** gives rise to a very different kind of theory of justice.

The popular name for this alternative theory is **libertarianism,** and it has recently become a powerful force in American politics. The basic idea, an "entitlement theory," puts the right to private property first and foremost, and couples with it a deep skepticism as to the wisdom or fairness of government. The original entitlement theory was developed by John Locke, who argued that the right to private property was so basic that it preceded any social conventions or laws and existed quite independent of any government or state. What gave a person the right to a piece of property, Locke argued, was that he had "mixed his labor with it," in other words, worked with it and improved it and so had the right to it. In today's terms—where what is at stake consists mainly of salaries and what we can buy with them (Locke was thinking mainly of land)—we would say that a person has the basic right to keep what he or she earns. Very recently, Locke's theory has been updated considerably and argued forcefully by John Rawls' younger Harvard colleague, **Robert Nozick.** In *Anarchy, State and Utopia,* Nozick argues for the entitlement theory and against any attempt to set "patterns" of fair distribution, for the enforcement of any such pattern must result in the violation of people's rights.

FROM *ANARCHY, STATE AND UTOPIA* BY **ROBERT NOZICK**

Our main conclusions about the state are that a minimal state, limited to the narrow functions of protection against force, theft, fraud, enforcement of contracts, and so on, is justified; that any more extensive state will violate persons' rights to not be forced to do certain things, and is unjustified; and that the minimal state is inspiring as well as right.

Individuals have rights, and there are things no person or group may do to them (without violating their rights). So strong and far-reaching are these rights that they raise the question of what, if anything, the state and its officials may do. How much room do individual rights leave for the state? . . . Our main conclusions about the state are that a minimal state, limited to the narrow functions of protection against force, theft, fraud, enforcement of contracts, and so on, is justified; that any more extensive state will violate persons' rights to not be forced to do certain things, and is unjustified; and that the minimal state is inspiring as well as right. Two noteworthy implications are that the state may not use its coercive apparatus for the purpose of getting some citizens to aid others, or in order to prohibit activities to people for their *own* good or protection.

◆◆◆

THE ENTITLEMENT THEORY

The subject of justice in holdings consists of three major topics. The first is the *original acquisition of holdings,* the appropriation of unheld things. This includes the issues of how unheld things may come to be held, the process, or processes, by which unheld things may come to be held, the things that may come to be held by these processes, the extent of what comes to be held by a particular process, and so on. We shall refer to the complicated truth about this topic, which we shall not formulate here, as the principle of justice in acquisition. The second topic concerns the *transfer of holdings* from one person to another. By what processes may a person transfer holdings to another? How may a person acquire a holding from another who holds it? Under this topic come general descriptions of voluntary exchange, and gift and (on the other hand) fraud, as well as reference to particular conventional details fixed upon in a given society. The complicated truth about this subject (with placeholders for conventional details) we shall call the principle of justice in transfer. (And we shall suppose it also includes principles governing how a person may divest himself of a holding, passing it into an unheld state.)

If the world were wholly just, the following inductive definition would exhaustively cover the subject of justice in holdings.

1. A person who acquires a holding in accordance with the principle of justice in acquisition is entitled to that holding.
2. A person who acquires a holding in accordance with the principle of justice in transfer, from someone else entitled to the holding, is entitled to the holding.
3. No one is entitled to a holding except by (repeated) applications of 1 and 2.

The complete principle of distributive justice would say simply that a distribution is just if everyone is entitled to the holdings they possess under the distribution.

A distribution is just if it arises from another just distribution by legitimate means. The legitimate means of moving from one distribution to another are specified by the principle of justice in transfer. The legitimate first "moves" are specified by the principle of justice in acquisition. Whatever arises from a just situation by just steps is itself just. . . .

Not all actual situations are generated in accordance with the two principles of justice in holdings: the principle of justice in acquisition and the principle of justice in transfer. Some people steal from others, or defraud them, or enslave them, seizing their product and preventing them from living as they choose, or forcibly exclude others from competing in exchanges. None of these are permissible modes of transition from one situation to another. And some persons acquire holdings by means not sanctioned by the principle of justice in acquisition. The existence of past injustice (previous violations of the first two principles of justice in holdings) raises the third major topic under justice in holdings: the rectification of injustice in holdings. If past injustice has shaped present holdings in various ways, some identifiable and some not, what now, if anything, ought to be done to rectify these injustices? What obligations do the performers of injustice have toward those whose position is worse than it would have been had the injustice not been done? Or, than it would have had compensation been paid promptly? How, if at all, do things change if the beneficiaries and those made worse off are not the direct parties in the act of injustice, but, for example, their descendants? Is an injustice done to someone whose holding was itself based upon an unrectified injustice? How far back must one go in wiping clean the historical slate of injustices? What may victims of injustice permissibly do in order to rectify the injustices being done to them, including the many injustices done by persons acting through their government? I do not know of a thorough or theoretically sophisticated treatment of such issues. Idealizing greatly, let us suppose theoretical investigations will produce a principle of rectification. This principle uses historical information about previous situations and injustices done in them (as defined by the first two principles of justice and rights against interference), and information about the actual course of events that flowed from these injustices, until the present, and it yields a description (or descriptions) of holdings in the society. . . .

HISTORICAL PRINCIPLES AND END-RESULT PRINCIPLES

The general outlines of the entitlement theory illuminate the nature and defects of other conceptions of distributive justice. The entitlement theory of justice in distribution is *historical;* whether a distribution is just depends upon how it came about. In contrast, *current time-slice principles* of justice hold that the justice of a distribution is determined by how things are distributed (who has what) as judged by some *structural* principle(s) of just distribution. A utilitarian who judges between any two distributions by seeing which has the greater sum of utility and, if the sums tie, applies some fixed equality criterion to choose the more equal distribution, would hold a current time-slice principle of justice. As would someone who had a fixed schedule of trade-offs between the sum of happiness and equality. According to a current time-slice principle, all that needs to be looked at, in judging the justice of a distribution, is who ends up with what; in comparing any two distributions one need look only at the matrix presenting the distributions. No further information need be fed into a principle of justice. It is a consequence of such principles of justice that any two structurally identical distributions are equally just. (Two distributions are structurally identical if they present the same profile, but perhaps have different persons occupying the particular slots. My having ten and your having five, and my having five and your having ten are structurally identical distributions.) Welfare economics is the theory of current time-slice principles of justice. The subject is conceived as operating on matrices representing only current information about distribution. This, as well as some of the usual conditions (for example, the choice of distribution is invariant under relabeling of columns), guarantees that welfare economics will be a current time-slice theory, with all of its inadequacies.

Most persons do not accept current time-slice principles as constituting the whole story about distributive shares. They think it relevant in assessing the justice of a situation to consider not only the distribution it embodies, but also how that distribution came about. If some persons are in prison for murder or war crimes, we do not say that to assess the justice of the distribution in the society we must look only at what this person has, and that person has, and that person has, . . . at the current time. We think it relevant to ask whether someone did something so that he *deserved* to be punished, deserved to have a lower share. Most will agree to the relevance of further information with regard to punishments and penalties. Consider also desired things. One traditional socialist view is that workers are entitled to the product and full fruits of their labor; thay have earned it; a distribution is unjust if it does not give the workers what they are entitled to. Such entitlements are based upon some past history. No socialist holding this view would find it comforting to be told that because the actual distribution *A* happens to coincide structurally with the one he desires *D*, therefore is no less just than *D;* . . . This socialist rightly, in my view, holds onto the notions of earning, producing, entitlement, desert, and so forth, and he rejects current time-slice principles that look only to the structure of the resulting set of holdings. . . . His mistake lies in his view of what entitlements arise out of what sorts of productive processes.[10]

5. Justice or Care: A Feminist Perspective

The debate about justice has gone on for almost 2,500 years. But it might be noted that most of the voices in the debate have been male voices, and this raises the question whether there is some male bias to the perspective in which justice has been debated, or, indeed, some male bias in the very notion of justice itself. Cheshire Calhoun has argued that this is the case. Here is an excerpt of her argument.

FROM "JUSTICE, CARE, GENDER BIAS" BY CHESHIRE CALHOUN

Carol Gilligan poses two separable, though in her work not separate, challenges to moral theory. The first is a challenge to the adequacy of current moral theory that is dominated by the ethics of justice. The ethics of justice, on her view, excludes some dimensions of moral experience, such as contextual decision making, special obligations, the moral motives of compassion and sympathy, and the relevance of considering one's own integrity in making moral decisions. The second is a challenge to moral theory's presumed gender neutrality. The ethics of justice is not gender neutral, she argues, because it advocates ideals of agency, moral motivation, and correct moral reasoning which women are less likely than men to achieve; and because the moral dimensions excluded from the ethics of justice are just the ones figuring more prominently in women's than men's moral experience.

The adequacy and gender bias charges are, for Gilligan, linked. She claims that the ethics of justice and the ethics of care are two different moral orientations. Whereas individuals may use both orientations, the shift from one to the other requires a Gestalt shift, since "the terms of one perspective do not contain the terms of the other." The exclusion of the care perspective from the ethics of justice simultaneously undermines the adequacy of the ethics of justice (it cannot give a complete account of moral life) and renders it gender-biased.

---

[10] Robert Nozick, *Anarchy, State and Utopia* (Cambridge, MA: Harvard University Press, 1974).

Some critics have responded by arguing that there is no logical incompatibility between the two moral orientations. Because the ethics of justice does not in principle exclude the ethics of care (even if theorists within the justice tradition have had little to say about care issues), it is neither inadequate nor gender-biased. Correctly applying moral rules and principles, for instance, requires, rather than excludes, knowledge of contextual details. Both orientations are crucial to correct moral reasoning and an adequate understanding of moral life. Thus, the ethics of justice and the ethics of care are not in fact rivaling, alternative moral theories. The so-called ethics of care merely makes focal issues that are already implicitly contained in the ethics of justice.

> *The exclusion of the care perspective from the ethics of justice simultaneously undermines the adequacy of the ethics of justice . . . and renders it gender-biased.*

Suppose the two are logically compatible. Would the charge of gender bias evaporate? Yes, so long as gender neutrality only requires that the ethics of justice could, consistently, make room for the central moral concerns of the ethics of care. But perhaps gender neutrality requires more than this. Since the spectre of gender bias in theoretical knowledge is itself a moral issue, we would be well advised to consider the question of gender bias more carefully before concluding that our moral theory speaks in an androgynous voice. Although we can and should test the ethics of justice by asking whether it could consistently include the central moral issues in the ethics of care, we might also ask what ideologies of the moral life are likely to result from the repeated inclusion or exclusion of particular topics in moral theorizing.

Theorizing that crystallizes into a tradition has nonlogical as well as logical implications. In order to explain why a tradition has the contours it does, one may need to suppose general acceptance of particular beliefs that are not logically entailed by any particular theory and might be denied by individual theorists were those beliefs articulated. When behavioral researchers, for example, focus almost exclusively on aggression and its role in human life, neglecting other behavioral motives, their doing so has the nonlogical implication that aggression is, indeed, the most important behavioral motive. This is because only a belief like this would explain the rationality of this pattern of research. Such nonlogical implications become ideologies when politically loaded (as the importance of aggression is when coupled with observations about women's lower level of aggression).

When understood as directed at moral theory's nonlogical implications, the gender-bias charge takes a different form. Even if the ethics of justice could consistently accommodate the ethics of care, the critical point is that theorists in the justice tradition have not said much, except in passing, about the ethics of care, and are unlikely to say much in the future without a radical shift in theoretical priorities; and concentrating almost exclusively on rights of noninterference, impartiality, rationality, autonomy, and principles creates an ideology of the moral domain which has undesirable political implications for women. This formulation shifts the justice-care debate from one about logical compatibility to a debate about which theoretical priorities would improve the lot of women.

B. INDIVIDUAL RIGHTS AND FREEDOM

If our concern were only the smooth workings of society, almost any government would do—the stronger the better, the more authoritarian, the more efficient. But efficiency is only one of several concerns and probably not the most important. You might argue that the public interest could be served by such a government, but it is clear that justice and individual rights could not. The importance of the social contract theory (and consent-of-the governed theories in general) is the clear emphasis on justice and rights. However, the social contract theory by itself is not entirely clear about the status of individual rights, as Nozick makes clear in his criticism of Rawls. Those rights concerning freedom are of particular concern here. How much personal freedom does the social contract guarantee us? Thus any discussion of justice and the state must include some special concern for the status of basic freedoms and **unalienable rights** (that is, rights that no one and no government may take away), such as freedom to speak one's political opinions without harassment, freedom to worship (or not worship) without being penalized or punished, freedom to defend oneself against attack ("the right to bear arms" is a controversial case), and the freedom to pursue one's own interests (where these do not interfere with the rights of others). In addition, we can add the right not to be imprisoned without reason, or accused without a fair trial, or punished unduly for a crime committed. Our best-known list of such freedoms and rights is the American Bill of Rights, appended to the main body of the Constitution as a kind of contractual guarantee of personal rights.

But even if the importance of such rights is indisputable, the precise formulation and extent of those rights are highly debatable. We speak of "unalienable rights," but should such rights be left unrestricted, for example, even in wartime? It is clear, to mention the most common example, that freedom of speech does not extend so far as the right to falsely yell "fire" in a crowded theater. Freedom of speech, therefore, like other rights, is limited by considerations of public welfare and utility. But how limited? Is mere annoyance to the government sufficient, or general boredom among the populace? Similarly, we can go back to the difficult examples we raised in earlier sections. Are the rights against imprisonment and harsh punishment always valid against overwhelming public interest? For example, are they valid in the case of a criminal who has committed crimes repeatedly? Or, to take a difficult example, is "free enterprise" an "unalienable" right in our society? Or is free enterprise rather a theory (and a debatable one) that suggests that public interest and justice will best be served by open competition and a free market? But that theory evolved before modern monopolies developed and before it was obvious that "free" markets could be manipulated so as not to be either free or in the public interest at all. Is that "freedom" still a right? Or should it also be tempered by other concerns?

One of the most important basic rights is the presumed right to own private property. John Locke, writing just after the English ("Glorious") Revolution of 1688, listed three basic rights that would become the main ingredients of both the American Declaration of Independence and a still-prominent political philosophy called liberalism. Foremost among them were "life, liberty, and the right to own private property." (The original draft of the American Declaration included just these three, but Jefferson replaced the last with the less committal "pursuit of happiness.") For Locke, private property is the bulwark of freedom and the basis of other human rights. One's own body is private property in the most basic sense; no one else has the authority to violate or use it without permission. Most contemporary societies recognize this right to one's own body as fundamental. But then Locke adds that the right to own property that one has helped cultivate with his or her body ("hath mixed his labour with it") is also basic to freedom and human dignity. The Protestant work ethic emerges very powerfully in this view, in which work and rights are treated together, the first being our way of earning the second:

FROM *THE SECOND TREATISE ON GOVERNMENT*
BY **JOHN LOCKE**

Though the earth and all inferior creatures be common to all men, yet every man has a *property* in his own *person*. This nobody has any right to but himself. The *labour* of his body and the *work* of his hands, we may say, are properly his. Whatsoever, then, he removes out of the state that nature hath provided and left it in, he hath mixed his labour with it, and joined to it something that is his own, and thereby makes it his property. It being by him removed from the common state nature placed it in, it hath by this labour something annexed to it that excludes the common right of other men. For his labour being the unquestionable property of the labourer, no man but he can have a right to what that is once joined to, at least where there is enough, and as good left in common for others.

For his labour being the unquestionable property of the labourer, no man but he can have a right to what that is once joined to, at least where there is enough, and as good left in common for others.

He that is nourished by the acorns he picked up under an oak, or the apples he gathered from the trees in the wood, has certainly appropriated them to himself. Nobody can deny but the nourishment is his. I ask, then, when did they begin to be his? when he digested? or when he ate? or when he boiled? or when he brought them home? or when he picked them up? And 'tis plain, if the first gathering made them not his, nothing else could. That labour put a distinction between them and common. That added something to them more than Nature, the common mother of all, had done, and so they became his private right. And will any one say he had not right to those acorns or apples he thus appropriated because he had not the consent of all mankind to make them his? Was it a robbery thus to assume to himself what belonged to all in common? If such a consent as that was necessary, man had starved, notwithstanding the plenty God had given him. We see in commons, which remain so by compact, that 'tis the taking any part of what is common, and removing it out of the state Nature leaves it in, which begins the property, without which the common is of no use. And the taking of this or that part does not depend on the express consent of all the commoners. Thus, the grass my horse has bit, the turfs my servant has cut, and the ore I have digged in any place, where I have a right to them in common with others, become my property without the assignation or consent of any body. The labour that was mine, removing them out of that common state they were in, hath fixed my property in them.

And thus, I think, it is very easy to conceive, without any difficulty, how labour could at first begin a title of property in the common things of nature, and how the spending it upon our uses bounded it; so that there could then be no reason of quarrelling about title, nor any doubt about the largeness of possession it gave. Right and conveniency went together. For as a man had a right to all he could employ his labour upon, so he had no temptation to labour for more than he could make use of. This left no room for controversy about the title, nor for encroachment on the right of others. What portion a man carved to himself was easily seen; and it was useless as well as dishonest to carve himself too much, or take more than he needed.[11]

It is important to point out that discussions of rights should never be set apart from discussions of political duties and obligations. As the several versions of the social contract make clear, these are always part of one and the same agreement— certain rights in return for certain obligations. To discuss freedom of speech, for example, without also discussing the obligation to be well informed and logically coherent, is to provide a dangerously one-sided view of the problem. One way of developing this idea of an exchange of rights and obligations has been to distinguish two different senses of "freedom": a *negative* freedom from interference and a *positive* freedom to realize one's own potential and find one's place in society. Freedom from interference may be necessary for a person to enjoy life and contribute to the welfare of those around him or her, but a person also needs positive goods—health and education, for example. Thus freedom takes on a double meaning, freedom *from* interference but freedom *to* participate in society too. Since positive freedom also

---

[11] John Locke, *The Second Treatise on Government* (New York: Hafner, 1956).

includes a person's being able to take on responsibilities, some philosophers have pointed out a paradox in the idea of being "free to perform obligations."

The idea that one is "free to perform obligations" may sound odd to us because we are so used to talking exclusively about freedom from constraints and the demands made by authority. But one theme that has recurred since the ancient Greeks is that all rights and "freedoms from" must be coupled with duties and obligations and the freedom to perform them. In Rousseau, for example, the citizen's obligations to the state are just as important as the state's obligations to its citizens. Many philosophers are concerned that simple freedom from constraint leaves people without direction or morality and can easily degenerate into chaos and anarchy. Thus these philosophers stress the necessity of laws and guidelines as an essential part of freedom. This is why they call it "positive" freedom since it necessarily includes "positive" goods (health and education) as well as a set of roles, duties, obligations, and constraints. This notion can be abused easily, however, for "positive freedom" can be made compatible with the most authoritarian state. (The Soviet Union, for example, often used the term *freedom* in this "positive" sense.) But despite possible abuses, it is important to see that there is more to freedom than simple freedom from interference. Whenever someone demands freedom, it is important to ask not only "from what?" but also "for what?"

It is also worth distinguishing several different kinds of rights. We can distinguish between "negative" and "positive" rights as well as freedoms; one has a right not to be interfered with, and one has rights *to* certain goods that society can provide. We have mostly been discussing negative rights (the right to be left alone, the right not to be arrested without good reason). But there are positive rights that are equally important, although they are often more controversial in this society, for example, the right to a minimal income regardless of the work one performs, the right to adequate health care regardless of one's ability to pay for it. Many rights are clearly localized to a particular state or a particular community, as, for example, the right of university regents to free football game tickets and lunches at taxpayers' expense. These rights exist by convention only and cannot be generalized from one community to another.

Then, more generally, there are **civil rights,** rights that are guaranteed in a particular state. One example can be the right to equal treatment despite differences in skin color or sex or religion, as required by various state and federal laws. These are clearly much more important than the conventional rights, and they have a clearly moral basis. For that reason, even though they are defined by reference to a particular state and society, they are often generalized to other societies as well. Insofar as they are generalized in this way, they become *moral* rights or **human rights,** extendable to all people, in any society, regardless of the laws and customs of the society in which they live. Some apparent human rights have been hotly debated: for example, whether the U.S. government has the moral authority to interfere with the harsh abuses of human rights in, say, China or Castro's Cuba. If the right in question is harsh punishment for a seemingly minor crime, it might be argued that their system of punishment is simply more severe than ours, and we should not apply our values. If the right in question is the ability of citizens to speak out against the government without threat of imprisonment or worse, a strong argument has been made that the

U.S. government does indeed have that moral authority (whether or not it wishes to risk the consequences is another matter). But if the right in question is one of those basic human rights against torture or debasement or pointless murder, then it can be argued that everyone has a moral obligation to defend such rights. Human rights are those that transcend all social and national boundaries; they demand that people deserve certain treatment just because they are human, regardless of all else.

A right is a kind of demand, the demand that one is owed something by society and the state, usually a certain sort of consideration or treatment. But most of the rights we have been discussing are in fact rights to freedom or to liberty, that is, the right to be left alone and not interfered with. A belief in individual freedom forms the basis of the liberal political philosophy, which is defined most of all by a commitment to the right of each individual to be free to do whatever he or she wishes as long as it doesn't interfere with similar rights of others. The classic statement of this position is another pamphlet by John Stuart Mill, *On Liberty* (1859). In it, he defends the rights of individuals and minorities against the tyranny of democratic majorities, for Mill sees that liberty can be as endangered in a democracy as it can in an authoritarian state. Mill goes on to offer a "very simple principle," that individual liberty is to be considered inviolable except when other people are threatened with harm.

from *ON LIBERTY*
by **JOHN STUART MILL**

The object of this Essay is to assert one very simple principle, as entitled to govern absolutely the dealings of society with the individual in the way of compulsion and control, whether the means used be physical force in the form of legal penalties, or the moral coercion of public opinion. That principle is, that the sole end for which mankind are warranted, individually or collectively, in interfering with the liberty of action of any of their number, is self-protection. That the only purpose for which power can be rightfully exercised over any member of a civilised community, against his will, is to prevent harm to others. His own good, either physical or moral, is not a sufficient warrant. He cannot rightfully be compelled to do or forbear because it will be better for him to do so, because it will make him happier, because, in the opinions of others, to do so would be wise, or even right. These are good reasons for remonstrating with him, or reasoning with him, or persuading him, or entreating him, but not for compelling him, or visiting with any evil in case he do otherwise. To justify that, the conduct from which it is desired to deter him must be calculated to produce evil to some one else. The only part of the conduct of any one, for which he is amenable to society, is that which concerns others. In the part which merely concerns himself, his independence is, of right, absolute. Over himself, over his own body and mind, the individual is sovereign.

It is, perhaps, hardly necessary to say that this doctrine is meant to apply only to human beings in the maturity of their faculties. We are not speaking of children, or of young persons below the age which the law may fix as that of manhood or womanhood. Those who are still in a state to require being taken care of by others, must be protected against their own actions as well as against external injury. For the same reason, we may leave out of consideration those backward states of society in which the race itself may be considered as in its nonage. The early difficulties in the way of spontaneous progress are so great, that there is seldom any choice of means for overcoming them; and a ruler full of the spirit of improvement is warranted in the use of any expedients that will attain an end, perhaps otherwise unattainable. Despotism is a legitimate mode of government in dealing with barbarians, provided the end be their improvement,[12] and the means justified by actually affecting that end. Liberty, as a principle, has no application to any state of things anterior to the time when mankind have become capable of being improved by free and equal discussion.

It is proper to state that I forego any advantage which could be derived to my argument from the idea of abstract right, as a thing independent of utility. I regard utility as the ultimate appeal on all ethical questions; but it must be utility in the largest sense, grounded on the permanent interests of a man as a progressive being. Those interests, I contend, authorise the subjection of individual spontaneity to external control, only in respect to those actions of each, which concern the interest of other people. If any one does an act hurtful to others, there is a *prima facie* case for punishing him, by law, or, where legal penalties are not safely applicable, by general disapprobation. There are also many positive acts for the benefit of others, which he may rightfully be compelled to perform; such as to give evidence in a court of justice; to bear his fair share in the common defence, or in any other joint work necessary to the interest of the society of which he enjoys the protection; and to perform certain acts of individual beneficence, such as saving a fellow creature's life, or interposing to protect the defenceless against ill-usage, things which whenever it is obviously a man's duty to do, he may rightfully be made responsible to society for not doing. A person may cause evil to others not only by his actions but by his inaction, and in either case is justly accountable to them for the injury. The latter case, it is true, requires a much more cautious exercise of compulsion than the former. To make any one answerable for doing evil to others is the rule; to make him answerable for not preventing evil is, comparatively speaking, the exception. Yet there are many cases clear enough and grave enough to justify that exception. In all things which regard the external relations of the individual, he is *de jure* amenable to those whose interests are concerned, and, if need be, to society as their protector. There are often good reasons for not holding him to the responsibility; but these reasons must arise from the special expediencies of the case: either because it is a kind of case in which he is on the whole likely to act better, when left to his own discretion, than when controlled in any way in which society have it in their

---

[12] Notice the political implications for this qualification, however, in "underdeveloped" countries and colonies. The principle of *paternalism*—that one ought to take care of those who cannot take care of themselves—is easily abused and therefore dangerous.

power to control him; or because the attempt to exercise control would produce other evils, greater than those which it would prevent. When such reasons as these preclude the enforcement of responsibility, the conscience of the agent himself should step into the vacant judgment seat, and protect those interests of others which have no external protection; judging himself all the more rigidly, because the case does not admit of his being made accountable to the judgment of his fellow creatures.

But there is a sphere of action in which society, as distinguished from the individual, has, if any, only an indirect interest; comprehending all that portion of a person's life and conduct which affects only himself, or if it also affects others, only with their free, voluntary, and undeceived consent and participation. When I say only himself, I mean directly, and in the first instance; for whatever affects himself, may affect others through himself; and the objection which may be grounded on this contingency, will receive consideration in the sequel. This, then, is the appropriate region of human liberty. It comprises, first, the inward domain of consciousness; demanding liberty of conscience in the most comprehensive sense; liberty of thought and feeling; absolute freedom of opinion and sentiment on all subjects, practical or speculative, scientific, moral, or theological. The liberty of expressing and publishing opinions may seem to fall under a different principle, since it belongs to that part of the conduct of an individual which concerns other people; but, being almost of as much importance as the liberty of thought itself, and resting in great part on the same reasons, is practically inseparable from it. Secondly, the principle requires liberty of tastes and pursuits; of framing the plan of our life to suit our own character; of doing as we like, subject to such consequences as may follow: without impediment from our fellow creatures, so long as what we do does not harm them, even though they should think our conduct foolish, perverse, or wrong. Thirdly, from this liberty of each individual, follows the liberty, within the same limits, of combination among individuals; freedom to unite, for any purpose not involving harm to others: the persons combining being supposed to be of full age, and not forced or deceived.

The only freedom which deserves the name, is that of pursuing our own good in our own way, so long as we do not attempt to deprive others of theirs, or impede their efforts to obtain it.

No society in which these liberties are not, on the whole, respected, is free, whatever may be its form of government and unqualified. The only freedom which deserves the name, is that of pursuing our own good in our own way, so long as we do not attempt to deprive others of theirs, or impede their efforts to obtain it. Each is the proper guardian of his own health, whether bodily, *or* mental and spiritual. Mankind are greater gainers by suffering each other to live as seems good to themselves, than by compelling each to live as seems good to the rest.[13]

---

[13] John Stuart Mill, *On Liberty* (London: Longmans, 1859).

Mill's main concern in his essay is the extent to which government and public interest have authority over individuals and individual actions. If an action harms other people or presents a public menace, then government does have the authority to prevent it or punish a person for doing it. But if an action is not harmful to others, the government has no such authority. In the question of freedom of speech, for example, this means that governments have no authority to censor some comment or publication unless it clearly harms other people, not merely annoys or personally offends them. Mill is particularly concerned with protecting individuals against "the tyranny of the majority." The public interest is authoritative to "a limit," but that limit does not include interfering with personal affairs or opinions.

C. FIGHTING FOR RIGHTS AND JUSTICE

In an ideal state, both government and populace would respect and uphold individual rights and justice. But neither governments nor people in general are ideal, and often, although both government and people give lip service to the importance of rights and justice, in practice they fall far short. In our own founding documents, for instance, it is clearly stated that "all men are created equal," but not only did the phrase "all men" not include half of the adult American population, its women, but this was written at a time when America legally included the right to own slaves (and the Declaration's primary author, Thomas Jefferson, was a slave owner himself). Although the laws permitting slavery were eliminated with the American Civil War, the segregation of the races and consequent violations of individual rights and justice continue in America until this day. But not only may a good country have bad laws and bad customs; worse, sometimes the law of the land itself violates the most basic tenets of rights and justice. South Africa, until 1993, was a nation whose very foundation was based on the separation of whites and nonwhites, at the cost of severe political, economic, social, and personal disadvantages for the latter.

In all such circumstances, whether the problem is not living up to noble principles and precepts, or living under the scope of bad laws, or living in a country whose very foundation violates human rights and justice, there is the painful necessity of fighting for these basic human values. It is wonderful for those of us who can take our rights and justice more or less for granted, though never let us forget, as many have reminded us, that the cost of such good fortune is "eternal vigilance" and that injustice anywhere can affect justice and well-being everywhere. But for those who find themselves directly confronting bad laws and evil practices, the philosophy of rights and justice provides the personal strength necessary to engage in such battles. In the five readings that follow, we see this philosophy at work in various ways in the words of some of the heroes of the previous century or so. We begin with **Frederick Douglass,** the nineteenth century abolitionist who was himself a former slave. The context of Douglass' argument may at first seem both shocking and surprising. In this selection, he defends a friend's decision to buy his own freedom (and that means, to obey the laws treating slaves as property) rather than to violate the law and run away.

Douglass' defense throws a great deal of light on the dilemma of African-Americans under the yoke of our most inhumane historical institution.

"IN DEFENSE OF PURCHASING FREEDOM"
BY FREDERICK DOUGLASS

22, St. Ann's Square, Manchester,
December 22, 1846

Dear Friend:

. . . I am in England, my family are in the United States. My sphere of usefulness is in the United States; my public and domestic duties are there; and there it seems my duty to go. But I am *legally* the property of Thomas Auld, and if I go to the United States, (no matter to what part, for there is no City of Refuge there, no spot sacred to freedom there,) Thomas Auld, *aided by the American Government,* can seize, bind and fetter, and drag me from my family, feed his cruel revenge upon me, and doom me to unending slavery. In view of this simple statement of facts, a few friends, desirous of seeing me released from the terrible liability, and to relieve my wife and children from the painful trepidation, consequent upon the liability, and to place me on an equal footing of safety with all other anti-slavery lecturers in the United States, and to enhance my usefulness by enlarging the field of my labors in the United States, have nobly and generously paid Hugh Auld, the agent of Thomas Auld, £150—in consideration of which, Hugh Auld (acting as his agent) and the Government of the United States agree, that I shall be free from all further liability.

These, dear friend, are the facts of the whole transaction. The principle here acted on by my friends, and that upon which I shall act in receiving the manumission papers, I deem quite defensible.

First, *as to those who acted as my friends, and their actions.* The actuating motive was, to secure me from a liability full of horrible forebodings to myself and family. With this object, I will do you the justice to say, I believe you fully unite, although some parts of your letters would seem to justify a different belief.

Then, as to the measure adopted to secure this result. Does it violate a fundamental principle, or does it not? This is the question, and to my mind the only question of importance, involved in the discussion, I believe that, on our part, no just or holy principle has been violated.

Before entering upon the argument in support of this view, I will take the liberty (and I know you will pardon it) to say, I think you should have pointed out some principle violated in the transaction, before you proceeded to exhort me to repentance. . . .

The principle which you appear to regard as violated by the transaction in question, may be stated as follows:—*Every man has a natural and inalienable right to himself.* The inference from this is, *"that man cannot hold property in man"*—and as man cannot hold property in man, neither can Hugh Auld nor the

United States have any right of property in me—and having no right of property in me, they have no right to sell me—and, having no right to sell me, no one has a right to buy me. I think I have now stated the principle, and the inference from the principle, distinctly and fairly. Now, the question upon which the whole controversy turns is, simply, this: does the transaction, which you condemn, really violate this principle? I own that, to a superficial observer, it would seem to do so. But I think I am prepared to show, that, so far from being a violation of that principle, it is truly a noble vindication of it. Before going further, let me state here, briefly, what sort of a purchase would have been a violation of this principle, which, in common with yourself, I reverence, and am anxious to preserve inviolate.

1st. It would have been a violation of that principle, had those who purchased me done so, *to make me a slave, instead of a freeman.* And,

2ndly. It would have been a violation of that principle, had those who purchased me done so with a view to compensate the slaveholder, for what he and they regarded as his rightful property.

In neither of these ways was my purchase effected. My liberation was, in their estimation, of more value than £150; the happiness and repose of my family were, in their judgment, more than paltry gold. The £150 was paid to the remorseless plunderer, not because he had any just claim to it, but to induce him to give up his legal claim to something which they deemed of more value than money. It was not to compensate the slaveholder, but to release me from his power; not to establish my *natural right* to freedom, but to release me from all legal liabilities to slavery. And all this, you and I, and the slaveholders, and all who know anything of the transaction, very well understand. The very letter to Hugh Auld, proposing terms of purchase, informed him that those who gave, *denied his right to it.* The error of those, who condemn this transaction, consists in their confounding the crime of buying men *into slavery,* with the meritorious act of buying men out of slavery, and the purchase of legal freedom with abstract right and natural freedom. They say, "If you BUY, you recognize the right to sell. If you receive, you recognize the right of the giver to give." And this has a show of truth, as well as of logic. But a few plain cases will show its entire fallacy.

There is now, in this country, a heavy duty on corn. The government of this country has imposed it; and though I regard it a most unjust and wicked imposition, no man of common sense will charge me with endorsing or recognizing the right of this government to impose this duty, simply because, to prevent myself and family from starving, I buy and eat this corn.

Take another case:—I have had dealings with a man. I have owed him one hundred dollars, and have paid it; I have lost the receipt. He comes upon me the second time for the money. I know, and he knows, he has no right to it; but he is a villain, and has me in his power. The law is with him, and against me. I must pay or be dragged to jail. I choose to pay the bill a second time. To say I sanctioned his right to rob me, because I preferred to pay rather than go to jail, is to utter an absurdity, to which no sane man would give heed. And yet the principle of action, in each of these cases, is the same. The man might indeed say, the claim is unjust—and declare, I will rot in jail, before I will pay it. But this would not, certainly, be demanded by any principle of truth, justice, or humanity. . . .

As to the expediency of the measures, different opinions may well prevail; but in regard to the principle, I feel it difficult to conceive of two opinions. I am free to say, that, had I possessed one hundred and fifty pounds, I would have seen Hugh Auld *kicking,* before I would have given it to him. I would have waited till the emergency came, and only given up the money when nothing else would do. But my friends thought it best to provide against the contingency; they acted on their own responsibility, and I am not disturbed about the result. But, having acted on a true principle, I *do not feel free to disavow their proceedings.*

In conclusion, let me say, I anticipate no such change in my position as you predict. I shall be Frederick Douglass still, and once a slave still. I shall neither be made to forget nor cease to feel the wrongs of my enslaved fellow-countrymen. My knowledge of slavery will be the same, and my hatred of it will be the same. By the way, I have never made my own person and suffering the theme of public discourse, but have always based my appeal upon the wrongs of the three millions now in chains; and these shall still be the burthen of my speeches. You intimate that I may reject the papers, and allow them to remain in the hands of those friends who have effected the purchase, and thus avail myself of the security afforded to them, without sharing any part of the responsibility of the transaction. My objection to this is one of honor. I do not think it would be very honorable on my part, to remain silent during the whole transaction, and giving it more than my silent approval; and then, when the thing is completed, and I am safe, attempt to play the *hero,* by throwing off all responsibility in the matter. It might be said, and said with great propriety, "Mr. Douglass, your indignation is very good, and has but one fault, and that is, *it comes too late!*" It would be a show of bravery when the danger is over. From every view I have been able to take the subject, I am persuaded to receive the papers, if presented,—not, however, as a proof of my right to be free, for *that is self-evident,* but as a proof that my friends have been legally robbed of £150, in order to secure that which is the birth-right of every man. And I will hold up those papers before the world, in proof of the plundering character of the American government. It shall be the brand of infamy, stamping the nation, in whose name the deed was done, as a great aggregation of hypocrites, thieves and liars,—and their condemnation is just. They declare that all men are created equal, and have a natural and inalienable right

> *I am persuaded to receive the papers — not, however, as a proof of my right to be free, for* **that is self-evident,** *but as a proof that my friends have been legally robbed of £150, in order to secure that which is the birth-right of every man.*

to liberty, while they rob me of £150, as a condition of my enjoying this natural and inalienable right. It will be their condemnation, in their own hand-writing, and may be held up to the world as a means of humbling that haughty republic into repentance.

I agree with you, that the contest which I have to wage is against the government of the United States. But the representative of that government is the slave-holder, *Thomas Auld*. He is commander-in-chief of the army and navy. The whole civil and naval force of the nation are at his disposal. He may command all these to his assistance, and bring them all to bear upon me, until I am made entirely subject to this will, or submit to be robbed myself, or allow my friends to be robbed, of seven hundred and fifty dollars. And rather than be subject to his will, I have submitted to be robbed, or allowed my friends to be robbed, of the seven hundred and fifty dollars.

Sincerely yours,
Frederick Douglass [14]

The great American essayist, **Henry David Thoreau,** did not agree with Socrates or with Douglass. In his famous essay "Civil Disobedience" he defended his decision not to pay his taxes. He claimed that for a person to obey the laws of government which behaved unjustly was the same as his or her behaving unjustly him or herself. While "lesser men"—degraded, immoral, and unthinking pawns of government—might go along year after year, casting their impotent and thoughtless vote, no man of moral character would do so, claimed Thoreau. Being such a man himself, he absolved himself of any obligations toward his country other than to "do what he believed right."

"CIVIL DISOBEDIENCE"
BY **HENRY DAVID THOREAU**

RESISTANCE TO CIVIL GOVERNMENT [15]

I heartily accept the motto,—"That government is best which governs least;" and I should like to see it acted up to more rapidly and systematically. Carried out, it finally amounts to this, which also I believe,—"That government is best which governs not at all;" and when men are prepared for it, that will be the kind of government which they will have. Government is at best but an expedient; but most governments are usually, and all governments are sometimes, inexpedient. The objections which have been brought against a standing army, and they are

---

[14] Frederick Douglass, *Selected Writings,* ed. Michael Meyer (New York: Modern Library, 1984).

[15] Henry David Thoreau, "Resistance to Civil Government," 1849, rpt. in the *Norton Anthology of American Literature* (New York: Norton, 1990).

many and weighty, and deserve to prevail, may also at least be brought against a standing government. The standing army is only an arm of the standing government. The government itself, which is only the mode which the people have chosen to execute their will, is equally liable to be abused and perverted before the people can act through it. Witness the present Mexican war, the work of comparatively a few individuals using the standing government as their tool; for, in the outset, the people would not have consented to this measure.

This American government,—what is it but a tradition, though a recent one, endeavoring to transmit itself unimpaired to posterity, but each instant losing some of its integrity? It has not the vitality and force of a single living man; for a single man can bend it to his will. It is a sort of wooden gun to the people themselves; and, if ever they should use it in earnest as a real one against each other, it will surely split. But it is not the less necessary for this; for the people must have some complicated machinery or other, and hear its din, to satisfy that idea of government which they have. Governments show thus how successfully men can be imposed on, even impose on themselves, for their own advantage. It is excellent, we must allow; yet this government never of itself furthered any enterprise, but by the alacrity with which it got out of its way. *It* does not keep the country free. *It* does not settle the West. *It* does not educate. The character inherent in the American people has done all that has been accomplished; and it would have done somewhat more, if the government had not sometimes got in its way. For government is an expedient by which men would fain succeed in letting one another alone; and, as has been said, when it is most expedient, the governed are most let alone by it. Trade and commerce, if they were not made of India rubber, would never manage to bound over the obstacles which legislators are continually putting in their way; and, if one were to judge these men wholly by the effects of their actions, and not partly by their intentions, they would deserve to be classed and punished with those mischievous persons who put obstructions on the railroads.

Must the citizen ever for a moment, or in the least degree, resign his conscience to the legislator? Why has every man a conscience, then?

But, to speak practically and as a citizen, unlike those who call themselves no-government men, I ask for, not at once no government, but *at once* a better government. Let every man make known what kind of government would command his respect, and that will be one step toward obtaining it.

After all, the practical reason why, when the power is once in the hands of the people, a majority are permitted, and for a long period continue, to rule, is not because they are most likely to be in the right, nor because this seems fairest to the minority, but because they are physically the strongest. But a government in which the majority rule in all cases cannot be based on justice, even as far as men understand it. Can there not be a government in which majorities do not virtually decide right and wrong, but conscience?—in which majorities decide only those questions to which the rule of expediency is applicable? Must the citizen ever for a moment, or in the least degree, resign his conscience to the legislator? Why has every man a conscience, then? I think that we should be men first, and subjects afterward. It is not desirable to cultivate a respect for the law, so much as for the right. The only obligation which I have a right to assume, is to do at any time what I think right. It is truly enough said, that a corporation has no conscience; but a corporation of conscientious men is a corporation *with* a conscience. Law never made men a whit more just; and, by means of their respect for it, even the well-disposed are daily made the agents of injustice. A common and natural result of an undue respect for law is, that you may see a file of soldiers, colonel, captain, corporal, privates, powder-monkeys and all, marching in admirable order over hill and dale to the wars, against their wills, aye, against their common sense and consciences, which makes it very steep marching indeed, and produces a palpitation of the heart. They have no doubt that it is a damnable business in which they are concerned; they are all peaceably inclined. Now, what are they? Men at all? or small moveable forts and magazines, at the service of some unscrupulous man in power? . . .

All voting is a sort of gaming, like chequers or backgammon, with a slight moral tinge to it, a playing with right and wrong, with moral questions; and betting naturally accompanies it. The character of the voters is not staked. I cast my vote, perchance, as I think right; but I am not vitally concerned that that right should prevail. I am willing to leave it to the majority. Its obligation, therefore, never exceeds that of expediency. Even voting *for the right* is *doing* nothing for it. It is only expressing to men feebly your desire that it should prevail. A wise man will not leave the right to the mercy of chance, nor wish it to prevail through the power of the majority. There is but little virtue in the action of masses of men. When the majority shall at length vote for the abolition of slavery, it will be because they are indifferent to slavery, or because there is but little slavery left to be abolished by their vote. *They* will then be the only slaves. Only *his* vote can hasten the abolition of slavery who asserts his own freedom by his vote.

◆◆◆

Under a government which imprisons any unjustly, the true place for a just man is also a prison. The proper place to-day, the only place which Massachusetts has provided for her freer and less desponding spirits, is in her prisons, to be put out and locked out of the State by her own act, as they have already put themselves out by their principles. It is there that the fugitive slave, and the Mexican prisoner on parole, and the Indian come to plead the wrongs of his race, should find them; on that separate, but more free and honorable ground, where the State places those who are not *with* her but *against* her,—the only house in a slave-state in which a free man can abide with honor. If any think that their influence would be lost there, and their voices no longer afflict the ear of the State, that they would not be as an enemy within its walls, they do not know by how much truth is stronger than error, nor how much more eloquently and effectively he can combat injustice who has experienced a little in his own person.

Cast your whole vote, not a strip of paper merely, but your whole influence. A minority is powerless while it conforms to the majority; it is not even a minority then; but it is irresistible when it clogs by its whole weight. If the alternative is to keep all just men in prison, or give up war and slavery, the State will not hesitate which to choose. If a thousand men were not to pay their tax-bills this year, that would not be a violent and bloody measure, as it would be to pay them, and enable the State to commit violence and shed innocent blood. This is, in fact, the definition of a peaceable revolution, if any such is possible. If the tax-gatherer, or any other public officer, asks me, as one has done, "But what shall I do?" my answer is, "If you really wish to do any thing, resign your office." When the subject has refused allegiance, and the officer has resigned his office, then the revolution is accomplished. But even suppose blood should flow. Is there not a sort of blood shed when the conscience is wounded? Through this wound a man's real manhood and immortality flow out, and he bleeds to an everlasting death. I see this blood flowing now.

◆ ◆ ◆

I have paid no poll-tax for six years. I was put into a jail once on this account, for one night; and, as I stood considering the walls of solid stone, two or three feet thick, the door of wood and iron, a foot thick, and the iron grating which strained the light, I could not help being struck with the foolishness of that institution which treated me as if I were mere flesh and blood and bones, to be locked up. I wondered that it should have concluded at length that this was the best use it could put me to, and had never thought to avail itself of my services in some way. I saw that, if there was a wall of stone between me and my townsmen, there was a still more difficult one to climb or break through, before they could get to be as free as I was. I did not for a moment feel confined, and the walls seemed a great waste of stone and mortar. I felt as if I alone of all my townsmen had paid my tax. They plainly did not know how to treat me, but behaved like persons who are underbred. In every threat and in every compliment there was a blunder; for they thought that my chief desire was to stand the other side of that stone wall. I could not but smile to see how industriously they locked the door on my meditations, which followed them out again without let or hinderance, and *they* were really all that was dangerous. As they could not reach me, they had resolved to punish my body; just as boys, if they cannot come at some person against whom they have a spite, will abuse his dog. I saw that the State was half-witted, that it was timid as a lone woman with her silver spoons, and that it did not know its friends from its foes, and I lost all my remaining respect for it, and pitied it.

Thus the State never intentionally confronts a man's sense, intellectual or moral, but only his body, his senses. It is not armed with superior wit or honesty, but with superior physical strength. I was not born to be forced. I will breathe after my own fashion. Let us see who is the strongest. What force has a multitude? They only can force me who obey a higher law than I. They force me to become like themselves. I do not hear of *men* being *forced* to live this way or that by masses of men. What sort of life were that to live? When I meet a government

which says to me, "Your money or your life," why should I be in haste to give it
my money? It may be in a great strait, and not know what to do: I cannot help
that. It must help itself; do as I do. It is not worth the while to snivel about it. I
am not responsible for the successful working of the machinery of society. I am
not the son of the engineer. I perceive that, when an acorn and a chestnut fall
side by side, the one does not remain inert to make way for the other, but both
obey their own laws, and spring and grow and flourish as best they can, till one,
perchance, overshadows and destroys the other. If a plant cannot live according
to its nature, it dies; and so a man.

A little more than a hundred years later, in 1963, Martin Luther King, Jr., used
similar reasoning in his decision to participate in the civil rights protests in Birmingham, Alabama. King was famous for his advocacy of nonviolent protest; nonetheless, King did believe in protest. In fact, he claims in the following famous "Letter
from Birmingham Jail" that disobeying the law was his moral—and Christian—
obligation.

FROM "LETTER FROM BIRMINGHAM JAIL"
BY THE REV. MARTIN LUTHER KING, JR.

I think I should indicate why I am here in Birmingham, since you have been
influenced by the view which argues against "outsiders coming in." I have the
honor of serving as president of the Southern Christian Leadership Conference,
an organization operating in every southern state, with headquarters in Atlanta,
Georgia. We have some eighty-five affiliated organizations across the South, and
one of them is the Alabama Christian Movement for Human Rights. Frequently
we share staff, educational and financial resources with our affiliates. Several
months ago the affiliate here in Birmingham asked us to be on call to engage in a
nonviolent direct-action program if such were deemed necessary. We readily
consented, and when the hour came we lived up to our promise. So I, along with
several members of my staff, am here because I was invited here. I am here because I have organizational ties here.

But more basically, I am in Birmingham because injustice is here. Just as the
prophets of the eighth century B.C. left their villages and carried their "thus
saith the Lord" far beyond the boundaries of their home towns, and just as the
Apostle Paul left his village of Tarsus and carried the gospel of Jesus Christ to
the far corners of the Greco-Roman world, so am I compelled to carry the gospel
of freedom beyond my own home town. Like Paul, I must constantly respond to
the Macedonian call for aid

Moreover, I am cognizant of the interrelatedness of all communities and
states. I cannot sit idly by in Atlanta and not be concerned about what happens
in Birmingham. Injustice anywhere is a threat to justice everywhere. We are
caught in an inescapable network of mutuality, tied in a single garment of destiny. Whatever affects one directly, affects all indirectly. Never again can we

afford to live with the narrow, provincial "outside agitator" idea. Anyone who lives inside the United States can never be considered an outsider anywhere within its bounds.

You deplore the demonstrations taking place in Birmingham. But your statement, I am sorry to say, fails to express a similar concern for the conditions that brought about the demonstration. I am sure that none of you would want to rest content with the superficial kind of social analysis that deals merely with effects and does not grapple with underlying causes. It is unfortunate that demonstrations are taking place in Birmingham, but it is even more unfortunate that the city's white power structure left the Negro community with no alternative.

Injustice anywhere is a threat to justice everywhere. We are caught in an inescapable network of mutuality, tied in a single garment of destiny. Whatever affects one directly, affects all indirectly.

In any nonviolent campaign there are four basic steps: collection of the facts to determine whether injustices exist; negotiation; self-purification; and direct action. We have gone through all these steps in Birmingham. There can be no gainsaying the fact that racial injustice engulfs this community. Birmingham is probably the most thoroughly segregated city in the United States. Its ugly record of brutality is widely known. Negroes have experienced grossly unjust treatment in the courts. There have been more unsolved bombings of Negro homes and churches in Birmingham than in any other city in the nation. These are the hard, brutal facts of the case. On the basis of these conditions, Negro leaders sought to negotiate with the city fathers. But the latter consistently refused to engage in good-faith negotiation.

Then, last September, came the opportunity to talk with leaders of Birmingham's economic community. In the course of the negotiations, certain promises were made by the merchants—for example, to remove the stores' humiliating racial signs. On the basis of these promises, the Reverend Fred Shuttlesworth and the leaders of the Alabama Christian Movement for Human Rights agreed to a moratorium on all demonstrations. As the weeks and months went by, we realized that we were the victims of a broken promise. A few signs, briefly removed, returned; the others remained.

As in so many past experiences, our hopes had been blasted, and the shadow of deep disappointment settled upon us. We had no alternative except to prepare for direct action, whereby we would present our very bodies as a means of laying our case before the conscience of the local and the national community. Mindful of the difficulties involved, we decided to undertake a process of self-purification. We began a series of workshops on nonviolence, and we repeatedly asked ourselves: "Are you able to accept blows without retaliating?" "Are you able to endure the ordeal of jail?" We decided to schedule our direct-action program for the Easter season, realizing that except for Christmas, this is the main shopping period of the year. Knowing that a strong economic-withdrawal program would be the by-product of direct action, we felt that this would be the best time to bring pressure to bear on the merchants for the needed change.

Then it occurred to us that Birmingham's mayoralty election was coming up in March, and we speedily decided to postpone action until after election day. When we discovered that the Commissioner of Public Safety, Eugene "Bull" Connor, had piled up enough votes to be in the run-off, we decided again to postpone action until the day after the run-off so that the demonstrations could not be used to cloud the issues. Like many others, we waited to see Mr. Connor defeated, and to this end we endured postponement after postponement. Having aided in this community need, we felt that our direct-action program could be delayed no longer.

You may well ask: "Why direct action? Why sit-ins, marches and so forth? Isn't negotiation a better path?" You are quite right in calling for negotiation. Indeed, this is the very purpose of direct action. Nonviolent direct action seeks to create such a crisis and foster such a tension that a community which has constantly refused to negotiate is forced to confront the issue. It seeks so to dramatize the issue that it can no longer be ignored. My citing the creation of tension as part of the work of the nonviolent-resister may sound rather shocking. But I must confess that I am not afraid of the word "tension." I have earnestly opposed violent tension, but there is a type of constructive, nonviolent tension which is necessary for growth. Just as Socrates felt that it was necessary to create a tension in the mind so that individuals could rise from the bondage of myths and half-truths to the unfettered realm of creative analysis and objective appraisal, so must we see the need for nonviolent gadflies to create the kind of tension in society that will help men rise from the dark depths of prejudice and racism to the majestic heights of understanding and brotherhood.

The purpose of our direct-action program is to create a situation so crisis-packed that it will inevitably open the door to negotiation. I therefore concur with you in your call for negotiation. Too long has our beloved Southland been bogged down in a tragic effort to live in monologue rather than dialogue.

◆◆◆

We know through painful experience that freedom is never voluntarily given by the oppressor; it must be demanded by the oppressed. Frankly, I have yet to engage in a direct-action campaign that was "well timed" in the view of those who have not suffered unduly from the disease of segregation. For years now I have heard the word "Wait!" It rings in the ear of every Negro with piercing familiarity. This "Wait" has almost always meant "Never." We must come to see, with one of our distinguished jurists, that "justice too long delayed is justice denied."

You express a great deal of anxiety over our willingness to break laws. This is certainly a legitimate concern. Since we so diligently urge people to obey the Supreme Court's decision of 1954 outlawing segregation in the public schools, at first glance it may seem rather paradoxical for us consciously to break laws. One may well ask: "How can you advocate breaking some laws and obeying others?" The answer lies in the fact that there are two types of laws: just and unjust. I would be the first to advocate obeying just laws. One has not only a legal but a moral responsibility to obey just laws. Conversely, one has a moral responsibility to disobey unjust laws. I would agree with St. Augustine that "an unjust law is no law at all."

Now, what is the difference between the two? How does one determine whether a law is just or unjust? A just law is a man-made code that squares with the moral law or the law of God. An unjust law is a code that is out of harmony with the moral law. To put it in the terms of St. Thomas Aquinas: An unjust law is a human law that is not rooted in eternal law and natural law. Any law that uplifts human personality is just. Any law that degrades human personality is unjust. All segregation statutes are unjust because segregation distorts the soul and damages the personality. It gives the segregator a false sense of superiority and the segregated a false sense of inferiority. Segregation, to use the terminology of the Jewish philosopher Martin Buber, substitutes an "I-it" relationship for an "I-thou" relationship and ends up relegating persons to the status of things. Hence segregation is not only politically, economically and sociologically unsound, it is morally wrong and sinful. Paul Tillich has said that sin is separation. Is not segregation an existential expression of man's tragic separation, his awful estrangement, his terrible sinfulness? Thus it is that I can urge men to obey the 1954 decision of the Supreme Court, for it is morally right; and I can urge them to disobey segregation ordinances, for they are morally wrong.

Let us consider a more concrete example of just and unjust laws. An unjust law is a code that a numerical or power majority group compels a minority group to obey but does not make binding on itself. This is *difference* made legal. By the same token, a just law is a code that a majority compels a minority to follow and that it is willing to follow itself. This is *sameness* made legal.

Let me give another explanation. A law is unjust if it is inflicted on a minority that, as a result of being denied the right to vote, had no part in enacting or devising the law. Who can say that the legislature of Alabama which set up that state's segregation laws was democratically elected? Throughout Alabama all sorts of devious methods are used to prevent Negroes from becoming registered voters, and there are some counties in which, even though Negroes constitute a majority of the population, not a single Negro is registered. Can any law enacted under such circumstances be considered democratically structured?

Sometimes a law is just on its face and unjust in its application. For instance, I have been arrested on a charge of parading without a permit. Now, there is nothing wrong in having an ordinance which requires a permit for a parade. But such an ordinance becomes unjust when it is used to maintain segregation and to deny citizens the First-Amendment privilege of peaceful assembly and protest.

◆ ◆ ◆

Oppressed people cannot remain oppressed forever. The yearning for freedom eventually manifests itself, and that is what has happened to the American Negro. Something within has reminded him of his birthright of freedom, and something without has reminded him that it can be gained. Consciously or unconsciously, he has been caught up by the *Zeitgeist,* and with his black brothers of Africa and his brown and yellow brothers of Asia, South America and the Caribbean, the United States Negro is moving with a sense of great urgency toward the promised land of racial justice. If one recognizes this vital urge that has engulfed the Negro community, one should readily understand why public demonstrations are taking place. The Negro has many pent-up resentments and latent frustrations, and he must release them. So let him march; let him make prayer pilgrimages to the city hall; let him go on freedom rides—and try to understand why he must do so. If his repressed emotions are not released in nonviolent ways, they will seek expression through violence; this is not a threat but a fact of history. So I have not said to my people: "Get rid of your discontent." Rather, I have tried to say that this normal and healthy discontent can be channeled into the creative outlet of nonviolent direct action. And now this approach is being termed extremist.

But though I was initially disappointed at being categorized as an extremist, as I continued to think about the matter I gradually gained a measure of satisfaction from the label. Was not Jesus an extremist for love: "Love your enemies, bless them that curse you, do good to them that hate you, and pray for them which despitefully use you, and persecute you." Was not Amos an extremist for justice: "Let justice roll down like waters and righteousness like an ever-flowing stream." Was not Paul an extremist for the Christian gospel: "I bear in my body the marks of the Lord Jesus." Was not Martin Luther an extremist: "Here I stand; I cannot do otherwise, so help me God." And John Bunyan: "I will stay in jail to the end of my days before I make a butchery of my conscience." And Abraham Lincoln: "This nation cannot survive half slave and half free." And Thomas Jefferson: "We hold these truths to be self-evident, that all men are created equal . . . ." So the question is not whether we will be extremists, but what kind of extremists we will be. Will we be extremists for hate or for love? Will we be extremists for the preservation of injustice or for the extension of justice? In that dramatic scene on Calvary's hill three men were crucified. We must never forget that all three were crucified for the same crime—the crime of extremism. Two were extremists for immorality, and thus fell below their environment. The other, Jesus Christ, was an extremist for love, truth, and goodness, and therefore rose above his environment. Perhaps the South, the nation and the world are in dire need of creative extremists.[16]

Malcolm X, a contemporary of King, believed in taking a far more aggressive stand against unjust government. He was one of the leaders of the "Black Nationalist" movement, which pursued not just justice, but an independent and separate state, for black people of all nations. Malcolm X's famous phrase "by any means necessary" indicated his rejection of King's (or Thoreau's) nonviolence and "civility" of disobedience. Rather, Malcolm X argued, building on Thomas Hobbes, that those

---

[16]Martin Luther King, Jr., "Letter from Birmingham Jail," rpt. as Chapter 5 of *Why We Can't Wait* (New York: New American Library, 1988 [reprint]).

mistreated by an unjust government have the right and the obligation to violate the laws of that government. Consider the following harsh words:

> *. . . I'm not standing here speaking to you as an American, or a patriot, or a flag-saluter, or a flag-waver — no, not I. I'm speaking as a victim of this American system. And I see America through the eyes of the victim. I don't see any American dream; I see an American nightmare.*

FROM **"THE BALLOT OR THE BULLET"** BY **MALCOLM X**

I am one who doesn't believe in deluding myself. I'm not going to sit at your table and watch you eat, with nothing on my plate, and call myself a diner. Sitting at the table doesn't make you a diner, unless you eat some of what's on that plate. Being here in America doesn't make you an American. Why, if birth made you American, you wouldn't need any legislation, you wouldn't need any amendments to the Constitution, you wouldn't be faced with civil-rights filibustering in Washington, D.C., right now. They don't have to pass civil-rights legislation to make a Polack an American.

No, I'm not an American. I'm one of the 22 million black people who are the victims of Americanism. One of the 22 million black people who are the victims of democracy, nothing but disguised hypocrisy. So, I'm not standing here speaking to you as an American, or a patriot, or a flag-saluter, or a flag-waver—no, not I. I'm speaking as a victim of this American system. And I see America through the eyes of the victim. I don't see any American dream; I see an American nightmare. . . .

Let the world know how bloody his hands are. Let the world know the hypocrisy that's practiced over here. Let it be the ballot or the bullet. Let him know that it must be the ballot or the bullet.[17]

Finally, we have **Nelson Mandela**'s heroic defiance of apartheid (racial separation) in South Africa, emerging in victory in 1993. Like Socrates in the *Apology,* Mandela makes his bold testament in the context of a trial for his life.

FROM *LONG WALK TO FREEDOM* BY **NELSON MANDELA**

Many years ago, when I was a boy brought up in my village in the Transkei, I listened to the elders of the tribe telling stories about the good old days before

---

[17] Malcolm X, "The Ballot or the Bullet," rpt. in *Malcolm X Speaks* (New York: Grove Press, 1965).

the arrival of the white man. Then our people lived peacefully, under the democratic rule of their kings and their amapakati [literally "insiders," but meaning those closest in rank to the king], and moved freely and confidently up and down the country without let or hindrance. The country was our own, in name and right. We occupied the land, the forests, the rivers; we extracted the mineral wealth beneath the soil and all the riches of this beautiful country. We set up and operated our own government, we controlled our own arms and we organized our trade and commerce. The elders would tell tales of the wars fought by our ancestors in defense of the Fatherland, as well as the acts of valor by generals and soldiers during these epic days. . . .

The structure and organization of early African societies in this country fascinated me very much and greatly influenced the evolution of my political outlook. The land, then the main means of production, belonged to the whole tribe and there was no individual ownership whatsoever. There were no classes, no rich or poor and no exploitation of man by man. All men were free and equal and this was the foundation of government. Recognition of this general principle found expression in the constitution of the council, variously called "Imbizo" or "Pitso" or "Kgotla," which governs the affairs of the tribe. The council was so completely democratic that all members of the tribe could participate in its deliberations. Chief and subject, warrior and medicine man, all took part and endeavored to influence its decisions. It was so weighty and influential a body that no step of any importance could ever be taken by the tribe without reference to it.

There was much in such a society that was primitive and insecure and it certainly could never measure up to the demands of the present epoch. But in such a society are contained the seeds of revolutionary democracy in which none will be held in slavery or servitude, and in which poverty, want and insecurity shall be no more. This is the history which, even today, inspires me and my colleagues in our political struggle.

◆◆◆

I told the court how I had joined the African National Congress and how its policy of democracy and nonracialism reflected my own deepest convictions. I explained how as a lawyer I was often forced to choose between compliance with the law and accommodating my conscience.

◆◆◆

I would say that the whole life of any thinking African in this country drives him continuously to a conflict between his conscience on the one hand and the law on the other. This is not a conflict peculiar to this country. The conflict arises for men of conscience, for men who think and who feel deeply in every country. Recently in Britain, a peer of the realm, Earl [Bertrand] Russell, probably the most respected philosopher of the Western world, was sentenced and convicted for precisely the type of activities for which I stand before you today—for following his conscience in defiance of the law, as a protest against the nuclear weapons policy being pursued by his own government. He could do no other than to oppose the law and to suffer the consequences for it. Nor can I. Nor can many Africans in this country. The law as it is applied, the law as it has been developed over a long period of history, and especially the law as it is written and designed by the Nationalist government is a law which, in our views, is immoral, unjust, and intolerable. Our consciences dictate that we must protest against it, that we must oppose it and that we must attempt to alter it . . . Men, I think, are not capable of doing nothing, of saying nothing, of not reacting to injustice, of not protesting against oppression, of not striving for the good society and the good life in the ways they see it.

◆ ◆ ◆

I recounted in detail the numerous times the government had used the law to hamper my life, career, and political work, through bannings, restrictions, and trials.

◆ ◆ ◆

I was made, by the law, a criminal, not because of what I had done, but because of what I stood for, because of what I thought, because of my conscience. Can it be any wonder to anybody that such conditions make a man an outlaw of society? Can it be wondered that such a man, having been outlawed by the government, should be prepared to lead the life of an outlaw, as I have led for some months, according to the evidence before this court?

> *I was made, by the law, a criminal, not because of what I had done, but because of what I stood for, because of what I thought, because of my conscience.*

It has not been easy for me during the past period to separate myself from my wife and children, to say good-bye to the good old days when, at the end of a strenuous day at an office I could look forward to joining my family at the dinner table, and instead to take up the life of a man hunted continuously by the police, living separated from those who are closest to me, in my own country, facing continually the hazards of detection and of arrest. This has been a life infinitely more difficult than serving a prison sentence. No man in his right senses would voluntarily choose such a life in preference to the one of normal, family, social life which exists in every civilized community.

But there comes a time, as it came in my life, when a man is denied the right to live a normal life, when he can only live the life of an outlaw because the government has so decreed to use the law to impose a state of outlawry upon him. I was driven to this situation, and I do not regret having taken the decisions that I did take. Other people will be driven in the same way in this country, by this very same force of police persecution and of administrative action by the government, to follow my course, of that I am certain.

◆ ◆ ◆

I enumerated the many times that we had brought our grievances before the government and the equal number of times that we were ignored or shunted aside. I described our stay-away of 1961 as a last resort after the government showed no signs of taking any steps to either talk with us or meet our demands. It was the government that provoked violence by employing violence to meet our nonviolent demands. I explained that because of the government's actions we had taken a more militant stance. I said that I had been privileged throughout my political life to fight alongside colleagues whose abilities and contributions were far greater than my own. Many others had paid the price of their beliefs before me, and many more would do so after me.

Before sentencing, I informed the court that whatever sentence the state imposed, it would do nothing to change my devotion to the struggle.

◆ ◆ ◆

I do not believe, Your Worship, that this court, in inflicting penalties on me for the crimes for which I am convicted should be moved by the belief that penalties will deter men from the course that they believe is right. History shows that penalties do not deter men when their conscience is aroused, nor will they deter my people or the colleagues with whom I have worked before.

I am prepared to pay the penalty even though I know how bitter and desperate is the situation of an African in the prisons of this country. I have been in these prisons and I know how gross is the discrimination, even behind the prison wall, against Africans. . . . Nevertheless these considerations do not sway me from the path that I have taken nor will they sway others like me. For to men, freedom in their own land is the pinnacle of their ambitions, from which nothing can turn men of conviction aside. More powerful than my fear of the dreadful conditions to which I might be subjected in prison is my hatred for the dreadful conditions to which my people are subjected outside prison throughout this country. . . .

Whatever sentence Your Worship sees fit to impose upon me for the crime for which I have been convicted before this court, may it rest assured that when my sentence has been completed I will still be moved, as men are always moved, by their conscience; I will still be moved by my dislike of the race discrimination against my people when I come out from serving my sentence, to take up again, as best I can, the struggle for the removal of those injustices until they are finally abolished once and for all. . . .

I have done my duty to my people and to South Africa. I have no doubt that posterity will pronounce that I was innocent and that the criminals that should have been brought before this court are the members of the government.

◆ ◆ ◆

When I had finished, the magistrate ordered a ten-minute recess to consider the sentence. I turned and looked out at the crowd before exiting the courtroom. I had no illusions about the sentence I would receive. Exactly ten minutes later, in a courtroom heavy with tension, the magistrate pronounced sentence: three years for inciting people to strike and two years for leaving the country without a passport; five years in all, with no possibility of parole. It was a stern sentence and there was wailing among the spectators. As the court rose, I turned to the gallery and again made a clenched fist, shouting "Amandla!" three times. Then, on its own, the crowd began to sing our beautiful anthem, "Nkosi Sikelel' iAfrika." People sang and danced and the women ululated as I was led away. The uproar among the gallery made me forget for a moment that I would be going to prison to serve what was then the stiffest sentence yet imposed in South Africa for a political offense.

Downstairs, I was permitted a brief good-bye to Winnie, and on this occasion she was not at all grim: she was in high spirits and shed no tears. She seemed confident, as much a comrade as a wife. She was determined to brace me. As I was driven away in the police van I could still hear the people outside singing "Nkosi Sikelel' iAfrika."[18]

D. ON THE ORIGINS OF GOOD AND EVIL

At the bottom of the ongoing debates about justice and the role of society in constituting and enforcing justice, a deeper debate about human nature is always just under the surface. In the Western tradition, we know this debate by way of two thousand years of arguments about so-called original sin, that is, the idea that people are essentially flawed just by virtue of the fact that they are human. If this is so, if people are, for instance, naturally selfish, then that fact would seem to dictate corrective governmental or cultural sanctions. Hobbes' view of man in the state of nature makes this quite clear. On the other hand, if one has a more benign view of human nature, as, for example, in the philosophy of Jean-Jacques Rousseau, then the sanctions of the state should be more modest, perhaps even minimal. But here we will look at a different version of that debate, carried out for an even longer period of time, in the philosophies of ancient China. On the one hand, there is the philosophy of **Mencius,** a disciple of the great Chinese philosopher Confucius, who argues that humanity is basically benevolent, that every person has within a sense of compassion for others. Against this view, there is the later philosopher **Hsun Tsu,** who argues to the contrary that people are naturally selfish and cultivation is necessary to correct their evil dispositions.

FROM *MENCIUS*
TRANS. **D. C. LAU**

6. Mencius said, 'No man is devoid of a heart sensitive to the suffering of others. Such a sensitive heart was possessed by the Former Kings and this manifested itself in compassionate government. With such a sensitive heart behind compassionate government, it was as easy to rule the Empire as rolling it on your palm.

'My reason for saying that no man is devoid of a heart sensitive to the suffering of others is this. Suppose a man were, all of a sudden, to see a young child on the verge of falling into a well. He would certainly be moved to compassion, not because he wanted to get in the good graces of the parents, nor because he wished to win the praise of his fellow villagers or friends, nor yet because he disliked the cry of the child. From this it can be seen that whoever is devoid of

---

[18] Nelson Mandela, *Long Walk to Freedom: The Autobiography of Nelson Mandela* (Boston: Little, Brown, 1994), pp. 329–333.

the heart of compassion is not human, whoever is devoid of the heart of shame is not human, whoever is devoid of the heart of courtesy and modesty is not human, and whoever is devoid of the heart of right and wrong is not human. The heart of compassion is the germ of benevolence; the heart of shame, of dutifulness; the heart of courtesy and modesty, of observance of the rites; the heart of right and wrong, of wisdom. Man has these four germs just as he has four limbs. For a man possessing these four germs to deny his own potentialities is for him to cripple himself; for him to deny the potentialities of his prince is for him to cripple his prince. If a man is able to develop all these four germs that he possesses, it will be like a fire starting up or a spring coming through. When these are fully developed, he can take under his protection the whole realm within the Four Seas, but if he fails to develop them, he will not be able to serve his parents.'

7. Mencius said, 'Is the maker of arrows really more unfeeling than the maker of armour? He is afraid lest he should fail to harm people, whereas the maker of armour is afraid lest he should fail to protect them. The case is similar with the sorcerer-doctor and the coffin-maker. For this reason one cannot be too careful in the choice of one's calling.

'Confucius said, "The best neighbourhood is where benevolence is to be found. Not to live in such a neighbourhood when one has the choice cannot by any means be considered wise." Benevolence is the high honour bestowed by Heaven and the peaceful abode of man. Not to be benevolent when nothing stands in the way is to show a lack of wisdom. A man neither benevolent nor wise, devoid of courtesy and dutifulness, is a slave. A slave ashamed of serving is like a maker of bows ashamed of making bows, or a maker of arrows ashamed of making arrows. If one is ashamed, there is no better remedy than to practise benevolence. Benevolence is like archery: an archer makes sure his stance is correct before letting fly the arrow, and if he fails to hit the mark, he does not hold it against his victor. He simply seeks the cause within himself.' [19]

FROM **HUMAN NATURE IS EVIL**
BY **HSUN TSU**

The nature of man is evil; his goodness is acquired.

His nature being what it is, man is born, first, with a desire for gain. If this desire is followed, strife will result and courtesy will disappear. Second, man is born with envy and hate. If these tendencies are followed, injury and cruelty will abound and loyalty and faithfulness will disappear. Third, man is born with passions of the ear and eye as well as the love of sound and beauty. If these passions are followed, excesses and disorderliness will spring up and decorum and righteousness will disappear. Hence to give rein to man's original nature and to yield to man's emotions will assuredly lead to strife and disorderliness, and he will revert to a state of barbarism. Therefore it is only under the influence of teachers

---

[19] From *Mencius,* trans. D. C. Lau (Penguin, 1970).

and laws and the guidance of the rules of decorum and righteousness that courtesy will be observed, etiquette respected, and order restored. From all this it is evident that the nature of man is evil and that his goodness is acquired.

Crooked wood needs to undergo steaming and bending by the carpenter's tools; then only is it straight. Blunt metal needs to undergo grinding and whetting; then only is it sharp. Now the original nature of man is evil, so he must submit himself to teachers and laws before he can be just; he must submit himself to the rules of decorum and righteousness before he can be orderly. On the other hand, without teachers and laws, men are biased and unjust; without decorum and righteousness, men are rebellious and disorderly. In ancient times the sage-kings knew that man's nature was evil and therefore biased and unjust, rebellious and disorderly. Thereupon they created the codes of decorum and righteousness and established laws and ordinances in order to bend the nature of man and set it right, and in order to transform his nature and guide it. All men are thus made to conduct themselves in a manner that is orderly and in accordance with the Way. At present, those men who are influenced by teachers and laws, who have accumulated culture and learning, and who are following the paths of decorum and righteousness, are the gentlemen. On the other hand those who give rein to their nature, who indulge in their willfulness, and who disregard decorum and righteousness, are the inferior men. From all this it is evident that the nature of man is evil and that his goodness is acquired.

> *Crooked wood needs to undergo steaming and bending by the carpenter's tools; then only is it straight. Blunt metal needs to undergo grinding and whetting; then only is it sharp. Now the original nature of man is evil, so he must submit himself to teachers and laws before he can be just. . . .*

Mencius says: "The reason man is ready to learn is that his nature is originally good." I reply: This is not so. This is due to a lack of knowledge about the original nature of man and of understanding of the distinction between what is natural and what is acquired. Original nature is a heavenly endowment; it cannot be learned, and it cannot be striven after. As to rules of decorum and righteousness, they have been brought forth by the sages, they can be attained by learning, and they can be achieved by striving. That which cannot be learned and cannot be striven after and rests with Heaven is what I call original nature. That which can be attained by learning and achieved by striving and rests with man is what I call acquired character. This is the distinction between original nature and acquired character. Now by the nature of man, the eye has the faculty of seeing and the ear has the faculty of hearing. But the keenness of the faculty of sight is inseparable from the eye, and the keenness of the faculty of hearing is inseparable from the ear. It is evident that keenness of sight and keenness of hearing cannot be learned.

Mencius says: "The original nature of man is good; but because men all ruin it and lose it, it becomes evil." I reply: In this he is gravely mistaken. Regarding the nature of man, as soon as he is born, he tends to depart from its original state and depart from its natural disposition, and he is bent on ruining it and losing it. From all this, it is evident that the nature of man is evil and that his goodness is acquired.

To say that man's original nature is good means that it can become beautiful without leaving its original state and it can become beneficial without leaving its natural disposition. This is to maintain that beauty pertains to the original state and disposition and goodness pertains to the heart and mind in the same way as the keenness of the faculty of sight is inseparable from the eye and the keenness of the faculty of hearing is inseparable from the ear, just as we say that the eye is keen in seeing or the ear is keen in hearing. Now as to the nature of man, when he is hungry he desires to be filled, when he is cold he desires warmth, when he is tired he desires rest. This is man's natural disposition. But now a man may be hungry and yet in the presence of elders he dare not be the first to eat. This is because he has to yield precedence to someone. He may be tired and yet he dare not take a rest. This is because he has to labor in the place of someone. For a son to yield to his father and a younger brother to yield to his older brother, for a son to labor in the place of his father and a younger brother to labor in the place of his older brother—both of these kinds of actions are opposed to man's original nature and contrary to man's feeling. Yet they are the way of the filial son and in accordance with the rules of decorum and righteousness. It appears if a person follows his natural disposition he will show no courtesy, and if he shows courtesy he is acting contrary to his natural disposition. From all this it is evident that the nature of man is evil and that his goodness is acquired.

It may be asked: "If man's original nature is evil, whence do the rules of decorum and righteousness arise?" I reply: All rules of decorum and righteousness are the products of the acquired virtue of the sage and not the products of the nature of man. Thus, the potter presses the clay and makes the vessel—but the vessel is the product of the potter's acquired skill and not the product of his original nature. Or again, the craftsman hews pieces of wood and makes utensils—but utensils are the product of the carpenter's acquired skills and not the product of his original nature. The sage gathers many ideas and thoughts and becomes well versed in human affairs, in order to bring forth the rules of decorum and righteousness and establish laws and institutions. So then the rules of decorum and righteousness and laws and institutions are similarly the products of the acquired virtue of the sage and not the products of his original nature. . . .

Man wishes to be good because his nature is evil. If a person is unimportant he wishes to be important, if he is ugly he wishes to be beautiful, if he is confined he wishes to be at large, if he is poor he wishes to be rich, if he is lowly he wishes to be honored—whatever a person does not have within himself, he seeks from without. But the rich do not wish for wealth and the honorable do not wish for position, for whatever a person has within himself he does not seek from without. From this it may be seen that man wishes to be good because his nature is evil. Now the original nature of man is really without decorum and righteousness, hence he strives to learn and seeks to obtain them. . . .

Straight wood does not require the carpenter's tools to be straight; by nature it is straight. Crooked wood needs to undergo steaming and bending by the carpenter's tools and then only will it be straight; by nature it is not straight. As the nature of man is evil, it must be submitted to the government of the sage-kings and the reforming influence of the rules of decorum and righteousness; then only will everyone issue forth in orderliness and be in accordance with goodness. From all this it is evident that the nature of man is evil and that his goodness is acquired.

It may be objected: "Decorum and righteousness and the accumulation of acquired virtues must be in the nature of man so that the sage could bring them forth." I reply: This is not so. Now the potter pounds and molds the clay and produces earthenware. Are the earthenware and clay then in the nature of the potter? The workman hews a piece of wood and makes utensils. Are furniture and wood then in the nature of the carpenter? So it is with the sage and decorum and righteousness; he produces them in the same way as earthenware is produced. Are decorum and righteousness and the accumulation of acquired virtues then in the original nature of man? As far as the nature of man is concerned, the sage-kings Yao and Shun have the same nature as the wicked King Chieh and robber Chih; the gentleman has the same nature as the inferior man. Should we now regard decorum and righteousness and the accumulation of acquired virtues as being in the nature of man, then why should we prize the sage-kings Yao and Yü and why should we prize the gentlemen? We prize Yao, Yü, and the gentlemen because they were able to transform nature and produce acquired virtue, and from acquired virtue decorum and righteousness issued forth. . . .

There is a saying: "The man on the street can become a Yü." How would you account for that? I reply: All that made Yü what he was was that he instituted humanity and righteousness, laws, and government. However, there are principles by which humanity and righteousness, laws and government can be known and practiced. At the same time any man on the street has the faculty for knowing them and has the capacity for practicing them. Thus it is evident that he can become a Yü. Should we assume there were really no principles by which humanity and righteousness, laws and government could be known and practiced, then even Yü would not be able to know them or practice them. Or, should we assume the man on the street really had no faculty for knowing humanity and righteousness, laws and government, or the capacity for practicing them, then the man cannot know, on the one hand, the proper relation between father and son and, on the other, the proper discipline between sovereign and minister. Thus it is evident that the man on the street does have the faculty for knowing and the capacity for practicing these virtues. Now let the man on the street take his faculty for knowing and his capacity for practicing humanity and righteousness, laws and government and bring them to bear upon the principles by which these virtues can be known and can be practiced—then it is self-evident that he can become a Yü. Yes, let the man on the street pursue the path of knowledge and devote himself to learning, with concentration of mind and a singleness of purpose; let him think, search, examine, and re-examine, day in and day out, with persistence and patience—let him thus accumulate good works without cease, then he may be counted among the gods and may form a triad with Heaven and earth. Hence sagehood is a state that any man can achieve by cumulative effort.[20]

SUMMARY AND CONCLUSION

In some areas of philosophy, the question arises, "What does this have to do with everyday life?" In political philosophy, as in moral philosophy, the connection between philosophy and "everyday life" is obvious. It is no coincidence that the major revolutions of the eighteenth and nineteenth centuries came soon after a flurry of philosophical radicalism. And we know that much of the world is divided and ruled according to rival political philosophies at the present time.

What is always at issue is the concept of justice. The ideas that people are equal and should be treated equally, that people have natural or human rights that no one and no government can take away from them, that people should equally share the material goods of society—these have all been the subject of constant debate, and sometimes wars and revolutions, for most of modern times. Then too, the nature of the state itself has been part of that debate as well as the stage on which the debate has been carried out. How much should the state serve the people and how much the people serve the state? What constitutes a good state? And when, if ever, do people have the right to overthrow the state, or a particular government, or a particular law? We cannot even begin to give adequate answers to these complex questions in the context of a general introduction to philosophy; but neither can we avoid asking them in the world as it is today.

GLOSSARY

alienation In Marx, the unnatural separation of a person from the products he or she makes, from other people, or from oneself.

anarchism The view that no government has the legitimate authority to coerce people and that the public interest and individual rights can only be served without a state of any kind.

authority That which controls; usually, that which has the right to control. (For example, the government has the authority to tax your income.)

civil rights Those rights that are determined by a particular state and its laws; constitutional rights, for example, are civil rights in this sense, guaranteed by the law of the land.

democracy That form of government in which policies or at least the makers of policy are chosen by popular mandate.

---

[20] Hsun Tsu from *Sourcebook in Chinese Philosophy,* Wing-Tsit Chan, ed. (Princeton, NJ: Princeton University Press, 1991).

distributive justice The ideal of everyone receiving his or her fair share. For example, concerns over ownership of land, just wages, and fair prices are all matters of distributive justice.

egalitarianism The view that all people are equal in rights and respect.

entitlement A right; for instance, a right to own property.

equality In political philosophy, the nondiscriminatory treatment of every person, regardless of sex, race, religion, physical or mental abilities, wealth, social status, and so forth.

fascism The view that the best government is the strongest, and that the government has the right—and perhaps the duty—to control the lives of every citizen for the sake of the most efficient society.

freedom See *liberty*.

government The instrument of authority; that body that rules, passes and enforces laws, and so forth.

human rights Those rights that are considered to be universal, "unalienable," and common to every person regardless of where or when he or she lives. For example, freedom from torture and degradation would be a human right.

justice In the general sense, the virtues of an ideal society. In the more particular sense, the balance of public interest and individual rights, the fair sharing of the available goods of society, the proper punishment of criminals, and the fair restitution of victims of crime and misfortune within society.

legitimacy The right to have authority; sanctioned power (for example, through the grace of God, by means of legal succession, by appeal to justice, or to the general consent of the people governed).

liberty (political freedom) The ability to act without restraint or threat of punishment. For example, the ability to travel between states without a passport, the ability to speak one's opinions without prosecution, or the ability to work for or choose one's own profession or career. This ability, however, is not mere physical or mental ability; one might have the liberty to travel or to try to become a doctor without having the means to do so. It is also important to distinguish this political sense of liberty or freedom from the metaphysical or causal sense discussed previously. Whether our acts are really free in that sense must be distinguished from the question whether we are constrained or free to act in this political sense. The first refers to the causes of human behavior; the second refers only to the existence of legislation and political forces constraining our behavior.

retributive justice "Getting even" or "an eye for an eye."

rights Demands that a member of society is entitled to make upon his or her society. Everyone, for example, has a right to police protection. Some people, by virtue of their position, have special rights; for example, congressmen have the right to send mail to their constituents without paying postage.

social contract An agreement, tacit or explicit, that all members of society shall abide by the laws of the state in order to maximize the public interest and ensure cooperation among themselves. It is important that such a contract need never have actually been signed in history; what is important is that every member of a society, by choosing to remain in that society, implicitly makes such an agreement.

society A group of people with common historical and cultural ties; usually but not always, members of the same state and ruled by the same government.

sovereign Independent. A sovereign state is one that is subject to the laws of no other state. A sovereign is a person (for example, a king) who is not subject or answerable to the commands of anyone else. A people are sovereign when their wishes are ultimate in the same way and not subject to commands by anyone else or any government. (To say that a people is sovereign is not to say that the will of any individual or group is sovereign within it.)

state The center of authority in a society, for example, the largest political unit in a society. Usually a state is a nation, for example, the United States, Germany, and so on. Usually, but not always, coextensive with a society, and usually, but not always, distinguished by a single form of government and a single government (for example, the U.S. federal government).

unalienable rights Those rights that no one and no government can take away, for example, the right of a person to protect his or her own life. In other words, *human rights.*

BIBLIOGRAPHY AND FURTHER READING

Plato, *The Republic,* trans. Francis M. Cornford (Oxford: Oxford University Press, 1941), is still standard reading for the basics and some thought-provoking alternatives in political philosophy. See also Aristotle, *Politics,* in *The Basic Works of Aristotle,* ed. R. McKeon (New York: Random House, 1941). Our own national documents, the Declaration of Independence and the Constitution, are always important reading. John Stuart Mill, *On Liberty,* ed. C. Shields (New York: Bobbs-Merrill, 1956), has long been the classic defense of liberalism. Michael Oakeshott, *Rationalism in Politics* (New York: Basic Books, 1962) is an important challenge to liberal philosophy. See also Robert Nisbet, *Conservatism: Dream and Reality* (Minneapolis: University of Minnesota Press, 1986). Karl Marx's *Communist Manifesto,* trans. S. Moore (Chicago: Regnery, 1969), and his *Early Writings,* trans. T. Bottomore (New York: McGraw-Hill, 1963), are essential reading for beginning students in political philosophy. Niccolò Machiavelli, *The Prince,* trans. C. Detmold (New York: Airmont, 1965), and Jean-Jacques Rousseau, *The Social Contract* (New York: Dutton, 1950) are both important and rewarding reading. For more general discussions of the philosophy of politics, see F. Olafson, ed., *Justice and Social Policy* (Englewood Cliffs, NJ: Prentice-Hall, 1961); G. Sabine, *A History of Political Theory,* 3rd ed. (New York: Holt, Rinehart and Winston, 1961); and P. Laslett and W. G. Runciman, eds. *Philosophy, Politics and Society* (Oxford: Blackwell, 1964). See also *Selected Writings of Frederick Douglass,* ed. M. Myer (New York: Random House, 1984). *The Autobiography of Malcolm X,* coauthored with Alex Haley (New York: Ballantine, 1987), and Martin Luther King, Jr., *A Testament of Hope,* ed. James M. Washington (New York: Harper & Row, 1986).

BEAUTY

A thing of beauty is a joy forever.

JOHN KEATS

Philosophy is not just the study of the True and the Good but also of the Beautiful.[1] The study of philosophy would surely be incomplete if it included the subjects of knowledge and reality but ignored the very real fulfillment that comes from what is unreal—stories, paintings, and artificially produced sounds—whose sole purpose seems to be that we enjoy them for what they are. Our sense of value would be truncated indeed if the study of philosophy included only moral values and ignored all matters artistic, giving no importance to what we term "aesthetic experience"—especially the experience of beauty.

What is art? What is its purpose, its role in human life? What is good art; what is bad art? And what, despite the endeavor, isn't art at all? How do we tell the difference? Is it true, as David Hume argued two centuries ago, that "there is no disputing over tastes"—that in matters of art there is only your opinion and another's opinion, with no standard for choosing between them?

These are the compelling questions faced by the philosophical study of **aesthetics,** and they remain as difficult and intractable as the eternal questions faced by metaphysics, ethics, and epistemology. Moreover, art, unlike philosophy, is clearly an important achievement in virtually every society. But what art means in different societies—or, indeed, whether it is even conceived of as "art"—differs considerably from culture to culture.

---

[1] I am most grateful to Kathleen Higgins for her extensive help in the preparation of this chapter.

A. PLATO AND THE TRANSCENDENCE
OF BEAUTY

When we experience a work of art that is remarkably beautiful and moving, we sometimes say that it is "heavenly" or "out of this world." Indeed, we often think of beauty as a form of perfection not to be expected in our imperfect lives. Consequently, any rare glimpse of (more or less) perfect beauty contrasts sharply with the mundane experiences of daily life. It is as if we are permitted a fleeting view of another world—an eternal world, a perfect world. Taken literally, this is Plato's conception of the nature of the beautiful. Beauty exists in a world apart from us, is unchanging, and manifests itself only in rare and fleeting instances.

Of course, beauty exists outside of art and works of art. Plato, perhaps paradoxically, distrusted the beauty that could be found in art, even the spectacular art of the recent Golden Age of Athens. But he appreciated other forms of beauty, for example, beauty found in people such as Socrates (who was not at all physically beautiful—in fact, he was said to be quite ugly). Given that beautiful people were manifestations of a heavenly or "transcendent" ideal of beauty, to experience true beauty was profoundly more wonderful than any mere earthly experience. In Shakespeare's *Romeo and Juliet,* Romeo thinks of Juliet and muses, "Beauty too rich for use, for earth too dear." Romeo has experienced the Platonic vision. He believes that he has encountered in his beloved a transcendent beauty more wondrous than any other beauty on earth.

Although Romeo thinks that his experience is unique, as members of Shakespeare's audience we accept Romeo's reaction as a universal kind of experience—in fact, an experience described by Plato two thousand years before Romeo's literary birth. Plato also connects love and the vision of the beautiful, especially in his dialogue *The Symposium.* Plato, like Romeo, speaks of beauty that is too wondrous for this world; unlike Romeo, Plato presents the concept as more than an expression of his own emotions. In fact, Plato takes a philosophical approach to the idea of beauty: he is not concerned primarily with his own experience, but with the role of beauty and love in the larger scheme of reality.

Plato conceived of Beauty as a transcendent Form. His Forms (Chapter 1) are the ideal entities that comprise the transcendent "World of Being." The things that exist in our material "world of becoming" are real to a lesser degree than the Forms, and they are real only because they participate in the Forms. In other words, the true being of any thing in this world is the ideal Form that shapes its structure. Insight into true reality occurs when we recognize the ideal Form behind the imperfect appearance of things in this world. And just as there are Forms for the "True" and the "Good" and for "Justice," there is an ideal Form of Beauty. We recognize the manifestation of this ideal Form of Beauty when we experience and fall in love with things and persons that are beautiful.

We come to know the Form of Beauty through the beautiful beings and things of this world. For example, when we recognize the beauty of another human being, we catch a glimpse of the transcendent Beauty in which that person participates. This is what happens when we fall in love. Our normal behavior and attitudes are disrupted completely when we fall in love because we are recognizing something that exists on another plane of reality. Of all the Forms, the Form of Beauty attracts us most naturally. Thus, the experience of falling in love is one of life's most beautiful.

Love, then, paves the way toward insight into the Form of Beauty. If we come to recognize that it is the Form of Beauty that we experience and love in another, our response to beauty becomes the initial step toward insight into the realm of Forms in general. But such insight is, as we have seen, a matter of "recollection." And because first experiences with beauty involve an encounter with an order of reality entirely different from the one to which we are accustomed, we are often confused by the first experience we have with love. We tend to think, like Romeo, that the beauty we encounter is uniquely characteristic of the beloved person (or, in the case of art, of the beautiful work of art). We do not realize initially that the beauty of our beloved is identical to the beauty of every other beautiful person or thing. It is only when we recognize that beauty in all its earthly manifestations is identical that we gain genuine insight into the Form of Beauty.

In Plato's *Symposium,* Socrates describes the stages involved in gaining insight into the Form of Beauty. Socrates tells the audience that a woman named Diotima taught him the mysteries of love. According to Diotima, true love begins with love of one person but reaches a higher level of development when the lover comes to love all that is beautiful. Ultimately, in loving all that is beautiful, the lover comes to realize that he or she loves only one thing, absolute Beauty itself. Socrates recounts what Diotima told him:

FROM *THE SYMPOSIUM*
BY **PLATO**

He who would proceed aright in this matter should begin in youth to visit beautiful forms; and first, if he be guided by his instructor aright, to love one such form only—out of that he should create fair thoughts; and soon he will of himself perceive that the beauty of one form is akin to the beauty of another; and then if beauty of form in general is his pursuit, how foolish would he be not to recognize that the beauty in every form is one and the same! And when he perceives this he will abate his violent love of the one, which he will despise and deem a small thing, and will become a lover of all beautiful forms; in the next stage he will consider that the beauty of the mind is more honourable than the beauty of the outward form. So that if a virtuous soul have but a little comeliness, he will be content to love and tend him, and will search out and bring to the birth thoughts which may improve the young, until he is compelled to contemplate and see the beauty of institutions and laws, and to understand that the beauty of them all is of one family, and that personal beauty is a trifle; and after laws and institutions he will go on to the sciences, that he may see their beauty, being not like a servant in love with the beauty of one youth or man or institution, himself a slave mean and narrow-minded, but drawing towards and contemplating the vast sea of beauty, he will create many fair and noble thoughts and notions in boundless love of wisdom; until on that shore he grows and waxes strong, and at last the vision is revealed to him of a single science, which is the science of beauty everywhere. To this I will proceed; please to give me your very best attention:

"He who has been instructed thus far in the things of love, and who has learned to see the beautiful in due order and succession, when he comes toward the end will suddenly perceive a nature of wondrous beauty (and this, Socrates, is the final cause of all our former toils)—a nature which in the first place is everlasting, not growing and decaying, or waxing and waning; secondly, not fair in one point of view and foul in another, or at one time or in one relation or at one place fair, at another time or in another relation or at another place foul, as if fair to some and foul to others, or in the likeness of a face or hands or any other part of the bodily frame, or in any form of speech or knowledge, or existing in any other being, as for example, in an animal, or in heaven, or in earth, or in any other place: but beauty absolute, separate, simple, and everlasting, which without diminution and without increase, or any change, is imparted to the ever-growing and perishing beauties of all other things. He who from these ascending under the influence of true love, begins to perceive that beauty, is not far from the end. And the true order of going, or being led by another, to the things of love, is to begin from the beauties of earth and mount upwards for the sake of that other beauty, using these as steps only, and from one going on to two, and from two to all fair forms, and from fair forms to fair practices, and from fair practices to fair notions, until from fair notions he arrives at the notion of absolute beauty, and at last knows what the essence of beauty is. This, my dear Socrates . . . is that life above all others which man should live. In the contemplation of beauty absolute; a beauty which if you once beheld, you would see not to be after the measure of gold, and garments, and fair boys and youths, whose presence now entrances you; and you and many a one would be content to live seeing them only and conversing with them without meat or drink, if that were possible—you only want to look at them and to be with them. But what if man had eyes to see the true beauty—the divine beauty, I mean, pure and clear and unalloyed, not clogged with the pollutions of mortality and all the colours and vanities of

And the true order of going, or being led by another, to the things of love, is to begin from the beauties of earth and mount upwards for the sake of that other beauty, using these as steps only, and from one going on to two, and from two to all fair forms, and from fair forms to fair practices, and from fair practices to fair notions, until from fair notions he arrives at the notion of absolute beauty, and at last knows what the essence of beauty is.

human life—thither looking, and holding converse with the true beauty simple and divine? Remember how in that communion only, beholding beauty with the eye of the mind, he will be enabled to bring forth, not images of beauty, but realities (for he has hold not of an image but of a reality), and bringing forth and nourishing true virtue to become the friend of God and be immortal, if mortal man may. Would that be an ignoble life?"[2]

The beauty of a particular person, according to Diotima's doctrine, is our starting point for discovering absolute Beauty. Our ultimate goal in loving the beauty of another is not to win that person's love, but for our soul to see the eternal Form of Beauty and to contemplate Beauty continuously. Plato's vision of what love should lead us toward is thus very different from Romeo's vision of what he wants. Romeo believes he loves Juliet, a particular woman. But Plato's Socrates would say that what Romeo really loves is Beauty itself, the Beauty he sees shining through Juliet.

Even Plato seems to have mixed feelings about the impersonal vision of love that Diotima describes. For in continuing the *Symposium,* Plato follows Socrates' speech with a speech by a drunken Alcibiades, who waxes eloquent on his particular and passionate love for Socrates. Some commentators have suggested that Plato means to imply that Socrates' story of love is too abstract, and that it must be balanced by recognition of the importance of the particular person who is loved. So too, we should ask whether a work of art is beautiful in itself or beautiful as a representation of abstract Beauty. If our spiritual development is furthered when we recognize that beauty is the same wherever we recognize it, it might seem that Plato would do better to emphasize our love of beauty in various nonhuman things. Even if we recoil from the idea that the uniqueness of the individual one loves is not important ultimately, we might well see some point to the idea that various beautiful objects in the world have something important in common. Why, then, does Plato not focus his attention on beautiful objects? In particular, why does Plato not suggest that works of Art guide us toward insight into Beauty itself?

The Form of Beauty is unambivalently wondrous for Plato—works of art are not. In fact, Plato is extremely suspicious of art. At times Plato criticizes artists for not knowing what they are doing; at other times he insists that what artists are doing is dangerous to the audience of their works. Plato emphasizes the beauty of human beings in his account of Beauty because he thinks that love of another is the primary way that most people gain insight into a higher spiritual realm. Yet, by contrast, Plato thinks that works of art tend to impress us with the wrong thing entirely: with the appearances of this world and with unenlightened talent. Beauty is one thing; art is something very different.

Plato's suspicion of art is complicated, however. For despite harsh judgments about the damage art can do, it is clear that Plato both admires some art and links it to a higher spiritual dimension. One of the clearest indications of Plato's ambivalence toward art is his treatment of poetry in his dialogue entitled *The Ion.* In *The Ion,* Socrates discusses poetic talent with Ion, a poetic interpreter by profession. Ion observes

---

[2] Plato, *The Symposium,* trans. Benjamin Jowett (Oxford: Oxford University Press, 1892).

that he moves audiences tremendously whenever he interprets Homer, but that his art seems quite feeble when he attempts to interpret any other poet. Socrates convinces Ion that his ability is not appropriately called an "art" at all; for if he performed with an art, he would know the rules to apply to *all* poetic material. Art, according to Socrates, is a kind of knowledge that can be applied by one who knows it to all appropriate materials, But Ion does not possess this kind of knowledge. Instead, Ion performs Homer well because he is divinely inspired.

FROM *THE ION*
BY **PLATO**

SOCRATES: I do see, Ion, and I'm going to announce to you what I think that is. As I said earlier, that's not a subject you've mastered—speaking well about Homer; it's a divine power that moves you, as a "Magnetic" stone moves iron rings. [That's what Euripides called it: most people call it "Heracleian."] This stone not only pulls those rings, if they're iron, it also puts power *in* the rings, so that they in turn can do just what the stone does—pull other rings—so that there's sometimes a very long chain of iron pieces and rings hanging from one another. And the power in all of them depends on this stone. In the same way, the Muse makes some people inspired herself, and then through those who are inspired a chain of other enthusiasts is suspended. You know, none of the epic poets, if they're good, are masters of their subject; they are inspired, possessed, and that is how they utter all those beautiful poems. The same goes for lyric poets if they're good: just as the Corybantes are not in their right minds when they dance, lyric poets, too, are not in their right minds when they make those beautiful lyrics, but as soon as they sail into harmony and rhythm they are possessed by Bacchic frenzy. Just as Bacchus worshippers when they are possessed draw honey and milk from rivers, but not when they are in their right minds—the soul of a lyric poet does this too, as they say themselves. For of course poets tell us that they gather songs at honey-flowing springs, from glades and gardens of the Muses, and that they bear songs to us as bees carry honey, flying like bees. And what they say is true. For a poet is an airy thing, winged and holy, and he is not able to make poetry until he becomes inspired and goes out of his mind and his intellect is no longer in him. As long as a human being has his intellect in his possession he will always lack the power to make

> *In this more than anything, then, I think, the god is showing us, so that we should be in no doubt about it, that these beautiful poems are not human, not even **from** human beings, but are divine and from gods; that poets are nothing but representatives of the gods, possessed by whoever possesses them.*

poetry or sing prophecy. Therefore because it's not by mastery that they make poems or say many lovely things about their subjects (as you do about Homer)—but because it's by a divine gift—each poet is able to compose beautifully only that for which the Muse has aroused him: one can do dithyrambs, another encomia, one can do dance songs, another, epics, and yet another, iambics; and each of them is worthless for the other types of poetry. You see, it's not mastery that enables them to speak those verses, but a divine power, since if they knew how to speak beautifully on one type of poetry by mastering the subject, they could do so for all the others also. That's why the god takes their intellect away from them when he uses them as his servants, as he does prophets and godly diviners, so that we who hear should know that *they* are not the ones who speak those verses that are of such high value, for their intellect is not in them: the god himself is the one who speaks, and he gives voice through them to us. The best evidence for this account is Tynnichus from Chalcis, who never made a poem anyone would think worth mentioning, *except* for the praise-song everyone sings, almost the most beautiful lyric-poem there is, and simply, as he says himself, "an invention of the Muses." In this more than anything, then, I think, the god is showing us, so that we should be in no doubt about it, that these beautiful poems are not human, not even *from* human beings, but are divine and from gods; that poets are nothing but representatives of the gods, possessed by whoever possesses them. To show *that,* the god deliberately sang the most beautiful lyric poem through the most worthless poet. Don't you think I'm right, Ion?[3]

The poet and his interpreters are in touch with the divine. Divine intervention by the Muses transports the poet from his ordinary state and empowers him to utter "his oracles." Plato suggests in this passage that poets do speak the truth about higher reality when they are possessed by the gods. Through the image of the magnet, Plato suggests that such truths or insights are communicated through the poet to the interpreter to the audience. Thus, what is communicated to the audience is of divine origin and presumably of value for spiritual insight. Nevertheless, although the poetry generated by divine possession is favorably cast in *The Ion,* the powers of the poet are not. Socrates, while acknowledging Ion's divine possession, discounts Ion the poet. Ion is a mere vessel employed by the gods; his soul has not regained knowledge of the Forms. Were Ion performing with knowledge—if Ion himself had insight—his ability would not be limited to Homer's poetry. But Ion does not possess knowledge nor control the art he claims to practice. Divine possession, not Ion himself, controls Ion's performance. Ion the poet operates in ignorance and has no control over his talent whatever.

Plato's ambivalence toward art is even more evident in *The Republic.* There Socrates discourses on the ignorance of artists, arguing at length for censorship of poetry—which might seem surprising in light of Socrates' suggestion in *The Ion* that

---

[3] Plato, *The Ion,* trans. Paul Woodruff (Indianapolis, IN: Hackett, 1983).

the poet is divinely inspired. In order to understand Socrates' harsh stance in *The Republic,* we must understand the concerns that motivate the Socrates of this dialogue.

In *The Republic,* Socrates and some of his disciples are concerned with the qualities that make a good state. Socrates' comments on the dangers of art arise in connection with this concern. Plato's suspicion of art revealed in this context derives from his beliefs about art's powers to distract citizens from their proper roles in the good state. As Plato understands it, the good state is one in which individuals serve their own particular function and in this manner promote the good of the whole. Ideally, citizens of the good state perform these functions in harmony with each other.

For harmony to exist in the external social order, the souls of the citizens must be in a state of harmony. An individual soul attains a state of harmony when each element of that soul performs its proper function, unimpeded by any other element. The state of harmony is achieved when reason—one of the three components of the soul—rules over the remaining components, the appetites and the spirited element. Ruling over the remaining two elements is reason's appropriate function, and the functions of the remaining elements are coordinated properly only when reason plays this role. Similarly, on the political level, the elements of the state can operate in coordination with one another only when the state is ruled in accordance with reason.

This vision of the good state and of the citizens who comprise it makes art problematic for two reasons: the first concerns reason's function, the second concerns art's capacity to arouse passion. Reason, in Plato's view, is the faculty that discerns true realities behind appearances. Our reliance on reason to rule our soul involves willingness to forego attention to appearances and to turn our attention to the deeper truths that appearances obscure. The arts, however, direct attention to appearances. For this reason, Socrates in *The Republic* disparages all imitative art as being a distraction from divine insight. Imitative art copies the appearance of material things, which themselves are appearances that disguise the true reality of the Forms. Consequently, this kind of art is "thrice removed from the truth." Socrates considers art's distance from truth with his disciples:

FROM ***THE REPUBLIC***
BY **PLATO**

But I do not mind saying to you, that all poetical imitations are ruinous to the understanding of the hearers, and that the knowledge of their true nature is the only antidote to them.

Explain the purport of your remark.

Well, I will tell you, although I have always from my earliest youth had an awe and love of Homer, which even now makes the words falter on my lips, for he is the great captain and teacher of the whole of that charming tragic company; but a man is not to be reverenced more than the truth, and therefore I will speak out.

Very good, he said. . . .

Let us take any common instance; there are beds and tables in the world—plenty of them, are there not?

Yes.

But there are only two ideas or forms of them—one the idea of a bed, the other of a table.

True.

And the maker of either of them makes a bed or he makes a table for our use, in accordance with the idea—that is our way of speaking in this and similar instances—but no artificer makes the ideas themselves: how could he?

Impossible. . . .

The painter is a creator of appearances, is he not?

Of course.

But then I suppose you will say that what he creates is untrue. And yet there is a sense in which the painter also creates a bed?

Yes, he said, but not a real bed.

And what of the maker of the bed? were you not saying that he too makes, not the idea which, according to our view, is the essence of the bed, but only a particular bed?

Yes, I did.

Then if he does not make that which exists he cannot make true existence, but only some semblance of existence; and if any one were to say that the work of the maker of the bed, or of any other workman, has real existence, he could hardly be supposed to be speaking the truth.

At any rate, he replied, philosophers would say that he was not speaking the truth. . . .

Well then, here are three beds: one existing in nature, which is made by God, as I think that we may say—for no one else can be the maker?

No.

There is another which is the work of the carpenter?

Yes.

And the work of the painter is a third?

Yes.

Beds, then, are of three kinds, and there are three artists who superintend them: God, the maker of the bed, and the painter?

Yes, there are three of them. . . .

Shall we, then, speak of Him as the natural author or maker of the bed?

Yes, he replied; inasmuch as by the natural process of creation He is the author of this and of all other things.

And what shall we say of the carpenter—is not he also the maker of the bed?

Yes.

But would you call the painter a creator and maker?

Certainly not.

Yet if he is not the maker, what is he in relation to the bed?

I think, he said, that we may fairly designate him as the imitator of that which the others make.

Good, I said; then you call him who is third in the descent from nature an imitator?

Certainly, he said.

And the tragic poet is an imitator, and therefore, like all other imitators, he is thrice removed from the king and from the truth?

That appears to be so.[4]

Thus, Plato contends, the imitative arts endanger their audience's ability to attend to true reality, for the arts direct attention to appearances and away from realities. In addition, art, especially poetry, has the dangerous potential to arouse passion. Nevertheless, Plato does not view passion as undesirable in itself; in fact, as we have seen, he believes that passion for beauty is the first developmental stage toward insight into the Forms. But when passion is not limited and controlled properly, Plato believes that passion can inspire the person who experiences it to disregard reason. The consequences are disastrous, both to the person's inner harmony and to his or her respect for the rule of reason in the state.

Passion, in Plato's opinion, also can distract citizens from attending to their functions in the community. In particular, poetry can endanger the state in this way, especially when it depicts characters who are unsuitable role models. Even Homer's depictions of the gods often present the gods engaged in unworthy behavior that could inspire the impressionable to socially undesirable aims and lifestyles. Plato concludes that poetry should be strictly censored, convinced as he is that poetry has the power to harm even the state's best citizens.

When in misfortune we feel a natural hunger and desire to relieve our sorrow by weeping and lamentation, and that this feeling which is kept under control in our own calamities is satisfied and delighted by the poets;—the better nature in each of us, not having been sufficiently trained by reason or habit, allows the sympathetic element to break loose because the sorrow is another's; and the spectator fancies that there can be no disgrace to himself in praising and pitying any one who comes telling him what a good man he is, and making a fuss about his troubles; he thinks that the pleasure is a gain, and why should he be supercilious and lose this and the poem too? Few persons ever reflect, as I should imagine, that from the evil of other men something of evil is communicated to themselves. And so the feeling of sorrow which has gathered strength at the sight of the misfortunes of others is with difficulty repressed in our own.

How very true!

And does not the same hold also of the ridiculous? There are jests which you would be ashamed to make yourself, and yet on the comic stage, or indeed in private, when you hear them, you are greatly amused by them, and are not at all disgusted at their unseemliness;—the case of pity is repeated;—there is a principle in human nature which is disposed to raise a laugh, and this which you once restrained by reason, because you were afraid of being thought a buffoon, is now let out again; and having stimulated the risible faculty at the theatre, you are betrayed unconsciously to yourself into playing the comic poet at home.

---

[4] Plato, *The Republic,* trans. Benjamin Jowett (Indianapolis, IN: Hackett, 1974). All subsequent quotations from Plato's *The Republic* are from this edition unless otherwise noted.

> *And the same may be said of lust and anger and all the other affections, of desire and pain and pleasure, which are held to be inseparable from every action — in all of them poetry feeds and waters the passions instead of drying them up; she lets them rule, although they ought to be controlled, if mankind are ever to increase in happiness and virtue.*

Quite true, he said.

And the same may be said of lust and anger and all the other affections, of desire and pain and pleasure, which are held to be inseparable from every action—in all of them poetry feeds and waters the passions instead of drying them up; she lets them rule, although they ought to be controlled, if mankind are ever to increase in happiness and virtue.

I cannot deny it.

Therefore, Glaucon, I said, whenever you meet with any of the eulogists of Homer declaring that he has been the educator of Hellas, and that he is profitable for education and for the ordering of human things, and that you should take him up again and again and get to know him and regulate your whole life according to him, we may love and honour those who say these things—they are excellent people, as far as their lights extend; and we are ready to acknowledge that Homer is the greatest of poets and first of tragedy writers; but we must remain firm in our conviction that hymns to the gods and praises of famous men are the only poetry which ought to be admitted into our State. For if you go beyond this and allow the honeyed muse to enter, either in epic or lyric verse, not law and the reason of mankind, which by common consent have ever been deemed best, but pleasure and pain will be the rulers in our State.

Despite this lengthy indictment of poetry, Plato's conclusions are again mixed. Already, in the next sentence of the dialogue, Socrates suggests the possibility of a conciliation between truth, the good state, and poetry.

> Notwithstanding this, let us assure our sweet friend and the sister arts of imitation, that if she will only prove her title to exist in a well-ordered State we shall be delighted to receive her—we are very conscious of her charms; but we may not on that account betray the truth.

B. ARISTOTLE AND THE SELF-SUFFICIENCY OF ART

The metaphysical differences between Plato and Aristotle are apparent in their respective aesthetics. Plato links beauty to the transcendent and judges art harshly when art fails to illuminate transcendent truth. By contrast, Aristotle focuses instead on the observable characteristics of art as a phenomenon in this world. Aristotle, concerned with art as a mode of Becoming, is interested in how artworks come about and in the process of intelligence that guides their formation. Beauty is, for Aristotle, an eminent feature of things in this world, which can be studied through examination of the structure of beautiful things.

Because Aristotle is concerned with art as a phenomenon in this world, he does not emphasize the same things that Plato emphasizes. Although Aristotle describes poetic talent as a gift (in *The Poetics*), he does not describe artistic creation as an intervention of the divine. Instead, Aristotle sees art as the product of human intentions, and he believes that some account can be given of the specific elements that comprise a good work of art. Artworks are products of "art" in the exact sense that Socrates denied art to Ion. Art is the capacity to make, involving a true course of reasoning. In other words, art is a kind of rational knowledge that a proficient artist knows how to employ in case after case.

Aristotle also differs from Plato in his account of art's desirable function. Plato sees art as valuable only insofar as it can serve an extra-artistic function. Aristotle, by contrast, believes that the arts are valuable in themselves. Although Aristotle, like Plato, discusses the role of art (especially music) in education, he does not believe that the arts have primarily a functional purpose. Instead, according to Aristotle, the arts are self-sufficient activities that contribute dignity to life and that give us a sense of the joy to be found in contemplation for its own sake. In addition, the arts also provide innocent amusement and relaxation from toil. However, the primary purpose of art is not to complement some extra-artistic purpose, but simply to give us something to cherish and contemplate in our leisure. For example, Aristotle sees imitative art as an innocent pleasure. He observes that we learn through imitating, and that we take great pleasure in learning (which includes, in this case, grasping what is being imitated). Aristotle also points out that we take a natural delight in imitations of all sorts. Imitative art, far from being inherently pernicious, springs from a natural human aptitude.

Aristotle's most important discussion of art occurs in *The Poetics;* in particular, his theory of tragedy has been tremendously influential. Proceeding from his definition of tragedy, consider Aristotle's succinct analysis.

FROM *THE POETICS*
BY **ARISTOTLE**

A tragedy then, is the imitation of an action that is serious and also, as having magnitude, complete in itself; in language with pleasurable accessories, each kind brought in separately in the parts of the work; in a dramatic, not in a narrative form; with incidents arousing pity and fear, wherewith to accomplish its catharsis of such emotions. Here by "language with pleasurable accessories" I mean that with rhythm and harmony or song superadded; and by "the kinds separately" I mean that some portions are worked out with verse only, and others in turn with song.

Aristotle, beginning with a discussion of plot and focusing on the magnitude of the tragic work, proceeds to analyze the elements of tragedy.

> We have laid it down that a tragedy is an imitation of an action that is complete in itself, as a whole of some magnitude; for a whole may be of no magnitude to speak of. Now a whole is that which has beginning, middle, and end. A beginning is that which is not itself necessarily after anything else, and which has naturally something else after it; an end is that which is naturally after something itself, either as its necessary or usual consequent, and with nothing else after it; and a middle, that which is by nature after one thing and has also another after it. A well-constructed Plot, therefore, cannot either begin or end at any one point one likes; beginning and end in it must be of the forms just described. Again: to be beautiful, a living creature, and every whole made up of parts, must not only present a certain order in its arrangement of parts, but also be of a certain definite magnitude. Beauty is a matter of size and order, and therefore impossible either (1) in a very minute creature, since our perception becomes indistinct as it approaches instantaneity; or (2) in a creature of vast size—one, say, 1,000 miles long—as in that case, instead of the object being seen all at once, the unity and wholeness of it is lost to the beholder. Just in the same way, then, as a beautiful whole made up of parts, or a beautiful living creature, must be of some size, but a size to be taken in by the eye, so a story or Plot must be of some length, but of a length to be taken in by the memory. As for the limit of its length, so far as that is relative to public performances and spectators, it does not fall within the theory of poetry. If they had to perform a hundred tragedies, they would be timed by water-clocks, as they are said to have been at one period. The limit, however, set by the actual nature of the thing is this: the longer the story, consistently with its being comprehensible as a whole, the finer it is by reason of its magnitude. As a rough general formula, "a length which allows of the hero passing by a series of probable or necessary stages from misfortune to happiness, or from happiness to misfortune," may suffice as a limit for the magnitude of the story.[5]

Aristotle may appear to be stating the obvious. In fact, his precepts on magnitude establish one of the most significant principles of traditional Western aesthetics— the principle of **closure**. According to the principle of closure, an artwork should have clear, well-defined limits and should not "begin or end at any point one likes." Instead, it should present something that is complete in itself.

In comparing a tragedy to a living creature, Aristotle also proposes a model that dominates the traditional Western understanding of the artwork—the model of Organic Life. The composition of an artwork should resemble that of a living organism. Each of the elements should serve the "life" of the work as a whole, and the functions of the elements should operate in harmony. The observer should get the impression that every element in the work is exactly as it should be, and that no

---

[5] Aristotle, *The Poetics,* from *The Works of Aristotle,* ed. W. D. Ross (Oxford: Clarendon Press, 1908). The subsequent quotation from Aristotle's *The Poetics* is from this edition.

elements should distract from the Unified Effect of the work as a whole. Closely related to this idea is the notion of Aesthetic Necessity, the idea that the composition of the work should be so perfectly structured and the elements so perfectly coordinated in serving the effect of the whole that any change would be a change for the worse. Aristotle makes this point as well. "[I]n poetry the story, as an imitation of action, must represent one action, a complete whole, with its several incidents so closely connected that the transposal or withdrawal of any one of them will disjoin and dislocate the whole."

Aristotle goes on to suggest appropriate techniques for unifying the tragedy. Simply tracing the events in one person's life does not unify a play, for many unrelated incidents transpire in a single individual's life. Instead, the unity of a tragedy should come from presenting the play as a single action. Aristotle believes that to accomplish this the playwright should limit the material to the events of one twenty-four hour period.

Aristotle again departs from Plato in his further comments on the material employed in tragedy. Far from thinking that an "ancient quarrel" exists between poetry and philosophy, Aristotle argues that poetry is itself philosophical.

The distinction between historian and poet is not in the one writing prose and the other verse . . . it consists really in this, that the one describes the thing that has been, and the other a kind of thing that might be.

From what we have said it will be seen that the poet's function is to describe, not the thing that has happened, but a kind of thing that might happen, i.e. what is possible as being probable or necessary. The distinction between historian and poet is not in the one writing prose and the other verse—you might put the work of Herodotus into verse, and it would still be a species of history; it consists really in this, that the one describes the thing that has been, and the other a kind of thing that might be. Hence poetry is something more philosophic and of graver import than history, since its statements are of the nature rather of universals, whereas those of history are singulars. By a universal statement I mean one as to what such or such a kind of man will probably or necessarily say or do—which is the aim of poetry, though it affixes proper names to the characters; by a singular statement, one as to what, say, Alcibiades did or had done to him.

Aristotle analyzed each of the elements indicated in his definition of tragedy, treating some at greater length than others. Other than Aristotle's comments on plot, his most influential remarks probably are those dealing with the effects of tragedy on the audience. Yet these remarks are terse and ambiguous. The definition of tragedy states that the incidents portrayed should arouse "pity and fear" in order to effect a catharsis of these emotions. Later on Aristotle states that although pity and fear can be aroused by the spectacle of the play, the more artistic method is to arouse them "by the very structure and incidents of the play." So desirable is it that the incidents provoke these emotions that Aristotle insists, "The Plot . . . should be so framed that, even without seeing the things take place, he who simply hears the account of them shall be filled with horror and pity at the incidents."

Elsewhere, in *The Rhetoric*, Aristotle elaborates on what these peculiarly tragic emotions involve. Fear arises from a mental picture of destructive or painful evil that we believe might befall us in the future. And we experience pity when such an evil befalls someone who does not deserve it, and when we recognize that the same thing might befall us or someone close to us. The tragic emotions of pity and fear are aroused, therefore, only when we feel some identification with the tragic hero's circumstances. In essence, we must identify with the tragic hero's vulnerability.

The tragedy aims to inspire pity and fear in its audience, but at the same time it aims to transform its audience by means of **catharsis.** Although the precise meaning of "catharsis" has been debated since Aristotle suggested this idea, presumably he means that the tragic emotions are either purged or purified. The burden of our sense of vulnerability is lightened as a result of our sympathetic co-suffering with the tragic hero. Perhaps Aristotle believes that we master our feelings of insecurity and vulnerability by expressing them vicariously through the play.

As one who is concerned primarily with the phenomena and mechanisms of this world, Aristotle admires verisimilitude in tragic depiction. He claims that characters should be lifelike and consistent with themselves, and that the poet should persuade the audience that the events portrayed are necessary or probable. Nonetheless, Aristotle is not a radical realist; the tragedy should, in his view, resemble life but also ennoble it. The tragic hero should be somewhat idealized, and even the impossible can be presented successfully as long as it appears to be the probable outcome of events. Again, Aristotle departs from Plato with respect to appearances. Tragedy can make good use of appearances to achieve a tragic effect, as Aristotle sees it. And while the ultimate aim of tragedy, and all poetry, is to reveal universal truths about human beings, these truths might be conveyed more forcefully by means of the idealized or the imaginary than by means of the unvarnished truth.

C. THE DISPUTE ABOUT TASTES

Both Plato and Aristotle profoundly affected later Western thought about beauty and art. Plato's suspicion of art—reinforced by Christian suspicion of sensual enjoyment—lingered in theoretical treatments of the subject for many centuries, and it colors popular Western thinking about art to this day. On the other hand, Aristotle's principles and models for successful art remain paradigmatic through recent times, and even departures from his general theories often rework Aristotelian models.

From the early Christian period through the medieval period, art was judged primarily on its ability to reveal truth in some fashion. **Plotinus** (ca. A.D. 204–270), a neo-Platonic philosopher, argued that art can provoke insight into the Forms more effectively than nature can. To recognize beauty in anything is, in his view, already to be attuned to true reality. Thus, beautiful art should be seen not as a distraction but as a vehicle to transcendent truth. In this capacity art can be more valuable than beautiful nature, for art—enlightened by human insight—can be designed with the explicit intention of illuminating the underlying reality to its audience.

Influenced by such neo-Platonic ideas, St. Augustine attempted to establish the legitimacy of art for Christians. In Augustine's view the artistic beholder can gain insight into the divine mind by contemplating beauty. For underlying both God's creation in general, and all beautiful art and nature, is numerical proportion and harmony. Thus, it is appropriate for the Christian to contemplate such beauty. For by means of the senses, beauty reveals something of God's nature to the mind. The arts, therefore, can bring us closer to God. And because the arts reflect the harmonious structure that underlies God's creative power, the arts can be used to symbolize the transcendent. The idea that art can be used to symbolize levels of reality that are not themselves sensuous dominated the medieval perspective on art as well.

David Hume, while adopting an extreme subjectivist stance toward aesthetic judgments, proposed another explanation of the fact that some aesthetic judgments are better than others. Hume is especially influential in the history of aesthetics, for it is Hume, in particular, whom Kant set out to refute in his aesthetic theory. Consider Hume's analysis of the problem that among different aesthetic observers there are extreme divergences of taste.

FROM "OF THE STANDARD OF TASTE" BY DAVID HUME

It is natural for us to seek a *Standard of Taste;* a rule, by which the various sentiments of men may be reconciled; at least, a decision, afforded, confirming one sentiment, and condemning another.

There is a species of philosophy, which cuts off all hopes of success in such an attempt, and represents the impossibility of ever attaining any standard of taste. The difference, it is said, is very wide between judgment and sentiment. All sentiment is right; because sentiment has a reference to nothing beyond itself, and is always real, wherever a man is conscious of it. But all determinations of the understanding are not right; because they have a reference to something beyond themselves, to wit, real matter of fact; and are not always conformable to that standard. Among a thousand different opinions which different men may entertain of the same subject, there is one, and but one, that is just and true; and the only difficulty is to fix and ascertain it. On the contrary, a thousand different sentiments, excited by the same object, are all right: Because no sentiment represents what is really in the object. It only marks a certain conformity or relation between the object and the organs or faculties of the mind; and if that conformity did not really exist, the sentiment could never possibly have being. Beauty is no quality in things themselves: It exists merely in the mind which contemplates them; and each mind perceives a different beauty. One person may even perceive deformity, where another is sensible of beauty; and every individual ought to acquiesce in his own sentiment, without pretending to regulate those of others. To seek the real beauty, or real deformity, is as fruitless an enquiry, as to pretend to ascertain the real sweet or real bitter. According to the disposition of the organs, the same object may be both sweet and bitter; and the proverb has justly determined it to be fruitless to dispute concerning tastes. It is very natural, and even quite necessary, to extend this axiom to mental, as well as bodily taste; and thus common sense, which is so often at variance with philosophy, especially with the skeptical kind, is found, in one instance at least, to agree in pronouncing the same decision.

But though this axiom, by passing into a proverb, seems to have attained the sanction of common sense; there is certainly a species of common sense which opposes it, at least serves to modify and restrain it. Whoever would assert an equality of genius and elegance between OGILBY and MILTON, or BUNYAN and ADDISON, would be thought to defend no less an extravagance, than if he had maintained a mole-hill to be as high as TENERIFFE, or a pond as extensive as the ocean. Though there may be found persons, who give the preference to the former authors; no one pays attention to such a taste; and we pronounce without scruple the sentiment of these pretended critics to be absurd and ridiculous. The principle of the natural equality of tastes is then totally forgot, and while we admit it on some occasions, where the objects seem near an equality, it appears an extravagant paradox, or rather a palpable absurdity, where objects so disproportioned are compared together.[6]

Although Hume believes it a reasonable principle of common sense that some aesthetic judgments are simply faulty, he refuses to conclude that any a priori rules can ground the validity of some judgments against their rivals.

It is evident that none of the rules of composition are fixed by reasonings *a priori,* or can be esteemed abstract conclusions of the understanding, from comparing those habitudes and relations of ideas, which are eternal and immutable. Their foundation is the same with that of all the practical sciences, experience; nor are they any thing but general observations, concerning what has been universally found to please in all countries and in all ages. Many of the beauties of poetry and even of eloquence are founded on falsehood and fiction, on hyperboles, metaphors, and an abuse or perversion of terms from their natural meaning. To check the sallies of the imagination, and to reduce every expression to geometrical truth and exactness, would be the most contrary to the laws of criticism; because it would produce a work, which, by universal experience, has been found the most insipid and disagreeable. But though poetry can never submit to exact truth, it must be confined by rules of art, discovered to the author

---

[6] David Hume, "Of the Standard of Taste," from *Essays, Moral, Political and Literary,* ed. T. H. Green (London: Longmans, Green and Co., 1882). All subsequent quotations of Hume's "Of the Standard of Taste" are from this edition unless otherwise noted.

either by genius or observation. If some negligent or irregular writers have pleased, they have not pleased by their transgressions of rule or order, but in spite of these transgressions: They have possessed other beauties, which were conformable to just criticism; and the force of these beauties has been able to overpower censure, and give the mind a satisfaction superior to the disgust arising from the blemishes.

How then can we criticize any taste as deplorable? Hume argues that we judge beauty much as we judge morality: we judge by means of a peculiarly aesthetic sentiment. Although each of us judges subjectively, the sentiment by which we judge is a natural and human one. Thus, we can expect considerable agreement among those whose sensibilities have been nurtured properly. Agreement about what is beautiful indicates that the aesthetic sentiment, which beauty naturally arouses, in the human soul has been aroused in various observers by a particular object.

However, Hume realizes that this account does not yet explain the considerable disagreement that we observe among those who pass aesthetic judgments. Hume goes on to explain that many contingencies interfere with the arousal of aesthetic sentiment by appropriate objects.

A perfect serenity of mind, a recollection of thought, a due attention to the object; if any of these circumstances be wanting, our experiment will be fallacious, and we shall be unable to judge of the catholic and universal beauty.

But though all the general rules of art are founded only on experience and on the observation of the common sentiments of human nature, we must not imagine, that, on every occasion, the feelings of men will be conformable to these rules. Those finer emotions of the mind are of a very tender and delicate nature, and require the concurrence of many favourable circumstances to make them play with facility and exactness, according to their general and established principles. The least exterior hindrance to such small springs, or the least internal disorder, disturbs their motion, and confounds the operation of the whole machine. When we would make an experiment of this nature, and would try the force of any beauty or deformity, we must choose with care a proper time and place, and bring the fancy to a suitable situation and disposition. A perfect serenity of mind, a recollection of thought, a due attention to the object; if any of these circumstances be wanting, our experiment will be fallacious, and we shall be unable to judge of the catholic and universal beauty. The relation, which nature has placed between the form and the sentiment will at least be more obscure; and it will require greater accuracy to trace and discern it. We shall be able to ascertain its influence not so much from the operation of each particular beauty, as from the durable admiration, which attends those works, that have survived all the caprices of mode and fashion, all the mistakes of ignorance and envy.

Rather surprisingly, we find Hume suggesting that if we really want to know whether or not a thing can appropriately be called beautiful, we should consult the experience of others. Durable admiration is a good indication of the aesthetic quality of an artwork, whereas our personal judgments of a work might well be distorted by our condition of mind or our prejudices. Hume rests his claim to the validity of particular aesthetic judgments, then, on the collective experience of generations, not on the particular experience of an individual on a particular occasion. He does not, therefore, believe that everyone has equally valid tastes.

Hume does, however, believe that the criterion for calling something beautiful is ultimately a subjective one. A thing is appropriately called beautiful if and only if it provokes aesthetic sentiment in appropriately disposed competent judges. What matters, then, is not so much the character of the object as the state of mind occasioned in the observer. Of course, the characteristics of the aesthetic object are relevant to whether or not it occasions aesthetic sentiment in the observer. Hume even indicates some of the objective characteristics commonly observed in artworks that have inspired durable admiration. But the test of an object's beauty is the experience it provokes in an observer. In this respect, as we are about to see, Hume resembles Kant. In general, modern Western aesthetics have turned their attention from the characteristics of the object to consideration of the state of mind that beauty and art occasion.

D. KANT: DISPUTES ABOUT TASTE RESOLVED

In his aesthetic work, Kant's primary concern is essentially the same as Hume's. He is interested in how our subjective aesthetic judgments are valid and in how we can claim that some such judgments are better than others. In the *Critique of Judgment,* Kant's explicit task is to establish aesthetic judgment on an **intersubjective** basis. However, although the problems that concern Kant resemble those that interest Hume, here as elsewhere Kant takes Hume as his target. Specifically, Kant sets out to refute Hume's idea that our disputes over taste can only be resolved empirically, and that such resolution is only a matter of consulting the empirical judgments of many aesthetic observers over time.

Kant wonders how it is that the judgment of the beautiful carries with it an expectation that others besides the subject will agree with the judgment. This is perplexing because a judgment that a thing is beautiful means that it provokes aesthetic pleasure within us. We cannot legitimately convince others of the correctness of our aesthetic judgment by providing them with conceptual arguments; argument is beside the point of whether we experience such pleasure or not.

But where does this universality of aesthetic experience come from if not from compelling argument? It comes from our capacity to contemplate suitable objects with our mental faculties in the extraordinary but intrinsically satisfying mode of operation that Kant describes as **free play.** The faculties that are involved in free play are the very faculties that Kant takes to be essential to the possibility of human cognition: imagination and understanding.

In his *Critique of Pure Reason,* Kant characterizes the respective roles of **imagination** and **understanding** for ordinary knowledge. Imagination gathers together the stuff of our experience into definite images or representations. On the basis of these representations, understanding forms definite concepts.

Consider a concrete example. In approaching a flower from the standpoint of cognition, the representation of the flower that the imagination presents to the understanding is "understood" by means of a definite concept (e.g., a petunia). Once the understanding has determined the appropriate concept with which to designate the represented object, the process of cognition is complete.

In aesthetic experience, the same two faculties (imagination and understanding) again operate together. However, the end result is not a determinate concept. Instead, the two faculties interact in free play. In this case, again, the imagination forms a representation of the object. But unlike the case of cognition, the representation generated by imagination is not enshrined cognitively by a definite concept. Indeed, in aesthetic experience, we feel that no definite concept could define adequately what we observe. Thus, the two faculties do not neatly finish their work in aesthetic experience. Instead, they "play" by mutually enlivening one another.

When we view the petunia aesthetically, our minds are not statically contemplative, but actively so. We leap from focusing on one aspect of the flower's form to focusing on another. In the midst of all this we find our understanding sufficiently engaged that often we do seek words to communicate the features of what we notice: "Isn't the way that petal curves interesting? It almost seems flirtatious." Such comments do not *explain* our enjoyment—in this case, of the flower's form. Yet they do reveal that our understanding in its own peculiar way is at work while our imagination is reworking its presentation.

The understanding's shifting emphasis, too, seems to encourage imagination to further reformulation of the image that it impresses on the mind. Imagination may present us with a differently focused representation of the petunia in light of the understanding's sensuous description "flirtatious." Because no conceptual classification confines the imagination, it can attend to more and more features of the object. It thus enhances our experience of the object's particularity as opposed to its generically classifiable features.

Against Hume, Kant argues that the convergence of our judgments about beauty are not merely empirical accidents but the necessary consequence of the very mental faculties we possess. Kant's defense of this claim depends again on the fact that the faculties employed in aesthetic experience are the very ones employed in cognition. Insofar as we can communicate with others—something that we assume in the case of all human beings and something that depends on our common ability to form concepts—we assume their reliance on the same processes of cognition as those we employ. In making this assumption, we assess that their cognitive faculties do function harmoniously.

But to the extent that we have presupposed this, we have presupposed in every human being the active capacity for aesthetic experience. For aesthetic experience depends only on the active, harmonious free play of the cognitive faculties. As Kant says later in the *Critique of Judgment,* the pleasure accompanying aesthetic experience is a satisfaction taken simply in the "harmonious (subjectively purposive) activity of the two cognitive powers in their freedom." Kant feels justified therefore in calling taste a kind of "common sense," for this "sense" is a responsive, harmonious condition of the cognitive faculties that can be activated in any aware human being.

Kant describes a judgment that a thing is beautiful as a necessary judgment. He does not mean that everyone empirically agrees that a thing is beautiful. Kant means that when we claim an object is beautiful, we mean it is an example of the sort of thing that can be contemplated aesthetically by any mentally healthy human being. If someone disagrees with our particular judgment that a thing is beautiful, we might discuss the disagreement as a consequence of his or her being preoccupied with practical concerns or by a private mood. But if someone never agreed with anyone that anything were beautiful, we would be right to believe that the person lacked something basic to a human being.

Kant makes two other important points about the nature of the beautiful: aesthetic experience of a beautiful object, he tells us, involves a stance of disinterestedness. The basic idea is that our enjoyment of the beautiful does not provoke any personal interest on our part. However, our enjoyment of the sensuously pleasing provokes an interest in sensuously appropriating the object. Our enjoyment of a T-bone steak, for example, essentially involves our experience of desire to eat it. Appreciation of the beautiful, by contrast, inspires no desire with respect to the object. Instead, we are content simply to contemplate the object.

Kant's other point is that an aesthetic judgment of a beautiful object involves contemplation of mere form. Kant has been described as a formalist because he believes aesthetic contemplation considers form alone. Even in the case of art, Kant contends that consideration of the content is irrelevant and even distracting from aesthetic contemplation. The sensuous satisfaction we might take in the materials of art are also, in Kant's view, irrelevant to aesthetic satisfaction. Kant goes so far in defending this claim that he insists that in painting it is the delineation only, not the colors (which might please or displease us on a purely sensuous level) that we consider when we are judging the work aesthetically. Kant also argues against the view that our emotional response to art has anything to do with the aesthetic satisfaction we take in it.

When we contemplate a beautiful object aesthetically, Kant tells us, we observe what he calls **purposiveness without a purpose.** The object, in other words, forms an organic unity that coheres as if toward a definite *telos,* or purpose. Kant accepts the Aristotelian model of the beautiful object as akin to a living organism. But although the elements of the beautiful object seem to function together toward a unifying purpose, we do not, in contemplating, discover what it is. If we did discover a definite purpose, it would provide the key to a conceptual account of the arrangement of elements in a beautiful object. A botanical account of the parts of a flower would be a conceptual explanation of the function of each element with respect to a definite end (the continued life of the flower). But no such definite, objectively identifiable end accounts for the aesthetic form of an object. We recognize only that the parts cohere without being able to explain why.

Although primarily we associate the concept of aesthetic beauty with art, the history of the subject often looks elsewhere. Plato took as his example of beauty the beautiful *person;* Kant's analysis of the beautiful focused primarily on *nature* rather than art. Kant, however, does consider art at some length. He considers art essentially to be representational, and therefore he believes that concepts mediate our appreciation of art. In other words, our impression of the kind of thing being represented is crucial to our judgment of whether or not it is well portrayed.

Nevertheless, while Kant believes that both artist and observer are constrained by their conceptions of the things being represented by art, he does not believe that concepts dictate recipes for art. Great art is a product of genius, not conceptual construction. Artistic genius is a natural faculty for producing "aesthetic ideas." These ideas are not conceptual and well defined in nature; instead they are generative, occasioning imaginative thought, but no particular thought. They are intuitive, and they guide the activity of the artist. Great artistic talent, on Kant's model, is thus a bit like poetic inspiration on Plato's. The artist can neither explain the origin of his or her ideas nor give a knowledgeable account of why his or her masterpiece takes the precise form that it does.

In tying artistic creation to genius, to some extent Kant sides with the empiricists. But Kant does not believe that unbridled genius is itself artistically desirable. If the ideas of the genius are not subjected to controlled forms, there is danger that the artistic product will be unintelligible to the artist's audience. Thus, Kant insists that *taste* must govern genius if works of art are to remain purposive. (Taste is the faculty of judging that a thing is beautiful.) Thus, in order for a genius to create artworks of value, the genius must examine and shape his productions from a critical posture.

Kant concludes his account of the beautiful with the suggestion that to us beauty symbolizes morality. By stimulating the free play of our faculties of imagination and understanding, beauty naturally reminds us of another situation in which we are free: our legislation of the moral law as free and rational agents. In the case of the moral law, another mental faculty, that of reason freely determines the morally ideal. And insofar as we behave in accordance with this moral ideal, we are free from determination by inclination. We are not constrained by the moral law; we are constrained by inclinations that naturally overtake us. When we resist natural inclinations and guide our lives only by our own rational faculties, we are truly free. Our sense of freedom in aesthetic experience naturally reminds us of our moral freedom; and in Kant's own view, this is beauty's highest accomplishment.

E. AFTER KANT: ART, SOCIETY, AND SELF-AWARENESS

Friedrich Schiller (1759–1805), who was influenced strongly by Kantian aesthetics, further developed the idea that beauty symbolizes morality. Schiller, in his *Letters on the Aesthetic Education of Man,* argued against the view of some of his contemporaries that concern for beauty is a distraction from the more serious, political concerns of life. To the contrary, Schiller contends, beauty first makes us capable of becoming good citizens.

In early life, Schiller argues, we conceive of the external world as an adversary that we must force to give us what we want. But when we begin to experience beauty, we learn that our interests and the external world can coincide harmoniously. This experience provides our first step toward personal and political maturity. For only when we have come to believe that the external world sometimes will cooperate with us are we willing to cooperate with the external world.

Beauty intimates to us the possibility of social harmony, for it allows us to conceive of peaceful coexistence with others that does not involve constraint on anyone's part. Schiller believes that this intuition of a world of cooperation and mutual freedom among ourselves and others is indispensable for any lasting political solution to the tensions among human beings. Thus, Schiller believes that it is our political responsibility to make beauty central in the education of our young.

Much later in the nineteenth century, **Count Lev Nikolayevich Tolstoy** (1828–1910) similarly argued that the value of art lay in its social/political function. But the function that Tolstoy had in mind was quite different from that of Schiller. Art serves its purpose, in Tolstoy's view, when art sincerely communicates emotion and thereby promotes feelings of community among people. Tolstoy, however, believed that most of the art of his culture did not serve its proper function. The art of the socially elite aimed only to give pleasure to its audience. By contrast, the art of the common people had the appropriate aim of sincere communication of feeling. Thus, Tolstoy's theory of art's purpose was not simply idealistic, but also quite critical of contemporary artistic practice.

1. G. W. F. Hegel

Nineteenth-century aesthetics did not, however, focus exclusively on the social/political function that art might serve. Rather, the most powerful theories of beauty emphasized the capacity of art to make human beings understand themselves. Foremost among such theorists was G. W. F. Hegel. Although Hegel did not believe that self-consciousness is a purely personal matter, he did believe that art is a vehicle that human beings have employed to become conscious of a shared spirit. Art, as Hegel understood it, is born of an attempt by human beings to humanize the materials that they find around them. In give creative form to such materials, they make them less alien from themselves. Moreover, because the forms that human beings use to give shape to these materials stem from the human mind, artworks embody the ideas of the mind in an external form. In this way art makes the ideas of the mind present to those who make it. Observing art, human beings can come to know themselves.

Artworks are under obligation to a sensuous medium. Yet ultimately they are addressed, not to the senses, but to the mind. So art's primary function is a spiritual one. However, because art involves a sensuous medium, tensions can exist between the medium and the spiritual idea that shapes it. For Hegel, the human spirit is always historically located, and its expressions reveal their historical context. Art, as an expression of the human spirit, has a history. Some of the developments of that history can be understood in terms of gradual human progress in learning to shape the materials of the world in accordance with the mind. Hegel describes three basic stages in art's development, which he distinguishes on the basis of their artworks' physical form to adequately embody the ideal spiritual content behind it.

FROM *THE PHILOSOPHY OF FINE ART*
BY **G. W. F. HEGEL**

We have here to consider *three* relations of the Idea to its external process of configuration.

(a) First, the origin of artistic creation proceeds from the Idea when, being itself still involved in defective definition and obscurity, or in vicious and untrue determinacy, it becomes embodied in the shapes of art. As indeterminate, it does not as yet possess in itself that individuality which the Ideal demands. Its abstract character and onesidedness leaves its objective presentment still defective and contingent. Consequently this first type of art is rather a mere search after plastic configuration than a power of genuine representation. . . .

(b) In the *second* type of art, which we propose to call "*Classical,*" the twofold defect of symbolic art is annulled. Now the symbolic configuration is imperfect, because, first, the Idea here only enters into consciousness in *abstract* determinacy or indeterminateness: and, secondly, by reason of the fact that the coalescence of import with embodiment can only throughout remain defective, and in its turn also wholly abstract. The classical art-type solves both these difficulties. It is, in fact, the free and adequate embodiment of the Idea in the shape which, according to its notional concept, is uniquely appropriate to the Idea itself. . . . Such a configuration, which the Idea essentially possesses as spiritual, and indeed as individually determinate spiritually, when it must perforce appear as a temporal phenomenon, is the *human form.* Personification and anthropomorphism have frequently been abused as a degradation of the spiritual. But art, in so far as its function is to bring to vision the spiritual in sensuous guise, must advance to such anthropomorphism, inasmuch as Spirit is only adequately presented to perception in its bodily presence. . . .

(c) The *romantic* type of art annuls the completed union of the Idea and its reality, and occurs, if on a higher plane, to the difference and opposition of both sides, which remained unovercome in symbolic art. The classical type of art no doubt attained the highest excellence of which the sensuous embodiment of art is capable. The defect, such as it is, is due to the defect which obtains in art itself throughout, the limitations of its entire province, that is to say. The limitation consists in this, that art in general and, agreeably to its fundamental idea, accepts for its object Spirit, the notion of which is infinite concrete universality, under the guise of sensuously concrete form. In the classical type it sets up the perfected coalescence of spiritual and sensuous existence as adequate conformation of both. As a matter of fact, however, in this fusion mind itself is not represented agreeably to its *true notional concept.* . . .

To escape from such a condition the romantic type of art once more cancels that inseparable unity of the classical type, by securing a content which passes beyond the classical stage and its mode of expres-

[Art] must deliver itself to the inward life, which coalesces with its object simply as though this were none other than itself, in other words, to the intimacy of soul, to the heart, the emotional life . . .

sion. . . . [I]n this third stage the object of art consists in the free and concrete presence of spiritual activity, whose vocation it is to appear as such a presence or activity for the inner world of conscious intelligence. In consonance with such an object art cannot merely work for sensuous perception. It must deliver itself to the inward life, which coalesces with its object simply as though this were none other than itself, in other words, to the intimacy of soul, to the heart, the emotional life, which as the medium of Spirit itself essentially strives after freedom, and seeks and possesses its reconciliation only in the inner chamber of spirit. It is this inward or ideal world which constitutes the content of the romantic sphere. . . .

This we may take to be in general terms the character of the symbolic, classical, and romantic types of art, which in fact constitute the three relations of the Idea to its embodiment in the realm of human art. They consist in the aspiration after the attainment and transcendency of the Ideal, viewed as the true concrete notion of beauty.[7]

In the Romantic stage of art's development, Hegel concludes, the ideal content is too completely spiritualized to be fully embodied by any physical form whatsoever. Thus, the significant spiritual concerns of the Romantic age eventually turn away from art as a primary vehicle of expression. Hegel concludes,

[I]t certainly is the case that Art is no longer able to discover the satisfaction of spiritual wants, which previous epochs and nations have sought for in it and exclusively found in it, a satisfaction which, at least on the religious side, was associated with art in the most intimate way. The fair days of Greek art, as also the golden time of the later middle ages, are over. . . . [A]rt is and remains for us, on the side of its highest possibilities, a thing of the past.[8]

Reflective thought, in Hegel's view, has replaced art as the vehicle for humanity's most significant spiritual contents and as the means by which humanity comes to

---

[7] G. W. F. Hegel, *The Philosophy of Fine Art*, trans. B. Bosanquet (London: Routledge and Kegan-Paul, 1905).

[8] G. W. F. Hegel, *Introduction to Aesthetics*, trans. B. Bosanquet (London: Routledge and Kegan-Paul, 1905).

know itself. Although art remains a source of enjoyment to modern human beings, it is no longer central to the pursuit of their central spiritual concerns.

2. Arthur Schopenhauer

Arthur Schopenhauer (1788–1860) does not share Hegel's sense of "the end of art." Schopenhauer, like Hegel, sees art as a medium through which human beings can gain insight into themselves. But Schopenhauer considers this self-awareness to be a private experience that any individual, at any historical period, might have, and of no less value now than for the ancients.

Schopenhauer's theory of art is bound intimately to his metaphysical theory. Accepting Kant's distinction between the noumenal and the phenomenal world, Schopenhauer is unwilling to accept Kant's view that we cannot come to know the noumenal reality behind phenomena. On the contrary, Schopenhauer argues, we know the noumenal world directly. The fundamental, noumenal reality is a turbulent, chaotic **Will**; and we directly experience this Will in our individual wills.

This fate may seem happier than that proposed by Kant when he denies us any knowledge of the thing-in-itself. But for Schopenhauer, this is not a happy fate at all. The Will, the ultimate reality, is a turbulent cauldron of struggle within itself. The phenomenal world, which is the Will's manifestation, is accordingly a vale of struggle and turbulence. The various phenomena struggle among themselves, and even a single being's individual will struggles within itself. Desire, which each of us experiences as the basic manifestation of our nature, is our immediate experience of the dissatisfaction and the internal tension of the will.

From the standpoint of our ordinary outlook on things, we are unaware of our true situation as regards our desires. We believe that we will be content once we gain what we want, although all of our experience shows us differently. And we do not consider those who obstruct us as being in the same position that we are, motivated by blind desire and incapable of doing otherwise. However, occasionally ethical insight indicates the fallacy of this usual way of thinking. When ethical insight overtakes us, we recognize that we are all in the same situation and that we cannot violate another being's will without violating ourselves. Schopenhauer interprets this kind of insight as a recognition that we are all one thing, namely, the Will. However, most of us do not change our lives as a result of such insight, but instead continue blindly through our lives, swinging like a pendulum between desire and (when we occasionally are satisfied) boredom.

The only way out of such misery is to renounce desire. Schopenhauer, one of the first Germans to become interested in Buddhism, adopted the Buddhist beliefs that desire causes suffering and that suffering ceases only with cessation of desire. Schopenhauer realized that the ascetic life that he proposed as the means to this end would not attract many of his readers. Indeed, if one considers his biography, it seems not to have greatly attracted Schopenhauer himself.

What did attract Schopenhauer was beauty. He believed that for himself and for most others, beauty alone provides a respite from what he calls "the penal servitude of willing." In the aesthetic experience we comport ourselves without motive or desire toward the object that we contemplate. We cease to be our ordinary willing selves and become instead "pure will-less subjects of knowledge." What we come to know in experience of the beautiful is the universal essence of the thing that we behold. Schopenhauer believes that we contemplate the Platonic Form of the beautiful thing, although he interprets the Forms as various hierarchical levels through which the Will manifests itself. When we contemplate aesthetically, both the beholder and the object become universal. The beholder ceases to be his or her private self with personal, willful motives, and the object beheld becomes its universal essence. In aesthetic experience we leave willing behind.

In the case of art, as in the case of beautiful nature, the observer contemplates the eternal Forms behind phenomena. The aim of art is to communicate knowledge of the Forms. Artistic talent, or genius, is an unusually developed ability to contemplate the universal in phenomena. Because the talented artist has this ability, he or she is able to present objects of the world in a manner that makes the universal present to the audience. (The exception to this rule is music. Music does not represent phenomenal things in a universal light. Instead it portrays the movements of the will directly. Music, alone among the arts, bypasses the Platonic Forms and portrays the deeper reality that Schopenhauer believes is behind them.)

In the case both of beautiful art and beautiful nature, we expand our awareness of our own nature. Schopenhauer believes that the Platonic Forms are more real than the phenomenal things of our world; he thinks that our ordinary sense of ourselves as private, separate individualities is illusory. The Platonic Forms are themselves aspects of the Will. Thus, to the extent that aesthetic experience illuminates them, it illuminates our fundamental nature, which is the Will itself. Schopenhauer suggests that aesthetic experience is akin to ethical insight, and that frequent aesthetic experience is potentially good for our ethical orientation. Unfortunately, however, any insight we might gain from aesthetic experience is, for most of us, transient. As soon as aesthetic contemplation is over, most of us are immediately back in the willful fray.

3. Friedrich Nietzsche

Nietzsche believed that aesthetic experience not only gives us insight into our true nature but also that it justifies life. Nietzsche postulates two aesthetic principles, the **Dionysian** and the **Apollonian.** Each of these principles guides a particular kind of aesthetic experience. Dionysian principle fashions art that is frenzied and chaotic; Dionysian experience communicates to the beholder a sense of our fundamental union with the dynamic reality of life. Apollonian principle depicts phenomena through beautiful, idealizing images; Apollonian experience communicates to the beholder a sense that the things of the world are clearly delineated and orderly. The paradigmatic Dionysian art is music; the paradigmatic Apollonian art is sculpture.

Thus, the Dionysian and the Apollonian principles each reveal something important about one's nature as a human being. The Dionysian principle reminds the individual of his participation in the dynamic flux of life. The Apollonian principle reinforces the individual's usual sense that he or she, like everything else, is separate and self-contained. Although Nietzsche concurs with Schopenhauer that this perspective is ultimately an illusion, he believes that it is a necessary illusion. We must, Nietzsche believes, behave as independent agents and believe that the world is relatively stable in order to accomplish the practical tasks essential to our sustained existence. Thus, both Apollonian and Dionysian perspectives remind us of something important about ourselves in relation to the world.

The Apollonian and Dionysian principles also remind us that life is worth living despite the suffering that it involves. Discussing the religion of the ancient Greeks, Nietzsche observes that the pantheon of gods and goddesses was invented by the Greeks under the sway of the Apollonian principle, for the gods and goddesses amounted to beautiful, idealizing images for aspects of human life. The gods, Nietzsche contends, justified human life by living it.

The Dionysian principle, too, had a role in the theodicy of the ancient Greeks. Nietzsche believes that the ancient Greeks used tragedy to reconcile the Apollonian and Dionysian modes of self-understanding. The subject matter of tragedy was explicitly the suffering of an individual, the tragic hero. In identifying with the tragic hero, the audience adopted the Apollonian perspective, which takes seriously the individual character of existence. Prior to the tragic catastrophe that befalls him, the tragic hero is preoccupied with individual pursuits.

The tragic catastrophe reveals the inherent fragility of individual existence and individual pursuits. From the Apollonian standpoint, the tragic hero has lost virtually everything. The audience is reminded of an important aspect of individual life—that it is inherently vulnerable.

At this point, however, the Dionysian principle reminds the audience that a human being's individual character is not the only aspect of his being. For even when he has suffered terribly as an individual, the tragic hero comes to recognize that he is still a part of the larger flux of being. This was what happened when the tragic hero made peace with the larger world order. The larger, Dionysian flux is so powerful and enthralling that this recognition is deeply joyous and sustaining.

Thus, when the Apollonian illusion that life is orderly and safe for the individual is destroyed, the tragic hero experiences the Dionysian insight that life is wonderful and joyous anyway. The ultimate purpose of tragedy was a spiritual one. It recalled its audience to an understanding of both Apollonian and Dionysian aspects of their lives, and it revealed the Dionysian truth that suffering is no argument against life's meaning.

By positing two aesthetic principles, Nietzsche challenged the traditional assumption that art had a single aim. Nietzsche's Apollonian principle embodied many traditional values, such as the aspiration for beautiful form and the desirability of closure. But his Dionysian principle made values of dynamism and chaos. Although the values of the Apollonian principle were compatible with disinterested contemplation, the Dionysian principle promoted interested participation. Nietzsche suggests with his duality that aesthetic experience can take more than one form, and that the various forms it can take might all be valuable to its audience's understanding of itself and its world.

F. ART AND REALITY IN THE TWENTIETH CENTURY

The twentieth century has produced many additional challenges to traditional aesthetics both from artistic and theoretical corners. Artists of various media deliberately have shirked such time-honored aesthetic values as closure and organic unity. Visual artists no longer necessarily aspire toward representation, and a large percentage of modern composers resist traditional tonal harmony as an organizing feature of their works. Meanwhile, philosopher **Arthur Danto** agrees with Hegel that the "death of art" is upon us. Reflective thought, Danto contends, has become both the formative agent and the aim of most modern art. Art is no longer a definitively spiritual activity.

Other twentieth-century challenges to the traditional conception of art have been radical reconsiderations of the tradition's assessment of art's relation to reality. **José Ortega y Gasset** attributes the unpopularity of the twentieth century to its predominant concern to "dehumanize" art. Ortega y Gasset sees this aspiration as a radical abandonment of the idea that art should illuminate reality. Art, in his view, inspires sentiments unrelated to those of everyday reality, and dehumanized art exists only for its own sake.

FROM *THE DEHUMANIZATION OF ART*
BY **JOSÉ ORTEGA Y GASSET**

With the objects of modern pictures no intercourse is possible. By divesting them of their aspect of "lived" reality the artist has blown up the bridges and burned the ships that could have taken us back to our daily world.

Far from going more or less clumsily toward reality, the artist is seen going against it. He is brazenly set on deforming reality, shattering its human aspect, dehumanizing it. With the things represented on traditional paintings we could have imaginary intercourse. Many a young Englishman has fallen in love with Gioconda. With the objects of modern pictures no intercourse is possible. By divesting them of their aspect of "lived" reality the artist has blown up the bridges and burned the ships that could have taken us back to our daily world. He leaves us locked up in an abstruse universe, surrounded by objects with which human dealings are inconceivable, and thus compels us to improvise other forms of intercourse completely distinct from our ordinary ways with things. We must invent unheard-of gestures to fit those singular figures. This new way of life which presupposes the annulment of spontaneous life is precisely what we call understanding and enjoyment of art. Not that this life lacks sentiments and passions, but those sentiments and passions evidently belong to a flora other than that which covers the hills and dales of primary and human life. What those ultra-objects[9] evoke in our inner artist are secondary passions, specifically aesthetic sentiments.

It may be said that, to achieve this result, it would be simpler to dismiss human forms—man, house, mountain—altogether and to construct entirely original figures. But, in the first place, this is not feasible.[10] Even in the most abstract ornamental line a stubborn reminiscence lurks of certain "natural" forms. Secondly—and this is the crucial point—the art of which we speak is inhuman not only because it contains no things human, but also because it is an explicit act of dehumanization. In his escape from the human world the young artist cares less for the "*terminus ad quem*," the startling fauna at which he arrives, than for the "*terminus a quo*," the human aspect which he destroys. The question is not to paint something altogether different from a man, a house, a mountain, but to paint a man who resembles a man as little as possible; a house that preserves of a house exactly what is needed to reveal the metamorphosis; a cone miraculously emerging—as the snake from his slough—from what used to be a mountain. For the modern artist, aesthetic pleasure derives from such a triumph over human matter. That is why he has to drive home the victory by presenting in each case the strangled victim.[11]

John Dewey, by contrast, argues that art's distance from reality in the twentieth century is an illusion, largely created by our tendency to insist on a radical dichotomy between the aesthetic and the rest of our lives. If most of the twentieth-century art audience does not discover illumination of the everyday in art, this is because they fail to recognize the germ of the aesthetic in the everyday.

In everyday experience we encounter tensions that aim at equilibrium and their ultimate resolutions. The basic rhythm of organic existence results from an organism's falling out of step with its environment and the restoration of equilibrium between the two. Art is thus built on the same pattern as the necessary rhythm of organic life. Our natural delight in artistic resolution of tensions is rooted in the satisfaction we feel when our own being, after being in tension with the environment, has reached a new and more highly developed state of adjustment than it has ever attained. This fundamentally biological satisfaction, according to Dewey, is itself a kind of aesthetic delight.

Dewey contends that the kind of significance we give to meaningful experiences in our lives also is an aesthetic significance. When we describe a situation in our past

---

[9]"Ultraism" is one of the most appropriate names that have been coined to denote the new sensibility.

[10]An attempt has been made in this extreme sense—in certain works by Picasso— but it has failed signally.

[11]José Ortega y Gasset, *The Dehumanization of Art and Other Essays* (Princeton, N.J.: Princeton University Press, 1948).

as "an experience," we are describing it as something unified. The tensions involved in the situation have run their course to completion and, as a result, the experience exhibits a kind of closure. As we recall "an experience" of this sort, we sense that the elements that compose it are integrated by a kind of pervasive emotion that Dewey describes as an "aesthetic quality." An aesthetic quality is a particular, unrepeatable feeling that we associate with the experience as a whole. Thus, the traditional aesthetic principles of closure and organic unity characterize the experiences that we designate as particularly significant in our lives.

As Dewey sees it, experiences of this sort are the primary unit of life. When we consider what makes our lives meaningful and significant, such experiences come to mind. We find an experience that we designate "an experience" intrinsically satisfying, even if the contents of the experience were less than comfortable at the time.

Observing the kinship between the experiences of life that are most meaningful to us and aesthetic experiences we have in connection with art, Dewey argues that aesthetic experience presents a challenge to philosophy. Our aim throughout life—the aim that philosophy desirably helps us reach—is to reconstruct our everyday experiences so that they become more determinate, harmonious, and meaningful. Art develops and accentuates what is characteristically valuable in the everyday. Art presents tensions that build to a culmination and resolution; aesthetic qualities that unify the effect of an artwork's materials dominate our experience of art. Therefore, if philosophy is to illuminate experience in general, it should examine art—which reveals experience in its integrity.

FROM *ART AS EXPERIENCE*
BY **JOHN DEWEY**

THE CHALLENGE TO PHILOSOPHY

Esthetic experience is imaginative. This fact, in connection with a false idea of the nature of imagination, has obscured the larger fact that all *conscious* experience has of necessity some degree of imaginative quality. For while the roots of every experience are found in the interaction of a live creature with its environment, that experience becomes conscious, a matter of perception, only when meanings enter it that are derived from prior experiences. Imagination is the only gateway through which these meanings can find their way into a present interaction; or rather, as we have just seen, the conscious adjustment of the new and the old *is* imagination. Interaction of a living being with an environment is found in vegetative and animal life. But the experience enacted is human and conscious only as that which is given here and now is extended by meanings and values drawn from what is absent in fact and present only imaginatively.[12]

---

[12] "Mind denotes a whole system of meanings as they are embodied in the workings of organic life. . . . Mind is a constant luminosity; consciousness is intermittent, a series of flashes of different intensities."

There is always a gap between the here and now of direct interaction and the past interactions whose funded result constitutes the meanings with which we grasp and understand what is now occurring. Because of this gap, all conscious perception involves a risk; it is a venture into the unknown, for as it assimilates the present to the past it also brings about some reconstruction of that past. When past and present fit exactly into one another, when there is only recurrence, complete uniformity, the resulting experience is routine and mechanical; it does not come to consciousness in perception. The inertia of habit overrides adaptation of the meaning of the here and now with that of experiences, without which there is no consciousness, the imaginative phase of experience.

Mind, that is the body of organized meanings by means of which events of the present have significance for us, does not always enter into the activities and undergoings that are going on here and now. Sometimes it is baffled and arrested. Then the stream of meanings aroused into activity by the present contact remain aloof. Then it forms the matter of reverie, of dream; ideas are floating, not anchored to any existence as its property, its possession of meanings. Emotions that are equally loose and floating cling to these ideas. The pleasure they afford is the reason why they are entertained and are allowed to occupy the scene; they are attached to existence only in a way that, as long as sanity abides, is felt to be only fanciful and unreal.

In every work of art, however, these meanings are actually embodied in a material which thereby becomes the medium for their expression. This fact constitutes the peculiarity of all experience that is definitely esthetic. Its imaginative quality dominates, because meanings and values that are wider and deeper than the particular here and now in which they are anchored are realized by way of *expressions* although not by way of an object that is physically efficacious in relation to other objects. Not even a useful object is produced except by the intervention of imagination. Some existent material was perceived in the light of relations and possibilities not hitherto realized when the steam engine was invented. But when the imagined possibilities were embodied in a new assemblage of natural materials, the steam engine took its place in nature as an object that has the same physical effects as those belonging to any other physical object. Steam did the physical work and produced the consequences that attend any expanding gas under definite physical conditions. The sole difference is that the conditions under which it operates have been arranged by human contrivance.

> *The work of art . . . is not only the outcome of imagination, but operates imaginatively rather than in the realm of physical existences. What it does is to concentrate and enlarge an immediate experience.*

The work of art, however, unlike the machine, is not only the outcome of imagination, but operates imaginatively rather than in the realm of physical existences. What it does is to concentrate and enlarge an immediate experience. The formed matter of esthetic experience directly *expresses,* in other words, the meanings that are imaginatively evoked; it does not, like the material brought into new relations in a machine, merely provide *means* by which purposes over and beyond the existence of the object may be executed. And yet the meanings imaginatively summoned, assembled, and integrated are embodied in material existence that here and now interacts with the self. The work of art is thus a challenge to the performance of a like act of evocation and organization, through imagination, on the part of the one who experiences it. It is not just a stimulus to and means of an overt course of action.[13]

G. THE OTHER HALF OF THE PICTURE: FEMINIST AESTHETICS

Feminists have argued, in aesthetics as in other branches of philosophy, that there are considerable differences between the way men and women experience art, and so too, considerable differences between male and female artists. So, too, as we all know, there are important and interesting cultural differences in conceptions of art and beauty. In the following section, **Marilyn French** discusses feminist aesthetics.

"IS THERE A FEMINIST AESTHETIC?"
BY **MARILYN FRENCH**

It is questionable whether the terms and issues of traditional aesthetics are applicable to feminist art. Some critics claim traditional aesthetic principles are universal, and that art is "above" sex, or at least, that sex is irrelevant to it. There is an art which is specifically feminist: that much is clear. Some, by virtue of its feminism, would deny it the title *art,* arguing that its political interest violates aesthetic standards. An aesthetic like Susanne Langer's, which defines what art creates and is indeed universal, fits feminist art as well as any other (Langer 1953). But most aesthetics are more prescriptive, and therefore more political: feminism has taught us that all critical approaches imply political standards, however tacitly. Before we can evaluate feminist art by any aesthetic principles, we need a definition of the art. In what follows, I will discuss the characteristics of feminist art as I understand them. For the sake of brevity, I will limit myself to the art I know best, literature, but the principles have parallels in the other arts.

The clearest proof of the existence of a feminist aesthetics is the distaste or rage feminists feel on encountering works that violate it. Sometimes a negative

---

[13]John Dewey, *Art as Experience* (New York: G. P. Putnam, 1934).

response seems to refer to subject matter—for example, I loathe lingering loving descriptions of mutilations of female bodies; yet when a writer like Andrea Dworkin treats such a theme, I feel it to be not offensive, but only unpleasant— it falls within the boundaries of "taste." So it is less subject-matter (content) than treatment (style) that is at issue. . . . Perhaps all a prescriptive aesthetic can be is a set of principles describing a particular style, a taste.

There are two fundamental, related principles that mark a work of art as feminist: 1.) It approaches reality from a feminist perspective; and 2.) it endorses female experience. Each principle has several ramifications, so is more complicated than it sounds.

In a work with a feminist perspective, the narrational point of view, the point of view lying behind the characters and events, penetrates, demystifies, or challenges patriarchal ideologies. So much has been written about patriarchy in the last two decades that one tends to assume readers understand the term; yet I have met highly educated people who do not understand the feminist use of the term, so I'll explain it briefly. Patriarchy is a way of thinking, a set of assumptions that has been translated into various structures or ideologies. The assumptions are, first: males are superior to females. Their superiority may be granted by a deity or by nature, but it is absolute in conferring on men authority over women. Second: males have individual destinies; they are promised domination, a surrogate godhead, transcendence over the natural world through power in heroism, sainthood, or some form of transcendent paternity—founding a dynasty, an institution, a religion, or a state, or creating an enduring work of art or technology. Third: the form taken by patriarchy is hierarchy, a structure designed to maintain and transmit power from spiritual father to spiritual son. This form absolutely excludes females unless they "make themselves male" (the requirement Jesus places on women entering "the Life" in the gnostic Gospel of Thomas) (1977). Women control biological transmission, the ability to bring forth young passed from mother to daughter. Having this power, they must be excluded from institutional power—which was modeled on the biological sort—if they are not to overwhelm men. Females have only a "natural" destiny: interchangeable parts of nature's cycles, they are maids (in both senses), who become mothers, and finally widows (or hags), in which avatar they are expendable.

Finally, domination is divine, so to pursue it is noble, heroic, glorious. The material to be dominated is, essentially, nature—all women; the body and emotions; "bestial" men; and natural processes, the flux and transitoriness of time, material decay, life itself. Patriarchal works focus on individual males who pursue glory; lonely, self-made and self-defeating, men are isolated from community and exiled forever from the "female" fate of happiness.

Since almost all modern worlds are patriarchal, feminist literature necessarily depicts patriarchy. But it does not underwrite its standards. Feminist literature may show patriarchal attitudes destroying a character or a world, but the narrative does not approve the destruction. When, in *The Faerie Queene,* Guyon destroys the luscious female world called The Bower of Bliss, Spenser, who has used his highest imaginative skills to create the Bower, judiciously approves its ruin. This is true also of Vergil in *The Aeneid*. The poet sighs about the tears of things (*lacrimae rerum*), regretting that beauty and feeling (Dido and sexual love for instance) are destroyed in the pursuit of glory, yet approves Aeneas's desertion of Dido, and his slaughter of those who oppose his domination. Aeneas's destiny is to found Rome; it overrides humanitarian or emotional concerns. Clearly, despite their feelings, both poets uphold patriarchy.

It is less clear where Tolstoy stands in *Anna Karenina*, or Austen in *Pride and Prejudice*. Both authors accept the patriarchal societies in which they live. Yet the pity Tolstoy lavishes on Anna, and the acute irony with which Austen pricks upper-class pretention and the unctuous ambition of the middle-classes, subvert patriarchal standards. This sympathy is not in the eye of the reader; it is built-in. Tolstoy's novel induces readers to feel the world lessened by Anna's death, rather than to feel that it was necessary, like Dido's, to a greater purpose. Austen's heroines maintain self-respect and integrity (wholeness) even as they triumph within a patriarchal structure. Many works of the past three centuries stretch patriarchal standards in this way; they are not feminist, but do not wholly support patriarchy either.

The feminist perspective is partly a reversal of patriarchal views. Feminism sees women as at least equal to men, humanly if not politically or economically; it considers transcendence illusory or factitious and pursuit of power a fatally doomed enterprise, since it cannot ever be satisfied, and usually or always involves the destruction of vital qualities and even life itself. Domination is not divine but lethal to dominator and dominated. It harms the dominator by cutting him off from trust and mutuality, the foundations of friendship and love, the two primary values; it harms the dominated by forcing them into dependency, which precludes truth in relationships. Domination creates false forms of friendship (society) and love (conventional marriage) which mask power relations. And feminist art focuses on people as wholes; the human is made up of body and emotion as well as mind and spirit; she is also part of a community, connected to others; and—on the broadest level—to nature in both positive and negative aspects.

The second principle is equally complicated. To endorse women's experience, feminist art must present it honestly, wholly. This is difficult because literature, like all art, is made up of conventions which are particularly marked in the area of gender. Just as it would be startling to observe a painting of a male nude reclining seductively à la Maja, or Olympe, or of a clothed female Picasso contemplating a naked male with emphatic genitals, literary shifts in presentation of gender startle, distracting attention from

> *. . . feminist art focuses on people as wholes; the human is made up of body and emotion as well as mind and spirit; she is also part of a community, connected to others; and— on the broadest level— to nature in both positive and negative aspects.*

what is being shown to *the fact* that it is shown. A work's political impact obliterates its other features. This means that either considerable time—decades or even centuries—must elapse before readers can concentrate on what is being shown, or the work will be forgotten without this ever happening. And conventions governing female characters in literature are extraordinarily powerful and tenacious.

One convention holds women's work trivial, insignificant, uninteresting. Indeed, even men's work was considered an inappropriate subject for literature until recently. Yet work fills our lives; domestic work *is* most women's entire life and takes up considerable time even for women who also work outside the home. What such work means to one's sense of self, of the larger world; how it affects a woman's relation to her children, mates, lovers, friends; its pleasures, pains, the personal and political consequences of endless work for which one is not paid: these experiences remain relatively unexplored because of convention.

Conventionally, women's stories had happy endings, usually marriage to a prince and living happily ever after—unless the heroine is guilty of a sexual transgression, in which case she is required to die. This convention has stretched to allow sexual women to survive, but readers still complain when a "good" woman does not live happily ever after. The assumption behind this convention seems to be that the world is ruled by a male bar of justice. All female characters come up before this bar, and males being just, grant the good ones happiness—a female, not a male condition (male heroes almost never live happily ever after). It the author does not grant a virtuous female character eternal felicity, either she doesn't deserve it or the male bar is not just. Since in a patriarchal world the latter is unthinkable, her virtue must be deceptive. So male critics pore over Shakespeare's Cordelia searching for the hidden flaw that explains her fate and alter Edith Wharton's perception of her heroines (who *are* flawed), making them responsible for their own unhappiness.

If the definition of a "good" woman no longer involves chastity, heroines are still required to be sweet, vulnerable, *likeable*. Readers do not expect sweetness or honesty of male protagonists: they don't even have to be likeable: consider the heroes of *Under the Volcano, Notes from Underground, Look Back in Anger.* Authoritative, angry, rebellious heroines make most readers impatient; they tend to blame the character for not finding a way to be happy. I think about Andrea Dworkin's *Ice and Fire,* which could not at first find an American publisher, or my own *The Bleeding Heart,* which female and male reviewers (if not readers) uniformly condemned. Actual women, we ourselves, may walk around in a constant state of rage and yet reject heroines like us. The most lethal combination is authority and sexuality; it is almost impossible to depict a woman with both except as a villain. . . .

These principles may sound limiting, as if feminist work could deal only and always with the middle ground, the mundane, the probable, eschewing flights of fancy, excessive characters, extremes of good and evil. This is not at all the case, although precisely that middle ground needs examination. Consider that for the 2500+ years of its existence, Western philosophy has looked at life strictly from a male perspective, and strictly as if men were constituted only of intellect, ambition, and political concern; as if they never had to deal with upset stomachs, irritation at their children, emotional dependency, hunger, or distress at growing bald. As Nietzsche pointed out, philosophy has ignored and dismissed the life of the body and the emotions, and—I would add—social involvement with women and children. It has been able to show men transcending only by pretending that the mundane does not exist and that other people do not matter.[14]

H. ART AND CULTURE:
JAPAN AND AFRICA

The category of "art" is in fact a relatively recent European invention. Cultures have been producing art for many thousands of years, of course, from the cave paintings in Lascaux, France, to the rich productions of sculptures, paintings, weavings, and utensils in virtually every one of the world's cultures, whether urban and aesthetically sophisticated or a peasant culture in which aesthetics must serve daily necessity. But the idea of art as a separate and particularly precious realm, the "art for art's sake" of the late nineteenth century, is relatively rare. In most societies, art serves the purpose of religion, or social ritual and identification, or practical utility. Art is also *expression*—of emotion, of desire, of interpersonal as well as personal needs. Perhaps most universal, however, is the role of art in *play,* as our imaginative and joyful attempt to recreate our world. In the following sections, **Mara Miller** talks about gender equality in Japanese art and **Isidore Okpewho** discusses the role of *play* and spirituality in African art.

ON JAPANESE EROTIC ART
BY **MARA MILLER**

The Japanese Self differs from the Western paradigm in two critical respects: it is constructed intersubjectively, rather than by opposition to an objectified Other, and it is equally feminine and masculine: it does not privilege the male position. The arts not only bear witness to this distinctively Japanese Self, they also play an important role in its constitution. . . .

The woodblock prints of the Ukiyo-e school of the Edo period (1600–1868) illustrate that the Japanese do have a strong tradition of individual Selfhood, that Selfhood and the Subject position are neither the exclusive privilege of men nor modeled on male experience, that this Selfhood is intersubjectively constituted and premised upon confidence in knowledge of the Other, and that art both illustrates and contributes to the construction of this Self. . . .

---

[14] Marilyn French, "Is There a Feminist Aesthetic?" in *Hypatia* 5 no. 2 (Summer 1990).

There are four ways in which Japanese artistic practices differ from the Western with regard to this paradigmatic correspondence between gender and status as Subject or Object. First, men are depicted not only as Subjects, but as Objects. Second, women are depicted not only as Objects but, far more commonly, as Subjects. In addition, both are shown in intersubjective relation, that is, in the act of mutual acknowledgement of the Subjecthood of the Other (with simultaneous acknowledgement of their own Subjecthood). Finally, the female gaze is recognized and incorporated; men are expected to be able to identify with a female Subject as well as a male one and vice versa. This situation may reflect the realities, if not the statistical norms, of real life; it certainly does *not* reflect the contemporary Confucianist ideology expounded by the government.

The middle-class Ukiyo-e audiences craved images of the heroes of their new popular culture: actors of the Kabuki theater and *bijin* (literally "beautiful women") and courtesans of the pleasure quarters. Although the stylization of these images is undeniable, so is a fascination with realism. From this realism emerges a type of portraiture distinctly different from that of the West, in that it is primarily interested neither in physical resemblance nor in the character of the person, but in those aspects of the person which reveal what we might call the "intended" self, the self-fashioned self, the self as it has decided to reveal itself to others.

Precursors of this understanding of the Self are found in the portraits of classical poets (male and female) dating from the Kamakura period on, like the portrait of the female poet Ono no Komachi (c. 850) . . . by the sixteenth-century Rimpa artist Sakai Hoitsu. The face is turned away from the viewer; it conveys no information of interest. Individuality resides in the set of the body and the costume—the elegance of the twelve-layer kimono is crucial—and in the words of the poet, written alongside the poet's name in expressive calligraphy. Ukiyo-e portraits of contemporary actual people capitalize upon this tradition of indicating Selfhood as a combination of name, posture or deportment, costume, and one's work. They understand the achieved Selfhood of such personages to be a complex comprised of individual identity (identifiable facial features, inscription of the actor's or courtesan's name, etc.), public persona (both as a function of social role—identifying insignia such as the actor's family's crest or the name of the courtesan's house, that help to determine for the viewer the social position—and as a set of choices made by the individual as to how to present herself or himself), and the person's mood or intention at a particular moment. . . .

Superficially some prints of beautiful women or *bijin* seem to exemplify the woman-as-object model. . . . In such works the female body is presented as spectacle, an ideal beauty without claims on or by the non-visual reality, a perfect scopophilic object, passively awaiting the male, and with gentle curves that invite completion by the viewer. . . .

Yet although among Japanese types of female beauty Harunobu's girl is one of the most compliant and vulnerable, she is not deprived of indicators of autonomy, as a comparable Western fragile beauty would be. The autonomy of

Harunobu's innocents is indicated by their position—frequently standing, and often outside, in public space—meeting lovers or . . . visiting shrines. . . . The aesthetic choices in their clothing and environments inform us of their tastes, education, abilities, and preferences. The gentle curves of the subtle kimono designs, each based on nature but alluding also to the season and to a wealth of literary references, suggest their temperaments. Books on the floor bespeak their literacy—which of course would include in this context familiarity with the classical novels, poetry and diaries written by women and men. . . .

Nowhere does the difference between the Western Self and the Japanese Self emerge more clearly than in erotic art or *Shunga* ("Spring pictures"). This difference is that between the Subject constructed by a relation (of dominance) to an Object and the Subject constructed intersubjectively, in relation to an Other conceived and encountered as a Subject.

Nowhere does the difference between the Western Self and the Japanese Self emerge more clearly than in erotic art or **Shunga.** *This difference is that between the Subject constructed by a relation (of dominance) to an Object and the Subject constructed intersubjectively, in relation to an Other conceived and encountered as a Subject.*

In explicitly erotic prints women are *not* restricted to the role of passive object of male desire. They quite clearly appear as active desiring Subjects. Women are sometimes shown in positions of submission, but more often stand and sit upright or lie with a man who is also lying down. Either the woman or the man may be on top; they may be intertwined, with neither dominant. Poses characteristic of Western erotica—the woman lying on her back with her hands behind her head, fully exposed to the viewer, or lying with her head fallen back in abandon, as if her neck were broken—are not seen in Japan until after contact with the West.

These women are not only active, and avoiding either extreme of dominance or submission, but they are desiring. They actively reach out for the man and fondle his genitals, they curl their toes with rapture. It is impossible to mistake their enjoyment.

The disempowerment of the nude Western sex object is missing in the Japanese examples. Nudity is important in the Western context because it signals the permission given the male viewer: deprived of social status, her nudity indicating not merely her agreement to the male gaze/fantasy/act but often a wantonness that makes her agreement beside the point, the woman is vulnerable. In Japan, on the other hand, the vulnerability of nudity is not only unnecessary but undesirable. (And nudity per se is not sexy in Japan; it was common in public bathing.) What is desirable in woman to a Japanese man is a Subject with whom to interact, not an Object on whom to project one's own fantasy. Clothing—the choice and combination of patterns, the colors, the references—is vital to the revelation of one's Subjecthood.

The encounter with the Other as full Subject is signaled by the mutual gaze into each other's eyes. All of these prints show the couple looking at each other. In Shunga, it is not only the male who gazes at the female; the woman gazes back. Or rather, the Gaze (as it is called in representational theory) or the Look (as it is called in philosophy) is mutual—neither looks at an Object, but into another Subject, with a look that creates the other as Subject rather than diminishing her or him to the status of Object. . . .

Not only in Shunga but generally, Japanese representations differ from Western ones in facilitating the female gaze as well as the male gaze. The Gaze is not only erotic. . . .

Women assume the right to gaze in other ways as well. They are frequently voyeurs in sexual scenes. They examine other women on the streets, especially in the work of Kiyonaga who is famous for his complex social situations.[15]

ON TRADITIONAL AFRICAN ART
BY **ISIDORE OKPEWHO**

Those who look for religion or worldview behind everything in traditional art have often ignored the basic *play* interest of the artist. Thus in nearly every study of traditional African art, nothing whatsoever is said about the numerous pieces of phallic or erotic sculpture that can be found in many African villages which have a lively tradition of plastic art. Where mention is made of such pieces, there is usually an effort to connect them with rites of initiation or of fertility, which are happily treated as "religious." Nor, in the countless anthologies with which the market of African folklore is glutted, do we find very much by way of ribald verse; yet ask any youth in a typical African village to recite you his favorite verses, and the chances are the majority of them have to do with sex.

An even more illuminating fact is that, in some of the more popular African tales which have anything to do with traditional religion, the religious element is frequently superseded by the play interest of the narrator, especially in the fervid context of the open performance. A useful illustration of this interest is provided by *The Mwindo Epic.* . . . Mwindo's pursuit of his errant father takes him mostly through the underworld regions, and the quest is obstructed by two hostile divinities, Muisa and Sheburungu; the latter of these, as the editors of the epic tell us, is "one of the epithets under which the supreme divinity of fire, Nyamurairi, is known." These are not inconsequential figures of a vague pantheon, but deities accompanied by the full appurtenances of worship. They are grouped along with other gods in the Nyanga cult system, and of them we are told:

---

[15] Mara Miller, "Desiring Women: The Aesthetics of Japanese Erotic Art," in *Aesthetics in Perspective,* ed. Kathleen M. Higgins (Fort Worth: Harcourt Brace, 1996).

All these divinities, together with the ancestors, are known under the generic term bashumbu. Shrines are made and plantains are grown for them, women are dedicated and married to them, sheep and hunting dogs are consecrated to them, prayers are said to them, and distinctive cultural paraphernalia for each of them are kept by their adepts. They manifest themselves in dreams and oracles and are responsible for good and evil in Nyanga life."

Thus among the Nyanga, at least, it would be considered preposterous for anyone (unless he was himself a divinity, and Mwindo is not a divinity) to be portrayed as contending against and overcoming the gods of the traditional pantheon. But Mwindo gets into a severe physical confrontation with Muisa. In the first round, Muisa levels Mwindo with his magic belt (*karemba*). Mwindo recovers, and with the aid of his own magic *conga*-scepter, smashes Muisa to the ground. With Sheburungu there is only a battle of wits—the *wiki* game. The god wins against Mwindo; but the hero, finding that ordinary human wits are of no use against a divinity, throws his magic *conga*-scepter into the bargain and wins.

For a human character to fight and win against a divinity is, we must agree, contrary to the spirit in which a society's religious life is conducted. Even when Mwindo is translated into the sky by the lightning-god Nkuba and warned against further heroic excesses, the warning is unconnected with his fights and victories against Muisa and Sheburungu, particularly as Nkuba himself had helped Mwindo part of the way in those confrontations. Again, let us look closely at Nkuba's conduct in this connection. Early in the story he takes sides with the enemies of Mwindo, but the hero always wins. Then Nkuba turns and becomes an ally of the hero in his struggles with some of his other enemies including Muisa and Sheburungu. But the final confrontation with Nkuba comes when Mwindo kills a dragon which is sacred to Nkuba, and consequently incurs the anger of his erstwhile ally. Though the denouement of the story seems to portray the hero as an overreacher, it is evident that the case for this rests only on his offense against Nkuba, and does not at all include his earlier acts of ostensible "impiety." The explanation offered by the editors, that "there was an excuse for the hero as long as he was the victim of his father's unjust decisions and actions," is inadequate. Sheburungu, over whom the hero had earlier triumphed, is, as the same editors tell us, the supreme creator-god as well as god of fire; and there is really nothing in the tale or in the editorial notes that puts Nkuba in a superior position to Sheburungu in the Nyanga cult system.

> *In the live, bubbling atmosphere wherein the Mwindo has been performed, what was normally a matter of serious concern for the community has become subject to the play instincts of the artist.*

The implications are quite obvious, particularly if we take into consideration, as we should, the lively context of the heroic song. In the live, bubbling atmosphere wherein the Mwindo has been performed, what was normally a matter of serious concern for the community has become subject to the play instincts of the artist. We may not go so far as Lévi-Strauss in maintaining that "myths operate in men's minds without their being aware of the fact"; for those obtrusive "religious" details and strophic comments which punctuate the song argue a certain presence of mind. But it is quite clear that, in this mythopoeic context, both the bard and his audience have been drawn into an experience not altogether germane to the spirit of worship or ritual. The figures of the cult belief have been subjected to patterns of behavior which tend sometimes to detract from the awe in which they are traditionally held, especially in a tale like Mwindo whose dramatic resources are evidently as much comical as serious. An audience treated to such a song will in no way consider its pious instincts offended by the bard's strange picture, particularly when they reflect that the human beings with whom the gods are fabled to be contending are not exactly like their next-door neighbors. True, in their theological beliefs they know that the gods are responsible for evil as well as good, and indeed the whimsical nature of the gods which is revealed by these songs may well mirror some of their convictions. But they are unaccustomed, in their sober theological thinking, to conceive of divinity in the peculiar dramatic circumstances in which the myth-maker puts it, and are well content to grant a heart-warming evening's performance the benefit of its strange content and outlook. Clearly in such a situation, the artistic play-drive has got the better of the religious instinct.

♦♦♦

Religion and ritual are not unimportant in the evolution of African art. What is objectionable is the popular notion that religion is always the starting point.

♦♦♦

But the artist has a further level of realism for what has been called "the spirit-regarding order." Art critics have repeatedly and erroneously called this kind of art "abstract." But in this category of art, the traditional artist is addressing himself not to ideas as such, or abstractions, but to spirits and deities vividly conceived. The distinction is worth emphasizing, because abstraction properly belongs to an age that has lost considerable faith in the perceptible real—an age, as it were, of disbelief. Those horrendous shapes that feature in the folk myth and the plastic arts are as real as the forests and the sequestered shrines that they inhabit. The *chi wara* of the Bambara is not simply "fecundity" as an abstract idea; it was a spirit sent down by the Creator to promote fecundity. But, although you cannot accurately picture a spirit, the Bambara have too vivid a sense of the real to be lost in imprecisions. So they portray the *chi wara* in the stylized form of a denizen of the fecund environment, the antelope, worn as a mask during their ritual dances.

It would be mistaken to call a figure abstract simply because it combined selective images in a composite form and was treated with some stylization. Those figures are vivid elements of a people's living myth. Allecto with serpents for her hair is not an abstract idea of fury; she *is* a Fury. The same applies to our ceremonial masks. They are the artist's vivid portrait of an ancestral or a genial presence—the figures, as Senghor tells us in his "Prayer to Masks," *through whom the spirit breathes.* But since the artist cannot claim exact knowledge of the outlines of a spirit's physiognomy, he endeavors to strike a just balance between his limitations and his sense of the real; those masks are a biomorphic response to the various forms and natures of the spirits concerned. It is remarkable how close those portraits of spirits can be.[16]

SUMMARY AND CONCLUSION

Philosophy includes the study of the Beautiful as well as the metaphysical, epistemological, and ethical concerns for the True and the Good. The experience of the beautiful usually is referred to as "aesthetics" and, typically, it is bound up with the study of art and artworks. But Plato took as his example the beautiful person and distrusted art; Kant took as his paradigm the beauty of nature and its ultimate significance, the inspiration to be moral. Foremost among the concerns that have dominated aesthetics since ancient times are the questions of how one can justify an aesthetic judgment and what is the place of art in society. Plato gave the first question a powerful answer, suggesting that our sense of beauty is in fact the recognition of a transcendent Form of Beauty. But he answered the second question with considerable suspicion, and ever since art has seemed at least to some philosophers to be more of a distraction than an important addition to social life.

Aristotle countered that art plays a vital role in everyday life, both as innocent entertainment and as a model of a kind of perfection. Christian thought often sided with Plato on this question, but modern thought tended to move back toward Aristotle. David Hume raised the serious challenge as to whether there could be any "objective" decision about the quality of art; Immanuel Kant answered Hume by saying that it is the very nature of our mental faculties that explains taste and our sense of beauty. Hegel, Schopenhauer, and Nietzsche defended the view that art provides a means of self-awareness, and therein lies its importance. The twentieth century has raised new questions as art has become more abstract and less representational—which José Ortega y Gasset calls "dehumanization" but John Dewey defends as a fundamental human experience. Finally, a new awareness of non-Western art and of gender in Western art has aroused contemporary sensibilities and created new challenges.

GLOSSARY

aesthetics The study of beauty and the experience of the beautiful.
Apollonian (Nietzsche) The rational principle in art, Form.

---

[16] Isidore Okpewho, "Principles of Traditional African Art," in *Aesthetics in Perspective,* ed. Kathleen M. Higgins (Fort Worth: Harcourt Brace, 1996).

catharsis (Aristotle) The purging (or purifying) of emotion through art.

closure Coming to a satisfactory end or conclusion, self-contained.

Dionysian (Nietzsche) The irrational principle in art, energy, willfulness.

free play (Kant) The interplay between the imagination and the understanding that produces the sense of beauty.

imagination (Kant) That mental faculty responsible for the production (and reproduction) of representations.

intersubjective Experience shared by different subjects.

purposiveness without a purpose (Kant) The idea that the elements of a beautiful object seem to cohere as if toward a purpose, but we can find no definite purpose. For example, a sunset seems to us a unified aesthetic phenomenon, but there obviously is no "purpose" to a sunset.

understanding (Kant) The faculty that provides determinate concepts to experience.

will (Schopenhauer) The ultimate irrational force that art allows us to escape (temporarily).

BIBLIOGRAPHY AND FURTHER READING

Plato, *Symposium,* trans. Paul Woodruff and Alexander Nehamas (Indianapolis, IN: Hackett, 1989). Plato, *The Republic,* trans. G. M. A. Grube (Indianapolis, IN: Hackett, 1974). Plato, *The Ion,* trans. Paul Woodruff (Indianapolis, IN: Hackett, 1983). Aristotle, *Poetics,* trans. W. D. Ross (Oxford: Clarendon Press, 1946). Immanuel Kant, *Critique of Judgment,* trans. W. Pluhar (Indianapolis, IN: Hackett, 1987). David Hume, "Of the Standard of Taste" in *Essays on Morality, Politics and Literature,* ed. T. H. Green (London: Longmans, 1882). G. W. F. Hegel, *Art, Religion, Philosophy,* ed. J. Glenn Gray (New York: Harper & Row, 1970). G. W. F. Hegel, *Aesthetics: Lectures on Fine Arts,* trans. T. M. Knox (2 vols.) (New York: Oxford University Press, 1975). Friedrich Nietzsche, *The Birth of Tragedy,* trans. Walter Kaufmann (New York: Random House, 1967). José Ortega y Gasset, *The Dehumanization of Art and Other Essays* (Princeton: Princeton University Press, 1948). Arthur Schopenhauer, *The World As Will and Idea,* trans. E. F. J. Payne (2 vols.) (New York: Dover, 1958). Leo Tolstoy, *What is Art?* trans. Louise and Aylmer Maude (New York: Oxford University Press, 1930). Two general anthologies are A. Hofstadter and R. Kuhns, eds., *Philosophies of Art and Beauty* (Chicago: Chicago University Press, 1964), and R. Stern and E. Robinson, eds. *Changing Concepts of Art* (New York: Haven, 1983). For a recent treatment of the philosophy of art, see Arthur Danto, *Transfiguration of the Commonplace* (Cambridge, MA: Harvard University Press, 1981). For a comprehensive general anthology, see Kathleen M. Higgins, *Aesthetics in Perspective* (Fort Worth: Harcourt Brace, 1996).

BRIEF BIOGRAPHIES

Al-Ghazali, Mohammad (1058–1111) Islamic philosopher and theologian, known especially for his criticisms of Aristotelianism and Avicenna. His most famous work was called *The Incoherence of the Philosophers.*

Anaximander (611–547? B.C.) Pre-Socratic philosopher who taught that reality is ultimately composed of an indeterminate something that we can never know directly through experience.

Anaximenes (6th century B.C.) Pre-Socratic philosopher who taught that the basic element of reality was air and that all things in the universe are different forms of air.

Anselm, Saint (1033–1109) Archbishop of Canterbury and author of the ontological argument for God's existence. He was one of the main defenders of the intellect and "understanding" against the then current anti-intellectualism of the Church. He is best known for his *Monologion* and *Proslogion,* in which the ontological argument is developed.

Aquinas, St. Thomas (1225–1274) Architect of the most comprehensive theological structure of the Roman Catholic Church, the *Summa Theologica,* which has long been recognized as the "official" statement of orthodox Christian beliefs by many theologians. Aquinas drew many of his arguments from Aristotle, as can be seen in his "five ways" of demonstrating the existence of God.

Aristippus (435?–356? B.C.) One of the Cynics and a student of Socrates, who taught that the good life consists solely of immediate pleasures.

Aristotle (384–322 B.C.) One of the greatest Western philosophers, Aristotle was born in northern Greece (Stagira). His father was the physician to Philip, king of Macedonia, and he himself was to become the tutor to Philip's son, Alexander the Great. For eighteen years Aristotle was a student in Plato's academy in Athens, where he learned and parted from Plato's views. After Plato's death, he turned to the study of biology, and many of his theories ruled Western science until the Renaissance. He was with Alexander until 335 B.C., when he returned to Athens to set up his own school, the Lyceum. After Alexander's death, the anti-Macedonian sentiment in Athens forced Aristotle to flee (commenting that the Athenians would not sin twice against philosophy). In addition to his biological studies, Aristotle virtually created the sciences of logic and linguistics, developed extravagant theories in physics and astronomy, and made significant contributions to metaphysics, ethics, politics, and aesthetics. His *Metaphysics* is still a basic text on the subject, and *Nicomachean Ethics* codified ancient Greek morality. This latter work stresses individual virtue and excellence for a small elite of Greek citizens. The best life of all, according to Aristotle, is the life of contemplation, that is, the life of a philosopher, for it is the most self-contained and the "closest to the gods." But such contemplation must be together with the pleasures of life, honor, wealth, and virtuous action.

Augustine, St. (354–430) The main figure in the development of medieval Christian thought from its roots in classical Greece and Rome. Augustine was born in North Africa and lived during the decline of the Roman Empire. After exploring various pagan beliefs, he was converted to Christianity and became Bishop of Hippo in North Africa. He is best known for his theological treatise *The City of God* and for his very personal *Confessions.*

Austin, John Langshaw (1911–1960) Oxford "ordinary-language" philosopher who had enormous influence on the development of "therapeutic" philosophy through attention to the details and nuances of everyday speech.

Baumgarten, Alexander Gottlieb (1714–1762) German aesthetician, influential in the years immediately preceding Immanuel Kant.

Bentham, Jeremy (1748–1832) A leader in the legal reform movement in England and the founding father of that ethical position called utilitarianism. His *principle of utility,* which says that one should act to produce the greatest good for the greatest number of people, was the central theme of utilitarianism and slowly worked its way into the confusion of rules and statutes that constituted the English legal system of his day. His best-known work is his *Introduction to the Principles of Morals and Legislation* (1789).

Bergson, Henri (1859–1941) French philosopher who argued that the world should be conceived in terms of duration and change, and as an old man, stood up to the Nazis in occupied Paris.

Berkeley, Bishop George (1685–1753) Wrote virtually all the works that made him famous before he turned twenty-eight. He was born, raised, and educated in Ireland, and as a student he immersed himself in the writings of the important philosophers of the time, particularly Locke, Newton, and some of the French metaphysicians. In later life, Berkeley became an educational missionary, visiting America and Bermuda, and then a bishop, eventually moving to Oxford. Unlike Locke and Hume, whose interests spread across the whole of philosophy, science, and human affairs, Berkeley restricted himself to a single problem— perception—and his entire philosophy is aptly summarized in his famous phrase "to be is to be perceived" (*esse est percipi*). His arguments for this position are most thoroughly outlined in his *Treatise Concerning the Principles of Human Knowledge* (1710).

Blanshard, Brand (1892–1987) Contemporary idealist and main American defender of the coherence theory of truth.

Bradley, Francis Herbert (1846–1924) The best-known and perhaps the most brilliant of the "British idealists" working at the turn of the century. He is best known for his work *Appearance and Reality* (1893), in which he argues a very strong version of the coherence theory of truth.

Buddha (6th century B.C.) The "Awakened One"; a name for the founder of the Buddhist religion; the ancient Indian prince, Siddharta Gautama, after his enlightenment.

Butler, Bishop Joseph (1692–1752) Powerful English clergyman who formulated what are still recognized as the standard arguments against psychological egoism in his *Fifteen Sermons* (1726).

Calhoun, Cheshire teaches philosophy at Colby College in Maine.

Churchland, Paul (1942–) American philosopher at the University of California, San Diego; specialist in cognitive science and the interplay between philosophy, computer science, and neurology.

Confucius (6th–5th century B.C.) Ancient Chinese sage and founder of the Confucian religion. His doctrine sought "gentlemanly conduct," which was to be achieved through adherence to ritual.

Corvino, John teaches philosophy at Wayne State University in Detroit and is the author of *Same Sex.*

Cynics (4th century B.C.) Group of post-Socratic philosophers who taught that the good life was a life of complete autonomy. Therefore they minimized the social values of success, wealth, and honor and focused their attention on what makes a person wholly self-sufficient. For Diogenes, this consisted of the simplest life possible, based upon simple pleasures and simple virtues. For Aristippus, this consisted of a life of immediate pleasure.

Democritus (5th century B.C.) Pre-Socratic philosopher who taught that reality is divisible into small "atoms," which combine to make up all things but which themselves are eternal and indivisible.

Derrida, Jacques (1930–) French philosopher and founder of the school of "deconstruction." He teaches at the Ecole Normal Superior in France, but is occasionally a visiting lecturer at American universities. He has taught at Yale, Cornell, and the University of California at Irvine.

Descartes, René (1596–1650) French philosopher who is usually considered the "father of modern philosophy." He was raised in the French aristocracy and educated at the excellent Jesuit College of La Flèche. He became skilled in the classics, law, and medicine; however, he decided that they fell far short of proper knowledge, and so he turned to modern science and mathematics. His first book was a defense of Copernicus, which he prudently did not publish. He discovered, while still a young man, the connections between algebra and geometry (which we now call "analytic geometry") and used this discovery as a model for the rest of his career. Basing the principles of philosophy and theology on a similar mathematical basis, he was able to develop a method in philosophy that could be carried through according to individual reason and no longer depended upon appeal to authorities whose insights and methods were questionable. In *Discourse on Method* (1637), he set out these basic principles, which he had already used in *Meditations on First Philosophy* (not published until 1641), to reexamine the foundations of philosophy. He sought a basic premise from which, as in a geometrical proof, he could deduce all those principles that could be known with certainty.

Dewey, John (1859–1952) American pragmatist and social critic, reformer. Author of a great many influential books on education as well as the central topics of philosophy.

d'Holbach, Baron Paul Henri (1723–1789) French philosopher and one of the leaders of the Enlightenment. An ardent materialist and atheist, he represented the most radical fringe of the brilliant free-thinkers of prerevolutionary France.

Diogenes (412?–323? B.C.) Cynic philosopher who lived an extremely simple life. Offered anything he wanted by Alexander the Great, he replied, "Get out of my light."

Douglass, Frederick (1818–1895) American abolitionist and freed slave; he became one of this country's greatest speakers and writers about freedom.

Edwards, Jonathan (1703–1758) American philosopher and Calvinist theologian. President at the time of his death of what is now Princeton University.

Epicurus (342?–270 B.C.) Greek philosopher who argued that the good life was pleasure, but not just the immediate pleasure talked about by Aristippus. Some pleasures last longer than others; some have a lower price than others. Accordingly, he taught self-control and avoidance of violent pleasures, which often caused more pain than ultimate pleasure. Ultimately what was most pleasurable, according to Epicurus, was a life of peace and quiet. Today we use the word "Epicurean" to describe someone who often indulges in pleasures, particularly sophisticated pleasures (gourmet food, for example).

Fichte, Johann Gottlieb (1762–1814) German philosopher, student of Immanuel Kant, who turned Kant's "transcendental" philosophy into a practically oriented and relativistic "ethical idealism." He taught that "the kind of philosophy a man chooses depends upon the kind of man he is." One of the first German nationalists.

Frankfurt, Harry American moral philosopher, currently teaching at Princeton University.

Frege, Gottlob (1848–1925) Brilliant logician whose work on the foundations of arithmetic inspired Bertrand Russell and Alfred North Whitehead and turned the current of logical thinking from the Mill-like empiricism that was then reigning (in Germany as well as England) to a hardheaded mathematical discipline. He is often said to have been the pioneer and innovator of modern mathematical logic. Most important, perhaps, is his *Foundations of Arithmetic* (1884).

Gadamer, Hans-Georg (1900–) Leading German promoter of hermeneutics.

Goodman, Nelson (1906–1998) Contemporary American pragmatist who, together with W. V. O. Quine, has made pragmatism once again a dominant force in philosophy.

Grosz, Elizabeth Director of the Institute for Critical and Cultural Studies at Monash University, Grosz has published several texts in feminist philosophy.

Hanh, Thich Nhat Vietnamese Buddhist monk, peace activist, and writer. He currently lives in France and occasionally teaches in the United States.

Hartshorne, Charles (1897–) is Professor Emeritus of philosophy at the University of Texas at Austin and the author of a great many books over his long and distinguished career.

Hegel, Georg Wilhelm Friedrich (1770–1831) German philosopher who, during the age of Napoleon, wrote his *Phenomenology of Spirit* (1807), which was the single most powerful influence in European philosophy—after Kant's works—for the next hundred years. He argued that there were many different views of the world, that none of them should be thought to be wholly correct or incorrect in exclusion of the others, but that these various views could still be compared and evaluated according to a "dialectic," in which some views are shown to be more developed, more inclusive, and more adequate than others.

Heidegger, Martin (1889–1976) German phenomenologist and student of Edmund Husserl, whose rebellion against his teacher began the "existential" movement in phenomenology. His best-known work is *Being and Time* (1927). Although focusing on metaphysics and phenomenology, this work is also one of the first existentialist studies of "human nature."

Held, Virginia American philosopher, specializing in feminist epistemology. She currently teaches at the City University of New York Graduate Center.

Heraclitus (5th century B.C.) Pre-Socratic philosopher who taught that the basic element of reality was fire and that all things are in constant flux but yet are unified by an underlying logic or *logos*.

Hobbes, Thomas (1588–1679) The author of *Leviathan* (1651) and one of England's first great modern philosophers. He is generally credited with the formulation of the theory of the "social contract" for the establishment of governments and society, and he was one of the first philosophers to base his theory of government on a conception of man prior to his "civilization," in what he called "the state of nature." This was, according to Hobbes, "solitary, poor, nasty, brutish, and short." Therefore, people were motivated to become part of society for their mutual protection. Hobbes also defended a materialist conception of the universe. Even the human mind, he argued, was nothing more than "matter in motion."

Hospers, John (1918–) Former professor of philosophy at the University of Southern California, articulate follower of Ayn Rand, and one-time Libertarian candidate for President of the United States.

Hsun Tsu (298–230 BCE) was a Confucian philosopher who emphasized the importance of culture in replacing man's natural selfishness with virtue.

Hume, David (1711–1776) Often admired as the outstanding genius of British philosophy. Born in Scotland (Edinburgh), where he spent much of his life, he often traveled to London and Paris. After a vacation in France, he wrote the *Treatise of Human Nature* (1739). He achieved notoriety as well as literary fame in his lifetime, was involved in scandals, and was proscribed by the Church. He was refused professorships at the leading universities for his "heresies." Yet he was, by all accounts, an utterly delightful man who never lost his sense of humor. He was "the life of the party" in London, Edinburgh, and Paris, and he has long set the standard of the ideal thinker for British philosophers. Hume's *Enquiry Concerning the Principles of Morals* (1751) created as much of a stir in the intellectual world as his *Enquiry Concerning Human Understanding* (1748). Like the latter book, the book on morality was a rewriting of his youthful *Treatise,* which never received the attention it deserved. Hume's thesis in moral philosophy was as skeptical and shocking as his thesis in epistemology. There is no knowledge of right and wrong and no rational defense of moral principles. These are based upon sentiment or feeling and, as such, cannot be defended by argument.

Husserl, Edmund (1859–1938) German-Czech philosopher and mathematician who was the founder of phenomenology, a modern form of rational intuitionism. With Gottlob Frege, he fought against the empiricist view of necessary truth defended by John Stuart Mill and developed an alternative view in which matters of necessity were not matters of ordinary experience but rather of a special kind of intuition. His best-known works are *Ideas* (Vol. 1) (1913) and *Cartesian Meditations* (1931).

Ibn-Rushd (Averroës) (1126–1198) Spanish Islamic theologian, generally considered to be the last Islamic Aristotelian.

Irigaray, Luce French feminist philosopher. Her work incorporates literary criticism, feminism, and philosophy. Her best known works are *Speculum of the Other Woman* and *This Sex Which Is Not One.*

James, William (1842–1910) Perhaps the greatest American philosopher (and psychologist) to this day. He developed the particularly American philosophy of pragmatism from the brilliant but obscure formulations of his colleague at Harvard, Charles Sanders Peirce, into a popular and still very powerful intellectual force. James was born in New York City and graduated from Harvard with a medical degree, but he decided to teach (at Harvard) rather than to practice medicine. His best-known work in philosophy, besides his work called *Pragmatism: A New Name for Some Old Ways of Thinking* (1907), is *The Varieties of Religious Experience* (1902). He also established himself as one of the fathers of modern psychology with his *Principles of Psychology* (1890).

Kane, Robert teaches philosophy at the University of Texas at Austin. He is the author of *Through the Moral Maze, The Importance of Free Will* and other books and many articles.

Kant, Immanuel (1724–1804) German philosopher, probably the greatest philosopher since Plato and Aristotle, who lived his entire life in a small town in East Prussia (Königsberg). He was a professor at the university there for more than thirty years; he never married, and his neighbors said that his habits were so regular that they could set their watches by him. (A later German poet said, "It is hard to write about Kant's life, for he had no life.") Yet, from a safe distance, he was one of the most persistent defenders of the French Revolution and, in philosophy, created no less a revolution himself. His philosophical system, embodied in three huge volumes called *Critique of Pure Reason* (1781), *Critique of Practical Reason* (1788), and *Critique of Judgment* (1790), changed the thinking of philosophers as much as the revolution changed France. His central thesis was the defense of what he called "synthetic *a priori*" judgments (and their moral and religious equivalents) by showing their necessity for all human experience. In this way, he escaped from Hume's skepticism and avoided the dead-end intuitionism of his rational predecessors.

Kierkegaard, Søren (1813–1855) Danish philosopher and theologian who is generally recognized as the father of existentialism and the founder of many varieties of contemporary religious irrationalism. Kierkegaard dedicated himself to religious writing after a short and not altogether successful attempt at the wild life and a brief engagement, which he broke off in order to devote himself to his work. The basic tenet of Kierkegaard's philosophy was the need for each individual to choose his own way of life. Christianity, as one of the possible choices, could not be considered anything other than just such a choice, a passionate choice, which had nothing to do with doctrines, churches, social groups, and ceremonies.

King, Martin Luther, Jr. (1929–1968) American Baptist minister, civil rights leader, and Nobel Prize Laureate. He was assassinated in 1968.

Leibniz, Gottfried Wilhelm von (1646–1716) Leibniz has been called "the last of the universal geniuses." He was one of the inventors of the calculus, the father of modern formal linguistics, the inventor of a primitive computer, a military strategist (who may have influenced Napoleon), a physicist who in his own time was thought to be the rival of Newton, and most of all a great philosopher. He grew up in Leipzig but traveled considerably (to Paris and Amsterdam and all over Germany). He spoke personally with most of the great philosophers of his time and debated with them constantly. His metaphysics is a curious combination of traditional theology and a radical alternative to the physical doctrines of Newton, to whose philosophy he had once been attracted but which he had given up as "absurd." His short *Monadology* (1714) is a summary of his mature metaphysical theories.

Lloyd, Genevieve Feminist philosopher, currently at the University of New South Wales in Australia.

Locke, John (1632–1704) Spent his early life in the English countryside, including many years at Oxford where he taught philosophy and the classics until he earned a medical degree and turned to medicine. Much of Locke's mature life, however, was spent in politics, and he joined a more or less revolutionary group that was fighting for the overthrow of the government. He was forced to flee England in 1683, and he lived in Holland until the Glorious Revolution of 1688. For his part in the struggle, he received a government position, although he spent most of his time writing his two *Treatises on Government* (1689) to justify the revolution and its political principles and defending his *Essay Concerning Human Understanding* (1690), which he had written while in exile. He is generally credited as not only the founder of British empiricism but the father of modern political liberalism as well.

Logical positivism (from roughly 1929 until the Nazis proscribed it in 1938) A powerful school of philosophy that originated in Vienna with a group of scientists and philosophers of anti-Nazi, liberal, antimetaphysical, and scientific persuasion—the "Vienna Circle." Against the horrendous mythologies and superstitions propagandized by the Nazis, using the old metaphysics as a tool, these philosophers used the clarity of science to dispel nonsense and to defend common sense. Accordingly, the group was broken by the Nazis, and most of its members, except for Moritz Schlick, who was shot by an insane student, left for the United States, England, and Holland. The main thrust of logical positivism is its total rejection of metaphysics in favor of a strong emphasis on science and verifiability through experience. The method of the logical positivists, accordingly, is strongly empiricist (they actually called themselves "logical empiricists") and has much in common with the method of Hume, according to which all knowledge is to be defended either as a matter of empirical fact to be verified (that is, confirmed) through experience or as a matter of logic and language to be demonstrated through analysis. Arithmetic and geometry, for the logical positivists, consist of analytic truths.

MacKinnon, Catherine American professor of law, known particularly for her writings on philosophy of law and feminism.

Malcolm X (1925–1965) Outspoken leader of the black nationalist movement in this country. He was assassinated in 1965, upon his return from a trip to the Middle East.

Mandela, Nelson was until recently the President of South Africa and remains the hero of the Republic.

Marcuse, Herbert (1898–1979) Twentieth-century philosopher of the "Frankfurt School," which sought inter-disciplinary Marxist social criticism. He emigrated to the United States during WWII, and taught during his later years at the University of California at LaJolla.

Marx, Karl (1818–1883) German philosopher and social theorist who formulated the philosophical basis for one of the most cataclysmic political ideologies of the twentieth century.

He received a doctorate in philosophy but could not teach in Germany because of his radical views. He spent most of his life abroad, in Paris, Brussels, and London, developing his theories and writing for various journals and newspapers (including the *New York Herald Tribune*). His savage attacks on established beliefs and advocacy of revolution were constant throughout his life and forced him into exile. As a young man he wrote a devastating critique of G. W. F. Hegel, whom he had studied and followed as a young student, and whose concept of "dialectic" he used in developing a powerful social-political philosophy of class conflict and economic determination.

Mead, Margaret (1901–1978) American anthropologist and author. Her two most famous works are *Coming of Age in Samoa* and *Sex and Temperament in Three Primitive Societies*.

Mencius (372–289 BCE) was a Confucian philosopher who emphasized man's natural compassion and virtue.

Merleau-Ponty, Maurice (1908–1961) French "existentialist," the most serious of the existential phenomenologists who followed Husserl in France. His most important work is his *Phenomenology of Perception* (1945). He is also well known for his political writings and his art criticism. In his early *Structure of Behavior* (1942), he argued that the human body cannot be considered merely another "fragment of matter," in other words, merely a body, but must be viewed as the center of our experience.

Michaels, Meredith (1950–) American philosopher, Smith College.

Mill, John Stuart (1806–1873) Son of James Mill, also a philosopher, and one of the documented geniuses of modern history. His intellectual feats by the age of ten would have been to the credit of most scholars at the age of sixty. He pushed himself so hard, however, that he suffered a nervous breakdown in 1826, at the age of twenty, and turned his attention from the "hard" sciences to poetry and political reform. He is best known for his moral and political writings, particularly *On Liberty* (1859) and *Utilitarianism* (1861). His logic and epistemology are the best to be found in the British empiricist tradition of the nineteenth century. His views on mathematics, for example, became one of those positions that every writer on the subject had either to accept or to fight forcefully.

Nāgārjuna (2nd century A.D.) Late ancient Indian skeptic, he claimed that knowledge of causation and substance was impossible.

Nagel, Thomas (1937–) American philosopher at New York University and a broadranging thinker who has written on a spectrum of topics from sex and death to political philosophy and racism in South Africa. He is the author of *Mortal Questions* and *The View from Nowhere*.

Narayan, Uma Educated in India and the United States, she teaches philosophy at Vassar College.

Nietzsche, Friedrich (1844–1900) German philosopher who declared himself the archenemy of traditional morality and Christianity and spent much of his life writing polemics against them. His most sustained and vicious attack (partly included in the text) is in one of his last books, *Antichrist* (1888). Although generally known as an immoralist (a name he chose for himself), Nietzsche's moral philosophy is actually an attack on one conception of morality in order to replace it with another. The morality he attacked was the morality of traditional Christianity as defined by Kant. The morality he sought to defend was the ancient morality of personal excellence, as defined by Aristotle. He referred to the first as "slave morality," suggesting that it was suitable only for the weak and servile, and to the latter as "master morality," suggesting that it was the morality of the strong and independent few.

Nishitani, Keiji (1900–) Japanese philosopher, a representative of the "Kyoto School," founded by Kitaro Nishida (1870–1945). Their work was devoted to incorporating Western thought, especially existentialism, with Buddhism.

Nozick, Robert (1938–) American philosopher at Harvard University; author of an influential book on political philosophy, *Anarchy, State and Utopia* and *Philosophical Explanations.*

Okpewho, Isidore A specialist in oral literature, Okpewho teaches in the English department of the University of Ibadan in Nigeria.

Ortega y Gasset, José (1883–1955) Spanish philosopher and author of the controversial book *The Revolt of the Masses.* He also wrote widely on metaphysics and aesthetics, and published a book on the subject of romantic love.

Ortner, Sherry American anthropologist, best known for her work in cross-cultural gender distinctions.

Parmenides (5th century B.C.) Pre-Socratic philosopher who taught that reality was eternal and unchanging and that therefore we could not know it as such.

Pascal, Blaise (1623–1662) French scientist and philosopher with mildly mystical tendencies. He stressed confidence in the "heart" rather than in reason, and many of his best-known writings are concerned with the problems of religious faith. However, he was also one of the inventors of the computer and a famous mathematician. His best-known work is *Pensées* ("Thoughts") (1669).

Plato (427–347 B.C.) Plato was born into a family of wealth and political power. But in Athens he fell under the influence of Socrates and turned his talents to philosophy. He conceived of a "philosopher-king," the ideal wise ruler, who certainly did not exist in Athens. He was disillusioned by Socrates' execution and devoted his life to continuing his work. Plato set up the Academy for this purpose and spent the rest of his life teaching there. He first set down his reminiscences of Socrates' life and death, and, using the dialogue form, with Socrates as his mouthpiece, he extended Socrates' thought into entirely new areas, notably, metaphysics and the theory of knowledge. Plato incorporated a theory of morality into his metaphysics and politics, particularly in *The Republic.* Like all Greeks, he saw ethics as part of politics and the good life for the individual in terms of the strength and harmony of the society. In *The Republic,* accordingly, Socrates argues against the various views of selfishness and hedonism that would interfere with such a conception. Virtue, he argues, is the harmony of the individual soul as well as the harmony of the individual within the society. It is still difficult, since we have nothing from Socrates himself, to know how much is original Plato and how much is transcribed Socrates.

Pythagoras (6th–5th century B.C.) The religious mystic who believed that numbers were the essence of all things. One of the Pre-Socratics.

Quine, Willard Van Orman (1908–) Contemporary American pragmatist whose early attacks on logical positivism and its basic tenets have been responsible for several of the dominant concerns of recent American philosophy. His attack on Immanuel Kant's distinction between "analytic" and "synthetic" sentences, for example, along with the more traditional distinction between necessity and contingency, have thrown the entire philosophical enterprise into considerable turmoil. According to Quine, there are no indubitably "necessary" statements or beliefs, just those that happen, at a particular point in our knowledge and interests, to hold a relatively protected place in the overall system of our beliefs for ostensibly practical reasons. He is the author of *Word and Object* (1960) and many other works in logic and the philosophy of language.

Rawls, John (1921–) Author of *A Theory of Justice* (1971) and professor of philosophy at Harvard University.

Rorty, Richard American philosopher, currently teaching at Stanford University .

Rousseau, Jean-Jacques (1712–1778) Stormy Enlightenment philosopher who fought with most of his peers (including David Hume) and developed a dramatic conception of "natural morality," which he contrasted to what he saw as the fraud and hypocrisy of contemporary civilized man. He formulated a picture of man in "the state of nature," before civilization, in which his "natural goodness" was not yet "corrupted" by society. The key to this idea was his conception of moral sentiment, which was innate in all people and not learned from society. His writings were condemned, and he spent much of his life running from the police. He died in total poverty, but only a few years after his death his political ideas became the central ideology of the French Revolution.

Russell, Bertrand (1872–1970) One of the greatest philosophers of our century. As a young man, he wrote, with Alfred North Whitehead, a book called *Principia Mathematica* (1903), which set the stage for modern logic and foundations of mathematics and gave logic a central role as a philosophical tool. He wrote an enormous number of philosophical books on virtually every topic, including several notorious polemics in favor of what was branded "free love" and atheism. He was a persistent and harsh critic of religion in general and Christianity in particular, as a source of what he called superstition and legitimized murder. Russell was a committed pacifist during World War I and wrote at least one of his most famous books while sitting in prison for his antiwar activities. Like his famous predecessor, David Hume (with whom he has much in common), Russell was too controversial for most universities, and a famous court case prevented him from teaching at the City College of New York. He won the Nobel prize in 1950.

Ryle, Gilbert (1900–1978) Oxford "ordinary-language" philosopher whose book *The Concept of Mind* (1949) set the stage for several decades of debate over his quasi-behavioristic resolution of the mind-body problem. His main thesis is that the distinction between mind and body rests on what he calls a "category mistake," that is, wrongly believing something to be one kind of thing when it is really another. In particular, it has been thought that mental events were events on a par with, but wholly different from, bodily events. Instead, Ryle argues, to talk about mind is to talk about behavioral dispositions and abilities. (To say that a person *wants* to do something is to say that he *would* do that if given the opportunity.)

Sartre, Jean-Paul (1905–1980) Contemporary French philosopher who began as a literary writer and a phenomenologist, in the style of Edmund Husserl, but who converted that austere philosophy to his own radical ends. He is generally regarded as the main proponent of the philosophy of "existentialism." Sartre's existentialism is a moral philosophy as well as a philosophy of freedom. It denies that there is any such thing as "human nature" and therefore insists that "man makes himself." That is, through our various choices and moral commitments we define what we want humanity to be. According to Sartre, we do not simply find moral principles upon which we should act, but rather we *choose* those moral principles *through our acting*. Thus Sartre's moral philosophy places most of its emphasis on action and minimizes the importance of moral deliberation and all that sort of moralizing in which we simply talk about what is good, rather than simply a "good will" as in Kant. In his novels and plays, Sartre's characters are always torn by alternative identities, suffering just because they cannot make up their minds. In his greatest work, *Being and Nothingness* (1943), Sartre argues that everyone "is who he is not, and is not who he is," by which he means (in a paradoxical phrase) that our identity is never simply the totality of facts ("facticity") that are true of us; we always identify ourselves with our plans and intentions for the future (our "transcendence") as well, which means that so long as we are alive, we have no fixed "identity" at all.

Schiller, Friedrich (1759–1805) German playwright and philosopher. Schiller followed Kant in philosophy and Goethe in literature, combining the influence of the two in his *Letters on the Aesthetic Education of Mankind.*

Schopenhauer, Arthur (1788–1860) German philosopher; famous pessimist and man of letters. His main work, *The World as Will and Idea,* was an elaboration on Kant's philosophy. Yet instead of Kant's rationality, irrationality of the will became the centerpiece of Schopenhauer's philosophy. The book was first published in 1819, but did not become popular and earn its author the fame he much desired until the second half of the nineteenth century.

Searle, John (1932–) American philosopher at the University of California, Berkeley, the best-known proponent of "speech–act theory" in the philosophy of language and the author of many controversial books and articles, including a series of attacks on the ambitions of cognitive science and computer models of the mind.

Shaffer, Jerome (1929–) American philosopher, presently teaching at the University of Connecticut. One of the best-known critics of the now influential "identity theory" of mind and body.

Shaftsbury, Earl of (1671–1713) Scottish "moral sentiment" theorist; defended and studied the role of such emotions as sympathy and compassion in moral life.

Smart, J. J. C. (1920–) Australian philosopher late of the Australian National University in Canberra. Classic defender of the mind–body "identity theory."

Socrates (470–399 B.C.) Athenian philosopher with a gift for rhetoric and debating. He had a notoriously poor marriage, had several children, and lived in poverty most of his life. Socrates began his studies in the physical sciences but soon turned to the study of human nature, morality, and politics. He became famous debating with the many "sophists" who wandered about giving practical training in argument and persuasion (the ancient equivalent of law school). Socrates found their general skepticism intolerable and urged a return to the absolute ideals of wisdom, virtue, justice, and the good life. In his philosophy, he approached these questions as matters of finding the exact definitions of these concepts in order to clarify our pursuit of them. In doing so, he developed a brilliant technique of dialogue or "dialectic" in which he would discover these definitions by constant debating, forcing his opponents or students to advance varying theories, which he in turn would knock down. In the process, the correct definition would slowly emerge. In his not always tactful search for truth, however, Socrates made many enemies, who eventually had him condemned to death, a cruel and unfair verdict he accepted with dignity.

Spinoza, Benedictus de (1632–1677) Spinoza was born Baruch ben Michael, the son of Jewish refugees from the Spanish Inquisition. He was born and grew up in Amsterdam, a relative haven of toleration in a world still dangerous because of religious hatreds. He studied to be a rabbi, making himself familiar with Christian theology as well. He was always a recluse who wandered about the country making a living by grinding lenses, and was later ostracized by his fellow Jews for his heretical beliefs. His best-known book is *Ethics* (1677); it is a radical reinterpretation of God as identical to the universe (pantheism) and a protracted argument concerning the uselessness of human struggle in the face of a thoroughly determined universe.

Stoics (4th century B.C., with revisions until the 1st century A.D.) An ancient movement in philosophy that taught self-control and minimized passion, with a willingness to endure whatever fate has in store. Some believers were Zeno of Citium in Greece (not the same as Zeno of the paradoxes), Seneca, and Marcus Aurelius in Rome.

Strawson, Peter Frederick (1919–) Contemporary Oxford philosopher whose book *Individuals* (1959) was responsible for reintroducing systematic metaphysics into current British philosophy. He called his metaphysics "descriptive," however, by which he meant to insist that it was only to be construed as an analysis and description of "our conceptual framework," not of "reality-in-itself." In the third chapter of that book, Strawson argues the thesis that the distinction between mind and body can be made only after we have recognized the primary category of "persons." Persons are not conglomerates of minds and bodies, and we can talk of minds and bodies only because we first have a way of specifying the different attributes of a person.

Tao Te Ching Poets (including Lao Tsu) (5th century B.C.) Ancient Chinese mystics whose doctrine was that the "Tao" or "Way" was the ineffable underpinning of existence.

Tarski, Alfred American logician who formulated the still controversial "semantic theory of truth" in 1944.

Thales (6th century B.C.) The first known Greek philosopher, who taught that all things were ultimately composed of water.

Thoreau, Henry David (1817–1862) American essayist, naturalist, and philosopher; a champion of individualism. His most famous work was *Walden.*

Tillich, Paul (1886–1965) German-born philosopher who spent many of his later years teaching in the United States. He is among the best known of those modern theologians who, like the Romantics of the last century, place the emphasis on emotion and "concern" rather than on reason in religion. In Tillich's theology, God is no longer the transcendent judge of the scriptures but simply the symbol of our "ultimate concern." He is the author of *Systematic Theology* (1953–63), *The Dynamics of Faith* (1957), and *The Courage to Be* (1952).

Watson, John (1878–1958) American psychologist generally recognized as the founder of behaviorism. He attacked the notion of "consciousness" as a remnant of the age-old religious belief in the "soul" and urged that we give up what he called such "magical" nonsense in favor of a purely scientific view, which allows us to talk sensibly only about observables, in other words, human behavior rather than the human "mind." He is the author of *Behaviorism* (1924).

Whitehead, Alfred North (1861–1947) Famous logician who, together with Bertrand Russell, established the basis of modern logic and who late in life turned to metaphysics. In place of the concept of substance, however, he argued for a concept of process, a universe in constant evolutionary change.

Wittgenstein, Ludwig (1889–1951) Austrian-born philosopher who became the single most powerful influence on twentieth-century "analytic" philosophy. He entered philosophy as an engineer, studied with Bertrand Russell, and wrote the book *Tractatus Logico-Philosophicus* (1922), which inspired logical positivism. Giving up philosophy for a number of years and changing his mind about his arguments in the *Tractatus,* he returned to philosophy at Cambridge and developed that "therapeutic" brand of philosophy that became known as "ordinary-language" philosophy. In his later works, culminating in his *Philosophical Investigations* (1953, published posthumously), Wittgenstein initiated a devastating attack on Cartesian dualism and the problems it carried with it. His so-called private language argument, in fact culled from a series of aphorisms, argues that even if there were such "private" occurrences as mental events, we should have no way of talking about them and no way of knowing about them, even in our own case. But although he is often described as a "behaviorist," Wittgenstein is better described as one of those philosophers who was groping for an entirely new conception of a "person" or at least attempting to reject all the old ones.

Zarathustra (Zoroaster) (6th century B.C.) Ancient Persian reformer and prophet of the first monotheistic religion, Zoroastrianism.

Zeno of Elea (5th century B.C.) Pre-Socratic philosopher and student of Parmenides who taught that motion was unreal and developed a series of brilliant paradoxes in order to prove it.

LITERARY CREDITS

INTRODUCTION

Excerpt from *The Clouds,* in *The Complete Plays of Aristophanes,* ed. by Moses Hadas, © 1962 by Bantam Books, a division of Random House, Inc.

Plato, *The Apology,* in *The Trial and Death of Socrates,* 2nd ed., trans. G.M.A. Grube, © 1975 Hackett Publishing Company. Reprinted with permission.

Plato, *The Crito,* in *The Trial and Death of Socrates,* 2nd ed., trans. G.M.A. Grube, © 1975 Hackett Publishing Company. Reprinted with permission.

Excerpt from *Tao Te Ching* by Lao Tsu.

Excerpt from *Discourse on Method* by Rene Descartes, trans. Elizabeth S. Haldane & G.R.T. Ross, 1911. Reprinted with the permission of Cambridge University Press.

CHAPTER I

Reprinted by permission of the publishers and the Loeb Classical Library from ARISTOTLE: METAPHYSICS, VOLUME XVII translated by H. Tredennick, Cambridge, Mass.: Harvard University Press, 1933.

From Karl Jaspers, *Basic Philosophical Writings–Selections.* Edited, translated and with introductions by Edith Ehrlich, Leonard H. Ehrlich, and George B. Pepper. (Athens, OH: Ohio University Press), pp. 382–387.

Excerpt from *The Ion,* trans. by Paul Woodruff, © 1983. Includes trans. of Heraclitus.

From Parmenides, *Fragments* (B2; B3; B6; 11 1–2; B8 11 3–9), trans. Paul Woodruff. Reprinted by permission of the author.

Brhadaranyaha 1.3.28, Brhadaranyaha 4.3.32, Isa Upanisad 406, Brhadaranyaha 5.1.1, Brhadaranyaha 3.7.3–3.7.23 passion. Chandogya 6.11 and Katha 1.25–27, 2.11–12, and 2.20–23. Trans. Stephen Phillips.

Yasna, from the Zend-Avesta, Part III, trans. L.H. Mills; part of the series, *The Sacred Books of the East,* ed. F. Max Muller (Westport, CT: Greenwood Press, 1972 [Oxford, 1887]). From the Yashts, from Zend-Avesta, Part II, trans. James Darmesteter; part of the series, *The Sacred Books of the East,* ed. F. Max Muller (Motilal Banarsidall: Delhi, 1965 [Oxford, 1883]).

The Analects of Confucius, trans. & annotated by Arthur Waley (New York: Vintage, 1938).

From *The Way of Life: An American Version,* trans. Witter Bynner (New York, The John Day Co., 1944). Sections 1, 18, 14, 33, and 57, respectively.

The "Fire-Sermon," from Maha-Vagga, Reprinted by permission of the publishers from BUDDHISM IN TRANSLATION by Henry Clark Warren, Cambridge, Mass.: Harvard University Press, Copyright 1896, 1953 by the President and Fellows of Harvard College.

Reprinted from Plato, *The Symposium,* translated by Alexander Nehamas and Paul Woodruff. Copyright © 1989 by A. Nehamas and P. Woodruff. All rights reserved. Reprinted by permission of Hackett Publishing Company, Inc.

Plato, *The Republic,* Bk. VII, trans. G.M.A. Grube. Copyright 1974 Hackett Publishing Company. Reprinted with permission.

Plato, *The Meno*, trans. G.M.A. Grube. Copyright 1976 Hackett Publishing Company. Reprinted with permission.

Aristotle, *Metaphysics*, T.1.1003a21, Z.1.1028a10, trans. W. D. Ross (Oxford: Oxford University Press, 1924).

Aristotle, *Physics*, II.1.193a9; II.1.193, I.8.191a24; trans. W. D. Ross (Oxford: Oxford University Press, 1936).

"On Substance," by Rene Descartes, from *Principles of Philosophy* in *The Philosophical Works of Descartes,* eds. E. Haldane & G.R.T. Ross,1911. Reprinted with the permission of Cambridge University Press.

Benedictus de Spinoza, from *Ethics* in *The Rationalists,* trans. R.H.M. Elwes (New York: Doubleday, 1960).

Gottfried Wilhelm von Leibniz, from *Monadology,* in *The Rationalists,* trans. George Montgomery (New York: Doubleday, 1968).

CHAPTER 2

John Wisdom, "Gods," in *Proceedings of the Aristotelian Society,* XLV (London: Harrison & Sons, 1944–45).

Albert Einstein, "Religion and Science," in *Ideas and Opinions,* trans. Sonia Bargmann (New York: Crown, 1954).

Keiji Nishitani, "What Is Religion?" from RELIGION AND NOTHINGNESS. Edited/translated by Jan Van Bragt. Copyright © 1982 Keiji Nishitani. Published by University of California Press.

St. Anselm, *Proslogion,* in *A Scholastic Miscellany,* vol. 10, The Library of Christian Classics, ed. and trans. Eugene R. Fairweather, 1956. Used by permission of Westminster John Knox Press.

Rene Descartes, "Meditation IV" in *Meditations on First Philosophy* in *The Philosophical Works of Descartes,* trans. Elizabeth S. Haldane and G.R.T. Ross,1911. Reprinted with the permission of Cambridge University Press.

Immanuel Kant, *The Critique of Pure Reason,* rev. 2nd ed., trans. Max Müller (London: Macmillan, 1927).

St. Thomas Aquinas, *Summa Theologica,* trans. Fathers of the English Dominican Province (New York: Benziger, Bruce & Glencoe, 1948).

David Hume, *Dialogues on Natural Religion,* ed. Norman Kemp Smith (Oxford: Oxford University Press, 1935).

Immanuel Kant, *Critique of Practical Reason,* trans. Lewis White. © 1992. Reprinted by permission of Prentice-Hall, Inc., Upper Saddle River, NJ.

William James, "The Will to Believe," in *The Will to Believe and Other Essays in Popular Philosophy* (New York: Longmans, Green, 1896).

Blaise Pascal, Pensees, #233 (New York: Modern Library, 1941).

St. Augustine, *Confessions,* Bk VII, trans. R.S. Pine-Coffin. Copyright © 1961 by R.S. Pine-Coffin. (Penguin Classics, 1961), pp. 136–149. Copyright © R.S. Pine-Coffin, 1961. Reprinted by permission of Penguin Books, Ltd.

Gita 1.31b-35, 3.9–12, 3.15, 4.6–8, 4.11, 4.14–19, 4.22–24, 4.31–33, 4.36–37, and 4.42b. Translated by Steve Phillips.

Ibn-Rushd, On the Philsophic Study of God, from *Averroes on the Harmonyh of Religion and Philosophy,* trans. By G.F. Hourani, (London: Luzac & Co.).

From THE BROTHERS KARAMAZOV by Fyodor Dostoevsky, translated by Andrew R. MacAndrew. Translation copyright © 1970 by Bantam, a division of Bantam Doubleday Dell Publishing Group, Inc. Used by permission of Bantam Books, a division of Random House, Inc.

Mohammad Al-Ghazali, *The Deliverance from Error,* from THE FAITH AND PRACTICE OF al-GHAZALI, translated by William Montgomery watt, 1951. Reprinted by permission of the translator.

Søren Kierkegaard, *Concluding Unscientific Postscript,* trans. David F. Swenson and Walter Lowrie. Copyright © 1992 by Princeton University Press. Reprinted by permission of Princeton University Press.

Søren Kierkegaard, *Philosophical Fragments,* trans. David Swenson Copyright © 1985 by Princeton University Press. Reprinted by permission of Princeton University Press.

From THE DYNAMICS OF FAITH by Paul Tillich. Copyright © 1957 by Paul Tillich. Renewed © 1985 by Hannah Tillich. Reprinted by permission of HarperCollins Publishers, Inc.

Karl Marx, *Critique of Hegel's Philosophy of Right* in *Early Writings,* trans. T. Bottomore. Copyright © 1963. Reprinted by permission of The McGraw-Hill Companies.

Friedrich Nietzsche, *Beyond Good and Evil,* trans. Walter Kaufmann (New York: Random House, 1966).

"The Antichrist" by Friedrich Nietzsche, from THE PORTABLE NIETZSCHE, edited by Walter Kaufmann, translated by Walter Kaufmann, copyright 1954 by The Viking Press, renewed © 1982 by Viking Penguin Inc. Used by permission of Viking Penguin, a division of Penguin Putnam Inc.

"The Joyful Wisdom." Reprinted with the permission of Scribner, a Division of Simon & Schuster from THE COMPLETE WORKS OF FRIEDRICH NIETZSCHE. Translated under the General Editorship of Oscar Levy (Russell & Russell, NY, 1964).

From THE FUTURE OF AN ILLUSION by Sigmund Freud, translated by James Strachey. Translation copyright © 1961 by James Strachey, renewed 1989 by Alix Strachey. Reprinted by permission of W.W. Norton & Company, Inc.

CHAPTER 3

Bertrand Russell, *The Problems of Philosophy* (Oxford: Oxford University Press, 1912).

Plato, from the *Theatetus,* trans. By F.M. Cornford, reprinted in *The Collected Dialogues of Plato,* eds. Edith Hamilton and Huntington Cairnes, Bollingen Series (Princeton: Princeton University Press, 1980), p. 61

Rene Descartes, *Meditations on First Philosophy,* in *The Philosophical Works of Descartes,* trans. Elizabeth S. Haldane and G.R.T. Ross, 1911. Reprinted with the permission of Cambridge University Press.

John Locke, from *An Essay Concerning Human Understanding,* A. C. Fraser (Oxford: Clarendon Press, 1894).

"Leibniz's Rebuttal" from *New Essays on Human Understanding* by Gottfried Wilhelm von Leibniz, trans. A. G. Langley. Reprinted by permission of Open Court Publishing Company, a division of Carus Publishing Company, Peru, IL. Copyright 1949 by Open Court Publishing.

John Locke, from *An Essay Concerning Human Understanding,* A. C. Fraser (Oxford: Clarendon Press, 1894).

Bishop George Berkeley, *Treatise Concerning The Principles of Human Knowledge,* (New York: Bobbs-Merrill, 1957). © 1957. Reprinted by permission of Prentice-Hall, Inc., Upper Saddle River, NJ

Bertrand Russell, *A History of Western Philosophy* (New York: Simon and Schuster, 1945).

David Hume, *A Treatise of Human Nature,* from *An Enquiry Concerning Human Understanding,* 2nd ed., ed. L.A. Selby-Bigge (Oxford: Oxford University Press, 1902).

From the *Madhyamaka-Karikas* from *Nagarjuna: The Philosophy of the Middle,* trans. David J. Kalupuhana (Albany: SUNY Press, 1986).

Uma Narayan, "The Project of Feminist Epistemology: Perspectives from a Non-Western Feminist" in *Gender/Body/Knowledge*, eds. Alison M. Jagger and Susan R. Bordo. Copyright © 1989 by Rutgers, The State University. Reprinted by permission.

CHAPTER 4

Immanuel Kant, *The Critique of Pure Reason*, rev. 2nd ed., trans. Max Müller (London: Macmillan, 1927).

Brand Blanshard, *The Nature of Thought* (New York: Macmillan, 1941).

Charles Peirce, "How to Make Our Ideas Clear," in *Popular Science Monthly* (January 1878).

William James, *Pragmatism: A New Name for Some Old Ways of Thinking* (New York: Longmans, Green, 1907.)

Alfred Tarski, "The Semantic Theory of Truth," in *Philosophy and Phenomenological Research* 4, no. 3 (March 1944). Reprinted by permission of Jan Tarski.

Immanuel Kant, PROLEGOMENA TO ANY FUTURE METAPHYSICS, trans. Lewis White Beck. Copyright 1957. Reprinted by permission of Prentice-Hall, Inc., Upper Saddle River, NJ.

G.W.F. Hegel, *The Phenomenology of Spirit*, trans. A.V. Miller, (New York: Oxford University Press, 1977).

G.W.F. Hegel, REASON IN HISTORY, trans. Robert S. Hartman, © 1953. Reprinted by permission of Prentice-Hall, Inc., Upper Saddle River, NJ.

Arthur Schopenhauer, *The World as Will and Representation*, pp. 275, *et supra*. Translated by E.F. Payne. Copyright © 1966 by Dover Publications, Inc. Reprinted by permission.

Friedrich Nietzsche, *Human-All-Too-Human, Gay Science*, and *Beyond Good and Evil* in *The Nietzsche Reader*, trans. R.J. Hollingdale (Penguin Classics, 1977), pp. 53–55, 58–60, 63. Copyright © R.J. Hollingdale 1961, 1969. Reprinted by permission of Penguin Books, Ltd.

Edmund Husserl, *The 1929 Paris Lectures*, trans. Peter Koestenbaum (Hague: Nijhoff, 1975). Reprinted with kind permission from Kluwer Academic Publishers.

Richard Rorty, "Solidarity or Objectivity?" from *Consequences of Pragmatism: Essays 1972–1980*. From PHILOSOPHICAL PAPERS, VOL. 1: Objectivity, Relativism, and Truth. Reprinted with the permission of Cambridge University Press.

Isamu Nagami, "Cultural Gaps: Why Do We Misunderstand?" from *Liberation Ethics: Essays in Religious and Social Ethics in Honor of Gibson Winter*, eds. Charles Amjad-Ali and W. Alvin Pitcher. Copyright © 1985. Reprinted by permission of the Center for the Scientific Study of Religion.

Elizabeth Grosz, "Philosophy," in *Feminist Knowledge: Critique and Construct*, ed. Sneja Gunew (London: Routledge, 1990).

CHAPTER 5

Rene Descartes, "Meditation VI," in Meditations on First Philosophy, in *The Philosophical Works of Descartes*, trans. Elizabeth S. Haldane and G.R.T. Ross, 1911. Reprinted with the permission of Cambridge University Press.

John Locke, *An Essay Concerning Human Understanding*, ed. A.C. Fraser (Oxford: Clarendon Press, 1894).

David Hume, *A Treatise of Human Nature*, ed. L.A. Selby-Bigge (Oxford: Oxford University Press, 1888).

Immanuel Kant, PROLEGOMENA TO ANY FUTURE METAPHYSICS, trans. Lewis White Beck. Copyright 1957. Reprinted by permission of Prentice-Hall, Inc., Upper

(New York: John Day, 1944).

CHAPTER 6

Rene Descartes, "Meditation VI," in *Meditations on First Philosophy,* in *The Philosophical Works of Descartes,* trans. Elizabeth S. Haldane and G.R.T. Ross, 1911. Reprinted with the permission of Cambridge University Press.

Rene Descartes, "Letter of Dedication to the Dean of Doctors of the Faculty of Scared Theology of Paris," in *Meditations on First Philosophy,* trans. Donald A. Cress (Indianapolis, IN: Hackett, 1979). Reprinted by permission.

Rene Descartes, "The Passions of the Soul," in *The Philosophical Works of Descartes,* trans. Elizabeth S. Haldane and G.R.T. Ross. Copyright1911. Reprinted with the permission of Cambridge University Press.

The Economist, July 20, 1996, "Science Does It With Feeling," pp. 2071–73. © 1996 The Economist Newspaper Group, Inc. Reprinted with permission. Further reproduction prohibited. www.economist.com

Gilbert Ryle, *The Concept of Mind.* Copyright 1949. Reprinted by permission of Routledge Publishers, Ltd.

J.J.C. Smart, "Sensations and Brain Processes," in *Philosophical Review* 68 (1959), pp. 141–56. Copyright 1959 Cornell University. Reprinted by permission of the publisher.

Jerome Shaffer, *Philosophy of Mind.* Copyright © 1994. Reprinted by permission of Prentice-Hall, Inc., Upper Saddle River, NJ.

Paul M. Churchland, *Matter and Consciousness: A Contemporary Introduction to the Philosophy of Mind* (Cambridge, MA: MIT Press, 1988), pp. 43–49.

John R. Searle, "The Myth of the Computer" in the *New York Review of Books.* Reprinted with permission from *The New York Review of Books.* Copyright © 1982 NYREV, Inc.

Sigmund Freud, *New Introductory Lectures on Psychoanalysis,* ed. and trans. James Strachey (New York: Norton, 1964).

Thomas Nagel, *Mortal Questions.* Copyright © 1979. Reprinted with the permission of Cambridge University Press.

Reprinted by permission of the publishers and the Loeb Classical Library from ARISTOTLE: MINOR WORKS, VOLUME XIV, translated by W.S. Hett, Cambridge, Mass.: Harvard University Press, 1936.

William James, "Does Consciousness Exist?" in *Journal of Philosophy, Psychology and Scientific Methods,* September 1, 1904.

CHAPTER 7

Sophocles, *Oedipus the King,* trans. H.D.F. Kitto, rpt. In Barnet, Berman, Burton, *Types of Drama,* 3rd ed. (Boston: Little, Brown).

Keiji Nishitani, RELIGION AND NOTHINGNESS. Edited/translated by Jan Van Bragt copyright © 1982 Keiji Nishitani. Published by University of California Press.

St. Augustine, *On Free Choice of Will,* trans. Anna S. Benjamin and L.H. Hackstaff, © 1964. Reprinted by permission of Prentice-Hall, Inc., Upper Saddle River, NJ.

Sir Mohammed Iqbal, *The Reconstruction of Religious Thought in Islam* (London: Oxford University Press, 1934).

Jacqueline Trimier, "African Philosophy," from *World Philosophy,* ed. R.C. Solomon and K. Higgins. Reprinted by permission of the author.

Jonathan Edwards, "Freedom of the Will," from *The Works of President Edwards, In Four Volumes,* Vol. 2 (New York: Leavitt and Allen, 1856).

pany. Reprinted by permission.

Bishop Joseph Butler, FIVE SERMONS, © 1950. Reprinted by permission of Prentice-Hall, Inc., Upper Saddle River, NJ.

Aristotle, *Nichomachean Ethics,* trans. F. H. Peters, 8th ed. (1901).

David Hume, *Enquiry Concerning the Principles of Morals* (La Salle, IL: Open Court, 1912).

Jean-Jacques Rousseau, *Emile,* trans. Barbara Foxley, J.M. Dent, Ltd.

Immanuel Kant, *Fundamental Principles of the Metaphysics of Morals,* trans. T.K. Abbott (New York: Longmans, Green, 1898).

Reprinted with permission of The Free Press, a Division of Simon & Schuster, from THE PRINCIPLES OF MORALS AND LEGISLATION by Jeremy Bentham. Introduction by Laurence J. LaFleur. Copyright 1948 by Hafner Publishing Company, Inc.

John Stuart Mill, *Utilitarianism Text and Critical Essays.* Copyright © 1990. Reprinted by permission of Prentice-Hall, Inc., Upper Saddle River, NJ.

Reprinted with the permission of Scribner, a Division of Simon & Schuster from THE COMPLETE WORKS OF FRIEDRICH NIETZSCHE. Translated under the General Editorship of Oscar Levy (Russell & Russell, NY, 1964).

Jean-Paul Sartre, *Existentialism as a Humanism,* trans. Philip Mairet (New York: Philosophical Library, 1949). Reprinted by permission.

Virginia Held, "Feminist Transformations of Moral Theory," in *Philosophy and Phenomenological Research,* Vol. L, Supplement (Fall 1990). Copyright © 1990 by Brown University. Reprinted by permission of the publisher.

John Corvino, *Same Sex: Debating the Ethics, Science, and Culture of Homosexuality* (Lanham, MA: Rowman & Littlefield, 1997), pp. 4–7. Reprinted by permission.

CHAPTER 9

Plato, *The Republic,* Bk. VI, trans. G.M.A. Grube (Indianapolis, IN: Hackett, 1974). Reprinted by permission.

Aristotle, *Nichomachean Ethics,* trans. W.D. Ross (Oxford: Oxford University Press, 1925).

David Hume, *Enquiry Concerning the Principles of Morals* (La Salle, IL: Open Court, 1912).

John Stuart Mill, *UTILITARIANISM TEXT AND CRITICAL ESSAYS,* by J.S. Mills, © 1990. Reprinted by permission of Prentice-Hall, Inc., Upper Saddle River, NJ.

Thomas Hobbes, *Leviathan* (New York: Hafner, 1926).

Jean-Jacques Rousseau, *The Social Contract and Discourses,* trans. G.D.H. Cole. J.M. Dent, Ltd.

John Rawls, "Justice as Fairness," in *The Philosophical Review* 67 (April 1958). Copyright 1958 Cornell University. Reprinted by permission of the publisher.

From ANARCHY, STATE AND UTOPIA by Robert Nozick. Copyright © 1974 by Basic Books, Inc. Reprinted by permission of Basic Books, a member of Perseus Books, L.L.C.

Cheshire Calhoun, "Justice, Care, Gender, Bias" from *What Is the Right Thing for Me to Do?* Reprinted by permission of the author.

Reprinted with permission of The Free Press, a Division of Simon & Schuster, from TWO TREATISES OF GOVERNMENT by John Locke. Edited, with Introduction, by Thomas J. Cook. Copyright 1947 by Hafner Publishing Company, Inc.

John Stuart Mill, *On Liberty,* (London: Longmans, 1859).

Frederick Douglass, *Selected Writings,* ed. Michael Meyer (New York: Modern Library, 1984).

Henry David Thoreau, "Resistance to Civil Government," 1849.

Martin Luther King, Jr., "Letter from Birmingham Jail." Reprinted by arrangement with The Heirs to the Estate of Martin Luther King, Jr., c/o Writers House, Inc. as agent for the proprietor. Copyright 1967 by Matin Luther King, Jr., copyright renewed 1995 by the Es-

INDEX

A posteriori, 255
A priori, 252, 255, 273–277, 547
Abrahamic religions, 130
Absolute space, 113
Absolute time, 114
Absolutism, 279, 296, 298
  ethical, 492–496
Absurd, the, 172
Accident, 84
Action-at-a-distance (Newton), 113
Ad hominem arguments, 33–34
Aesthetics, 649–692. *See also* Beauty
African art, 688–691
"African philosophy" (Trimier), 431–432
Agnosticism, 124
Al-Ghazali, 167–168
Allah. *See* Islam
Altruism, 501, 504
Analects (Confucius), 62–63
Analogy, argument by, 29–30
Analytic truths, 252–255
Anarchism, 581
Anarchy, State and Utopia (Nozick), 612–615
Anaximander, 50
Anaximenes, 50–51
Androgyny, 359–360
"Androgyny as a Progressive Ideal for Human Development" (Ferguson), 359–360
Animism, 53
Anselm, Saint, 133–135, 141, 162
Antecedent conditions, 436
Anthropomorphism, 131–132
Antichrist, The (Nietzsche), 177–178
Apeiron, 50
Apollonian aesthetics, 675–676
Apology, The (Plato), 2–4, 13–14
Appearance/reality distinction, 54
Aquinas, Saint Thomas, 84, 141–145, 490
Argument, 12–13, 18–37
  by analogy, 29–30
  by counter-example, 26, 30–32
  deductive, 21–26, 30, 32

from design, 144, 145, 164
  inductive, 21, 26–29, 30
  reductio ad absurdum, 32
Aristophanes, 1–2
Aristotle, 10, 46, 56, 80–88, 143, 144, 329
  on art and beauty, 659–663
  categories of, 81–82
  on causation, 86–88
  on contemplation, 516–518
  cosmology of, 85–88
  on essence, 84–86
  on freedom, 452–454
  on justice, 579–580, 584–585
  on law of contradiction, 254
  metaphysics of, 80–88
  on matter, 84
  on morality, 488, 504–518, 553–556
  on the soul, 414
  on substance, 81–85, 97
  teleological views of, 84–88
  on tragedy, 660–663
  and virtue, 504–518
Art, 649–692. *See also* Beauty
Art as Experience (Dewey), 679–681
Artificial intelligence. *See* Functionalism
Asceticism, 14
Ash'arites, 429
Assumption, 12
"At the Audobon" (Malcolm X), 355
Atheism, 124
Atoms, 52
Attributes (Spinoza), 97
Augustine, Saint, 68, 153–154, 427, 489, 664
Austen, Jane, 683
Authority, 580, 621–624
Autonomy, 491, 518–519
Averroës. *See* Ibn-Rushd
"Axial Period" (Jaspers), 47–48
Axioms, 18, 97

Bad faith (Sartre), 344–346
"Ballot or the Bullet, The" (Malcolm X), 354–355, 637
Barth, Karl, 141